THE

PROSE AND POETRY

OF

EUROPE AND AMERICA:

CONSISTING OF

LITERARY GEMS AND CURIOSITIES,

AND CONTAINING

THE CHOICE AND BEAUTIFUL PRODUCTIONS

OF MANY OF

THE MOST POPULAR WRITERS OF THE PAST AND PRESENT AGE;

BEING

A RARE AND VALUABLE WORK

FOR THE

LIBRARY OR THE BOUDOIR, AND AN ELEGANT GIFT-BOOK FOR ALL SEASONS

COMPILED

BY G. P. MORRIS AND N. P. WILLIS.

COMPLETE IN ONE VOLUME.

NEW-YORK:
LEAVITT & ALLEN,
(SUCCESSORS TO LEAVITT & CO.),
NO. 27 DEY-STREET.
1853.

PREFACE.

If you have ever looked with the feeling of paternity on the first green buds of a plantation of choice trees, dear reader, you can comprehend the pleasure with which we turned over the leaves of this volume—the product of much care and pains-taking. The work is now completed, and fit for a choice cabinet, or fitter still for the occupancy of a centre-table, to be taken up in any mood, and read at any length, or with any degree of abstraction. What rich variety in its contents! What more delightful than such a book, every word of which is part of a choice treasure of literature? What better idea was ever started than that of these sands of gold, sifted from the flood of English literature—a rescue of capital things, wastefully adrift, and giving a number of the most brilliant prose tales ever written? Here are gems from the master-spirits of the by-gone time—and here is sweet and earnest Barry Cornwall. What is there, in the way of lyric poetry, better worth keeping by you? And here are Pinckney's finished poems, that have been scattered over the world, untraceable to their author, till now; and the deathless efforts at invention, by the three magicians of fancy, Drake, Praed and Keats; and the poems which are the marrow of Moore's immortality; and the long lost and splendid "Angel of the World," by Croly, coupled with the enchanting narrative of "The Rimini," by Leigh Hunt. And who will not rejoice in our bringing together the inimitable songs of the bard of poor Jack, immortal and heart-stirring Dibdin? Who that has feeling or taste, piety or love of purity, will not thank us for the incomparable sacred poetry embodied in this work—for Saturday evening and Sunday reading, inestimable treasures; and also for the beautiful selections from Goldsmith, Byron, Wordsworth, Scott, Montgomery, Hood, Campbell, Breton, Mrs. Hemans, Miss Landon, and a host of others, whose productions adorn this delightful volume? What book, published in this, or any other country, ever boasted so rich and novel a variety? Here we have succeeded in getting into presentable shape, such choice productions as we used to lend upon bond and mortgage, so precious were our copies of them, and so fearful were we that they would never be returned. We have been years and years in making these selections, and this Library is our pride. With the assurance that the work contains nothing which is not amply worthy of preservation, it is submitted to the public as a treasure of rare story, poetry and moral, well worth every one's owning.

THIS VOLUME

CONTAINS

SELECTIONS FROM THE WORKS OF THE FOLLOWING AUTHORS

AND

MANY ANONYMOUS PRODUCTIONS OF STERLING MERIT,

HERE COLLECTED FOR THE FIRST TIME.

Acton, Eliza
Akenside, Mark
Addy, Mrs.
Amelia,
Addison,
Arne, Michael
Ainsley, Hugh
Adams, Jean
Austin, Dr.

Beckforth, William
Breton, Nicholas
Barton B.
Bryant, W. C.
Bulwer, E. L.
Bird, James
Byron, Lord
Brown, M. A.
Bowering, Dr
Bayley, T. H
Barrets, E. S
Beaumont and Fletcher
Boyse, Samuel
Burns, Robert
Burleigh, William
Buchanan, Rev. H
Bonna, A. R.
Buchanan, John
Brown, J.
Barton, Bernerd
Ballentine, James
Blanier, Miss

Croly, Rev. George
Campbell, Thomas
Cowley, William
Clare, J.
Cornwall, Barry
Cowper, William
Campion, Thomas
Carraw, Thomas
Cowley, Abraham
Cunningham, John
Crabbe
Coleridge
Conder, Josiah
Cherry, Andrew
Cobb, James
Cockburn, Mrs
Clurie, Rev. John
Crawford, Archibald
Cramer, Julian

Drake, Joseph Rodman
Dale, Rev. T.
Downing, Mrs.
Dibdin, Charles
Dibdin T.
Delta
Dacre, Lady
Daniel, Samuel
Dryden, John
Doane, Bishop
Dickerson, E.
Douglas
D'Arfrey, John
Dunlop, Dr.

Ettrick Shepherd
Elliott, E.
East, William

Fletcher, Miss
Fitzadam, J.
Florian
Fletcher, Phineas
Fletcher, Giles
Fraser, Robert
Ferrier, Miss

Gregory, Dr.
Goldsmith, Oliver
Gay, John
Gillespie, Rev. W.
Good, J. M.
Grant, Edward
Grant, Mrs
Gilfillan, R.
Grinfield, J.

Heber, Bishop
Hauff, Wilhelm
Hood, Thomas
Hemans, Mrs.
Hervey, J. K.
Hart, J.
Hogg, James
Herrick, Robert
Howitt, William
Huie, Dr
Hodson, W.
Howitt, Mary
Hall, S. C.
Hamilton, R.
Hallet, George

Irving, Washington
Imlah, John
Johnson, Dr. Samuel
Jonson, Ben
Jenyns, Soame
Jewsbury, Miss
Johnson, Miles
Jeffreys, C.

Keats, John
Knowles, J. Sheridan
Kappa, J.
Keble, C.

Landon, Miss E L.
Lyle, Thomas
Lovelace, Richard
Lyndsay, Lady Anne
Laidlaw, William

Moore, Thomas
Montgomery, James
Malcolm, John
Montgomery, Robert
Mitford, Miss
Milman, Dr.
Milton, John
Mason, William
Moir, D. M.
Macaulay, T. B.
Muller, F.
Marriot, A.
Marsden, John
Macneil, Hector
Monk Lewis
May, John
Mackay, Charles

Norton, Hon. Mrs.
Neele, Henry
Nicholas, T. G.
Noel, Rt. Hon. B.

Praed, William Macworth
Percival, J. K.
Pembroke, Earl of
Peterborough, Earl of
Prior, Matthew
Pierpont, Rev. John
Peabody
Plauché, J. R.
Pollok
Paul, W.
Percy
Pinckney, Edward Coate
Redding, Cyrus
Rogers, Samuel
Rochester, Lord
Randolph, Thomas
Roscoe, William
Raffles, Rev. T.
Richardson, C. H.
Read, William
Ramsay, Allan
Riddle, Rev. H. S.

Scribe, Eugene
Smith, Horace
Shakspeare, William
Spenser
Swain, Charles
Southey, Robert
Shelley, P. B.
Scott, Sir Walter
Suckling, Sir John
Stanley, Thomas
Somerville, William
Sedley, Sir Charles
Shenstone, William
Southwell, William
Sigourney, Mrs.
Stewart, Mrs Dovale
Spittall, Dr

Taylor, Emily
Tennyson, Alfred
Tannahill, Robert
Townsend, H.
Thomson, James
Taylor, Miss Jane
Toplady
Thomson, C. W.
Tucker, D.
Thorn, William

Walker, Mrs.
Wordsworth, William
White, Henry Kirk
Wilson, Mrs. C. B.
Watts, Dr A. A.
Waller, Edmund
Wolfe, Rev. Charles
Wastell, D.
Wilson, Professor
Walton, C.
Willard, Mrs.
Wesley, Rev. ohn
Walker, John
Wilson, Alexander
Wilson, W

CONTENTS.

CONTENTS.

CONTENTS.

CONTENTS.

THE MIRROR LIBRARY.

JUDITH, OR THE OPERA BOX,

BY EUGENE SCRIBE.

One evening—if I remember rightly, it was at the end of 1831—there was a great crowd at the Opera, for Taglioni was to dance. The spectators had crowded themselves on the steps of the orchestra, and the extra stools furnished for the friends of the conductor formed a sort of barricade which I found it difficult to surmount, amidst cries of "Hush, hush! silence, silence!" from the enthusiastic amateurs whom I disturbed. For when Taglioni dances, one not only gazes but listens. It seems as if the eye were not sufficient to admire with. I found myself in an awkward position, forced to stand amidst a group of my friends whom I met there by appointment, and who were too much crowded to make room for me, when a young man rose and offered me his seat, which I declined, not wishing to deprive him of the pleasure of the spectacle.

"It is no deprivation," he said—"I am going out."

I accepted his offer with thanks; and my obliging neighbour cast a last look at the stage before taking his departure, stopped an instant, and leaning his back against the box of General Claparede, seemed to look for some one in the distance, and then, sinking gradually into a profound revery, thought no more of retiring.

He was right in saying I did not deprive him of the view; for, turning his back to the stage—seeing nothing—hearing nothing—he appeared entirely to forget where he was. I examined him attentively. It was impossible to imagine a face more handsome or expressive. Dressed simply and elegantly, there was something noble and distinguished in all his movements. He seemed about five-and-twenty. His fine black eyes were fixed incessantly on a front box of the second tier with an indefinable expression of melancholy and despair. Involuntarily I turned in that direction, and I saw that the box was empty.

"He expects somebody who has not come," I said.—"She has deceived him—she is ill—or her father has prevented her, and he loves and expects in vain. Poor young man!" And I watched as attentively as he. I pitied him, and would have given the world to see the door of the box opened; but it remained closed.

The ballette was about to end; and while the inferior dancers were performing, conversation as usual proceeded almost aloud. Among other things, we talked of *Robert le Diable*, which was then in rehearsal, and was about to appear in a few days. My friends made all sorts of inquiries—about the music—the ballettes—the situations, etc., and begged very earnestly to attend the last rehearsals. A rehearsal seems so strange and wonderful to those unaccustomed to it! I promised to introduce them, and we all rose up to go away, for the curtain was about to fall: and as I found myself near my unknown friend, who remained still motionless in the same place, I expressed my regret that I had accepted his offer, and my gratification if I could do any thing to oblige him in return.

"You can do so quite easily," he replied; "I have just gathered that you are M. Meyerbeer."

"I have not that honour—"

"At any rate, you are one of the authors of *Robert le Diable?*"

"After a sort," I said; "I wrote the words."

"Well, then," he rejoined, "let me be present at the rehearsal to-morrow."

"We are so little prepared as yet, that I can only venture to ask my friends."

"That is one reason more for my repeating the request."

"And," I said, "I am delighted you have repeated it on those terms."

He shook my hand, and the hour was fixed for the following day.

He was exact to his appointment. We walked for a few minutes about the stage before the rehearsal commenced. He spoke gravely, yet pleasantly and cleverly; but it was easy to perceive that it needed an effort to keep up the conversation, and that he was pre-occupied with other thoughts. Our goddesses of the dance and of the song began to arrive one after another. Several times I perceived him tremble, and once his agitation was so great that he had to support himself on the side scenes. I began to suspect he was a rejected lover of one of our Clios or Terpsichores—a suspicion which his extreme handsomeness and his style altogether rendered by no means probable; and in reality I was mistaken. He spoke to no one—went near no one—and no one knew who he was.

The rehearsal began. I looked for him in the orchestra among the amateurs. He was not there; and though the body of the house was somewhat dark, I thought I saw him in the front box which he had gazed on so constantly the night before. I was anxious to make sure of this, and at the end of the rehearsal, after the admirable trio of the fifth act, I ascended to the second tier. Meyerbeer, who had something to say to me, accompanied me. We arrived at the box, of which the door was half open, and saw the unknown with his head resting on his hands. At our approach, he turned quickly round and rose up. His pale face was covered with tears. Meyerbeer was overjoyed; and, without saying a word, shook his hand most kindly, as if to thank him. The unknown, trying to conceal his embarrassment, muttered some words of compliment in such a vague and unconnected manner, that he saw he had not listened to the performance, and that for two hours he had been thinking of any thing rather than the music. Meyerbeer whispered to me in despair—"The wretch has not heard a note!"

We all three descended the stairs; and crossing the large beautiful court which leads to the Rue Grange Bataliere, the unknown bowed to M. Sausseret, who at that time had the letting of the seats.

I went to M. Sausseret. "You know that handsome young fellow who has just left me?"

"M. Arthur—Rue du Helder—No. 9. I know nothing more. He has engaged a box on the second tier for this winter."

"He was there this moment," I said.

"Then he seems to use it in the morning only, for he never goes near it at night. The box is always empty."

And in fact, the whole week the door was never opened. The box remained deserted.

The first appearance of *Robert* was now near, and on such occasions a poor devil of an author is overwhelmed with applications for boxes and tickets. You may imagine what time he has to attend to his play, and the changes and curtailments that may be required. He has to answer letters and claims that pour in upon him from all quarters, and it is invariably the ladies who are most exacting on such nights. "You were to have got me two boxes, and I have only got one." "You promised me No. 10, next to the General's, and they have sent me No. 15, next to Madame D———, whom I detest, and who casts me into the shade with her diamonds." A first night is a time when you get into scrapes with your best friends, who, perhaps, overlook it in a few days if your piece "takes," but who nurse their indignation a long time if you are damned; so that you are punished both by them and the public at the same time. Misfortunes never come alone. Well, then, on the morning of the first night of *Robert,* I had promised a box to some ladies; but the manager took it away from me to give it to—a journalist. I complained. He replied, "'Tis for a journalist. You understand? A journalist who hates you, but who has promised—thanks to my politeness in giving him your box—to speak favourably of the music."

It was impossible to resist an argument like this, and the box was given up. But where was I to bestow my fair friends, whose wrath was a much more serious matter to me than that of the journalist? I luckily remembered my unknown acquaintance, and went to his residence. His room was very simple and unostentatious, particularly for a man who had a box at the Opera.

"My dear sir," I said, "I come to ask you a great favour."

"Say on."

"Do you intend to be present at the first representation of *Robert le Diable?* In your box, I mean."

He appeared embarrassed, and replied with some hesitation, "I should be very happy—but—it is impossible."

"Have you disposed of it?"

"No."

"Will you give it up to me? You will get me out of an awkward predicament."

His trouble seemed to increase every moment. He *could* not refuse me; and at last, as if making a great effort to command himself, he said, "I agree, but upon one condition—that you put nobody into that box but *men.*"

"Impossible, my dear sir, I ask it expressly to accommodate some ladies."

He was silent for a while. "And among those ladies," he said, "is there any one you love?"

"Undoubtedly," I replied.

"Then take the box," he said, "for I leave Paris today."

I made a motion expressive of interest and curiosity, and he seemed to divine my thoughts; for he took me by the hand, and said, "You no doubt perceive that certain fond and sad remembrances attach themselves to that box. I can communicate them to no one. Of what use is it to complain when one is miserable and hopeless, and when it is all by his own fault?"

That night the first representation of *Robert* took place, and my friend Meyerbeer achieved a triumph which resounded all through Europe. Since that time, many other events, literary and political—many other successes and many failures have occurred. I saw no more of M. Arthur—I thought of him no more. I had forgotten him.

A night or two ago, I found myself once more in the orchestra, at the right side of the Opera. It was not to see *Robert*—it was to see the *Huguenots.* Five years had passed away.

"You come late," said one of my friends, a professor of civil law, who has as much "esprit" at night as erudition in the morning.

"And you are very wrong in so doing," added a little man dressed in black, with a sharp voice and a powdered head, as he tapped me on the shoulder. I turned round, and saw M. Baraton, the notary of my family.

"You here!" I cried—"and your office—"

"Sold it three months ago—I am rich—I am a widower—I am sixty years old—I have been twenty years married, and thirty years a notary—I think I am entitled to a little enjoyment."

"And he has now been a subscriber to the Opera for eight days," said the professor of civil law.

"Ay, to be sure; I like to laugh; I like comedy, and so I have bought an admission here."

"And why not at the Fran ais?"

"Oh! not half so amusing as here—one sees and hears the most extraordinary things in the world. These gentlemen know every thing—there is not a box of which they do not know the history."

"Indeed!" I cried, and mechanically turned towards the box on the second tier, which had so excited my curiosity some years before. What was my amazement! That night it was empty as before; and the only empty one in the whole house!

I was delighted to have a history to tell, and in a few words related all that I have now told you. I was listened to with attention: my friends were lost in conjecture—the professor tried to recall some ancient recollections—the little notary smiled most maliciously.

"Well, gentlemen," I said to them, "which of you (who know every thing) can unriddle this enigma for us; who can tell us the story of that mysterious box?"

They were all silent, even the professor, who passed his hand over his brow as if to refresh his recollection of some anecdote, and would probably have finished by inventing one appropriate to the occasion, if the notary had given him time.

"Who will tell you that story?" he exclaimed, with an air of triumph, "who but I?—I know the whole particulars."

"You, M. Baraton?"

"To be sure."

"Go on, then—go on,"—and we all drew near to listen.

"Go on, M. Baraton."

"Well, then," said the little notary, with an important look, and taking a pinch of snuff, "which of you was acquainted with—"

But at that moment the first crash of the overture began—and M. Baraton, who piqued himself on not losing a single note, stopped immediately, and said—"After the first act, gentlemen."

"Gentlemen," said the notary, when the first act of the *Huguenots* was finished, "Queen Marguerite has to be dressed with all her maids of honour—the castle and gardens of Chenonceaux have to be got ready; and the interval will be long enough, I think, to enable me to tell you the story you wish to hear." And after a placid pinch of snuff, which gave him time to collect his thoughts, M. Baraton commenced in these words:—

"Which of you, gentlemen, was acquainted with the little Judith?"

We all looked at each other, and the oldest frequenter of the orchestra was puzzled.

"The little Judith," he went on, "who some seven or eight years ago was brought out as a figurante in the ballette?"

"Stay," said the professor of civil law, with somewhat of a pedantic air, "a little blonde who was one of the pages in the Muette?"

"She was dark," said the notary: "as to the part yo.

attribute to her, I have no positive document on the subject, and prefer relying on your immense erudition."

The professor bowed.

"But, whether dark or fair, there was one thing that nobody disputed, and that was, that the little Judith was a charming creature. And another point, which appeared undeniable, was, that her aunt, Madame Bonnivet, was portress in the Rue Richelieu, in the house of an old gentleman, whose confidential manager she had once been; some said his cook: but Madame Bonnivet disdained the impeachment, and went on, quietly plying her knitting-needles, and managing for the different lodgers, while her niece even already began making conquests. For it was impossible to pass the porter's lodge without being struck with the extraordinary beauty of little Judith, who was scarcely twelve years old. Her eyes even then were the finest in the world; her teeth like pearls; her form exquisitely graceful; and in whatever dress she wore, she had the most *distingué* air imaginable; and, to crown all, an expressive, clear, and open countenance, with something radiant and coquettish in its very innocence. In short, she gave promise of one of those glorious combinations of grace and beauty, enough to turn people's heads, and, as a poet would say, to change the fate of empires.

People paid Madame Bonnivet so many compliments every day on the loveliness of her niece, that she determined to make considerable sacrifices for her education. She sent her, therefore, to a charity school, where little girls were taught to read and write—an enormous amount of instruction, the advantages of which were soon felt by Madame Bonnivet herself; who, in her capacity of portress, had found it rather difficult to make out the different addresses, and to send the letters and parcels to their respective destinations. Judith took this duty on herself, to the universal satisfaction of all concerned; and Madame Bonnivet being now persuaded that with such an education, superadded to so much beauty, her niece was sure to make a sensation in the world, she waited impatiently for an opening. It was not long before an opportunity presented itself. M. Rosambeau, the ballette-master, who rented one of the attics, offered to give little Judith some lessons; and, in a few days after, Madame Bonnivet communicated in confidence to all the ladies of her acquaintance, that her niece had been accepted as one of the *corps de ballet* of the Opera—a piece of news which of course was spread far and wide, and flew rapidly from door to door along the whole extent of the Rue Richelieu.

Here, then, was little Judith installed at the Opera, taking lessons every morning of M. Rosambeau, and coming on at night—totally unnoticed amidst the groups of young girls, naiads, or pages, as the professor justly observed a few minutes ago.

Judith was innocence itself, though belonging to the stage; for she had been brought up in a respectable house, where all the lodgers were decent Benedicks. Her aunt, who was as watchful as a dragon, never left her; accompanied her to the theatre in the morning, brought her home at night, and even remained whole days in the green-room knitting her stockings, while her niece took lessons and practised her steps. You wonder what became all this time of the large house in the Rue Richelieu. I can't exactly say; but people believe that a friend of Madame Bonnivet undertook all her duties there, in the expectation of the little Judith making a catch; for you are aware, gentlemen, that no one goes on the Opera boards unless with the hope of making a catch—gaining a settlement, or however you choose to express that great object of an actress's ambition. In this way they leave the stage—they are rich—they reform; and the good aunt—for all pretty dancers, you may have remarked, have invariably aunts of the highest respectability—marries her niece, now weaned from the vanities of tin spangles and paste diamonds, to a flourishing stockbroker, or—"

"A retired notary," added the professor.

M. Baratou shrugged his shoulders. "Of course," he said: "but at that time thoughts of such prodigious advancement had never entered into the heads of either Madame Bonnivet or her niece. Ambition grows on us by degrees."

"But Judith," I said—"what became of Judith?" for I saw the curtain about to rise.

"Judith! I'm coming to her directly. Madame Bonnivet, in spite of all her caution, could not hinder her niece from talking with her companions. In the mornings in the green-room, and, above all, at night when they were on the stage—a region where the aunt found it impossible to follow—Judith heard some things that astonished her.

One of the nymphs or sylphides, her companions, whispered in her ear—"See, Judith, look in the orchestra—at the right—how hard he is looking at me."

"Who?" said Judith.

"That handsome young man with the cashmere vest don't you see him?"

"What does it all mean?"

"I've struck him."

"Struck him?" said Judith, astonished.

"Ha, ha!" said the nymph, "what a simpleton you are! Girls, here's a curiosity—she has never had an admirer!"

"All her aunt's fault," said another of the sylphs.

"Indeed! Well, if I had an aunt so ridiculous, I would—"

"Hush, hush; you know nothing about it," replied the other, who seemed a few years older; "she perhaps has serious intentions about little Judith, and, to keep her from the dangers of love, is going to give her to a protector."

"She!" rejoined the other, "she hasn't wit enough to get her one. Such good fortune would be too much to expect."

Judith did not lose a syllable, but had not courage to ask anybody for an explanation. But she understood enough to see she was looked down upon, and she naturally had an intense desire to avenge herself, to humble her companions, and fill them with rage and envy. Accordingly, when Madame Bonnivet informed her on their return, with a solemn face, that she would introduce her to a protector—a noble and rich protector—her first sensation was one of joyful surprise; and her aunt, who had not expected such a reception for her news, proceeded in rapture.

"Yes, my darling niece, an admirable person in all respects—a person who will secure your happiness, and a provision for your aunt; and indeed he can't do less, after all the trouble and expense your education has cost me."

Here the good aunt wiped away a few tears; and Judith, who was moved at the appearance of so much tenderness, only ventured to ask who was the protector, and how she had deserved such generosity.

"You shall know in good time," replied the aunt; "but in the meanwhile your companions will die with spite."

This was the very thing Judith wanted; and great indeed was the surprise when the intelligence became known in the green-room.

"Is it possible? a creature like that! a figurante—a chorus-girl, and I a first dancer—'tis disgusting!"

"Quite right!" said the others: "she is so good; she deserves her good luck, she is so sweet and pretty" And, in short, if it had been a marriage to a duke, they could not have made more exclamations, or envied her advancement more sincerely. And there could no longer be any doubt upon the subject, when her aunt appeared that evening in a magnificent shawl of Ternaux. But who could this protector be?—some rich old curmudgeon—some gouty old bachelor, or worn-out old *roué?* But to all these questions Judith maintained a prudent reserve; one great reason of which probably was, that she did not know a syllable about the matter.

In a few days she had quitted the porter's lodge to live with her aunt in a charming suite of rooms in the Rue de Provence—a bed-room furnished splendidly, and a boudoir so tasteful, so elegantly fitted up, that the aunt never ventured to approach it; she preferred sitting in the dining-parlour, or indeed in the kitchen; she felt so much more at her ease there than elsewhere. But day after day passed on, and nobody appeared, which struck Judith as something rather strange; for Judith was without education, but not without sense. Her candour and *naïveté* proceeded from innocence, not from stupidity; and after thinking over her position for some time, she would have given the world for somebody to consult—for some one to defend her against this protector whom she did not know, and whom she feared and hated. It is true, the only idea she had formed of him was of an ugly old man; for her companions had prepared her for nothing else by their conversations. She accordingly trembled, and had almost f[illegible]d with agitation, when, on the fifth day, her aunt threw open the door and announced the expected visitor.

Judith would have risen to receive him with proper respect, but her limbs shook, and she sank back again upon the sofa. When at length she raised her eyes, she saw standing before her a handsome young man of twenty-two or twenty-three years old, of a noble and elegant appearance, who looked at her with a kind and benevolent expression. In one instant she felt she was safe. A person who looked at her with so soft a smile would be her defender from all evil, and from him she would have nothing to fear.

"Mademoiselle," he said, in a calm and respectful tone; but perceiving that Madame Bonnivet was still in the room, he made her a sign, and she immediately remembered she had orders to give about the dinner—"Mademoiselle, you are here at home; I hope you will be happy; but pardon me if I have the honour of seeing you but seldom—other engagements will prevent me the pleasure. I therefore lay claim to but one title—that of your friend; to but one privilege—that of satisfying your slightest wish."

Judith did not reply; but the beating of her heart lifted up the light muslin of her pelerin.

"As to your aunt," and this he said with a scarcely perceptible tone of contempt, "she will hereafter be at your command; for I wish that you should give your commands to every one here, commencing with myself."

He then went near her, and took her hand, which he lifted to his lips, and seeing that the hand still trembled—"Have I alarmed you?" he said; "be assured that I shall never repeat my visit except when you desire it—adieu, Judith!"

And he went away, leaving the poor girl in a state of emotion which she could not comprehend. All day long she thought of nothing but the handsome stranger with his beautiful black eyes. She had not ventured to look at him, and yet nothing he had done, not a movement had escaped her. She was uneasy, and lost her spirits; her complexion grew pale, and her aunt smiled.

When the stranger was spoken of, she blushed the deepest scarlet, and her aunt smiled again.

But he returned no more, and she could not ask him to return. What had she to complain of?—apartments beautifully furnished—servants and carriage at her command—she had not a want in the world!

On the other hand, her companions in the theatre, seeing her so brilliantly dressed, and so radiant in beauty, overwhelmed her with questions. But those very questions made her have suspicions that there was something unusual in the whole transaction—that she was treated with a sort of disdain; and she avoided the conversation as much as she could, and never told her aunt even how very respectfully she had been addressed. One night when the house was crowded, she perceived the stranger in the royal box looking at her. She nearly screamed with joy, and made a dancer miss the proper time, who was just then whirling a pirouette.

"What's the matter?" said Nathalie, one of her friends who held the other end of a garland.

"'Tis he! there he is!"

"Is it possible! Count Arthur de V———, one of the young nobles of the court of Charles X., and moreover the handsomest of them all! You have nothing to complain of with such a friend to see you every day."

Judith made no reply. She was too happy. Arthur, to the great scandal of all who saw it, bowed to her from the king's box; and, better still, when the ballette was finished, just when she was about to ascend to her dressing-room, Arthur came to the side scenes, and said quite audibly, so as to be heard by the lord chamberlain, who had the direction of the opera—"Will you allow me the honour of conducting you home?"

"'Tis too much honour for me," stammered Judith, without perceiving what a laugh her answer excited.

"Make haste, then. I will wait for you on the stage."

She lost no time, you may be sure, in changing her dress; and, on returning, she found Arthur in conversation with a group of fashionables, and with M. Lubert, the manager, to whom he recommended Judith very warmly, and then gave her his arm before them all, and conducted her down the performers' staircase. At the door his carriage was ready to receive them; they got in, and, as it was cold, he pulled up the glass, and put her shawl over her shoulders. How beautiful she was—so glad—so gratified; but the gladness did not last long. The distance is so short between the Rue Grange Batelière and the Rue de Provence, and the horses went so fast! The carriage stopped; Arthur got out and offered his hand to Judith. They went up stairs together, and arrived at the door of her apartments. He rang the bell respectfully took his leave, and disappeared.

Judith could not sleep. The conduct of the count appeared so rude. He might at least have entered her room, and sat down for a moment. She knew very little, to be sure, of the manners of high society; but she thought that would have been more polite than to leave her so suddenly at the door. She was feverish and disturbed; and at daybreak got out of bed, and went to the window to get cool. There, before her door, still stood the carriage with the fast gray horses; they pawed the ground with cold and impatience; the coachman was asleep on his box.

"Excuse me, gentlemen," said the notary, when he had reached this part of his story; "the next act is just beginning, and I don't wish to lose a word of the opera—when the curtain falls—"

The next morning, and the next again, Judith opened her window at daybreak. The count's carriage was always at the door! It was evident that he sent it in the same manner almost every night, and she could not imagine the reason of such a proceeding; and, as to asking him for an explanation, she could not have ventured on such presumption for the world. And, besides, she hardly ever saw him, except on opera nights in a box on the second tier, which he had taken for the season. He never came upon the stage; he never again offered to conduct her home. What, then, was to be done?

Luckily for her, her companions did him an injustice, and accused him of treating her ill. She was delighted, for she had now an excuse for writing to him; and accordingly she indited an epistle, beseeching him to come to her apartments. It was by no means an easy task to write a letter; so it took poor Judith the whole day. She began it over again, and made fifty foul copies before she achieved one to her mind. One of these must have dropped out of her bag; for, in the evening, she heard the young authors and others who were free of the orchestra, laughing immoderately at an ill-spelt, ill-written note, as they handed it about from one to the other. She was forced to hear their explosions of merriment, their satirical remarks, and the resolution they came to, to insert the unsigned note (the author of which was luckily unknown) in one of the newspapers, as a model for the De Sevignes of the ballette. What were the terror and agony of Judith, *not* at hearing her letter turned into ridicule, but to think that the count would have the same feelings of contempt when he read the unfortunate note, which she would have purchased back again with her life. She was accordingly more dead than alive, when on the following morning Arthur entered her room.

"I am come, dear Judith—I lost no time when I received your letter;" and that fatal, that horrible letter he held in his hand—"What is it you require?"

"What I require—Monsieur le Comte? I don't know how to tell it you—but that letter—itself—since you have read it—if indeed you have been able to make it out—"

"Very easily, my dear girl," replied the count with a slight smile.

"Ah!" cried Judith, in despair. "that letter is enough

to show you that I am a poor girl without talent, without education, who is ashamed of her ignorance and wishes to remove it. But how am I to do it? If you do not come to my assistance—if you refuse to help me with your advice—with your support—"

"What is it you wish?"

"Give me masters, and you will see if I am not industrious, if I do not profit by their lessons."

"But when can they come to you?"

"Any time—one thought keeps me anxious by day and sleepless at night."

"What thought?"

"The thought of the opinion you must have of me. You must despise me, and look on me as unworthy of your notice; and you are right," she continued, hurriedly. "I know how contemptible I am—I know myself—and I wish, if possible, to have no cause to blush for myself or to be a disgrace to you."

The count looked at her with amazement, and said—"I shall do as you require; you shall have any masters you want."

Next day Judith had a master to teach her writing, and history, and geography. You should have seen the ardour she studied with; and her natural abilities developed themselves with incredible rapidity. At first she liked it for Arthur's sake, and then she liked it for its own. It was her pleasantest enjoyment, her consolation under all her anxieties. She submitted to the fines for absence, to stay at home and devote herself to her books all day. Her companion said, "Judith has gone mad—she will lose her engagement—she is very foolish."

But Judith worked the harder, saying, "I shall make myself worthy of him at last; he will see what efforts I make to improve myself." But, alas! he could see nothing of the kind; for whenever he came Judith was so agitated, and stammered and hesitated so much, and became so confused, that he thought all the lessons were thrown away upon her. The effect of the knowledge she had acquired was to make her feel more bitterly how stupid and ridiculous he must think her; and that conviction rendered her still more constrained and embarrassed, and hindered the display of her real sentiments, so innocent and so tender: and Arthur, as might be expected, came but seldom. Sometimes he remained a short time with her after the ballette; but when twelve o'clock sounded, he always took his leave. She ventured to ask him—"When shall I see you?"

"I will tell you at the opera, to-morrow."

But how was this to be done? He was almost always in his box on the second tier; and when he intended to visit her on the following morning, he lifted his right hand to his ear, and that was as much as to say, I will come to the Rue de Provence.

And Judith would watch for him all the day—she admitted nobody—not even her aunt, that she might have the pleasure of seeing him entirely to herself.

In spite of the reserve of the count, she had made one discovery, and that was, that he had some sorrow that weighed him down. What could the sorrow be? She could not bring herself to ask him, and yet she would have been so delighted to have been able to share it with him. But that was a happiness she did not dare to hope for—and yet she shared it, though she did not know what it was. So, when the count asked her, as he often did, "What is the matter, Judith?—have you any grief to vex you?"—if she had dared, she would have answered, "Yours!"

One day a horrible idea occurred to her: She muttered to herself, in despair—"He loves another—yes! yes! he loves another! Why does he bring me here?—what can be his object? It is from no love to me; because, if he loved me—" Judith fixed her eyes on a large mirror, and she certainly looked so young, so blooming, so beautiful, no wonder she remained sunk in a revery. The door of her boudoir was opened quickly; Arthur walked in—he had an air of trouble and chagrin, such as she had never seen before.

"Judith," he said, "dress yourself immediately. You shall go with me to the Tuileries."

"Is it possible?"

"Yes. The weather is delightful; all Paris will be there."

"And will you take me there?" cried Judith, enraptured; for the count had never walked out with her, or given her his arm in public.

"To be sure. I will take you there before the whole world!—in the great avenue," said the count hurriedly, walking about the room—"come along, Madame Bonnivet," he added, quickly, to the old aunt, who at that moment came in; "dress your niece as splendidly as you can; and, above every thing, be quick!"

Madame Bonnivet made preparations for taking off the morning dress that Judith wore; but she blushed, and made a sign that Arthur was still in the room.

"Tush, tush!" said the aunt, "are we to be on such ceremony with monsieur the count!" and without any more ado she unlaced the gown, and it tumbled on the floor.

Judith did not know where to look, or what to do, and was quite oppressed with shame.

But, alas! her modesty was altogether useless on this occasion. Arthur never looked near her. Absorbed by one idea that seemed to excite his rage and indignation, he traversed the apartment with great rapidity, and in one of his turns threw down a little vase made of shells, which broke in a thousand pieces.

"Oh, what a pity!" exclaimed Judith, forgetting at that moment the state of her toilet.

"Yes, indeed," echoed the aunt—"it cost five hundred francs, at the least."

"Not for that!—not for that!" said Judith—"but because it came from *him*——"

"Well, are you ready?" cried Arthur, impatiently, who had not heard a word of their reflections on the vase.

"In one moment—aunt, my shawl; now, my gloves."

"And your mantle," said Arthur; "you have forgotten it, and you will find it cold."

"Oh, no!"

"Your hand is burning," said Madame Bonnivet; "you are feverish, my child; I don't think you ought to go."

"I am well—quite well," said Judith, hurrying on—"let us go—let us go; I would not stay at home for all the world."

The carriage was at the door. They got in, and drove down the Boulevards—at noon-day—together! And, to complete the happiness of the elated Judith, she saw two of her companions in the Rue de la Paix, and bowed to them with the gracious condescension which extreme happiness produces—two principal performers, who on that occasion were trudging humbly on foot.

The carriage stopped at the gate of the Rue de Rivoli. Judith took the count's arm, and they promenaded in the principal allée. It was a fête day. All the rank and fashion of Paris had assembled; the crowd was immense.

In a moment Arthur and his companion were the objects of universal observation. They were both so handsome, it was impossible to avoid remarking them. Every one turned round to look at them, and ask who they were.

"'Tis the young Count Arthur de V."

"Are they married?"

Judith trembled at the question with a sensation of pleasure—and of pain at the same time—that she could not account for.

"No, indeed," said a grand-looking lady, in a disdainful tone—while she caressed a little spaniel in her arms, and was attended by two footmen in superb liveries—"Monsieur the count is not married; my lord, his uncle, wo'n't hear of it."

"Then who is that beautiful creature with him? His sister, perhaps?"

"O, you wrong him, I assure you. She is his mistress—an opera girl. At least, I think I have heard so."

Luckily, Judith did not hear the old dowager's remarks; for at that moment the Baron de Blangi, who walked behind them, said to his brother the Chevalier—"'Tis little Judith."

"What! the girl Arthur is so fond of?"

"He has gone mad about her—he ruins himself."

"He is quite right," replied the chevalier. "Who would not do the same? How beautiful she is!"

"Take care; you'll fall in love with her."

"I'm that already. Come, and let us see her close."

"If the crowd will let us."

And the crowd that kept following her went on making remarks of the same kind, and Arthur heard them. For the first time he looked at Judith as she deserved to be looked at, and was astonished to find her so beautiful.—The walk, the company, and above all, the consciousness of being admired, had given her cheeks and eyes an unusual glow; and then she was sixteen years old, and loved, and fancied, for the first time, that she was loved in return; and these are admirable reasons for looking one's best. The sensation created by her appearance was immense; but when she saw the look of admiration that Arthur fixed on her, all her triumph sank into insignificance, the praises of the crowd were forgotten, and she went home that day exclaiming—"What a happy girl I am!"

Next morning, Judith received two letters. The first was a *carte blanche* from the Baron de Blangi. She threw it into the fire, and forgot it in a moment.

The second bore a signature which Judith read over twice, as she could hardly believe her eyes; but she could not doubt the reality. It was signed "The Bishop of ——," and was in these terms:

"Mademoiselle,—You appeared publicly yesterday at the Tuileries with my nephew, Count Arthur de V——, and by so doing, put the finishing stroke to a scandal, the consequences of which are incalculable. Although, in punishment for the sins of men, God has permitted our ancient powers to be diminished, we have still enough left to enable us to punish your audacity. I therefore give you notice that if you do not put a stop to any similar scandal, I have sufficient credit with the Lord Chamberlain to have you dismissed from the Opera. If, on the other hand, you give up my nephew at once and forever, we offer you (for the motive will sanctify the means) two thousand louis, and the absolution of all your sins," etc., etc., etc.

Judith was at first annihilated on perusing that dreadful letter; but she soon took courage, and collecting all her energies, replied in the following words:

"My Lord,—You use me harshly, and yet I can declare before God and to you, that I have nothing for which to reproach myself. 'Tis so, I declare most solemnly: and yet, my lord, in this there is no merit attributable to me. I owe it entirely to him who has spared and respected me. Yes, my lord, your nephew is innocent of the wrongs you impute to him; and if to love be criminal in the sight of heaven, it is a crime of which I am guilty, and in which Arthur is not an accomplice.

"Hear, then, the resolution I have taken.

"I shall say to him—what I have never ventured to say to him for myself—but for you, my lord, I will take courage and say to him, 'Arthur, do you love me?'—And if—as I believe, as I fear—he shall answer, 'No, Judith, I do not love you,' then, my lord, I shall obey you. I shall separate myself from him—I shall never see him more: and I hope, my lord, you will think of me too highly to offer me any thing as a reward, and that you will not add degradation to despair. The latter is sufficient for one who resolves to die. But if heaven, if my good angel, if the happiness of my life shall lead him to say, 'I love you, Judith,'—ah! 'tis a sinful thing I am about to say to you, and you will most justly pour your maledictions on my head; but mark me, my lord, there is no power on earth that shall hinder me from being his—from sacrificing every thing to him. I will brave all, even your indignation; for, after all, what can you do? At most, you can take my life; and why should I hesitate to die if I could only feel assured I have been beloved?

"Pardon me, my lord, if this letter should offend you. It is written by a poor girl who is ignorant of the world and of her duty; but who hopes to find some mitigation of your anger in consideration of that ignorance—the openness of her confession—and, above all, in the profound respect with which she has the honour to remain," etc., etc., etc.

Judith sealed the letter, and sent it without consulting with any one upon the subject; and from that moment, being determined to know her fate, she waited impatiently for the next visit of the count. She saw him in his box, but he seemed sombre and pre-occupied. He made no sign to her—he never looked near her. At last, on the following night, he made the usual signal, and Judith now felt certain that she should see him in the morning, and put an end to the state of suspense and misery, which she felt was more intolerable than the worst that could befall her.

But in the morning, the chasseur of the count made his appearance with an apology from his master on the plea of business of the most urgent importance, and with an intimation, at the same time, that he would come that night to supper. To supper! he who had always taken his leave so early! The aunt seemed wonderfully pleased with the arrangement, and Judith remained sunk in deep thought.

At eleven o'clock, the most elegant little supper that could be procured was all ready by the zeal of Madame Bonnivet. As to Judith, she saw nothing—she heard nothing—she expected. All the faculties of her soul were absorbed in that one idea. But eleven o'clock came—half past eleven—twelve—and no Arthur. The whole night elapsed; he came not, and she expected still; and the next day passed, and the following days, and yet Arthur came not. She heard nothing of him—she saw him no more. What then was the meaning of all this? What had become of him?

"Gentlemen," said the little notary, interrupting his narration, "the curtain is just rising—After the next act."

"Gentlemen," said the little notary, when the third act of the *Huguenots* was concluded, "I suppose you are anxious to make out what has happened to our friend young Arthur, and above all, to discover who he is."

"You should have begun with that," said I.

"I have a right to arrange my story as I choose"

"And besides," added the professor, "one shouldn't be very critical on the conduct of a story at the Opera: nobody attends to it."

"A very lucky thing for the authors of the words," said the little notary, with a bow to me; and satisfied with his hint, he went on with his account.

Count Arthur de V——— is descended from a very ancient and distinguished family in the south. His mother, left a widow very young, had no child besides, and was poorly provided for; but she had a brother who was immensely rich. This brother, Monseigneur the Abbe de V———, was one of the most influential prelates at the court of Louis XVIII., and afterwards at that of Charles X.; and we know very well what was the influence of the clergy at that time; an influence that governed the kingdom, the sovereign himself, and even the army. The Abbe de V——— was of a cold and haughty disposition, selfish and severe, but an excellent relation notwithstanding; for he was ambitious for himself, and for every one that belonged to him. He charged himself with his nephew's education, introduced him at court, and procured the restoration to his sister of some portion of the property that had been confiscated during the emigration. The mother died, blessing the name of her brother, and enjoining her son to be obedient in all things to his uncle. Arthur, who adored his mother, swore obedience to her injunctions when she was dying; and it was the more easy for him to perform his vow, from the circumstance that, from his earliest years, he had always been accustomed to receive his uncle's commands with the most unhesitating submission.

Sedate, quiet, and bashful, yet full of courage and generosity, Arthur had always had a strong inclination for a military life: partly for the uniform and the epaulettes, but principally, perhaps, because in the palace of his uncle he saw nothing but gowns and cassocks. He ventured one day, but with great shyness, to make his uncle acquainted with his wishes; but the prelate knit his brows, and answered, harshly and decidedly, he had other views for him.

The Abbe de V——— had been advanced to a bishopric, and he hoped for more. He had a good chance for the hat of a cardinal; and he was desirous of making his nephew share in his good fortune, and felt sure of being able to secure him the highest dignities of the church.—In short, the church was at that time the surest avenue to wealth and power. Arthur did not dare openly to resist the terrible ascendant of his uncle; but he secretly vowed that he would never be a bishop. The king, in the mean time, had been spoken to on the subject, and had expressed his warmest approbation. Arthur was to enter the seminary in a few months as a matter of form, to take orders, and go through the lower offices to the highest dignities of his new profession as rapidly as possible. He remembered the promise he had given to his mother, and, besides, everybody would have accused him of ingratitude if he ran directly counter to the wishes of his uncle; and as he therefore did not dare to oppose his designs at once, he endeavoured to find out some method of forcing the bishop to resign them of his own accord. He could think of no better means to effect his purpose than some good dashing scandal, that might render him unworthy of the venerable profession into which they tried to force him against his will. But this was not so easy a matter as might be supposed. Whether it rose from Arthur's natural disposition or from his education, he had a fund of moral feeling that prevented him from being a libertine; and Arthur took as much pains to make himself a rake as might have sufficed to make him a bishop. But he had a number of friends who introduced him to their gayeties. The racketing and sprees of his companions were insipid and disgusting; and he turned his attention to the ladies of the court, as a better means of gaining what he wished. But the ladies of that court avoided the slightest appearance of impropriety; not that they extended their dislike to any thing beyond appearance, and a glaring, unmistakeable impropriety was all that Arthur desired. A ray of light broke in upon his despair, when one of his friends said to him,

"Take an opera girl for your mistress; everybody will know it."

"What! I?" exclaimed Arthur, flushing with indignation at the first thought of such a proceeding; "I mix myself up with such a set!"

"You need have nothing to do with them. These matters are easily arranged. The *éclat* of a mistress is all you require. Take one: you may do as you like afterwards, but your point will be gained at once."

"Well, I consent."

You know already how the matter was arranged between Arthur and the aunt. Measures were taken to have the bishop informed of the scandal. He took no notice. He was told that every night his nephew's carriage was stationed in the Rue de Provence; and Arthur hoped every day for a blow-up with his benefactor, when he had resolved to throw all the blame on an uncontrollable passion which rendered him unworthy of the sacred office, and he could by no means account for his uncle's *sang froid* and placid forbearance. It was the calm that precedes the storm.

One morning, his lordship said to him, "The king has been displeased with you for some time. I know not wherefore."

"I guess the reason," replied the nephew.

"I have no wish to know it, sir. His majesty has deigned to overlook it, but insists on your entering the seminary in two days."

"I! uncle? Imp——"

"They are the king's orders; and your objections must be made to him, not to me," said the prelate haughtily, and turned away.

Arthur, almost out of his senses with rage, hurried off to Judith—took her to the Tuileries—paraded her as his mistress before all the world, on the very evening before he was to start for the seminary. This time it was impossible to pretend ignorance of so very glaring a scandal, or to think of forcing the hero of it into the church—at any rate for a long time. The bishop wrote the letter I have repeated to you to Judith, and the king sent an order to the count to leave Paris within twenty-four hours. It was impossible to disobey. Luckily, he was acquainted with one of the sons of M. de Bourmont, and went off on the following night with the expedition to Algiers.

"Since the choice of the place of my exile," he said, "is left to me, I shall choose one where glory is to be gained."

He went off at night with the utmost secrecy, for as his motions were watched; and if they had suspected his destination, he was afraid they would have hindered his departure. He wrote a few lines to Judith, to tell her he was only to be absent a few days; but that note, insignificant as it was, was intercepted, and never reached her. The bishop had great interest with the police. A week afterwards, Arthur was at sea. On the twentieth day he disembarked in Africa, was one of the first at the storming of the fort, and was wounded at the side of his gallant friend, young Bourmont, who was killed at the moment of victory. Arthur was for a long time in danger. For two months his life was despaired of; and when he recovered, his fortune, his hopes, and those of his uncle, had all disappeared, in three days, with the monarchy of Charles X.

The bishop could not bear up against such a disaster. Ill, and suffering in mind and body, he was unable to follow the exiled court as he desired. Disappointment and vexation inflamed his blood. A dangerous fever was produced by all these miseries, and not knowing what to do in the state of irritation into which he had worked himself, he revenged himself for the revolution of July on his unfortunate nephew. Arthur, still weak from his wounds, arrived in Paris; and it is here that I became connected with the story, (said the notary, somewhat elevating his voice.) The count came to me about the succession. I had long been his notary, and that of his family. We proceeded first to break the seals. I will not trouble you with professional details; but in taking an inventory of all the papers deposited in his lordship's escritoire, a letter struck my eye with the signature, "Judith, danseuse à l'Opera." The letter of an opera dancer in the desk of a bishop! I would have destroyed it out of respect to the church; but Arthur had already got hold of it, and from the emotion it produced, I fancied for a moment—heaven forgive me for the thought!—that the uncle and nephew had been rivals unknown to each other.

"Poor girl, poor girl!" exclaimed Arthur, "what nobleness! what generosity! what a treasure I possessed! There, there!" he said to me, "read that;" and when I came to the sentence—"If to love be criminal in the sight of heaven, it is a crime of which I am guilty, and in which Arthur is not an accomplice——"

"'Tis true!" exclaimed Arthur, who had tears glistening in his eyes—"She loved me with all her soul, and I never perceived it, and never thought of loving *her*—and she was sixteen years old! and pure and beautiful!—for you have no idea, M. Baraton, how beautiful she is—the most beautiful woman in Paris."

"I have no manner of doubt of it," I replied; "but, if you please, we will go on with the inventory."

"As you please;" and he continued to read fragments of the letter aloud. "If heaven, if my good angel, if the happiness of my life shall lead him to say, I love you Judith—ah! 'tis a sinful thing I am about to say to you and you will most justly pour your maledictions on my head; but mark me, my lord, there is no power on earth that shall hinder me from being his—from sacrificing every thing to him."

"And I misunderstood her! I rejected a love like this! I only was to blame: but I will repair my fault—I will sacrifice my life to her—I will own her before the world; I shall be proud of her, and introduce her to my friends—to you yourself, M. Baraton—who don't listen to a syllable I am saying, but keep poring over those musty papers!"

Papers, indeed! It was his uncle's will I had discovered, which disinherited him, and disposed of his enormous fortune among hospitals and other charitable foundations. I told Arthur the contents—but he did not show the least disappointment, and began to read Judith's letter again and again.

"You shall see her, M. Baraton—you shall see my beautiful Judith—you shall dine with her this very day!"

"But these papers—this will," I said.

"Well—I have nothing more to do with them," he said, with a smile; "but Judith will love me. Adieu

M. Baraton, adieu. I shall find with her more happiness than I lose with these papers. Adieu;" and he left me, while his eyes beamed with joy and anticipation.

"Strange young man!" I said to myself—"to be consoled by a pretty face for the loss of such a succession!" and I finished the inventory.

An hour or two afterwards, I was about to go home, when Arthur rushed in like a madman.

"She is not there—she is gone—I have lost her!"

"What! she's false, then?"

"Who told you so? Unsay the word—or——" He had taken tight hold of me by the collar.

"I know nothing about it."

"So much the better," he said. "Three months ago she disappeared—she has left the opera."

"What did her companions tell you?"

"They told me nonsensical stories—some said she had been carried off—another told me, with the utmost coolness, she had resolved to destroy herself."

"Possible enough," I said. "Since the revolution of July, suicide has come greatly into fashion."

"Say it not—say it not!" cried Arthur; "you will drive me mad! I went to her apartments in the Rue de Provence, but she had left them, without saying where she was going."

"No trace?"

"The rooms are to let; they have never been occupied since."

"And you found nothing in them?"

"Nothing——except that in her aunt's room, on the ground floor, th's card, intended for some trunk, with the address, 'To Madame Bonnivet, Bordeaux'—and now that I remember, she comes from that neighbourhood."

"Well."

"Take all the management of my affairs—make what arrangement you like."

"What are you going to do?"

"Follow her traces—or rather those of her aunt."

"In your present state of health you wouldn't start for Bordeaux?"

"This hour!" He started that evening; and——But here the fourth act of the *Huguenots* began, and the notary listened in silence.

Arthur remained six months at Bordeaux, making every possible inquiry about Madame Bonnivet, but nobody could give him the slightest information. He advertised for her in the newspapers—and at last an old lady, with whom it appeared she had lodged, came and informed him that his search was now useless, for Madame Bonnivet had been dead two months.

"And her niece?" exclaimed Arthur.

"She was not with her—but the aunt lived very comfortably, and had an annuity of a hundred louis."

"Where did it come from?"

"Nobody knew."

"Did she ever speak of her niece?"

"Sometimes she mentioned her name—but instantly checked herself, as if there was some secret to be concealed."

And this was all that Arthur had been able to ascertain by the most careful inquiry. He came back in despair; for, since he had lost Judith, his attachment had grown into a passion. It was the one idea of his existence. He bitterly recalled the minutes—so few and unobserved at the time—he had passed beside her. Every look, every smile, rushed back upon his memory—he visited every spot where she had been—he never missed the opera.

He wished to occupy her apartments in the Rue de Provence; but unluckily they had been engaged by a stranger, who did not live in them. He thought at all events he would go and look at them—the porter had not the keys, and the doors and window-shutters continued firmly closed! Arthur, as you may suppose, took very little interest in his own affairs, but they gave great uneasiness to me. Disinherited by his uncle, he had nothing left but the small property of his mother—about fifteen thousand livres a year. He had squandered half of it, first in his expenses with Judith, and next in his endeavours to discover what had become of her; for he grudged nothing to attain his object. At the slightest hint, he sent out couriers all over the world, but always without success; and he kept constantly saying to me—"'Tis useless!—she is dead!" In our meetings upon business, he spoke to me of nothing but her—and I could hardly slip in a word about the state of his affairs. At last I got him persuaded to sell off every thing, and pay his debts; but it was a great sacrifice for him to part with the lands that came to him from his mother. But it was indispensable. He owed nearly two hundred thousand francs, and the interest would very soon have swallowed up the remainder of his estate. Bills, therefore, were printed; advertisements inserted in the newspapers, and, on the very evening before the sale was to take place, I received a communication from one of my legal brethren, which filled me with joy and surprise. Fate seemed at last to have grown tired of persecuting poor Arthur.

A certain M. de Corval, a man of very indifferent character, who had owed his mother a very considerable sum, now desired to pay it, with full interest from the time it had become due—making in all the sum of a hundred thousand crowns; and the notary he employed brought me the full amount in gold and bank-notes. I rushed off to tell the good news to Arthur, but he seemed neither glad nor sorry. As long as Judith was not talked of, every thing else was indifferent to him. As for me, I lost no time in giving a receipt, paying off our creditors, and every thing went on swimmingly, with the exception of one very curious incident.

One day Arthur met M. de Corval, who had behaved so honourably, and thanked him in the kindest terms. At the very moment when that gentleman had begun to excuse himself, on the plea of some recent losses, for being still unable to pay what he owed——

"But you paid me last month a hundred thousand crowns."

"I!"

"I have no further claim on you—you owe me nothing."

"'Tis impossible!"

"Ask my notary."

The debtor—who was such no longer—hurried to me, and could not conceal his amazement.

"You are a lucky man," I said.

"M. Arthur still more so," he replied, very testily—"for I had made up my mind, as I could not possibly pay, it was exactly the same as if I did not owe; and this business does not make me a farthing richer; but the case is very different with him—he may think himself exceedingly fortunate."

"What!—then," I said, "you really don't know where the money came from?"

"I have no notion," replied M. de Corval; "but if the same party should offer to pay off any more of my debts, I hope you will let me know; it will be pleasant to have some benefit for myself."

We were more amazed than ever. I went to the notary who had transacted the business. The letter which instructed him to pay me the money bore the post-mark "Havre," and the hand it was written in was unknown to us all; but Arthur uttered an exclamation of joy when he saw the seal, half-broken as it was. It was Judith's. He had presented to her a seal in former days, with the motto, "Toujours seul"—and there it was upon the letter.

"The letter has come from Judith!" he said, and dropped it on the floor.

"Well, then," I replied, "you see she is still alive, and has not forgotten you—you ought to be delighted."

Arthur was furious. He would have liked better if she had been dead. "For why does she conceal herself? Why, since she knows where I live, does she not come to me? She is not worthy to see me—she loves me no longer—she has forgotten me!"

"The letter," I suggested, "proves the reverse."

"And what right has she to insult me with her benefits? Where has she got her riches? How has she had the audacity to offer them to me? And since when has she considered me base enough to accept them? I won't have the money—take it back again!"

"With all my heart," I said? "but what am I to do with it?"

"What you like—I refuse it."

"You can't refuse it now. Your debts are paid with it—your estate cleared—thanks to the hundred thousand crowns."

"I instruct you to sell my lands—realize that sum, which I shall never touch, and keep it till I find some means of returning it."

"But think what a state your affairs will be in."

"That is of no consequence. Faithless as she is, I cannot repent of having ruined myself for Judith; but to be enriched by her is a degradation I cannot submit to. Sell every thing!"

And, in spite of all my remonstrances, he persisted in his resolution. The estate was sold—the first three hundred thousand francs were deposited with me, and the surplus was sufficient to buy an annuity of six thousand livres for Arthur in the national funds—and that was the whole of his fortune.

He lived in this way for two years, striving to banish a recollection that weighed upon his heart Sombre and melancholy, he forswore all society. He saw me almost every day, and spoke of nothing but Judith. He told me he had forgotten her—that he despised her; and yet the only places he went to were those which recalled her to his recollection most vividly. One day, or rather one night, there was a masked ball at the opera. Alone, in spite of the crowd, he walked in silence through all the noise of the assembly—he went on the stage where he had seen Judith so often—then wandering among the corridors, he ascended slowly to the box on the second tier where he had sat so often in those happy days, and from which he had given the signal of a visit to the Rue de Provence on the following morning. The door of the box was open. A female in an elegant domino was sitting there alone, and apparently sunk in deep thought. At sight of Arthur she started, rose up, and would have left the box: but, scarcely able to support herself, she leaned on one of the sides, and sank down upon the sofa. Her agitation attracted Arthur's notice, and he went forward and offered his assistance.

Without answering, she rejected his offer with a motion of her hand. "The heat has made you ill," he said, with an emotion which he could not master; "if you will take off your mask for a moment——"

She refused his assistance again, and contented herself with throwing back the hood of her domino, which had covered her head.

Arthur saw the beautiful black hair falling in ringlets on her shoulder. It was exactly in the same style that Judith wore it—that graceful attitude, that exquisitely elegant form—the shape, the manners—that undefinable charm which we may feel, but cannot account for—all were there!

She rose up at last.

Arthur started. It was now his turn to feel faint—but instantly summoning all his strength, he whispered—

"Judith! Judith! 'tis you!"

She would have left the box—

"Stay, stay! for heaven's sake! and let me tell you that I am the most unhappy of men; that I never knew you, even when you deserved all my love!"

She trembled.

"Yes, you deserved it then, and I did not know it; and now I love you, Judith! I love nobody but you—I shall love you for ever, even now that you are unfaithful—now that you have forgotten me!"

She tried to answer, but could not. She laid her hand on her heart, as if to justify herself.

"And how, then, can I account for your absence; and above all, for your benefits—those benefits which have made me blush for you, and which I have rejected! Yes, Judith! I desire them not—I wish for nothing but you, and your love! And if it be, indeed, true that you have not forgotten me, and that you love me still, come to me! It is love only I can give you now. for I have no longer a fortune to offer you! Ah, you hesitate—you answer not—I understand your silence! Farewell—for ever!"

He was turning to depart, but Judith held him by the hand.

"Speak, then, Judith! Speak, I entreat you!"

The poor girl could not. Sobs choked her voice.

Arthur fell at her feet—she had not spoken; but she was in tears—and Arthur felt that she was justified.

"You love me, then, still? you love nobody but me?"

"No one!" she said, and gave him her hand.

"And how am I to believe you?—what proof can I have?"

"Time."

"What can I do?"

"Wait!"

"And what token of your love?"

She dropped the bouquet which she held in her hand; and while Arthur stooped to pick it up, she darted through the corridor and disappeared.

He followed her—saw her at a distance among the crowd—lost her again—and had nearly recovered her traces once more, when, on arriving at the lobby, he saw her leap into a magnificent chariot, which went off at a full gallop!

"Gentlemen," said the notary, interrupting his narrative, "'tis very late—I am an early man—and, with your permission, will finish the rest of my story next opera night."

On the following Wednesday we were all in the orchestra punctual to our appointment, but the notary did not make his appearance. The opera was "*Robert*," and it recalled to my recollection my first meeting with Arthur. I now understood his melancholy and pre-occupation, and fancied that if Meyerbeer himself had been aware of his story, he would have pardoned his inattention even to the inimitable trio. But was Arthur at that moment in a less miserable condition? Was he better qualified to appreciate good music? Was he happy, and had he discovered the beautiful Judith? We were still ignorant of the causes that kept them apart; and the absence of our little historian added to our impatience. He arrived at last at the end of the second act, and never was so enthusiastic a reception given to a favourite actor, or dancer, after three months' absence, as we now gave M. Baraton. "You've come at last, my good friend—here—sit down—we've kept your place. How late you are!"

"I have been present at the signatures of a contract," replied the notary—"I say *present* at the signatures, but not professionally. I have given up the shop; and, thank heaven! I owe nothing."

"Yes you do—you owe us——"

"A *dénouement*," said the professor.

"Ah, the history of Judith—well." M. Baraton took the seat that had been kept for him, and continued his tale:—

She had said "Wait!"—and, for some days, Arthur was patient enough—he hoped every hour for a letter or a rendezvous. "I shall see her again!" he exclaimed—"she will come to me again!" But days and weeks passed on, and Judith never came. Six months passed this way—a year—and at last two years rolled by. I felt anxious about Arthur, and sometimes I was even uneasy about his sanity. The scene at the masked ball had affected him strangely. There were moments when he believed that he was labouring under some hallucination. He fancied it was all a dream—an illusion; and he began to have doubts of every thing he heard or saw. It was with difficulty that our utmost care restored him from a dangerous illness, into which hope deferred had thrown him. He never would touch the money advanced by Judith; and his own fortune, I told you, amounted only to six thousand livres a year. Of these he spent four thousand in subscribing for a box at the opera—the box on the second tier, where he had encountered Judith the night of the masked ball. He went there every evening, as long as he had any hopes of seeing her again; and when he sank into despair, he could not summon courage to enter it. He felt himself, when he sat in it, "*seul, toujours seul*"—and the feeling of loneliness made him wretched. All he could do was to come occasionally to the orchestra; and, after looking long and earnestly at the box on the opposite side, he would say, "She is not there!" and leave the theatre. This was his course of life, only diversified by an occasional journey into the country, when he fancied he had obtained some trace of the lost one; but he always came back disconsolate to Paris, and resumed his old habits. It was to meet him more frequently that I secured a seat here by the year. Last week he had come—he had seated himself in the orchestra—not at this side, but at the other. On that occasion—hopeless and wretched—he had turned his back to the house, and was sunk in his own miserable reflections. But a sudden sensation among those around him, aroused him from his revery.

A young lady of the most exquisite beauty, and magnificently dressed, had come into a box, and the whole artillery of opera-glasses was turned upon her in a moment. Nothing was heard but exclamations of "What a beautiful creature!—how brilliant!—how graceful!"

"What age should you think her, sir?" said one.

"Twenty-one or twenty-two," said another.

"Bah! she isn't eighteen."

"Do you know who she is, then?"

"No, sir; this is her first appearance at the opera—for I'm a subscriber, and know every face that has made a sensation here since the year—hem——"

And it seemed that nobody knew any thing about her. At last a gentleman of very distinguished appearance bowed to her. Every one worried him with questions who she was.

"'Tis Lady Inggerton—the wife of a rich English nobleman."

"Indeed!—so young—and so rich!"

And it was whispered about that she had been nobody once—a poor girl that was about to throw herself into the water in a fit of despair; and that, after being rescued by the old nobleman, she gained his heart so entirely, that he persuaded her to marry him, to enable him to leave her his enormous fortune—which he had actually done.

"The deuse! If she's a widow, she's a glorious catch!"

Her time of mourning is just expired, and, of course, all the young fellows, both in England and France, are making up to her.

"No doubt," said the young man who had been making these inquiries, pulling up his neckcloth; "and do you know, my good fellow, I rather think her ladyship is looking in this direction."

"Nonsense!"

"'Tis no nonsense, I assure you—I appeal to this gentleman;" and he addressed himself to Arthur, who had heard nothing of the conversation, and had to be informed of the whole matter.

Arthur raised his eyes, and in the box in the second tier, that box that used to be his, he saw—

Ah! people don't die of surprise and joy, for Arthur is still alive; he felt his heart beat quick. 'Twas she!—'twas Judith!—but at the same time he continued motionless; he did not dare to stir; he was afraid of awakening.

"You know her, then, sir?" inquired his neighbour.

Arthur made no reply, for at that instant his eyes met Judith's!—he saw hers lighting up with joy—and what was he to think? My heavens! how did his brain keep from turning, when he saw the hand of Judith—that hand so white and beautiful—raised slowly to her ear, (the very signal that in other days he used to give to her,) and play with the emerald drops that he had presented to her! Luckily, as I said before, people don't die of happiness; but Arthur felt some vague idea that he should go mad. He hid his face in his hands a moment, to convince himself it was not an illusion; and when he looked up again, the vision had vanished! Judith had disappeared!

A tremour took possession of his limbs—a hand of iron crushed his heart: but when he remembered what he had seen—what he had heard—and that she had given him a signal known only to themselves, he darted from his place; he left the orchestra, and hurried into the street, saying, "If I deceive myself this time—if I am again mistaken—I shall either go mad or blow my brains out!" And having come to this sage resolution, he walked steadily to the Rue de Provence; he knocked at the door, (which was instantly opened,) and asked for—Judith!

"Madame is within, sir," said the porteress, very quietly.

Arthur almost fainted, and had to support himself on the baluster. He went up to the second floor, crossed the well-known rooms, and opened the door of the boudoir. It was furnished exactly as it was six years before.

The supper he had ordered before his departure was there, all laid on the table. There were seats set for two; and Judith, sitting on a sofa, said to him the moment he entered, "You come late, Arthur," and held out her hand.

Arthur fell at her feet.

Here the notary stopped short.

"Well!" we all exclaimed, "go on."

"What more have I to tell you?" said M. Baraton, with a knowing smile. "I have just come from dining with them. The ceremony took place to-day."

"They are married, then?"

"To be sure."

"A widow is a kind of animal," said one of the circle, "who—"

"Has very little resemblance to Judith," interposed the notary; "for a curious part of the story that I have not told you is, that the old peer, her husband, never called her any thing but his daughter."

At that moment the box on the second tier opened—Judith came in, wrapped up in her ermined mantle, and leaning on the arm of her lover—her husband.

And a round of exclamations might be heard among the audience—

"How lovely she is!"

"A lucky dog!"

THE BEGGAR-GIRL OF THE PONT-DES-ARTS.

BY WILHELM HAUFF.

Any one who may have chanced to have lodged at the "King of England," in Stuttgart, in the year 1824, or to have strolled in the spacious gardens in front, must have noticed certain figures who attracted general attention. There were, among others, two men, who, it seemed, did not belong to the population of Stuttgart, and would have been more at home on the Prado or the *plaza de Peros* at Seville. Imagine a tall, thin, elderly man, with iron-gray hair, deepset, burning eyes, a hawk nose, and thin, compressed lips. His walk is slow and stately; and if you have a lively fancy, you cannot but wish him, instead of his black frock-coat, a slashed doublet and Spanish cloak, to complete the picture. When you look at his black silk breeches and stockings, the huge roses in his shoes, the long sword by his side, and the high-pointed hat pressed down on his forehead; and that servant, with a step as stately as his master's, does not his heavy yet roguish face, his parti-coloured dress, and the boldness with which he stares at every thing, remind us of the servants in Spanish plays, who follow their master like his shadow, far below him in manners, his equals in pride, his superiors in cunning? Under his arm he carries his master's cloak and umbrella, and in his hand is a silver segar-box, a flint and steel. Every one stopped to look at this pair as they moved slowly along. It was Don Pedro de San Montanjo Ligez, chamberlain of the crown prince of ———, who was living in Stuttgart at the time, and his servant.

A very trifling circumstance often makes a man conspicuous. This was the case with young Froben. He had been in town about six months, and used to come into the gardens every day at two o'clock precisely, and walk three times round the lake, and then five times up and down the broad walk. He passed by all the splendid equipages and pretty women, by all the crowd of senators, aulic counsellors and *militaires*, without being noticed, for he looked like an every-day personage of some eight and twenty or thirty. But ever since one afternoon, when he happened to meet Don Pedro, when the latter greeted him cordially, took his arm, and walked up and down with him a few times in earnest discourse, he was looked upon with a good deal of curiosity and even respect. Yes, the proud reserved Spaniard treated him with marked distinction. The very prettiest of the young ladies began to observe that he was not ugly, that there was even something interesting in his features, and the senators and counsellors began to ask who he might be? Some young officers professed to be able to answer this question, and stated that he now and then took a steak for a dinner, lived in —— street, and rode a very pretty horse. They then enumerated the good qualities of his horse with great accuracy, and this led them to a discussion on horse-flesh in general, which is said to have been profound and valuable.

After this, Froben was often seen in company with the Don, especially at night in his hotel, where they sat and talked apart from the other guests, Diego standing behind his master's chair and serving them with segars and Xeres. No one could divine the subject of these long conversations.

What was it but the fine gallery of Messrs. Boiserée and Bertram, in which they had first become acquainted? These hospitable gentlemen had given our young friend permission to visit their collection as often as he chose, and he availed himself of it most liberally. In rain, in snow, and in fine weather he came; he often looked ill, but still he came. We should estimate Herr von Froben's taste too highly, however, if we supposed he was busy in studying or copying the admirable works of the Flemish school. He came in softly, bowed in silence, and hurried to a distant room, which contained one single picture. This he examined long, and then left the gallery in silence. The proprietors had too much delicacy to inquire into the cause of his extraordinary affection for the picture, but they could not but wonder at it. Often, when he went out, the tears stood in his eyes.

The picture had no great value as a work of art. It represented a lady partly in the Spanish and partly in the old German costume. A blooming, cheerful face, with clear, loving eyes, finely chiselled lips and rounded chin, stood boldly out from the back-ground. The forehead was adorned by a profusion of hair and a little hat, with heavy white feathers, placed somewhat archly on one side. The dress, which was high in the neck, was loaded with rich chains, and bore testimony to its owner's wealth as well as modesty.

"I suppose he is in love with the picture," thought the proprietor; "but if so, he loves without hope, for it is at least three hundred years old." By and by it seemed as though Froben was not the only admirer of the portrait. One day the prince of P—— visited the gallery with his suite. His chamberlain, Don Pedro, when he saw this painting, uttered a cry of surprise, and seemed overcome by astonishment. When the prince left the gallery, Don Pedro was not to be found: at last he was discovered standing with folded arms and in deep thought before the picture. He asked where it came from, and was told that it was painted by a celebrated artist several hundred years before, and had been obtained by accident. "Oh, no," he cried, "it is new; it is not a hundred years old: tell me, pray tell me, when you got it—where can I find her?"

He was old and looked too venerable to be laughed at for his burst of passion; but when he was again told that the picture was supposed to be painted by Lucas Cranach, he shook his head gravely: "Gentlemen," said he, laying his hand upon his heart, "Don Pedro de San Montanjo Ligez believes you to be honourable men. You are not picture-dealers, and have no interest to misrepresent the age of this picture. But unless I am greatly deceived, I know the lady who is here represented." He made a ceremonious bow, and left the gallery. "Really," thought the proprietor, "if we were not so certain about the age of this picture, I should be in doubt. At any rate, unless I am greatly deceived, as the Spaniard says, this is not his last visit to our collection."

And so it happened. As soon as the gallery was opened, Don Pedro de San Montanjo Ligez stepped gravely and majestically in, sweeping past the long rows of paintings towards the lady in the hat and feathers. He was vexed to find the ground already occupied. A young man stood there, gazed at the picture, stepped back to a window to watch the flights of the clouds, and then came up, and gazed again. He was vexed—but had to be patient. He busied himself with the other paintings, but kept turning his head every moment to see whether the young gentleman had not gone. But he stood there firm as a wall, and seemed lost in thought. The Spaniard coughed to arouse him, but he kept dreaming on; he moved his foot roughly, the young man looked round at him a moment vacantly, and then turned to fasten again on the picture. "San Pedro! Santiago de Compostella! what a tedious amateur!" muttered he, and left the room angrily, feeling that the disappointment had deprived him of all enjoyment for that day. The next day, before the clock had done striking twelve, he mounted the gallery stairs in dignified haste, and made for the well-known picture, and, by good luck, he was the first and only visiter, and free to look his fill. He gazed long and fixedly at the picture; his eye grew dim, he drew his hand across his shaggy eyelashes and murmured, "Oh, Laura!" A sigh was plainly heard as an echo to this exclamation—he turned round in surprise—the same young man stood near him, looking earnestly at the portrait. Vexed at the interruption, he nodded a careless salutation; the young man returned it with less coldness but equal pride. The Spaniard determined to sit his troublesome neighbour out, but in vain—for to his amazement, the young stranger took a chair and sat down a few paces off, so as to be at his ease. "The fool! I really believe he is making sport of my gray hairs," said Don Pedro, and left the room in great indignation. In the ante-chamber he met one of the proprietors of the collection. He tendered him his thanks for his politeness, but at the same time could not help saying a word about the disturber of his peace. "You may have noticed," he remarked, "that one of your pictures has a special value in my eyes. I came, on your invitation, to see this, to spend my time before it undisturbed, and now a mischievous young man watches my movements, comes whenever I come, and spends whole hours, merely to vex me, before a painting that he has no interest in."

The owner smiled. "I am not so certain as to that: the contrary seems to be the case, for this is not the first day that he has devoted to that picture."

"Who is he?"

"A certain Herr von Froben, who has been here six months. Ever since he saw the portrait in question, he has been in the habit of coming every day at the same hour to pay his respects to it. You see at any rate that he must feel an interest in the picture, since he has been so constant a visiter to it for so long a time."

"What! six months!" cried the old man; "I have done him wrong in my thoughts, God forgive me! I really fear that I have behaved rudely to him. And he is a *caballero*, you say? No, it shall never be said of Pedro de Ligez that he was rude to a stranger. Tell him—but no, I will speak to him myself."

The next day he found Froben at his post. The young man stepped aside to make room for his senior, who bowed ceremoniously as he addressed him, "If I am not mistaken, Señor, I have seen you looking at this picture before. So it is with me: I take great interest in this picture, and am never tired of looking at it."

Froben was surprised, and hesitated a little as he answered, "I admit it has peculiar merit in my eyes—for—since—as there is something in it which I greatly admire." The Spaniard looked at him inquiringly, and Froben added, more calmly, "It is singular what effect a painting will sometimes produce. Thousands pass by this picture, find the drawing correct, and praise its colouring, but it does not affect them profoundly, while one person may find in it a deep hidden meaning, he cannot tear himself away, he feels chained to the spot, and returns to it again and again."

"You may be right," replied the old man, thoughtfully, "but I conceive this applies only to great compositions, in which the artist sought to express a profound conception. Many pass by, and at last the true expression is felt by some one, who is then lost in admiration. But will this hold true of such heads?"

The young man coloured. "Why not? the fine outlines of the face, this noble forehead, this thoughtful eye, his sweet mouth, are not these finely conceived and expressed? Is there not something attractive in the features which—"

"Certainly. She was unquestionably a very pretty woman; the family is remarkable for beauty."

"What family?" asked Froben, doubting whether his new acquaintance was in his right mind. "This is a fancy piece, and some hundred years old."

"What? do you too believe that silly story? Between ourselves, the owners are mistaken this time: I know the lady."

"For God's sake! do you know her?—Where is she now?—Who is she?"

"I should rather say, I *did* know her," replied the old man, raising his moist eye to the painting. "Yes, I knew her in Valencia, twenty years ago—a long time! It is Doña Laura Tortosi."

"Twenty years ago!" repeated Froben, sadly; "no, it is not she!"

"Why?" cried Don Pedro; "do you suppose, then, the painter invented these features? Even without knowing the Tortosi family, do you not see it must be a family portrait? I say it is Doña Laura, as I knew her many years since."

"It may be like her—in which case she must be a very lovely person—but as for this piece, the records prove that it was hanging in the church of St. Mary Magdalen at least a hundred and fifty years ago."

"Then may the fiend pluck out my eyes!" exclaimed the Spaniard, seizing his hat and rushing from the room. "It is a device of the evil one to torture me;" and the tears stood in his eyes.

One evening, when the two gentlemen were sitting in the parlour of the "King of England," Don Pedro suddenly said, "The crowd here prevents all conversation; will you help me empty a bottle of Ximenes in my apartment?"

"With pleasure."

"Wait a moment till I prepare to receive you. I will send for you."

In a few minutes, Diego appeared with a silver candlestick in each hand, and bowed gravely to Froben, as the signal to follow him. On entering, he found his host had laid aside his frock-coat, and appeared in a close-fitting black doublet and ample scarlet mantle. A sword with golden hilt was buckled by his side.

"Welcome, Don Frobenio," was his salutation. "I have long desired a moment's friendly conversation with you. Whenever I paid a visit to my Laura's likeness, I found you there before me. And excuse me playing the spy, but I could not help seeing that you felt more deeply interested in the picture than you have ever been willing to confess."

Froben blushed, for the old man's glance was keen and penetrating. He told him: "It is true, and you are right in supposing it is not the painting, but the subject that attracts me. Alas! it reminds me of the sweetest yet most unhappy hour of my life! You will smile when I tell you that I once saw a lady who is very like that picture: that I saw her but *once*, and yet that I never shall forget her."

"Alas! it is my case, too!" murmured the Spaniard.

"You will laugh outright, however," continued Froben, "when I confess that I am able to speak as to only half of her face. I do not know whether she is a blond or a brunette—whether she has a high or a low forehead, blue eyes or black, I really don't know. But the finely shaped nose, the lovely mouth, the chiselled chin—these I behold in the picture, the same as I once beheld the reality!"

"Strange!—and can you remember so distinctly those features which are generally more easily forgotten than the eyes and the hair; and after seeing them only once, too?"

"Ah, Don Pedro! lips that we have once kissed, such lips we do not soon forget. I will tell you how it happened."

"Stop—not a word!" exclaimed the Spaniard. "You would have a right to think me ill-bred, if I asked a cavalier for his secret, without first communicating my own I will tell you what I know of the lady.

"Señor, I was born in Granada, of a noble family, by whom I was instructed in religion and in science, and destined to the profession of arms. When I had reached the rank of captain, I was sent to my uncle, a stern old veteran, who commanded in Valencia. A great change had taken place in his household since I saw him last. I was surprised when he introduced an elderly lady to me as his second wife, and still more agreeably so, when I was made acquainted with a beautiful young one, whom he called his daughter Laura, my cousin.

"You have seen her, Don Frobenio. That picture is a faithful copy of her lovely features, at least so far as it was possible for earthly art to imitate them. I need not say that I loved her. My affection was open and joyous; there were none of those barriers between us that usually separate lovers in my country. My uncle loved me as a son, and if I understood his hints rightly, was not unwilling to make me so. On my father's part, there could be no objection, for Laura was of a noble as well as wealthy family. You may judge how violent my love must have been, as I loved where there were no obstacles to feed the flame. As for the lady, she allowed me to confess my sentiments, my uncle gave his consent, and we were to be married as soon as he could obtain a majority for me. About this time I became intimate with a captain in the Swiss Guard, and we were soon the closest friends. He was a fair-haired, handsome youth, with a delicate complexion and light-blue eyes. He would have been too effeminate for a soldier, but for his renown in arms. This made him so much the more dangerous. His style of beauty was one so new among us, that when he talked about the ice and snow of Switzerland, many a lady sighed to think that his heart seemed equally cold.

"One day a friend, who knew of my engagement, gave me to understand, in mysterious circumlocution, that I had better marry my cousin at once, as otherwise something unpleasant might happen. I made further inquiries, and learned Doña Laura was in the habit of meeting a stranger at a friend's house. I could not believe it, and yet a jealous pang remained; I determined to watch her closely. That very afternoon she left us, saying that she wished to see a friend. A little while afterwards, I followed her, and kept watch by the door of the house. A fury seized me as I saw a man, wrapped in a mantle, stealing along at nightfall in the shade of the buildings. As the figure approached me, I seized hold of its dress, and cried, 'Whoever you are, give me your honour that you do not come here to visit Laura de Tortosi?' 'Who dares to question me thus?' said a deep voice. His accent betrayed the stranger, and I felt a painful foreboding. 'It is Captain de San Montanjo Ligez,' I replied, and pulled the cloak from before his face, and saw my friend, the Swiss Captain. He stood there like a culprit, without speaking. I drew my sword, and motioned to him to do the same. 'I have no arms but a dagger,' he said. I was about to pass my blade through his body, but could not do it as he stood there helpless before me. I appointed the next morning for our meeting, and he left the place. I kept guard at the door till Laura's litter was brought, and I saw her enter it. The torture of mind I felt would not let me sleep, and at midnight I heard a knock at my door. It was Laura's old servant, who handed me a letter, and retired. Señor! heaven forbid that you should ever receive such a letter! She told me that she loved the Swiss long before she knew me—that she had kept it a secret, knowing how her mother detested foreigners, and that she had been forced to accept my proposals in spite of herself. She took all the blame to herself; she protested solemnly that Tannensee had often wanted to confess the truth to me, and would have done it but for her entreaties. She intimated that the family would be disgraced unless I furnished them with the means of flight. She begged me not to seek a meeting with him, for that if he fell, she, his wife, would not survive him. She ended by appealing to my magnanimity, declaring that she always esteemed, though she could not love me. You can conceive that such an epistle threw cold water on the flame of my love; and it cooled my anger, too, in part. But, as I had been deceived, I felt that honour required me to be at our rendezvous the next morning. The Captain felt, perhaps, how deeply he had injured me, for, though the better swordsman, he merely defended himself, and it was not his fault that I ran my hand, here between the thumb and finger, on his sword, so that I could fight no longer. While they were binding up the wound, I handed him Laura's letter. He begged and implored me to forgive him; I did it, but with a heavy heart.

"The story of my love is ended, Don Frobenio; for, five days afterwards, Laura and the Swiss Captain had disappeared."

"And with your assistance?"

"I did all I could to help them. My aunt was deeply grieved; but it was better that she should never see her daughter, than to have disgrace come upon our house."

"Noble-hearted man!" cried Froben, "what must it not have cost you! In truth, it was a hard trial."

"It was, indeed!" said the old man, smiling bitterly. "At first, I thought the wound would never heal; but time does wonders, my young friend! I have never since seen or heard of her; only once the papers mentioned Colonel Tannensee as an officer under Napoleon, who had distinguished himself at Brienne. But when I came here, and saw my Laura before me, the same as she was twenty years ago, the old wounds opened afresh, and—you know yourself, I used to go every day to see her."

Don Pedro had told his story with all the gravity of an old Castilian. When he had ended, he took off his hat, stroked his beard, and said, "I have told you, Don Frobenio, a story which I have confided to but a few; not to lead you to imitate my confidence, though your secret would be as safe in my breast as the ashes of our kings in the Escurial. I will confess I am anxious to ask why you take such an interest in the lady; but curiosity is unbecoming a man of my years, and I say no more."

Froben answered, "I will tell you my little adventure with pleasure. It does not reveal a lady's secret, and ends, in fact, where other tales usually begin. But, with your permission, as it is now so late, we will leave it till to-morrow."

"As you please," said the Spaniard.

The next day, Froben was in the gallery, as usual, before the picture. He waited a whole hour; but the old man did not make his appearance. He walked up and down the grounds, but looked in vain for the well-known black breeches and pointed hat. At the hotel, his absence was explained. "They are all gone, his highness and all. Despatches came at midnight, and the prince and his suite set off before day-break." Don Pedro had left a card, on the back of which was written in pencil, "Farewell, my dear Don Frobenio, you still owe me your story: kiss Doña Laura for me." He smiled at the commission, but soon felt that his old friend's absence left him solitary. There was nothing now to detain him in Stuttgart, and he left the city as quietly as he had entered it.

Froben pursued his journey along the Rhine. His head was still full of the romantic ideas that the portrait had called into being. As he drew near the lovely plain of the Neckar, he began to forget these fantastic visions, and to remember the object of his journey. It was a visit to a friend, in whose company he had travelled through France and England. Similarity of character did not form the ground of their friendship. The Baron von Faldner was somewhat rough and rude, and even his travels had not polished him. He was one of those who, because they neglect books, think they can do without them, and persuade themselves that they are what they call "practical men;" that is, universal geniuses, who know every thing without studying it, and are perfect masters of business, agriculture, housekeeping, and the like. He was happy, because he did not know his own deficiencies; but self-conceit made him overbearing in company, and a tyrant at home. "I wonder if he still says, 'I told you so,'" thought Froben. "He always used to speak thus, even if he had prophesied the contrary the minute before, and there was no undeceiving him."—His estate lay in one of the loveliest valleys of the Rhine, and our traveller could not but hope that the beauties by which he was surrounded had tended to soften his natural harshness.

He entered the park, and saw his friend at a distance. He seemed to be disputing with an old man, who was busy digging round a tree. "I don't care if you have done it that way for a hundred years, and not fifty; you must transplant the tree as I tell you." The old man put on his cap with a sigh, looked at the noble tree with a sad eye, and set to work hastily, and, as it seemed, unwillingly. The Baron whistled a tune as he turned away, and saw a stranger, who held out his hand to him with a smile. "What's your wish?" he asked hastily.

"Don't you know me then, Faldner? Have your trees made you forget London and Paris?"

"Froben! is it possible?" cried the host as he embraced him. "But how thin and pale you look. That comes from your sitting and studying so much: but you never would take advice. I always told you it would not answer for you."

"Think a moment, my dear fellow. Didn't you always tell me that I would never do for a sportsman or farmer, and that I must take to law or diplomacy?"

"Ah, I see you are troubled with your old complaint, want of memory. Did not I tell you—"

"Let it pass, and tell me where you have been since we parted."

The Baron's story was a short one, wholly made up of complaints of bad weather and stupid servants. He gave him to understand that he was a great proficient in farming, but found all his neighbours and people very obstinate. He confessed that he lived a life of care and trouble, of vexation and quarrel. His friend could see plainly that he still rode his hobby, and could not rein it in.

It was now Froben's turn, and he said in a few words that he had been attached to one or two embassies, had got tired of them, and asked for a long leave of absence, and was now seeing the world.

"Happy fellow!" cried Faldner, "I much envy you. Here to-day and there to-morrow, nothing to tie you down, and as free as air. I only wish I could live like you."

"But why not? Look out for a good overseer, saddle your horse, and set off with me."

"Ah, you don't understand," answered Faldner, embarrassed. "If I am away only one day, every thing goes wrong. Besides, I have done a foolish thing—but no matter. However, my travelling days are over."

A servant came up just then to say that his mistress was returned, and asked where tea should be served? "Up stairs," said Faldner, in some confusion. "What! are you a married man?" asked Froben, "and haven't told me of it yet! Well, I congratulate, and so forth; but pray, tell me—I should as soon have thought of the sky's falling—how long since?"

"About six months," said the Baron in a low tone, and looking at the ground; "but why should you wonder at it? You ought to know that in such a large establishment—"

"Certainly, it is very natural and proper; but I remember how you used to talk about marriage. I never supposed you would find anybody to suit you."

"No, excuse me. I always told you—"

"To be sure, I admit it," answered Froben, with a smile; "and *I* always told you that with your romantic fancies of ideal perfection, you would always live a bachelor. As there is a lady in the case, I can't appear in my travelling dress, so you will excuse me a few moments. Farewell till we meet again."

Just as he left him, a tall and graceful lady came up, and asked the Baron hastily, "Whom were you talking with just now? Who was it that said, 'Farewell, till we meet again'?"

The Baron started up and gazed on his wife with astonishment at seeing the delicate paleness of her cheek suffused with crimson "It is too bad, Josephine," he cried. "How often have I told you that Hufeland forbids violent exercise to people of your constitution? You have been walking here from the house, I suppose, and got warm, and now you want to sit down in the cool air. I have to tell you every thing twenty times over, as I would to a child. You ought to be ashamed of yourself."

"Oh, don't be angry with me," said his wife in a trembling voice. "I only came out to meet you, and rode all the way."

"Your cheeks condemn you," was the answer. "Must I be for ever talking to you? No shawl, either, and so late! What is the use of my flinging away money for such nonsense if you don't wear them? It's enough to make a man mad. You will not do any thing to please me. Your self-will wears me out completely. It's enough—"

"Pray, forgive me, Franz," said she, wiping away the big tears from her eyes. "I have not seen you all day long, and I wanted to surprise you, and forgot all about a shawl. You will forgive me—you will forgive your wife, won't you?"

"Yes, yes, that's enough; now leave me alone. You know I don't like such scenes. And in tears, too! Do for heaven's sake break yourself of this foolish habit of crying at any thing and every thing. We have a guest to-day—Froben, who travelled with me. Behave yourself as you ought—do you hear me? See that nothing is wanting, for I don't like to have to keep house besides all my other business."

He walked before her to the castle in silence.

When Faldner showed Froben to his room, he could not refrain from congratulating his host on his choice. "Really, Franz, I never saw her equal. You were always a lucky fellow, but I never thought you would get such a prize, with your strange ideas."

"Yes, yes; she is well enough," answered the Baron, dryly, as he snuffed the candle; "a man can't have every thing, and ought not to expect it in this world."

"Why! I hope and trust you are not insensible to such excellence. I have seen many women in my day, but never one of such perfect beauty! What eyes! What a figure! And I do not know but that I admire her cultivated mind and delicate taste even still more highly."

"You seem quite captivated," rejoined Faldner, laughing, "but you have read too much; you are not a practical man; I always told you so. Believe me, a smart, active housekeeper is worth more than what you call your accomplished women. Good-night—thank your stars that you are a freeman, and—don't be in a hurry to choose."

Froben had not failed to observe how anxiously she had watched her husband's looks, and how much she seemed to stand in awe of him. He felt that so ill-assorted a union must have been the work of interest, and not of affection, and that so delicate, so sensitive a creature, was ill-fitted to bear the humours of her stern and selfish lord. He sat, plunged in such thoughts, till he began to reproach himself for them. "I have been false to my first love to-night," thought he. "Another image has filled my thoughts, and I have given way to ideas that are perhaps sinful, certainly idle!" With these words, he unrolled the engraving from the beloved picture in his bosom, which he always carried with him; but what was his surprise as he noticed the wonderful resemblance it bore to the Baroness Von Faldner? As to hair and eyes, he could not speak; but the mouth, nose, chin, and throat were surprisingly alike. "What!" thought he, "can she be my friend's wife?—she whom I saw but once, and imperfectly, yet whom I love, and shall love for ever! The stature and the figure, too, the same! Her eyes were fixed on me the whole evening, as though she had seen me before. But it is all folly. The proud Baron of Faldner, with his high ideas of nobility and pure descent, would never have stooped to wed a beggar girl!"

The next morning, when Froben came down to the drawing-room, he found himself alone. His host had ridden out to view the estate, and his lady was busied with household affairs. He took up carelessly the cards that lay on the mantel. Among them was his friend's wedding-card, on which he saw, "Baron Von Faldner and Josephine Von Tannensee."

The name surprised him. It was the very name of the Swiss officer who had figured in Don Pedro's story. He had hardly time to collect his thoughts, disturbed by this coincidence, when Josephine appeared. She apologized for her husband's absence, adding, "His life is always a laborious and anxious one; but I really believe, he is so accustomed to a press of business, that he would not be contented without it."

"Is there more than usual to be attended to on the estate?"

"No, he is always so; he is never at rest; and he spends the whole day, from morning to night, among his workmen."

"You must often feel solitary, I should suppose, during his absence."

"Solitary!" she repeated, and her voice trembled a little, "no—memory is the companion of those who are alone; and besides," she added, with an effort at a smile, "in so large an establishment as ours, there are a thousand things to be attended to—so that I do not, *must* not, feel lonesome."

The slight accent of sorrow with which she spoke, impressed Froben deeply; and he paused a while before he answered. "Women, now-a-days, possess talents and acquirements which can be developed in society alone. And I have often thought how unhappy one of your sex would be, supposing her to possess a cultivated mind, a taste for reading and for intellectual society, if she finds no kindred spirit in her domestic circle, and yet is confined to it."

Josephine blushed, and our hero could not but feel that he had unconsciously reminded her of her own situation. To give the conversation a more general character, she replied, "We country ladies, of course, enjoy such pleasures less frequently, but still we are not so lonely as you might suppose; we visit each other often—only see what a pile of cards there is on the mantel there."

"That reminds me," said Froben, "that I was guilty of a petty larceny just now;" and he produced the wedding-card. "Will you believe it, that I did not know of my friend's marriage till last night? The card first informed me of your name. It is Tennensee, I find."

"Yes," she answered, with a smile, "and I was no loser in exchanging so insignificant a name for the noble one of Faldner."

"If your father was, as I suppose, Colonel Von Tennensee, you cannot call it insignificant."

She blushed. "My dear father! They tell me the Emperor esteemed him a gallant officer, and he died a general. I never knew him."

"Was he not a Swiss?"

She looked at him with some surprise. "If I am not mistaken, my mother told me he was."

"And was not your mother named Laura, and of a Spanish family?" She turned pale. "Laura was her name, but—what do you know about her? Spanish! no, she spoke German, and was of that nation."

To account for this curiosity, Froben told the story of his meeting with Don Pedro, and his firm belief that she was the daughter of that Laura whom the Spaniard had loved so warmly. He enlarged on the rank and wealth of her newly-found relative, but Josephine betrayed no pleasure at the discovery; on the contrary, she leaned her head on her hand and burst into tears.

"What have I done!" cried Froben, in despair. "It was all my folly—a mere conjecture only. Your relatives can decide that better, I—"

"Alas! it is my evil fate to have no kindred," said she. "Happy are they who can look back to a long line of honourable ancestors: who have kind and good relatives, endeared to them by the ties of blood. I was an only child, and I have always lived among strangers. My father, I heard, quarrelled with his relations in Switzerland, because they wanted him to marry a rich heiress at home; and when my mother died, there was not a soul in the world to whom I could say, Have pity on me!"

Froben was anxious, as well as affected at her grief. "Was not your mother's name Tortosi?" he asked.

"She was called Laura Von Tortheim."

"The names are the same: and I believe you will now have no cause to complain of being alone in the world. One kinsman, at least, you have, and one of the most excellent of men. Faldner will be delighted when he hears of our discovery."

Her tears began to flow afresh. "You do not know my husband," she replied. "You have no idea how suspicious he is. Every thing must go on regularly and soberly; and he detests any thing like a surprise, or a change, from the very bottom of his soul. I had to regard it as a favour," she added, bitterly, "as a favour, that a man of such an ancient family would make me his wife, and be satisfied with the few papers I had to show my birth. He tells me every day that he might have married into the first houses—or else, that my family is only newly ennobled—that he knows nothing about my mother, and that some of the Tennensees have even turned merchants."

It was plain that she had married from poverty, not choice, and that her brutal husband treated her with rudeness and cruelty. Faldner's return to dinner cut short the conversation.

His wife came forward to meet him, but he passed hastily by her. "Is it not enough to drive a man mad, Froben?" were his first words. "I have spent a fortune in getting a steam-engine from England, and it won't work at all! Something has been left out or lost. I brought down an engineer from Mentz, to put it up. I showed him the drawings. There is the whole story, all lettered and numbered, and yet the bungler cannot put it up!"

Faldner ate little, but drank freely; and his displeasure gradually gave way to boisterous mirth. At the close of the meal, Josephine gathered courage and addressed him. "I had a singular conversation with our guest this morning, which has led to the discovery of a kinsman of mine." Froben repeated the story, not without some anxiety as to the effect it would produce; but, contrary to his expectations, the Baron seemed delighted. "'Tis as clear as day!" he cried; "Tortheim and Tortosi—all the same thing. And you say the old chap is rich, my dear fellow? Rich, and a bachelor, and always talking about his Laura! Zounds! Josephine, there's a chance for lots of piastres!"

Josephine was not much pleased, perhaps, at his coarse way of expressing himself; but she answered calmly, "This will account for the snatches of Spanish songs that always floated in my mind, and also for my having been brought up a Catholic." With these words she retired.

"Write to the old man, will you, Froben? and tell him you have found his Laura's daughter. I always told Countess Landstrom that, even though my wife had nothing, I was sure she would bring luck to the house. How much do you suppose the Don will cut up?"

Froben changed colour. "How should I know? Do you suppose I asked him? But what were you saying about Countess Landstrom?"

"Oh, it was there I met my wife. You know I'm a practical man. I might have married the richest girl in the country; but I said to myself, All is not gold that glitters. Josephine was a kind of companion to the Countess. She was busy all day long, making tea, sewing, overseeing the servants, watering flowers, and every thing. I thought she would make a good housekeeper, and though I could not find out much about her family, I married her."

"And you are as happy as the day is long."

"Why, so so; she has nothing of a practical turn; but I lock up all her books, and make her keep house. But come, let us look at my unlucky steam-engine."

As the gentlemen were mounting their horses, Froben saw Josephine at a window waving her handkerchief. "The Baroness is saluting you," he said; but his host only laughed, and rode on. "Why do you support her in all that sentimental folly, so that we must kiss and flourish handkerchiefs whenever I am going away for a few hours? It is enough to spoil any woman; and whenever you marry, do as I do. You never say where you are going. Your horse is brought round. 'Where are you going, dear?' she asks two or three times. You say nothing, but put on your gloves. 'How can you go away and leave me here all alone?' she asks, and lays her hand on your shoulder. You pick up your whip and say, 'I am going to so-and-so; there is something to be done to-day. Adieu; and if I don't come back by supper-time, don't wait for me.' She is shocked—you whistle; she goes to the window and flourishes her handkerchief—you ride straight on, and take no notice of her. That makes a woman respect you. After two or three such scenes, my wife gave up asking me any question, I assure you."

The engineer was at work, but had made no progress Faldner grew violent, and called him a bungler and a rogue. The man's face was crimson with resentment, but he suppressed it. "I will engage to put any machine in order, but I must have my own way about it, and in this case—"

"I've been helping you a little, and that I suppose has put you out? I have seen half a dozen such machines, and I know perfectly well that the large wheels work on the cylinder, and the small ones above—"

"This is of another pattern, however, as the drawings show."

"What do I care for drawings? I'm deceived all round—cheated by everybody."

Froben, meanwhile, had been examining the drawings carefully, and said at last, "I will lay a bet that it is all as it should be. F and H here go with I, and this connects the stamping-mill with the machine."

"To be sure it does!" cried the engineer, triumphantly. "This makes the whole thing easy." The Baron laughed to conceal his surprise, and left the management to his friend, expressing little faith in his success. He was deceived, however, for in a very short time the machine was put up and at work.

This restored him to good humour, and he gave a little entertainment in honour of his success. Cheerful and good-humoured as he seemed, it did not escape Froben that he persecuted his wife incessantly. She did every thing wrong, and he drove her, without remorse, from the kitchen to the parlour and back again. His visitors were delighted with her grace and beauty, and the old ladies were loud in their praises of her good housewifery. "See now," the Baron whispered to his friend, "what wonders good discipline will do! She has got along very well to-day, with a little help from me, of course. But she'll mend—she'll mend." The general mirth and the good wine elevated his spirits still higher, and it was soon high time to leave the table, as he and some of his friends were indulging in some excellent jokes, which were rather too broad for the delicate ears of the ladies. Sport of every kind was now the order of the day, and even the good old-fashioned game of forfeits was tolerated. It chanced to be Froben's turn to redeem his favour, and Josephine, who fixed the forfeits, decided that he should tell some *true* passage in his life. The choice was loudly applauded, most of all by Faldner, and when he saw Froben hesitate, he cried, "Come, begin! or I will for you, and tell your piquant adventure with the beggar-girl of the *Pont-des-Arts.*"

Froben blushed and looked displeased; but the company, who suspected that some good jest was at the bottom of the allusion, cried, "The story!—the story of the *Pont-des-Arts!*" And he made up his mind to tell it, chiefly to avoid any indiscretion on the part of his host, who was warmed with wine. Faldner promised, if the narrator departed from the truth in any respect, to bring him back to it, as he was himself a witness of the adventure.

"I do not know," began Froben, "whether you are aware that some years ago our friend Faldner and I travelled together, and lived in Paris in the same house. Our studies were the same—we visited the same circles—in a word, we were inseparable. We had a mutual friend, Doctor M——, a fellow-countryman, who lived in the *Rue Taranne*, which, as you know, lies on the left bank of the Seine, and leads into the *Rue Dominique*. Our regular evening walk was through the Champs Elysées, across to the Fauxbourg St. Germain, and thence to our friends, where we often sat till very late, chatting about Germany, France, and what not. We lived, I ought to add, in the *Place des Victoires*, a good way off from the *Rue Taranne*, and we generally came home by the *Pont-des-Arts*, so as to cross the Louvre, and save time. One night—it was after eleven—it had rained a little, and the wind blew chilly and keen, especially along the river. We were going from Quai Malaquois across the Pont-des-Arts. The bridge is only for foot passengers, and of course, at that time of night, every thing was quite still around it. We walked across in silence, wrapping our cloaks around us; and I was just hurrying down the steps on the other side, when I saw an extraordinary sight. A tall, slim female stood leaning against the side of the bridge. A little black hat was tied close before her face, which was still more completely hidden by a green veil: she wore a black silk cloak, and the wind betrayed a delicate, youthful figure; a little hand holding a plate peeped out of the cloak. In front stood a little lantern, whose flickering light showed a small neat foot. There is no place, perhaps, where the contrast between the greatest splendour and the lowest depths of misery is as striking as in Paris; but still you meet few beggars. They seldom attack you forwardly, and you never find them follow you up or persecute you with their demand. A blind old man sometimes sits or kneels at the corner of the street, holding out his hand quietly, and leaves it to the passer-by to notice his look of entreaty or not. The most affecting of all, as I thought, were the shame-faced ones, who stand motionless, almost breathless, in a corner, with their faces covered, and a taper burning before them. Many of my acquaintances assured me that they were generally people of the better class, who had become so much reduced that they must either go to labour, or if they were ashamed, or unable to work for their daily bread, chose this last resource before ending their lives and sorrows in the Seine. The female figure at the bridge which enchained my attention was of this class. I eyed her more closely; her limbs seemed to tremble with the cold even more than the flickering light in her lantern; but she was silent, and let her sorrow and the cold night-wind speak for her. I felt in my pockets, but I had no small change, and not even a single franc. I turned to Faldner and asked him to lend me some; but he was out of temper, as it seemed, at my keeping him waiting in the cold; and he called to me in German, 'Leave the beggar alone, and come home to bed—I'm almost frozen.' 'Give me a couple of sous, my dear fellow,' I said; but he pulled me by the cloak and tried to drag me away. The veiled figure before me spoke in a trembling but sweet-toned voice, and, to our surprise, in good German, 'O, gentlemen, have pity on me!' The tone and the language made such an impression on me, that I again asked him for some money: he laughed—'Very well; there is a couple of francs,' said he; 'try your luck with the girl if you choose, but let me go to sleep.' He gave me the money and walked away. I was really confused, for she must have heard what Faldner said; and the unhappy are the last that I should wish to insult. I drew nearer to her, irresolutely. 'My girl,' I said, 'you have chosen a poor stand: there will be few people coming by here to-night.' She did not answer aloud, but whispered after a while, 'May those few have pity on the unfortunate!' This answer surprised me, it was so natural, yet so apt. Her graceful attitude and the tone of her voice indicated a person of education. 'We are fellow-countrymen,' I said; 'let me ask if I cannot do something more for you than this mere passing assistance.' 'We are very poor,' she answered, and this time more boldly, 'and my mother is sick and has no one to help her.' Without reflection, and led only by the vague feeling that attracted me to her, I said, 'Show me where she is.' She was silent and seemed embarrassed. 'You must consider this as my honest wish to aid you, if I can,' I said. 'Come, then, sir,' she rejoined, picked up her lantern, blew it out, and hid it and the plate under her cloak."

"What," cried the Baron, bursting into a laugh, as Froben seemed to pause, "do you mean to stop here? Do you want to deceive me now, as you tried to then? Thus far, ladies and gentlemen, he has spoken the exact historical truth. He supposed, probably, that I was far away; but I was standing some two paces off from this moving, good Samaritan dialogue, under the portal of the Louvre, and witnessed the whole affair. Whether the conversation is truly reported or not, I cannot say, for the confounded wind made me lose it; but I saw the damsel blow out her lantern, and go back with him over the bridge. The night was so cold that I did not follow up his adventure; but, after all, I will bet that he did not find mamma sick, or any thing of the kind; but the fair dame was only singing the old siren-song to a new tune." He laughed loudly at his own wit, and the men joined him; the ladies looked down, and Josephine seemed displeased both at her husband's remarks and her guest's strange story; for her fingers trembled so that she could hardly hold her plate; and she eyed the narrator with a look which he felt himself bound to interpret in a way little honourable to himself: "I cannot allow my friend here," he continued in a loud voice that silenced the company, "to put such an interpretation on my conduct: allow me, therefore, to proceed, and by my life,"—and as he spoke his colour grew deeper and his eyes brightened, "I will tell you nothing but the truth."

"The girl crossed the bridge I had just passed over. I had time enough to look at her, as I walked silently by her side, or rather behind her. Her figure, so far as I could see for her cloak, and more particularly her voice, were quite youthful. Her gait was quick, but easy. I offered her my arm, but she would not take it. At the corner of the bridge she turned into the *Rue Mazarin*. 'Has your mother been sick long?' I asked her, stepping up alongside, and trying to get a peep at her face. 'For two years,' she answered, with a deep sigh; 'but for a week past she has been much worse.' 'Have you been there often before now?' 'Where?' she asked. 'On the bridge.' 'This is the first time,' was her answer. 'You did not choose a good place, then; the other avenues are more frequented.' I was sorry, even while saying so; for I felt that it must hurt her deeply, and she whispered and sobbed in reply, 'I am a stranger here, and—I was ashamed to go into the crowd.' How great must be the misery, I said to myself, that can force such a creature to ask alms! It is true, some such thoughts as Faldner had expressed, occurred to me now and then; but I set myself against them—they were too unnatural. If she really belonged to that wretched class of women, why should she hide her features, and stand in such a lonely place? Why should she take such care to conceal a figure which, so far as I could judge from a few hasty glimpses, was a fine one? No—it could be nothing but real wretchedness, and that shame of unmerited poverty which makes it so touching. 'Has your mother a physician?' I asked, after a while. 'She had; but when we got to be too poor to buy medicines, he wanted to send her to the *Hôpital des Incurables*, and I could not bear *that*. Oh, heavens! my dear mother in a hospital!' She wept at this, and raised her handkerchief to her eyes: as the plate and lantern which she held in the other hand prevented her from keeping her cloak close folded, the wind blew it aside, and I saw that I was not mistaken; her figure was tall and graceful, her dress plain; but, as far as I could notice, perfectly neat. She caught at her cloak, and, in assisting her, I felt the touch of a soft, white hand.

"By this time we had walked through the Rue Magasin, St. Germain, Ecole de Médecine, and a few little alleys, when all at once she stopped short, and said she had lost her way. She said she lived in *Rue St. Severin.* I was puzzled, for I did not know where to find it myself. I saw a light in a brandy-shop in a cellar, and went down to ask the way, leaving her alone. When I came up, I heard voices speaking loud, and saw, by the dim light of a street lamp, that the girl was struggling with two gentlemen, one of whom had seized her hand, while the other had hold of her cloak; they were laughing and talking to her. I suspected what was going on, and pulled the cloak out of his grasp. She clung to my arm, sobbing and speechless. 'Gentlemen,' I said, 'you see you are mistaken. Let go the lady's cloak this moment!' 'Ah! excuse me, sir,' said the stranger, 'I see you have a prior right to the lady,' and they went off laughing. We walked on, and the poor girl clung to my arm as though she was afraid of falling down in the street. 'Courage, courage!' I said, 'St. Severin is only a little way off, and you'll soon be at home.' When we reached the street, she stopped short. 'No, sir, you must not go any farther with me,' said she. 'Why not, pray, since you have brought me so far with you already? I beg of you not to suspect me of an improper motive.' I had unconsciously taken her hand, and perhaps pressed it; she withdrew it hastily, and added, 'Forgive me my rudeness in bringing you so far out of your way. I beg of you, leave me now!' I understood that the advances of the strangers had wounded her deeply, and perhaps even made her suspicious of me, and this had a great effect upon me. I took out the silver I had got from Faldner, and was going to hand it to her, but the thought of the trifling aid this small sum would afford, made me withdraw my hand, and I gave her what little gold I had about me. Her hand trembled as she took it: she seemed to suppose it was silver, thanked me in an unsteady but sweet voice, and was going away. 'Stop,' said I, 'I hope your mother will be better; but she may perhaps be in want of something, and, my girl, you are not the right person for such night excursions as this. Will you not be in front of the *Ecole de Médecine* this day week at the same hour, so that I can hear how your mother is?' She seemed to hesitate, but at last said 'Yes.' 'And put on that hat with the green veil, so that I may know you again.' She promised to do so, thanked me again, ran hastily up the street, and was lost in the darkness."

"When I awoke the next morning, my adventure seemed like a dream. But Faldner, who came soon, and began to rally me with his usual delicacy, removed all doubts. The thing seemed to me, when considered in the clear light of the morning, altogether too fabulous to be told to my skeptical friend. We have reached, now-a-days, a pitch of delicacy which borders closely on indelicacy; we had often rather seem wild and debauched, than singular or unused to the ways of the world. I was disturbed by some undefinable feeling, even more than by Faldner's jokes. I reproached myself for not having got a sight of her face, at any rate. 'Why this excessive delicacy?' I said to myself; 'really, for a couple of Napoleons, it would not have been too much just to ask her to raise her veil for a moment.' And yet when I reflected on her whole deportment, which, simple as it was, was wholly free from vulgarity, I was forced, half unwillingly, to own that I did right. The voice alone is a sufficient distinction between good-breeding and rudeness; and the sweet tones I had listened to *must* belong to a person of some education and refinement. I could not get rid of these thoughts all day long; and at night, when I visited a brilliant circle of ladies, I was accompanied in my mind by the poor girl in her black hat, green veil, and impenetrable cloak. The rest of the week I kept blaming myself for my folly, and yet indulging in it. It seemed as though the capital of the civilized world, with all its attractions, had nothing worth noticing except the *Pont-des-Arts.* At last the Friday came. I used every stratagem to get rid of Faldner and the rest of my friends, and set out as soon as it was dark. It was an hour's walk, and I had time enough for reflection; and I determined to see her face at any rate, and to make up my mind what to think of her. I had started off so early, that it was only ten when I reached the *Ecole de Médecine*—a full hour before my time. I stepped into a café, and tumbled over a file of newspapers: at last it struck eleven.

"There were few people about, and no green veil to be seen anywhere. Suppose she should not come, thought I, as I walked up and down for the tenth time. The half hour struck, and I began to grumble at my own folly, when I saw something green, under a lamp some thirty paces off. I hurried up—and it was she. 'Good evening,' said I, 'I am glad you are come—I was afraid you would not keep your appointment.' She bowed low, without taking my hand, and walked by my side. She seemed deeply moved. 'Sir, my noble-hearted countrymen,' said she, 'I could not but keep my word, if only to thank you. Be assured it is not in order to make fresh demands on your benevolence. Oh, how richly, how generously you have treated us! Can a daughter's heartfelt thanks, can my sick mother's prayers and blessings be any return for it?' 'Don't say a word about it,' answered I; 'how is your mother?' 'I believe I may begin to hope again the physician does not speak, decidedly, but she feels stronger. Oh, how much I thank you! Your liberal present enabled me to buy her strengthening food; and, believe me, sir, the thought that such good men are still to be found in the world has done her almost as much service.' 'What did your mother say to you when you came home?' I inquired. 'She was very anxious, as it was so late; she had been very unwilling to let me go out, and was afraid of some mischief happening. I told her every thing; but when I untied my handkerchief and drew out the presents you gave me, and there was gold among them—gold among the copper and silver—she was astonished, and—' She stopped and seemed unable to go on. I could guess that her mother had suspected something wrong, and I put some more questions; but she answered, with touching frankness, 'that her mother said their generous countryman must be either a prince or an angel.' 'I am neither the one nor the other,' I replied; 'but how much have you left?—any thing?' 'Oh, yes,' said she, confidently; but it did not escape me that she sighed unconsciously at the same time. 'How much is there left?' I asked, and more peremptorily. 'Oh, we paid our bill at the apothecary's, and a month's rent, and I bought something for mother to eat, and there is something left yet!' How wretchedly they must live, thought I, when out of this trifle they can pay for medicines and a month's rent, and buy food for a week! 'I want you to tell me exactly how much there is left,' I continued. 'Sir!' was her reply, as she drew back a step. 'My good girl, you do not, or you will not understand me. I ask you seriously what you expect to do when this little sum is gone? have you any prospect of assistance?' 'No, none!' was the sad answer. 'Think of your mother, and do not reject my aid,' I added. I offered her my hand, and she pressed it to her heart gratefully. 'Come with me, then,' said I; 'I do not come straight from home, and am unluckily without money; be good enough to go a little way with me, and I will give you something for your mother.' She went with me in silence; and though I was pleased with the thought of having her with me, I felt almost hurt that she should go with me so readily, by night, to a gentleman's lodgings—but it was not so. After walking a few hundred paces, she drew her arm out of mine. 'No, no, I must not, I cannot,' she cried, bursting into tears. 'Why not?—what is the matter?' asked I. 'I will not go further—I cannot go with you.' 'Upon my word,' I cried, with some anger, 'you really have very little confidence in me; if it was not for your mother I would quit you at once, for you insult me.' She took my hand and pressed it fervently. 'Have I offended you? God knows I did not mean it. Pardon a poor ignorant girl. You are so generous, how could I think of offending you?' 'Come along, then,' I rejoined, 'we have no time to lose' it is late, and we are a good way off.' But she stopped short and said, 'No, nothing shall tempt me to go further.' 'What are you afraid of? There is no one here—you may go with me in safety.' But she only repeated, 'I beg you, for God's sake, to leave me!' I knew very well that if I painted her mother's need in lively colours, she would go with me, but I was moved at her suffering. 'Well, then, stay,' I told her; 'but stop, do you understand needle-work?'

"'Oh, yes, sir,' she said, drying her tears.

"'Here is a white handkerchief—can you hem and mark a half dozen such for me?'

"She looked at it, and answered, 'With pleasure, sir, and do it neatly, too.'

"To my mortification, I had to produce money, though I had pretended to have none about me.

"Here, buy six of them; can you have three ready by next Sunday?' She promised to do it, and I gave her something more for her mother. She thanked me warmly, and seemed to be pleased that I had given her work, for she kept chattering on about how neatly she would do the handkerchiefs, and once she asked me if I would have a border *à l'Anglaise*. I said yes to every thing, but held her fast as she was leaving me. 'There is something else you must do to oblige me; you can do it, and that easily,' I remarked.

"'And pray what is it? I will gladly do any thing for you,' was her answer.

"'Let me, then, lift that envious veil and see your face, that I may have some recollection of this night.'

"She slipped aside, and only held her veil tighter. 'Do not, I beg of you,' she said, seeming to struggle with herself at the time; 'you have the sweet remembrance of your bounty; my mother strictly forbade me to lift my veil, and, besides, I assure you I am as ugly as darkness itself. I would only frighten you!'

"Her resistance only roused my curiosity still more; a really ugly woman, I thought, would never say so of herself. I tried to catch her veil, but she slipped away like an eel, crying, '*Dimanche à revoir*,' and was gone. She stopped some fifty yards off, waved my white handkerchief, and said, 'Good-night,' in her silvery voice."

"The next week I busied myself in thinking what the girl's rank in life could be. The more I dwelt on her choice language and delicate feelings, the higher I was inclined to place her. I determined to ascertain that point at any rate, and not to be put off again so easily as in the matter of the veil. The Sunday came, and you may remember that afternoon, Faldner, which we spent at Montmorenci. You wanted to stay late, and I urged you to go home early, and finally went off without you. You did not believe the excuse I gave, that I could not bear the night air; but you did not dream of a rendezvous with the beggar-girl of the *Pont-des-Arts*—and how could you? She was the first on the ground this time, and as she had the handkerchiefs to give me, she was beginning to fear I had missed her. She kept talking on with almost childlike delight, and, as I fancied, with more confidence than before, while showing me her work by the light of a street lamp. She seemed delighted to hear me praise her needle-work.

"'See,' said she, 'I have worked in your name, too,' pointing to E. V. F. beautifully embroidered in the corner. She wanted to give me back a handful of silver, and nothing but my declaring that I should feel insulted by her doing so, induced her to take it again. I ordered something else, as I saw that this way of giving charity was most agreeable to her feelings. Her mother was not worse, though still confined to her bed. When we had disposed of this subject, I asked her directly what was her family and condition. Her story, which was told in a few words, is so common a one in France that I suppose it is the burden of every beggar's petition. Her father was an officer in the *grande armée*, who had been put upon half-pay after the restoration, had joined the emperor in the hundred days, and fallen with the guard at Waterloo. His widow lost his pension, and lived afterwards poorly and wretchedly. For two years they had subsisted on the remains of their little property, and had just reached that lowest degree of misery, when no resource remains but to quit the world at once. I asked her if she could not have assisted her mother in some other way.

"'You mean by going out to service?' inquired she, without the least embarrassment; 'certainly; but I could not do it. Before my mother fell sick, I was too young, hardly fourteen, and when she got so bad that she could not leave her bed, I had to remain with her. If she had continued well, I would gladly have forgotten our former situation, and would have gone to a milliner's, or got a situation as governess, for I have been well educated, sir but it could not be.'

"I again begged her to raise her veil, but in vain. The allusion she made to her age rendered me, I will confess, still more anxious to see her face. She could not be much over sixteen; but she begged me so earnestly to excuse her; she said her mother had given her such good reasons for avoiding it that it could not be. After this, we used to meet twice a week. I had always some work for her, and she was always ready with it at the appointed time. The more closely I adhered to the deportment I had always showed towards her, the more distant and respectful I was, the more frank and confiding did she become. She even confessed to me that, when at home, she was always thinking of our next meeting; and did not I do the same? Day and night I thought only of this singular creature, whose refined taste, amiable softness, and peculiar situation made her every day more interesting to me. Meantime, spring had arrived, and with it the time at which I had promised Faldner to join him in a trip to England. Many may think what I say silly, but it is the fact, that I thought of our journey with reluctance. Paris had nothing to interest me longer, but the beggar-girl had so captivated my senses that I looked forward with sorrow to our separation. I could not avoid going without making myself a laughing-stock—for no other sufficient reason for putting off our excursion could be devised. I was ashamed of myself, too, and reproached myself with my own folly. I determined to go, but certainly no one ever took so little pleasure in seeing England as I did."

"I told her of my intention a week beforehand; she trembled and wept. I told her to ask her mother for permission to visit her, and she gave it. The next time, however, she told me, with great concern, that her mother begged me to give up the idea, as a visit, in her present frame of mind, would overcome her I thought of it only as a means of seeing my fair one by daylight, and unveiled, so I requested this favour again. She wished me to come again before going away, and promised to obtain her mother's permission. I shall never forget that evening. She came, and my first question was whether she had agreed to it; she said yes, and raised her veil herself. The moon shone bright, and I looked under her hat with trembling eagerness. It seemed, however, that the permission to unveil was only a partial one, for she wore what is called a Venetian mask, which hides the upper part of the face. But how beautiful, how finished were the features that I saw! A small, delicate nose, blooming cheeks, a lovely mouth, a perfect chin, and a graceful, dazzling white neck. As to her eyes, I could not satisfy myself, but I fancied they were dark and fiery. She blushed as I gazed long and transportedly at her. 'Do not be angry with me, sir,' said she, 'for wearing this half-mask; my mother would not allow it at all at first, and, after all, it was only on this condition. I felt provoked at it myself; but she gave me good reasons for it, and I saw the force of them.'

"'And pray what were her reasons?' I asked.

"'Oh, sir,' cried she, mournfully, 'you will live for ever in our hearts, but you must forget us, nevertheless; you must never, never see me again, or if you do, must not recognise me!'

"'Do you suppose, then, that I shall not recollect these fine features, even if I should not see your eyes or forehead?'

"'My mother thinks you will not,' was her answer; 'she says it is very hard to remember a face that we have only seen half of.'

"'And why must I not see you—not recognise you?'

"She wept again, and clasped my hand as she replied, 'It must not be! You will not care about ever meeting the poor beggar-girl again, and—no, my mother was right, it is better thus!'

"I told her that my journey would be a short one—that I should probably be back in Paris in two months, and that I hoped to meet her again. She only wept more bitterly, and shook her head. I asked why she doubted it.

"'I feel that this is the last time I shall ever see you,' she told me. 'I do not think my mother will live long: our physician told me so yesterday—and then all is over! And even if she should live, when you go to London you'll soon forget such a poor, wretched creature as I am.' Her grief affected me deeply. I tried to console her; I promised solemnly that I never would forget her. I made her promise to be in the same place on the first and fifteenth of every month to meet me. She promised it, smiling through her tears, as if she felt little hope of it. 'Farewell, then, till we meet again!' I said, as I clasped her in my arms, and put a small plain ring on her finger; 'farewell!—think of me sometimes, and do not forget the first and fifteenth.'

"'How could I forget it!' she answered, looking up to me tearfully. 'But I shall never see you again; you are bidding me adieu for ever.'

"I could not refrain from kissing her soft lips. She blushed, but did not resist. I slipped a bank-note into her hand—she eyed me anxiously, and clung closer to me. 'Farewell, till we meet again!' I said, as she gently freed herself from my embrace. The moment of parting seemed to give her courage; she threw her arms around me, and I felt a warm kiss on her lips as she said, passionately, 'For ever—farewell for ever!' and disappeared.

"I have never seen her since. After a stay of three months, I returned to Paris; on the fifteenth, I repaired to the *Place de l'Ecole de Médecine*, and waited there over an hour; but my fair one did not appear. I went there again and again, on the first and fifteenth of every month; many a time, too, I strode through the *Rue St. Severin*, and looked up to the windows, and inquired for a poor German lady with one daughter; but I never heard of them again, and the sweet girl was right when she bade me farewell, 'for ever.'"

Our hero told his tale with a degree of earnestness that added to its effect, and it plainly produced a deep impression, at least on the feminine portion of the company. Josephine wept, and many of the ladies wiped their eyes by stealth. The gentlemen had grown serious, and seemed to listen with much interest; only the Baron smiled meaningly, and touched his neighbour's elbow every now and then, and whispered something in his ear. When Froben paused, he broke into a loud laugh. "That's what I call getting cleverly out of the scrape!" he cried. "I always said our friend was a deep one. Only see how the ladies are moved—the dog! and my wife there is whining, as though the priest had refused her absolution. Capital, upon my word! Truth and fiction! Yes, yes, you have been copying Göthe—truth and fiction! It's a capital joke!"

Froben felt hurt, and answered, in some displeasure, "I told you at first that I intended to avoid fiction, and tell nothing but the truth, and I hope you will not refuse to believe it such."

"Heaven forbid!" replied the Baron, laughingly. "The truth is, you made your own arrangement with the girl, and now you have built up a little romance out of your visits to her. But you told the story well—that I won't deny."

The young man's colour changed; he noticed that Josephine's eyes were fixed anxiously upon her husband; he thought he saw that she was of Faldner's opinion, and he was unwilling to be deprived of her esteem by this vulgar wit. "I beg you to say no more about it," he went on; "I have never yet had any reason to put a false colouring on any action of mine, and I cannot allow others to do it for me. I tell you, for the last time, on my word, every thing happened just as I have told it."

"Then, heaven pity you!" answered Faldner, clapping his hands; "for, if so, your exaggerated delicacy and theoretical weakness made you throw away a couple of hundred francs on a cunning street-walker, who took you in with an every-day story about poverty and a sick mother, and you got nothing for it but one poor kiss! Poor devil, to be made such a fool of in Paris!"

This insinuation, and the loud laughter with which it was greeted, provoked our hero still further. He was about to leave the company in a towering passion, when he was arrested by an unexpected sight. Josephine rose up slowly, pale as a corpse, and seemed about to make some reply to her husband, but sank down lifeless. Everybody sprang up and ran about in confusion; the ladies assisted her, the gentlemen asked each other how it had happened so suddenly. Froben came near fainting himself, in alarm, and the Baron muttered curses upon the weak nerves of women, and their fastidious delicacy, that makes them faint so easily—all was confusion. Josephine came to herself in a few minutes; she wished to retire to her room, and all the ladies crowded after her, all busy, and all curious; a hundred remedies were proposed, all of which had been found specifics in cases of fainting, and finally it was unanimously resolved that the Baroness' great exertions to entertain her guests, and the cares of her household, had produced the unpleasant accident, aided, perhaps, by the embarrassments she must have felt at the very improper language her husband had allowed himself to use.

The Baron was busy, in the mean time, in bringing back the company to order. He pledged his guests, and endeavoured to quiet their apprehensions by all the arguments he could devise. "It's nothing but a new-fangled notion," said he; "every lady of rank has weak nerves, and if she has not, she fears she will be taken for ill-bred; this fainting away is the fashion. Another notion is, that we must never call any thing by its right name; every thing must be so delicate, devout, lady-like, and proprietyfied, that its enough to drive a man mad. She is angry now, because I indulged in an innocent jest—because I did not melt away in sympathy at this most tender and affecting story, but, instead, ventured to throw out a few practical suggestions! Why, there's no harm in such things among ourselves! And as for you, friend Froben, I thought you were too sensible a man to take offence so easily."

The person he addressed had disappeared, and repaired to his chamber, out of humour with himself and with the world. He was at a loss how to account for what happened, and his mind, half indignant at his friend's coarseness, half alarmed at Josephine's accident, was too much moved to admit of calm reflection. "Will not *she* believe me?" he thought to himself, "will she give more weight to her husband's sneers than to the plain, unadorned truth with which I told my story? What meant the strange glances she cast upon me while I was speaking? How could this adventure affect her so deeply as to make her turn pale and tremble? Does she really respect me, and was she offended at his rudeness, which must have lowered me so much in her eyes? And what did she mean to say, when she rose, to check Faldner's vulgarity? or to defend me even?" He paced up and down his room as he thought thus, and his eyes fell upon the engraving of his beloved picture. He unrolled it, and eyed it with a bitter smile. "And how could I let a feeling of shame induce me to open my heart to beings who understand nothing about matters of which the fashionable world is ignorant: vice and meanness seem to them more proper, more natural, than unusual virtue. How could I forget myself so far as to speak of those lips and cheeks to stocks and stones! Poor, poor girl! how far nobler art thou, in thy low estate, than these butterflies, who know real suffering and honest poverty only from report, and who treat as a fable every virtue that rises above their own level! Where art thou now? and dost thou think of thy friend, and those evenings that made him so happy!" These thoughts changed the current of his feelings, and grief took the place of anger.

The next morning Froben turned over in his mind the events of the day before, and was debating with himsel whether or not he should leave the house, when his door opened, and the Baron entered, crest-fallen and ashamed. "You did not come to table last night, nor this morning," he began; "you are angry; but be reasonable, and pardon me; I had drunk too much wine, and you know my weakness when I am heated; I cannot forbear joking. I have been punished enough already in having my fête end so, and making me the talk of the neighbourhood for a month to come. Don't make me more miserable; let us be friendly as before."

"Let the affair rest," said Froben, gloomily, as he offered him his hand, "I do not like to discuss such subjects; but to-morrow I must leave you; I cannot stay here longer."

"Don't be such a fool," said Faldner, who had not expected this, "to be off for such a trifle; but I always said you were a hot-headed fellow. No, you can't go; you know you must wait at any rate till we get an answer from the Don. As for our friends you need not be uneasy, for they all gave me a famous scolding, especially the women, and said you were right, and I was to blame for all."

"How is the Baroness?" asked Froben, to change the subject.

"Oh, perfectly well; she was only a little frightened for fear of some difficulty between us; she is waiting breakfast for you; come down and be reasonable. I must be off to the mill. It's all forgotten, is it not?"

"Certainly, only let us drop the subject," was his answer, and he followed the Baron, who, full of pleasure at their speedy reconciliation, informed his lady of what had passed, and hastened to the mill. To Froben it seemed that every thing was changed; perhaps the change was in himself only. Josephine's features, her whole deportment, seemed different. A settled melancholy, a tender sorrow seemed to have settled upon her features, yet her smile, as she welcomed him, was sweet and kind. She ascribed her illness of the day before to over-exertion, and seemed to wish to avoid the subject. But Froben, who set so high a value on her good opinion, could not consent to her refraining from all allusion to his story, and he told her, "I cannot suffer you to elude me so, Baroness! I think little of the opinions of others. What do I care if they choose to measure me by their own standard! But really I should be deeply grieved if you should come to a false conclusion, or even entertain for a moment opinions which must lower me greatly in your esteem. I beg of you, tell me honestly what you think of me and of my story?"

She eyed him for some time; her fine eyes filled with tears, as she took his hand and replied—"What I think of it, Froben? If the whole world should doubt it, *I* at least know that you have spoken the truth. You are not aware how well I know you!"

His colour rose with pleasure as he kissed her hand. "How good it is in you not to misunderstand me," was his answer. "And indeed every word I said was the exact truth."

"And this girl," she continued, "is it she of whom you were speaking lately? Don't you remember when we were talking of Jean Paul's Clotilda, and you owned to me that you were in love, and without hope? Is it she?"

"It is," he answered gloomily. "No, you must not laugh at this folly; you can feel too deeply to think it ridiculous. I know how much may be said against this fancy. I have often blamed myself as a fool, a dreamer chasing a shadow. I do not even know whether she loves me in return."

"She does!" cried Josephine, involuntarily; but blushing at what she said, she added, "she must love you: believe me, such noble conduct must have made a deep impression on the heart of a girl of sixteen; and in all her language, as you have told it, there lurks, unless I am greatly mistaken, a very considerable degree of love."

Our hero listened to her words with delight. "How often I have said so to myself, when I was without hope, and looked back sadly to the past!" he rejoined. "But to what purpose? Only to make myself more unhappy. I have often struggled with myself, have often sought to distract myself in the crowd, to occupy my mind with a press of business. That fair unhappy figure always hovered before my eyes, and to see her once more was all I craved. I desire it still; I may confess it to you, for you can understand and respect my feelings; and I set out on a journey only because my longing desire to search for her and to look upon her drove me from home. And when I reflect upon it, it sometimes seems to me as if she might yet be mine! You turn away your head. Oh, I understand; you think I ought not to marry any one who was sunk so low in poverty, of such doubtful descent; you are thinking of the opinions of the world, and I have often thought over it myself, but, so true as I live, if I were to find her again such as I left her, I would take counsel only of my heart. Would you censure me severely for doing so?"

She did not answer; her head was turned aside, and rested on her hand. Without moving, she handed him a book, and asked him to read for her He took it, looking at her inquiringly; for the first time he could not understand her behaviour; but she made a sign to him to read, and he obeyed, though he would rather have poured out the fulness of his heart still further. He read at first without attention, but after awhile the subject attracted him, and drew his thoughts more and more away from their conversation, and finally so engrossed him that he did not observe that the Baroness turned upon him a look of sadness, that her glances were fixed tenderly upon him, and that her eyes often filled with tears, which it was not easy to repress. By the time he had done, Josephine had recovered herself so far that she could talk composedly about the author; but he still fancied that her voice trembled at times, and the kind familiarity with which she had always treated her husband's friend had disappeared, and he would have felt unhappy, except that the warm feelings expressed in her eyes made him doubt the accuracy of his observation.

As the Baron was not expected till evening, and his lady had retired to her apartments, Froben resolved to sleep away the sultry noon-day heat till dinner-time. He threw himself down on a mossy bank in the arbour which the many pleasing hours he had spent there with his amiable hostess had endeared to him, and was soon asleep. He had left his cares behind, they did not pursue him into the land of dreams; pleasant recollections only came, and mingled and shaped themselves into new and bright images; the young girl of the *Rue St. Severin* hovered before him with her sweet voice, and began to talk of her mother; he scolded her for staying away so long, as he had never failed to look for her on the first and fifteenth of every month; he tried to steal a kiss to punish her, she resisted; he raised her veil, and saw Don Pedro, dressed in his love's clothes, and Diego his servant ready to burst with laughing at the trick. Then fancy, at one bold leap, placed him in the picture-gallery in Stuttgart. The paintings had been differently arranged, he looked through all the rooms for his favourite portrait, but in vain, it was not to be found; he began to weep and to complain loudly, when the attendant came up, and asked him to be quiet and not wake the pictures, as they were all asleep just then. All at once he saw it hanging in a corner, not as before a half-length, but large as life; it looked mischievously at him, then stepped out of the frame and embraced her bewildered adorer; he felt a long, warm kiss on his lips. It sometimes happens when we are dreaming, that we think we awake, and say to ourselves it was all a dream, and so it was with him. He thought that the kiss wakened him, and that he opened his eyes, and lo! a blooming face, that seemed a well-known one, bent over him. He closed his eyes again, faint with the delicious feeling of the warm breath, the sweet kisses that he drank in; he heard a noise, he opened his eyes again, and he saw a figure in a black hat and cloak, with a green veil, flit away. As she turned a corner she looked round at him again; it was the features of his beloved, and she wore the same envious mask. "Ah! it's only a dream!" he said, laughing at himself, and tried to shut his eyes again, but the consciousness of being awake, the rustling of the leaves in the wind, and the plashing of the fountains were so plain that he was soon fully aroused. The strange and well-defined shape of his dream stood lifelike before his mind, he looked towards the corner, round which she vanished, towards the spot where she stood and bent over him, and he thought he yet felt her kisses on his lips. "Has it come to this, then," he thought, not without alarm, "that I dream by day, and think I see her before me! To what madness will this lead? No, I never should have believed that any one could dream so vividly. It is a sickness of the brain, a fever of the fancy, and I am almost disposed to believe that dreams can leave foot-prints behind them, for those in the sand here are not the marks of my foot." His glance fell on the bench where he had lain, and he saw a folded paper; he took it up in great surprise. There was no direction, it was folded like a billet-doux; he debated a moment whether to open it or not, but curiosity prevailed, he opened it, and—a ring fell out. He held it in his hand while he ran over the letter hastily. "Often am I near thee, my noble benefactor, often am I near thee, filled with that inexpressible love which gratitude inspires, and which will end only with life. I know thy noble heart beats for me alone: thou hast wandered through distant countries to meet me, but in vain—forget an unhappy creature—for what avails it? There is happiness in the thought of being thine, and thine only, but it cannot be! For ever! was the word I said even then; I love, indeed, but fate condemns us to live asunder; only in your memory is she allowed to live as The Beggar-Girl of the Pont-des-Arts."

Our hero a second time fancied he was dreaming; he looked round inquiringly, but the well-known objects around him—the arbour, the trees, the distant castle, were all in their places, and he saw that he was really awake. And the letter was there—a real epistle, and no creation of fancy. "Perhaps some one is playing me a trick," he thought; "it must be so, it is Josephine's work, and the figure I saw was only a masquerade." He felt the ring lying in his hand, and turned pale as he examined it. No, *here* was no trick, it was the self-same ring he gave his beloved when he bade her farewell for ever. Though at first tempted to indulge in superstitious feelings, the idea that finally gained the mastery was, that this token of his mistress indicated that she must be near at hand. The idea was rapture; he would not allow himself to doubt; he would see her, and that soon. He pressed the ring to his lips and rushed out of the arbour. His glances wandered in every direction in hopes of seeing her. But he looked in vain. He asked the workmen in the garden, the servants in the castle, whether they had seen any strange lady. They had seen no one. He sat down to table in perfect bewilderment. It was in vain that Faldner sought to learn the cause of his embarrassment; that the Baroness asked whether it was the scene of yesterday that disturbed him; his only answer was, "that something had happened which he should certainly call a miracle, if his reason did not overcome his superstitious feelings."

This strange occurrence, and the language of the note, which he read over ten times a day, made him very thoughtful. He began to consider whether it was possible for heavenly beings to mingle among men. He had often laughed at the enthusiasts who believe in appearances and messages from another world, and divine spirits that wait on man, as firmly as they do in the Gospel. He had often proved the physical impossibility of such apparitions, but what was he to think now? He determined to forget it all, and the very next moment wearied himself with efforts to render the recollection still more vivid. The next day it happened again that Josephine was too busy in household affairs to entertain him, and he repaired to the well-known arbour. He read, and as he did so, the thought that perhaps she might appear again, distracted his attention. The mid-day heat was exhausting; he tried to keep himself awake; he read with more zeal and exertion, but his head gradually fell back, the book dropped from his hands, and he fell asleep.

He awoke at about the same hour as on the day before, but no green-veiled figure was in sight; he laughed at himself for having expected her, and rose up sad and discontented to return to the castle. All at once he saw a white handkerchief lying near him, which he did not remember to have placed there; he looked at it, and was sure it was his, for it was marked with his initials. "How did this get here?" he asked himself, in amazement, as he saw that it was one of the handkerchiefs which his beloved had hemmed for him, and which he always kept as sacredly as if they had been holy reliques. "Is this another token?" thought he, as he opened it in the hope of finding another billet-doux. He was disappointed, but he noticed something embroidered in one of the corners, and on examining it he read the words, "For ever!" "She has been here then!" he exclaimed, "and I have slept through it all like a sluggard! Why this new token? why repeat those sad words which have made me so unhappy already?" He again asked all the servants if they had seen any stranger in the garden. They all said No; and the old gardener added, that no one had been in the garden for three hours but her ladyship. "And how was she dressed?" asked Froben, in great surprise. "Oh, sir, that's more than I can tell you," was the answer; "she is always dressed like a lady, but what she wore I can't tell you, by the same token, as she passed, she nodded in her friendly way, and said, 'Good-day, Jacob.'" Our hero took him aside. "I entreat you to tell me," he whispered, "did she wear a green veil? had she large black goggles?" The old man looked at him suspiciously and shook his head. "Black goggles! her ladyship wear black goggles! Why, how can you say so? her eyes are as clear and sharp as a chamois', and she to wear black goggles like the old women at church! No, no, sir, you must not let such foolish ideas get into your brain; and excuse me, sir, but the sun is so hot I think you had better put on a hat for fear of a stroke of the sun." So said the old gardener and walked away, touching his forehead with his forefinger, to hint to the other servants that he was afraid there was something wrong in the young gentleman's upper story.

The only way Froben could account for this mysterious proceeding was, that it was unaccountable; and this strange way of sporting with his affections and his honour occupied him so much, that he did not see many things which otherwise would hardly have escaped his notice. Josephine's eyes were red when they met at table. The Baron was cross and silent, and seemed to be obliged to give vent to the ill-humour which clouded his brow and eye, by an occasional curse at his wife's bad cookery and worse housekeeping. She made no answer; sometimes she cast a glance at Froben, as though imploring his assistance or consolation; alas, she did not notice that her husband watched those looks, and that they made the red spot on his cheek grow deeper. As for Froben, he thought it nothing unusual, and did not even take the trouble to ask the Baroness the reason of her husband's ill-humour; nor did he think it strange that she grew more reserved in Faldner's presence, and when his friend forced him to accompany him on his visits to his farms, and spend the whole day with him in measuring, viewing, and calculating, he only ascribed it to his restless activity. One day, however, he was a little surprised at his behaviour. Faldner was waiting for him to ride out, booted and spurred. He feigned slight illness as an excuse, and on his adding, unsuspectingly, "Besides, you know I must stay and read to your wife sometimes," the Baron cried out in high anger, "No, I will not have any more reading Every thing is going wrong already without that. I don't want to have her head filled with such romantic notions as I've seen a sample of lately. Read to yourself, my dear fellow, and excuse me if I dispose of my wife otherwise. Go down into the garden, Josephine, there are some vegetables to be got ready for dinner, and afterwards be good enough to go to the clergyman's; you have owed them a visit this long time." Saying this, he took up his whip and walked away. "What does this mean? what is the matter with him to-day?" Froben asked in astonishment, seeing that Josephine had hard work to keep from sobbing. "Oh, he is always so," was her answer: "your visit made a little difference at first, but he is now himself again." "But, for heaven's sake!" cried Froben, "send one of your servants into the garden." "I must not," she answered decidedly, "I must see to it myself," "And the visit to the clergyman's!" "You have heard that I *must* pay it; let us say no more about it. But yourself seemed changed within these few days; you are not so cheerful as you were. Do you find it disagreeable here? Have either my husband or myself done any thing that is unpleasant?"

Froben was confused: he was on the point of telling her his strange adventure in the garden; but the idea of exposing his weakness to her restrained him. "I received letters from —— lately, and if my humour seems changed, they are the cause," was his answer. She looked at him doubtingly; a reply seemed to hover upon her lips, but it seemed as if she was hurt at the want of confidence his looks expressed, and she suppressed it. She rang for her maid, and descended to the garden without inviting him to accompany her.

Some hours later he walked into the garden, and on asking for the Baroness, was told that she had gone to the clergyman's. He hastened to the arbour, and sat down with a beating heart. He was determined to keep awake this time. "I will see," said he, "whether this being that hovers round my steps so strangely will bring me a third token. I will pretend to sleep, and by my life, if it comes again, I will find out what it is!" He read till noon, then lay down upon the seat and closed his eyes. He was more than once nearly overpowered by sleep, but expectation, uneasiness, and his firm resolution to shake off the heavy dew of slumber kept him awake. He had lain so for perhaps half an hour, when the shrubbery rustled. He half opened his eyes, and saw how two white hands parted the branches gently, so as to get a view of the sleeper. Then light, light steps were pressed upon the gravel. He looked by stealth at the entrance of the arbour, and his heart was ready to burst with impatient joy, when he saw his beloved in her black cloak and hat, the green veil thrown back, and the black half mask before the upper part of her sweet face.

She approached on tiptoe. He saw that a deeper glow tinged her cheeks as she drew nearer. She eyed the sleeper fixedly, sighed deeply, and seemed to wipe away a tear. Then she came up to him, bent down, her breath was upon his lips—she bent yet lower, and her mouth rested upon his as gently as the rosy morning alights upon the hill.

He could not restrain himself longer; he threw his arms around her, and she sank upon her knees with a short cry of terror. He sprang up in great alarm, supposing that she had fainted; but it was not so. Filled with delight at finding her again, he raised her up, and drew her to a seat beside him. He covered her face with glowing kisses; he clasped her closer and closer. "No; this is no vision of fancy. I hold thee in my arms as I once did; I love thee as I did then, and am happy, for thou lovest me too!" Her cheeks were crimson—she made no answer, but tried to free herself from his embrace. "No, this time I will not let you go," he cried; "I will hold you fast this time; and no power on earth shall tear me from you. Come, away with this envious mask—I will see the whole of that lovely face—ah! I have often beheld it in my dreams!" She seemed to wish to resist—she drew her breath heavily, and struggled with him; but our hero's ecstasy of delight at this unexpected discovery soon made him the conqueror. He held her arms with one hand, with the other he threw back her hat, untied the mask, and saw——his friend's wife. "Josephine!" he cried in despair, as though an abyss opened before him. She sat beside him pale, stupified, and speechless, and only said with a sad smile, "Yes, Josephine." "Have *you* been trifling with me so?" he asked; and all his hopes and his happiness vanished. "You might have spared me this masquerade. But," as a new idea flashed upon him, "tell me, for heaven's sake, where did you get this ring, this handkerchief?"

She blushed, wept, and hid her face. "This will not do, I must have an answer." He went on—"The ring and handkerchief are mine—how did they come into your hands?"

"From thee!" was all she whispered. A new light came upon him; it almost dazzled him, but he embraced her, and gazed at her with looks of love and wonder. "You—you are she, and it is no dream!" he exclaimed. "Did I hear aright? Did you say that you were my beloved girl? Oh, heavens! what a cloud was upon my eyes! Yes, these are her cheeks, this her mouth, and this is not the first time I have kissed it!" She looked at him with loving eyes. "What would have become of me without you, noble-hearted man!" she went on; and the light of her eyes was quenched in tears. "I bring you the blessing of my dying mother; you made her last days quiet, and relieved her from the load of misery that lay so heavy on her. How can I ever thank you? what would I have been without you? But," and she hid her face in her hands, "what *am* I now? the wife of another, the wife of thy friend!" He saw that her bosom heaved with grief, and streams of tears flowed through her fingers. He felt how deeply she must love him, and he never thought of reproaching her for having given herself to another. "It is so," said he gloomily, drawing her closer, as though he feared to lose her, "it is so; let us think that it must be so, otherwise we should have been too happy. But in this minute you are wholly mine; fancy that you are once more coming across the Place de l'Ecole de Médecine, and that I am waiting for you. O, come! embrace me as you did then! Oh, embrace me for once, only once!" She hung upon his neck, lost in recollection; the remembrance of the present gradually melted away; bright and cheering thoughts rose up; a sweet smile played upon her lips and dimpled her cheeks. "And did you not know me?" she asked. "And did you not know me?" he asked in return. "Ah!" she said, "I watched your features closely, and thought they were printed on my heart; yet I did not know you. Perhaps it was because I only saw you at night, always wrapped in a cloak, with your hat pulled over your eyes. The first night you came, when you called to Faldner, 'Farewell till we meet again,' I thought I knew the tone, but I laughed at myself for my folly. But the moment you named the *Pont-des-Arts*, I saw that your face brightened, and I felt that it was you. That you did not recognise me is not wonderful; I have grown very pale since then, have I not?"

"Josephine! where were my senses, where was mine eye, mine ear, that I did not know you? The first time we met a pleasing alarm seized me, you were so like the portrait which chance led me to love, because it was so like you; but the discovery of your mother's family led me astray; I beheld in you only the daughter of the lovely Doña Laura de Tortosi, and my spirit wandered far away in search of yourself."

"O heavens," she cried, "is it true, is it possible! can you love me still?" "Can I not,—but must I, ought I?' was his sad answer. "You are the Baroness von Faldner—tell me, tell me how this happened? Could you not wait a little while for me!"

She dried her tears, and made an effort to compose herself before she answered him thus:—"It seemed as though ill-fortune had contrived every thing so as to make me as unhappy as possible. When you left us, I had no friend. From the very first moment, when you asked your companion for money in our dear mother-tongue, my heart was yours; and when you supplied our wants with such nobleness of mind and delicacy, I wanted to clasp you to my heart, and to confess that I worshipped you almost as a being of a higher order. When you left us, I wept bitterly, for a painful foreboding told me that we should never meet again. My mother died suddenly a week afterwards. The money you gave us enabled me to pay for her interment, and to discharge our little debts. A lady, the Countess Landskrau, who lived in the neighbourhood, heard of us and sent for me. She examined me as to my education, looked carefully at my mother's papers, and seemed satisfied. I became her companion, and we left Paris. I will not tell you how my heart bled at the idea; in a fortnight you would return, and I would have had a chance of seeing you again! It was not to be, Edward: I never heard of you afterwards. I did not even know your name, and thought you must have long since forgotten the beggar-girl. I lived on the bounty of strangers. I had to endure many mortifications. When the Countess came to live here, and Faldner paid court to me, when I saw that the Countess innocently regarded it as an excellent match, that she was very probably tired of me—I had been happy only once in my life, and could not hope ever to be so again—every thing else was indifferent to me, and I became his wife."

"Poor creature! Why, with your tender heart, your delicate sensibilities, your many claims to a more dignified station at least, why were you fated to be *his* wife? But so it is, and I cannot, must not remain here a single day longer. Rough as he is, I have once called him friend; I am now his guest, and even if this was not, we can never be happy!"

He spoke in deep sorrow, and he kissed her eyes only to avoid being yet more unmanned by the grief he read in them.

"Oh, stay but one day," she whispered; "I have but just found you, and yet you want to leave me. When you are gone, the door of happiness is closed to me for ever, and I want a few recollections to live upon in the wide desert in which my lot is cast."

"I will confess every thing to Faldner," cried Froben; "he will cast you off, and then I may claim you. My house is not so finely situated as his castle; you can take in all my estate from its roof; but within my domains you shall be queen, and I your first and truest slave!"

She only shook her head. "Such are your doctrines. I was brought up and married in the holy Catholic church, and nothing but death can ever make me free. How often our wishes are at variance with our duty!"

"Farewell, then, for ever," he added gloomily; "but till to-morrow, and then for ever!"

"For ever," she whispered, and clung to his breast.

"What, do I find you here, miserable strumpet?" cried at this moment a third person who stood near them. Both sprang up in terror; before them, trembling and gnashing his teeth with rage, stood the Baron, holding in one hand a paper, in the other a whip, which he was about to let fall on the fair shoulders of his unhappy wife. Froben interposed, took the whip from him, and flung it away, saying, "I beg of you not to make a scene here; your people are in the garden, and such violence would only disgrace you and your house."

"What!" cried Faldner, "is not my house enough disgraced already by this wretched creature—this beggar that I have entertained in it? Do you suppose I don't know your hand-writing?" he asked, showing her the paper; "here is a sweet letter to the gay gallant, the hero of the romance. So I was fated to marry a lady who had first been under your care, and when you are tired of her, honest Faldner is at hand to make her Her Ladyship; then, some six months after or so, the first friend comes, by mere accident, on a visit, just to renew an old acquaintance. As to that, *you* shall answer me, villain; as for this pauper, she may take her plate and lantern and go back to the *Pont-des-Arts*, or live on your wages. My servants shall horsewhip her out of the castle!"

The man of breeding has, at such times, a decided advantage over a vulgar adversary, whose anger makes him lose reason and self-command, and consequently bewilders. One glance at Josephine, who lay pale and trembling on the mossy bank, told Froben what was to be done. He gave her his arm, and led her to the castle. The Baron eyed them with rage; he was on the point of calling his servants to execute his threat, but was kept back by the fear of making his disgrace still more public. He hurried up to the parlour, where he found Josephine lying in tears on the sofa, hiding her face in the pillow, and Froben standing silently at a window. He ran around the room in fury; he cursed himself for having married such a creature. "If there is any law left in the country, I will be rid of her!" he cried: "she has given me false certificates; the pauper represented herself to be of noble birth—the marriage is null and void!"

"That is certainly the best thing you can do," rejoined Froben, "if you only set about it in the right way."

"Ha, sir!" roared the Baron, "are you laughing at me, after bringing on me this disgrace? Come along we don't need a court of law to separate us—that can be done in a moment; come along!"

Josephine, understanding what he meant, sprang up she flung herself at his feet, and begged him to punish her alone; she assured him that Froben was innocent; she confessed that she had written the letter, and declared that he had not discovered who she was till that morning. Our hero interrupted her, and led her back to the sofa. "Before taking such a step as you hint at, I generally make my arrangements, and I advise you to do the same," he said, coolly. "First of all, the Baroness must leave the castle, for I will not suffer her to remain here when I am not present to protect her from your ill-treatment."

"You act as if you felt yourself at home," replied the Baron, ironically; "but I had nearly forgotten madame was once your property. Where shall we take the sweet creature, then? To the poor-house, to a hospital, or to the next hedge, to follow her trade?"

Froben did not answer him; turning to Josephine, he asked, "Does the Countess still live in the neighbourhood? Cannot you find a home there for a few days?"

"I will go to her," she murmured.

"Very well; Faldner will have the goodness to send you there, and you can remain till Faldner finds out how unjust he has been towards us?"

Josephine went to the Countess's. Froben advised her to make her visit a short one, promising to inform her of her husband's movements, and to persuade him, if possible, to a reconciliation. "No!" she cried, passionately, "within these walls I will never appear again. I turn my back upon them for ever. Believe me, a woman can bear much, and I have been very patient, but to-day he has insulted me too deeply to be forgotten. Even if I have to go back to the *Pont-des-Arts*, to beg for a couple of sous, I would rather do it than submit to such insults from such a man. My father was a gallant soldier and esteemed officer of the Empire, and his daughter cannot stoop to be Faldner's maid-servant."

Froben began packing up when she left, and was busy writing a letter or two when Faldner entered his room. He was surprised to see his host, and expected a new burst of passion. But it was not so; he only said, "The more I read this unlucky letter, which I found in your room this forenoon, the more am I convinced that you are not to blame in this wretched affair—that is, that you did not know the person; that I found my wife in your arms I freely forgive you, for that woman ceased to belong to me the moment she wrote that silly letter."

"I am glad, for the sake of our old friendship," answered Froben, "that you view the matter in this light; and, moreover, it enables me to speak coolly with you. In the first place, I give you my word that neither to-day nor ever before did any thing pass between us which would cast the least reflection on your honour; that she was a poor girl once, that she was compelled to ask for charity—"

"No, no; say at once that she went round begging," cried Faldner, "and strolled about the streets and squares of that wicked Paris by night, to earn money. I might have had the honour of her acquaintance then, if I had chosen it, for I was present at the moving scene on the *Pont-des-Arts*. No; even if I could believe what you tell me, I am still disgraced: the Faldner family and a beggar-girl!"

"Her father and mother were of noble birth—"

"Stuff, nonsense! What a fool I was for letting myself be taken in so! I might as well have married the bar-maid at the village ale-house, if she carried a beer-glass in her coat of arms, and brought me false registers!"

"That is a matter of small consequence in my eyes; the main point is, that from the very first you treated her like a servant and not a wife. She could not love you—you are not suited for each other."

"That is the right word," replied the Baron; "we are not suited to each other; the Baron Von Faldner and a beggar-girl cannot suit each other. I am very glad now that I followed my own ideas, and always treated her so; it was what she deserved. I always said there was something vulgar about her."

His rudeness irritated our hero, and he was about to

make a sharp answer, but checked himself for Josephine's sake. The Baron informed him that he meant to bring the whole affair before the civil tribunal, and allege mutual aversion as a reason for divorce. * * * * * * * * * * It is true that, with the different religious faith of the two lovers, neither of them could indulge the hopes of a new union; but Josephine, sad as her future prospects might be, preferred any thing to the disgraceful treatment to which she had been subjected. As for her husband, though a feeling of remorse sometimes attacked him in a solitary hour, he sought diversion in business, and consolation in the thought that nobody was acquainted with the stain his escutcheon had suffered in making a beggar-girl of doubtful character the Baroness Von Faldner.

A few weeks after these events, Froben was walking up and down the bridge at Mentz. While he was lost in thought, a travelling-carriage rolled past him, whose strange appearance attracted general notice. Our hero's eyes were fastened more strongly on the servant upon the box, whose cheerful brown face seemed as familiar to him as the gaudy colours of his livery. As the carriage approached slowly, the servant noticed him in turn, and cried, "Santiago de Compostella!—there he is himself!" He jumped down, opened the coach door, and out peeped the well-known features of Don Pedro. Our hero hastened to greet him, and the old man embraced him joyfully. "Where is she?—where is my Laura's daughter? In the name of the Holy Mary, is she here?—tell me—tell me at once!" Froben was at a loss what to say: he merely told him that she was then living near the city, and that he should see her the next morning.

Tears of joy stood in the Spaniard's eyes. "How much am I indebted to you, my dear young friend, for giving me news of her!" he cried. "As soon as I could get leave of absence, Diego got the coach ready, and I drove twenty miles a day, so great was my impatience! And is she living happily?—does she look like her mother?" Froben avoided answering these questions till he had led Don Pedro to his lodgings. The generous juice of Xeres was produced, Diego handed him a cigar and a light, as usual, and, as soon as he was comfortably settled, our hero began to tell his story. The Spaniard listened with deep interest; to Diego's great vexation, he let his cigar go out, for the first time in twenty years, and when Froben came to the violent scene between Faldner and his unhappy wife, his southern blood began to boil; he pulled his hat down on his forehead, wrapped his cloak round the left arm, and cried, with flashing eyes, "Bring me my long rapier, Diego; as true as I am a good Christian and a Spanish cavalier, I will have the wretch's life; I will run him through, if he had a crucifix on his breast: I will make an end of him without the sacrament and without absolution, that I will! My rapier, I say, Diego!" Our hero tried to sooth the old man, exhausted by his own violence, and showed him that this was useless, as Josephine was no longer in her oppressor's power. The next morning they went to the Countess. It was a moving sight to look upon, as the old man embraced Josephine's blooming, youthful figure, and eyed every feature closely, till his own stern expression relaxed, and with what deep emotion he kissed her eyes and lips. "Yes, you are my Laura's daughter!" he exclaimed; "You have nothing of your father but his golden hair; in all your features you are a Tortosi! Be henceforth my daughter, my dear child: I am rich—I have no kinsmen; you are nearer and dearer to me than any one else on earth, and no one else has so good a claim to you!" The sidelong glances Josephine sometimes cast at Froben seemed to express some doubt as to this last assertion, but she kissed his hand respectfully, and called him her second father.

The joy of meeting lasted but a short time. Don Pedro related that business called him back to Portugal, and that he did not see why Josephine might not go with him at once; he was so firmly attached to every doctrine of the church that he did not conceive the possibility of Froben's seeking to wed Josephine, the divorced wife of another. (What the views of the lovers may have been as to this point, we have not learned; we only know that Froben sometimes hinted at the propriety of her turning Lutheran, which she declined sadly, but firmly.) Our hero then proposed to her to let Don Pedro depart, and to remain in Germany, promising to remain her friend, if he could not be her husband. This, too, she declined, confessing frankly that she feared her own weakness too much, and that now her misfortunes had made her so proud that she could not bear the idea of lowering herself in the eyes of one whom she esteemed as much as she loved him. She had other and nobler reasons, too. "Why," she thought to herself, "should he waste the flower of his life in devotion to an unfortunate creature who can never be his? Why should he give up the prospect of domestic happiness, of a family and a home, for my sake? No; time will assuage his grief, and he will one day forget an unhappy woman who will think of him, love him, and pray for him to the last moment of her life."

It seemed, therefore, as though Josephine's prophetic farewell, "for ever," was yet to receive its fulfilment. Don Pedro and his newly-found kinswoman left the Countess's estate, to take shipping in Holland. Froben, who was kept alive only by the hope of soon joining them in Portugal, accompanied them on their journey, and when she begged him not to prolong the pain of separation, he entreated her, in return, "only to the sea, and then—farewell!"

In the month of August, in the same year, an English ship was lying at Ostem, bound for Portugal. About nine o'clock, on a lovely cloudless morning, a shot was fired from the vessel, as a signal for the passengers to embark. A boat came off to the shore, and took away a number, with their baggage. Before it returned, there came down to the beach a party of four persons, evidently of a superior rank to the other passengers. A tall, elderly man stepped majestically in front; he wore a broad-leafed hat, and his cloak hung so gracefully from his shoulders, that one of the sailors swore "if the old fellow wasn't a Spaniard, he'd eat him." After him came a young gentleman, escorting a lady. He looked pale, and seemed trying to conquer his own grief, in order to speak some words of comfort to the lady in hers. Her features were disfigured by weeping, and her lips pressed convulsively together A hat with waving feathers, a costly dress of heavy silk, with rich chains on neck and bosom, seemed ill-suited for a sea-voyage, and seemed to indicate that she had only come to see the young man off. Behind the pair came a servant, who wore his black hair in a Spanish net, and carried a huge umbrella under his arm.

When they reached the shore, the lady clung to her companion so closely that the feathers she wore hid his face and his tears from the eyes of the spectators. The old man stood a little way off, wrapped in his mantle, and looking at the sea. His eye glistened, either with a tear or the reflection from the waves. The boat came plashing up; a plank was thrown out; the old man shook his young friend's hand heartily, and walked rapidly over it, followed by Diego. The young people embraced each other again, and the gentleman prepared to lead her to the boat. "For ever!" she whispered, with a melancholy smile. "For ever!" sighed the young man in reply She stood, by this time, on the plank; the mate, a bluff Englishman, stood ready to receive her, and had already stretched out his broad hand, and was getting ready some well-meant commonplace consolation. Then she turned her dark eye away from the boundless ocean, and it rested on her lover. He stood with outstretched arms on the shore—in his features the rapture of love was mingled with the anguish of parting. Then she seemed as if she could control herself no longer—she sprang to the shore, and in a moment hung upon our hero's neck. "No—I cannot go across the sea!" she cried; "I will stay here: I will do any thing you ask me; I will abandon a faith that prevents my being yours. You are now my country, my kindred, my all: I will stay in Germany!"

"Josephine! my Josephine!" exclaimed Froben, pressing her to his heart in a storm of delight; "mine, then, for ever! Heaven has inspired you; for, oh! the pain of parting would have killed me!" They were close-locked in each other's arms when the Spaniard came on shore to part them. "Come, children," he said, "one leave-taking ought to have contented you; come, Josephine, it's of no use to wait; the ship is going to fire for the last time." "Let them fire a broadside, if they choose, Don Pedro," cried Froben, joyfully; "she stays here—she stays with me." "What do I hear?" rejoined the Spaniard, gravely; "I hope it is not as the cavalier supposes; will you not follow your kinsman, Josephine?"

"No!" she answered boldly. "As I stood there in the boat, and looked at the ocean that was soon to divide us, a voice within told me what I ought to do; my mother showed me the way; she followed the man of her heart through the wide world: she left father and mother. I know what I ought to do; here stands the man to whom I owe the peace of my mother's last moments; life, honour, every thing; and shall I leave him? Greet, for me, the graves of my ancestors in Valencia, Don Pedro, and tell them there is yet one of the Tortosi blood left who values love more than life."

Don Pedro was moved. "Follow your heart, then; perhaps it prompts you better than an old man like me could do. I know that, at least, you will be happy in the arms of this cavalier, and I know the honour of our family is as dear to him as his own. But, Don Frobenio, what will you say to your proud kindred when you present to them this child of misfortune? Will you have the courage to endure the sneers of the world?"

"Farewell, Don Pedro," answered our hero, boldly, holding out one hand to the Spaniard, while with the other he clasped his mistress; "be of good courage, and do not doubt me. I will show her to the world, and when any one asks, 'Pray, who was she?' I will reply, with pride, '*The Beggar-girl of the Pont-des-Arts!*'"

THE PIC-NIC PARTY.

BY HORACE SMITH.

To give a pic-nic party a fair chance of success, it must be almost impromptu: projected at twelve o'clock at night at the earliest, executed at twelve o'clock on the following day at the latest; and even then the odds are fearfully against it. The climate of England is not remarkable for knowing its own mind; nor is the weather "so fixed in its resolve" but that a bright August moon, suspended in a clear sky, may be lady-usher to a morn of fog, sleet, and drizzle. Then, again—but this being tender ground, we will only hint at the possibility of such a change—a lady of the intended party might quit the drawing-room at night in the sweetest humour imaginable, and make her appearance at breakfast in a less amiable mood, or, perhaps, "prefer taking breakfast in her own room,"—from which notice husbands sometimes infer that such a change has taken place.

Mr. Claudius Bagshaw, a retired silk mercer, in the vicinity of London, determined, notwithstanding all these arguments, to have a pic-nic party on the twenty-fourth of August, his wedding-day. On the third of July, Mr. Claudius Bagshaw, after eating his breakfast and reading the Morning Post, looked out of his parlour window to watch the horticultural pursuits of his better part. Mr. Bagshaw had become a member of one of the "march-of-intellect-societies," and was confident that the pic-nic would turn out a very pleasant thing.

"How fortunate we shall be, dear," said Mr. Bagshaw, "how happy we shall be, if the weather should be as fine on our wedding-day as it is now."

"True, love," replied Mrs. Bagshaw; "but this is only the third of July and, as the anniversary of our happy day is the twenty-fourth of August, the weather *may* change."

This proposition Mr. Bagshaw did not attempt to deny.

The Bagshaws were the happiest couple in the world. Being blessed with the negative blessing of no offspring, the stream of their affections was not diverted into little channels, but ebbed and flowed in one uninterrupted tide reciprocally from bosom to bosom. They never disputed, they never quarrelled. Yes, they did sometimes, but then it was from a mutual over-anxiety to please. Each was afraid to pronounce a choice, or a preference, lest it might be disagreeable to the other; and hence there occasionally did arise little bickerings, and tiffings, and miffings, which were quite as unpleasant in their effects, and sometimes as difficult to settle, as quarrels originating in less amiable causes.

"But," said Mr. Bagshaw, referring to the barometer, "the instrument for indicating the present state and probable changes of the weather, still maintains its elevation; and I tell you what, dear, if the weather should be *preposterous* on the twenty-fourth of August, suppose, instead of going into the north, as we did last year, we migrate into Kent or Surrey? Instead of dining at Hampstead, as we did last year, shall we go to Greenwich, or to Putney, and eat little fishes?"

"Whichever you like, love," was the lady's answer to the so-intended question.

"But I put it to your choice, dear."

"Either—or neither—please yourself, love, and you are sure you will please me."

"Pshaw! but it is for the gratification of your—or, more properly speaking, for your gratification. I submit to you an alternative for the purpose of election; and you know, Jane, I repudiate indifference, even as concerning or applying to trifles."

"You know, Claudius, we have but one wish, and that is to please each other; so do you decide."

"But, Mrs. Bagshaw, I must promulgate a request that —having, as I have, no desire but to please you—you will——"

"How, sir! would you force me to choose, when I am so obedient as to choose that you should have the choice entirely your own way? This treatment of me is monstrous!"

And here Mrs. Bagshaw did what is usual and proper for ladies to do on such occasions—she burst into tears.

"Why, then, madam, to use a strong expression, I must say that——"

But a loud rap at the street-door prevented the utterance of an "expression," the force of which would doubtless have humbled Mrs. Claudius Bagshaw down to the very dust.

"Claudius," said the lady, hastily drying her eyes, "that is uncle John's knock. We'll go to Gre—Put—Greenwich, love."

"That's well, dear; and be assured, love, that nothing is so adverse to the constitution of what Locke emphatically calls the human mind, philosophically considered, as to persevere in that state of indecision which—that—whereof—but we will not go to either; uncle John shall select the locality."

Uncle John was a bachelor of fifty-five, possessing twelve thousand pounds, a strong disinclination to part with any of them, a good heart, and a bad temper.

"Good morning t'ye, good folks; as usual, I perceive, billing and cooing."

The Bagshaws had by this time got together in a cor

ner of the garden, and were lovingly occupied in trimming the same pot of sweet peas.

"Quite the contrary, uncle John," said Mrs. Bagshaw. "Claudius and I have just had one of our most desperate quarrels."

And here the happy pair giggled, and exchanged looks which were meant to imply that *their* most desperate quarrels were mere kitten's play; and that uncle John did so interpret them, he made manifest by a knowing shake of his fore-finger.

"The fact is, sir, Jane and I talk of commemorating the annual recurrence of the anniversary of our wedding-day, at some place a *leetle* farther in the country; but our minds are in a perfect vacuum concerning the identity of the spot. Now, sir, will you reduce the place to a mathematical certainty, and be one of the party?"

"Why—um—no; these things are expensive; we come home at night with a guinea a-piece less in our pockets, and I don't see the good of that."

"I have it!" cried Bagshaw; "we'll make it a pic-nic; that *won't* be expensive."

"Then I'm with you, Bagshaw, with all my heart—and it shall be *al fresco*."

"There or anywhere else you please, sir," gravely replied the learned member of the universal-knowledge-warehouse.

"Uncle John means in the open air, Claudius; that *will* be delightful."

"Charming!" rejoined Bagshaw.

It may be inquired why uncle John, who objected to the disbursement of a guinea for a day's pleasure, should so readily have yielded at the suggestion of a pic-nic. Uncle John possessed a neat little morocco pocket-case, containing a dozen silver spoons, and silver-handled knives and forks, and although we are told that these implements are of later invention than fingers, there is, nevertheless, a very general bias in their favour, for the purpose to which they are applied. Now, uncle John being aware of the prevalence of their employment, it was for this reason he never objected to make one of a pic-nic party; for, whilst others contributed chickens, pigeon-pies, or wines—it being the principle of such parties that each member should furnish something to the feast—uncle John invariably contributed the use of his knives, forks, and spoons.

The whole morning was spent in debating on who should be invited to partake of this "pleasantest thing that ever was," and examining into their several pretensions, and their powers of contributing to the amusements of the day; when, at length, the honour of nomination was conferred upon the persons following, and for the reasons assigned:

Sir Thomas and Lady Grouts—because of their title, which would give an air to the thing—(Sir Thomas, formerly a corn-chandler, having been knighted for carrying up an address in the late reign.) Miss Euphemia Grouts, daughter, No. 1—who would bring her guitar. Miss Corinna Grouts, ditto, No. 2—because she would sing.

Mr. and Mrs. Snodgrass—Mr. Snodgrass being vice-president of the grand junction march-of-intellect-society. Mr. Frederick Snodgrass, their son, (lately called to the chancery bar,) who would bring his flute.

Messrs. Wrench and son, (eminent dentists.) The father to be invited because he was charming company, and the son, a dead bore, because the father would be offended if he were not. And, lastly,

Miss Snubbleston, a rich maiden lady of forty-four, for no other earthly qualification whatever than her carriage, which (to use Bagshaw's words) would carry herself and *us three*, and also transplant a large portion of the provender to the place of rendezvous.

Bagshaw having made out a fair copy of this list, somewhat in the shape of a bill of parcels, this, the first step towards the "pleasantest thing that ever was," was taken with entire satisfaction.

"Why, Bagshaw," exclaimed uncle John, who had cast up the numbers, "including our three selves, we shall be thirteen!"

The member of the institution perceived the cause of his alarm! but having been lectured out of *prejudices* respecting matters of greater moment than this, he prepared a look of ineffable contempt as his only reply; however, happening to think of uncle John's twelve thousand pounds, he suppressed it, and just contented himself with,

"And what then, sir?"

"Why, *then*, sir, that is a risk I won't run; and unless we can manage to——I have it! the very man. How came we to forget him? *The—very—man!* You know Jack Richards?"

The last four words were delivered in a tone implying the utter impossibility of any human creature being unacquainted with Jack Richards.

"Not in the least, sir. I never heard of him."

"What! never heard of Ja——. The thing is impossible; everybody knows Jack Richards. The very thing for us; such a wit! such a wag!—he is the life and soul of every thing. Should he be unengaged for the twenty-fourth of August. But he is so caught up! I was invited to meet him at dinner last Sunday at Jones's, but he didn't come. Such a disappointment to us! However, I shall meet him on Thursday at the Tims's, if he should but keep his promise, and then—"

"But, uncle," said Mrs. Bagshaw, "hadn't you better send him an invitation at once?"

"I'll do better still, my dear; I'll call at his lodgings, and if I find him hanging loose, I'll bring him to dine with you to-day." Then, turning to Bagshaw, he added, "That a man like *you* shouldn't know Jack Richards, is surprising!"

As this was evidently pointed at Mr. Claudius Bagshaw in his capacity of member of a learned body, Bagshaw pursed up his mouth into a mock-modesty smile, and slightly bowed. Off went uncle John in quest of Jack Richards; and, that the pleasantest thing in the world might not suffer by delay, off went Mr. Bagshaw to apprize the Snodgrasses, the Groutses, and the rest of the nominees; and, more important still, off went the lady to the poulterer's, to inquire whether he was likely to have any nice pigeons for a pie, about the twenty-third of next month. The dinner-hour arrived, and so did uncle John, but with a face of unspeakable wo.

"I feared how it would be."

"What! can't he be with us on the twenty-fourth?" inquired both the Bagshaws at the same instant.

"He will if he can; but he won't promise. But to-day—! However, it serves us right; we were unwise to indulge a hope of his coming at so short a notice. He has almost engaged himself to you for Sunday fortnight, though. What a creature it is!—he has given me such a pain in my side!"

"Something he said that almost killed you with laughing? Repeat it, uncle, repeat it."

"Why, no, he didn't say any thing particular; but he has a knack of poking one in the ribs, in his comical way, and sometimes he hurts you."

We intended to describe Jack Richards at length; uncle John's accidental notice of this trait has, most probably, rendered that trouble unnecessary. Indeed, we feel that we need scarcely add to it, that he can sing a devilish good song, (and everybody knows what is meant by that,) and imitated the inimitable Mathews' imitations of the actors, not even excepting his imitation of Tate Wilkinson's imitation of Garrick.

Except the uncertainty of Jack Richards, the result of the morning's occupation was satisfactory. Bagshaw, still retaining his old business-like habits of activity and industry, had contrived to wait on every person named in the list, all of whom had promised their attendance! and Mrs. Bagshaw had received from the poulterer a positive assurance that he would raise heaven and earth to supply her with pigeons on the twenty-third of the ensuing August!

Committees were forthwith summoned. First, a committee to consider of the whereabout. At this, after an evening of polite squabbling, which had nearly put an end to the project altogether, Twickenham meadows received the honour of selection—*nem. con.* as Bagshaw said. Next, lest it should happen, as it did once happen, for want of such preconcert, that a pic-nic party of ten found themselves at their place of meeting with ten fillets of veal and ten hams, Mr. Bagshaw called a committee of "provender." Here it was settled that the Snodgrasses should contribute four chickens and a tongue; the Bagshaws, their pigeon-pie; Wrench and son, a ham; Sir Thomas Grouts, a hamper of his own *choice* wine; Miss Snubbleston, a basket of fruit and pastry; uncle John, his silver spoons, knives, and forks; and Jack Richards—his charming company. And lastly, came the committee for general purposes! At this important meeting, it was agreed that the party proceed to Twickenham by water; that to save the trouble of loading and unloading, Miss Snubbleston's carriage convey the hampers, &c. direct to the place appointed—the said carriage, moreover, serving to bring the ladies to town, should the evening prove cold; that, for the *water-music*, the following programme be adopted: 1. On reaching Vauxhall bridge, the concert to commence with Madame Pasta's grand scena in "Medea," previous to the murder of the children, by Miss Corinna Grouts. 2. Nicholson's grand flute concerto in five sharps, by Mr. Frederick Snodgrass. 3. Grand aria, with variations, guitar, by Miss Euphemia Grouts. 4. Sweet Bird; accompaniment, flute obligato, Miss C. G. and Mr. F. S.—and 5. The Dettingen Te Deum, (arranged for three voices, by Mr. F. S.) by Miss Euphemia, Miss Corinna, and Mr. Frederick Snodgrass. The "interstices," as Mr. Bagshaw called them, to be filled up by the amusing talents of the elder Wrench and uncle John's friend. And, lastly, that the company do assemble at Mr. Bagshaw's on the morning of the twenty-fourth of August, at ten o'clock, *precisely*, in order to have the advantage of the tide both ways.

Three days prior to the important twenty-fourth, Mr. Bagshaw went to engage the boat, but, in a squabble with the boatman, Mr. B. got a black eye. This was the first mishap.

Restless and impatient though you be, depend upon it, there is not a day of the whole three hundred and sixty-five will put itself, in the slightest degree, out of the way, or appear one second before its appointed time, for your gratification. Oh, that people would consider this, and wait events with patience! Certainly Mr. Bagshaw did not. The night of the twenty-third to him appeared an age. His repeater was in his hand every ten minutes. He thought the morning would never dawn—but he was mistaken; it did; and as fine a morning as if it had been made on purpose to favour his excursion. By six o'clock he was dressed!—by eight the contributions from all the members had arrived, and were ranged in the passage. There was their own pigeon-pie, carefully packed in brown paper and straw; Sir Thomas's hamper of his own choice wine; and the rest. Every thing promised fairly. The young ladies and Mr. Frederick had had thirty rehearsals of their grand arias and concertos, and were perfect to a demi-semiquaver; Jack Richards would *certainly* come; and the only drawback upon Mr. Bagshaw's personal enjoyment—but nothing in this world is perfect—was the necessity he was under of wearing his green shade, which would totally deprive him of the pleasure of contemplating the beauties of the Thames' scenery—a thing he had set his heart upon. Nine! ten!

"No one here yet! Jane, my love, we shall infallibly lose the tide;" and for the next quarter of an hour the place of the poor repeater was no sinecure.

A knock! Mr. and Mrs. Snodgrass and Mr. Frederick. Another! The whole family of the Groutses. Next came Mr. Charles Wrench.

"Bless us! Mr. Charles," said Bagshaw, "where is your father?"

Now, Mr. Wrench, senior, was an agreeable old dentist, always gay, generally humorous, sometimes witty; he could *sketch* characters as well as *draw* teeth; and, on occasions of this kind, was invaluable. The son was a mere donkey; a silly, simpering, well-dressed young gentleman, the owner of no more than the eighth of an idea, and of a very fine set of teeth, which he constantly exhibited like a sign or advertisement of his shop. Appended to every thing he uttered were a preface and postscript, in the form of a sort of billy-goat grin.

"He! he! he! he! Fayther regrets emezingly he caint come, being called to attend the Duchess of Dilborough. He! he! he! he!"

As we have already said that it was in pure compliment to the father that the son was invited, and not at all for the sake of his own company, his presence was a grievous aggravation of the disappointment.

The next knock announced Miss Snubbleston. But where was her carriage? Why, it had been newly varnished, and they might scratch her panels with the hampers; and then she was afraid of her springs. So here was Miss Snubbleston without her carriage, for the convenience of which alone she had been invited, considered by the rest in exactly the same light as young Mr. Wrench without old Mr. Wrench—*id est*, a damper. A new arrangement was the necessary consequence; and the baskets, under the superintendence of a servant, were jolted down in a hackney coach, to be embarked at Westminster. But Miss Snubbleston brought with her a substitute, which was by no means a compensation. Cupid, her wretched, little, barking, yelping, Dutch pug, had eaten something that had dis agreed with him, and his fair mistress would not "for worlds" have left him at home while he was so indisposed. Well, no one chose to be the first to object to the intruder, so Cupid was received.

ARRIVAL OF JACK RICHARDS.

"But where can uncle John and his friend be? We shall lose the tide, that's certain," was scarcely uttered by Mr. Bagshaw, when in came our uncle, together with the long-expected Jack Richards.

The usual introductions over, Mr. Richards saluted everybody with the self-sufficient swagger of a vulgar lion.

"The day smiles auspicious, sir," said Bagshaw, who thought it requisite he should throw off something fine to so celebrated a person.

"Smile?—a broad grin, I call it, sir." And here was a general laugh.

"Oh, excellent!"

"Capital!"

Uncle John, proud of his friend, whispered in Bagshaw's ear, "You see, Jack's beginning." And now hats and gloves were in motion.

"You have got your flute, Frederick?"

"Yes, mother," was the reply.

"Lau, ma," cried Miss Corinna, "if I haven't come without 'Sweet Bird,' and my scena from 'Medea,' I declare."

As these were indispensable to the amusements of the day, a servant was dispatched for them. He couldn't be gone longer than half an hour. Half an hour! thought Bagshaw; 'tis eleven now; and the tide——. But the servant was absent a few minutes beyond the half hour, and poor Bagshaw suffered severely from that gnawing impatience, amounting almost to pain, which every mother's son of us has experienced upon occasions of greater—or less importance than this. They were again at the very point of starting, when a message was brought to Mrs. Snodgrass that little Master Charles had cut his thumb dreadfully! What was to be done? Mrs. Snodgrass vowed she shouldn't be easy in her mind the whole day, unless she knew the extent of the mischief; and as they *only* lived in Euston-square, and she could be there and back again in twenty minutes, she would herself go see what really was the matter—and away she went. Twenty minutes! During all this time, Bagshaw—but who would attempt to describe anguish indescribable? At length he was relieved by the return of Mrs. Snodgrass; but, to the horror and consternation of himself and of all present, she introduced the aforesaid Master Charles—an ugly, ill-tempered, blubbering little brat of seven years old, with a bloated red face, scrubby white hair, and red eyes; and with the interesting appendage of a thick slice of bread and butter in his hand.

"I'm sure you'll pardon this liberty," said the affectionate mamma: "but poor Charley has cut himself very much, and he would not be pacified till I consented to take him with us. He has promised to be very good. There, don't cry any more, darling!" and, accordingly, the urchin roared with tenfold vigour. There were no particular manifestations of joy at this arrival; and it is just possible, although nothing was uttered to that effect, that there did exist a general and cordial wish that young Master Snodgrass were sprawling at the bottom of the deepest well in England. Uncle John, indeed, did utter something about the pug and the child—two such nuisances—people bringing their brats into grown up company.

At length the procession set out: the Bagshaws, uncle John and Jack Richards bringing up the rear in a hackney-coach. On reaching the corner of the street, Mrs. Bagshaw called out to the driver to stop.

"What is the matter, dear?" said Bagshaw.

"Your eye-lotion, love."

"Well, never mind that, sweet."

"Claudius, I shall be miserable if you go without it. Dr. Nooth desired you would use it every two hours. I must insist—now, for my sake, love—such an eye as he has got, Mr. Richards!"

So away went Bagshaw to the Lake of Lausanne Lodge for the lotion, which, as it always happens when folks are in a hurry, it took him a quarter of an hour to find.

They were now fairly on the road.

"What a smell of garlick!" exclaimed uncle John; "it is intolerable!"

"Dear me!" said Mr. Richards, "do you perceive it? 'Tis a fine Italian sausage I bought at Morel's, as my contribution. We shall find it an excellent relish in the country;" and he exhibited his purchase, enveloped in a brown paper.

"Pha! shocking!—'tis a perfect nuisance! Put it into your pocket again, or throw it out at the window." But Mr. Richards preferred obeying the first command.

Apropos of contributions—"Uncle, have you brought your spoons?"

"Here they are," replied uncle, at the same time drawing from his pocket a parcel in size and form very closely resembling Mr. Richards's offensive contribution.

On arriving at Westminster Bridge, they found the rest of the party already seated in the barge, and the first sound that saluted their ears was an intimation that, owing to their being two hours behind time, (it was now past twelve,) they should hardly save the tide.

"I knew it would be so," said Bagshaw, with more of discontent than he had thought to experience, considering the pains he had taken that every thing should be well-ordered.

As uncle John was stepping into the boat, Richards, with great dexterity, exchanged parcels with him, putting the Italian sausage into uncle John's pocket and the spoons into his own; enhancing the wit of the manœuvre by whispering to the Bagshaws, who, with infinite delight, had observed it.

"Hang me," said Richards, "but he shall have enough of the garlick!"

The old gentleman was quite unconscious of the operation, as Richards adroitly diverted his attention from it by giving him one of his facetious pokes in the ribs, which nearly bent him double, and drew a roar of laughter from every one else.

Just as they were pushing off, their attention was attracted by a loud howling. It proceeded from a large Newfoundland dog which was standing at the water's edge.

"Confound it!" cried Richards, "that's my Carlo! He has followed me, unperceived, all the way from home—I would not lose him for fifty pounds. I must take him back—pray put me ashore. This is very provoking—though he is *a very quiet dog!*"

There was no mistaking this hint. Already were there two nuisances on board—master Charles and the Dutch pug: but as they were to choose between Jack Richards with his dog, or no Jack Richards, (or in other words, no life and soul of the party,) it was presently decided that Carlo should be invited to a seat on the hampers, which were stowed at the head of the boat—uncle John having first extracted from Mr. Richards an assurance that their new guest would lie there as still as a mouse. This complaisance was amply rewarded by a speedy display of Mr. Richards' powers of entertainment. As soon as they reached the middle of the river Jack Richards suddenly jumped up, for the purpose of frightening Miss Snubblestone; a jest at which everybody else would have laughed, had not their own lives been endangered by it. Even his great admirer suggested to him that once of that was enough. His next joke was one of a more intellectual character. Though he had never till this day seen Sir Thomas, he had accidentally heard something about his former trade.

"What is the difference between Lord Eldon and Sir Thomas Grouts?" Nobody could tell.

"One is an ex-chancellor—the other is an ex-chandler." Everybody laughed, except the Grouts family.

This was succeeded by another thrust in uncle John's side; after which came a pun, which we shall not record, as the effect of it was to force the ladies to cough and look into the water, the gentlemen to look at each other, and Mrs. Snodgrass to whisper to Mrs. Bagshaw—

"Who *is* this Mr. Richards?"

Indeed, there would have been no end to his pleasantries had they not been interrupted by a request that Miss Corinna would open the concert, as they were fast approaching Vauxhall bridge. Mr. Bagshaw (looking at the programme, which he had drawn out on paper ruled with red and blue lines) objected to this, as it would disturb the previous arrangement, according to which the concert was not to commence till they were *through* the bridge. This objection was overruled, and the fair Corinna unrolled the music, for which the servant had been dispatched with so much haste. Miss Corinna screamed! What was the matter?

"They had not sent the grand scena from Medea, af ter all, but a wrong piece!" And the pains she had taken to be perfect in it!

"Could not Miss Corinna sing it from memory?"

"Impossible!"

"How careless of you, Corinna! then sing what they have sent."

"Why, ma," said Corinna, with tears in her eyes, and holding up the unfortunate sheets, "why bless me, ma, I can't sing the overture to Der Freyschutz!"

The difficulty of such a performance being readily admitted, Mr. Frederick Snodgrass declared himself but too happy to comply with the calls for his concerto in five sharps, which stood next on the list; and with the air of one well satisfied that an abundance of admiration and applause would reward his efforts, he drew forth his flute, when, lo! one of the joints was missing! This accident was nearly fatal to the musical entertainments of the day; for not only was the concerto thereby rendered impracticable, but "Sweet Bird," with the flute-accompaniment obligato, was put *hors de combat*. Disappointment having, by this, been carried to its uttermost bounds, the announcement that two strings of the guitar had gone, was received with an indifference almost stoical; and every one was grateful to Miss Euphemia for so *willingly* undertaking (the whispered menaces of Lady Grouts being heard by nobody but the young lady herself) to do all that could be done under such untoward circumstances. She would endeavour to accompany herself through a little ballad; but she failed.

Mr. Claudius Bagshaw, with all his literature, science, and philosophy, now, for the first time, wondered how any thing could fail, so much trouble having been taken to insure success. Drawing forth his repeater, he a-hem'd, and just muttered—

"Unaccountable! Hem! upon my word! One o'clock, and no pleasure yet!"

"One o'clock," echoed his spouse; "then 'tis time for your eye, dear!" and Bagshaw was compelled not only to suffer his damaged optics to be dabbled by his tormentingly affectionate wife, but to submit again to be hoodwinked, in spite of his entreaties to the contrary, and his pathetic assurances that he had not yet seen a bit of the prospect; a thing he had set his heart upon.

Now occurred a dead silence of some minutes. A steamboat rushed by. Bagshaw seized this opportunity to make a display of his scientific acquirements; and this he did with the greater avidity, as he had long wished to astonish vice-president Snodgrass. Besides, in the event of his offering to deliver a course of lectures at the institution, the vice-president might bear evidence to his capabilities for the purpose—his acquaintance not only with the facts, but with the terms of science. Whether those terms were always correctly applied, we confess ourselves not sufficiently learned to pronounce.

"How wondrous is the science of mechanism! how

variegated its progeny, how simple, yet how compound! I am propelled to the consideration of this subject by having optically perceived that ingenious nautical instrument, which has just now flown along like a mammoth, that monster of the deep! You ask me how are steam-boats propagated? in other words, how is such an infinite and immoveable body inveigled along its course? I will explain it to you. It is by the power of friction: that is to say, the two wheels, or paddles, turning diametrically, or at the same moment, on the axioms, and repressing by the rotundity of their motion the action of the menstruum in which the machine floats,—water being, in a philosophical sense, a powerful non-conductor,—it is clear, that in proportion as is the revulsion so is the progression; and as is the centrifugal force, so is the—"

"Pooh!" cried uncle John impatiently, "let us have some music."

"I have an apprehension, Bagshaw," said the vice-president,—"that I should not presume to dispute with you—that you are wrong in your theory of the centrifugal force of the axioms. However, we will discuss that point at the Grand-Junction. But come, Frederick, the 'Dettingen te deum.'"

Frederick and the young ladies having, by many rehearsals, perfected themselves in the performance of this piece, instantly complied. Scarcely had they reached the fourth bar, when Jack Richards, who had not for a long time perpetrated a joke, produced a harsh, brassy-toned, German colina, and "blew a blast so loud and shrill," that the Dutch pug began to bark, Carlo to howl, and the other nuisance, master Charles, to cry. The German colina was of itself bad enough, but these congregated noises were intolerable. Uncle John aimed a desperate blow with a large apple, which he was just about to bite, at the head of Carlo, who, in order to give his lungs fair play, was standing on all fours on the hampers. The apple missed the dog, and went some distance beyond him into the water. Mr. Carlo, attributing to uncle John a kinder feeling than that which actually prompted the proceeding, looked upon it as a good-natured expedient to afford him an opportunity of adding his mite to the amusements of the day, by displaying a specimen of his training. Without waiting for a second hit, he plunged into the river, seized the apple, and, paddling up the side of the boat with the prize triumphantly exhibited in his jaws, to the consternation of the whole party, he scrambled in between uncle John and his master, dropped the apple upon the floor, distributed a copious supply of Thames' water amongst the affrighted beholders, squeezed his way through them as best he could, and, with an air of infinite self-satisfaction, resumed his place on the hampers.

Had Mr. Jack Richards, the owner of the dog, been at the bottom of the Thames a week before this delightful twenty-fourth, not one of the party, Mr. Richards himself excepted, would have felt in the slightest degree concerned; but since, with a common regard to politeness, they could not explicitly tell him so, they contented themselves with bestowing upon Mr. Carlo every term of opprobrium, every form of execration, which good-manners will allow—leaving it to the sagacity of "the life and soul of the company" to apply them to himself, if so it might be agreeable to him. Poor fellow! he felt the awkwardness of his situation, and figuratively, as well as literally speaking, this exploit of his dog threw a *damp* upon him, as it had done upon every one else.

For some time the pic-nics pursued their way in solemn silence. At length Bagshaw, perceiving that there would be very little pleasure if matters were allowed to go on in this way, exclaimed—

"An intelligent observer, not imbued with the knowledge of our intentions, would indicate us to be a combination of perturbed spirits, rowed by Charon across the river Tiber."

In cases of this kind, the essential is to break the ice. Conversation was now resumed.

"Ah! ha!" said the vice-president, "Sion-house."

"The residuum of the Northumberlands," said Claudius, "one of the most genealogical and antique families in England."

And here, having put forth so much classical and historical lore, almost in a breath, he marked his own satisfaction by a short, single cough. The vice-president *said* nothing, but he thought to himself, "There is much more in this Bagshaw than I suspected."

Jack Richards was up again.

"Come, what's done can't be helped; but, upon my soul! I am sorry at being the innocent cause of throwing cold water on the party."

"Cold water, indeed! look at me, sir," said Miss Snubbleston, with tears in her eyes, and exhibiting her *ci-devant* shoulder-of-mutton sleeves, which, but half an hour before, as stiff and stately as starch could make them, were now hanging loose and flabby about her skinny arms.

"Too bad, Jack," said uncle John, "to bring that cursed Carlo of yours!"

Carlo, perceiving that he was the subject of conversation, was instantly on his legs, his eye steadily fixed upon uncle John, evidently expecting a signal for a second plunge. The alarm was general, and every tongue joined in the scream of "Lie down, sir! lie down!"

Uncle John, who had been more than once offended by the odour from his friend's garlic sausage, and who had on each and every such occasion vented an exclamation of disgust, to the great amusement of Mr. Richards, (who chuckled with delight to think of the exchange he had secretly effected,) here, in the very middle of the stream, resolved to rid himself of the annoyance. Unperceived by any one, he gently drew the parcel from Richards' coat-pocket, and let it drop into the water! Like king Richard's pierced coffin, once in, it soon found the way to the bottom. Uncle John could scarcely restrain his inclination to laugh aloud; however, he contrived to assume an air of indifference, and whistled part of a tune.

ARRIVAL AT TWICKENHAM, AND THE CATASTROPHE.

Arrived at Twickenham, the boatmen were ordered to pull up to a beautiful meadow, sloping down to the water's edge. There was no time to lose—they had no pleasure yet—so Bagshaw entreated that every one "would put his shoulder to the wheel, and be on the *qui rala.*" In an instant a large heavy hamper were landed, but as, in compliance with Bagshaw's request, every one did something to *help*, a scene of confusion was the consequence, and numerous pieces of crockery were invalided ere the cloth was properly spread, and the dishes, plates, and glasses distributed. But for the feast. Mr. Snodgrass's basket was opened, and out of it were taken four remarkably fine chickens, and a tongue—uncooked! There was but one mode of accounting for this trifling omission. Mr. Snodgrass's Betty was a downright matter-of-fact person, who obeyed orders to the very letter. Having been told, the evening before, to get four fine chickens for roasting, together with a tongue, and to pack them, next morning, in a basket, she did so literally and strictly; but, as she had received no distinct orders to dress them, to have done so she would have deemed an impertinent departure from her instructions. Well; since people in a high state of civilization, like Mr. Claudius Bagshaw and his friends, cannot eat raw chickens, they did the only thing they could under the circumstances—they grumbled exceedingly, and put them back again into the basket. This was a serious deduction in the important point of quantity, and uncle John felt a slight touch of remorse at having thrown, as he thought, his friend's Italian sausage into the Thames. However, there was still provision in the garrison. But the run of luck in events, as at a game of whist, may be against you; and when it is so, be assured that human prudence and foresight—remarkable as even Mrs. Bagshaw's, who bespoke her pigeons seven weeks before she wanted them—avail but little. When the packages were first stowed in the boat, the pigeon-pie was inadvertently placed at the bottom, and every thing else, finishing with the large heavy hamper of crockery, with Carlo on that, upon it; so that when it was taken up it appeared a chaotic mass of pie-crust, broken china, pigeons, brown paper, beef-steak, eggs, and straw!

"Now this is enough to provoke a saint!" said Bagshaw; and no one attempting to deny the position, with this salvo for his own character of philosophic patience, he indulged himself in the full expression of his vexation and sorrow. After a minute examination, he declared the pie to be "a complete squash," and that nobody could venture to eat it but at the imminent risk of being choked. As he was about to throw it over the hedge, Miss Snubbleston, seized with an unusual fit of generosity, called out to him—

"What *are* you doing? Though it isn't fit for us to eat, it will be quite a treat to the poor watermen. I dare say, poor souls, the[illegible] don't often get pigeon-pie."

But the good gen[illegible] of Mr. Carlo prevailed; and the truth of the adage, "'[illegible] an ill wind that blows nobody good," was confirmed in his mind as he found himself busily employed in the ingenious operation of separating pigeon from porcelain. It was, doubtless, extremely ill-bred in one dog not to invite another. and Cupid expressed his sense of the slight by a long-continued yell, which drew down upon him, from the equally disappointed bipeds of the company, sundry wishes, the positive accomplishment of which would not have tended much to his personal happiness. The next basket was opened. Things were not altogether in a desperate state. Mr. Wrench's ham was in perfect order, and that, with Miss Snubbleston's salad, and some bread, and—could it be possible! After so much preparation, and Mr. Bagshaw's committee of "provender" to boot, that no one should have thought of so obvious a requisite as bread! There would not be time to send Mr. Bagshaw to Twickenham town to procure some, for it was getting late, and if they lost the tide, they should be on the water till midnight, and they did not like the appearance of the sky, which was by no means so blue as it had hitherto been. However, the want of bread did not *much* signify; they could make a shift with Miss Snubbleston's biscuits and poundcakes. But uncle John did not come out on an excursion of pleasure to make shift; no more did Bagshaw, no more did any of the others. There was nothing else to be done; so where is Miss Snubbleston's basket? And where is Master Charles? gracious! Don't be alarmed, the precious rarity is in no danger. He was soon discovered behind a tree, whither he had dragged the fruit and cakes, and was engaged with all his might and main, in an endeavour, with a piece of stick, to force out an apple. In this attempt, as it was presently seen, the interesting child had cracked a bottle, the contents of which, merely a preparation of oil, vinegar, and mustard for the salad, were quietly dribbling through the pound-cakes, biscuits, and fruit. Similar aspirations to those which had lately been so cordially expressed for the Dutch pug, were now most devoutly formed in behalf of Master Charles.

"This comes of bringing their plaguey brats with them," said uncle and Bagshaw.

Whilst this scene was going on, Jack Richards, perceiving that the service of the table was incomplete, bethought him of uncle John's silver handled knives and forks, and spoons; he felt first in one pocket, and then in the other, then he ran down to search the boat, then he rummaged the baskets.

"Jack, my boy," hallooed uncle John, "don't trouble yourself, you'll never see *that* again."

"What, sir?"

"I could not bear the smell of it any longer, so I slyly drew it out of your pocket, and dexterously let it fall into the deepest part of the Thames."

And here uncle John chuckled, and looked about him for applause.

"Bless me, sir! Don't say so—why—bless my heart—you don't know—before we got into the boat, I put the sausage into your pocket, and your case of cutlery into my own!"

There was a general burst of laughter against uncle John. He turned as pale as—nay, paler, than any thing that has ever yet been dragged into the comparison; for an instant he stood stock-still, then thrust his hand into his pocket, drew forth the unfortunate substitute, and at the same time exclaiming D——tion! dashed it violently to the ground. He next buttoned his coat from the bottom to the top, pulled down his cuffs, whispered to his no longer admired Jack Richards, "You shall hear from me, Mr. ——;" and saying aloud to Bagshaw, "This comes of your confounded party of pleasure, sir," away he went. and returned to town outside a Twickenham coach; resolving by the way to call out *that* Mr. Richards, and to eject the Bagshaws from the snug corner they held in his last will and testament.

This explosion seemed to have banished pleasure for that day. They were all, more or less, out of humour; and instead of making the best of things, as they had hitherto done, they now made the worst of them. Sir Thomas's hamper of *his choice wine* (which, by the by, he purchased at a cheap shop for the occasion) was opened; and slices of ham were cut with the only knife and fork. Jack Richards tried to be facetious, but it would not do. He gave Bagshaw a poke in the ribs, which was received with a very formal, "Sir, I must beg—." To Mr. Wrench, junior, he said—

"You have not spoken much to-day—but you have made amends for your silence—d'ye take?—Your *ham* is good, though your *tongue* is not worth much!"

Instead of laughing, Mr. Wrench simpered something about impertinent liberties and satisfaction. On being invited by Sir Thomas to a second glass of his old East India, he said that one was a dose—had rather not double the *Cape;* and at the first glass of champaigne, he inquired whether there had been a plentiful supply of gooseberries that year. In short, whether it were that the company knew not how to appreciate his style of wit and pleasantry, or that he was in reality a very disagreeable person, the fact is that—but hold! let us say nothing ill of him; he died last week, at Folkestone, of a surfeit of goose, in the forty-ninth year of his age. For the consolation of such as were amused by him, and regret his loss, be it remembered that there are still to be found many Jack Richards in this world.

As we have said, they now resolved to make the worst of every thing; the grass was damp, the gnats were troublesome, Carlo's nose was in everybody's face, Cupid's teeth at everybody's calves, and Master Charles was ill of the many sour apples; it was growing late, and no good could come of sitting longer in the open air. They re-embarked. By the time they reached Putney it was pitch dark, and the tide was setting against them. They moved on in mute impatience, for there was a slight sprinkling of rain. It now fell in torrents. Master Charles grew frightened and screamed. Cupid yelped and Carlo howled. Accompanied the rest of the way by these pleasing sounds, at one in the morning (two hours and a half later than they intended) they arrived at Westminster-stairs, dull, dreary, drowsy, discontented, and drenched.

THE WIFE.

BY WASHINGTON IRVING

The treasures of the deep are not so precious
As are the concealed comforts of a man
Lock'd up in woman's love. I scent the air
Of blessings, when I come but near the house.
What a delicious breath marriage sends forth—
The violet bed 's not sweeter!

MIDDLETON.

I HAVE often had occasion to remark the fortitude with which women sustain the most overwhelming reverses of fortune. Those disasters which break down the spirit of a man, and prostrate him in the dust, seem to call forth all the energies of the softer sex, and give such intrepidity and elevation to their character, that at times it approaches to sublimity. Nothing can be more touching, than to behold a soft and tender female, who had been all weakness and dependence, and alive to every trivial roughness, while treading the prosperous paths of life, suddenly rising in mental force to be the comforter and supporter of her husband under misfortune, and abiding, with unshrinking firmness, the bitterest blasts of adversity.

As the vine, which has long twined its graceful foliage about the oak, and been lifted by it into sunshine, will, when the hardy plant is rifted by the thunderbolt, cling round it with its caressing tendrils, and bind up its shattered boughs; so is it beautifully ordered by Providence, that woman, who is the mere dependant and ornament of man in his happier hours, should be his stay and solace when smitten with sudden calamity; winding herself into the rugged recesses of his nature, tenderly supporting the drooping head, and binding up the broken heart.

I was once congratulating a friend, who had around him a blooming family, knit together in the strongest affection. "I can wish you no better lot," said he, with enthusiasm, "than to have a wife and children. If you are prosperous, there they are to share your prosperity; if otherwise, there they are to comfort you." And, indeed, I have observed that a married man falling into misfortune, is more apt to retrieve his situation in the world than a single one; partly, because he is more stimulated to exertion by the necessities of the helpless and beloved beings who depend upon him for subsistence; but chiefly, because his spirits are soothed and relieved by domestic endearments, and his self-respect kept alive by finding, that though all abroad is darkness and humiliation, yet there is still a little world of love at home, of which he is the monarch. Whereas, a single man is apt to run to waste and self-neglect; to fancy himself lonely and abandoned, and his heart to fall to ruin, like some deserted mansion, for want of an inhabitant.

These observations call to mind a little domestic story, of which I was once a witness. My intimate friend, Leslie, had married a beautiful and accomplished girl, who had been brought up in the midst of fashionable life. She had, it is true, no fortune, but that of my friend was ample; and he delighted in the anticipation of indulging her in every elegant pursuit, and administering to those delicate tastes and fancies that spread a kind of witchery about the sex.—"Her life," said he, "shall be like a fairy tale."

The very difference in their characters produced a harmonious combination; he was of a romantic, and somewhat serious cast; she was all life and gladness. I have often noticed the mute rapture with which he would gaze upon her in company, of which her sprightly powers made her the delight; and how, in the midst of applause, her eye would still turn to him, as if there alone she sought favor and acceptance. When leaning on his arm, her slender form contrasted finely with his tall manly person. The fond confiding air with which she looked up to him seemed to call forth a flush of triumphant pride and cherishing tenderness, as if he doated on his lovely burthen for its very helplessness. Never did a couple set forward on the flowery path of early and well-suited marriage with a fairer prospect of felicity.

It was the misfortune of my friend, however, to have embarked his property in large speculations; and he had not been married many months, when, by a succession of sudden disasters it was swept from him, and he found himself reduced to almost penury. For a time he kept his situation to himself, and went about with a haggard countenance, and a breaking heart. His life was but a protracted agony; and what rendered it more insupportable was the necessity of keeping up a smile in the presence of his wife; for he could not bring himself to overwhelm her with the news. She saw, however, with the quick eyes of affection, that all was not well with him. She marked his altered looks and stifled sighs, and was not to be deceived by his sickly and vapid attempts at cheerfulness. She tasked all her sprightly powers and tender blandishments to win him back to happiness; but she only drove the arrow deeper into his soul. The more he saw cause to love her, the more torturing was the thought that he was soon to make her wretched. A little while, thought he, and the smile will vanish from that cheek—the song will die away from those lips—the lustre of those eyes will be quenched with sorrow—and the happy heart which now beats lightly in that bosom, will be weighed down, like mine, by the cares and miseries of the world.

At length he came to me one day, and related his whole situation in a tone of the deepest despair. When I had heard him through, I inquired, "Does your wife know all this?" At the question he burst into an agony of tears. "For God's sake!" cried he, "if you have any pity on me, don't mention my wife; it is the thought of her that drives me almost to madness!"

"And why not?" said I, "She must know it sooner or later: you cannot keep it long from her, and the intelligence may break upon her in a more startling manner than if imparted by yourself; for the accents of those we love soften the harshest tidings. Besides, you are depriving yourself of the comforts of her sympathy; and not merely that, but also endangering the only bond that can keep hearts together—an unreserved community of thought and feeling. She will soon perceive that something is secretly preying upon your mind; and true love will not brook reserve: it feels undervalued and outraged, when even the sorrows of those it loves are concealed from it."

"Oh, but, my friend! to think what a blow I am to give to all her future prospects—how I am to strike her very soul to the earth, by telling her that her husband is a beggar!—that she is to forego all the elegancies of life—all the pleasures of society—to shrink with me into indigence and obscurity! To tell her that I have dragged her down from the sphere in which she might have continued to move in constant brightness—the light of every eye—the admiration of every heart!—How can she bear poverty? She has been brought up in all the refinements of opulence How can she bear neglect? She has been the idol of society. Oh, it will break her heart—it will break her heart!"

I saw his grief was eloquent, and I let it have its flow; for sorrow relieves itself by words. When his paroxysm had subsided, and he had relapsed into moody silence, I resumed the subject gently, and urged him to break his situation at once to his wife. He shook his head mournfully, but positively.

"But how are you to keep it from her? It is necessary she should know it, that you may take the steps proper to the alteration of your circumstances. You must change your style of living—nay," observing a pang to pass across his countenance, "don't let that afflict you. I am sure you have never placed your happiness in outward show—you have yet friends, warm friends, who will not think the worse of you for being less splendidly lodged: and surely it does not require a palace to be happy with Mary—" "I could be happy with her," cried he convulsively, "in a hovel!—I could go down with her into poverty and the dust!—I could—I could—God bless her!—God bless her!" cried he, bursting into a transport of grief and tenderness.

"And believe me, my friend," said I, stepping up, and grasping him warmly by the hand, "believe me, she can be the same with you. Ay, more: it will be a source of pride and triumph to her—it will call forth all the latent energies and fervent sympathies of her nature; for she will rejoice to prove that she loves you for yourself. There is in every true woman's heart a spark of heavenly fire, which lies dormant in the broad daylight of prosperity; but which kindles up, and beams and blazes in the dark hour of adversity. No man knows what the wife of his bosom is—no man knows what a ministering angel she is—until he has gone with her through the fiery trials of this world."

There was something in the earnestness of my manner, and the figurative style of my language, that caught the excited imagination of Leslie. I knew the auditor I had to deal with; and following up the impression I had made, I finished by persuading him to go home and unburthen his sad heart to his wife.

I must confess, notwithstanding all I had said, I felt some little solicitude for the result. Who can calculate on the fortitude of one whose whole life has been a round of pleasures? Her gay spirits might revolt at the dark, downward path of low humility, suddenly pointed out before her, and might cling to the sunny regions in which they had hitherto revelled. Besides, ruin in fashionable life is accompanied by so many galling mortifications, to which, in other ranks, it is a stranger.—In short, I could not meet Leslie, the next morning, without trepidation. He had made the disclosure.

"And how did she bear it?"

"Like an angel! It seemed rather to be a relief to her mind, for she threw her arms round my neck, and asked if this was all that had lately made me unhappy.—But, poor girl," added he, "she cannot realize the change we must undergo. She has no idea of poverty but in the abstract: she has only read of it in poetry, where it is allied to love. She feels as yet no privation: she suffers no loss of accustomed conveniencies nor elegancies. When we come practically to experience its sordid cares, its paltry wants, its petty humiliations—then will be the real trial."

"But," said I, "now that you have got over the severest task, that of breaking it to her, the sooner you let the world into the secret the better. The disclosure may be mortifying; but then it is a single misery, and soon over; whereas you otherwise suffer it, in anticipation, every hour in the day. It is not poverty, so much as pretence, that harasses a ruined man—the struggle between a proud mind and an empty purse—the keeping up a hollow show that must soon come to an end. Have the courage to appear poor, and you disarm poverty of its sharpest sting." On this point I found Leslie perfectly prepared. He had no false pride himself, and as to his wife, she was only anxious to conform to their altered fortunes.

Some days afterwards, he called upon me in the evening. He had disposed of his dwelling-house, and taken a small cottage in the country, a few miles from town. He had been busied all day in sending out furniture. The new establishment required few articles, and those of the simplest kind. All the splendid furniture of his late residence had been sold, excepting his wife's harp. That, he said, was too closely associated with the idea of herself; it belonged to the little story of their loves; for some of the sweetest moments of their courtship were those when he had leaned over that instrument, and listened to the melting tones of her voice. I could not but smile at this instance of romantic gallantry in a doating husband.

He was now going out to the cottage, where his wife had been all day, superintending its arrangement. My feelings had become strongly interested in the progress of this family story, and as it was a fine evening, I offered to accompany him.

He was wearied with the fatigues of the day, and as we walked out, fell into a fit of gloomy musing.

"Poor Mary!" at length broke, with a heavy sigh, from his lips.

"And what of her," asked I, "has any thing happened to her?"

"What," said he, darting an impatient glance, "is it nothing to be reduced to this paltry situation—to be caged in a miserable cottage—to be obliged to toil almost in the menial concerns of her wretched habitation?"

"Has she then repined at the change?"

"Repined! she has been nothing but sweetness and good humour. Indeed, she seems in better spirits than I have ever known her; she has been to me all love, and tenderness, and comfort!"

"Admirable girl!" exclaimed I. "You call yourself poor, my friend; you never were so rich—you never knew the boundless treasures of excellence you possessed in that woman."

"Oh! but, my friend, if this first meeting at the cottage were over, I think I could then be comfortable. But this is her first day of real experience: she has been introduced into an humble dwelling—she has been employed all day in arranging its miserable equipments—she has for the first time known the fatigues of domestic employment—she has for the first time looked around her on a home destitute of every thing elegant—almost of every thing convenient; and may now be sitting down, exhausted and spiritless, brooding over a prospect of future poverty."

There was a degree of probability in this picture that I could not gainsay, so we walked on in silence.

After turning from the main road, up a narrow lane, so thickly shaded by forest trees as to give it a complete air of seclusion, we came in sight of the cottage. It was humble enough in its appearance for the most pastoral poet; and yet it had a pleasing rural look. A wild vine had overrun one end with a profusion of foliage; a few trees threw their branches gracefully over it; and I observed several pots of flowers tastefully disposed about the door, and on the grass plot in front. A small wicket-gate opened upon a footpath that wound through some shrubbery to the door. Just as we approached, we heard the sound of music—Leslie grasped my arm; we paused and listened. It was Mary's voice, singing, in a style of the most touching simplicity, a little air of which her husband was peculiarly fond.

I felt Leslie's hand tremble on my arm. He stepped forward, to hear more distinctly. His step made a noise on the gravel walk. A bright beautiful face glanced out at the window, and vanished—a light footstep was heard—and Mary came tripping forth to meet us. She was in a pretty rural dress of white; a few wild flowers were twisted in her fine air; a fresh bloom was on her cheek; her whole countenance beamed with smiles—I had never seen her look so lovely.

"My dear George," cried she, "I am so glad you are come; I have been watching and watching for you; and running down the lane, and looking out for you. I've set out a table under a beautiful tree behind the cottage; and I've been gathering some of the most delicious strawberries, for I know you are fond of them—and we have such excellent cream—and every thing is so sweet and still here.—Oh!" said she, putting her arm within his, and looking up brightly in his face, "Oh, we shall be so happy!"

Poor Leslie was overcome.—He caught her to his bosom—he folded his arms round her—he kissed her again and again—he could not speak, but the tears gushed into his eyes; and he has often assured me, that though the world has since gone prosperously with him, and his life has indeed been a happy one, yet never has he experienced a moment of more exquisite felicity.

THE EPICUREAN.

BY THOMAS MOORE.

A LETTER TO THE TRANSLATOR, FROM ——, Esq.

Cairo, June 19, 1800.

My dear Sir,

During a visit lately paid by me to the monastery of St. Macarius—which is situated, as you know, in the Valley of the Lakes of Natron—I was lucky enough to obtain possession of a curious Greek manuscript, which, in the hope that you may be induced to translate it, I herewith transmit to you. Observing one of the monks very busily occupied in tearing up into a variety of fantastic shapes some papers which had the appearance of being the leaves of old books, I inquired of him the meaning of his task, and received the following explanation:—

The Arabs, it seems, who are as fond of pigeons as the ancient Egyptians, have a superstitious notion that, if they place in their pigeon-houses small scraps of paper, written over with learned characters, the birds are always sure to thrive the better for the charm; and the monks, who are never slow in profiting by superstition, have, at all times, a supply of such amulets for purchasers.

In general, the fathers of the monastery have been in the habit of scribbling these fragments themselves; but a discovery lately made by them, saves all this trouble. Having dug up (as my informant stated) a chest of old manuscripts, which, being chiefly on the subject of alchemy, must have been buried in the time of Dioclesian, "we thought," added the monk, "that we could not employ such rubbish more properly, than in tearing it up, as you see, for the pigeon-houses of the Arabs."

On my expressing a wish to rescue some part of these treasures from the fate to which his indolent fraternity had consigned them, he produced the manuscript which I have now the pleasure of sending you—the only one, he said, remaining entire—and I very readily paid the price which he demanded for it.

You will find the story, I think, not altogether uninteresting; and the coincidence, in many respects, of the curious details in Chapter VI., with the description of the same ceremonies in the Romance of *Sethos*, will, I have no doubt, strike you. Hoping that you may be induced to give a translation of this Tale to the world,

I am, my dear Sir, very truly yours, ——

CHAPTER I.

It was in the fourth year of the reign of the late Emperor Valerian, that the followers of Epicurus, who were at that time numerous in Athens, proceeded to the election of a person to fill the vacant Chair of their sect;—and, by the unanimous voice of the School, I was the individual chosen for their Chief. I was just then entering on my twenty-fourth year, and no instance had ever before occurred, of a person so young being selected for that high office. Youth, however, and the personal advantages that adorn it, could not but rank among the most agreeable recommendations to a sect that included within its circle all the beauty as well as the wit of Athens, and which, though dignifying its pursuits with the name of philosophy, was little else than a plausible pretext for the more refined cultivation of pleasure.

The character of the sect had, indeed, much changed since the time of its wise and virtuous founder, who, while he asserted that Pleasure is the only Good, inculcated also that Good is the only source of Pleasure. The purer part of this doctrine had long evaporated, and the temperate Epicurus would have as little recognised his own sect in the assemblage of refined voluptuaries who now usurped its name, as he would have known his own quiet Garden in the luxurious groves and bowers among which the meetings of the School were now held.

Many causes concurred, at this period, besides the attractiveness of its doctrines, to render our School by far the most popular of any that still survived the glory of Greece. It may generally be observed, that the prevalence, in one half of a community, of very rigid notions on the subject of religion, produces the opposite extreme of laxity and infidelity in the other; and this kind of re-action it was that now mainly contributed to render the doctrines of the Garden the most fashionable philosophy of the day. The rapid progress of the Christian faith had alarmed all those, who, either from piety or worldliness, were interested in the continuance of the old established creed—all who believed in the Deities of Olympus, and all who lived by them. The natural consequence was, a considerable increase of zeal and activity, throughout the constituted authorities and priesthood of the whole Heathen world. What was wanting in sincerity of belief was made up in rigour;—the weakest parts of the Mythology were those, of course, most angrily defended, and any reflections, tending to bring Saturn, or his wife Ops, into contempt, were punished with the utmost severity of the law.

In this state of affairs, between the alarmed bigotry of the declining Faith and the simple, sublime austerity of her rival, it was not wonderful that those lovers of ease and pleasure, who had no interest, reversionary or otherwise, in the old religion, and were too indolent to inquire into the sanctions of the new, should take refuge from the severities of both in the arms of a luxurious philosophy, which, leaving to others the task of disputing about the future, centred all its wisdom in the full enjoyment of the present.

The sectaries of the Garden had, ever since the death of their founder, been accustomed to dedicate to his memory the twentieth day of every month. To these monthly rites had, for some time, been added a grand annual Festival, in commemoration of his birth. The feasts given on this occasion by my predecessors in the Chair, had been invariably distinguished for their taste and splendour; and it was my ambition, not merely to imitate this example, but even to render the anniversary, now celebrated under my auspices, so lively and brilliant as to efface the recollection of all that had preceded it.

Seldom, indeed, had Athens witnessed so bright a scene. The grounds that formed the original site of the Garden had received, from time to time, considerable additions; and the whole extent was now laid out with that perfect taste, which understands how to wed Nature with Art, without sacrificing any of her simplicity to the alliance. Walks, leading through wildernesses of shade and fragrance—glades, opening, as if to afford a play-ground for the sunshine—temples, rising on the very spots where Imagination herself would have called them up, and fountains and lakes, in alternate motion and repose, either wantonly courting the verdure, or calmly sleeping in its embrace—such was the variety of feature that diversified these fair gardens; and, animated as they were on this occasion, by all the living wit and loveliness of Athens, it afforded a scene such as my own youthful fancy, rich as it was then in images of luxury and beauty, could hardly have anticipated.

The ceremonies of the day began with the very dawn, when, according to the form of simpler and better times, those among the disciples who had apartments within the Garden, bore the image of our Founder in procession from chamber to chamber, chanting verses in praise of what had long ceased to be objects of our imitation—his frugality and temperance.

Round a beautiful lake, in the centre of the Garden, stood four white Doric temples, in one of which was collected a library containing all the flowers of Grecian literature; while, in the remaining three, Conversation, the Song, and the Dance, held, uninterrupted by each other, their respective rites. In the Library stood busts of all the most illustrious Epicureans, both of Rome and Greece—Horace, Atticus, Pliny the elder, the poet Lucretius, Lucian, and the lamented biographer of the Philosophers, lately lost to us, Diogenes Laertius. There were also the portraits, in marble, of all the eminent female votaries of the School—Leontium and her fair daughter Danae, Themista, Philenis, and others.

It was here that, in my capacity of Heresiarch, on the morning of the Festival, I received the felicitations of the day from some of the fairest lips of Athens; and, in pronouncing the customary oration to the memory of our Master (in which it was usual to dwell upon the doctrines he had inculcated,) endeavoured to attain that art, so useful before such an audience, of lending to the gravest subjects a charm, which secures them listeners even among the simplest and most volatile.

Though study, as may be supposed, engrossed but little the nights or mornings of the Garden, yet all the lighter parts of learning—that portion of its attic honey, for which the bee is not compelled to go very deep into the flower—was somewhat zealously cultivated by us. Even here, however, the young student had to encounter that kind of distraction, which is, of all others, the least favourable to composure of thought; and, with more than one of my fair disciples there used to occur such scenes as the following, which a poet of the Garden, taking his picture from the life, thus described:—

"As o'er the lake, in evening's glow,
That temple threw its lengthening shade,
Upon the marble steps below
There sate a fair Corinthian maid,
Gracefully o'er some volume bending;
While, by her side, the youthful Sage
Held back her ringlets, lest, descending,
They should o'er-shadow all the page."

But it was for the evening of that day, that the richest of our luxuries were reserved. Every part of the Garden was illuminated, with the most skilful variety of lustre; while over the Lake of the Temples were scattered wreaths of flowers, through which boats, filled with beautiful children, floated, as through a liquid parterre.

Between two of these boats a mock combat was perpetually carried on;—their respective commanders, two blooming youths, being habited to represent Eros and Anteros: the former, the Celestial Love of the Platonists, and the latter, that more earthly spirit, which usurps the name of Love among the Epicureans. Throughout the whole evening their conflict was maintained with various success; the timid distance at which Eros kept aloof from his lively antagonist being his only safeguard against those darts of fire, with showers of which the other assailed him, but which, falling short of their mark upon the lake, only scorched the few flowers on which they fell, and were extinguished.

In another part of the gardens, on a wide glade, illuminated only by the moon, was performed an imitation of the torch-race of the Panathenæa by young boys chosen for their fleetness, and arrayed with wings, like Cupids; while, not far off, a group of seven nymphs, with each a star on her forehead, represented the movements of the planetary choir, and embodied the dream of Pythagoras into real motion and song.

At every turning some new enchantment broke unexpectedly on the eye or ear; and now, from the depth of a dark grove, from which a fountain at the same time issued, there came a strain of sweet music, which, mingling with the murmur of the water, seemed like the voice of the spirit that presided over its flow; while, at other times, the same strain appeared to come breathing from among flowers, or was heard suddenly from under ground, as if the foot had just touched some spring that set its melody in motion.

It may seem strange that I should now dwell upon all these trifling details; but they were to me full of the future; and every thing connected with that memorable night—even its long-repented follies—must for ever live fondly and sacredly in my memory. The festival concluded with a banquet, at which, as master of the Sect, I presided; and being, myself, in every sense, the ascendant spirit of the whole scene, gave life to all around me, and saw my own happiness reflected in that of others.

CHAPTER II.

The festival was over;—the sounds of the song and dance had ceased, and I was now left in those luxurious gardens, alone. Though so ardent and active a votary of pleasure, I had, by nature, a disposition full of melancholy;—an imagination that, even in the midst of mirth and happiness, presented saddening thoughts, and threw the shadow of the future over the gayest illusions of the present. Melancholy was, indeed, twin-born in my soul with Passion; and not even in the fullest fervour of the latter were they ever separated. From the first moment that I was conscious of thought and feeling, the same dark thread had run across the web; and images of death and annihilation came to mingle themselves with even the most smiling scenes through which love and enjoyment led me. My very passion for pleasure but deepened these gloomy thoughts. For, shut out, as I was by my creed, from a future life, and having no hope beyond the narrow horizon of this, every minute of earthly delight assumed, in my eyes a mournful preciousness; and pleasure, like the flower of the cemetery, grew but more luxuriant from the neighbourhood of death.

This very night my triumph, my happiness, had seemed complete. I had been the presiding genius of that voluptuous scene. Both my ambition and my love of pleasure had drunk deep of the rich cup for which they thirsted. Looked up to as I was by the learned, and admired and loved by the beautiful and the young, I had seen, in every eye that met mine, either the acknowledgment of bright triumphs already won, or the promise of others, still brighter, that awaited me. Yet, even in the midst of all this, the same dark thoughts had presented themselves;—the perishableness of myself and all around me had recurred every instant to my mind. Those hands I had prest—those eyes, in which I had seen sparkling a spirit of light and life that ought never to die—those voices, that had spoken of eternal love—all, all I felt, were but a mockery of the moment, and would leave nothing eternal but the silence of their dust!

Oh, were it not for this sad voice,
Stealing amid our mirth to say,
That all in which we most rejoice,
Ere night may be the earth-worm's prey;
But for this bitter—only this—
Full as the world is brimm'd with bliss,
And capable as feels my soul
Of draining to its depth the whole,
I should turn earth to heaven, and be,
If bliss made gods, a deity!

Such was the description I gave of my own feelings in one of those wild, passionate songs, to which this mixture of mirth and melancholy, in a spirit so buoyant, naturally gave birth.

And seldom had my heart so fully surrendered itself to this sort of vague sadness as at that very moment, when as I paced thoughtfully among the fading lights and flowers of the banquet, the echo of my own step was all that now sounded, where so many gay forms had lately been revelling. The moon was still up, the morning had not yet glimmered, and the calm glories of the night still rested on all around. Unconscious whither my pathway led, I continued to wander along, till I, at length, found myself before that fair statue of Venus, with which the chisel of Alcamenes had embellished our Garden;—that image of deified woman, the only idol to which I had ever yet bent the knee. Leaning against the pedestal of the statue, I raised my eyes to heaven, and fixing them sadly and intently on the ever-burning stars, as if seeking to read the mournful secret in their light, asked, wherefore was it that Man alone must fade and perish, while they so much less wonderful, less godlike than he, thus still lived on in radiance unchangeable and for ever! "Oh, that there were some spell, some talisman," I exclaimed, "to make the spirit that burns within us deathless as those stars, and opes to it a career like theirs, as bright and inextinguishable throughout all time!"

While thus indulging in wild and melancholy fancies, I felt that lassitude which earthly pleasure, however sweet, still leaves behind, come insensibly over me, and at length sunk at the base of the statue to sleep.

But even in sleep, the same fancies continued to haunt me; and a dream, so distinct and vivid, as to leave behind it the impression of reality, thus presented itself to my mind. I found myself suddenly transported to a wide and desolate plain, where nothing appeared to breathe, or move, or live. The very sky that hung above it looked pale and extinct, giving the idea, not of darkness, but of light that had become dead;—and had that whole region been the remains of some older world, left broken up and sunless, it could not have presented an aspect more quenched and desolate. The only thing that bespoke life, throughout this melancholy waste, was a small spark of light, that at first glimmered in the distance, but, at length, slowly approached the bleak spot where I stood. As it drew nearer, I could see that its small but steady gleam came from a taper in the hand of an ancient and venerable man, who now stood, like a pale messenger from the grave, before me. After a few moments of awful silence, during which he looked at me with a sadness that thrilled my very soul, he said "Thou, who seekest eternal life, go unto the shores of the dark Nile—go unto the shores of the dark Nile, and thou wilt find the eternal life thou seekest!"

No sooner had he uttered these words than the death-like hue of his cheek at once brightened into a smile of more than earthly promise; while the small torch he held in his hand sent forth a glow of radiance, by which suddenly the whole surface of the desert was illuminated;—the light spreading even to the distant horizon's edge, along whose line I could now see gardens, palaces, and spires, all as bright as the rich architecture of the clouds at sunset. Sweet music, too, came floating in every direction through the air, and, from all sides, such varieties of enchantment broke upon me, that, with the excess alike of harmony and of radiance, I awoke.

That infidels should be superstitious is an anomaly neither unusual nor strange. A belief in superhuman agency seems natural and necessary to the mind; and, if not suffered to flow in the obvious channels, it will find a vent in some other. Hence, many who have doubted the existence of a God, have yet implicitly placed themselves under the patronage of Fate or the stars. Much the same inconsistency I was conscious of in my own feelings. Though rejecting all belief in a Divine Providence, I had yet a faith in dreams, that all my philosophy could not conquer. Nor was experience wanting to confirm me in my delusion; for, by some of those accidental coincidences, which make the fortune of soothsayers and prophets, dreams, more than once, had been to me—

Oracles, truer far than oak,
Or dove, or tripod, ever spoke.

It was not wonderful, therefore, that the vision of that night—touching, as it did, a chord so ready to vibrate—should have affected me with more than ordinary power, and even sunk deeper into my memory with every effort I made to forget it. In vain did I mock at my own weakness; such self-derision is seldom sincere. In vain did I pursue my accustomed pleasures. Their zest was, as usual, for ever new; but still, in the midst of all my enjoyment, came the cold and saddening consciousness of mortality, and, with it, the recollection of that visionary promise, to which my fancy, in defiance of reason, still continued to cling.

At times indulging in reveries, that were little else than a continuation of my dream, I even contemplated the possible existence of some mighty secret, by which youth, if not perpetuated, might be at least prolonged, and that dreadful vicinity of death, within whose circle love pines and pleasure sickens, might be for a while averted. "Who knows," I would ask, "but that in Egypt, that region of wonders, where Mystery hath yet unfolded but half her treasures—when still remain, undeciphered, upon the pillars of Seth, so many written secrets of the antediluvian world—who can tell but that some powerful charm, some amulet, may there lie hid, whose discovery, as this phantom hath promised, but awaits my coming—some compound of the same pure atoms, that form the essence of the living stars, and whose infusion into the frame of man might render him also unfading and immortal!"

Thus fondly did I sometimes speculate, in those vague moods of mind, when the life of excitement in which I was engaged, acting upon a warm heart and vivid fancy, produced an intoxication of spirit, during which I was not wholly myself. This bewilderment, too, was not a little increased by the constant struggle I experienced between my own natural feelings, and the cold, mortal creed of my sect—in endeavouring to escape from whose deadening bondage I but broke loose into the realms of fantasy and romance.

Even in my soberest moments, however, that strange vision for ever haunted me; and every effort I made to chase it from my recollection was unavailing. The deliberate conclusion, therefore, to which I at last came, was, that to visit Egypt was now my only resource; that without seeing that land of wonders, I could not rest, nor until convinced of my folly by disappointment, be reasonable. Without delay, accordingly, I announced to my friends of the Garden, the intention I had formed to pay a visit to the land of Pyramids. To none of them, however, did I dare to confess the vague, visionary impulse that actuated me;—knowledge being the object that I alleged, while Pleasure was that for which they gave me credit. The interests of the School, it was feared, might suffer by my absence; and there were some tenderer ties, which had still more to fear from separation. But for the former inconvenience a temporary remedy* was provided; while the latter a skilful distribution of vows and sighs alleviated. Being furnished with recommendatory letters to all parts of Egypt, I set sail in the summer of the year 257, A. D., for Alexandria.

CHAPTER III.

To one, who so well knew how to extract pleasure from every moment on land, a sea-voyage, however smooth and favourable, appeared the least agreeable mode of losing time that could be devised. Often, indeed, did my imagination, in passing some isle of those seas, people it with fair forms and loving hearts, to which most willingly would I have paused to offer homage. But the wind blew direct towards the land of Mystery; and, still more, I heard a voice within me, whispering for ever, "On."

As we approached the coast of Egypt, our course became less prosperous; and we had a specimen of the benevolence of the divinities of the Nile, in the shape of a storm, or rather whirlwind, which had nearly sunk our vessel, and which the Egyptians on board declared to be the work of their deity, Typhon. After a day and night of danger, during which we were driven out of our course to the eastward, some benigner influence prevailed above; and, at length, as the morning freshly broke, we saw the beautiful city of Alexandria rising from the sea, with its proud Palace of Kings, its portico of four hundred columns, and the fair Pillar of Pillars, towering in the midst to heaven.

After passing in review this splendid vision, we shot rapidly round the Rock of Pharos, and, in a few minutes, found ourselves in the harbour of Eunostus. The sun had risen, but the light on the Great Tower of the Rock was still burning; and there was a languor in the first waking movements of that voluptuous city—whose houses and temples lay shining in silence around the harbour—that sufficiently attested the festivities of the preceding night.

We were soon landed on the quay; and, as I walked through a line of palaces and shrines, up the street which leads from the sea to the Gate of Canopus, fresh as I was from the contemplation of my own lovely Athens, I yet felt a glow of admiration at the scene around me, which its novelty, even more than its magnificence, inspired. Nor were the luxuries and delights, which such a city promised, among the least of the considerations upon which my fancy dwelt. On the contrary, every thing around me seemed prophetic of love and pleasure. The very forms of the architecture, to my Epicurean imagination, appeared to call up images of living grace; and even the dim seclusion of the temples and groves spoke only of tender mysteries to my mind. As the whole bright scene grew animated around me, I felt that though Egypt might not enable me to lengthen life, she could teach the next best art—that of multiplying its enjoyments.

The population of Alexandria, at this period, consisted of the most motley miscellany of nations, religions and sects that had ever been brought together in one city. Besides the school of the Grecian Platonist was seen the oratory of the cabalistic Jew; while the church of the Christian stood, undisturbed, over the crypts of the Egyptian Hierophant. Here, the adorer of Fire, from the East, laughed at the less elegant superstition of the worshipper of cats, from the West. Here Christianity, too, had learned to emulate the pious vagaries of Paganism; and while, on one side, her Ophite professor was seen bending his knee gravely before a serpent, on the other, a Nicosian Christian was heard contending, with no less gravity, that there could be no chance whatever of salvation out of the pale of the Greek alphabet. Still worse, the uncharitableness of Christian schism was already, with equal vigour, distinguishing itself; and I heard every where, on my arrival, of the fierce rancour and hate, with which the Greek and Latin churchmen were then persecuting each other, because, forsooth, the one fasted on the seventh day of the week, and the others fasted upon the fourth and sixth!

To none, however, of these different creeds and sects, except in as far as they furnished food for ridicule, had I time to pay much attention. I was now in the most luxurious city of the universe, and accordingly gave way, without reserve, to the various seductions that surrounded me. My reputation, both as a philosopher and a man of pleasure, had preceded my coming; and Alexandria, the second Athens of the world, welcomed me as her own. I found my celebrity, indeed, act as a talisman, that opened all hearts and doors at my approach. The usual novitiate of acquaintance was dispensed with in my favour, and not only intimacies, but loves and friendships, ripened as rapidly in my path, as vegetation springs up where the Nile has flowed. The dark beauty of the Egyptian women possessed a novelty in my eyes that enhanced its other charms; and the hue left by the sun on their rounded cheeks seemed but an earnest of the genial ardour he must have kindled in their hearts—

Th' imbrowning of the fruit, that tells,
How rich within the soul of sweetness dwells.

Some weeks had now passed in such constant and ever-changing pleasures, that even the melancholy voice deep within my heart, though it still spoke, was but seldom listened to, and soon died away in the sound of the siren songs that surrounded me. At length, as the novelty of these gay scenes wore off, the same vague and gloomy bodings began to mingle with all my joys; and an incident that occurred, at this time, during one of my gayest revels, conduced still more to deepen their gloom.

The celebration of the annual festival of Serapis happened to take place during my stay, and I was, more than once, induced to mingle with the gay multitudes that flocked to the shrine at Canopus on the occasion. Day and night, as long as this festival lasted, the great canal, which led from Alexandria to Canopus, was covered with boats full of pilgrims of both sexes, all hastening to avail themselves of this pious license, which lent the zest of a religious sanction to pleasure, and gave a holyday to the follies and passions of earth, in honour of heaven.

I was returning, one lovely night, to Alexandria. The north wind, that welcome visiter, had cooled and freshened the air, while the banks, on either side of the stream, sent forth, from groves of orange and henna, the most delicious odours. As I had left all the crowd behind me at Canopus, there was not a boat to be seen on the canal but my own; and I was just yielding to the thoughts which solitude at such an hour inspires, when my reveries were suddenly broken by the sound of some female voices, coming mingled with laughter and screams, from the garden of a pavilion, that stood, brilliantly illuminated, upon the bank of the canal.

On rowing nearer, I perceived that both the mirth and the alarm had been caused by the efforts of some playful girls to reach a hedge of jasmine which grew near the water, and in bending towards which they had nearly fallen into the stream. Hastening to proffer my assistance, I soon recognised the voice of one of my fair Alexandrian friends; and, springing on the bank, was surrounded by the whole group, who insisted on my joining their party in the pavilion: and, having flung around me, as fetters, the tendrils of jasmine, which they had just plucked, conducted me, no unwilling captive, to the banquet-room.

I found here an assemblage of the very flower of Alexandrian society. The unexpectedness of the meeting added new zest to it on both sides; and seldom had I ever felt more enlivened myself, or succeeded better in infusing life and gaiety into others.

Among the company were some Greek women, who according to the fashion of their country, wore veils; but, as usual, rather to set off than to conceal their beauty, some bright gleams of which were constantly escaping from under the cloud. There was, however, one female, who particularly attracted my attention, on whose head was a chaplet of dark-coloured flowers, and who sat veiled and silent during the whole of the banquet. She took no share, I observed, in what was passing around: the viands and the wine were by her untouched, nor did a word that was spoken seem addressed to her ear. This abstraction from a scene so sparkling with gaiety, though apparently unnoticed by any one but myself, struck me as mysterious and strange. I inquired of my fair neighbour the cause of it, but she looked grave, and was silent.

In the mean time, the lyre and the cup went round; and a young maid from Athens, as if inspired by the presence of her countryman, took her lute, and sung to it some of the songs of Greece, with a warmth of feeling that bore me back to the banks of the Ilissus, and, even in the bosom of present pleasure, drew a sigh from my heart for that which had passed away. It was day-break ere our delighted party rose, and most unwillingly re-embarked to return to the city.

We were scarce afloat, when it was discovered that the lute of the young Athenian had been left behind; and, with a heart still full of its sweet sounds, I most readily sprang on shore to seek it. I hastened at once to the banquet-room, which was now dim and solitary, except that—there, to my utter astonishment, was still seated that silent figure, which had awakened so much my curiosity during the evening. A vague feeling of awe came over me, as I now slowly approached it. There was no motion, no sound of breathing in that form;—not a leaf of the dark chaplet upon its brow stirred. By the light of a dying lamp which stood on the table before the figure, I raised, with a hesitating hand, the veil; and saw —what my fancy had already anticipated—that the shape underneath was lifeless, was a skeleton! Startled and shocked, I hurried back with the lute to the boat, and was almost as silent as that shape itself during the remainder of the voyage.

This custom among the Egyptians of placing a mummy, or skeleton, at the banquet-table, had been for some time disused, except at particular ceremonies; and, even on such occasions, it had been the practice of the luxurious Alexandrians to disguise this memorial of mortality in the manner just described. But to me, who was wholly unprepared for such a spectacle, it gave a shock from which my imagination did not speedily recover. This silent and ghastly witness of mirth seemed to embody, as it were, the shadow in my own heart. The features of the grave were thus stamped upon the idea that had long haunted me, and this picture of what I was *to be* now associated itself constantly with the sunniest aspect of what I *was*.

The memory of the dream now recurred to me more livelily than ever. The bright, assuring smile of that venerable Spirit, and his words, "Go to the shores of the dark Nile, and thou wilt find the eternal life thou seekest," were for ever present to my mind. But as yet, alas, I had done nothing towards realizing the proud promise. Alexandria was not Egypt;—the very soil on which it now stood was not in existence, when already Thebes and Memphis had numbered ages of glory.

"No," I exclaimed; "it is only beneath the Pyramids of Memphis, or in the mystic Halls of the Labyrinth, those holy arcana are to be found, of which the antediluvian world has made Egypt its heir, and among which—blest thought!—the key to eternal life may lie."

Having formed my determination, I took leave of my many Alexandrian friends, and departed for Memphis.

CHAPTER IV.

EGYPT was, perhaps, of all others, the country most calculated, from that mixture of the melancholy and the voluptuous, which marked the character of her people, her religion, and her scenery, to affect deeply a fancy and temperament like mine, and keep both for ever tremblingly alive. Wherever I turned, I beheld the desert and the garden, mingling together their desolation and bloom. I saw the love-bower and the tomb standing side by side, as if, in that land, Plea sure and Death kept hourly watch upon each other. In the very luxury of the climate there was the same saddening influence. The monotonous splendour of the days, the solemn radiance of the nights—all tended to cherish that ardent melancholy, the offspring of passion and of thought, which had been so long the familiar inmate of my soul.

When I sailed from Alexandria, the inundation of the Nile was at its full. The whole valley of Egypt lay covered by its blood; and, as, looking around me, I saw in the light of the setting sun, shrines, palaces, and monuments, encircled by the waters, I could almost fancy that I beheld the sinking island of Atalantis, on the last evening its temples were visible above the wave. Such varieties too, of animation as presented themselves on every side!—

While, far as sight could reach, beneath as clear
And blue a heaven as ever bless'd this sphere,
Gardens, and pillar'd streets, and porphyry domes,
And high-built temples, fit to be the homes
Of mighty gods—and pyramids, whose hour
Outlasts all time, above the waters tower!

Then, too, the scenes of pomp and joy that make
One theatre of this vast peopled lake,
Where all that Love, Religion, Commerce gives
Of life and motion, ever moves and lives.
Here, up the steps of temples, from the wave
Ascending, in procession slow and grave,
Priests, in white garments, go, with sacred wands
And silver cymbals gleaming in their hands:
While, there, rich barks—fresh from those sunny tracts
Far off, beyond the sounding cataracts—
Glide with their precious lading to the sea,
Plumes of bright birds, rhinoceros' ivory,
Gems from the Isle of Meröe, and those grains
Of gold, wash'd down by Abyssinian rains.

Here, where the waters wind into a bay
Shadowy and cool, some pilgrims on their way
To Saïs or Bubastus, among beds
Of lotus-flowers, that close above their heads,
Push their light barks, and hid, as in a bower
Sing, talk, or sleep away the sultry hour;
While, haply, not far off, beneath a bank
Of blossoming acacias, many a prank
Is play'd in the cool current by a train
Of laughing nymphs, lovely as she, whose chain
Around two conquerors of the world was cast,
But, for a third too feeble, broke at last!

Enchanted with the whole scene, I lingered delightedly on my voyage, visiting all those luxurious and venerable places, whose names have been consecrated by the wonder of ages. At Sais I was present during the Festival of Lamps, and read, by the blaze of innumerable lights, those sublime words on the temple of Neitha:—"I am all that has been, that is, and that will be, and no man hath ever lifted my veil." I wandered among the prostrate obelisks of Heliopolis, and saw, not without a sigh, the sun smiling over her ruins, as if in mockery of the mass of perishable grandeur, that had once called itself, in its pride, "The City of the Sun." But to the Isle of the Golden Venus was, I own, my fondest pilgrimage;—and there, as I rambled through its shades, where bowers are the only temples, I felt how far more worthy to form the shrine of a Deity are the ever-living stems of the garden and the grove, than the most precious columns the inanimate quarry can supply.

Every where new pleasures, new interests awaited me; and though Melancholy stood, as usual, for ever near, her shadow fell but half-way over my vagrant path, leaving the rest but more welcomely brilliant from the contrast. To relate my various adventures, during this short voyage, would only detain me from events, far, far more worthy of record. Amidst all this endless variety of attractions, the great object of my journey had been forgotten;—the mysteries of this land of the sun still remained, to me, as much mysteries as ever, and as yet I had been initiated in nothing but its pleasures.

It was not till that memorable evening, when I first stood before the Pyramids of Memphis, and beheld them towering aloft, like the watch-towers of Time, from whose summit, when about to expire, he will look his last—it was not till this moment that the great secret announced in my dream again rose, in all its inscrutable darkness upon my thoughts. There was a solemnity in the sunshine resting upon those monuments—a stillness, as of reverence, in the air that breathed around them, which seemed to steal, like the music of past times, into my heart. I thought what myriads of the wise, the beautiful, and the brave, had sunk into dust since earth first saw those wonders; and, in the sadness of my soul, I exclaimed,—"Must man alone, then, perish? must minds and hearts be annihilated, while pyramids endure? Oh, Death, Death! even upon these everlasting tablets—the only approach to immortality that kings themselves could purchase—thou hast written our doom awfully, and intelligibly, saying, 'There is for man no eternal mansion, but the grave!'"

My heart sunk at the thought; and, for the moment, I yielded to that desolate feeling, which overspreads the soul that hath no light from the future. But again the buoyancy of my nature prevailed, and again, the willing dupe of vain dreams, I deluded myself into the belief of all that my heart most wished, with that happy facility which enables imagination to stand in the place of happiness. "Yes," I cried, "immortality *must* be within man's reach, and, as wisdom alone is worthy of such a blessing, to the wise alone must the secret have been revealed. It is said, that deep under yonder pyramid, has lain for ages concealed the Table of Emerald, on which the Thrice-Great Hermes, in times before the flood, engraved the secret of Alchemy, which gives gold at will. Why, then, may not the mightier, the more god-like secret, that gives *life* at will, be recorded there also? It was by the power of gold, of endless gold, that the kings, who now repose in those massy structures, scooped earth to its very centre, and raised quarries into the air, to provide for themselves tombs that might outstand the world. Who can tell but that the gift of immortality was also theirs? who knows but that they themselves, triumphant over decay, still live;—those mighty mansions, which we call tombs, being rich and everlasting palaces, within whose depths, concealed from this withering world, they still wander, with the few Elect who have been sharers of their gift, through a sunless, but ever illuminated, elysium of their own? Else, wherefore those structures? wherefore that subterranean realm, by which the whole valley of Egypt is undermined? Why, else, those labyrinths, which none of earth hath ever beheld—which none of heaven, except that God, who stands, with finger on his hushed lip, hath ever trodden?"

While thus I indulged in fond dreams, the sun, already half sunk beneath the horizon, was taking calmly and gloriously, his last look of the Pyramids—as he had done, evening after evening, for ages, till they had grown familiar to him as the earth itself. On the side turned to his ray they now presented a front of dazzling whiteness, while, on the other, their great shadows, lengthening away to the eastward, looked like the first steps of Night, hastening to envelope the hills of Araby in her shade.

No sooner had the last gleam of the sun disappeared, than on every house-top in Memphis, gay, gilded banners were seen waving aloft, to proclaim his setting—while, at the same moment, a full burst of harmony was heard to peal from all the temples along the shores.

Startled from my musings by these sounds, I at once recollected, that, on that very evening, the great festival of the Moon was to be celebrated. On a little island, half-way over between the gardens of Memphis and the eastern shore, stood the temple of that goddess,

whose beams
Bring the sweet time of night-flowers and dreams.
Not the cold Dian of the North, who chains
In vestal ice the current of young veins;
But she, who haunts the gay, Bubastian grove,
And owns she sees, from her bright heaven above,
Nothing on earth to match that heaven, but love!

Thus did I exclaim, in the words of one of their own Egyptian poets, as, anticipating the various delights of the festival, I cast away from my mind all gloomy thoughts; and, hastening to my little bark, in which I now lived the life of a Nile bird, on the waters, steered my course to the island-temple of the Moon.

CHAPTER V.

THE rising of the Moon, slow and majestic, as if conscious of the honours that awaited her upon earth, was welcomed with a loud acclaim from every eminence, where multitudes stood watching for her first light. And seldom had that light risen upon a more beautiful scene. The city of Memphis—still grand, though no longer the unrivalled Memphis, that had borne away from Thebes the crown of supremacy, and worn it undisputed through ages—now, softened by the mild moonlight that harmonized with her decline, shone forth among her lakes, her pyramids, and her shrines, like one of those dreams of human glory that must ere long pass away. Even already ruin was visible around her. The sands of the Libyan desert were gaining upon her like a sea; and there, among solitary columns and sphinxes, already half sunk from sight, Time seemed to stand waiting, till all that now flourished around him should fall beneath his desolating hand, like the rest.

On the waters all was gaiety and life. As far as eye could reach, the lights of innumerable boats were seen studding, like rubies, the surface of the stream. Vessels of every kind—from the light coracle, built for shooting down the cataracts, to the large yacht that glides slowly to the sound of flutes—all were afloat for this sacred festival, filled with crowds of the young and the gay, not only from Memphis and Babylon, but from cities still farther removed from the festal scene.

As I approached the island, I could see, glittering through the trees on the bank, the lamps of the pilgrims hastening to the ceremony. Landing in the direction which those lights pointed out, I soon joined the crowd; and, passing through a long alley of sphinxes, whose spangling marble gleamed out from the dark sycamores around them, reached in a short time the grand vestibule of the temple, where I found the ceremonies of the evening already commenced.

In this vast hall, which was surrounded by a double range of columns, and lay open over-head to the stars of heaven, I saw a group of young maidens, moving in a sort of measured step, between walk and dance, round a small shrine, upon which stood one of those sacred birds, that, on account of the variegated colour of their wings, are dedicated to the worship of the moon. The vestibule was dimly lighted—there being but one lamp of naphtha hung on each of the great pillars that encircled it. But, having taken my station beside one of those pillars, I had a clear view of the young dancers, as in succession they passed me.

The drapery of all was white as snow; and each wore loosely, beneath the bosom, a dark-blue zone, or bandelet, studded, like the skies at midnight, with small silver stars. Through their dark locks was wreathed the white lily of the Nile—that sacred flower being accounted no less welcome to the moon, than the golden blossoms of the bean-flower are known to be to the sun. As they passed under the lamp, a gleam of light flashed from their bosoms, which, I could perceive, was the reflection of a small mirror, that, in the manner of the women of the East, each of the dancers wore beneath her left shoulder.

There was no music to regulate their steps; but, as they gracefully went round the bird on the shrine, some to the beat of the castanet, some to the shrill ring of a sistrum—which they held uplifted in the attitude of their own divine Isis—continued harmoniously to time the cadence of their feet; while others, at every step, shook a small chain of silver, whose sound, mingling with those of the castanets and sistrums, produced a wild but not unpleasing harmony.

They seemed all lovely; but there was one—whose face the light had not yet reached, so downcast she held it—who attracted, and, at length, riveted all my looks and thoughts. I know not why, but there was a something in those half-seen features—a charm in the very shadow, that hung over their imagined beauty—which took my fancy more than all the out-shining loveliness of her companions. So enchained was I by this coy mystery, that her alone, of all the group, could I either see or think of—her alone I watched, as, with the same downcast brow, she glided gently and aerially round the altar, as if her presence, like that of a spirit, was something to be felt, not seen.

Suddenly, while I gazed, the loud crash of a thousand cymbals was heard;—the massy gates of the Temple flew open, as if by magic, and a flood of radiance from the illuminated aisle filled the whole vestibule; while, at the same instant, as if the light and the sounds were born together, a peal of rich harmony came mingling with the radiance.

It was then—by that light, which shone full upon the young maiden's features, as, starting at the sudden blaze, she raised her eyes to the portal, and as quickly let fall their lids again—it was then I beheld, what even my own ardent imagination, in its most vivid dreams of beauty, had never pictured. Not Psyche herself, when pausing or the threshold of heaven, while its first glories fell on her dazzled lids, could have looked more purely beautiful, or blushed with a more innocent shame. Often as I had felt the power of looks, none had ever entered into my soul so deeply. It was a new feeling—a new sense—coming as suddenly upon me as that radiance into the vestibule, and, at once filling my whole being;—and had that bright vision but lingered another moment before my eyes, I should in my transport have wholly forgotten who I was and where, and thrown myself, in prostrate adoration, at her feet.

But scarcely had that gush of harmony been heard, when the sacred bird, which had, till now, been standing motionless as an image, spread wide his wings and flew into the Temple; while his graceful young worshippers, with a fleetness like his own, followed—and she, who had left a dream in my heart never to be forgotten, vanished along with the rest. As she went rapidly past the pillar against which I leaned, the ivy that encircled it caught in her drapery, and disengaged some ornament, which fell to the ground. It was the small mirror which I had seen shining on her bosom. Hastily and tremulously I picked it up, and hurried to restore it; but she was already lost to my eyes in the crowd.

In vain did I try to follow;—the aisles were already filled, and numbers of eager pilgrims pressed towards the portal. But the servants of the Temple denied all further entrance, and still, as I presented myself, their white wands barred the way. Perplexed and irritated amid that crowd of faces, regarding all as enemies that impeded my progress, I stood on tiptoe, gazing into the busy aisles, and with a heart beating as I caught, from time to time, a glimpse of some spangled zone, or lotus wreath, which led me to fancy that I had discovered the fair object of my search. But it was all in vain;—in every direction, files of sacred nymphs were moving, but nowhere could I discover her whom alone I sought.

In this state of breathless agitation did I stand for some time—bewildered with the confusion of faces and lights, as well as with the clouds of incense that rolled around me—till, fevered and impatient, I could endure it no longer. Forcing my way out of the vestibule into the cool air, I hurried back through the alley of sphinxes to the shore, and flung myself into my boat.

There lies, to the north of Memphis, a solitary lake, (which at this season of the year, mingles with the rest of the waters,) upon whose shores stands the Necropolis, or City of the Dead—a place of melancholy grandeur, covered over with shrines and pyramids, where many a kingly head, proud even in death, has lain awaiting through long ages the resurrection of its glories. Through a range of sepulchral grots underneath, the humbler denizens of the tomb are deposited—looking out on each successive generation that visits them, with the same face and features they wore centuries ago. Every plant and tree, consecrated to death, from the asphodel-flower to the mystic plaintain, lends its sweetness or shadow to this place of tombs; and the only noise that disturbs its eternal calm, is the low humming sound of the priests at prayer, when a new inhabitant is added to the Silent City.

It was towards this place of death that, in a mood of mind, as usual, half gloomy, half bright, I now, almost unconsciously, directed my bark. The form of the young Priestess was continually before me. That one bright look of hers, the very remembrance of which was worth all the actual smiles of others, never for a moment left my mind. Absorbed in such thoughts, I continued to row on, scarce knowing whither I went, till, at length, startled to find myself within the shadow of the City of the Dead, I looked up, and beheld, rising in succession before me, pyramid beyond pyramid, each towering more loftily than the other—while all were out-topped in grandeur by one, upon whose summit the bright moon rested as on a pedestal.

Drawing nearer to the shore, which was sufficiently elevated to raise this silent city of tombs above the level of the inundation, I rested my oar, and allowed the boat to rock idly upon the water; while, in the mean time, my thoughts, left equally without direction, were allowed to fluctuate as idly. How vague and various were the dreams that then floated through my mind—that bright vision of the temple still mingling itself with all! Sometimes she stood before me, like an aerial spirit, as pure as if that element of music and light, into which I had seen her vanish, was her only dwelling. Sometimes, animated with passion, and kindling into a creature of earth, she seemed to lean towards me with looks of tenderness, which it were worth worlds, but for one instant, to inspire; and again—as the dark fancies, that ever haunted me, recurred—I saw her cold, parched, and blackening, amid the gloom of those eternal sepulchres before me

Turning away, with a shudder, from the cemetery at this thought, I heard the sound of an oar plying swiftly through the water, and, in a few moments, saw, shooting past me towards the shore, a small boat in which sat two female figures, muffled up and veiled. Having landed them not far from the spot where, under the shadow of a tomb on the bank, I lay concealed, the boat again departed, with the same fleetness, over the flood.

Never had the prospect of a lively adventure come more welcome to me than at this moment, when my busy fancy was employed in weaving such chains for my heart, as threatened a bondage, of all others the most difficult to break. To become enamoured thus of a creature of my own imagination, was the worst, because the most lasting, of follies. It is only reality that can afford any chance of dissolving such spells, and the idol I was now creating to myself must for ever remain ideal. Any pursuit, therefore, that seemed likely to divert me from such thoughts—to bring back my imagination to earth and reality, from the vague region in which it had been wandering, was a relief far too seasonable not to be welcomed with eagerness.

I had watched the course which the two figures took, and, having hastily fastened my boat to the bank, stepped gently on shore, and, at a little distance, followed them. The windings through which they led were intricate; but, by the bright light of the moon, I was enabled to keep their forms in view, as, with rapid step, they glided among the monuments. At length, in the shade of a small pyramid, whose peak barely surmounted the plane-trees that grew nigh, they vanished from my sight. I hastened to the spot, but there was not a sign of life around; and, had my creed extended to another world, I might have fancied these forms were spirits, sent down from thence to mock me—so instantaneously had they disappeared. I searched through the neighbouring grove, but all there was still as death. At length, in examining one of the sides of the pyramid, which, for a few feet from the ground, was furnished with steps, I found, midway between peak and base, a part of its surface, which, although presenting to the eye an appearance of smoothness, gave to the touch, I thought, indications of a concealed opening.

After a variety of efforts and experiments, I, at last, more by accident than skill, pressed the spring that commanded this hidden aperture. In an instant the portal slid aside, and disclosed a narrow stairway within, the two or three first steps of which were discernable by the moonlight, while the rest were all lost in utter darkness. Though it was difficult to conceive that the persons whom I had been pursuing would have ventured to pass through this gloomy opening, yet to account for their disappearance otherwise was still more difficult. At all events, my curiosity was now too eager in the chase to relinquish it;—the spirit of adventure, once raised, could not be so easily laid. Accordingly, having sent up a gay prayer to that bliss-loving Queen whose eye alone was upon me, I passed through the portal, and descended into the pyramid.

CHAPTER VI.

At the bottom of the stairway I found myself in a low, narrow passage, through which, without stooping almost to the earth, it was impossible to proceed. Though leading through a multiplicity of dark windings, this way seemed but little to advance my progress—its course, I perceived, being chiefly circular, and gathering, at every turn, but a deeper intensity of darkness.

"Can any thing," thought I, "of human kind sojourn here?"—and had scarcely asked myself the question, when the path opened into a long gallery, at the farthest end of which a gleam of light was visible. This welcome glimmer appeared to issue from some cell or alcove, in which the right-hand wall of the gallery terminated, and, breathless with expectation, I stole gently towards it.

Arrived at the end of the gallery, a scene presented itself to my eyes, for which my fondest expectations of adventure could not have prepared me. The place from which the light proceeded was a small chapel, of whose interior, from the dark recess in which I stood, I could take, unseen myself, a full and distinct view. Over the walls of this oratory were painted some of those various symbols, by which the mystic wisdom of the Egyptians loves to shadow out the History of the Soul; the winged globe with a serpent—the rays descending from above, like a glory—and the Theban beetle, as he comes forth after the waters have passed away, and the first sunbeam falls on his regenerated wings.

In the middle of the chapel, on a low altar of granite, lay a lifeless female from, enshrined within a case of crystal—as it is the custom to preserve the dead in Ethiopia—and looking as freshly beautiful as if the soul had but a few hours departed. Among the emblems of death, on the front of the altar, were a slender lotus branch broken in two, and a small bird just winging its flight from the spray.

To these memorials of the dead, however, I paid but little attention; for there was a living object there upon which my eyes were now intently fixed.

The lamp, by which the whole of the chapel was illuminated, was placed at the head of the pale image in the shrine; and between its light and me stood a female form, bending over the monument, as if to gaze upon the silent features within. The position in which this figure was placed, intercepting a strong light, afforded me, at first, but an imperfect and shadowy view of it. Yet even at this mere outline I felt my heart beat high—and memory had no less share, as it proved, in this feeling than imagination. For, on the head changing its position, so as to let a gleam fall upon the features, I saw, with a transport which had almost led me to betray my lurking-place, that it was she—the young worshipper of Isis—the same, the very same, whom I had seen, brightening the holy place where she stood, and looking like an inhabitant of some purer world.

The movement, by which she had now afforded me an opportunity of recognizing her, was made in raising from the shrine a small cross of silver, which lay directly over the bosom of the lifeless figure. Bringing it close to her lips, she kissed it with a religious fervour; then turning her eyes mournfully upwards, held them fixed with a degree of inspired earnestness, as if, at that moment, in direct communion with Heaven, they saw neither roof, nor any other earthly barrier, between them and the skies.

What a power is there in innocence! whose very helplessness is its safeguard—in whose presence even Passion himself stands abashed, and turns worshipper at the very altar which he came to despoil! She, who, but a short hour before, had presented herself to my imagination as something I could have risked immortality to win—she, whom gladly, from the floor of her own lighted temple, in the very face of its proud ministers, I would have borne away in triumph and dared all punishments, divine and human, to make her mine—that very creature was now before me, as if thrown by fate itself, into my power—standing there, beautiful and alone, with nothing but her innocence for her guard! Yet, no—so touching was the purity of the whole scene, so calm and august that protection which the dead extended over the living, that every earthly feeling was forgotten as I gazed, and love itself became exalted into reverence.

But, entranced as I felt in witnessing such a scene, thus to enjoy it by stealth seemed to me a wrong, a sacrilege—and, rather than let her eyes encounter the flash of mine, or disturb, by a whisper, that sacred silence, in which Youth and Death held communion through undying Love, I would have suffered my heart to break, without a murmur, where I stood. Gently, as if life itself depended on my every movement, I stole away from that tranquil and holy scene—leaving it still holy and tranquil as I had found it—and, gliding back through the same passages and windings by which I had entered, reached again the narrow stairway, and re-ascended into light.

The sun had just risen, and, from the summit of the Arabian hills, was pouring down his beams into that vast valley of waters—as if proud of last night's homage to his own divine Isis, now fading away in the superior splendour of her Lord. My first impulse was to fly at once from this dangerous spot, and in new loves and pleasures seek forgetfulness of the wondrous scene I had just witnessed. "Once," I exclaimed, "out of the circle of this enchantment, I know too well my own susceptibility to new impressions, to feel any doubt that I shall soon break the spell that is now around me."

But vain were all my efforts and resolves. Even while swearing to fly that spot, I found my steps still lingering fondly round the pyramid—my eyes still turned towards the portal which severed this enchantress from the world of the living. Hour after hour did I wander through that City of

Silence, till, already, it was mid-day, and, under the sun's meridian eye, the mighty pyramid of pyramids stood, like a great spirit, shadowless.

Again did those wild and passionate feelings, which, for the moment, her presence had subdued into reverence, return to take possession of my imagination and my senses. I even reproached myself for the awe, that had held me spell-bound before her. "What," thought I, "would my companions of the Garden say, did they know that their chief—he whose path Love had strewed with trophies—was now pining for a simple Egyptian girl, in whose presence he had not dared to utter a single sigh, and who had vanquished the victor, without even knowing her triumph!"

A blush came over my cheek at the humiliating thought, and I determined, at all risks, to await her coming. That she should be an inmate of those gloomy caverns seemed inconceivable; nor did there appear to be any egress out of their depths but by the pyramid. Again, therefore, like a sentinel of the dead, did I pace up and down among those tombs, contrasting mournfully the burning fever in my own veins with the cold quiet of those who lay slumbering around.

At length the intense glow of the sun over my head, and, still more, that ever restless agitation in my heart, became too much for even strength like mine to endure. Exhausted, I threw myself down at the base of the pyramid—choosing my place directly under the portal, where, even should slumber surprise me, my heart, if not my ear, might still keep watch, and her footstep, light as it was, could not fail to awake me.

After many an ineffectual struggle against drowsiness, I at length sunk into sleep—but not into forgetfulness. The same image still haunted me, in every variety of shape, with which imagination, assisted by memory, could invest it. Now, like the goddess Neitha, upon her throne at Sais, she seemed to sit, with the veil just raised from that brow which till then no mortal had ever beheld—and now, like the beautiful enchantress Rhodope, I saw her rise from out the pyramid in which she had dwelt for ages,—

> "Fair Rhodope, as story tells,
> The bright unearthly nymph, who dwells
> 'Mid sunless gold and jewels hid,
> The Lady of the Pyramid!"

So long had my sleep continued, that, when I awoke, I found the moon again resplendent above the horizon. But all around was looking tranquil and lifeless as before; nor did a print on the grass betray that any foot had passed there since my own. Refreshed, however, by my long rest, and with a fancy still more excited by the mystic wonders of which I had been dreaming, I now resolved to revisit the chapel in the pyramid, and put an end, if possible, to this strange mystery that haunted me.

Having learned, from the experience of the preceding night, the inconvenience of encountering those labyrinths without a light, I now hastened to provide myself with a lamp from my boat. Tracking my way back with some difficulty to the shore, I there found not only my lamp, but also some dates and dried fruits, of which I was always provided with store, for my roving life upon the waters, and which, after so many hours of abstinence, were now a most welcome and necessary relief.

Thus prepared, I again ascended the pyramid, and was proceeding to search out the secret spring, when a loud, dismal noise was heard at a distance, to which all the melancholy echoes of the cemetery gave answer. The sound came, I knew, from the Great Temple on the shore of the lake, and was the sort of shriek which its gates—the Gates of Oblivion as they are called—used always to send forth from their hinges, when opening at night, to receive the newly-landed dead.

I had, more than once before, heard that sound, and always with sadness; but at this moment, it thrilled through me like a voice of ill omen, and I almost doubted whether I should not abandon my enterprise. The hesitation, however, was but momentary;—even while it passed through my mind, I had touched the spring of the portal. In a few seconds more, I was again in the passage beneath the pyramid; and, being enabled by the light of my lamp to follow the windings more rapidly, soon found myself at the door of the small chapel in the gallery.

I entered, still awed, though there was now, alas, nought living within. The young Priestess had vanished like a spirit into the darkness; and all the rest remained as I had left it on the preceding night. The lamp still stood burning upon the crystal shrine; the cross was lying where the hands of the young mourner had placed it, and the cold image, within the shrine, wore still the same tranquil look, as if resigned to the solitude of death—of all lone things the loneliest. Remembering the lips that I had seen kiss that cross, and kindling with the recollection, I raised it passionately to my own;—but the dead eyes, I thought, met mine, and, awed and saddened in the midst of my ardour, I replaced the cross upon the shrine.

I had now lost every clue to the object of my pursuit, and, then with all that sullen satisfaction which certainty, even when unwelcome, brings, was about to retrace my steps slowly to earth, when, as I held forth my lamp, on leaving the chapel, I perceived that the gallery, instead of terminating here, took a sudden and snake-like bend to the left, which had before eluded my observation, and which seemed to give promise of a pathway still farther into those recesses. Re-animated by this discovery, which opened a new source of hope to my heart, I cast, for a moment, a hesitating look at my lamp, as if to inquire whether it would be faithful through the gloom I was about to encounter, and then, without further consideration, rushed eagerly forward.

CHAPTER VII.

THE path led, for a while, through the same sort of narrow windings as those which I had before encountered in descending the stairway; and at length opened, in a similar manner, into a straight and steep gallery, along each side of which stood, closely ranged and upright, a file of lifeless bodies, whose glassy eyes appeared to glare upon me preternaturally as I passed.

Arrived at the end of this gallery, I found my hopes, for the second time, vanish; as the path, it was manifest, extended no further. The only object I was able to discern, by the glimmering of my lamp, which now burned, every minute, fainter and fainter, was the mouth of a large well, that lay gaping before me—a reservoir of darkness, black and unfathomable. It now crossed my memory that I had once heard of such wells, as being used occasionally for passages by the priests. Leaning down, therefore, over the edge, I examined anxiously all within, in order to see if it afforded the means of a descent into the chasm; but the sides, I could perceive, were hard and smooth as glass, being varnished all over with that sort of dark pitch, which the Dead Sea throws out on its slimy shore.

After a more attentive scrutiny, however, I observed, at the depth of a few feet, a sort of iron step, projecting dimly from the side, and, below it, another, which, though hardly perceptible, was just sufficient to encourage an adventurous foot to the trial. Though all hope of tracing the young Priestess was now at an end—it being impossible that female foot should have ventured on this descent—yet, as I had engaged so far in the adventure, and there was, at least, a mystery to be unravelled, I determined, at all hazards, to explore the chasm. Placing my lamp, therefore, (which was hollowed at the bottom, so as to be worn like a helmet,) firmly upon my head, and having thus both hands at liberty for exertion, I set my foot cautiously on the iron step, and descended into the well.

I found the same footing, at regular intervals, to a considerable depth; and had already counted near a hundred of these steps, when the ladder altogether ceased, and I could descend no further. In vain did I stretch down my foot in search of support—the hard slippery sides were all that it encountered. At length, stooping my head, so as to let the light fall below, I observed an opening or window directly above the step on which I stood; and, taking for granted that the way must lie in that direction, contrived to clamber, with no small difficulty, through the aperture.

I now found myself on a rude and narrow stairway, the steps of which were cut out of the living rock, and wound spirally downward in the same direction as the well. Almost dizzy with the descent, which seemed as if it would never end, I, at last, reached the bottom, where a pair of massy iron gates were closed directly across my path, as if wholly to forbid any further progress. Massy and gigantic, however, as they were, I found, to my surprise, that the hand of an infant might have opened them with ease—so readily did their stupendous folds give way to my touch,

"Light as a lime-bush, that receives
Some wandering bird among its leaves."

No sooner, however, had I passed through, than the astounding din, with which the gates clashed together again, was such as might have awakened death itself. It seemed as if every echo throughout that vast, subterranean world, from the Catacombs of Alexandria to Thebes' Valley of Kings, had caught up and repeated the thundering sound.

Startled as I was by the crash, not even this supernatural clangour could divert my attention from the sudden light that now broke around me—soft, warm, and welcome, as are the stars of his own South to the eyes of the mariner who has long been wandering through the cold seas of the North. Looking for the source of this splendour, I saw, through an archway opposite, a long illuminated alley, stretching away as far as the eye could reach, and fenced, on one side, with thickets of odoriferous shrubs; while along the other extended a line of lofty arcades, from which the light, that filled the whole area, issued. As soon, too, as the din of the deep echoes had subsided, there stole gradually on my ear a strain of choral music, which appeared to come mellowed and sweetened in its passage, through many a spacious hall within those shining arcades; while among the voices I could distinguish some female tones, which, towering high and clear above all the rest, formed the spire, as it were, into which the harmony tapered as it rose.

So excited was my fancy by this sudden enchantment, that—though never had I caught a sound from the fair Egyptian's lips—I yet persuaded myself that the voice I now heard was hers, sounding highest and most heavenly of all that choir, and calling to me, like a distant spirit from its sphere. Animated by this thought, I flew forward to the archway, but found, to my mortification, that it was guarded by a trellis-work, whose bars, though invisible at a distance, resisted all my efforts to force them.

While occupied in these ineffectual struggles, I perceived, to the left of the archway, a dark cavernous opening, which seemed to lead in a direction parallel to the lighted arcades. Notwithstanding, however, my impatience, the aspect of this passage, as I looked shudderingly into it, chilled my very blood. It was not so much darkness, as a sort of livid and ghastly twilight, from which a damp, like that of death-vaults, exhaled, and through which, if my eyes did not deceive me, pale, phantom-like shapes were, at that very moment, hovering.

Looking anxiously round, to discover some less formidable outlet, I saw, over the vast folding-gates through which I had just passed, a blue, tremulous flame, which, after playing for a few seconds over the dark ground of the pediment, settled gradually into characters of light, and formed the following words:—

You, who would try
 Yon terrible track,
To live, or to die,
 But ne'er to look back—

You, who aspire
 To be purified there,
By the terrors of Fire,
 Of Water, and Air—

If danger, and pain,
 And death, you despise,
On—for again
 Into light you shall rise;

Rise into light
 With that Secret Divine,
Now shrouded from sight
 By the Veils of the Shrine!

But if——

Here the letters faded away into a dead blank, more awfully intelligible than the most eloquent words.

A new hope now flashed across me. The dream of the Garden, which had been for some time almost forgotten, returned freshly to my mind. "Am I, then," I exclaimed, "in the path to the promised mystery? and shall the great secret of Eternal Life *indeed* be mine?"

"Yes!" seemed to answer out of the air, that spirit-voice, which still was heard at a distance crowning the choir with its single sweetness. I hailed the omen with transport. Love and Immortality, both beckoning me onward—who would give even a thought to fear, with two such bright hopes in prospect? Having invoked and blessed that unknown enchantress, whose steps had led me to this abode of mystery and knowledge, I instantly plunged into the chasm.

Instead of that vague, spectral twilight, which had at first met my eye, I now found, as I entered, a thick darkness, which, though far less horrible, was, at this moment, still more disconcerting, as my lamp, which had been, for some time, almost useless, was now fast expiring. Resolved, however, to make the most of its last gleam, I hastened, with rapid step, through this gloomy region, which appeared to be wider and more open to the air than any I had yet passed. Nor was it long before the sudden appearance of a bright blaze in the distance announced to me that my first great Trial was at hand. As I drew nearer, the flames before me burst high and wide on all sides;—and the awful spectacle that then presented itself was such as might have daunted hearts far more accustomed to dangers than mine.

There lay before me, extending completely across my path, a thicket, or grove, of the most combustible trees of Egypt—tamarind, pine, and Arabian balm; while around their stems and branches were coiled serpents of fire, which, twisting themselves rapidly from bough to bough, spread the contagion of their own wild-fire as they went, and involved tree after tree in one general blaze. It was, indeed, rapid as the burning of those reed-beds of Ethiopia, whose light is often seen brightening, at night, the distant cataracts of the Nile.

Through the middle of this blazing grove, I could now perceive my only pathway lay. There was not a moment, therefore, to be lost—for the conflagration gained rapidly on either side, and already the narrowing path between was strewed with vivid fire. Casting away my now useless lamp, and holding, my robe as some slight protection over my head I ventured, with trembling limbs, into the blaze.

Instantly, as if my presence had given new life to the flames, a fresh outbreak of combustion arose on all sides The trees clustered into a bower of fire above my head, while the serpents that hung hissing from the red branches shot showers of sparkles down upon me as I passed. Never were decision and activity of more avail:—one minute later, and I must have perished. The narrow opening, of which I had so promptly availed myself, closed instantly behind me; and as I looked back, to contemplate the ordeal which I had passed, I saw that the whole grove was already one mass of fire.

Rejoiced to have escaped this first trial, I instantly plucked from one of the pine-trees a bough that was but just kindled, and with this for my only guide, hastened breathlessly forward. I had advanced but a few paces, when the path turned suddenly off, leading downwards, as I could perceive by the glimmer of my brand, into a more confined region, through which a chilling air, as if from some neighbouring waters, blew over my brow. Nor had I proceeded far in this course, when the sound of torrents—mixed, as I thought, from time to time, with shrill wailings, resembling the cries of persons in danger or distress—fell mournfully upon my ear. At every step the noise of the dashing waters increased, and I now perceived that I had entered an immense rocky cavern, through the middle of which, headlong as a winter-torrent, the dark flood, to whose roar I had been listening, poured its waters; while upon its surface floated grim spectre-like shapes, which, as they went by, sent forth those dismal shrieks I had heard—as if in fear of some awful precipice towards whose brink they were hurrying.

I saw plainly that across that torrent must be my course. It was, indeed, fearful; but in courage and perseverance now lay my only hope. What awaited me on the opposite shore, I knew not; for all there was immersed in impenetrable gloom, nor could the feeble light which I carried send its glimmer half so far. Dismissing, however, all thoughts but that of pressing onward, I sprung from the rock on which I stood into the flood, trusting that, with my right hand, I should be able to buffet the current, while, with the other, as long as a gleam of my brand remained, I might hold it aloft to guide me safely to the shore.

Long, formidable, and almost hopeless was the struggle I had now to maintain; and more than once, overpowered by the rush of the waters, I had given myself up, as destined to follow those pale, death-like apparitions, that still went past me, hurrying onward, with mournful cries, to find their doom in some invisible gulf beyond

At length, just as my strength was nearly exhausted, and the last remains of the pine branch were dropping from my hand, I saw, outstretching towards me into the water, a light double balustrade, with a flight of steps between, ascending, almost perpendicularly, from the wave, till they seemed lost in a dense mass of clouds above. This glimpse—for it was nothing more, as my light expired in giving it—lent new spring to my courage. Having now both hands at liberty, so desperate were my efforts, that, after a few minutes' struggle, I felt my brow strike against the stairway, and, in an instant, my feet were on the steps.

Rejoiced at my escape from that perilous flood, though I knew not whither the stairway led, I promptly ascended the steps. But this feeling of confidence was of short duration. I had not mounted far, when, to my horror, I perceived that each successive step, as my foot left it, broke away from beneath me, leaving me in mid-air, with no other alternative than that of still mounting by the same momentary footing, and with the appalling doubt whether it would even endure my tread.

And thus did I, for a few seconds, continue to ascend, with nothing beneath me but that awful river, in which—so tranquil had it now become—I could hear the plash of the falling fragments, as every step in succession gave way from under my feet. It was a most fearful moment—but even still worse remained. I now found the balustrade, by which I had held during my ascent, and which had hitherto appeared to be firm, growing tremulous in my hand, while the step, to which I was about to trust myself, tottered under my foot. Just then, a momentary flash, as if of lightning, broke around me; and I saw, hanging out of the clouds, so as to be barely within my reach, a huge brazen ring. Instinctively I stretched forth my arm to seize it, and, at the same instant, both balustrade and steps gave way beneath me, and I was left swinging by my hands in the dark void. As if, too, this massy ring, which I grasped, was by some magic power linked with all the winds in heaven, no sooner had I seized it than, like the touching of a spring, it seemed to give loose to every variety of gusts and tempests, that ever strewed the sea-shore with wrecks or dead; and, as I swung about, the sport of this elemental strife, every new burst of its fury threatened to shiver me, like a storm-sail, to atoms!

Nor was even this the worst;—for, still holding, I know not how, by the ring, I felt myself caught up, as if by a thousand whirlwinds, and then round and round, like a stone-shot in a sling, continued to be whirled in the midst of all this deafening chaos, till my brain grew dizzy, my recollection became confused, and I almost fancied myself on that wheel of the infernal world, whose rotations Eternity alone can number!

Human strength could no longer sustain such a trial. I was on the point, at least, of loosing my hold, when suddenly the violence of the storm moderated;—my whirl through the air gradually ceased, and I felt the ring slowly descend with me, till—happy as a shipwrecked mariner at the first touch of land—I found my feet once more upon firm ground.

At the same moment, a light of the most delicious softness filled the whole air. Music, such as is heard in dreams, came floating at a distance; and as my eyes gradually recovered their powers of vision, a scene of glory was revealed to them, almost too bright for imagination, and yet living and real. As far as the sight could reach, enchanting gardens were seen, opening away through long tracts of light and verdure, and sparkling every where with fountains, that circulated, like streams of life, among the flowers. Not a charm was here wanting, that the fancy of poet or prophet, in their warmest pictures of Elysium, have ever yet dreamed or promised. Vistas, opening into scenes of indistinct grandeur—streams, shining out at intervals, in their shadowy course—and labyrinths of flowers, leading, by mysterious windings, to green, spacious glades full of splendour and repose. Over all this, too, there fell a light, from some unseen source, resembling nothing that illumines our upper world—a sort of golden moonlight, mingling the warm radiance of day with the calm and melancholy lustre of night.

Nor were there wanting inhabitants for this sunless Paradise. Through all the bright gardens were seen wandering, with the serene air and step of happy spirits, groups both of young and old, of venerable and of lovely forms, bearing, most of them, the Nile's white flowers on their heads, and branches of the eternal palm in their hands; while, over the verdant turf, fair children and maidens went dancing to aerial music, whose source was, like that of the light, invisible, but which filled the whole air with its mystic sweetness.

Exhausted as I was by the painful trials I had undergone, no sooner did I perceive those fair groups in the distance, than my weariness, both of frame and spirit, was forgotten. A thought crossed me that she, whom I sought, might haply be among them; and notwithstanding the feeling of awe, with which that unearthly scene inspired me, I was about to fly, on the instant, to ascertain my hope. But while in the act of making the effort, I felt my robe gently pulled, and turning round, beheld an aged man before me, whom, by the sacred hue of his garb, I knew at once to be a Hierophant. Placing a branch of the consecrated palm in my hand, he said, in a solemn voice, "Aspirant of the Mysteries, welcome!"—then, regarding me for a few seconds with grave attention, added, in a tone of courteousness and interest, "The victory over the body hath been gained! Follow me, young Greek, to thy resting-place."

I obeyed the command in silence—and the Priest, turning away from this scene of splendour, into a secluded pathway, where the light gradually faded as we advanced, led me to a small pavilion, by the side of a whispering stream, where the very spirit of slumber seemed to preside, and, pointing silently to a bed of dried poppy-leaves, left me to repose.

CHAPTER VIII.

THOUGH the sight of that splendid scene, whose glories opened upon me like a momentary glimpse into another world, had, for an instant, re-animated my strength and spirit, yet, so completely was my whole frame subdued by fatigue, that, even had the form of the young Priestess herself then stood before me, my limbs would have sunk in the effort to reach her. No sooner had I fallen on my leafy couch, than sleep, like a sudden death, came over me; and I lay, for hours, in that deep and motionless rest, which not even a shadow of life disturbs.

On awaking I saw, beside me, the same venerable personage, who had welcomed me to this subterranean world on the preceding night. At the foot of my couch stood a statue, of Grecian workmanship, representing a boy, with wings, seated gracefully on a lotus-flower, and having the forefinger of his right hand pressed to his lips. This action, together with the glory round his brows, denoted, as I already knew, the God of Silence and Light.

Impatient to know what further trials awaited me, I was about to speak, when the Priest exclaimed anxiously, "Hush!" —and, pointing to the statue at the foot of the couch, said,—"Let the spell of that Spirit be upon thy lips, young stranger, till the wisdom of thy instructors shall think fit to remove it. Not unaptly doth the same deity preside over Silence and Light; since it is only out of the depth of contemplative silence, that the great light of the soul, Truth, can arise!"

Little used to the language of dictation or instruction, I was now preparing to rise, when the Priest again restrained me; and, at the same moment, two boys, beautiful as the young Genii of the stars, entered the pavilion. They were habited in long garments of the purest white, and bore each a small golden chalice in his hand. Advancing towards me, they stopped on opposite sides of the couch, and one of them, presenting to me his chalice of gold, said, in a tone between singing and speaking,—

"Drink of this cup—Osiris sips
The same in his halls below;
And the same he gives, to cool the lips
Of the Dead who downward go.

"Drink of this cup—the water within
Is fresh from Lethe's stream;
'Twill make the past, with all its sin,
And all its pain and sorrows, seem
Like a long-forgotten dream!

"The pleasure, whose charms
Are steep'd in wo;
The knowledge, that harms
The soul to know;

"The hope, that, bright
As the lake of the waste,
Allures the sight,
But mocks the taste:

"The love, that binds
Its innocent wreath,
Where the serpent winds,
In venom, beneath;—

"All that, of evil or false, by thee
Hath ever been known or seen,
Shall melt away in this cup, and be
Forgot, as it never had been!"

Unwilling to throw a slight on this strange ceremony, I leaned forward, with all due gravity, and tasted the cup; which I had no sooner done than the young cup-bearer on the other side, invited my attention; and, in his turn, presenting the chalice which he held, sung, with a voice still sweeter than that of his companion, the following strain:—

"Drink of this cup—when Isis led
Her boy, of old, to the beaming sky,
She mingled a draught divine, and said—
'Drink of this cup, thou'lt never die!'

"Thus do I say and sing to thee,
Heir of that boundless heaven on high,
Though frail, and fall'n, and lost thou be,
Drink of this cup, thou'lt never die!"

Well as I had hitherto kept my philosophy on its guard against the illusions with which, I knew, this region abounded, the young cup-bearer had here touched a spring of imagination, over which my philosophy, as has been seen, had but little control. No sooner had the words, "thou shalt never die," struck on my ear, than the dream of the Garden came fully to my mind; and, starting half-way from the couch, I stretched forth my hands to the cup. But, recollecting myself instantly, and fearing that I had betrayed to others a weakness fit only for my own secret indulgence, I sunk back again, with a smile of affected indifference, on my couch—while the young minstrel, but little interrupted by my movement, still continued his strain, of which I heard but the concluding words:—

"And Memory, too, with her dreams shall come
Dreams of a former, happier day,
When Heaven was still the Spirit's home,
And her wings had not yet fallen away;

"Glimpses of glory, ne'er forgot,
That tell, like gleams on a sunset sea,
What once hath been, what now is not,
But, oh! what again shall brightly be."

Though the assurances of immortality contained in these verses would at any other moment—vain and visionary as I thought them—have sent my fancy wandering into reveries of the future, the effort of self-control I had just made enabled me to hear them with indifference.

Having gone through the form of tasting his second cup, I again looked anxiously to the Hierophant, to ascertain whether I might be permitted to rise. His assent having been given, the young pages brought to my couch a robe and tunic, which, like their own, were of linen of the purest white; and having assisted to clothe me in this sacred garb, they then placed upon my head a chaplet of myrtle, in which the symbol of Initiation, a golden grasshopper, was seen shining out from among the dark leaves.

Though sleep had done much to refresh my frame, something more was still wanting to restore its strength; and it was not without a smile at my own reveries I reflected, how much more welcome than even the young page's cup of immortality was the unpretending, but real, repast now set before me—fresh fruits from the Isle of Gardens in the Nile, the delicate flesh of the desert antelope, and wine from the Vineyard of the Queens at Anthylla, which one of the pages fanned with a palm-leaf, to keep it cool.

Having done justice to these dainties, it was with pleasure I heard the proposal of the Priest, that we should walk forth together, and meditate among the scenes without. I had not forgotten the splendid Elysium that last night welcomed me—those rich gardens, that soft unearthly music and light, and, above all, those fair forms I had seen wandering about—as if, in the very midst of happiness, still seeking it. The hope, which had then occurred to me, that, among those bright groups might haply be found the young maiden I sought, now returned with increased strength. I had little doubt that my guide was leading me to the same Elysian scene, and that the form, so fit to inhabit it, would again appear before my eyes.

But far different, I found, was the region to which he now conducted me;—nor could the whole world have produced a scene more gloomy, or more strange. It wore the appearance of a small, solitary valley, enclosed, on every side, by rocks, which seemed to rise, almost perpendicularly, till they reached the very sky;—for it was, indeed, the blue sky that I saw shining between their summits, and whose light, dimmed thus and nearly lost in its long descent, formed the melancholy daylight of this nether world. Down the side of these rocky walls descended a cataract whose source was upon earth, and on whose waters, as they rolled glassily over the edge above, a gleam of radiance rested, showing how brilliant and pure was the sunshine they had left behind. From thence, gradually growing darker, and frequently broken by alternate chasms and projections, the stream fell, at last, in a pale and thin mist—the phantom of what it had been on earth—into a small lake that lay at the base of the rock to receive it.

Nothing was ever so bleak and saddening as the appearance of this lake. The usual ornaments of the waters of Egypt were not wanting to it: the tall lotus here uplifted her silvery flowers, and the crimson flamingo floated over the tide. But they looked not the same as in the world above;—the flower had exchanged its whiteness for a livid hue, and the wings of the bird hung heavy and colourless. Every thing wore the same half-living aspect; and the only sounds that disturbed the mournful stillness were the wailing cry of a heron among the sedges, and that din of the falling waters, in their midway struggle, above.

There was, indeed, an unearthly sadness in the whole scene, of which no heart, however light, could resist the influence. Perceiving how much I was affected by it, "Such scenes," remarked the Priest, "are best suited to that solemn complexion of mind, which becomes him who approaches the Great Mystery of futurity. Behold"—and, in saying thus he pointed to the opening over our heads, through which, though the sun had but just passed his meridian, I could perceive a star or two twinkling in the heavens—"in the same manner as from this gloomy depth we can see those fixed stars, which are invisible now to the dwellers on the bright earth, even so, to the sad and self-humbled spirit, doth many a mystery of heaven reveal itself, of which they, who walk in the light of the proud world, know not!"

He now led me towards a rustic seat or alcove, beside which stood an image of that dark Deity, that God without a smile, who presides over the silent kingdom of the Dead. The same livid and lifeless hue was upon his features, that hung over everything in this dim valley; and, with his right hand, he pointed directly downwards, to denote that his melancholy kingdom lay there. A plantain—that favourite tree of the genii of Death—stood behind the statue, and spread its branches over the alcove, in which the Priest now seated himself, and made a sign that I should take my place by his side.

After a long pause, as if of thought and preparation,—"Nobly," said he, "young Greek, hast thou sustained the first trials of Initiation. What still remains, though of vital import to the soul, brings with it neither pain nor peril to the body. Having now proved and chastened thy mortal frame by the three ordeals of Fire, of Water, and of Air, the next task to which we are called is the purification of thy spirit—the effectual cleansing of that inward and immortal part, so as to render it fit for the reception of the last luminous revealment, when the Veils of the Sanctuary shall be thrown aside, and the Great Secret of Secrets unfolded to thy view!—Towards this object, the primary and most important step is, instruction. What the three purifying elements thou hast passed through have done for thy body instruction will effect for——"

"But that lovely maiden!" I exclaimed, bursting from my silence, having fallen, during his speech, into a deep reverie, in which I had forgotten him, myself, the Great Secret, every thing—but her.

Startled by this profane interruption, he cast a look of alarm towards the statue, as if fearful lest the God should have heard my words. Then, turning to me, in a tone of mild solemnity, "It is but too plain," said he, "that thoughts of the upper world, and of its vain, shadowy delights, still engross thee far too much, to allow the lessons of Truth to sink profitably into thy heart. A few hours of meditation amid this solemn scenery—of that wholesome meditation, which purifies, by saddening—may haply dispose thee to receive, with due feelings of reverence, the holy and imperishable knowledge we have in store for thee. With this hope I now leave thee to thy own thoughts, and to that God, before whose calm and mournful eye all the vanities of the world, from which thou comest, wither!"

Thus saying, he turned slowly away, and passing behind the statue, towards which he had pointed during the last sentence, suddenly, and, as if by enchantment, disappeared from my sight.

CHAPTER IX.

BEING now left to my own solitary thoughts, I was fully at leisure to reflect, with some degree of coolness, upon the inconveniences, if not dangers, of the situation into which my love of adventure had hurried me. However prompt my imagination was always to kindle, in its own ideal sphere, I have ever found that, when brought into contact with reality, it as suddenly cooled;—like those meteors, that appear to be stars, while in the air, but the moment they touch earth, are extinguished. And such was the feeling of disenchantment that now succeeded to the wild dreams in which I had been indulging. As long as Fancy had the field of the future to herself, even immortality did not seem too distant a race for her. But when human instruments interposed, the illusion all vanished. From mortal lips the promise of immortality seemed a mockery, and even imagination had no wings that could carry beyond the grave.

Nor was this disappointment the only feeling that pained and haunted me;—the imprudence of the step, on which I had ventured, now appeared in its full extent before my eyes. I had here thrown myself into the power of the most artful priesthood in the world, without even a chance of being able to escape from their toils, or to resist any machinations with which they might beset me. It appeared evident, from the state of preparation in which I had found all that wonderful apparatus, by which the terrors and splendours of Initiation are produced, that my descent into the pyramid was not unexpected. Numerous, indeed, and active as were the spies of the Sacred College of Memphis, it could little be doubted that all my movements, since my arrival, had been watchfully tracked; and the many hours I had employed in wandering and exploring around the pyramid, betrayed a curiosity and spirit of adventure which might well suggest to these wily priests the hope of inveigling an Epicurean into their toils.

I was well aware of their hatred to the sect of which I was Chief;—that they considered the Epicureans as, next to the Christians, the most formidable enemies of their craft and power. "How thoughtless, then," I exclaimed, "to have placed myself in a situation, where I am equally helpless against fraud and violence, and must either pretend to be the dupe of their impostures, or else submit to become the victim of their vengeance!" Of these alternatives, bitter as they both were, the latter appeared by far the more welcome. It was with a blush that I even looked back upon the mockeries I had already yielded to; and the prospect of being put through still further ceremonials, and of being tutored and preached to by hypocrites whom I so much despised, appeared to me, in my present mood of mind, a trial of patience, compared to which the flames and whirlwinds I had already encountered were pastime.

Often and impatiently did I look up, between those rocky walls, to the bright sky that appeared to rest upon their summits, as, pacing round and round, through every part of the valley, I endeavoured to find some outlet from its gloomy precincts. But vain were all my endeavours;—that rocky barrier, which seemed to end but in heaven, interposed itself every where. Neither did the image of the young maiden, though constantly in my mind, now bring with it the least consolation or hope. Of what avail was it that she, perhaps, was an inhabitant of this region, if I could neither behold her smile, nor catch the sound of her voice—if, while among preaching priests I wasted away my hours, her presence was, alas, diffusing its enchantments elsewhere.

At length, exhausted, I lay down by the brink of the lake, and gave myself up to all the melancholy of my fancy. The pale semblance of day-light, which had hitherto glimmered around, grew, every moment, more dim and dismal. Even the rich gleam, at the summit of the cascade, had faded; and the sunshine, like the water, exhausted in its descent, had now dwindled into a ghostly glimmer, far worse than darkness. The birds upon the lake, as if about to die with the dying light, sunk down their heads; and, as I looked to the statue, the deepening shadows gave such an expression to its mournful features as chilled my very soul.

The thought of death, ever ready to present itself to my imagination, now came, with a disheartening weight, such as I had never before felt. I almost fancied myself already in the dark vestibule of the grave—removed, for ever, from the world above, and with nothing but the blank of an eternal sleep before me. It had happened, I knew, frequently, that the visitants of this mysterious realm were, after their descent from earth, never seen or heard of;—being condemned, for some failure in their initiatory trials, to pine away their lives in those dark dungeons, with which as well as with altars, this region abounded. Such, I shuddered to think, might probably be my own destiny; and so appalling was the thought, that even the courage by which I had been hitherto sustained died within me, and I was already giving myself up to helplessness and despair.

At length, after some hours of this gloomy musing, I heard a rustling in the sacred grove behind the statue; and, soon after, the sound of the Priest's voice—more welcome than I had ever thought such voice could be—brought the assurance that I was not yet wholly abandoned. Finding his way to me through the gloom, he now led me to the same spot, on which we had parted so many hours before; and, addressing me in a voice that retained no trace of displeasure, bespoke my attention, while he should reveal to me some of those divine truths, by whose infusion, he said, into the soul of man, its purification can alone be effected.

The valley had now become so dark, that we could no longer, as we sat, discern each other's faces. There was a melancholy in the voice of my instructor that well accorded with the gloom around us: and, saddened and subdued, I now listened with resignation, if not with interest, to those sublime, but, alas, I thought, vain tenets, which, with all the warmth of a true believer, this Hierophant expounded to me.

He spoke of the pre-existence of the soul—of its abode, from all eternity, in a place of splendour and bliss, of which whatever we have most beautiful in our conceptions here is but a dim transcript, a clouded remembrance. In the blue depths of ether, he said, lay that "Country of the Soul"—its boundary alone visible in the line of milky light, which, as by a barrier of stars, separates it from the dark earth. "Oh, realm of purity! Home of the yet unfallen Spirit!—where, in the days of her first innocence, she wandered; ere yet her beauty was soiled by the touch of earth, or her resplendent wings had withered away. Methinks I see," he cried, "at this moment, those fields of radiance—I look back, through the mists of life, into that luminous world, where the souls that have never lost their high, heavenly rank, still soar, without a stain, above the shadowless stars, and there dwell together in infinite perfection and bliss!"

As he spoke these words, a burst of pure, brilliant light, like a sudden opening of heaven, broke through the valley; and, as soon as my eyes were able to endure the splendour, such a vision of glory and loveliness opened upon them, as took even my sceptical spirit by surprise, and made it yield, at once, to the potency of the spell.

Suspended, as I thought, in air, and occupying the whole of the opposite region of the valley, there appeared an immense orb of light, within which, through a haze of radiance, I could see distinctly fair groups of young female spirits, who, in silent, but harmonious movement, like that of the stars, wound slowly through a variety of fanciful evolutions; seeming, as they linked and unlinked each other's arms, to form a living labyrinth of beauty and grace. Though their feet appeared to glide along a field of light, they had also wings, of the most brilliant hue, which, like rainbows over waterfalls, when played with by the breeze, reflected, every moment, a new variety of glory.

As I stood, gazing with wonder, the orb, with all its ethereal inmates, began gradually to recede into the dark void, lessening, as it went, and becoming more bright, as it lessened;—till, at length, distant, to all appearance, as a retiring comet, this little world of Spirits, in one small point of intense radiance, shone its last and vanished. "Go," exclaimed the rapt Priest, "ye happy souls, of whose dwelling a glimpse is thus given to our eyes,—go, wander, in your orb, through the boundless heaven, nor ever let a thought of this perishable world come to mingle its dross with your divine nature, or allure you down earthward to that mortal fall by which spirits, no less bright and admirable, have been ruined!"

A pause ensued, during which, still under the influence of wonder, I sent my fancy wandering after the inhabitants of that orb—almost wishing myself credulous enough to believe in a heaven, of which creatures, so much like those I had worshipped on earth, were inmates.

At length, the Priest, with a mournful sigh at the sad contrast he was about to draw between the happy spirits we had just seen and the fallen ones of earth, resumed again his melancholy History of the Soul. Tracing it gradually, from the first moment of earthward desire to its final eclipse in the shadows of this world, he dwelt upon every stage of its darkening descent, with a pathos that sent sadness into the very depths of the heart. The first downward look of the spirit towards earth—the tremble of her wings on the edge of Heaven—the giddy slide, at length, down that fatal descent—and the Leathern cup, midway in the sky, of which when she has once tasted, Heaven is forgot—through all these gradations he traced mournfully her fall, to that last stage of darkness, when wholly immersed in this world, her celestial nature becomes changed, she no longer can rise above earth, nor even remember her former home, except by glimpses so vague, that, at length, mistaking for hope what is only, alas! recollection, she believes those gleams to be a light from the Future, not the Past.

"To retrieve this ruin of the once-blessed soul—to clear away from around her the clouds of earth, and, restoring her lost wings, facilitate their return to Heaven—such," said the reverend man, "is the great task of our religion, and such the triumph of those divine Mysteries, in whose inmost depths the life and essence of that holy religion lie treasured. However sunk, and changed, and clouded may be the Spirit, yet as long as a single trace of her original light remains, there is still hope that ——"

Here the voice of the Priest was interrupted by a strain of mournful music, of which the low, distant breathings had been, for some minutes, audible, but which now gained upon the ear too thrillingly to let it listen to any more earthly sound. A faint light too at that instant broke through the valley—and I could perceive, not far from the spot where we sat, a female figure, veiled, and crouching to earth, as if subdued by sorrow, or under the influence of shame.

The feeble light, by which I saw her, came from a pale, moon-like meteor which had gradually formed itself in the air as the music approached, and now shed over the rocks and the lake a glimmer as cold as that by which the Dead, in their own kingdom, gaze upon each other. The music, too, which appeared to rise from out of the lake, full of the breath of its dark waters, spoke a despondency in every note which no language could express;—and as I listened to its tones, and looked upon that fallen Spirit, (for such, the holy man whispered, was the form before us,) so entirely did the illusion of the scene take possession of me, that, with almost painful anxiety, I now awaited the result.

Nor had I gazed long before that form rose slowly from its drooping position;—the air around it grew bright, and the pale meteor over-head assumed a more cheerful and living light. The veil, which had before shrouded the face of the figure, became every minute more transparent, and the features, one by one, gradually disclosed themselves. Having tremblingly watched the progress of the apparition, I now started from my seat, and half exclaimed, "It is she!" In another minute, this veil had, like a thin mist, melted away, and the young priestess of the Moon stood, for the third time, revealed before my eyes!

To rush instantly towards her was my first impulse—but the arm of the Priest held me firmly back. The fresh light, which had begun to flow in from all sides, collected itself in a flood of glory around the spot where she stood. Instead of melancholy music, strains of the most exalted rapture were heard; and the young maiden, buoyant as the inhabitants of the fairy orb, amid a blaze of light like that which fell upon her in the Temple, ascended slowly into the air.

"Stay, beautiful vision, stay!" I exclaimed, as, breaking from the hold of the Priest, I flung myself prostrate on the ground—the only mode by which I could express the admiration, even to worship, with which I was filled. But the vanishing spirit heard me not:—receding into the darkness, like that orb, whose heavenward track she seemed to follow, her form lessened by degrees away, till she was seen no more; while, gazing, till the last luminous speck had disappeared, I allowed myself unconsciously to be led away by my reverend guide, who, placing me once more on my bed of poppy-leaves, left me there to such repose as it was possible, after such a scene, to enjoy.

CHAPTER X.

The apparition with which I had been blessed in that Valley of Visions—for so the place where I had witnessed these wonders was called—brought back to my heart all the hopes and fancies in which, during my descent from earth, I had indulged. I had now seen once more that matchless creature, who had been my guiding star into this mysterious realm; and that she was destined to be, in some way, connected with the further revelations that awaited me, I saw no reason to doubt. There was a sublimity, too, in the doctrines of my reverend teacher, and even a hope in the promises of immortality held out by him, which, in spite of reason, won insensibly both upon my fancy and my pride.

The Future, however, was now but of secondary consideration;—the Present, and that deity of the Present, woman, were the objects that engrossed my whole soul. It was, indeed, for the sake of such beings alone that I considered immortality desirable, nor, without them, would eternal life have appeared to me worth a single prayer. To every further trial of my patience and faith, I now made up my mind to submit without a murmur. Some kind chance, I fondly persuaded myself, might yet bring me nearer to the object of my adoration, and enable me to address, as mortal woman, one who had hitherto been to me but as a vision, a shade.

The period of my probation, however, was nearly at an end. Both frame and spirit had now stood the trial; and as the crowning test of the purification of the latter was that power of seeing into the world of spirits, with which I had proved myself, in the Valley of Visions, to be endowed, there now remained, to complete my Initiation, but this one night more, when, in the Temple of Isis, and in the presence of her unveiled image, the last grand revelation of the Secret of Secrets was to be laid open to me.

I passed the morning of this day in company with the same venerable personage, who had, from the first, presided over the ceremonies of my instruction, and who, to inspire me with due reverence for the [illegible] and magnificence of his religion, now conducted me through the long range of illuminated galleries and shrines, that extend under the site upon which Memphis and the Pyramids stand, and form a counterpart under ground to that mighty city of temples upon earth.

He then descended with me, still lower, into those winding crypts, where lay the Seven Tables of stone, found by Hermes in the valley of Hebron. "On these tables," said he, "is written all the knowledge of the antediluvian race—the decrees of the stars from the beginning of time, the annals of a still earlier world, and all the marvellous secrets, both of heaven and earth, which would have been,

but for this key,
Lost in the Universal Sea.'"

Returning to the region, from which we had descended, we next visited, in succession, a series of small shrines representing the various objects of adoration throughout Egypt, and thus furnishing to the Priest an occasion for explaining the mysterious nature of animal worship, and the refined doctrines of theology that lay veiled under its forms. Every shrine was consecrated to a particular faith, and contained a living image of the deity which it adored. Beside the goat of Mendes, with his refulgent star upon his breast, I saw the crocodile, as presented to the eyes of its idolator at Arsinoe, with costly gems in its loathsome ears, and rich bracelets of gold encircling its feet. Here, floating through a tank in the centre of a temple, the sacred carp of Lepidotum showed its silvery scales; while, there, the Isiac serpents trailed languidly over the altar, with that sort of movement which is thought most favourable to the aspirations of their votaries. In one of the small chapels we found a beautiful child, employed in feeding and watching over those golden beetles, which are adored for their brightness, as emblems of the sun; while, in another, stood a sacred ibis upon its pedestal, so like, in plumage and attitude, to the bird of the young Priestess, that most gladly would I have knelt down and worshipped it for her sake.

After visiting all these various shrines, and hearing the reflections which they suggested, I was next led by my guide to the Great Hall of the Zodiac, on whose ceiling was delineated, in bright and undying colours, the map of the firmament, as it appeared at the first dawn of time. Here, in pointing out the track of the sun among the spheres, he spoke of the analogy that exists between moral and physical darkness—of the sympathy with which all spiritual creatures regard the sun, so as to sadden and decline when he sinks into his wintry hemisphere, and to rejoice when he resumes his own empire of light. Hence, the festivals and hymns, with which most of the nations of the earth are wont to welcome the resurrection of his orb in spring, as an emblem and pledge of the re-ascent of the soul to heaven. Hence, the songs of sorrow, the mournful ceremonies—like those Mysteries of the Night, upon the Lake of Sais—in which they brood over its autumnal descent into the shades, as a type of the Spirit's fall into this world of death.

In discourses such as these the hours passed away; and though there was nothing in the light of this sunless region to mark to the eye the decline of day, my own feelings told me that the night drew near;—nor, in spite of my incredulity, could I refrain from a slight flutter of hope, as that promised moment of revelation drew nigh, when the Mystery of Mysteries was to be made all my own. This consummation, however, was less near than I expected. My patience had still further trials to encounter. It was necessary, I now found, that, during the greater part of the night, I should keep watch in the Sanctuary of the Temple, alone and in utter darkness—thus preparing myself, by meditation, for the awful moment, when the irradiation from behind the sacred Veils was to burst upon me.

At the appointed hour, we left the Hall of the Zodiac, and proceeded through a long line of marble galleries, where the lamps were more thinly scattered as we advanced, till, at length, we found ourselves in total darkness. Here the Priest, taking me by the hand, and leading me down a flight of steps, into a place where the same deep gloom prevailed, said, with a voice trembling, as if from excess of awe,—"Thou art now within the Sanctuary of our goddess, Isis, and the veils, that conceal her sacred image, are before thee!"

After exhorting me earnestly to that train of thought, which best accorded with the spirit of the place where I stood, and, above all, to that full and unhesitating faith, with which alone, he said, the manifestation of such mysteries should be approached, the holy man took leave of me, and re-ascended the steps;—while so spell-bound did I feel by that deep darkness, that the last sound of his footsteps died upon my ear, before I ventured to stir a limb from the position in which he had left me.

The prospect of the long watch I had now to look forward to was dreadful. Even danger itself, if in an active form, would have been far preferable to this sort of safe, but dull, probation, by which patience was the only virtue put to the proof. Having ascertained how far the space around me was free from obstacles, I endeavoured to beguile the time by pacing up and down within those limits, till I became tired of the monotonous echoes of my own tread. Finding my way, then, to what I felt to be a massive pillar, and, leaning wearily against it, I surrendered myself to a train of thoughts and feelings, far different from those with which the good Hierophant had hoped to inspire me.

"If these priests," thought I, "possess really the secret of life, why are they themselves the victims of death? why sink into the grave with the cup of immortality in their hands? But no, safe boasters, the eternity they so lavishly promise is reserved for *another*, a future world—that ready resource of all priestly promises—that depository of the airy pledges of all creeds. Another world!—alas! where doth it lie? or, what spirit hath ever come to say that Life is there?"

The conclusion at which, half sadly, half passionately, I arrived, was that, life being but a dream of the moment never to come again, every bliss so vaguely promised for hereafter ought to be secured by the wise man here. And, as no heaven I had ever heard of from these visionary priests opened half such certainty of happiness as that smile which I beheld last night—"Let me," I exclaimed, impatiently, striking the massy pillar till it rung, "let me but make that beautiful Priestess my own, and I here willingly exchange for her every chance of immortality, that the combined wisdom of Egypt's Twelve Temples can offer me!"

No sooner had I uttered these words, than a tremendous peal, like that of thunder, rolled over the Sanctuary, and seemed to shake its very walls. On every side, too, a succession of blue, vivid flashes pierced, like lances of light, through the gloom, revealing to me, at intervals, the mighty dome in which I stood—its ceiling of azure, studded with stars—its colossal columns, towering aloft,—and those dark, awful veils, whose massy drapery hung from the roof to the floor, covering the rich glories of the Shrine beneath their folds.

So weary had I grown of my tedious watch, that this stormy and fitful illumination, during which the Sanctuary seemed to rock to its base, was by no means an unwelcome interruption of the monotonous trial my patience had to suffer. After a short interval, however, the flashes ceased;—the sounds died away, like exhausted thunder, through the abyss, and darkness and silence, like that of the grave, succeeded.

Resting my back once more against the pillar, and fixing my eyes upon that side of the Sanctuary from which the promised irradiation was to burst, I now resolved to await the awful moment in patience. Resigned, and almost immovable, I had remained thus for nearly another hour, when suddenly along the edges of the mighty Veils, I perceived a thin rim of light, as if from some brilliant object under them;—resembling that border which encircles a cloud at sunset, when the rich radiance from behind is escaping at its edges.

This indication of concealed glories grew every instant more strong; till, at last, vividly marked as it was upon the darkness, the narrow fringe of lustre almost pained the eye—giving a promise of a fulness of splendour too bright to be endured. My expectations were now wound to the highest pitch, and all the scepticism, into which I had been cooling down my mind, was forgotten. The wonders that had been presented to me since my descent from earth—that glimpse into Elysium on the first night of my coming—those visitants from the land of Spirits in the mysterious valley—all led me to expect, in this last and brightest revelation, such visions of glory and knowledge as might transcend even fancy itself, nor leave a doubt that they belonged less to earth than heaven.

While, with an imagination thus excited, I stood waiting the result, an increased gush of light still more awakened my attention; and I saw with an intenseness of interest, which made my heart beat aloud, one of the corners of the mighty Veil raised slowly from the floor. I now felt that the Great Secret, whatever it might be, was at hand. A vague hope even crossed my mind—so wholly had imagination now resumed her empire—that the splendid promise of my dream was on the very point of being realized!

With surprise, however, and, for the moment, with some disappointment, I perceived, that the massy corner of the Veil was but lifted sufficiently from the ground to allow a female figure to emerge from under it—and then fell over its mystic splendours as utterly dark as before. By the strong light, too, that issued when the drapery was raised, and illuminated the profile of the emerging figure, I either saw, or fancied that I saw, the same bright features, that had already so often mocked me with their momentary charm, and seemed destined, indeed, to haunt my fancy as unavailingly as even the fond vain dream of Immortality itself.

Dazzled as I had been by that short gush of splendour, and distrusting even my senses, when under the influence of so much excitement, I had but just begun to question myself as to the reality of my impression, when I heard the sounds of light footsteps approaching me through the gloom. In a second or two more, the figure stopped before me, and, placing the end of a riband gently in my hand, said, in a tremulous whisper, "Follow, and be silent."

So sudden and strange was the adventure, that, for a moment, I hesitated—fearing that my eyes might possibly have been deceived as to the object they had seen. Casting a look towards the Veil, which seemed bursting with its luminous secret, I was almost doubting to which of the two chances I should commit myself, when I felt the riband in my hand pulled softly at the other extremity. This movement, like a touch of magic, at once decided me. Without any further deliberation, I yielded to the silent summons, and following my guide, who was already at some distance before me, found myself led up the same flight of marble steps, by which the Priest had conducted me into the Sanctuary. Arrived at their summit, I felt the pace of my conductress quicken, and giving one more look to the Veiled Shrine, whose glories we left burning uselessly behind us, hastened onward into the gloom, full of confidence in the belief, that she, who now held the other end of that clue, was one whom I was ready to follow devotedly through the world.

CHAPTER XI.

With such rapidity was I hurried along by my unseen guide, full of wonder at the speed with which she ventured through these labyrinths, that I had but little time left for reflection upon the strangeness of the adventure to which I had committed myself. My knowledge of the character of the Memphian priests, as well as some fearful rumours that had reached me, concerning the fate that often attended unbelievers in their hands, awakened a momentary suspicion of treachery in my mind. But, when I recalled the face of my guide, as I had seen it in the small chapel, with that divine look, the very memory of which brought purity into the heart, I found my suspicions all vanish, and felt shame at having harboured them but an instant.

In the mean while, our rapid course continued without any interruption, through windings even more capriciously intricate than any I had yet passed, and whose thick gloom seemed never to have been broken by a single glimmer of light. My unseen conductress was still at some distance before me, and the slight clue, to which I clung as if it were Destiny's own thread, was still kept, by the speed of her course, at full stretch between us. At length, suddenly stopping, she said, in a breathless whisper, "Seat thyself here;" and, at the same moment, led me by the hand to a sort of low car, in which, obeying her brief command, I lost not a moment in placing myself, while the maiden, no less promptly, took her seat by my side.

A sudden click, like the touching of a spring, was then heard, and the car—which, as I had felt in entering it, leaned half-way over a steep descent—on being let loose from its station, shot down, almost perpendicularly, into the darkness, with a rapidity which, at first, nearly deprived me of breath. The wheels slid smoothly and noiselessly in grooves, and the impetus, which the car acquired in descending, was sufficient, I perceived, to carry it up an eminence that succeeded—from the summit of which it again rushed down another declivity, even still more long and precipitous than the former. In this manner we proceeded, by alternate falls and rises, till, at length, from the last and steepest elevation, the car descended upon a level of deep sand, where, after running for a few yards, it by degrees lost its motion, and stopped.

Here the maiden, alighting again, placed the riband in my hands—and again I followed her, though with more slowness and difficulty than before, as our way now led up a flight of damp and time-worn steps, whose ascent seemed to the wearied and insecure foot interminable. Perceiving with what languor my guide advanced, I was on the point of making an effort to assist her progress, when the creak of an opening door above, and a faint gleam of light which, at the same moment, shone upon her figure, apprised me that we were at last arrived within reach of sunshine.

Joyfully I followed through this opening, and, by the dim light, could discern that we were now in the sanctuary of a vast, ruined temple—having entered by a secret passage under the pedestal, upon which an image of the idol of the place once stood. The first movement of the young maiden, after closing again the portal under the pedestal, was, without even a single look towards me, to cast herself down upon her knees, with her hand clasped and uplifted, as if in thanksgiving or prayer. But she was unable, evidently, to sustain herself in this position;—her strength could hold out no longer. Overcome by agitation and fatigue, she sunk senseless upon the pavement.

Bewildered as I was myself, by the strange events of the night, I stood for some minutes looking upon her in a state of helplessness and alarm. But, reminded, by my own feverish sensations, of the reviving effects of the air, I raised her gently in my arms, and crossing the corridor that surrounded the sanctuary, found my way to the outer vestibule of the Temple. Here, shading her eyes from the sun, I placed her, reclining upon the steps, where the cool north-wind, then blowing freshly between the pillars, might play, with free draught, over her brow.

It was, indeed—as I now saw, with certainty—the same beautiful and mysterious girl, who had been the cause of my descent into that subterranean world, and who now, under such strange and unaccountable circumstances, was my guide back again to the realms of day. I looked around to discover where we were, and beheld such a scene of grandeur, as, could my eyes have been then attracted to any object but the pale form reclining at my side, might well have induced them to dwell on its splendid beauties.

I was now standing, I found, on the small island in the centre of Lake Mœris; and that sanctuary, where we had just emerged from darkness, formed part of the ruins of an ancient temple, which was, (as I have since learned,) in the grander days of Memphis, a place of pilgrimage for worshippers from all parts of Egypt. The fair Lake, itself, out of whose waters once rose pavilions, palaces, and even lofty pyramids, was still, though divested of many of these wonders, a scene of interest and splendour such as the whole world could not equal. While the shores still sparkled with mansions and temples, that bore testimony to the luxury of a living race,—the voice of the Past, speaking out of unnumbered ruins, whose summits, here and there, rose blackly above the wave, told of times long fled, and generations long swept away, before whose giant remains all the glory of the present stood humbled. Over the southern bank of the Lake hung the dark relics of the Labyrinth;—its twelve Royal Palaces representing the mansions of the Zodiac—its thundering portals and constellated halls, having left nothing now behind but a few frowning ruins, which, contrasted with the soft groves of acacia and olive around them, seemed to rebuke the luxuriant smiles of nature, and threw a melancholy grandeur over the whole scene.

The effects of the air, in re-animating the young Priestess, were less speedy than I had expected;—her eyes were still closed, and she remained pale and insensible. Alarmed, I now rested her head (which had been, for some time, supported by my arm) against the base of one of the columns, with my cloak for its pillow, while I hastened to procure some water from the Lake. The temple stood high, and the descent to the shore was precipitous. But, my Epicurean habits having but little impaired my activity, I soon descended, with the lightness of a desert deer, to the bottom. Here, plucking from a lofty bean-tree, whose flowers stood, shining like gold, above the water, one of those large hollowed leaves that serve as cups for the Hebes of the Nile, I filled it from the Lake, and hurried back with the cool draught towards the Temple. It was not, however, without some difficulty that I at last succeeded in bearing my rustic chalice steadily up the steep; more than once did an unlucky slip waste all its contents, and as often did I return impatiently to refill it.

During this time, the young maiden was fast recovering her animation and consciousness; and, at the moment when I appeared above the edge of the steep, was just rising from the steps, with her hand pressed to her forehead, as if confusedly recalling the recollection of what had occurred. No sooner did she observe me, than a short cry of alarm broke from her lips. Looking anxiously round, as though she sought for protection, and half-audibly uttering the words, "Where is he?" she made an effort, as I approached, to retreat into the Temple.

Already, however, I was by her side, and taking her hand, as she turned away from me, gently in mine, asked, "Whom dost thou seek, fair Priestess?"—thus, for the first time, breaking the silence she had enjoined, and in a tone that might have re-assured the most timid spirit. But my words had no effect in calming her apprehension. Trembling, and with her eyes still averted towards the Temple, she continued in a voice of suppressed alarm, "Where *can* he be?—that venerable Athenian, that philosopher, who ——"

"Here, here," I exclaimed, anxiously, interrupting her—"behold him still by thy side—the same, the very same, who saw thee steal from under the Veils of the Sanctuary, whom thou hast guided by a clue through those labyrinths below, and who now only waits his command from those lips, to devote himself through life and death to thy service." As I spoke these words, she turned slowly round, and looking timidly in my face, while her own burned with blushes, said, in a tone of doubt and wonder, "Thou!" and then hid her eyes in her hands.

I knew not how to interpret a reception so unexpected. That some mistake or disappointment had occurred was evident; but so inexplicable did the whole adventure appear to me, that it was in vain to think of unravelling any part of it. Weak and agitated, she now tottered to the steps of the Temple, and there seating herself, with her forehead against the cold marble, seemed for some moments absorbed in the most anxious thought; while silent and watchful I awaited her decision, though, at the same time, with a feeling which the result proved to be prophetic—that my destiny was, from thenceforth, linked inseparably with hers.

The inward struggle by which she was agitated, though violent, was not of long continuance. Starting suddenly from her seat, with a look of terror towards the Temple, as if the fear of immediate pursuit had alone decided her, she pointed eagerly towards the East, and exclaimed, "To the Nile, without delay!"—clasping her hands, after she had thus spoken, with the most suppliant fervour, as if to soften the abruptness of the mandate she had given, and appealing to me at the same time, with a look that would have taught Stoics themselves tenderness.

I lost not a moment in obeying the welcome command. With a thousand wild hopes naturally crowding upon my fancy, at the thoughts of a voyage, under such auspices, I descended rapidly to the shore, and hailing one of those boats that ply upon the Lake for hire, arranged speedily for a passage down the canal to the Nile. Having learned, too, from the boatman, a more easy path up the rock, I hastened back to the Temple for my fair charge; and, without a word or look, that could alarm, even by its kindness, or disturb the innocent confidence which she now evidently reposed in me, led her down by the winding path to the boat.

Every thing around looked sunny and smiling as we embarked. The morning was in its first freshness, and the path of the breeze might clearly be traced over the Lake, as it went wakening up the waters from their sleep of the night. The gay, golden-winged birds that haunt these shores, were, in every direction, skimming along the Lake; while, with a graver consciousness of beauty, the swan and the pelican were seen dressing their white plumage in the mirror of its wave. To add to the liveliness of the scene, there came, at intervals, on the breeze, a sweet tinkling of musical instruments from boats at a distance, employed thus early in pursuing the fish of these waters, that allow themselves to be decoyed into the nets by music.

The vessel I had selected for our voyage was one of those small pleasure-boats or yachts—so much in use among the luxurious navigators of the Nile—in the centre of which rises a pavilion of cedar or cypress wood, adorned richly on the outside, with religious emblems, and gaily fitted up, within, for feasting and repose. To the door of this pavilion I now led my companion, and, after a few words of kindness—tempered cautiously with as much reserve as the deep tenderness of my feeling towards her would admit—left her to court that restoring rest, which the agitation of her spirits so much required.

For myself, though repose was hardly less necessary to me, the state of ferment in which I had been so long kept, appeared to render it hopeless. Having thrown myself on the deck of the vessel, under an awning which the sailors had raised for me, I continued, for some hours, in a sort of vague day-dream—sometimes passing in review the scenes of that subterranean drama, and sometimes, with my eyes fixed in drowsy vacancy, receiving passively the impressions of the bright scenery through which we passed.

The banks of the canal were then luxuriantly wooded. Under the tufts of the light and towering palm were seen the orange and the citron, interlacing their boughs; while, here and there, huge tamarisks thickened the shade, and, at the very edge of the bank, the willow of Babylon stood bending its graceful branches into the water. Occasionally, out of the depth of these groves, there shone a small temple or pleasure-house; while, now and then, an opening in their line of foliage allowed the eye to wander over extensive fields, all covered with beds of those pale, sweet roses, for which this district of Egypt is so celebrated.

The activity of the morning hour was visible in every direction. Flights of doves and lapwings were fluttering among the leaves; and the white heron, which had been roosting all night in some date-tree, now stood sunning its wings upon the green bank, or floated, like living silver, over the flood. The flowers, too, both of land and water, looked all just freshly awakened;—and, most of all, the superb lotus, which, having risen along with the sun from the wave, was now holding up her chalice for a full draught of his light.

Such were the scenes that now successively presented themselves, and mingled with the vague reveries that floated through my mind, as our boat, with its high, capacious sail, swept along the flood. Though the occurrences of the last few days could not but appear to me one continued series of wonders, yet by far the greatest marvel of all was, that she, whose first look had sent wild-fire into my heart—whom I had thought of ever since with a restlessness of passion, that would have dared all danger and wrong to obtain its object—*she* was now at this moment resting sacredly within that pavilion, while guarding her, even from myself, I lay motionless at its threshold.

Meanwhile, the sun had reached his meridian height. The busy hum of the morning had died gradually away, and all around was sleeping in the hot stillness of noon. The Nile-goose, having folded up her splendid wings, was lying motionless on the shadow of the sycamores in the water. Even the nimble lizards upon the bank appeared to move less nimbly, as the light fell on their gold and azure hues. Overcome as I was with watching, and weary with thought, it was not long before I yielded to the becalming influence of the hour. Looking fixedly at the pavilion—as if once more to assure myself that I was in no dream or trance, but that the young Egyptian was really there—I felt my eyes close as I gazed, and in a few minutes sunk into a profound sleep.

CHAPTER XII.

It was by the canal through which we now sailed, that, in the more prosperous days of Memphis, the commerce of Upper Egypt and Nubia was transported to her magnificent Lake, and from thence, having paid tribute to the queen of cities, was poured forth again, through the Nile, into the ocean. The course of this canal to the river was not direct, but ascending in a south-easterly direction towards the Said; and in calms, or with adverse winds, the passage was tedious. But as the breeze was now blowing freshly from the north, there was every prospect of our reaching the river before nightfall. Rapidly, too, as our galley swept along the flood, its motion was so smooth as to be hardly felt; and the quiet gurgle of the waters, and the drowsy song of the boatman at the prow, were the only sounds that disturbed the deep silence which prevailed.

The sun, indeed, had nearly sunk behind the Libyan hills, before the sleep, into which these sounds had contributed to lull me, was broken; and the first object on which my eyes rested, in waking, was that fair young Priestess—seated within a porch which shaded the door of the pavilion, and bending intently over a small volume that lay unrolled on her lap.

Her face was but half-turned towards me; and as she once or twice, raised her eyes to the warm sky whose light fell, softened through the trellis, over her cheek, I found all those feelings of reverence, which she had inspired we with in the chapel, return. There was even a purer and holier charm around her countenance, thus seen by the natural light of day, than in those dim and unhallowed regions below. She was now looking, too, direct to the glorious sky, and her pure eyes and that heaven, so worthy of each other, met.

After contemplating her for a few moments, with little less than adoration, I rose gently from my resting-place, and approached the pavilion. But the mere movement had startled her from her devotion, and, blushing and confused, she covered the volume with the folds of her robe.

In the art of winning upon female confidence, I had long, of course, been schooled; and, now that to the lessons of gallantry the inspiration of love was added, my ambition to please and to interest could hardly fail, it may be supposed, of success. I soon found, however, how much less fluent is the heart than the fancy, and how very different may be the operations of making love and feeling it. In the few words of greeting now exchanged between us, it was evident that the gay, the enterprising Epicurean was little less embarrassed than the secluded Priestess;—and, after one or two ineffectual efforts to converse, the eyes of both turned bashfully away, and we relapsed into silence.

From this situation—the result of timidity on one side, and of a feeling altogether new on the other—we were, at length, relieved, after an interval of estrangement, by the boatmen announcing that the Nile was in sight. The countenance of the young Egyptian brightened at this intelligence: and the smile with which I congratulated her upon the speed of our voyage was responded to by another from her, so full of gratitude, that already an instinctive sympathy seemed established between us.

We were now on the point of entering that sacred river, of whose sweet waters the exile drinks in his dreams—for a draught of whose flood the royal daughters of the Ptolemies, when far away, on foreign thrones, have been known to sigh in the midst of their splendour. As our boat, with slackened sail, was gliding into the current, an inquiry from the boatmen, whether they should anchor for the night in the Nile, first reminded me of the ignorance in which I still remained, with respect to the motive or destination of our voyage. Embarrassed by their question, I directed my eyes towards the Priestess, whom I saw waiting for my answer with a look of anxiety, which this silent reference to her wishes at once dispelled. Unfolding eagerly the volume with which I had seen her so much occupied, she took from between its folds a small leaf of papyrus, on which there appeared to be some faint lines of drawing, and after looking upon it thoughtfully for a few moments, placed it, with an agitated hand, in mine.

In the mean time, the boatmen had taken in their sail, and the yacht drove slowly down the river with the current; while, by a light which had been kindled at sunset on the deck, I stood examining the leaf that the Priestess had given me—her dark eyes fixed anxiously on my countenance all the while. The lines traced upon the papyrus were so faint as to be almost invisible, and I was for some time wholly unable to form a conjecture as to their import. At length, however, I succeeded in making out that they were a sort of map, or outlines—traced slightly and unsteadily with a Memphian reed—of a part of that mountainous ridge by which Upper Egypt is bounded to the east, together with the names, or rather emblems, of the chief towns in its immediate neighbourhood.

It was thither, I now saw clearly, that the young Priestess wished to pursue her course. Without further delay, therefore, I ordered the boatmen to set our yacht before the wind, and ascend the current. My command was promptly obeyed: the white sail again rose into the region of the breeze, and the satisfaction that beamed in every feature of the fair Egyptian showed that the quickness with which I had attended to her wishes was not unfelt by her. The moon had now risen; and though the current was against us, the Etesian wind of the season blew strongly up the river, and we were soon floating before it, through the rich plains and groves of the Said.

The love with which this simple girl had inspired me, was partly, perhaps, from the mystic scenes and situations in which I had seen her, not unmingled with a tinge of superstitious awe, under the influence of which I felt the natural buoyancy of my spirit repressed. The few words that had passed between us on the subject of our route had somewhat loosened this spell; and what I wanted of vivacity and confidence was more than compensated by the tone of deep sensibility which love had awakened in their place.

We had not proceeded far, before the glittering of lights at a distance, and the shooting up of fire-works, at intervals, into the air, apprized us that we were then approaching one of those night-fairs, or marts, which it is the custom, at this season, to hold upon the Nile. To me the scene was familiar, but to my young companion it was evidently a new world; and the mixture of alarm and delight with which she gazed, from under her veil, upon the busy scene into which we now sailed, gave an air of innocence to her beauty, which still more heightened its every charm.

It was one of the widest parts of the river; and the whole surface, from one bank to the other, was covered with boats. Along the banks of a green island, in the middle of the stream, lay anchored the galleys of the principal traders—large floating bazaars, bearing each the name of its owner, emblazoned in letters of flame, upon the stern. Over their decks were spread out, in gay confusion, the products of the loom and needle of Egypt—rich carpets of Memphis, and likewise those variegated veils, for which the female embroiderers of the Nile are so celebrated, and to which the name of Cleopatra lends a traditional charm. In each of the other galleys was exhibited some branch of Egyptian workmanship—vases of the fragrant porcelain of On—cups of that frail crystal, whose hues change like those of the pigeon's plumage—enamelled amulets graven with the head of Anubis, and necklaces and bracelets of the black beans of Abyssinia.

While Commerce was thus displaying her various luxuries in one quarter, in every other, the spirit of Pleasure, in all its countless shapes, swarmed over the waters. Nor was the festivity confined to the river alone; as along the banks of the island and on the shores, illuminated mansions were seen glittering through the trees, from whence sounds of music and merriment came. In some of the boats were bands of minstrels, who, from time to time, answered each other, like echoes, across the wave; and the notes of the lyre, the flageolet, and the sweet lotus-wood flute, were heard, in the pauses of revelry, dying along the waters.

Meanwhile, from other boats stationed in the least lighted places, the workers of fire sent forth their wonders into the air. Bursting out suddenly from time to time, as if in the very exuberance of joy, these sallies of flame appeared to reach the sky, and there, breaking into a shower of sparkles, shed such a splendour around, as brightened even the white Arabian hills—making them shine as doth the brow of Mount Atlas at night, en the fire from his own bosom is playing around its snows.

he opportunity this mart afforded us, of providing ourselves with some less remarkable habiliments than those in which we had escaped from that nether world, was too seasonable not to be gladly taken advantage of by both. For myself, the strange mystic garb which I wore was sufficiently concealed by my Grecian mantle, which I had fortunately thrown round me on the night of my watch. But the thin veil of my companion was a far less efficient disguise. She had, indeed, flung away the golden beetles from her hair; but the sacred robe of her order was still too visible, and the stars of the bandelet shone brightly through her veil.

Most gladly, therefore, did she avail herself of this opportunity of a change; and, as she took from out a casket—which, with the volume I had seen her reading, appeared to be her only treasure—a small jewel, to give in exchange for the simple garments she had chosen, there fell out at the same time, the very cross of silver which I had seen her kiss, as may be remembered, in the monumental chapel, and which was afterwards pressed to my own lips. This link between us, (for such it now appeared to my imagination) called up again in my heart all the burning feelings of that moment;—and, had I not abruptly turned away, my agitation would but too plainly have betrayed itself.

The object, for which we had delayed in this gay scene, having been accomplished, the sail was again spread, and we proceeded on our course up the river. The sounds and the lights we had left behind died gradually away, and we now floated along in moonlight and silence once more. Sweet dews, worthy of being called "the tears of Isis," fell refreshingly through the air, and every plant and flower sent its fragrance to meet them. The wind, just strong enough to bear us smoothly against the current, scarce stirred the shadow of the tamarisks on the water. As the inhabitants from all quarters were collected at the night-fair, the Nile was more than usually still and solitary. Such a silence, indeed, prevailed, that, as we glided near the shore, we could hear the rustling of the acacias, as the chameleons ran up their stems. It was, altogether, such a night as only the climate of Egypt can boast, when the whole scene around lies lulled in that sort of bright tranquillity, which may be imagined to light the slumbers of those happy spirits, who are said to rest in the Valley of the Moon, on their way to heaven.

By such a light, and at such an hour, seated, side by side, on the deck of that bark, did we pursue our course up the lonely Nile—each a mystery to the other—our thoughts, our objects, our very names, a secret;—separated, too, till now, by destinies so different; the one, a gay voluptuary of the Garden of Athens; the other, a secluded Priestess of the Temples of Memphis;—and the only relation yet established between us being that dangerous one of love, passionate love, on one side, and the most feminine and confiding dependence on the other.

The passing adventure of the night-fair had not only dispelled a little our mutual reserve, but had luckily furnished us with a subject on which we could converse without embarrassment. From this topic I took care to lead her, without any interruption, to others—being fearful lest our former silence should return, and the music of her voice again be lost to me. It was only, indeed, by thus indirectly unburdening my heart that I was enabled to avoid the disclosure of all I thought and felt; and the restless rapidity with which I flew from subject to subject was but an effort to escape from the only one in which my heart was really interested.

"How bright and happy," said I—pointing up to Sothis, the fair Star of the Waters, which was just then shining brilliantly over our heads—"How bright and happy this world ought to be, if, as your Egyptian sages assert, yon pure and beautiful luminary was its birth-star!" Then, still leaning back, and letting my eyes wander over the firmament, as if seeking to disengage them from the fascination which they dreaded—"To the study," I exclaimed, "for ages, of skies like this, may the pensive and mystic character of your nation be traced. That mixture of pride and melancholy which naturally arises at the sight of those eternal lights shining out of darkness;—that sublime, but saddened, anticipation of a Future, which steals sometimes over the soul in the silence of such an hour, when, though Death appears to reign in the deep stillness of earth, there are yet those beacons of Immortality burning in the sky."

Pausing, as I uttered the word "immortality," with a sigh to think how little my heart echoed to my lips, I looked in the face of my companion, and saw that it had lighted up, as I spoke, into a glow of holy animation, such as Faith alone gives;—such as Hope herself wears, when she is dreaming of heaven. Touched by the contrast, and gazing upon her with mournful tenderness, I found my arms half opened, to clasp her to my heart, while the words died away inaudibly on my lips,—"Thou, too, beautiful maiden! must thou, too, die for ever?"

My self-command, I felt, had nearly deserted me. Rising abruptly from my seat, I walked to the middle of the deck, and stood, for some moments, unconsciously gazing upon one of those fires, which—according to the custom of all who travel by night on the Nile—our boatmen had kindled, to scare away the crocodiles from the vessel. But it was in vain that I endeavoured to compose my spirit. Every effort I made but more deeply convinced me, that, till the mystery which hung round that maiden should be solved—till the secret, with which my own bosom laboured, should be disclosed —it was fruitless to attempt even a semblance of tranquillity.

My resolution was therefore taken;—to lay open, at once, the feelings of my own heart, as far as such revealment might be hazarded, without startling the timid innocence of my companion. Thus resolved, I resumed my seat, with more composure, by her side; and taking from my bosom the small mirror which she had dropped in the Temple, and which I had ever since worn suspended round my neck, presented it with a trembling hand to her view. The boatmen had just kindled one of their night-fires near us, and its light, as she leaned forward to look at the mirror, fell upon her face.

The quick blush of surprise with which she recognised it to be hers, and her look of bashful yet eager inquiry, in raising her eyes to mine, were appeals to which I was not, of course, tardy in answering. Beginning with the first moment when I saw her in the Temple, and passing hastily, but with words that burned as they went, over the impression which she had then left upon my heart and fancy, I proceeded to describe the particulars of my descent into the pyramid —my surprise and adoration at the door of the chapel—my encounter with the Trials of Initiation, so mysteriously prepared for me, and all the various visionary wonders I had witnessed in that region, till the moment when I had seen her stealing from under the Veils to approach me.

Though, in detailing these events, I had said but little of the feelings they had awakened in me—though my lips had sent back many a sentence, unuttered, there was still enough that could neither be subdued nor disguised, and which, like that light from under the veils of her own Isis, glowed through every word that I spoke. When I told of the scene in the chapel—of the silent interview which I had witnessed between the dead and the living—the maiden leaned down her head and wept, as from a heart full of tears. It seemed a pleasure to her, however, to listen; and, when she looked at me again, there was an earnest and affectionate cordiality in her eyes, as if the knowledge of my having been present at that mournful scene had opened a new source of sympathy and intelligence between us. So neighbouring are the fountains of Love and of Sorrow, and so imperceptibly do they often mingle their streams.

Little, indeed, as I was guided by art or design, in my manner and conduct towards this innocent girl, not all the most experienced gallantry of the Garden could have dictated a policy half so seductive as that which my new master, Love, now taught me. The same ardour which, if shown at once, and without reserve, might probably have startled a heart so little prepared for it, being now checked and softened by the timidity of real love, won its way without alarm, and, when most diffident of success, was then most surely on its way to triumph. Like one whose slumbers are gradually broken by sweet music, the maiden's heart was awakened without being disturbed. She followed the course of the charm, unconscious whither it led, nor was even aware of the flame she had lighted in another's bosom, till startled by the reflection of its glimmering in her own.

Impatient as I was to appeal to her generosity and sympathy, for a similar proof of confidence to that which I had just given, the night was now too far advanced for me to impose upon her such a task. After exchanging a few words, in which, though little met the ear, there was, on both sides, a tone and manner that spoke far more than language, we took a lingering leave of each other for the night, with every prospect, I fondly hoped, of being still together in our dreams.

CHAPTER XIII.

It was so near the dawn of day when we parted that we found the sun sinking westward when we rejoined each other. The smile, so frankly cordial, with which she met me, might have been taken for the greeting of a long-mellowed friendship, did not the blush and the cast-down eyelid that followed betray symptoms of a feeling newer and less calm. For myself, lightened as I was, in some degree, by the avowal which I had made, I was yet too conscious of the new aspect thus given to our intercourse, not to feel some little alarm at the prospect of returning to the theme. We were both, therefore, alike willing to allow our attention to be diverted, by the variety of strange objects that presented themselves on the way, from a subject that evidently both were alike unwilling to approach.

The river was now all stirring with commerce and life Every instant we met with boats descending the current, so wholly independent of aid from sail or oar, that the mariners sat idly on the deck as they shot along, either singing or playing upon their double-reeded pipes. The greater number of these boats came laden with those large emeralds, from the mine in the desert, whose colours, it is said, are brightest at the full of the moon; while some brought cargoes of frankincense from the acacia groves near the Red Sea. On the decks of others, that had been, as we learned, to the Golden Mountains beyond Syene, were heaped blocks and fragments of that sweet-smelling wood, which is yearly washed down, by the Green Nile of Nubia, at the season of the floods.

Our companions up the stream were far less numerous. Occasionally a boat, returning lightened from the fair of last night, shot rapidly past us, with those high sails that catch every breeze from over the hills;—while, now and then, we overtook one of those barges full of bees, that are sent at this season to colonise the gardens of the south, and take advantage of the first flowers after the inundation has passed away.

For a short time, this constant variety of objects enabled us to divert so far our conversation as to keep it from lighting upon the one, sole subject, round which it constantly hovered. But the effort, as might be expected, was not long successful. As evening advanced, the whole scene became more solitary. We less frequently ventured to look upon each other, and our intervals of silence grew more long.

It was near sunset, when, in passing a small temple on the shore, whose porticoes were now full of the evening light, we saw issuing from a thicket of acanthus near it, a train of young maidens gracefully linked together in the dance by stems of the lotus held at arms' length between them. Their tresses were also wreathed with this gay emblem of the season, and in such profusion were its white flowers twisted around their waists and arms, that they might have been taken, as they lightly bounded along the bank, for Nymphs of the Nile, then freshly risen from their bright gardens under the wave.

After looking for a few minutes at this sacred dance, the maiden turned away her eyes, with a look of pain, as if the remembrances it recalled were of no welcome nature. This momentary retrospect, this glimpse into the past, appeared to offer a sort of clue to the secret for which I panted;—and accordingly I proceeded, as gradually and delicately as my impatience would allow, to avail myself of the opening Her own frankness, however, relieved me from the embarrassment of much questioning. She appeared even to feel that the confidence I sought was due to me; and beyond the natural hesitation of maidenly modesty, not a shade of reserve or evasion appeared.

To attempt to repeat, in her own touching words, the simple story which she now related to me, would be like endeavouring to note down some unpremeditated strain of music, with all those fugitive graces, those felicities of the moment, which no art can restore, as they first met the ear. From a feeling, too, of humility, she had omitted in her short narrative several particulars relating to herself, which I afterwards learned;—while others, not less important, she but slightly passed over, from a fear of offending the prejudices of her heathen hearer.

I shall, therefore, give her story, not as she, herself, sketched it, but as it was afterwards filled up by a pious and venerable hand—far, far more worthy than mine of being associated with the memory of such purity.

STORY OF ALETHE.

"The mother of this maiden was the beautiful Theora of Alexandria, who, though a native of that city, was descended from Grecian parents. When very young, Theora was one of the seven maidens selected to note down the discourses of the eloquent Origen, who, at that period, presided over the School of Alexandria, and was in all the fulness of his fame, both among Pagans and Christians. Endowed richly with the learning of both creeds, he brought the natural light of philosophy to illustrate the mysteries of faith, and was then only proud of his knowledge of the wisdom of this world, when he found it minister usefully to the triumph of divine truth.

"Although he had courted in vain the crown of martyrdom, it was held, through his whole life, suspended over his head; and, in more than one persecution, he had shown himself cheerfully ready to die for that holy faith which he lived but to testify and uphold. On one of these occasions, his tormentors, having habited him like an Egyptian priest, placed him upon the steps of the Temple of Serapis, and commanded that he should, in the manner of the Pagan ministers, present palm-branches to the multitude who went up into the shrine. But the courageous Christian disappointed their views. Holding forth the branches with an unshrinking hand, he cried aloud, 'Come hither, and take the branch,—not of an Idol Temple, but of Christ.'

"So indefatigable was this learned Father in his studies, that, while composing his Commentary on the Scriptures, he was attended by seven scribes or notaries, who relieved each other in recording the dictates of his eloquent tongue; while the same number of young females, selected for the beauty of their penmanship, were employed in arranging and transcribing the precious leaves

"Among the scribes so selected was the fair young Theora, whose parents, though attached to the Pagan worship, were not unwilling to profit by the accomplishments of their daughter, thus occupied in a task, which they looked on as purely mechanical. To the maid herself, however, her employment brought far other feelings and consequences. She read anxiously as she wrote, and the divine truths, so eloquently illustrated, found their way, by degrees, from the page to her heart. Deeply, too, as the written words affected her, the discourses from the lips of the great teacher himself, which she had frequent opportunities of hearing, sunk still more deeply into her mind. There was, at once, a sublimity and gentleness in his views of religion, which, to the tender hearts and lively imaginations of women, never failed to appeal with convincing power. Accordingly, the list of his female pupils was numerous; and the names of Barbara, Juliana, Herais, and others, bear honourable testimony to his influence over that sex.

"To Theora the feeling with which his discourses inspired her, was like a new soul—a consciousness of spiritual existence, never before felt. By the eloquence of the comment she was awakened into admiration of the text; and when, by the kindness of a Catechumen of the school, who had been struck by her innocent zeal, she, for the first time, became possessor of a copy of the Scriptures, she could not sleep for thinking of her sacred treasure. With a mixture of pleasure and fear she hid it from all eyes, and was like one who had received a divine guest under her roof, and felt fearful of betraying its divinity to the world.

"A heart so awake would have been with ease secured to the faith, had her opportunities of hearing the sacred word continued. But circumstances arose to deprive her of this advantage. The mild Origen, long harassed and thwarted in his labours by the tyranny of Demetrius, Bishop of Alexandria, was obliged to relinquish his school, and fly from Egypt. The occupation of the fair scribe, was, therefore, at an end: her intercourse with the followers of the new faith ceased; and the glowing enthusiasm of her heart gave way to more worldly impressions.

"Among other earthly feelings, love conduced not a little to wean her thoughts from the true religion. While still very young, she became the wife of a Greek adventurer, who had come to Egypt as a purchaser of that rich tapestry, in which the needles of Persia are rivalled by the looms of the Nile. Having taken his young bride to Memphis, which was still the great mart of this merchandise, he there, in the midst of his speculations, died—leaving his widow on the point of becoming a mother, while, as yet, but in her nineteenth year.

"For single and unprotected females it has been, at all times, a favourite resource, to seek for employment in the service of some of those great temples by which so large a portion of the wealth and power of Egypt is absorbed. In most of these institutions there exists an order of Priestesses, which, though not hereditary, like that of the Priests, is provided for by ample endowments, and confers that dignity and station, with which, in a government so theocratic, Religion is sure to invest even her humblest handmaids. From the general policy of the Sacred College of Memphis, we may take for granted, that an accomplished female, like Theora, found but little difficulty in being elected one of the Priestesses of Isis; and it was in the service of the subterranean shrines that her ministry chiefly lay.

"Here, a month or two after her admission, she gave birth to Alethe, who first opened her eyes among the unholy pomps and specious miracles of this mysterious region. Though Theora, as we have seen, had been diverted by other feelings from her first enthusiasm for the Christian faith, she had never wholly forgot the impression then made upon her. The sacred volume, which the pious Catechumen had given her, was still treasured with care; and, though she seldom opened its pages, there was always an idea of sanctity associated with it in her memory, and often would she sit to look upon it with reverential pleasure, recalling the happiness she had felt when it was first made her own.

"The leisure of her new retreat, and the lone melancholy of widowhood, led her still more frequently to indulge in such thoughts, and to recur to those consoling truths which she had heard in the school of Alexandria. She now began to peruse eagerly the sacred volume, drinking deep of the fountain of which she before but tasted, and feeling—what thousands of mourners, since her, have felt—that Christianity is the true and only religion of the sorrowful.

"This study of her secret hours became still more dear to her, as well from the peril with which, at that period, it was attended, as from the necessity she felt herself under of concealing from those around her the precious light that had been thus kindled in her own heart. Too timid to encounter the fierce persecution, which awaited all who were suspected of a leaning to Christianity, she continued to officiate in the pomps and ceremonies of the Temple:—though, often, with such remorse of soul, that she would pause, in the midst of the rites, and pray inwardly to God, that he would forgive this profanation of his Spirit.

"In the meantime her daughter, the young Alethe, grew up still lovelier than herself, and added, every hour, both to her happiness and her fears. When arrived at a sufficient age, she was taught, like the other children of the priestesses, to take a share in the service and ceremonies of the shrines The duty of some of these young servitors was to look after the flowers for the altar;—of others, to take care that the sacred vases were filled every day with fresh water from the Nile. The task of some was to preserve, in perfect polish, those silver images of the Moon which the priests carried in processions; while others were, as we have seen, employed in feeding the consecrated animals, and in keeping their plumes and scales bright for the admiring eyes of their worshippers.

"The office allotted to Alethe—the most honourable of these minor ministries—was to wait upon the sacred birds of the Moon, to feed them daily with those eggs from the Nile which they loved, and provide for their use that purest water, which alone these delicate birds will touch. This employment was the delight of her childish hours; and that ibis, which Alciphron (the Epicurean) saw her dance round in the Temple, was, of all the sacred flock, her especial favourite, and had been daily fondled and fed by her from infancy.

"Music, as being one of the chief spells of this enchanted region, was an accomplishment required of all its ministrants, and the harp, the lyre, and the sacred flute, sounded nowhere so sweetly as through these subterranean gardens. The chief object, indeed, in the education of the youth of the Temple, was to fit them, by every grace of art and nature, to give effect to the illusion of those shows and phantasms, in which the entire charm and secret of Initiation lay.

"Among the means employed to support the old system of superstition, against the infidelity and, still more, the new Faith that menaced it, was an increased display of splendour and marvels in those mysteries for which Egypt has so long been celebrated. Of these ceremonies so many imitations had, under various names, multiplied throughout Europe, that at length the parent superstition ran a risk of being eclipsed by its progeny; and, in order still to rank as the first Priesthood in the world, it became necessary for those of Egypt to remain still the best impostors

"Accordingly, every contrivance that art could devise, or labour execute—every resource that the wonderful knowledge of the Priests, in pyrotechny, mechanics, and dioptrics, could command—was brought into action to heighten the effect of their Mysteries, and give an air of enchantment to every thing connected with them.

"The final scene of beatification—the Elysium, into which the Initiate was received—formed, of course, the leading attraction of these ceremonies; and to render it captivating alike to the senses of the man of pleasure, and the imagination of the spiritualist, was the great object to which the attention of the Sacred College was devoted. By the influence of the Priests of Memphis over those of the other Temples they had succeeded in extending their subterranean frontier, both to the north and south, so as to include, within their ever-lighted Paradise, some of the gardens excavated for the use of the other Twelve Shrines.

"The beauty of the young Alethe, the touching sweetness of her voice, and the sensibility that breathed throughout her every look and movement, rendered her a powerful auxiliary in such appeals to the imagination. She had been, accordingly, in her very childhood, selected from among her fair companions, as the most worthy representative of spiritual loveliness, in those pictures of Elysium—those scenes of another world—by which not only the fancy, but the reason, of the excited Aspirants was dazzled.

"To the innocent child herself these shows were pastime. But to Theora, who knew too well the imposition to which they were subservient, this profanation of all that she loved was a perpetual source of horror and remorse. Often would she—when Alethe stood smiling before her, arrayed, perhaps, as a spirit of the Elysian world—turn away, with a shudder, from the happy child, almost fancying she saw already the shadows of sin descending over that innocent brow, as she gazed upon it.

"As the intellect of the young maid became more active and inquiring, the apprehensions and difficulties of the mother increased. Afraid to communicate her own precious secret, lest she should involve her child in the dangers that encompassed it, she yet felt it to be no less a cruelty than a crime to leave her wholly immersed in the darkness of Paganism. In this dilemma, the only resource that remained to her was to select, and disengage from the dross that surrounded them, those pure particles of truth which lie at the bottom of all religions;—those feelings, rather than doctrines, of which God has never left his creatures destitute, and which, in all ages, have furnished, to those who sought after it, some clue to his glory.

"The unity and perfect goodness of the Creator; the fall of the human soul into corruption, its struggles with the darkness of this world, and its final redemption and re-ascent to the source of all spirit;—these natural solutions of the problem of our existence. these elementary grounds of all religion and virtue, which Theora had heard illustrated by her Christian teacher, lay also, she knew, veiled under the theology of Egypt; and to impress them, in their abstract purity, upon the mind of her susceptible pupil, was, in default of more heavenly lights, her sole ambition and care.

"It was generally their habit, after devoting their mornings to the service of the Temple, to pass their evenings and nights in one of those small mansions above ground, allotted, within the precincts of the Sacred College, to some of the most favoured Priestesses. Here, out of the reach of those gross superstitions, which pursued them, at every step, below, she endeavoured to inform, as far as she could venture, the mind of her beloved girl; and found it lean as naturally and instinctively to truth, as plants long shut up in darkness will, when light is let in upon them, incline themselves to its rays.

"Frequently, as they sat together on the terrace at night, admiring that glorious assembly of stars, whose beauty first misled mankind into idolatry, she would explain to the young listener by what gradations of error it was that the worship, thus transferred from the Creator to the creature, sunk still lower and lower in the scale of being, till man, at length, presumed to deify man, and by the most monstrous of inversions, heaven was made the mere mirror of earth, reflecting back all its most earthly features.

"Even in the Temple itself, the anxious mother would endeavour to interpose her purer lessons among the idolatrous ceremonies in which they were engaged. When the favourite ibis of Alethe took its station upon the shrine, and the young maiden was seen approaching, with all the gravity of worship, the very bird which she had played with but an hour before—when the acacia-bough, which she herself had plucked, seemed to acquire a sudden sacredness in her eyes, as soon as the priest had breathed upon it—on all such occasions Theora, though with fear and trembling, would venture to suggest to the youthful worshipper the distinction that should be drawn between the sensible object of adoration, and that spiritual, unseen Deity, of which it was but the remembrancer or type.

"With sorrow, however, she soon discovered that, in thus but partially letting in light upon a mind far too ardent to rest satisfied with such glimmerings, she but bewildered the heart which she meant to guide, and cut down the feeble hope around which its faith twined, without substituting any other support in its place. As the beauty, too, of Alethe began to attract all eyes, now fears crowded upon the mother's heart;—fears, in which she was but too much justified by the characters of some of those around her.

"In this sacred abode, as may easily be conceived, morality did not always go hand in hand with religion. The hypocritical and ambitious Orcus, who was, at this period, High Priest of Memphis, was a man, in every respect, qualified to preside over a system of such splendid fraud. He had reached that effective time of life, when enough of the warmth and vigour of youth remains to give animation to the counsels of age. But, in his instance, youth had left only the baser passions behind, while age but brought with it a more refined maturity of mischief. The advantages of a faith appealing almost wholly to the senses, were well understood by him; nor had he failed either to discover that, in order to render religion subservient to his own interests, he must shape it adroitly to the interests and passions of others.

"The state of anxiety and remorse in which the mind of the hapless Theora was kept by the scenes, however artfully veiled, which she daily witnessed around her, became at length intolerable. No perils that the cause of truth could bring with it would be half so dreadful as this endurance of sinfulness and deceit. Her child was, as yet, pure and innocent; but, without that sentinel of the soul, Religion, how long might she continue so?

"This thought at once decided her: all other fears vanished before it. She resolved instantly to lay open to Alethe the whole secret of her soul; to make this child, who was her only hope on earth, the sharer of all her hopes in heaven, and then fly with her, as soon as possible, from this unhallowed spot, to the far desert—to the mountains—to any place, however desolate, where God and the consciousness of innocence might be with them.

"The promptitude with which her young pupil caught from her the divine truths was even beyond what she expected. It was like the lighting of one torch at another, so prepared was Alethe's mind for the illumination. Amply, indeed, was the anxious mother now repaid for all her misery, by this perfect communion of love and faith, and by the delight with which she saw her beloved child—like the young antelope, when first led by her dam to the well—drink thirstily by her side, at the source of all life and truth.

"But such happiness was not long to last. The anxieties that Theora had suffered began to prey upon her health. She felt her strength daily decline; and the thoughts of leaving, alone and unguarded in the world, that treasure which she had just devoted to Heaven, gave her a feeling of despair which but hastened the ebb of life. Had she put in practice her resolution of flying from this place, her child might have been now beyond the reach of all she dreaded, and in the solitude of the desert would have found at least safety from wrong. But the very happiness she had felt in her new task diverted her from this project;—and it was now too late, for she was already dying.

"She still continued, however, to conceal the state of her health from the tender and sanguine girl, who, though observing the traces of disease on her mother's cheek, little knew that they were the hastening footsteps of death, nor even thought of the possibility of ever losing what was so dear to her. Too soon, however, the moment of separation arrived; and while the anguish and dismay of Alethe were in proportion to the security in which she had indulged, Theora, too felt, with bitter regret, that she had sacrificed to her fond consideration much precious time, and that there now remained but a few brief and painful moments, for the communication of all those wishes and instructions on which the future destiny of the young orphan depended.

"She had, indeed, time for little more than to place the

sacred volume solemnly in her hands; to implore that she would, at all risks, fly from this unholy place; and, pointing in the direction of the mountains of the Said, to name, with her last breath, the venerable man, to whom, under Heaven, she looked for the protection and salvation of her child.

"The first violence of feeling to which Alethe gave way was succeeded by a fixed and tearless grief, which rendered her insensible, for some time, to the dangers of her situation. Her sole comfort consisted in visiting that monumental chapel where the beautiful remains of Theora lay. There, night after night, in contemplation of those placid features, and in prayers for the peace of the departed spirit, did she pass her lonely and—however sad they were—happiest hours. Though the mystic emblems that decorated that chapel were but ill-suited to the slumber of a Christian, there was one among them, the Cross, which, by a remarkable coincidence, is an emblem alike common to the Gentile and the Christian—being, to the former, a shadowy type of that immortality, of which, to the latter, it is a substantial and assuring pledge.

"Nightly, upon this cross, which she had often seen her lost mother kiss, did she breathe forth a solemn and heartfelt vow, never to abandon the faith which that departed spirit had bequeathed to her. To such enthusiasm, indeed, did her heart at such moments rise, that, but for the last injunctions from those pallid lips, she would, at once, have avowed her perilous secret, and boldly pronounced the words, 'I am a Christian,' among those benighted shrines!

"But the will of her, to whom she owed more than life, was to be obeyed. To escape from this haunt of superstition must now, she felt, be her first object; and in planning the means of effecting it, her mind, day and night, was employed. It was with a loathing not to be concealed, that she now found herself compelled to resume her idolatrous services at the shrine. To some of the offices of Theora she succeeded, as is the custom, by inheritance; and in the performance of these tasks—sanctified as they were in her eyes by the pure spirit she had seen engaged in them—there was a sort of melancholy pleasure in which her sorrow found relief. But the part she was again forced to take, in the scenic shows of the Mysteries, brought with it a sense of degradation and wrong which she could no longer endure.

"Already had she formed, in her own mind, a plan of escape, in which her acquaintance with all the windings of this mystic realm gave her confidence, when the solemn reception of Alciphron, as an Initiate, took place.

"From the first moment of the landing of that philosopher at Alexandria, he had become an object of suspicion and watchfulness to the inquisitorial Orcus, whom philosophy, in any shape, naturally alarmed, but to whom the sect over which the young Athenian presided was particularly obnoxious. The accomplishments of Alciphron, his popularity, wherever he went, and the bold freedom with which he indulged his wit at the expense of religion, were all faithfully reported to the High Priest by his spies, and awakened in his mind no kindly feelings towards the stranger. In dealing with an infidel, such a personage as Orcus could know no other alternative but that of either converting or destroying him; and though his spite, as a man, would have been more gratified by the latter proceeding, his pride, as a priest, led him to prefer the triumph of the former.

"The first descent of the Epicurean into the pyramid became speedily known, and the alarm was immediately given to the priests below. As soon as they had discovered that the young philosopher of Athens was the intruder, and that he not only still continued to linger round the pyramid, but was observed to look often and wistfully towards the portal, it was concluded that his curiosity would impel him to try a second descent; and Orcus, blessing the good chance which had thus brought the wild bird into his net, resolved not to suffer an opportunity so precious to be wasted.

"Instantly, the whole of that wonderful machinery, by which the phantasms and illusions of Initiation are produced, were put in active preparation throughout that subterranean realm; and the increased stir and vigilance awakened among its inmates, by this more than ordinary display of the resources of priestcraft, rendered the accomplishment of Alethe's purpose, at such a moment, peculiarly difficult. Wholly ignorant of the important share which it had been her own fortune to take in attracting the young philosopher down to this region, she but heard of him vaguely, as the Chief of a great Grecian sect, who had been led, by either curiosity or accident, to expose himself to the first trials of Initiation; and whom the priests, she could see, were endeavouring to ensnare in their toils, by every art and lure with which their dark science had gifted them.

"To her mind, the image of a philosopher, such as Alciphron had been represented to her, came associated with ideas of age and reverence; and, more than once, the possibility of his being made instrumental to her deliverance flashed a hope across her heart in which she could not refrain from indulging. Often had she been told by Theora of the many Gentile sages, who had laid their wisdom down humbly at the foot of the Cross; and though this Initiate, she feared, could hardly be among the number, yet the rumours which she had gathered from the servants of the Temple, of his undisguised contempt for the errors of Heathenism, led her to hope she might find tolerance, if not sympathy, in her appeal to him.

"Nor was it solely with a view to her own chance of deliverance that she thus connected him in her thoughts with the plan which she meditated. The look of proud and self-gratulating malice, with which the High Priest had mentioned this 'Infidel,' as he styled him, when giving her instructions in the scene she was to act before the philosopher in the valley, too plainly informed her of the dark destiny that hung over him. She knew how many were the hapless candidates for Initiation who had been doomed to a durance worse than that of the grave, for but a word, a whisper, breathed against the sacred absurdities that they witnessed; and it was evident to her that the venerable Greek (for such her fancy represented Alciphron) was no less interested in escaping from the snares and perils of this region than herself.

"Her own resolution was, at all events, fixed. That visionary scene, in which she had appeared before Alciphron—little knowing how ardent were the heart and imagination over which her beauty, at that moment, exercised its influence—was, she solemnly resolved, the very last unholy service, that superstition or imposture should ever command of her.

"On the following night the Aspirant was to watch in the Great Temple of Isis. Such an opportunity of approaching and addressing him might never come again. Should he, from compassion for her situation, or a sense of the danger of his own, consent to lend his aid to her flight, most gladly would she accept it—well assured that no danger or treachery she might risk could be half so odious and fearful as those which she left behind. Should he, on the contrary, reject the proposal, her determination was equally fixed—to trust to that God whose eye watches over the innocent, and go forth alone.

"To reach the island in Lake Mœris was her first great object; and there occurred fortunately, at this time, a mode of effecting her purpose, by which both the difficulty and dangers of the attempt would be much diminished. The day of the annual visitation of the High Priest to the Place of Weeping—as that island in the centre of the Lake is called—was now fast approaching; and Alethe knew that the self-moving car, by which the High Priest and one of the Hierophants are conveyed down to the chambers under the Lake, stood then waiting in readiness. By availing herself of this expedient, she would gain the double advantage both of facilitating her own flight, and retarding the speed of her pursuers.

"Having paid a last visit to the tomb of her beloved mother, and wept there, long and passionately, till her heart almost failed in the struggle—having paused, too, to give a kiss to her favourite ibis, which, although too much a Christian to worship, she was still child enough to love—she went early, with a trembling step, to the Sanctuary, and there hid herself in one of the recesses of the Shrine. Her intention was to steal out from thence while it was yet dark, and before the illumination of the great Statue behind the Veils had begun. But her fears delayed her till it was almost too late;—already was the image lighted up, and still she remained trembling in her hiding-place.

"In a few minutes more the mighty Veils would have been withdrawn, and the glories of that scene of enchantment laid open—when, at length, summoning all her courage, and taking advantage of a momentary absence of those epmloyed in preparing this splendid mockery, she stole from under the Veil, and found her way, through the gloom, to the Epicurian. There was then no time for explanation;—she had but to trust to the simple words, 'Follow, and be silent;' and the implicit readiness with which she found them obeyed filled her with no less surprise than the philosopher himself had felt in hearing them.

"In a second or two they were on their way through the

subterranean windings, leaving the ministers of Isis to waste their splendours on vacancy, through a long series of miracles and visions which they now exhibited—unconscious that he, whom they were taking such pains to dazzle, was already, under the guidance of the young Christian, far removed beyond the reach of their deceiving spells."

CHAPTER XIV.

Such was the singular story, of which this innocent girl now gave me, in her own touching language, the outline.

The sun was just rising as she finished her narrative. Fearful of encountering the expression of those feelings with which, she could not but observe, I was affected by her recital, scarcely had she concluded the last sentence, when, rising abruptly from her seat, she hurried into the pavilion, leaving me with the words fast crowding for utterance to my lips.

Oppressed by the various emotions thus sent back upon my heart, I lay down on the deck in a state of agitation, that defied even the most distant approaches of sleep. While every word she had uttered, every feeling she expressed, but ministered new fuel to that flame which consumed me, and to describe which, passion is far too weak a word, there was also much of her recital that disheartened and alarmed me. To find a Christian thus under the garb of a Memphian Priestess, was a discovery that, had my heart been less deeply interested, would but have more powerfully stimulated my imagination and pride. But, when I recollected the austerity of the faith she had embraced—the tender and sacred tie, associated with it in her memory, and the devotion of woman's heart to objects thus consecrated—her very perfections but widened the distance between us, and all that most kindled my passion at the same time chilled my hopes.

Were we to be left to each other, as on this silent river, in such undisturbed communion of thoughts and feelings, I knew too well, I thought, both her sex's nature and my own, to feel a doubt that love would ultimately triumph. But the severity of the guardianship to which I must resign her—that of some monk of the desert, some stern Solitary—the influence such a monitor would gain over her mind—and the horror with which, ere long, he might teach her to regard the reprobate infidel upon whom she now smiled—in all this prospect I saw nothing but despair. After a few short hours, my dream of happiness would be at an end, and such a dark chasm must then open between our fates, as would dissever them, wide as earth from heaven, asunder.

It was true, she was now wholly in my power. I feared no witnesses but those of earth, and the solitude of the desert was at hand. But though I acknowledged not a heaven, I worshipped her who was, to me, its type and substitute. If, at any moment, a single thought of wrong or deceit, towards one so sacred arose in my mind, one look from her innocent eyes averted the sacrilege. Even passion itself felt a holy fear in her presence—like the flame trembling in the breeze of the sanctuary—and Love, pure Love, stood in the place of Religion.

As long as I knew not her story, I could indulge, at least, in dreams of the future. But, now—what expectation, what prospect remained? My single chance of happiness lay in the hope, however delusive, of being able to divert her thoughts from the fatal project she meditated; of weaning her, by persuasion and argument, from that austere faith, which I had before hated and now feared; and of attaching her, perhaps, alone and unlinked as she was in the world, to my own fortunes for ever!

In the agitation of these thoughts, I had started from my resting place, and continued to pace up and down, under a burning sun, till, exhausted both by thought and feeling, I sunk down, amid that blaze of light, into a sleep, which to my fevered brain seemed a sleep of fire.

On awaking, I found the veil of Alethe laid carefully over my brow; while she, herself, sat near me, under the shadow of the sail, looking anxiously upon that leaf, which her mother had given her, and employed apparently in comparing its outlines with the course of the river, as well as with the forms of the rocky hills by which we were passing. She looked pale and troubled, and rose eagerly to meet me, as if she had long and impatiently waited for my waking.

Her heart, it was plain, had been disturbed from its security, and was beginning to take alarm at its own feelings. But, though vaguely conscious of the peril to which she was exposed, her reliance, as is usual in such cases, increased with her danger, and upon me, far more than on herself, did she seem to depend for saving her. To reach, as soon as possible, her asylum in the desert, was now the urgent object of her entreaties and wishes; and the self-reproach which she expressed at having, for a single moment, suffered her thoughts to be diverted from this sacred purpose, not only revealed the truth, that she *had* forgotten it, but betrayed even a glimmering consciousness of the cause.

Her sleep, she said, had been broken by ill-omened dreams. Every moment the shade of her mother had stood before her, rebuking, with mournful looks, her delay, and pointing, as she had done in death, to the eastern hills. Bursting into tears at this accusing recollection, she hastily placed the leaf, which she had been examining, in my hands, and implored that I would ascertain, without a moment's delay, what portion of our voyage was still unperformed, and in what space of time we might hope to accomplish it.

I had, still less than herself, taken note of either place or distance; and could we have been left to glide on in this dream of happiness, should never have thought of pausing to ask where it would end. But such confidence was far too sacred to be deceived; and, reluctant as I naturally felt, to enter on an inquiry, which might soon dissipate even my last hope, her wish was sufficient to supersede even the selfishness of love, and on the instant I proceeded to obey her will.

There stands on the eastern bank of the Nile, to the north of Antinoe, a high and steep rock, impending over the flood, which has borne, for ages, from a prodigy connected with it, the name of the Mountain of the Birds. Yearly, it is said, at a certain season and hour, large flocks of birds assemble in the ravine, of which this rocky mountain forms one of the sides, and are there observed to go through the mysterious ceremony of inserting each its beak into a particular cleft of the rock, till the cleft closes upon one of their number, when all the rest of the birds take wing, and leave the selected victim to die.

Through the ravine, rendered famous by this charm—for such the multitude consider it—there ran, in ancient times, a canal from the Nile, to some great and forgotten city, now buried in the desert. To a short distance from the river this canal still exists, but, after having passed through the defile, its scanty waters disappear, and are wholly lost under the sands.

It was in the neighbourhood of this place, as I could collect from the delineations on the leaf—where a flight of birds represented the name of the mountain—that the abode of the Solitary, to whom Alethe was about to consign herself, was situated. Little as I knew of the geography of Egypt, it at once struck me, that we had long since left this mountain behind; and, on inquiring of our boatmen, I found my conjecture confirmed. We had, indeed, passed it, on the preceding night; and, as the wind had been, ever since, blowing strongly from the north, and the sun was already sinking towards the horizon, we must be now, at least, a day's sail to the southward of the spot.

This discovery, I confess, filled my heart with a feeling of joy which I found it difficult to conceal. It seemed as if fortune was conspiring with love in my behalf, and, by thus delaying the moment of our separation, afforded me a chance at least of happiness. Her look and manner, too, when informed of our mistake, rather encouraged than chilled this secret hope. In the first moment of astonishment her eyes opened upon me with a suddenness of splendour, under which I felt my own wink as though lightning had crossed them.—But she again, as suddenly, let their lids fall, and, after a quiver of her lip, which showed the conflict of feeling then going on within, crossed her arms upon her bosom, and looked down silently upon the deck; her whole countenance sinking into an expression, sad, but resigned, as if she now felt that fate was on the side of wrong, and saw Love already stealing between her soul and heaven.

I was not slow, of course, in availing myself of what I fancied to be the irresolution of her mind. But, still, fearful of exciting alarm by any appeal to feelings of regard or tenderness, I but addressed myself to her imagination, and to that love of novelty and wonders, which is ever ready to be awakened within the youthful breast. We were now approaching that region of miracles, Thebes. "In a day or two," said I, "we shall see, towering above the waters, the colossal Avenue of Sphinxes, and the bright Obelisks of the Sun. We shall visit the plain of Memnon, and behold those mighty statues that fling their shadows at sunrise over the Libyan hills;

We shall hear the image of the Son of the Morning responding to the first touch of light. From thence, in a few hours, a breeze like this will transport us to those sunny islands near the cataracts; there, to wander, among the sacred palm-groves of Philæ, or sit, at noontide hour, in those cool alcoves, which the waterfall of Syene shadows under its arch. Oh, who is there that, with scenes of such loveliness within reach, would turn coldly away to the bleak desert, and leave this fair world, with all its enchantments, shining unseen and unenjoyed? At least"—I added, taking tenderly her hand in mine—"let a few more days be stolen from the dreary fate to which thou hast devoted thyself, and then ——"

She had heard but the last few words—the rest had been lost upon her. Startled by the tone of tenderness into which, in despite of all my resolves, I had suffered my voice to soften, she looked for an instant with passionate earnestness into my face; then, dropping upon her knees with her clasped hands upraised, exclaimed—"Tempt me not, in the name of God I implore thee, tempt me not to swerve from my sacred duty. Oh! take me instantly to that desert mountain, and I will bless thee for ever."

This appeal, I felt, could not be resisted—even though my heart were to break for it. Having silently intimated my assent to her prayer, by a slight pressure of her hand as I raised her from the deck, I proceeded immediately, as we were still in full career, for the south, to give orders that our sail should be instantly lowered, and not a moment lost in retracing our course.

In giving these directions, however, it, for the first time, occurred to me, that, as I had hired this yacht in the neighbourhood of Memphis, where it was probable the flight of the young Priestess would be most vigilantly tracked, we should run the risk of betraying to the boatmen the place of her retreat;—and there was now a most favourable opportunity for taking precautions against this danger. Desiring therefore, that we should be landed at a small village on the shore, under pretence of paying a visit to some shrine in the neighbourhood, I there dismissed our barge, and was relieved from fear of further observation, by seeing it again set sail, and resume its course fleetly up the current.

From the boats of all descriptions that lay idle beside the bank, I now selected one, in every respect, suited to my purpose—being, in its shape and accommodations, a miniature of our former vessel, but, at the same time, so light and small as to be manageable by myself alone, and requiring, with the advantage of the current, little more than a hand to steer it. This boat I succeeded, without much difficulty, in purchasing, and, after a short delay, we were again afloat down the current;—the sun just then sinking, in conscious glory, over his own golden shrines, in the Libyan waste.

The evening was calmer and more lovely than any that had yet smiled upon our voyage; and, as we left the shore, a strain of sweet melody came soothingly over our ears. It was the voice of a young Nubian girl, whom we saw kneeling before an acacia, upon the bank, and singing, while her companions stood around, the wild song of invocation, which, in her country, they address to that enchanted tree:—

"Oh! Abyssinian tree,
We pray, we pray to thee,
By the glow of thy golden fruit,
And the violet hue of thy flower
And the greeting mute
Of thy bough's salute
To the stranger who seeks thy bower.

"Oh! Abyssinian tree,
How the traveller blesses thee,
When the night no moon allows,
And the sunset hour is near,
And thou bend'st thy boughs
To kiss his brows,
Saying, 'Come, rest thee here.'
Oh! Abyssinian tree,
Thus bow thy head to me!"

In the burden of this song the companions of the young Nubian joined; and we heard the words, "Oh! Abyssinian tree," dying away on the breeze, long after the whole group had been lost to our eyes.

Whether, in the new arrangement which I had made for our voyage, any motive, besides those which I professed, had a share, I can scarcely, even myself—so bewildered were then my feelings—determine. But no sooner had the current borne us away from all human dwellings, and we were alone on the waters, with not a soul near, than I felt how closely such solitude draws hearts together, and how much more we seemed to belong to each other, than when there were eyes around us

The same feeling, but without the same sense of its danger, was manifest in every look and word of Alethe. The consciousness of the one great effort which she had made appeared to have satisfied her heart on the score of duty—while the devotedness with which she saw I attended to her every wish, was felt with all that trusting gratitude which, in woman, is the day-spring of love. She was, therefore, happy, innocently happy; and the confiding, and even affectionate, unreserve of her manner, while it rendered my trust more sacred, made it also far more difficult.

It was only, however, upon subjects unconnected with our situation or fate, that she yielded to such interchange of thought, or that her voice ventured to answer mine. The moment I alluded to the destiny that awaited us, all her cheerfulness fled, and she became saddened and silent. When I described to her the beauty of my own native land—its founts of inspiration and fields of glory—her eyes sparkled with sympathy, and sometimes even softened into fondness. But when I ventured to whisper, that, in that glorious country, a life full of love and liberty awaited her; when I proceeded to contrast the adoration and bliss she might command, with the gloomy austerities of the life to which she was hastening—it was like the coming of a sudden cloud over a summer sky. Her head sunk, as she listened;—I waited in vain for an answer; and when, half playfully reproaching her for this silence, I stooped to take her hand, I could feel the warm tears fast falling over it.

But even this—feeble as was the hope it held out—was still a glimpse of happiness. Though it foreboded that I should lose her, it also whispered that I was loved. Like that lake, in the land of Roses, whose waters are half-sweet, half-bitter, I felt my fate to be a compound of bliss and pain—but its very pain well worth all ordinary bliss.

And thus did the hours of that night pass along; while every moment shortened our happy dream, and the current seemed to flow with a swifter pace than any that ever yet hurried to the sea. Not a feature of the whole scene but lives, at this moment, freshly in my memory;—the broken starlight on the water;—the rippling sound of the boat, as, without oar or sail, it went, like a thing of enchantment, down the stream;—the scented fire, burning beside us upon the deck, and then that face, on which its light fell, revealing, at every moment, some new charm—some blush or look, more beautiful than the last!

Often, while I sat gazing, forgetful of all else, in this world, our boat, left wholly to itself, would drive from its course, and bearing us away to the bank, get entangled in the water flowers, or be caught in some eddy, ere I perceived where we were. Once, too, when the rustling of my oar among the flowers, had startled away from the bank some wild antelopes, that had stolen, at that still hour, to drink of the Nile, what an emblem did I think it of the young heart then beside me—tasting, for the first time, of hope and love, and so soon alas, to be scared from their sweetness for ever!

CHAPTER XV.

The night was now far advanced—the bend of our course towards the left, and the closing in of the eastern hills upon the river, gave warning of our approach to the hermit's dwelling. Every minute now appeared like the last of existence; and I felt a sinking of despair at my heart, which would have been intolerable, had not a resolution that suddenly, and as if by inspiration, occurred to me, presented a glimpse of hope, which, in some degree, calmed my feelings.

Much as I had, all my life, despised hypocrisy—the very sect I had embraced being chiefly recommended to me by the war they continued to wage upon the cant of all others—it was, nevertheless, in hypocrisy that I now scrupled not to take refuge from that calamity which to me was far worse than either shame or death, my separation from Alethe. In my despair I adopted the humiliating plan—deeply humiliating as I felt it to be, even amid the joy with which I welcomed it—of offering myself to this hermit, as a convert to his faith, and thus becoming the fellow-disciple of Alethe under his care

From the moment I resolved upon this plan my spirit felt lightened. Though having fully before my eyes the mean labyrinth of imposture into which it would lead me, I thought of nothing but the chance of our continuing still together. In this hope, all pride, all philosophy, was forgotten, and every thing seemed tolerable, but the prospect of losing her.

Thus resolved, it was with somewhat less reluctant feelings that I now undertook, at the anxious desire of my companion, to ascertain the site of that well-known mountain in the neighbourhood of which the anchoret's dwelling lay. We had already passed one or two stupendous rocks, which stood, detached, like fortresses, over the river's brink, and which in some degree corresponded with the description on the leaf. So little was there of life now stirring along the shores, that I had begun almost to despair of any assistance from inquiry, when, on looking to the western bank, I saw a boatman among the sedges, towing his small boat, with some difficulty, up the current. Hailing him as we passed, I asked,—"Where stands the Mountain of the Birds?"—and he had hardly time, as he pointed above us, to answer "There," when we perceived that we were just then entering into the shadow, which this mighty rock flings across the whole of the flood

In a few moments we had reached the mouth of the ravine, of which the Mountain of the Birds forms one of the sides, and through which the scanty canal from the Nile flows. At the sight of this awful chasm, within some of whose dreary recesses (if we had rightly interpreted the leaf) the dwelling of the Solitary was to be found, our voices sunk at once into a low whisper, while Alethe turned round to me with a look of awe and eagerness, as if doubtful whether I had not already disappeared from her side. A quick movement, however, of her hand towards the ravine, told too plainly that her purpose was still unchanged. Immediately checking, therefore, with my oars, the career of my boat, I succeeded, after no small exertion, in turning it out of the current of the river, and steering into this bleak and stagnant canal.

Our transition from life and bloom to the very depth of desolation was immediate. While the water on one side of the ravine lay buried in shadow, the white skeleton-like crags of the other stood aloft in the pale glare of moonlight. The sluggish stream through which we moved yielded sullenly to the oar, and the shriek of a few water birds, which we had roused from their fastnesses, was succeeded by a silence, so dead and awful, that our lips seemed afraid to disturb it by a breath; and half-whispered exclamations, "How dreary!"—"How dismal!"—were almost the only words exchanged between us.

We had proceeded for some time through this gloomy defile, when, at a short distance before us, among the rocks upon which the moonlight fell, we could perceive, on a ledge elevated but a little above the canal, a small hut or cave, which, from a tree or two planted around it, had some appearance of being the abode of a human being. "This, then," thought I, "is the home to which she is destined!"—A chill of despair came again over my heart, and the oars, as I sat gazing, lay motionless in my hands.

I found Alethe, too, whose eyes had caught the same object, drawing closer to my side than she had yet ventured. Laying her hand agitatedly upon mine, "We must here," said she, "part for ever." I turned to her as she spoke; there was a tenderness, a despondency, in her countenance, that at once saddened and inflamed my soul. "Part!" I exclaimed, passionately—"No!—the same God shall receive us both. Thy faith, Alethe, shall, from this hour, be mine; and I will live and die in this desert with thee!"

Her surprise, her delight, at these words was like a momentary delirium. The wild, anxious smile, with which she looked into my face, as if to ascertain whether she had indeed heard my words aright, bespoke a happiness too much for reason to bear. At length, the fulness of her heart found relief in tears; and, murmuring forth an incoherent blessing on my name, she let her head fall languidly and powerlessly on my arm. The light from our boat-fire shone upon her face. I saw her eyes, which she had closed for a moment, again opening upon me with the same tenderness, and—merciful Providence, how I remember that moment!—was on the point of bending down my lips towards hers, when, suddenly, in the air above us, as if coming direct from heaven, there burst forth a strain of choral music, that with its solemn sweetness filled the whole valley.

Breaking away from my caress at these supernatural sounds, the maiden threw herself trembling upon her knees, and, not daring to look up, exclaimed wildly, "My mother, oh my mother!"

It was the Christian's morning hymn that we heard;—the same as I learned afterwards, that, on their high terrace at Memphis, she had been taught by her mother to sing to the rising sun.

Scarcely less startled than my companion, I looked up, and saw, at the very summit of the rock above us, a light, appearing to come from a small opening or window, through which those sounds likewise, that had appeared to me so supernatural, issued. There could be no doubt, that we had now found—if not the dwelling of the anchorite—at least, the haunt of some of the Christian brotherhood of these rocks, by whose assistance we could not fail to find the place of his retreat.

The agitation, into which Alethe had been thrown by the first burst of that psalmody, soon yielded to the softening recollections which it brought back; and a calm came over her brow, such as it had never before worn, since we met. She seemed to feel as if she had now reached her destined haven and hailed, as the voice of heaven itself, those solemn sounds by which she was welcomed to it.

In her tranquillity, however, I was very far from yet sympathising. Full of impatience to learn all that awaited her as well as myself, I pushed our boat close to the base of the rock, so as to bring it directly under that lighted window on the summit, to explore my way up to which was now my immediate object. Having hastily received my instructions from Alethe, and made her repeat again the name of the Christian whom we sought, I sprang upon the bank, and was not long in discovering a sort of path, or stairway, cut rudely out of the rock, and leading, as I found, by easy windings, up the steep.

After ascending for some time, I arrived at a level space or ledge, which the hand of labour had succeeded in converting into a garden, and which was planted, here and there, with fig-trees and palms. Around it, too, I could perceive, through the glimmering light, a number of small caves or grottos, into some of which, human beings might find an entrance; while others appeared of no larger dimensions than those tombs of the Sacred Birds which are seen ranged around Lake Mœris.

I was still, I found, but half-way up the ascent, nor was there visible any further means of continuing my course, as the mountain from hence rose, almost perpendicularly, like a wall. At length, however, on exploring more closely, I discovered behind the shade of a fig-tree, a large ladder of wood, resting firmly against the rock, and affording an easy and safe ascent up the steep.

Having ascertained thus far, I again descended to the boat for Alethe, whom I found trembling already at her short solitude; and having led her up the stairway to this quiet garden, left her lodged there securely, amid its holy science, while I pursued my way upward to the light upon the rock.

At the top of the long ladder I found myself on another ledge or platform, somewhat smaller than the first, but planted, in the same manner, with trees, and, as I could perceive by the mingled light of morning and the moon, embellished with flowers. I was now near the summit;—there remained but another short ascent, and, as a ladder against the rock, supplied, as before, the means of scaling it, I was in a few minutes at the opening from which the light issued.

I had ascended gently, as well from a feeling of awe at the whole scene, as from an unwillingness to disturb rudely the rites on which I intruded. My approach, therefore, being unheard, an opportunity was, for some moments, afforded me of observing the group within, before my appearance at the window was discovered.

In the middle of the apartment, which seemed to have been once a Pagan oratory, there was collected an assembly of about seven or eight persons, some male, some female, kneeling in silence round a small altar;—while, among them, as if presiding over their solemn ceremony, stood an aged man, who, at the moment of my arrival, was presenting to one of the female worshippers an alabaster cup, which she applied, with profound reverence, to her lips. The venerable countenance of the minister, as he pronounced a short prayer over her head, wore an expression of profound feeling that showed how wholly he was absorbed in that rite; and when she had drank of the cup—which I saw had engraven on its side the image of a head, with a glory round it—the holy man bent down and kissed her forehead.

After this parting salutation, the whole group rose silently from their knees; and it was then, for the first time, that by a cry of terror from one of the women, the appearance of a stranger at the window was discovered. The whole assembly seemed startled and alarmed, except him, that superior person, who, advancing from the altar, with an unmoved look, raised the latch of the door adjoining to the window, and admitted me.

There was, in this old man's features, a mixture of elevation and sweetness, of simplicity and energy, which commanded at once attachment and homage; and half-hoping, half-fearing, to find in him the destined guardian of Alethe, I looked anxiously in his face, as I entered, and pronounced the name "Melanius!"—"Melanius is my name, young stranger," he answered; "and whether in friendship or in enmity thou comest, Melanius blesses thee." Thus saying, he made a sign with his right hand above my head, while, with involuntary respect, I bowed beneath the benediction.

"Let this volume," I replied, "answer for the peacefulness of my mission"—at the same time placing in his hands the copy of the Scriptures which had been his own gift to the mother of Alethe, and which her child now brought as the credential of her claims on his protection. At the sight of this sacred pledge, which he instantly recognized, the solemnity which had at first marked his reception of me, softened into tenderness. Thoughts of other times appeared to pass through his mind; and as, with a sigh of recollection, he took the book from my hands, some words on the outer leaf caught his eye. They were few—but contained, most probably, the last wishes of the dying Theora; for, as he read them over eagerly, I saw tears in his aged eyes. "The trust," he said, with a faltering voice, "is precious and sacred, and God will enable, I hope, his servant to guard it faithfully."

During this short dialogue, the other persons of the assembly had departed—being, as I afterwards learned, brethren from the neighbouring bank of the Nile, who came thus secretly before daybreak, to join in worshipping their God. Fearful lest their descent down the rock might alarm Alethe, I hurried briefly over the few words of explanation that remained, and leaving the venerable Christian to follow at his leisure, hastened anxiously down to rejoin the young maiden.

CHAPTER XVI.

Melanius was one of the first of those zealous Christians of Egypt, who, following the recent example of the hermit, Paul, bade farewell to all the comforts of social existence, and betook themselves to a life of contemplation in the desert. Less selfish, however, in his piety, than most of these ascetics, Melanius forgot not the world in leaving it. He knew that man was not born to live wholly for himself; that his relation to human kind was that of the link to the chain, and that even his solitude should be turned to the advantage of others. In flying, therefore, from the din and disturbance of life, he sought not to place himself beyond the reach of its sympathies, but selected a retreat where he could combine all the advantages of solitude with those opportunities of being useful to his fellow-men, which a neighbourhood to their populous haunts would afford.

That taste for the gloom of subterranean recesses, which the race of Misraim inherit from their Ethiopian ancestors, had, by hollowing out all Egypt into caverns and crypts, supplied these Christian anchorets with an ample choice of retreats. Accordingly, some found a shelter in the grottos of Elethya;—others, among the royal tombs of the Thebaid. In the middle of the Seven Valleys, where the sun rarely shines, a few have fixed their dim and melancholy retreat; while others have sought the neighbourhood of the red Lakes of Nitria, and there, like those Pagan solitaries of old, who fixed their dwelling among the palm-trees near the Dead Sea, pass their whole lives in musing amidst the sterility of nature, and seem to find, in her desolation, peace.

It was on one of those mountains of the Said, to the east of the river, that Melanius, as we have seen, chose his place of seclusion—having all the life and fertility of the Nile on one side, and the lone, dismal barrenness of the desert on the other. Half way down this mountain, where it impends over the ravine, he found a series of caves or grottos dug out of the rock, which had, in other times, ministered to some purpose of mystery, but whose use had long been forgotten, and their recesses abandoned.

To this place, after the banishment of his great master, Origen, Melanius, with a few faithful followers, retired, and there, by the example of his innocent life, as well as by his fervid eloquence, succeeded in winning crowds of converts to his faith. Placed, as he was, in the neighbourhood of the rich city, Antinoe, though he mingled not with its multitude, his name and his fame were ever among them, and to all who sought after instruction or consolation, the cell of the hermit was always open.

Notwithstanding the rigid abstinence of his own habits, he was yet careful to provide for the comforts of others. Content with a rude pallet of straw, himself, he had always for the stranger a less homely resting place. From his grotto, the wayfaring and the indigent never went unrefreshed; and, with the aid of some of his brethren, he had formed gardens along the ledges of the mountain, which gave an air of life and cheerfulness to his rocky dwelling, and supplied him with the chief necessaries of such a climate—fruit and shade.

Though the acquaintance he had formed with the mother of Alethe, during the short period of her attendance at the school of Origen, was soon interrupted, and never afterwards renewed, the interest which he had then taken in her fate was far too lively to be forgotten. He had seen the zeal with which her young heart welcomed instruction; and the thought that so promising a candidate for heaven should have relapsed into idolatry, came often, with disquieting apprehension, over his mind.

It was, therefore, with true pleasure, that, but a year or two before Theora's death, he had learned by a private communication from her, transmitted through a Christian embalmer of Memphis, that "not only had her own heart taken root in the faith, but that a new bud had flowered with the same divine hope; and that, ere long, he might see them both transplanted to the desert."

The coming, therefore, of Alethe was far less a surprise to him, than her coming thus alone was a shock and a sorrow; and the silence of their first meeting showed how painfully both remembered that the tie which had brought them together was no longer of this world—that the hand, which should have been then joined with theirs, was now mouldering in the tomb. I now saw, that even religion like his was not proof against the sadness of mortality. For, as the old man put aside the ringlets from her forehead, and contemplated in that clear countenance the reflection of what her mother had been, there mingled a mournfulness with his piety, as he said, "Heaven rest her soul!" which showed how little even the certainty of a heaven for those we love can reconcile us to the pain of having lost them on earth.

The full light of day had now risen upon the desert, and our host, reminded, by the faint looks of Alethe, of the many anxious hours we had passed without sleep, proposed that we should seek, in the chambers of the rock, such rest as a hermit's dwelling could offer. Pointing to one of the largest of these openings, as he addressed me—"Thou wilt find," he said, "in that grotto a bed of fresh doum leaves, and may the consciousness of having protected the orphan sweeten thy sleep!"

I felt how dearly this praise had been earned, and already almost repented of having deserved it There was a sadness in the countenance of Alethe, as I took leave of her, to which the forebodings of my own heart but too faithfully responded; nor could I help fearing, as her hand parted lingeringly from mine, that I had, by this sacrifice, placed her beyond my reach for ever.

Having lighted for me a lamp, which, in these recesses, even at noon, is necessary, the holy man led me to the entrance of the grotto. And here, I blush to say, my career of hypocrisy began. With the sole view of obtaining another glance at Alethe, I turned humbly to solicit the benediction of the Christian, and, having conveyed to her, while bending reverently down, as much of the deep feelings of my soul as looks could express, I then, with a desponding spirit, hurried into the cavern.

A short passage led me to the chamber within—the walls of which I found covered, like those of the grottos of Lycopolis, with paintings, which, though executed long ages ago, looked as fresh as if their colours were but laid on yesterday. They were, all of them, representations of rural and domestic scenes; and, in the greater number, the melancholy imagination of the artist had called in, as usual, the presence of Death, to throw his shadow over the picture.

My attention was particularly drawn to one series of subjects, throughout the whole of which the same group—consisting of a youth, a maiden, and two aged persons, who appeared to be the father and mother of the girl—were represented in all the details of their daily life. The looks and attitudes of the young people denoted that they were lovers:

and, sometimes, they were seen sitting under a canopy of flowers, with their eyes fixed on each other's faces, as though they could never look away; sometimes, they appeared walking along the banks of the Nile,—

> ——— on one of those sweet nights
> When Isis, the pure star of lovers, lights
> Her bridal crescent o'er the holy stream-
> When wandering youths and maidens watch her beam,
> And number o'er the nights she hath to run,
> Ere she again embrace her bridegroom sun.

Through all these scenes of endearment the two elder persons stood by;—their calm countenances touched with a share of that bliss, in whose perfect light the young lovers were basking. Thus far, all was happiness;—but the sad lesson of mortality was yet to come. In the last picture of the series, one of the figures was missing. It was that of the young maiden, who had disappeared from among them. On the brink of a dark lake stood the three who remained; while a boat, just departing for the City of the Dead, told too plainly the end of their dream of happiness.

This memorial of a sorrow of other times—of a sorrow, ancient as death itself—was not wanting to deepen the melancholy of my mind, or to add to the weight of the many bodings that pressed upon it.

After a night, as it seemed, of anxious and unsleeping thought, I rose from my bed, and returned to the garden. I found the Christian alone—seated, under the shade of one of his trees, at a small table, on which there lay a volume unrolled, while a beautiful antelope was sleeping at his feet. Struck by the contrast which he presented to those haughty priests, whom I had seen surrounded by the pomp and gorgeousness of temples, "Is this, then," thought I, "the faith before which the world now trembles—its temple the desert, its treasury a book, and its High Priest the solitary dweller of the rock?"

He had prepared for me a simple but hospitable repast, of which fruits from his own garden, the white bread of Olyra, and the juice of the honey-cane, formed the most costly luxuries. His manner to me was even more cordial and fatherly than before; but the absence of Alethe, and, still more, the ominous reserve, with which he not only, himself, refrained from all mention of her name, but eluded the few inquiries, by which I sought to lead to it, seemed to confirm all the apprehensions I had felt in parting from her.

She had acquainted him, it was evident, with the whole history of our flight. My reputation as a philosopher—my desire to become a Christian—all was already known to the zealous anchoret, and the subject of my conversion was the very first on which he entered. Oh, pride of philosophy, how wert thou then humbled, and with what shame did I stand in the presence of that venerable man, not daring to let my eyes encounter his, while, with unhesitating trust in the sincerity of my intention, he welcomed me to a participation of his holy hope, and imprinted the Kiss of Charity on my infidel brow!

Embarrassed as I could not but feel by the humiliating consciousness of hypocrisy, I was even still more perplexed by my almost total ignorance of the real tenets of the faith to which I professed myself a convert. Abashed and confused, and with a heart sick at its own deceit, I listened to the animated and eloquent gratulations of the Christian, as though they were words in a dream, without any link or meaning; nor could disguise, but by the mockery of a reverent bow, at every pause, the total want of self-possession, and even of speech, under which I laboured.

A few minutes more of such trial, and I must have avowed my imposture. But the holy man perceived my embarrassment;—and, whether mistaking it for awe, or knowing it to be ignorance, relieved me from my perplexity by, at once, changing the theme. Having gently awakened his antelope from its sleep, "You have doubtless," he said, "heard of my brother-anchoret, Paul, who, from his cave in the marble mountains, near the Red Sea, sends hourly the blessed 'sacrifice of thanksgiving' to heaven. Of *his* walks, they tell me, a lion is the companion; but, for me," he added, with a playful and significant smile, "who try my powers of taming but on the gentler animals, this feeble child of the desert is a far fitter playmate." Then, taking his staff, and putting the time-worn volume which he had been perusing into a large goat-skin pouch, that hung by his side, "I will now," said he, "conduct thee over my rocky kingdom, that thou mayest see in what drear and barren places that 'sweet fruit of the spirit' Peace, may be gathered."

To speak of peace to a heart throbbing, as mine did, at that moment, was like talking of some distant harbour to the mariner sinking at sea. In vain did I look around for some sign of Alethe;—in vain make an effort even to utter her name. Consciousness of my own deceit, as well as a fear of awakening in the mind of Melanius any suspicion that might tend to frustrate my only hope, threw a fetter over my spirit, and checked my tongue. In humble silence, therefore, I followed; while the cheerful old man, with slow, but firm step, ascended the rock, by the same ladders which I had mounted on the preceding night.

During the time when the Decian Persecution was raging, many Christians, as he told me, of the neighbourhood, had taken refuge under his protection, in these grottos; and the small chapel upon the summit, where I had found his flock at prayer, was, in those awful times of suffering, their usual place of retreat, where, by drawing up those ladders, they were enabled to secure themselves from pursuit.

The view, from the top of the rock, extending on either side, embraced the two extremes of fertility and desolation; nor could the Epicurean and the Anchoret, who now stood gazing from that height, be at any loss to indulge their respective tastes, between the living luxuriance of the world on one side, and the dead, pulseless repose of the desert on the other. When we turned to the river, what a picture of animation presented itself! Near us to the south, were the graceful colonnades of Antinoe, its proud, populous streets, and triumphal monuments. On the opposite shore, rich plains, all teeming with cultivation to the water's edge, seemed to offer up, as from verdant altars, their fruits to the sun; while, beneath us, the Nile,

> — the glorious stream,
> That late between the banks was seen to glide
> With shrines and marble cities, on each side,
> Glittering, like jewels strung along a chain—
> Had now sent forth its waters, and o'er plain
> And valley, like a giant from his bed
> Rising with outstretch'd limbs, superbly spread.

From this scene, on one side of the mountain, we had but to turn round our eyes to the other, and it was as if Nature herself had become suddenly extinct;—a wide waste of sands, bleak and interminable, wearying out the sun with its sameness of desolation;—black, burnt-up rocks, that stood as barriers, at which life stopped;—while the only signs of animation, past or present, were the foot-prints, here and there, of an antelope or ostrich, or the bones of dead camels, as they lay whitening at a distance, marking out the track of the caravans over the waste.

After listening, while he contrasted, in a few eloquent words, the two regions of life and death on whose confines we stood, I again descended with my guide to the garden that we had left. From thence, turning into a path along the mountain-side, he led me to another row of grottos, facing the desert, which had been once, he said, the abode of these brethren in Christ, who had fled with him to this solitude from the crowded world—but which death had, within a few short months, rendered tenantless. A cross of red stone, and a few faded trees, were the only traces these solitaries had left behind.

A silence of some minutes succeeded, while we descended to the edge of the canal; and I saw opposite, among the rocks, that solitary cave, which had so chilled me with its aspect on the preceding night. Beside the bank we found one of those rustic boats, which the Egyptians construct of planks of white thorn, bound rudely together with bands of papyrus. Placing ourselves in this boat, and rather impelling than rowing it across, we made our way through the foul and shallow flood, and landed directly under the site of the cave.

This dwelling was situated, as I have already mentioned, on a ledge of the rock; and, being provided with a sort of window, or aperture, to admit the light of heaven, was accounted, I found, far more cheerful than the grottos on the other side of the ravine. But there was a dreariness in the whole region around, to which light only lent additional horror. The dead whiteness of the rocks, as they stood, like ghosts, in the sunshine;—that melancholy pool, half-lost in the sands; all gave to my mind the idea of a wasting world. To dwell in a place so desolate seemed to me a living death; and when the Christian, as we entered the cave, said, "Here is to be thy home," prepared as I had been for the worst, all my resolution gave way;—every feeling of disappointed passion and humbled pride, which had been gathering round my heart for the last few hours, found a vent at once, and I burst into tears.

Accustomed to human weakness and, perhaps guessing at some of the sources of mine, the good Hermit, without appearing to take any notice of this emotion, proceeded to expatiate, with a cheerful air, on, what he called, the comforts of my dwelling. Sheltered from the dry, burning wind of the south, my porch would inhale, he said, the fresh breeze of the Dog-star. Fruits from his own mountain-garden should furnish my repast. The well of the neighbouring rock would supply my beverage; and "here," he continued—lowering his voice into a more solemn tone, as he placed upon the table the volume which he had brought—"here, my son, is that 'well of living waters,' in which alone thou wilt find lasting refreshment or peace!" Thus saying, he descended the rock to his boat; and, after a few plashes of his oar had died upon my ear, the solitude and silence that reigned around me was complete.

CHAPTER XVII.

What a fate was mine!—but a few weeks since, presiding over that gay Festival of the Garden, with all the luxuries of existence tributary in my train; and now—self-humbled into a solitary outcast—the hypocritical pupil of a Christian anchoret—without even the excuse of religious fanaticism, or any other madness, but that of love, wild love, to extenuate my fall! Were there a hope that by this humiliating waste of existence, I might purchase now and then a momentary glimpse of Alethe, even the depths of the desert, with such a chance, would be welcome. But to live—and live thus—*without* her, was a misery which I neither foresaw nor could endure.

Hating even to look upon the den to which I was doomed, I hurried out into the air, and found my way, along the rocks, to the desert. The sun was going down, with that blood-red hue, which he so often wears, in this climate, at his setting. I saw the sands, stretching out, like a sea to the horizon, as if their waste extended to the very verge of the world—and, in the bitterness of my feelings, rejoiced to see so large a portion of creation rescued, even by this barren liberty, from the encroaching grasp of man. The thought seemed to relieve my wounded pride, and, as I wandered over the dim and boundless solitude, to be thus free even amidst blight and desolation, appeared to me a blessing.

The only living thing I saw was a restless swallow, whose wings were of the same hue with the gray sands over which he fluttered. "Why (thought I) may not the mind, like this bird, partake of the colour of the desert, and sympathise in its austerity, its freedom, and its calm?"—thus vainly endeavouring, between despondence and defiance, to encounter with some degree of fortitude what yet my heart sickened to contemplate. But the effort was unavailing. Overcome by that vast solitude, whose repose was not the slumber of peace, but rather the sullen and burning silence of hate, I felt my spirit give way, and even love itself yielded to despair.

Taking my seat on a fragment of a rock, and covering my eyes with my hands, I made an effort to shut out the overwhelming prospect. But all in vain—it was still before me, with every additional horror that fancy could suggest; and when, again looking forth, I beheld the last red ray of the sun, shooting across the melancholy and lifeless waste, it appeared to me like the light of that comet which once desolated this world, and thus luridly shone out over the ruin that it had made!

Appalled by my own gloomy imaginations, I turned towards the ravine; and, notwithstanding the disgust with which I had fled from my dwelling, was not ill pleased to find my way, over the rocks, to it again. On approaching the cave, to my astonishment, I saw a light within. At such a moment, any vestige of life was welcome, and I hailed the unexpected appearance with pleasure. On entering, however, I found the chamber all as lonely as I had left it. The light I had seen came from a lamp that burned brightly on the table; beside it was unfolded the volume which Melanius had brought, and upon the open leaves—oh, joy and surprise—lay the well-known cross of Alethe!

What hand, but her own, could have prepared this reception for me?—The very thought sent a hope into my heart, before which all despondency fled. Even the gloom of the desert was forgotten, and my rude cave at once brightened into a bower. She had here reminded me, by this sacred memorial, of the vow which I had pledged to her under the Hermit's rock; and I now scrupled not to reiterate the same daring promise, though conscious that through hypocrisy alone I could fulfil it.

Eager to prepare myself for my task of imposture, I sat down to the volume, which I now found to be the Hebrew Scriptures; and the first sentence, on which my eyes fell, was—"The Lord hath commanded the blessing, even Life for evermore!" Startled by these words, in which it appeared to me as if the Spirit of my dream had again pronounced his assuring prediction, I raised my eyes from the page, and repeated the sentence over and over, as if to try whether in these sounds there lay any charm or spell, to re-awaken that faded illusion in my soul. But, no—the rank frauds of the Memphian priesthood had dispelled all my trust in the promises of religion. My heart had again relapsed into its gloom of scepticism, and, to the word of "Life," the only answer it sent back was, "Death!"

Being impatient, however, to possess myself of the elements of a faith, upon which—whatever it might promise for hereafter—I felt that all my happiness here depended, I turned over the pages with an earnestness and avidity, such as never even the most favourite of my studies had awakened in me. Though, like all who seek but the surface of learning, I flew desultorily over the leaves, lighting only on the more prominent and shining points, I yet found myself, even in this undisciplined career, arrested, at every page, by the awful, the supernatural sublimity, the alternate melancholy and grandeur of the images that crowded upon me.

I had, till now, known the Hebrew theology but through the platonising refinement of Philo;—as, in like manner, for my knowledge of the Christian doctrine I was indebted to my brother Epicureans, Lucian and Celsus. Little, therefore, was my mind prepared for the simple majesty, the high tone of inspiration—the poetry, in short, of heaven that breathed throughout these oracles. Could admiration have kindled faith, I should, that night, have been a believer; so elevated, so awed, was my imagination by that wonderful book—its warnings of wo, its announcements of glory, and its unrivalled strains of adoration and sorrow.

Hour after hour, with the same eager and desultory curiosity, did I turn over the leaves;—and when, at length, I lay down to rest, my fancy was still haunted by impressions it had received. I went again through the various scenes of which I had read; again called up, in sleep, the bright images that had passed before me; and when awakened at early dawn by the solemn Hymn from the chapel, imagined that I was still listening to the sound of the winds, sighing mournfully through the harps of Israel on the willows.

Startling from my bed, I hurried out upon the rock, with a hope that, among the tones of that morning choir, I might be able to distinguish the sweet voice of Alethe. But the strain had ceased;—I caught only the last notes of the Hymn, as, echoing up that lonely valley, they died away into the silence of the desert.

With the first glimpse of light I was again eagerly at my study, and, notwithstanding the frequent distraction both of my thoughts and looks towards the distant, half-seen grottos of the Anchoret, continued my task with unabating perseverance throughout the day. Still alive, however, only to the eloquence, the poetry of what I studied, of its claims to authority, as a history, I never once paused to consider. My fancy alone being interested by it, to fancy alone I referred all that it contained; and, passing rapidly from annals to prophecy, from narration to song, regarded the whole but as a tissue of oriental allegories, in which the deep melancholy of Egyptian associations was interwoven with the rich and sensual imagery of the East.

Towards sunset I saw the venerable Hermit, on his way, across the canal, to my cave. Though he was accompanied only by his graceful antelope, which came snuffing the wild air of the desert, as if scenting its home, I felt his visit, even thus, to be a most welcome relief. It was the hour, he said, of his evening ramble up the mountain—of his accustomed visit to those cisterns of the rock, from which he drew nightly his most precious beverage. While he spoke, I observed in his hand one of those earthen cups, in which it is the custom of the inhabitants of the wilderness to collect the fresh dew among the rocks. Having proposed that I should accompany him in his walk, he proceeded to lead me, in the direction of the desert, up the side of the mountain that rose above my dwelling and which formed the southern wall or screen of the defile.

Near the summit we found a seat, where the old man paused to rest. It commanded a full view over the desert, and was by the side of one of those hollows in the rock, those natural reservoirs, in which are treasured the dews of night for the refreshment of the dwellers in the wilderness. Having learned from me how far I had advanced in my study—"In yonder light," said he, pointing to a small cloud in the east, which had been formed on the horizon by the haze of the desert, and was now faintly reflecting the splendours of sunset—"in the midst of that light stands Mount Sinai, of whose glory thou hast read; upon whose summit was the scene of one of those awful revelations, in which the Almighty has renewed from time to time his communication with Man, and kept alive the remembrance of his own Providence in this world."

After a pause, as if absorbed in the immensity of the subject, the holy man continued his sublime theme. Looking back to the earliest annals of time, he showed how constantly every relapse of the human race into idolatry has been followed by some manifestation of Divine power, chastening the strong and proud by punishment, and winning back the humble by love. It was to preserve, he said, unextinguished upon earth, that great and vital truth—the Creation of the world by one Supreme Being, that God chose, from among the nations, an humble and enslaved race—that he brought them out of their captivity "on eagles' wings," and, still surrounding every step of their course with miracles, has placed them before the eyes of all succeeding generations, as the depositories of his will and the ever-during memorials of his power.

Passing, then, in review the long train of inspired interpreters, whose pens and whose tongues were made the echoes of the Divine voice, he traced throughout the events of successive ages, the gradual unfolding of the dark scheme of Providence—darkness without, but all light and glory within. The glimpses of a coming redemption, visible even through the wrath of Heaven;—the long series of prophecy through which this hope runs, burning and alive, like a spark along a chain;—the slow and merciful preparation of the hearts of mankind for the great trial of their faith and obedience that was at hand, not only by miracles that appealed to the living, but by prophecies launched into the future to carry conviction to the yet unborn;—"through all these glorious and beneficent gradations we may track," said he, "the manifest footsteps of a Creator, advancing to his grand, ultimate end—the salvation of his creatures."

After some hours devoted to these holy instructions, we returned to the ravine, and Melanius left me at my cave; praying, as he parted from me—with a benevolence which I but ill, alas! deserved—that my soul might, under these lessons, be "as a watered garden," and, ere long, "bear fruit unto life eternal."

Next morning, I was again at my study, and even more eager in the awakening task than before. With the commentary of the Hermit freshly in my memory, I again read through, with attention, the Book of the Law. But in vain did I seek the promise of immortality in its pages. "It tells me," said I, "of a God coming down to earth, but of the ascent of Man to heaven it speaks not. The rewards, the punishments it announces, lie all on this side of the grave; nor did even the Omnipotent offer to his own chosen servants a hope beyond the impassable limits of this world. Where, then, is the salvation of which the Christian spoke? or, if Death be at the root of the faith, can Life spring out of it?"

Again, in the bitterness of disappointment, did I mock at my own willing self-delusion—again rail at the arts of that traitress, Fancy, ever ready, like the Delilah of this wondrous book, to steal upon the slumbers of Reason, and deliver him up, shorn and powerless, to his foes. If deception, thought I, be necessary, at least let me not practice it on myself;—in the desperate alternative before me, let me rather be even hypocrite than dupe.

These self-accusing reflections, cheerless as they rendered my task, did not abate, for a single moment, my industry in pursuing it. I read on and on, with a sort of sullen apathy, neither charmed by style, nor transported by imagery—the fatal blight in my heart having communicated itself to my imagination and taste. The curses and the blessings, the glory and the ruin, which the historian recorded, and the prophet had predicted, seemed all of this world—all temporal and earthly. That mortality, of which the fountain-head had tasted, tinged the whole stream; and when I read the words, "all are of the dust, and all turn to dust again," a feeling, like the wind of the desert, came witheringly over me. Love, Beauty, Glory, every thing most bright and worshipped upon earth, appeared to be sinking before my eyes, under this dreadful doom, into one general mass of corruption and silence.

Possessed by the image of desolation I had thus called up, I laid my head upon the book, in a paroxysm of despair Death, in all his most ghastly varieties, passed before me; and I had continued thus for some time, as under the influence of a fearful vision, when the touch of a hand upon my shoulder roused me. Looking up, I saw the Anchoret standing by my side;—his countenance beaming with that sublime tranquillity, which a hope, beyond this earth, alone can bestow. How I did envy him!

We again took our way to the seat upon the mountain—the gloom within my own mind making every thing around more gloomy. Forgetting my hypocrisy in my feelings, I proceeded at once to make an avowal to him of all the doubts and fears which my study of the morning had awakened.

"Thou art yet, my son," he answered, "but on the threshhold of our faith. Thou hast seen but the first rudiments of the Divine plan;—its full and consummate perfection hath not yet opened upon thy mind. However glorious that manifestation of Divinity on Mount Sinai, it was but the forerunner of another, still more glorious, which, in the fulness of time, was to burst upon the world; when all, that before had seemed dim and incomplete, was to be perfected, and the promises, shadowed out by the 'spirit of prophecy,' realized;—when the seal of silence, under which the future had so long lain, was to be broken, and the glad tidings of life and immortality proclaimed to the world!"

Observing my features brighten at these words, the pious man continued. Anticipating some of the holy knowledge that was in store for me, he traced, through all its wonders and mercies, the great work of Redemption, dwelling in detail upon every miraculous circumstance connected with it—the exalted nature of the Being, by whose ministry it was accomplished, the noblest and first created of the Sons of God, inferior only, to the one, self-existent Father;—the mysterious incarnation of this heavenly messenger;—the miracles that authenticated his divine mission;—the example of obedience to God and love to man, which he set, as a shining light, before the world for ever;—and, lastly and chiefly, his death and resurrection, by which the covenant of mercy was sealed, and "life and immortality brought to light."

"Such," continued the Hermit, "was the Mediator, promised through all time, to 'make reconciliation for iniquity,' to change death into life, and bring 'healing on his wings' to a darkened world. Such was the last crowning dispensation of that God of benevolence, in whose hands sin and death are but instruments of everlasting good; and who, through apparent evil and temporary retribution, bringing all things 'out of darkness into his marvellous light,' proceeds watchfully and unchangingly to the great, final object of his providence—the restoration of the whole human race to purity and happiness!"

With a mind astonished, if not touched, by these discourses, I returned to my cave, and found the lamp, as before, ready lighted to receive me. The volume which I had been hitherto studying, was replaced by another, which lay open upon the table, with a branch of fresh palm between its leaves. Though I could not doubt to whose gentle and guardian hand I was indebted for this invisible watchfulness over my studies, there was yet a something in it, so like spiritual interposition, that it struck me with awe;—and never more than at this moment, when, on approaching the volume, I saw, as the light glistened over its silver letters, that it was the very Book of Life of which the Hermit had spoken!

The midnight hymn of the Christians had sounded through the valley, before I had yet raised my eyes from that sacred volume; and the second hour of the sun found me again over its pages.

CHAPTER XVIII.

In this mode of existence I had now passed some days;—my mornings devoted to reading, my nights to listening, under the wide canopy of heaven, to the holy eloquence of Melanius.

The perseverance with which I inquired, and the quickness with which I learned, soon succeeded in deceiving my benevolent instructor, who mistook curiosity for zeal, and knowledge for belief Alas! cold, and barren, and earthly was that knowledge—the word without the spirit, the shape without the life. Even when, as a relief from hypocrisy, I persuaded myself that I believed, it was but a brief delusion, a faith, whose hope crumbled at the touch—like the fruit of the desert-shrub, shining and empty!

But, though my soul was still dark, the good Hermit saw not into its depths. The very facility of my belief, which might have suggested some doubt of its sincerity, was but regarded, by his innocent zeal, as a more signal triumph of the truth. His own ingenuousness led him to a ready trust in others; and the examples of such conversion as that of the philosopher, Justin, who, during a walk by the sea-shore, received the light into his soul, had prepared him for illuminations of the spirit, even more rapid than mine.

During all this time, I neither saw nor heard of Alethe;—nor could my patience have endured through so long a privation, had not those mute vestiges of her presence, that welcomed me every night on my return, made me feel that I was still living under her gentle influence, and that her sympathy hung round every step of my progress. Once, too, when I ventured to speak her name to Melanius, though he answered not my inquiry, there was a smile, I thought, of promise upon his countenance, which love, far more alive than faith, was ready to interpret as it desired.

At length—it was on the sixth or seventh evening of my solitude, when I lay resting at the door of my cave, after the study of the day—I was startled by hearing my name called loudly from the opposite rocks; and looking up, saw, upon the cliff near the deserted grottos, Melanius and—oh! I *could not* doubt—my Alethe by his side!

Though I had never, since the first night of my return from the desert, ceased to flatter myself with the fancy that I was still living in her presence, the actual sight of her once more made me feel for what a long age we had been separated. She was clothed all in white, and, as she stood in the last remains of the sunshine, appeared to my too prophetic fancy like a parting spirit, whose last footsteps on earth that pure glory encircled.

With a delight only to be imagined, I saw them descend the rocks, and, placing themselves in the boat, proceed directly towards my cave. To disguise from Melanius the mutual delight with which we again met was impossible;—nor did Alethe even attempt to make a secret of her joy. Though blushing at her own happiness, as little could her frank nature conceal it, as the clear waters of Ethiopia can hide their gold. Every look, every word, bespoke a fulness of affection, to which, doubtful as I was of our tenure of happiness, I knew not how to respond.

I was not long, however, left ignorant of the bright fate that awaited me; but, as we wandered or rested among the rocks, learned every thing that had been arranged since our parting. She had made the Hermit, I found, acquainted with all that had passed between us; had told him, without reserve, every incident of our voyage—the avowals, the demonstrations of affection on one side, and the deep sentiment that gratitude had awakened on the other. Too wise to regard affections so natural with severity—knowing that they were of heaven, and but made evil by man—the good Hermit had heard of our attachment with pleasure; and, fully satisfied as to the honour and purity of my views, by the fidelity with which I had delivered my trust into his hands, saw, in my affection for the young orphan, but a providential resource against that friendless solitude in which his death must soon leave her.

As, listening eagerly, I collected these particulars from their discourse, I could hardly trust my ears. It seemed a happiness too great to be true, to be real; nor can words convey any idea of the joy, the shame, the wonder with which I listened, while the holy man himself declared that he awaited but the moment, when he should find me worthy of becoming a member the Christian Church, to give me also the hand of Alethe in that sacred union, which alone sanctifies love, and makes the faith, which it pledges, holy. It was but yesterday, he added, that his young charge, herself, after a preparation of prayer and repentance, such as even her pure spirit required, had been admitted, by the sacred ordinance of baptism, into the bosom of the faith;—and the white garment she wore, and the ring of gold on her finger, "were symbols," he added, "of that New Life into which she had been initiated."

I raised my eyes to hers as he spoke, but withdrew them again, dazzled and confused. Even her beauty, to my imagination, seemed to have undergone some brightening change; and the contrast between that open and happy countenance, and the unblest brow of the infidel that stood before her, abashed me into a sense of unworthiness, and almost checked my rapture.

To that night, however, I look back, as an epoch in my existence. It proved that sorrow is not the only awakener of devotion, but that joy may sometimes quicken the holy spark into life. Returning to my cave, with a heart full, even to oppression, of its happiness, I could find no other relief to my overcharged feelings, than that of throwing myself on my knees, and uttering, for the first time in my life, a heart-felt prayer, that if, indeed, there were a Being who watched over mankind, he would send down one ray of his truth into my darkened soul, and make it worthy of the blessings, both here and hereafter, proffered to it!

My days now rolled on in a perfect dream of happiness. Every hour of the morning was welcomed as bringing nearer and nearer the blest time of sunset, when the Hermit and Alethe never failed to visit my now charmed cave, where her smile left, at each parting, a light that lasted till her return. Then, our rambles, together, by starlight, over the mountain; our pauses, from time to time, to contemplate the wonders of the bright heaven above us; our repose by the cistern of the rock; and our silent listening, through hours that seemed minutes, to the holy eloquence of our teacher;—all, all was happiness of the most heart-felt kind, and such as even the doubts, the cold lingering doubts, that still hung, like a mist, around my heart, could neither cloud nor chill.

As soon as the moonlight nights returned, we used to venture into the desert; and those sands, which had lately looked so desolate, in my eyes, now assumed even a cheerful and smiling aspect. To the light, innocent heart of Alethe, every thing was a source of enjoyment. For her, even the desert had its jewels and flowers; and, sometimes, her delight was to search among the sands for those beautiful pebbles of jasper that abound in them;—sometimes her eyes would sparkle with pleasure on finding, perhaps, a stunted marigold, or one of those bitter, scarlet flowers, that lend their dry mockery of ornament to the desert. In all these pursuits and pleasures the good Hermit took a share—mingling occasionally with them the reflections of a benevolent piety, that lent its own cheerful hue to all the works of creation, and saw the consoling truth, "God is Love," written legibly every where

Such was, for a few weeks, my blissful life. Oh, mornings of hope! oh, nights of happiness! with what melancholy pleasure do I retrace your flight, and how reluctantly pass to the sad events that followed.

During this time, in compliance with the wishes of Melanius, who seemed unwilling that I should become wholly estranged from the world, I used occasionally to pay a visit to the neighbouring city, Antinoe, which, being the capital of the Thebaid, is the centre of all the luxury of Upper Egypt. But here, so changed was my every feeling by the all-absorbing passion which now possessed me, that I sauntered along, wholly uninterested by either the scenes or the people that surrounded me, and, sighing for that rocky solitude where my Alethe breathed, felt *this* to be the wilderness, and *that* the world.

Even the thoughts of my own native Athens, that at every step were called up, by the light Grecian architecture of this imperial city, did not awaken one single regret in my heart—one wish to exchange even an hour of my desert for the best luxuries and honours that awaited me in the Garden. I saw the arches of triumph;—I walked under the superb portico, which encircles the whole city with its marble shade;—I stood in the Circus of the Sun, by whose rose-coloured pillars the mysterious movements of the Nile are measured;—on all these proud monuments of glory and art, as well as on the gay multitude that enlivened them, I looked with an unheeding eye. If they awakened in me any thought, it was the mournful idea, that, one day, like Thebes and Heliopolis, this pageant would pass away, leaving nothing behind but a few mouldering ruins—like sea-shells found where the ocean has been—to tell that the great tide of Life was once there!

But, though indifferent thus to all that had formerly attracted me, there were subjects, once alien to my heart, on which it was now most tremblingly alive; and some rumours which had reached me, in one of my visits to the city, of an expected change in the policy of the Emperor towards the Christians, filled my mind with apprehensions as new as they were dreadful to me.

The toleration and even favour which the Christians enjoyed, during the first four years of the reign of Valerian, had removed from them all fear of a renewal of those horrors, which they had experienced under the rule of his predecessor, Decius. Of late, however, some less friendly dispositions had manifested themselves. The bigots of the court taking alarm at the rapid spread of the new faith, had succeeded in filling the mind of the monarch with that religious jealousy, which is the ever-ready parent of cruelty and injustice. Among these counsellors of evil was Macrianus, their Prætorian Prefect, who was by birth an Egyptian, and had long made himself notorious—so akin is superstition to intolerance—by his addiction to the dark practices of demon-worship and magic.

From this minister, who was now high in the favour of Valerian, the new measures of severity against the Christians were expected to emanate. All tongues, in all quarters, were busy with the news. In the streets, in the public gardens, on the steps of the temples, I saw, everywhere, groups of inquirers collected, and heard the name of Macrianus upon every tongue. It was dreadful, too, to observe, in the countenances of those who spoke, the variety of feeling with which the rumour was discussed, according as they feared or desired its truth—according as they were likely to be among the torturers or the victims.

Alarmed, though still ignorant of the whole extent of the danger, I hurried back to the ravine, and, going at once to the grotto of Melanius, detailed to him every particular of the intelligence I had collected. He listened to me with a composure, which I mistook, alas! for confidence in his own security; and, naming the hour for our evening walk, retired into his grotto.

At the accustomed time, accompanied by Alethe, he came to my cave. It was evident that he had not communicated to her the intelligence which I had brought, for never hath brow worn such happiness as that which now played around hers:—it was alas! *not* of this earth. Melanius, himself, though composed, was thoughtful; and the solemnity, almost approaching to melancholy, with which he placed the hand of Alethe in mine—in the performance, too, of a ceremony that *ought* to have filled my heart with joy—saddened and alarmed me. This ceremony was our betrothment—the act of plighting our faith to each other, which we now solemnized on the rock before the door of my cave, in the face of that calm, sunset heaven, whose one star stood as our witness. After a blessing from the Hermit upon our spousal pledge, I placed the ring—the earnest of our future union—on her finger; and, in the blush, with which she surrendered to me her whole heart at that instant, forgot every thing but my happiness, and felt secure even against fate!

We took our accustomed walk that evening, over the rocks and on the desert. So bright was the moon—more like the daylight indeed of other climes—that we could plainly see the tracks of the wild antelopes in the sand; and it was not without a slight tremble of feeling in his voice, as if some melancholy analogy occurred to him as he spoke, that the good Hermit said, "I have observed, in the course of my walks, that wherever the track of that gentle animal appears, there is, almost always, found the foot-print of a beast of prey near it." He regained, however, his usual cheerfulness before we parted, and fixed the following evening for an excursion, on the other side of the ravine, to a point looking, he said, "towards that northern region of the desert, where the hosts of the Lord encamped on their departure out of bondage."

Though, when Alethe was present, all my fears even for herself were forgotten in that perpetual element of happiness, which encircled her like the air that she breathed, no sooner was I alone, than vague terrors and bodings crowded upon me. In vain did I endeavour to reason away my fears, by dwelling only on the most cheering circumstances—on the reverence with which Melanius was regarded, even by the Pagans, and the inviolate security with which he had lived through the most perilous periods, not only safe himself, but affording sanctuary in the depths of his grottos to others. Though somewhat calmed by these considerations, yet, when at length I sunk off to sleep, dark, horrible dreams took possession of my mind. Scenes of death and of torment passed confusedly before me; and, when I awoke, it was with the fearful impression that all these horrors were real.

CHAPTER XIX.

At length, the day dawned—that dreadful day! Impatient to be relieved from my suspense, I threw myself into my boat—the same in which we had performed our happy voyage—and, as fast as oars could speed me, hurried away to the city. I found the suburbs silent and solitary, but, as I approached the Forum, loud yells, like those of barbarians in combat, struck on my ear, and, when I entered it—great God, what a spectacle presented itself! The imperial edict against the Christians had arrived during the night, and already the wild fury of bigotry was let loose.

Under a canopy, in the middle of the Forum, was the tribunal of the Governor. Two statues—one of Apollo, the other of Osiris—stood at the bottom of the steps that led up to his judgment seat. Before these idols were shrines, to which the devoted Christians were dragged from all quarters by the soldiers and mob, and there compelled to recant, by throwing incense into the flame, or, on their refusal, hurried away to torture and death. It was an appalling scene;—the consternation, the cries of some of the victims—the pale, silent resolution of others;—the fierce shouts of laughter that broke from the multitude, when the dropping of the frankincense on the altar proclaimed some denier of Christ; and the fiend-like triumph with which the courageous Confessors, who avowed their faith, were led away to the flames;—never could I have conceived such an assemblage of horrors!

Though I gazed but for a few minutes, in those minutes I felt and fancied enough for years. Already did the form of Alethe appear to flit before me through that tumult;—I heard them shout her name;—her shriek fell on my ear; and the very thought so palsied me with terror, that I stood fixed and statue-like on the spot.

Recollecting, however, the fearful preciousness of every moment, and that—perhaps, at this very instant—some emissaries of blood might be on their way to the Grottos, I rushed wildly out of the Forum, and made my way to the quay.

The streets were now crowded; but I ran headlong through the multitude, and was already under the portico leading down to the river—already saw the boat that was to bear me to Alethe—when a Centurion stood sternly in my path, and I was surrounded and arrested by soldiers! It was in vain that I implored, that I struggled with them as for life, assuring them that I was a stranger—that I was an Athenian—that I was—*not* a Christian. The precipitation of my flight was sufficient evidence against me, and unrelentingly, and by force, they bore me away to the quarters of their Chief.

It was enough to drive me at once to madness! Two hours, two frightful hours, was I kept waiting the arrival of the Tribune of their Legion—my brain burning with a thousand fears and imaginations, which every passing minute made but more likely to be realized. All I could collect, too, from the conversations of those around me, but added to the agonizing apprehensions with which I was racked. Troops, it was said, had been sent in all directions through the neighbourhood, to bring in the rebellious Christians, and make them bow before the Gods of the Empire. With horror, too, I heard of Orcus—Orcus, the High Priest of Memphis—as one of the principal instigators of this sanguinary edict, and as here present in Antinoe, animating and directing its execution.

In this state of torture I remained till the arrival of the Tribune. Absorbed in my own thoughts, I had not perceived his entrance;—till, hearing a voice, in a tone of friendly surprise, exclaim, "Alciphron!" I looked up, and in this legionary Chief recognised a young Roman of rank, who had held a military command, the year before, at Athens, and was one of the most distinguished visitors of the Garden. It was no time, however, for courtesies:—he was proceeding with all cordiality to greet me, but, having heard him order my instant release, I could wait for no more. Acknowledging his kindness but by a grasp of the hand, I flew off, like one frantic, through the streets, and, in a few minutes was on the river.

My sole hope had been to reach the grottos before any of the detached parties should arrive, and, by a timely flight across the desert, rescue, at least, Alethe from their fury. The ill-fated delay that had occurred rendered this hope almost desperate; but the tranquillity I found every where as I proceeded down the river, and my fond confidence in the sacredness of the Hermit's retreat, kept my heart from sinking altogether under its terrors.

Between the current and my oars, the boat flew, with the speed of wind, along the waters, and I was already near the rocks of the ravine, when I saw, turning out of the canal, into the river, a barge crowded with people, and glittering with arms! How did I ever survive the shock of that sight? The oars dropped, as if struck out of my hands, into the water, and I sat, helplessly gazing, as that terrific vision approached. In a few minutes, the current brought us together;—and I saw, on the deck of the barge, Alethe herself and the Hermit surrounded by soldiers!

We were already passing each other, when, with a desperate effort, I sprang from my boat and lighted upon the edge of their vessel. I knew not what I did, for despair was my only prompter. Snatching at the sword of one of the soldiers, as I stood tottering on the edge, I had succeeded in wresting it out of his hands, when, at the same moment I received a thrust of a lance from one of his comrades, and fell backward into the river. I can just remember rising again and making a grasp at the side of the vessel;—but the shock, and the faintness from my wound, deprived me of all consciousness, and a shriek from Alethe, as I sank, is all I can recollect of what followed.

Would I had then died!—Yet, no, A mighty Being—I should have died in darkness, and, I have lived to know Thee!

On returning to my senses, I found myself reclined on a couch, in a splendid apartment, the whole appearance of which being Grecian, I, for a moment, forgot all that had passed, and imagined myself in my own home at Athens. But too soon the whole dreadful certainty flashed upon me; and, starting wildly—disabled as I was—from my couch, I called loudly and with the shriek of a maniac, upon Alethe.

I was in the house, I then found, of my friend and disciple, the young Tribune, who had made the Governor acquainted with my name and condition, and had received me under his roof, when brought bleeding and insensible, to Antinoe. From him I now learned at once—for I could not wait for details—the sum of all that had happened in that dreadful interval. Melanius was no more—Alethe still alive, but in prison!

"Take me to her"—I had but time to say—"take me to her instantly, and let me die by her side"—when, nature again failing under such shocks, I relapsed into insensibility. In this state I continued for near an hour, and, on recovering, found the Tribune by my side. The horrors, he said, of the Forum were, for that day, over,—but what the morrow might bring, he shuddered to contemplate. His nature, it was plain, revolted from the inhuman duties in which he was engaged. Touched by the agonies he saw me suffer, he, in some degree, relieved them, by promising that I should, at nightfall, be conveyed to the prison, and, if possible, through his influence, gain access to Alethe. She might yet, he added, be saved, could I succeed in persuading her to comply with the terms of the edict, and make sacrifice to the Gods.—"Otherwise," said he, "there is no hope;—the vindictive Orcus, who has resisted even this short respite of mercy, will, to-morrow, inexorably demand his prey."

He then related to me, at my own request—though every word was torture—all the harrowing details of the proceeding before the Tribunal. "I have seen courage," said he, "in its noblest forms, in the field; but the calm intrepidity with which that aged hermit endured torments—which it was hardly less torment to witness—surpassed all that I could have conceived of human fortitude."

My poor Alethe, too—in describing to me her conduct, the brave man wept like a child. Overwhelmed, he said, at first by her apprehensions for my safety, she had given way to a full burst of womanly weakness. But no sooner was she brought before the Tribunal, and the declaration of her faith was demanded of her, than a spirit almost supernatural seemed to animate her whole form. "She raised her eyes," said he, calmly, but with fervour, to heaven, while a blush was the only sign of mortal feeling on her features:—and the clear, sweet, and untrembling voice, with which she pronounced her own doom, in the words, 'I am a Christian!' sent a thrill of admiration and pity throughout the multitude. Her youth, her loveliness, affected all hearts, and a cry of 'Save the young maiden!' was heard in all directions."

The implacable Orcus, however, would not hear of mercy. Resenting, as it appeared, with all his deadliest rancour, not only her own escape from his toils, but the aid with which she had, so fatally to his views, assisted mine, he demanded loudly and in the name of the insulted sanctuary of Isis, her instant death. It was but by the firm intervention of the Governor, who shared the general sympathy in her fate, that the delay of another day was granted to give a chance to the young maiden of yet recalling her confession, and thus affording some pretext for saving her.

Even in yielding, with evident reluctance, to this respite, the inhuman Priest would yet accompany it with some mark of his vengeance. Whether for the pleasure (observed the Tribune) of mingling mockery with his cruelty, or as a warning to her of the doom she must ultimately expect, he gave orders that there should be tied round her brow one of those chaplets of coral, with which it is the custom of young Christian maidens to array themselves on the day of their martyrdom;—"and, thus fearfully adorned," said he, "she was led away, amidst the gaze of the pitying multitude, to prison."

With these harrowing details the short interval till nightfall—every minute of which seemed an age—was occupied. As soon as it grew dark, I was placed upon a litter—my wound, though not dangerous, requiring such a conveyance—and, under the guidance of my friend, I was conducted to the prison. Through his interest with the guard, we were without difficulty admitted, and I was borne into the chamber where the maiden lay immured. Even the veteran guardian of the place seemed touched with compassion for his prisoner, and supposing her to be asleep, had the litter placed gently near her.

She was half reclining, with her face hid beneath her hands, upon a couch—at the foot of which stood an idol, over whose hideous features a lamp of naphtha, that hung from the ceiling, shed a wild and ghastly glare. On a table before the image was a censer, with a small vessel of incense beside it—one grain of which, thrown voluntarily into the flame, would, even now, save that precious life. So strange, so fearful was the whole scene, that I almost doubted its reality. Alethe! my own happy Alethe! *can* it, I thought, be thou that I look upon?

She now slowly, and with difficulty, raised her head from the couch, on observing which, the kind Tribune withdrew, and we were left alone. There was a paleness, as of death, over her features; and those eyes which, when I last saw them, were but too bright, too happy for this world, looked dim and sunken. In raising herself up, she put her hand, as if from pain, to her forehead, whose marble hue but appeared more death-like from those red bands that lay so awfully across it.

After wandering for a minute vaguely, her eyes at length rested upon me—and, with a shriek, half-terror, half-joy, she sprung from the couch, and sunk upon her knees by my side. She had believed me dead; and, even now, scarcely trusted her senses. "My husband! my love!" she exclaimed; "oh if thou comest to call me from this world, behold I am ready!" In saying thus, she pointed wildly to that ominous wreath, and then dropped her head down upon my knee, as if an arrow had pierced it.

"Alethe!" I cried—terrified to the very soul by that mysterious pang—and, as if the sound of my voice had re-animated her, she looked up, with a faint smile, in my face. Her thoughts, which had evidently been wandering, became collected; and in her joy at my safety, her sorrow at my suffering, she forgot entirely the fate that impended over herself. Love, innocent love, alone occupied all her thoughts; and the warmth, the affection, the devotedness with which she spoke—oh how, at any other moment, I would have blessed, have lingered upon every word!

But the time flew fast—that dreadful morrow was approaching. Already I saw her writhing in the hands of the torturer—the flames, the racks, the wheels, were before my eyes! Half frantic with the fear that her resolution was fixed, I flung myself from the litter in an agony of weeping, and supplicated her, by the love she bore me, by the happiness that awaited us, by her own merciful God, who was too good to require such a sacrifice—by all that the most passionate anxiety could dictate, I implored that she would avert from us the doom that was coming, and—but for once—comply with the vain ceremony demanded of her.

Shrinking from me, as I spoke—but with a look more of sorrow than reproach—"What, thou, too!" she said, mournfully—"thou, into whose inmost spirit I had fondly hoped the same light had entered as into my own! No, never be thou leagued with them who would tempt me to 'make shipwreck of my faith!' Thou, who couldst alone bind me to life, use not, I entreat thee, thy power; but let me die, as He I serve, hath commanded—die for the Truth. Remember the holy lessons we heard together on those nights, those happy nights, when both the present and future smiled upon us—when even the gift of eternal life came more welcome to my soul, from the glad conviction that thou wert to be a sharer in its blessings;—shall I forfeit now that divine privilege? shall I deny the true God, whom we then learned to love?

"No, my own betrothed," she continued—pointing to the two rings on her finger—"behold these pledges—they are both sacred. I should have been as true to thee as I am now to heaven,—nor in that life to which I am hastening shall our love be forgotten. Should the baptism of fire, through which I shall pass to-morrow, make me worthy to be heard before the throne of Grace, I will intercede for thy soul—I will pray that it may yet share with mine that 'inheritance, immortal and undefiled,' which Mercy offers, and that thou—and my dear mother—and I——"

She here dropped her voice; the momentary animation, with which devotion and affection had inspired her, vanished; —and there came a darkness over all her features, a livid darkness—like the approach of death—that made me shudder through every limb. Seizing my hand convulsively, and looking at me with a fearful eagerness, as if anxious to hear some consoling assurance from my own lips—"Believe me," she continued, "not all the torments they are preparing for me—not even this deep, burning pain in my brow, to which they will hardly find an equal—could be half so dreadful to me as the thought that I leave thee, without——"

Here her voice again failed; her head sunk upon my arm, and—merciful God, let me forget what I then felt—I saw that she was dying! Whether I uttered any cry, I know not;—but the Tribune came rushing into the chamber, and, looking on the maiden, said, with a face full of horror, "It is but too true!"

He then told me in a low voice, what he had just learned from the guardian of the prison, that the band round the young Christian's brow was—oh horrible!—a compound of the most deadly poison—the hellish invention of Orcus, to satiate his vengeance, and make the fate of his poor victim secure. My first movement was to untie that fatal wreath—but it would not come away—it would not come away!

Roused by the pain, she again looked in my face; but, unable to speak, took hastily from her bosom the small silver cross which she had brought with her from my cave. Having pressed it to her own lips, she held it anxiously to mine, and, seeing me kiss the holy symbol with fervour, looked happy, and smiled. The agony of death seemed to have passed away;—there came suddenly over her features a heavenly light, some share of which I felt descending into my own soul, and, in a few minutes more, she expired in my arms.

Here ends the Manuscript; but, on the outer cover is found, in the handwriting of a much later period, the following Notice, extracted, as it appears, from some Egyptian martyrology:

"Alciphron — an Epicurean philosopher, converted to Christianity, A.D. 257, by a young Egyptian maiden, who suffered martyrdom in that year. Immediately upon her death, he betook himself to the desert, and lived a life, it is said, of much holiness and penitence. During the persecution under Dioclesian, his sufferings for the faith were most exemplary; and being at length, at an advanced age, condemned to hard labour, for refusing to comply with an Imperial edict, he died at the Brass Mines of Palestine, A.D. 297.

"As Alciphron held the opinions maintained since by Arius, his memory has not been spared by Athanasian writers, who, among other charges, accuse him of having been addicted to the superstitions of Egypt. For this calumny, however, there appears to be no better foundation than a circumstance, recorded by one of his brother monks, that there was found after his death, a small metal mirror, like those used in the ceremonies of Isis, suspended around his neck."

REUBEN AND ROSE.

A TALE OF ROMANCE.

The darkness that hung upon Willumberg's walls
Had long been remember'd with awe and dismay;
For years not a sunbeam had play'd in its halls,
And it seem'd as shut out from the regions of day.

Though the valleys were brightened by many a beam,
Yet none could the woods of that castle illume;
And the lightning, which flash'd on the neighbouring stream,
Flew back, as if fearing to enter the gloom!

"Oh! when shall this horrible darkness disperse!"
Said Willumberg's lord to the Seer of the Cave;—
'It can never dispel," said the wizard of verse,
"Till the bright star of chivalry sinks in the wave!"

And who was the bright star of chivalry then?
Who *could* be but Reuben, the flow'r of the age?
For Reuben was first in the combat of men,
Though Youth had scarce written his name on her page.

For Willumberg's daughter his young heart had beat,—
For Rose, who was bright as the spirit of dawn,
When with wand dropping diamonds, and silvery feet,
It walks o'er the flow'rs of the mountain and lawn.

Must Rose, then, from Reuben, so fatally sever?
Sad, sad were the words of the Seer of the Cave,
That darkness should cover that castle for ever,
Or Reuben be sunk in the merciless wave!

To the wizard she flew, saying, "Tell me, oh, tell!
Shall my Reuben no more be restored to my eyes?"
"Yes, yes—when a spirit shall toll the great bell
Of the mould'ring abbey, your Reuben shall rise!"

Twice, thrice he repeated "Your Reuben shall rise!"
And Rose felt a moment's release from her pain;
And wip'd, while she listen'd, the tears from her eyes,
And hop'd she might yet see her hero again.

That hero could smile at the terrors of death,
When he felt that he died for the sire of his Rose;
To the Oder he flew, and there, plunging beneath,
In the depth of the billows soon found his repose.—

How strangely the order of destiny falls!—
Not long in the waters the warrior lay,
When a sunbeam was seen to glance over the walls,
And the castle of Willumberg bask'd in the ray!

All, all but the soul of the maid was in light,
There sorrow and terror lay gloomy and blank;
Two days did she wander, and all the long night,
In quest of her love, on the wide river's bank.

Oft, oft did she pause for the toll of the bell,
And heard but the breathings of night in the air;
Long, long did she gaze on the watery swell,
And saw but the foam of the white billow there.

And often as midnight its veil would undraw,
As she look'd at the light of the moon in the stream
She thought 'twas his helmet of silver she saw,
As the curl of the surge glitter'd high in the beam.

And now the third night was begemming the sky;
Poor Rose, on the cold, dewy margent reclin'd,
There wept till the tear almost froze in her eye,
When—hark!—'twas the bell that came deep in the wind

She startled, and saw, through the glimmering shade,
A form o'er the waters in majesty glide;
She knew 'twas her love, though his cheek was decay'd,
And his helmet of silver was washed by the tide.

Was this what the Seer of the Cave had foretold?—
Dim, dim through the phantom the moon shot a gleam
'Twas Reuben, but, ah! he was deathly and cold,
And fleeted away like the spell of a dream!

Twice, thrice did he rise, and as often she thought
From the bank to embrace him, but vain her endeavour!
Then, plunging beneath, at a billow she caught
And sunk to repose on its bosom for ever!

A FATHER'S LEGACY TO HIS DAUGHTERS.

BY DR. GREGORY.

My Dear Girls,

You had the misfortune to be deprived of your mother, at a time of life when you were insensible of your loss, and could receive little benefit, either from her instruction, or her example. Before this comes to your hands, you will likewise have lost your father.

I have had many melancholy reflections on the forlorn and helpless situation you must be in, if it should please God to remove me from you before you arrive at that period of life, when you will be able to think and act for yourselves. I know mankind too well. I know their falsehood, their dissipation, their coldness to all the duties of friendship and humanity. I know the little attention paid to helpless infancy. You will meet with few friends disinterested enough to do you a good office, when you are incapable of making them any return, by contributing to their interest or their pleasure, or to the gratification of their vanity.

I have been supported under the gloom naturally arising from these reflections, by a reliance on the goodness of that Providence which has hitherto preserved you, and given me the most pleasing prospect of the goodness of your dispositions; and by the secret hope, that your mother's virtues will entail a blessing on her children.

The anxiety I have for your happiness has made me resolve to throw together my sentiments, relating to your future conduct in life. If I live for some years, you will receive them with much greater advantage, suited to your different geniuses and dispositions. If I die sooner, you must receive them in this very imperfect manner; the last proof of my affection.

You will all remember your father's fondness, when perhaps every other circumstance relating to him is forgotten. This remembrance, I hope, will induce you to give a serious attention to the advices I am now going to leave with you. I can request this with the greater confidence, as my sentiments on the most interesting points that regard life and manners, were entirely correspondent to your mother's, whose judgment and taste I trusted much more than my own.

You must expect that the advice which I shall give you will be very imperfect, as there are many nameless delicacies in female manners, of which none but a woman can judge.

You will have one advantage by attending to what I am going to leave with you; you will hear, at least for once in your lives, the genuine sentiments of a man, who has no interest in flattering or deceiving you. I shall throw my reflections together without any studied order, and shall only, to avoid confusion, range them under a few general heads.

You will see, in a little treatise of mine, just published, in what an honorable point of view I have considered your sex; not as domestic drudges, or the slaves of our pleasure, but as our companions and equals; as designed to soften and polish our manners: and as Thompson finely says,

> To raise the virtues, animate the bliss,
> And sweeten all the toils of human life.

I shall not repeat what I have there said on this subject, and shall only observe, that from the view I have given of your natural character and place in society, there arises a certain propriety of conduct peculiar to your sex. It is this peculiar propriety of female manners of which I intend to give you my sentiments, without touching on those general rules of conduct by which men and women are equally bound.

While I explain to you that system of conduct which I think will tend most to your honor and happiness, I shall, at the same time, endeavor to point out those virtues and accomplishments which render you most respectable and most amiable in the eyes of my own sex.

RELIGION.

Though the duties of religion, strictly speaking, are equally binding on both sexes, yet certain differences in their natural character and education, render some vices in your sex odious. The natural hardness of our hearts, and strength of our passions, inflamed by the uncontrolled license we are too often indulged with in our youth, are apt to render our manners more dissolute, and make us less susceptible of the finer feelings of the heart. Your superior delicacy, your modesty, and the usual severity of your education, preserve you, in a great measure, from any temptation to those vices to which we are most subjected. The natural softness and sensibility of your dispositions particularly fit you for the practice of those duties where the heart is chiefly concerned. And this along with the natural warmth of your imaginations, renders you peculiarly susceptible of the feelings of devotion.

There are many circumstances in your situation that peculiarly require the supports of religion to enable you to act in them with spirit and propriety. Your whole life is often a life of suffering. You cannot plunge into business, or dissipate yourselves in pleasure and riot, as men too often do, when under the pressure of misfortunes. You must bear your sorrows in silence, unknown and unpitied. You must often put on a face of serenity and cheerfulness, when your hearts are torn with anguish, or sinking in despair. Then your only resource is in the consolations of religion. It is chiefly owing to these that you bear domestic misfortunes better than we do.

But you are sometimes in very different circumstances, that equally require the restraints of religion. The natural vivacity, and perhaps the natural vanity of your sex, are very apt to lead you into a dissipated state of life, that deceives you, under the appearance of innocent pleasure; but which in reality wastes your spirits, impairs your health, weakens all the superior faculties of your minds, and often sullies your reputations. Religion, by checking this dissipation and rage for pleasure, enables you to draw more happiness, even from those very sources of amusement, which when too frequently applied to, are often productive of satiety and disgust.

Religion is rather a matter of sentiment than reasoning. The important and interesting articles of faith are sufficiently plain. Fix your attention on these, and do not meddle with controversy. If you get into that, you plunge into a chaos, from which you will never be able to extricate yourselves. It spoils the temper, and, I suspect, has no good effect upon the heart.

Avoid all books, and all conversation, that tend to shake your faith on those great points of religion which should serve to regulate your conduct, and on which your hopes of future and eternal happiness depend.

Never indulge yourselves in ridicule on religious subjects; nor give countenance to it in others, by seeming diverted with what they say. This, to people of good breeding, will be a sufficient check.

I wish you to go no farther than the scriptures for your religious opinions. Embrace those you find clearly revealed. Never perplex yourselves about such as you do not understand, but treat them with silent and becoming reverence. I would advise you to read only such religious books as are addressed to the heart, such as inspire pious and devout affections, such as are proper to direct you in your conduct, and not such as tend to entangle you in the endless maze of opinions and systems.

Be punctual in the stated performance of your private devotions, morning and evening. If you have any sensibility or imagination, this will establish such an intercourse between you and the Supreme Being, as will be of infinite consequence to you in life. It will communicate an habitual cheerfulness to your tempers; give a firmness and steadiness to your virtue, and enable you to go through all the vicissitudes of human life with propriety and dignity.

I wish you to be regular in your attendance on public worship, and in receiving the communion. Allow nothing to interrupt your public or private devotions, except the performance of some active duty in life, to which they should always give place. In your behavior at public worship observe an exemplary attention and gravity.

That extreme strictness which I recommend to you in these duties, will be considered by many of your acquaintance as a superstitious attachment to forms; but in the advice I give you on this and other subjects, I have an eye to the spirit and manners of the age. There is a levity and dissipation in the present manners, a coldness and listlessness in whatever relates to religion, which can not fail to infect you, unless you purposely cultivate in your minds a contrary bias, and make the devotional taste habitual.

Avoid all grimace and ostentation in your religious duties. They are the usual cloaks of hypocrisy; at least they show a weak and vain mind.

Do not make religion a subject of common conversation in mixed companies. When it is introduced, rather seem to decline it. At the same time, never suffer any person to insult you by any foolish ribaldry on your religious opinions, but show the same resentment you would naturally do on being offered any other personal insult. But the surest way to avoid this, is by a modest reserve on the subject, and by using no freedom with others about their religious sentiments.

Cultivate an enlarged charity for all mankind, however they may differ from you in their religious opinions. That difference may probably arise from causes in which you had no share, and from which you can derive no merit.

Show your regard to religion by a distinguishing respect to all its ministers, of whatever persuasion, who do not by their lives dishonor their professions; but never allow them the direction of your consciences, lest they taint you with the narrow spirit of their party.

The best effect of your religion will be a diffusive humanity to all in distress. Set apart a certain proportion of your income as sacred to charitable purposes. But in this, as well as in the practice of every other duty, carefully avoid ostentation. Vanity is always defeating her own purposes. Fame is one of the natural rewards of virtue. Do not pursue her, and she will follow you.

Do not confine your charity to giving money. You may have many opportunities of showing a tender and compassionate spirit, where your money is not wanted. There is a false and unnatural refinement in sensibility, which makes some people shun the sight of every object in distress. Never indulge this, especially where your friends or acquaintances are concerned. Let the days of their misfortunes, when the world forgets or avoids them, be the season for you to exercise your humanity and friendship. The sight of human misery softens the heart, and makes it better; it checks the pride of health and prosperity, and the distress it occasions is amply compensated by the consciousness of doing your duty, and by the secret endearments which nature has annexed to all our sympathetic sorrows.

Women are greatly deceived when they think they recommend themselves to our sex by their indifference to religion. Even those men who are themselves unbelievers, dislike infidelity in you. Every man who knows human nature connects a religious taste in your sex with softness and sensibility of heart; at least, we always consider the want of it as a proof of that hard and masculine spirit, which of all your faults we dislike the most. Besides, men consider your religion as one of their principal securities for that female virtue in which they are most interested. If a gentleman pretends an attachment to any of you, and endeavors to shake your religious principles, be assured he is either a fool, or has designs on you which he dares not openly avow.

You will probably wonder at my having educated you in a church different from my own. The reason was plainly this: I looked on the differences between our churches to be of no real importance, and that a preference of one to the other was a mere matter of taste. Your mother was educated in the church of England, and had an attachment to it, and I had a prejudice in favor of everything she liked. It never was her desire that you should be baptized by a clergyman of the church of England, or be educated in that church. On the contrary, the delicacy of her regard to the smallest circumstances that could affect me in the eye of the world, made her anxiously insist it might be otherwise. But I could not yield to her in that kind of generosity. When I lost her, I became still more determined to educate you in that church, as I feel a secret pleasure in doing everything that appears to me to express my affection and veneration for her memory. I draw but a very faint and imperfect picture of what your mother was, while I endeavor to point out what you should be.

NOTE. The reader will remember, that such observations as respect equally both sexes, are all along as much as possible avoided.

CONDUCT AND BEHAVIOR.

ONE of the chief beauties in a female character is that modest reserve, that retiring delicacy, which avoids the public eye, and is disconcerted even at the gaze of admiration. I do not wish you to be insensible to applause. If you were, you must become, if not worse, at least less amiable women. But you may be dazzled by that admiration, which yet rejoices your heart.

When a girl ceases to blush, she has lost the most powerful charm of beauty. That extreme sensibility which it indicates, may be a weakness and incumbrance in our sex, as I have too often felt, but in yours it is peculiarly engaging. Pedants who think themselves philosophers, ask why a woman should blush when she is conscious of no crime? It is a sufficient answer, that nature has made you to blush when you are guilty of no fault, and has forced us to love you because you do so. Blushing is so far from being necessarily an attendant on guilt, that it is the usual companion of innocence.

This modesty, which I think so essential in your sex, will naturally dispose you to be rather silent in company, especially in a large one. People of sense and discernment will never mistake such silence for dulness. One may take a share in conversation without uttering a syllable. The expression in the countenance shows it, and this never escapes an observing eye.

I should be glad that you had an easy dignity in your behavior at public places, but not that confident ease, that unabashed countenance, which seems to set the company at defiance. If, while a gentleman is speaking to you, one of superior rank addresses you, do not let your eager attention and visible preference betray the flutter of your heart. Let your pride on this occasion preserve you from that meanness into which your vanity would sink you. Consider that you expose yourselves to the ridicule of the company, and affront one gentleman only to swell the triumph of another, who, perhaps, thinks he does you honor in speaking to you.

Converse with men even of the first rank, with that dignified modesty, which may prevent the approach of the most distant familiarity, and consequently prevent them from feeling themselves your superiors.

Wit is the most dangerous talent you can possess. It must be guarded with great discretion and good-nature, otherwise it will create you many enemies. It is perfectly consistent with softness and delicacy, yet they are seldom found united. Wit is so flattering to vanity, that those who possess it become intoxicated, and lose all self-command.

Humor is a different quality. It will make your company much solicited; but be cautious how you indulge it. It is often a great enemy to delicacy, and a still greater one to dignity of character. It may sometimes gain you applause, but will never procure you respect.

Be even cautious in displaying your good sense. It will be thought you assume a superiority over the rest of the company. But if you happen to have any learning, keep it a profound secret, especially from the men, who generally look with a jealous and malignant eye on a woman of great parts and a cultivated understanding.

A man of real genius and candor is far superior to this meanness. But such a one will seldom fall in your way; and if by accident he should, do not be anxious to show the full extent of your knowledge. If he has any opportunities of seeing you, he will soon discover it to himself; and if you have any advantages of person or manner, and keep your own secret, he will probably give you credit for a great deal more than you possess. The great art of pleasing in conversation, consists in making the company pleased with themselves. You will more readily hear than talk yourselves into their good graces.

Beware of detraction, especially where your own sex are concerned. You are generally accused of being particularly addicted to this vice—I think unjustly. Men are full as guilty of it when their interests interfere. As your interests more frequently clash, and as your feelings are quicker than ours, your temptations to it are more frequent. For this reason, be particularly tender of the reputation of your own sex, especially when they happen to rival you in our regards. We look on this as the strongest proof of dignity and true greatness of mind.

Show a compassionate sympathy to unfortunate women, especially to those who are rendered so by the villany of men. Indulge a secret pleasure, I may say pride, in being the friends and refuge of the unhappy, but without the vanity of showing it.

Consider every species of indelicacy in conversation, as shameful in itself, and as highly disgusting to us. All double entendre is of this sort. The dissoluteness of men's education allows them to be diverted with a kind of wit, which yet they have delicacy enough to be shocked at, when it comes from your mouths, or even when you hear it without pain and contempt. Virgin purity is of that delicate nature, that it can not hear certain things without contamination. It is always in your power to avoid these. No man but a brute or a fool will insult a woman with conversation which he sees gives her pain; nor will he dare do it if she resent the injury with a becoming spirit. There is a dignity in conscious virtue which is able to awe the most shameless and abandoned of men.

You will be reproached, perhaps, with prudery. By prudery is usually meant an affectation of delicacy. Now I do not wish you to affect delicacy—I wish you to possess it. At any rate, it is better to run the risk of being thought ridiculous than disgusting.

The men will complain of your reserve. They will assure you that a franker behavior would make you more amiable. But trust me, they are not sincere when they tell you so. I acknowledge, that on some occasions it might render you more agreeable as companions, but it would render you less amiable as women—an important distinction which many of your sex are not aware of. After all, I wish you to have great ease and openness in your conversation. I only point out some considerations which ought to regulate your behavior in that respect.

Have a sacred regard to truth. Lying is a mean and despicable vice. I have known some women of excellent parts, who were so much addicted to it that they could not be trusted in the relation of any story, especially if it contained anything of the marvellous, or if they themselves were the heroines of the tale. This weakness did not proceed from a bad heart, but was merely the effect of vanity, or an unbridled imagination. I do not mean to censure that lively embellishment of a humorous story, which is only intended to promote innocent mirth.

There is a certain gentleness of spirit and manners extremely engaging in your sex; not that indiscriminate attention, that unmeaning simper, which smiles on all alike. This arises, either from an affectation of softness, or from perfect insipidity.

There is a species of refinement in luxury just beginning to prevail among the gentlemen of this country, to which our ladies are yet as great strangers as any women upon earth; I hope for the honor of the sex they may ever continue so; I mean the luxury of eating. It is a despicable, selfish vice in men, but in your sex it is beyond expression indelicate and disgusting.

Every one who remembers a few years back, is sensible of a very striking change in the attention and respect formerly paid by the gentlemen to the ladies. Their drawing-rooms are deserted, and after dinner and supper the gentlemen are impatient till they retire. How they came to lose this respect, which nature and politeness so well entitle them to, I shall no here particularly inquire. The revolutions of manners in any country depend on causes very various and complicated. I shall only observe, that the behavior of the ladies in the last age was very reserved and stately. It would now be reckoned ridiculously stiff and formal. Whatever it was, it had certainl the effect of making them more respected

A fine woman, like other fine things in nature, has her proper point of view, from which she may be seen to most advantage. To fix this point requires great judgment, and an intimate knowledge of the human heart. By the present mode of female manners, the ladies seem to expect that they shall regain their ascendency over us by the fullest display of their personal charms, by being always in our eye at public places, by conversing with us with the same unreserved freedom as we do with one another; in short, by resembling us as nearly as they possibly can. But a little time and experience will show the folly of this expectation and conduct.

The power of a fine woman over the hearts of men, even of the finest parts, is even beyond what she conceives. They are sensible of the pleasing illusion, but they can not, nor do they wish to dissolve it. But if she is determined to dispel the charm, it certainly is in her power; she may soon reduce the angel to a very ordinary girl.

There is a native dignity, an ingenuous modesty, to be expected in your sex, which is your natural protection from the familiarities of the men, and which you should feel previous to the reflection that it is your interest to keep yourselves sacred from all personal freedoms. The many nameless charms and endearments of beauty should be reserved to bless the arms of the happy man to whom you give your heart, but who, if he has the least delicacy, will despise them, if he knows they have been prostituted to fifty men before him. The sentiment, that a woman may allow all innocent freedoms, provided her virtue is secure, is both grossly indelicate and dangerous, and has proved fatal to many of your sex.

Let me now recommend to your attention that elegance, which is not so much a quality of itself, as the high polish of every other. It is what diffuses an ineffable grace over every look, every motion, every sentence you utter. It is partly a personal quality, in which respect it is the gift of nature; but I speak of it principally as a quality of the mind. In a word, it is the perfection of taste in life and manners—every virtue and every excellence, in their most graceful and amiable forms.

You may think, perhaps, I want to throw every spark of nature out of your composition, and to make you entirely artificial. Far from it. I wish you to possess the most perfect simplicity of heart and manners. I think you may possess dignity without pride, affability without meanness, and simple elegance without affectation. Milton had my idea, when he says of Eve,

"Grace was in all her steps, Heaven in her eye,
In every gesture dignity and love."

AMUSEMENTS.

EVERY period of life has amusements which are natural and proper to it. You may indulge the variety of your tastes in these, while you keep within the bounds of that propriety which is suitable to your sex.

Some amusements are conducive to health, as various kinds of exercise; some are connected with qualities really useful, as different kinds of women's work, and all the domestic concerns of a family; some are elegant accomplishments, as dress, dancing, music, and drawing. Such books as improve your understanding, enlarge your knowledge, and cultivate your taste, may be considered in a higher point of view than mere amusements. There are a variety of others, which are neither useful nor ornamental, such as play of different kinds.

I would particularly recommend to you those exercises that oblige you to be much abroad in the open air, such as walking, and riding on horseback. This will give vigor to your constitutions, and a bloom to your complexions. If you accustom yourselves to go abroad always in chairs and carriages, you will soon become so enervated as to be unable to go out of doors without them. They are like most articles of luxury, useful and agreeable when judiciously used, but when made habitual they become both insipid and pernicious.

An attention to your health is a duty you owe to yourselves and to your friends. Bad health seldom fails to have an influence on the spirits and temper. The finest geniuses, the most delicate minds have very frequently a correspondent delicacy of bodily constitutions, which they are too apt to neglect. Their luxury lies in reading and late hours, equal enemies to health and beauty.

But though good health be one of the greatest blessings in life, never make a boast of it, but enjoy it in grateful silence. We so naturally associate the idea of female softness and delicacy with a correspondent delicacy of constitution, that when a woman speaks of her great strength, her extraordinary appetite, her ability to bear excessive fatigue, we recoil at the description in a way she is little aware of.

The intention of your being taught needlework, knitting, and such like, is not on account of the intrinsic value of all you can do with your hands, which is trifling, but to enable you to judge more perfectly of that kind of work, and to direct the execution of it in others. Another principal end is to enable you to fill up, in a tolerably agreeable way, some of the many solitary hours you must necessarily pass at home. It is a great article in the happiness of life, to have your pleasures as independent of others as possible. By continually gadding about in search of amusement, you lose the respect of all your acquaintances, whom you oppress with those visits, which by a more discreet management might have been courted.

The domestic economy of a family is entirely a woman's province, and furnishes a variety of subjects for the exertion both of good sense and good taste. If you ever come to have the charge of a family, it ought to engage much of your time and attention; nor can you be excused from this by any extent of fortune, though with a narrow one the ruin that follows the neglect of it may be more immediate.

I am at the greatest loss what to advise you in regard to books. There is no impropriety in your reading history, or cultivating any art or science to which genius or accident leads you. The whole volume of Nature lies open to your eye, and furnishes an infinite variety of entertainment. If I was sure that Nature had given you such strong principles of taste and sentiment as would remain with you, and influence your future conduct, with the utmost pleasure would I endeavor to direct your reading in such a way as might form that taste to the utmost perfection of truth and elegance. "But when I reflect how easy it is to warm a girl's imagination, and how difficult deeply and permanently to affect her heart; how readily she enters into every refinement of sentiment, and how easily she can sacrifice them to vanity or convenience;" I think I may very probably do you an injury by artificially creating a taste, which, if Nature never gave it you, would only serve to embarrass your future conduct. I do not want to *make* you anything; I want to know what Nature has made you, and to perfect you on her plan. I do not wish you to have sentiments that might perplex you; I wish you to have sentiments that may uniformly and steadily guide you, and such as your hearts so thoroughly approve, that you would not forego them for any consideration this world could offer.

Dress is an important article in female life. The love of dress is natural to you, and therefore it is proper and reasonable. Good sense will regulate your expense in it, and good taste will direct you to dress in such a way as to conceal any blemishes, and set off your beauties, if you have any, to the greatest advantage. But much delicacy and judgment are required in the application of this rule. A fine woman shows her charms to most advantage, when she seems most to conceal them. The finest bosom in nature is not so fine as what imagination forms. The most perfect elegance of dress appears always the most easy, and the least studied.

Do not confine your attention to dress to public appearances. Accustom yourself to an habitual neatness, so that in the most careless undress, in your unguarded hours, you may have no reason to be ashamed of your appearance. You will not easily believe how much we consider your dress as expressive of your characters. Vanity, levity, slovenliness, folly, appear through it. An elegant simplicity is an equal proof of taste and delicacy.

In dancing, the principal points you are to attend to, are ease and grace. I would have you dance with spirit; but never allow yourself to be so far transported with mirth, as to forget the delicacy of your sex. Many a girl, dancing in the gayety and innocence of her heart, is thought to discover a spirit she little dreams of.

I know no entertainment that gives such pleasure to any person of sentiment or humor, as the theatre. But I am sorry to say that there are few English comedies a lady can see, without a shock to delicacy. You will not readily suspect the comments gentlemen make on your behavior on such occasions. Men are often best acquainted with the most worthless of your sex, and from them too readily form their judgment of the rest. A virtuous girl often hears very indelicate things with a countenance nowise embarrassed, because in truth she does not understand them. Yet this is, most ungenerously, ascribed to that command of features and that ready presence of mind, which you are thought to possess in a degree far beyond us; or, by still more malignant observers, it is ascribed to hardened effrontery.

Sometimes a girl laughs with all the simplicity of unsuspecting innocence, for no other reason but being infected with other people's laughing; she is then believed to know more than she should do. If she does happen to understand an improper thing, she suffers a very complicated distress; she feels her modesty hurt in the most sensible manner, and at the same time is ashamed of appearing conscious of the injury. The only way to avoid these inconveniences, is never to go to a play that is particularly offensive to delicacy. Tragedy subjects you to no such distress. Its sorrows will soften and ennoble your hearts.

I need say little about gaming, the ladies in this country being as yet almost strangers to it. It is a ruinous and incurable vice; and as it leads to all the selfish and turbulent passions, is peculiarly odious in your sex. I have no objection to your playing a little at any kind of game, as a variety in your amusements, provided that what you can possibly lose is such a trifle as can neither interest nor hurt you.

In this, as well as in all important points of conduct, show a determined resolution and steadiness. This is not in the least inconsistent with that softness and gentleness so amiable in your sex. On the contrary, it gives that spirit to a mild and sweet disposition, without which it is apt to degenerate into insipidity. It makes you respectable in your own eyes, and dignifies you in ours.

FRIENDSHIP, LOVE, MARRIAGE.

THE luxury and dissipation that prevail in genteel life, as they corrupt the heart in many respects, so they render it incapable of warm, sincere, and steady friendship. A happy choice of friends will be of the utmost consequence to you, as they may assist you by their advice and good offices. But the immediate gratification which friendship affords to a warm, open, and ingenuous heart, is of itself a sufficient motive to court it.

In the choice of your friends, have principal regard to goodness of heart and fidelity. If they possess taste and genius, that will still make them more agreeable and useful companions. You have particular reason to place confidence in those who have shown affection for you in your early days, when you were incapable of making them any return. This is an obligation for which you can not be too grateful; when you read this, you will naturally think of your mother's friend, to whom you owe so much.

If you have the good fortune to meet with any who deserve the name of friends, unbosom yourselves to them with the most unsuspicious confidence. It is one of the world's maxims, never to trust any person with a secret, the discovery of which could give you any pain; but it is the maxim of a little mind and a cold heart, unless where it is the effect of frequent disappointments and bad usage. An open temper, if restrained by tolerable prudence, will make you on the whole much happier than a reserved suspicious one, although you may sometimes suffer by it. Coldness and distrust are but the too certain consequences of age and experience; but they are unpleasant feelings, and need not be anticipated before their time.

But however open you may be in talking of your own affairs, never disclose the secrets of one friend to another. These are sacred deposites, which do not belong to you, nor have you any right to make use of them.

There is another case in which I suspect it is proper to be secret, not so much from motives of prudence as delicacy. I mean love matters. Though a woman has no reason to be ashamed of an attachment to a man of merit, yet nature, whose authority is superior to philosophy, has annexed a sense of shame to it. It is even long before a woman of delicacy dares avow to her own heart that she loves; and when all the subterfuges of ingenuity to conceal it from herself fail, she feels a violence done both to her pride and to her modesty. This, I should imagine, must always be the case where she is not sure of a return to her attachment.

In such a situation, to lay the heart open to any person whatever, does not appear to me consistent with the perfection of female delicacy. But perhaps I am in the wrong. At the same time I must tell you, that, in point of prudence, it concerns you to attend well to the consequences of such a discovery. These secrets, however important in your own estimation, may appear very trifling to your friend, who possibly will not enter into your feelings, but may rather consider them as a subject of pleasantry. For this reason, love secrets are of all others the worst kept. But the consequences to you may be very serious, as no man of spirit and delicacy ever valued a heart much hackneyed in the ways of love.

If, therefore, you must have a friend to pour out your heart to, be sure of her honor and secresy. Let her not be a married woman, especially if she live happily with her husband. There are certain unguarded moments, in which such a woman, though the best and worthiest of her sex, may let hints escape, which, at other times, or to any other person than her husband, she would be incapable of; nor will a husband in this case feel himself under the same obligation of secresy and honor, as if you had put your confidence originally in himself, especially on a subject which the world is apt to treat so lightly.

If all other circumstances are equal, there are obvious advantages in your making friends of one another. The ties of blood, and your being so much united in one common interest, form an additional bond of union to your friendship. If your brothers should have the good fortune to have hearts susceptible to friendship, to possess truth, honor, sense, and delicacy of sentiment, they are the fittest and most unexceptionable confidants. By placing confidence in them, you will receive every advantage which you could hope for from the friendship of men, without any of the inconveniences that attend such connexions with our sex.

Beware of making confidants of your servants. Dignity, not properly understood, very readily degenerates into pride, which enters into no friendships, because it can not bear an equal, and is so fond of flattery as to grasp at it even from servants and dependants. The most intimate confidants, therefore, of proud people, are valets de chambre and waiting-women. Show the utmost humanity to your servants; make their situation as comfortable to them as possible; but if you make them your confidants you spoil them and debase yourselves.

Never allow any person, under the pretended sanction of friendship, to be so familiar as to lose a proper respect for you. Never allow them to tease you on any subject that is disagreeable, or where you have once taken your resolution. Many will tell you that this reserve is inconsistent with the freedom which friendship allows. But a certain respect is as necessary in friendship as in love. Without it you may be liked as a child, but you will never be beloved as an equal.

The temper and dispositions of the heart in your sex make you enter more readily and warmly into friendships than men. Your natural propensity to it is so strong, that you often run into intimacies which you soon have sufficient cause to repent of, and this makes your friendships so very fluctuating.

Another great obstacle to the sincerity as well as the steadiness of your friendships, is the great clashings of your interests in the pursuits of love, ambition, or vanity. For these reasons, it should appear at first view more eligible for you to contract your friendships with the men. Among other obvious advantages of an easy intercourse between the two sexes, it occasions an emulation and exertion in each to excel and be agreeable; hence their respective excellencies are mutually communicated and blended. As their interests in no degree interfere, there can be no foundation for jealousy or suspicion of rivalship. The friendship of a man for a woman is always blended with a tenderness which he never feels for one of his own sex, even where love is in no degree concerned. Besides, we are conscious of a natural title you have to our protection and good offices, and therefore we feel an additional obligation of honor to serve you, and to observe an inviolable secrecy whenever you confide in us.

But apply these observations with great caution. Thousands of women of the best hearts and the finest parts have been ruined by men who approached them under the specious name of friendship. But supposing a man to have the most uudoubted honor, yet his friendship to a woman is so near akin to love, that if she be very agreeable in her person she will probably very soon find a lover where she only wished to meet a friend. Let me here, however, warn you against that weakness so common among vain women, the imagination that every man who takes particular notice of you is a lover. Nothing can expose you more to ridicule than the taking up a man on the suspicion of being your lover, who, perhaps, never thought of you in that view, and giving yourselves those airs so common among silly women on such occasions.

There is a kind of unmeaning gallantry much practised by some men, which, if you have any discernment, you will find really harmless. Men of this sort will attend you to public places, and be useful to you by a number of little observances, which those of a superior class do not so well understand, or have not leisure to regard, or perhaps are too proud to submit to. Look on the compliments of such men as words of course, which they repeat to every agreeable woman of their acquaintance. There is a familiarity they are apt to assume, which a proper dignity in your behavior will be easily able to check.

There is a different species of men whom you may like as agreeable companions, men of worth, taste, and genius, whose conversation in some respects may be superior to what you generally meet with among your own sex. It will be foolish in you to deprive yourselves of a useful and agreeable acquaintance, merely because idle people say he is your lover. Such a man may like your company without having any design on your person.

People whose sentiments, and particularly whose tastes correspond, naturally like to associate together, although neither of them have the most distant view of any further connexion. But as this similarity of minds often gives rise to a more tender attachment than friendship, it will be prudent to keep a watchful eye over yourselves, lest your hearts become too far engaged before you are aware of it. At the same time, I do not think that your sex, at least in this part of the world, have much of that sensibility which disposes to such attachments. What is commonly called love among you is gratitude, and a partiality to the man who prefers you to the rest of your sex; and such a man you often marry, with little of either personal esteem or affection. Indeed, without an unusual share of natural sensibility, and very peculiar good fortune, a woman in this country has very little probability of marrying for love.

It is a maxim laid down among you, and a very prudent one it is, that love is not to begin on your part, but is to be entirely the consequence of our attachment to you. Now supposing a woman to have sense and taste, she will not find many men to whom she can possibly be supposed to bear any considerable share of esteem. Among these few it is a very great chance if any of them distinguishes her particularly. Love, at least with us, is exceedingly capricious, and will not always fix where reason says it should. But supposing one of them should become particularly attached to her, it is still extremely improbable that he should be the man in the world her heart most approved of.

As, therefore, Nature has not given you that unlimited range in your choice which we may enjoy, she has wisely and benevolently assigned to you a greater flexibility of taste on this subject. Some agreeable qualities recommend a gentleman to your common good liking and friendship. In the course of his acquaintance he contracts an attachment to you. When you perceive it, it excites your gratitude; this gratitude rises into a preference, and this preference perhaps at last advances to some degree of attachment, especially if it meets with crosses and difficulties, for these, and a state of suspense, are very great excitements to attachment, and are the food of love in both sexes. If attachment was not excited in your sex in this manner, there is not one of a million of you that could ever marry with any degree of love.

A man of taste and delicacy marries a woman because he loves her more than any other. A woman of equal taste and delicacy marries him because she esteems him, and because he gives her that preference. But if a man unfortunately becomes attached to a woman whose heart is secretly pre-engaged, his attachment. instead of obtaining a suitable return, is particularly offensive, and if he persists to tease her, he makes himself equally the object of her scorn and aversion.

The effects of love among men are diversified by their different tempers. An artful man may counterfeit every one of them so as easily to impose on a young girl of an open, generous, and feeling heart, if she is not extremely on her guard. The finest parts in such a girl may not always prove sufficient for her security. The dark and crooked paths of cunning, are unsearchable and inconceivable to an honorable and elevated mind.

The following, I apprehend, are the most genuine effects of an honorable passion among the men, and the most difficult to counterfeit. A man of delicacy often betrays his passion by his too great anxiety to conceal it, especially if he has little hopes of success. True love, in all its stages, seeks concealment, and never expects success. It renders a man not only respectful, but timid to the highest degree in his behavior to the woman he loves. To conceal the awe he stands in of her, he may sometimes affect pleasantry, but it sits awkwardly on him, and he quickly relapses into seriousness, if not into dulness. He magnifies all her real perfections in his imagination, and is either blind to her failings, or converts them into beauties. Like a person conscious of guilt, he is jealous that every eye observes him; and to avoid this, he shuns all the little observances of common gallantry.

His heart and his character will be improved in every respect by his attachment. His manners will become more gentle, and his conversation more agreeable; but diffidence and embarrassment will always make him appear to disadvantage in the company of his mistress. If the fascination continue long, it will totally depress his spirit, and extinguish every active, vigorous, and manly principle of his mind. You will find this subject beautifully and pathetically painted in Thomson's Spring.

When you observe in a gentleman's behavior the marks which I have described above, reflect seriously what you are to do. If his attachment is agreeable to you, I leave you to do as nature, good sense, and delicacy, shall direct you. If you love him, let me advise you never to discover to him the full extent of your love—no, not although you marry him. That sufficiently shows your preference, which is all he is entitled to know. If he has delicacy, he will ask for no stronger proof of your affection, for your sake; [illegible] has sense, he will not ask for his own. This is an unpleasant truth, but it is my duty to let you know it; violent love can not subsist, at least can not be expressed for any time together, on both sides; otherwise the certain consequence, however concealed, is satiety and disgust. Nature, in this case, has laid the reserve on you.

If you see evident proofs of a gentleman's attachment and you are determined to shut your heart against him, as you ever hope to be used with generosity by the person who shall engage your own heart, treat him honorably and humanely. Do not let him linger in miserable suspense, but be anxious to let him know your sentiments with regard to him.

However people's hearts may deceive them, there is scarcely a person that can love for any time, without at least some distant hope of success. If you really wish to undeceive a lover, you may do it in a variety of ways. There is a certain species of easy familiarity in your behavior, which may satisfy him, if he has any discernment left, that he has nothing to hope for. But perhaps your particular temper may not admit of this. You may easily show that you want to avoid his company; but if he is a man whose friendship you wish to preserve, you may not choose this method, because then you lose him in every capacity. You may get a common friend to explain matters to him, or fall in with many other devices, if you are seriously anxious to put him out of suspense.

But if you are resolved against every such method, at least do not shun opportunities of letting him explain himself. If you do this, you act barbarously and unjustly. If he brings you to an explanation, give him a polite, but resolute and decisive answer. In whatever way you convey your sentiments to him, if he is a man of spirit and delicacy, he will give you no further trouble, nor apply to your friends for their intercession. This last is a method of courtship which every man of spirit will disdain. He will never whine nor sue for your pity. That would mortify him almost as much as your scorn. In short, you may possibly break such a heart, but you can not bend it. Great pride always accompanies delicacy, however concealed under the appearance of the utmost gentleness and modesty, and is the passion of all others the most difficult to conquer.

There is a case where a woman may coquet justifiably to the utmost verge which her conscience will allow. It is where a gentleman purposely declines to make his addresses, till such time as he thinks himself perfectly sure of her consent. This at bottom is intended to force a woman to give up the undoubted privilege of her sex, the privilege of her refusing; it is intended to force her to explain herself, in effect, before the gentleman deigns to do it, and by this means to oblige her to violate the modesty and delicacy of her sex, and to invert the clearest order of nature. All this sacrifice is proposed to be made merely to gratify a most despicable vanity in a man who would degrade the very woman whom he wishes to make his wife.

It is of great importance to distinguish whether a gentleman who has the appearance of being your lover delays to speak explicitly, from the motive I have mentioned, or from a diffidence inseparable from true attachment. In the one case, you can scarcely use him too ill; in the other, you ought to use him with great kindness; and the greatest kindness you can show him, if you are determined not to listen to his addresses, is to let him know it as soon as possible.

I know the many excuses with which women endeavor to justify themselves to the world, and to their own consciences, when they act otherwise. Sometimes they plead ignorance, or at least uncertainty of the gentleman's real sentiments. That may often be the case. Sometimes they plead decorums of their sex, which enjoin an equal behavior to all men, and forbid them to consider any man as a lover, till he has directly told them so. Perhaps few women carry their ideas of female delicacy and decorum so far as I do. But I must say you are not entitled to plead the obligation of these virtues, in opposition to the superior ones of gratitude, justice, and humanity. The man is entitled to all these, who prefers you to the rest of your sex, and perhaps whose greatest weakness is this very preference. The truth of the matter is, vanity and the love of admiration are so prevailing passions among you, that you may be considered to make a very great sacrifice when you give up a lover, till every art of coquetry fails to keep him, or till he forces you to an explanation. You can be fond of the love when you are indifferent to, or even despise the lover.

But the deepest and most artful coquetry is employed by women of superior taste and sense, to engage and fix the heart of a man whom the world and they themselves esteem, although they are determined never to marry him. But his conversation amuses them, and his attachment is the highest gratification to their vanity; nay, they can sometimes be gratified with the utter ruin of his fortune, fame, and happiness. God forbid I should ever think so of all of your sex. I know many of them have principles, have generosity and dignity of soul, that elevate them above the worthless vanity I have been speaking of.

Such a woman, I am persuaded, may always convert a lover, if she can not give her affections, into a warm and steady friend, provided he is a man of sense, resolution, and candor. If she explains herself to him with a generous openness and freedom, he must feel the stroke as a man; but he will likewise bear it as a man; what he suffers he will suffer in silence. Every sentiment of esteem will remain: but love, though it requires very little food, and is easily surfeited with too much, yet it requires some. He will view her in the light of a married woman; and though passion subsides, yet a man of a candid and generous heart always retains a tenderness for a woman he has once loved, and who has used him well, beyond what he feels for any other of her sex.

If he has not confided his own secret to anybody, he has an undoubted title to ask you not to divulge it. If a woman chooses to trust any of her companions with her own unfortunate attachments, she may, as it is her own affair alone; but if she has any generosity or gratitude, she will not betray a secret which does not belong to her.

Male coquetry is much more inexcusable than female, as well as more pernicious; but it is rare in this country. Very few men will give themselves the trouble to gain or retain any woman's affections, unless they have views on her either of an honorable or dishonorable kind. Men employed in the pursuits of business, ambition, or pleasure, will not give themselves the trouble to engage a woman's affections merely from the vanity of conquest, and of triumphing over the heart of an innocent and defenceless girl. Besides, people never value much what is entirely in their power. A man of parts, sentiment, and address, if he lays aside all regard to truth and humanity, may engage the hearts of fifty women at the same time, and may likewise conduct his coquetry with so much art, as to put it out of the power of any of them to specify a single expression that could be said to be directly expressive of love.

This ambiguity of behavior, this art of keeping one in suspense, is the great secret of coquetry in both sexes. It is the more cruel in us, because we can carry it what length we please, and continue it as long as we please, without your being so much as at liberty to complain or expostulate; whereas we can break our chain, and force you to explain, whenever we become impatient of our situation.

I have insisted the more particularly on this subject of courtship, because it may most readily happen to you at that early period of life when you can have little experience or knowledge of the world, when your passions are warm, and your judgments not arrived at such full maturity as to be able to correct them. I wish you to possess such high principles of honor and generosity as will render you incapable of deceiving, and at the same time to possess that acute discernment which may secure you against being deceived.

A woman, in this country, may easily prevent the first impressions of love, and every motive of prudence and delicacy should make her guard against them, till such time as she has received the most convincing proof of the attachment of a man of such merit as will justify a reciprocal regard. Your hearts, indeed, may be shut inflexibly and permanently against all the merit a man can possess. That may be your misfortune, but can not be your fault. In such a situation, you would be equally unjust to yourself and your lover, if you gave him your hand when your heart revolted against him. But miserable will be your fate if you allow an attachment to steal on you before you are sure of a return, or, what is infinitely worse, where are wanting those qualities which alone can insure happiness in a married state.

I know nothing that renders a woman more despicable, than her thinking it essential to happiness to be married. Beside the gross indelicacy of the sentiment, it is a false one, as thousands of women have experienced. But if it was true, the belief that it is so, and the consequent impatience to be married, is the most effectual way to prevent it.

You must not think from this, that I do not wish you to marry. On the contrary, I am of opinion, that you may attain a superior degree of happiness in a married state to what you can possibly find in any other. I know the forlorn and unprotected situation of an old maid, the chagrin and peevishness which are apt to infect their tempers, and the great difficulty of making a transition with dignity and cheerfulness from the period of youth, beauty, admiration, and respect, into the calm, silent, unnoticed retreat of declining years.

I see some unmarried women of active, vigorous minds, and a great vivacity of spirits, degrading themselves, sometimes by entering into a dissipated course of life unsuitable to their years, and exposing themselves to the ridicule of girls who might have been their grand-children, sometimes by oppressing their acquaintances by impertinent intrusion into their private affairs, and sometimes by being the propagators of scandal and defamation. All this is owing to an exuberant activity of spirit, which, if it had found employment at home, would have rendered them respectable and useful members of society.

I see other women in the same situation, gentle, modest, blessed with sense, taste, delicacy. and every milder feminine virtue of the heart, but of weak spirits, bashful, and timid; I see such women sinking into obscurity and insignificance, and gradually losing every elegant accomplishment, for this evident reason, that they are not united to a partner who has sense, and worth, and taste to know their value—one who is able to draw forth their concealed qualities, and show them to advantage; who can give that support to their feeble spirits which they stand so much in need of, and who, by his affection and tenderness, might make such a woman happy in exerting every talent, and accomplishing herself in every elegant art that could contribute to his amusement.

In short, I am of opinion, that a married state, if entered into from proper motives of esteem and affection, will be the happiest for yourselves, and make you most respectable in the eyes of the world, and the most useful members of society. But I must confess I am not enough of a patriot to wish you to marry for the good of the public. I wish you to marry for no other reason but to make yourselves happier. When I am so particular in my advices about your conduct, I own my heart beats with the fond hope of making you worthy the attachment of men who will deserve you, and be sensible of your merit. But Heaven forbid you should ever relinquish the ease and independence of a single life, to become the slaves of a fool or a tyrant's caprice.

As these have been always my sentiments, I shall do you but justice when I leave you in such independent circumstances as may lay you under no temptation to do from necessity what you would never do from choice. This will likewise save you from that cruel mortification to a woman of spirit—the suspicion that a gentleman thinks he does you an honor or a favor when he asks you for his wife. If I live till you arrive at that age when you shall be capable to judge for yourselves, and do not strangely alter my sentiments, I shall act toward you in a very different manner from what most parents do. My opinion has always been, that when that period arrives the parental authority ceases.

I hope I shall always treat you with that affection and easy confidence which may dispose you to look on me as your friend. In that capacity alone I shall think myself entitled to give you my opinion; in the doing of which I should think myself highly criminal if I did not to the utmost of my power endeavor to divest myself of all personal vanity, and all prejudices in favor of my particular taste. If you did not choose to follow my advice, I should not on that account cease to love you as my children. Though my right to your obedience was expired, yet I should think nothing could release me from the ties of nature and humanity.

You may perhaps imagine that the reserved behavior which I recommend to you, and your appearing seldom at public places, must cut off all opportunities of your being acquainted with gentlemen; I am very far from intending this. I advise you to no reserve but what will render you more respected and beloved by our sex. I do not think public places suited to make people acquainted together. They can only be distinguished there by their looks and external behavior. But it is in private companies alone where you can expect easy and agreeable conversation, which I should never wish you to decline. If you do not allow gentlemen to become acquainted with you, you can never expect to marry with attachment on either side. Love is very seldom produced at first sight, at least it must have, in that case, a very unjustifiable foundation. True love is founded on esteem, in a correspondence of taste and sentiments, and steals on the heart imperceptibly.

There is one advice I shall leave you, to which I beg your particular attention; before your affections become in the least engaged to any man, examine your tempers, your tastes, and your hearts, very severely, and settle it in your own minds, what are the requisites to your happiness in a married state; and as it is almost impossible that you should get everything you wish, come to a steady determination what you are to consider as essential, and what may be sacrificed.

If you have hearts disposed by nature for love and friendship, and possess those feelings which enable you to enter into all the refinements and delicacies of these attachments, consider well, for Heaven's sake, and as you value your future happiness, before you give them any indulgence. If you have the misfortune (for a very great misfortune it commonly is to your sex) to have such a temper and such sentiments deeply rooted in you, if you have spirit and resolution to resist the solicitations of vanity, the persecution of friends (for you will have lost the only friend that would never persecute you), and can support the prospect of the many inconveniences attending the state of an old maid, which I formerly pointed out, then you may indulge yourselves in that kind of sentimental reading and conversation, which is most correspondent to your feelings.

But if you find, on a strict self-examination, that marriage is absolutely essential to your happiness, keep the secret inviolable in your own bosoms, for the reason I formerly mentioned; but shun as you would the most fatal poison, all that species of reading and conversation which warms the imagination, which engages and softens the heart, and raises the taste above the level of common life. If you do otherwise, consider the terrible conflict of passions this may afterward raise in your breasts.

If this refinement once takes deep root in your minds, and you do not obey its dictates, but marry from vulgar and mercenary views, you may never be able to eradicate it entirely, and then it will imbitter all your married days. Instead of meeting with sense, delicacy, tenderness, a lover, a friend, an equal companion, in a husband, you may be tired with insipidity and dulness; shocked with indelicacy, or mortified by indifference. You will find none to compassionate, or even understand your sufferings; for your husbands may not use you cruelly, and may give you as much money for your clothes, personal expense, and domestic necessaries, as is suitable to their fortunes. The world therefore would look on you as unreasonable women, who did not deserve to be happy, if you were not so. To avoid these complicated evils, if you are determined at all events to marry, I would advise you to make all your reading and amusements of such a kind, as do not affect the heart nor the imagination, except in the way of wit or humor.

I have no view by these advices to lead your tastes; I only want to persuade you of the necessity of knowing your own minds, which, though seemingly very easy, is what your sex seldom attain on many important occasions in life, but particularly on this of which I am speaking. There is not a quality I more anxiously wish you to possess, than that collected, decisive spirit which rests on itself, which enables you to see where your true happiness lies, and to pursue it with the most determined resolution. In matters of business, follow the advice of those who know them better than yourselves, and in whose integrity you can confide; but in matters of taste, that depend on your own feelings, consult no one friend whatever, but consult your own hearts.

If a gentleman makes his address to you, or gives you reason to believe he will do so, before you allow your affections to be engaged, endeavor in the most prudent and secret manner, to procure from your friends every necessary piece of information concerning him; such as his character for sense, his morals, his temper, fortune, and family; whether it is distinguished for parts and worth, or for folly, knavery, and loathsome hereditary diseases. When your friends inform you of these, they have fulfilled their duty. If they go further, they have not that deference for you which a becoming dignity on your part would effectually command.

Whatever your views are in marrying, take every possible precaution to prevent their being disappointed. If fortune, and the pleasures it brings are your aim, it is not sufficient that the settlements of a jointure and children's provision be ample, and properly secured; it is necessary that you should enjoy the fortune during your own life. The principal security you can have for this will depend on your marrying a good natured, generous man, who despises money, and who will let you live where you can best enjoy that pleasure, that pomp and parade of life, for which you married him.

From what I have said you will easily see that I could never pretend to advise whom you should marry; but I can with great confidence advise whom you should not marry.

Avoid a companion that may entail any hereditary disease on your posterity, particularly (that most dreadful of all human calamities) madness. It is the height of imprudence to run into such a danger, as in my opinion highly criminal.

Do not marry a fool; he is the most intractable of all animals; he is led by his passions and caprices, and is incapable of hearing the voice of reason. It may probably too hurt your vanity, to have husbands for whom you have reason to blush and tremble every time they open their lips in company. But the worst circumstance that attends a fool, is his constant ieal ousy of his wife being thought to govern him. This renders it impossible to lead him, and he is continually doing absurd and disagreeable things, for no other reason but to show he dares do them.

A rake is always a suspicious husband, because he has only known the most worthless of your sex. He likewise entails the worst diseases on his wife and children, if he has the misfortune to have any.

If you have a sense of religion yourselves, do not think of husbands who have none. If they have tolerable understandings, they will be glad that you have religion, for their own sakes, and for the sake of their families; but it will sink you in their esteem. If they are weak men, they will be continually teasing and shocking you about your principles. If you have children, you will suffer the most bitter distress, in seeing all your endeavors to form their minds to virtue and piety, all your endeavors to secure their present and eternal happiness, frustrated, and turned into ridicule.

As I look on your choice of a husband to be of the greatest consequence to your happiness, I hope you will make it with the utmost circumspection. Do not give way to a sudden sally of passion, and dignify it with the name of love. Genuine love is not founded in caprice; it is founded in nature, on honorable views, on virtue, on similarity of tastes and sympathy of souls.

If you have these sentiments, you will never marry any one when you are not in that situation in point of fortune, which is necessary to the happiness of either of you. What that competency may be, can only be determined by your own tastes. It would be ungenerous in you to take advantage of a lover's attachment to plunge him into distress; if he has any honor, no personal gratification will ever tempt him to enter into any connexion which will render you unhappy. If you have as much between you as to satisfy all your reasonable demands, it is sufficient.

I shall conclude with endeavoring to remove a difficulty which must naturally occur to any woman of reflection on the subject of marriage. What is to become of all these refinements of delicacy, that dignity of manners, which checked all familiarities, and suspended desire in respectful and awful admiration? In answer to this I shall only observe, that if motives of interest or vanity have had any share in your resolution to marry, none of these chimerical notions will give you any pain, nay, they will very quickly appear as ridiculous in your own eyes as they probably always did in the eyes of your husbands. They have been sentiments which floated in your imaginations, but have never reached your hearts. But if these sentiments have been truly genuine, and if you have had the singular happy fate to attach those who understand them, you have no reason to be afraid.

Marriage, indeed, will at once dispel the enchantment raised by external beauty; but the virtues and graces that first warmed the heart, that reserve and delicacy which always left the lover with something further to wish, and often made him doubtful of your sensibility or attachment, may and ought ever to remain.

The tumult of passion will necessarily subside; but it will be succeeded by an endearment that affects the heart in a more equal, more sensible, and tender manner. But I must check myself, and not indulge in descriptions that may mislead you, and that too sensibly awake the remembrance of my happier days, which, perhaps, it were better for me to forget for ever.

I have thus given you my opinion on some of the most important articles of your future life, chiefly calculated for that period when you are just entering the world. I have endeavored to avoid some peculiarities of opinion, which, from their contradiction to the general practice of the world I might reasonably have suspected were not so well founded. But in writing to you, I am afraid my heart has been too warmly interested to allow me to keep this resolution This may have produced some embarrassment, and some seeming contradictions. What I have written has been the amusement of some solitary hours, and has served to divert some melancholy reflections. I am conscious I undertook a task to which I was very unequal; but I have discharged a part of my duty You will at least be pleased with it, as the last mark of your father's love and attention.

TRIALS AND TEMPTATIONS OF WOMAN.

If it be true, that the sight of a great man manfully struggling against trouble is enough to make the gods shed tears, that of a virtuous woman bearing sorrow with patience and fortitude might well bring angels from heaven to cheer and comfort her.

Almost synonymous with suffering is the name of woman; for though the troubles which man and woman have to bear, may, if considered in the abstract, be much the same in amount, yet if reference be made to woman's sensibility, whether of mind or body, the suffering must fall much heavier upon her than upon man. She is so formed as not to be firm enough to withstand, or yet flexible enough to bend to the blast of affliction.

Man has indeed vast trials and troubles; but then he has both a mind and a body constitutionally fitted to grapple with them; whereas a woman has to bear the same amount of affliction with a temperament the very reverse. So fair, so fragile, as women are, are they to be exposed against the jarring winds which affliction lets loose, and which spread desolation and sorrow wheresoever they sweep? Are the sensibilities and the feelings which so adorn the female heart to be stung by grief, when they seem only fitted for gayety and joy?

Women are naturally buoyant and light-hearted—the eye beaming with brightness, and the cheek usually wearing a smile; but this must bring equally a sense of pain, for the heart most easily pleased is soonest saddened. If they were more indifferent to pleasure there would be a greater callousness to pain. It is this very sensitiveness of their nature which makes pain so much more easily felt, as the brightest mirror is the soonest sullied.

In every station she can occupy, is a woman exposed to trial and to trouble; and the more she is bound to others, the more is she exposed to sorrow in her own person.

The happiest and most endearing of all the terms which can be applied to woman, is undoubtedly that of mother. But who can tell a mother's trials—a mother's troubles, sorrows, or afflictions? Take a mother in her happiest moments; see her encircled by her children, with whom she is playing. "One she kisses upon its cheek, and clasps another to her bosom; one she sets upon her knee, and finds a seat upon her foot for another." There is, then, to her, joy unmingled with sorrow, and pleasure free from pain. She has forgotten the anguish she suffered in giving these children birth; she thinks not of the many sleepless nights she passed while she was watching and guarding the helplessness of infancy. The gay smile and the happy look she wears, attest the pleasure she feels; but they also tell how deep would be the suffering if aught of evil were to happen to her offspring. And, ere long, it may be the sore stroke comes, and one of her children is laid upon a bed of sickness. And a very sore trial is this to a mother; her fond pictures of the future are blasted in an instant, and she has to attend upon the child, pallid and pained by sickness, with whom she was so fondly playing but a short period before. Who but a mother can know a mother's feelings, when called upon to discharge a duty like this? How much anxiety, how much watchfulness is displayed; how eagerly she notes the irregular and feverish breathings of her child! And often does it happen that sickness not only comes to one child, but that it runs through the whole group. Before many days the mother will detect the hectic spot brightening on another fair cheek—too surely presaging the increase of her troubles, her anxieties, and her pains. But she relaxes nothing of her solicitude or care. With her amount of hardships appears to increase her power to overcome them; and, amid this disease and these trials, she maintains her usual calmness and serenity of mind.

A brief time passes away, and the darkened windows of that house proclaim that one of its inmates is a corpse. It is the brightest and the fairest that death hath laid low. Of the two that sickened, one is fast returning to health and joy—the other lies cold and dead.

While there remained life, hope still lingered; but when the one went out the other fled. And now has a mother to mourn over a departed child—this trial of trials, how shall a woman's heart bear up against so much as this? Oh! the mother will stand at the side of her pale child, and will fix a deep and penetrating look upon those calm and placid features, which, ere mortality begins to settle them, look more like marble than death; and she will impress a burning kiss upon its cheek, too cold, alas! to be warmed by this fondest token. She may not speak; but her ears—these, which form the most powerful of oratory—these tell how the heart is wrung with anguish, how riven with grief.

And not only does an affliction like this bring with it poignancy of grief and deepness of sorrow—how severe a trial is it also of temper! The hardest of all things is to bear affliction with a right mind; and many a secret thought is likely to arise in a mother's mind when standing by the side of a dead child, suggesting the idea that God has dealt hardly and harshly in inflicting so severe a blow; and a murmur may arise that the even-handed justice of God has not been shown in her case, and that the dispensations of his providence are not always right. It is a hard task, and therefore a very severe trial, to bear affliction with patience and resignation; for the heart of a mother so bereaved feels that a severer, and as she thinks, a more unjust stroke, has been dealt upon her than upon others. She will call to mind the youth, the innocence of her departed child; and all these will seem to her so many reasons why death should have been kept away. But she will not think how many mothers have been similarly bereaved, and how many scalding tears they have shed over children death has thus stricken—for grief to all but a resigned and patient temper is selfish. Under these trials, therefore, the heart should bend with patience to the will of God. And though the eye may still weep, and the heart be sorrowed, yet in the midst of all, by recognising in the affliction the hand of a father, the lips may breathe forth with perfect sincerity, "The Lord gave, and the Lord hath taken away: blessed be the name of the Lord."

But all the duties of a mother are so many trials, to watch and train her children, to guard the waywardness of youth, to teach, to admonish, to instruct, to advise—all are attended with hardships, and, therefore, all are trials. She will find so many things to try her own temper—she will have to maintain so strict a guard over herself, lest her own conduct disproving those things she teaches, that which she plants with one hand she may be plucking up with the other. And a severer trial than all these frequently assails a mother—for those are labors she delights in, and the pleasure she feels in performing them compensates for the difficulty of the tasks. But when a mother sees that all these instructions have been thrown away, and that a child is entering a path which conducts to ruin, then will her trial be most severe and poignant, and, in the bitterness of her grief, she would wish rather to have seen a son coffined and buried, had he been virtuous, than that he should live to dishonor God, disgrace his parents, and ruin himself. And it will add considerably to her grief when she calls to mind how imperfect at best many of her instructions must have been; she will think that more might still have been done—though there was very much—to try to wean him from his attachment to bad companions, and to base and unworthy pursuits.

And to the deep grief which is ever to be felt by the recklessness and immorality of a child, will be added the painful thoughts arising from the knowledge that though she taught and instructed to the best of her power, yet that if she had thought more deeply she might have followed a better method, and that the ill success may be partly chargeable upon herself. And this is, perhaps, one of the sorest trials a mother can have befall her; for she charges herself, in all probability undeservedly, with having, through negligence or improper management, suffered evil habits to obtain the ascendency in the mind of her child; so that over and above the pain which she feels on account of him who manifests a proneness to evil, there will be added the pain derived from the thought that much of this proneness is chargeable upon herself. And the nobler the mind, the more will this feeling rise, for it is the invariable characteristic of great minds to think humbly of themselves.

These, then, are all so many causes of trial to a mother, and they are so numerous and manifest, that the history of a mother might be told in these few words: 'She is born to trouble."

Nor are the temptations to which a mother is exposed much less numerous than her trials. Surrounded by those who are entirely dependant upon her, is she not tempted to manifest a degree of pride and arrogance, to treat her children as if with life they had derived everything else from her, so that her will was law, and no opinion tenable which she did not entertain? And this is a temptation by which many, very many, mothers are overcome, so that their children seem at home to be complete ciphers, and only enjoy life when out of their mother's presence.

How much, too, is a mother tempted to a frequent display of anger! So many vexations and crosses are continually pressing upon her, that she must frequently be tempted to display pique and irritability Again, from the continued demand upon her attention, she is liable to lose patience, and hastily and hurriedly to perform a duty, or perhaps altogether to neglect it.

These are all so many temptations to the display of an unholy and unamiable disposition to which a mother is exposed. She should therefore keep a guard upon her actions, and set a watch upon her lips, lest she perform some action in a moment of anger, or utter some expression when her temper is excited, which will in calmer hours bring with it regret and repentance. Knowing how much depends upon her a mother should be careful in everything she says and does; and then will the trials she has undergone, and the temptations she has resisted, become bright jewels in her crown of immortality.

Equally to a wife is life a source of trial. The character and disposition of each inmate in her house may be a great source of trial; but it is a husband who brings it down upon her head in its poignancy and bitterness. It is on him that all her affections are centred; and when she finds that but little love is yielded her in return, then must she undergo a severe trial. If he should prove unkind and inconstant, requiring that she be solicitous for his comforts, though he may show but small concern for hers—if he indulge in habits of sensuality and debauchery, preferring the midnight revel, with its voluptuous pleasures, to the calm attractiveness of home—there will be a severe trial inflicted on a wife—a trial of patience, of temper, of virtue, and of love.

But if the reverse is the case, and a wife finds the husband of her love to be also the truest and dearest friend she has, she may still be exposed to trial and trouble. If they be so firmly linked to each other that one heart seems to beat in both breasts, then will every pain which befalls the one be equally a trial to the other. A wife will have to bear all a husband's pain—she will have to share all his troubles and all his sorrows; and the burden will fall heavier upon her, from her temper being so much more susceptible, for the mere seeing a husband's heart grieved will be a trial to her own. There can not then be a trial he has to undergo which is not equally a trial to her, nor can any of those numerous casualties which so often befall humanity happen to him without her participating in their perplexity and trouble. And thus, as the world is always presenting something of disappointment and care, will a wife be continually having many trials. But more than all these, and far heavier and harder, will be those to which she may be brought by sickness and death; these heir-looms of humanity, which no amount of prudence can guard against, bring with them the severest trials, and cause the greatest hardships to be undergone.

How hard is the trial inflicted upon a wife who has to minister to the wants of a husband when lying upon a bed of sickness! Sickness, like sorrow, makes the heart selfish, and many will be the peevish whims she may be called upon to gratify; many an unreasonable request is sure to be made by the invalid; and over and above these, the trial of seeing one she loves in pain: and thus she will have many things to try her temper, for her patience, her kindness, and her love, are sure to be tasked to the utmost.

But alas! sickness is too often the stepping-stone to death, and perhaps before many days that loved husband may be numbered among the dead. This is the hardest of all trials. The midnight watchings—the unremitting attention, the sick-chamber requires—the want of sleep,—all these a wife could have borne with patience and resignation; but death—this has bereaved her of all that she held dearest—this has riven her heart, and the gushing tears which roll down her cheek proclaim how deeply flowed the stream of affection.

The most inconsolable of all things is the heart of a widow in the first days of her bereavement, and therefore is this affliction which brings so much grief the severest of all trials. It is vain to tell her that time will soften her grief, and that sorrow is unavailing, benefiting not the dead, and only injuring the living; it is equally useless to say that sorrow will not bring back the dead to life. The heart of the widow would answer, in the words of the philosopher of old, —"It is for that very reason I am shedding tears." For a time at least she will remain deaf to all consolation—nay, she will wish even that consolation should not be offered, for she will not for a moment entertain the thought that her departed husband can ever be forgotten, or that she shall regard at any time as less severe the blow which deprived her of that truest of her earthly friends. She will call to mind all the scenes and events in which they bore a part,—the joyousness of youth—the deepness of their loves—the actions in which they both participated—the sorrows no less than the joys which they shared together—and all these will be so many different voices to tell of the greatness of her bereavement, declaring the hardness of the trial she is called upon to undergo.

And, under a trial like this, where shall the widowed heart find comfort? Friends may gather around her, eager to show their sympathy, and striving to cheer her in these troublous hours. But the sympathy of friends is unsatisfactory at best, even when most kind; for it only tells of the greatness of the loss, and brings nothing to cheer or make resigned under the affliction. They may tell her that death is unavoidable—that time will mitigate the grief—that the retrospect of her conduct is such, that she can not charge herself with neglect to her husband—and that, therefore, she should not take his death so much to heart. But all such sympathy as this is unavailing. It is like attempting to bring back the glories of the day after the sun has gone down, by exhibiting the blackness of night; and, in the one case as in the other, in place of being reconciled, the mind the more regrets the loss of former brightness.

And as affliction is hard to bear at all, so is it yet harder to meet it in a right and proper frame of mind. Many a murmur will be breathed—many a secret thought is likely to arise, on the inequality of God's dealings; and a comparison to be drawn between herself and others, who seem blessed with everything of health and happiness. It is only by and through a genuine practical religion that affliction can be borne patiently and resignedly; for religion teaches the ends and uses of affliction, and thus prepares the mind to encounter it with patience. It does not seek to wrap up the heart in the rigidity of stoicism—it does not forbid the shedding of tears, or the manifestation of sorrow; for tears are the balm to a wounded spirit, and Christians have an example they may follow, in that their Master wept. But while not forbidding—nay, even encouraging—the grief of the heart to flow in drops from the eyes, religion tells us that all afflictions are sent for a good end, and that the heart should not repine or murmur when they come, for that it is the hand of a Father who deals the blow—not for the pleasure of giving pain, but because afflictive dispensations are a means to lead the heart from earth to heaven—from the evanescent and perishable, to the eternal and everlasting.

It were easy to speak further of the trials which still attach themselves to the female heart, illustrating them by the tears which fall from the eyes of a daughter who stands over the grave where a loved parent sleeps, or by those shed by a sister over the ashes of a brother. But, without going further into detail upon these points, we may say with truth, that the amount of her suffering is of fearful extent and of bitter poignancy.

It is hardly too much to say that the life of a woman is a life of trial—so continual is the demand upon her energy and firmness, when constitutionally she is made yielding and submissive. How much of patience is woman called upon to endure! how many secret cares which the world knows not of, are locked up in her breast! and though the eye beams with brightness and the cheek may wear a smile, yet the heart is disquieted and troubled—grief, like a canker-worm, is eating at the core, though the bud be still beautiful.

In all the duties of women, great trials are inflicted upon them—principally trials of the mind—those of temper, of resolution, and of kindness; and all these have to be encountered singly and silently—there is no applause to follow success—no mighty crowds surround them to stimulate to exertion, and to urge on to victory; but in the secret depths of their own hearts the struggle is carried on; there is it that the strife takes place, and human eyes see nothing of the conflict, nor is anything divulged of the difficulty of the war.

How many trials are also inflicted by the unamiable dispositions, which, more or less, have a lodgment in every heart! What a fierce struggle with nature is it when any strive to conquer a disposition which they know to be wrong, but which has been so engrafted in them as to have "grown with their growth and strengthened with their strength!" Suppose the disposition which it is wished to conquer be passion—what numberless battles will have to be fought before victory is obtained! To such a disposition, at the mere utterance of a word, the heart takes fire, and, in an instant, the brow is wrapped in darkness, as in a thunder-cloud, and the eye flashes forth its lightning, and truly difficult is it to so have the heart under control under circumstances of sudden irritation, that the feelings shall be subdued and kept under. Suppose pride or vanity to be the characteristic feature of the disposition; but, sensible of the impropriety, an attempt is made to subdue it: what a revolution will have to be effected ere the proud mind can be brought to humility, or the vain to think others as good or better than themselves!

In these and in similar instances the trials are very difficult to be overcome, not only because the struggle is acquiring a mastery over nature—which of itself is sufficiently a trial—but also because, while the struggle is carried on, there will not be breathed, to cheer the combatant, a word of encouragement, of support, or of commendation.

To woman, as to man, come sickness and death, and these both have their trials. What a demand upon patience and resignation is made when the body is pained by sickness and enfeebled by disease! What a trial, when the prospect of dissolution is present to the view—when pain is severing the silken cords which bind soul to body, and the world is receding quickly from the view! It may have been a female's part to have tended the sick-bed of a relative, and to have cheered and comforted when the death-struggle came on; and in these she may have displayed the noblest and the best feelings which adorn human nature. But when she herself comes to the point of death, far different may be the feelings which agitate her breast. It is one thing to see sickness and death, but quite another to have to meet them.

It is of all things the most solemn and awful to die. A trial is then made of every principle which has been held by the mind—the world then begins to be regarded in its true light—actions are brought to their proper standard, and only those who have prepared for death can meet their last enemy with complacency; for, "as the production of the metal proveth the work of the alchymist, so is death the test of our lives, the essay which showeth the standard of all our actions."

And this is a trial all have to submit to. In life it happens that many afflictions descend upon one individual, whereas others scarcely know what trouble is—but death is the appointed lot of all. It comes in a thousand forms and a thousand different ways, but it surely comes. And only those who have lived in preparation for death die with a bright hope of immortality.

It is the buoyancy of woman's nature which gives yet greater keenness to the trials by which she is encompassed. Possessing a mind naturally imaginative and lively, and a disposition which makes her concentrate all her energies upon every object which engages her attention, she thereby brings upon herself much trouble. A disposition which is constantly imagining, suffers troubles which perhaps have no existence, for the brightest cloud soon assumes the blackness of night, and imagined trouble is often far harder to bear than real, and by every energy being roused, disappointments are sure to have very frequently to be encountered, and from these causes commonly arise to woman many and severe trials.

The temptations to which women are exposed are almost as numerous as their trials, especially during the season of youth, when the heart is most light and the cheek wears its fairest teint. From the homage which the world pays to beauty, they are led to vanity, and tempted to pursuits which procure them flatteries and homage. Hence they are induced to enlist themselves in the companionship of those who think pleasure the greatest good, and its pursuit the noblest occupation. And if a woman yield to this first temptation, others quickly rise up around her. She will see that much which she had been accustomed to consider high and noble is counted of no great worth by the world's votaries. Truth might have been regarded as a holy thing, and to speak anything false was like profanation to the lips; but in the world she will find that flatteries take the place of truth, and in order to stand well with others, and to have admirers around her, a young woman may soon exchange her love of truth for the sake of uttering things she does not feel—hollow flatteries and empty praise.

The female sex are exposed to many temptations, from their having but few objects of interest to engage their attention. From the period of leaving school to that of marriage, the life of a female is generally little more than a blank. She leaves school with expanded faculties, high hopes, beating expectations, and ardor of application, but not a suitable object upon which to expend them—and thus she wastes lofty thoughts, and brilliant purposes, and surprising powers, on the dull earth or the deaf air; she seems like some glorious temple, beautiful in architecture, costly in ornaments, rich in splendor, and radiant with light, but wanting a shrine upon which to burn incense, and a God to adore.

At first fancy becomes busy, peopling the air with images, building up imaginary structures, and depicting events in which themselves act the part of a heroine; but, by degrees, this feeling cools down, or becomes overwrought, and then follows a state of inactivity which at last ends in complete *ennui*. Then are various remedies tried to restore the lost spirits, and the temptations with which they will be assailed with will be those which lead them to seek pleasure, perhaps, in these most unsatisfactory ones—in the constantly spending the evenings at parties, in the ball-room, or at the theatre.

It is commonly said that women have but few temptations in common with the other sex. It may be true that they have not many from the great world without; but they have many, very many, from the little world within. Every thought which suggests the following the expedient in place of the right is a powerful temptation; every suggestion to the pride of display, or to the passion for flattery or applause, is a temptation; every secret longing after unpossessed good—every desire to shine pre-eminent in beauty all are so many temptations which scatter roses before the feet, but bring ruin in their train.

Surrounded by trials and environed by temptations, woman stands trials the hardest to bear, and temptations the most difficult to overcome; and to meet these she is endowed with a weak and delicate frame, and with a mind in which fortitude appears to hold but a small place. And yet the disasters which almost break down the spirit of man are borne patiently, energetically, and nobly, by the softer sex, as though trouble had a magical power over the female heart, on the mere touch of which, woman rose from weakness and dependance, to be a guide, a comforter, and a support.

It was once a matter of debate, whether women ought to be educated, and, proud of his own learning, man bounded off, by a broad line of demarcation, female intellect from his own. But if he wants to know how trouble is to be endured or temptation resisted, let him cast aside his speculations of science, let him shut up his books on the strength of human intellect, and the greatness of human understanding, let him banish from his sight his wild and visionary theories, in which there exist as much fiction as truth, and let him go to woman—woman whom, in his pride and his intolerance he hardly thought worth educating, and there he will find that what intellect has failed to accomplish, has been achieved by the moral affections alone.

Having pointed out some of the trials and temptations to which woman is liable while endeavoring to discharge the obligations which society imposes on her, we will now proceed to show the consolation that religion affords in affliction.

If we take life as it is, divested of all hope of the future, a more gloomy picture could scarcely be imagined. We come into a world, which, at every step we turn, presents sorrow and disappointment. Each makes for himself an idea of happiness, and all set forth on the pursuit of the fancied good; but all find that their happiness existed in imagination only, and that the pursuit thereof was like that of a boy chasing a butterfly, which is no sooner grasped than the bright hues come off in the hand; while, on the other hand, there arises to the mind a long train of troubles which ourselves must encounter, and the still more lengthened ones which would befall those we love best. Misfortune, and pain, and death, haunt our footsteps, and hardly will one difficulty be overcome, ere another, as from the ashes of the former, will arise, like a cloud in the west to dim the brightness of the day. At every turn we take, at every point we reach, we find that trouble and perplexity are assailing us. It is only when religion is taken into account, that the justness of God's dealings with the human family becomes apparent. The god of the savage is a god of wrath and revenge, delighting in slaughter, and revelling in blood. The god of the skeptic is a being who, after having once given laws, allows all to go on without interference or control. But the God of the Christian is a God of love—a God who, while concerned in ordering the movement of systems, has a thought for the lowliest and the meanest of the creatures he has formed. It is this great truth which religion inculcates, and is a truth in which, as creatures subjected to sorrow, and pain, and death, we have the greatest possible interest; for without this truth being fully understood, affliction will never be regarded under a proper point of view, or be borne with a right spirit.

There is a mother bending in tearful agony over the lifeless form of her only child. The bitterness of grief is present to her in its most poignant form; and as she presses her lips to the pale, cold cheek of her beloved child, she feels that the blow has been unjustly dealt, and that the bud should have been left to become a flower ere it was smitten by the blast. It will be thus that she reasons: "Oh! if I had been God, should I not have spared this fairest flower? Should I have let the blast of death sweep over it, and bring down the young, the beautiful, the innocent, to the cold grave? Could I have dimmed the lustre of those eyes, which, blue as the midnight heavens, were, like those heavens, the habitation of love? Could I have faded the color of that fair cheek, than which the rose's teints were scarcely more beautiful? Could I have destroyed all that beauty, withered all that fairness, and brought so soon the dread curse which condemns dust to return to its kindred dust?"

It is thus a mother might be supposed to complain when she sees the child of her love lying cold and still. She will probably think that much of injustice has been done alike to herself and to her child in thus destroying the fondest hopes of the one, and the life of the other. But if we may suppose the Almighty as desiring to vindicate the justness of his own actions, it would be thus, we may imagine, the reply would be made: "In your sorrow, oh! fond mother, you accuse me of injustice and partiality, dealing affliction in undue measure to one, and granting happiness beyond a common share to another. But to all created things which live upon your globe have I thus dealt. Do not the evidences which are to be gathered from every beast, every bird, and every insect, attest that all has been done which could give to the things which I have created the greatest possible amount of enjoyment? Where the life is brief, is it not bright? and to those creatures which die when the sun goes down, has not their life been a day of sunshine? And why with the human family should it be supposed that I deal more hardly than with the insect of a day? Have I not endowed the human race with vast powers and surprising faculties, far beyond those I have given to the rest of earth's tenants, giving to them an immortal soul, and destining them to dwell in that high kingdom where my own throne is set, when their present life is ended? All that I have done for human-kind, the love I have manifested for them, bearing with their ingratitude, and with the contempt manifested toward my commandments, ought to have been sufficient to have brought all hearts to be centred on myself. I sent into the world prophets and wise men, gifted with supernatural powers, and endued with a prescience belonging only to myself, and even went so far as to assume humanity myself, that the bright heritage forfeited by apostacy might be regained. And, for all that has been done, for all that has been borne, I ask no hard service. Love and obedience are all that is demanded;—love to myself, which, while it is my due, is the highest honor bestowed upon humanity, and obedience to my laws, the infringement of which is sure to bring misery to the transgressor.

"But so degraded is the human heart, that even with the best, earth still holds them in restraint. Some links are binding down the heart—some dear friend has the affections, and the heart is weaned from myself. But as I know the frailty of humanity, I deal with it as gently as I can. Removing the ties and breaking the links which bind to earth, I thus seek to bring the heart back to myself. If affliction be sent, it is to show the perishableness of everything earthly; if sickness, to bring back the heart to look for support where alone it is to be found.

"You arraign me unjustly in accusing me of harshly dealing with you. It is true, death has overtaken your child in the bright dawn of love: but that child was to you an idol, occupying every thought, and causing you to forget God. You put the gift in the place of the Giver, and set your affections upon that so entirely as to exclude from your thoughts obligations yet more binding. But now that your child is no more, you will, when time has softened down your grief, attend once more to the duties of religion.

Recognising a Father's hand in the chastisement, you will learn to set your affections on brighter objects and on more endearing things.

"A mother's love—it is a holy feeling. I, who gave that love, know best its depth and fervency. But even that feeling may be abused. It may descend to idolatry, and then the thoughts are turned completely from their God.

"But if, to turn the mother's heart to religious duties, I have permitted that her child should fall under the power of the destroyer, have I herein dealt unjustly? Am I not the God of life? can I, therefore, be pleased with death? In taking the young from the world, I but remove them to a happier land. The bright bud which childhood wears, is not always certain of blooming as brightly; and in all cases are they taken from the evil to come. Life is not always happiness, nor early death a curse. If your child had lived, temptations would have assailed it, which it would not have overcome: troubles and sorrows would have crowded upon it, and life would have presented little of enjoyment, and very much of suffering. Will you then arraign my dispensations, declaring them unjust and harsh, when the stroke which seemed to destroy, has saved you both?—saved you in that your heart will return to think of God; and saved your child, by removing it before the world had thrown round it its attractions, which would have engrossed its soul, and brought its ruin."

It is under this view that the Bible presents the dealings of God, and under no other creed than Christianity is there to be gathered anything of comfort or consolation. It is only the thought that God's purposes are always for the best, which can cheer under suffering, comfort under trouble, and deprive death of its sting. Sorrow is deprived of much of its bitterness by regarding the affliction as sent by a Being whose attributes are those of benevolence and love.

The doctrine of a particular Providence is a doctrine fraught with the greatest consolation to mankind, who are born to sorrow. Not only is it that nothing can happen but what God permits—nothing can happen but what he enjoins. The notion of God should not be, that he has lit up the sun, and given the winds power to roam through the world; but rather that his glance is in every beam, and his breath in every breeze. The idea should not be entertained, that after having given life to men, God concerns himself no more with his creatures; but rather that through his special interference is it that breath follows breath, and pulse succeeds pulse; so that in every trouble and in every joy—in every hope which rises to cheer, and in every doubt which darkens, the hand of God may be discerned, producing out of a thousand seeming ills, and a thousand apparent discrepancies, not only a general, but an individual good.

And how much of consolation is there to a heart when deeply stricken with sorrow, to be able to feel that all afflictions are set for a wise purpose, and that there is a bright kingdom hereafter, where pain shall have no entrance! It would go far to dry a mother's tears, which the death of her child has caused to flow, if she could be thus persuaded to regard the dealings of God. It would be to take half the bitterness from sorrow, if she could be made to feel that in allowing death to take her child, God has been dealing both kindly and gently, in that he has removed it from the world when the heart was innocent, and pain and sorrow scarcely known.

When the mind is impressed with religion, there is always a calmness and serenity, prosperity does not elate, nor adversity depress; and the reason of this is, that both are considered as coming from God—the one as well as the other counted as ministering to good.

No doubt afflictions presented in the taking away by death of those held the dearest, and those the most loved, though not the only ones befalling humanity, are the hardest to be borne. The tears which fall from mourners' eyes, whether it be a parent over a child, a wife over a husband, a child over a parent, or a sister over a brother or a sister—these speak of afflictions the bitterest and most trying; for other losses may again be made up, but when death bereaves us of those we love, who shall bring back the departed? tears can not do it—grief has no power—prayers avail not. "We shall go to them, but they will not return to us," is the conviction forced upon every mind which has thought upon God. And how sweet is the thought that the dead will again be seen—that those long mourned for on earth will be met again in a brighter land! This feeling is of itself sufficient to dry the eye and cheer the heart. Brief may be the separation—a journey would almost have parted them for as long a lapse of time, and then those endearing ties of friendship and love, which bound but for a moment and then were severed, shall be reunited in that land where nothing dies. That such will be the case, Religion assures us; while Hope raises her radiant finger and points upward to the skies.

But not only in these cases is the power of religion felt—in others less severe its influence is apparent. Is it the loss of property which is grieving the heart? has worldly substance crumbled away, leaving but scanty means of subsistence, in place of the hitherto comparatively large resources and ample revenue? The voice of religion is heard—"If earthly riches make to themselves wings and fly away, are there not yet riches more enduring stored in heaven? Earthly riches are fleeting and transient; heavenly, firm, and abiding. Earthly possessions can but be enjoyed for a few years; heavenly are eternal." And does it not, then, take much from the hardness of poverty to think that abundance may soon again be the portion—and abundance which never grows less, and knows no change?

In whatever form trouble may come—in whatever shape or under whatever aspect religion still brings a comfort and a support; there is not a sorrow which it can not cheer, nor a doubt which it can not remove, nor a difficulty which it can not prepare for; it bids us "cast all our care upon God, for he careth for us."

And not only is religion a guide through life—it is also that which teaches us how death may be best prepared for. The calmest and happiest death-beds are those which have religion to cheer. We do not always expect that nothing of weakness will be displayed even by those whose lives have been most exemplary, and whose hearts have been firmly fixed upon God. The breaking up of this earthly house—the tearing down the curious fastenings, that the soul may quit its tenement—this of itself is almost sufficient to bring dismay and fear. And the liberated spirit, where shall it find a home? It must travel, a lonely and a widowed thing, through the vastness of immensity; the place of its future abode "eye hath not seen," and of all the souls which have quitted human bodies, not one has returned to tell of the land in which it dwells. And that body, too, which is so "fearfully and wonderfully made," and which has been guarded with so much care, is to be taken down, joint from joint and limb from limb, to become a plaything for the winds and a sport for the elements, and to mingle with its kindred dust and ashes.

No marvel is it, with such thoughts as these, that the mind should display something of weakness. It might even be considered marvellous if no weakness were exhibited, considering how fearful a thing death is, and what a vast change it will effect.

But to those who have made religion the guide of life, death is not fearful. The spirit, it is true, must quit its habitation; but the knowledge that it return to the God who gave it, destroys the pain which the thought of its separation would otherwise give. And the body, this must return to the grave; but the thought of the great glories which await it hereafter, more than compensate for the dishonor attending dissolution. And so it comes to pass, that while weeping friends stand around, vainly striving to hide their grief, the dying person contemplates the death which is so fast approaching, with calmness and complacency, and after having bid all those who are gathered round the bedside an affectionate farewell, and entreated them to mitigate their sorrow, yields the last breath with the bright hope of a glorious immortality.

If thus religion were made the guide of life, we should not be so cast down when sorrow came. Having our thoughts fixed on a higher and better land, our words would be those of that honest Hibernian, who, on being told that the house in which he dwelt was on fire, replied, "What care I for the house, I am but a lodger!" We should feel that we were but lodgers on earth; that our home was heaven; and little, therefore, should we be moved by those calamities which befall us, except so far as to make our affections become more firmly centred on our happy home. If we were fairly to regard earth and all belonging to it, we should not suffer all our affections to be engrossed by it; for an individual is but as a speck or an atom—a bubble in the ocean. And little as a single individual is counted, less is the concern manifested when death shall have ended his worldly career. The morrow after he shall have quitted this lower world, the sun will rise as brightly, the birds will sing as sweetly, and the flowers bloom as beautifully as ever. Nature never puts on the garb of mourning, nor ever drops a tear. Why, then, should we maintain such a vast attachment to this world, which cares not for our presence while living, nor mourns our loss when dead? a world, moreover, which cheats us at every turn, giving shadows for substances, and phantoms for realities, and which gives so long a train of troubles and pains. And yet, knowing all this, still the world has a vast influence over us; and though in every other instance we put off a present small good for a future great one, in this particular we prefer the present and insignificant to the future and glorious, so that if it were not for the afflictive dispensations of Providence, we should never carry our thoughts beyond the present narrow limits, and the future would be kept entirely from our view. These keep the mind from entirely resting on earth, by the continual display of the transitoriness and unsatisfactoriness of its possession. Were it not for the hope of a glorious hereafter, we should be creatures who were always grasping at the unsubstantial, and pursuing the visionary—mariners without a compass—travellers without a guide—catching at shadows, and attempting to track the course of meteors; and as all our endeavors to procure the fancied good would be utterly unavailing, we should meet with nothing but continual disappointment. The afflictive dispensations of Providence, at the same time, lead the mind to see how hollow, at best, are the pleasures earth has to bestow, and to draw the mind thence to heaven. But if affliction be not borne with a right spirit, it works harm in place of good; if the heart be not softened, it is sure to become hardened. Afflictions never leave us entirely as they find us; and when they do not reform, they make us callous. The mind will never retain exactly the same position after as before the discipline of Providence; and if we do not go forward we are certain to retrograde. But it seems to be counted of all things the most desperate of wickedness to continue in a state of irreligion after afflictions have been sent; for of Ahaz is this testimony left, as if to mark him off from all others: "And in the time of his distress did he trespass against the Lord: this is that king Ahaz." Many were the evil actions of this king, but through none is he marked out for obloquy and shame; the ban is fixed upon him for having *in distress* trespassed against his God. So generally true is it, that when suffering and trouble come the heart turns to God, that it certainly seems to show a degree of desperation and hardihood to sin in the time of distress.

Those who are impressed with a firm sense of religion are seldom ruffled by the events of time. Such are mostly contented; for whatever their stations, they look round the globe and see yet many worse off than themselves—many who wander through the world deserted and forlorn, with none to sooth or cheer them under the severest affliction—without a home, without a friend. They then look up to the bright heavens above, and reflect that but a few brief years and their habitation will be in that glorious land. When friends forsake, they have still the bright flowers and the green trees, upon which they can place their affections; and more than all, they still have their God; so that in no case can they be downcast or disheartened—that they have always something to cheer and something to enjoy.

It was religion which supported the propagators of Christianity in its earliest days, urging them to brave danger, persecution, and death; it was religion which supported martyrs at the stake and the scaffold, when doomed to seal the charter of their faith with their blood; it has been religion which has supported so many under trials the most severe, and afflictions the most bitter; it has been religion which has cheered the poor in their destitution, the orphan in his loneliness, the widow in her sorrow, the suffering in their pain; and, more than all, it has been religion which has taken the bitterness from death, making it almost a blessing more than a curse, compelling the tyrant to perform the part of a friend rather than that of a destroyer; so that not only with complacency but even with gladness, have many sunk to that sleep which shall last till the judgment-day, when they will arise in glory, and as they enter heaven declare with joy that religion was happiness.

God has given religion to be our guide, and promised his grace to be our support; and so enwoven is religion with the best feelings of the human heart, that vice instinctively pays respect to virtue, and confesses a superiority and excellence in real religion; so much so, that the vicious man would become the virtuous, if it were not that habits of dissipation had so bound him—habits which, like the poisoned vest of Hercules, can only be pulled off by tearing the skin from the bone.

It is only by religion—for religion is virtue—that we can be happy either here or hereafter; for God has so linked happiness with holiness, that, like twin sisters, where the one is, the other strays not far distant. By the power of religion we are enabled to overcome the evils of our nature, and to live in obedience to the law of God; evil habits may be overcome, evil dispositions cured, and a fitness for heaven be obtained, even on this side of the grave.

The first, the brightest, and the best of all acquirements, is real religion; for by this is effected love to God, and peace and good-will to mankind Nothing of malice or envy will be displayed or encouraged—no outbreaks of temper tolerated, no falseness or dissimulation allowed; but that charity which thinketh no evil, and attempteth all good, will be enthroned in the heart and exhibited in the conduct of all who are endeavoring to become followers of "those who through faith and patience now inherit the promises."

LALLA ROOKH.

PREFACE.

The Poem, or Romance, of Lalla Rookh having now reached its twentieth edition, a short account of the origin and progress of a work which has been hitherto, at least, so very fortunate in its course, may not be deemed, perhaps, superfluous or misplaced.

It was about the year 1812 that, impelled far more by the encouraging suggestions of friends than by any confident promptings of my own ambition, I was induced to attempt a Poem upon some Oriental subject, and of those quarto dimensions which Scott's late triumphs in that form had then rendered the regular poetical standard. A negotiation on the subject was opened with the Messrs. Longman in the same year, but, from some causes which have now escaped my recollection, led to no decisive result; nor was it till a year or two after, that any further steps were taken in the matter,—their house being the only one, it is right to add, with which, from first to last, I held any communication upon the subject.

On this last occasion, an old friend of mine, Mr. Perry, kindly offered to lend me the aid of his advice and presence in the interview which I was about to hold with the Messrs. Longman, for the arrangement of our mutual terms; and what with the friendly zeal of my negotiator on the one side, and the prompt and liberal spirit with which he was met on the other, there has seldom occurred any transaction in which Trade and Poesy have shone out so advantageously in each other's eyes. The short discussion that then took place between the two parties, may be comprised in a very few sentences. "I am of opinion," said Mr. Perry,—enforcing his view of the case by arguments which it is not for me to cite,—"that Mr. Moore ought to receive for his Poem the largest price that has been given, in our day, for such a work." "That was," answered the Messrs. Longman, "three thousand guineas." "Exactly so," replied Mr. Perry, "and no less a sum ought he to receive."

It was then objected, and very reasonably, on the part of the firm, that they had never yet seen a single line of the Poem; and that a perusal of the work ought to be allowed to them, before they embarked so large a sum in the purchase. But no;—the romantic view which my friend Perry took of the matter was, that this price should be given as a tribute to reputation already acquired, without any condition for a previous perusal of the new work. This high tone, I must confess, not a little startled and alarmed me; but, to the honour and glory of Romance,—as well on the publishers' side as the poet's,—this very generous view of the transaction was, without any difficulty, acceded to, and the firm agreed, before we separated, that I was to receive three thousand guineas for my Poem.

At the time of this agreement, but little of the work, as it stands at present, had yet been written. But the ready confidence in my success shown by others, made up for the deficiency of that requisite feeling within myself; while a strong desire not wholly to disappoint this "auguring hope," became almost a substitute for inspiration. In the year 1815, therefore, having made some progress in my task, I wrote to report the state of the work to the Messrs. Longman, adding, that I was now most willing and ready, should they desire it, to submit the manuscript for their consideration. Their answer to this offer was as follows:—"We are certainly impatient for the perusal of the Poem; but solely for our gratification. Your sentiments are always honourable."*

I continued to pursue my task for another year, being likewise occasionally occupied with the Irish Melodies, two or three numbers of which made their appearance during the period employed in writing Lalla Rookh. At length, in the year 1816, I found my work sufficiently advanced to be placed in the hands of the publishers. But the state of distress to which England was reduced in that dismal year, by the exhausting effects of the series of wars she had just then concluded, and the general embarrassment of all classes, both agricultural and commercial, rendered it a juncture the least favourable that could well be conceived for the first launch into print of so light and costly a venture as Lalla Rookh. Feeling conscious, therefore, that, under such circumstances, I should act but honestly in putting it in the power of the Messrs. Longman to reconsider the terms of their engagement with me,—leaving them free to postpone, modify, or even, should such be their wish, relinquish it altogether, I wrote them a letter to that effect, and received the following answer:—"We shall be most happy in the pleasure of seeing you in February. We agree with you, indeed, that the times are most inauspicious for 'poetry and thousands;' but we believe that your poetry would do more than that of any other living poet at the present moment."†

The length of time I employed in writing the few stories strung together in Lalla Rookh will appear, to some persons, much more than was necessary for the production of such easy and "light o' love" fictions. But, besides that I have been, at all times, a far more slow and pains-taking workman than would ever be guessed, I fear, from the result, I felt that, in this instance, I had taken upon myself a more than ordinary responsibility, from the immense stake risked by others on my chance of success. For a long time, therefore, after the agreement had been concluded, though generally at work with a view to this task, I made but

* April 10, 1815

† November 9, 1816

very little real progress in it; and I have still by me the beginnings of several stories, continued, some of them, to the length of three or four hundred lines, which, after in vain endeavouring to mould them into shape, I threw aside, like the tale of Cambuscan, "left half-told." One of these stories, entitled The Peri's Daughter, was meant to relate the loves of a nymph of this aërial extraction with a youth of mortal race, the rightful prince of Ormuz, who had been, from his infancy, brought up in seclusion, on the banks of the river Amou, by an aged guardian named Mohassan. The story opens with the first meeting of these destined lovers, then in their childhood; the Peri having wafted her daughter to this holy retreat, in a bright enchanted boat, whose first appearance is thus described:—

* * * * * *

For, down the silvery tide afar,
There came a boat, as swift and bright
  As shines in heav'n some pilgrim-star,
That leaves its own high home, at night,
To shoot to distant shrines of light.

"It comes, it comes," young Orian cries,
And panting to Mohassan flies.
Then down upon the flowery grass
Reclines to see the vision pass;
With partly joy and partly fear,
To find its wondrous light so near,
And hiding oft his dazzled eyes
Among the flowers on which he lies.

* * * * * *

Within the boat a baby slept,
Like a young pearl within its shell;
  While one, who seem'd of riper years,
  But not of earth, or earth-like spheres,
Her watch beside the slumberer kept;
Gracefully waving, in her hand,
  The feathers of some holy bird,
  With which, from time to time, she stirr'd
The fragrant air, and coolly fann'd
The baby's brow, or brush'd away
  The butterflies that, bright and blue
As on the mountains of Malay,
  Around the sleeping infant flew.

And now the fairy boat hath stopp'd
Beside the bank—the nymph has dropp'd
Her golden anchor in the stream:

* * * * * *

A song is sung by the Peri in approaching, of which the following forms a part:—

My child she is but half divine,
Her father sleeps in the Caspian water;
    Sea-weeds twine
    His funeral shrine,
But he lives again in the Peri's daughter.
Fain would I fly from mortal sight
  To my own sweet bowers of Peristan;
But there the flowers are all too bright
  For the eyes of a baby born of man.
On flowers of earth her feet must tread;
  So hither my light-wing'd bark hath brought her;
    Stranger, spread
    Thy leafiest bed,
To rest the wandering Peri's daughter.

In another of these inchoate fragments, a proud female saint, named Banou, plays a principal part; and her progress through the streets of Cufa, on the night of a great illuminated festival, I find thus described:

It was a scene of mirth that drew
A smile from ev'n the Saint Banou,
As, through the hush'd, admiring throng,
She went with stately steps along,
And counted o'er, that all might see,
The rubies of her rosary.
But none might see the worldly smile
That lurk'd beneath her veil, the while:—
Alla forbid! for who would wait
Her blessing at the temple's gate,—
What holy man would ever run
To kiss the ground she knelt upon,
If once, by luckless chance, he knew
She look'd and smiled as others do?
Her hands were join'd, and from each wrist,
By threads of pearl and golden twist,
Hung relics of the saints of yore,
And scraps of talismanic lore,—
Charms for the old, the sick, the frail,
Some made for use, and all for sale.
On either side the crowd withdrew,
To let the Saint pass proudly through;
While turban'd heads of every hue,
Green, white, and crimson bow'd around,
And gay tiaras touch'd the ground,—
As tulip-bells, when o'er their beds
The musk-wind passes, bend their heads.
Nay, some there were among the crowd
Of Moslem heads that round her bow'd,
So fill'd with zeal, by many a draught
Of Shiraz wine, profanely quaff'd,
That, sinking low in reverence then,
They never rose till morn again.

There are yet two more of these unfinished sketches one of which extends to a much greater length than I was aware of; and, as far as I can judge from a hasty renewal of my acquaintance with it, is not incapable of being yet turned to account.

In only one of these unfinished sketches, the tale of the Peri's Daughter, had I yet ventured to invoke that most home-felt of all my inspirations, which has lent to the story of The Fire-worshippers its main attraction and interest. That it was my intention, in the concealed Prince of Ormuz, to shadow out some impersonation of this feeling, I take for granted from the prophetic words supposed to be addressed to him by his aged guardian:—

Bright child of destiny! even now
I read the promise on that brow,
That tyrants shall no more defile
The glories of the Green-Sea Isle,
But Ormuz shall again be free,
And hail her native Lord in thee!

In none of the other fragments do I find any trace of this sort of feeling, either in the subject or the personages of the intended story; and this was the reason, doubtless, though hardly known, at the time, to myself, that, finding my subjects so slow in kindling my own sympathies, I began to despair of their ever touching the hearts of others; and felt often inclined to say,

"Oh no, I have no voice or hand
For such a song in such a land."

Had this series of disheartening experiments been carried on much further, I must have thrown aside the work in despair. But at last, fortunately, as it proved, the thought occurred to me of founding a story on the fierce struggle so long maintained between the Ghebers,* or ancient Fire-worshippers of Persia, and their haughty Moslem masters. From that moment, a new and deep interest in my whole task took possession of me. The cause of tolerance was again my inspiring theme; and the spirit that had spoken in the melodies of Ireland soon found itself at home in the East.

Having thus laid open the secrets of the workshop to account for the time expended in *writing* this work, I must also, in justice to my own industry, notice the pains I took in long and laboriously *reading* for it. To form a store-house, as it were, of illustration purely Oriental, and so familiarize myself with its various treasures, that, as quick as Fancy in her airy spiritings required the assistance of fact, the memory was ready, like another Ariel, at her "strong bidding," to furnish materials for the spell-work,—such was, for a long while, the sole object of my studies; and whatever time and trouble this preparatory process may have cost me, the effects resulting from it, as far as the humble merit of truthfulness is concerned, have been such as to repay me more than sufficiently for my pains. I have not forgotten how great was my pleasure, when told by the late Sir James Mackintosh that he was once asked by Colonel Wilks, the historian of British India, "whether it was true that Moore had never been in the East?" "Never," answered Mackintosh. "Well, that shows me," replied Colonel Wilks,

* Voltaire, in his tragedy of "Les Guèbres," written with a similar under-current of meaning, was accused of having transformed his Fire-worshippers into Jansenists:—"Quelques figuristes," he says "prétendent que les Guèbres sont les Jansénistes."

"that reading over D'Herbelot is as good as riding on the back of a camel."

I need hardly subjoin to this lively speech, that although D'Herbelot's valuable work was, of course, one of my manuals, I took the whole range of all such Oriental reading as was accessible to me; and became, for the time, indeed, far more conversant with all relating to that distant region, than I have ever been with the scenery, productions, or modes of life of any of those countries lying most within my reach. We know that D'Anville, though never in his life out of Paris, was able to correct a number of errors in a plan of the Troad taken by De Choiseul, on the spot; and, for my own very different, as well as far inferior, purposes, the knowledge I had thus acquired of distant localities, seen only by me in day-dreams, was no less ready and useful.

An ample reward for all this painstaking has been found in such welcome tributes as I have just cited; nor can I deny myself the gratification of citing a few more of the same description. From another distinguished authority on Eastern subjects, the late Sir John Malcolm, I had myself the pleasure of hearing a similar opinion publicly expressed;—that eminent person having remarked, in a speech spoken by him at a Literary Fund Dinner, that together with those qualities of the poet which he much too partially assigned to me, was combined also "the truth of the historian."

Sir William Ouseley, another high authority, in giving his testimony to the same effect, thus notices an exception to the general accuracy for which he gives me credit:—"Dazzled by the beauties of this composition,* few readers can perceive, and none surely can regret, that the poet, in his magnificent catastrophe, has forgotten, or boldly and most happily violated, the precept of Zoroaster, above noticed, which held it impious to consume any portion of a human body by fire, especially by that which glowed upon their altars." Having long lost, I fear, most of my Eastern learning, I can only cite, in defence of my catastrophe, an old Oriental tradition, which relates that Nimrod, when Abraham refused, at his command, to worship the fire, ordered him to be thrown into the midst of the flames.† A precedent so ancient for this sort of use of the worshipped element, appears, for all purposes at least of poetry, to be fully sufficient.

In addition to these agreeable testimonies, I have also heard, and need hardly add, with some pride and pleasure, that parts of this work have been rendered into Persian, and have found their way to Ispahan. To this fact, as I am willing to think it, allusion is made in some lively verses, written many years since, by my friend Mr. Luttrell:—

"I'm told, dear Moore, your lays are sung,
(Can it be true, you lucky man?)
By moonlight, in the Persian tongue,
Along the streets of Ispahan."

That some knowledge of the work may have really reached that region, appears not improbable from a passage in the Travels of Mr. Frazer, who says, that "being delayed for some time at a town on the shores of the Caspian, he was lucky enough to be able to amuse himself with a copy of Lalla Rookh, which a Persian had lent him."

Of the description of Balbec, in "Paradise and the Peri," Mr. Carne, in his Letters from the East, thus speaks:—"The description in Lalla Rookh of the plain and its ruins, is exquisitely faithful. The minaret is on the declivity near at hand, and there wanted only the muezzin's cry to break the silence."

* The Fire-worshippers.

† Tradunt autem Hebræi hanc fabulam quod Abraham in ignem missus sit quia ignem adorare noluit.—St. Hieron. *in Quæst. in Genesim.*

I shall now tax my readers' patience with but one more of these generous vouchers. Whatever of vanity there may be in citing such tributes, they show, at least, of what great value, even in poetry, is that prosaic quality, industry; since, as the reader of the foregoing pages is now fully apprized, it was in a slow and laborious collection of small facts, that the first foundations of this fanciful Romance were laid.

The friendly testimony I have just referred to, appeared some years since in the form in which I now give it, and, if I recollect right, in the Athenæum:—

"I embrace this opportunity of bearing my individual testimony (if it be of any value) to the extraordinary accuracy of Mr. Moore, in his topographical, antiquarian, and characteristic details, whether of costume, manners, or less-changing monuments, both in his Lalla Rookh and in the Epicurean. It has been my fortune to read his Lalla Rookh in Persia itself; and I have perused the Epicurean, while all my recollections of Egypt and its still existing wonders are as fresh as when I quitted the banks of the Nile for Arabia: I owe it, therefore, as a debt of gratitude (though the payment is most inadequate) for the great pleasure I have derived from his productions, to bear my humble testimony to their local fidelity.

"J. S. B."

Among the incidents connected with this work, I must not omit to notice the splendid Divertissement, founded upon it, which was acted at the Château Royal of Berlin, during the visit of the Grand Duke Nicholas to that capital in the year 1822. The different stories composing the work were represented in Tableaux Vivans and songs; and among the crowd of royal and noble personages engaged in the performances, I shall mention those only who represented the principal characters, and whom I find thus enumerated in the published account of the Divertissement.*

"Fadladin, Grand-Nasir,	*Comte Haack, (Maréchal de Cour.)*
Aliris, Roi de Bucharie, . .	*S. A. I. Le Grand Duc.*
Lalla Roûkh, ...	*S. A. I. La Grand Duchesse.*
Aurungzeb, le Grand Mogol,	*S. A. R. Le Prince Guillaume, frère du Roi.*
Abdallah, Père d'Aliris,	*S. A. R. Le Duc de Cumberland.*
La Reine, son épouse,	*S. A. R. La Princesse Louise Radzivill."*

Besides these and other leading personages, there were also brought into action, under the various denominations of Seigneurs et Dames de Bucharie, Dames de Cachemire, Seigneurs et Dames dansans à la Fête des Roses, &c., nearly 150 persons.

Of the manner and style in which the Tableaux of the different stories are described in the work from which I cite, the following account of the performance of Paradise and the Peri will afford some specimen:—

"La décoration répresentoit les portes brillantes du Paradis, entourées de nuages. Dans le premier tableau on voyoit la Péri, triste et desolée, couchée sur le seuil des portes fermées, et l'Ange de lumière qui lui addresse des consolations et des conseils. Le second représente le moment, où la Peri, dans l'espoir que ce don lui ouvrira l'entrée du Paradis, recueille la dernière goutte de sang que vient de verser le jeune guerrier Indien. . . . . .

"La Péri et l'Ange de lumière répondoient pleinement à l'image et à l'idée qu'on est tenté de se faire de ces deux individus, et l'impression qu'a faite généralement la suite des tableaux de cet épisode délicat et intéressant est loin de s'effacer de notre souvenir."

In this grand Fête, it appears, originated the trans

* Lalla Roûkh, Divertissement mêlé de Chants et de Danses, Berlin, 1822. The work contains a series of coloured engravings, representing groups, processions, &c., in different Oriental costumes.

lation of Lalla Rookh into German verse, by the Baron de la Motte Fouqué; and the circumstances which led him to undertake the task are described by himself, in a Dedicatory Poem to the Empress of Russia, which he has prefixed to his translation. As soon as the performance, he tells us, had ended, Lalla Rookh (the Empress herself) exclaimed with a sigh, "Is it, then, all over? are we now at the close of all that has given us so much delight? and lives there no poet who will impart to others, and to future times, some notion of the happiness we have enjoyed this evening?" On hearing this appeal, a Knight of Cachmere (who is no other than the poetical Baron himself) comes forward and promises to attempt to present to the world "the Poem itself in the measure of the original:"—whereupon Lalla Rookh, it is added, approvingly smiled.

LALLA ROOKH.

TO

SAMUEL ROGERS, ESQ.

THIS EASTERN ROMANCE IS INSCRIBED,

BY HIS VERY GRATEFUL AND AFFECTIONATE FRIEND,

THOMAS MOORE.

May 19, 1817.

LALLA ROOKH.

In the eleventh year of the reign of Aurungzebe, Abdalla, King of the Lesser Bucharia, a lineal descendant from the Great Zingis, having abdicated the throne in favour of his son, set out on a pilgrimage to the shrine of the Prophet; and, passing into India through the delightful valley of Cashmere, rested for a short time at Delhi on his way. He was entertained by Aurungzebe in a style of magnificent hospitality, worthy alike of the visiter and the host, and was afterwards escorted with the same splendour to Surat, where he embarked for Arabia.* During the stay of the Royal Pilgrim at Delhi, a marriage was agreed upon between the Prince, his son, and the youngest daughter of the Emperor, Lalla Rookh;†—a Princess described by the poets of her time as more beautiful than Leila,‡ Shirine,§ Dewildé,‖ or any of those heroines whose names and loves embellish the songs of Persia and Hindostan. It was intended that the nuptials should be celebrated at Cashmere; where the young King, as soon as the cares of empire would permit, was to meet, for the first time, his lovely bride, and after a few months' repose in that enchanting valley, conduct her over the snowy hills into Bucharia.

The day of Lalla Rookh's departure from Delhi was as splendid as sunshine and pageantry could make it. The bazars and baths were all covered with the richest tapestry; hundreds of gilded barges upon the Jumna floated with their banners shining in the water; while through the streets groups of beautiful children went strewing the most delicious flowers around, as in that Persian festival called the Scattering of the Roses;¶ till every part of the city was as fragrant as if a caravan of musk from Khoten had passed through it. The Princess, having taken leave of her kind father, who at parting hung a cornelian of Yemen round her neck, on which was inscribed a verse from the Koran, and having sent a considerable present to the Fakirs, who kept up the Perpetual Lamp in her sister's tomb, meekly ascended the palankeen prepared for her; and, while Aurungzebe stood to take a last look from his balcony, the procession moved slowly on the road to Lahore.

Seldom had the Eastern world seen a cavalcade so superb. From the gardens in the suburbs to the imperial palace, it was one unbroken line of splendour. The gallant appearance of the Rajahs and Mogul lords, distinguished by those insignia of the Emperor's favor,* the feathers of the egret of Cashmere in their turbans, and the small silver-rimmed kettle drums at the bows of their saddles;—the costly armour of their cavaliers, who vied, on this occasion, with the guards of the great Keder Khan,† in the brightness of their silver battle-axes, and the massiness of their maces of gold;—the glittering of the gilt pine-apples‡ on the tops of the palankeens;—the embroidered trappings of the elephants, bearing on their backs small turrets in the shape of little antique temples, within which the ladies of Lalla Rookh lay as it were enshrined;—the rose-coloured veils of the Princess's own sumptuous litter,§ at the front of which a fair young female slave sat fanning her through the curtains, with feathers of the Argus pheasant's wing;‖—and the lovely troop of Tartarian and Cashmerian maids of honour, whom the young king had sent to accompany his bride, and who rode on each side of the litter, upon small Arabian horses;—all was brilliant, tasteful, and magnificent, and pleased even the critical and fastidious Fadladeen, Great Nazir or Chamberlain of the Haram, who was borne in his palankeen immediately after the Princess, and considered himself not the least important personage of the pageant.

These particulars of the visit of the King of Bucharia to Aurungzebe are found in *Dow's History of Hindostan*, vol. iii. p. 392.

† Tulip cheek.

‡ The mistress of Mejnoun, upon whose story so many Romances in all the languages of the East are founded.

§ For the loves of this celebrated beauty with Khosrou and with Ferhad, see *D'Herbelot, Gibbon, Oriental Collections*, &c.

‖ "The history of the loves of Dewildé and Chizer, the son of the Emperor Alla, is written in an elegant poem, by the noble Chusero."—*Ferishta.*

¶ Gul Reazee.

* "One mark of honour or knighthood bestowed by the Emperor is the permission to wear a small kettle drum at the bows of their saddles, which at first was invented for the training of hawks, and to call them to the lure, and is worn in the field by all sportsmen to that end."—*Fryer's* Travels.

"Those on whom the King has conferred the privilege, must wear an ornament of jewels on the right side of the turban, surmounted by a high plume of the feathers of a kind of egret. This bird is found only in Cashmere, and the feathers are carefully collected for the King, who bestows them on his nobles."—*Elphinstone's* Account of Caubul.

† "Khedar Khan, the Khakan, or King of Turquestan, beyond the Gihon, (at the end of the eleventh century,) whenever he appeared abroad was preceded by seven hundred horsemen with silver battle-axes, and was followed by an equal number bearing maces of gold. He was a great patron of poetry, and it was he who used to preside at public exercises of genius, with four basins of gold and silver by him to distribute among the poets who excelled."—*Richardson's* Dissertation prefixed to his Dictionary.

‡ "The kubdeh, a large golden knob, generally in the shape of a pine-apple, on the top of the canopy over the litter or palanquin."—*Scott's* Notes on the Bahardanush.

§ In the Poem of Zohair, in the Moallakat, there is the following lively description of "a company of maidens seated on camels."

"They are mounted in carriages covered with costly awnings, and with rose-coloured veils, the linings of which have the hue of crimson Andem-wood.

"When they ascend from the bosom of the vale, they sit forward on the saddle-cloth with every mark of a voluptuous gayety.

"Now, when they have reached the brink of yon blue, gushing rivulet, they fix the poles of their tents like the Arab with a settled mansion."

‖ See *Bernier's* description of the attendants on Rauchanara-Begum in her progress to Cashmere.

FADLADEEN was a judge of every thing,—from the pencilling of a Circassian's eyelids, to the deepest questions of science and literature; from the mixture of a conserve of rose-leaves, to the composition of an epic poem: and such influence had his opinion upon the various tastes of the day, that all the cooks and poets of Delhi stood in awe of him. His political conduct and opinions were founded upon that line of Sadi—"Should the Prince at noon-day say, It is night, declare that you behold the moon and stars;" and his zeal for religion, of which Aurungzebe was a munificent protector,* was about as disinterested as that of the goldsmith who fell in love with the diamond eyes of the idol of Jaghernaut.†

During the first days of their journey, LALLA ROOKH, who had passed all her life within the shadow of the Royal Gardens of Delhi,‡ found enough in the beauty of the scenery through which they passed to interest her mind, and delight her imagination; and when at evening, or in the heat of the day, they turned off from the high road to those retired and romantic places which had been selected for her encampments,—sometimes on the banks of a small rivulet, as clear as the waters of the Lake of Pearl;§ sometimes under the sacred shade of a Banyan tree, from which the view opened upon a glade covered with antelopes; and often in those hidden, embowered spots, described by one from the Isles of the West,|| as "places of melancholy, delight, and safety, where all the company around was wild peacocks and turtle-doves;"—she felt a charm in these scenes, so lovely and so new to her, which, for a time, made her indifferent to every other amusement. But LALLA ROOKH was young, and the young love variety; nor could the conversation of her Ladies and the Great Chamberlain, FADLADEEN, (the only persons, of course, admitted to her pavilion,) sufficiently enliven those many vacant hours, which were devoted neither to the pillow nor the palankeen. There was a little Persian slave who sung sweetly to the Vina, and who, now and then, lulled the Princess to sleep with the ancient ditties of her country, about the loves of Wamak and Ezra,¶ the fair-haired Zal and his mistress Rodahver;** not forgetting the combat of Rustam with the terrible White Demon.†† At other times she was amused by those graceful dancing-girls of Delhi, who had been permitted by the Bramins of the Great Pagoda to attend her, much to the horror of the good Mussulman FADLADEEN, who could see nothing graceful or agreeable in idolaters, and to whom the very tinkling of their golden anklets‡‡ was an abomination.

* This hypocritical Emperor would have made a worthy associate of certain Holy Leagues. "He held the cloak of religion (says Dow) between his actions and the vulgar; and impiously thanked the Divinity for a success which he owed to his own wickedness. When he was murdering and persecuting his brothers and their families, he was building a magnificent mosque at Delhi, as an offering to God for his assistance to him in the civil wars. He acted as high priest at the consecration of this temple, and made a practice of attending divine service there in the humble dress of a Fakeer. But when he lifted one hand to the Divinity, he, with the other, signed warrants for the assassination of his relations."—*History of Hindostan*, vol. iii. p. 335. See also the curious letter of Aurungzebe, given in the *Oriental Collections*, vol. i. p. 320.

† "The idol at Jagnernat has two fine diamonds for eyes. No goldsmith is suffered to enter the Pagoda, one having stole one of these eyes, being locked up all night with the Idol."—*Tavernier.*

‡ See a description of these Royal Gardens in "An Account of the present state of Delhi, by Lieut. W. Franklin."—*Asiat. Resear.* vol. iv. p. 417.

§ "In the neighbourhood is Notte Gill, or the Lake of Pearl, which receives this name from its pellucid water."—*Pennant's* Hindostan.

"Nasir Jung encamped in the vicinity of the Lake of Tonoor, amused himself with sailing on that clear and beautiful water, and gave it the fanciful name of Motee Talah, 'the Lake of Pearls,' which it still retains."—*Wilks's* South of India.

|| Sir Thomas Roe, Ambassador from James I. to Jehanguire.

¶ "The romance Wemakweazra, written in Persian verse, which contains the loves of Wamak and Ezra, two celebrated lovers who lived before the time of Mahomet."—*Note on the Oriental Tales.*

** Their amour is recounted in the Shah-Namêh of Ferdousi; and there is much beauty in the passage which describes the slaves of Rodahver sitting on the bank of the river and throwing flowers into the stream, in order to draw the attention of the young Hero who is encamped on the opposite side.—See *Champion's* translation.

†† Rustam is the Hercules of the Persians. For the particulars of his victory over the Seped Deeve, or White Demon, see *Oriental Collections*, vol. ii. p. 45. Near the city of Shirauz is an immense quadrangular monument, in commemoration of this combat, called the Kelaat-i-Deev Sepeed, or Castle of the White Giant, which Father Angelo, in his Gazophilacium Persicum, p. 127, declares to have been the most memorable monument of antiquity which he had seen in Persia.—See *Ouseley's* Persian Miscellanies.

‡‡ "The women of the Idol, or dancing girls of the Pagoda, have little golden bells, fastened to their feet, the soft harmonious tinkling of which vibrates in unison with the exquisite melody of their voices."—*Maurice's* Indian Antiquities.

"The Arabian courtesans, like the Indian women, have little golden bells fastened round their legs, neck, and elbows, to the sound of which they dance before the King. The Arabian princesses wear golden rings on their fingers, to which little bells are suspended, as well as in the flowing tresses of their hair, that their superior rank may be known, and they themselves receive in passing the homage due to them."—See *Calmet's* Dictionary, art. Bells.

But these and many other diversions were repeated till they lost all their charm, and the nights and noon-days were beginning to move heavily, when, at length, it was recollected that, among the attendants sent by the bridegroom, was a young poet of Cashmere, much celebrated throughout the Valley for his manner of reciting the Stories of the East, on whom his Royal Master had conferred the privilege of being admitted to the pavilion of the Princess, that he might help to beguile the tediousness of the journey by some of his most agreeable recitals. At the mention of a poet, FADLADEEN elevated his critical eyebrows, and, having refreshed his faculties with a dose of that delicious opium* which is distilled from the black poppy of the Thebais, gave orders for the minstrel to be forthwith introduced into the presence.

The Princess, who had once in her life seen a poet from behind the screens of gauze in her Father's hall, and had conceived from that specimen no very favourable ideas of the Caste, expected but little in this new exhibition to interest her;—she felt inclined, however, to alter her opinion on the very first appearance of FERAMORZ. He was a youth about LALLA ROOKH's own age, and graceful as that idol of women, Crishna,†—such as he appears to their young imaginations, heroic, beautiful, breathing music from his very eyes, and exalting the religion of his worshippers into love. His dress was simple, yet not without some marks of costliness; and the Ladies of the Princess were not long in discovering that the cloth, which encircled his high Tartarian cap, was of the most delicate kind that the shawl-goats of Tibet supply.‡ Here and there, too, over his vest, which was confined by a flowered girdle of Kashan, hung strings of fine pearl, disposed with an air of studied negligence; nor did the exquisite embroidery of his sandals escape the observation of these fair critics; who, however they might give way to FADLADEEN upon the unimportant topics of religion and government, had the spirit of martyrs in every thing relating to such momentous matters as jewels and embroidery.

For the purpose of relieving the pauses of recitation by music, the young Cashmerian held in his hand a kitar,—such as, in old times, the Arab maids of the West used to listen to by moonlight in the gardens of the Alhambra,—and having premised, with much humility, that the story he was about to relate was founded on the adventures of that Veiled Prophet of Khorassan,§ who, in the year of the Hegira 163, created such alarm throughout the Eastern Empire, made an obeisance to the Princess, and thus began:—

THE

VEILED PROPHET OF KHORASSAN.||

IN that delightful Province of the Sun,
The first of Persian lands he shines upon,
Where all the loveliest children of his beam,
Flow'rets and fruits, blush over ev'ry stream,¶
And, fairest of all streams, the MURGA roves
Among MEROU's** bright palaces and groves;—
There on that throne, to which the blind belief
Of millions raised him, sat the Prophet-Chief,

* "Abou-Tige, ville de la Thebaïde, où il croît beaucoup de pavot noir, dont se fait le meilleur opium."—*D'Herbelot.*

† The Indian Apollo. "He and the three Râmas are described as youths of perfect beauty; and the princesses of Hindustân were all passionately in love with Chrishna, who continues to this hour the darling God of the Indian women."—*Sir W. Jones*, on the Gods of Greece, Italy, and India.

‡ See *Turner's* Embassy for a description of this animal, "the most beautiful among the whole tribe of goats." The material for the shawls (which is carried to Cashmere) is found next the skin.

§ For the real history of this Impostor, whose original name was Hakem ben Haschem, and who was called Mocanna from the veil of silver gauze (or, as others say, golden) which he always wore, see *D'Herbelot.*

|| Khorassan signifies, in the old Persian language, Province or Region of the Sun.—*Sir W. Jones.*

¶ "The fruits of Meru are finer than those of any other place; and one cannot see in any other city such palaces with groves, and streams and gardens."—*Ebn Haukal's* Geography.

** One of the royal cities of Khorassan.

The Great MOKANNA. O'er his features hung
The Veil, the Silver Veil, which he had flung
In mercy there, to hide from mortal sight
His dazzling brow, till man could bear its light.
For, far less luminous, his votaries said,
Were ev'n the gleams, miraculously shed
O'er MOUSSA'S* cheek,† when down the Mount he trod,
All glowing from the presence of his God!

On either side, with ready hearts and hands,
His chosen guard of bold Believers stands;
Young fire-eyed disputants, who deem their swords,
On points of faith, more eloquent than words;
And such their zeal, there's not a youth with brand
Uplifted there, but, at the Chief's command,
Would make his own devoted heart its sheath,
And bless the lips that doom'd so dear a death!
In hatred to the Caliph's hue of night,‡
Their vesture, helms and all, is snowy white;
Their weapons various—some equipp'd, for speed,
With javelins of the light Kathaian reed;§
Or bows of buffalo horn and shining quivers
Fill'd with the stems‖ that bloom on IRAN'S rivers;¶
While some, for war's more terrible attacks,
Wield the huge mace and pond'rous battle-axe;
And as they wave aloft in morning's beam
The milk-white plumage of their helms, they seem
Like a chenar-tree grove** when winter throws
O'er all its tufted heads his feath'ring snows.

Between the porphyry pillars, that uphold
The rich moresque-work of the roof of gold,
Aloft the Harem's curtain'd galleries rise,
Where through the silken network, glancing eyes
From time to time, like sudden gleams that glow
Through autumn clouds, shine o'er the pomp below.—
What impious tongue, ye blushing saints, would dare
To hint that aught but Heav'n hath placed you there?
Or that the loves of this light world could bind,
In their gross chain, your Prophet's soaring mind?
No—wrongful thought!—commission'd from above
To people Eden's bowers with shapes of love,
(Creatures so bright, that the same lips and eyes
They wear on earth will serve in Paradise,)
There to recline among Heav'n's native maids,
And crown th' Elect with bliss that never fades—
Well hath the Prophet-Chief his bidding done;
And ev'ry beauteous race beneath the sun,
From those who kneel at BRAHMA'S burning founts,††
To the fresh nymphs bounding o'er YEMEN'S mounts;
From PERSIA'S eyes of full and fawn-like ray,
To the small, half-shut glances of KATHAY;‡‡
And GEORGIA'S bloom, and AZAB'S darker smiles,
And the gold ringlets of the Western Isles;
All, all are there;—each Land its flower hath given,
To form that fair young Nursery for Heav'n!

But why this pageant now? this arm'd array?
What triumph crowds the rich Divan to-day
With turban'd heads, of ev'ry hue and race,
Bowing before that veil'd and awful face,
Like tulip-beds,§§ of diff'rent shape and dyes,
Bending beneath th' invisible West-wind's sighs!
What new-made mystery now, for Faith to sign,
And blood to seal, as genuine and divine,
What dazzling mimicry of God's own power
Hath the bold Prophet plann'd to grace this hour.

Not such the pageant now, though not less proud;
Yon warrior youth, advancing from the crowd,
With silver bow, with belt of broider'd crape,
And fur-bound bonnet of Bucharian shape,*
So fiercely beautiful in form and eye,
Like war's wild planet in a summer sky;
That youth to-day,—a proselyte, worth hordes
Of cooler spirits and less practised swords,
Is come to join, all bravery and belief,
The creed and standard of the heav'n-sent Chief.

Though few his years, the West already knows
Young AZIM'S fame;—beyond the Olympian snows,
Ere manhood darken'd o'er his downy cheek,
O'erwhelm'd in fight, and captive to the Greek,†
He linger'd there, till peace dissolved his chains.
Oh, who could, ev'n in bondage, tread the plains
Of glorious GREECE, nor feel his spirit rise
Kindling within him? who, with heart and eyes,
Could walk where liberty had been, nor see
The shining footprints of her Deity,
Nor feel those godlike breathings in the air,
Which mutely told her spirit had been there?
Not he, that youthful warrior,—no, too well
For his soul's quiet work'd th' awak'ning spell;
And now, returning to his own dear land,
Full of those dreams of good that, vainly grand,
Haunt the young heart,—proud views of human kind,
Of men to Gods exalted and refined,—
False views, like that horizon's fair deceit,
Where earth and heav'n but *seem*, alas, to meet:—
Soon as he heard an Arm Divine was raised
To right the nations, and beheld, emblazed
On the white flag, MOKANNA'S host unfurl'd,
Those words of sunshine, "Freedom to the World,"
At once his faith, his sword, his soul obey'd
Th' inspiring summons; every chosen blade
That fought beneath that banner's sacred text
Seem'd doubly edged, for this world and the next;
And ne'er did Faith with her smooth bandage bind
Eyes more devoutly willing to be blind,
In virtue's cause;—never was soul inspired
With livelier trust in what it most desired,
Than his, th' enthusiast there, who kneeling, pale
With pious awe, before that Silver Veil,
Believes the form, to which he bends his knee,
Some pure, redeeming angel, sent to free
This fetter'd world from every bond and stain,
And bring its primal glories back again!

Low as young AZIM knelt, that motley crowd
Of all earth's nations sunk the knee and bow'd,
With shouts of "ALLA!" echoing long and loud;
While high in air, above the Prophet's head,
Hundreds of banners, to the sunbeam spread,
Waved like the wings of the white birds that fan
The flying throne of star-taught SOLIMAN.‡
Then thus he spoke:—"Stranger, though new the frame
"Thy soul inhabits now, I've track'd its flame
"For many an age,§ in ev'ry chance and change

* Moses.

† "Ses disciples assuroient qu'il se couvroit le visage, pour ne pas éblouir ceux qui l'approchoient par l'éclat de son visage comme Moïse." *D'Herbelot.*

‡ Black was the colour adopted by the Caliphs of the House of Abbas, in their garments, turbans, and standards.—"Il faut remarquer ici touchant les habits blancs des disciples de Hakem, que la couleur des habits, des coîffures et des étendarts des Khalifes Abassides étant la noire, ce chef de Rebelles ne pouvoit pas choisir une que lui fût plus opposée."—*D'Herbelot.*

§ "Our dark javelins, exquisitely wrought of Khathaian reeds, slender and delicate."—*Poem of Amru.*

‖ Pichula, used anciently for arrows by the Persians.

¶ The Persians call this plant Gaz. The celebrated shaft of Isfendiar, one of their ancient heroes, was made of it. "Nothing can be more beautiful than the appearance of this plant in flower during the rains on the banks of rivers, where it is usually interwoven with a lovely twining asclepias."—*Sir W. Jones*, Botanical Observations on Select Indian Plants.

** The oriental plane. "The chenar is a delightful tree; its bole is of a fine white and smooth bark; and its foliage, which grows in a tuft at the summit, is of a bright green."—*Morier's* Travels.

†† The burning fountains of Brahma near Chittogong, esteemed as holy.—*Turner.*

‡‡ China.

§§ "The name of tulip is said to be of Turkish extraction, and given to the flower on account of its resembling a turban."—*Beckmann's* History of Inventions.

* "The inhabitants of Bucharia wear a round cloth bonnet, shaped much after the Polish fashion, having a large fur border. They tie their kaftans about the middle with a girdle of a kind of silk crape, several times round the body."—*Account of Independent Tartary, in Pinkerton's Collection.*

† In the war of the Caliph Mahadi against the Empress Irene, for an account of which vide *Gibbon*, vol. x.

‡ This wonderful Throne was called The Star of the Genii. For a full description of it, see the Fragment, translated by Captain Franklin, from a Persian MS. entitled "The History of Jerusalem." *Oriental Collections*, vol. i. p. 235.—When Soliman travelled, the eastern writers say, "He had a carpet of green silk on which his throne was placed, being of a prodigious length and breadth, and sufficient for all his forces to stand upon, the men placing themselves on his right hand, and the spirits on his left; and that when all were in order, the wind, at his command, took up the carpet, and transported it, with all that were upon it, wherever he pleased: the army of birds at the same time flying over their heads, and forming a kind of canopy to shade them from the sun." *Sale's* Koran, vol. ii. p. 214. note.

§ The transmigration of souls was one of his doctrines.—Vide *D'Herbelot.*

"Of that existence, through whose varied range,—
"As through a torch-race, where, from hand to hand
"The flying youths transmit their shining brand,
"From frame to frame the unextinguish'd soul
"Rapidly passes, till it reach the goal!

"Nor think 'tis only the gross Spirits, warm'd
"With duskier fire and for earth's medium form'd,
"That run this course;—Beings, the most divine,
"Thus deign through dark mortality to shine.
"Such was the Essence that in ADAM dwelt,
"To which all Heav'n, except the Proud One, knelt:*
"Such the refined Intelligence that glow'd
"In MOUSSA's† frame,—and, thence descending, flow'd
"Through many a Prophet's breast;‡ in ISSA§ shone,
"And in MOHAMMED burn'd; till, hast'ning on,
"(As a bright river that, from fall to fall
"In many a maze descending, bright through all,
"Finds some fair region where, each labyrinth past,
"In one full lake of light it rests at last,)
"That Holy Spirit, settling calm and free
"From lapse or shadow, centres all in me!"

Again, throughout th' assembly, at these words,
Thousands of voices rung: the warriors' swords
Were pointed up to heaven; a sudden wind
In th' open banners play'd, and from behind
Those Persian hangings, that but ill could screen
The Harem's loveliness, white hands were seen
Waving embroider'd scarfs, whose motion gave
A perfume forth—like those the Houris wave
When beck'ning to their bow'rs th' immortal Brave.

"But these," pursued the Chief, "are truths sublime,
"That claim a holier mood and calmer time
"Than earth allows us now;—this sword must first
"The darkling prison-house of Mankind burst,
"Ere Peace can visit them, or Truth let in
"Her wakening daylight on a world of sin.
"But then,—celestial warriors, then, when all
"Earth's shrines and thrones before our banner fall;
"When the glad Slave shall at these feet lay down
"His broken chain, the tyrant Lord his crown,
"The Priest his book, the Conqueror his wreath,
"And from the lips of Truth one mighty breath
"Shall, like a whirlwind, scatter in its breeze
"That whole dark pile of human mockeries;—
"Then shall the reign of mind commence on earth,
"And starting fresh as from a second birth,
"Man, in the sunshine of the world's new spring,
"Shall walk transparent, like some holy thing!
"Then, too, your Prophet from his angel brow
"Shall cast the Veil that hides its splendours now,
"And gladden'd Earth shall, through her wide expanse,
"Bask in the glories of this countenance!

"For thee, young warrior, welcome!—thou hast yet
"Some tasks to learn, some frailties to forget,
"Ere the white war-plume o'er thy brow can wave;—
"But, once my own, mine all, till in the grave!"

The pomp is at an end—the crowds are gone—
Each ear and heart still haunted by the tone
Of that deep voice, which thrill'd like ALLA's own!
The Young all dazzled by the plumes and lances,
The glitt'ring throne, and Harem's half-caught glances;
The Old deep pond'ring on the promised reign
Of peace and truth: and all the female train
Ready to risk their eyes, could they but gaze
A moment on that brow's miraculous blaze!

But there was one, among the chosen maids,
Who blush'd behind the gallery's silken shades,
One, to whose soul the pageant of to-day
Has been like death:—you saw her pale dismay,
Ye wond'ring sisterhood, and heard the burst
Of exclamation from her lips, when first
She saw that youth, too well, too dearly known,
Silently kneeling at the Prophet's throne.

Ah ZELICA! there *was* a time, when bliss
Shone o'er thy heart from ev'ry look of his;
When but to see him, hear him, breathe the air
In which he dwelt, was thy soul's fondest prayer
When round him hung such a perpetual spell,
Whate'er he did, none ever did so well.
Too happy days! when, if he touch'd a flow'r
Or gem of thine, 'twas sacred from that hour;
When thou didst study him till every tone
And gesture and dear look became thy own,—
Thy voice like his, the changes of his face
In thine reflected with still lovelier grace,
Like echo, sending back sweet music, fraught
With twice the aërial sweetness it had brought!
Yet now he comes,—brighter than even he
E'er beam'd before,—but, ah! not bright for thee
No—dread, unlook'd for, like a visitant
From th' other world, he comes as if to haunt
Thy guilty soul with dreams of lost delight,
Long lost to all but mem'ry's aching sight:—
Sad dreams! as when the Spirit of our Youth
Returns in sleep, sparkling with all the truth
And innocence once ours, and leads us back,
In mournful mockery, o'er the shining track
Of our young life, and points out every ray
Of hope and peace we've lost upon the way!
Once happy pair!—In proud BOKHARA's groves,
Who had not heard of their first youthful loves?
Born by that ancient flood,* which from its spring
In the dark Mountains swiftly wandering,
Enrich'd by ev'ry pilgrim brook that shines
With relics from BUCHARIA's ruby mines,
And, lending to the CASPIAN half its strength,
In the cold Lake of Eagles sinks at length;—
There, on the banks of that bright river born,
The flow'rs, that hung above its wave at morn,
Bless'd not the waters, as they murmur'd by,
With holier scent and lustre, than the sigh
And virgin-glance of first affection cast
Upon their youth's smooth current, as it pass'd.
But war disturb'd this vision,—far away
From her fond eyes summon'd to join th' array
Of PERSIA's warriors on the hills of THRACE,
The youth exchanged his sylvan dwelling-place
For the rude tent and war-field's deathful clash;
His ZELICA's sweet glances for the flash
Of Grecian wild-fire, and Love's gentle chains
For bleeding bondage on BYZANTIUM's plains.

Month after month, in widowhood of soul
Drooping, the maiden saw two summers roll
Their suns away—but, ah, how cold and dim
Ev'n summer suns, when not beheld with him!
From time to time ill-omen'd rumours came,
Like spirit-tongues, mutt'ring the sick man's name,
Just ere he dies:—at length those sounds of dread
Fell with'ring on her soul, "AZIM is dead!"
Oh Grief, beyond all other griefs, when fate
First leaves the young heart lone and desolate
In the wide world, without that only tie
For which it loved to live or fear'd to die;—
Lorn as the hung-up lute, that ne'er hath spoken
Since the sad day its master-chord was broken!

Fond maid, the sorrow of her soul was such,
Ev'n reason sunk,—blighted beneath its touch;
And though, ere long, her sanguine spirit rose

* "And when we said unto the angels, Worship Adam, they all worshipped him except Eblis, (Lucifer,) who refused."—*The Koran*, chap. ii.

† Moses.

‡ This is according to D'Herbelot's account of the doctrines of Mocanna:—"Sa doctrine étoit, que Dieu avoit pris une forme et figure humaine, depuis qu'il eut commandé aux Anges d'adorer Adam, le premier des hommes. Qu'après la Mort d'Adam, Dieu étoit apparu sous la figure de plusieurs Prophètes, et autres grands hommes qu'il avoit choisis, jusqu'à ce qu'il prit celle d'Abu Moslem, Prince de Khorassan, lequel professoit l'erreur de la Tenassukhiah ou Métempsychose; et qu'après la mort de ce Prince, la Divinité étoit passée, et descendue en sa personne."

§ Jesus.

* The Amoo, which rises in the Belur Tag, or Dark Mountains, and running nearly from east to west, splits into two branches; one of which falls into the Caspian Sea, and the other into Aral Nahr, or the Lake of Eagles.

Above the first dead pressure of its woes,
Though health and bloom return'd, the delicate chain
Of thought, once tangled, never clear'd again.
Warm, lively, soft as in youth's happiest day,
The mind was still all there, but turn'd astray ;—
A wand'ring bark, upon whose pathway shone
All stars of heaven, except the guiding one !
Again she smiled, nay, much and brightly smiled,
But 'twas a lustre, strange, unreal, wild ;
And when she sung to her lute's touching strain,
'Twas like the notes, half-ecstasy, half pain,
The bulbul* utters, ere her soul depart,
When, vanquish'd by some minstrel's pow'rful art,
She dies upon the lute whose sweetness broke her heart.

Such was the mood in which that mission found
Young Zelica,—that mission, which around
The Eastern world, in every region blest
With woman's smile, sought out its loveliest,
To grace that galaxy of lips and eyes
Which the Veil'd Prophet destined for the skies :—
And such quick welcome as a spark receives
Dropp'd on a bed of Autumn's wither'd leaves,
Did every tale of these enthusiasts find
In the wild maiden's sorrow-blighted mind.
All fire at once the madd'ning zeal she caught ;—
Elect of Paradise ! blest, rapturous thought !
Predestined bride, in heaven's eternal dome,
Of some brave youth—ha ! durst they say "of *some*
No—of the one, one only object traced
In her heart's core too deep to be effaced ;
The one whose mem'ry, fresh as life, is twined
With every broken link of her lost mind ;
Whose image lives, though Reason's self be wreck'd,
Safe 'mid the ruins of her intellect !

Alas, poor Zelica ! it needed all
The fantasy, which held thy mind in thrall,
To see in that gay Harem's glowing maids
A sainted colony for Eden's shades ;
Or dream that he,—of whose unholy flame
Thou wert too soon the victim,—shining came
From Paradise, to people its pure sphere
With souls like thine, which he hath ruin'd here !
No—had not reason's light totally set,
And left thee dark, thou hadst an amulet
In the loved image, graven on thy heart,
Which would have saved thee from the tempter's art,
And kept alive, in all its bloom of breath,
That purity, whose fading is love's death !—
But lost, inflamed,—a restless zeal took place
Of the mild virgin's still and feminine grace ;
First of the Prophet's favourites, proudly first
In zeal and charms,—too well th' Impostor nursed
Her soul's delirium, in whose active flame,
Thus lighting up a young, luxuriant frame,
He saw more potent sorceries to bind
To his dark yoke the spirits of mankind,
More subtle chains than hell itself e'er twined.
No art was spared, no witch'ry ;—all the skill
His demons taught him was employ'd to fill
Her mind with gloom and ecstasy by turns—
That gloom, through which Phrensy but fiercer burns ;
That ecstasy, which from the depth of sadness
Glares like the maniac's moon, whose light is madness !

'Twas from a brilliant banquet, where the sound
Of poesy and music breathed around,
Together picturing to her mind and ear
The glories of that heav'n, her destined sphere,
Where all was pure, where every stain that lay
Upon the spirit's light should pass away,
And, realizing more than youthful love
E'er wish'd or dream'd, she should for ever rove
Through fields of fragrance by her Azim's side,
His own bless'd, purified, eternal bride !—
'Twas from a scene, a witching trance like this,
He hurried her away, yet breathing bliss,
To the dim charnel-house ;—through all its steams
Of damp and death, led only by those gleams
Which foul Corruption lights, as with design
To show the gay and proud *she* too can shine—
And, passing on through upright ranks of Dead,
Which to the maiden, doubly crazed by dread,
Seem'd, through the bluish death-light round them cast
To move their lips in mutt'rings as she pass'd—
There, in that awful place, when each had quaff'd
And pledged in silence such a fearful draught,
Such—oh ! the look and taste of that dread bowl
Will haunt her till she dies—he bound her soul
By a dark oath, in hell's own language framed,
Never, while earth his mystic presence claim'd,
While the blue arch of day hung o'er them both,
Never, by that all-imprecating oath,
In joy or sorrow from his side to sever.—
She swore, and the wide charnel echoed, "Never, never '

From that dread hour, entirely, wildly giv'n
To him and—she believed, lost maid !—to heav'n ;
Her brain, her heart, her passions all inflamed,
How proud she stood, when in full Harem named
The Priestess of the Faith !—how flash'd her eyes
With light, alas, that was not of the skies,
When round, in trances, only less than hers,
She saw the Harem kneel, her prostrate worshippers.
Well might Mokanna think that form alone
Had spells enough to make the world his own :—
Light, lovely limbs, to which the spirit's play
Gave motion, airy as the dancing spray,
When from its stem the small bird wings away :
Lips in whose rosy labyrinth, when she smiled,
The soul was lost ; and blushes, swift and wild
As are the momentary meteors sent
Across th' uncalm, but beauteous firmament.
And then her look—oh ! where's the heart so wise
Could unbewilder'd meet those matchless eyes ?
Quick, restless, strange, but exquisite withal,
Like those of angels, just before their fall ;
Now shadow'd with the shames of earth—now cross'd
By glimpses of the Heav'n her heart had lost ;
In ev'ry glance there broke, without control,
The flashes of a bright, but troubled soul,
Where sensibility still wildly play'd,
Like lightning, round the ruins it had made.

And such was now young Zelica—so changed
From her who, some years since, delighted ranged
The almond groves that shade Bokhara's tide,
All life and bliss, with Azim by her side !
So alter'd was she now, this festal day,
When, 'mid the proud Divan's dazzling array,
The vision of that Youth whom she had loved,
Had wept as dead, before her breathed and moved ,
When—bright, she thought, as if from Eden's track
But half-way trodden, he had wander'd back
Again to earth, glist'ning with Eden's light—
Her beauteous Azim shone before her sight.

O Reason ! who shall say what spells renew,
When least we look for it, thy broken clew !
Through what small vistas o'er the darken'd brain
Thy intellectual day-beam bursts again ;
And how, like forts, to which beleaguerers win
Unhoped-for entrance through some friend within,
One clear idea, waken'd in the breast
By mem'ry's magic, lets in all the rest.
Would it were thus, unhappy girl, with thee !
But though light came, it came but partially ;
Enough to show the maze, in which thy sense
Wander'd about—but not to guide it thence ;
Enough to glimmer o'er the yawning wave,
But not to point the harbour which might save.
Hours of delight and peace, long left behind,
With that dear form came rushing o'er her mind ;
But oh ! to think how deep her soul had gone
In shame and falsehood since those moments shone ;
And, then, her oath—*there* madness lay again,
And, shudd'ring, back she sunk into her chair

* The nightingale.

Of mental darkness, as if blest to flee
From light, whose every glimpse was agony!
Yet, *one* relief this glance of former years
Brought, mingled with its pain,—tears, floods of tears,
Long frozen at her heart, but now like rills
Let loose in spring-time from the snowy hills,
And gushing warm, after a sleep of frost,
Through valleys where their flow had long been lost.

Sad and subdued, for the first time her frame
Trembled with horror, when the summons came
(A summons proud and rare, which all but she,
And she, till now, had heard with ecstasy)
To meet Mokanna at his place of prayer,
A garden oratory, cool and fair,
By the stream's side, where still at close of day
The Prophet of the Veil retired to pray;
Sometimes alone—but, oft'ner far, with one,
One chosen nymph to share his orison.

Of late none found such favour in his sight
As the young Priestess; and though, since that night
When the death-caverns echoed every tone
Of the dire oath that made her all his own,
Th' Impostor, sure of his infatuate prize,
Had, more than once, thrown off his soul's disguise,
And utter'd such unheav'nly, monstrous things,
As ev'n across the desp'rate wanderings
Of a weak intellect, whose lamp was out,
Threw startling shadows of dismay and doubt;—
Yet zeal, ambition, her tremendous vow,
The thought, still haunting her, of that bright brow,
Whose blaze, as yet from mortal eye conceal'd,
Would soon, proud triumph! be to her reveal'd,
To her alone;—and then the hope, most dear,
Most wild of all, that her transgression here
Was but a passage through earth's grosser fire,
From which the spirit would at last aspire,
Ev'n purer than before,—as perfumes rise
Through flame and smoke, most welcome to the skies—
And that when Azim's fond, divine embrace
Should circle her in heav'n, no dark'ning trace
Would on that bosom he once loved remain,
But all be bright, be pure, be *his* again!—
These were the wild'ring dreams, whose curst deceit
Had chain'd her soul beneath the tempter's feet,
And made her think ev'n damning falsehood sweet.
But now that Shape, which had appall'd her view,
That Semblance—oh how terrible, if true!
Which came across her phrensy's full career
With shock of consciousness, cold, deep, severe,
As when, in northern seas, at midnight dark,
An isle of ice encounters some swift bark,
And, startling all its wretches from their sleep,
By one cold impulse hurls them to the deep;—
So came that shock not phrensy's self could bear,
And waking up each long-lull'd image there,
But check'd her headlong soul, to sink it in despair!

Wan and dejected, through the ev'ning dusk,
She now went slowly to that small kiosk,
Where, pondering alone his impious schemes,
Mokanna waited her—too wrapp'd in dreams
Of the fair-rip'ning future's rich success,
To heed the sorrow, pale and spiritless,
That sat upon his victim's downcast brow,
Or mark how slow her step, how alter'd now
From the quick, ardent Priestess, whose light bound
Came like a spirit's o'er th' unechoing ground,—
From that wild Zelica, whose every glance
Was thrilling fire, whose ev'ry thought a trance!

Upon his couch the Veil'd Mokanna lay,
While lamps around—not such as lend their ray,
Glimm'ring and cold, to those who nightly pray
In holy Koom,* or Mecca's dim arcades,—
But brilliant, soft, such lights as lovely maids
Look loveliest in, shed their luxurious glow
Upon his mystic Veil's white glitt'ring flow.
Beside him, 'stead of beads and books of pray'r,
Which the world fondly thought he mused on there,
Stood Vases, fill'd with Kishmee's* golden wine,
And the red weepings of the Shiraz vine;
Of which his curtain'd lips full many a draught
Took zealously, as if each drop they quaff'd,
Like Zemzem's Spring of Holiness,† had pow'r
To freshen the soul's virtues into flow'r!
And still he drank and ponder'd—nor could see
Th' approaching maid, so deep his revery;
At length, with fiendish laugh, like that which broke
From Eblis at the Fall of Man, he spoke:—
"Yes, ye vile race, for hell's amusement given,
"Too mean for earth, yet claiming kin with heav'n;
"God's images, forsooth! such gods as he
"Whom India serves, the monkey deity;‡—
"Ye creatures of a breath, proud things of clay,
"To whom if Lucifer, as grandams say,
"Refused, though at the forfeit of heaven's light,
"To bend in worship, Lucifer was right!§
"Soon shall I plant this foot upon the neck
"Of your foul race, and without fear or check,
"Luxuriating in hate, avenge my shame,
"My deep-felt, long-nursed loathing of man's name!
"Soon at the head of myriads, blind and fierce
"As hooded falcons, through the universe
"I'll sweep my dark'ning, desolating way,
"Weak man my instrument, curst man my prey!

"Ye wise, ye learn'd, who grope your dull way on
"By the dim twinkling gleams of ages gone,
"Like superstitious thieves, who think the light
"From dead men's marrow guides them best at night‖—
"Ye shall have honours—wealth—yes, Sages, yes—
"I know, grave fools, your wisdom's nothingness;
"Undazzled it can track yon starry sphere,
"But a gilt stick, a bauble blinds it here.
"How I shall laugh, when trumpeted along,
"In lying speech, and still more lying song,
"By these learn'd slaves, the meanest of the throng;
"Their wits bought up, their wisdom shrunk so small
"A sceptre's puny point can wield it all!

"Ye too, believers of incredible creeds,
"Whose faith enshrines the monsters which it breeds;
"Who, bolder ev'n than Nemrod, think to rise,
"By nonsense heap'd on nonsense, to the skies;
"Ye shall have miracles, ay, sound ones too,
"Seen, heard, attested, ev'ry thing—but true.
"Your preaching zealots, too inspired to seek
"One grace of meaning for the things they speak;
"Your martyrs, ready to shed out their blood,
"For truths too heav'nly to be understood;
"And your State Priests, sole venders of the lore,
"That works salvation;—as, on Ava's shore,
"Where none *but* priests are privileged to trade
"In that best marble of which Gods are made;¶
"They shall have mysteries—ay, precious stuff,
"For knaves to thrive by—mysteries enough;

* The cities of Com (or Koom) and Cashan are full of mosques, mausoleums, and sepulchres of the descendants of Ali, the Saints of Persia. *Chardin.*

* An island in the Persian Gulf, celebrated for its white wine.

† The miraculous well at Mecca; so called, says Sale, from the murmuring of its waters.

‡ The god Hannaman.—"Apes are in many parts of India highly venerated, out of respect to the god Hannaman, a deity partaking of the form of that race."—*Pennant's* Hindoostan.

See a curious account, in *Stephen's Persia*, of a solemn embassy from some part of the Indies to Goa, when the Portuguese were there, offering vast treasures for the recovery of a monkey's tooth, which they held in great veneration, and which had been taken away upon the conquest of the kingdom of Jafanapatan.

§ This resolution of Eblis not to acknowledge the new creature, man, was, according to Mahometan tradition, thus adopted:—"The earth (which God had selected for the materials of his work) was carried into Arabia to a place between Mecca and Tayef, where, being first kneaded by the angels, it was afterwards fashioned by God himself into a human form, and left to dry for the space of forty days, or, as others say, as many years; the angels, in the meantime, often visiting it, and Eblis (then one of the angels nearest to God's presence, afterwards the devil) among the rest: but he, not contented with looking at it, kicked it with his foot till it rung, and knowing God designed that creature to be his superior, took a secret resolution never to acknowledge him as such."—*Sale*, on the Koran.

‖ A kind of lantern formerly used by robbers, called the Hand of Glory, the candle for which was made of the fat of a dead malefactor. This, however, was rather a western than an eastern superstition.

¶ The material of which images of Gaudma (the Birman Deity) are made, is held sacred. "Birmans may not purchase the marble in mass, but are suffered, and indeed encouraged, to buy figures of the Deity ready made."—*Syme's* Ava, vol. ii. p. 376

"Dark, tangled doctrines, dark as fraud can weave,
"Which simple votaries shall on trust receive,
"While craftier feign belief, till they believe.
"A Heav'n too ye must have, ye lords of dust,—
"A splendid Paradise, pure souls, ye must:
"That Prophet ill sustains his holy call,
"Who finds not heav'ns to suit the tastes of all;
"Houris for boys, omniscience for sages,
"And wings and glories for all ranks and ages.
"Vain things!—as lust or vanity inspires,
"The heav'n of each is but what each desires,
"And, soul or sense, whate'er the object be,
"Man would be man to all eternity!
"So let him—Eblis!—grant this crowning curse,
"But keep him what he is, no Hell were worse."

"Oh my lost soul!" exclaim'd the shudd'ring maid,
Whose ears had drunk like poison all he said:—
Mokanna started—not abash'd, afraid,—
He knew no more of fear than one who dwells
Beneath the tropics knows of icicles!
But, in those dismal words that reach'd his ear,
"Oh my lost soul!" there was a sound so drear,
So like that voice, among the sinful dead,
In which the legend o'er Hell's Gate is read,
That, new as 'twas from her, whom naught could dim
Or sink till now, it startled even him.

"Ha, my fair Priestess!"—thus, with ready wile,
Th' Impostor turn'd to greet her—"thou, whose smile
"Hath inspiration in its rosy beam
"Beyond th' Enthusiast's hope or Prophet's dream;
"Light of the Faith! who twin'st religion's zeal
"So close with love's, men know not which they feel,
"Nor which to sigh for, in their trance of heart,
"The heav'n thou preachest or the heav'n thou art!
"What should I be without thee? without thee
"How dull were power, how joyless victory!
"Though borne by angels, if that smile of thine
"Bless'd not my banner, 'twere but half divine.
"But—why so mournful, child? those eyes that shone
"All life last night—what!—is their glory gone?
"Come, come—this morn's fatigue hath made them pale,
"They want rekindling—suns themselves would fail
"Did not their comets bring, as I to thee,
"From light's own fount supplies of brilliancy.
"Thou seest this cup—no juice of earth is here,
"But the pure waters of that upper sphere,
"Whose rills o'er ruby beds and topaz flow,
"Catching the gem's bright colour as they go.
"Nightly my Genii come and fill these urns—
"Nay, drink—in ev'ry drop life's essence burns;
"'Twill make that soul all fire, those eyes all light—
"Come, come, I want thy loveliest smiles to-night:
"There is a youth—why start?—thou saw'st him then;
"Look'd he not nobly? such the godlike men
"Thou'lt have to woo thee in the bow'rs above;—
"Though *he*, I fear, hath thoughts too stern for love,
"Too ruled by that cold enemy of bliss
"The world calls virtue—we must conquer this;
"Nay, shrink not, pretty sage! 'tis not for thee
"To scan the mazes of Heav'n's mystery:
"The steel must pass through fire, ere it can yield
"Fit instruments for mighty hands to wield.
"This very night I mean to try the art
"Of powerful beauty on that warrior's heart.
"All that my Harem boasts of bloom and wit,
"Of skill and charms, most rare and exquisite,
"Shall tempt the boy;—young Mirzala's blue eyes,
"Whose sleepy lid like snow on violets lies;
"Arouya's cheeks, warm as a spring-day sun,
"And lips that, like the seal of Solomon,
"Have magic in their pressure; Zeba's lute,
"And Lilla's dancing feet, that gleam and shoot
"Rapid and white as sea-birds o'er the deep—
"All shall combine their witching powers to steep
"My convert's spirit in that soft'ning trance,
"From which to heav'n is but the next advance;—
"That glowing, yielding fusion of the breast,
"On which Religion stamps her image best.
"But hear me, Priestess!—though each nymph of these
"Hath some peculiar, practised power to please,
"Some glance or step which, at the mirror tried,
"First charms herself, then all the world beside;
"There still wants *one*, to make the vict'ry sure,
"One who in every look joins every lure:
"Through whom all beauty's beams concentred pass,
"Dazzling and warm, as through love's burning glass;
"Whose gentle lips persuade without a word,
"Whose words, ev'n when unmeaning, are adored.
"Like inarticulate breathings from a shrine,
"Which our faith takes for granted are divine.
"Such is the nymph we want, all warmth and light,
"To crown the rich temptations of to-night;
"Such the refined enchantress that must be
"This hero's vanquisher,—and thou art she!"

With her hands clasp'd, her lips apart and pale,
The maid had stood, gazing upon the Veil
From which these words, like south winds through a fence
Of Kerzrah flow'rs, came fill'd with pestilence;*
So boldly utter'd, too! as if all dread
Of frowns from her, of virtuous frowns, were fled,
And the wretch felt assured that, once plunged in,
Her woman's soul would know no pause in sin!

At first, though mute she listen'd, like a dream
Seem'd all he said: nor could her mind, whose beam
As yet was weak, penetrate half his scheme.
But when, at length, he utter'd, "Thou art she!"
All flash'd at once, and shrieking piteously,
"Oh not for worlds!" she cried—"Great God! to whom
"I once knelt innocent, is this my doom?
"Are all my dreams, my hopes of heav'nly bliss,
"My purity, my pride, then come to this,—
"To live, the wanton of a fiend! to be
"The pander of his guilt—oh infamy!
"And sunk, myself, as low as hell can steep
"In its hot flood, drag others down as deep!
"Others—ha! yes—that youth who came to-day—
"*Not* him I loved—not him—oh! do but say,
"But swear to me this moment 'tis not he,
"And I will serve, dark fiend, will worship even thee!"

"Beware, young raving thing;—in time beware,
"Nor utter what I cannot, must not bear,
"Ev'n from *thy* lips. Go—try thy lute, thy voice,
"The boy must feel their magic;—I rejoice
"To see those fires, no matter whence they rise,
"Once more illuming my fair Priestess' eyes;
"And should the youth, whom soon those eyes shall warm,
"*Indeed* resemble thy dead lover's form,
"So much the happier wilt thou find thy doom,
"As one warm lover, full of life and bloom,
"Excels ten thousand cold ones in the tomb.
"Nay, nay, no frowning, sweet!—those eyes were made
"For love, not anger—I must be obey'd."

"Obey'd!—'tis well—yes, I deserve it all—
"On me, on me Heav'n's vengeance cannot fall
"Too heavily—but Azim, brave and true
"And beautiful—must *he* be ruin'd too?
"Must *he* too, glorious as he is, be driven
"A renegade like me from Love and Heaven?
"Like me?—weak wretch, I wrong him—not like me,
"No—he's all truth and strength and purity!
"Fill up your madd'ning hell-cup to the brim,
"Its witch'ry, fiends, will have no charm for him.
"Let loose your glowing wantons from their bow'rs,
"He loves, he loves, and can defy their powers!
"Wretch as I am, in *his* heart still I reign
"Pure as when first we met, without a stain!
"Though ruin'd—lost—my mem'ry, like a charm
"Left by the dead, still keeps his soul from harm
"Oh! never let him know how deep the brow
"He kiss'd at parting is dishonour'd now;
"Ne'er tell him how debased, how sunk is she,
"Whom once he loved—once!—*still* loves dotingly.

* "It is commonly said in Persia, that if a man breathe in the hot south wind, which in June or July passes over that flower, (the Kerzereh,) it will kill him."—*Thevenot*

"Thou laugh'st, tormentor,—what!—thou'lt brand my name?
"Do, do—in vain—he'll not believe my shame—
"He thinks me true, that naught beneath God's sky
"Could tempt or change me, and—so once thought I.
"But this is past—though worse than death my lot,
"Than hell—'tis nothing while *he* knows it not.
"Far off to some benighted land I'll fly,
"Where sunbeam ne'er shall enter till I die;
"Where none will ask the lost one whence she came,
"But I may fade and fall without a name.
"And thou—curst man or fiend, whate'er thou art,
"Who found'st this burning plague-spot in my heart,
"And spread'st it—oh, so quick!—through soul and frame,
"With more than demon's art, till I became
"A loathsome thing, all pestilence, all flame!—
"If when I'm gone——"

"Hold, fearless maniac, hold,
"Nor tempt my rage—by Heaven, not half so bold
"The puny bird, that dares with teasing hum
"Within the crocodile's stretch'd jaws to come;*
"And so thou'lt fly, forsooth?—what!—give up all
"Thy chaste dominion in the Harem Hall,
"Where now to Love and now to ALLA given,
"Half mistress and half saint, thou hang'st as even
"As doth MEDINA'S tomb, 'twixt hell and heaven!
"Thou'lt fly?—as easily may reptiles run,
"The gaunt snake once hath fix'd his eyes upon;
'As easily, when caught, the prey may be
'Pluck'd from his loving folds, as thou from me.
"No, no, 'tis fix'd—let good or ill betide,
"Thou'rt mine till death, till death MOKANNA'S bride!
"Hast thou forgot thy oath?"—

At this dread word,
The Maid, whose spirit his rude taunts had stirr'd
Through all its depths, and roused an anger there,
That burst and lighten'd even through her despair—
Shrunk back, as if a blight were in the breath
That spoke that word, and stagger'd pale as death.

"Yes, my sworn bride, let others seek in bow'rs
"Their bridal place—the charnel vault was ours!
"Instead of scents and balms, for thee and me
"Rose the rich steams of sweet mortality;
"Gay, flick'ring death-lights shone while we were wed,
"And, for our guests, a row of goodly Dead,
"(Immortal spirits in their time, no doubt,)
"From reeking shrouds upon the rite look'd out!
"That oath thou heard'st more lips than thine repeat—
"That cup—thou shudd'rest, Lady—was it sweet?
"That cup we pledged, the charnel's choicest wine,
"Hath bound thee—ay—body and soul all mine;
"Bound thee by chains that, whether blest or curst,
"No matter now, not hell itself shall burst!
"Hence, woman, to the Harem, and look gay,
"Look wild, look—any thing but sad; yet stay—
"One moment more—from what this night hath pass'd,
"I see thou know'st me, know'st me *well* at last.
"Ha! ha! and so, fond thing, thou thought'st all true,
"And that I love mankind?—I do, I do—
"As victims, love them; as the sea-dog dotes
"Upon the small, sweet fry that round him floats;
"Or, as the Nile-bird loves the slime that gives
"That rank and venomous food on which she lives!—†

"And, now thou seest my *soul's* angelic hue,
"'Tis time these *features* were uncurtain'd too;—
"This brow, whose light—oh rare celestial light!
"Hath been reserved to bless thy favour'd sight;
"These dazzling eyes, before whose shrouded might
"Thou'st seen immortal Man kneel down and quake—
"Would that they *were* heaven's lightnings for his sake!

* The humming-bird is said to run this risk for the purpose of picking the crocodile's teeth. The same circumstance is related of the lapwing, as a fact to which he was witness, by *Paul Lucas*, Voyage fait en 1714.

The ancient story concerning the Trochilus, or humming-bird, entering with impunity into the mouth of the crocodile, is firmly believed at Java.—*Barrow's Cochin China.*

† Circum eandem ripas (Nili, viz.) ales est Ibis. Ea serpentium populatur ova, gratissimamque ex his escam nidis suis refert.—*Solinus.*

"But turn and look—then wonder, if thou wilt,
"That I should hate, should take revenge, by guilt,
"Upon the hand, whose mischief or whose mirth
"Sent me thus maim'd and monstrous upon earth;
"And on that race who, though more vile they be
"Than mowing apes, are demi-gods to me!
"Here—judge if hell, with all its power to damn,
"Can add one curse to the foul thing I am!"

He raised his veil—the Maid turn'd slowly round,
Look'd at him—shriek'd—and sunk upon the ground.

ON their arrival, next night, at the place of encampment, they were surprised and delighted to find the groves all around illuminated; some artists of Yamtcheou* having been sent on previously for the purpose. On each side of the green alley which led to the Royal Pavilion, artificial sceneries of bamboo-work† were erected, representing arches, minarets, and towers, from which hung thousands of silken lanterns, painted by the most delicate pencils of Canton. Nothing could be more beautiful than the leaves of the mango-trees and acacias, shining in the light of the bamboo scenery, which shed a lustre round as soft as that of the nights of Peristan.

LALLA ROOKH, however, who was too much occupied by the sad story of ZELICA and her lover to give a thought to any thing else, except, perhaps, him who related it, hurried on through this scene of splendour to her pavilion,—greatly to the mortification of the poor artists of Yamtcheou,—and was followed with equal rapidity by the Great Chamberlain, cursing, as he went, that ancient Mandarin, whose parental anxiety in lighting up the shores of the lake, where his beloved daughter had wandered and been lost, was the origin of these fantastic Chinese illuminations.‡

Without a moment's delay, young FERAMORZ was introduced, and FADLADEEN, who could never make up his mind as to the merits of a poet till he knew the religious sect to which he belonged, was about to ask him whether he was a Shia or a Sooni, when LALLA ROOKH impatiently clapped her hands for silence, and the youth, being seated upon the musnud near her, proceeded:—

PREPARE thy soul, young AZIM!—thou hast braved
The bands of GREECE, still mighty though enslaved;
Hast faced her phalanx, arm'd with all its fame,
Her Macedonian pikes and globes of flame;
All this hast fronted, with firm heart and brow;
But a more perilous trial waits thee now,—
Woman's bright eyes, a dazzling host of eyes
From every land where woman smiles or sighs;
Of every hue, as Love may chance to raise
His black or azure banner in their blaze;
And each sweet mode of warfare, from the flash
That lightens boldly through the shadowy lash,
To the sly, stealing splendours, almost hid,
Like swords half-sheathed, beneath the downcast lid;
Such, AZIM, is the lovely, luminous host
Now led against thee; and let conqu'rors boast

* "The feast of Lanterns is celebrated at Yamtcheou with more magnificence than anywhere else: and the report goes, that the illuminations there are so splendid, that an Emperor once, not daring openly to leave his Court to go thither, committed himself, with the Queen and several Princesses of his family, into the hands of a magician, who promised to transport them thither in a trice. He made them in the night to ascend magnificent thrones that were borne up by swans, which in a moment arrived at Yamtcheou. The Emperor saw at his leisure all the solemnity, being carried upon a cloud that hovered over the city and descended by degrees; and came back again with the same speed and equipage, nobody at Court perceiving his absence."—*The Present State of China*, p. 156.

† See a description of the nuptials of Vizier Alee in the *Asiatic Annual Register of* 1804.

‡ "The vulgar ascribe it to an accident that happened in the family of a famous Mandarin, whose daughter, walking one evening upon the shore of a lake, fell in and was drowned; this afflicted father, with his family, ran thither, and, the better to find her, he caused a great company of lanterns to be lighted. All the inhabitants of the place thronged after him with torches. The year ensuing they made fires upon the shores the same day; they continued the ceremony every year, every one lighted his lantern, and by degrees it commenc[illegible] a custom."—*Present State of China.*

Their fields of fame; he who in virtue arms
A young, warm spirit against beauty's charms,
Who feels her brightness, yet defies her thrall,
Is the best, bravest conqu'ror of them all.

Now, through the Harem chambers, moving lights
And busy shapes proclaim the toilet's rites;—
From room to room the ready handmaids hie,
Some skill'd to wreath the turban tastefully,
Or hang the veil, in negligence of shade,
O'er the warm blushes of the youthful maid,
Who, if between the folds but *one* eye shone,
Like SEBA's Queen, could vanquish with that one:*
While some bring leaves of Henna, to imbue
The fingers' ends with a bright roseate hue,†
So bright, that in the mirror's depth they seem
Like tips of coral branches in the stream;
And others mix the Kohol's jetty dye,
To give that long, dark languish to the eye,‡
Which makes the maids, whom kings are proud to cull
From fair Circassia's vales, so beautiful.
All is in motion; rings, and plumes, and pearls,
Are shining ev'rywhere:—some younger girls
Are gone by moonlight to the garden-beds,
To gather fresh, cool chaplets for their heads;—
Gay creatures! sweet, though mournful, 'tis to see
How each prefers a garland from that tree
Which brings to mind her childhood's innocent day,
And the dear fields and friendships far away.
The maid of INDIA, blest again to hold
In her full lap the Champac's leaves of gold,§
Thinks of the time when, by the GANGES' flood,
Her little playmates scatter'd many a bud
Upon her long, black hair, with glossy gleam
Just dripping from the consecrated stream;
While the young Arab, haunted by the smell
Of her own mountain flow'rs, as by a spell,—
The sweet Elcaya,|| and that courteous tree
Which bows to all who seek its canopy,¶
Sees, call'd up round her by these magic scents,
The well, the camels, and her father's tents;
Sighs for the home she left with little pain,
And wishes ev'n its sorrows back again!

Meanwhile, through vast illuminated halls,
Silent and bright, where nothing but the falls
Of fragrant waters, gushing with cool sound
From many a jasper fount, is heard around,
Young AZIM roams bewilder'd,—nor can guess
What means this maze of light and loneliness.
Here, the way leads, o'er tesselated floors
Or mats of CAIRO, through long corridors,
Where, ranged in cassolets and silver urns,
Sweet wood of aloe or of sandal burns;
And spicy rods, such as illume at night
The bow'rs of TIBET,** send forth odorous light
Like Peris' wands, when pointing out the road
For some pure Spirit to its blest abode:—
And here, at once, the glittering saloon
Bursts on his sight, boundless and bright as noon;
Where, in the midst, reflecting back the rays
In broken rainbows, a fresh fountain plays
High as th' enamell'd cupola, which tow'rs
All rich with Arabesques of gold and flow'rs:
And the mosaic floor beneath shines through
The sprinkling of that fountain's silv'ry dew,
Like the wet, glist'ning shells, of ev'ry dye,
That on the margin of the Red Sea lie.

Here too he traces the kind visitings
Of woman's love in those fair, living things
Of land and wave, whose fate—in bondage thrown
For their weak loveliness—is like her own!
On one side gleaming with a sudden grace
Through water, brilliant as the crystal vase
In which it undulates, small fishes shine,
Like golden ingots from a fairy mine;—
While, on the other, latticed lightly in
With odoriferous woods of COMORIN,*
Each brilliant bird that wings the air is seen;—
Gay, sparkling loories, such as gleam between
The crimson blossoms of the coral tree†
In the warm isles of India's sunny sea:
Mecca's blue sacred pigeon,‡ and the thrush
Of Hindostan,§ whose holy warblings gush,
At evening, from the tall pagoda's top;—
Those golden birds that, in the spice-time, drop
About the gardens, drunk with that sweet food||
Whose scent hath lured them o'er the summer flood;¶
And those that under Araby's soft sun
Build their high nests of budding cinnamon;**
In short, all rare and beauteous things, that fly
Through the pure element, here calmly lie
Sleeping in light, like the green birds†† that dwell
In Eden's radiant fields of asphodel!

So on, through scenes past all imagining,
More like the luxuries of that impious King,‡‡
Whom Death's dark Angel, with his lightning torch,
Struck down and blasted ev'n in Pleasure's porch,
Than the pure dwelling of a Prophet sent,
Arm'd with Heaven's sword, for man's enfranchisement-
Young AZIM wander'd, looking sternly round,
His simple garb and war-boots' clanking sound
But ill according with the pomp and grace
And silent lull of that voluptuous place.

"Is this, then," thought the youth, "is this the way
"To free man's spirit from the dead'ning sway
"Of worldly sloth,—to teach him while he lives,
"To know no bliss but that which virtue gives,
"And when he dies, to leave his lofty name
"A light, a landmark on the cliffs of fame?
"It was not so, Land of the generous thought
"And daring deed, thy godlike sages taught;
"It was not thus, in bowers of wanton ease,
"Thy Freedom nursed her sacred energies;
"Oh! not beneath th' enfeebling, with'ring glow
"Of such dull lux'ry did those myrtles grow,
"With which she wreathed her sword, when she would dare
"Immortal deeds; but in the bracing air
"Of toil,—of temperance,—of that high, rare,
"Ethereal virtue, which alone can breathe
"Life, health, and lustre into Freedom's wreath.

* "Thou hast ravished my heart with one of thine eyes."—*Sol. Song.*

† "They tinged the ends of her fingers scarlet with Henna, so that they resembled branches of coral."—*Story of Prince Futtun in Bahardanush.*

‡ "The women blacken the inside of their eyelids with a powder named the black Kohol."—*Russel.*

"None of these ladies," says *Shaw*, "take themselves to be completely dressed till they have tinged the hair and edges of their eyelids with the powder of lead-ore. Now, as this operation is performed by dipping first into the powder a small wooden bodkin of the thickness of a quill, and then drawing it afterwards through the eyelids over the ball of the eye, we shall have a lively image of what the Prophet (Jer. iv. 30) may be supposed to mean by *rending the eyes with painting*. This practice is no doubt of great antiquity; for besides the instance already taken notice of, we find that where Jezebel is said (2 Kings ix. 30) *to have painted her face*, the original words are *she adjusted her eyes with the powder of lead ore*."—*Shaw's* Travels.

§ "The appearance of the blossoms of the gold-coloured Champac on the black hair of the Indian women has supplied the Sanscrit poets with many elegant allusions."—See *Asiatic Researches*, vol. iv.

|| A tree famous for its perfume, and common on the hills of Yemen. —*Niebuhr.*

¶ Of the genus mimosa, "which droops its branches whenever any person approaches it, seeming as if it saluted those who retire under its shade."—*Ibid.*

** "Cloves are a principal ingredient in the composition of the perfumed rods, which men of rank keep constantly burning in their presence."—*Turner's* Tibet.

* "C'est d'où vient le bois d'aloës, que les Arabes appellent Oud Comari, et celui du sandal, qui s'y trouve en grande quantité."—*D'Herbelot.*

† "Thousands of variegated loories visit the coral-trees."—*Barrow.*

‡ "In Mecca there are quantities of blue pigeons, which none will affright or abuse, much less kill."—*Pitt's* Account of the Mahometans.

§ "The Pagoda Thrush is esteemed among the first choristers of India. It sits perched on the sacred pagodas, and from thence delivers its melodious song."—*Pennant's* Hindostan.

|| *Tavernier* adds, that while the Birds of Paradise lie in this intoxicated state, the emmets come and eat off their legs; and that hence it is they are said to have no feet.

¶ Birds of Paradise, which, at the nutmeg season, come in flights from the southern isles to India; and "the strength of the nutmeg," says *Tavernier*, "so intoxicates them that they fall dead drunk to the earth."

** "That bird which liveth in Arabia, and buildeth its nest with cinnamon."—*Brown's* Vulgar Errors.

†† "The spirits of the martyrs will be lodged in the crops of green birds."—*Gibbon*, vol. ix. p. 21.

‡‡ Shedad, who made the delicious gardens of Irim, in imitation of Paradise, and was destroyed by lightning the first time he attempted to enter them.

" Who, that surveys this span of earth we press,—
" This speck of life in time's great wilderness,
" This narrow isthmus 'twixt two boundless seas,
" The past, the future, two eternities !—
" Would sully the bright spot, or leave it bare,
" When he might build him a proud temple there,
" A name, that long shall hallow all its space,
" And be each purer soul's high resting-place ?
" But no—it cannot be, that one, whom God
" Has sent to break the wizard Falsehood's rod,—
" A Prophet of the Truth, whose mission draws
" Its rights from Heav'n, should thus profane its cause
" With the world's vulgar pomps ;—no, no,—I see—
" He thinks me weak—this glare of luxury
" Is but to tempt, to try the eaglet gaze
" Of my young soul—shine on, 'twill stand the blaze !"

So thought the youth ;—but, ev'n while he defied
This witching scene, he felt its witch'ry glide
Through ev'ry sense. The perfume breathing round,
Like a pervading spirit ;—the still sound
Of falling waters, lulling as the song
Of Indian bees at sunset, when they throng
Around the fragrant Nilica, and deep
In its blue blossoms hum themselves to sleep ;*
And music, too—dear music ! that can touch
Beyond all else the soul that loves it much—
Now heard far off, so far as but to seem
Like the faint, exquisite music of a dream ;
All was too much for him, too full of bliss,
The heart could nothing feel, that felt not this ;
Soften'd he sunk upon a couch, and gave
His soul up to sweet thoughts, like wave on wave
Succeeding in smooth seas, when storms are laid ;
He thought of Zelica, his own dear maid,
And of the time when, full of blissful sighs,
They sat and look'd into each other's eyes,
Silent and happy—as if God had giv'n
Naught else worth looking at on this side heav'n.

" Oh, my loved mistress, thou, whose spirit still
" Is with me, round me, wander where I will—
" It is for thee, for thee alone I seek
" The paths of glory ; to light up thy cheek
" With warm approval—in that gentle look,
" To read my praise, as in an angel's book,
" And think all toils rewarded, when from thee
" I gain a smile worth immortality !
" How shall I bear the moment, when restored
" To that young heart where I alone am Lord,
" Though of such bliss unworthy,—since the best
" Alone deserve to be the happiest :—
" When from those lips, unbreathed upon for years,
" I shall again kiss off the soul-felt tears,
" And find those tears warm as when last they started,
" Those sacred kisses pure as when we parted.
" O my own life !—why should a single day,
" A moment keep me from those arms away ?"

While thus he thinks, still nearer on the breeze
Come those delicious, dream-like harmonies,
Each note of which but adds new, downy links
To the soft chain in which his spirit sinks.
He turns him tow'rd the sound, and far away
Through a long vista, sparkling with the play
Of countless lamps,—like the rich track which Day
Leaves on the waters, when he sinks from us,
So long the path, its light so tremulous ;—
He sees a group of female forms advance,
Some chain'd together in the mazy dance
By fetters, forged in the green sunny bow'rs,
As they were captives to the King of Flow'rs ;†
And some disporting round, unlink'd and free,
Who seem'd to mock their sisters' slavery ;
And round and round them still, in wheeling flight
Went, like gay moths about a lamp at night ;
While others waked, as gracefully along
Their feet kept time, the very soul of song
From psalt'ry, pipe, and lutes of heav'nly thrill,
Or their own youthful voices, heav'nlier still.
And now they come, now pass before his eye.
Forms such as Nature moulds, when she would vie
With Fancy's pencil, and give birth to things
Lovely beyond its fairest picturings.
Awhile they dance before him, then divide,
Breaking, like rosy clouds at even-tide
Around the rich pavilion of the sun,—
Till silently dispersing, one by one,
Through many a path that from the chamber leads
To gardens, terraces, and moonlight meads,
Their distant laughter comes upon the wind,
And but one trembling nymph remains behind,—
Beck'ning them back in vain, for they are gone,
And she is left in all that light alone ;
No veil to curtain o'er her beauteous brow,
In its young bashfulness more beauteous now ;
But a light golden chain-work round her hair,*
Such as the maids of Yezd† and Shiras wear,
From which, on either side, gracefully hung
A golden amulet in the Arab tongue,
Engraven o'er with some immortal line
From Holy Writ, or bard scarce less divine ;
While her left hand, as shrinkingly she stood,
Held a small lute of gold and sandal-wood,
Which, once or twice, she touch'd with hurried strain,
Then took her trembling fingers off again.
But when at length a timid glance she stole
At Azim, the sweet gravity of soul
She saw through all his features calm'd her fear,
And, like a half-tamed antelope, more near,
Though shrinking still, she came ;—then sat her down
Upon a musnud's‡ edge, and, bolder grown,
In the pathetic mode of Isfahan§
Touch'd a preluding strain, and thus began :—

There's a bower of roses by Bendemeer's‖ stream,
And the nightingale sings round it all the day long ;
In the time of my childhood 'twas like a sweet dream,
To sit in the roses and hear the bird's song.

That bower and its music I never forget,
But oft when alone, in the bloom of the year,
I think—is the nightingale singing there yet ?
Are the roses still bright by the calm Bendemeer ?

No, the roses soon wither'd that hung o'er the wave,
But some blossoms were gather'd, while freshly they shone,
And a dew was distill'd from their flowers, that gave
All the fragrance of summer when summer was gone.

Thus memory draws from delight, ere it dies,
An essence that breathes of it many a year ;
Thus bright to my soul, as 'twas then to my eyes,
Is that bower on the banks of the calm Bendemeer !

" Poor maiden !" thought the youth, " if thou wert sent,
" With thy soft lute and beauty's blandishment,
" To wake unholy wishes in this heart,
" Or tempt its troth, thou little know'st the art.
" For though thy lip should sweetly counsel wrong,
" Those vestal eyes would disavow its song.
" But thou hast breathed such purity, thy lay
" Returns so fondly to youth's virtuous day,
" And leads thy soul—if e'er it wander'd thence—
" So gently back to its first innocence,
" That I would sooner stop the unchain'd dove,

* "My Pandits assure me that the plant before us (the Nilica) is their Sephalica, thus named because the bees are supposed to sleep on its blossoms."—*Sir W. Jones.*

† "They deferred it till the King of Flowers should ascend his throne of enamelled foliage. —*The Bahardanush.*

* "One of the head-dresses of the Persian women is composed of a light golden chain-work, set with small pearls, with a thin gold plate pendent, about the bigness of a crown-piece, on which is impressed an Arabian prayer, and which hangs upon the cheek below the ear."—*Hanway's* Travels.

† "Certainly the women of Yezd are the handsomest women in Persia. The proverb is, that to live happy a man must have a wife of Yezd, eat the bread of Yezdecas, and drink the wine of Shiraz."—*Tavernier.*

‡ Musnuds are cushioned seats usually reserved for persons of distinction.

§ The Persians, like the ancient Greeks, call their musical modes or Perdas by the names of different countries or cities, as the mode of Isfahan, the mode of Irak, &c.

‖ A river which flows near the ruins of Chilminar.

"When swift returning to its home of love,
"And round its snowy wing new fetters twine,
"Than turn from virtue one pure wish of thine!"

Scarce had this feeling pass'd, when, sparkling through
The gently open'd curtains of light blue
That veil'd the breezy casement, countless eyes,
Peeping like stars through the blue evening skies,
Look'd laughing in, as if to mock the pair*
That sat so still and melancholy there:—
And now the curtains fly apart, and in
From the cool air, 'mid showers of jessamine
Which those without fling after them in play,
Two lightsome maidens spring,—lightsome as the
Who live in th' air on odours,—and around
The bright saloon, scarce conscious of the ground,
Chase one another, in a varying dance
Of mirth and languor, coyness and advance,
Too eloquently like love's warm pursuit:—
While she, who sung so gently to the lute
Her dream of home, steals timidly away,
Shrinking as violets do in summer's ray,—
But takes with her from AZIM's heart that sigh,
We sometimes give to forms that pass us by
In the world's crowd, too lovely to remain,
Creatures of light we never see again!

Around the white necks of the nymphs who danced
Hung carcanets of orient gems, that glanced
More brilliant than the sea-glass glitt'ring o'er
The hills of crystal on the Caspian shore;*
While from their long, dark tresses, in a fall
Of curls descending, bells as musical
As those that, on the golden-shafted trees
Of EDEN, shake in the eternal breeze,†
Rung round their steps, at ev'ry bound more sweet,
As 'twere th' ecstatic language of their feet.
At length the chase was o'er, and they stood wreath'd
Within each other's arms; while soft there breathed
Through the cool casement, mingled with the sighs
Of moonlight flow'rs, music that seem'd to rise
From some still lake, so liquidly it rose;
And, as it swell'd again at each faint close,
The ear could track, through all that maze of chords
And young sweet voices, these impassion'd words:

A SPIRIT there is, whose fragrant sigh
 Is burning now through earth and air;
Where cheeks are blushing, the Spirit is nigh,
 Where lips are meeting, the Spirit is there!

His breath is the soul of flow'rs like these,
 And his floating eyes—oh! *they* resemble‡
Blue water-lilies,§ when the breeze
 Is making the stream around them tremble.

Hail to thee, hail to thee, kindling pow'r!
 Spirit of Love, Spirit of Bliss!
Thy holiest time is the moonlight hour,
 And there never was moonlight so sweet as this.

By the fair and brave
 Who blushing unite,
Like the sun and wave,
 When they meet at night;

By the tear that shows
 When passion is nigh,
As the rain-drop flows
 From the heat of the sky;

By the first love-beat
 Of the youthful heart,
By the bliss to meet,
 And the pain to part;

By all that thou hast
 To mortals given,
Which—oh, could it last,
 This earth were heaven.

We call thee hither, entrancing Power!
 Spirit of Love! Spirit of Bliss!
Thy holiest time is the moonlight hour,
 And there never was moonlight so sweet as this.

Impatient of a scene, whose lux'ries stole,
Spite of himself, too deep into his soul,
And where, 'midst all that the young heart loves most,
Flow'rs, music, smiles, to yield was to be lost,
The youth had started up, and turn'd away
From the light nymphs, and their luxurious lay,
To muse upon the pictures that hung round,—*
Bright images, that spoke without a sound,
And views, like vistas into fairy ground.
But here again new spells came o'er his sense:—
All that the pencil's mute omnipotence
Could call up into life, of soft and fair,
Of fond and passionate, was glowing there;
Nor yet too warm, but touch'd with that fine art
Which paints of pleasure but the purer part;
Which knows ev'n Beauty when half-veil'd is best,—
Like her own radiant planet of the west,
Whose orb when half-retired looks loveliest.†
There hung the history of the Genii-King,
Traced through each gay, voluptuous wandering
With her from SABA's bowers, in whose bright eyes
He read that to be blest is to be wise;—‡
Here fond ZULEIKA§ woos with open arms
The Hebrew boy, who flies from her young charms,
Yet, flying, turns to gaze, and, half undone,
Wishes that Heav'n and she could *both* be won;
And here MOHAMMED, born for love and guile,
Forgets the Koran in his MARY's smile;—
Then beckons some kind angel from above
With a new text to consecrate their love.||

With rapid step, yet pleased and ling'ring eye,
Did the youth pass these pictured stories by,
And hasten'd to a casement, where the light
Of the calm moon came in, and freshly bright
The fields without were seen, sleeping as still
As if no life remain'd in breeze or rill.
Here paused he, while the music, now less near,
Breathed with a holier language on his ear,
As though the distance, and that heav'nly ray
Through which the sounds came floating, took away
All that had been too earthly in the lay.

Oh! could he listen to such sounds unmoved,
And by that light—nor dream of her he loved?

---

* "To the north of us (on the coast of the Caspian, near Badku) was a mountain, which sparkled like diamonds, arising from the sea-glass and crystals with which it abounds."—*Journey of the Russian Ambassador to Persia*, 1746.

† "To which will be added the sound of the bells, hanging on the trees, which will be put in motion by the wind proceeding from the throne of God, as often as the blessed wish for music."—*Sale*.

‡ "Whose wanton eyes resemble blue water-lilies, agitated by the breeze."—*Jayadeva*.

§ The blue lotus, which grows in Cashmere and in Persia

* It has been generally supposed that the Mahometans prohibit all pictures of animals; but *Toderini* shows that, though the practice is forbidden by the Koran, they are not more averse to painted figures and images than other people. From Mr. Murphy's work, too, we find that the Arabs of Spain had no objection to the introduction of figures into painting.

† This is not quite astronomically true. "Dr. Hadley (says Keil) has shown that Venus is brightest when she is about forty degrees removed from the sun; and that then but *only a fourth part* of her lucid disk is to be seen from the earth."

‡ For the loves of King Solomon (who was supposed to preside over the whole race of Genii) with Balkis, the Queen of Sheba or Saba, see *D'Herbelot*, and the *Notes on the Koran*, chap. 2.

"In the palace which Solomon ordered to be built against the arrival of the Queen of Saba, the floor or pavement was of transparent glass, laid over running water, in which fish were swimming." This led the Queen into a very natural mistake, which the Koran has not thought beneath its dignity to commemorate. "It was said unto her, 'Enter the palace.' And when she saw it she imagined it to be a great water; and she discovered her legs, by lifting up her robe to pass through it. Whereupon Solomon said to her, 'Verily, this is the place evenly floored with glass.'"—Chap. 27.

§ The wife of Potiphar, thus named by the Orientals.

The passion which this frail beauty of antiquity conceived for her young Hebrew slave has given rise to a much-esteemed poem in the Persian language, entitled *Yusef van Zelikha*, by *Noureddin Jami*; the manuscript copy of which, in the Bodleian Library at Oxford, is supposed to be the finest in the whole world."—*Note upon Nott's Translation of Hafez*.

|| The particulars of Mahomet's amour with Mary, the Coptic girl, in justification of which he added a new chapter to the Koran, may be found in *Gagnier's Notes upon Abulfeda*, p. 151.

Dream on, unconscious boy! while yet thou mayst;
'Tis the last bliss thy soul shall ever taste.
Clasp yet awhile her image to thy heart,
Ere all the light, that made it dear, depart.
Think of her smiles as when thou saw'st them last,
Clear, beautiful, by naught of earth o'ercast;
Recall her tears, to thee at parting giv'n,
Pure as they weep, *if* angels weep, in Heav'n.
Think, in her own still bower she waits thee now,
With the same glow of heart and bloom of brow,
Yet shrined in solitude—thine all, thine only,
Like the one star above thee, bright and lonely.
Oh! that a dream so sweet, so long enjoy'd,
Should be so sadly, cruelly destroy'd!

The song is hush'd, the laughing nymphs are flown,
And he is left, musing of bliss, alone;—
Alone?—no, not alone—that heavy sigh,
That sob of grief, which broke from some one nigh—
Whose could it be?—alas! is misery found
Here, even here, on this enchanted ground?
He turns, and sees a female form, close veil'd,
Leaning, as if both heart and strength had fail'd,
Against a pillar near;—not glitt'ring o'er
With gems and wreaths, such as the others wore,
But in that deep-blue, melancholy dress,*
Bokhara's maidens wear in mindfulness
Of friends or kindred, dead or far away;—
And such as Zelica had on that day
He left her—when, with heart too full to speak,
He took away her last warm tears upon his cheek.

A strange emotion stirs within him,—more
Than mere compassion ever waked before;
Unconsciously he opes his arms, while she
Springs forward, as with life's last energy,
But, swooning in that one convulsive bound,
Sinks, ere she reach his arms, upon the ground;—
Her veil falls off—her faint hands clasp his knees—
'Tis she herself!—'tis Zelica he sees!
But, ah, so pale, so changed—none but a lover
Could in that wreck of beauty's shrine discover
The once-adored divinity—ev'n he
Stood for some moments mute, and doubtingly
Put back the ringlets from her brow, and gazed
Upon those lids, where once such lustre blazed,
Ere he could think she was *indeed* his own,
Own darling maid, whom he so long had known
In joy and sorrow, beautiful in both;
Who, ev'n when grief was heaviest—when loth
He left her for the wars—in that worst hour
Sat in her sorrow like the sweet night-flow'r,†
When darkness brings its weeping glories out,
And spreads its sighs like frankincense about.

"Look up, my Zelica—one moment show
"Those gentle eyes to me, that I may know
"Thy life, thy loveliness is not all gone,
"But *there*, at least, shines as it ever shone.
"Come, look upon thy Azim—one dear glance,
"Like those of old, were heav'n! whatever chance
"Hath brought thee here, oh, 'twas a blessed one!
"There—my loved lips—they move—that kiss hath run
"Like the first shoot of life through every vein,
"And now I clasp her, mine, all mine again.
"Oh the delight—now, in this very hour,
"When, had the whole rich world been in my pow'r,
"I should have singled out thee, only thee,
"From the whole world's collected treasury—
"To have thee here—to hang thus fondly o'er
"My own, best, purest Zelica once more!"

It was indeed the touch of those fond lips
Upon her eyes that chased their short eclipse,
And, gradual as the snow, at Heaven's breath,
Melts off and shows the azure flow'rs beneath,
Her lids unclosed, and the bright eyes were seen
Gazing on his—not, as they late had been,
Quick, restless, wild, but mournfully serene;
As if to lie, ev'n for that tranced minute,
So near his heart, had consolation in it;
And thus to wake in his beloved caress
Took from her soul one half its wretchedness.
But, when she heard him call her good and pure,
Oh, 'twas too much—too dreadful to endure.
Shudd'ring she broke away from his embrace,
And, hiding with both hands her guilty face,
Said, in a tone whose anguish would have riv'n
A heart of very marble, "Pure!—oh Heav'n!"

That tone—those looks so changed—the withering blight,
That sin and sorrow leave where'er they light;
The dead despondency of those sunk eyes,
Where once, had he thus met her by surprise,
He would have seen himself, too happy boy,
Reflected in a thousand lights of joy;
And then the place,—that bright, unholy place,
Where vice lay hid beneath each winning grace
And charm of lux'ry, as the viper weaves
Its wily cov'ring of sweet balsam leaves,—*
All struck upon his heart, sudden and cold
As death itself;—it needs not to be told—
No, no—he sees it all, plain as the brand
Of burning shame can mark—whate'er the hand
That could from Heav'n and him such brightness sever,
'Tis done—to Heav'n and him she's lost forever!
It was a dreadful moment; not the tears,
The ling'ring, lasting misery of years
Could match that minute's anguish—all the worst
Of sorrow's elements in that dark burst
Broke o'er his soul, and, with one crash of fate,
Laid the whole hopes of his life desolate.

"Oh! curse me not," she cried, as wild he toss'd
His desp'rate hand tow'rds Heav'n—"though I am lost
"Think not that guilt, that falsehood made me fall,
"No, no—'twas grief, 'twas madness did it all!
"Nay, doubt me not—though all thy love hath ceased—
"I know it hath—yet, yet believe, at least,
"That every spark of reason's light must be
"Quench'd in this brain, ere I could stray from thee
"They told me thou wert dead—why, Azim, why
"Did we not, both of us, that instant die
"When we were parted? oh! couldst thou but know
"With what a deep devotedness of wo
"I wept thy absence—o'er and o'er again
"Thinking of thee, still thee, till thought grew pain,
"And mem'ry, like a drop that, night and day,
"Falls cold and ceaseless, wore my heart away;
"Didst thou but know how pale I sat at home,
"My eyes still turn'd the way thou wert to come,
"And, all the long, long night of hope and fear,
"Thy voice and step still sounding in my ear—
"Oh God! thou wouldst not wonder that, at last,
"When every hope was all at once o'ercast,
"When I heard frightful voices round me say,
"*Azim is dead!*—this wretched brain gave way,
"And I became a wreck, at random driven,
"Without one glimpse of reason or of Heav'n—
"All wild—and even this quenchless love within
"Turn'd to foul fires to light me into sin!—
"Thou pitiest me—I knew thou wouldst—that sky
"Hath naught beneath it half so lorn as I.
"The fiend, who lured me hither—hist! come near,
"Or thou too, *thou* art lost, if he should hear—
"Told me such things—oh! with such dev'lish art,
"As would have ruin'd ev'n a holier heart—
"Of thee, and of that ever-radiant sphere,
"Where bless'd at length, if I but served *him* here,
"I should forever live in thy dear sight,
"And drink from those pure eyes eternal light.
"Think, think how lost, how madden'd I must be,
"To hope that guilt could lead to God or thee!

* 'Deep blue is their mourning colour."—*Hanway.*
† The sorrowful nyctanthes, which begins to spread its rich odour after sunset.

* "Concerning the vipers, which Pliny says were frequent among the balsam-trees, I made very particular inquiry; several were brought me alive both to Yambo and Jidda."—*Bruce.*

"Thou weep'st for me—do weep—oh, that I durst
"Kiss off that tear!—but, no—these lips are curst,
"They must not touch thee;—one divine caress,
"One blessed moment of forgetfulness
"I've had within those arms, and *that* shall lie
"Shrined in my soul's deep mem'ry till I die;
"The last of joy's last relics here below,
"The one sweet drop, in all this waste of wo,
"My heart has treasured from affection's spring,
"To sooth and cool its deadly withering!
"But thou—yes, thou must go—forever go;
"This place is not for thee—for thee! oh no:
"Did I but tell thee half, thy tortured brain
"Would burn like mine, and mine go wild again!
"Enough, that Guilt reigns here—that hearts, once good,
"Now tainted, chill'd, and broken, are his food.—
"Enough, that we are parted—that there rolls
"A flood of headlong fate between our souls,
"Whose darkness severs me as wide from thee
"As hell from heav'n, to all eternity!"

"ZELICA, ZELICA!" the youth exclaim'd,
In all the tortures of a mind inflamed
Almost to madness—"by that sacred Heav'n,
"Where yet, if pray'rs can move, thou'lt be forgiven,
"As thou art here—here, in this writhing heart,
"All sinful, wild, and ruin'd as thou art!
"By the remembrance of our once pure love,
"Which, like a church-yard light, still burns above
"The grave of our lost souls—which guilt in thee
"Cannot extinguish, nor despair in me!
"I do conjure, implore thee to fly hence—
"If thou hast yet one spark of innocence,
Fly with me from this place—"
"With thee! oh bliss!
"'Tis worth whole years of torment to hear this.
"What! take the lost one with thee?—let her rove
"By thy dear side, as in those days of love,
"When we were both so happy, both so pure?—
"Too heav'nly dream! if there's on earth a cure
"For the sunk heart, 'tis this—day after day
"To be the blest companion of thy way;
"To hear thy angel eloquence—to see
"Those virtuous eyes forever turn'd on me;
"And, in their light re-chasten'd silently,
"Like the stain'd web that whitens in the sun,
"Grow pure by being purely shone upon!
"And thou wilt pray for me—I know thou wilt—
"At the dim vesper hour, when thoughts of guilt
"Come heaviest o'er the heart, thou'lt lift thine eyes,
"Full of sweet tears, unto the dark'ning skies,
"And plead for me with Heav'n, till I can dare
"To fix my own weak, sinful glances there;
"Till the good angels, when they see me cling
"Forever near thee, pale and sorrowing,
"Shall for thy sake pronounce my soul forgiven,
"And bid thee take thy weeping slave to Heav'n!
"Oh yes, I'll fly with thee——"
Scarce had she said
These breathless words, when a voice deep and dread
As that of MONKER, waking up the dead
From their first sleep—so startling 'twas to both—
Rung through the casement near, "Thy oath! thy oath!"
Oh Heav'n! the ghastliness of that Maid's look!—
"'Tis he," faintly she cried, while terror shook
Her inmost core, nor durst she lift her eyes,
Though through the casement, now, naught but the skies
And moonlight fields were seen, calm as before—
"'Tis he, and I am his—all, all is o'er—
"Go—fly this instant, or thou'rt ruin'd too—
"My oath, my oath, oh God! 'tis all too true,
"True as the worm in this cold heart it is—
"I am MOKANNA's bride—his, AZIM, his—
"The Dead stood round us while I spoke that vow,
"Their blue lips echo'd it—I hear them now!
"Their eyes glared on me while I pledged that bowl,
"'Twas burning blood—I feel it in my soul!
"And the Veil'd Bridegroom—hist! I've seen to-night
"What angels know not of—so foul a sight,
"So horrible—oh! never mayst thou see
"What *there* lies hid from all but hell and me!
"But I must hence—off, off, I am not thine,
"Nor Heav'n's, nor Love's, nor aught that is divine—
"Hold me not—ha! think'st thou the fiends that sever
"Hearts, cannot sunder hands?—thus, then—forever!"

With all that strength which madness lends the weak
She flung away his arm; and with a shriek,
Whose sound, though he should linger out more years
Than wretch e'er told, can never leave his ears,
Flew up through that long avenue of light,
Fleetly as some dark, ominous bird of night,
Across the sun, and soon was out of sight!

LALLA ROOKH could think of nothing all day but the misery of these two young lovers. Her gayety was gone, and she looked pensively even upon FADLADEEN. She felt, too, without knowing why, a sort of uneasy pleasure in imagining that AZIM must have been just such a youth as FERAMORZ; just as worthy to enjoy all the blessings, without any of the pangs, of that illusive passion which too often, like the sunny apples of Istkahar,* is all sweetness on one side, and all bitterness on the other.

As they passed along a sequestered river after sunset, they saw a young Hindoo girl upon the bank,† whose employment seemed to them so strange, that they stopped their palankeens to observe her. She had lighted a small lamp filled with oil of cocoa, and placing it in an earthen dish, adorned with a wreath of flowers, had committed it with a trembling hand to the stream; and was now anxiously watching its progress down the current, heedless of the gay cavalcade which had drawn up beside her. LALLA ROOKH was all curiosity;—when one of her attendants, who had lived upon the banks of the Ganges, (where this ceremony is so frequent that often, in the dusk of the evening, the river is seen glittering all over with lights like the Oton-Tala, or Sea of Stars,‡) informed the Princess that it was the usual way in which the friends of those who had gone on dangerous voyages offered up vows for their safe return. If the lamp sunk immediately, the omen was disastrous; but if it went shining down the stream, and continued to burn till entirely out of sight, the return of the beloved object was considered as certain.

LALLA ROOKH, as they moved on, more than once looked back to observe how the young Hindoo's lamp proceeded; and while she saw with pleasure that it was still unextinguished, she could not help fearing that all the hopes of this life were no better than that feeble light upon the river. The remainder of the journey was passed in silence. She now, for the first time, felt that shade of melancholy which comes over the youthful maiden's heart, as sweet and transient as her own breath upon a mirror; nor was it till she heard the lute of FERAMORZ touched lightly at the door of her pavilion, that she waked from the revery in which she had been wandering. Instantly her eyes were lighted up with pleasure; and after a few unheard remarks from FADLADEEN upon the indecorum of a poet seating himself in the presence of a Princess, every thing was arranged as on the preceding evening, and all listened with eagerness while the story was thus continued:—

WHOSE are the gilded tents that crowd the way
Where all was waste and silent yesterday?
This City of War which, in a few short hours,
Hath sprung up here,§ as if the magic powers

---

* "In the territory of Istkahar there is a kind of apple, half of which is sweet and half sour."—*Ebn Haukal.*

† For an account of this ceremony, see *Grandpré's* Voyage in the Indian Ocean.

‡ "The place where the Whangho, a river of Thibet, rises, and where there are more than a hundred springs which sparkle like stars; whence it is called Hotun-nor, that is, the Sea of Stars."—*Description of Thibet in Pinkerton.*

§ "The Lescar or Imperial Camp is divided, like a regular town, into squares, alleys, and streets, and from a rising ground furnishes one of the most agreeable prospects in the world. Starting up in a few hours in an uninhabited plain, it raises the idea of a city built by enchantment. Even those who leave their houses in cities to follow the prince in his progress are frequently so charmed with the Lescar, when situated in a beautiful and convenient place, that they cannot prevail with themselves to re-

Of Him who, in the twinkling of a star,
Built the high pillar'd halls of CHILMINAR,*
Had conjured up, far as the eye can see,
This world of tents, and domes, and sun-bright armory:
Princely pavilions, screen'd by many a fold
Of crimson cloth, and topp'd with balls of gold:—
Steeds, with their housings of rich silver spun,
Their chains and poitrels glitt'ring in the sun;
And camels tufted o'er with Yemen's shells,†
Shaking in every breeze their light-toned bells!

But yester-eve, so motionless around,
So mute was this wide plain, that not a sound
But the far torrent, or the locust bird‡
Hunting among the thickets, could be heard;—
Yet hark! what discords now, of ev'ry kind,
Shouts, laughs, and screams, are revelling in the wind;
The neigh of cavalry;—the tinkling throngs
Of laden camels and their drivers' songs;—§
Ringing of arms, and flapping in the breeze
Of streamers from ten thousand canopies;—
War-music, bursting out from time to time,
With gong and tymbalon's tremendous chime;
Or, in the pause, when harsher sounds are mute,
The mellow breathings of some horn or flute,
That far off, broken by the eagle note
Of th' Abyssinian trumpet,‖ swell and float.

Who leads this mighty army?—ask ye "who?"
And mark ye not those banners of dark hue,
The Night and Shadow,¶ over yonder tent?—
It is the CALIPH's glorious armament.
Roused in his Palace by the dread alarms,
That hourly came, of the false Prophet's arms,
And of his host of infidels, who hurl'd
Defiance fierce at Islam** and the world,—
Though worn with Grecian warfare, and behind
The veils of his bright Palace calm reclined,
Yet brook'd he not such blasphemy should stain,
Thus unrevenged, the evening of his reign;
But, having sworn upon the Holy Grave††
To conquer or to perish, once more gave
His shadowy banners proudly to the breeze,
And, with an army nursed in victories,
Here stands to crush the rebels that o'er-run
His blest and beauteous Province of the Sun.

Ne'er did the march of MAHADI display
Such pomp before;—not ev'n when on his way
To MECCA's Temple, when both land and sea
Were spoil'd to feed the Pilgrim's luxury;‡‡
When round him, 'mid the burning sands, he saw
Fruits of the North in icy freshness thaw,
And cool'd his thirsty lip, beneath the glow
Of MECCA's sun, with urns of Persian snow:—*
Nor e'er did armament more grand than that
Pour from the kingdoms of the Caliphat.
First, in the van, the People of the Rock,†
On their light mountain steeds, of royal stock:‡
Then, chieftains of DAMASCUS, proud to see
The flashing of their swords' rich marquetry;—§
Men, from the regions near the VOLGA's mouth,
Mix'd with the rude, black archers of the South;
And Indian lancers, in white-turban'd ranks,
From the far SINDE, or ATTOCK's sacred banks,
With dusky legions from the Land of Myrrh,‖
And many a mace-arm'd Moor and Mid-sea islander

Nor less in number, though more new and rude
In warfare's school, was the vast multitude
That, fired by zeal, or by oppression wrong'd,
Round the white standard of th' impostor throng'd.
Beside his thousands of Believers—blind,
Burning and headlong as the Samiel wind—
Many who felt, and more who fear'd to feel
The bloody Islamite's converting steel,
Flock'd to his banner;—Chiefs of th' UZBEK race,
Waving their heron crests with martial grace;¶
TURKOMANS, countless as their flocks, led forth
From th' aromatic pastures of the North;
Wild warriors of the turquoise hills,**—and those
Who dwell beyond the everlasting snows
Of HINDOO KOSH,†† in stormy freedom bred,
Their fort the rock, their camp the torrent's bed.
But none, of all who own'd the Chief's command,
Rush'd to that battle-field with bolder hand,
Or sterner hate, than IRAN's outlaw'd men,
Her Worshippers of Fire‡‡—all panting then
For vengeance on th' accursed Saracen;
Vengeance at last for their dear country spurn'd,
Her throne usurp'd, and her bright shrines o'erturn'd
From YEZD's§§ eternal mansion of the Fire,
Where aged saints in dreams of Heav'n expire:
From BADKU, and those fountains of blue flame
That burn into the CASPIAN,‖‖ fierce they came,
Careless for what or whom the blow was sped,
So vengeance triumph'd, and their tyrants bled

Such was the wild and miscellaneous host,
That high in air their motley banners toss'd
Around the Prophet-Chief—all eyes still bent
Upon that glittering Veil, where'er it went,
That beacon through the battle's stormy flood,
That rainbow of the field, whose showers were blood!

Twice hath the sun upon their conflict set,
And risen again, and found them grappling yet;
While streams of carnage in his noontide blaze
Smoke up to Heav'n—hot as that crimson haze,

---

move. To prevent this inconvenience to the court, the Emperor, after sufficient time is allowed to the tradesmen to follow, orders them to be burnt out of their tents."—*Dow's* Hindostan.

Colonel Wilks gives a lively picture of an Eastern encampment:—"His camp, like that of most Indian armies, exhibited a motley collection of covers from the scorching sun and dews of the night, variegated according to the taste or means of each individual, by extensive enclosures of coloured calico surrounding superb suites of tents; by ragged clothes or blankets stretched over sticks or branches; palm-leaves hastily spread over similar supports; handsome tents and splendid canopies; horses, oxen, elephants, and camels; all intermixed without any exterior mark of order or design, except the flags of the chiefs, which usually mark the centres of a congeries of these masses; the only regular part of the encampment being the streets of shops, each of which is constructed nearly in the manner of a booth at an English fair."—*Historical Sketches of the South of India.*

* The edifices of Chilminar and Balbec are supposed to have been built by the Genii, acting under the orders of Jan ben Jan, who governed the world long before the time of Adam.

† "A superb camel, ornamented with strings and tufts of small shells."—*Ali Bey.*

‡ A native of Khorassan, and allured southward by means of the water of a fountain between Shiraz and Ispahan, called the Fountain of Birds, of which it is so fond that it will follow wherever that water is carried.

§ "Some of the camels have bells about their necks, and some about their legs, like those which our carriers put about their fore-horses' necks, which together with the servants (who belong to the camels, and travel on foot) singing all night, make a pleasant noise, and the journey passes away delightfully."—*Pitt's* Account of the Mahometans.

"The camel-driver follows the camels singing, and sometimes playing upon his pipe; the louder he sings and pipes, the faster the camels go. Nay, they will stand still when he gives over his music."—*Tavernier.*

‖ "This trumpet is often called, in Abyssinia, *nesser cano*, which signifies the Note of the Eagle."—*Note of Bruce's Editor.*

¶ The two black standards borne before the Caliphs of the House of Abbas were called, allegorically, The Night and The Shadow.—See *Gibbon.*

** The Mahometan religion.

†† "The Persians swear by the Tomb of Shah Besade, who is buried at Casbin; and when one desires another to asseverate a matter, he will ask him, if he dare swear by the Holy Grave."—*Struy.*

‡‡ Mahadi, in a single pilgrimage to Mecca, expended six millions of dinars of gold.

* Nivem Meccam apportavit, rem ibi aut nunquam aut raro visam.—*Abulfeda.*

† The inhabitants of Hejaz or Arabia Petræa, called by an Eastern writer, "The People of the Rock."—*Ebn Haukal.*

‡ "Those horses, called by the Arabians Kochlani, of whom a written genealogy has been kept for 2000 years. They are said to derive their origin from King Solomon's steeds."—*Niebuhr.*

§ "Many of the figures on the blades of their swords are wrought in gold or silver, or in marquetry with small gems."—*Asiat. Misc.* v. i.

‖ Azab or Saba.

¶ "The chiefs of the Uzbek Tartars wear a plume of white heron's feathers in their turbans."—*Account of Independent Tartary.*

** In the mountains of Nishapour and Tous (in Khorassan) they find turquoises.—*Ebn Haukal.*

†† For a description of these stupendous ranges of mountains, see *Elphinstone's Caubul.*

‡‡ The Ghebers or Guebres, those original natives of Persia who adhered to their ancient faith, the religion of Zoroaster, and who, after the conquest of their country by the Arabs, were either persecuted at home, or forced to become wanderers abroad.

§§ "Yezd, the chief residence of those ancient natives, who worship the Sun and the Fire, which latter they have carefully kept lighted, without being once extinguished for a moment, about 3000 years, on a mountain near Yezd, called Ater Quedah, signifying the House or Mansion of the Fire. He is reckoned very unfortunate who dies off that mountain."—*Stephen's Persia.*

‖‖ "When the weather is hazy, the springs of Naphtha (on an island near Baku) boil up the higher, and the Naphtha often takes fire on the surface of the earth, and runs in a flame into the sea to a distance almost incredible."—*Hanway on the Everlasting Fire at Baku.*

By which the prostrate Caravan is awed,*
In the red Desert, when the wind's abroad.
"On, Swords of God!" the panting CALIPH calls,—
"Thrones for the living—Heav'n for him who falls!"—
"On, brave avengers, on," MOKANNA cries,
"And EBLIS blast the recreant slave that flies!"
Now comes the brunt, the crisis of the day—
They clash—they strive—the CALIPH's troops give way.
MOKANNA's self plucks the black Banner down,
And now the Orient World's Imperial crown
Is just within his grasp—when, hark, that shout!
Some hand hath check'd the flying Moslem's rout;
And now they turn, they rally—at their head
A warrior, (like those angel youths who led,
In glorious panoply of Heav'n's own mail,
The Champions of the Faith through BEDER's vale,)†
Bold as if gifted with ten thousand lives,
Turns on the fierce pursuers' blades, and drives
At once the multitudinous torrent back—
While hope and courage kindle in his track;
And, at each step, his bloody falchion makes
Terrible vistas through which vict'ry breaks!
In vain MOKANNA, 'midst the general flight,
Stands, like the red moon, on some stormy night,
Among the fugitive clouds that, hurrying by,
Leave only her unshaken in the sky—
In vain he yells his desp'rate curses out,
Deals death promiscuously to all about,
To foes that charge and coward friends that fly,
And seems of *all* the Great Arch-enemy.
The panic spreads—"A miracle!" throughout
The Moslem ranks, "a miracle!" they shout,
All gazing on that youth, whose coming seems
A light, a glory, such as breaks in dreams;
And ev'ry sword, true as o'er billows dim
The needle tracks the load-star, following him!

Right tow'rds MOKANNA now he cleaves his path,
Impatient cleaves, as though the bolt of wrath
He bears from Heav'n withheld its awful burst
From weaker heads, and souls but half-way curst,
To break o'er Him, the mightiest and the worst!
But vain his speed—though, in that hour of blood,
Had all God's seraphs round MOKANNA stood,
With swords of fire, ready like fate to fall,
MOKANNA's soul would have defied them all;
Yet now, the rush of fugitives, too strong
For human force, hurries ev'n *him* along:
In vain he struggled 'mid the wedged array
Of flying thousands—he is borne away;
And the sole joy his baffled spirit knows,
In this forced flight, is—murd'ring as he goes!
As a grim tiger, whom the torrent's might
Surprises in some parch'd ravine at night,
Turns, ev'n in drowning, on the wretched flocks,
Swept with him in that snow-flood from the rocks,
And, to the last, devouring on his way,
Bloodies the stream he hath not power to stay.

"Alla illa Alla!"—the glad shout renew—
"Alla Akbar!"‡—the Caliph's in MEROU.
Hang out your gilded tapestry in the streets,
And light your shrines and chant your ziraleets.§
The Swords of God have triumph'd—on his throne
Your Caliph sits, and the veil'd Chief hath flown.
Who does not envy that young warrior now,
To whom the Lord of Islam bends his brow,
In all the graceful gratitude of power,
For his throne's safety in that perilous hour?
Who doth not wonder, when, amidst th' acclaim
Of thousands heralding to heaven his name—
'Mid all those holier harmonies of fame,
Which sound along the path of virtuous souls,
Like music round a planet as it rolls,—
He turns away—coldly, as if some gloom
Hung o'er his heart no triumphs can illume;—
Some sightless grief, upon whose blasted gaze
Though glory's light may play, in vain it plays.
Yes, wretched AZIM! thine is such a grief,
Beyond all hope, all terror, all relief;
A dark, cold calm, which nothing now can break,
Or warm or brighten,—like that Syrian Lake,*
Upon whose surface morn and summer shed
Their smiles in vain, for all beneath is dead!—
Hearts there have been o'er which this weight of wo
Came by long use of suff'ring, tame and slow;
But thine, lost youth! was sudden—over thee
It broke at once, when all seem'd ecstasy;
When Hope look'd up, and saw the gloomy Past
Melt into splendour, and Bliss dawn at last—
'Twas then, ev'n then, o'er joys so freshly blown,
This mortal blight of misery came down;
Ev'n then, the full warm gushings of thy heart
Were check'd—like fount drops, frozen as they start-
And there, like them, cold, sunless relics hang,
Each fix'd and chill'd into a lasting pang.

One sole desire, one passion now remains
To keep life's fever still within his veins,
Vengeance! dire vengeance on the wretch who cast
O'er him and all he loved the ruinous blast.
For this, when rumours reach'd him in his flight
Far, far away, after that fatal night,—
Rumours of armies, thronging to th' attack
Of the Veil'd Chief,—for this he wing'd him back,
Fleet as the vulture speeds to flags unfurl'd,
And, when all hope seem'd desp'rate, wildly hurl'd
Himself into the scale, and saved a world.
For this he still lives on, careless of all
The wreaths that Glory on his path lets fall;
For this alone exists—like lightning fire,
To speed one bolt of vengeance, and expire!

But safe as yet that Spirit of Evil lives;
With a small band of desp'rate fugitives,
The last sole stubborn fragment, left unriv'n,
Of the proud host that late stood fronting Heav'n,
He gain'd MEROU—breathed a short curse of blood
O'er his lost throne—then pass'd the JIHON's flood,†
And gath'ring all whose madness of belief
Still saw a Saviour in their down-fall'n Chief,
Raised the white banner within NEKSHEB's gates,‡
And there, untamed, th' approaching conq'ror waits.

Of all his Harem, all that busy hive
With music and with sweets sparkling alive,
He took but one, the partner of his flight,
One—not for love—not for her beauty's light—
No, ZELICA stood with'ring 'midst the gay,
Wan as the blossom that fell yesterday
From th' Alma tree and dies, while overhead
To-day's young flow'r is springing in its stead.§
Oh, not for love—the deepest Damn'd must be
Touch'd with Heaven's glory, ere such fiends as he
Can feel one glimpse of Love's divinity.
But no, she is his victim;—*there* lie all
Her charms for him—charms that can never pall,
As long as hell within his heart can stir,
Or one faint trace of Heaven is left in her.
To work an angel's ruin,—to behold
As white a page as Virtue e'er unroll'd
Blacken, beneath his touch, into a scroll
Of damning sins, seal'd with a burning soul—
This is his triumph; this the joy accurst,
That ranks him among demons all but first:

* *Savary* says of the south wind, which blows in Egypt from February to May, "Sometimes it appears only in the shape of an impetuous whirlwind, which passes rapidly, and is fatal to the traveller, surprised in the middle of the deserts. Torrents of burning sand roll before it, the firmament is enveloped in a thick veil, and the sun appears of the colour of blood. Sometimes whole caravans are buried in it."

† In the great victory gained by Mahomed at Beder, he was assisted, say the Mussulmans, by three thousand angels, led by Gabriel, mounted on his horse Hiazum.—See *The Koran and its Commentators.*

‡ The Tecbir, or cry of the Arabs. "Alla Akbar!" says Ockley, means, "God is most mighty."

§ The ziraleet is a kind of chorus, which the women of the East sing upon joyful occasions.—*Russel.*

* The Dead Sea, which contains neither animal nor vegetable life.

† The ancient Oxus.

‡ A city of Transoxiana.

§ "You never can cast your eyes on this tree, but you meet there either blossoms or fruit; and as the blossom drops, underneath on the ground (which is frequently covered with these purple-coloured flowers) others come forth in their stead" &c. &c.—*Nieuhoff.*

This gives the victim, that before him lies
Blighted and lost, a glory in his eyes,
A light like that with which hell-fire illumes
The ghastly, writhing wretch whom it consumes!

But other tasks now wait him—tasks that need
All the deep daringness of thought and deed
With which the Dives* have gifted him—for mark,
Over yon plains, which night had else made dark,
Those lanterns, countless as the winged lights
That spangle INDIA's fields on show'ry nights,—†
Far as their formidable gleams they shed,
The mighty tents of the beleaguerer spread,
Glimm'ring along th' horizon's dusky line,
And thence in nearer circles, till they shine
Among the founts and groves, o'er which the town
In all its arm'd magnificence looks down.
Yet, fearless, from his lofty battlements
MOKANNA views that multitude of tents;
Nay, smiles to think that, though entoil'd, beset,
Not less than myriads dare to front him yet;—
That friendless, throneless, he thus stands at bay,
Ev'n thus a match for myriads such as they.
"Oh for a sweep of that dark Angel's wing,
"Who brush'd the thousands of th' Assyrian King‡
"To darkness in a moment, that I might
"People Hell's chambers with yon host to-night!
"But, come what may, let who will grasp the throne,
"Caliph or Prophet, Man alike shall groan;
"Let who will torture him, Priest—Caliph—King—
"Alike this loathsome world of his shall ring
"With victims' shrieks and howlings of the slave,—
"Sounds that shall glad me ev'n within my grave!"
Thus, to himself—but to the scanty train
Still left around him, a far different strain:—
"Glorious Defenders of the sacred Crown
"I bear from Heav'n, whose light nor blood shall [illegible]
"Nor shadow of earth eclipse;—before whose ge[illegible]
"The paly pomp of this world's diadems,
"The crown of GERASHID, the pillar'd throne
"Of PARVIZ,§ and the heron crest that shone,‖
"Magnificent o'er ALI's beauteous eyes,¶
"Fade like the stars when morn is in the skies:
"Warriors, rejoice—the port to which we've pass'd
"O'er Destiny's dark wave, beams out at last!
"Vict'ry's our own—'tis written in that Book
"Upon whose leaves none but the angels look,
"That ISLAM's sceptre shall beneath the power
"Of her great foe fall broken in that hour,
"When the moon's mighty orb, before all eyes,
"From NEKSHEB's Holy Well portentously shall rise!
"Now turn and see!"——

They turn'd, and, as he spoke,
A sudden splendour all around them broke,
And they beheld an orb, ample and bright,
Rise from the Holy Well,** and cast its light
Round the rich city and the plain for miles,—††
Flinging such radiance o'er the gilded tiles
Of many a dome, and fair-roof'd imaret,
As autumn suns shed round them when they set.

Instant from all who saw th' illusive sign
A murmur broke—"Miraculous! divine!"
The Gheber bow'd, thinking his idol star
Had waked, and burst impatient through the bar
Of midnight, to inflame him to the war;
While he of MOUSSA's creed saw, in that ray,
The glorious Light which, in his freedom's day,
Had rested on the Ark,* and now again
Shone out to bless the breaking of his chain.

"To victory!" is at once the cry of all—
Nor stands MOKANNA loit'ring at that call;
But instant the huge gates are flung aside,
And forth, like a diminutive mountain-tide
Into the boundless sea, they speed their course
Right on into the Moslem's mighty force.
The watchmen of the camp,—who, in their rounds
Had paused, and even forgot the punctual sounds
Of the small drum with which they count the nigh[t]†
To gaze upon that supernatural light,—
Now sink beneath an unexpected arm,
And in a death-groan give their last alarm
"On for the lamps, that light yon lofty screen,‡
"Nor blunt your blades with massacre so mean;
"*There* rests the Caliph—speed—one lucky lance
"May now achieve mankind's deliverance."
Desp'rate the die—such as they only cast,
Who venture for a world, and stake their last.
But Fate's no longer with him—blade for blade
Springs up to meet them through the glimm'ring [illegible]
And, as the clash is heard, new legions soon
Pour to the spot, like bees of KAUZEROON§
To the shrill timbrel's summons,—till, at length,
The mighty camp swarms out in all its strength.
And back to NEKSHEB's gates, covering the plain
With random slaughter, drives the adventurous train;
Among the last of whom the Silver Veil
Is seen glitt'ring at times, like the white sail
Of some toss'd vessel, on a stormy night,
Catching the tempest's momentary light!

And hath not *this* brought the proud spirit low?
Nor dash'd his brow, nor check'd his daring? No
Though half the wretches, whom at night he led
To thrones and vict'ry, lie disgraced and dead,
Yet morning hears him, with unshrinking crest,
Still vaunt of thrones, and vict'ry to the rest;—
And they believe him!—oh, the lover may
Distrust that look which steals his soul away;—
The babe may cease to think that it can play
With Heaven's rainbow;—alchymists may doubt
The shining gold their crucible gives out;
But Faith, fanatic Faith, once wedded fast
To some dear falsehood, hugs it to the last.

And well th' Impostor knew all lures and arts
That LUCIFER e'er taught to tangle hearts;
Nor, 'mid these last bold workings of his plot
Against men's souls, is ZELICA forgot.
Ill-fated ZELICA! had reason been
Awake, through half the horrors thou hast seen,
Thou never couldst have borne it—Death had come
At once, and taken thy wrung spirit home.
But 'twas not so—a torpor, a suspense
Of thought, almost of life, came o'er the intense
And passionate struggles of that fearful night,
When her last hope of peace and heav'n took flight:
And though, at times, a gleam of phrensy broke,—
As through some dull volcano's vale of smoke
Ominous flashings now and then will start,

---

* The Demons of the Persian mythology.

† Carreri mentions the fire-flies in India during the rainy season.—See his Travels.

‡ Sennacherib, called by the Orientals King of Moussal.—*D'Herbelot.*

§ Chosroes. For the description of his Throne or Palace, see *Gibbon* and *D'Herbelot.*

There were said to be under this Throne or Palace of Khosrou Parviz a hundred vaults filled with "treasures so immense, that some Mahometan writers tell us, their Prophet, to encourage his disciples, carried them to a rock, which at his command opened, and gave them a prospect through it of the treasures of Khosrou."—*Universal History.*

‖ "The crown of Gerashid is cloudy and tarnished before the heron tuft of thy turban."—From one of the elegies or songs in praise of Ali, written in characters of gold round the gallery of Abbas's tomb.—See *Chardin.*

¶ The beauty of Ali's eyes was so remarkable, that whenever the Persians would describe any thing as very lovely, they say it is Ayn Hali, or the Eyes of Ali.—*Chardin.*

** We are not told more of this trick of the Impostor, than that it was "une machine, qu'il disoit être la Lune." According to Richardson, the miracle is perpetuated in Nekscheb.—"Nakshab, the name of a city in Transoxiana, where they say there is a well, in which the appearance of the moon is to be seen night and day."

†† "Il amusa pendant deux mois le peuple de la ville de Nekhscheb, en faisant sortir toutes les nuits du fond d'un puits un corps lumineux semblable à la Lune, qui portoit sa lumière jusqu'à la distance de plusieurs milles."—*D'Herbelot.* Hence he was called Sazendéhmah, or the Moon-maker.

* The Shechinah, called Sakînat in the Koran.—See *Sale's Note*, chap. ii.

† The parts of the night are made known as well by instruments of music, as by the rounds of the watchmen with cries and small drums.—See *Burder's Oriental Customs*, vol. i. p. 119.

‡ The Serrapurda, high screens of red cloth, stiffened with cane, used to enclose a considerable space round the royal tents.—*Notes on the Bahardanush.*

The tents of princes are generally illuminated. Norden tells us that the tent of the Bey of Girge was distinguished from the other tents by forty lanterns being suspended before it.—See *Harmer's* Observations on Job.

§ "From the groves of orange-trees at Kauzeroon the bees cull a celebrated honey."—*Morier's Travels.*

Which sh w the fire's still busy at its heart;
Yet was she mostly wrapp'd in solemn gloom,—
Not such as AZIM'S, brooding o'er its doom,
And calm without, as is the brow of death,
While busy worms are gnawing underneath—
But in a blank and pulseless torpor, free
From thought or pain, a seal'd-up apathy,
Which left her oft, with scarce one living thrill
The cold, pale victim of her tort'rer's will.

Again, as in MEROU, he had her deck'd
Gorgeously out, the Priestess of the sect;
And led her glitt'ring forth before the eyes
Of his rude train, as to a sacrifice,—
Pallid as she, the young, devoted Bride
Of the fierce NILE, when deck'd in all the pride
Of nuptial pomp, she sinks into his tide.*
And while the wretched maid hung down her head,
And stood, as one just risen from the dead,
Amid that gazing crowd, the fiend would tell
His credulous slaves it was some charm or spell
Possess'd her now,—and from that darken'd trance
Should dawn ere long their Faith's deliverance.
Or if, at times, goaded by guilty shame,
Her soul was roused, and words of wildness came,
Instant the bold blasphemer would translate
Her ravings into oracles of fate,
Would hail Heav'n's signals in her flashing eyes,
And call her shrieks the language of the skies!

But vain at length his arts—despair is seen
Gath'ring around; and famine comes to glean
All that the sword had left unreap'd:—in vain
At morn and eve across the northern plain
He looks impatient for the promised spears
Of the wild hordes and TARTAR mountaineers;
They come not—while his fierce beleaguerers pour
Engines of havoc in, unknown before,†
And horrible as new;‡—javelins, that fly
Enwreath'd with smoky flames through the dark sky,
And red-hot globes, that, opening as they mount,
Discharge, as from a kindled Naphtha fount,§
Showers of consuming fire o'er all below;
Looking, as through th' illumined night they go,
Like those wild birds‖ that by the Magians oft,
At festivals of fire, were sent aloft
Into the air, with blazing fagots tied
To their huge wings, scatt'ring combustion wide
All night the groans of wretches who expire,
In agony, beneath these darts of fire,
Ring through the city—while, descending o'er
Its shrines and domes and streets of sycamore,—
Its lone bazars, with their bright cloths of gold,
Since the last peaceful pageant left unroll'd,—
Its beauteous marble baths, whose idle jets
Now gush with blood,—and its tall minarets,
That late have stood up in the evening glare
Of the red sun, unhallow'd by a prayer;
O'er each, in turn, the dreadful flame-bolts fall,
And death and conflagration throughout all
The desolate city hold high festival!

MOKANNA sees the world is his no more;—
One sting at parting, and his grasp is o'er.
"What!—drooping now?"—thus, with unblushing cheek
He hails the few, who yet can hear him speak,
Of all those famish'd slaves around him lying,
And by the light of blazing temples dying;—
"What!—drooping now?—now, when at length we press
"Home o'er the very threshold of success;
"When ALLA from our ranks hath thinn'd away
"Those grosser branches, that kept out his ray
"Of favour from us, and we stand at length
"Heirs of his light and children of his strength,
"The chosen few, who shall survive the fall
"Of Kings and Thrones, triumphant over all!
"Have you then lost, weak murm'rers as you are,
"All faith in him, who was your Light, your Star?
"Have you forgot the eye of glory, hid
"Beneath this Veil, the flashing of whose lid
"Could, like a sun-stroke of the desert, wither
"Millions of such as yonder Chief brings hither?
"Long have its lightnings slept—too long—but now
"All earth shall feel th' unveiling of this brow!
"To-night—yes, sainted men! this very night
"I bid you all to a fair festal rite,
"Where—having deep refresh'd each weary limb
"With viands, such as feast Heaven's cherubim,
"And kindled up your souls, now sunk and dim,
"With that pure wine the Dark-eyed Maids above
"Keep, seal'd with precious musk, for those they love,*—
"I will myself uncurtain in your sight
"The wonders of this brow's ineffable light;
"Then lead you forth, and with a wink disperse
"Yon myriads, howling through the universe!"

Eager they listen—while each accent darts
New life into their chill'd and hope-sick hearts;
Such treach'rous life as the cool draught supplies
To him upon the stake, who drinks and dies!
Wildly they point their lances to the light
Of the fast sinking sun, and shout "To-night!"—
"To-night," their Chief re-echoes in a voice
Of fiend-like mockery that bids hell rejoice.
Deluded victims!—never hath this earth
Seen mourning half so mournful as their mirth.
Here, to the few, whose iron frames had stood
This racking waste of famine and of blood,
Faint, dying wretches clung, from whom the shout
Of triumph like a maniac's laugh broke out:
There, others, lighted by the smould'ring fire,
Danced, like wan ghosts about a funeral pyre,
Among the dead and dying, strew'd around;—
While some pale wretch look'd on, and from his wound
Plucking the fiery dart by which he bled,
In ghastly transport waved it o'er his head!

'Twas more than midnight now—a fearful pause
Had follow'd the long shouts, the wild applause,
That lately from those Royal Gardens burst,
Where the Veil'd demon held his feast accurst,

* "A custom still subsisting at this day, seems to me to prove that the Egyptians formerly sacrificed a young virgin to the God of the Nile; for they now make a statue of earth in shape of a girl, to which they give the name of the Betrothed Bride, and throw it into the river."—*Savary.*

† That they knew the secret of the Greek fire among the Mussulmans early in the eleventh century, appears from *Dow's* Account of Mamood I. "When he arrived at Moultan, finding that the country of the Jits was defended by great rivers, he ordered fifteen hundred boats to be built, each of which he armed with six iron spikes, projecting from their prows and sides, to prevent their being boarded by the enemy, who were very expert in that kind of war. When he had launched this fleet, he ordered twenty archers into each boat, and five others with fire balls, to burn the craft of the Jits, and naphtha to set the whole river on fire."

The *agnee aster*, too, in Indian poems the Instrument of Fire, whose flame cannot be extinguished, is supposed to signify the Greek Fire.—See *Wilks's* South of India, vol. i. p. 471.—And in the curious Javan poem, the *Brata Yudha*, given by *Sir Stamford Raffles* in his History of Java, we find, "He aimed at the heart of Soéta with the sharp-pointed Weapon of Fire."

The mention of gunpowder as in use among the Arabians, long before its supposed discovery in Europe, is introduced by *Ebn Fadhl*, the Egyptian geographer, who lived in the thirteenth century. "Bodies," he says, "in the form of scorpions, bound round and filled with nitrous powder, glide along, making a gentle noise; then exploding, they lighten, as it were, and burn. But there are others which, cast into the air, stretch along like a cloud, roaring horribly, as thunder roars, and on all sides vomiting out flames, burst, burn, and reduce to cinders whatever comes in their way." The historian *Ben Abdalla*, in speaking of the sieges of Abulualid in the year of the Hegira 712, says, "A fiery globe, by means of combustible matter, with a mighty noise suddenly emitted, strikes with the force of lightning, and shakes the citadel."—See the extracts from *Casiri's* Biblioth. Arab. Hispan. in the Appendix to *Berington's* Literary History of the Middle Ages.

‡ The Greek fire, which was occasionally lent by the emperors to their allies. "It was," *says* Gibbon, "either launched in red-hot balls of stone and iron, or darted in arrows and javelins, twisted round with flax and tow, which had deeply imbibed the inflammable oil."

§ See *Hanway's* Account of the Springs of Naphtha at Baku (which is called by *Lieutenant Pottinger* Joala Mookee, or, the Flaming Mouth) taking fire and running into the sea. *Dr. Cooke*, in his Journal, mentions some wells in Circassia, strongly impregnated with this inflammable oil, from which issues boiling water. "Though the weather," he adds, "was now very cold, the warmth of these wells of hot water produced near them the verdure and flowers of spring."

Major Scott Waring says that naphtha is used by the Persians, as we are told it was in hell, for lamps.

. . . . many a row
Of starry lamps and blazing cressets, fed
With naphtha and asphaltus, yielding light
As from a sky.

‖ "At the great festival of fire, called the Sheb Sezè, they used to set fire to large bunches of dry combustibles, fastened round wild beasts and birds, which being then let loose, the air and earth appeared one great illumination; and as these terrified creatures naturally fled to the woods for shelter, it is easy to conceive the conflagrations they produced."—*Richardson's* Dissertation.

* "The righteous shall be given to drink of pure wine, sealed: the seal whereof shall be musk."—*Koran*, chap. lxxxiii.

When Zelica—alas, poor ruin'd heart,
In ev'ry horror doom'd to bear its part!—
Was bidden to the banquet by a slave,
Who, while his quiv'ring lip the summons gave,
Grew black, as though the shadows of the grave
Compass'd him round, and, ere he could repeat
His message through, fell lifeless at her feet!
Shuddering she went—a soul-felt pang of fear,
A presage that her own dark doom was near,
Roused ev'ry feeling, and brought Reason back
Once more to writhe her last upon the rack.
All round seem'd tranquil—ev'n the foe had ceased,
As if aware of that demoniac feast,
His fiery bolts; and though the heav'ns look'd red,
'Twas but some distant conflagration's spread.
But hark—she stops—she listens—dreadful tone!
'Tis her Tormentor's laugh—and now, a groan,
A long death-groan comes with it:—can this be
The place of mirth, the bower of revelry?
She enters—Holy ALLA, what a sight
Was there before her! By the glimm'ring light
Of the pale dawn, mix'd with the flare of brands
That round lay burning, dropp'd from lifeless hands,
She saw the board in splendid mockery spread,
Rich censers breathing—garlands overhead—
The urns, the cups, from which they late had quaff'd,
All gold and gems, but—what had been the draught?
Oh! who need ask, that saw those livid guests,
With their swoll'n heads sunk black'ning on their breasts,
Or looking pale to Heav'n with glassy glare,
As if they sought but saw no mercy there;
As if they felt, though poison rack'd them through,
Remorse the deadlier torment of the two!
While some, the bravest, hardiest in the train
Of their false Chief, who on the battle-plain
Would have met death with transport by his side,
Here mute and helpless gasp'd;—but, as they died,
Look'd horrible vengeance with their eyes' last strain,
And clinch'd the slack'ning hand at him in vain.

Dreadful it was to see the ghastly stare,
The stony look of horror and despair,
Which some of these expiring victims cast
Upon their souls' tormentor to the last;—
Upon that mocking Fiend, whose veil, now raised,
Show'd them, as in death's agony they gazed,
Not the long promised light, the brow, whose beaming
Was to come forth, all conquering, all redeeming,
But features horribler than Hell e'er traced
On its own brood;—no Demon of the Waste,*
No church-yard Ghole, caught lingering in the light
Of the blest sun, e'er blasted human sight
With lineaments so foul, so fierce as those
Th' Impostor now, in grinning mock'ry, shows:—
"There, ye wise Saints, behold your Light, your Star—
"Ye *would* be dupes and victims, and ye *are*.
"Is it enough? or must I, while a thrill
"Lives in your sapient bosoms, cheat you still?
"Swear that the burning death ye feel within
"Is but the trance with which Heaven's joys begin;
"That this foul visage, foul as e'er disgraced
"Ev'n monstrous man, is—after God's own taste;
"And that—but see!—ere I have half-way said
"My greetings through, th' uncourteous souls are fled.
"Farewell, sweet spirits! not in vain ye die,
"If EBLIS loves you half so well as I.—
"Ha, my young bride!—'tis well—take thou thy seat;
"Nay come—no shuddering—didst thou never meet
"The Dead before?—they graced our wedding, sweet;
"And these, my guests to-night, have brimm'd so true
"Their parting cups, that *thou* shalt pledge one too.
"But—how is this?—all empty?—all drunk up?
"Hot lips have been before thee in the cup,
"Young bride—yet stay—one precious drop remains,
"Enough to warm a gentle Priestess' veins;—
"Here, drink—and should thy lover's conquering arms
"Speed hither, ere thy lip lose all its charms,
"Give him but half this venom in thy kiss,
"And I'll forgive my haughty rival's bliss!

"For *me*—I too must die—but not like these
"Vile, rankling things, to fester in the breeze;
"To have this brow in ruffian triumph shown,
"With all death's grimness added to its own,
"And rot to dust beneath the taunting eyes
"Of slaves, exclaiming, 'There his Godship lies!'
"No—cursed race—since first my soul drew breath,
"They've been my dupes, and *shall* be even in death.
"Thou seest yon cistern in the shade—'tis fill'd
"With burning drugs, for this last hour distill'd:—*
"There will I plunge me in that liquid flame—
"Fit bath to lave a dying Prophet's frame!—
"There perish, all—ere pulse of thine shall fail—
"Nor leave one limb to tell mankind the tale.
"So shall my votaries, wheresoe'er they rave,
"Proclaim that Heav'n took back the Saint it gave;—
"That I've but vanish'd from this earth awhile,
"To come again, with bright, unshrouded smile!
"So shall they build me altars in their zeal,
"Where knaves shall minister, and fools shall kneel;
"Where Faith may mutter o'er her mystic spell,
"Written in blood—and Bigotry may swell
"The sail he spreads for Heav'n with blasts from hell!
"So shall my banner, through long ages, be
"The rallying sign of fraud and anarchy;—
"Kings yet unborn shall rue MOKANNA's name,
"And, though I die, my spirit, still the same,
"Shall walk abroad in all the stormy strife,
"And guilt, and blood, that were its bliss in life.
"But, hark! their batt'ring engine shakes the wall—
"Why, *let* it shake—thus I can brave them all.
"No trace of me shall greet them, when they come,
"And I can trust thy faith, for—thou'lt be dumb.
"Now mark how readily a wretch like me,
"In one bold plunge commences Deity!"

He sprung and sunk, as the last words were said—
Quick closed the burning waters o'er his head.
And ZELICA was left—within the ring
Of those wide walls the only living thing;
The only wretched one, still cursed with breath,
In all that frightful wilderness of death!
More like some bloodless ghost—such as, they tell,
In the Lone Cities of the Silent† dwell,
And there, unseen of all but ALLA, sit
Each by its own pale carcass, watching it.

But morn is up, and a fresh warfare stirs
Throughout the camp of the beleaguerers.
Their globes of fire (the dread artill'ry lent
By GREECE to conquering MAHADI) are spent;
And now the scorpion's shaft, the quarry sent
From high balistas, and the shielded throng
Of soldiers swinging the huge ram along,
All speak th' impatient Islamite's intent
To try, at length, if tower and battlement
And bastioned wall be not less hard to win,
Less tough to break down than the hearts within.
First in impatience and in toil is he,
The burning AZIM—oh! could he but see
Th' Impostor once alive within his grasp,
Not the gaunt lion's hug, nor boa's clasp,
Could match that gripe of vengeance, or keep pace
With the fell heartiness of Hate's embrace!

Loud rings the pond'rous ram against the walls;
Now shake the ramparts, now a buttress falls,
But still no breach—"Once more, one mighty swing
"Of all your beams, together thundering!"

* "The Afghauns believe each of the numerous solitudes and deserts of their country to be inhabited by a lonely demon, whom they call the Ghoolee Beeabau, or Spirit of the Waste. They often illustrate the wildness of any sequestered tribe, by saying, they are as wild as the Demon of the Waste."—*Elphinstone's Caubul.*

* "Il donna du poison dans le vin à tous ses gens, et se jeta lui-même ensuite dans une cuve pleine de drogues brûlantes et consumantes, afin qu'il ne restât rien de tous les membres de son corps, et que ceux qui restoient de sa secte puissent croire qu'il étoit monté au ciel, ce qui ne manqua pas d'arriver."—*D'Herbelot.*

† "They have all a great reverence for burial grounds, which they sometimes call by the poetical name of Cities of the Silent, and which they people with the ghosts of the departed, who sit each at the head of his own grave, invisible to mortal eyes."—*Elphinstone.*

There—the wall shakes—the shouting troops exult,
"Quick, quick discharge your weightiest catapult
"Right on that spot, and NEKSHEB is our own!"
'Tis done—the battlements come crashing down,
And the huge wall, by that stroke riven in two,
Yawning, like some old crater, rent anew,
Shows the dim, desolate city smoking through.
But strange! no signs of life—naught living seen
Above, below—what can this stillness mean?
A minute's pause suspends all hearts and eyes—
"In through the breach," impetuous AZIM cries;
But the cool CALIPH, fearful of some wile
In this blank stillness, checks the troops awhile,—
Just then, a figure, with slow step, advanced
Forth from the ruin'd walls, and, as there glanced
A sunbeam over it, all eyes could see
The well-known Silver Veil!—"'Tis He, 'tis He,
"MOKANNA, and alone!" they shout around;
Young AZIM from his steed springs to the ground—
"Mine, Holy Caliph! mine," he cries, "the task
"To crush yon daring wretch—'tis all I ask."
Eager he darts to meet the demon foe,
Who still across wide heaps of ruin slow
And falteringly comes, till they are near;
Then, with a bound, rushes on AZIM's spear,
And, casting off the Veil in falling, shows—
Oh!—'tis his ZELICA's life-blood that flows!

"I meant not, AZIM," soothingly she said,
As on his trembling arm she lean'd her head,
And, looking in his face, saw anguish there
Beyond all wounds the quiv'ring flesh can bear—
"I meant not *thou* shouldst have the pain of this:—
"Though death, with thee thus tasted, is a bliss
"Thou wouldst not rob me of, didst thou but know,
"How oft I've pray'd to God I might die so!
"But the Fiend's venom was too scant and slow;—
"To linger on were madd'ning—and I thought
"If once that Veil—nay, look not on it—caught
"The eyes of your fierce soldiery, I should be
"Struck by a thousand death-darts instantly.
"But this is sweeter—oh! believe me, yes—
"I would not change this sad, but dear caress,
"This death within thy arms I would not give
"For the most smiling life the happiest live!
"All, that stood dark and drear before the eye
"Of my stray'd soul, is passing swiftly by;
"A light comes o'er me from those looks of love,
"Like the first dawn of mercy from above;
"And if thy lips but tell me I'm forgiv'n,
"Angels will echo the bless'd words in Heav'n!
"But live, my AZIM;—oh! to call thee mine
"Thus once again! *my* AZIM—dream divine!
"Live, if thou ever lov'dst me, if to meet
"Thy ZELICA hereafter would be sweet,
"Oh, live to pray for her—to bend the knee
"Morning and night before that Deity,
"To whom pure lips and hearts without a stain,
"As thine are, AZIM, never breathed in vain,—
"And pray that he may pardon her,—may take
"Compassion on her soul for thy dear sake,
"And, naught rememb'ring but her love to thee,
"Make her all thine, all His, eternally!
"Go to those happy fields where first we twined
"Our youthful hearts together—every wind
"That meets thee there, fresh from the well-known flow'rs,
"Will bring the sweetness of those innocent hours
"Back to my soul, and thou mayst feel again
"For thy poor ZELICA as thou didst then.
"So shall thy orisons, like dew that flies
"To Heav'n upon the morning's sunshine, rise
"With all love's earliest ardour to the skies!
"And should they—but, alas, my senses fail—
"Oh for one minute!—should thy prayers prevail—
"If pardon'd souls may, from that World of Bliss,
"Reveal their joy to those they love in this—
"I'll come to thee—in some sweet dream—and tell—
"Oh Heav'n—I die—dear love! farewell, farewell!"

Time fleeted—years on years had pass'd away,
And few of those who on that mournful day,
Had stood, with pity in their eyes, to see
The maiden's death, and the youth's agony,
Were living still—when, by a rustic grave,
Beside the swift Amoo's transparent wave,
An aged man, who had grown aged there
By that lone grave, morning and night in prayer,
For the last time knelt down—and, though the shade
Of death hung dark'ning over him, there play'd
A gleam of rapture on his eye and cheek,
That brighten'd even Death—like the last streak
Of intense glory on th' horizon's brim,
When night o'er all the rest hangs chill and dim.
His soul had seen a Vision, while he slept;
She, for whose spirit he had pray'd and wept
So many years, had come to him, all dress'd
In angel smiles, and told him she was bless'd!
For this the old man breathed his thanks, and died
And there, upon the banks of that loved tide,
He and his ZELICA sleep side by side.

THE story of the Veiled Prophet of Khorassan being ended, they were now doomed to hear FADLADEEN's criticisms upon it. A series of disappointments and accidents had occurred to this learned Chamberlain during the journey. In the first place, those couriers stationed, as in the reign of Shah Jehan, between Delhi and the Western coast of India, to secure a constant supply of mangoes for the Royal Table, had, by some cruel irregularity, failed in their duty; and to eat any mangoes but those of Mazagong was, of course, impossible.* In the next place, the elephant, laden with his fine antique porcelain,† had, in an unusual fit of liveliness, shattered the whole set to pieces:—an irreparable loss, as many of the vessels were so exquisitely old, as to have been used under the Emperors Yan and Chun, who reigned many ages before the dynasty of Tang. His Koran, too, supposed to be the identical copy between the leaves of which Mahomet's favourite pigeon used to nestle, had been mislaid by his Koran-bearer three whole days; not without much spiritual alarm to FADLADEEN, who, though professing to hold with other loyal and orthodox Mussulmans, that salvation could only be found in the Koran, was strongly suspected of believing in his heart, that it could only be found in his own particular copy of it. When to all these grievances is added the obstinacy of the cooks, in putting the pepper of Canara into his dishes instead of the cinnamon of Serendib, we may easily suppose that he came to the task of criticism with, at least, a sufficient degree of irritability for the purpose.

"In order," said he, importantly swinging about his chaplet of pearls, "to convey with clearness my opinion of the story this young man has related, it is necessary to take a review of all the stories that have ever——" —"My good FADLADEEN!" exclaimed the Princess, interrupting him, "we really do not deserve that you should give yourself so much trouble. Your opinion of the poem we have just heard, will, I have no doubt, be abundantly edifying, without any further waste of your valuable erudition."—"If that be all," replied the critic,—evidently mortified at not being allowed to show how much he knew about every thing, but the subject immediately before him,—"if that be all that is required, the matter is easily dispatched." He then proceeded to analyze the poem in that strain, (so well known to the unfortunate bards of Delhi,) whose censures were an infliction from which few

---

* "The celebrity of Mazagong is owing to its mangoes, which are certainly the best fruit I ever tasted. The parent-tree, from which all those of this species have been grafted, is honoured during the fruit-season by a guard of sepoys; and, in the reign of Shah Jehan, couriers were stationed between Delhi and the Mahratta coast, to secure an abundant and fresh supply of mangoes for the royal table."—*Mrs. Graham's* Journal of a Residence in India.

† This old porcelain is found in digging, and "if it is esteemed, it is not because it has acquired any new degree of beauty in the earth, but because it has retained its ancient beauty; and this alone is of great importance in China, where they give large sums for the smallest vessels which were used under the Emperors Yan and Chun, who reigned many ages before the dynasty of Tang, at which time porcelain began to be used by the Emperors," (about the year 442.)—*Dunn's* Collection of Curious Observations, &c.;—a bad translation of some parts of the Lettres Edifiantes et Curieuses of the Missionary Jesuits.

recovered, and whose very praises were like the honey extracted from the bitter flowers of the aloe. The chief personages of the story were, if he rightly understood them, an ill-favoured gentleman, with a veil over his face;—a young lady, whose reason went and came, according as it suited the poet's convenience to be sensible or otherwise;—and a youth in one of those hideous Bucharian bonnets, who took the aforesaid gentleman in a veil for a Divinity. "From such materials," said he, "what can be expected?—after rivalling each other in long speeches and absurdities, through some thousands of lines as indigestible as the filberts of Berdaa, our friend in the veil jumps into a tub of aquafortis; the young lady dies in a set speech, whose only recommendation is that it is her last; and the lover lives on to a good old age, for the laudable purpose of seeing her ghost, which he at last happily accomplishes, and expires. This, you will allow, is a fair summary of the story; and if Nasser, the Arabian merchant, told no better, our Holy Prophet (to whom be all honour and glory!) had no need to be jealous of his abilities for story-telling."*

With respect to the style, it was worthy of the matter;—it had not even those politic contrivances of structure, which make up for the commonness of the thoughts by the peculiarity of the manner, nor that stately poetical phraseology by which sentiments mean in themselves, like the blacksmith's† apron converted into a banner, are so easily gilt and embroidered into consequence. Then, as to the versification, it was, to say no worse of it, execrable: it had neither the copious flow of Ferdosi, the sweetness of Hafez, nor the sententious march of Sadi; but appeared to him, in the uneasy heaviness of its movements, to have been modelled upon the gait of a very tired dromedary. The licenses, too, in which it indulged, were unpardonable;—for instance this line, and the poem abounded with such;—

Like the faint, exquisite music of a dream.

"What critic that can count," said **Fadladeen**, "and has his full complement of fingers to count withal, would tolerate for an instant such syllabic superfluities?"—He here looked round, and discovered that most of his audience were asleep; while the glimmering lamps seemed inclined to follow their example. It became necessary, therefore, however painful to himself, to put an end to his valuable animadversions for the present, and he accordingly concluded, with an air of dignified candour, thus:—"Notwithstanding the observations which I have thought it my duty to make, it is by no means my wish to discourage the young man:—so far from it, indeed, that if he will but totally alter his style of writing and thinking, I have very little doubt that I shall be vastly pleased with him."

Some days elapsed, after this harangue of the Great Chamberlain, before **Lalla Rookh** could venture to ask for another story. The youth was still a welcome guest in the pavilion—to *one* heart, perhaps, too dangerously welcome;—but all mention of poetry was, as if by common consent, avoided. Though none of the party had much respect for **Fadladeen**, yet his censures, thus magisterially delivered, evidently made an impression on them all. The Poet, himself, to whom criticism was quite a new operation, (being wholly unknown in that Paradise of the Indies, Cashmere,) felt the shock as it is generally felt at first, till use has made it more tolerable to the patient;—the Ladies began to suspect that they ought not to be pleased, and seemed to conclude that there must have been much good sense in what **Fadladeen** said, from its having set them all so soundly to sleep;—while the self-complacent Chamberlain was left to triumph in the idea of having, for the hundred and fiftieth time in his life, extinguished a Poet. **Lalla Rookh** alone—and Love knew why—persisted in being delighted with all she had heard, and in resolving to hear

* "La lecture de ces Fables plaisoit si fort aux Arabes, que, quand Mahomet les entretenoit de l'Histoire de l'Ancien Testament, ils les méprisoient, lui disant que celles que Nasser leur racontoient étoient beaucoup plus belles. Cette préférence attira à Nasser la malédiction de Mahomet et de tous ses disciples."—*D'Herbelot.*

† The blacksmith Gao, who successfully resisted the tyrant Zohak, and whose apron became the Royal Standard of Persia.

more as speedily as possible. Her manner, however, of first returning to the subject was unlucky. It was while they rested during the heat of noon near a fountain, on which some hand had rudely traced those well-known words from the Garden of Sadi,—"Many, like me, have view'd this fountain, but they are gone, and their eyes are closed forever!"—that she took occasion, from the melancholy beauty of this passage, to dwell upon the charms of poetry in general. "It is true," she said, "few poets can imitate that sublime bird, which flies always in the air, and never touches the earth:*—it is only once in many ages a Genius appears, whose words, like those on the Written Mountain, last forever:†—but still there are some as delightful, perhaps, though not so wonderful, who, if not stars over our head, are at least flowers along our path, and whose sweetness of the moment we ought gratefully to inhale, without calling upon them for a brightness and a durability beyond their nature. In short," continued she, blushing, as if conscious of being caught in an oration, "it is quite cruel that a poet cannot wander through his regions of enchantment, without having a critic forever, like the Old Man of the Sea, upon his back!"‡ **Fadladeen**, it was plain, took this last luckless allusion to himself, and would treasure it up in his mind as a whetstone for his next criticism. A sudden silence ensued; and the Princess, glancing a look at **Feramorz**, saw plainly she must wait for a more courageous moment.

But the glories of Nature, and her wild, fragrant airs playing freshly over the current of youthful spirits, will soon heal even deeper wounds than the dull Fadladeens of this world can inflict. In an evening or two after, they came to the small Valley of Gardens, which had been planted by order of the Emperor for his favourite sister Rochinara, during their progress to Cashmere, some years before; and never was there a more sparkling assemblage of sweets, since the Gulzar-e-Irem, or Rose-Bower of Irem. Every precious flower was there to be found that poetry, or love, or religion, has ever consecrated; from the dark hyacinth, to which Hafez compares his mistress's hair,§ to the *Cámalatá*, by whose rosy blossoms the heaven of Indra is scented.|| As they sat in the cool fragrance of this delicious spot, and **Lalla Rookh** remarked that she could fancy it the abode of that Flower-loving Nymph whom they worship in the temples of Kathay,¶ or of one of those Peris, those beautiful creatures of the air, who live upon perfumes, and to whom a place like this might make some amends for the Paradise they have lost,—the young Poet, in whose eyes she appeared, while she spoke, to be one of the bright spiritual creatures she was describing, said hesitatingly that he remembered a Story of a Peri, which, if the Princess had no objection, he would venture to relate. "It is," said he, with an appealing look to **Fadladeen**, "in a

* "The Huma, a bird peculiar to the East. It is supposed to fly constantly in the air, and never touch the ground; it is looked upon as a bird of happy omen; and that every head it overshades will in time wear a crown."—*Richardson.*

In the terms of alliance made by Fuzzel Oola Khan with Hyder in 1760, one of the stipulations was, "that he should have the distinction of two honorary attendants standing behind him, holding fans composed of the feathers of the humma, according to the practice of his family."—*Wilks's* South of India. He adds in a note:—"The Humma is a fabulous bird. The head over which its shadow once passes will assuredly be circled with a crown. The splendid little bird suspended over the throne of Tippo Sultaun, found at Seringapatam in 1799, was intended to represent this poetical fancy."

† "To the pilgrims to Mount Sinai we must attribute the inscriptions, figures, &c. on those rocks, which have from thence acquired the name of the Written Mountain."—*Volney.* M. Gebelin and others have been at much pains to attach some mysterious and important meaning to these inscriptions; but Niebuhr, as well as Volney, thinks that they must have been executed at idle hours by the travellers to Mount Sinai, "who were satisfied with cutting the unpolished rock with any pointed instrument; adding to their names and the date of their journeys some rude figures, which bespeak the hand of a people but little skilled in the arts."—*Niebuhr.*

‡ The Story of Sinbad.

§ See *Nott's* Hafez, Ode v.

|| "The Cámalatá (called by Linnæus, Ipomæa) is the most beautiful of its order, both in the colour and form of its leaves and flowers; its elegant blossoms are 'celestial rosy red, Love's proper hue,' and have justly procured it the name of Cámalatá, or Love's Creeper."—*Sir W. Jones.*

"Cámalatá may also mean a mythological plant, by which all desires are granted to such as inhabit the heaven of Indra; and if ever flower was worthy of Paradise, it is our charming Ipomæa."—*Ib.*

¶ "According to Father Premare, in his tract on Chinese Mythology, the Mother of Fo-hi was the daughter of heaven, surnamed Flower-loving; and as the nymph was walking alone on the bank of a river, she found herself encircled by a rainbow, after which she became pregnant, and, at the end of twelve years, was delivered of a son radiant as herself."—*Asiat. Res.*

lighter and humbler strain than the other:" then, striking a few careless but melancholy chords on his kitar, he thus began:—

PARADISE AND THE PERI.

One morn a Peri at the gate
Of Eden stood, disconsolate;
And as she listen'd to the Springs
  Of Life within, like music flowing,
And caught the light upon her wings
  Through the half-open portal glowing,
She wept to think her recreant race
Should e'er have lost that glorious place!

"How happy," exclaim'd this child of air,
"Are the holy Spirits who wander there,
  "'Mid flowers that never shall fade or fall;
"Though mine are the gardens of earth and sea
"And the stars themselves have flowers for me,
  "One blossom of Heaven out-blooms them all

"Though sunny the Lake of cool Cashmere,
"With its plane-tree Isle reflected clear,*
  "And sweetly the founts of that Valley fall;
"Though bright are the waters of Sing-su-hay,
"And the golden floods that thitherward stray,†
"Yet—oh, 'tis only the Blest can say
  "How the waters of Heaven outshine them all!

"Go, wing thy flight from star to star,
"From world to luminous world, as far
  "As the universe spreads its flaming wall:
"Take all the pleasures of all the spheres,
"And multiply each through endless years,
  "One minute of Heaven is worth them all!"

The glorious Angel, who was keeping
The gates of Light, beheld her weeping;
And, as he nearer drew and listen'd
To her sad song, a tear-drop glisten'd
Within his eyelids, like the spray
  From Eden's fountain, when it lies
On the blue flow'r, which—Bramins say—
  Blooms nowhere but in Paradise.‡

"Nymph of a fair but erring line!"
Gently he said—"One hope is thine.
"'Tis written in the Book of Fate,
  "*The Peri yet may be forgiv'n,*
"*Who brings to this Eternal gate*
  "*The Gift that is most dear to Heav'n!*
Go, seek it, and redeem thy sin—
"'Tis sweet to let the pardon'd in."

Rapidly as comets run
To th' embraces of the Sun;—
Fleeter than the starry brands
Flung at night from angel hands§
At those dark and daring sprites
Who would climb th' empyreal heights,
Down the blue vault the Peri flies,
  And, lighted earthward by a glance
That just then broke from morning's eyes,
  Hung hov'ring o'er our world's expanse.

But whither shall the Spirit go
To find this gift for Heav'n?—"I know
"The wealth," she cries, "of every urn
"In which unnumber'd rubies burn,
"Beneath the pillars of Chilminar;*
"I know where the Isles of Perfume are,†
"Many a fathom down in the sea,
"To the south of sun-bright Araby;‡
"I know, too, where the Genii hid
"The jewell'd cup of their King Jamshid,§
"With life's elixir sparkling high—
"But gifts like these are not for the sky.
"Where was there ever a gem that shone
"Like the steps of Alla's wonderful Throne?
"And the Drops of Life—oh! what would they be
"In the boundless Deep of Eternity?"

While thus she mused, her pinions fann'd
The air of that sweet Indian land,
Whose air is balm; whose ocean spreads
O'er coral rocks, and amber beds;||
Whose mountains, pregnant by the beam
Of the warm sun, with diamonds teem;
Whose rivulets are like rich brides,
Lovely, with gold beneath their tides;
Whose sandal groves and bowers of spice
Might be a Peri's Paradise!
But crimson now her rivers ran
  With human blood—the smell of death
Came reeking from those spicy bowers,
And man, the sacrifice of man,
  Mingled his taint with every breath
Upwafted from th' innocent flowers.
Land of the Sun! what foot invades
Thy Pagods and thy pillar'd shades—¶
Thy cavern shrines, and Idol stones,
Thy Monarchs and their thousand Thrones?**
'Tis He of Gazna††—fierce in wrath
  He comes, and India's diadems
Lie scatter'd in his ruinous path.—
  His bloodhounds he adorns with gems,
Torn from the violated necks
  Of many a young and loved Sultana;‡‡
  Maidens, within their pure Zenana,
  Priests in the very fane he slaughters,
And choaks up with the glittering wrecks
  Of Golden shrines the sacred waters!

Downward the Peri turns her gaze,
And, through the war-field's bloody haze,
Beholds a youthful warrior stand,
  Alone beside his native river,—
The red blade broken in his hand,
  And the last arrow in his quiver.
"Live," said the Conqu'ror, "live to share
"The trophies and the crowns I bear!"
Silent that youthful warrior stood—
Silent he pointed to the flood
All crimson with his country's blood,

* "Numerous small islands emerge from the Lake of Cashmere. One is called Char Chenaur, from the plane trees upon it."—*Foster.*

† "The Altan Kol or Golden River of Tibet, which runs into the Lakes of Sing-su hay, has abundance of gold in its sands, which employs the inhabitants all the summer in gathering it."—*Description of Tibet in Pinkerton.*

‡ "The Brahmins of this province insist that the blue campac flowers only in Paradise."—*Sir W. Jones.* It appears, however, from a curious letter of the Sultan of Menangcabow, given by Marsden, that one place on earth may lay claim to the possession of it. "This is the Sultan, who keeps the flower champaka that is blue, and to be found in no other country but his, being yellow elsewhere."—*Marsden's* Sumatra.

§ "The Mahometans suppose that falling stars are the firebrands wherewith the good angels drive away the bad, when they approach too near the empyrean or verge of the heavens."—*Fryer.*

* The Forty Pillars; so the Persians call the ruins of Persepolis. It is imagined by them that this palace and the edifices at Balbec were built by Genii, for the purpose of hiding in their subterraneous caverns immense treasures, which still remain there.—*D'Herbelot, Volney.*

† *Diodorus* mentions the Isle of Panchaia, to the south of Arabia Felix, where there was a temple of Jupiter. This island, or rather cluster of isles, has disappeared, "sunk (says *Grandpré*) in the abyss made by the fire beneath their foundations."—*Voyage to the Indian Ocean.*

‡ The Isles of Panchaia.

§ "The cup of Jamshid, discovered, they say, when digging for the foundations of Persepolis."—*Richardson.*

|| "It is not like the Sea of India, whose bottom is rich with pearls and ambergris, whose mountains of the coast are stored with gold and precious stones, whose gulfs breed creatures that yield ivory, and among the plants of whose shores are ebony, red wood, and the wood of Hairzan, aloes, camphor, cloves, sandal-wood, and all other spices and aromatics; where parrots and peacocks are birds of the forest, and musk and civet are collected upon the lands."—*Travels of two Mohammedans.*

¶
. . . . in the ground
The bended twigs take root, and daughters grow
About the mother-tree, *a pillar'd shade,*
High over arch'd, and echoing walks between.
MILTON.

For a particular description and plate of the Banyan-tree, see *Cordiner's* Ceylon.

** "With this immense treasure Mamood returned to Ghizni, and in the year 400 prepared a magnificent festival, where he displayed to the people his wealth in golden thrones and in other ornaments, in a great plain without the city of Ghizni."—*Firishta.*

†† "Mahmood of Gazna, or Ghizni, who conquered India in the beginning of the 11th century."—See his History in *Dow* and *Sir J. Malcolm.*

‡‡ "It is reported that the hunting equipage of the Sultan Mahmood was so magnificent, that he kept 400 greyhounds and bloodhounds, each of which wore a collar set with jewels, and a covering edged with gold and pearls."—*Universal History,* vol. iii.

Then sent his last remaining dart,
For answer, to th' Invader's heart.

False flew the shaft, though pointed well;
The Tyrant lived, the Hero fell!—
Yet mark'd the Peri where he lay,
And, when the rush of war was past,
Swiftly descending on a ray
Of morning light, she caught the last—
Last glorious drop his heart had shed,
Before his free-born spirit fled!

"Be this," she cried, as she wing'd her flight,
"My welcome gift at the Gates of Light.
"Though foul are the drops that oft distil
"On the field of warfare, blood like this,
"For Liberty shed, so holy is,*
"It would not stain the purest rill,
"That sparkles among the Bowers of Bliss!
"Oh, if there be, on this earthly sphere,
"A boon, an offering Heaven holds dear,
"'Tis the last libation Liberty draws
"From the heart that bleeds and breaks in her cause!"

"Sweet," said the Angel, as she gave
The gift into his radiant hand,
"Sweet is our welcome of the Brave
"Who die thus for their native Land.—
"But see—alas!—the crystal bar
"Of Eden moves not—holier far
"Than even this drop the boon must be,
"That opes the gates of Heaven for thee!"

Her first fond hope of Eden blighted,
Now among Afric's lunar Mountains,†
Far to the South, the Peri lighted;
And sleek'd her plumage at the fountains
Of that Egyptian tide—whose birth
Is hidden from the sons of earth
Deep in those solitary woods,
Where oft the Genii of the Floods
Dance round the cradle of their Nile,
And hail the new-born Giant's smile.‡
Thence over Egypt's palmy groves,
Her grots, and sepulchres of Kings,§
The exiled Spirit sighing roves;
And now hangs listening to the doves
In warm Rosetta's vale‖—now loves
To watch the moonlight on the wings
Of the white pelicans that break
The azure calm of Mœris' Lake.¶
'Twas a fair scene—a Land more bright
Never did mortal eye behold!
Who could have thought, that saw this night
Those valleys and their fruits of gold
Basking in Heaven's serenest light;—
Those groups of lovely date-trees bending
Languidly their leaf-crown'd heads,
Like youthful maids, when sleep descending
Warns them to their silken beds;—**
Those virgin lilies, all the night
Bathing their beauties in the lake,
That they may rise more fresh and bright,
When their beloved Sun's awake;—
Those ruin'd shrines and towers that seem
The relics of a splendid dream;
Amid whose fairy loneliness
Naught but the lapwing's cry is heard,
Naught seen but (when the shadows, flitting
Fast from the moon, unsheath its gleam,)
Some purple-wing'd Sultana* sitting
Upon a column, motionless
And glitt'ring like an Idol bird!—
Who could have thought, that there, even there,
Amid those scenes so still and fair,
The Demon of the Plague hath cast
From his hot wing a deadlier blast,
More mortal far than ever came
From the red Desert's sands of flame!
So quick, that ev'ry living thing
Of human shape, touch'd by his wing,
Like plants, where the Simoom hath pass'd,
At once falls black and withering!
The sun went down on many a brow,
Which, full of bloom and freshness then,
Is rankling in the pest-house now,
And ne'er will feel that sun again.
And, oh! to see th' unburied heaps
On which the lonely moonlight sleeps—
The very vultures turn away,
And sicken at so foul a prey!
Only the fierce hyæna stalks†
Throughout the city's desolate walks‡
At midnight, and his carnage plies:—
Wo to the half-dead wretch, who meets
The glaring of those large blue eyes§
Amid the darkness of the streets!

"Poor race of men!" said the pitying Spirit,
"Dearly ye pay for your primal Fall—
"Some flow'rets of Eden ye still inherit,
"But the trail of the Serpent is over them all!"

She wept—the air grew pure and clear
Around her, as the bright drops ran;
For there's a magic in each tear,
Such kindly Spirits weep for man!

Just then beneath some orange trees,
Whose fruit and blossoms in the breeze
Were wantoning together, free,
Like age at play with infancy—
Beneath that fresh and springing bower,
Close by the lake, she heard the moan
Of one who, at this silent hour,
Had thither stol'n to die alone.
One who in life where'er he moved,
Drew after him the hearts of many;
Yet now, as though he ne'er were loved,
Dies here unseen, unwept by any!
None to watch near him—none to slake
The fire that in his bosom lies,
With ev'n a sprinkle from that lake,
Which shines so cool before his eyes.
No voice, well known through many a day,
To speak the last, the parting word,
Which, when all other sounds decay.
Is still like distant music heard;—
That tender farewell on the shore
Of this rude world, when all is o'er,
Which cheers the spirit, ere its bark
Puts off into the unknown Dark.

* Objections may be made to my use of the word Liberty in this, and more especially in the story that follows it, as totally inapplicable to any state of things that has ever existed in the East; but though I cannot, of course, mean to employ it in that enlarged and noble sense which is so well understood at the present day, and, I grieve to say, so little acted upon, yet it is no disparagement to the word to apply it to that national independence, that freedom from the interference and dictation of foreigners, without which, indeed, no liberty of any kind can exist; and for which both Hindoos and Persians fought against their Mussulman invaders with, in many cases, a bravery that deserved much better success.

† "The Mountains of the Moon, or the Montes Lunæ of antiquity, at the foot of which the Nile is supposed to arise."—*Bruce.*

"Sometimes called," says *Jackson*, "Jibbel Kumrie, or the white or lunar-coloured mountains; so a white horse is called by the Arabians a moon-coloured horse."

‡ "The Nile, which the Abyssinians know by the names of Abey and Alaway, or the Giant."—*Asiat. Research.* vol. 1. p. 387.

§ "See Perry's View of the Levant for an account of the sepulchres in Upper Thebes, and the numberless grots, covered all over with hieroglyphics in the mountains of Upper Egypt.

‖ "The orchards of Rosetta are filled with turtle-doves."—*Sonnini.*

¶ Savary mentions the pelicans upon Lake Mœris.

** "The superb date-tree, whose head languidly reclines, like that of a handsome woman overcome with sleep."—*Dafard el Hadad.*

* "That beautiful bird, with plumage of the finest shining blue, with purple beak and legs, the natural and living ornament of the temples and palaces of the Greeks and Romans, which, from the stateliness of its port, as well as the brilliancy of its colours, has obtained the title of Sultana."—*Sonnini.*

† Jackson, speaking of the plague that occurred in West Barbary, when he was there, says, "The birds of the air fled away from the abodes of men. The hyænas, on the contrary, visited the cemeteries," &c.

‡ "Gondar was full of hyænas from the time it turned dark, till the dawn of day, seeking the different pieces of slaughtered carcasses, which this cruel and unclean people expose in the streets without burial, and who firmly believe that these animals are Falashta from the neighbouring mountains, transformed by magic, and come down to eat human flesh in the dark in safety."—*Bruce.*

§ Ibid.

Deserted youth! one thought alone
Shed joy around his soul in death—
That she, whom he for years had known,
And loved, and might have call'd his own,
Was safe from this foul midnight's breath,—
Safe in her father's princely halls,
Where the cool airs from fountain falls,
Freshly perfumed by many a brand
Of the sweet wood from India's land,
Were pure as she whose brow they fann'd.

But see—who yonder comes by stealth,*
This melancholy bow'r to seek,
Like a young envoy, sent by Health,
With rosy gifts upon her cheek?
'Tis she—far off, through moonlight dim,
He knew his own betrothed bride,
She, who would rather die with him,
Than live to gain the world beside!—
Her arms are round her lover now,
His livid cheek to hers she presses,
And dips, to bind his burning brow,
In the cool lake her loosen'd tresses.
Ah! once, how little did he think
An hour would come, when he should shrink
With horror from that dear embrace,
Those gentle arms, that were to him
Holy as is the cradling place
Of Eden's infant cherubim!
And now he yields—now turns away,
Shudd'ring as if the venom lay
All in those proffer'd lips alone—
Those lips that, then so fearless grown,
Never until that instant came
Near his unask'd, or without shame.
"Oh! let me only breathe the air,
"The blessed air, that's breathed by thee,
"And, whether on its wings it bear
"Healing or death, 'tis sweet to me!
"There—drink my tears, while yet they fall—
"Would that my bosom's blood were balm,
"And, well thou know'st, I'd shed it all,
"To give thy brow one minute's calm.
"Nay, turn not from me that dear face—
"Am I not thine—thy own loved bride—
"The one, the chosen one, whose place,
"In life or death, is by thy side?
"Think'st thou that she, whose only light,
"In this dim world, from thee hath shone,
"Could bear the long, the cheerless night,
"That must be hers when thou art gone?
"That I can live, and let thee go,
"Who art my life itself?—No, no—
"When the stem dies, the leaf that grew
"Out of its heart must perish too!
"Then turn to me, my own love, turn,
"Before, like thee, I fade and burn;
"Cling to these yet cool lips, and share
"The last pure life that lingers there!"
She fails—she sinks—as dies the lamp
In charnel airs, or cavern-damp,
So quickly do his baleful sighs
Quench all the sweet light of her eyes.
One struggle—and his pain is past—
Her lover is no longer living!
One kiss the maiden gives, one last,
Long kiss, which she expires in giving!

"Sleep," said the PERI, as softly she stole
The farewell sigh of that vanishing soul,
As true as e'er warm'd a woman's breast—
"Sleep on, in visions of odour rest,
"In balmier airs than ever yet stirr'd
"Th' enchanted pile of that lonely bird,
"Who sings at the last his own death-lay,†
"And in music and perfume dies away!"

Thus saying, from her lips she spread
Unearthly breathings through the place,
And shook her sparkling wreath, and shed
Such lustre o'er each paly face,
That like two lovely saints they seem'd,
Upon the eve of doomsday taken
From their dim graves, in odour sleeping
While that benevolent PERI beam'd
Like their good angel, calmly keeping
Watch o'er them till their souls would waker

But morn is blushing in the sky;
Again the PERI soars above,
Bearing to Heav'n that precious sigh
Of pure, self-sacrificing love.
High throbb'd her heart, with hope elate,
Th' Elysian palm she soon shall win,
For the bright Spirit at the gate
Smiled as she gave that off'ring in;
And she already hears the trees
Of Eden, with their crystal bells
Ringing in that ambrosial breeze
That from the throne of ALLA swells;
And she can see the starry bowls
That lie around that lucid lake,
Upon whose banks admitted Souls
Their first sweet draught of glory take!*

But, ah! even PERIS' hopes are vain—
Again the Fates forbade, again
Th' immortal barrier closed—"Not yet,"
The Angel said, as, with regret,
He shut from her that glimpse of glory—
"True was the maiden, and her story,
"Written in light o'er ALLA's head,
"By seraph eyes shall long be read.
"But, PERI, see—the crystal bar
"Of Eden moves not—holier far
"Than ev'n this sigh the boon must be
"That opes the Gates of Heav'n for thee"

Now, upon SYRIA's land of roses†
Softly the light of Eve reposes,
And, like a glory, the broad sun
Hangs over sainted LEBANON;
Whose head in wintry grandeur tow'rs,
And whitens with eternal sleet,
While summer, in a vale of flow'rs,
Is sleeping rosy at his feet.

To one, who look'd from upper air
O'er all th' enchanted regions there,
How beauteous must have been the glow,
The life, the sparkling from below!
Fair gardens, shining streams, with ranks
Of golden melons on their banks,
More golden where the sun-light falls;—
Gay lizards glittering on the walls‡
Of ruin'd shrines, busy and bright
As they were all alive with light;
And, yet more splendid, numerous flocks
Of pigeons, settling on the rocks,
With their rich restless wings, that gleam
Variously in the crimson beam
Of the warm West,—as if inlaid
With brilliants from the mine, or made
Of tearless rainbows, such as span
Th' unclouded skies of PERISTAN.
And then the mingling sounds that come,
Of shepherd's ancient reed,§ with hum

* This circumstance has been often introduced into poetry;—by Vincentius Fabricius, by Darwin, and lately, with very powerful effect, by Mr. Wilson.

† "In the East, they suppose the Phœnix to have fifty orifices in his bill, which are continued to his tail; and that, after living one thousand years, he builds himself a funeral pile, sings a melodious air of different harmonies through his fifty organ-pipes, flaps his wings with a velocity which sets fire to the wood, and consumes himself."—*Richardson.*

* "On the shores of a quadrangular lake stand a thousand goblets, made of stars, out of which souls predestined to enjoy felicity drink the crystal wave."—From *Châteaubriand's* Description of the Mahometan Paradise, in his *Beauties of Christianity.*

† Richardson thinks that Syria had its nam from Suri, a beautiful and delicate species of rose, for which that country has been always famous, hence, Suristan, the Land of Roses.

‡ "The number of lizards I saw one day in the great court of the Temple of the Sun at Balbec amounted to many thousands; the ground, the walls, and stones of the ruined buildings, were covered with them."—*Bruce.*

§ "The Syrinx or Pan's pipe is still a pastoral instrument in Syria—*Russel.*

Of the wild bees of PALESTINE,*
Banqueting through the flow'ry vales;
And, JORDAN, those sweet banks of thine,
And woods, so full of nightingales.†

But naught can charm the luckless PER
Her soul is sad, her wings are weary—
Joyless she sees the Sun look down
On that great Temple, once his own,‡
Whose lonely columns stand sublime,
Flinging their shadows from on high,
Like dials, which the wizard, Time,
Had raised to count his ages by!

Yet haply there may lie conceal'd
Beneath those Chambers of the Sun,
Some amulet of gems, anneal'd
In upper fires, some tablet seal'd
With the great name of SOLOMON,
Which, spell'd by her illumined eyes,
May teach her where, beneath the moon,
In earth or ocean, lies the boon,
The charm that can restore so soon
An erring Spirit to the skies.

Cheer'd by this hope she bends her thither;-
Still laughs the radiant eye of Heaven,
Nor have the golden bowers of Even
In the rich West begun to wither;—
When, o'er the vale of BALBEC winging
Slowly, she sees a child at play,
Among the rosy wild-flow'rs singing,
As rosy and as wild as they;
Chasing, with eager hands and eyes,
The beautiful blue damsel-flies,§
That flutter'd round the jasmine stems,
Like winged flow'rs or flying gems:—
And, near the boy, who tired with play
Now nestling 'mid the roses lay,
She saw a wearied man dismount
From his hot steed, and on the brink
Of a small imaret's rustic fount‖
Impatient fling him down to drink.
Then swift his haggard brow he turn'd
To the fair child, who fearless sat,
Though never yet hath day-beam burn'd
Upon a brow more fierce than that,—
Sullenly fierce—a mixture dire,
Like thunder clouds, of gloom and fire;
In which the PERI's eye could read
Dark tales of many a ruthless deed;
The ruin'd maid—the shrine profaned—
Oaths broken—and the threshold stain'd
With blood of guests!—*there* written, all,
Black as the damning drops that fall
From the denouncing Angel's pen,
Ere Mercy weeps them out again.

Yet tranquil now that man of crime
(As if the balmy evening time
Soften'd his spirit) look'd and lay,
Watching the rosy infant's play:—
Though still, whene'er his eye by chance
Fell on the boy, its lurid glance
Met that unclouded, joyous gaze,
As torches, that have burnt all night
Through some impure and godless rite,
Encounter morning's glorious rays.

But, hark! the vesper calls to pray'r,
As slow the orb of daylight sets,
Is rising sweetly on the air,
From SYRIA's thousand minarets.

The boy has started from the bed
Of flow'rs, where he had laid his head,
And down upon the fragrant sod
Kneels* with his forehead to the south,
Lisping th' eternal name of God
From Purity's own cherub mouth,
And looking, while his hands and eyes
Are lifted to the glowing skies,
Like a stray babe of Paradise,
Just lighted on that flow'ry plain,
And seeking for its home again.
Oh! 'twas a sight—that Heav'n—that child—
A scene, which might have well beguiled
Ev'n haughty EBLIS of a sigh
For glories lost and peace gone by!

And how felt *he*, the wretched Man
Reclining there—while memory ran
O'er many a year of guilt and strife,
Flew o'er the dark flood of his life,
Nor found one sunny resting-place,
Nor brought him back one branch of grace?
"There *was* a time," he said, in mild,
Heart-humbled tones—"thou blessed child!
"When, young and haply pure as thou,
"I look'd and pray'd like thee—but now—"
He hung his head—each nobler aim,
And hope, and feeling, which had slept
From boyhood's hour, that instant came
Fresh o'er him, and he wept—he wept!

Blest tears of soul-felt penitence!
In whose benign, redeeming flow
Is felt the first, the only sense
Of guiltless joy that guilt can know

"There's a drop," said the PERI, "that dow. from the moon
"Falls through the withering airs of June
"Upon EGYPT's land,† of so healing a pow'r,
"So balmy a virtue, that ev'n in the hour
"That drop descends, contagion dies,
"And health reanimates earth and skies!—
"Oh, is it not thus, thou man of sin,
"The precious tears of repentance fall?
"Though foul thy fiery plagues within,
"One heavenly drop hath dispell'd th[illegible]

And now—behold him kneeling there
By the child's side, in humble pray'r,
While the same sunbeam shines upon
The guilty and the guiltless one,
And hymns of joy proclaim through He[illegible]
The triumph of a Soul Forgiv'n!

'Twas when the golden orb had set,
While on their knees they linger'd yet,
There fell a light more lovely far
Than ever came from sun or star,
Upon the tear that, warm and meek,
Dew'd that repentant sinner's cheek.
To mortal eye this light might seem
A northern flash or meteor beam—
But well the enraptured PERI knew
'Twas a bright smile the Angel threw
From Heaven's gate, to hail that tear
Her harbinger of glory near!

"Joy, joy forever! my task is done—
"The gates are pass'd, and Heav'n is won.

* "Wild bees, frequent in Palestine, in hollow trunks or branches of trees, and the clefts of rocks. Thus it is said, (Psalm lxxxi.) '*honey out of the stony rock.*'"—*Burder's* Oriental Customs.

† "The river Jordan is on both sides beset with little, thick, and pleasant woods, among which thousands of nightingales warble all together."—*Thevenot.*

‡ The Temple of the Sun at Balbec.

§ "You behold there a considerable number of a remarkable species of beautiful insects, the elegance of whose appearance and their attire procured for them the name of Damsels."—*Sonnini.*

‖ Imaret, "hospice où on loge et nourrit, gratis, les pélerins pendant trois jours."—*Toderini, translated by the Abbé de Cournand.* See also *Castellan's* Mœurs des Othomans, tom. v. p. 145.

* "Such Turks as at the common hours of prayer are on the road, or so employed as not to find convenience to attend the mosques, are still obliged to execute that duty; nor are they ever known to fail, whatever business they are then about, but pray immediately when the hour alarms them, whatever they are about, in that very place they chance to stand on; insomuch that when a janissary, whom you have to guard you up and down the city, hears the notice which is given him from the steeples, he will turn about, stand still, and beckon with his hand, to tell his charge he must have patience for awhile; when, taking out his handkerchief, he spreads it on the ground, sits cross legged thereupon, and says his prayers, though in the open market, which, having ended, he leaps briskly up, salutes the person whom he undertook to convey, and renews his journey with the mild expression of *Ghell gohnnum ghell*, or, Come, dear, follow me."—*Aaron Hill's* Travels.

† The Nucta, or Miraculous Drop, which falls in Egypt precisely on St. John's day, in June, and is supposed to have the effect of stopping the plague.

"Oh! am I not happy? I am, I am—
  "To thee, sweet Eden! how dark and sad
"Are the diamond turrets of SHADUKIAM,*
  "And the fragrant bowers of AMBERABAD!

"Farewell, ye odours of Earth, that die
"Passing away like a lover's sigh;—
"My feast is now of the Tooba Tree,†
"Whose scent is the breath of Eternity!

"Farewell, ye vanishing flowers, that shone
  "In my fairy wreath, so bright and brief;—
"Oh! what are the brightest that e'er have blown,
"To the lote-tree, springing by ALLA's throne,‡
  "Whose flowers have a soul in ev'ry leaf.
"Joy, joy forever!—my task is done—
"The gates are pass'd, and Heav'n is won!"

"AND this," said the Great Chamberlain, "is poetry! this flimsy manufacture of the brain, which in comparison with the lofty and durable monuments of genius, is as the gold filigree-work of Zamara beside the eternal architecture of Egypt!" After this gorgeous sentence, which, with a few more of the same kind, FADLADEEN kept by him for rare and important occasions, he proceeded to the anatomy of the short poem just recited. The lax and easy kind of metre in which it was written ought to be denounced, he said, as one of the leading causes of the alarming growth of poetry in our times. If some check were not given to this lawless facility, we should soon be overrun by a race of bards as numerous and as shallow as the hundred and twenty thousand Streams of Basra.§ They who succeeded in this style deserved chastisement for their very success;—as warriors have been punished, even after gaining a victory, because they had taken the liberty of gaining it in an irregular or unestablished manner. What, then, was to be said to those who failed? to those who presumed, as in the present lamentable instance, to imitate the license and ease of the bolder sons of song, without any of that grace or vigour which gave a dignity even to negligence;—who, like them, flung the jereed‖ carelessly, but not, like them, to the mark;—"and who," said he, raising his voice to excite a proper degree of wakefulness in his hearers, contrive to appear heavy and constrained in the midst of all the latitude they allow themselves, like one of those young pagans that dance before the Princess, who is ingenious enough to move as if her limbs were fettered, in a pair of the lightest and loosest drawers of Masulipatam!"

It was but little suitable, he continued, to the grave march of criticism to follow this fantastical Peri, of whom they had just heard, through all her flights and adventures between earth and heaven; but he could not help adverting to the puerile conceitedness of the Three Gifts which she is supposed to carry to the skies,—a drop of blood, forsooth, a sigh, and a tear! How the first of these articles was delivered into the Angel's "radiant hand" he professed himself at a loss to discover; and as to the safe carriage of the sigh and the tear, such Peris and such poets were beings by far too incomprehensible for him even to guess how they managed such matters. "But, in short," said he, "it is a waste of time and patience to dwell longer upon a thing so incurably frivolous,—puny even among its own puny race, and such as only the Banyan Hospital¶ for Sick Insects should undertake."

In vain did LALLA ROOKH try to soften this inexorable critic; in vain did she resort to her most eloquent commonplaces,—reminding him that poets were a timid and sensitive race, whose sweetness was not to be drawn forth, like that of the fragrant grass near the Ganges, by crushing and trampling upon them;*—that severity often extinguished every chance of the perfection which it demanded; and that, after all, perfection was like the Mountain of the Talisman,—no one had ever yet reached its summit.† Neither these gentle axioms, nor the still gentler looks with which they were inculcated, could lower for one instant the elevation of FADLADEEN's eyebrows, or charm him into any thing like encouragement, or even toleration, of her poet. Toleration, indeed, was not among the weaknesses of FADLADEEN:—he carried the same spirit into matters of poetry and of religion, and, though little versed in the beauties or sublimities of either, was a perfect master of the art of persecution in both. His zeal was the same, too, in either pursuit; whether the game before him was pagans or poetasters,—worshippers of cows, or writers of epics.

They had now arrived at the splendid city of Lahore, whose mausoleums and shrines, magnificent and numberless, where Death appeared to share equal honours with Heaven, would have powerfully affected the heart and imagination of LALLA ROOKH, if feelings more of this earth had not taken entire possession of her already. She was here met by messengers, dispatched from Cashmere who informed her that the King had arrived in the Valley, and was himself superintending the sumptuous preparations that were then making in the Saloons of the Shalimar for her reception. The chill she felt on receiving this intelligence,—which to a bride whose heart was free and light would have brought only images of affection and pleasure,—convinced her that her peace was gone forever, and that she was in love, irretrievably in love, with young FERAMORZ. The veil had fallen off in which this passion at first disguises itself, and to know that she loved was now as painful as to love *without* knowing it had been delicious. FERAMORZ, too,—what misery would be his, if the sweet hours of intercourse so imprudently allowed them should have stolen into his heart the same fatal fascination as into hers;—if, notwithstanding her rank, and the modest homage he always paid to it, even *he* should have yielded to the influence of those long and happy interviews, where music, poetry, the delightful scenes of nature,—all had tended to bring their hearts close together, and to waken by every means that too ready passion, which often, like the young of the desert-bird, is warmed into life by the eyes alone!‡ She saw but one way to preserve herself from being culpable as well as unhappy, and this, however painful, she was resolved to adopt. FERAMORZ must no more be admitted to her presence. To have strayed so far into the dangerous labyrinth was wrong, but to linger in it, while the clew was yet in her hand, would be criminal. Though the heart she had to offer to the King of Bucharia might be cold and broken, it should at least be pure; and she must only endeavour to forget the short dream of happiness she had enjoyed,—like that Arabian shepherd, who, in wandering into the wilderness, caught a glimpse of the Gardens of Irim, and then lost them again forever!§

The arrival of the young Bride at Lahore was celebrated in the most enthusiastic manner. The Rajas and Omras in her train, who had kept at a certain distance during the journey, and never encamped nearer to the Princess than was strictly necessary for her safeguard,

---

* The Country of Delight—the name of a province in the kingdom of Jinnistan, or Fairy Land, the capital of which is called the City of Jewels. Amberabad is another of the cities of Jinnistan.

† The tree Tooba, that stands in Paradise, in the palace of Mahomet. See *Sale's Prelim. Disc.* Tooba, says *D'Herbelot*, signifies beatitude, or eternal happiness.

‡ Mahomet is described, in the 53d chapter of the Koran, as having seen the angel Gabriel "by the lote-tree, beyond which there is no passing: near it is the Garden of Eternal Abode." This tree, say the commentators, stands in the seventh Heaven, on the right hand of the Throne of God.

§ "It is said that the rivers or streams of Basra were reckoned in the time of Pelal ben Abi Bordeh, and amounted to the number of one hundred and twenty thousand streams."—*Ebn Haukal.*

‖ The name of the javelin with which the Easterns exercise. See *Castellan, Mœurs des Othomans*, tom. iii. p. 161.

¶ "This account excited a desire of visiting the Banyan Hospital, as I had heard much of their benevolence to all kinds of animals that were either sick, lame, or infirm, through age or accident. On my arrival, there were presented to my view many horses, cows, and oxen, in one apartment; in another, dogs, sheep, goats, and monkeys, with clean straw for them to repose on. Above-stairs were depositories for seeds of many sorts, and flat, broad dishes for water, for the use of birds and insects."—*Parson's* Travels.

It is said that all animals know the Banyans, that the most timid approach them, and that birds will fly nearer to them than to other people.'—See *Grandpré.*

* "A very fragrant grass from the banks of the Ganges, near Heridwar, which in some places covers whole acres, and diffuses, when crushed, a strong odour."—*Sir W. Jones* on the Spikenard of the Ancients.

† "Near this is a curious hill, called Koh Talism, the Mountain of the Talisman, because, according to the traditions of the country, no person ever succeeded in gaining its summit."—*Kinneir.*

‡ "The Arabians believe that the ostriches hatch their young by only looking at them."—*P. Vansleb, Relat. d'Egypte.*

§ See *Sale's Koran*, note, vol. ii. p. 484.

here rode in splendid cavalcade through the city, and distributed the most costly presents to the crowd. Engines were erected in all the squares, which cast forth showers of confectionery among the people; while the artisans, in chariots* adorned with tinsel and flying streamers, exhibited the badges of their respective trades through the streets. Such brilliant displays of life and pageantry among the palaces, and domes, and gilded minarets of Lahore, made the city altogether like a place of enchantment;—particularly on the day when LALLA ROOKH set out again upon her journey, when she was accompanied to the gate by all the fairest and richest of the nobility, and rode along between ranks of beautiful boys and girls, who kept waving over their heads plates of gold and silver flowers,† and then threw them around to be gathered by the populace.

For many days after their departure from Lahore, a considerable degree of gloom hung over the whole party. LALLA ROOKH, who had intended to make illness her excuse for not admitting the young minstrel, as usual, to the pavilion, soon found that to feign indisposition was unnecessary;—FADLADEEN felt the loss of the good road they had hitherto travelled, and was very near cursing Jehan-Guire (of blessed memory!) for not having continued his delectable alley of trees,‡ at least as far as the mountains of Cashmere;—while the Ladies, who had nothing now to do all day but to be fanned by peacocks' feathers and listen to FADLADEEN, seemed heartily weary of the life they led, and, in spite of all the Great Chamberlain's criticisms, were so tasteless as to wish for the poet again. One evening, as they were proceeding to their place of rest for the night, the Princess, who, for the freer enjoyment of the air, had mounted her favourite Arabian palfrey, in passing by a small grove heard the notes of a lute from within its leaves, and a voice, which she but too well knew, singing the following words:—

TELL me not of joys above,
  If that world can give no bliss,
Truer, happier than the Love
  Which enslaves our souls in this.

Tell me not of Houris' eyes;—
  Far from me their dangerous glow,
If those looks that light the skies
  Wound like some that burn below.

Who, that feels what Love is here,
  All its falsehood—all its pain—
Would, for even Elysium's sphere,
  Risk the fatal dream again?

Who, that 'midst a desert's heat
  Sees the waters fade away,
Would not rather die than meet
  Streams again as false as they?

The tone of melancholy defiance in which these words were uttered, went to LALLA ROOKH's heart;—and, as she reluctantly rode on, she could not help feeling it to be a sad but still sweet certainty, that FERAMORZ was to the full as enamoured and miserable as herself.

The place where they encamped that evening was the first delightful spot they had come to since they left Lahore. On one side of them was a grove full of small Hindoo temples, and planted with the most graceful trees of the East; where the tamarind, the cassia, and the silken plantains of Ceylon were mingled in rich contrast with the high fan-like foliage of the Palmyra,—that favourite tree of the luxurious bird that lights up the chambers of its nest with fire-flies.§ In the middle of the lawn where the pavilion stood there was a tank surrounded by small mangoe-trees, on the clear cold waters of which floated multitudes of the beautiful red lotus;* while at a distance stood the ruins of a strange and awful-looking tower, which seemed old enough to have been the temple of some religion no longer known, and which spoke the voice of desolation in the midst of all that bloom and loveliness. This singular ruin excited the wonder and conjectures of all. LALLA ROOKH guessed in vain, and the all-pretending FADLADEEN, who had never till this journey been beyond the precincts of Delhi, was proceeding most learnedly to show that he knew nothing whatever about the matter, when one of the Ladies suggested that perhaps FERAMORZ could satisfy their curiosity. They were now approaching his native mountains, and this tower might perhaps be a relic of some of those dark superstitions, which had prevailed in that country before the light of Islam dawned upon it. The Chamberlain, who usually preferred his own ignorance to the best knowledge that any one else could give him, was by no means pleased with this officious reference; and the Princess, too, was about to interpose a faint word of objection, but, before either of them could speak, a slave was dispatched for FERAMORZ, who, in a very few minutes, made his appearance before them—looking so pale and unhappy in LALLA ROOKH's eyes, that she repented already of her cruelty in having so long excluded him.

That venerable tower, he told them, was the remains of an ancient Fire-Temple, built by those Ghebers or Persians of the old religion, who, many hundred years since, had fled hither from their Arab conquerors,† preferring liberty and their altars in a foreign land to the alternative of apostasy or persecution in their own. It was impossible, he added, not to feel interested in the many glorious but unsuccessful struggles, which had been made by these original natives of Persia to cast off the yoke of their bigoted conquerors. Like their own Fire in the Burning Field at Bakou,‡ when suppressed in one place, they had but broken out with fresh flame in another; and, as a native of Cashmere, of that fair and Holy Valley, which had in the same manner become the prey of strangers,§ and seen her ancient shrines and native princes swept away before the march of her intolerant invaders, he felt a sympathy, he owned, with the sufferings of the persecuted Ghebers, which every monument like this before them but tended more powerfully to awaken.

It was the first time that FERAMORZ had ever ventured upon so much *prose* before FADLADEEN, and it may easily be conceived what effect such prose as this must have produced upon that most orthodox and most pagan-hating personage. He sat for some minutes aghast, ejaculating only at intervals, "Bigoted conquerors!—sympathy with Fire-worshippers!"‖—while FERAMORZ, happy to take advantage of this almost speechless horror of the Chamberlain, proceeded to say that he knew a melancholy story, connected with the events of one of those struggles of the brave Fire-worshippers against their Arab masters, which, if the evening was not too far advanced, he should have much pleasure in being allowed to relate to the Princess. It was impossible for LALLA ROOKH to refuse;—he had never before looked half so animated; and when he spoke of the Holy Valley his eyes had sparkled, she thought, like the talismanic characters on the scimitar of Solomon. Her consent was therefore most readily granted; and while FADLADEEN sat in unspeakable dismay, expecting treason and abomination in every line, the poet thus began his story of the Fire-worshippers:—

* Oriental Tales.

† Ferishta. "Or rather," says *Scott*, upon the passage of Ferishta, from which this is taken, "small coins, stamped with the figure of a flower. They are still used in India to distribute in charity, and, on occasion, thrown by the purse-bearers of the great among the populace."

‡ The fine road made by the Emperor Jehan-Guire from Agra to Lahore, planted with trees on each side. This road is 250 leagues in length. It has "little pyramids or turrets," says *Bernier*, "erected every half league, to mark the ways, and frequent wells to afford drink to passengers, and to water the young trees."

§ "The Baya, or Indian Gross-beak."—*Sir W. Jones.*

* "Here is a large pagoda by a tank, on the water of which float multitudes of the beautiful red lotus: the flower is larger than that of the white water lily, and is the most lovely of the nymphæas I have seen."—*Mrs. Graham's* Journal of a Residence in India.

† "On les voit persécutés par les Khalifes se retirer dans les montagnes du Kerman: plusieurs choisirent pour retraite la Tartarie et la Chine; d'autres s'arrêtèrent sur les bords du Gange, à l'est de Delhi."—*M. Anquetil*, Mémoires de l'Académie, tom. xxxi. p. 346.

‡ The "Ager ardens," described by *Kempfer, Amœnitat. Exot.*

§ "Cashmere (says its historians) had its own princes 4000 years before its conquest by Akbar in 1585. Akbar would have found some difficulty to reduce this paradise of the Indies, situated as it is within such a fortress of mountains, but its monarch, Yusef-Khan, was basely betrayed by his Omrahs."—*Pennant.*

‖ Voltaire tells us that in his Tragedy "Les Guèbres," he was generally supposed to have alluded to the Jansenists. I should not be surprised if this story of the Fire-worshippers were found capable of a similar doubleness of application.

THE FIRE-WORSHIPPERS.

'Tis moonlight over Oman's Sea;*
Her banks of pearl and palmy isles
Bask in the night-beam beauteously,
And her blue waters sleep in smiles.
'Tis moonlight in Harmozia's† walls,
And through her Emir's porphyry halls,
Where, some hours since, was heard the swell
Of trumpet and the clash of zel,‡
Bidding the bright-eyed sun farewell;—
The peaceful sun, whom better suits
The music of the bulbul's nest,
Or the light touch of lovers' lutes,
To sing him to his golden rest.
All hush'd—there's not a breeze in motion;
The shore is silent as the ocean.
If zephyrs come, so light they come,
Nor leaf is stirr'd nor wave is driven;—
The wind-tower on the Emir's dome§
Can hardly win a breath from heaven.

Ev'n he, that tyrant Arab, sleeps
Calm, while a nation round him weeps;
While curses load the air he breathes,
And falchions from unnumber'd sheaths
Are starting to avenge the shame
His race hath brought on Iran's|| name.
Hard, heartless Chief, unmoved alike
'Mid eyes that weep, and swords that strike;—
One of that saintly, murd'rous brood,
To carnage and the Koran given,
Who think through unbelievers' blood
Lies their directest path to heav'n;—
One, who will pause and kneel unshod
In the warm blood his hand hath pour'd,
To mutter o'er some text of God
Engraven on his reeking sword;—¶
Nay, who can coolly note the line,
The letter of those words divine,
To which his blade, with searching art,
Had sunk into its victim's heart!

Just Alla! what must be thy look,
When such a wretch before thee stands
Unblushing, with thy Sacred Book,—
Turning the leaves with blood-stain'd hands,
And wresting from its page sublime
His creed of lust, and hate, and crime;—
Ev'n as those bees of Trebizond,
Which, from the sunniest flow'rs that glad
With their pure smile the gardens round,
Draw venom forth that drives men mad.**

Never did fierce Arabia send
A satrap forth more direly great;
Never was Iran doom'd to bend
Beneath a yoke of deadlier weight.
Her throne had fall'n—her pride was crush'd—
Her sons were willing slaves, nor blush'd,
In their own land,—no more their own,—
To crouch beneath a stranger's throne.
Her tow'rs, where Mithra once had burn'd,
To Moslem shrines—oh shame!—were turn'd,
Where slaves, converted by the sword,
Their mean, apostate worship pour'd,
And cursed the faith their sires adored.
Yet has she hearts, 'mid all this ill,
O'er all this wreck high buoyant still
With hope and vengeance;—hearts that yet—

* The Persian Gulf, sometimes so called, which separates the shores of Persia and Arabia.

† The present Gombaroon, a town on the Persian side of the Gulf.

‡ A Moorish instrument of music.

§ "At Gombaroon and other places in Persia, they have towers for the purpose of catching the wind, and cooling the houses."—*Le Bruyn.*

|| "Iran is the true general name for the empire of Persia."—*Asiat. Res. Disc.* 5.

¶ "On the blades of their scimitars some verse from the Koran is usually inscribed."—*Russel.*

** "There is a kind of Rhododendros about Trebizond, whose flowers the bee feeds upon, and the honey thence drives people mad."—*Tournefort.*

Like gems, in darkness, issuing rays
They've treasured from the sun that's set,—
Beam all the light of long-lost days!
And swords she hath, nor weak nor slow
To second all such hearts can dare;
As he shall know, well, dearly know,
Who sleeps in moonlight lux'ry there,
Tranquil as if his spirit lay
Becalm'd in Heav'n's approving ray.
Sleep on—for purer eyes than thine
Those waves are hush'd, those planets shine;
Sleep on, and be thy rest unmoved
By the white moonbeam's dazzling power;—
None but the loving and the loved
Should be awake at this sweet hour

And see—where, high above those rocks
That o'er the deep their shadows fling,
Yon turret stands;—where ebon locks,
As glossy as a heron's wing
Upon the turban of a king,*
Hang from the lattice, long and wild,—
'Tis she, that Emir's blooming child,
All truth and tenderness and grace,
Though born of such ungentle race;—
An image of Youth's radiant Fountain
Springing in a desolate mountain!†

Oh what a pure and sacred thing
Is Beauty, curtain'd from the sight
Of the gross world, illumining
One only mansion with her light!
Unseen by man's disturbing eye,—
The flow'r that blooms beneath the sea,
Too deep for sunbeams, doth not lie
Hid in more chaste obscurity.
So, Hinda, have thy face and mind,
Like holy myst'ries, lain enshrined.
And oh, what transport for a lover
To lift the veil that shades them o'er!
Like those who, all at once, discover
In the lone deep some fairy shore,
Where mortal never trod before,
And sleep and wake in scented airs
No lip had ever breathed but theirs.

Beautiful are the maids that glide,
On summer-eves, through Yemen's‡ dales,
And bright the glancing looks they hide
Behind their litters' roseate veils;—
And brides, as delicate and fair
As the white jasmine flow'rs they wear,
Hath Yemen in her blissful clime,
Who, lull'd in cool kiosk or bow'r,§
Before their mirrors count the time,||
And grow still lovelier ev'ry hour.
But never yet hath bride or maid
In Araby's gay Harem smiled,
Whose boasted brightness would not fade
Before Al Hassan's blooming child

Light as the angel shapes that bless
An infant's dream, yet not the less

* "Their kings wear plumes of black herons' feathers upon the right side, as a badge of sovereignty."—*Hanway.*

† "The Fountain of Youth, by a Mahometan tradition, is situated in some dark region of the East."—*Richardson.*

‡ Arabia Felix.

§ "In the midst of the garden is the chiosk, that is, a large room commonly beautified with a fine fountain in the midst of it. It is raised nine or ten steps, and enclosed with gilded lattices, round which vines, jessamines, and honeysuckles, make a sort of green wall; large trees are planted round this place, which is the scene of their greatest pleasures."—*Lady M. W. Montagu.*

|| The women of the East are never without their looking-glasses. "In Barbary," says *Shaw*, "they are so fond of their looking-glasses, which they hang upon their breasts, that they will not lay them aside, even when after the drudgery of the day they are obliged to go two or three miles with a pitcher or a goat's skin to fetch water."—*Travels.*
In other parts of Asia they wear little looking-glasses on their thumbs. "Hence (and from the lotus being considered the emblem of beauty) is the meaning of the following mute intercourse of two lovers before their parents:—

"'He, with salute of def'rence due,
A lotus to his forehead press'd:
She raised her mirror to his view,
Then turn'd it inward to her breast.'"

Asiatic Miscellany, vol ii

Rich in all woman's loveliness;—
With eyes so pure, that from their ray
Dark Vice would turn abash'd away,
Blinded like serpents, when they gaze
Upon the em'rald's virgin blaze;—*
Yet fill'd with all youth's sweet desires,
Mingling the meek and vestal fires
Of other worlds with all the bliss,
The fond, weak tenderness of this:
A soul, too, more than half divine,
Where, through some shades of earthly feeling,
Religion's soften'd glories shine,
Like light through summer foliage stealing,
Shedding a glow of such mild hue,
So warm, and yet so shadowy too,
As makes the very darkness there
More beautiful than light elsewhere.

Such is the maid who, at this hour,
Hath risen from her restless sleep,
And sits alone in that high bow'r,
Watching the still and shining deep.
Ah! 'twas not thus,—with tearful eyes
And beating heart,—she used to gaze
On the magnificent earth and skies,
In her own land, in happier days.
Why looks she now so anxious down
Among those rocks, whose rugged frown
Blackens the mirror of the deep?
Whom waits she all this lonely night?
Too rough the rocks, too bold the steep,
For man to scale that turret's height!—

So deem'd at least her thoughtful sire,
When high, to catch the cool night-air,
After the day-beam's with'ring fire,†
He built her bow'r of freshness there,
And had it deck'd with costliest skill,
And fondly thought it safe as fair;—
Think, reverend dreamer! think so still,
Nor wake to learn what Love can dare;—
Love, all-defying Love, who sees
No charm in trophies won with ease;—
Whose rarest, dearest fruits of bliss
Are pluck'd on Danger's precipice!
Bolder than they, who dare not dive
For pearls, but when the sea's at rest,
Love, in the tempest most alive,
Hath ever held that pearl the best
He finds beneath the stormiest water.
Yes—Araby's unrivall'd daughter,
Though high that tow'r, that rock-way rude,
There's one who, but to kiss thy cheek,
Would climb th' untrodden solitude
Of Ararat's tremendous peak,‡
And think its steeps, though dark and dread,
Heav'n's pathways, if to thee they led!
Ev'n now thou seest the flashing spray,
That lights his oar's impatient way;
Ev'n now thou hear'st the sudden shock
Of his swift bark against the rock,
And stretchest down thy arms of snow,
As if to lift him from below!
Like her to whom, at dead of night,
The bridegroom, with his locks of light,§
Came, in the flush of love and pride,
And scaled the terrace of his bride;—
When, as she saw him rashly spring,
And midway up in danger cling,
She flung him down her long black hair,
Exclaiming, breathless, "There, love, there!"
And scarce did manlier nerve uphold
The hero Zal in that fond hour,
Than wings the youth who, fleet and bold,
Now climbs the rocks to Hinda's bower
See—light as up their granite steeps
The rock-goats of Arabia clamber,*
Fearless from crag to crag he leaps,
And now is in the maiden's chamber.

She loves—but knows not whom she loves,
Nor what his race, nor whence he came;—
Like one who meets, in Indian groves,
Some beauteous bird without a name,
Brought by the last ambrosial breeze,
From isles in th' undiscover'd seas,
To show his plumage for a day
To wond'ring eyes, and wing away!
Will *he* thus fly—her nameless lover?
Alla forbid! 'twas by a moon
As fair as this, while singing over
Some ditty to her soft Kanoon,†
Alone, at this same witching hour,
She first beheld his radiant eyes
Gleam through the lattice of the bow'r,
Where nightly now they mix their sighs;
And thought some spirit of the air
(For what could waft a mortal there?)
Was pausing on his moonlight way
To listen to her lonely lay!
This fancy ne'er hath left her mind:
And—though, when terror's swoon had pass'd,
She saw a youth, of mortal kind,
Before her in obeisance cast,—
Yet often since, when he hath spoken
Strange, awful words,—and gleams have broken
From his dark eyes, too bright to bear,
Oh! she hath fear'd her soul was giv'n
To some unhallow'd child of air,
Some erring Spirit cast from heav'n,
Like those angelic youths of old,
Who burn'd for maids of mortal mould,
Bewilder'd left the glorious skies,
And lost their heav'n for woman's eyes.
Fond girl! nor fiend nor angel he
Who woos thy young simplicity;
But one of earth's impassion'd sons,
As warm in love, as fierce in ire,
As the best heart whose current runs
Full of the Day God's living fire.

But quench'd to-night that ardour seems,
And pale his cheek, and sunk his brow;—
Never before, but in her dreams,
Had she beheld him pale as now:
And those were dreams of troubled sleep,
From which 'twas joy to wake and weep;
Visions, that will not be forgot,
But sadden every waking scene,
Like warning ghosts, that leave the spot
All wither'd, where they once have been.

"How sweetly," said the trembling maid,
Of her own gentle voice afraid,
So long had they in silence stood,
Looking upon that tranquil flood—
"How sweetly does the moon-beam smile
"To-night upon yon leafy isle!
"Oft, in my fancy's wanderings,
"I've wish'd that little isle had wings,
"And we, within its fairy bow'rs,

* "They say that if a snake or serpent fix his eyes on the lustre of those stones (emeralds) he immediately becomes blind."—*Ahmed ben Abdalaziz*, Treatise on Jewels.

† "At Gombaroon and the Isle of Ormus it is sometimes so hot, that the people are obliged to lie all day in the water."—*Marco Polo.*

‡ This mountain is generally supposed to be inaccessible. *Struy* says, "I can well assure the reader that their opinion is not true, who suppose this mount to be inaccessible." He adds, that "the lower part of the mountain is cloudy, misty, and dark, the middlemost part very cold, and like clouds of snow, but the upper regions perfectly calm."—It was on this mountain that the Ark was supposed to have rested after the Deluge, and part of it, they say, exists there still, which Struy thus gravely accounts for:—"Whereas none can remember that the air on the top of the hill did ever change or was subject either to wind or rain, which is presumed to be the reason that the Ark has endured so long without being rotten."—See *Carreri's* Travels, where the doctor laughs at this whole account of Mount Ararat.

§ In one of the books of the Shâh Nâmeh, when Zal, (a celebrated hero of Persia, remarkable for his white hair,) comes to the terrace of his mistress Rodahver at night, she lets down her long tresses to assist him in his ascent;—he, however, manages it in a less romantic way by fixing his crook in a projecting beam.—See *Champion's Ferdosi.*

* "On the lofty hills of Arabia Petræa are rock-goats."—*Niebuhr.*

† "Canun, espèce de psaltérion, avec des cordes de boyaux; les dames en touchent dans le sérail, avec des décailles armées de pointes de cooc."—*Toderini, translated by De Cournand.*

"Were wafted off to seas unknown,
"Where not a pulse should beat but ours,
"And we might live, love, die alone!
"Far from the cruel and the cold,—
"Where the bright eyes of angels only
"Should come around us, to behold
"A paradise so pure and lonely.
"Would this be world enough for thee?"—
Playful she turn'd, that he might see
The passing smile her cheek put on;
But when she mark'd how mournfully
His eyes met hers, that smile was gone;
And, bursting into heart-felt tears,
"Yes, yes," she cried, "my hourly fears,
"My dreams have boded all too right—
"We part—forever part—to-night!
"I knew, I knew it *could* not last—
"'Twas bright, 'twas heav'nly, but 'tis past!
"Oh! ever thus, from childhood's hour,
"I've seen my fondest hopes decay;
"I never loved a tree or flow'r,
"But 'twas the first to fade away.
"I never nursed a dear gazelle,
"To glad me with its soft black eye,
"But when it came to know me well,
"And love me, it was sure to die!
"Now too—the joy most like divine
"Of all I ever dreamt or knew,
"To see thee, hear thee, call thee mine,—
"Oh misery! must I lose *that* too?
"Yet go—on peril's brink we meet;—
"Those frightful rocks—that treach'rous sea—
"No, never come again—though sweet,
"Though heav'n, it may be death to thee.
"Farewell! and blessings on thy way,
"Where'er thou goest, beloved stranger!
"Better to sit and watch that ray,
"And think thee safe, though far away,
"Than have thee near me, and in danger!"

"Danger!—oh tempt me not to boast—"
The youth exclaim'd—"thou little know'st
"What he can brave, who, born and nursed
"In Danger's paths, has dared her worst;
"Upon whose ear the signal-word
"Of strife and death is hourly breaking;
"Who sleeps with head upon the sword
"His fever'd hand must grasp in waking.
"Danger!—"
"Say on—thou fear'st not then,
"And we may meet—oft meet again?"

"Oh! look not so—beneath the skies
"I now fear nothing but those eyes.
"If aught on earth could charm or force
"My spirit from its destined course,—
"If aught could make this soul forget
"The bond to which its seal is set,
"'Twould be those eyes; they, only they,
"Could melt that sacred seal away!
"But no—'tis fix'd—*my* awful doom
"Is fix'd—on this side of the tomb
"We meet no more;—why, why did Heav'n
"Mingle two souls that earth has riv'n,
"Has rent asunder wide as ours?
"Oh, Arab maid, as soon the Powers
"Of Light and Darkness may combine,
"As I be link'd with thee or thine!
"Thy Father————"
"Holy ALLA save
"His gray head from that lightning glance!
"Thou know'st him not—he loves the brave;
"Nor lives there under heaven's expanse
"One who would prize, would worship thee
"And thy bold spirit, more than he.
"Oft when, in childhood, I have play'd
"With the bright falchion by his side,
"I've heard him swear his lisping maid
"In time should be a warrior's bride.
"And still, whene'er at Harem hours,
"I take him cool sherbets and flow'rs,
"He tells me, when in playful mood,
"A hero shall my bridegroom be,
"Since maids are best in battle woo'd,
"And won with shouts of victory!
"Nay, turn not from me—thou alone
"Art form'd to make both hearts thy own.
"Go—join his sacred ranks—thou know'st
"Th' unholy strife these Persians wage:
"Good Heaven, that frown!—even now thou glow'st
"With more than mortal warrior's rage.
"Haste to the camp by morning's light,
"And when that sword is raised in fight,
"Oh still remember, Love and I
"Beneath its shadow trembling lie!
"One vict'ry o'er those Slaves of Fire,
"Those impious Ghebers, whom my sire
"Abhors——"
"Hold, hold—thy words are death—"
The stranger cried, as wild he flung
His mantle back, and show'd beneath
The Gheber belt that round him clung.—*
"Here, maiden, look—weep—blush to see
"All that thy sire abhors in me!
"Yes—*I* am of that impious race,
"Those Slaves of Fire who, morn and even,
"Hail their Creator's dwelling-place
"Among the living lights of heaven:†
"Yes—*I* am of that outcast few,
"To IRAN and to vengeance true,
"Who curse the hour your Arabs came
"To desolate our shrines of flame,
"And swear, before God's burning eye,
"To break our country's chains, or die!
"Thy bigot sire,—nay, tremble not,—
"He, who gave birth to those dear eyes,
"With me is sacred as the spot
"From which our fires of worship rise!
"But know—'twas he I sought that night,
"When, from my watch-boat on the sea,
"I caught this turret's glimm'ring light,
"And up the rude rocks desp'rately
"Rush'd to my prey—thou know'st the rest—
"I climb'd the gory vulture's nest,
"And found a trembling dove within;—
"Thine, thine the victory—thine the sin—
"If Love hath made one thought his own,
"That Vengeance claims first—last—alone!
"Oh! had we never, never met,
"Or could this heart even now forget
"How link'd, how bless'd we might have been,
"Had fate not frown'd so dark between!
"Hadst thou been born a Persian maid,
"In neighbouring valleys had we dwelt,
"Through the same fields in childhood play'd,
"At the same kindling altar knelt,—
"Then, then, while all those nameless ties,
"In which the charm of Country lies,
"Had round our hearts been hourly spun,
"Till IRAN's cause and thine were one;
"While in thy lute's awak'ning sigh
"I heard the voice of days gone by,
"And saw, in ev'ry smile of thine,
"Returning hours of glory shine;—

* They (the Ghebers) lay so much stress on their cushee or girdle, as not to dare to be an instant without it.—*Grose's* Voyage.—"Le jeune homme nia d'abord la chose; mais, ayant été dépouillé de sa robe, et la large ceinture qu'il portoit comme Ghèbre," &c. &c.—*D'Herbelot* art. Agduani. "Pour se distinguer des Idolâtres de l'Inde, les Guèbres se ceignent tous d un cordon de laine, ou de poil de chameau."—*Encyclopédie Francoise.*

D'Herbelot says this belt was generally of leather.

† "They suppose the Throne of the Almighty is seated in the sun, and hence their worship of that luminary."—*Hanway.* "As to fire, the Ghebers place the spring-head of it in that globe of fire, the Sun, by them called Mythras, or Mihir, to which they pay the highest reverence, in gratitude for the manifold benefits flowing from its ministerial omniscience. But they are so far from confounding the subordination of the Servant with the majesty of its Creator, that they not only attribute no sort of sense or reasoning to the sun or fire, in any of its operations, but consider it as a purely passive blind instrument, directed and governed by the immediate impression on it of the will of God; but they do not even give that luminary, all-glorious as it is, more than the second rank amongst his works, reserving the first for that stupendous production of Divine power, the mind of man."—*Grose.* The false charges brought against the religion of these people by their Mussulman tyrants is but one proof among many of the truth of this writer's remark, that "calumny is often added to oppression, if but for the sake of justifying it."

"While the wrong'd Spirit of our land
"Lived, look'd, and spoke her wrongs through thee,—
"God! who could then this sword withstand?
"Its very flash were victory!
"But now—estranged, divorced forever,
"Far as the grasp of Fate can sever;
"Our only ties what love has wove,—
"In faith, friends, country, sunder'd wide,
"And then, then only, true to love,
"When false to all that's dear beside!
"Thy father IRAN's deadliest foe—
"Thyself, perhaps, even now—but no—
"Hate never look'd so lovely yet!
"No—sacred to thy soul will be
"The land of him who could forget
"All but that bleeding land for thee.
"When other eyes shall see, unmoved,
"Her widows mourn, her warriors fall,
"Thou'lt think how well one Gheber loved,
"And for *his* sake thou'lt weep for all!
"But look ——"
With sudden start he turn'd,
And pointed to the distant wave,
Where lights, like charnel meteors, burn'd
Bluely, as o'er some seaman's grave:
And fiery darts, at intervals,*
Flew up all sparkling from the main,
As if each star that nightly falls,
Were shooting back to heaven again.

"My signal lights!—I must away—
"Both, both are ruin'd, if I stay.
"Farewell—sweet life! thou cling'st in vain—
"Now, Vengeance, I am thine again!"
Fiercely he broke away, nor stopp'd,
Nor look'd—but from the lattice dropp'd
Down 'mid the pointed crags beneath,
As if he fled from love to death.
While pale and mute young HINDA stood,
Nor moved, till in the silent flood
A momentary plunge below
Startled her from her trance of wo;
Shrieking she to the lattice flew,
"I come—I come—if in that tide
"Thou sleep'st to-night, I'll sleep there too,
"In death's cold wedlock, by thy side.
"Oh! I would ask no happier bed
"Than the chill wave my love lies under:—
"Sweeter to rest together dead,
"Far sweeter, than to live asunder!"
But no—their hour is not yet come—
Again she sees his pinnace fly,
Wafting him fleetly to his home,
Where'er that ill-starr'd home may lie;
And calm and smooth it seem'd to win
Its moonlight way before the wind,
As if it bore all peace within,
Nor left one breaking heart behind!

THE Princess, whose heart was sad enough already, could have wished that FERAMORZ had chosen a less melancholy story; as it is only to the happy that tears are a luxury. Her Ladies, however, were by no means sorry that love was once more the Poet's theme; for, whenever he spoke of love, they said, his voice was as sweet as if he had chewed the leaves of that enchanted tree, which grows over the tomb of the musician, Tan-Sein.†

Their road all the morning had lain through a very dreary country;—through valleys, covered with a low bushy jungle, where, in more than one place, the awful signal of the bamboo-staff*, with the white flag at its top, reminding the traveller that, in that very spot, the tiger had made some human creature his victim. It was, therefore, with much pleasure that they arrived at sunset in a safe and lovely glen, and encamped under one of those holy trees, whose smooth columns and spreading roofs seem to destine them for natural temples of religion. Beneath this spacious shade, some pious hands had erected a row of pillars ornamented with the most beautiful porcelain†, which now supplied the use of mirrors to the young maidens, as they adjusted their hair in descending from the palankeens. Here, while, as usual, the Princess sat listening anxiously, with FADLADEEN in one of his loftiest moods of criticism by her side, the young Poet, leaning against a branch of the tree, thus continued his story:

THE morn hath risen clear and calm,
And o'er the Green Sea‡ palely shines,
Revealing BAHREIN's§ groves of palm,
And lighting KISHMA's§ amber vines.
Fresh smell the shores of ARABY,
While breezes from the Indian Sea
Blow round SELAMA's§ sainted cape,
And curl the shining flood beneath,—
Whose waves are rich with many a grape,
And cocoa-nut and flow'ry wreath,
Which pious seamen, as they pass'd,
Had tow'rd that holy headland cast—
Oblations to the Genii there
For gentle skies and breezes fair!
The nightingale now bends her flight¶
From the high trees, where all the night
She sung so sweet, with none to listen;
And hides her from the morning star
Where thickets of pomegranate glisten
In the clear dawn,—bespangled o'er
With dew, whose night-drops would not stain
The best and brightest scimitar**
That ever youthful Sultan wore
On the first morning of his reign.

And see—the Sun himself!—on wings
Of glory up the East he springs.
Angel of Light! who from the time
Those heavens began their march sublime,
Hath first of all the starry choir
Trod in his Maker's steps of fire!
Where are the days, thou wondrous sphere,
When IRAN, like a sun-flow'r, turn'd
To meet that eye where'er it burn'd?—
When, from the banks of BENDEMEER
To the nut-groves of SAMARCAND,
Thy temples flamed o'er all the land?
Where are they? ask the shades of them
Who on CADESSIA's†† bloody plains,
Saw fierce invaders pluck the gem
From IRAN's broken diadem,
And bind her ancient faith in chains:—
Ask the poor exile, cast alone
On foreign shores, unloved, unknown,

---

* "The Mamelukes that were in the other boat, when it was dark, used to shoot up a sort of fiery arrows into the air, which in some measure resembled lightning or falling stars."—*Baumgarten.*

† "Within the enclosure which surrounds this monument (at Gualior) is a small tomb to the memory of Tan-Sein, a musician of incomparable skill, who flourished at the court of Akbar. The tomb is overshadowed by a tree, concerning which a superstitious notion prevails, that the chewing of its leaves will give an extraordinary melody to the voice."—*Narrative of a Journey from Agra to Ouzein, by W. Hunter, Esq.*

* "It is usual to place a small white triangular flag, fixed to a bamboo staff of ten or twelve feet long, at the place where a tiger has destroyed a man. It is common for the passengers also to throw each a stone or brick near the spot, so that in the course of a little time a pile equal to a good wagon-load is collected. The sight of these flags and piles of stones imparts a certain melancholy, not perhaps altogether void of apprehension."—*Oriental Field Sports*, vol. ii.

† The Ficus Indica is called the Pagod Tree and Tree of Councils; the first, from the idols placed under its shade; the second, because meetings were held under its cool branches. In some places it is believed to be the haunt of spectres, as the ancient spreading oaks of Wales have been of fairies; in others are erected beneath the shade pillars of stone, or posts, elegantly carved, and ornamented with the most beautiful porcelain to supply the use of mirrors."—*Pennant.*

‡ The Persian Gulf.—"To dive for pearls in the Green Sea, or Persian Gulf."—*Sir W. Jones.*

§ Islands in the Gulf.

‖ Or Selemeh, the genuine name of the headland at the entrance of the Gulf, commonly called Cape Musseldom. "The Indians, when they pass the promontory, throw cocoa-nuts, fruits, or flowers into the sea, to secure a propitious voyage."—*Morier.*

¶ "The nightingale sings from the pomegranate-groves in the day-time, and from the loftiest trees at night."—*Russel's Aleppo.*

** In speaking of the climate of Shiraz, Franklin says, "The dew is of such a pure nature, that if the brightest scimitar should be exposed to it all night, it would not receive the least rust."

†† The place where the Persians were finally defeated by the Arabs, and their ancient monarchy destroyed.

Beyond the Caspian's Iron Gates,*
  Or on the snowy Mossian mountains,
Far from his beauteous land of dates,
  Her jasmine bow'rs and sunny fountains:
Yet happier so than if he trod
His own beloved, but blighted, sod,
Beneath a despot stranger's nod!—
Oh, he would rather houseless roam
  Where Freedom and his God may lead,
Than be the sleekest slave at home
  That crouches to the conqu'ror's creed!

Is Iran's pride then gone forever,
  Quench'd with the flame in Mithra's caves!—
No—she has sons, that never—never—
  Will stoop to be the Moslem's slaves,
  While heav'n has light or earth has graves;—
Spirits of fire, that brood not long,
But flash resentment back for wrong;
And hearts where, slow but deep, the seeds
Of vengeance ripen into deeds,
Till, in some treach'rous hour of calm,
They burst, like Zeilan's giant palm,†
Whose buds fly open with a sound
That shakes the pigmy forests round!
Yes, Emir! he, who scaled that tow'r,
  And, had he reach'd thy slumb'ring breast,
Had taught thee, in a Gheber's pow'r
  How safe ev'n tyrant heads may rest—
Is one of many, brave as he,
Who loathe thy haughty race and thee;
Who, though they know the strife is vain,
Who, though they know the riven chain
Snaps but to enter in the heart
Of him who rends its links apart,
Yet dare the issue,—blest to be
Ev'n for one bleeding moment free,
And die in pangs of liberty!
Thou know'st them well—'tis some moons since
  Thy turban'd troops and blood-red flags,
Thou satrap of a bigot Prince,
  Have swarm'd among these Green Sea crags;
Yet here, ev'n here, a sacred band
Ay, in the portal of that land
Thou, Arab, dar'st to call thy own,
Their spears across thy path have thrown;
Here—ere the winds half wing'd thee o'er—
Rebellion braved thee from the shore.

Rebellion! foul, dishonouring word,
  Whose wrongful blight so oft has stain'd
The holiest cause that tongue or sword
  Of mortal ever lost or gain'd.
How many a spirit, born to bless,
  Hath sunk beneath that with'ring name,
Whom but a day's, an hour's success
  Had wafted to eternal fame!
As exhalations, when they burst
From the warm earth, if chill'd at first,
If check'd in soaring from the plain,
Darken to fogs and sink again;—
But, if they once triumphant spread
Their wings above the mountain-head,
Become enthroned in upper air,
And turn to sun-bright glories there!

And who is he, that wields the might
  Of Freedom on the Green Sea brink,
Before whose sabre's dazzling light‡
  The eyes of Yemen's warriors wink?
Who comes, embower'd in the spears
Of Kerman's hardy mountaineers?
Those mountaineers that truest, last,

* Derbend.—"Les Turcs appelent cette ville Demir Capi, Porte de Fer; ce sont les Caspiæ Portæ des anciens.—*D'Herbelot.*

† The Talpot or Talipot tree. "This beautiful palm-tree, which grows in the heart of the forests, may be classed among the loftiest trees, and becomes still higher when on the point of bursting forth from its leafy summit. The sheath which then envelops the flower is very large, and, when it bursts, makes an explosion like the report of a cannon. —*Thunberg.*

‡ "When the bright cimitars make the eyes of our heroes wink." —*The Moallakat, Poem of Amru.*

  Cling to their country's ancient rites,
As if that God, whose eyelids cast
  Their closing gleam on Iran's heights,
Among her snowy mountains threw
The last light of his worship too!

'Tis Hafed—name of fear, whose sound
  Chills like the mutt'ring of a charm!—
Shout but that awful name around,
  And palsy shakes the manliest arm.
'Tis Hafed, most accursed and dire
(So rank'd by Moslem hate and ire)
Of all the rebel Sons of Fire!
Of whose malign, tremendous pow'r
The Arabs, at their mid-watch hour,
Such tales of fearful wonder tell,
That each affrighted sentinel
Pulls down his cowl upon his eyes,
Lest Hafed in the midst should rise!
A man, they say, of monstrous birth,
A mingled race of flame and earth,
Sprung from those old, enchanted kings,*
  Who in their fiery helms, of yore,
A feather from the mystic wings
  Of the Simoorgh resistless wore;
And gifted by the Fiends of Fire,
Who groan'd to see their shrines expire,
With charms that, all in vain withstood,
Would drown the Koran's light in blood!

Such were the tales, that won belief,
  And such the colouring Fancy gave
To a young, warm, and dauntless Chief,—
  One who, no more than mortal brave,
Fought for the land his soul adored,
  For happy homes and altars free,
His only talisman, the sword,
  His only spell-word, Liberty!
One of that ancient hero line,
Along whose glorious current shine
Names, that have sanctified their blood;
As Lebanon's small mountain-flood
Is render'd holy by the ranks
Of sainted cedars on its banks.†
'Twas not for him to crouch the knee
Tamely to Moslem tyranny;
'Twas not for him, whose soul was cast
In the bright mould of ages past,
Whose melancholy spirit, fed
With all the glories of the dead,
Though framed for Iran's happiest years,
Was born among her chains and tears!—
'Twas not for him to swell the crowd
Of slavish heads, that shrinking bow'd
Before the Moslem, as he pass'd,
Like shrubs beneath the poison-blast—
No—far he fled—indignant fled
  The pageant of his country's shame;
While every tear her children shed
  Fell on his soul like drops of flame;
And, as a lover hails the dawn
  Of a first smile, so welcomed he
The sparkle of the first sword drawn
  For vengeance and for liberty!

But vain was valour—vain the flower
Of Kerman, in that deathful hour,
Against Al Hassan's whelming power,—
In vain they met him, helm to helm,
Upon the threshold of that realm
He came in bigot pomp to sway,

* Tahmuras, and other ancient Kings of Persia; whose adventures in Fairy-land among the Peris and Dives may be found in Richardson's curious Dissertation. The griffin Simoorgh, they say, took some feathers from her breast for Tahmuras, with which he adorned his helmet, and transmitted them afterwards to his descendants.

† This rivulet, says Dandini, is called the Holy River from the "cedar-saints" among which it rises.

In the *Lettres Edifiantes*, there is a different cause assigned for its name of Holy. "In these are deep caverns, which formerly served as so many cells for a great number of recluses, who had chosen these retreats as the only witnesses upon earth of the severity of their penances. The tears of these pious penitents gave the river of which we have just treated the name of the Holy River."—See *Châteaubriand's Beauties of Christianity*

And with their corpses block'd his way—
In vain—for every lance they raised,
Thousands around the conqueror blazed;
For every arm that lined their shore,
Myriads of slaves were wafted o'er,—
A bloody, bold, and countless crowd,
Before whose swarm as fast they bow'd
As dates beneath the locust cloud.

There stood—but one short league away
From old HARMOZIA's sultry bay—
A rocky mountain, o'er the Sea
Of OMAN beetling awfully;*
A last and solitary link
Of those stupendous chains that reach
From the broad Caspian's reedy brink
Down winding to the Green Sea beach.
Around its base the bare rocks stood,
Like naked giants, in the flood,
As if to guard the Gulf across;
While, on its peak, that braved the sky,
A ruin'd Temple tower'd so high
That oft the sleeping albatross†
Struck the wild ruins with her wing,
And from her cloud-rock'd slumbering
Started—to find man's dwelling there
In her own silent fields of air!
Beneath, terrific caverns gave
Dark welcome to each stormy wave
That dash'd, like midnight revellers, in;—
And such the strange, mysterious din
At times throughout those caverns roll'd,—
And such the fearful wonders told
Of restless sprites imprison'd there,
That bold were Moslem, who would dare,
At twilight hour, to steer his skiff
Beneath the Gheber's lonely cliff.‡

On the land side, those tow'rs sublime,
That seem'd above the grasp of Time,
Were sever'd from the haunts of men
By a wide, deep, and wizard glen,
So fathomless, so full of gloom,
No eye could pierce the void between:
It seem'd a place where Gholes might come
With their foul banquets from the tomb,
And in its caverns feed unseen.
Like distant thunder, from below,
The sound of many torrents came,
Too deep for eye or ear to know
If 'twere the sea's imprison'd flow,
Or floods of ever-restless flame.
For, each ravine, each rocky spire
Of that vast mountain stood on fire;§
And, though forever past the days
When God was worshipp'd in the blaze
That from its lofty altar shone,—
Though fled the priests, the vot'ries gone,
Still did the mighty flame burn on,‖
Through chance and change, through good and ill,
Like its own God's eternal will,
Deep, constant, bright, unquenchable!

Thither the vanquish'd HAFED led
His little army's last remains;—
"Welcome, terrific glen!" he said,
"Thy gloom, that Eblis' self might dread,
"Is Heav'n to him who flies from chains!"
O'er a dark, narrow bridge-way, known
To him and to his Chiefs alone,
They cross'd the chasm and gain'd the tow'rs,—
"This home," he cried, "at least is ours;—
"Here we may bleed, unmock'd by hymns
"Of Moslem triumph o'er our head;
"Here we may fall, nor leave our limbs
"To quiver to the Moslem's tread.
"Stretch'd on this rock, while vultures' beaks
"Are whetted on our yet warm cheeks,
"Here—happy that no tyrant's eye
"Gloats on our torments—we may die!"—

'Twas night when to those towers they came
And gloomily the fitful flame,
That from the ruin'd altar broke,
Glared on his features, as he spoke:—
"'Tis o'er—what men could do, we've done—
"If IRAN *will* look tamely on,
"And see her priests, her warriors driven
"Before a sensual bigot's nod,
"A wretch who shrines his lust in heav'n,
"And makes a pander of his God;
"If her proud sons, her high-born souls,
"Men, in whose veins—oh last disgrace!
"The blood of ZAL and RUSTAM* rolls,—
"If they *will* court this upstart race,
"And turn from MITHRA's ancient ray,
"To kneel at shrines of yesterday;
"If they *will* crouch to IRAN's foes,
"Why, let them—till the land's despair
"Cries out to Heav'n, and bondage grows
"Too vile for ev'n the vile to bear!
"Till shame at last, long hidden, burns
"Their inmost core, and conscience turns
"Each coward tear the slave lets fall
"Back on his heart in drops of gall.
"But *here*, at least, are arms unchain'd,
"And souls that thraldom never stain'd;—
"This spot, at least, no foot of slave
"Or satrap ever yet profaned;
"And though but few—though fast the wave
"Of life is ebbing from our veins,
"Enough for vengeance still remains.
"As panthers, after set of sun,
"Rush from the roots of LEBANON
"Across the dark-sea robber's way,†
"We'll bound upon our startled prey:
"And when some hearts that proudest swell
"Have felt our falchion's last farewell;
"When Hope's expiring throb is o'er,
"And ev'n Despair can prompt no more,
"This spot shall be the sacred grave
"Of the last few who, vainly brave,
"Die for the land they cannot save!"

His chiefs stood round—each shining blade
Upon the broken altar laid—
And though so wild and desolate
Those courts, where once the Mighty sate
Nor longer on those mould'ring tow'rs
Was seen the feast of fruits and flow'rs,
With which of old the Magi fed
The wand'ring Spirits of their dead;‡
Though neither priest nor rites were there,
Nor charmed leaf of pure pomegranate;§

* This mountain is my own creation, as the "stupendous chain," of which I suppose it a link, does not extend quite so far as the shores of the Persian Gulf. "This long and lofty range of mountains formerly divided Media from Assyria, and now forms the boundary of the Persian and Turkish empires. It runs parallel with the river Tigris and Persian Gulf, and almost disappearing in the vicinity of Gomberoon (Harmozia) seems once more to rise in the southern districts of Kerman, and following an easterly course through the centre of Meckraun and Balouchistan, is entirely lost in the deserts of Sinde."—*Kinnier's* Persian Empire.

† These birds sleep in the air. They are most common about the Cape of Good Hope.

‡ "There is an extraordinary hill in this neighbourhood called Kohé Gubr, or the Guebre's mountain. It rises in the form of a lofty cupola, and on the summit of it, they say, are the remains of an Atush Kudu or Fire Temple. It is superstitiously held to be the residence of Deeves or Sprites, and many marvellous stories are recounted of the injury and witchcraft suffered by those who essayed in former days to ascend or explore it."—*Pottinger's* Beloochistan.

§ The Ghebers generally built their temples over subterraneous fires.

‖ "At the city of Yezd, in Persia, which is distinguished by the appellation of the Darûb Abadut, or Seat of Religion, the Guebres are permitted to have an Atush Kudu or Fire Temple (which, they assert, has had the sacred fire in it since the days of Zoroaster) in their own compartment of the city; but for this indulgence they are indebted to the avarice, not the tolerance of the Persian government, which taxes them at twenty-five rupees each man."—*Pottinger's* Beloochistan.

* Ancient heroes of Persia. Among the Guebres there are some who boast their descent from Rustam."—*Stephen's* Persia.

† See Russel's account of a panther's attacking travellers in the night on the sea-shore about the roots of Lebanon.

‡ "Among other ceremonies, the Magi used to place upon the tops of high towers various kinds of rich viands, upon which it was supposed the Peris and the spirits of their departed heroes regaled themselves."—*Richardson.*

§ In the ceremonies of the Ghebers round their Fire, as described by Lord, "the Daroo," he says, "giveth them water to drink, and a pomegranate leaf to chew in the mouth, to cleanse them from inward uncleanness."

Nor hymn, nor censer's fragrant air,
  Nor symbol of their worshipp'd planet;*
Yet the same God that heard their sires
Heard *them*, while on that altar's fires
They swore† the latest, holiest deed
Of the few hearts still left to bleed,
Should be, in IRAN's injured name,
To die upon that Mount of Flame—
The last of all her patriot line,
Before her last untrampled Shrine.

Brave, suff'ring souls! they little knew
How many a tear their injuries drew
From one meek maid, one gentle foe,
Whom love first touch'd with others' wo—
Whose life, as free from thought as sin,
Slept like a lake, till Love threw in
His talisman, and woke the tide,
And spread its trembling circles wide.
Once, EMIR! thy unheeding child,
'Mid all this havoc, bloom'd and smiled—
Tranquil as on some battle plain
  The Persian lily shines and tow'rs,‡
Before the combat's redd'ning stain
  Hath fall'n upon her golden flow'rs.
Light-hearted maid, unawed, unmoved,
While Heav'n but spared the sire she loved,
Once at thy evening tales of blood
Unlist'ning and aloof she stood—
And oft, when thou hast paced along
  Thy Harem halls with furious heat,
Hast thou not cursed her cheerful song,
  That came across thee, calm and sweet,
Like lutes of angels, touch'd so near
Hell's confines, that the damn'd can hear!

Far other feelings Love hath brought—
  Her soul all flame, her brow all sadness,
She now has but the one dear thought,
  And thinks that o'er, almost to madness!
Oft doth her sinking heart recall
His words—"for *my* sake weep for all;"
And bitterly, as day on day
  Of rebel carnage fast succeeds,
She weeps a lover snatch'd away
  In ev'ry Gheber wretch that bleeds.
There's not a sabre meets her eye,
  But with his life-blood seems to swim;
There's not an arrow wings the sky,
  But fancy turns its point to him.
No more she brings with footstep light
AL HASSAN's falchion for the fight;
And—had he look'd with clearer sight,
Had not the mists, that ever rise
From a foul spirit, dimm'd his eyes—
He would have mark'd her shudd'ring frame,
When from the field of blood he came,
The falt'ring speech—the look estranged—
Voice, step, and life, and beauty changed—
He would have mark'd all this, and known
Such change is wrought by Love alone!

Ah! not the Love, that should have bless'd
So young, so innocent a breast;
Not the pure, open, prosp'rous Love,
That, pledged on earth and seal'd above,
Grows in the world's approving eyes,
  In friendship's smile and home's caress,
Collecting all the heart's sweet ties
  Into one knot of happiness!
No, HINDA, no—thy fatal flame
Is nursed in silence, sorrow, shame;—
  A passion, without hope or pleasure,
In thy soul's darkness buried deep,
  It lies like some ill-gotten treasure,—
Some idol, without shrine or name,
O'er which its pale-eyed votaries keep
Unholy watch, while others sleep.

Seven nights have darken'd OMAN's sea,
  Since last, beneath the moonlight ray,
She saw his light oar rapidly
  Hurry her Gheber's bark away,—
And still she goes, at midnight hour,
To weep alone in that high bow'r,
And watch, and look along the deep
For him whose smiles first made her weep,
But watching, weeping, all was vain,
She never saw his bark again.
The owlet's solitary cry,
The night-hawk, flitting darkly by,
  And oft the hateful carrion bird,
Heavily flapping his clogg'd wing,
Which reek'd with that day's banqueting—
  Was all she saw, was all she heard.

'Tis the eighth morn—AL HASSAN's brow
  Is brighten'd with unusual joy—
What mighty mischief glads him now,
  Who never smiles but to destroy?
The sparkle upon HERKEND's Sea,
When toss'd at midnight furiously,*
Tells not of wreck and ruin nigh,
More surely than that smiling eye!
"Up, daughter, up—the KERNA's† breath
"Has blown a blast would waken death,
"And yet thou sleep'st—up, child, and see
"This blessed day for Heaven and me,
"A day more rich in Pagan blood
"Than ever flash'd o'er OMAN's flood.
"Before another dawn shall shine,
"His head—heart—limbs—will all be mine,
"This very night his blood shall steep
"These hands all over ere I sleep!"

"*His* blood!" she faintly scream'd—her mind
Still singling *one* from all mankind—
"Yes—spite of his ravines and tow'rs,
"HAFED, my child, this night is ours.
"Thanks to all conqu'ring treachery,
  "Without whose aid the links accurst,
"That bind these impious slaves, would be
  "Too strong for ALLA's self to burst!
"That rebel fiend, whose blade has spread
"My path with piles of Moslem dead,
"Whose baffling spells had almost driv'n
"Back from their course the Swords of Heav'n,
"This night, with all his band, shall know,
"How deep an Arab's steel can go,
"When God and Vengeance speed the blow.
"And—Prophet! by that holy wreath
"Thou wor'st on OHOD's field of death,‡
"I swear, for ev'ry sob that parts
"In anguish from these heathen hearts,
"A gem from PERSIA's plunder'd mines
"Shall glitter on thy Shrine of Shrines.
"But, ha!—she sinks—that look so wild—
"Those vivid lips—my child, my child,
"This life of blood befits not thee,
"And thou must back to ARABY.
  "Ne'er had I risk'd thy timid sex
"In scenes that man himself might dread,
"Had I not hoped our ev'ry tread
  "Would be on prostrate Persian necks—
"Curst race, they offer swords instead!

* "Early in the morning they (the Parsees or Ghebers at Oulam) go in crowds to pay their devotions to the Sun, to whom upon all the altars there are spheres consecrated, made by magic, resembling the circles of the sun, and when the sun rises, these orbs seem to be inflamed, and to turn round with a great noise. They have every one a censer in their hands, and offer incense to the sun."—*Rabbi Benjamin*.

† "Nul d'entre eux oseroit se parjurer, quand il a pris à témoin cet élément terrible et vengeur."—*Encyclop. Francoise*.

‡ "A vivid verdure succeeds the autumnal rains, and the ploughed fields are covered with a Persian lily, of a resplendent yellow colour."—*Russel's* Aleppo

* "It is observed, with respect to the Sea of Herkend, that when it is tossed by tempestuous winds it sparkles like fire."—*Travels of Two Mohammedans*.

† A kind of trumpet;—it "was that used by Tamerlane, the sound of which is described as uncommonly dreadful, and so loud as to be heard at the distance of several miles."—*Richardson*.

‡ "Mohammed had two helmets, an interior and exterior one; the latter of which, called Al Mawashah, the fillet, wreath, or wreathed garland, he wore at the battle of Ohod."—*Universal History*.

"But cheer thee, maid,—the wind that now
"Is blowing o'er thy feverish brow,
"To-day shall waft thee from the shore;
"And e'er a drop of this night's gore
"Have time to chill in yonder tow'rs,
"Thou'lt see thy own sweet Arab bow'rs."

His bloody boast was all too true;
There lurk'd one wretch among the few
Whom HAFED's eagle eye could count
Around him on that Fiery Mount,—
One miscreant, who for gold betray'd
The pathway through the valley's shade
To those high tow'rs, where Freedom stood
In her last hold of flame and blood.
Left on the field that dreadful night,
When, sallying from their Sacred height,
The Ghebers fought hope's farewell fight,
He lay—but died not with the brave;
That sun, which should have gilt his grave,
Saw him a traitor and a slave;—
And, while the few, who thence return'd
To their high rocky fortress, mourn'd
For him among the matchless dead
They left behind on glory's bed,
He lived, and, in the face of morn,
Laugh'd them and Faith and Heav'n to scorn.

Oh for a tongue to curse the slave,
  Whose treason, like a deadly blight,
Comes o'er the councils of the brave,
  And blast's them in their hour of might!
May Life's unblessed cup for him
Be drugg'd with treach'ries to the brim,—
With hopes that but allure to fly,
  With joys, that vanish while he sips,
Like Dead Sea fruits that tempt the eye,
  But turn to ashes on the lips!*
His country's curse, his children's shame,
Outcast of virtue, peace, and fame,
May he, at last, with lips of flame
On the parch'd desert thirsting die,—
While lakes, that shone in mockery nigh,†
Are fading off, untouch'd, untasted,
Like the once glorious hopes he blasted!
And, when from earth his spirit flies,
  Just Prophet, let the damn'd-one dwell
Full in the sight of Paradise,
  Beholding heav'n, and feeling hell!

LALLA ROOKH had, the night before, been visited by a dream which, in spite of the impending fate of poor HAFED, made her heart more than usually cheerful during the morning, and gave her cheeks all the freshened animation of a flower that the Bid-musk has just passed over.‡ She fancied that she was sailing on that Eastern Ocean, where the sea-gipsies, who live forever on the water,§ enjoy a perpetual summer in wandering from isle to isle, when she saw a small gilded bark approaching her. It was like one of those boats which the Maldivian islanders send adrift, at the mercy of winds and waves, loaded with perfumes, flowers, and odoriferous wood, as an offering to the Spirit whom they call King of the Sea. At first, this little bark appeared to be empty, but, on coming nearer——

She had proceeded thus far in relating the dream to her Ladies, when FERAMORZ appeared at the door of the pavilion. In his presence, of course, every thing else was forgotten, and the continuance of the story was instantly requested by all. Fresh wood of aloes was set to burn in the cassolets;—the violet sherbets* were hastily handed round, and after a short prelude on his lute, in the pathetic measure of Nava,† which is always used to express the lamentations of absent lovers, the Poet thus continued:—

THE day is low'ring—stilly black
Sleeps the grim wave, while heav'n's rack,
Dispersed and wild, 'twixt earth and sky
Hangs like a shatter'd canopy.
There's not a cloud in that blue plain
  But tells of storm to come or past;—
Here, flying loosely as the mane
  Of a young war-horse in the blast;—
There, roll'd in masses dark and swelling,
As proud to be the thunder's dwelling!
While some, already burst and riv'n,
Seem melting down the verge of heav'n;
As though the infant storm had rent
  The mighty womb that gave him birth,
And, having swept the firmament,
  Was now in fierce career for earth.

On earth 'twas yet all calm around,
A pulseless silence, dread, profound,
More awful than the tempest's sound.
The diver steer'd for ORMUS' bowers,
And moor'd his skiff till calmer hours;
The sea-birds, with portentous screech,
Flew fast to land;—upon the beach
The pilot oft had paused, with glance
Turn'd upward to that wild expanse;—
And all was boding, drear, and dark
As her own soul, when HINDA's bark
Went slowly from the Persian shore.—
No music timed her parting oar,‡
Nor friends upon the less'ning strand
Linger'd, to wave the unseen hand,
Or speak the farewell, heard no more.—
But lone, unheeded, from the bay
The vessel takes its mournful way,
Like some ill-destined bark that steers
In silence through the Gate of Tears.§

And where was stern AL HASSAN then?
Could not that saintly scourge of men

---

* "They say that there are apple-trees upon the sides of this sea, which bear very lovely fruit, but within are all full of ashes."—*Thevenot.* The same is asserted of the oranges there; vide *Witman's* Travels in Asiatic Turkey.

"The Asphalt Lake, known by the name of the Dead Sea, is very remarkable on account of the considerable proportion of salt which it contains. In this respect it surpasses every other known water on the surface of the earth. This great proportion of bitter tasted salts is the reason why neither animal nor plant can live in this water."—*Klaproth's* Chemical Analysis of the Water of the Dead Sea, Annals of Philosophy, January, 1813. *Hasselquist*, however, doubts the truth of this last assertion, as there are shell-fish to be found in the lake.

Lord Byron has a similar allusion to the fruits of the Dead Sea, in that wonderful display of genius, his third Canto of Childe Harold—magnificent beyond any thing, perhaps, that even *he* has ever written.

† "The Suhrab or Water of the Desert is said to be caused by the rarefaction of the atmosphere from extreme heat; and, which augments the delusion, it is most frequent in hollows, where water might be expected to lodge. I have seen bushes and trees reflected in it with as much accuracy as though it had been the face of a clear and still lake."—*Pottinger.*

"As to the unbelievers, their works are like a vapour in a plain, which the thirsty traveller thinketh to be water, until when he cometh thereto he findeth it to be nothing."—*Koran*, chap. 24.

‡ "A wind which prevails in February, called Bidmusk, from a small and odoriferous flower of that name."—"The wind which blows these flowers commonly lasts till the end of the month."—*Le Bruyn.*

§ "The Biajús are of two races: the one is settled on Borneo, and are a rude but warlike and industrious nation, who reckon themselves the original possessors of the island of Borneo. The other is a species of sea-gipsies or itinerant fishermen, who live in small covered boats, and enjoy a perpetual summer on the eastern ocean, shifting to leeward from island to island, with the variations of the monsoon. In some of their customs this singular race resemble the natives of the Maldivia islands. The Maldivians annually launch a small bark, loaded with perfumes, gums, flowers, and odoriferous wood, and turn it adrift at the mercy of wind and waves, as an offering to the *Spirit of the Winds;* and sometimes similar offerings are made to the spirit whom they term *the King of the Sea.* In like manner the Biajús perform their offering to the god of evil, launching a small bark, loaded with all the sins and misfortunes of the nation, which are imagined to fall on the unhappy crew that may be so unlucky as first to meet with it."—*Dr. Leyden* on the Language and Literature of the Indo-Chinese Nations.

* "The sweet-scented violet is one of the plants most esteemed, particularly for its great use in Sorbet, which they make of violet sugar."—*Hasselquist.*

"The Sherbet they most esteem, and which is drunk by the Grand Signor himself, is made of violets and sugar."—*Tavernier.*

† "Last of all she took a guitar, and sung a pathetic air in the measure called Nava, which is always used to express the lamentations of absent lovers."—*Persian Tales.*

‡ "The Easterns used to set out on their longer voyages with music."—*Harmer.*

§ "The Gate of Tears, the straits or passage into the Red Sea, commonly called Babelmandel. It received this name from the old Arabians, on account of the danger of the navigation, and the number of shipwrecks by which it was distinguished; which induced them to consider as dead, and to wear mourning for all who had the boldness to hazard the passage through it into the Ethiopic ocean."—*Richardson.*

From bloodshed and devotion spare
One minute for a farewell there?
No—close within, in changeful fits
Of cursing and of pray'r, he sits
In savage loneliness to brood
Upon the coming night of blood,—
With that keen, second-scent of death,
By which the vulture snuffs his food
In the still warm and living breath!*
While o'er the wave his weeping daughter
Is wafted from these scenes of slaughter,—
As a young bird of BABYLON,†
Let loose to tell of vict'ry won,
Flies home, with wing, ah! not unstain'd
By the red hands that held her chain'd.

And does the long-left home she seeks
Light up no gladness on her cheeks?
The flow'rs she nursed—the well-known groves,
Where oft in dreams her spirit roves—
Once more to see her dear gazelles
Come bounding with their silver bells;
Her birds' new plumage to behold,
And the gay, gleaming fishes count,
She left, all filleted with gold,
Shooting around their jasper fount;‡
Her little garden mosque to see,
And once again, at evening hour,
To tell her ruby rosary§
In her own sweet acacia bow'r.—
Can these delights, that wait her now,
Call up no sunshine on her brow?
No,—silent, from her train apart,—
As even now she felt at heart
The chill of her approaching doom,—
She sits, all lovely in her gloom
As a pale Angel of the Grave;
And o'er the wide, tempestuous wave,
Looks, with a shudder, to those tow'rs,
Where, in a few short awful hours,
Blood, blood, in streaming tides shall run,
Foul incense for to-morrow's sun!
"Where art thou, glorious stranger! thou,
"So loved, so lost, where art thou now?
"Foe—Gheber—infidel—whate'er
"Th' unhallow'd name thou'rt doom'd to bear,
"Still glorious—still to this fond heart
"Dear as its blood, whate'er thou art!
"Yes—ALLA, dreadful ALLA! yes—
"If there be wrong, be crime in this,
"Let the black waves that round us roll,
"Whelm me this instant, ere my soul,
"Forgetting faith—home—father—all—
"Before its earthly idol fall,
"Nor worship ev'n Thyself above him—
"For, oh, so wildly do I love him,
"Thy Paradise itself were dim
"And joyless, if not shared with him!"
Her hands were clasp'd—her eyes upturn'd,
Dropping their tears like moonlight rain;
And, though her lip, fond raver! burn'd
With words of passion, bold, profane,
Yet was there light around her brow,
A holiness in those dark eyes,
Which show'd—though wand'ring earthward now—
Her spirit's home was in the skies.
Yes—for a spirit pure as hers
Is always pure, ev'n while it errs;
As sunshine, broken in the rill,
Though turn'd astray, is sunshine still!
So wholly had her mind forgot
All thoughts but one, she heeded not

* "I have been told that whensoever an animal falls down dead, one or more vultures, unseen before, instantly appear."—*Pennant.*

† "They fasten some writing to the wings of a Bagdat or Babylonian pigeon."—*Travels of certain Englishmen.*

‡ "The Empress of Jehan-Guire used to divert herself with feeding tame fish in her canals, some of which were many years afterwards known by fillets of gold, which she caused to be put around them."—*Harris.*

§ "Le Tespih, qui est un chapelet, composé de 99 petites boules d'agathe, de jaspe, d'ambre, de corail, ou d'autre matière précieuse. J'en ai vu un superbe au Seigneur Jerpos; il étoit de belles et grosses perles parfaites et égales, estimé trente mille piasters."—*Toderini.*

The rising storm—the wave that cast
A moment's midnight, as it pass'd—
Nor heard the frequent shout, the tread
Of gath'ring tumult o'er her head—
Clash'd swords and tongues that seem'd to vie
With the rude riot of the sky.
But, hark!—that war-whoop on the deck—
That crash, as if each engine there,
Mast, sails, and all, were gone to wreck,
'Mid yells and stampings of despair!
Merciful Heaven! what *can* it be?
'Tis not the storm, though fearfully
The ship has shudder'd as she rode
O'er mountain-waves—"Forgive me, God.
"Forgive me"—shriek'd the maid, and knelt
Trembling all over—for she felt
As if her judgment-hour was near;
While crouching round, half dead with fear,
Her handmaids clung, nor breathed, nor stirr'd.
When, hark!—a second crash—a third—
And now, as if a bolt of thunder
Had riven the labouring planks asunder,
The deck falls in—what horrors then!
Blood, waves, and tackle, swords and men
Come mix'd together through the chasm,—
Some wretches in their dying spasm
Still fighting on—and some that call
"For GOD and IRAN!" as they fall!

Whose was the hand that turn'd away
The perils of th' infuriate fray,
And snatch'd her breathless from beneath
This wilderment of wreck and death?
She knew not—for a faintness came
Chill o'er her, and her sinking frame
Amid the ruins of that hour
Lay, like a pale and scorched flow'r
Beneath the red volcano's show'r.
But, oh! the sights and sounds of dread
That shock'd her ere her senses fled!
The yawning deck—the crowd that strove
Upon the tott'ring planks above—
The sail, whose fragments, shivering o'er
The strugglers' heads, all dash'd with gore,
Flutter'd like bloody flags—the clash
Of sabres, and the lightning's flash
Upon their blades, high toss'd about
Like meteor brands*—as if throughout
The elements one fury ran,
One gen'ral rage, that left a doubt
Which was the fiercer, Heaven or man!

Once too—but no—it could not be—
'Twas fancy all—yet once she thought,
While yet her fading eyes could see,
High on the ruin'd deck she caught
A glimpse of that unearthly form,
That glory of her soul,—even then,
Amid the whirl of wreck and storm,
Shining above his fellow-men,
As, on some black and troublous night,
The Star of EGYPT,† whose proud light
Never hath beam'd on those who rest
In the White Islands of the West,‡
Burns through the storm with looks of flame
That put Heaven's cloudier eyes to shame.
But no—'twas but the minute's dream—
A fantasy—and ere the scream
Had half-way pass'd her pallid lips,
A death-like swoon, a chill eclipse
Of soul and sense its darkness spread
Around her, and she sunk, as dead

How calm, how beautiful comes on
The stilly hour, when storms are gone;
When warring winds have died away,
And clouds, beneath the glancing ray,
Melt off, and leave the land and sea

* The meteors that Pliny calls "faces."

† "The brilliant Canopus, unseen in European climates."—*Brown.*

‡ See Wilford's learned Essays on the Sacred Isles in the West.

Sleeping in bright tranquillity,—
Fresh as if Day again were born,
Again upon the lap of Morn!—
When the light blossoms, rudely torn,
And scatter'd at the whirlwind's will,
Hang floating in the pure air still,
Filling it all with precious balm,
In gratitude for this sweet calm;—
And every drop the thunder-show'rs
Have left upon the grass and flow'rs
Sparkles, as 'twere that lightning-gem*
Whose liquid flame is born of them!
When, 'stead of one unchanging breeze,
  There blow a thousand gentle airs,
  And each a diff'rent perfume bears,—
As if the loveliest plants and trees
Had vassal breezes of their own
To watch and wait on them alone,
And waft no other breath than theirs:
When the blue waters rise and fall,
In sleepy sunshine mantling all;
And ev'n that swell the tempest leaves
Is like the full and silent heaves
Of lovers' hearts, when newly blest,
Too newly to be quite at rest.

Such was the golden hour that broke
Upon the world, when Hinda woke
From her long trance, and heard around
No motion but the water's sound
Rippling against the vessel's side,
As slow it mounted o'er the tide.—
But where is she?—her eyes are dark,
Are wilder'd still—is this the bark,
The same, that from Harmozia's bay
Bore her at morn—whose bloody way
The sea-dog track'd?—no—strange and new
Is all that meets her wond'ring view.
Upon a galliot's deck she lies,
  Beneath no rich pavilion's shade,—
No plumes to fan her sleeping eyes,
  Nor jasmine on her pillow laid,
But the rude litter, roughly spread
With war-cloaks, is her homely bed,
And shawl and sash, on javelins hung,
For awning o'er her head are flung.
Shudd'ring she look'd around—there lay
  A group of warriors in the sun,
Resting their limbs, as for that day
  Their ministry of death were done.
Some gazing on the drowsy sea,
Lost in unconscious revery;
And some, who seem'd but ill to brook
That sluggish calm, with many a look
To the slack sail impatient cast,
As loose it flagg'd around the mast.

Blest Alla! who shall save her now?
  There's not in all that warrior band
One Arab sword, one turban'd brow
  From her own faithful Moslem land.
Their garb—the leathern belt† that wraps
  Each yellow vest‡—that rebel hue—
The Tartar fleece upon their caps—§
  Yes—yes—her fears are all too true,
And Heav'n hath, in this dreadful hour,
Abandon'd her to Hafed's power;
Hafed, the Gheber!—at the thought
  Her very heart's blood chills within;
He, whom her soul was hourly taught
  To loathe, as some foul fiend of sin,
Some minister, whom Hell had sent,
To spread its blast, where'er he went,

And fling, as o'er our earth he trod,
His shadow betwixt man and God!
And she is now his captive,—thrown
In his fierce hands, alive, alone;
His th' infuriate band she sees,
All infidels—all enemies!
What was the daring hope that then
Cross'd her like lightning, as again,
With boldness that despair had lent,
  She darted through that armed crowd
A look so searching, so intent,
  That even the sternest warrior bow'd
Abash'd, when he her glances caught,
As if he guess'd whose form they sought.
But no—she sees him not—'tis gone,
The vision that before her shone
Through all the maze of blood and storm,
Is fled—'twas but a phantom form—
One of those passing, rainbow dreams,
Half light, half shade, which Fancy's beams
Paint on the fleeting mists that roll
In trance or slumber round the soul.

But now the bark, with livelier bound,
  Scales the blue wave—the crew's in motion,
The oars are out, and with light sound
  Break the bright mirror of the ocean,
Scatt'ring its brilliant fragments round.
And now she sees—with horror sees,
  Their course is tow'rd that mountain-hold,—
Those tow'rs that make her life-blood freeze,
Where Mecca's godless enemies
  Lie, like beleaguer'd scorpion's, roll'd
  In their last deadly, venomous fold!
Amid th' illumined land and flood
Sunless that mighty mountain stood;
Save where, above its awful head,
There shone a flaming cloud, blood-red,
As 'twere the flag of destiny
Hung out to mark where death would be!

Had her bewilder'd mind the pow'r
Of thought in this terrific hour,
She well might marvel where or how
Man's foot could scale that mountain's brow
Since ne'er had Arab heard or known
Of path but through the glen alone.—
But every thought was lost in fear,
When, as their bounding bark drew near
The craggy base, she felt the waves
Hurry them tow'rd those dismal caves,
That from the Deep in windings pass
Beneath that Mount's volcanic mass;—
And loud a voice on deck commands
To low'r the mast and light the brands!—
Instantly o'er the dashing tide
Within a cavern's mouth they glide,
Gloomy as that eternal Porch
  Through which departed spirits go:—
Not ev'n the flare of brand and torch
  Its flick'ring light could further throw
  Than the thick flood that boil'd below.
Silent they floated—as if each
Sat breathless, and too awed for speech
In that dark chasm, where even sound
Seem'd dark,—so sullenly around
The goblin echoes of the cave
Mutter'd it o'er the long black wave
As 'twere some secret of the grave!

But soft—they pause—the current turns
  Beneath them from its onward track;—
Some mighty, unseen barrier spurns
  The vexed tide, all foaming, back,
And scarce the oars' redoubled force
Can stem the eddy's whirling force;
When, hark!—some desp'rate foot has sprung
Among the rocks—the chain is flung—
The oars are up—the grapple clings,
And the toss'd bark in moorings swings.

* A precious stone of the Indies, called by the ancients Ceraunium, because it was supposed to be found in places where thunder had fallen. Tertullian says it has a glittering appearance, as if there had been fire in it; and the author of the Dissertation in Harris's Voyages, supposes it to be the opal.

† *D'Herbelot*, art. Agduani.

‡ "The Guebres are known by a dark yellow colour, which the men affect in their clothes."—*Thevenot*.

§ "The Kolah, or cap, worn by the Persians, is made of the skin of the sheep of Tartary."—*Waring*.

Just then, a day-beam through the shade
Broke tremulous—but, ere the maid
Can see from whence the brightness steals,
Upon her brow she shudd'ring feels
A viewless hand, that promptly ties
A bandage round her burning eyes;
While the rude litter where she lies,
Uplifted by the warrior throng,
O'er the steep rocks is borne along.

Blest power of sunshine!—genial Day,
What balm, what life is in thy ray!
To feel thee is such real bliss,
That had the world no joy but this,
To sit in sunshine calm and sweet,—
It were a world too exquisite
For man to leave it for the gloom,
The deep, cold shadow of the tomb.
Ev'n HINDA, though she saw not where
Or whither wound the perilous road,
Yet knew by that awak'ning air,
Which suddenly around her glow'd,
That they had ris'n from darkness then,
And breathed the sunny world again!
But soon this balmy freshness fled—
For now the steepy labyrinth led
Through damp and gloom—'mid crash of boughs,
And fall of loosen'd crags that rouse
The leopard from his hungry sleep,
Who, starting, thinks each crag a prey,
And long is heard, from steep to steep,
Chasing them down their thund'ring way!
The jackal's cry—the distant moan
Of the hyæna, fierce and lone—
And that eternal sadd'ning sound
Of torrents in the glen beneath,
As 'twere the ever-dark Profound
That rolls beneath the Bridge of Death!
All, all is fearful—ev'n to see,
To gaze on those terrific things
She now but blindly hears, would be
Relief to her imaginings;
Since never yet was shape so dread,
But Fancy, thus in darkness thrown,
And by such sounds of horror fed,
Could frame more dreadful of her own.

But does she dream? has Fear again
Perplex'd the workings of her brain,
Or did a voice, all music, then
Come from the gloom, low whisp'ring near—
"Tremble not, love, thy Gheber's here?"
She *does* not dream—all sense, all ear,
She drinks the words, "Thy Gheber's here."
'Twas his own voice—she could not err—
Throughout the breathing world's extent
There was but *one* such voice for her,
So kind, so soft, so eloquent!
Oh, sooner shall the rose of May
Mistake her own sweet nightingale,
And to some meaner minstrel's lay
Open her bosom's glowing veil,*
Than Love shall ever doubt a tone,
A breath of the beloved one!

Though blest, 'mid all her ills, to think
She has that one beloved near,
Whose smile, though met on ruin's brink,
Hath power to make even ruin dear,—
Yet soon this gleam of rapture, cross'd
By fears for him, is chill'd and lost.
How shall the ruthless HAFED brook
That one of Gheber blood should look,
With aught but curses in his eye,
On her, a maid of ARABY—
A Moslem maid—the child of him,
Whose bloody banner's dire success
Hath left their altars cold and dim,
And their fair land a wilderness!
And, worse than all, that night of blood
Which comes so fast—Oh! who shall stay
The sword that once hath tasted food
Of Persian hearts, or turn its way?
What arm shall then the victim cover,
Or from her father shield her lover?

"Save him, my God!" she inly cries—
"Save him this night—and if thine eyes
"Have ever welcomed with delight
"The sinner's tears, the sacrifice
"Of sinners' hearts—guard him this night,
"And here, before thy throne, I swear
"From my heart's inmost core to tear
"Love, hope, remembrance, though they be
"Link'd with each quiv'ring life-string there,
"And give it bleeding all to Thee!
"Let him but live,—the burning tear,
"The sighs, so sinful, yet so dear,
Which have been all too much his own,
"Shall from this hour be Heaven's alone.
"Youth pass'd in penitence, and age
"In long and painful pilgrimage,
"Shall leave no traces of the flame
"That wastes me now—nor shall his name
"E'er bless my lips, but when I pray
"For his dear spirit, that away
"Casting from its angelic ray
"Th' eclipse of earth, he, too, may shine
"Redeem'd, all glorious and all Thine!
"Think—think what victory to win
"One radiant soul like his from sin,—
"One wand'ring star of virtue back
"To its own native, heaven-ward track!
"Let him but live, and both are Thine,
"Together thine—for, bless'd or cross'd,
"Living or dead, his doom is mine,
"And, if *he* perish, both are lost!

THE next evening LALLA ROOKH was entreated by her Ladies to continue the relation of her wonderful dream; but the fearful interest that hung round the fate of HINDA and her lover had completely removed every trace of it from her mind; much to the disappointment of a fair seer or two in her train, who prided themselves on their skill in interpreting visions, and who had already remarked, as an unlucky omen, that the Princess, on the very morning after the dream, had worn a silk dyed with the blossoms of the sorrowful tree, Nilica.*

FADLADEEN, whose indignation had more than once broken out during the recital of some parts of this heterodox poem, seemed at length to have made up his mind to the infliction; and took his seat this evening with all the patience of a martyr, while the Poet resumed his profane and seditious story as follows:—

To tearless eyes and hearts at ease
The leafy shores and sun-bright seas,
That lay beneath that mountain's height,
Had been a fair enchanting sight.
'Twas one of those ambrosial eves
A day of storm so often leaves
At its calm setting—when the West
Opens her golden bowers of rest,
And a moist radiance from the skies
Shoots trembling down, as from the eyes

* A frequent image among the oriental poets. "The nightingales warbled their enchanting notes, and rent the thin veils of the rose-bud and the rose."—*Jami*.

* "Blossoms of the sorrowful Nyctanthes give a durable colour to silk."—*Remarks on the Husbandry of Bengal*, p. 200. Nilica is one of the Indian names of this flower.—*Sir W. Jones*. The Persians call it Gul.—*Carreri*.

Of some meek penitent, whose last,
Bright hours atone for dark ones past
And whose sweet tears, o'er wrong forgiv'n,
Shine, as they fall, with light from heav'n!

'Twas stillness all—the winds that late
  Had rush'd through KERMAN'S almond groves,
And shaken from her bow'rs of date
  That cooling feast the traveller loves,*
Now, lull'd to languor, scarcely curl
  The Green Sea wave, whose waters gleam
Limpid, as if her mines of pearl
  Were melted all to form the stream:
And her fair islets, small and bright,
  With their green shores reflected there,
Look like those PERI isles of light,
  That hang by spell-work in the air.

But vainly did those glories burst
On HINDA'S dazzled eyes, when first
The bandage from her brow was taken,
And, pale and awed as those who waken
In their dark tombs—when, scowling near,
The Searchers of the Grave† appear,—
She shudd'ring turn'd to read her fate
  In the fierce eyes that flash'd around;
And saw those towers all desolate
  That o'er her head terrific frown'd,
As if defying ev'n the smile
Of that soft heav'n to gild their pile.
In vain with mingled hope and fear,
She looks for him whose voice so dear
Had come, like music, to her ear—
Strange, mocking dream! again 'tis fled
And oh, the shoots, the pangs of dread
That through her inmost bosom run,
  When voices from without proclaim
" HAFED, the Chief"—and, one by one,
  The warriors shout that fearful name!
He comes—the rock resounds his tread—
How shall she dare to lift her head,
Or meet those eyes whose scorching glare
Not YEMEN'S boldest sons can bear?
In whose red beam, the Moslem tells,
Such rank and deadly lustre dwells,
As in those hellish fires that light
The mandrake's charnel leaves at night.‡
How shall she bear that voice's tone,
At whose loud battle-cry alone
Whole squadrons oft in panic ran,
Scatter'd like some vast caravan,
When, stretch'd at evening round the well,
They hear the thirsting tiger's yell.

Breathless she stands, with eyes cast down,
Shrinking beneath the fiery frown,
Which, fancy tells her, from that brow
Is flashing o'er her fiercely now:
And shudd'ring as she hears the tread
  Of his retiring warrior band.—
Never was pause so full of dread;
  Till HAFED with a trembling hand
Took hers, and, leaning o'er her, said,
" HINDA;"—that word was all he spoke,
And 'twas enough—the shriek that broke
  From her full bosom, told the rest.—
Panting with terror, joy, surprise,
The maid but lifts her wond'ring eyes,
  To hide them on her Gheber's breast!
'Tis he, 'tis he—the man of blood,
The fellest of the Fire-fiend's brood,
HAFED, the demon of the fight,
Whose voice unnerves, whose glances blight,—
Is her own loved Gheber, mild
And glorious as when first he smiled
In her lone tow'r, and left such beams
Of his pure eye to light her dreams,
That she believed her bower had giv'n
Rest to some wanderer from heav'n!

Moments there are, and this was one
Snatch'd like a minute's gleam of sun
Amid the black Simoom's eclipse—
  Or, like those verdant spots that bloom
Around the crater's burning lips,
  Sweet'ning the very edge of doom!
The past—the future—all that Fate
Can bring of dark or desperate
Around such hours, but makes them cast
Intenser radiance while they last!

Ev'n he, this youth—though dimm'd and gone
Each star of Hope that cheer'd him on—
His glories lost—his cause betray'd—
IRAN, his dear-loved country, made
A land of carcasses and slaves,
One dreary waste of chains and graves!
Himself but ling'ring, dead at heart,
  To see the last, long struggling breath
Of Liberty's great soul depart,
  Then lay him down and share her death—
Ev'n he, so sunk in wretchedness,
  With doom still darker gath'ring o'er him,
Yet, in this moment's pure caress,
  In the mild eyes that shone before him,
Beaming that bless'd assurance, worth
All other transports known on earth,
That he was loved—well, warmly loved—
Oh! in this precious hour he proved
How deep, how thorough-felt the glow
Of rapture, kindling out of wo;—
How exquisite one single drop
Of bliss, thus sparkling to the top
Of mis'ry's cup—how keenly quaff'd,
Though death must follow on the draught!

She, too, while gazing on those eyes
  That sink into her soul so deep,
Forgets all fears, all miseries,
  Or feels them like the wretch in sleep,
Whom fancy cheats into a smile,
Who dreams of joy, and sobs the while.
The mighty Ruins where they stood,
  Upon the mount's high, rocky verge
Lay open tow'rds the ocean flood,
  Where lightly o'er the illumined surge
Many a fair bark that, all the day,
Had lurk'd in shelt'ring creek or bay,
Now bounded on, and gave their sails,
Yet dripping, to the ev'ning gales;
Like eagles, when the storm is done,
Spreading their wet wings in the sun.
The beauteous clouds, though daylight Star
Had sunk behind the hills of LAR,
Were still with ling'ring glories bright,
As if, to grace the gorgeous West,
  The Spirit of departing Light
That eve had left his sunny vest
  Behind him, ere he wing'd his flight.
Never was scene so form'd for love!
Beneath them waves of crystal move
In silent swell—Heav'n glows above,
And their pure hearts, to transport giv'n,
Swell like the wave, and glow like Heav'n.

But ah! too soon that dream is past—
  Again, again her fear returns;—
Night, dreadful night, is gath'ring fast,
  More faintly the horizon burns,
And every rosy tint that lay
On the smooth sea hath died away.
Hastily to the dark'ning skies
A glance she casts—then wildly cries,
At night, he said—and, look, 'tis near—
" Fly, fly—if yet thou lov'st me, fly—

* "In parts of Kerman, whatever dates are shaken from the trees by the wind they do not touch, but leave them for those who have not any, or for travellers."—*Ebn Haukal.*

† "The two terrible angels, Monkir and Nakir, who are called 'the Searchers of the Grave,' in the 'Creed of the orthodox Mahometans,' given by Ockley, vol. ii.

‡ "The Arabians call the mandrake 'the Devil's candle,' on account of its shining appearance in the night."—*Richardson.*

"Soon will his murd'rous band be here,
"And I shall see thee bleed and die.—
"Hush! heard'st thou not the tramp of men
"Sounding from yonder fearful glen?—
"Perhaps ev'n now they climb the wood—
"Fly, fly—though still the West is bright,
"He'll come—oh! yes—he wants thy blood—
"I know him—he'll not wait for night!"

In terrors ev'n to agony
She clings around the wond'ring Chief;—
"Alas, poor wilder'd maid! to me
"Thou ow'st this raving trance of grief.
"Lost as I am, naught ever grew
"Beneath my shade but perish'd too—
"My doom is like the Dead Sea air,
"And nothing lives that enters there!
"Why were our barks together driv'n
"Beneath this morning's furious heav'n?
Why, when I saw the prize that chance
"Had thrown into my desp'rate arms,—
"When, casting but a single glance
"Upon thy pale and prostrate charms,
"I vow'd (though watching viewless o'er
"Thy safety through that hour's alarms)
"To meet th' unmanning sight no more—
"Why have I broke that heart-wrung vow?
"Why weakly, madly met thee now?—
"Start not—that noise is but the shock
"Of torrents through yon valley hurl'd—
"Dread nothing here—upon this rock
"We stand above the jarring world,
"Alike beyond its hope—its dread—
"In gloomy safety, like the Dead!
"Or, could ev'n earth and hell unite
"In league to storm this Sacred Height,
"Fear nothing thou—myself, to-night,
"And each o'erlooking star that dwells
"Near God will be thy sentinels;—
"And, ere to-morrow's dawn shall glow,
"Back to thy sire——"

"To-morrow!—no—"
The maiden scream'd—"thou'lt never see
"To-morrow's sun—death, death will be
"The night-cry through each reeking tower,
"Unless we fly, ay, fly this hour!
"Thou art betray'd—some wretch who knew
"That dreadful glen's mysterious clew—
"Nay, doubt not—by yon stars, 'tis true—
"Hath sold thee to my vengeful sire;
"This morning, with that smile so dire
"He wears in joy, he told me all,
"And stamp'd in triumph through our hall,
"As though thy heart already beat
"Its last life-throb beneath his feet.
"Good Heav'n, how little dream'd I then
"His victim was my own loved youth!-
"Fly—send—let some one watch the glen—
"By all my hopes of heav'n 'tis truth!"

Oh! colder than the wind that freezes
Founts, that but now in sunshine play'd,
Is that congealing pang which seizes
The trusting bosom, when betray'd.
He felt it—deeply felt—and stood,
As if the tale had froz'n his blood,
So mazed and motionless was he;—
Like one whom sudden spells enchant,
Or some mute, marble habitant
Of the still Halls of ISHMONIE!*

But soon the painful chill was o'er,
And his great soul, herself once more,
Look'd from his brow in all the rays
Of her best, happiest, grandest days.

Never, in moment most elate,
Did that high spirit loftier rise;—
While bright, serene, determinate,
His looks are lifted to the skies,
As if the signal lights of Fate
Were shining in those awful eyes!
'Tis come—his hour of martyrdom
In IRAN's sacred cause is come;
And, though his life hath pass'd away,
Like lightning on a stormy day,
Yet shall his death-hour leave a track
Of glory, permanent and bright,
To which the brave of after-times,
The suff'ring brave, shall long look back
With proud regret,—and by its light
Watch through the hours of slav'ry's night
For vengeance on th' oppressor's crimes.
This rock, his monument aloft,
Shall speak the tale to many an age;
And hither bards and heroes oft
Shall come in secret pilgrimage,
And bring their warrior sons, and tell
The wond'ring boys where HAFED fell;
And swear them on those lone remains
Of their lost country's ancient fanes,
Never—while breath of life shall live
Within them—never to forgive
Th' accursed race, whose ruthless chain
Hath left on IRAN's neck a stain
Blood, blood alone can cleanse again.

Such are the swelling thoughts that now
Enthrone themselves on HAFED's brow;
And ne'er did Saint of ISSA* gaze
On the red wreath, for martyrs twined,
More proudly than the youth surveys
That pile, which through the gloom behind
Half lighted by the altar's fire,
Glimmers—his destined funeral pyre?
Heap'd by his own, his comrades' hands,
Of ev'ry wood of odorous breath,
There, by the Fire-God's shrine it stands,
Ready to fold in radiant death
The few still left of those who swore
To perish there, when hope was o'er—
The few, to whom that couch of flame,
Which rescues them from bonds and shame,
Is sweet and welcome as the bed
For their own infant Prophet spread,
When pitying Heav'n to roses turn'd
The death-flames that beneath him burn'd†

With watchfulness the maid attends
His rapid glance, where'er it bends—
Why shoot his eyes such awful beams?
What plans he now? what thinks or dreams
Alas! why stands he musing here,
When ev'ry moment teems with fear?
"HAFED, my own beloved Lord,"
She kneeling cries—"first, last adored!
"If in that soul thou'st ever felt
"Half what thy lips impassion'd swore,
"Here, on my knees that never knelt
"To any but their God before,
"I pray thee, as thou lov'st me, fly—
"Now, now—ere yet their blades are nigh.
"Oh haste—the bark that bore me hither
"Can waft us o'er yon dark'ning sea,
"East—west—alas, I care not whither,
"So thou art safe, and I with thee!
"Go where we will, this hand in thine,

* For an account of Ishmonie, the petrified city in Upper Egypt, where it is said there are many statues of men, women, &c., to be seen to this day, see *Perry's View of the Levant.*

* Jesus.

† The Ghebers say that when Abraham, their great Prophet, was thrown into the fire by order of Nimrod, the flame turned instantly into "a bed of roses, where the child sweetly reposed."—*Tavernier.*

Of their other Prophet, Zoroaster, there is a story told in *Dion Prusæus*, Orat. 36, that the love of wisdom and virtue leading him to a solitary life upon a mountain, he found it one day all in a flame, shining with celestial fire, out of which he came without any harm, and instituted certain sacrifices to God, who, he declared, then appeared to him.—V. de *Patrick* on Exodus. iii. 2.

"Those eyes before me smiling thus,
"Through good and ill, through storm and shine,
"The world's a world of love for us!
"On some calm, blessed shore we'll dwell,
"Where 'tis no crime to love too well;—
"Where thus to worship tenderly
"An erring child of light like thee
"Will not be sin—or, if it be,
"Where we may weep our faults away,
"Together kneeling, night and day,
"Thou, for *my* sake, at ALLA's shrine,
"And I—at *any* God's, for thine!"

Wildly these passionate words she spoke—
Then hung her head, and wept for shame;
Sobbing, as if a heart-string broke
With every deep-heaved sob that came.
While he, young, warm—oh! wonder not
If, for a moment, pride and fame,
His oath—his cause—that shrine of flame,
And IRAN's self are all forgot
For her whom at his feet he sees
Kneeling in speechless agonies.
No, blame him not, if Hope awhile
Dawn'd in his soul, and threw her smile
O'er hours to come—o'er days and nights,
Wing'd with those precious, pure delights
Which she, who bends all beauteous there,
Was born to kindle and to share.
A tear or two, which, as he bow'd
To raise the suppliant, trembling stole,
First warn'd him of this dang'rous cloud
Of softness passing o'er his soul.
Starting, he brush'd the drops away,
Unworthy o'er that cheek to stray;—
Like one who, on the morn of fight,
Shakes from his sword the dews of night,
That had but dimm'd, not stain'd its light,
Yet, though subdued th' unnerving thrill,
Its warmth, its weakness linger'd still,
So touching in its look and tone,
That the fond, fearing, hoping maid
Half counted on the flight she pray'd,
Half thought the hero's soul was grown
As soft, as yielding as her own,
And smiled and bless'd him, while he said,—
"Yes—if there be some happier sphere,
"Where fadeless truth like ours is dear,—
"If there be any land of rest
"For those who love and ne'er forget,
"Oh! comfort thee—for safe and bless'd
"We'll meet in that calm region yet!

Scarce had she time to ask her heart
If good or ill these words impart,
When the roused youth impatient flew
To the tow'r-wall, where, high in view,
A pond'rous sea-horn* hung, and blew
A signal, deep and dread as those
The storm-fiend at his rising blows.—
Full well his Chieftains, sworn and true
Through life and death, that signal knew;
For 'twas th' appointed warning blast,
Th' alarm, to tell when hope was past,
And the tremendous death-die cast!
And there, upon the mould'ring tower,
Hath hung this sea-horn many an hour,
Ready to sound o'er land and sea
That dirge-note of the brave and free.

They came—his Chieftains at the call
Came slowly round, and with them all—
Alas, how few!—the worn remains
Of those who late o'er KERMAN's plains
Went gaily prancing to the clash
Of Moorish zel and tymbalon,
Catching new hope from every flash
Of their long lances in the sun,
And, as their coursers charged the wind,
And the white ox-tails stream'd behind,*
Looking, as if the steeds they rode,
Were wing'd, and every Chief a God!
How fall'n, how alter'd now! how wan
Each scarr'd and faded visage shone
As round the burning shrine they came;—
How deadly was the glare it cast,
As mute they paused before the flame
To light their torches as they pass'd!
'Twas silence all—the youth hath plann'd
The duties of his soldier-band;
And each determined brow declares
His faithful Chieftains well know theirs.

But minutes speed—night gems the skies—
And oh, how soon, ye blessed eyes
That look from heaven, ye may behold
Sights that will turn your star-fires cold!
Breathless with awe, impatience, hope,
The maiden sees the veteran group
Her litter silently prepare,
And lay it at her trembling feet;—
And now the youth, with gentle care,
Hath placed her in the shelter'd seat,
And press'd her hand—that ling'ring press
Of hands, that for the last time sever;
Of hearts, whose pulse of happiness,
When that hold breaks, is dead forever
And yet to *her* this sad caress
Gives hope—so fondly hope can err!
'Twas joy, she thought, joy's mute excess—
Their happy flight's dear harbinger;
'Twas warmth—assurance—tenderness—
'Twas any thing but leaving her.

"Haste, haste!" she cried, "the clouds grow dark,
"But still, ere night, we'll reach the bark;
"And by to-morrow's dawn—oh bliss!
"With thee upon the sun-bright deep,
"Far off, I'll but remember this,
"As some dark vanish'd dream of sleep;
"And thou——" but ah!—he answers not—
Good Heav'n!—and does she go alone?
She now has reach'd that dismal spot,
Where, some hours since, his voice's tone
Had come to sooth her fears and ills,
Sweet as the angel ISRAFIL's,†
When every leaf on Eden's tree
Is trembling to his minstrelsy—
Yet now—oh, now, he is not nigh.—
"HAFED! my HAFED!—if it be
"Thy will, thy doom this night to die,
"Let me but stay to die with thee,
"And I will bless thy loved name
"Till the last life-breath leaves this frame
"Oh! let our lips, our cheeks be laid
"But near each other while they fade;
"Let us but mix our parting breaths,
"And I can die ten thousand deaths!
"You too, who hurry me away
"So cruelly, one moment stay—
"Oh! stay—one moment is not much—
"He yet may come—for *him* I pray—
"HAFED! dear HAFED!"—all the way
In wild lamentings that would touch
A heart of stone, she shriek'd his name
To the dark woods—no HAFED came:—
No—hapless pair—you've look'd your last:—
Your hearts should both have broken then
The dream is o'er—your doom is cast—
You'll never meet on earth again!

Alas for him, who hears her cries!
Still half-way down the steep he stands,
Watching with fix'd and feverish eyes
The glimmer of those burning brands,

* "The shell called Siiankos, common to India, Africa, and the Mediterranean, and still used in many parts as a trumpet for blowing alarms or giving signals: it sends forth a deep and hollow sound."—*Pennant.*

* "The finest ornament for the horses is made of six large flying tassels of long white hair, taken out of the tails of wild oxen, that are to be found in some places of the Indies."—*Thevenot.*

† "The angel Israfil, who has the most melodious voice of all God's creatures."—*Sale*

That down the rocks, with mournful ray,
Light all he loves on earth away!
Hopeless as they who, far at sea,
By the cold moon have just consign'd
The corse of one, loved tenderly,
To the bleak flood they leave behind;
And on the deck still ling'ring stay,
And long look back with sad delay,
To watch the moonlight on the wave,
That ripples o'er that cheerless grave.

But see—he starts—what heard he then?
That dreadful shout!—across the glen
From the land-side it comes, and loud
Rings through the chasm; as if the crowd
Of fearful things that haunt that dell,
Its Gholes and Dives and shapes of hell,
Had all in one dread howl broke out,
So loud, so terrible that shout!
"They come—the Moslems come!"—he cries,
His proud soul mounting to his eyes,—
"Now, Spirits of the Brave, who roam
Enfranchised through yon starry dome,
Rejoice—for soul's of kindred fire
Are on the wing to join your choir!"
He said—and, light as bridegrooms bound
To their young loves, reclimb'd the steep
And gain'd the Shrine—his Chiefs stood round—
Their swords, as with instinctive leap,
Together, at that cry accursed,
Had from their sheaths like sunbeams burst.
And hark!—again—again it rings;
Near and more near its echoings
Peal through the chasm—oh! who that then
Had seen those list'ning warrior-men,
With their swords grasp'd, their eyes of flame
Turn'd on their Chief—could doubt the shame,
Th' indignant shame with which they thrill
To hear those shouts, and yet stand still;

He read their thoughts—they were his own—
"What! while our arms can wield these blades,
"Shall we die tamely? die alone?
"Without one victim to our shades,
"One Moslem heart, where, buried deep,
"The sabre from its toil may sleep?
"No—God of IRAN's burning skies!
"Thou scorn'st th' inglorious sacrifice.
"No—though of all earth's hope bereft,
"Life, swords, and vengeance still are left.
"We'll make yon valley's reeking caves
"Live in the awe-struck minds of men,
"Till tyrants shudder, when their slaves
"Tell of the Gheber's bloody glen.
"Follow, brave hearts!—this pile remains
"Our refuge still from life and chains;
"But his the best, the holiest bed,
"Who sinks entomb'd in Moslem dead!"

Down the precipitous rocks they sprung,
While vigour, more than human, strung
Each arm and heart.—Th' exulting foe
Still through the dark defiles below,
Track'd by his torches' lurid fire,
Wound slow, as through GOLCONDA's vale*
The mighty serpent, in his ire,
Glides on with glitt'ring, deadly trail.
No torch the Ghebers need—so well
They know each myst'ry of the dell,
So oft have, in their wanderings,
Cross'd the wild race that round them dwell,
The very tigers from their delves
Look out, and let them pass, as things
Untamed and fearless like themselves!

There was a deep ravine, that lay
Yet darkling in the Moslem's way;
Fit spot to make invaders rue
The many fall'n before the few.

* See Hoole upon the Story of Sinbad

The torrents from that morning's sky
Had fill'd the narrow chasm breast-high,
And, on each side, aloft and wild,
Huge cliffs and toppling crags were piled,—
The guards with which young Freedom lines
The pathway to her mountain-shrines.
Here, at this pass, the scanty band
Of IRAN's last avengers stand;
Here wait, in silence like the dead,
And listen for the Moslem's tread
So anxiously, the carrion-bird
Above them flaps his wing unheard!

They come—that plunge into the water
Gives signal for the work of slaughter.
Now, Ghebers, now—if e'er your blades
Had point or prowess, prove them now—
Wo to the file that foremost wades!
They come—a falchion greets each brow,
And, as they tumble, trunk on trunk,
Beneath the gory waters sunk,
Still o'er their drowning bodies press
New victims quick and numberless;
Till scarce an arm in HAFED's band,
So fierce their toil, hath power to stir,
But listless from each crimson hand
The sword hangs, clogg'd with massacre
Never was horde of tyrants met
With bloodier welcome—never yet
To patriot vengeance hath the sword
More terrible libations pour'd!

All up the dreary, long ravine,
By the red, murky glimmer seen
Of half-quench'd brands, that o'er the flood
Lie scatter'd round and burn in blood,
What ruin glares! what carnage swims!
Heads, blazing turbans, quiv'ring limbs,
Lost swords that, dropp'd from many a hand,
In that thick pool of slaughter stand;
Wretches who wading, half on fire
From the toss'd brands that round them fly,
'Twixt flood and flame in shrieks expire;—
And some who, grasp'd by those that die,
Sink woundless with them, smother'd o'er
In their dead brethren's gushing gore!

But vainly hundreds, thousands bleed,
Still hundreds, thousands more succeed;
Countless as tow'rds some flame at night
The North's dark insects wing their flight,
And quench or perish in its light,
To this terrific spot they pour—
Till, bridged with Moslem bodies o'er,
It bears aloft their slipp'ry tread,
And o'er the dying and the dead,
Tremendous causeway! on they pass.
Then, hapless Ghebers, then, alas!
What hope was left for you? for you,
Whose yet warm pile of sacrifice
Is smoking in their vengeful eyes;—
Whose swords how keen, how fierce they knew,
And burn with shame to find how few?

Crush'd down by that vast multitude,
Some found their graves where first they stood;
While some with hardier struggle died,
And still fought on by HAFED's side,
Who, fronting to the foe, trod back
Tow'rds the high towers his gory track;
And, as a lion swept away
By sudden swell of JORDAN's pride
From the wild covert where he lay,*
Long battles with th' o'erwhelming tide,
So fought he back with fierce delay,
And kept both foes and fate at bay.

* "In this thicket upon the banks of the Jordan several sorts of wild beasts are wont to harbour themselves, whose being washed out of the covert by the overflowings of the river, gave occasion to that allusion of Jeremiah, *he shall come up like a lion from the swelling of Jordan.*"—*Maundrell's Aleppo.*

But whither now? their track is lost,
Their prey escaped—guide, torches gone—
By torrent beds and labyrinths cross'd,
The scatter'd crowd rush blindly on—
"Curse on those tardy lights that wind,"
They panting cry, "so far behind;
"Oh for a bloodhound's precious scent,
"To track the way the Gheber went!"
Vain wish—confusedly along
They rush, more desp'rate as more wrong;
Till, wilder'd by the far-off lights,
Yet glitt'ring up those gloomy heights,
Their footing, mazed and lost, they miss,
And down the darkling precipice
Are dash'd into the deep abyss;
Or midway hung, impaled on rocks,
A banquet, yet alive, for flocks
Of rav'ning vultures,—while the dell
Re-echoes with each horrible yell.

Those sounds—the last, to vengeance dear,
That e'er shall ring in HAFED's ear,—
Now reach'd him, as al t, alone,
Upon the steep way breathless thrown,
He lay beside his reeking blade,
Resign'd, as if life's task were o'er,
Its last blood-offering amply paid,
And IRAN's self could claim no more.
One only thought, one ling'ring beam
Now broke across his dizzy dream
Of pain and weariness—'twas she,
His heart's pure planet, shining yet
Above the waste of memory,
When all life's other lights were set.
And never to his mind before
Her image such enchantment wore.
It seem'd as if each thought that stain'd,
Each fear that chill'd their loves was past,
And not one cloud of earth remain'd
Between him and her radiance cast;—
As if to charms before so bright,
New grace from other worlds was given,
And his soul saw her by the light
Now breaking o'er itself from heav'n!
A voice spoke near him—'twas the tone
Of a loved friend, the only one
Of all his warriors, left with life
From that short night's tremendous strife.—
"And must we then, my Chief, die here?
"Foes round us, and the Shrine so near?"
These words have roused the last remains
Of life within him—"What! not yet
"Beyond the reach of Moslem chains!"
The thought could make ev'n Death forget
His icy bondage—with a bound
He springs, all bleeding, from the ground,
And grasps his comrade's arm, now grown
Ev'n feebler, heavier than his own,
And up the painful pathway leads,
Death gaining on each step he treads.
Speed them, thou God, who heard'st their vow!
They mount—they bleed—oh save them now—
The crags are red they've clamber'd o'er,
The rock-weed's dripping with their gore;—
Thy blade too, HAFED, false at length,
Now breaks beneath thy tott'ring strength!
Haste, haste—the voices of the Foe
Come near and nearer from below—
One effort more—thank Heav'n! 'tis past,
They've gain'd the topmost steep at last.
And now they touch the temple's walls,
Now HAFED sees the Fire divine—
When, lo!—his weak, worn comrade falls
Dead on the threshold of the shrine.
"Alas, brave soul, too quickly fled!
"And must I leave thee with'ring here,
"The sport of every ruffian's tread,
"The mark for every coward's spear?
"No, by yon altar's sacred beams!"
He cries, and, with a strength that seems
Not of this world, uplifts the frame
Of the fall'n Chief, and tow'rds the flame
Bears him along;—with death-damp hand
The corpse upon the pyre he lays,
Then lights the consecrated brand,
And fires the pile, whose sudden blaze
Like lightning bursts o'er OMAN's Sea.—
"Now, Freedom's God! I come to Thee,"
The youth exclaims, and with a smile
Of triumph vaulting on the pile,
In that last effort, ere the fires
Have harm'd one glorious limb, expires!

What shriek was that on OMAN's tide?
It came from yonder drifting bark,
That just hath caught upon her side
The death-light—and again is dark.
It is the boat—ah, why delay'd?—
That bears the wretched Moslem maid,
Confided to the watchful care
Of a small veteran band, with whom
Their gen'rous Chieftain would not share
The secret of his final doom,
But hoped when HINDA, safe and free.
Was render'd to her father's eyes,
Their pardon, full and prompt, would be
The ransom of so dear a prize.—
Unconscious, thus, of HAFED's fate,
And proud to guard their beauteous freight,
Scarce had they clear'd surfy waves
That foam around those frightful caves,
When the cursed war-whoops, known so well
Came echoing from the distant dell—
Sudden each oar, upheld and still,
Hung dripping o'er the vessel's side.
And, driving at the current's will,
They rock'd along the whisp'ring tide;
While every eye, in mute dismay,
Was tow'rd that fatal mountain turn'd,
Where the dim altar's quiv'ring ray
As yet all lone and tranquil burn'd.

Oh! 'tis not, HINDA, in the pow'r
Of Fancy's most terrific touch
To paint thy pangs in that dread hour—
Thy silent agony—'twas such
As those who feel could paint too well,
But none e'er felt and lived to tell!
'Twas not alone the dreary state
Of a lorn spirit, crush'd by fate,
When, though no more remains to dread,
The panic chill will not depart;—
When, though the inmate Hope be dead,
Her ghost still haunts the mould'ring hear
No—pleasures, hopes, affections, gone,
The wretch may bear, and yet live on,
Like things, within the cold rock found
Alive, when all's congeal'd around.
But there's a blank repose in this,
A calm stagnation, that were bliss
To the keen, burning, harrowing pain,
Now felt through all thy breast and brain;—
That spasm of terror, mute, intense,
That breathless, agonized suspense,
From whose hot throb, whose deadly aching.
The heart hath no relief but breaking!

Calm is the wave—heav'n's brilliant lights
Reflected dance beneath the prow;—
Time was when, on such lovely nights,
She who is there, so desolate now,
Could sit all cheerful, though alone,
And ask no happier joy than seeing
That star-light o'er the waters thrown—
No joy but that, to make her blest,
And the fresh, buoyant sense of Being,
Which bounds in youth's yet careless breast,—
Itself a star, not borrowing light,
But in its own glad essence bright.
How different now!—but, hark, again
The yell of havoc rings—brave men!
In vain, with beating hearts, ye stand

On the bark's edge—in vain each hand
Half draws the falchion from its sheath ;
All's o'er—in rust your blades may lie :—
He, at whose word they'ye scatter'd death,
Ev'n now, this night, himself must die!
Well may ye look to yon dim tower,
And ask, and wond'ring guess what means
The battle-cry at this dead hour—
Ah ! she could tell you—she, who leans
Unheeded there, pale, sunk, aghast,
With brow against the dew-cold mast ;—
Too well she knows—her more than life,
Her soul's first idol and its last,
Lies bleeding in that murd'rous strife.

But see—what moves upon the height ?
Some signal !—'tis a torch's light.
What bodes its solitary glare ?
In gasping silence tow'rd the Shrine
All eyes are turn'd—thine, Hinda, thine
Fix their last fading life-beams there.
'Twas but a moment—fierce and high
The death-pile blazed into the sky,
And far away, o'er rock and flood
Its melancholy radiance sent ;
While Hafed, like a vision stood
Reveal'd before the burning pyre,
Tall, shadowy, like a Spirit of Fire
Shrined in its own grand element!
"'Tis he !"—the shudd'ring maid exclaims,—
But, while she speaks, he's seen no more ;
High burst in air the funeral flames,
And Iran's hopes and hers are o'er!

One wild, heart-broken shriek she gave ;
Then sprung, as if to reach that blaze,
Where still she fix'd her dying gaze,
And, gazing, sunk into the wave,—
Deep, deep,—where never care or pain
Shall reach her innocent heart again!

Farewell—farewell to thee, Araby's daughter,
(Thus warbled a Peri beneath the dark sea,)
No pearl ever lay, under Oman's green water,
More pure in its shell than thy Spirit in thee.

Oh ! fair as the sea-flower close to thee growing,
How light was thy heart till Love's witchery came,
Like the wind of the south,* o'er a summer lute blowing,
And hush'd all its music, and wither'd its frame!

But long, upon Araby's green sunny highlands,
Shall maids and their lovers remember the doom
Of her, who lies sleeping among the Pearl Islands,
With naught but the sea-star† to light up her tomb.

And still, when the merry date-season is burning,‡
And calls to the palm-groves, the young and the old,
The happiest there, from their pastime returning
At sunset, will weep when thy story is told.

The young village-maid, when with flow'rs she dresses
Her dark flowing hair for some festival day,
Will think of thy fate till, neglecting her tresses,
She mournfully turns from the mirror away.

Nor shall Iran, beloved of her Hero ! forget thee—
Though tyrants watch over her tears as they start,
Close, close by the side of that Hero she'll set thee,
Embalm'd in the innermost shrine of her heart.

Farewell—be it ours to embellish thy pillow
With ev'ry thing beauteous that grows in the deep ;
Each flow'r of the rock and each gem of the billow
Shall sweeten thy bed and illumine thy sleep.

Around thee shall glisten the loveliest amber
That ever the sorrowing sea-bird has wept ;*
With many a shell, in whose hollow-wreath'd chamber
We, Peris of Ocean, by moonlight have slept.

We'll dive where the gardens of coral lie darkling,
And plant all the rosiest stems at thy head ;
We'll seek where the sands of the Caspian are sparkling,
And gather their gold to strew over thy bed.

Farewell—farewell—until Pity's sweet fountain
Is lost in the hearts of the fair and the brave,
They'll weep for the Chieftain who died on that mountain,
They'll weep for the Maiden who sleeps in this wave

The singular placidity with which Fadladeen had listened, during the latter part of this obnoxious story surprised the Princess and Feramorz exceedingly ; and even inclined towards him the hearts of these unsuspicious young persons, who little knew the source of a complacency so marvellous. The truth was, he had been organizing, for the last few days, a most notable plan of persecution against the poet, in consequence of some passages that had fallen from him on the second evening of recital,—which appeared to this worthy Chamberlain to contain language and principles, for which nothing short of the summary criticism of the Chabuk‡ would be advisable. It was his intention, therefore, immediately on their arrival at Cashmere, to give information to the King of Bucharia of the very dangerous sentiments of his minstrel ; and if, unfortunately, that monarch did not act with suitable vigour on the occasion, (that is, if he did not give the Chabuk to Feramorz, and a place to Fadladeen,) there would be an end, he feared, of all legitimate government in Bucharia. He could not help, however, auguring better both for himself and the cause of potentates in general ; and it was the pleasure arising from these mingled anticipations that diffused such unusual satisfaction through his features, and made his eyes shine out like poppies of the desert, over the wide and lifeless wilderness of that countenance.

Having decided upon the Poet's chastisement in this manner, he thought it but humanity to spare him the minor tortures of criticism. Accordingly, when they assembled the following evening in the pavilion, and Lalla Rookh was expecting to see all the beauties of her bard melt away, one by one, in the acidity of criticism, like pearls in the cup of the Egyptian queen,—he agreeably disappointed her, by merely saying, with an ironical smile, that the merits of such a poem deserved to be tried at a much higher tribunal : and then suddenly passed off into a panegyric, upon all Mussulman sovereigns, more particularly his august and Imperial master, Aurungzebe,—the wisest and best of the descendants of Timur—who, among other great things he had done for mankind, had given to him, Fadladeen, the very profitable posts of Betel-carrier, and Taster of Sherbets to the Emperor, Chief Holder of the Girdle of Beautiful Forms,§ and Grand Nazir, or Chamberlain of the Harem.

They were now not far from that Forbidden River,‖ beyond which no pure Hindoo can pass ; and were re-

---

* "This wind (the Samoor) so softens the strings of lutes, that they can never be tuned while it lasts."—*Stephen's Persia.*

† "One of the greatest curiosities found in the Persian Gulf is a fish which the English call Star-fish. It is circular, and at night very luminous, resembling the full moon surrounded by rays."—*Mirza Abu Taleb.*

‡ For a description of the merriment of the date-time, of their work, their dances, and their return home from the palm-groves at the end of autumn with the fruits, see *Kempfer, Amœnitat. Exot.*

* Some naturalists have imagined that amber is a concretion of the tears of birds.—See *Trevoux, Chambers.*

† "The bay Kieselarke, which is otherwise called the Golden Bay the sand whereof shines as fire."—*Struy.*

‡ "The application of whips or rods."—*Dubois.*

§ Kempfer mentions such an officer among the attendants of the King of Persia, and calls him "formæ corporis estimator." His business was, at stated periods, to measure the ladies of the Harem by a sort of regulation-girdle, whose limits it was not thought graceful to exceed. If any of them outgrew this standard of shape, they were reduced by abstinence till they came within proper bounds.

‖ The Attock.

"Akbar on his way ordered a fort to be built upon the Nilab, which he called Attock, which means in the Indian language Forbidden ; for, by the superstition of the Hindoos, it was held unlawful to cross that river."—*Dow's* Hindostan.

posing for a time in the rich valley of Hussun Abdaul, which had always been a favourite resting-place of the Emperors in their annual migrations to Cashmere. Here often had the Light of the Faith, Jehan-Guire, been known to wander with his beloved and beautiful Nourmahal; and here would LALLA ROOKH have been happy to remain forever, giving up the throne of Bucharia and the world, for FERAMORZ and love in this sweet lonely valley. But the time was now fast approaching when she must see him no longer,—or, what was still worse, behold him with eyes whose every look belonged to another; and there was a melancholy preciousness in these last moments, which made her heart cling to them as it would to life. During the latter part of the journey, indeed, she had sunk into a deep sadness, from which nothing but the presence of the young minstrel could awake her. Like those lamps in tombs, which only light up when the air is admitted, it was only at his approach that her eyes became smiling and animated. But here, in this dear valley, every moment appeared an age of pleasure; she saw him all day, and was, therefore, all day happy,—resembling, she often thought, that people of Zinge,* who attribute the unfading cheerfulness they enjoy to one genial star that rises nightly over their heads.†

The whole party, indeed, seemed in their liveliest mood during the few days they passed in this delightful solitude. The young attendants of the Princess, who were here allowed a much freer range than they could safely be indulged with in a less sequestered place, ran wild among the gardens and bounded through the meadows lightly as young roes over the aromatic plains of Tibet. While FADLADEEN, in addition to the spiritual comfort derived by him from a pilgrimage to the tomb of the saint from whom the valley is named, had also opportunities of indulging, in a small way, his taste for victims, by putting to death some hundreds of those unfortunate little lizards,‡ which all pious Mussulmans make it a point to kill;—taking for granted, that the manner in which the creature hangs its head is meant as a mimicry of the attitude in which the Faithful say their prayers.

About two miles from Hussun Abdaul were those Royal Gardens,§ which had grown beautiful under the care of so many lovely eyes, and were beautiful still, though those eyes could see them no longer. This place, with its flowers and its holy silence, interrupted only by the dipping of the wings of birds in its marble basins filled with the pure water of those hills, was to LALLA ROOKH all that her heart could fancy of fragrance, coolness, and almost heavenly tranquillity. As the Prophet said of Damascus, "it was too delicious;"‖—and here, in listening to the sweet voice of FERAMORZ, or reading in his eyes what yet he never dared to tell her, the most exquisite moments of her whole life were passed. One evening, when they had been talking of the Sultana Nourmahal, the Light of the Harem,¶ who had so often wandered among these flowers, and fed with her own hands, in those marble basins, the small shining fishes of which she was so fond,** the youth in order to delay the moment of separation, proposed to recite a short story, or rather rhapsody, of which this adored Sultana was the heroine. It related, he said, to the reconcilement of a sort of lovers' quarrel which took place between her and the Emperor during a Feast of Roses at Cashmere; and would remind the Princess of that difference between Haroun-al-Raschid and his fair mistress Marida,* which was so happily made up by the soft strains of the musician, Moussali. As the story was chiefly to be told in song, and FERAMORZ had unluckily forgotten his own lute in the valley, he borrowed the vina of LALLA ROOKH's little Persian slave, and thus began:—

* "The inhabitants of this country (Zinge) are never afflicted with sadness or melancholy; on this subject the Sheikh *Abu-al-Kheir-Azhari* has the following distich:—

"'Who is the man without care or sorrow, (tell) that I may rub my hand to him.

"'(Behold) the Zingians, without care or sorrow, frolicksome with tipsiness and mirth.'

"The philosophers have discovered that the cause of this cheerfulness proceeds from the influence of the star Soheil, or Canopus, which rises over them every night."—*Extract from a Geographical Persian Manuscript called Heft Aklim, or the Seven Climates, translated by W. Ouseley, Esq.*

† The star Soheil, or Canopus.

‡ "The lizard Stellio. The Arabs call it Hardun. The Turks kill it, for they imagine that by declining the head it mimics them when they say their prayers."—*Hasselquist.*

§ For these particulars respecting Hussun Abdaul I am indebted to the very interesting introduction of Mr. Elphinstone's work upon Caubul.

‖ "As you enter at that Bazar, without the gate of Damascus, you see the Green Mosque, so called because it hath a steeple faced with green glazed bricks, which render it very resplendent; it is covered at top with a pavilion of the same stuff. The Turks say this mosque was made in that place, because Mahomet being come so far, would not enter the town, saying it was too delicious."—*Thevenot.* This reminds one of the following pretty passage in Isaac Walton. "When I sat last on this primrose bank, and looked down these meadows, I thought of them as Charles the Emperor did of the city of Florence, 'that they were too pleasant to be looked on, but only on holidays.'"

¶ Nourmahal signifies Light of the Harem. She was afterwards called Nourjehan, or the Light of the World.

** See the third note on p. 38.

Who has not heard of the Vale of CASHMERE,
With its roses the brightest that earth ever gave,†
Its temples, and grottoes, and fountains as clear
As the love-lighted eyes that hang over their wave?

Oh! to see it at sunset,—when warm o'er the Lake
Its splendour at parting a summer eve throws,
Like a bride, full of blushes, when ling'ring to take
A last look of her mirror at night ere she goes!
When the shrines through the foliage are gleaming half shown,
And each hallows the hour by some rites of its own.
Here the music of pray'r from a minaret swells,
Here the Magian his urn, full of perfume, is swinging,
And here, at the altar, a zone of sweet bells
Round the waist of some fair Indian dancer is ringing.‡
Or to see it by moonlight,—when mellowly shines
The light o'er its palaces, gardens, and shrines;
When the water-falls gleam, like a quick fall of stars,
And the nightingale's hymn from the Isle of Chenars
Is broken by laughs and light echoes of feet
From the cool, shining walks where the young people meet.—
Or at morn, when the magic of daylight awakes
A new wonder each minute, as slowly it breaks,
Hills, cupolas, fountains, call'd forth every one
Out of darkness, as if just born of the Sun.
When the Spirit of Fragrance is up with the day,
From his Harem of night-flow'rs stealing away;
And the wind, full of wantonness woos like a lover
The young aspen-trees,§ till they tremble all over.
When the East is as warm as the light of first hopes,
And Day, with his banner of radiance unfurl'd,
Shines in through the mountainous portal‖ that opes,
Sublime, from that Valley of bliss to the world!

But never yet, by night or day,
In dew of spring or summer's ray,
Did the sweet Valley shine so gay
As now it shines—all love and light,
Visions by day and feasts by night!
A happier smile illumes each brow,
With quicker spread each heart uncloses,
And all is ecstasy,—for now
The Valley holds its Feast of Roses;¶
The joyous Time, when pleasures pour
Profusely round, and, in their shower,
Hearts open, like the Season's Rose,—
The Flow'ret of a hundred leaves,**
Expanding while the dew-fall flows,
And every leaf its balm receives.

* "Haroun Al Raschid, cinquième Khalife des Abassides, s'étant un jour brouillé, avec une de ses maîtresses nommée Maridah, qu'il aimoit cependant jusqu'à l'excès, et cette mésintelligence ayant déjà durée quelque tems, commença à s'ennuyer. Giafar Barmaki, son favori, qui s'en appercût, commanda à Abbas ben Ahnaf, excellent poëte de ce tems là, de composer quelques vers sur le sujet de cette brouillerie. Ce poëte exécuta l'ordre de Giafar, qui fit chanter ces vers par Moussali en présence du Khalife, et ce prince fut tellement touché de la tendresse des vers du poëte, et de la douceur de la voix du musicien, qu'il alla aussitôt trouver Maridah, et fit sa paix avec elle."—*D'Herbelot.*

† "The rose of Kashmere for its brilliancy and delicacy of odour has long been proverbial in the East."—*Forster.*

‡ "Tied round her waist the zone of bells, that sounded with ravishing melody."—*Song of Jayadeva.*

§ "The little isles in the Lake of Cachemire are set with arbours and large-leaved aspen-trees, slender and tall."—*Bernier.*

‖ "The Tuckt Suliman, the name bestowed by the Mahommetans on this hill, forms one side of a grand portal to the Lake."—*Forster.*

¶ "The Feast of Roses continues the whole time of their remaining in bloom."—See *Pietro de la Valle.*

** "Gul sad berk, the Rose of a hundred leaves. I believe a particular species."—*Ouseley.*

'Twas when the hour of evening came
  Upon the Lake, serene and cool,
When Day had hid his sultry flame
  Behind the palms of BARAMOULE,*
When maids began to lift their heads,
Refresh'd from their embroider'd beds,
Where they had slept the sun away,
And waked to moonlight and to play.
All were abroad—the busiest hive
On BELA'S† hills is less alive,
When saffron beds are full in flow'r,
Than look'd the Valley in that hour.
A thousand restless torches play'd
Through every grove and island shade;
A thousand sparkling lamps were set
On every dome and minaret;
And fields and pathways, far and near,
Were lighted by a blaze so clear,
That you could see, in wand'ring round,
The smallest rose-leaf on the ground.
Yet did the maids and matrons leave
Their veils at home that brilliant eve;
And there were glancing eyes about,
And cheeks that would not dare shine out
  In open day, but thought they might
Look lovely then, because 'twas night.
And all were free and wandering,
  And all exclaim'd to all they met,
That never did the summer bring
  So gay a Feast of Roses yet:—
The moon had never shed a light
  So clear as that which bless'd them there;
The roses ne'er shone half so bright,
  Nor they themselves look'd half so fair.

And what a wilderness of flow'rs!
It seem'd as though from all the bow'rs
And fairest fields of all the year,
The mingled spoil were scatter'd here.
The Lake, too, like a garden breathes,
  With the rich buds that o'er it lie,—
As if a shower of fairy wreaths
  Had fall'n upon it from the sky!
And then the sounds of joy,—the beat
Of tabors and of dancing feet;—
The minaret-crier's chant of glee
Sung from his lighted gallery,‡
And answered by a ziraleet
From neighbouring Harem, wild and sweet;—
The merry laughter, echoing
From gardens, where the silken swing§
Wafts some delighted girl above
The top leaves of the orange-grove;
Or from those infant groups at play
Among the tents‖ that line the way,
Flinging, unawed by slave or mother,
Handfuls of roses at each other.—
Then, the sounds from the Lake,—the low whisp'ring in boats,
  As they shoot through the moonlight;—the dipping of oars,
And the wild, airy warbling that ev'ry where floats,
  Through the groves, round the islands, as if all the shores,
Like those of KATHAY, utter'd music, and gave
An answer in song to the kiss of each wave.¶

* *Bernier.*

† A place mentioned in the Toozek Jehangeery, or Memoirs of Jehan-Guire, where there is an account of the beds of saffron-flowers about Cashmere.

‡ "It is the custom among the women to employ the Maazeen to chant from the gallery of the nearest minaret, which on that occasion is illuminated, and the women assembled at the house respond at intervals with a ziraleet or joyous chorus."—*Russel.*

§ "The swing is a favourite pastime in the East, as promoting a circulation of air, extremely refreshing in those sultry climates."—*Richardson.*

"The swings are adorned with festoons. This pastime is accompanied with music of voices and of instruments, hired by the masters of the swings."—*Thevenot.*

‖ "At the keeping of the Feast of Roses we beheld an infinite number of tents pitched, with such a crowd of men, women, boys, and girls, with music, dances," &c. &c.—*Herbert.*

¶ "An old commentator of the Chou-King says, the ancients having remarked that a current of water made some of the stones near its banks send forth a sound, they detached some of them, and being charmed with the delightful sound they emitted, constructed King or musical instruments of them."—*Grosier.*

This miraculous quality has been attributed also to the shore of Attica. "Hujus littus, ait Capella, concentum musicum illisis terræ undis reddere, quod propter tantam eruditionis vim puto dictum."—*Ludov. Vives in Augustin. de Civitat. Dei.* lib. xviii. c. 8.

But the gentlest of all are those sounds, full of feeling,
That soft from the lute of some lover are stealing,—
Some lover, who knows all the heart-touching power
Of a lute and a sigh in this magical hour.
Oh! best of delights as it ev'ry where is
To be near the loved *One*,—what a rapture is his
Who in moonlight and music thus sweetly may glide
O'er the Lake of CASHMERE, with that *One* by his side!
If woman can make the worst wilderness dear,
Think, think what a Heav'n she must make of CASHMERE!

So felt the magnificent Son of ACBAR,*
When from pow'r and pomp and the trophies of war
He flew to that Valley, forgetting them all
With the light of the HAREM, his young NOURMAHAL.
When free and uncrown'd as the Conqueror roved
By the banks of that lake, with his only beloved,
He saw, in the wreaths she would playfully snatch
From the hedges, a glory his crown could not match,
And preferr'd in his heart the least ringlet that curl'd
Down her exquisite neck to the throne of the world.

There's a beauty, forever unchangingly bright,
Like the long, sunny lapse of a summer-day's light,
Shining on, shining on, by no shadow made tender,
Till Love falls asleep in its sameness of splendour.
This *was* not the beauty—oh, nothing like this,
That to young NOURMAHAL gave such magic of bliss!
But that loveliness, ever in motion, which plays
Like the light upon autumn's soft shadowy days,
Now here and now there, giving warmth as it flies
From the lip to the cheek, from the cheek to the eyes;
Now melting in mist and now breaking in gleams,
Like the glimpses a saint hath of Heav'n in his dreams
When pensive, it seem'd as if that very grace,
That charm of all others, was born with her face!
And when angry,—for ev'n in the tranquillest climes
Light breezes will ruffle the blossoms sometimes—
The short, passing anger but seem'd to awaken
New beauty, like flow'rs that are sweetest when shaken.
If tenderness touch'd her, the dark of her eye
At once took a darker, a heav'nlier dye,
From the depth of whose shadow, like holy revealings
From innermost shrines, came the light of her feelings.
Then her mirth—oh! 'twas sportive as ever took wing
From the heart with a burst, like the wild-bird in spring;
Illumed by a wit that would fascinate sages,
Yet playful as Peris just loosed from their cages.†
While her laugh, full of life, without any control
But the sweet one of gracefulness, rung from her soul;
And where it most sparkled no glance could discover,
In lip, cheek, or eyes, for she brighten'd all over,—
Like any fair lake that the breeze is upon,
When it breaks into dimples and laughs in the sun
Such, such were the peerless enchantments, that gave
NOURMAHAL the proud Lord of the East for her slave:
And though bright was his Harem,—a living parterre
Of the flow'rs‡ of this planet—though treasures were there,
For which SOLIMAN'S self might have giv'n all the store
That the navy from OPHIR e'er wing'd to his shore,
Yet dim before *her* were the smiles of them all,
And the Light of his Harem was young NOURMAHAL!

  But where is she now, this night of joy,
  When bliss is every heart's employ?—
  When all around her is so bright,
  So like the visions of a trance,
  That one might think, who came by chance
  Into the vale this happy night,
  He saw that City of Delight§
  In Fairy-land, whose streets and tow'rs
  Are made of gems and light and flow'rs!

* Jehan-Guire was the son of the Great Acbar.

† In the wars of the Dives with the Peris, whenever the former took the latter prisoners, "they shut them up in iron cages, and hung them on the highest trees. Here they were visited by their companions, who brought them the choicest odours."—*Richardson.*

‡ In the Malay language the same word signifies women and flowers

§ The capital of Shadukiam. See the first note on p. 28

Where is the loved Sultana? where,
When mirth brings out the young and fair,
Does she, the fairest hide her brow,
In melancholy stillness now?

Alas!—how light a cause may move
Dissension between hearts that love!
Hearts that the world in vain had tried,
And sorrow but more closely tied;
That stood the storm when waves were rough,
Yet in a sunny hour fall off,
Like ships that have gone down at sea,
When heav'n was all tranquillity!
A something, light as air—a look,
  A word unkind or wrongly taken—
Oh! love, that tempests never shook,
  A breath, a touch like this hath shaken.
And ruder words will soon rush in
To spread the breach that words begin;
And eyes forget the gentle ray
They wore in courtship's smiling day;
And voices lose the tone that shed
A tenderness round all they said;
Till fast declining, one by one,
The sweetnesses of love are gone,
And hearts so lately mingled, seem
Like broken clouds,—or like the stream,
That smiling left the mountain's brow
  As though its waters ne'er could sever,
Yet ere it reach the plain below,
  Breaks into floods that part forever.

Oh, you, that have the charge of Love,
  Keep him in rosy bondage bound,
As in the Fields of Bliss above
  He sits with flow'rets fetter'd round;*
Loose not a tie that round him clings,
Nor ever let him use his wings;
For ev'n an hour, a minute's flight
Will rob the plumes of half their light.
Like that celestial bird,—whose nest
  Is found beneath far Eastern skies,—
Whose wings, though radiant when at rest,
  Lose all their glory when he flies!†

Some diff'rence of this dang'rous kind,—
By which, though light, the links that bind
The fondest hearts may soon be riv'n;
Some shadow in Love's summer heav'n,
Which, though a fleecy speck at first,
May yet in awful thunder burst;—
Such cloud it is that now hangs over
The heart of the Imperial Lover,
And far hath banish'd from his sight
His Nourmahal, his Harem's Light!
Hence is it, on this happy night,
When pleasure through the fields and groves
Has let loose all her world of loves,
And every heart has found its own,
He wanders joyless and alone,
And weary as that bird of Thrace,
Whose pinion knows no resting-place.‡

In vain the loveliest cheeks and eyes
This Eden of the Earth supplies
  Come crowding round—the cheeks are pale,
The eyes are dim:—though rich the spot
With ev'ry flow'r this earth has got,
  What is it to the nightingale,
If there his darling rose is not?§
In vain the Valley's smiling throng
Worship him as he moves along;
He heeds them not—one smile of hers
Is worth a world of worshippers.
They but the Star's adorers are,
She is the Heav'n that lights the Star!

Hence is it, too, that Nourmahal,
  Amid the luxuries of this hour
Far from the joyous festival,
  Sits in her own sequester'd bow'r,
With no one near to sooth or aid,
  But that inspired and wondrous maid,
Namouna, the Enchantress;—one,
O'er whom his race the golden sun
For unremember'd years has run,
Yet never saw her blooming brow
Younger or fairer than 'tis now.
Nay, rather,—as the west wind's sigh
Freshens the flow'r it passes by,—
Time's wing but seem'd, in stealing o'er,
To leave her lovelier than before.
Yet on her smiles a sadness hung,
And when, as oft she spoke or sung
Of other worlds, there came a light
From her dark eyes so strangely bright,
That all believed nor man nor earth
Were conscious of Namouna's birth!

All spells and talismans she knew,
  From the great Mantra,* which around
The Air's sublimer Spirits drew,
  To the gold gems† of Afric, bound
Upon the wand'ring Arab's arm,
To keep him from the Siltim's‡ harm.
And she had pledged her powerful art,—
Pledged it with all the zeal and heart
Of one who knew, though high her sphere,
What 'twas to lose a love so dear,—
To find some spell that should recall
Her Selim's§ smile to Nourmahal!

'Twas midnight—through the lattice, wreath'd
With woodbine, many a perfume breathed
From plants that wake when others sleep,
From timid Jasmine buds, that keep
Their odour to themselves all day,
But, when the sunlight dies away,
Let the delicious secret out
To every breeze that roams about;—
When thus Namouna:—"'Tis the hour
"That scatters spells on herb and flow'r,
"And garlands might be gather'd now,
"That, twined around the sleeper's brow,
"Would make him dream of such delights,
"Such miracles and dazzling sights,
"As Genii of the Sun behold,
"At evening from their tents of Gold
"Upon th' horizon—where they play
"Till twilight comes, and, ray by ray,
"Their sunny mansions melt away.
"Now, too, a chaplet might be wreath'd
"Of buds o'er which the moon has breathed,
"Which worn by her, whose love has stray'd,
  "Might bring some Peri from the skies,
"Some sprite, whose very soul is made
  "Of flow'rets' breaths and lovers' sighs,
"And who might tell——"

"For me, for me,"
Cried Nourmahal impatiently,—
"Oh! twine that wreath for me to-night."
Then, rapidly, with foot as light
As the young musk-roe's, out she flew,
To cull each shining leaf that grew
Beneath the moonlight's hallowing beams,
For this enchanted Wreath of Dreams.

* See the representation of the Eastern Cupid, pinioned closely round with wreaths of flowers, in *Picart's* Cérémonies Religieuses.

† "Among the birds of Tonquin is a species of Goldfinch, which sings so melodiously that it is called the Celestial Bird. Its wings, when it is perched, appear variegated with beautiful colours, but when it flies they lose all their splendour."—*Grosier*.

‡ "As these birds on the Bosphorus are never known to rest, they are called by the French 'les âmes damnées.'"—*Dalloway*.

§ "You may place a hundred handfuls of fragrant herbs and flowers before the nightingale, yet he wishes not, in his constant heart, for more than the sweet breath of his beloved rose."—*Jami*

* "He is said to have found the great *Mantra*, spell or talisman, through which he ruled over the elements and spirits of all denominations."—*Wilford*.

† "The gold jewels of Jinnie, which are called by the Arabs El Herez, from the supposed charm they contain."—*Jackson*.

‡ "A demon, supposed to haunt woods, &c. in a human shape."—*Richardson*.

§ The name of Jehan-Guire before his accession to the throne.

Anemones and Seas of Gold,*
And new-blown lilies of the river,
And those sweet flow'rets, that unfold
Their buds on CAMADEVA's quiver ;†—
The tube-rose, with her silv'ry light,
That in the Gardens of Malay
Is call'd the Mistress of the Night,‡
So like a bride, scented and bright,
She comes out when the sun's away ;—
Amaranths, such as crown the maids
That wander through ZAMARA's shades ;§
And the white moon-flow'r, as it shows,
On SERENDIB's high crags, to those
Who near the isle at evening sail,
Scenting her clove-trees in the gale ;
In short, all flow'rets and all plants,
From the divine Amrita tree,||
That blesses heaven's inhabitants
With fruits of immortality,
Down to the basil tuft,¶ that waves
Its fragrant blossom over graves,
And to the humble rosemary,
Whose sweets so thanklessly are shed
To scent the desert** and the dead :—
All in that garden bloom, and all
Are gather'd by young NOURMAHAL,
Who heaps her baskets with the flow'rs
And leaves, till they can hold no more ;
Then to NAMOUNA flies, and show'rs
Upon her lap the shining store.

With what delight th' Enchantress views
So many buds, bathed with the dews
And beams of that bless'd hour !—her glance
Spoke something, past all mortal pleasures,
As, in a kind of holy trance,
She hung above those fragrant treasures,
Bending to drink their balmy airs,
As if she mix'd her soul with theirs.
And 'twas, indeed, the perfume shed
From flow'rs and scented flame, that fed
Her charmed life—for none had e'er
Beheld her taste of mortal fare,
Nor ever in aught earthly dip,
But the morn's dew, her roseate lip.
Fill'd with the cool, inspiring smell,
Th' Enchantress now begins her spell,
Thus singing as she winds and weaves
In mystic form the glittering leaves :—

I know where the winged visions dwell
That around the night-bed play ;
I know each herb and flow'ret's bell,
Where they hide their wings by day
Then hasten we, maid,
To twine our braid,
To-morrow the dreams and flowers will fade.

The image of love, that nightly flies
To visit the bashful maid,
Steals from the jasmine flower, that sighs
Its soul, like her, in the shade.
The dream of a future, happier hour,
That alights on misery's brow,
Springs out of the silv'ry almond-flow'r,
That blooms on a leafless bough.*
Then hasten we, maid,
To twine our braid,
To-morrow the dreams and flowers will fade

The visions, that oft to worldly eyes
The glitter of mines unfold,
Inhabit the mountain-herb,† that dyes
The tooth of the fawn like gold.
The phantom shapes—oh touch not them
That appal the murd'rer's sight,
Lurk in the fleshly mandrake's stem,
That shrieks, when pluck'd at night !
Then hasten we, maid,
To twine our braid,
To-morrow the dreams and flowers will fade

The dream of the injured, patient mind,
That smiles with the wrongs of men,
Is found in the bruised and wounded rind
Of the cinnamon, sweetest then.
Then hasten we, maid,
To twine our braid,
To-morrow the dreams and flowers will fade

No sooner was the flow'ry crown
Placed on her head, than sleep came down,
Gently as nights of summer fall,
Upon the lids of NOURMAHAL ;—
And, suddenly, a tuneful breeze,
As full of small, rich harmonies
As ever wind, that o'er the tents
Of AZAB‡ blew, was full of scents,
Steals on her ear, and floats and swells,
Like the first air of morning creeping
Into those wreathy, Red Sea shells,
Where Love himself, of old, lay sleeping ;§
And now a Spirit, form'd, 'twould seem,
Of music and of light,—so fair,
So brilliantly his features beam,
And such a sound is in the air
Of sweetness when he waves his wings,—
Hovers around her, and thus sings :

From CHINDARA's|| warbling fount I come,
Call'd by that moonlight garland's spell ;
From CHINDARA's fount, my fairy home,
Where in music, morn and night, I dwell.
Where lutes in the air are heard about,
And voices are singing the whole day long
And every sigh the heart breathes out
Is turn'd, as it leaves the lips, to song !
Hither I come
From my fairy home,
And if there's a magic in Music's strain,
I swear by the breath
Of that moonlight wreath,
Thy Lover shall sigh at thy feet again.

For mine is the lay that lightly floats,
And mine are the murm'ring, dying notes,
That fall as soft as snow on the sea,
And melt in the heart as instantly :—

* Hemasagara, or the Sea of Gold, with flowers of the brightest gold colour."—*Sir W. Jones.*

† "This tree (the Nagacesara) is one of the most delightful on earth, and the delicious odour of its blossoms justly gives them a place in the quiver of Camadeva, or the God of Love."—*Sir W. Jones.*

‡ "The Malayans style the tube-rose (Polianthes tuberosa) Sandal Malam, or the Mistress of the Night."—*Pennant.*

§ The people of the Batta country in Sumatra, (of which Zamara is one of the ancient names,) "when not engaged in war, lead an idle, inactive life, passing the day in playing on a kind of flute, crowned with garlands of flowers, among which the globe-amaranthus, a native of the country, mostly prevails."—*Marsden.*

|| "The largest and richest sort (of the Jambu, or rose-apple) is called Amrita, or immortal, and the mythologists of Tibet apply the same word to a celestial tree, bearing ambrosial fruit."—*Sir W. Jones.*

¶ Sweet bazil, called Rayhan in Persia, and generally found in churchyards

The women in Egypt go, at least two days in the week, to pray and weep at the sepulchres of the dead ; and the custom then is to throw upon the tombs a sort of herb which the Arabs call *rihan*, and which is our sweet basil."—*Maillet*, Lett. 10.

** "In the Great Desert are found many stalks of lavender and rosemary."—*Asiat. Res*

* "The almond-tree with white flowers, blossoms on the bare branches."—*Hasselquist.*

† An herb on Mount Libanus, which is said to communicate a yellow golden hue to the teeth of the goats and other animals that graze upon it.

Niebuhr thinks this may be the herb which the Eastern alchymists look to as a means of making gold. "Most of those alchymical enthusiasts think themselves sure of success, if they could but find out the herb, which gilds the teeth and gives a yellow colour to the flesh of the sheep that eat it. Even the oil of this plant must be of a golden colour. It is called *Haschischat ed dab.*"

Father Jerome Dandini, however, asserts that the teeth of the goats at Mount Libanus are of a *silver* colour ; and adds, "this confirms to me that which I observed in Candia : to wit, that the animals that live on Mount Ida eat a certain herb, which renders their teeth of a golden colour ; which, according to my judgment, cannot otherwise proceed than from the mines which are under ground."—*Dandini*, Voyage to Mount Libanus.

‡ The myrrh country.

§ "This idea (of deities living in shells) was not unknown to the Greeks, who represent the young Nerites, one of the Cupids, as living in shells on the shores of the Red Sea."—*Wilford.*

|| "A fabulous fountain, where instruments are said to be constantly playing."—*Richardson.*

And the passionate strain that, deeply going,
  Refines the bosom it trembles through,
As the musk-wind, over the water blowing,
  Ruffles the wave, but sweetens it too.

Mine is the charm, whose mystic sway
The Spirits of past Delight obey;—
Let but the tuneful talisman sound,
And they come, like Genii, hov'ring round.
And mine is the gentle song that bears
  From soul to soul, the wishes of love,
As a bird, that wafts through genial airs
  The cinnamon-seed from grove to grove.*
'Tis I that mingle in one sweet measure
The past, the present, and future of pleasure;†
When Memory links the tone that is gone
  With the blissful tone that's still in the ear;
And Hope from a heavenly note flies on
  To a note more heavenly still that is near.

The warrior's heart, when touch'd by me,
Can as downy soft and as yielding be
As his own white plume, that high amid death
Through the field has shone—yet moves with a breath!
And, oh, how the eyes of Beauty glisten,
  When Music has reach'd her inward soul,
Like the silent stars, that wink and listen
  While Heaven's eternal melodies roll.
    So hither I come
    From my fairy home,
And if there's a magic in Music's strain,
    I swear by the breath
    Of that moonlight wreath,
Thy lover shall sigh at thy feet again.

'Tis dawn—at least that earlier dawn,
Whose glimpses are again withdrawn,‡
As if the morn had waked, and then
Shut close her lids of light again.
And Nourmahal is up, and trying
  The wonders of her lute, whose strings—
Oh, bliss!—now murmur like the sighing
  From that ambrosial Spirit's wings.
And then, her voice, 'tis more than human—
  Never, till now, had it been given
To lips of any mortal woman
  To utter notes so fresh from heaven;
Sweet as the breath of angel sighs,
  When angel sighs are most divine.—
"Oh! let it last till night," she cries,
  "And he is more than ever mine."
And hourly she renews the lay,
  So fearful lest its heav'nly sweetness
Should, ere the evening, fade away,—
  For things so heav'nly have such fleetness!
But, far from fading, it but grow
Richer, diviner as it flows;
  Till rapt she dwells on every string,
    And pours again each sound along,
  Like Echo, lost and languishing,
    In love with her own wondrous song.

That evening, (trusting that his soul
  Might be from haunting love released
By mirth, by music, and the bowl,)
  Th' imperial Selim held a feast
In his magnificent Shalimar:—*
In whose Saloons, when the first star
Of evening o'er the waters trembled,
The Valley's loveliest all assembled;
All the bright creatures that, like dreams,
Glide through its foliage, and drink beams
Of beauty from its founts and streams;†
And all those wand'ring minstrel-maids,
Who leave—how *can* they leave?—the shades
Of that dear Valley, and are found
  Singing in gardens of the South‡
Those songs, that ne'er so sweetly sound
  As from a young Cashmerian's mouth.

There, too, the Harem's inmates smile;—
  Maids from the West, with sun-bright hair
And from the Garden of the Nile,
  Delicate as the roses there;—§
Daughters of Love from Cyprus' rocks,
With Paphian diamonds in their locks;—‖
Light Peri forms, such as they are
On the gold meads of Candahar;¶
And they, before whose sleepy eyes,
  In their own bright Kathaian bow'rs,
Sparkle such rainbow butterflies,
  That they might fancy the rich flow'rs,
That round them in the sun lay sighing,
Had been by magic all set flying.**

Every thing young, every thing fair
From East and West is blushing there,
Except—except—oh, Nourmahal!
Thou loveliest, dearest of them all,
The one, whose smile shone out alone,
Amidst a world the only one;
Whose light, among so many lights,
Was like that star on starry nights,
The seaman singles from the sky,
To steer his bark forever by!
Thou wert not there—so Selim thought,
  And every thing seem'd drear without thee,
But, ah! thou wert, thou wert,—and brought
  Thy charm of song all fresh about thee.
Mingling unnoticed with a band
Of lutanists from many a land,

---

* "The Pompadour pigeon is the species, which, by carrying the fruit of the cinnamon to different places, is a great disseminator of this valuable tree."—See *Brown's* Illustr., Tab. 19.

† "Whenever our pleasure arises from a succession of sounds, it is a perception of a complicated nature, made up of a *sensation* of the present sound or note, and an *idea* or remembrance of the foregoing, while their mixture and concurrence produce such a mysterious delight, as neither could have produced alone. And it is often heightened by an anticipation of the succeeding notes. Thus Sense, Memory, and Imagination, are conjunctively employed."—*Gerrard* on Taste.

This is exactly the Epicurean theory of Pleasure, as explained by Cicero:—"Quocirca corpus gaudere tamdiu, dum præsentem sentiret voluptatem; animum et præsentem percipere pariter cum corporo et prospicere venientem, nec præteritam præterfluere sinere."

Madame de Staël accounts upon the same principle for the gratification we derive from *rhyme*:—"Elle est l'image de l'espérance et du souvenir. Un son nous fait désirer celui qui doit lui répondre, et quand le second retentit il nous rappelle celui qui vient de nous échapper."

‡ "The Persians have two mornings, the Soobhi Kazim and the Soobhi Sadig, the false and the real day-break. They account for this phenomenon in a most whimsical manner. They say that as the sun rises from behind the Kohi Qaf (Mount Caucasus) it passes a hole perforated through that mountain, and that darting its rays through it, it is the cause of the Soobhi Kazim, or this temporary appearance of day-break. As it ascends, the earth is again veiled in darkness, until the sun rises above the mountain, and brings with it the Soobhi Sadig, or real morning."—*Scott Waring*. He thinks Milton may allude to this, when he says—

"Ere the blabbing Eastern scout,
The nice morn on the Indian steep
From her cabin'd loop-hole peep."

* "In the centre of the plain, as it approaches the Lake, one of the Delhi Emperors, I believe Shah Jehan, constructed a spacious garden called the Shalimar, which is abundantly stored with fruit-trees and flowering shrubs. Some of the rivulets which intersect the plain are led into a canal at the back of the garden, and flowing through its centre, or occasionally thrown into a variety of water-works, compose the chief beauty of the Shalimar. To decorate this spot the Mogul Princes of India have displayed an equal magnificence and taste; especially Jehan Gheer, who, with the enchanting Noor Mahl, made Kashmire his usual residence during the summer months. On arches thrown over the canal are erected, at equal distances, four or five suits of apartments, each consisting of a saloon, with four rooms at the angles, where the followers of the court attend, and the servants prepare sherbets, coffee, and the hookah. The frame of the doors of the principal saloon is composed of pieces of a stone of a black colour, streaked with yellow lines, and of a closer grain and higher polish than porphyry. They were taken, it is said, from a Hindoo temple, by one of the Mogul princes, and are esteemed of great value."—*Forster*.

† "The waters of Cachemir are the more renowned from its being supposed that the Cachemirians are indebted for their beauty to them."—*Ali Yezdi*.

‡ "From him I received the following little Gazzel, or Love Song, the notes of which he committed to paper from the voice of one of those singing girls of Cashmere, who wander from that delightful valley over the various parts of India."—*Persian Miscellanies*.

§ "The roses of the Jinan Nile, or Garden of the Nile, (attached to the Emperor of Morocco's palace,) are unequalled, and mattresses are made of their leaves for the men of rank to recline upon."—*Jackson*.

‖ "On the side of a mountain near Paphos there is a cavern which produces the most beautiful rock-crystal. On account of its brilliancy it has been called the Paphian diamond."—*Mariti*.

¶ "There is a part of Candahar, called Peria, or Fairy Land."—*Thevenot*. In some of those countries to the north of India, vegetable gold is supposed to be produced.

** "These are the butterflies which are called in the Chinese language Flying Leaves. Some of them have such shining colours, and are so variegated, that they may be called flying flowers; and indeed they are always produced in the finest flower gardens."—*Dunn*

And veil'd by such a mask as shades
The features of young Arab maids,—*
A mask that leaves but one eye free,
To do its best in witchery,—
She roved, with beating heart, around,
And waited, trembling, for the minute,
When she might try if still the sound
Of her loved lute had magic in it.

The board was spread with fruits and wine;
With grapes of gold, like those that shine
On Casbin's hills;†—pomegranates full
Of melting sweetness, and the pears,
And sunniest apples‡ that Caubul
In all its thousand gardens§ bears;—
Plantains, the golden and the green,
Malaya's nectar'd mangusteen;‖
Prunes of Bokhara, and sweet nuts
From the far groves of Samarcand,
And Basra dates, and apricots,
Seed of the sun,¶ from Iran's land;—
With rich conserve of Visna cherries,**
Of orange flowers, and of those berries
That, wild and fresh, the young gazelles
Feed on in Erac's rocky dells.††
All these in richest vases smile,
In baskets of pure santal-wood,
And urns of porcelain from that isle‡‡
Sunk underneath the Indian flood,
Whence oft the lucky diver brings
Vases to grace the halls of kings.
Wines, too, of every clime and hue,
Around their liquid lustre threw;
Amber Rosolli,§§—the bright dew
From vineyards of the Green-Sea gushing;‖‖
And Shiraz wine, that richly ran
As if that jewel, large and rare,
The ruby for which Kublai-Khan
Offer'd a city's wealth,¶¶ was blushing,
Melted within the goblets there!

And amply Selim quaffs of each,
And seems resolved the flood shall reach
His inward heart,—shedding around
A genial deluge, as they run,
That soon shall leave no spot undrown'd,
For Love to rest his wings upon.
He little knew how well the boy,
Can float upon a goblet's streams,
Lighting them with his smile of joy;—
As bards have seen him in their dreams,
Down the blue Ganges laughing glide
Upon a rosy lotus wreath,***
Catching new lustre from the tide
That with his image shone beneath.

But what are cups, without the aid
Of song to speed them as they flow?
And see—a lovely Georgian maid,
With all the bloom, the freshen'd glow
Of her own country maidens' looks,
When warm they rise from Teflis' brooks *
And with an eye, whose restless ray,
Full, floating, dark—oh, he, who knows
His heart is weak, of Heav'n should pray
To guard him from such eyes as those!
With a voluptuous wildness flings
Her snowy hand across the strings
Of a syrinda,† and thus sings:—

Come hither, come hither—by night and by day,
We linger in pleasures that never are gone:
Like the waves of the summer, as one dies away,
Another as sweet and as shining comes on.
And the love that is o'er, in expiring, gives birth
To a new one as warm, as unequall'd in bliss
And, oh! if there be an Elysium on earth,
It is this, it is this.‡

Here maidens are sighing, and fragrant their sigh
As the flow'r of the Amra just oped by a bee;§
And precious their tears as that rain from the sky,‖
Which turns into pearls as it falls in the sea.
Oh! think what the kiss and the smile must be worth
When the sigh and the tear are so perfect in bliss.
And own if there be an Elysium on earth,
It is this, it is this.

Here sparkles the nectar, that, hallow'd by love,
Could draw down those angels of old from their sphere,
Who for wine of this earth¶ left the fountains above,
And forgot heav'n's stars for the eyes we have here.
And, bless'd with the odour our goblet gives forth,
What Spirit the sweets of his Eden would miss?
For, oh! if there be an Elysium on earth,
It is this, it is this.

The Georgian's song was scarcely mute,
When the same measure, sound for sound,
Was caught up by another lute,
And so divinely breathed around,
That all stood hush'd and wondering,
And turn'd and look'd into the air,
As if they thought to see the wing
Of Israfil,** the Angel, there;—
So pow'rfully on ev'ry soul
That new, enchanted measure stole.
While now a voice, sweet as the note
Of the charm'd lute, was heard to float
Along its chords, and so entwine
Its sounds with theirs, that none knew whether
The voice or lute was most divine,
So wondrously they went together:—

There's a bliss beyond all that the minstrel has told,
When two, that are link'd in one heav'nly tie,
With heart never changing, and brow never cold,
Love on through all ills, and love on till they die!
One hour of a passion so sacred is worth
Whole ages of heartless and wand'ring bliss;
And, oh! if there *be* an Elysium on earth,
It is this, it is this.

'Twas not the air, 'twas not the words,
But that deep magic in the chords
And in the lips, that gave such pow'r
As Music knew not till that hour.
At once a hundred voices said,
"It is the mask'd Arabian maid!"
While Selim, who had felt the strain
Deepest of any, and had lain

* The Arabian women wear black masks with little clasps prettily ordered."—*Carreri*. Niebuhr mentions their showing but one eye in conversation.

† "The golden grapes of Casbin."—*Description of Persia*.

‡ "The fruits exported from Cabul are apples, pears, pomegranates," &c.—*Elphinstone*.

§ "We sat down under a tree, listened to the birds, and talked with the son of our Mehmaundar about our country and Caubul, of which he gave an enchanting account: that city and its 100,000 gardens," &c.—*Id.*

‖ "The mangusteen, the most delicate fruit in the world; the pride of the Malay islands."—*Marsden*.

¶ "A delicious kind of apricot, called by the Persians tokmek-shems, signifying sun's seed."—*Description of Persia*.

** "Sweetmeats, in a crystal cup, consisting of rose leaves in conserve, with lemon of Visna cherry, orange flowers," &c.—*Russel*.

†† "Antelopes cropping the fresh berries of Eruc."—The *Moallakat*, Poem of Tarafa.

‡‡ "Mauri-ga-Sima, an island near Formosa, supposed to have been sunk in the sea for the crimes of its inhabitants. The vessels which the fishermen and divers bring up from it are sold at an immense price in China and Japan."—See *Kempfer*.

§§ Persian Tales.

‖‖ The white wine of Kishma.

¶¶ "The king of Zeilan is said to have the very finest ruby that was ever seen. Kublai-Khan sent and offered the value of a city for it, but the King answered he would not give it for the treasure of the world." *Marco Polo*.

*** The Indians feign that Cupid was first seen floating down the Ganges on the Nymphæa Nelumbo.—See *Pennant*.

* Teflis is celebrated for its natural warm baths.—See *Ebn Haukal*.

† "The Indian Syrinda, or guitar."—*Symez*.

‡ "Around the exterior of the Dewan Khafs (a building of Shah Allum's) in the cornice are the following lines in letters of gold upon a ground of white marble—'*If there be a paradise upon earth, it is this, it is this.*'"—*Francklin*.

§ "Delightful are the flowers of the Amra trees on the mountain-tops, while the murmuring bees pursue their voluptuous toil."—*Song of Jayadeva*.

‖ "The Nisan or drops of spring rain, which they believe to produce pearls if they fall into shells."—*Richardson*.

¶ For an account of the share which wine had in the fall of the angels, see *Mariti*.

** The Angel of Music. See note † p. 43.

Some minutes rapt, as in a trance,
After the fairy sounds were o'er,
Too inly touch'd for utterance,
Now motion'd with his hand for more :—

Fly to the desert, fly with me,
Our Arab tents are rude for thee;
But, oh! the choice what heart can doubt,
Of tents with love, or thrones without?

Our rocks are rough, but smiling there
Th' acacia waves her yellow hair,
Lonely and sweet, nor loved the less
For flow'ring in a wilderness.

Our sands are bare, but down their slope
The silv'ry-footed antelope
As gracefully and gaily springs
As o'er the marble courts of kings.

Then come—thy Arab maid will be
The loved and lone acacia-tree,
The antelope, whose feet shall bless
With their light sound thy loneliness.

Oh! there are looks and tones that dart
An instant sunshine through the heart,—
As if the soul that minute caught
Some treasure it through life had sought;

As if the very lips and eyes,
Predestined to have all our sighs,
And never be forgot again,
Sparkled and spoke before us then!

So came thy ev'ry glance and tone
When first on me they breathed and shone;
New, as if brought from other spheres,
Yet welcome as if loved for years.

Then fly with me—if thou hast known
No other flame, nor falsely thrown
A gem away, that thou hadst sworn
Should ever in thy heart be worn.

Come, if the love thou hast for me,
Is pure and fresh as mine for thee,—
Fresh as the fountain under ground,
When first 'tis by the lapwing found.*

But if for me thou dost forsake
Some other maid, and rudely break
Her worshipp'd image from its base,
To give to me the ruin'd place;—

Then, fare thee well—I'd rather make
My bower upon some icy lake
When thawing suns begin to shine,
Than trust to love so false as thine!

There was a pathos in this lay,
That, ev'n without enchantment's art,
Would instantly have found its way
Deep into SELIM's burning heart;
But, breathing, as it did, a tone
To earthly lutes and lips unknown;
With every chord fresh from the touch
Of Music's Spirit,—'twas too much!
Starting, he dash'd away the cup,—
Which, all the time of this sweet air,
His hand had held, untasted, up,
As if 'twere fix'd by magic there,—
And naming her, so long unnamed,
So long unseen, wildly exclaim'd,
"Oh NOURMAHAL! oh NOURMAHAL!
"Hadst thou but sung this witching strain,
"I could forget—forgive thee all,
"And never leave those eyes again."

* The Hudhud, or Lapwing, is supposed to have the power of discovering water under ground.

The mask is off—the charm is wrought—
And SELIM to his heart has caught,
In blushes, more than ever bright,
His NOURMAHAL, his Harem's Light!
And well do vanish'd frowns enhance
The charm of every brighten'd glance;
And dearer seems each dawning smile
For having lost its light awhile:
And, happier now for all her sighs,
As on his arm her head reposes,
She whispers him, with laughing eyes,
"Remember, love, the Feast of Roses!"

FADLADEEN, at the conclusion of this light rhapsody, took occasion to sum up his opinion of the young Cashmerian's poetry,—of which, he trusted, they had that evening heard the last. Having recapitulated the epithets, "frivolous"—"inharmonious"—"nonsensical," he proceeded to say that, viewing it in the most favourable light, it resembled one of those Maldivian boats, to which the Princess had alluded in the relation of her dream,*—a slight, gilded thing, sent adrift without rudder or ballast, and with nothing but vapid sweets and faded flowers on board. The profusion, indeed, of flowers and birds, which this poet had ready on all occasions,—not to mention dews, gems, &c.—was a most oppressive kind of opulence to his hearers; and had the unlucky effect of giving to his style all the glitter of the flower-garden without its method, and all the flutter of the aviary without its song. In addition to this, he chose his subjects badly, and was always most inspired by the worst parts of them. The charms of paganism, the merits of rebellion,—these were the themes honoured with his particular enthusiasm; and, in the poem just recited, one of his most palatable passages was in praise of that beverage of the Unfaithful, wine;—"being, perhaps," said he, relaxing into a smile, as conscious of his own character in the Harem on this point, "one of those bards, whose fancy owes all its illumination to the grape, like that painted porcelain,† so curious and so rare, whose images are only visible when liquor is poured into it." Upon the whole, it was his opinion, from the specimens which they had heard, and which, he begged to say, were the most tiresome part of the journey, that—whatever other merits this well-dressed young gentleman might possess—poetry was by no means his proper avocation; "and indeed," concluded the critic, "from his fondness for flowers and for birds, I would venture to suggest that a florist or a bird-catcher is a much more suitable calling for him than a poet."

They had now begun to ascend those barren mountains, which separate Cashmere from the rest of India, and, as the heats were intolerable, and the time of their encampments limited to the few hours necessary for refreshment and repose, there was an end to all their delightful evenings, and LALLA ROOKH saw no more of FERAMORZ. She now felt that her short dream of happiness was over, and that she had nothing but the recollection of its few blissful hours, like the one draught of sweet water that serves the camel across the wilderness, to be her heart's refreshment during the dreary waste of life that was before her. The blight that had fallen upon her spirits soon found its way to her cheek, and her ladies saw with regret—though not without some suspicion of the cause—that the beauty of their mistress, of which they were almost as proud as of their own, was fast vanishing away at the very moment of all when she had most need of it. What must the King of Bucharia feel when, instead of the lively and beautiful LALLA ROOKH, whom the poets of Delhi had described as more perfect than the divinest images in the house of Azor,‡ he should

* See p. 37.

† "The Chinese had formerly the art of painting on the sides of porcelain vessels fish and other animals, which were only perceptible when the vessel was full of some liquor. They call this species Kia-tsin, that is, *azure is put in press*, on account of the manner in which the azure is laid on."—"They are every now and then trying to recover the art of this magical painting, but to no purpose."—*Dunn.*

‡ An eminent carver of idols, said in the Koran to be father to Abraham. "I have such a lovely idol as is not to be met with in the house of Azor."—*Hafiz.*

receive a pale and inanimate victim, upon whose cheek neither health nor pleasure bloomed, and from whose eyes Love had fled,—to hide himself in her heart?

If any thing could have charmed away the melancholy of her spirits, it would have been the fresh airs and enchanting scenery of that Valley, which the Persians so justly called the Unequalled.* But neither the coolness of its atmosphere, so luxurious after toiling up those bare and burning mountains,—neither the splendour of the minarets and pagodas, that shone out from the depth of its woods, nor the grottoes, hermitages, and miraculous fountains,† which make every spot of that region holy ground,—neither the countless waterfalls, that rush into the Valley from all those high and romantic mountains that encircle it, nor the fair city on the Lake, whose houses, roofed with flowers,‡ appeared at a distance like one vast and variegated parterre;—not all these wonders and glories of the most lovely country under the sun could steal her heart for a minute from those sad thoughts which but darkened, and grew bitterer every step she advanced.

The gay pomps and processions that met her upon her entrance into the Valley, and the magnificence with which the roads all along were decorated, did honour to the taste and gallantry of the young King. It was night when they approached the city, and, for the last two miles, they had passed under arches, thrown from hedge to hedge, festooned with only those rarest roses from which the Attar Gul, more precious than gold, is distilled and illuminated in rich and fanciful forms with lanterns of the triple-coloured tortoise-shell of Pegu.§ Sometimes, from a dark wood by the side of the road, a display of fire-works would break out, so sudden and so brilliant, that a Brahmin might fancy he beheld that grove, in whose purple shade the God of Battles was born, bursting into a flame at the moment of his birth;—while, at other times, a quick and playful irradiation continued to brighten all the fields and gardens by which they passed, forming a line of dancing lights along the horizon; like the meteors of the north as they are seen by those hunters,‖ who pursue the white and blue foxes on the confines of the Icy Sea.

These arches and fire-works delighted the Ladies of the Princess exceedingly; and with their usual good logic, they deduced from his taste for illuminations, that the King of Bucharia would make the most exemplary husband imaginable. Nor, indeed, could LALLA ROOKH herself help feeling the kindness and splendour with which the young bridegroom welcomed her;—but she also felt how painful is the gratitude, which kindness from those we cannot love excites; and that their best blandishments come over the heart with all that chilling and deadly sweetness, which we can fancy in the cold, odoriferous wind,¶ that is to blow over this earth in the last days.

The marriage was fixed for the morning after her arrival, when she was, for the first time, to be presented to the monarch in that Imperial Palace beyond the lake, called the Shalimar. Though never before had a night of more wakeful and anxious thought been passed in the Happy Valley, yet, when she rose in the morning, and her Ladies came around her, to assist in the adjustment of the bridal ornaments, they thought they had never seen her look half so beautiful. What she had lost of the bloom and radiancy of her charms was more than made up by that intellectual expression, that soul beaming forth from the eyes, which is worth all the rest of loveliness. When they had tinged her fingers with the Henna leaf, and placed upon her brow a small coronet of jewels, of the shape worn by the ancient Queens of Bucharia, they flung over her head the rose-coloured bridal veil, and she proceeded to the barge that was to convey her across the lake;—first kissing, with a mournful look, the little amulet of carnelian, which her father at parting had hung about her neck.

The morning was as fresh and fair as the maid on whose nuptials it rose, and the shining lake all covered with boats, the minstrels playing upon the shores of the islands, and the crowded summer-houses on the green hills around, with shawls and banners waving from their roofs, presented such a picture of animated rejoicing, as only she who was the object of it all, did not feel with transport. To LALLA ROOKH alone it was a melancholy pageant; nor could she have even borne to look upon the scene, were it not for a hope that, among the crowds around, she might once more perhaps catch a glimpse of FERAMORZ. So much was her imagination haunted by this thought, that there was scarcely an islet or boat she passed on the way, at which her heart did not flutter with the momentary fancy that he was there. Happy, in her eyes, the humblest slave upon whom the light of his dear looks fell!—In the barge immediately after the princess sat FADLADEEN, with his silken curtains thrown widely apart, that all might have the benefit of his august presence, and with his head full of the speech he was to deliver to the King, "concerning FERAMORZ, and literature, and the Chabuk, as connected therewith."

They now had entered the canal which leads from the Lake to the splendid domes and saloons of the Shalimar, and went gliding on through the gardens that ascended from each bank, full of flowering shrubs that made the air all perfume; while from the middle of the canal rose jets of water, smooth and unbroken, to such a dazzling height, that they stood like tall pillars of diamond in the sunshine. After sailing under the arches of various saloons, they at length arrived at the last and most magnificent, where the monarch awaited the coming of his bride; and such was the agitation of her heart and frame, that it was with difficulty she could walk up the marble steps, which were covered with cloth of gold for her ascent from the barge. At the end of the hall stood two thrones, as precious as the Cerulean Throne of Coolburga*, on one of which sat ALIRIS, the youthful King of Bucharia, and on the other was, in a few minutes, to be placed the most beautiful Princess in the world. Immediately upon the entrance of LALLA ROOKH into the saloon, the monarch descended from his throne to meet her; but scarcely had he time to take her hand in his, when she screamed with surprise, and fainted at his feet. It was FERAMORZ himself that stood before her!—FERAMORZ was, himself, the Sovereign of Bucharia, who in this disguise had accompanied his young bride from Delhi, and having won her love as an humble minstrel, now amply deserved to enjoy it as a King.

The consternation of FADLADEEN at this discovery was, for the moment, almost pitiable. But change of opinion is a resource too convenient in courts for this experienced

* Kachmire be Nazeer.—*Forster.*

† "The pardonable superstition of the sequestered inhabitants has multiplied the places of worship of Mahadeo, of Beschan, and of Brama. All Cashmere is holy land, and miraculous fountains abound."—*Major Rennel's* Memoirs of a Map of Hindostan.

Jehan Guire mentions "a fountain in Cashmere called Tirnagh, which signifies a snake; probably because some large snake had formerly been seen there."—"During the lifetime of my father, I went twice to this fountain, which is about twenty coss from the city of Cashmere. The vestiges of places of worship and sanctity are to be traced without number amongst the ruins and the caves, which are interspersed in its neighbourhood."—*Toozek Jehangeery.*—Vide *Asiat. Misc.*, vol. ii.

There is another account of Cashmere by Abul-Fazil, the author of the Ayin-Acbaree, "who," says *Major Rennel*, "appears to have caught some of the enthusiasm of the valley, by his description of the holy places in it."

‡ "On a standing roof of wood is laid a covering of fine earth, which shelters the building from the great quantity of snow that falls in the winter season. This fence communicates an equal warmth in winter, as a refreshing coolness in the summer season, when the tops of the houses, which are planted with a variety of flowers, exhibit at a distance the spacious view of a beautifully-chequered parterre."—*Forster.*

§ "Two hundred slaves there are, who have no other office than to hunt the woods and marshes for triple-coloured tortoises for the King's Vivary. Of the shells of these also lanterns are made."—*Vincent le Blanc's* Travels.

‖ For a description of the Aurora Borealis as it appears to these hunters, vide *Encyclopædia.*

¶ This wind, which is to blow from Syria Damascena, is, according to the Mahometans, one of the signs of the Last Day's approach.

Another of the signs is, "Great distress in the world, so that a man when he passes by another's grave shall say, Would to God I were in his place!"—*Sale's* Preliminary Discourse.

* "On Mahommed Shaw's return to Koolburga (the capital of Dekkan) he made a great festival, and mounted this throne with much pomp and magnificence, calling it Firozeh or Cerulean. I have heard some old persons, who saw the throne Firozeh in the reign of Sultan Mamood Bhamenee, describe it. They say that it was in length nine feet, and three in breadth; made of ebony, covered with plates of pure gold, and set with precious stones of immense value. Every prince of the house of Bhamenee, who possessed this throne, made a point of adding to it some rich stones; so that when, in the reign of Sultan Mamood, it was taken to pieces, to remove some of the jewels to be set in vases and cups, the jewellers valued it at one crore of oons, (nearly four millions sterling.) I learned also that it was called Firozeh from being partly enamelled of a sky-blue colour, which was in time totally concealed by the number of jewels." *Ferishta.*

courtier not to have learned to avail himself of it. His criticisms were all, of course, recanted instantly: he was seized with an admiration of the King's verses, as unbounded as, he begged him to believe, it was disinterested; and the following week saw him in possession of an additional place, swearing by all the Saints of Islam that never had there existed so great a poet as the Monarch ALIRIS, and, moreover, ready to prescribe his favourite regimen of the Chabuk for every man, woman, and child that dared to think otherwise.

Of the happiness of the King and Queen of Bucharia, after such a beginning, there can be but little doubt; and, among the lesser symptoms, it is recorded of LALLA ROOKH, that, to the day of her death, in memory of their delightful journey, she never called the King by any other name than FERAMORZ.

SONGS WRITTEN IN AMERICA IN 1806–7.

I KNEW BY THE SMOKE.

I KNEW by the smoke, that so gracefully curl'd
Above the green elms, that a cottage was near,
And I said, "If there's peace to be found in the world,
A heart that was humble might hope for it here!"

It was noon, and on flowers that languish'd around
In silence reposed the voluptuous bee;
Every leaf was at rest, and I heard not a sound
But the woodpecker tapping the hollow beech-tree.

And "Here in this lone little wood," I exclaim'd,
"With a maid who was lovely to soul and to eye,
"Who would blush when I praised her, and weep if I blamed,
"How blest could I live, and how calm could I die!

"By the shade of yon sumach, whose red berry dips
"In the gush of the fountain, how sweet to recline,
"And to know that I sigh'd upon innocent lips,
"Which had never been sigh'd on by any but mine!"

CANADIAN BOAT SONG.

FAINTLY as tolls the evening chime
Our voices keep tune and our oars keep time.
Soon as the woods on shore look dim,
We'll sing at St. Ann's our parting hymn.
Row, brothers, row, the stream runs fast,
The Rapids are near and the daylight's past.

Why should we yet our sail unfurl?
There is not a breath the blue wave to curl;
But, when the wind blows off the shore,
Oh! sweetly we'll rest our weary oar.
Blow, breezes, blow, the stream runs fast,
The Rapids are near and the daylight's past.

Utawas' tide! this trembling moon
Shall see us float over thy surges soon.
Saint of this green isle! hear our prayers,
Oh, grant us cool heavens and favouring airs.
Blow, breezes, blow, the stream runs fast,
The Rapids are near and the daylight's past.

ALONE BY THE SCHUYLKILL.

ALONE by the Schuylkill a wanderer roved,
And bright were its flowery banks to his eye;
But far, very far were the friends that he loved,
And he gazed on its flowery banks with a sigh.

Oh Nature, though blessed and bright are thy rays,
O'er the brow of creation enchantingly thrown,
Yet faint are they all to the lustre that plays
In a smile from the heart that is fondly our own.

Nor long did the soul of the stranger remain
Unblest by the smile he had languish'd to meet;
Though scarce did he hope it would sooth him again,
Till the threshold of home had been press'd by his feet.

But the lays of his boyhood had stol'n to their ear,
And they loved what they knew of so humble a name
And they told him, with flattery welcome and dear,
That they found in his heart something better than fame.

Nor did woman—oh woman! whose form and whose soul
Are the spell and the light of each path we pursue;
Whether sunn'd in the tropics or chill'd at the pole,
If woman be there, there is happiness too:-

Nor did she her enamoring magic deny,—
That magic his heart had relinquish'd so long,—
Like eyes he had loved was *her* eloquent eye,
Like them did it soften and weep at his song.

Oh, blest be the tear, and in memory oft
May its sparkle be shed o'er the wand'rer's dream,
Thrice blest be that eye, and may passion as soft,
As free from a pang, ever mellow its beam!

The stranger is gone—but he will not forget,
When at home he shall talk of the toils he has known,
To tell, with a sigh, what endearments he met,
As he stray'd by the wave of the Schuylkill alone

THE LAKE OF THE DISMAL SWAMP.

"They tell of a young man, who lost his mind upon the death of a girl he loved, and who, suddenly disappearing from his friends, was never afterwards heard of. As he had frequently said, in his ravings, that the girl was not dead, but gone to the Dismal Swamp, it is supposed he had wandered into that dreary wilderness, and had died of hunger, or been lost in some of its dreadful morasses."—*Anon.*

"La Poésie a ses monstres comme la nature."—D'ALEMBERT.

"THEY made her a grave, too cold and damp
"For a soul so warm and true;
"And she's gone to the Lake of the Dismal Swamp,
"Where, all night long, by a fire-fly lamp,
"She paddles her white canoe.

"And her fire-fly lamp I soon shall see,
"And her paddle I soon shall hear;
"Long and loving our life shall be,
"And I'll hide the maid in a cypress-tree,
"When the footstep of death is near."

Away to the Dismal Swamp he speeds—
His path was rugged and sore,
Through tangled juniper, beds of reeds,
Through many a fen, where the serpent feeds,
And man never trod before.

And, when on the earth he sunk to sleep,
If slumber his eyelids knew,
He lay, where the deadly vine doth weep
Its venomous tear and nightly steep
The flesh with blistering dew!

And near him the she-wolf stirr'd the brake,
And the copper-snake breathed in his ear,
Till he starting cried, from his dream awake,
"Oh! when shall I see the dusky Lake,
"And the white canoe of my dear?"

He saw the Lake, and a meteor bright
Quick over its surface play'd—
"Welcome," he said, "my dear one's light."
And the dim shore echoed, for many a night,
The name of the death-cold maid.

Till he hollow'd a boat of the birchen bark,
  Which carried him off from shore;
Far, far he follow'd the meteor spark,
The wind was high and the clouds were dark,
  And the boat return'd no more.

But oft, from the Indian hunter's camp,
  This lover and maid so true
Are seen at the hour of midnight damp
To cross the Lake by a fire-fly lamp,
  And paddle their white canoe!

THE SNOW SPIRIT.

No, ... 'er did the wave in its elements steep
  An island of lovelier charms;
It blooms in the giant embrace of the deep,
  Like Hebe in Hercules' arms.
The blush of your bowers is light to the eye,
  And their melody balm to the ear;
But the fiery planet of day is too nigh,
  And the Snow Spirit never comes here.

The down from his wing is as white as the pearl
  That shines through thy lips when they part,
And it falls on the green earth as melting, my girl,
  As a murmur of thine on the heart.
Oh! fly to the clime, where he pillows the death,
  As he cradles the birth of the year;
Bright are your bowers and balmy their breath,
  But the Snow Spirit cannot come here.

How sweet to behold him, when borne on the gale,
  And brightening the bosom of morn,
He flings, like the priest of Diana, a veil
  O'er the brow of each virginal thorn.
Yet think not the veil he so chillingly casts
  Is the veil of a vestal severe;
No, no, thou wilt see, what a moment it lasts,
  Should the Snow Spirit ever come here.

But fly to his region—lay open thy zone,
  And he'll weep all his brilliancy dim,
To think that a bosom, as white as his own,
  Should not melt in the daybeam like him.
Oh! lovely the print of those delicate feet
  O'er his luminous path will appear—
Fly, fly, my beloved! this island is sweet,
  But the Snow Spirit cannot come here.

THE FIRE-FLY.

At morning, when the earth and sky
  Are glowing with the light of spring,
We see thee not, thou humble fly!
  Nor think upon thy gleaming wing.

But when the skies have lost their hue,
  And sunny lights no longer play,
Oh then we see and bless thee too
  For sparkling o'er the dreary way.

Thus let me hope, when lost to me
  The lights that now my life illume,
Some milder joys may come, like thee,
  To cheer, if not to warm, the gloom!

THE STEERSMAN'S SONG.

When freshly blows the northern gale,
  And under courses snug we fly;
Or when light breezes swell the sail,
  And royals proudly sweep the sky;
'Longside the wheel, unwearied still
  I stand, and, as my watchful eye
Doth mark the needle's faithful thrill,
  I think of her I love, and cry,
            Port, my boy, port!

When calms delay, or breezes blow
  Right from the point we wish to steer;
When by the wind close-haul'd we go,
  And strive in vain the port to near;
I think 'tis thus the fates defer
  My bliss with one that's far away,
And while remembrance springs to her,
  I watch the sails and sighing say,
            Thus, my boy! thus

But see, the wind draws kindly aft,
  All hands are up the yards to square,
And now the floating stu'n-sails waft
  Our stately ship through waves and air.
Oh! then I think that yet for me
  Some breeze of fortune thus may spring,
Some breeze to waft me, love, to thee—
  And in that hope I smiling sing,
            Steady, boy! so.

A BEAM OF TRANQUILLITY SMILED IN THE WEST.

A beam of tranquillity smiled in the west,
  The storms of the morning pursued us no more,
And the wave, while it welcomed the moment of rest,
  Still heaved, as remembering ills that were o'er.

Serenely my heart took the hue of the hour,
  Its passions were sleeping, were mute as the dead;
And the spirit becalm'd but remember'd their power,
  As the billow the force of the gale that was fled.

I thought of those days, when to pleasure alone
  My heart ever granted a wish or a sigh;
When the saddest emotion my bosom had known,
  Was pity for those who were wiser than I.

I reflected, how soon in the cup of Desire
  The pearl of the soul may be melted away;
How quickly, alas, the pure sparkle of fire
  We inherit from heav'n, may be quench'd in the clay

And I pray'd of that Spirit who lighted the flame,
  That Pleasure no more might its purity dim;
So that, sullied but little, or brightly the same,
  I might give back the boon I had borrow'd from him

How blest was the thought! it appear'd as if Heav'n
  Had already an opening to Paradise shown;
As if, passion all chasten'd and error forgiven.
  My heart then began to be purely its own

I look'd to the west, and the beautiful sky,
  Which morning had clouded, was clouded no more.
"Oh! thus," I exclaim'd, "may a heavenly eye
  "Shed light on the soul that was darken'd before!"

WELL—PEACE TO THY HEART.

Well—peace to thy heart, though another's it be,
And health to that cheek, though it bloom not for me!
To-morrow I sail for those cinnamon groves,
Where nightly the ghost of the Carribee roves,
And, far from the light of those eyes, I may yet
Their allurements forgive and their splendour forget

Farewell to Bermuda, and long may the bloom
Of the lemon and myrtle its valleys perfume;
May spring to eternity hallow the shade,
Where Ariel has warbled and Waller has stray'd.
And thou—when, at dawn, thou shalt happen to roam
Through the lime-cover'd alley that leads to thy home,
Where oft, when the dance and the revel were done,
And the stars were beginning to fade in the sun,
I have led thee along, and have told by the way
What my heart all the night had been burning to say—
Oh! think of the past—give a sigh to those times,
And a blessing for me to that alley of limes.

THE CULPRIT FAY,

BY

JOSEPH RODMAN DRAKE.

"My visual orbs are purged from film, and, lo!
Instead of Anster's turnip-bearing vales
I see old fairy land's miraculous show!
  Her trees of tinsel kissed by freakish gales,
Her Ouphs that, cloaked in leaf-gold, skim the breeze,
  And fairies, swarming ——————"

TENNANT'S ANSTER FAIR.

I.

'Tis the middle watch of a summer's night—
The earth is dark, but the heavens are bright;
Naught is seen in the vault on high
But the moon, and the stars, and the cloudless sky,
And the flood which rolls its milky hue,
A river of light on the welkin blue.
The moon looks down on old Cronest,
She mellows the shades, on his shaggy breast,
And seems his huge gray form to throw
In a silver cone on the wave below;
His sides are broken by spots of shade,
By the walnut bough and the cedar made,
And through their clustering branches dark
Glimmers and dies the fire-fly's spark—
Like starry twinkles that momently break
Through the rifts of the gathering tempest's rack.

II.

The stars are on the moving stream,
  And fling, as its ripples gently flow,
A burnished length of wavy beam
  In an eel-like, spiral line below;
The winds are whist, and the owl is still,
  The bat in the shelvy rock is hid.
And naught is heard on the lonely hill
But the cricket's chirp, and the answer shrill
  Of the gauze-winged katy-did;
And the plaint of the wailing whip-poor-will,
  Who moans unseen, and ceaseless sings,
Ever a note of wail and wo,
  Till morning spreads her rosy wings,
And earth and sky in her glances glow.

III.

'Tis the hour of fairy ban and spell;
The wood-tick has kept the minutes well;
He has counted them all with click and stroke
Deep in the heart of the mountain-oak,
And he has awakened the sentry elve
  Who sleeps with him in the haunted tree,
To bid him ring the hour of twelve,
  And call the fays to their revelry;
Twelve small strokes on his tinkling bell—
('Twas made of the white snail's pearly shell;)
"Midnight comes, and all is well!
Hither, hither, wing your way!
'Tis the dawn of the fairy-day."

IV.

They come from beds of lichen green,
They creep from the mullen's velvet screen;
  Some on the backs of beetles fly
From the silver tops of moon-touched trees,
  Where they swung in their cobweb hammocks nigh,
And rocked about in the evening breeze;
  Some from the hum-bird's downy nest—
They had driven him out by elfin power,
  And, pillowed on plumes of his rainbow breast,
Had slumbered there till the charmed hour;
  Some had lain in the scoop of the rock,
With glittering ising-stars inlaid;
  And some had opened the four-o'clock,
And stole within its purple shade.
  And now they throng the moonlight glade,
Above—below—on every side,
  Their little minim forms arrayed
In the tricksy pomp of fairy pride!

V.

They come not now to print the lea,
In freak and dance around the tree,
Or at the mushroom board to sup,
And drink the dew from the buttercup;—
A scene of sorrow waits them now,
For an Ouphe has broken his vestal vow;
He has loved an earthly maid,
And left for her his woodland shade;
He has lain upon her lip of dew,
And sunned him in her eye of blue,
Fanned her cheek with his wing of air,
Played in the ringlets of her hair,
And, nestling on her snowy breast,
Forgot the lily-king's behest.
For this the shadowy tribes of air
  To the elfin court must haste away:—
And now they stand expectant there,
  To hear the doom of the culprit Fay.

VI.

The throne was reared upon the grass,
Of spice-wood and of sassafras;
On pillars of mottled tortoise-shell
Hung the burnished canopy—
And over it gorgeous curtains fell
Of the tulip's crimson drapery.
The monarch sat on his judgment-seat,
On his brow the crown imperial shone,
The prisoner Fay was at his feet,
And his peers were ranged around the throne.
He waved his sceptre in the air,
He looked around and calmly spoke;
His brow was grave and his eye severe,
But his voice in a softened accent broke:

VII.

"Fairy! Fairy! list and mark:
Thou hast broke thine elfin chain;
Thy flame-wood lamp is quenched and dark,
And thy wings are died with a deadly stain—
Thou hast sullied thine elfin purity
In the glance of a mortal maiden's eye,
Thou hast scorned our dread decree,
And thou shouldst pay the forfeit high,
But well I know her sinless mind
Is pure as the angel forms above,
Gentle and meek, and chaste and kind,
Such as a spirit well might love;
Fairy! had she spot or taint,
Bitter had been thy punishment.

Tied to the hornet's shardy wings;
Tossed on the pricks of nettles' stings;
Or seven long ages doomed to dwell
With the lazy worm in the walnut-shell;
Or every night to writhe and bleed
Beneath the tread of the centipede;
Or bound in a cobweb dungeon dim,
Your jailer a spider huge and grim,
Amid the carrion bodies to lie,
Of the worm, and the bug, and the murdered fly
These it had been your lot to bear,
Had a stain been found on the earthly fair.
Now list, and mark our mild decree—
Fairy, this your doom must be:

VIII.

"Thou shalt seek the beach of sand
Where the water bounds the elfin land;
Thou shalt watch the oozy brine
Till the sturgeon leaps in the bright moonshine,
Then dart the glistening arch below,
And catch a drop from his silver bow.
The water-sprites will wield their arms
And dash around, with roar and rave,
And vain are the woodland spirits' charms,
They are the imps that rule the wave.
Yet trust thee in thy single might:
If thy heart be pure and thy spirit right,
Thou shalt win the warlock fight.

IX.

"If the spray-bead gem be won,
The stain of thy wing is washed away:
But another errand must be done
Ere thy crime be lost for aye;
Thy flame-wood lamp is quenched and dark,
Thou must reillume its spark.
Mount thy steed and spur him high
To the heaven's blue canopy;
And when thou seest a shooting star,
Follow it fast, and follow it far—
The last faint spark of its burning train
Shall light the elfin lamp again.
Thou hast heard our sentence, Fay;
Hence! to the water-side, away!"

X.

The goblin marked his monarch well;
He spake not, but he bowed him low,
Then plucked a crimson colen-bell,
And turned him round in act to go.
The way is long, he can not fly,
His soiled wing has lost its power,
And he winds adown the mountain high,
For many a sore and weary hour.
Through dreary beds of tangled fern,
Through groves of nightshade dark and dern,
Over the grass and through the brake,
Where toils the ant and sleeps the snake;
Now over the violets azure flush
He skips along in lightsome mood;
And now he thrids the bramble-bush,
Till its points are dyed in fairy blood.
He has leaped the bog, he has pierced the brier,
He has swum the brook, and waded the mire,
Till his spirits sank, and his limbs grew weak,
And the red waxed fainter in his cheek.
He had fallen to the ground outright,
For rugged and dim was his onward track,
But there came a spotted toad in sight,
And he laughed as he jumped upon her back.
He bridled her mouth with a silkweed twist,
He lashed her sides with an osier thong;
And now, through evening's dewy mist,
With leap and spring they bound along,
Till the mountain's magic verge is past,
And the beach of sand is reached at last.

XI.

Soft and pale is the moony beam,
Moveless still the glassy stream;
The wave is clear, the beach is bright
With snowy shells and sparkling stones;
The shore-surge comes in ripples light,
In murmurings faint and distant moans;
And ever afar in the silence deep
Is heard the splash of the sturgeon's leap,
And the bend of his graceful bow is seen—
A glittering arch of silver sheen,
Spanning the wave of burnished blue,
And dripping with gems of the river-dew.

XII.

The elfin cast a glance around,
As he lighted down from his courser toad,
Then round his breast his wings he wound,
And close to the river's brink he strode;
He sprang on a rock, he breathed a prayer,
Above his head his arms he threw,
Then tossed a tiny curve in air,
And headlong plunged in the waters blue.

XIII.

Up sprung the spirits of the waves,
From the sea-silk beds in their coral caves,
With snail-plate armor snatched in haste,
They speed their way through the liquid waste.
Some are rapidly borne along
On the mailed shrimp or the prickly prong,
Some on the blood-red leeches glide,
Some on the stony star-fish ride,
Some on the back of the lancing squab,
Some on the sideling soldier-crab;
And some on the jellied quarl, that flings
At once a thousand streamy stings;
They cut the wave with the living oar,
And hurry on to the moonlight shore,
To guard their realms and chase away
The footsteps of the invading Fay.

XIV.

Fearlessly he skims along,
His hope is high, and his limbs are strong,

He spreads his arms like the swallow's wing,
And throws his feet with a frog-like fling;
His locks of gold on the waters shine,
At his breast the tiny foam-bees rise,
His back gleams bright above the brine,
And the wake-line foam behind him lies.
But the water-sprites are gathering near
To check his course along the tide;
Their warriors come in swift career
And hem him round on every side;
On his thigh the leech has fixed his hold,
The quarl's long arms are round him rolled,
The prickly prong has pierced his skin,
And the squab has thrown his javelin,
The gritty star has rubbed him raw,
And the crab has struck with his giant claw;
He howls with rage, and he shrieks with pain,
He strikes around, but his blows are vain;
Hopeless is the unequal fight,
Fairy! naught is left but flight.

XV.

He turned him round, and fled amain
With hurry and dash to the beach again,
He twisted over from side to side,
And laid his cheek to the cleaving tide;
The strokes of his plunging arms are fleet,
And with all his might he flings his feet,
But the water-sprites are round him still,
To cross his path and work him ill.
They bade the wave before him rise;
They flung the sea-fire in his eyes,
And they stunned his ears with the scallop-stroke,
With the porpoise heave and the drum-fish croak.
Oh! but a weary wight was he
When he reached the foot of the dogwood-tree.
—Gashed and wounded, and stiff and sore,
He laid him down on the sandy shore;
He blessed the force of the charmed line,
And he banned the water-goblin's spite,
For he saw around in the sweet moonshine
Their little wee faces above the brine,
Giggling and laughing with all their might
At the piteous hap of the Fairy wight.

XVI.

Soon he gathered the balsam dew
From the sorrel-leaf and the henbane bud;
Over each wound the balm he drew,
And with cobweb lint he stanched the blood.
The mild west wind was soft and low,
It cooled the heat of his burning brow,
And he felt new life in his sinews shoot,
As he drank the juice of the calamus root;
And now he treads the fatal shore,
As fresh and vigorous as before.

XVII.

Wrapped in musing stands the sprite:
'Tis the middle wane of night;
His task is hard, his way is far,
But he must do his errand right
Ere dawning mounts her beamy car,
And rolls her chariot wheels of light;
And vain are the spells of fairy-land;
He must work with a human hand.

XVIII.

He cast a saddened look around,
But he felt new joy his bosom swell,
When, glittering on the shadowed ground,
He saw a purple mussel-shell;
Thither he ran, and he bent him low,
He heaved at the stern and he heaved at the bow,
And he pushed her over the yielding sand,
Till he came to the verge of the haunted land.
She was as lovely a pleasure-boat
As ever fairy had paddled in,
For she glowed with purple paint without,
And shone with silvery pearl within;
A sculler's notch in the stern he made,
An oar he shaped of the bootle blade;
Then sprung to his seat with a lightsome leap,
And launched afar on the calm, blue deep.

XIX.

The imps of the river yell and rave;
They had no power above the wave,
But they heaved the billow before the prow,
And they dashed the surge against her side,
And they struck her keel with jerk and blow,
Till the gunwale bent to the rocking tide.
She wimpled about to the pale moonbeam,
Like a feather that floats on a wind-tossed stream;
And momently athwart her track
The quarl upreared his island back,
And the fluttering scallop behind would float,
And patter the water about the boat;
But he bailed her out with his colen-bell,
And he kept her trimmed with a wary tread,
While on every side like lightning fell
The heavy strokes of his bootle-blade.

XX.

Onward still he held his way,
Till he came where the column of moonshine lay,
And saw beneath the surface dim
The brown-backed sturgeon slowly swim;
Around him were the goblin train—
But he sculled with all his might and main,
And followed wherever the sturgeon led,
Till he saw him upward point his head;
Then he dropped his paddle-blade,
And held his colen-goblet up
To catch the drop in its crimson cup.

XXI.

With sweeping tail and quivering fin,
Through the wave the sturgeon flew,
And, like the heaven-shot javelin,
He sprung above the waters blue.
Instant as the star-fall light
He plunged him in the deep again,
But left an arch of silver bright,
The rainbow of the moony main.
It was a strange and lovely sight
To see the puny goblin there;
He seemed an angel form of light,
With azure wing and sunny hair,
Throned on a cloud of purple fair,
Circled with blue and edged with white,
And sitting at the fall of even
Beneath the bow of summer heaven.

XXII.

A moment, and its lustre fell;
But ere it met the billow blue,
He caught within his crimson bell
A droplet of its sparkling dew—
Joy to thee, Fay! thy task is done,
Thy wings are pure, for the gem is won—
Cheerly ply thy dripping oar,
And haste away to the elfin shore.

XXIII.

He turns, and, lo! on either side
The ripples on his path divide;
And the track o'er which his boat must pass
Is smooth as a sheet of polished glass.
Around, their limbs the sea-nymphs lave,
With snowy arms half swelling out,
While on the glossed and gleamy wave
Their sea-green ringlets loosely float;

They swim around with smile and song;
They press the bark with pearly hand,
And gently urge her course along,
Toward the beach of speckled sand;
And, as he lightly leaped to land,
They bade adieu with nod and bow,
Then gayly kissed each little hand,
And dropped in the crystal deep below.

XXIV.

A moment stayed the fairy there;
He kissed the beach and breathed a prayer;
Then spread his wings of gilded blue,
And on to the elfin court he flew;
As ever ye saw a bubble rise,
And shine with a thousand changing dies,
Till, lessening far, through ether driven,
It mingles with the hues of heaven;
As, at the glimpse of morning pale,
The lance-fly spreads his silken sail,
And gleams with blendings soft and bright,
Till lost in the shades of fading night;
So rose from earth the lovely Fay—
So vanished, far in heaven away!

* * * * * *

Up, Fairy! quit thy chick-weed bower,
The cricket has called the second hour,
Twice again, and the lark will rise
To kiss the streaking of the skies—
Up! thy charmed armor don,
Thou'lt need it ere the night be gone.

XXV.

He put his acorn helmet on;
It was plumed of the silk of the thistle-down;
The corslet plate that guarded his breast
Was once the wild bee's golden vest;
His cloak, of a thousand mingled dies,
Was formed of the wings of butterflies;
His shield was the shell of a lady-bug queen,
Studs of gold on a ground of green;
And the quivering lance which he brandished bright,
Was the sting of a wasp he had slain in fight.
Swift he bestrode his fire-fly steed;
He bared his blade of the bent grass blue;
He drove his spurs of the cockle-seed,
And away like a glance of thought he flew,
To skim the heavens, and follow far
The fiery trail of the rocket-star.

XXVI.

The moth-fly, as he shot in air,
Crept under the leaf, and hid her there;
The katy-did forgot its lay,
The prowling gnat fled fast away,
The fell mosqueto checked his drone,
And folded his wings till the Fay was gone,
And the wily beetle dropped his head,
And fell on the ground as if he were dead;
They crouched them close in the darksome shade,
They quaked all o'er with awe and fear,
For they had felt the blue-bent blade,
And writhed at the prick of the elfin spear;
Many a time, on a summer's night,
When the sky was clear and the moon was bright,
They had been roused from the haunted ground
By the yelp and bay of the fairy hound;
They had heard the tiny bugle-horn,
They had heard the twang of the maize-silk string,
When the vine-twig bows were tightly drawn,
And the needle-shaft through air was borne,
Feathered with down of the hum-bird's wing.
And now they deemed the courier ouphe,
Some hunter-sprite of the elfin ground;
And they watched till they saw him mount the roof
That canopies the world around;
Then glad they left their covert lair,
And freaked about in the midnight air

XXVII.

Up to the vaulted firmament
His path the fire-fly courser bent,
And at every gallop on the wind,
He flung a glittering spark behind;
He flies like a feather in the blast
Till the first light cloud in heaven is past.
But the shapes of air have begun their work,
And a drizzly mist is round him cast,
He can not see through the mantle murk,
He shivers with cold, but he urges fast;
Through storm and darkness, sleet and shade,
He lashes his steed and spurs amain
For shadowy hands have twitched the rein,
And flame-shot tongues around him played,
And near him many a fiendish eye
Glared with a fell malignity,
And yells of rage, and shrieks of fear,
Came screaming on his startled ear.

XXVIII.

His wings are wet around his breast,
The plume hangs dripping from his crest,
His eyes are blurred with the lightning's glare,
And his ears are stunned with the thunder's blare
But he gave a shout, and his blade he drew,
He thrust before and he struck behind,
Till he pierced their cloudy bodies through,
And gashed their shadowy limbs of wind;
Howling the misty spectres flew,
They rend the air with frightful cries,
For he has gained the welkin blue,
And the land of clouds beneath him lies.

XXIX.

Up to the cope careering swift,
In breathless motion fast,
Fleet as the swallow cuts the drift,
Or the sea-roc rides the blast,
The sapphire sheet of eve is shot,
The sphered moon is past,
The earth but seems a tiny blot
On a sheet of azure cast.
O! it was sweet, in the clear moonlight,
To tread the starry plain of even,
To meet the thousand eyes of night,
And feel the cooling breath of heaven!
But the elfin made no stop or stay
Till he came to the bank of the milky-way,
Then he checked his courser's foot,
And watched for the glimpse of the planet-shoot.

XXX.

Sudden along the snowy tide
That swelled to meet their footsteps' fall,
The sylphs of heaven were seen to glide,
Attired in sunset's crimson pall;
Around the Fay they weave the dance,
They skip before him on the plain,
And one has taken his wasp-sting lance,
And one upholds his bridle-rein;
With warblings wild they lead him on
To where, through clouds of amber seen,
Studded with stars, resplendent shone
The palace of the sylphid queen.
Its spiral columns, gleaming bright,
Were streamers of the northern light;
Its curtain's light and lovely flush
Was of the morning's rosy blush,
And the ceiling fair that rose aboon
The white and feathery fleece of noon.

XXXI.

But, O! how fair the shape that lay
Beneath a rainbow bending bright;
She seemed to the entranced Fay
The loveliest of the forms of light;

Her mantle was the purple rolled
  At twilight in the west afar;
'Twas tied with threads of dawning gold,
  And buttoned with a sparkling star.
Her face was like the lily roon
  That veils the vestal planet's hue;
Her eyes, two beamlets from the moon,
  Set floating in the welkin blue.
Her hair is like the sunny beam,
And the diamond gems which round it gleam
Are the pure drops of dewy even
That ne'er have left their native heaven.

XXXII.

She raised her eyes to the wondering sprite,
  And they leaped with smiles, for well I ween
Never before in the bowers of light
  Had the form of an earthly Fay been seen.
Long she looked in his tiny face;
  Long with his butterfly cloak she played;
She smoothed his wings of azure lace,
  And handled the tassel of his blade;
And as he told in accents low
The story of his love and wo,
She felt new pains in her bosom rise,
And the tear-drop started in her eyes.
And "O, sweet spirit of earth," she cried,
  "Return no more to your woodland height,
But ever here with me abide
  In the land of everlasting light!
Within the fleecy drift we'll lie,
  We'll hang upon the rainbow's rim;
And all the jewels of the sky
  Around thy brow shall brightly beam!
And thou shalt bathe thee in the stream
  That rolls its whitening foam aboon,
And ride upon the lightning's gleam,
  And dance upon the orbed moon!
We'll sit within the Pleiad ring,
  We'll rest on Orion's starry belt,
And I will bid my sylphs to sing
  The song that makes the dew-mist melt;
Their harps are of the umber shade,
  That hides the blush of waking day,
And every gleamy string is made
  Of silvery moonshine's lengthened ray;
And thou shalt pillow on my breast,
  While heavenly breathings float around,
And, with the sylphs of ether blest,
  Forget the joys of fairy ground."

XXXIII.

She was lovely and fair to see,
And the elfin's heart beat fitfully;
But lovelier far, and still more fair,
The earthly form imprinted there;
Naught he saw in the heavens above
Was half so dear as his mortal love,
For he thought upon her looks so meek,
And he thought of the light flush on her cheek;
Never again might he bask and lie
On that sweet cheek and moonlight eye,
But in his dreams her form to see,
To clasp her in his revery,
To think upon his virgin bride,
Was worth all heaven, and earth beside.

XXXIV.

"Lady," he cried, "I have sworn to-night,
On the word of a fairy-knight,
To do my sentence-task aright;
My honor scarce is free from stain,
I may not soil its snows again;
Betide me weal, betide me wo,
Its mandate must be answered now."
Her bosom heaved with many a sigh,
The tear was in her drooping eye;
But she led him to the palace-gate,
  And called the sylphs who hovered there,
And bade them fly and bring him straight
  Of clouds condensed a sable car.
With charm and spell she blessed it there,
From all the fiends of upper air;
Then round him cast the shadowy shroud,
And tied his steed behind the cloud;
And pressed his hand as she bade him fly
Far to the verge of the northern sky,
For by its wane and wavering light
There was a star would fall to-night.

XXXV.

Borne afar on the wings of the blast,
Northward away, he speeds him fast,
And his courser follows the cloudy wain
Till the hoof-strokes fall like pattering rain.
The clouds roll backward as he flies,
Each flickering star behind him lies,
And he has reached the northern plain,
And backed his fire-fly steed again,
Ready to follow in its flight
The streaming of the rocket-light.

XXXVI.

The star is yet in the vault of heaven,
  But it rocks in the summer gale;
And now 'tis fitful and uneven,
  And now 'tis deadly pale;
And now 'tis wrapped in sulphur-smoke,
  And quenched is its rayless beam,
And now with a rattling thunder-stroke
  It bursts in flash and flame.
As swift as the glance of the arrowy lance
  That the storm-spirit flings from high,
The star-shot flew o'er the welkin blue,
  As it fell from the sheeted sky.
As swift as the wind in its trail behind
  The elfin gallops along,
The fiends of the clouds are bellowing loud,
  But the sylphid charm is strong;
He gallops unhurt in the shower of fire,
  While the cloud-fiends fly from the blaze,
He watches each flake till its sparks expire,
  And rides in the light of its rays.
But he drove his steed to the lightning's speed,
  And caught a glimmering spark;
Then wheeled around to the fairy ground,
  And sped through the midnight dark.

* * * * * * * *

Ouphe and Goblin! Imp and Sprite!
  Elf of eve! and starry Fay!
Ye that love the moon's soft light,
  Hither, hither wend your way;
Twine ye in a jocund ring,
  Sing and trip it merrily,
Hand to hand, and wing to wing,
  Round the wild witch-hazel tree.

Hail the wanderer again
  With dance and song, and lute and lyre,
Pure his wing and strong his chain,
  And doubly bright his fairy fire.
Twine ye in an airy round,
  Brush the dew and print the lea;
Skip and gambol, hop and bound,
  Round the wild witch-hazel tree.

The beetle guards our holy ground,
  He flies about the haunted place,
And if mortal there be found,
  He hums in his ears and flaps his face;
The leaf-harp sounds our roundelay,
  The owlet's eyes our lanterns be;
Thus we sing, and dance, and play,
  Round the wild witch-hazel tree.

But, hark! from tower on tree-top high,
  The sentry-elf his call has made:
A streak is in the eastern sky,
  Shapes of moonlight! flit and fade!
The hill-tops gleam in morning's spring,
The sky-lark shakes his dappled wing,
The day-glimpse glimmers on the lawn,
The cock has crowed, and the Fays are gone.

LILLIAN,

BY

WILLIAM MACKWORTH PRAED.

ADVERTISEMENT.

The reader is requested to believe that the following statement is literally true; because the writer is well aware that the circumstances under which Lillian was composed are the only sources of its merits and the only apology for its faults.

At a small party at Cambridge some malicious belles endeavored to confound their sonnetteering friends, by setting unintelligible and inexplicable subjects for the exercise of their poetic talents. Among many others the Thesis was given out which is the motto of Lillian:

" A dragon's tail is flayed to warm
A headless maiden's heart,"

and the following poem was an attempt to explain the riddle.

The partiality with which it had been honored in manuscript, and the frequent applications which have been made to the author for copies, must be his excuse for having a few impressions struck off for *private circulation* among his friends.

It was written, however, with the sole view of amusing the ladies in whose circle the idea originated; and to them, with all due humility and devotion, it is inscribed.

Trinity College, Cambridge, *October* 26, 1822.

" A dragon's tail is flayed to warm
A headless maiden's heart."—Miss ——.

" And he's cleckit this great muckle bird out o' this wee egg:
he could wile the very flounders out o' the Frith."
Mr. Saddletree.

CANTO I.

I.

There was a dragon in Arthur's time,
When dragons and griffins were voted " prime,"
Of monstrous reputation:
Up and down, and far and wide,
He roamed about in his scaly pride;
And ever at morn and even-tide,
He made such rivers of blood to run
As shocked the sight of the blushing sun,
And deluged half the nation.
It was a pretty monster, too,
With a crimson head, and a body blue,
And wings of a warm and delicate hue,
Like the glow of a deep carnation;
And the terrible tail that lay behind,
Reached out so far as it twisted and twined,
That a couple of dwarfs, of wondrous strength,
Bore, when he travelled, its horrible length,
Like a duke's at the coronation.
His mouth had lost one ivory tooth,
Or the dragon had been in very sooth,
No insignificant charmer;
And that, —— alas! he had ruined it,
When on new-year's day, in a hungry fit,
He swallowed a tough and a terrible bit—
Sir Lob in his brazen armor.
Swift and light were his steps on the ground,
Strong and smooth was his hide around,
For the weapons which the peasants flung
Ever unfelt or unheeded rung,
Arrow, and stone, and spear,
As snow o'er Cynthia's window flits,
Or raillery of twenty wits
On a fool's unshrinking ear.

II.

In many a battle the beast had been,
Many a blow he had felt and given.
Sir Digore came with a menacing mein,
But he sent Sir Digore straight to heaven,
Stiff and stour were the arms he wore,
Huge the sword he was wont to clasp,
But the sword was little, the armor brittle,
Locked in the coil of the dragon's grasp

III.

He came on Sir Florice of Sesseny Land,
  Pretty Sir Florice from over the sea,
And smashed him all as he stepped on the sand,
  Cracking his head like a nut from the tree.
No one till now, had found, I trow,
  Anything good in the scented youth,
Who had taken much pains to be rid of his brains,
  Before they were sought by the dragon's tooth.

IV.

He came on the sheriff of Hereford,
  As he sat him down to his Sunday dinner;
And the sheriff he spoke but this brief word,
  "St. Francis be good to a corpulent sinner!"
Fat was he, as a sheriff might be,
  From the crown of his head to the tip of his toe;
But the sheriff was small, or nothing at all,
  When put in the jaws of the dragon foe.

V.

He came on the Abbot of Arnondale,
  As he kneeled him down to his morning devotion;
But the dragon he shuddered, and turned his tail
  About, "with a short uneasy motion."
Iron and steel, for an early meal,
  He stomached with ease, or the muse is a liar;
But out of all question, he failed in digestion,
  If ever he ventured to swallow a friar!

VI.

Monstrous brute!—his dread renown
Made whispers and terrors in country and town;
Nothing was babbled by boor or knight
But tales of his civic appetite.
At last, as after dinner he lay,
Hid from the heat of the solar ray
By boughs that had woven an arbor shady,
He chanced to fall in with the headless lady.
Headless! alas! 'twas a piteous gibe;
I'll drink Aganippe, and then describe.

VII.

Her father had been a stout yeoman,
Fond of his jest, and fond of his can,
  But never over-wise;
And once, when his cups had been many and deep,
He met with a dragon fast asleep,
  'Twas a faery in disguise.
In a dragon's form she had ridden the storm,
  The realm of the sky invading;
Sir Grahame's ship was stout and fast,
But the faery came on the rushing blast,
And shivered the sails, and shivered the mast,
And down went the gallant ship, at last,
  With all the crew and lading.
And the fay laughed out, to see the rout,
  As the last dim hope was fading;
And this she had done, in a love of fun,
  And a love of masquerading.
She lay that night in a sunny vale,
  And the yeoman found her sleeping;
Fiercely he smote her glittering tail,
But oh! his courage began to fail,
  When the fairy rose all weeping.
"Thou hast lopped," she said, "beshrew thine hand!
The fairest foot in fairy-land!

VIII.

"Thou hast an infant in thine home!
Never to her shall reason come
  For weeping or for wail,
Till she shall ride with a fearless face
  On a living dragon's scale,
And fondly clasp to her heart's embrace
  A living dragon's tail."
The faery's form from his shuddering sight
Flowed away in a stream of light.

IX.

Disconsolate that youth departed,
  Disconsolate and poor;
And wended, chill and broken-hearted,
  To his cottage on the moor;
Sadly and silently he knelt
  His lonely hearth beside;
Alas! how desolate he felt
  As he hid his face, and cried.
The cradle where the babe was laid
  Stood in its own dear nook,
But long—how long!—he knelt, and prayed,
  And did not dare to look.
He looked at last; his joy was there,
And slumbering with that placid air
Which only babes and angels wear.
Over the cradle he leaned his head;
The cheek was warm, and the lip was red;
And he felt, he felt, as he saw her lie,
A hope—which was a mockery.
The babe unclosed her eye's pale lid;
Why doth he start from the sight it hid?
He hath seen in the dim and fitful ray,
That the light of the soul hath gone away!
Sigh nor prayer he uttered there,
In mute and motionless despair,
But he laid him down beside his child,
And LILLIAN saw him die—and smiled.
The mother! she had gone before;
And in the cottage on the moor,
With none to watch her, and caress,
No arm to clasp, no voice to bless,
The witless child grew up alone,
And made all Nature's book her own.

X.

If, in the warm and passionate hour,
When Reason sleeps in Fancy's bower,
If thou hast ever, ever felt
A dream of delicate beauty melt
  Into thine heart's recess,
Seen by the soul, and seen by the mind,
  But indistinct in its loveliness,
Adored, and not defined;
A bright creation, a shadowy ray,
Fading and flitting in mist away,
Nothing to gaze on, and nothing to hear,
But something to cheat the eye and ear
With a fond conception and joy of both,
So that you might, that hour, be loath
To change for some one's sweetest kiss
Thy vision of unenduring bliss,
Or lose some one's sweetest tone,
The murmur thou drinkest all alone—
If such a vision hath ever been thine,
Thou hast a heart that may look on mine!

XI.

For, oh! the light of my saddened theme
Was like to naught but a poet's dream,
Or the forms that come on the twilight's wing,
Shaped by the soul's imagining.
Beautiful shade, with her tranquil air,
And her thin white arm, and her flowing hair,
And the light of her eye so coldly obscure,
And the hue of her cheek so pale and pure!
Reason and Thought she had never known,
Her heart was as cold as a heart of stone;
So you might guess from her eyes' dim rays,
And her idiot laugh, and her vacant gaze.
She wandered about all lone on the heather,
She and the wild heath-birds together;
For LILLIAN seldom spoke or smiled,
But she sang as sweet as a little child.

Into her song her dreams would throng,
  Silly, and wild, and out of place;
And yet that wild and roving song
  Entranced the soul in its desolate grace.
And hence the story had ever run,
That the fairest of dames was a headless one.

XII.

The pilgrim in his foreign weeds
  Would falter in his prayer;
And the monk would pause with his half-told beads
  To breathe a blessing there;
The knight would loose his vizor-clasp,
And drop the rein from his nerveless grasp,
And pass his hand across his brow
With a sudden sigh, and a whispered vow,
And marvel Flattery's tale was told,
From a lip so young, to an ear so cold.
She had seen her sixteenth winter out
When she met with the beast I was singing about:
The dragon, I told you, had dined that day;
So he gazed upon her as he lay
Earnestly looking, and looking long,
With his appetite weak, and his wonder strong.
Silent he lay in his motionless coil;
And the song of the lady was sweet the while—

  "Nonny Nonny! I hear it float,
  Innocent bird, thy tremulous note:
  It comes from thy home in the eglantine,
  And I stay this idle song of mine,
  Nonny Nonny! to listen to thine!

  "Nonny Nonny! 'LILLIAN sings
  The sweetest of all living things!'
  So Sir Launcelot averred;
  But surely Sir Launcelot never heard
  Nonny Nonny! the natural bird!"

XIII.

The dragon he lay in mute amaze,
Till something of kindness crept into his gaze;
He drew the flames of his nostrils in,
He veiled his claws with their speckled skin,
He curled his fangs in a hideous smile;
And the song of the lady was sweet the while—

  "Nonny Nonny! who shall tell
  Where the summer breezes dwell?
  Lightly and brightly they breathe and blow
  But whence they come and whither they go,
  Nonny Nonny! who shall know?

  "Nonny Nonny! I hear your tone,
  But I feel ye can not read mine own;
  And I lift my neck to your fond embraces,
  But who hath seen in your resting-places,
  Nonny Nonny! your beautiful faces?"

XIV.

A moment! and the dragon came
Crouching down to the peerless dame,
With his fierce red eye so fondly shining,
And his terrible tail so meekly twining,
And the scales on his huge limbs gleaming o'er
Gayer than ever they gleamed before.
She had won his heart, while she charmed his ear,
And LILLIAN smiled, and knew no fear.
And see, she mounts between his wings;
  (Never a queen had a gaudier throne,)
And fairy-like she sits and sings,
  Guiding the steed with a touch and a tone.
Aloft, aloft in the clear blue ether,
The dame and the dragon they soared together;
He bore her away on the breath of the gale—
The two little dwarfs held fast by the tail.

XV.

Fanny! a pretty group for drawing;
My dragon like a war-horse pawing,
My dwarfs in a fright, and my girl in an attitude,
Patting the beast in her soulless gratitude.
There; you may try it, if you will,
While I drink my coffee, and nib my quill.

LILLIAN.

CANTO II.

XVI.

THE sun shone out on hill and grove;
  It was a glorious day,
The lords and the ladies were making love,
  And the clowns were making hay;
But the town of Brentford marked with wonder
A lightning in the sky, and thunder,
And thinking ('twas a thinking town)
Some prodigy was coming down,
A mighty mob to Merlin went
To learn the cause of this portent;
And he, a wizard sage but comical,
Looked through his glasses astronomical,
And puzzled every foolish sconce
By this oracular response:—

XVII.

"Now the slayer doth not slay,
  Weakness flings her fear away,
  Power bears the powerless,
  Pity rides the pitiless;
  Are ye lovers? are ye brave?
  Hear ye this, and seek, and save!
He that would wed the loveliest maid,
  Must don the stoutest mail,
For the rider shall never be sound in the head
  Till the ridden be maimed in the tail.
Hey, diddle diddle! the cat and the fiddle!
  None but the lover can read me my riddle

XVIII.

How kind art thou, and oh! how mighty,
Cupid! thou son of Aphrodite!
By thy sole aid, in old romance,
Heroes and heroines sing and dance;
Of cane and rod there's little need;
They never learn to write or read;
Yet often, by thy sudden light,
Enamored dames contrive to write;
And often, in the hour of need,
Enamored youths contrive to read.
(I make a small digression here;
I merely mean to make it clear
That if Sir Eglamour had wit
To read and construe, bit by bit,
All that the wizard had expressed,
And start conjectures on the rest,

Cupid had sharpened his discerning,
The little god of love and learning,)
He revolved in his bed, what Merlin had said,
Though Merlin had labored to scatter a veil on't;
And found out the sense of the tail and the head,
Though none of his neighbors could made head or tail on't.

XIX.

Sir Eglamour was one o' the best
Of Arthur's table round;
He never set his spear in rest,
But a dozen went to the ground.
Clear and warm as the lightning flame,
His valor from his father came,
His cheek was like his mother's;
And his hazel eye more clearly shone
Than any I ever have looked upon,
Save Fanny's and two others!
With his spur so bright, and his rein so light,
And his steed so swift and ready,
And his skilful sword, to wound or ward,
And his spear so sure and steady;
He bore him like a British knight
From London to Penzance,
Avenged all weeping women's slight,
And made all giants dance.
And he had travelled far from home,
Had worn a mask at Venice,
Had kissed the bishop's toe at Rome,
And beat the French at tennis!
Hence he had many a courtly play,
And jeerings and gibes in plenty,
And he wrote more rhymes in a single day
That Byron or Bowles in twenty.

XX.

He clasped to his side his sword of pride,
His sword, whose native polish vied
With many a gory stain;
Keen and bright as a meteor-light,
But not so keen, and not so bright,
As Moultrie's* jesting vein.
And his shield he bound his arm around,
His shield, whose dark and dingy round
Naught human could get through;
Heavy and thick as a wall of brick,
But not so heavy and not so thick
As Robert's Review.†
With a smile and a jest he set out on the quest,
Clad in his stoutest mail,
With his helm of the best, and his spear in the rest,
To flay the dragon's tail.

XXI.

The warrior travelled wearily,
Many a league and many a mile;
And the dragon sailed in the clear blue sky;
And the song of the lady was sweet the while—
"My steed and I, my steed and I,
On in the path of the winds we fly,
And I chase the planets that wander at even,
And bathe my hair in the dews of heaven!
Beautiful stars, so thin and bright,
Exquisite visions of vapor and light,
I love ye all with a sister's love,
And I rove with ye wherever ye rove,
And I drink your changeless, endless song,
The music ye make as ye wander along!
Oh! let me be, as one of ye,
Floating for aye on your liquid sea;
And I'll feast with you on the purest rain,
To cool my weak and wildered brain,

* The Rev. John Moultrie, who, in 1823 (when many manuscript copies of "Lillian" were in circulation), wrote some beautiful and pathetic lyrics, some of which appeared in Knight's Quarterly Magazine.

† "My Grandmother's Review—the British." *Don Juan*. Roberts was the editor.—*Vide Byron's celebrated letter to him.*

And I'll give you the loveliest lock of my hair
For a little spot in your realm of air!"

XXII.

The dragon came down when the morn shone bright,
And slept in the beam of the sun;
Fatigued, no doubt, with his airy flight,
As I with my jingling one.
With such a monstrous adversary
Sir Eglamour was far too weary
To think of bandying knocks;
He came on his foe as still as death,
Walking on tiptoe, and holding his breath,
And instead of drawing his sword from his sheath,
He drew a pepper-box!

XXIII.

The pepper was as hot as flame,
The box of wondrous size;
He gazed one moment on the dame,
Then, with a sure and steady aim,
Full in the dragon's truculent phiz
He flung the scorching powder—whiz!
And darkened both his eyes!

XXIV.

Have you not seen a little kite
Rushing away on its paper wing,
To mix with the wild wind's quarrelling?
Up it soars with an arrowy flight,
Till, weak and unsteady,
Torn by the eddy,
It dashes to earth from its hideous height.
Such was the rise of the beast in his pain,
Such was his falling to earth again;
Upward he shot, but he saw not his path,
Blinded with pepper, and blinded with wrath;
One struggle—one vain one—of pain and emotion!
And he shot back again, "like a bird of the ocean!"
Long he lay, in a trance, that day,
And alas! he did not wake before
The cruel knight, with skill and might,
Had lopped and flayed the tail he wore.

XXV.

Twelve hours by the chime he lay in his slime,
More utterly blind, I trow,
Than a polypheme in the olden time,
Or a politician now.
He sped, as soon as he could see,
To the Paynim bowers of Rosalie;
For there the dragon had hope to cure,
By the tinkling rivulets ever pure,
By the glowing sun, and fragrant gale,
His wounded honor, and wounded tail!
He hied him away to the perfumed spot.
The little dwarfs clung—where the tail was [illegible]!

XXVI.

The damsel gazed on that young knight,
With something of terror, but more of delight;
Much she admired the gauntlets he wore,
Much the device that his buckler bore,
Much the feathers that danced on his crest,
But most the baldrick that shone on his breast.
She thought the dragon's pilfered scale
Was fairer far than the warrior's mail,
And she lifted it up with her weak white arm,
Unconscious of its hidden charm,
And round her throbbing bosom tied,
In mimickry of warlike pride.

XXVII.

Gone is the spell that bound her!
The talisman hath touched her heart,
And she leaps with a fearful and fawn-like start
As the shades of glamoury depart—

Strange thoughts are glimmering round her
Deeper and deeper her cheek is glowing,
Quicker and quicker her breath is flowing,
And her eye gleams out from its long dark lashes,
Fast and full, unnatural flashes;
For hurriedly and wild
Doth reason pour her hidden treasures,
Of human griefs, and human pleasures.
Upon her new-found child.
And "Oh!" she saith, "my spirit doth seem
To have risen to-day from a pleasant dream;
A long, long dream—but I feel it breaking!
Painfully sweet is the throb of waking."
And then she laughed, and wept again:
While, gazing on her heart's first rain,
Bound in his turn by a magic chain,
The silent youth stood there:
Never had either been so blest;—
You that are young may picture the rest,
You that are young and fair.
Never before, on this warm land,
Came Love and Reason hand in hand.

XXVIII.

When you were blest, in childhood's years,
With the brightest hopes, and the lightest fears,
Have you not wandered, in your dream,
Where a greener glow was on the ground,
And a clearer breath in the air around,
And a purer life in the gay sunbeam,
And a tremulous murmur in every tree,
And a motionless sleep on the quiet sea?
And have you not lingered, lingered still,
All unfettered in thought and will,
A fair and cherished boy;
Until you felt it pain to part
From the wild creations of your art,
Until your young and innocent heart
Seemed bursting with its joy?
And then, oh then, hath your waking eye
Opened in all its ecstasy,
And seen your mother leaning o'er you,
The loved and loving one that bore you,
Giving her own, her fond caress,
And looking her eloquent tenderness?
Was it not heaven to fly from the scene
Where the heart in the vision of night had been,
And drink, in one o'erflowing kiss,
Your deep reality of bliss?
Such was LILLIAN's passionate madness,
Such the calm of her waking gladness.

XXIX.

Enough! my tale is all too long:
Fair children, if the trifling song,
That flows for you to-night,
Hath stolen from you one gay laugh,
Or given your quiet hearts to quaff
One cup of young delight,
Pay ye the rhymer for his toils
In the coinage of your golden smiles,
And treasure up his idle verse
With the stories ye loved from the lips of your nurse.

THE EVE OF ST. AGNES,

BY

JOHN KEATS.

THE reader should give us three pearls, instead of three half-pence,* for this number of our publication, for it presents him with the *whole* of Mr. Keats's beautiful poem, entitled as above—to say nothing of our loving commentary.

St. Agnes was a Roman virgin, who suffered martyrdom in the reign of Diocletian. Her parents, a few days after her decease, are said to have had a vision of her, surrounded by angels, and attended by a white lamb, which afterward became sacred to her. In the Catholic church, formerly, the nuns used to bring a couple of lambs to her altar during mass. The superstition is (for we believe it is still to be found), that by taking certain measures of divination, damsels may get a sight of their future husbands in a dream. The ordinary process seems to have been by fasting. Aubrey (as quoted in "Brand's Popular Antiquities") mentions another, which is, to take a row of pins, and pull them out one by one, saying a Pater-noster; after which, upon going to bed, the dream is sure to ensue. Brand quotes Ben Jonson:—

"And on sweet St. Agnes' night,
Please you with the promised sight—
Some of husbands, some of lovers,
Which an empty dream discovers."

But another poet has now taken up the creed in good poetic earnest; and if the superstition should go out in every other respect, in his rich and loving pages it will live for ever.

I.

ST. AGNES' EVE—Ah! bitter chill it was;
The owl, for all his feathers, was a-cold:
The hare limped trembling through the frozen grass,
And silent was the flock in woolly fold;
Numb were the beadsman's fingers while he told
His rosary, and while his frosted breath,
Like pious incense, from a censer old,
Seemed taking flight for heaven without a death,
Past the sweet Virgin's picture, while his prayer he saith.

What a complete feeling of winter-time is here, together with an intimation of those Catholic elegancies, of which we are to have more in the poem!

"The owl with all his feathers was a-cold."

Could he have selected an image more warm and comfortable in itself, and, therefore, better contradicted by the season? We feel the plump, feathery bird in his nook, shivering in spite of his natural household warmth, and staring out at the strange weather. The hare limping through the chill grass is very piteous, and the "silent flock" very patient; and how quiet and gentle, as well as winterly, are all these circumstances, and fit to open a quiet and gentle poem! The breath of the pilgrim, likened to "pious incense," completes them, and is a simile in admirable "keeping," as the painters call it; that is to say, is thoroughly harmonious in itself, and with all that is going on. The breath of the pilgrim is visible, so is that of a censer; his object is religious, and so is the use of the censer; the censer, after its fashion, may be said to pray, and its breath, like the pilgrim's, ascends to heaven. Young students of poetry may, in this image alone, see what imagination is, under one of its most poetical forms, and how thoroughly it "tells." There is no part of it unfitting. It is not applicable in one point, and the reverse in another.

II.

His prayer he saith, this patient, holy man.
Then takes his lamp, and riseth from his knees,
And back returneth, meager, barefoot, wan,
Along the chapel aisle by slow degrees:
The sculptured dead on each side seemed to freeze,
Imprisoned in black purgatorial rails:
Knights, ladies, praying in dumb orat'ries,
He passeth by; and his weak spirit fails
To think how they may ache in icy hoods and mails.

The germe of this thought, or something like it, is in Dante, where he speaks of the figures that perform the part of sustaining columns in architecture. Keats had read Dante in Mr. Cary's translation, for which he had a great respect. He began to read him afterward in Italian, which language he was mastering with surprising quickness. A friend of ours has a copy of Ariosto, containing admiring marks of his pen. But the same thought may have originally struck one poet as well as another. Perhaps there are few that have not felt something like it, in seeing the figures upon tombs. Here, however, for the first time, we believe, in English poetry, is it expressed, and with what feeling and elegance! Most wintry as well as penitential is the word "aching" in "icy hoods and mails," and most felicitous the introduction of the Catholic idea in the word "purgatorial." The very color of the rails is made to assume a meaning, and to shadow forth the gloom of the punishment—

"*Imprisoned in black purgatorial* rails"

* The price of the journal in which the article first appeared.

III.

Northward he turneth through a little door,
And scarce three steps, ere music's golden tongue
Flattered to tears this aged man and poor;
But no; already had his death-bell rung;
The joys of all his life were said and sung:
His was harsh penance on St. Agnes' Eve:
Another way he went, and soon among
Rough ashes sat he, for his soul's reprieve;
And all night kept awake, for sinner's sake to grieve.

"*Flattered to tears* this aged man and poor."

This "flattered" is exquisite. A true poet is by nature a metaphysician; far greater in general than metaphysicians professed. He feels instinctively what the others get at by long searching. In this word "flattered" is the whole theory of the secret of tears; which are the tributes, more or less worthy, of self-pity to self-love. Whenever we shed tears, we take pity on ourselves; and we feel, if we do not consciously say so, that we deserve to have the pity taken. In many cases, the pity is just, and the self-love not to be construed unhandsomely. In many others, it is the reverse; and this is the reason why selfish people are so often found among the tear-shedders, and why they seem even to shed them for others. They imagine themselves in the situation of the others, as indeed the most generous must, before they can sympathize; but the generous console as well as weep. Selfish tears are niggardly of everything but themselves.

"Flattered to tears." Yes, the poor old man was moved by the sweet music to think that so sweet a thing was intended for his comfort as well as for others. He felt that the mysterious kindness of Heaven did not omit even his poor, old, sorry case in its numerous workings and visitations; and, as he wished to live longer, he began to think that his wish was to be attended to. He began to consider how much he had suffered wrongly or mysteriously—and how much better a man he was, with all his sins, than fate seemed to have taken him for. Hence he found himself deserving of tears and self-pity, and he shed them, and felt soothed by his poor, old, loving self. Not undeservedly either; for he was a pains-taking pilgrim, aged, patient, and humble, and willingly suffered cold and toil for the sake of something better than he could otherwise deserve; and so the pity is not exclusively on his own side: we pity him too, and would fain see him well out of that cold chapel, gathered into a warmer place than a grave. But it was not to be. We must, therefore, console ourselves with knowing, that this icy endurance of his was the last, and that he soon found himself at the sunny gate of heaven.

IV.

That ancient beadsman heard the prelude soft,
And so it chanced (for many a door was wide
From hurry to and fro) soon up aloft
The *silver-snarling trumpets* 'gan to chide;
The level chambers, ready with their pride,
Were glowing to receive a thousand guests:
The carved angels, ever eager-eyed,
Stared, where upon their heads the cornice rests,
With hair blown black, and wings put cross-wise on their breasts.

V.

At length burst in the argent revelry,
With plume, tiara, and all rich array,
Numerous as shadows haunting fairily
The brain, new stuffed, in youth, with triumphs gay
Of old romance. Those let us wish away,
And turn, sole-thoughted, to one Lady there,
Whose heart had brooded, all that wintry day,
On love, and winged St. Agnes' saintly care,
As she had heard old dames full many times declare.

VI.

They told her how, upon St. Agnes' Eve,
Young virgins might have visions of delight;
And soft adorings from their loves receive
Upon the honeyed middle of the night,
If ceremonies due they did aright;
As, supperless to bed they must retire,
And couch supine their beauties, lily white;
Nor look behind, nor sidewise, but require
Of heaven with upward eyes for all that they desire.

VII.

Full of this whim was thoughtful Madeline;
The music, yearning like a god in pain,
She scarcely heard; her maiden eyes divine
Fixed on the floor, saw many a sweeping train
Pass by—she heeded not at all; in vain
Came many a tiptoe, amorous cavalier,
And back retired; not cooled by high disdain.
But she saw not; her heart was otherwhere—
She sighed for Agnes' dreams, the sweetest of the year.

VIII.

She danced along with vague, regardless eyes,
Anxious her lips, her breathing quick and short;
The hallowed hour was near at hand; she sighs
Amid the timbrels, and the thronged résort
Of whisperers, in anger or in sport;
'Mid looks of love, defiance, hate, and scorn,
Hood-winked with faery fancy; all amort,
Save to St. Agnes and her lambs unshorn,
And all the bliss to be before to-morrow morn.

IX.

So, purposing each moment to retire,
She lingered still. Meantime, across the moors,
Had come young Porphyro, with heart on fire
For Madeline. Beside the portal doors,
Buttressed from moonlight, stands he, and implores
All saints to give him sight of Madeline,
But for one moment in the tedious hours,
That he might gaze, and worship all unseen,
Perchance speak, kneel, touch, kiss—in sooth such things have been.

X.

He ventures in; let no buzzed whisper tell,
All eyes be muffled, or a hundred swords
Will storm his heart, Love's fev'rous citadel.
For him those chambers held barbarian hordes,
Hyena foemen, and hot-blooded lords,
Whose very dogs would execrations howl
Against his lineage. Not one breast affords
Him any mercy, in that mansion foul.
Save one old beldame, weak in body and in soul.

XI.

Ah, happy chance! the aged creature came
Shuffling along with ivory-headed wand,
To where he stood, hid from the torches' flame,
Behind a broad hall-pillar, far beyond
The sound of merriment and chorus bland.
He startled her; but soon she knew his face,
And grasped his fingers in her palsied hand:
Saying, "Mercy, Porphyro! hie thee from this place;
They are all here to-night, the whole blood-thirsty race.

XII.

"Get hence! get hence! there's dwarfish Hildebrand,
He had a fever late, and in the fit
He cursed thee and thine, both house and land:
Then there's that old Lord Maurice, *not a whit*
More tame for his gray hairs—Alas, me! flit—

Flit like a ghost away."—"Ah, gossip dear,
We're safe enough; here in this arm-chair sit,
And tell me how—"—"Good saints! not here! not here!
Follow me, child, or else these stones will be thy bier."

XIII.

He followed through a lowly-arched way,
Brushing the cobwebs with his lofty plume;
And as she muttered, "Well-a—well-a-day!"
He found him *in a little moonlight room,*
Pale, latticed, chill, and silent as a tomb.
"Now tell me where is Madeline," said he,
"Oh, tell me, Angela, by the holy loom
Which none but secret Sisterhood may see,
When they St. Agnes' wool are weaving piously."

The poet does not make his "little moonlight room" comfortable, observe. The high taste of the exordium is kept up. All is still wintry. There is to be no comfort in the poem but what is given by love. All else may be willingly left to the cold walls.

XIV.

"St. Agnes! Ah! it is St. Agnes' Eve—
Yet men will murder upon holydays;
Thou must hold water in a witch's sieve,
And be the liege-lord of all elves and fays
To venture so: it fills me with amaze
To see thee, Porphyro!—St. Agnes' Eve!
God's help! my lady fair the conjuror plays
This very night: good angels her deceive!
But let me laugh awhile; I've mickle time to grieve."

XV.

Feebly she laugheth in the languid moon,
While Porphyro upon her face doth look,
Like puzzled urchin on an aged crone,
Who keepeth closed a wondrous riddle-book,
As spectacled she sits in chimney nook;
But soon his eyes grew brilliant, when she told
His lady's purpose; and he scarce could brook
Tears, at the thought of those enchantments cold,
And Madeline asleep in lap of legends old.

He almost shed tears of sympathy, to think how his treasure is exposed to the cold—and of delight and pride to think of her sleeping beauty, and her love for himself. This passage "asleep in the lap of legends old" is in the highest imaginative taste, fusing together the tangible and the spiritual, the real and the fanciful, the remote and the near. Madeline is asleep in her bed; but she is also asleep in accordance with the legends of the season; and therefore the bed becomes *their* lap as well as sleep's. The poet does not critically think of all this; he feels it: and thus should other young poets draw upon the prominent points of their feelings on a subject, sucking the essence out of them into analogous words, instead of beating about the bush for *thoughts,* and, perhaps, getting very clever ones, but confused—not the best, nor any one better than another. Such, at least, is the difference between the truest poetry and the degrees beneath it.

XVI.

Sudden a thought *came, like a full-blown rose,*
Flushing his brow; and in his pained heart
Made purple riot; then doth he propose
A stratagem, that makes the beldame start.
"A cruel man, and impious, thou art:
Sweet lady! let her pray, and sleep, and dream,
Alone with her good angels, far apart
From wicked men like thee. Go! go!—I deem
Thou canst not, surely, be the same that thou dost seem."

XVII.

"I will not harm her, by all saints I swear,"
Quoth Porphyro: "Oh, may I ne'er find grace,
When my weak voice shall whisper its last prayer,
If one of her soft ringlets I displace,
Or look with *ruffian-passion* in her face;
Good Angela, believe me by these tears,
Or I will, even in a moment's space,
Awake with horrid shout my foeman's ears,
And beard them, though they be more fang'd than wolves and bears."

XVIII.

"Ah! why wilt thou affright a feeble soul?
A poor, weak, palsy-stricken *church-yard* thing,
Whose passing-bell may ere the midnight toll;
Whose prayers for thee, each morn and evening,
Were never miss'd?" Thus plaining, doth she bring
A gentler speech from burning Porphyro;
So woful and of such deep sorrowing,
That Angela gives promise she will do
Whatever he shall wish, betide or weal or wo;

XIX.

Which was, to lead him in close secrecy,
Even to Madeline's chamber, and there hide
Him in a closet, of such privacy
That he might see her beauty unespied,
And win, perhaps, that night a peerless bride;
While legioned fairies paced the coverlet,
And pale enchantment held her sleepy-eyed.
Never on such a night have lovers met,
Since Merlin paid his demon all the monstrous debt.

What he means by Merlin's "monstrous debt," we can not say. Merlin, the famous enchanter, obtained King Uther his interview with the fair Iogerne; but though he was the son of a devil, and conversant with the race, we are aware of no debt that he owed them.

XX.

"It shall be as thou wishest," said the dame;
"All cates and dainties shall be stored there,
Quickly on this feast-night; by the tambor-frame
Her own lute thou wilt see; no time to spare,
For I am slow and feeble, and scarce dare
On such a catering trust my dizzy head;
Wait here, my child, with patience; kneel in prayer
The while: ah! thou must needs the lady wed;
Or may I never leave my grave among the dead."

XXI.

So saying, she hobbled off with busy fear;
The lovers endless minutes slowly passed,
The dame returned and whispered in his ear
To follow her; with aged eyes aghast
From fright of dim espial. Safe at last,
Through many a dusky gallery, they gain
The maiden's chamber, *silken, hushed, and chaste,*
Where Porphyro took covert, pleased amain:
His poor guide hurried back with agues in her brain.

XXII.

Her faltering hand upon the balustrade,
Old Angelo was feeling for the stair,
When Madeline, St. Agnes' charmed maid,
Rose, like a missioned spirit, unaware:
With silver taper's light, and pious care,
She turned, and down the aged gossip led
To a safe level matting. Now prepare
Young Porphyro, for gazing on that bed;
She comes, she comes again, like ring-dove frayed and fled.

XXIII.

Out went the taper as she hurried in;
Its little smoke in pallid moonshine died;
She closed the door, she panted all akin
To spirits of the air, and visions wide;
Nor uttered syllable, or, wo betide!
But to her heart her heart was voluble,
Paining with eloquence her balmy side:
As though a tongueless nightingale should swell
Her throat in vain, and die heart-stifled in her dell.

"Its little smoke in pallid moonshine died,"

is a verse in the taste of Chaucer, full of minute grace and truth. The smoke of the waxen taper seems almost as ethereal and fair as the moonlight, and both suit each other and the heroine. But what a lovely ine is the seventh, about the heart:—

"Paining with eloquence her balmy side."

And the nightingale! how touching the simile! The heart a "tongueless nightingale," dying in that dell of the bosom! What thorough sweetness, and perfection of lovely imagery! How one delicacy is heaped upon another! But for a burst of richness, noiseless, colored, suddenly enriching the moonlight, as if a door of heaven were opened, read the following:—

XXIV.

A casement high and triple-arched there was,
All garlanded with carven imageries
Of fruits and flowers, and bunches of knot-grass,
And diamonded with panes of quaint device,
Innumerable of stains and splendid dies,
As are the tiger-moth's deep damasked wings;
And in the midst, among thousand heraldries,
And TWILIGHT *saints, and dim emblazonings,*
A shielded 'scutcheon BLUSHED *with blood of queens and kings.*

Could all the pomp and graces of aristocracy, with Titian's and Raphael's aid to boot, go beyond the rich religion of this picture, with its "twilight saints," and its 'scutcheons "blushing with the blood of queens?" But we must not stop the reader:—

XXV.

Full on this casement shone the wintry moon,
And threw warm *gules* on Madeline's fair breast,
As down she knelt for heaven's grace and boon;
Rose-bloom fell on her hands together pressed,
And on her silver cross soft amethyst;
And on her hair a glory like a saint:
She seemed *a splendid angel, newly dressed*
Save wings, for heaven; Porphyro grew faint,
She knelt, so pure a thing, so free from mortal taint.

The lovely and innocent creature thus praying under the gorgeous painted window, completes the exceeding and unique beauty of this picture—one that will for ever stand by itself in poetry, as an addition to the stock. It would have struck a glow on the face of Shakspere himself. He might have put Imogen or Ophelia under such a shrine. How proper, as well as pretty, the heraldic term *gules*, considering the occasion! *Red* would not have been a fiftieth part so good. And with what elegant luxury he touches the "silver cross" with "amethyst," and the fair human hands with "rose color," the kin to their carnation! The lover's growing "faint," is one of the few inequalities which are to be found in the later productions of this great but young and over-sensitive poet. He had, at the time of writing his poems, the seeds of a mortal illness in him, and he, doubtless, wrote as he had felt—for he was also deeply in love; and extreme sensibility struggled in him with a great understanding. But our picture is not finished:—

XXVI.

Anon his heart revives; her vespers done,
Of all its wreathed pearls her hair she frees;
Unclasped her *warmed* jewels one by one;
Loosens her fragrant boddice; *by degrees*
Her rich attire creeps rustling to her knees;
Half hidden, *like a mermaid in sea-weed,*
Pensive awhile she dreams awake, and sees
In fancy fair St. Agnes in her bed,
But dares not look behind, or all the charm is fled.

How true and cordial the "*warmed* jewels!" and what matter of fact also, made elegant, is the rustling downward of the attire; and the mixture of dress and undress, and dishevelled hair, likened to a "mer maid in sea-weed!" But the next stanza is perhaps the most exquisite in the poem.

XXVII.

Soon, trembling in her soft and chilly nest,
In sort of wakeful swoon, perplexed she lay,
Until the poppied warmth of sleep oppressed
Her soothed limbs, and soul, fatigued away,
Flown, like a thought, until the morrow-day;
Blissfully havened both from joy and pain;
Clasped like a missal, where swart Paynims pray;
Blinded alike from sunshine and from rain,
AS THOUGH A ROSE SHOULD SHUT, AND BE A BUD AGAIN.

Can the beautiful go beyond this? We never saw it. And how the imagery rises! Flown like a *thought*—blissfully *havened*—clasped like a missal in a land of *Pagans:* that is to say, where Christian prayer-books must not be seen, and are, therefore, doubly cherished for the danger. And then, although nothing can surpass the preciousness of this idea, is the idea of the beautiful, crowning all—

"*Blinded alike from sunshine and from rain,*
As though a rose should shut, and be a bud again."

Thus it is that poetry, in its intense sympathy with creation, may be said to create anew, rendering its words almost as tangible as the objects they speak of, and individually more lasting; the spiritual perpetuity putting them on a level (not to speak it profanely) with the fugitive forms of the substance.

But we are to have more luxuries still, presently.

XXVIII.

Stolen to this paradise, and so entranced,
Porphyro gazed upon her empty dress,
And listened to her breathing, if it chanced
To wake into a slumberous tenderness;
Which when he heard, that minute did he bless,
And breathed himself; then from the closet crept,
Noiseless as fear in a wild wilderness,
And over the hushed carpet silent stept,
And 'tween the curtains peeped, where, lo! how fast she slept.

XXIX.

Then, by the bedside, where the faded moon
Made a dim silver twilight—soft he set
A table, and, half-anguished, threw thereon
A cloth of *woven crimson, gold, and jet:*—
O for some drowsy Morphean amulet!
The boisterous, midnight, festive, clarion,
The kettle-drum, and far-heard clarionet,
Affray his ears, though but in dying tone:—
The hall-door shuts again, and all the noise is gone.

XXX.

And still she slept *an azure-lidded sleep*
In blanched linen, smooth and lavendered,
While he from forth the closet brought a heap
Of candied apple, quince, and plum, and gourd,
With jellies soother than the creamy curd,
And lucent syrups, tinct with cinnamon:
Manna and dates, in argosy transferred
From Fez; *and spiced dainties, every one,*
From silken Samarcand to cedared Lebanon.

Here is delicate modulation, and super-refined epicurean nicety!

"Lucent syrups, tinct with cinnamon,"

make us read the line delicately, and at the tip-end, as it were, of one's tongue.

XXXI.

These delicates he heaped with glowing hand
On golden dishes, and in baskets bright
Of wreathed silver: sumptuous they stand
In the retired quiet of the night,
Filling the chilly room with perfume light.—
"And now, my love, my seraph fair awake!
Thou art my heaven, and I thine eremite:
Open thine eyes, for meek St. Agnes' sake,
Or I shall drowse beside thee, so my soul doth ache."

XXXII.

Thus whispering, his warm, unnerved arm
Sank in her pillow. Shaded was her dream
By the dusk curtains:—'twas a midnight charm
Impossible to melt as iced stream:
The lustrous salvers in the moonlight gleam;
Broad golden fringe upon the carpet lies;
It seemed he never, never could redeem
From such a steadfast spell his lady's eyes;
So mused awhile, entoiled in woofed phantasies.

XXXIII.

Awakening up, he took her hollow lute—
Tumultuous—and, in chords that tenderest be,
He played an ancient ditty, long since mute,
In Provence called, "La belle dame sans mercy:"
Close to her ear touching the melody;—
Wherewith disturbed she uttered a soft moan:
He ceased—she panted quick—and suddenly
Her blue affrayed eyes wide open shone:
Upon his knees he sank, pale as smooth-sculptured stone.

XXXIV.

Her eyes were open, but she still beheld,
Now wide awake, the vision of her sleep:
There was a painful change, that nigh expelled
The blisses of her dream so pure and deep,
At which fair Madeline began to weep,
And moan forth witless words with many a sigh;
While still her gaze on Porphyro would keep;
Who knelt, with joined hands and piteous eye,
Fearing to move or speak, she looked so dreamingly.

XXXV.

"Ah, Porphyro!" said she, "but even now
Thy voice was a sweet tremble in mine ear,
Made tuneable with every sweetest vow,
And those sad eyes were spiritual and clear;
How changed thou art! how pallid, chill, and drear—
Give me that voice again, my Porphyro,
Those looks immortal, those complainings dear;
Oh! leave me not in this eternal wo,
For if thou diest, my love, I know not where to go."

Madeline is half awake, and Porphyro reassures her with living kind looks, and an affectionate embrace.

XXXVI.

Beyond a mortal man impassioned far
At these voluptuous accents, he arose,
Ethereal, flushed, and like a throbbing star
Seen 'mid the sapphire heaven's deep repose;
Into her dream he melted, as the rose
Blendeth its odor with the violet—
Solution sweet. Meanwhile the frost wind blows
Like love's alarum, pattering the sharp sleet
Against the window panes: St. Agnes' moon hath set.

XXXVII.

'Tis dark; quick pattereth the flaw-blown sleet:
"This is no dream; my bride, my Madeline!"
'Tis dark; the iced gusts still rave and beat.
"No dream, alas! alas! and wo is mine;
Porphyro will leave me here to fade and pine;—
Cruel! what traitor could thee hither bring?
I curse not, for my heart is lost in thine,
Though thou forsakest a deceived thing;—
A dove, forlorn and lost, with sick unpruned wing."

XXXVIII.

"My Madeline! sweet dreamer! lovely bride!
Say, may I be for aye thy vassal blest?
Thy beauty's shield, heart-shaped, and vermeil-died?
Ah! silver shrine, here will I take my rest,
After so many hours of toil and quest—
A famished pilgrim, saved by a miracle,
Though I have found, I will not rob thy nest
Saving of thy sweet self; if thou thinkst well
To trust, fair Madeline, to no rude infidel."

With what a pretty wilful conceit the *costume* of the poem is kept up in the third line about the shield. The poet knew when to introduce apparent trifles forbidden to those who are void of real passion, and who, feeling nothing intensely, can intensify nothing.

XXXIX.

"Hark! 'tis an elfin-storm from faery land,
Of haggard seeming, but a boon indeed;
Arise—arise! the morning is at hand;
The bloated wassailers will never heed:—
Let us away, my love, with happy speed;
There are no ears to hear, or eyes to see—
Drowned all in Rhenish and the sleepy mead:
Awake! arise! my love, and fearless be,
For o'er the southern moors I have a home for thee."

XL.

She hurried at his words, beset with fears,
For there were sleeping dragons all around,
At glaring watch, perhaps, with ready spears—
Down the wide stairs a darkling way they found—
In all the house was heard no human sound.
A chain-drooped lamp was flickering by each door;
The arras, rife with horseman, hawk, and hound,
Fluttered in the besieging wind's uproar:
And the long carpets rose along the gusty floor.

This is a slip of the memory, for there were hardly carpets in those days. But the truth of the painting makes amends, as in the unchronological pictures of old masters.

XLI.

They glide, like phantoms, into the wide hall;
Like phantoms to the iron porch they glide,
Where lay the porter in uneasy sprawl,
With a huge empty flagon by his side;
The wakeful blood-hound rose and shook his hide,
But his sagacious eye an inmate owns:
By one, and one, the bolts full easy slide:
The chains lie silent on the footworn stones;
The key turns, and the door upon its hinges groans.

XLII.

And they are gone: ay, ages long ago
These lovers fled away *into the storm.*
That night the baron dreampt of many a wo,
And all his warrior-guests, with shade and form
Of witch, and demon, and large coffin-worm,
Were long be-nightmared. Angela the old
Died palsy-twitched, with meager face deform:
The beadsman, after thousand aves told,
For aye unsought-for, slept among his ashes cold.

Here endeth the young and divine poet, but not the delight and gratitude of his readers; for, as he sings elsewhere—

"A thing of beauty is a joy for ever."

NOTES,

BY N. P. WILLIS.

"THE ROCOCO" is the quaint, but, in fact, most descriptive name of an "Extra" now in press for the "Mirror Library." Those of your readers who have been lately in France will be familiar with the term *rococo*. The etymology of it has been matter of no little fruitless inquiry. It came into use about four or five years ago, when it was the rage to look up costly and old-fashioned articles of jewellery and furniture. A valuable stone, for example, in a beautiful but antique setting, was *rococo*. A beauty, who had the kind of face painted in the old pictures, was *rococo*. A chair, or a table of carved wood, costly once, but unfashionable for many a day, was *rococo*. Articles of *vertu* were looked up, and offered for sale with a view to the prevailing taste for *rococo*—highly-carved picture-frames, old but elaborately-made trinkets, rich brocades, etc., etc.—*things intrinsically beautiful and valuable, in short, but unmeritedly obsolete.* "THE ROCOCO," published by the proprietors of the New Mirror, answers this description exactly. It comprises the three most exquisite and absolute creations of pure imagination (in my opinion) that have been produced since Shakspere—"LILLIAN," by *Praed;* "THE CULPRIT FAY," by *Drake;* and "ST. AGNES' EVE," by *Keats*—all three of which have been overlaid and partially lost sight of in the torrent of new literature, but all three now to be had in fair type, *price one shilling!* The man who could read either of these three poems without feeling the chambers of his brain filled with intellectual incense—without feeling his eyes warm, his blood moved, and his inmost craving of novelty and melody deliciously ministered to—does not love poetry enough "to give a rose-tint to his russet cares." I declare, I think it is worth the outlay of a fever to get (by seclusion and depletion) the delicacy of nerve and perception to devour and relish, with intellectual nicety, these three subtly-compounded feasts of imagination.

Of these three poems, "THE CULPRIT FAY" is, by much, the most original in conception—though, in composition, it is far less artistic than "THE EVE OF ST. AGNES." The reader who feels patriotic on the subject of poetry will rejoice in the former poem, as being in its imagery and associations wholly American, as in its original design it is wholly unsuggested by any other poem. "It was composed," says his biography, "hastily among the Highlands of the Hudson, in the summer of 1819. The author was walking with some friends on a warm moonlight evening, when one of the party remarked that it would be difficult to write a faery poem, purely imaginative, without the aid of human characters. When the party was reassembled, two or three days afterward, 'THE CULPRIT FAY' was read to them, nearly as it is now printed.

"Drake placed a very modest estimate on his own productions, and it is believed that but a small portion of them have been preserved. When on his death-bed, a friend inquired of him what disposition he would have made with his poems—'O, burn them,' he replied, 'they are quite valueless.' Written copies of a number of them were, however, in circulation, and some had been incorrectly printed in the periodicals; and for this reason, Commodore Dekay, the husband of the daughter and only child of the deceased poet, published, in 1836, the single collection of them which has appeared. Drake was unassuming and benevolent in his manners and feelings, and he had an unfailing fountain of fine humor, which made him one of the most pleasant of companions."

The three authors of these three works of genius, died alike prematurely. Mr. Praed, author of "LILLIAN," (in whose company the writer had the pleasure of passing some time at the country-seat of a mutual friend in England), was in the plenitude of a brilliant political career, a member of parliament, and a man of fortune. He had been not long married when he died. Like Drake, he set but small value on his poetry. He kept it as a vein to amuse his friends, and the accomplished lady who was his entertainer at the house just alluded to, had a large manuscript volume of his poetry, worthy of any reputation, which was rigorously banned from publication by the author. He was a man of very grave demeanor, rather above the middle height, of a consumptive habit, pale and thoughtful looking. His intimate friends were very few, and in all his character, he was concentrative and retiring. The irreproachable purity of his life, and the lofty character of his ambitions and pursuits, gave him a weight and hedged him about with a dignity which made his career looked upon with unusual interest, and his death more than ordinarily mournful.

The history of KEATS is better known to the world than that of either of the others. His death is said to lie at the door of Lord Brougham—who wrote the criticism, in the agony of reading which Keats burst a blood-vessel. He had been an apothecary's boy, and the critic unfeelingly counselled him to "return to his gallipots." The writer visited his grave at Rome, and read there the epitaph he himself directed to be graven on the head-stone: "Here lies one whose name was written in water." It almost requires a poet to appreciate the unreachable delicacy of Keats's use of language. He plucks his epithets from the profoundest hiding-places of meaning and association. He wrote with a *nib inevitable*—its forked pursuit certain detection to the elusive, reluctant, indispensable *best word.* The sense of satisfaction aches while you read his poetry—so clear to the bottom of the capability of language drops his plummet word. The Italicised passages in the "Eve of St. Agnes" will be a guide to what we mean.

St. Agnes was a Roman virgin who suffered martyrdom in the reign of Diocletian. Her parents, a few days after her decease, are said to have had a vision of her surrounded by angels, and attended by a white lamb, which afterward became sacred to her. In the catholic church, formerly, the nuns used to bring a couple of lambs to her altar during mass. The superstition is, that *by taking certain measures of divination, on St. Agnes' Eve, damsels may get a sight of their future husbands in a dream* Keats's poem makes beautiful use of the superstition.

THE LOVES OF THE ANGELS.

BY

THOMAS MOORE.

PREFACE.

THE Eastern story of the angels Harut and Marut,* and the Rabbinical fictions of the loves of Uzziel and Shâmchazai,† are the only sources to which I need refer, for the origin of the notion on which this Romance is founded. In addition to the fitness of the subject for poetry, it struck me also as capable of affording an allegorical medium, through which might be shadowed out (as I have endeavored to do in the following stories) the fall of the Soul from its original purity‡—the loss of light and happiness which it suffers, in the pursuit of this world's perishable pleasures—and the punishments, both from conscience and divine justice, with which impurity, pride, and presumptuous inquiry into the awful secrets of Heaven, are sure to be visited. The beautiful story of Cupid and Psyche owes its chief charm to this sort of "veiled meaning," and it has been my wish (however I may have failed in the attempt) to communicate to the following pages the same *moral* interest.

Among the doctrines, or notions, derived by Plato from the East, one of the most natural and sublime is that which inculcates the pre-existence of the soul, and its gradual descent into this dark material world, from that region of spirit and light which it is supposed to have once inhabited, and to which, after a long lapse of purification and trial, it will return. This relief, under various symbolical forms, may be traced through almost all the Oriental theologies. The Chaldeans represent the Soul as originally endowed with wings, which fall away when it sinks from its native element, and must be reproduced before it can hope to return. Some disciples of Zoroaster once inquired of him, "How the wings of the Soul might be made to grow again?" "By sprinkling them," he replied, "with the Waters of Life." "But where are those Waters to be found?" they asked. "In the Garden of God," replied Zoroaster.

The mythology of the Persians has allegorized the same doctrine, in the history of those genii of light who strayed from their dwellings in the stars, and obscured their original nature by mixture with this material sphere; while the Egyptians, connecting it with the descent and ascent of the sun in the zodiac, considered Autumn as emblematic of the Soul's decline toward darkness, and the reappearance of Spring as its return to life and light.

* See note on page 3.

† Hyde de Relig. Vet. Persarum, p. 272.

‡ The account which Macrobius gives* of the downward journey of the Soul, through that gate of the zodiac which opens into the lower spheres, is a curious specimen of the wild fancies passed for philosophy in ancient times.

In the system of Manes, the luminous or spiritual principle owes its corruption, not to any evil tendency of its own, but to a violent inroad of the spirits of darkness, who, finding themselves in the neighborhood of this pure light, and becoming passionately enamored of its beauty, break the boundaries between them, and take forcible possession of it.†

* In Somn. Scipionis, cap. 12.

† See a Treatise "De la Religion des Perses," by the Abbé Foucher Mémoires de l'Académie, tom. xxxi., p. 456.

Besides the chief spirits of the Mahometan heaven, such as Gabriel, the angel of Revelations, Israfil, by whom the last trumpet is to be sounded, and Azrael, the angel of death, there were also a number of subaltern intelligences, of which tradition has preserved the names, appointed to preside over the different stages, or ascents, into which the celestial world was supposed to be divided.* Thus Kelail governs the fifth heaven; while Sadiel, the presiding spirit of the third, is also employed in steadying the motions of the earth, which would be in a constant state of agitation, if this angel did not keep his foot planted upon its orb.†

Among other miraculous interpositions in favor of Mahomet, we find commemorated in the pages of the Koran the appearance of five thousand angels on his side at the battle of Bedr.

The ancient Persians supposed that Ormuzd appointed thirty angels to preside successively over the days of the month, and twelve greater ones to assume the government of the months themselves; among whom Bahman (to whom Ormuzd committed the custody of all animals, except man), was the greatest. Mihr, the angel of the 7th month, was also the spirit that watched over the affairs of friendship and love; Chûr had the care of the disk of the sun; Mah was agent for the concerns of the moon; Isphandârmaz (whom Cazvin calls the Spirit of the Earth) was the tutelar genius of good and virtuous women, etc., etc. For all this the reader may consult the 19th and 20th chapters of Hyde de Relig. Vet. Persarum, where the names and attributes of these daily and monthly angels are with much minuteness and erudition explained. It appears, from the Zend-avesta, that the Persians had a certain office or prayer for every day of the month (addressed to the particular angel who presided over it), which they called the Sirouzé.

The Celestial Hierarchy of the Syrians, as described by Kircher, appears to be the most regularly graduated of any of these systems. In the sphere of the Moon they placed the angels, in that of Mercury the archangels, Venus and the Sun contained the Principalities and the Powers; and so on to the summit of the planetary system, where, in the sphere of Saturn, the Thrones had their station. Above this was the habitation of the Cherubim in the sphere of the fixed stars; and still higher, in the region of those stars which are so distant as to be imperceptible, the Seraphim, we are told, the most perfect of all celestial creatures, dwelt.

The Sabeans also (as D'Herbelot tells us) had their classes of angels, to whom they prayed as mediators, or intercessors; and the Arabians worshipped *female* angels, whom they called Benad Hasche, or, Daughters of God.

* "We adorned the lower heaven with lights. and placed therein a guard of angels."—*Koran*, chap. xli.

† See D'Herbelot, *passim*.

THE LOVES OF THE ANGELS.

'Twas when the world was in its prime,
When the fresh stars had just begun
Their race of glory, and young Time
Told his first birth-days by the sun ·
When, in the light of Nature's dawn
Rejoicing, men and angels met*
On the high hill and sunny lawn—
Ere sorrow came, or Sin had drawn
'Twixt man and heaven her curtain yet!
When earth lay nearer to the skies
Than in these days of crime and wo,
And mortals saw, without surprise,
In the mid-air, angelie eyes
Gazing upon this world below.

Alas, that Passion should profane,
Even then, the morning of the earth!
That, sadder still, the fatal stain
Should fall on hearts of heavenly birth—
And that from Woman's love should fall
So dark a stain, most sad of all!

One evening, in that primal hour,
On a hill's side, where hung the ray
Of sunset, brightening rill and bower,
Three noble youths conversing lay;
And, as they looked, from time to time,
To the far sky, where Daylight furled
His radiant wing, their brows sublime
Bespoke them of that distant world—
Spirits, who once, in brotherhood
Of faith and bliss, near Alla stood,
And o'er whose cheeks full oft had blown
The wind that breathes from Alla's throne,†
Creatures of light, such as *still* play,
Like motes in sunshine, round the Lord,
And through their infinite array
Transmit each moment, night and day,
The echo of his luminous word!

Of Heaven they spoke, and, still more oft,
Of the bright eyes that charmed them thence;
Till, yielding gradual to the soft
And balmy evening's influence—
The silent breathing of the flowers
The melting light that beamed above,
As on their first, fond, erring hours,
Each told the story of his love,
The history of that hour unblest,
When, like a bird, from its high nest
Won down by fascinating eyes,
For Woman's smile he lost the skies.

The First who spoke was one, with look
The least celestial of the three—
A Spirit of light mould, that took
The prints of earth most yieldingly;
Who, even in heaven, was not of those
Nearest the Throne,‡ but held a place
Far off, among those shining rows
That circle out through endless space,
And o'er whose wings the light from Him
In Heaven's centre falls most dim.

Still fair and glorious, he but shone
Among those youths th' unheavenliest one—
A creature, to whom light remained
From Eden still, but altered, stained,
And o'er whose brow not Love alone
A blight had, in his transit, cast,
But other, earthlier joys had gone,
And left their foot-prints as they passed.
Sighing, as back through ages flown,
Like a tomb-searcher, Memory ran,
Lifting each shroud that Time had thrown
O'er buried hopes, he thus began:—

* The Mahometans believe, says D'Herbelot, that in that early period of the world, "les hommes n'eurent qu'une seule religion, et furent souvent visités des Anges, qui leur donnoient la main."

† "To which will be joined the sound of the bells hanging on the trees, which will be put in motion by the wind proceeding from the Throne, so often as the Blessed wish for music." See *Sale's Koran, Prelim. Dissert*

‡ The ancient Persians supposed that this Throne was placed in the Sun, and that through the stars were distributed the various classes of Angels that encircled it.

The Basilidians supposed that there were three hundred and sixty-five orders of angels, "dont la perfection alloit en d'écroissant, à mesure qu'ils s'éloignoient de la première classe d'esprits placés dans le premier ciel." See *Dupuis, Orig. des Cultes*, tom. ii., p. 112

FIRST ANGEL'S STORY.

"'Twas in a land, that far away
Into the golden orient lies,
Where Nature knows not night's delay,
But springs to meet her bridegroom, Day,
Upon the threshold of the skies.
One morn, on earthly mission sent,*
And mid-way choosing where to light,
I saw, from the blue element—
Oh beautiful, but fatal sight!
One of earth's fairest womankind,
Half veiled from view, or rather shrined
In the clear crystal of a brook;
Which, while it hid no single gleam
Of her young beauties, made them look
More spirit-like, as they might seem
Through the dim shadowing of a dream.
Pausing in wonder I looked on,
While, playfully around her breaking
The waters, that like diamonds shone
She moved in light of her own making.
At length, as from that airy height
I gently lowered my breathless flight,
The tremble of my wings all o'er
(For through each plume I felt the thrill)
Startled her, as she reached the shore
Of that small lake—her mirror still—
Above whose brink she stood, like snow
When rosy with a sunset glow.
Never shall I forget those eyes!
The shame, the innocent surprise
Of that bright face, when in the air
Uplooking, she beheld me there,
It seemed as if each thought, and look,
And motion, were that minute chained
Fast to the spot, such root she took,
And—like a sunflower by a brook,
With face upturned—so still remained!

In pity to the wond'ring maid,
Though loath from such a vision turning,
Downward I bent, beneath the shade
Of my spread wings to hide the burning
Of glances, which—I well could feel—
For me, for her, too warmly shone;
But, ere I could again unseal
My restless eyes, or even steal
One sidelong look, the maid was gone—
Hid from me in the forest leaves,
Sudden as when, in all her charms
Of full-blown light, some cloud receives
The Moon into his dusky arms.

'Tis not in words to tell the power,
The despotism that, from that hour,

* It appears that, in most languages, the term employed for an angel means also a messenger. Firischteh, the Persian word for angel, is derived (says D'Herbelot) from the verb Firischtin, to send. The Hebrew term, too, Melak, has the same signification.

Passion held o'er me. Day and night
I sought around each neighboring spot;
And, in the chase of this sweet light,
My task, and heaven, and all forgot;
All, but the one, sole, haunting dream
Of her I saw in that bright stream.

Nor was it long, ere by her side
I found myself, whole happy days,
List'ning to words, whose music vied
With our own Eden's seraph lays,
When seraph lays are warmed by love,
But, wanting *that*, far, far above!
And looking into eyes where, blue
And beautiful, like skies seen through
The sleeping wave, for me there shone
A heaven, more worshipped than my own.
Oh what, while I could hear and see
Such words and looks, was heaven to me?
Though gross the air on earth I drew,
'Twas blessed, while she breathed it too;
Though dark the flowers, though dim the sky,
Love lent them light while she was nigh.
Throughout creation I but knew
Two separate worlds—the *one*, that small,
Beloved, and consecrated spot
Where LEA *was*—the other, all
The dull, wide waste, where she was *not!*

But vain my suit, my madness vain;
Though gladly, from her eyes to gain
One earthly look, one stray desire,
I would have torn the wings, that hung
Furled at my back, and o'er the Fire
In GEHIM's* pit their fragments flung;—
'Twas hopeless all—pure and unmoved
She stood, as lilies in the light
Of the hot noon but look more white;
And though she loved me, deeply loved,
'Twas not as man, as mortal—no,
Nothing of earth was in that glow—
She loved me but as one, of race
Angelic, from that radiant place
She saw so oft in dreams—that heaven,
To which her prayers at morn were sent,
And on whose light she gazed at even,
Wishing for wings, that she might go
Out of this shadowy world below,
To that free, glorious element?

Well I remember by her side
Sitting at rosy even-tide,
When—turning to the star, whose head
Looked out, as from a bridal bed,
At that mute, blushing hour—she said,
'Oh! that it were my doom to be
The Spirit of yon beauteous star,
Dwelling up there in purity,
Alone, as all such bright things are;
My sole employ to pray and shine,
To light my censer at the sun
And cast its fire toward the shrine
Of Him in heaven, th' Eternal one!'

So innocent the maid, so free
From mortal taint in soul and frame,
Whom 'twas my crime—my destiny—
To love, ay, burn for, with a flame,
To which earth's wildest fires are tame.

* The name given by the Mahometans to the infernal regions, over which, they say, the angel Tabhek presides.
By the seven gates of hell, mentioned in the Koran, the commentators understand seven different departments or wards, in which seven different sorts of sinners are to be punished. The first, called Gehennem, is for sinful Mussulmans; the second, Ladha, for Christian offenders; the third, Hothama, is appointed for Jews; and the fourth and fifth, called Sair and Sacar, are destined to receive the Sabæans and the worshippers of fire; in the sixth, named Gehim, those pagans and idolaters who admit a plurality of gods are placed; while into the abyss of the seventh, called Derk Asfal, or the Deepest, the hypocritical canters of *all* religions are thrown.

Had you but seen her look, when first
From my mad lips th' avowal burst;
Not angered—no—the feeling came
From depths beyond mere anger's flame—
It was a sorrow, calm as deep,
A mournfulness that could not weep,
So filled her heart was to the brink,
So fixed and frozen with grief, to think
That angel natures—that even I,
Whose love she clung to, as the tie
Between her spirit and the sky—
Should fall thus headlong from the height
Of all that heaven hath pure and bright!

That very night—my heart had grown
Impatient of its inward burning;
The term, too, of my stay was flown,
And the bright Watchers near the throne,
Already, if a meteor shone
Between them and this nether zone,
Thought 'twas their herald's wing returning
Oft did the potent spell-word, given
To Envoys hither from the skies,
To be pronounced, when back to heaven
It is their time or wish to rise,
Come to my lips that fatal day;
And once, too, was so nearly spoken,
That my spread plumage in the ray
And breeze of heaven began to play;
When my heart failed—the spell was broken-
The word unfinished died away,
And my checked plumes, ready to soar,
Fell slack and lifeless as before.
How could I leave a world which she,
Or lost or won, made all to me?
No matter where my wand'rings were,
So there she looked, breathed, moved about—
Wo, ruin, death, more sweet with her,
Than Paradise itself, without!

But, to return—that very day
A feast was held, where, full of mirth,
Came—crowding thick as flowers that play
In summer winds—the young and gay
And beautiful of this bright earth.
And she was there, and 'mid the young
And beautiful stood first, alone;
Though on her gentle brow still hung
The shadow I that morn had thrown—
The first, that ever shame or wo
Had cast upon its vernal snow.
My heart was maddened;—in the flush
Of the wild revel I gave way
To all that frantic mirth—that rush
Of desp'rate gayety, which they,
Who never felt how pain's excess
Can break out thus, think happiness!
Sad mimicry of mirth and life,
Whose flashes come but from the strife
Of inward passions—like the light
Struck out by clashing swords in fight.

Then, too, that juice of earth, the bane
And blessing of man's heart and brain—
That draught of sorcery, which brings
Phantoms of fair, forbidden things—
Whose drops, like those of rainbows, smile
Upon the mists that circle man,
Brightening not only Earth, the while,
But grasping Heaven, too, in their span!
Then first the fatal winecup rained
Its dews of darkness through my lips,*

* I have already mentioned that some of the circumstances of this story were suggested to me by the eastern legend of the two angels, Harut and Marut, as given by Mariti, who says that the author of Taalim founds upon it the Mahometan prohibition of wine.† I have since found that Mariti's version of the tale (which differs also from that of Dr Prideaux, in his life of Mahomet), is taken from the French Encyclopédie, in which work, under the head "Arot et Marot." the reader will find it.

† The Bahardanush tells the fable differently.

Casting whate'er of light remained
 To my lost soul into eclipse;
And filling it with such wild dreams,
 Such fantasies and wrong desires,
As, in the absence of heaven's beams,
 Haunt us for ever—like wild-fires,
 That walk this earth, when day retires.

Now hear the rest; our banquet done,
I sought her in th' accustomed bower,
Where late we oft, when day was gone,
And the world hushed, had met alone,
 At the same silent, moonlight hour.
Her eyes, as usual, were upturned
To her loved star, whose lustre burned
 Purer than ever on that night;
 While she, in looking, grew more bright,
 As though she borrowed of its light.

There was a virtue in that scene,
 A spell of holiness around,
Which, had my burning brain not been
 Thus maddened, would have held me bound,
 As though I trod celestial ground.
Even as it was, with soul all flame,
 And lips that burned in their own sighs,
I stood to gaze, with awe and shame—
The memory of Eden came
 Full o'er me when I saw those eyes;
And though too well each glance of mine
 To the pale, shrinking maiden proved
How far, alas! from aught divine,
Aught worthy of so pure a shrine,
 Was the wild love with which I loved,
Yet must she, too, have seen—oh yes,
 'Tis soothing but to *think* she saw
The deep, true, soul-felt tenderness,
 The homage of an Angel's awe
To her, a mortal, whom pure love
Then placed above him—far above—
And all that struggle to repress
A sinful spirit's mad excess,
Which worked within me at that hour,
 When, with a voice, where Passion shed
All the deep sadness of her power,
 Her melancholy power—I said,
'Then be it so; if back to heaven
 I must unloved, unpitied fly,
Without one blest memorial given
 To sooth me in that lonely sky;
One look, like those the young and fond
 Give when they're parting—which would be,
Even in remembrance, far beyond
 All heaven hath left of bliss for me!

Oh, but to see that head recline
 A minute on this trembling arm,
And those mild eyes look up to mine,
 Without a dread, a thought of harm!
To meet, but once, the thrilling touch
 Of lips too purely fond to fear me—
Or, if that boon be all too much,
 Even thus to bring their fragrance near me!
Nay, shrink not so—a look—a word—
 Give them but kindly, and I fly;
Already, see, my plumes have stirred,
 And tremble for their home on high.
Thus be our parting—cheek to cheek—
 One minute's lapse will be forgiven,
And thou, the next, shalt hear me speak
 The spell that plumes my wing for heaven!'

While thus I spoke, the fearful maid,
Of me, and of herself afraid,
Had shrinking stood, like flowers beneath
The scorching of the south-wind's breath:
But when I named—alas! too well,
 I now recall, though wildered then—
Instantly, when I named the spell,
 Her brow, her eyes uprose again,
And, with an eagerness, that spoke
The sudden light that o'er her broke,

'The spell, the spell!—oh, speak it now,
 And I will bless thee!' she exclaimed—
 Unknowing what I did, inflamed,
And lost already, on her brow
 I stamped one burning kiss, and named
The mystic word, till then ne'er told
To living creature of earth's mould!
Scarce was it said, when, quick as thought,
Her lips from mine, like echo, caught
The holy sound—her hands and eyes
Were instant lifted to the skies,
And thrice to heaven she spoke it out
 With that triumphant look Faith wears,
When not a cloud of fear or doubt,
 A vapor from this vale of tears,
 Between her and her God appears!

That very moment her whole frame
All bright and glorified became,
And at her back I saw unclose
Two wings, magnificent as those
 That sparkle around ALLA's Throne,
Whose plumes, as buoyantly she rose
 Above me, in the moonbeam shone
With a pure light, which—from its hue,
Unknown upon this earth—I knew
Was light from Eden, glist'ning through!
Most holy vision! ne'er before
 Did aught so radiant—since the day
When EBLIS, in his downfall, bore
 The third of the bright stars away—
Rise, in earth's beauty, to repair
That loss of light and glory there!

But did I tamely view her flight?
 Did not *I*, too, proclaim out thrice
The powerful words that were, that night—
Oh, even for heaven too much delight!—
 Again to bring us, eyes to eyes,
 And soul to soul, in Paradise?
I did—I spoke it o'er and o'er—
 I prayed, I wept, but all in vain;
For me the spell had power no more.
 There seemed around me some dark chain
Which still, as I essayed to soar,
 Baffled, alas! each wild endeavor:
Dead lay my wings, as they have lain
Since that sad hour, and will remain—
 So wills th' offended God—for ever!

It was to yonder star I traced
Her journey up th' illumined waste—
That isle in the blue firmament,
To which so oft her fancy went
 In wishes and in dreams before,
And which was now—such, Purity,
Thy blest reward—ordained to be
 Her home of light for evermore!
Once—or did I but fancy so?—
 Even in her flight to that fair sphere
'Mid all her spirit's new-felt glow,
A pitying look she turned below
 On him who stood in darkness here;
Him whom, perhaps, if vain regret
Can dwell in heaven, she pities yet;
And oft, when looking to this dim
And distant world, remembers him.

But soon that passing dream was gone;
Further and further off she shone,
Till lessened to a point, as small
 As are those specks that yonder burn—
Those vivid drops of light, that fall
 The last from Day's exhausted urn.
And when at length she merged, afar,
Into her own immortal star,
And when at length my straining sight
 Had caught her wing's last fading ray,
That minute from my soul the light
 Of heaven and love both passed away;
And I forgot my home, my birth,
 Profaned my spirit, sunk my brow,
And revelled in gross joys of earth,
 Till I became—what I am now!"

The Spirit bowed his head in shame;
A shame, that of itself would tell—
Were there not even those breaks of flame,
Celestial, through his clouded frame—
How grand the height from which he fell!
That holy Shame, which ne'er forgets
Th' unblenched renown it used to wear;
Whose blush remains, when Virtue sets,
To show her sunshine *has* been there.

Once only, while the tale he told,
Were his eyes lifted to behold
That happy stainless star, where she
Dwelt in her bower of purity!
One minute did he look, and then—
As though he felt some deadly pain
From its sweet light through heart and brain—
Shrunk back, and never looked again.

Who was the Second Spirit? he
With the proud front and piercing glance—
Who seemed when viewing heaven's expanse,
As though his far-sent eye could see
On, on into th' Immensity
Behind the veils of that blue sky,
Where Alla's grandest secrets lie?—
His wings, the while, though day was gone,
Flashing with many a various hue
Of light they from themselves alone,
Instinct with Eden's brightness, drew.
'Twas Rubi—once among the prime
And flower of those bright creatures, named
Spirits of Knowledge,* who o'er Time
And Space and Thought an empire claimed,
Second alone to Him, whose light
Was, even to theirs, as day to night;
'Twixt whom and them was distance far
And wide as would the journey be
To reach from any island star
The vague shores of Infinity!

'Twas Rubi, in whose mournful eye
Slept the dim light of days gone by;
Whose voice, though sweet, fell on the ear
Like echoes, in some silent place,
When first awaked for many a year;
And when he smiled, if o'er his face
Smile ever shone, 'twas like the grace
Of moonlight rainbows, fair, but wan,
The sunny life, the glory gone.
Even o'er his pride, though still the same,
A soft'ning shade from sorrow came;
And though at times his spirit knew
The kindlings of disdain and ire,
Short was the fitful glare they threw—
Like the last flashes, fierce but few,
Seen through some noble pile on fire!

Such was the Angel, who now broke
The silence that had come o'er all,
When he, the Spirit that last spoke,
Closed the sad hist'ry of his fall;
And, while a sacred lustre, flown
For many a day, relumed his cheek—
Beautiful, as in days of old;
And not those eloquent lips alone
But every feature seemed to speak—
Thus his eventful story told:—

* The Kerubiim, as the Mussulmans call them, are often joined indiscriminately with the Asrafil or Seraphim, under one common name of Azazil, by which all spirits who approach near the throne of Alla are designated.

SECOND ANGEL'S STORY.

"You both remember well the day,
When unto Eden's new-made bowers,
Alla convoked the bright array
Of his supreme angelic powers,
To witness the one wonder yet,
Beyond man, angel, star, or sun,
He must achieve, ere he could set
His seal upon the world, as done—
To see that last perfection rise,
That crowning of creation's birth,
When, 'mid the worship and surprise
Of circling angels, Woman's eyes
First opened upon heaven and earth;
And from their lids a thrill was sent,
That through each living spirit went,
Like first light through the firmament!

Can you forget how gradual stole
The fresh-awakened breath of soul
Throughout her perfect form—which seemed
To grow transparent, as there beamed
That dawn of Mind within, and caught
New loveliness from each new thought?
Slow as o'er summer's seas we trace
The progress of the noontide air,
Dimpling its bright and silent face
Each minute into some new grace
And varying heaven's reflections there—
Or, like the light of evening, stealing
O'er some fair temple, which all day
Hath slept in shadow, slow revealing
Its several beauties, ray by ray,
Till it shines out a thing to bless,
All full of light and loveliness.
Can you forget her blush when round
Through Eden's lone, enchanted ground
She looked, and saw, the sea—the skies—
And heard the rush of many a wing,
On high behests then vanishing;
And saw the last few angel eyes,
Still ling'ring—mine among the rest—
Reluctant leaving scenes so blest?
From that miraculous hour, the fate
Of this new, glorious Being dwelt
For ever, with a spell-like weight,
Upon my spirit—early, late,
Whate'er I did, or dreamed or felt,
The thought of what might yet befall
That matchless creature mixed with all.
Nor she alone, but her whole race
Through ages yet to come—whate'er
Of feminine, and fond, and fair,
Should spring from that pure mind and face,
All waked my soul's intensest care;
Their forms, souls, feelings, still to me
Creation's strangest mystery!

It was my doom, even from the first,
When witnessing the primal burst
Of Nature's wonders, I saw rise
Those bright creations in the skies—
Those worlds instinct with life and light,
Which man, remote, but sees by night—
It was my doom still to be haunted
By some new wonder, some sublime
And matchless work, that, for the time
Held all my soul, enchained, enchanted,
And left me not a thought, a dream,
A word, but on that only theme!

The wish to know—that endless thirst,
Which even by quenching is awaked,
And which becomes or blest or curst,
As is the fount whereat 'tis slaked—
Still urged me onward, with desire
Insatiate, to explore, inquire—
Whate'er the wondrous things might be,
That waked each new idolatry—
Their cause, aim, source, whence-ever sprung—

Their inmost powers, as though for me
Existence on that knowledge hung.

Oh what a vision were the stars,
When first I saw them burn on high,
Rolling along, like living cars
Of light, for gods to journey by!*
They were my heart's first passion—days
And nights, unwearied, in their rays
Have I hung floating, till each sense
Seemed full of their bright influence.
Innocent joy! alas, how much
Of misery had I shunned below,
Could I have still lived blest with such;
Nor, proud and restless burned to know
The knowledge that brings guilt and wo.
Often—so much I loved to trace
The secrets of this starry race—
Have I at morn and evening run
Along the lines of radiance spun
Like webs, between them and the sun,
Untwisting all the tangled ties
Of light into their different dies—
Then fleetly winged I off, in quest
Of those, the farthest, loneliest,
That watch, like winking sentinels,†
The void, beyond which Chaos dwells;
And there, with noiseless plume, pursued
Their track through that grand solitude,
Asking intently all and each
What soul within their radiance dwelt,
And wishing their sweet light were speech,
That they might tell me all they felt.

Nay, oft so passionate my chase
Of these resplendent heirs of space,
Oft did I follow—lest a ray
Should 'scape me in the farthest night—
Some pilgrim Comet, on his way
To visit distant shrines of light,
And well remember how I sung
Exultingly, when on my sight
New worlds of stars, all fresh and young,
As if just born of darkness, sprung!

Such was my pure ambition then,
My sinless transport, night and morn;
Ere yet this newer world of men,
And that most fair of stars was born
Which I, in fatal hour saw rise
Among the flowers of Paradise!
Thenceforth my nature all was changed,
My heart, soul, senses, turned below;
And he, who but so lately ranged
Yon wonderful expanse, where glow
Worlds upon worlds—yet found his mind
Even in that luminous range confined—
Now blest the humblest, meanest sod
Of the dark earth where Woman trod!
In vain my former idols glistened
From their far thrones; in vain these ears
To the once-thrilling music listened,
That hymned around my favorite spheres—

To earth, to earth each thought was given,
That in this half-lost soul had birth;
Like some high mount, whose head's in heaven,
While its whole shadow rests on earth!

Nor was it Love, even yet, that thralled
My spirit in his burning ties;
And less, still less could it be called
That grosser flame, round which Love flies
Nearer and nearer till he dies—
No, it was wonder, such as thrilled
At all God's works my dazzled sense;
The same rapt wonder, only filled
With passion, more profound, intense—
A vehement, but wandering fire,
Which, though nor love, nor yet desire—
Though through all womankind it took
Its range, as lawless lightnings run,
Yet wanted but a touch, a look,
To fix it burning upon *One*.

Then, too, the ever-restless zeal,
Th' insatiate curiosity
To know how shapes, so fair, must feel
To look, but once, beneath the seal
Of so much loveliness, and see
What souls belonged to such bright eyes—
Whether, as sunbeams find their way
Into the gem that hidden lies,
Those looks could inward turn their ray,
And make the soul as bright as they:
All this impelled my anxious chase,
And still the more I saw and knew,
Of Woman's fond, weak, conquering race,
Th' intenser still my wonder grew.

I had beheld their First, their EVE,
Born in that splendid Paradise,
Which sprung there solely to receive
The first light of her waking eyes.
I had seen purest angels lean
In worship o'er her from above;
And man—oh yes, had envying seen
Proud man possessed of all her love.
I saw their happiness, so brief,
So exquisite—her error, too,
That easy trust, that prompt belief
In what the warm heart wishes true;
That faith in words, when kindly said,
By which the whole fond sex is led—
Mingled with—what I durst not blame,
For 'tis my own—that zeal to *know*,
Sad, fatal zeal, so sure of wo;
Which, though from heaven all pure it came,
Yet stained, misused, brought sin and shame
On her, on me, on all below!

I had seen this; had seen Man, armed,
As his soul is, with strength and sense,
By her first words to ruin charmed;
His vaunted reason's cold defence,
Like an ice-barrier in the ray
Of melting summer, smiled away.
Nay, stranger yet, spite of all this—
Though by her counsels taught to err,
Though driven from Paradise for her,
(And *with* her—*that*, at least, was bliss),
Had I not heard him, ere he crost
The threshold of that earthly heaven,
Which by her wildering smile he lost—
So quickly was the wrong forgiven!
Had I not heard him, as he prest
The frail, fond trembler to a breast
Which she had doomed to sin and strife,
Call her—even then—his Life! his Life!*
Yes, such the love-taught name, the first,
That ruined Man to Woman gave,

* "C'est un fait indubitable que la plupart des anciens philosophes, soit Chaldéens, soit Grecs, nous ont donné les astres comme animés, et ont soutenu que les astres, qui nous éclairent, n'étoient que ou les chars, ou même les navires, des Intelligences qui les conduisoient. Pour les *Chars*, cela se lit partout; on n'a qu'ouvrir Pline, St. Clément," &c., &c.—*Mémoire Historique, sur le Sabiisme*, par M. FOURMONT.

A belief that the stars are either spirits or the vehicles of spirits, was common to all the religions and heresies of the East. Kircher has given the names and stations of the seven archangels, who were by the Cabala of the Jews distributed through the planets.

† According to the cosmogony of the ancient Persians, there were four stars set as sentinels in the four quarters of the heavens, to watch over the other fixed stars, and superintend the planets in their course. The names of these four sentinel stars are, according to the Boundesh, Taschter, for the east; Satevis, for the west; Venand, for the south; and Haftorang, for the north.

* Chavah, or, as it is in Arabic, Havah (the name by which Adam called the woman after their transgression), means "Life."

Even in his outcast hour, when curst
By her fond witchery, with that worst
And earliest boon of love, the grave!
She, who brought death into the world,
There stood before him, with the light
Of their lost Paradise still bright
Upon those sunny locks, that curled
Down her white shoulders to her feet—
So beautiful in form, so sweet
In heart and voice, as to redeem
The loss, the death of all things dear,
Except herself—and make it seem
Life, endless Life, while she was near!
Could I help wondering at a creature,
Thus circled round with spells so strong—
One, to whose ev'ry thought, word, feature,
In joy and wo, through right and wrong,
Such sweet omnipotence Heaven gave,
To bless or ruin, curse or save?

Nor did the marvel cease with her—
New Eves in all her daughters came,
As strong to charm, as weak to err,
As sure of man through praise and blame,
Whate'er they brought him, pride or shame,
He still th' unreasoning worshipper,
And they, throughout all time, the same,
Enchantresses of soul and frame,
Into whose hands, from first to last,
This world with all its destinies,
Devotedly by Heaven seems cast,
To save or ruin, as they please!
Oh, 'tis not to be told how long,
How restlessly I sighed to find
Some *one*, from out that witching throng,
Some abstract of the form and mind
Of the whole matchless sex, from which
In my own arms beheld, possest,
I might learn all the powers to witch,
To warm, and (if my fate unblest
Would have it) ruin, of the rest!
Into whose inward soul and sense
I might descend, as doth the bee
Into the flower's deep heart, and thence
Rifle, in all its purity,
The prime, the quintessence, the whole
Of wondrous Woman's frame and soul!

At length, my burning wish, my prayer—
(For such—oh what will tongues not dare,
When hearts go wrong?—this lip preferred)—
At length my ominous prayer was heard—
But whether heard in heaven or hell,
Listen—and thou wilt know *too* well.

There was a maid, of all who move
Like visions o'er this orb, most fit
To be a bright young angel's love,
Herself so bright, so exquisite!
The pride, too, of her step, as light
Along th' unconscious earth she went,
Seemed that of one, born with a right
To walk some heavenlier element,
And tread in places where her feet
A star at every step should meet.
'Twas not alone that loveliness
By which the wildered sense is caught—
Of lips, whose very breath could bless;
Of playful blushes, that seemed naught
But luminous escapes of thought;
Of eyes that, when by anger stirred,
Were fire itself, but, at a word
Of tenderness, all soft became
As though they could, like the sun's bird,
Dissolve away in their own flame—
Of form, as pliant as the shoots
Of a young tree, in vernal flower;
Yet round and glowing as the fruits,
That drop from it in summer's hour;
'Twas not alone this loveliness
That falls to loveliest woman's share,
Though, even here, her form could spare
From its own beauty's rich excess
Enough to make even *them* more fair—
But 'twas the Mind, outshining clear
Through her whole frame—the soul, still near,
To light each charm, yet independent
Of what it lighted, as the sun
That shines on flowers, would be resplendent
Were there no flowers to shine upon—
'Twas this, all this, in one combined—
Th' unnumbered looks and arts that form
The glory of young woman-kind,
Taken, in their perfection, warm,
Ere time had chilled a single charm,
And stamped with such a seal of Mind,
As gave to beauties, that might be
Too sensual else, too unrefined,
The impress of Divinity.

'Twas this—a union, which the hand
Of Nature kept for her alone,
Of everything most playful, bland,
Voluptuous, spiritual, grand,
In angel-natures and her own—
Oh this it was that drew me nigh
One, who seemed kin to heaven as I,
A bright twin-sister from on high—
One, in whose love, I felt, were given
The mixed delights of either sphere,
All that the spirit seeks in heaven,
And all the senses burn for here.

Had we—but hold—hear every part
Of our sad tale—spite of the pain
Remembrance gives, when the fixed dart
Is stirred thus in the wound again—
Hear every step, so full of bliss,
And yet so ruinous, that led
Down to the last, dark precipice,
Where perished both—the fallen, the dead!

From the first hour she caught my sight,
I never left her—day and night
Hovering unseen around her way,
And 'mid her loneliest musings near,
I soon could track each thought that lay,
Gleaming within her heart, as clear
As pebbles within brooks appear;
And there, among the countless things
That keep young hearts for ever glowing,
Vague wishes, fond imaginings,
Love-dreams, as yet no object knowing—
Light, winged hopes, that come when bid,
And rainbow joys that end in weeping;
And passions, among pure thoughts hid,
Like serpents under flowerets sleeping:
'Mong all these feelings—felt where'er
Young hearts are beating—I saw there
Proud thoughts, aspirings high—beyond
Whate'er yet dwelt in soul so fond—
Glimpses of glory, far away
Into the bright, vague future given;
And fancies, free and grand, whose play,
Like that of eaglets, is near heaven!
With this, too—what a soul and heart
To fall beneath the tempter's art!—
A zeal for knowledge, such as ne'er
Enshrined itself in form so fair,
Since that first, fatal hour, when Eve,
With every fruit of Eden blest,
Save one alone—rather than leave
That *one* unreached, lost all the rest.

It was in dreams that first I stole,
With gentle mastery o'er her mind—
In that rich twilight of the soul,
When reason's beam, half hid behind
The clouds of sleep, obscurely gilds
Each shadowy shape the Fancy builds—
'Twas then, by that soft light, I brought
Vague, glimmery visions to her view;—
Catches of radiance, lost when caught,
Bright labyrinths, that led to naught,
And vistas, with no pathway through;—

Dwellings of bliss, that opening shone,
  Then closed, dissolved, and left no truce—
All that, in short, could tempt Hope on,
  But give her wing no resting-place;
Myself the while, with brow, as yet,
Pure as the young moon's coronet,
Through every dream *still* in her sight,
  Th' enchanter of each mocking scene,
Who gave the hope, then brought the blight,
Who said, 'Behold, yon world of light,'
  Then sudden dropt a veil between!

At length, when I perceived each thought,
Waking or sleeping, fixed on naught
  But these illusive scenes, and me—
The phantom, who thus came and went
In half revealments only meant
  To madden curiosity—
When by such various arts I found
Her fancy to its utmost wound,
One night—'twas in a holy spot,
Which she for prayer had chose—a grot
Of purest marble, built below
Her garden beds, through which a glow
From lamps invisible then stole,
  Brightly pervading all the place—
Like that mysterious light, the soul,
  Itself unseen, sheds through the face.
There, at her altar, while she knelt,
And all that woman ever felt,
  When God and man both claimed her sighs—
Every warm thought, that ever dwelt,
  Like summer clouds, 'twixt earth and skies,
  Too pure to fall, too gross to rise,
  Spoke in her gestures, tones, and eyes—
Then, as the mystic light's soft ray
Grew softer still, as though its ray
Was breathed from her, I heard her say:—

'Oh idol of my dreams, whate'er
  Thy nature be—human, divine,
Or but half heavenly—still too fair,
  Too heavenly to be ever mine!

Wonderful Spirit, who dost make
  Slumber so lovely that it seems
No longer life to live awake,
  Since heaven itself descends in dreams,

Why do I ever lose thee? why,
  When on thy realms and thee I gaze,
Still drops that veil, which I could die,
  Oh gladly, but one hour to raise?

Long ere such miracles as thou
  And thine came o'er my thoughts, a thirst
For light was in this soul, which now
  Thy looks have into passion nursed.

There's nothing bright above, below,
  In sky—earth—ocean, that this breast,
Doth not intensely burn to know,
  And thee, thee, thee, o'er all the rest!

Then come, oh Spirit, from behind
  The curtains of thy radiant home,
If thou wouldst be as angel shrined,
  Or loved and clasped as mortal, come!

Bring all thy dazzling wonders here,
  That I may, waking, know and see;
Or waft me hence to thy own sphere
  Thy heaven or—ay, even *that* with thee!

Demon or God, who hold'st the book
  Of knowledge spread beneath thine eye,
Give me, with thee, but one bright look
  Into its leaves, and let me die!

By those ethereal wings, whose way
  Lies through an element, so fraught
With living Mind, that, as they play,
  Their every movement is a thought!

By that bright, wreathed hair, between
  Whose sunny clusters the sweet wind
Of Paradise so late hath been,
  And left its fragrant soul behind!

By those impassioned eyes, that melt
  Their light into the inmost heart:
Like sunset in the waters, felt
  As molten fire through every part—

I do implore thee, oh most bright
  And worshipped Spirit, shine but o'er
My waking, wondering eyes this night,
  This one blest night—I ask no more!'

Exhausted, breathless, as she said
These burning words, her languid head
Upon the altar's steps she cast,
As if that brain-throb were its last—

Till, startled by the breathing, nigh,
Of lips, that echoed back her sigh,
Sudden her brow again she raised:
  And there, just lighted on the shrine,
Beheld me—not as I had blazed
  Around her, full of light divine,
In her late dreams, but softened down
Into more mortal grace;—my crown
Of flowers, too radiant for this world,
  Left hanging on yon starry steep;
My wings shut up, like banners furled,
  When Peace hath put their pomp to sleep
  Or like autumnal clouds, that keep
Their lightnings sheathed, rather than mar
The dawning hour of some young star;
And nothing left, but what beseemed
  Th' accessible, though glorious mate
Of mortal woman—whose eyes beamed
  Back upon hers, as passionate;
Whose ready heart brought flame for flame,
Whose sin, whose madness was the same;
And whose soul lost, in that one hour,
  For her and for her love—oh more
Of heaven's light than even the power
  Of heaven itself could now restore!

And yet, that hour!"——

The Spirit here
  Stopped in his utterance, as if words
Gave way beneath the wild career
  Of his then rushing thoughts—like chords,
Midway in some enthusiast's song,
Breaking beneath a touch too strong;
While the clenched hand upon the brow
Told how remembrance throbbed there now!
But soon 'twas o'er—that casual blaze
From the sunk fire of other days—
That relic of a flame, whose burning
  Had been too fierce to be relumed,
Soon passed away, and the youth, turning
  To his bright listeners, thus resumed:—

"Days, months elapsed, and though what most
  On earth I sighed for was mine, all—
Yet—was I happy? God, thou know'st,
Howe'er they smile, and feign, and boast,
  What happiness is theirs, who fall!
'Twas bitterest anguish—made more keen
Even by the love, the bliss, between
Whose throbs it came, like gleams of hell
  In agonizing cross-light given
Athwart the glimpses, they who dwell
  In purgatory* catch of heaven!

* Called by the Mussulmans Al Araf—a sort of wall or partition which, according to the 7th chapter of the Koran, separates hell from paradise, and where they, who have not merits sufficient to gain them immediate admittance into heaven are supposed to stand for a certain period, alternately tantalized and tormented by the sights that are on either side presented to them.

Manes, who borrowed in many instances from the Platonists, placed his purgatories, or places of purification, in the Sun and Moon.—*Beausobre*, liv. iii., chap. 8.

The only feeling that to me
Seemed joy—or rather my sole rest
From aching misery—was to see
My young, proud, blooming LILIS blest.
She, the fair fountain of all ill
To my lost soul—whom yet its thirst
Fervidly panted after still,
And found the charm fresh as at first—
To see *her* happy—to reflect
Whatever beams still round me played
Of former pride, of glory wrecked,
On her, my Moon, whose light I made,
And whose soul worshipped even my shade—
This was, I own, enjoyment—this
My sole, last lingering glimpse of bliss.
And proud she was, fair creature !—proud,
Beyond what even most queenly stirs
In woman's heart, nor would have bowed
That beautiful young brow of hers
To aught beneath the First above,
So high she deemed her Cherub's love !

Then, too, that passion, hourly growing
Stronger and stronger—to which even
Her love, at times, gave way—of knowing
Everything strange in earth and heaven ;
Not only all that, full revealed,
Th' eternal ALLA loves to show,
But all that He hath wisely sealed
In darkness, for man *not* to know—
Even this desire, alas ! ill-starred
And fatal as it was, I sought
To feed each minute, and unbarred
Such realms of wonder on her thought,
As ne'er, till then, had let their light
Escape on any mortal's sight !
In the deep earth—beneath the sea—
Through caves of fire—through wilds of air—
Wherever sleeping Mystery
Had spread her curtain, we were there—
Love still beside us, as we went,
At home in each new element,
And sure of worship everywhere !

Then first was Nature taught to lay
The wealth of all her kingdoms down
At woman's worshipped feet, and say,
'Bright creature, this is all thine own !'
Then first were diamonds, from the night*
Of earth's deep centre brought to light,
And made to grace the conquering way
Of proud young beauty with their ray.

Then, too, the pearl from out its shell
Unsightly, in the sunless sea,
(As 'twere a spirit, forced to dwell
In form unlovely) was set free,
And round the neck of woman threw
A light it lent and borrowed too.
For never did this maid—whate'er
Th' ambition of the hour—forget
Her sex's pride in being fair ;
Nor that adornment, tasteful, rare,
Which makes the mighty magnet, set
In Woman's form, more mighty yet.
Nor was there aught within the range
Of my swift wing in sea or air,
Of beautiful, or grand, or strange,
That, quickly as her wish could change,
I did not seek, with such fond care,

* "Quelques gnomes désireux de devenir immortels, avoient voulu gagner les bonnes graces des nos filles, et leur avoient apporté des pierreries dont ils sont gardiens naturels : et ces auteurs ont cru, s'appuyans sur le livre d'Enoch mal-entendu, que c'étoient des pièges que les anges amoureux," &c., &c.—*Comte de Gabalis.*

As the fiction of the loves of angels with women gave birth to the fanciful world of sylphs and gnomes, so we owe to it also the invention of those beautiful Genii and Peris, which embellish so much the mythology of the East ; for in the fabulous histories of Caiöumarath, of Thamurath, &c., these spiritual creatures are always represented as the descendants of Seth, and called the Bani Alginn, or children of Giann.

That when I've seen her look above
At some bright star admiringly,
I've said, 'Nay, look not there, my love,*
Alas, I *can not* give it thee !'

But not alone the wonders found
Through Nature's realm—th' unveiled, material,
Visible glories, that abound,
Through all her vast, enchanted ground—
But whatsoe'er unseen, ethereal,
Dwells far away from human sense,
Wrapped in its own intelligence—
The mystery of that Fountain-head,
From which all vital spirit runs,
All breath of Life, where'er 'tis spread
Through men or angels, flowers or suns—
The workings of th' Almighty Mind,
When first o'er Chaos he designed
The outlines of this world ; and through
That depth of darkness—like the bow,
Called out of rain-clouds, hue by hue—†
Saw the grand, gradual picture grow ;
The covenant with human kind
By ALLA made‡—the chains of Fate
He round himself and them hath twined,
Till his high task he consummate—
Till good from evil, love from hate,
Shall be worked out through sin and pain,
And Fate shall loose her iron chain,
And all be free, be bright again !

Such were the deep-drawn mysteries,
And some, even more obscure, profound,
And wildering to the mind than these,
Which—far as woman's thought could sound,
Or a fallen, outlawed spirit reach—
She dared to learn, and I to teach.
Till—filled with such unearthly lore,
And mingling the pure light it brings
With much that fancy had, before,
Shed in false, tainted glimmerings—
Th' enthusiast girl spoke out, as one
Inspired, among her own dark race,
Who from their ancient shrines would run,
Leaving their holy rites undone,
To gaze upon her holier face.
And, though but wild the things she spoke,
Yet, 'mid that play of error's smoke
Into fair shapes by fancy curled,
Some gleams of pure religion broke—
Glimpses, that have not yet awoke,
But startled the still-dreaming world !
Oh, many a truth, remote, sublime,
Which Heaven would from the minds of men
Have kept concealed, till its own time,
Stole out in these revealments then—
Revealments dim, that have forerun,
By ages, the great Sealing One !||
Like that imperfect dawn, or light§
Escaping from the Zodiac's signs,
Which makes the doubtful east half bright,
Before the real morning shines !

Thus did some moons of bliss go by—
Of bliss to her, who saw but love
And knowledge throughout earth and sky ;
To whose enamored soul and eye,
I seemed—as is the sun on high—
The light of all below, above,

* I am aware that this happy saying of Lord Albemarle's loses much of its grace and playfulness, by being put into the mouth of any but a human lover.

† According to Whitehurst's theory, the mention of rainbows by an antediluvian angel is an anachronism ; as he says, "There was no rain before the flood, and consequently no rainbow, which accounts for the novelty of this sight after the Deluge."

‡ For the terms of this compact, of which the angels were supposed to be witnesses, see the chapter of the Koran, entitled Al Araf, and the article "Adam" in D'Herbelot.

|| In acknowledging the authority of the great Prophets who had preceded him, Mahomet represented his own mission as the final "*Seal*," or consummation of them all.

§ The Zodiacal Light.

The spirit of sea, and land, and air,
Whose influence, felt everywhere,
Spread from its centre, her own heart,
Even to the world's extremest part;
While through that world her reinless mind
Had now careered so fast and far,
That earth itself seemed left behind,
And her proud fancy, unconfined,
Already saw Heaven's gates ajar!

Happy enthusiast! still, oh still—
Spite of my own heart's mortal chill,
Spite of that double-fronted sorrow,
Which looks at once before and back,
Beholds the yesterday, the morrow,
And sees both comfortless, both black—
Spite of all this, I could have still
In her delight forgot all ill;
Or, if pain *would* not be forgot,
At least have borne and murmured not.
When thoughts of an offended Heaven,
Of sinfulness, which I—even I,
While down its steep most headlong driven—
Well knew could never be forgiven,
Came o'er me with an agony
Beyond all reach of mortal wo—
A torture kept for those who know,
Know *every* thing, and—worst of all—
Know and love Virtue while they fall!
Even then, her presence had the power
To sooth, to warm—nay, even to bless—
If ever bliss could graft its flower,
On stem so full of bitterness—
Even then her glorious smile to me
Brought warmth and radiance, if not balm;
Like moonlight o'er a troubled sea,
Brightening the storm it can not calm.

Oft, too, when that disheartening fear,
Which all who love, beneath yon sky,
Feel, when they gaze on what is dear—
The dreadful thought that it must die!
That desolating thought, which comes
Into men's happiest hours and homes;
Whose melancholy boding flings
Death's shadow o'er the brightest things,
Sicklies the infant's bloom, and spreads
The grave beneath young lovers' heads!
This fear, so sad to all—to me
Most full of sadness, from the thought
That I must still live on,* when she
Would, like the snow that on the sea
Fell yesterday, in vain be sought;
That Heaven to me this final seal
Of all earth's sorrow would deny,
And I eternally must feel
The death-pang, without power to die!
Even this, her fond endearments—fond
As ever cherished the sweet bond
'Twixt heart and heart—could charm away;
Before her look no clouds would stay,
Or, if they did, their gloom was gone,
Their darkness put a glory on!
But 'tis not, 'tis not for the wrong,
The guilty, to be happy long;
And she, too, now, had sunk within
The shadow of her tempter's sin,
Too deep for even Omnipotence
To snatch the fated victim thence!

Listen, and, if a tear there be
Left in your hearts, weep it for me.

'Twas on the evening of a day,
Which we in love had dreamed away;
In that same garden, where—the pride
Of seraph splendor laid aside,
And those wings furled, whose open light
For mortal gaze were else too bright—
I first had stood before her sight,
And found myself—oh, ecstasy,
Which even in pain I ne'er forget—
Worshipped as only God should be,
And loved as never man was yet!
In that same garden were we now,
Thoughtfully side by side reclining,
Her eyes turned upward, and her brow
With its own silent fancies shining.

It was an evening bright and still
As ever blushed on wave or bower,
Smiling from heaven, as if naught ill
Could happen in so sweet an hour.
Yet, I remember, both grew sad
In looking at that light—even she,
Of heart so fresh, and brow so glad,
Felt the still hour's solemnity,
And thought she saw, in that repose,
The death-hour not alone of light,
But of this whole fair world—the close
Of all things beautiful and bright—
The last, grand sunset, in whose ray
Nature herself died calm away!

At length, as though some livelier thought
Had suddenly her fancy caught,
She turned upon me her dark eyes,
Dilated into that full shape
They took in joy, reproach, surprise,
As 'twere to let more soul escape,
And, playfully as on my head
Her white hand rested, smiled and said:—

'I had, last night, a dream of thee,
Resembling those divine ones, given,
Like preludes to sweet minstrelsey,
Before thou cam'st thyself from heaven.

The same rich wreath was on thy brow,
Dazzling as if of starlight made;
And these wings, lying darkly now,
Like meteors round thee flashed and played.

Thou stoodst all bright, as in those dreams,
As if just wafted from above;
Mingling earth's warmth with heaven's beams,
A creature to adore and love.

Sudden I felt thee draw me near
To thy pure heart, where, fondly placed,
I seemed within the atmosphere
Of that exhaling light embraced;

And felt, methought, th' ethereal flame
Pass from thy purer soul to mine;
Till—oh, too blissful—I became,
Like thee, all spirit, all divine!

Say, why did dream so blest come o'er me,
If, now I wake, 'tis faded, gone?
When will my Cherub shine before me
Thus radiant, as in heaven he shone?

When shall I, waking, be allowed
To gaze upon those perfect charms,
And clasp thee once, without a cloud,
A chill of earth, within these arms?

Oh what a pride to say, this, this
Is my own Angel—all divine,
And pure, and dazzling as he is,
And fresh from heaven—he's mine, he's mine

Thinkst thou, were LILIS in thy place,
A creature of yon lofty skies,
She would have hid one single grace,
One glory from her lover's eyes?

No, no—then, if thou lov'st like me,
Shine out, young Spirit, in the blaze

* Pococke, however, gives it as the opinion of the Mahometan doctors, that all souls, not only of men and of animals, living either on land or in the sea, but of the angels also, must necessarily taste of death.

Of thy most proud divinity,
 Nor think thou'lt wound this mortal gaze.

Too long and oft I've looked upon
 Those ardent eyes, intense even thus—
Too near the stars themselves have gone,
 To fear aught grand or luminous.

Then doubt me not—oh, who can say
 But that this dream may yet come true,
And my blest spirit drink thy ray,
 Till it becomes all heavenly too?

Let me this once but feel the flame
 Of those spread wings, the very pride
Will change my nature, and this frame
 By the mere touch be deified!'

Thus spoke the maid, as one not used
To be by earth or heaven refused—
As one, who knew her influence o'er
 All creatures, whatsoe'er they were,
And, though to heaven she could not soar,
 At least would bring down heaven to her.
Little did she, alas, or I—
 Even I, whose soul, but half-way yet
Immerged in sin's obscurity
Was as the earth whereon we lie,
 O'er half whose disk the sun is set—
Little did we foresee the fate,
 The dreadful—how can it be told?
Such pain, such anguish to relate
 Is o'er again to feel, behold!
But, charged as 'tis, my heart must speak
Its sorrow out, or it will break!
Some dark misgivings *had*, I own,
 Passed for a moment through my breast—
Fears of some danger, vague, unknown,
 To one, or both—something unblest
 To happen from this proud request.
But soon these boding fancies fled;
 Nor saw I aught that could forbid
My full revealment, save the dread
 Of that first dazzle, when, unhid,
 Such light should burst upon a lid
Ne'er tried in heaven; and even this glare
She might, by love's own nursing care,
Be, like young eagles, taught to bear.
For well I knew, the lustre shed
From cherub wings, when proudliest spread,
Was, in its nature, lambent, pure,
 And innocent as is the light
The glow-worm hangs out to allure
 Her mate to her green bower at night.
Oft had I in the mid-air, swept
Through clouds in which the lightning slept,
As in its lair, ready to spring,
Yet waked it not—though from my wing
A thousand sparks fell glittering!
Oft too when round me from above
 The feathered snow, in all its whiteness,
Fell like the moultings of heaven's Dove—*
 So harmless, though so full of brightness,
Was my brow's wreath, that it would shake
From off its flowers each downy flake
As delicate, unmelted, fair,
And cool as they had lighted there.

Nay even with Lilis—had I not
 Around her sleep all radiant beamed,
Hung o'er her slumbers, nor forgot
 To kiss her eyelids, as she dreamed?
And yet, at morn, from that repose,
 Had she not waked, unscathed and bright,
As doth the pure, unconscious rose,
 Though by the firefly kissed all night.

Thus having—as, alas, deceived
By my sin's blindness, I believed—
No cause for dread, and those dark eyes
 Now fixed upon me, eagerly
As though th' unlocking of the skies
 Then waited but a sign from me—
How could I pause? how even let fall
 A word, a whisper that could stir,
In her proud heart a doubt, that all
 I brought from heaven belonged to her.
Slow from her side I rose, while she
Arose, too, mutely, tremblingly.
But not with fear—all hope and pride,
 She waited for the awful boon,
Like priestesses, at eventide,
 Watching the rise of the full moon,
Whose light, when once its orb hath shone,
'Twill madden them to look upon!

Of all my glories, the bright crown,
Which, when I last from heaven came down,
Was left behind me, in yon star
That shines from out those clouds afar—
Where, relic sad, 'tis treasured yet,
The downfallen angel's coronet!
Of all my glories, this alone
 Was wanting: but th' illumin'd brow,
 The sun-bright locks, the eyes that now
Had love's spell added to their own,
And poured a light till then unknown;
 Th' unfolded wings, that, in their play,
Shed sparkles bright as Alla's throne;
 All I could bring of heaven's array,
 Of that rich panoply of charms
A Cherub moves in, on the day
Of his best pomp, I now put on;
And, proud that in her eyes I shone
 Thus glorious, glided to her arms;
Which still (though, at a sight so splendid,
 Her dazzled brow had, instantly,
Sunk on her breast) were wide extended
 To clasp the form she durst not see!*
Great Heaven! how *could* thy vengeance ligh
So bitterly on one so bright?
How could the hand, that gave such charms,
Blast them again in love's own arms?
Scarce had I touched her shrinking frame
 When—oh most horrible! I felt
That every spark of that pure flame—
 Pure, while among the stars I dwelt—
Was now, by my transgressions, turned
Into gross, earthly fire, which burned,
Burned all it touched, as fast as eye
 Could follow the fierce, ravening flashes;
Till there—oh God, I still ask why
Such doom was hers? I saw her lie
 Blackening within my arms to ashes!
That brow, a glory but to see—
 Those lips, whose touch was what the first
Fresh cup of immortality
 Is to a new-made angel's thirst!
Those clasping arms, within whose round—
My heart's horizon—the whole bound
Of its hope, prospect, heaven was found!
Which, even in this dread moment, fond
 As when they first were round me cast,
Loosed not in death the fatal bond,
 But, burning, held me to the last!
All, all, that, but that morn, had seemed
As if Love's self there breathed and beamed.

* The Dove, or pigeon which attended Mahomet as his Familiar, and was frequently seen to whisper into his ear, was, if I recollect right, one of that select number of animals (including also the ant of Solomon, the dog of the Seven Sleepers, &c.), which were thought by the Prophet worthy of admission into Paradise.

"The Moslems have a tradition that Mahomet was saved (when he hid himself in a cave in Mount Shur) by his pursuers finding the mouth of the cave covered by a spider's web, and a nest built by two pigeons at the entrance, with two eggs unbroken in it, which made them think no one could have entered it. In consequence of this, they say, Mahomet enjoined his followers to look upon pigeons as sacred, and never to kill a spider."—*Modern Universal History*, vol. i.

* "Mohammed [says Sale,] though a prophet, was not able to bear the sight of Gabriel, when he appeared in his proper form, much less would others be able to support it."

Now, parched and black, before me lay,
Withering in agony away;
And mine, oh misery! mine the flame,
From which this desolation came;
I, the curst spirit, whose caress
Had blasted all that loveliness!

'Twas maddening! but now hear even worse—
Had death, death only, been the curse
I brought upon her—had the doom
But ended here, when her young bloom
Lay in the dust—and did the spirit
No part of that fell curse inherit,
'Twere not so dreadful—but, come near—
Too shocking 'tis for earth to hear—
Just when her eyes, in fading, took
  Their last, keen, agonized farewell,
And looked in mine with—oh, that look!
  Great vengeful Power, whate'er the hell
Thou mayst to human souls assign,
The memory of that look is mine!

In her last struggle, on my brow
  Her ashy lips a kiss imprest,
So withering!—I feel it now—
  'Twas fire—but fire, even more unblest
Than was my own, and like that flame,
The angels shudder but to name,
Hell's everlasting element!
  Deep, deep it pierced into my brain,
Madd'ning and torturing as it went;
  And here—mark here, the brand, the stain
It left upon my front—burnt in
By that last kiss of love and sin—
A brand, which all the pomp and pride
Of a fallen Spirit can not hide!

But is it thus, dread Providence—
  Can it, indeed, be thus, that she,
Who (but for *one* proud, fond offence)
  Had honored heaven itself, should be
Now doomed—I can not speak it—no,
Merciful ALLA! '*tis* not so—
Never could lips divine have said
The fiat of a fate so dread.
And yet, that look—so deeply fraught
  With more than anguish, with despair—
That new, fierce fire, resembling naught
  In heaven or earth—this scorch I bear!—
Oh—for the first time that these knees
  Have bent before thee since my fall,
Great Power, if ever thy decrees
  Thou couldst for prayer like mine recall,
Pardon that spirit, and on me,
  On me, who taught her pride to err,
Shed out each drop of agony
  Thy burning vial keeps for her!
See, too, where low beside me kneel
  Two other outcasts, who, though gone
And lost themselves, yet dare to feel
  And pray for that poor mortal one.
Alas! too well, too well they know
The pain, the penitence, the wo
That Passion brings upon the best,
The wisest, and the loveliest.
Oh, who is to be saved, if such
  Bright, erring souls are not forgiven;
So loath they wander, and so much
  Their very wand'rings lean toward heaven!
Again, I cry, Just Power, transfer
  That creature's sufferings all to me—
  Mine, mine the guilt, the torment be,
To save one minute's pain to her,
  Let mine last all eternity!"

He paused, and to the earth bent down
  His throbbing head; while they, who felt
That agony as 'twere their own,
  Those angel youths, beside him knelt,
And, in the night's still silence there,
  While mournfully each wand'ring air
Played in those plumes, that never more
To their lost home in heaven must soar,
Breathed inwardly the voiceless prayer,
Unheard by all but Mercy's ear—
And which if Mercy *did not* hear,
Oh, God would *not* be what this bright
  And glorious universe of his,
This world of beauty, goodness, light,
  And endless love, proclaims he *is!*
Not long they knelt, when, from a wood
That crowned that airy solitude,
They heard a low, uncertain sound,
As from a lute, that just had found
Some happy theme, and murmured round
The new-born fancy, with fond tone,
Scarce thinking aught so sweet its own!
Till soon a voice, that matched as well
  That gentle instrument, as suits
The sea-air to an ocean-shell
  (So kin its spirit to the lute's),
Tremblingly followed the soft strain,
Interpreting its joy, its pain,
  And lending the light wings of words
To many a thought, that else had lain
  Unfledged and mute among the chords.

All started at the sound—but chief
  The third young Angel, in whose face,
Though faded like the others, grief
  Had left a gentler, holier trace;
As if, even yet, through pain and ill,
Hope had not fled him—as if still
Her precious pearl, in sorrow's cup,
  Unmelted at the bottom lay,
To shine again, when, all drunk up,
  The bitterness should pass away.
Chiefly did he, though in his eyes
There shone more pleasure than surprise,
Turn to the wood, from whence that sound
  Of solitary sweetness broke;
Then, listening, look delighted round
  To his bright peers, while thus it spoke:
"Come, pray with me, my seraph love,
  My angel-lord, come pray with me;
In vain to-night my lip hath strove
To send one holy prayer above—
The knee may bend, the lip may move,
  But pray I can not, without thee!
I've fed the altar in my bower
  With droppings from the incense-tree;
I've sheltered it from wind and shower,
But dim it burns the livelong hour,
As if, like me, it had no power
  Of life or lustre, without thee!

A boat at midnight sent alone
  To drift upon the moonless sea,
A lute, whose leading chord is gone,
A wounded bird, that hath but one
Imperfect wing to soar upon,
  Are like what I am, without thee!

Then ne'er, my spirit-love, divide,
  In life or death, thyself from me;
But when again, in sunny pride,
Thou walkst through Eden, let me glide,
A prostrate shadow, by thy side—
  Oh happier thus than without thee!"

The song had ceased, when, from the wood
  Which, sweeping down that airy height,
Reached the lone spot whereon they stood—
  There suddenly shone out a light
From a clear lamp, which, as it blazed
Across the brow of one, who raised
Its flame aloft (as if to throw
The light upon that group below),
Displayed two eyes, sparkling between
The dusky leaves, such as are seen
By fancy only, in those faces,
  That haunt a poet's walk at even,
Looking from out their leafy places
  Upon his dreams of love and heaven.

'Twas but a moment—the blush, brought
O'er all her features at the thought
  Of being seen thus, late, alone,
By any but the eyes she sought,
  Had scarcely for an instant shone
  Through the dark leaves, when she was gone—
Gone, like a meteor that o'erhead
Suddenly shines, and, ere we've said,
"Behold, how beautiful!"—'tis fled.

Yet, ere she went, the words, "I come,
  I come, my NAMA," reached her ear,
  In that kind voice, familiar, dear,
Which tells of confidence, of home—
  Of habit, that hath drawn hearts near,
Till they grow *one*—of faith sincere,
And all that Love most loves to hear;
A music, breathing of the past,
  The present, and the time to be,
Where Hope and Memory, to the last,
  Lengthen out life's true harmony!
Nor long did he, whom call so kind
Summoned away, remain behind;
Nor did there need much time to tell
  What they—alas! more fallen than he
From happiness and heaven—knew well,
  His gentler love's short history!

Thus did it run—*not* as he told
  The tale himself, but as 'tis graved
Upon the tablets that, of old,
  By SETH* were from the deluge saved,
All written over with sublime
And sadd'ning legends of th' unblest,
But glorious Spirits of that time,
  And this young Angel's 'mong the rest.

THIRD ANGEL'S STORY.

AMONG the Spirits, of pure flame,
  That in th' eternal heavens abide—
Circles of light, that from the same
  Unclouded centre sweeping wide,
  Carry its beams on every side—
Like spheres of air that waft around
The undulations of rich sound,
Till the far-circling radiance be
Diffused into infinity!
First and immediate near the Throne
Of ALLA,† as if most his own,
The Seraphs stand‡—this burning sign
Traced on their banner, "Love divine!"

Their rank, their honors, far above
  Even those to high-browed Cherubs given,
Though knowing all;—so much doth love
  Transcend all Knowledge, even in heaven!
'Mong these was ZARAPH once—and none
  E'er felt affection's holy fire,
Or yearned toward th' Eternal One,
  With half such longing, deep desire.
Love was to his impassioned soul
  Not, as with others, a mere part
Of its existence, but the whole—
  The very life-breath of his heart!
Oft, when from ALLA's lifted brow
  A lustre came, too bright to bear,
And all the seraph ranks would bow,
  To shade their dazzled sight, nor dare
  To look upon th' effulgence there—
This Spirit's eyes would court the blaze
  (Such pride he in adoring took),
And rather lose, in that one gaze,
  The power of looking, than *not* look!
Then, too, when angel voices sung
The mercy of their God, and strung
Their harps to hail, with welcome sweet,
  That moment, watched for by all eyes,
When some repentant sinner's feet
  First touched the threshold of the skies,
Oh then how clearly did the voice
Of ZARAPH above all rejoice!
Love was in every buoyant tone—
  Such love, as only could belong
To the blest angels, and alone
  Could, even from angels, bring such song!

Alas, that it should e'er have been
  In heaven as 'tis too often here,
Where nothing fond or bright is seen,
  But it hath pain and peril near;
Where right and wrong so close resemble,
  That what we take for virtue's thrill
Is often the first downward tremble
  Of the heart's balance unto ill;
Where Love hath not a shrine so pure,
  So holy, but the serpent, Sin,
In moments, even the most secure,
  Beneath his altar may glide in!

So was it with that Angel—such
  The charm, that sloped his fall along,
From good to ill, from loving much,
  Too easy lapse, to loving wrong.
Even so that amorous Spirit, bound
By beauty's spell, where'er 'twas found,
From the bright things above the moon
  Down to earth's beaming eyes descended
Till love for the Creator soon
  In passion for the creature ended.

'Twas first at twilight, on the shore
  Of the smooth sea, he heard the lute
And voice of her he loved steal o'er
  The silver waters, that lay mute,
As loath, by even a breath, to stay
The pilgrimage of that sweet lay,
Whose echoes still went on and on,
Till lost among the light that shone
Far off, beyond the ocean's brim—
  There, where the rich cascade of day
Had, o'er th' horizon's golden rim,
  Into Elysium rolled away!

* Seth is a favorite personage among the Orientals, and acts a conspicuous part in many of their most extravagant romances. The Syrians pretended to have a Testament of this Patriarch in their possession, in which was explained the whole theology of angels, their different orders, &c., &c. The Curds, too (as Hyde mentions in his Appendix), have a book, which contains all the rites of their religion, and which they call Sohuph Sheit, or the Book of Seth.

In the same manner that Seth and Cham are supposed to have preserved these memorials of antediluvian knowledge, Xixuthrus is said in Chaldean fable to have deposited in Siparis, the city of the Sun, those monuments of science which he had saved out of the waters of a deluge.—See Jablonski's learned remarks upon these columns or tablets of Seth, which he supposes to be the same with the pillars of Mercury, or the Egyptian Thoth.—*Pantheon. Egypt.*, lib. v., cap. 5.

† The Mussulmans, says D'Herbelot, apply the general name, Mocarreboun, to all those spirits "qui approchent le plus près le Trône." Of this number are Mikail and Gebrail.

‡ The Seraphim, or Spirits of Divine Love.

There appears to be, among writers on the East, as well as among the Orientals themselves, considerable indecision with regard to the respective claims of Seraphim and Cherubim to the highest rank in the celestial hierarchy. The derivation which Hyde assigns to the word *Cherub* seems to determine the precedence in favor of that order of spirits: "Cherubim, *i. e.*, Propinqui Angeli, qui sc. Deo proprius quam alii accedunt; nam *Charab* est *i. q. Karab*, appropinquare" (p. 263). Al Beidawi, too, one of the commentators of the Koran, on that passage, "The angels, who bear the throne, and those who stand about it" (chap. xl.), says, "These are the Cherubim, the highest order of angels." On the other hand, we have seen, in a preceding note, that the Syrians place the sphere in which the Seraphs dwell at the very summit of all the celestial systems; and even among Mahometans, the words Azazil and Mocarreboun (which mean the spirits that stand nearest to the throne of Alla) are indiscriminately applied to both Seraphim and Cherubim.

Of God she sung, and of the mild
Attendant Mercy, that beside
His awful throne for ever smiled,
Ready, with her white hand, to guide
His bolts of vengeance to their prey—
That she might quench them on the way!
Of Peace—of that Atoning Love,
Upon whose star, shining above
This twilight world of hope and fear,
The weeping eyes of Faith are fixed
So fond, that with her every tear
The light of that love-star is mixed!—
All this she sung, and such a soul
Of piety was in that song,
That the charmed Angel, as it stole
Tenderly to his ear, along
Those lulling waters where he lay,
Watching the daylight's dying ray,
Thought 'twas a voice from out the wave,
An echo, that some sea-nymph gave
To Eden's distant harmony,
Heard faint and sweet beneath the sea!

Quickly, however, to its source,
Tracing that music's melting course,
He saw, upon the golden sand
Of the seashore, a maiden stand,
Before whose feet th' expiring waves
Flung their last offering with a sigh—
As, in the East, exhausted slaves
Lay down the far-brought gift, and die—
And, while her lute hung by her, hushed,
As if unequal to the tide
Of song, that from her lips still gushed,
She raised, like one beatified,
Those eyes, whose light seemed rather given
To be adored than to adore—
Such eyes, as may have looked *from* heaven,
But ne'er were raised to it before?

Oh Love, Religion, Music*—all
That's left of Eden upon earth—
The only blessings, since the fall
Of our weak souls, that still recall
A trace of their high, glorious birth—
How kindred are the dreams you bring!
How Love, though unto earth so prone,
Delights to take Religion's wing,
When time or grief hath stained his own!
How near to Love's beguiling brink,
Too oft, entranced Religion lies!
While Music, Music is the link
They *both* still hold by to the skies,
The language of their native sphere,
Which they had else forgotten here.

How then could ZARAPH fail to feel
That moment's witcheries?—one, so fair,
Breathing out music, that might steal
Heaven from itself, and rapt in prayer
That seraphs might be proud to share!
Oh, he *did* feel it, all too well—
With warmth, that far too dearly cost—
Nor knew he, when at last he fell,
To which attraction, to which spell,
Love, Music, or Devotion, most
His soul in that sweet hour was lost.

Sweet was the hour, though dearly won,
And pure, as aught of earth could be,
For then first did the glorious sun
Before religion's altar see
Two hearts in wedlock's golden tie
Self-pledged, in love to live and die.
Blest union! by that Angel wove,
And worthy from such hands to come;
Safe, sole asylum, in which Love,
When fallen or exiled from above,
In this dark world can find a home.

* "Les Egyptiens disent que la Musique est *Sœur de a Religion*"—*Voyages de Pythagore*, tom. i., p. 422.

And, though the Spirit had transgressed,
Had, from his station 'mong the blest
Won down by woman's smile, allowed
Terrestrial passion to breathe o'er
The mirror of his heart, and cloud
God's image, there so bright before—
Yet never did that Power look down
On error with a brow so mild;
Never did Justice wear a frown,
Through which so gently Mercy smiled.
For humble was their love—with awe
And trembling like some treasure kept,
That was not theirs by holy law—
Whose beauty with remorse they saw,
And o'er whose preciousness they wept.

Humility, that low, sweet root,
From which all heavenly virtues shoot,
Was in the hearts of both—but most
In NAMA's heart, by whom alone
Those charms for which a heaven was lost,
Seemed all unvalued and unknown;
And when her seraph's eyes she caught,
And hid hers glowing on his breast,
Even bliss was humbled by the thought—
"What claim have I to be so blest?"
Still less could maid, so meek, have nursed
Desire of knowledge—that vain thirst,
With which the sex hath all been cursed,
From luckless EVE to her, who near
The Tabernacle stole to hear
The secrets of the angels:* no—
To love as her own Seraph loved,
With Faith, the same through bliss and wo—
Faith, that, were even its light removed,
Could, like the dial, fixed remain,
And wait till it shone out again;
With Patience that, though often bowed
By the rude storm, can rise anew;
And Hope that, even from Evil's cloud,
Sees sunny Good half breaking through!
This deep, relying Love, worth more
In heaven than all a Cherub's lore—
This Faith, more sure than aught beside,
Was the sole joy, ambition, pride
Of her fond heart—th' unreasoning scope
Of all its views, above, below,
So true she felt it that to *hope*,
To *trust*, is happier than to *know*.

And thus in humbleness they trod,
Abashed, but pure before their God;
Nor e'er did earth behold a sight
So meekly beautiful as they,
When, with the altar's holy light
Full on their brows, they knelt to pray,
Hand within hand, and side by side,
Two links of love, awhile untied
From the great chain above, but fast
Holding together to the last!—
Two fallen Splendors,† from that tree,
Which buds with such eternally,‡

* Sara.

† An allusion to the Sephiroths, or Splendors of the Jewish Cabbala, represented as a tree, of which God is the crown or summit.

The Sephiroths are the higher orders of emanative beings in the strange and incomprehensible system of the Jewish Cabbala. They are called by various names, Pity, Beauty, etc., etc.; and their influences are supposed to act through certain canals, which communicate with each other.

‡ The reader may judge of the rationality of this Jewish system by the following explanation of part of the machinery:—"Les canaux qui sortent de la Miséricorde et de la Force, et qui vont aboutir à la Beauté, sont chargés d'un grand nombre d'Anges. Il y en a trente-cinq sur le canal de la Miséricorde, qui recompensent et qui couronnent la vertu des Saints," etc., etc.—For a concise account of the Cabalistic Philosophy, see Enfield's very useful compendium of Brucker.

"On les représente quelquefois sous la figure d'un arbre .... l'Ensoph qu'on met au-dessus de l'arbre Sephirotique ou les Splendeurs divins, est l'Infini."—*L'Histoire des Juifs*, liv. ix. 11.

Shaken to earth, yet keeping all
Their light and freshness in the fall.
Their only punishment (as wrong,
However sweet, must bear its brand),
Their only doom was this—that, long
As the green earth and ocean stand,
They both shall wander here—the same,
Throughout all time, in heart and frame—
Still looking to that goal sublime,
Whose light remote, but sure, they see;
Pilgrims of Love, whose way is Time,
Whose home is in Eternity!
Subject, the while, to all the strife,
True Love encounters in this life—
The wishes, hopes, he breathes in vain;
The chill, that turns his warmest sighs
To earthly vapor, ere they rise;
The doubt he feeds on, and the pain
That in his very sweetness lies:
Still worse, th' illusions that betray
His footsteps to their shining brink;
That tempt him, on his desert way
Through the bleak world, to bend and drink,
Where nothing meets his lips, alas!—
But he again must sighing pass
On to that far-off home of peace,
In which alone his thirst will cease.

All this they bear, but, not the less,
Have moments rich in happiness—
Blest meetings, after many a day
Of widowhood past far away,
When the loved face again is seen
Close, close, with not a tear between—
Confidings frank, without control,
Poured mutually from soul to soul;
As free from any fear or doubt
As is that light from chill or stain,
The sun into the stars sheds out,
To be by them shed back again!—
That happy minglement of hearts,
Where, changed as chymic compounds are,
Each with its own existence parts,
To find a new one, happier far!
Such are their joys—and, crowning all,
That blessed hope of the bright hour,
When, happy and no more to fall,
Their spirits shall, with freshened power,
Rise up rewarded for their trust
In Him, from whom all goodness springs,
And, shaking off earth's soiling dust
From their emancipated wings,
Wander for ever through those skies
Of radiance, where Love never dies!

In what lone region of the earth
These Pilgrims now may roam or dwell,
God and the Angels, who look forth
To watch their steps, alone can tell.
But should we, in our wanderings,
Meet a young pair, whose beauty wants
But the adornment of bright wings,
To look like heaven's inhabitants—
Who shine where'er they tread, and yet
Are humble in their earthly lot,
As is the wayside violet,
That shines unseen, and were it not
For its sweet breath, would be forgot—
Whose hearts, in every thought, are one,
Whose voices utter the same wills—
Answering, as Echo doth some tone
Of fairy music 'mong the hills,
So like itself, we seek in vain
Which is the echo, which the strain—
Whose piety is love, whose love,
Though close as 'twere their souls' embrace,
Is not of earth, but from above—
Like two fair mirrors, face to face,
Whose light, from one to th' other thrown,
Is heaven's reflection, not their own—
Should we e'er meet with aught so pure,
So perfect here, we may be sure
'Tis ZARAPH and his bride we see;
And call young lovers round, to view
The pilgrim pair, as they pursue
Their pathway toward eternity.

THE SYLPH'S BALL.

A SYLPH, as bright as ever sported
Her figure through the fields of air,
By an old swarthy Gnome was courted,
And, strange to say, he won the fair.

The annals of the oldest witch
A pair so sorted could not show,
But how refuse?—the Gnome was rich,
The Rothschild of the world below;

And Sylphs, like other pretty creatures,
Are told, betimes, they must consider
Love as an auctioneer of features,
Who knocks them down to the best bidder.

Home she was taken to his Mine—
A Palace, paved with diamonds all—
And, proud as Lady Gnome to shine,
Sent out her tickets for a Ball.

The *lower* world, of course, was there,
And all the best; but of the *upper*
The sprinkling was but shy and rare,
A few old Sylphids, who loved supper.

As none yet knew the wondrous Lamp
Of DAVY, that renowned Aladdin,
And the Gnome's Halls exhaled a damp,
Which accidents from fire were bad in;

The chambers were supplied with light
By many strange but safe devices;
Large fire-flies, such as shine at night
Among the Orient's flowers and spices;—

Musical flint-mills—swiftly played
By elfin hands—that, flashing round,
Like certain fire-eyed minstrel maids,
Gave out, at once, both light and sound.

Bologna stones, that drink the sun;
And water from that Indian sea,
Whose waves at night like wild-fire run—
Corked up in crystal carefully.

Glow-worms, that round the tiny dishes,
Like little lighthouses, were set up!
And pretty phosphorescent fishes,
That by their own gay light were eat up.

'Mong the few guests from Ether, came
That wicked Sylph, whom Love we call:
My Lady knew him but by name,
My Lord, her husband, not at all.

Some prudent Gnomes, 'tis said, apprized
That he was coming, and, no doubt,
Alarmed about his touch, advised
He should, by all means, be kept out.

But others disapproved this plan,
And, by his flame though somewhat frighted,
Thought Love too much a gentleman,
In such a dangerous place to light it.

However, *there* he was—and dancing
With the fair Sylph, light as a feather;
They looked like two fresh sunbeams, glancing,
At daybreak, down to earth together.

And all had gone off safe and well,
But for that plaguy torch, whose light,
Though not *yet* kindled—who could tell
How soon, how devilishly, it *might?*

And so it chanced—which, in those dark
  And fireless halls, was quite amazing;
Did we not know how small a spark
  Can set the torch of Love a-blazing.

Whether it came (when close entangled
  In the gay waltz) from her bright eyes,
Or from the *lucciole*, that spangled
  Her locks of jet—is all surmise;

But certain 'tis th' ethereal girl
  Did drop a spark, at some odd turning,
Which, by the waltz's windy whirl,
  Was fanned up into actual burning.

Oh for that Lamp's metallic gauze,
  That curtain of protecting wire,
Which DAVY delicately draws
  Around illicit, dangerous fire!—

The wall he sets 'twixt Flame and Air,
  (Like that which barred young Thisbe's bliss,)
Through whose small holes this dangerous pair
  May see each other, but not kiss.*

At first the torch looked rather bluely,
  A sign, they say, that no good boded—
Then quick the gas became unruly,
  And, crack! the ball-room all exploded.

Sylphs, Gnomes, and fiddlers, mixed together,
  With all their aunts, sons, cousins, nieces,
Like butterflies in stormy weather,
  Were blown—legs, wings, and tails—to pieces!

While, 'mid these victims of the torch,
  The Sylph, alas! too, bore her part—
Found lying, with a livid scorch,
  As if from lightning, o'er her heart!

• • • • • • • •

"Well done"—a laughing Goblin said—
  Escaping from this gaseous strife—
"'Tis not the *first* time Love has made
  A *blow-up* in connubial life!"

* ——"Partique dedêre
Oscula quisque suæ, non pervenientia contrà."—OVID.

GENIUS AND CRITICISM.

"Scripsit quidem fata, sed sequitur."—SENECA.

OF old, the Sultan Genius reigned,
  As Nature meant, supreme, alone;
With mind unchecked, and hands unchained,
  His views, his conquests were his own.

But power like his, that digs its grave
  With its own sceptre, could not last;
So Genius' self became the slave
  Of laws that Genius' self had passed.

As Jove, who forged the chain of Fate,
  Was, ever after, doomed to wear it;
His nods, his struggles all too late—
  "*Qui semel jussit, semper paret.*"

To check young Genius' proud career,
  The slaves, who now his throne invaded,
Made Criticism his prime Vizier,
  And from that hour his glories faded.

Tied down in Legislation's school,
  Afraid of even his own ambition,
His very victories were by rule,
  And he was great but by permission.

His most heroic deeds—the same,
  That dazzled, when spontaneous actions—
Now, done by law, seemed cold and tame,
  And shorn of all their first attractions.

If he but stirred to take the air,
  Instant, the Viz[illegible]at
"Good Lord, your Highness can't go there—
  Bless me, your Highness can't do that."

If, loving pomp, he chose to buy
  Rich jewels for his diadem,
"The taste was bad, the price was high—
  A flower were simpler than a gem."

To please them if he took to flowers—
  "What trifling, what unmeaning things!
Fit for a woman's toilet hours,
  But not at all the style for Kings."

If, fond of his domestic sphere,
  He played no more the rambling comet—
"A dull, good sort of a man, 'twas clear,
  But, as for great or brave, far from it."

Did he then look o'er distant oceans,
  For realms more worthy to enthrone him?
"Saint Aristotle, what wild notions!
  Serve a '*ne exeat regno*' on him."

At length, their last and worst to do,
  They round him placed a guard of watchmen
Reviewers, knaves in brown, or blue
  Turned up with yellow—chiefly Scotchmen;

To dog his footsteps all about,
  Like those in Longwood's prison-grounds,
Who at Napoleon's heels rode out,
  For fear the Conqueror should break bounds.

Oh for some Champion of his power,
  Some *Ultra* spirit, to set free,
As erst in Shakspere's sovereign hour,
  The thunders of his Royalty!—

To vindicate his ancient line,
  The first, the true, the only one,
Of Right, eternal and divine,
  That rules beneath the blessed sun.

IMITATION.

FROM THE FRENCH.

WITH women and apples both Paris and Adam
  Made mischief enough in their day:—
God be praised that the fate of mankind, my dear madam,
  Depends not on us, the same way.
For, weak as I am with temptation to grapple,
  The world would have doubly to rue thee;
Like Adam, I'd gladly take *from* thee the apple,
  Like Paris, at once give it *to* thee.

THE ANGEL OF THE WORLD.

BY

REV. GEORGE CROLY.

THERE's glory on thy mountains, proud Bengal,
When on their temples bursts the morning sun!
There's glory on thy marble-towered wall,
Proud Ispahan, beneath his burning noon!
There's glory—when his golden course is done,
Proud Istamboul, upon thy waters blue!
But fall'n Damascus, thine was beauty's throne,
In morn, and noon, and evening's purple dew,
Of all from Ocean's marge to mighty Himmalu.

East of the city stands a lofty mount,
Its brow with lightning delved and rent in sunder;
And through the fragments rolls a little fount,
Whose channel bears the blast of fire and thunder!
And there has many a pilgrim come to wonder;
For there are flowers unnumber'd blossoming,
With but the bare and calcined marble under;
Yet in all Asia no such colours spring,
No perfumes rich as in that mountain's rocky ring.

And some who pray'd the night out on the hill,
Have said they heard,—unless it was their dream,
Or the mere murmur of the babbling rill,—
Just as the morn-star shot its first slant beam,
A sound of music, such as they might deem
The song of spirits—that would sometimes sail
Close to their ear, a deep, delicious stream,
Then sweep away, and die with a low wail;
Then come again, and thus, till LUCIFER was pale.

And some, but bolder still, had dared to turn
That soil of mystery for hidden gold;
But saw strange, stifling blazes round them burn,
And died!—by few that venturous tale was told.
And wealth was found; yet, as the pilgrims hold,
Though it was glorious on the mountain's brow,
Brought to the plain it crumbled into mould,
The diamonds melted in the hand like snow;
So none molest that spot for gems or ingots now,

But one, and ever after, round the hill
He stray'd:—they said a meteor scorch'd his sight;
Blind, mad, a warning of Heaven's fearful will.
'Twas on the sacred evening of "The Flight,"
His spade turn'd up a shaft of marble white,
Fragment of some kiosk, the chapiter
A crystal circle, but at morn's first light
Rich forms began within it to appear,
Sceptred and wing'd, and then, it sank in water clear.

Yet once upon that guarded mount, no foot
But of the Moslem true might press a flower,
And of them none, but with some solemn suit
Beyond man's help, might venture near the bower:
For, in its shade, in beauty and in power,
For judgment sat the ANGEL OF THE WORLD:
Sent by the prophet, till the destined hour
That saw in dust Arabia's idols hurl'd,
Then to the skies again his wing should be unfurl'd.

It came at last. It came with trumpet's sounding,
It came with thunders of the atabal,
And warrior shouts, and Arab charger's bounding,
The SACRED STANDARD crown'd Medina's wall!
From palace-roof, and minaret's golden ball,
Ten thousand emerald banners floated free,
Beneath, like sunbeams, through the gateway tall,
The Emirs led their steel-mail'd chivalry,
And the whole city rang with sports and soldier glee.

This was the eve of eves, the end of war,
Beginning of dominion, first of time!
When, swifter than the shooting of a star,
Mohammed saw the Vision's pomps sublime!
Swept o'er the rainbow'd sea—the fiery clime,
Heard from the throne its will in thunders roll'd;
Then glancing on our world of woe and crime,
Saw from Arabia's sands his banner's fold
Wave o'er the brighten'd globe its sacred conquering gold.

The sun was slowly sinking to the West,
Pavilion'd with a thousand glorious dyes;
The turtle-doves were winging to the nest,
Along the mountain's soft declivities;
The fresher breath of flowers began to rise,
Like incense, to that sweet departing sun;
Faint as the hum of bees the city's cries:
A moment, and the lingering disk was gone;
Then were the Angels' task on earth's dim orbit done.

Oft had he gazed upon that lovely vale,
But never gazed with gladness such as now;
When on Damascus' roofs and turrets pale
He saw the solemn sunlight's fainter glow,
With joy he heard the Imaun's voices flow
Like breath of silver trumpets on the air;
The vintagers' sweet song, the camels' low,
As home they stalked from pasture, pair by pair,
Flinging their shadows tall in the steep sunset glare.

Then at his sceptre's wave a rush of plumes
Shook the thick dew-drops from the roses' dyes;
And, as embodying of their waked perfumes,
A crowd of lovely forms, with lightning eyes,
And flower-crown'd hair, and cheeks of Paradise,
Circled the bower of beauty on the wing;
And all the grove was rich with symphonies
Of seeming flute, and horn, and golden string,
That slowly rose, and o'er the Mount hung hovering

The Angel's flashing eyes were on the vault,
That now with lamps of diamond all was hung,
His mighty wings like tissues heavenly-wrought
Upon the bosom of the air were hung.
The solemn hymn's last harmonies were sung,
The sun was couching on the distant zone.
"Farewell" was breathing on the Angel's tongue,—
He glanced below. There stood a suppliant one!
The impatient Angel sank, in wrath, upon his throne

Yet all was quickly soothed,—"this labour past,
His coronet of tenfold light was won."
His glance again upon the form was cast,
That now seem'd dying on the dazzling stone;
He bade it rise and speak. The solemn tone
Of Earth's high Sovereign mingled joy with fear,
As summer vales of rose by lightning shown;
As the night-fountain in the desert drear;
His voice seem'd sudden life to that fall'n suppliant's ear.

The form arose—the face was in a veil,
The voice was low, and often check'd with sighs;
The tale it utter'd was a simple tale;
"A vow to close a dying parent's eyes,
And brought its weary steps from Tripolis;
The Arab in the Syrian mountains lay,
The caravan was made the robber's prize,
The pilgrim's little wealth was swept away,
Man's help was vain." Here sank the voice in soft decay.

"And this is Earth!" the Angel frowning said;
And from the ground he took a matchless gem,
And flung it to the mourner, then outspread
His pinions, like the lightning's rushing beam.
The pilgrims started at the diamond's gleam,
Glanced up in prayer, then, bending near the throne,
Shed the quick tears that from the bosom stream,
And tried to speak, but tears were there alone;
The pitying Angel said, "Be happy and begone."

The weeper raised the veil; a ruby lip
First dawn'd: then glow'd the young cheek's deeper hue,
Yet delicate as roses when they dip
Their odorous blossoms in the morning dew.
Then beam'd the eyes, twin stars of living blue;
Half shaded by the curls of glossy hair,
That turn'd to golden as the light wind threw
Their clusters in the Western golden glare,
Yet was her blue eye dim, for tears were standing there.

He look'd upon her, and her hurried gaze
Sought from his glance sweet refuge on the ground;
But o'er her cheek of beauty rush'd a blaze;
And, as the soul had felt some sudden wound,
Her bosom heaved above its silken bound.
He looked again; the cheek was deadly pale;
The bosom sank with one long sigh profound;
Yet still one lily hand upheld her veil,
And still one press'd her heart—that sigh told all its tale.

She stoop'd, and from the thicket pluck'd a flower,
And fondly kiss'd, and then with feeble hand
She laid it on the footstool of the bower;
Such was the ancient custom of the land.
Her sighs were richer than the rose they fann'd;
The breezes swept it to the Angel's feet;
Yet even that sweet slight boon, 'twas Heaven's command,
He must not touch, from her though doubly sweet,
No earthly gift must stain that hallow'd judgment-seat.

Still lay the flower upon the splendid spot,
The Pilgrim turn'd away, as smote with shame;
Her eye a glance of self-upbraiding shot;
'Twas in his soul, a shaft of living flame.
Then bow'd the humble one, and bless'd his name,
Cross'd her white arms, and slowly bade farewell.
A sudden faintness o'er the Angel came;
The voice rose sweet and solemn as a spell,
She bow'd her face to earth, and o'er it dropped her veil.

Beauty, what art thou, that thy slightest gaze
Can make the spirit from its centre roll;
Its whole long course, a sad and shadowy maze?
Thou midnight or thou noontide of the soul;
One glorious vision lighting up the whole
Of the wide world; or one deep, wild desire,
By day and night consuming, sad and sole;
Till Hope, Pride, Genius, nay, till Love's own fire,
Desert the weary heart, a cold and mouldering pyre.

Enchanted sleep, yet full of deadly dreams;
Companionship divine, stern solitude;
Thou serpent, colour'd with the brightest gleams
That e'er hid poison, making hearts thy food;
Woe to the heart that lets thee once intrude,
Victim of visions that life's purpose steal,
Till the whole struggling nature lies subdued,
Bleeding with wounds the grave alone must heal.
Proud Angel, was it thine that mortal woe to feel?

Still knelt the pilgrim, cover'd with her veil,
But all her beauty living on his eye;
Still hyacinth the clustering ringlets fell
Wreathing her forehead's polish'd ivory;
Her cheek unseen still wore the rose-bud's dye;
She sigh'd; he heard the sigh beside him swell,
He glanced around—no spirit hover'd nigh—
Touch'd the fall'n flower, and blushing, sigh'd "farewell"
What sound has stunn'd his ear? A sudden thunder-peal

He look'd on heaven, 'twas calm, but in the vale
A creeping mist had girt the mountain round,
Making the golden minarets glimmer pale;
It scaled the mount,—the feeble day was drown'd.
The sky was with its livid hue embrown'd,
But soon the vapours grew a circling sea,
Reflecting lovely from its blue profound
Mountain, and crimson cloud, and blossom'd tree;
Another heaven and earth in bright tranquillity.

And on its bosom swam a small chaloupe,
That like a wild swan sported on the tide.
The silken sail that canopied its poop
Show'd one that look'd an Houri in her pride;
Anon came spurring up the mountain's side
A warrior Moslem all in glittering mail,
That to his country's doubtful battle hied.
He saw the form, he heard the tempter's tale,
And answered with his own: for beauty will prevail.

But now in storm uprose the vast mirage;
Where sits she now who tempted him to roam?
How shall the skiff with that wild sea engage!
In vain the quivering helm is turn'd to home
Dark'ning above the piles of tumbling foam,
Rushes a shape of woe, and through the roar
Peals in the warrior's ear a voice of doom.
Down plunges the chaloupe.—The storm is o'er
Heavy and slow the corpse rolls onward to the shore.

The Angel's heart was smote—but that touch'd flower,
Now opening, breathed such fragrance subtly sweet,
He felt it strangely chain him to the bower.
He dared not then that pilgrim's eye to meet,
But gazed upon the small unsandal'd feet,
Shining like silver on the floor of rose;
At length he raised his glance;—the veil's light net
Had floated backward from her pencil'd brows,
Her eye was fix'd on Heaven, in sad, sublime repose.

A simple Syrian lyre was on her breast,
And on her crimson lip was murmuring
A village strain, that in the day's sweet rest
Is heard in Araby round many a spring,
When down the twilight vales the maidens bring
The flocks to some old patriarchal well;
Or where beneath the palms some desert-king
Lies, with his tribe around him as they fell!
The thunder burst again; a long, deep, crashing peal.

The Angel heard it not; as round the range
Of the blue hill-tops roar'd the volley on,
Uttering its voice with wild, ærial change;
Now sinking in a deep and distant moan,
Like the last echo of a host o'erthrown;
Then rushing with new vengeance down again,
Shooting the fiery flash and thunder-stone,
Till flamed, like funeral pyres, the mountain chain
The Angel heard it not; its wisdom all was vain.

He heard not even the strain, though it had changed
From the calm sweetness of the holy hymn.
His thoughts from depth to depth unconscious ranged,
Yet all within was dizzy, strange, and dim;
A mist seem'd spreading between heaven and him;
He sat absorb'd in dreams;—a searching tone
Came on his ear, oh how her dark eyes swim
Who breathed that echo of a heart undone,
The song of early joys, delicious, dear, and gone!

Again it changed.—But, now 'twas wild and grand,
The praise of hearts that scorn the world's control,
Disdaining all but Love's delicious band,
The chain of gold and flowers, the tie of soul
Again strange paleness o'er her beauty stole,
She glanced above, then stoop'd her glowing eye,
Blue as the star that glitter'd by the pole;
One tear-drop gleam'd, she dash'd it quickly by,
And dropp'd the lyre, and turn'd—as if she turn'd to die.

The night-breeze from the mountains had begun;
And as it wing'd among the clouds of even,
Where, like a routed king, the Sultan Sun
Still struggled on the fiery verge of heaven;
Their volumes in ten thousand shapes were driven;
Spreading away in boundless palace halls,
Whose lights from gold and emerald lamps were given;
Or airy citadels and battled walls;
Or sunk in valleys sweet, with silver waterfalls.

But, for those sights of heaven the Angel's heart
Was all unsettled: and a bitter sigh
Burst from his burning lip, and with a start
He cast upon the earth his conscious eye.
The whole horizon from that summit high
Spread out in vision, from the pallid line
Where old Palmyra's pomps in ruin lie,
Gilding the Arab sands, to where supine
The western lustre tinged thy spires, lost Palestine!

Yet, loveliest of the vision was the vale
That sloped beneath his own imperial bowers;
Sheeted with colours like an Indian mail,
A tapestry sweet of all sun-painted flowers,
Balsam, and clove, and jasmines scented showers,
And the red glory of the Persian rose,
Spreading in league on league around the towers,
Where, loved of Heaven, and hated of its foes,
The Queen of Cities shines, in calm and proud repose.

And still he gazed—and saw not that the eve
Was fading into night. A sudden thought
Struck to his dreaming heart, that made it heave;
Was he not there in Paradise?—that spot,
Was it not lovely as the lofty vault
That rose above him? In his native skies,
Could he be happy till his soul forgot,
Oh! how forget, the being whom his eyes
Loved as their light of light? He heard a tempest rise—

Was it a dream? the vale at once was bare,
And o'er it hung a broad and sulphurous cloud:
The soil grew red and rifted with its glare;
Down to their roots the mountain cedars bow'd;
Along the ground a rapid vapour flow'd,
Yellow and pale, thick seam'd with streaks of flame.
Before it sprang the vulture from the shroud;
The lion bounded from it scared and tame;
Behind it, dark'ning heaven, the mighty wirlwind came.

Like a long tulip bed, across the plain
A caravan approach'd the evening well,
A long, deep mass of turban, plume, and vane;
And lovely came its distant, solemn swell
Of song, and pilgrim-horn, and camel-bell.
The sandy ocean rose before their eye,
In thunder on their bending host it fell
Ten thousand lips sent up one fearful cry;
The sound was still'd at once, beneath its wave they lie.

But, two escaped, that up the mountain sprung,
And those the dead men's treasure downwards drew;
One, with slow steps; but beautiful and young
Was she, who round his neck her white arms threw
Away the tomb of sand like vapour flew.
There, naked lay the costly caravan,
A league of piles of silk and gems that threw
A rainbow light, and mid them stiff and wan,
Stretch'd by his camel's flank, their transient master, man.

The statelier wand'rer from the height was won,
And cap and sash soon gleam'd with plunder'd gold.
But, now the Desert rose, in pillars dun,
Glowing with fire like iron in the mould,
That wings with fiery speed, recoil'd, sprang, roll'd;
Before them waned the moon's ascending phase,
The clouds above them shrank the redd'ning fold:
On rush'd the giant columns blaze on blaze,
The sacrilegious died, wrapp'd in the burning haze.

The Angel sat enthroned within a dome
Of alabaster raised on pillars slight,
Curtain'd with tissues of no earthly loom;
For spirits wove the web of blossoms bright,
Woof of all flowers that drink the morning light,
And with their beauty figured all the stone
In characters of mystery and might,
A more than mortal guard around the throne,
That in their tender shade one glorious diamond shone

And every bud round pedestal and plinth,
As fell the evening, turn'd a living gem.
Lighted its purple lamp the hyacinth,
The dahlia pour'd its thousand-colour'd gleam,
A ruby torch the wond'ring eye might deem
Hung on the brow of some night-watching tower,
Where upwards climb'd the broad magnolia's stem.
An urn of lovely lustre every flower,
Burning before the king of that illumined bower.

And nestling in that arbour's leafy twine,
From cedar's top to violet's lowly bell,
Were birds, now hush'd, of plumage all divine,
That, as the quivering radiance on them fell,
Shot back such hues as stain the orient shell,
Touching the deep, green shades with light from eyes
Jacinth, and jet, and blazing carbuncle,
And gold-dropt coronets, and wings of dyes
Bathed in the living streams of their own Paradise.

The Angel knew the warning of that storm;
But saw the shudd'ring Minstrel's step draw near,
And felt the whole deep witchery of her form;
Her sigh was music's echo to his ear;
He loved—and what has love to do with fear?
Now night had droop'd on earth her raven wing,
But in the arbour all was splendour clear;
And, like twin spirits in its charmed ring,
Shone that sweet child of earth and that star-diadem'd king

For, whether 'twas the light's unusual glow,
Or that some dazzling change had on her come;
Her look, though lovely still, was loftier now,
Her tender cheek was flush'd with brighter bloom;
Yet in her azure eyebeam gather'd gloom,
Like evening's clouds across its own blue star,
Then would a sudden flash its depths illume;
And wore she but the wing and gemm'd tiar,
She seem'd instinct with might to make the clouds her car

She slowly raised her arm, that, bright as snow,
Gleam'd like a rising meteor through the air,
Shedding white lustre on her turban'd brow;
And gazed on heaven, as wrapt in solemn prayer;
She still look'd woman, yet more proudly fair;
And as she stood and pointed to the sky,
With that fix'd look of loveliness and care,
The Angel thought, and check'd it with a sigh,
He saw some Spirit fallen from immortality.

The silent prayer was done; and now she moved
Faint to his footstool, and, upon her knee,
Besought her lord, if in his heaven they loved,
That, as she never more his face must see,
She there might pledge her heart's fidelity.
Then turn'd, and pluck'd a cluster from the vine,
And o'er a chalice waved it, with a sigh,
Then stoop'd the crystal cup before the shrine.
In wrath the Angel rose—the guilty draught was wine!

She stood; she shrank; she totter'd. Down he sprang,
Clasp'd with one hand her waist, with one upheld
The vase—his ears with giddy murmurs rang;
His eye upon her dying cheek was spell'd;
Up to the brim the draught of evil swell'd
Like liquid rose, its odour touch'd his brain;
He knew his ruin, but his soul was quell'd;
He shudder'd—gazed upon her cheek again,
Press'd her pale lip, and to the last that cup did drain

Th' enchantress smiled, as still in some sweet dream,
Then waken'd in a long, delicious sigh,
And on the bending spirit fix'd the beam
Of her deep, dewy, melancholy eye.
The undone Angel gave no more reply
Than hiding his pale forehead in the hair
That floated on her neck of ivory,
And breathless pressing, with her ringlets fair,
From his bright eyes the tears of passion and despair.

The heaven was one blue cope, inlaid with gems
Thick as the concave of a diamond mine,
But from the north now fly pale, phosphor beams,
That o'er the mount their quivering net entwine;
The smallest stars through that sweet lustre shine
Then, like a routed host, its streamers fly:
Then, from the moony horizontal line
A surge of sudden glory floods the sky,
Ocean of purple waves, and molten lazuli

But wilder wonder smote their shrinking eyes:
A vapour plunged upon the vale from heaven,
Then, darkly gathering, tower'd of mountain size;
From its high crater column'd smokes were driven;
It heaved within, as if pent flames had striven
With mighty winds to burst their prison hold,
Till all the cloud-volcano's bulk was riven
With angry light, that seem'd in cataracts roll'd,
Silver, and sanguine steel, and streams of molten gold.

Then echoed on the winds a hollow roar,
An earthquake groan, that told convulsion near:
Out rush'd the burthen of its burning core,
Myriads of fiery globes, as day-light clear.
The sky was fill'd with flashing sphere on sphere,
Shooting straight upward to the zenith's crown.
The stars were blasted in that splendour drear,
The land beneath in wild distinctness shone,
From Syria's yellow sands to Libanus' summit-stone

The storm is on the embattled clouds receding,
The purple streamers wander pale and thin,
But o'er the pole a fiercer flame is spreading,
Wheel within wheel of fire, and far within
Revolves a stooping splendour crystalline.
A throne;—but who the sitter on that throne!
The Angel knew the punisher of sin.
Check'd on his lip the self-upbraiding groan,
And clasp'd his dying love, and joy'd to be undone.

And once, 'twas but a moment, on her cheek
He gave a glance, then sank his hurried eye,
And press'd it closer on her dazzling neck.
Yet, even in that swift gaze, he could espy
A look that made his heart's blood backwards fly.
Was it a dream? there echoed in his ear
A stinging tone—a laugh of mockery!
It was a dream—it must be. Oh! that fear,
When the heart longs to know, what it is death to hear.

He glanced again—her eye was upwards still,
Fix'd on the stooping of that burning car;
But through his bosom shot an arrowy thrill,
To see its solemn, stern, unearthly glare;
She stood a statue of sublime despair,
But on her lip sat scorn.—His spirit froze,—
His footstep reel'd,—his warm lip gasp'd for air;
She felt his throb,—and o'er him stoop'd with brows
As evening sweet, and kiss'd him with a lip of rose.

Again she was all beauty, and they stood
Still fonder clasp'd, and gazing with the eye
Of famine, gazing on the poison'd food
That it must feed on, or abstaining die.
There was between them now nor tear nor sigh;
Theirs was the deep communion of the soul;
Passions absorbing, bitter luxury;
What was to them or heaven or earth, the whole
Was in that fatal spot, where they stood sad, and sole.

The minstrel first shook off the silent trance;
And in a voice sweet as the murmuring
Of summer streams beneath the moonlight's glance,
Besought the desperate one to spread the wing
Beyond the power of his vindictive king.
Slave to her slightest word, he raised his plume.
For life or death, he reck'd not which, to spring;
Nay, to confront the thunder and the gloom.
She wildly kiss'd his hand, and sank, as in a tomb.

The Angel sooth'd her, "No! let Justice wreak
Its wrath upon them both, or him alone."
A flush of love's pure crimson lit her cheek;
She whisper'd, and his stoop'd ear drank the tone
With mad delight; "Oh, there is one way, one,
To save us both. Are there not mighty words,
Graved on the magnet-throne where Solomon
Sits ever guarded by the genii swords,
To give thy servant wings, like her resplendent Lords?"

This was the sin of sins! the first, last crime,
In earth and heaven, unnamed, unnameable;
This from his throne of light, before all time,
Had smitten Eblis, brightest, first that fell.
He started back.—"What urg'd him to rebel?
What led that soft seducer to his bower?
Could *she* have laid upon his soul that spell,
Young, lovely, fond; yet but an earthly flower?"
But for that fatal cup, he had been free that hour.

But still its draught was fever in his blood.
He caught the upward, humble, weeping gleam
Of woman's eye, by passion all subdued;
He sigh'd, and at his sigh he saw it beam:
Oh! the sweet frenzy of a lover's dream!
A moment's lingering, and they both must die.
The lightning round them shot a broader stream;
He felt her clasp his feet in agony;
He spoke the "Words of might",—the thunder gave reply

Away! away! the sky is one black cloud,
Shooting its lightnings down in spire on spire.
Around the mount its canopy is bow'd,
A fiery vault upraised on pillar'd fire;
The stars like lamps along its roof expire;
But through its centre bursts an orb of rays
The Angel knew the Avenger in his ire!
The hill-top smoked beneath the stooping blaze,
The culprits dared not there their guilty glances raise.

And words were utter'd from that whirling sphere,
That mortal sense might never hear and live.
They pierced like arrows through the Angel's ear;
He bow'd his head; 'twas vain to fly or strive.
Down comes the final wrath: the thunders give
The doubled peal,—the rains in cataracts sweep,
Broad bars of fire the sheeted deluge rive;
The mountain summits to the valley leap,
Pavilion, garden, grove, smoke up one ruin'd heap.

The storm stands still! a moment's pause of terror!
All dungeon-dark!—Again the lightnings yawn,
Shewing the earth as in a quivering mirror.
The prostrate Angel felt but that the one,
Whose love had lost him Paradise, was gone:
He dared not see her corpse!—he closed his eyes;
A voice burst o'er him, solemn as the tone
Of the last trump,—he glanced upon the skies,
He saw, what shook his soul with terror, shame, surprise

The Minstrel stood before him; two broad plumes
Spread from her shoulders on the burthen'd air;
Her face was glorious still, but love's young blooms
Had vanish'd for the hue of bold despair;
A fiery circle crown'd her sable hair;
And, as she look'd upon her prostrate prize,
Her eyeballs shot around a meteor glare,
Her form tower'd up at once to giant size,
'Twas Eblis! king of Hell's relentless sovereignties.

The tempter spoke—"Spirit, thou mightst have stood,
But thou hast fall'n a weak and willing slave.
Now were thy feeble heart our serpents' food,
Thy bed our burning ocean's sleepless wave,
But haughty Heaven controls the power it gave.
Yet art thou doom'd to wander from thy sphere,
Till the last trumpet reaches to the grave;
Till the Sun rolls the grand concluding year;
Till Earth is Paradise; then shall thy crime be clear"

The Angel listen'd,—risen upon one knee,
Resolved to hear the deadliest undismay'd
His star-dropt plume hung round him droopingly,
His brow, like marble, on his hand was staid.
Still through the auburn locks' o'erhanging shade
His face shone beautiful; he heard his ban;
Then came the words of mercy, sternly said;
He plunged within his hands his visage wan,
And the first wild, sweet tears from his heart-pulses ran.

The Giant grasp'd him as he fell to earth,
And his black vanes upon the air were flung,
A tabernacle dark;—and shouts of mirth
Mingled with shriekings through the tempest swung;
His arm around the fainting angel clung.
Then on the clouds he darted with a groan;
A moment o'er the mount of ruin hung,
Then burst through space, like the red comet's cone,
Leaving his track on heaven a burning, endless zone.

THE STORY OF RIMINI.

CANTO I.

THE COMING TO FETCH THE BRIDE FROM RAVENNA.

THE sun is up, and 'tis a morn of May
Round old Ravenna's clear-shown towers and bay,
A morn, the loveliest which the year has seen,
Last of the spring, yet fresh with all its green;
For a warm eve, and gentle rains at night,
Have left a sparkling welcome for the light,
And there's a crystal clearness all about;
The leaves are sharp, the distant hills look out;
A balmy briskness comes upon the breeze;
The smoke goes dancing from the cottage trees;
And when you listen, you may hear a coil
Of bubbling springs about the grassier soil;
And all the scene in short,—sky, earth, and sea,
Breathes like a bright-eyed face, that laughs out openly

'Tis nature, full of spirits, waked and springing:—
The birds to the delicious time are singing,
Darting with freaks and snatches up and down,
Where the light woods go seaward from the town;
While happy faces, striking through the green
Of leafy roads, at every turn are seen;
And the far ships, lifting their sails of white
Like joyful hands, come up with scatter'd light,
Come gleaming up, true to the wished-for day,
And chase the whistling brine, and swirl into the bay.

And well may all who can, come crowding there,
If peace returning, and processions rare,
And to crown all, a marriage in the spring
Can set enjoying fancies on the wing;
For on this sparkling day, Ravenna's pride,
The daughter of their prince, becomes a bride,
A bride, to ransom an exhausted land:
And he, whose victories have obtained her hand,
Has taken with the dawn, so flies report,
His promised journey to the expecting court,
With hasting pomp, and squires of high degree,
The bold Giovanni, lord of Rimini.

Already in the streets the stir grows loud
Of joy increasing and a bustling crowd.
With feet and voice the gathering hum contends,
Yearns the deep talk, the ready laugh ascends:
Callings, and clapping doors, and curs unite,
And shouts from mere exuberance of delight,
And armed bands, making important way,
Gallant and grave, the lords of holiday,
And nodding neighbors, greeting as they run,
And pilgrims, chanting in the morning sun.
With heaved-out tapestry the windows glow,
By lovely faces brought, that come and go;
Till, the work smoothed, and all the street attired,
They take their seats, with upward gaze admired;
Some looking down, some forwards or aside,
Some re-adjusting tresses newly tied,
Some turning a trim waist, or o'er the flow
Of crimson cloths hanging a hand of snow;
But all with smiles prepared, and garlands green,
And all in fluttering talk, impatient for the scene.

And hark! the approaching trumpets, with a start
On the smooth wind come dancing to the heart.
A moment's hush succeeds; and from the walls,
Firm and at once, a silver answer calls.
Then press the crowd; and all, who best can strive
In shuffling struggle, tow'rd the palace drive,
Where baluster'd and broad, of marble fair,
Its portico commands the public square;
For there Duke Guido is to hold his state
With his fair daughter, seated o'er the gate:—
But the full place rejects the invading tide;
And after a rude heave from side to side,
With angry faces turned, and feet regained,
The peaceful press with order is maintained,
Leaving the path-ways only for the crowd,
The space within for the procession proud.

For in this manner is the square set out:—
The sides, path-deep, are crowded round about,
And faced with guards, who keep the road entire;
And opposite to these a brilliant quire
Of knights and ladies hold the central spot,
Seated in groups upon a grassy plot;
The seats with boughs are shaded from above
Of early trees transplanted from a grove,
And in the midst, fresh whistling through the scene
A lightsome fountain starts from out the green,
Clear and compact, till, at its height o'er-run,
It shakes its loosening silver in the sun.

There, talking with the ladies, you may see,
As in some nest of faery poetry,
Some of the finest warriors of the court,—
Baptist, and Hugo of the princely port,
And Azo, and Obizo, and the grace
Of frank Esmeriald with his open face,
And Felix the Fine Arm, and him who well
Repays his lavish honors, Lionel,
Besides a host of spirits, nursed in glory,
Fit for sweet woman's love and for the poet's story

There too, in thickest of the bright-eyed throng
Stands the young father of Italian song,
Guy Cavalcanti, of a knightly race;
The poet looks out in his earnest face;
He with the pheasant's plume—there—bending now
Something he speaks around him with a bow,
And all the listening looks, with nods and flushes,
Break round him into smiles and sparkling blushes.

Another start of trumpets, with reply;
And o'er the gate a sudden canopy
Of snowy white disparts its draperied shade,
And Guido issues with the princely maid,
And sits;—the courtiers fall on either side;
But every look is fixed upon the bride,
Who pensive comes at first, and hardly hears
The enormous shout that springs as she appears;
Till, as she views the countless gaze below,
And faces that with grateful homage glow,

A home to leave, and husband yet to see,
Fade in the warmths of that great charity;
And hard it is, she thinks, to have no will;
But not to bless these thousands, harder still:
With that, a keen and quivering glance of tears
Scarce moves her patient mouth, and disappears;
A smile is underneath, and breaks away,
And round she looks and breathes, as best befits the day
What need I tell of lovely lips and eyes,
A perfect waist, and bosom's balmy rise?
There's not in all that crowd a gallant being,
Whom if his heart were whole, and rank agreeing,
It would not fire to twice of what he is,
To clasp her to his heart, and call her his.

While thus with tip-toe looks the people gaze,
Another shout the neighb'ring quarters raise:
The train are in the town, and gathering near,
With noise of cavalry, and trumpets clear;
A princely music, unbedinned with drums;
The mighty brass seems opening as it comes;
And now it fills, and now it shakes the air,
And now it bursts into the sounding square;
At which the crowd with such a shout rejoice,
Each thinks he's deafen'd with his neighbor's voice.
Then, with a long-drawn breath, the clangors die;
The palace trumpets give a last reply,
And clattering hoofs succeed, with stately stir
Of snortings proud and clinking furniture.
It seems as if the harnessed war were near;
But in their garb of peace the train appear,
Their swords alone reserved, but idly hung,
And the chains freed by which their shields were slung

First come the trumpeters, clad all in white
Except the breast, which wears a scutcheon bright.
By four and four they ride, on horses grey;
And as they sit along their easy way,
To the steed's motion yielding as they go,
Each plants his trumpet on his saddle-bow.

The heralds next appear, in vests attired
Of stiffening gold with radiant colors fired;
And then the pursuivants, who wait on these,
All dressed in painted richness to the knees:
Each rides a dappled horse, and bears a shield,
Charged with three heads upon a golden field.*

Twelve ranks of squires come after, twelve in one,
With forked pennons lifted in the sun,
Which tell, as they look backward in the wind,
The bearings of the knights that ride behind.
Their steeds are ruddy bay; and every squire
His master's color shows in his attire.

These past, and at a lordly distance, come
The knights themselves, and fill the quickening hum,
The flower of Rimini. Apart they ride,
Six in a row, and with a various pride;
But all as fresh as fancy could desire,
All shapes of gallantry on steeds of fire.

Differing in colors is the knight's array,
The horses, black and chesnut, roan and bay;—
The horsemen, crimson vested, purple, and white,—
All but the scarlet cloak for every knight,
Which thrown apart, and hanging loose behind,
Rests on the steed, and ruffles in the wind.
Instead of helm, in draperies they appear
Of folded cloth, depending by the ear:
And the steeds also make a mantled show;
The golden bits keep wrangling as they go:
With gold the bridles glance against the sun;
And the rich horse-cloths, ample every one,
Which, from the saddle-bow, dress half the steed,
Are some of them all thick with golden thread:
Others have spots, on grounds of different hue,
As burning stars upon a cloth of blue;
Or purple smearings, with a velvet light,
Rich from the glary yellow thickening bright;
Or a spring green, powdered with April posies;
Or flush vermilion, set with silver roses:
But all go sweeping back, and seem to dress
The forward march with loitering stateliness.

* The arms of the Malatesta family.

With various earnestness the crowd admire
Horseman and horse, the motion and the attire.
Some watch, as they go by, the riders' faces
Looking composure, and their knightly graces;
The life, the carelessness, the sudden heed,
The body curving to the rearing steed,
The patting hand, that best persuades the check,
And makes the quarrel up with a proud neck,
The travell'd hues of some, the bloom of those,
And scars, the keepsakes of admiring foes.

Others the horses and their pride explore,
Their jauntiness behind and strength before;
The flowing back, firm chest, and fetlocks clean,
The branching veins ridging the glossy lean,
The mane hung sleekly, the projecting eye
That to the stander near looks awfully,
The finished head, in its compactness free,
Small, and o'erarching to the lifted knee,
The start and snatch, as if they felt the comb,
With mouths that fling about the creamy foam,
The snorting turbulence, the nod, the champing,
The shift, the tossing, and the fiery tramping.

And now the Princess, pale and with fixed eye,
Perceives the last of those precursors nigh,
Each rank uncovering, as they pass in state,
Both to the courtly fountain and the gate.
And then a second interval succeeds
Of stately length, and then a troop of steeds
Milkwhite and unattired, Arabian bred,
Each by a blooming boy lightsomely led:
In every limb is seen their faultless race;
But sprightly malice glances in the face;
They doubt their masters in a foreign place:
Slender their spotless shapes, and meet the sight
With freshness, after all those colors bright:
And as with easy pitch their steps they bear,
The very ease seems something to beware:
The yielding head has still a wilful air.
These for a princely present are divined,
And show the giver is not far behind.

The talk increases now, and now advance,
Space after space, with many a sprightly prance,
The pages of the court, in rows of three;
Of white and crimson is their livery.
Space after space,—and still the train appear,—
A fervid whisper fills the general ear—
Ah—yes—no—'tis not he—but 'tis the squires
Who go before him when his pomp requires;
And now his huntsman shows the lessening train
Now the squire-carver, and the chamberlain,—
And now his banner comes, and now his shield
Borne by the squire that waits him to the field.
And then an interval,—a lordly space;—
A pin-drop silence strikes o'er all the place;
The princess, from a distance, scarcely knows
Which way to look; her color comes and goes,
And, with an impulse and affection free,
She lays her hand upon her father's knee,
Who looks upon her with a labored smile,
Gathering it up into his own the while,
When some one's voice, as if it knew not how
To check itself, exclaims, "The prince! now—now!"
And on a milk-white courser, like the air,
A glorious figure springs into the square,
Up, with a burst of thunder, goes the shout,
And rolls the trembling walls and peopled roofs about.

Never was nobler finish of fine sight;
'Twas like the coming of a shape of light;
And every lovely gazer, with a start,
Felt the quick pleasure smite across her heart.
The princess, who at first could scarcely see,
Though looking still that way from dignity,
Gathers new courage as the praise goes round,
And bends her eyes to learn what they have found
And see,—his horse obeys the check unseen;
And with an air 'twixt ardent and serene,
Letting a fall of curls about his brow,
He takes his cap off with a gallant bow;
Then for another and a deafening shout,

And scarfs are waved, and flowers come fluttering out,
And, shaken by the noise, the reeling air
Sweeps with a giddy whirl among the fair,
And whisks their garments, and their shining hair.

With busy interchange of wonder glows
The crowd, and loves his bravery as he goes,—
But on his shape the gentler sight attends,
Moves as he passes,—as he bends him, bends,—
Watches his air, his gesture, and his face,
And thinks it never saw such manly grace,
So fine are his bare throat, and curls of black,—
So lightsomely dropt in, his lordly back—
His thigh so fitted for the tilt or dance,
So heaped with strength, and turned with elegance;
But above all, so meaning is his look,
Full, and as readable as open book;
And such true gallantry the sex descries
In the frank lifting of his cordial eyes.

His haughty steed, who seems by turns to be
Vexed and made proud by that cool mastery,
Shakes at his bit, and rolls his eyes with care,
Reaching with stately step at the fine air;
And now and then, sideling his restless pace,
Drops with his hinder legs, and shifts his place,
And feels through all his frame a fiery thrill:
The princely rider on his back sits still,
And looks where'er he likes, and sways him at his will.

Surprise, relief, a joy scarce understood,
Something perhaps of very gratitude,
And fifty feelings, undefin'd and new,
Dance through the bride, and flush her faded hue
"Could I but once," she thinks, "securely place
A trust for the contents on such a case,
And know the spirit that should fill that dwelling,
This chance of mine would hardly be compelling."
Just then, the stranger, coming slowly round
By the clear fountain and the brilliant ground,
And bending, as he goes, with frequent thanks,
Beckons a follower to him from the ranks,
And loosening, as he speaks, from its light hold,
A dropping jewel with its chain of gold,
Sends it, in token he had loved him long,
To the young father of Italian song:
The youth smiles up, and with a lowly grace
Bending his lifted eyes and blushing face,
Looks after his new friend, who, scarcely gone
In the wide turning, nods and passes on.

This is sufficient for the destined bride;
She took an interest first, but now a pride:
And as the prince comes riding to the place,
Baring his head, and raising his fine face,
She meets his full obeisance with an eye
Of self-permission and sweet gravity;
He looks with touched respect, and gazes, and goes by.

CANTO II.

THE BRIDE'S JOURNEY TO RIMINI.

Pass we the followers, and their closing state
The court was entered by a hinder gate;
The duke and princess had retired before,
Joined by the knights and ladies at the door;
But something seemed amiss, and there ensued
Deep talk among the spreading multitude,
Who stood in groups, or paced the measured street,
Filling with earnest hum the noontide heat;
Nor ceased the wonder, as the day increased,
And brought no symptoms of a bridal feast,
No mass, no tilt, no largess for the crowd,
Nothing to answer that procession proud;
But a blank look, as if no court had been,
Silence without and secrecy within;
And nothing heard by listening at the walls,
But now and then a bustling through the halls,
Or the dim organ roused at gathering intervals.

The truth was this:—The bridegroom had not come,
But sent his brother, proxy in his room.
A lofty spirit the former was, and proud,
Little gallant, and had a sort of cloud
Hanging for ever on his cold address,
Which he mistook for sovereign manliness
But more of this hereafter. Guido knew
The prince's faults; and he was conscious too,
That sweet as was his daughter, and prepared
To do her duty, where appeal was barred,
She had a sense of marriage, just and free;
And where the match looked ill for harmony,
Might pause with firmness, and refuse to strike
A chord her own sweet music so unlike.
The old man therefore, kind enough at heart,
Yet fond, from habit, of intrigue and art,
And little formed for sentiments like these,
Which seemed to him mere maiden niceties
Had thought at once to gratify the pride
Of his stern neighbor, and secure the bride,
By telling him, that if, as he had heard,
Busy he was just then, 'twas but a word,
And he might send and wed her by a third,
Only the duke thus farther must presume,
For both their sakes,—that still a prince must come
The bride meantime was told, and not unmoved,
To look for one no sooner seen than loved;
And when Giovanni, struck with what he thought
Mere proof how his triumphant hand was sought,
Dispatched the wished-for prince, who was a creature
Formed in the very poetry of nature,
The effect was perfect, and the future wife
Caught in the elaborate snare, perhaps for life

One shock there was, however, to sustain,
Which nigh restored her to herself again.
She saw, when all were housed, in Guido's face
A look of liesurely surprise take place;
A little whispering followed for a while,
And then 'twas told her with an easy smile,
That Prince Giovanni, to his great chagrin,
Had been delayed by something unforeseen,
But rather than defer his day of bliss
(If his fair ruler took it not amiss)
Had sent his brother Paulo in his stead;
"Who," said old Guido, with a nodding head,
"May well be said to represent his brother,
For when you see the one, you know the other."

By this time Paulo joined them where they stood,
And seeing her in some uneasy mood,
Changed the mere cold respects his brother sent
To such a strain of cordial compliment,
And paid them with an air so frank and bright,
As to a friend appreciated at sight,
That air in short which sets you at your ease,
Without implying your perplexities,
That what with the surprise in every way,
The hurry of the time, the appointed day,
The very shame, which now appeared increased,
Of begging leave to have her hand released,
And above all, those tones, and smiles, and looks,
Which seemed to realize the dreams of books,
And helped her genial fancy to conclude
That fruit of such a stock must all be good,
She knew no longer how she could oppose:
Quick were the marriage-rights; and at the close,
The proxy, turning midst the general hush,
Kissed her meek lips, betwixt a rosy blush.

At last, about the vesper hour, a score
Of trumpets issued from the palace door,
The banners of their brass with favors tied,
And with a blast proclaimed the wedded bride.
But not a word the sullen silence broke,
Till something of a gift the herald spoke,
And with a bag of money issuing out,
Scattered the ready harvest round about;
Then burst the mob into a jovial cry,
And largess! largess! claps against the sky,
And bold Giovanni's name, the lord of Rimini.

The rest however still were looking on,
Careless and mute, and scarce the noise was gone,
When riding from the gate with banners reared,
Again the morning visitors appeared.
The prince was in his place; and in a car,

Before him, glistening like a farewell star,
Sate the dear lady with her brimming eyes;
And off they set, through doubtful looks and cries;
For some too shrewdly guessed, and some were vexed
At the dull day, and some the whole perplexed;
And all great pity thought it to divide
Two that seemed made for bridegroom and for bride.
Ev'n she, whose heart this strange, abrupt event
Had cross'd and sear'd with burning wonderment
Could scarce, at times, a starting cry forbear
At leaving her own home and native air;
Till passing now the limits of the town,
And on the last few gazers looking down,
She saw by the road-side an aged throng,
Who wanting power to bustle with the strong,
Had learnt their gracious mistress was to go,
And gathered there, an unconcerted show;
Bending they stood, with their old forehead's bare,
And the winds fingered with their reverend hair.
Farewell! farewell, my friends! she would have cried,
But in her throat the leaping accents died,
And, waving with her hand a vain adieu,
She dropt her veil, and backwarder withdrew,
And let the kindly tears their own good course pursue.

It was a lovely evening, fit to close
A lovely day, and brilliant in repose.
Warm, but not dim, a glow was in the air;
The softened breeze came smoothing here and there;
And every tree, in passing, one by one,
Gleamed out with twinkles of the golden sun:
For leafy was the road, with tall array,
On either side, of mulberry and bay,
And distant snatches of blue hills between;
And there the alder was with its bright green,
And the broad chestnut, and the poplar's shoot,
That like a feather waves from head to foot,
With, ever and anon, majestic pines;
And still from tree to tree, the early vines
Hung garlanding the way in amber lines.

Nor long the princess kept her from the view
Of that dear scenery with its parting hue:
For sitting now, calm from the gush of tears,
With dreaming eye fixed down, and half-shut ears,
Hearing, yet hearing not, the fervent sound
Of hoofs thick reckoning and the wheel's moist round,
A call of "slower!" from the farther part
Of the check'd riders, woke her with a start;
And looking up again, half sigh, half stare,
She lifts her veil, and feels the freshening air.

'Tis down a hill they go, gentle indeed,
And such, as with a bold and playful speed
Another time they would have scorned to measure;
But now they take with them a lovely treasure,
And feel they should consult her gentle pleasure.

And now with thicker shades the pines appear;
The noise of hoofs grows duller on the ear;
And quitting suddenly their gravelly toil,
The wheels go spinning o'er a sandy soil.
Here first the silence of the country seems
To come about her with its listening dreams,
And full of anxious thoughts, half freed from pain,
In downward musing she relapsed again,
Leaving the others, who had passed that way
In careless spirits of the early day,
To look about, and mark the reverend scene,
For awful tales renowned, and everlasting green.

A heavy spot the forest looks at first,
To one grim shade condemned, and sandy thirst,
Or only chequered, here and there, with bushes
Dusty and sharp, or plashy pools with rushes,
About whose sides the swarming insects fry,
Opening with noisome din, as they go by.
But entering more and more they quit the sand
At once, and strike upon a grassy land,
From which the trees, as from a carpet, rise
In knolls and clumps, with rich varieties.
A moment's trouble find the knights to rein
Their horses in, which, feeling turf again,
Thrill, and curvet, and long to be at large
To scour the space and give the winds a charge,
Or pulling tight the bridles, as they pass,
Dip their warm mouths into the freshening grass.
But soon in easy rank, from glade to glade,
Proceed they, coasting underneath the shade,
Some baring to the cool their placid brows,
Some looking upward through the glimmering boughs,
Or peering grave through inward-opening places,
And half prepared for glimpse of shadowy faces.
Various the trees and passing foliage here,—
Wild pear, and oak, and dusky juniper,
With briony between in trails of white,
And ivy, and the suckle's streaky light,
And moss, warm gleaming with a sudden mark,
Like growths of sunshine left upon the bark,
And still the pine, long-haired, and dark, and tall,
In lordly right, predominant o'er all.

Much they admire that old religious tree
With shaft above the rest up-shooting free,
And shaking, when its dark locks feel the wind,
Its wealthy fruit with rough Mosaic rind.
At noisy intervals, the living cloud
Of cawing rooks breaks o'er them, gathering loud
Like a wild people at a stranger's coming;
Then hushing paths succeed, with insects humming,
Or ring-dove, that repeats his pensive plea,
Or startled gull up-screaming towards the sea.
But scarce their eyes encounter living thing,
Save, now and then, a goat loose wandering,
Or a few cattle, looking up aslant
With sleepy eyes and meek mouths ruminant;
Or once, a plodding woodman, old and bent,
Passing with half indifferent wonderment,
Yet turning, at the last, to look once more;
Then feels his trembling staff, and onward as before

So ride they pleased,—till now the couching sun
Levels his final look through shadows dun;
And the clear moon, with meek o'er-lifted face,
Seems come to look into the silvering place.
Then first the bride waked up, for then was heard,
Sole voice, the poet's and the lover's bird,
Preluding first, as if the sounds were cast
For the dear leaves about her, till at last
With floods of rapture, in a perfect shower,
She vents her heart on the delicious hour.
Lightly the horsemen go, as if they'd ride
A velvet path, and hear no voice beside:
A placid hope assures the breath-suspending bride.

So ride they in delight through beam and shade;—
Till many a rill now passed, and many a glade,
They quit the piny labyrinths, and soon
Emerge into the full and day-like moon:
Chilling it seems; and pushing steed on steed,
They start them freshly with a homeward speed.
Then well-known fields they pass, and straggling cots
Boy-storied trees, and love-remember'd spots,
And turning last a sudden corner, see
The moon-lit towers of slumbering Rimini
The marble bridge comes heaving forth below
With a long gleam; and nearer as they go,
They see the still Marecchia, cold and bright,
Sleeping along with face against the light.
A hollow trample now,—a fall of chains,—
The bride has entered,—not a voice remains;—
Night, and a maiden silence, wrap the plains.

CANTO III.

THE FATAL PASSION.

Now why must I disturb a dream of bliss,
And bring cold sorrow 'twixt the wedded kiss?
How mar the face of beauty, and disclose
The weeping days that with the morning rose,
And bring the bitter disappointment in,—
The holy cheat, the virtue-binding sin,—
The shock, that told this lovely, trusting heart,
That she had given, beyond all power to part,
Her hope, belief, love, passion, to one brother,
Possession, (oh, the misery!) to another!

Some likeness was there 'twixt the two,—an air
At times, a cheek, a color of the hair,
A tone, when speaking of indifferent things;
Nor, by the scale of common measurings,
Would you say more perhaps, than that the one
Was more robust, the other finelier spun;
That of the two, Giovanni was the graver,
Paulo the livelier, and the more in favor.

Some tastes there were indeed, that would prefer
Giovanni's countenance as the martialler;
And 'twas a soldier's truly, if an eye
Ardent and cool at once, drawn-back and high,
An eagle's nose and a determined lip,
Were the best marks of manly soldiership.
Paulo's was fashioned in a different mould,
And surely the more fine: for though 'twas bold,
When boldness was required, and could put on
A glowing frown as if an angel shone,
Yet there was nothing in it one might call
A stamp exclusive or professional,—
No courtier's face, and yet its smile was ready,—
No scholar's, yet its look was deep and steady,—
No soldier's, for its power was all of mind,
Too true for violence, and too refined.
The very nose, lightly yet firmly wrought,
Showed taste; the forehead a clear-spirited thought;
Wisdom looked sweet and inward from his eye;
And round his mouth was sensibility:—
It was a face, in short, seemed made to show
How far the genuine flesh and blood could go;—
A morning glass of unaffected nature,—
Something, that baffled looks of loftier feature,—
The visage of a glorious human creature.

If any points there were, at which they came
Nearer together, 'twas in knightly fame,
And all accomplishments that art may know,—
Hunting, and princely hawking, and the bow,
The rush together in the bright-eyed list,
Fore-thoughted chess, the riddle rarely missed,
And the decision of still knottier points,
With knife in hand, of boar and peacock joints,—
Things, that might shake the fame that Tristan got,
And bring a doubt on perfect Launcelot.*
But leave we knighthood to the former part;
The tale I tell is of the human heart.

The worst of Prince Giovanni, as his bride
Too quickly found, was an ill-temper'd pride.
Bold, handsome, able (if he chose) to please,
Punctual and right in common offices,
He lost the sight of conduct's only worth,
The scattering smiles on this uneasy earth,
And on the strength of virtues of small weight,
Claimed tow'rds himself the exercise of great.
He kept no reckoning with his sweets and sours;—
He 'd hold a sullen countenance for hours,
And then, if pleased to cheer himself a space,
Look for the immediate rapture in your face,
And wonder that a cloud could still be there,
How small soever, when his own was fair.
Yet such is conscience,—so designed to keep
Stern, central watch, though all things else go sleep,
And so much knowledge of one's self there lies
Cored, after all, in our complacencies,
That no suspicion would have touched him more,
Than that of wanting on the generous score:
He would have whelmed you with a weight of scorn,
Been proud at eve, inflexible at morn,
In short, ill-tempered for a week to come,
And all to strike that desperate error dumb.
Taste had he, in a word, for high-turned merit,
But not the patience, nor the genial spirit·
And so he made, 'twixt virtue and defect,
A sort of fierce demand on your respect,
Which, if assisted by his high degree,
It gave him in some eyes a dignity,
And struck a meaner deference in the many,
Left him at last unloveable with any.

* The two famous knights of the Round Table, great huntsmen, and of course great carvers. Boars and peacocks, served up whole, the latter with the feathers on, were eminent dishes with the knights of old, and must have called forth all the exercise of this accomplishment.

From this complexion in the reigning brother
His younger birth perhaps had saved the other.
Born to a homage less gratuitous,
He learned to win a nobler for his house;
And both from habit and a genial heart,
Without much trouble of the reasoning art,
Found this the wisdom and the sovereign good
To be, and make, as happy as he could.
Not that he saw, or thought he saw, beyond
His general age, and could not be as fond
Of wars and creeds as any of his race,—
But most he loved a happy human face;
And wheresoe'er his fine, frank eyes were thrown,
He struck the looks he wished for, with his own.
So what but service leaped where'er he went!
Was there a tilt-day or a tournament,—
For welcome grace there rode not such another,
Nor yet for strength, except his lordly brother.
Was there a court-day, or a feast, or dance,
Or minstrelsy with roving plumes from France,
Or summer party to the greenwood shade,
With lutes prepared, and cloth on herbage laid,
And ladies' laughter coming through the air,—
He was the readiest and the blithest there;
And made the time so exquisitely pass
With stories told with elbow on the grass,
Or touched the music in his turn so finely,
That all he did, they thought, was done divinely

The lovely stranger could not fail to see
Too soon this difference, more especially
As her consent, too lightly now, she thought,
With hopes far different had been strangely bought,
And many a time the pain of that neglect
Would strike in blushes o'er her self-respect:
But since the ill was cureless, she applied
With busy virtue to resume her pride,
And hoped to value her submissive heart
On playing well a patriot daughter's part,
Trying her new-found duties to prefer
To what a father might have owed to her.
The very day too when her first surprise
Was full, kind tears had come into her eyes
On finding, by his care, her private room
Furnished, like magic, from her own at home;
The very books and all transported there,
The leafy tapestry, and the crimson chair,
The lute, the glass that told the shedding hours,
The little urn of silver for the flowers,
The frame for broidering, with a piece half done,
And the white falcon, basking in the sun,
Who, when he saw her, sidled on his stand,
And twined his neck against her trembling hand
But what had touched her nearest, was the thought,
That if 'twere destined for her to be brought
To a sweet mother's bed, the joy would be
Giovanni's too, and his her family:—
He seemed already father of her child,
And on the nestling pledge in patient thought she smiled
Yet then a pang would cross her, and the red
In either downward cheek startle and spread,
To think that he, who was to have such part
In joys like these, had never shared her heart;
But then she chased it with a sigh austere;
And did she chance, at times like these, to hear
Her husband's footstep, she would haste the more,
And with a double smile open the door,
And hope his day had worn a happy face;
Ask how his soldiers pleased him, or the chase,
Or what new court had sent to win his sovereign grace.

The prince, at this, would bend on her an eye
Cordial enough, and kiss her tenderly;
Nor, to say truth, was he in general slow
To accept attentions, flattering to bestow;
But then meantime he took no generous pains,
By mutual pleasing, to secure his gains;
He entered not, in turn, in her delights,
Her books, her flowers, her taste for rural sights;
Nay scarcely her sweet singing minded he,
Unless his pride was roused by company;
Or when to please him, after martial play,
She strained her lute to some old fiery lay

Of fierce Orlando, or of Ferumbras,
Or Ryan's cloak, or how by the red grass
In battle you might know where Richard was

Yet all the while, no doubt, however stern
Or cold at times, he thought he loved in turn,
And that the joy he took in her sweet ways,
The pride he felt when she excited praise,
In short, the enjoyment of his own good pleasure,
Was thanks enough, and passion beyond measure.

She, had she loved him, might have thought so too:
For what will love's exalting not go through,
Till long neglect, and utter selfishness,
Shame the fond pride it takes in its distress?
But ill prepared was she, in her hard lot,
To fancy merit where she found it not,—
She, who had been beguiled,—she, who was made
Within a gentle bosom to be laid,—
To bless and to be blessed,—to be heart-bare
To one who found his bettered likeness there,—
To think for ever with him, like a bride,—
To haunt his eye, like taste personified,—
To double his delight, to share his sorrow,
And like a morning beam, to wake him every morrow.

Paulo, meantime, who ever since the day
He saw her sweet looks bending o'er his way,
Had stored them up, unconsciously, as graces
By which to judge all other forms and faces,
Had learnt, I know not how, the secret snare,
Which gave her up, that evening, to his care.
Some babbler, may-be, of old Guido's court,
Or foolish friend had told him, half in sport:
But to his heart the fatal flattery went;
And grave he grew, and inwardly intent,
And ran back, in his mind, with sudden spring,
Look, gesture, smile, speech, silence, every thing,
E'en what before had seemed indifference,
And read them over in another sense.
Then would he blush with sudden self-disdain,
To think how fanciful he was, and vain;
And with half angry, half regretful sigh,
Tossing his chin, and feigning a free eye,
Breathe off, as 'twere, the idle tale, and look
About him for his falcon or his book,
Scorning that ever he should entertain
One thought that in the end might give his brother pain.

This start however came so often round,—
So often fell he in deep thought, and found
Occasion to renew his carelessness,
Yet every time the power grown less and less,
That by degrees, half wearied, half inclined,
To the sweet struggling image he resigned;
And merely, as he thought, to make the best
Of what by force would come about his breast,
Began to bend down his admiring eyes
On all her touching looks and qualities,
Turning their shapely sweetness every way,
Till 'twas his food and habit day by day,
And she became companion of his thought;
Silence her gentleness before him brought,
Society her sense, reading her books,
Music her voice, every sweet thing her looks,
Which sometimes seemed, when he sat fixed awhile,
To steal beneath his eyes with upward smile
And did he stroll into some lonely place,
Under the tress, upon the thick soft grass,
How charming, would he think, to see her here!
How heightened then, and perfect would appear
The two divinest things in earthly lot,
A lovely woman in a rural spot!

Thus daily went he on, gathering sweet pain
About his fancy, till it thrilled again:
And if his brother's image, less and less,
Startled him up from his new idleness,
'Twas not—he fancied,—that he reasoned worse,
Or felt less scorn of wrong, but the reverse.
That one should think of injuring another,
Or trenching on his peace,—this too a brother,—
And all from selfishness and pure weak wi ,
To him seemed marvellous and impossible

'Tis true thought he, one being more there was,
Who might meantime have weary hours to pass,
One weaker too to bear them,—and for whom?—
No matter;—he could not reverse her doom;
And so he sighed and smiled, as if one thought
Of paltering could suppose that *he* was to be caught

Yet if she loved him, common gratitude,
If not, a sense of what was fair and good,
Besides his new relationship and right,
Would make him wish to please her all he might
And as to thinking,—where could be the harm,
If to his heart he kept its secret charm?
He wished not to himself another's blessing,
But then he might console for not possessing;
And glorious things there were, which but to see
And not admire, were mere stupidity:
He might as well object to his own eyes
For loving to behold the fields and skies,
His neighbor's grove, or story-painted hall;
'Twas but the taste for what was natural;
Only his fav'rite thought was loveliest of them all.

Concluding thus and happier that he knew
His ground so well, near and more near he drew,
And, sanctioned by his brother's manner, spent
Hours by her side, as happy as well-meant.
He read with her, he rode, he train'd her hawk,
He spent still evenings in delightful talk,
While she sat busy at her broidery frame;
Or touched the lute with her, and when they came
To some fine part, prepared her for the pleasure,
And then with double smile stole on the measure

Then at the tournament,—who there but she
Made him more gallant still than formerly,
Couch o'er his tightened lance with double force,
Pass like the wind, sweeping down man and horse,
And franklier then than ever, midst the shout
And dancing trumpets ride, uncovered, round about?
His brother only, more than hitherto,
He would avoid, or sooner let subdue,
Partly from something strange unfelt before,
Partly because Giovanni sometimes wore
A knot his bride had worked him, green and gold:—
For in all things with nature did she hold;
And while 'twas being worked, her fancy was
Of sunbeams mingling with a tuft of grass.

Francesca from herself but ill could hide
What pleasure now was added to her side,—
How placidly, yet fast, the days flew on
Thus link'd in white and loving unison,
And how the chair he sat in, and the room,
Began to look, when he had failed to come.
But as she better knew the cause than he,
She seemed to have the more necessity
For struggling hard, and rousing all her pride;
And so she did at first; she even tried
To feel a sort of anger at his care:
But these extremes brought but a kind despair;
And then she only spoke more sweetly to him,
And found her failing eyes give looks that melted thro' him

Giovanni too, who felt relieved indeed
To see another to his place succeed,
Or rather filling up some trifling hours,
Better spent elsewhere, and beneath his powers,
Left the new tie to strengthen day by day,
Talked less and less, and longer kept away,
Secure in his self-love and sense of right,
That he was welcome most, come when he might
And doubtless, they, in their still finer sense,
With added care repaid this confidence,
Turning their thoughts from his abuse of it,
To what on their own parts was graceful and was fit.

Ah now, ye gentle pair,—now think awhile,
Now, while ye still can think, and still can smile;
Now, while your generous hearts have not been grieved
Perhaps with something not to be retrieved,
And ye have still, within, the power of gladness,
From self-resentment free, and retrospective madness!

So did they think—but partly from delay,
Partly from fancied ignorance of the way,

And most from feeling the bare contemplation,
Give them fresh need of mutual consolation,
They scarcely tried to see each other less,
And did but meet with deeper tenderness,
Living, from day to day, as they were used,
Only with graver thoughts, and smiles reduced,
And sighs more frequent, which, when one would heave,
The other longed to start up and receive.
For whether some suspicion now had crossed
Giovanni's mind, or whether he had lost
More of his temper lately, he would treat
His wife with petty scorns, and starts of heat,
And, to his own omissions proudly blind,
O'erlook the pains she took to make him kind,
And yet be angry, if he thought them less;
He found reproaches in her meek distress,
Forcing her silent tears, and then resenting,
Then almost angrier grown from half repenting,
And, hinting at the last, that some there were
Better perhaps than he, and tastefuller,
And these, for what he knew,—he little cared,—
Might please her, and be pleased, though he despaired.
Then would he quit the room, and half disdain
Himself for being in so harsh a strain,
And venting thus his temper on a woman;
Yet not the more for that changed he in common,
Or took more pains to please her, and be near:—
What! should he truckle to a woman's tear?

At times like these the princess tried to shun
The face of Paulo as too kind a one;
And shutting up her tears with final sigh,
Would walk into the air, and see the sky,
And feel about her all the garden green,
And hear the birds that shot the covert boughs between.

A noble range it was, of many a rood,
Walled round with trees, and ending in a wood:
Indeed the whole was leafy; and it had
A winding stream about it, clear and glad,
That danced from shade to shade, and on its way
Seemed smiling with delight to feel the day.
There was the pouting rose, both red and white,
The flamy heart's-ease, flushed with purple light,
Blush-hiding strawberry, sunny-colored box,
Hyacinth, handsome with its clustering locks,
The lady lily, looking gently down,
Pure lavender, to lay in bridal gown,
The daisy, lovely on both sides,—in short,
All the sweet cups to which the bees resort,
With plots of grass, and perfumed walks between
Of citron, honeysuckle, and jessamine,
With orange, whose warm leaves so finely suit,
And look as if they shade a golden fruit;
And midst the flowers, turfed round beneath a shade
Of circling pines, a babbling fountain played,
And 'twixt their shafts you saw the water bright,
Which through the darksome tops glimmer'd with show'ring light.
So now you walked beside an odorous bed
Of gorgeous hues, white, azure, golden, red;
And now turned off into a leafy walk,
Close and continuous, fit for lovers' talk;
And now pursued the stream, and as you trod
Onward and onward o'er the velvet sod,
Felt on your face an air, watery and sweet,
And a new sense in your soft-lighting feet;
And then perhaps you entered upon shades,
Pillowed with dells and uplands 'twixt the glades,
Through which the distant palace, now and then,
Looked lordly forth with many-windowed ken;
A land of trees, which reaching round about,
In shady blessing stretched their old arms out,
With spots of sunny opening, and with nooks,
To lie and read in, sloping into brooks,
Where at her drink you started the slim deer,
Retreating lightly with a lovely fear.
And all about, the birds kept leafy house,
And sung and sparkled in and out the boughs;
And all about, a lovely sky of blue
Clearly was felt, or down the leaves laughed through;
And here and there, in every part, were seats,
Some in the open walks, some in retreats;
With bowering leaves o'erhead, to which the eye
Looked up half sweetly and half awfully,—
Places of nestling green, for poets made,
Where, when the sunshine struck a yellow shade,
The rugged trunks, to inward peeping sight,
Thronged in dark pillars up the gold green light.

But 'twixt the wood and flowery walks, halfway,
And formed of both, the loveliest portion lay,
A spot, that struck you like enchanted ground:—
It was a shallow dell, set in a mound
Of sloping shrubs, that mounted by degrees,
The birch and poplar mixed with heavier trees;
From under which, sent through a marble spout,
Betwixt the dark wet green, a rill gushed out,
Whose low sweet talking seemed as if it said
Something eternal to that happy shade.
The ground within was lawn, with plots of flowers
Heaped towards the centre, and with citron bowers
And in the midst of all, clustered with bay
And myrtle, and just gleaming to the day,
Lurked a pavilion,—a delicious sight,—
Small, marble, well-proportioned, mellowy white,
With yellow vine-leaves sprinkled,—but no more,—
And a young orange either side the door.
The door was to the wood, forward, and square,
The rest was domed at top, and circular;
And through the dome the only light came in,
Tinged, as it entered, with the vine-leaves thin.

It was a beauteous piece of ancient skill,
Spared from the rage of war, and perfect still;
By some supposed the work of fairy hands,
Famed for luxurious taste, and choice of lands,—
Alcina, or Morgana,—who from fights
And errant fame enveigled amorous knights,
And lived with them in a long round of blisses,
Feasts, concerts, baths, and bower-enshaded kisses.
But 'twas a temple, as its sculpture told,
Built to the Nymphs that haunted there of old;
For o'er the door was carved a sacrifice
By girls and shepherds brought, with reverend eyes
Of sylvan drinks and food, simple and sweet,
And goats with struggling horns and planted feet.
And round about, ran on a line with this
In like relief, a world of Pagan bliss,
That showed, in various scenes, the nymphs themselves
Some by the water-side on bowery shelves
Leaning at will,—some in the water sporting
With sides half swelling forth, and looks of courting,—
Some in a flowery dell, hearing a swain
Play on his pipe, till the hills ring again,—
Some tying up their long moist hair,—some sleeping
Under the trees, with fauns and satyrs peeping,—
Or sidelong-eyed, pretending not to see
The latter in the brakes come creepingly,
While from their careless urns, lying aside
In the long grass, the straggling waters slide
Never, be sure, before or since was seen
A summer-house so fine in such a nest of green.

All the green garden, flower-bed, shade, and plot
Francesca loved, but most of all this spot.
Whenever she walked forth, wherever went,
About the grounds, to this at last she bent:
Here she had brought a lute and a few books;
Here would she lie for hours, with grateful looks
Thanking at heart the sunshine and the leaves,
The vernal rain-drops counting from the eaves,
And all that promising, calm smile we see
In nature's face, when we look patiently.
Then would she think of heaven; and you might hear
Sometimes when every thing was hushed and clear,
Her gentle voice from out those shades emerging,
Singing the evening anthem to the Virgin.
The gardeners and the rest, who served the place,
And blest whenever they beheld her face,
Knelt when they heard it, bowing and uncovered,
And felt as if in air some sainted beauty hovered

One day,—'twas on a summer afternoon,
When airs and gurgling brooks are best in tune,
And grasshoppers are loud, and day-work done,
And shades have heavy outlines in the sun,—

The princess came to her accustomed bower
To get her, if she could, a soothing hour,
Trying, as she was used, to leave her cares
Without, and slumberously enjoy the airs,
And the low-talking leaves, and that cool light
The vines let in, and all that hushing sight
Of closing wood seen through the opening door,
And distant plash of waters tumbling o'er,
And smell of citron blooms, and fifty luxuries more.

She tried, as usual, for the trial's sake,
For even that diminished her heart-ache;
And never yet, how ill soe'er at ease,
Came she for nothing 'midst the flowers and trees.
Yet how it was she knew not, but that day,
She seemed to feel too lightly borne away,—
Too much relieved,—too much inclined to draw
A careless joy from every thing she saw,
And looking round her with a new-born eye,
As if some tree of knowledge had been nigh,
To taste of nature, primitive and free,
And bask at ease in her heart's liberty.

Painfully clear those rising thoughts appeared,
With something dark at bottom that she feared;
And turning from the fields her thoughtful look,
She reached o'er head, and took her down a book,
And fell to reading with as fix'd an air,
As though she had been wrapt since morning there.

'Twas Launcelot of the Lake, a bright romance,
That, like a trumpet, made young pulses dance,
Yet had a softer note that shook still more;—
She had begun it but the day before,
And read with a full heart, half sweet, half sad,
How old King Ban was spoiled of all he had
But one fair castle: how one summer's day
With his fair queen and child he went away
To ask the great King Arthur for assistance;
How reaching by himself a hill at distance,
He turned to give his castle a last look,
And saw its far white face: and how a smoke,
As he was looking, burst in volumes forth,
And good King Ban saw all that he was worth,
And his fair castle, burning to the ground,
So that his wearied pulse felt over-wound,
And he lay down, and said a prayer apart
For those he loved, and broke his poor old heart.
Then read she of the queen with her young child
How she came up, and nearly had gone wild,
And how in journeying on in her despair,
She reached a lake and met a lady there,
Who pitied her, and took the baby sweet
Into her arms, when lo, with closing feet
She sprang up all at once, like bird from brake,
And vanished with him underneath the lake.
The mother's feelings we as well may pass:—
The fairy of the place that lady was,
And Launcelot (so the boy was called) became
Her inmate, till in search of knightly fame
He went to Arthur's court, and played his part
So rarely, and displayed so frank a heart,
That what with all his charms of look and limb,
The Queen Geneura fell in love with him:
And here, with growing interest in her reading,
The princess, doubly fixed, was now proceeding.

Ready she sat with one hand to turn o'er
The leaf, to which her thoughts ran on before,
The other propping her white brow, and throwing
Its ringlets out, under the skylight glowing.
So sat she fixed; and so observed was she
Of one, who at the door stood tenderly,—
Paulo,—who from a window seeing her
Go straight across the lawn, and guessing where,
Had thought she was in tears, and found, that day,
His usual efforts vain to keep away.
"May I come in?" said he:—it made her start,—
That smiling voice;—she colored, pressed her heart
A moment, as for breath, and then with free
And usual tone said, "O yes,—certainly."
There's went to be, at conscious times like these,
An affectation of a bright-eyed ease,
An air of something quite serene and sure,
As if to seem so, were to be, secure:
With this the lovers met, with this they spoke,
With this they sat down to the self-same book
And Paulo, by degrees, gently embraced
With one permitted arm her lovely waist;
And both their cheeks, like peaches on a tree,
Leaned with a touch together, thrillingly:
And o'er the book they hung, and nothing said,
And every lingering page grew longer as they read.

As thus they sat, and felt with leaps of heart
Their color change, they came upon the part
Where fond Geneura, with her flame long nurst,
Smiled upon Launcelot when he kissed her first:
That touch, at last, through every fibre slid;
And Paulo turned, scarce knowing what he did,
Only he felt he could no more dissemble,
And kissed her, mouth to mouth, all in a tremble.
Sad were those hearts, and sweet was that long kiss:
Sacred be love from sight, whate'er it is.
The world was all forgot, the struggle o'er,
Desperate the joy,—That day they read no more.

CANTO IV.

HOW THE BRIDE RETURNED TO RAVENNA

SORROW, they say, to one with true touched ear,
Is but the discord of a warbling sphere,
A lurking contrast, which though harsh it be,
Distils the next note more deliciously.
E'en tales like this, founded on real woe,
From bitter seed to balmy fruitage grow:
The woe was earthly, fugitive, is past;
The song that sweetens it, may always last.
And even they, whose shattered hearts and frames
Make them unhappiest of poetic names,
What are they, if they know their calling high
But crushed perfumes exhaling to the sky?
Or weeping clouds, that but a while are seen,
Yet keep the earth they haste to, bright and green?

Once, and but once,—nor with a scornful face
Tried worth will hear,—that scene again took place
Partly by chance they met, partly to see
The spot where they had last gone cheerfully,
But most, from failure of all self-support;—
And oh! the meeting in that loved resort!
No peevishness there was, no loud distress,
No mean retort of sorry selfishness;
But a mute gush of hiding tears from one
Clasped to the core of him, who yet shed none,—
And self-accusings then, which he began,
And into which her tearful sweetness ran;
And then kind looks, with meeting eyes again,
Starting to deprecate each other's pain;
Till half persuasions they could scarce do wrong,
And sudden sense of wretchedness, more strong,
And—why should I add more?—again they parted,
He doubly torn for her, and she nigh broken-hearted.

She never ventured in that spot again;
And Paulo knew it, but could not refrain;
He went again one day; and how it looked!
The calm, old shade!—his presence felt rebuked.
It seemed, as if the hopes of his young heart,
His kindness, and his generous scorn of art,
Had all been mere a dream, or at the best
A vain negation, that could stand no test;
And that on waking from his idle fit,
He found himself (how could he think of it!)
A selfish boaster and a hypocrite.

That thought before had grieved him; but the pain
Cut sharp and sudden now it came again.
Sick thoughts of late had made his body sick,
And pale he stood, and seemed to burst all o'er
Into moist anguish never felt before,
And with a dreadful certainty to know,
His peace was gone, and all to come was wo

Francesca too,—the being, made to bless,—
Destined by him to the same wretchedness,—
It seemed as if such whelming thoughts must find
Some props for them, or he should lose his mind.—
And find he did, not what the worse disease
Of want of charity calls sophistries,—
Nor what can cure a generous heart of pain,—
But humble guesses, helping to sustain.
He thought, with quick philosophy, of things
Rarely found out except through sufferings,—
Of habit, circumstance, design, degree,
Merit, and will, and thoughtful charity:
And these, although they pushed down as they rose,
His self-respect, and all those morning shows
Of true and perfect, which his youth had built,
Pushed with them too the worst of other's guilt;
And furnished him, at least, with something kind,
On which to lean a sad and startled mind:
Till youth, and natural vigor, and the dread
Of self-betrayal, and a thought that spread
From time to time in gladness o'er his face,
That she he loved could have done nothing base,
Helped to restore him to his usual life,
Though grave at heart, and with himself at strife;
And he would rise betimes, day after day,
And mount his favorite horse, and ride away
Miles in the country, looking round about,
As he glode by, to force his thoughts without;
And, when he found it vain, would pierce the shade
Of some enwooded field or closer glade.
And there dismounting, idly sit, and sigh
Or pluck the grass beside him with vague eye,
And almost envy the poor beast, that went
Cropping it, here and there, with dumb content.
But thus, at least, he exercised his blood,
And kept it livelier than inaction could;
And thus he earned for his thought-working head
The power of sleeping when he went to bed,
And was enabled still to wear away
That task of loaded hearts, another day.

But she, the gentler frame,—the shaken flower,
Plucked up to wither in a foreign bower,—
The struggling, virtue-loving, fallen she,
The wife that was, the mother that might be,—
What could she do, unable thus to keep
Her strength alive, but sit, and think, and weep,
For ever stooping o'er her broidery frame,
Half blind, and longing till the night-time came,
When worn and wearied out with the day's sorrow,
She might be still and senseless till the morrow?

And oh, the morrow, how it used to rise!
How would she open her despairing eyes,
And from the sense of the long lingering day,
Rushing upon her, almost turn away,
Loathing the light, and groan to sleep again!
Then sighing once for all, to meet the pain,
She would get up in haste, and try to pass
The time in patience, wretched as it was;
Till patience self, in her distempered sight,
Would seem a charm to which she had no right,
And trembling at the lip, and pale with fears,
She shook her head, and burst into fresh tears.
Old comforts now were not at her command:
The falcon reached in vain from off his stand;
The flowers were not refreshed; the very light,
The sunshine, seemed as if it shone at night;
The least noise smote her like a sudden wound;
And did she hear but the remotest sound
Of song or instrument about the place,
She hid with both her hands her streaming face.
But worse to her than all (and oh! thought she,
That ever, ever, such a worse should be!)
The sight of infant was, or child at play;
Then would she turn, and move her lips, and pray,
That heaven would take her, if it pleased, away.

I pass the meetings Paulo had with her:—
Calm were they in their outward character,
Or pallid efforts, rather, to suppress
The pangs within, that either's might be less;
And ended mostly with a passionate start
Of tears and kindness, when they came to part
Thinner he grew, she thought, and pale with care
"And I, 'twas I, that dashed his noble air!"
He saw her wasting, yet with placid show;
And scarce could help exclaiming in his woe,
"O gentle creature, look not at me so!"

But Prince Giovanni, whom her wan distress
Had touched, of late, with a new tenderness,
Which, to his fresh surprise, did but appear
To wound her more than when he was severe,
Began, with other helps perhaps, to see
Strange things, and missed his brother's company.
What a convulsion was the first sensation!
Rage, wonder, misery, scorn, humiliation,
A self-love, struck as with a personal blow,
Gloomy revenge, a prospect full of woe,
All rushed upon him, like the sudden view
Of some new world, foreign to all he knew,
Where he had waked and found disease's visions true

If any lingering hope, that he was wrong,
Smoothed o'er him now and then, 'twas not so long
Next night, as sullenly awake he lay,
Considering what to do the approaching day
He heard his wife say something in her sleep:—
He shook and listened;—she began to weep,
And moaning louder, seemed to shake her head,
Till all at once articulate, she said,
"He loves his brother yet—dear heaven, 'twas I—"
Then lower voiced—"only—*do* let me die."

The prince looked at her hastily;—no more;
He dresses, takes his sword, and through the door
Goes, like a spirit, in the morning air;—
His squire awaked attends; and they repair,
Silent as wonder, to his brother's room:—
His squire calls him up too; and forth they come.

The brothers meet,—Giovanni scarce in breath,
Yet firm and fierce, Paulo as pale as death.
"May I request, sir," said the prince, and frowned,
"Your ear a moment in the tilting ground?"
"*There*, brother?" answered Paulo, with an air
Surprised and shocked. "Yes, *brother*," cried he, "there."
The word smote crushingly; and paler still,
He bowed, and moved his lips, as waiting on his will.

Giovanni turned, and down the stairs they bend;
The squires, with looks of sad surprise, attend;
Then issue forth in the moist-striking air,
And toward the tilt-yard cross a planted square.

'Twas a fresh autumn dawn, vigorous and chill
The lightsome morning star was sparkling still,
Ere it turned in to heaven; and far away
Appeared the streaky fingers of the day.
An opening in the trees took Paulo's eye,
As mute his brother and himself went by:
It was a glimpse of the tall wooded mound,
That screened Francesca's favorite spot of ground
Massy and dark in the clear twilight stood,
As in a lingering sleep, the solemn wood;
And through the bowering arch, which led inside,
He almost fancied once, that he descried
A marble gleam, where the pavilion lay;—
Starting he turned, and looked another way.

Arrived, and the two squires withdrawn apart,
The prince spoke low, as with a laboring heart,
And said, "Before you answer what you can,
I wish to tell you, as a gentleman,
That what you may confess," (and as he spoke
His voice with breathless and pale passion broke)
"Will implicate no person known to you,
More than disquiet in its sleep may do."

Paulo's heart bled; he waved his hand, and bent
His head a little in acknowledgment.
"Say then, sir, if you can," continued he,
"One word will do—you have not injured me:
Tell me but so, and I shall bear the pain
Of having asked a question I disdain:—
But utter nothing, if not that one word;
And meet me this:"—he stopped and drew his sword

Paulo seemed firmer grown from his despair;
He drew a little back; and with the air
Of one who would do well, not from a right
To be well thought of, but in guilt's despite,
"I am," said he, "I know,—'twas not so ever—
But fight for it! and with a brother! Never."
"How!" with uplifted voice, exclaimed the other;
"The vile pretence! who asked you—with a *brother?*
Brother! O traitor to the noble name
Of Malatesta, I deny the claim.
What! wound it deepest? strike me to the core,
Me, and the hopes which I can have no more,
And then, as never Malatesta could,
Shrink from the letting a few drops of blood?"

"It is not so," cried Paulo, "'tis not so;
But I would save you from a further woe."

"A further woe, recreant!" retorted he:
"I know of none: yes, one there still may be;
Save me the woe, save me the dire disgrace
Of seeing one of an illustrious race
Bearing about a heart, which feared no law,
And a vile sword, which yet he dare not draw."

"Brother, dear brother!" Paulo cried, "nay, nay,
I'll use the word no more;—but *peace*, I pray!
You trample on a soul, sunk at your feet!"
"'Tis false;" exclaimed the prince; "'tis a retreat
To which you fly, when manly wrongs pursue,
And fear the grave you bring a woman to."

A sudden start, yet not of pride or pain,
Paulo here gave; he seemed to rise again;
And taking off his cap without a word,
He drew, and kissed the crossed hilt of his sword,
Looking to heaven;—then with a steady brow,
Mild, yet not feeble, said, "I'm ready now."

"A noble word!" exclaimed the prince, and smote
Preparingly on earth his firming foot:—
The squires rush in between, in their despair,
But both the princes tell them to beware.
"Back, Gerard," cries Giovanni; "I require
No teacher here, but an observant squire."
"Back, Tristan," Paulo cries; "fear not for me;
All is not worst that so appears to thee.
And here," said he, "a word." The poor youth came,
Starting in sweeter tears to hear his name:
A whisper, and a charge there seemed to be,
Given to him kindly, yet inflexibly:
Both squires then drew apart again, and stood
Mournfully both, each in his several mood,—
One half in rage, as to himself he speaks,
The other with the tears streaming down both his cheeks.

The prince attacked with nerve in every limb,
Nor seemed the other slow to match with him;
Yet as the fight grew warm, 'twas evident,
One fought to wound, the other to prevent:
Giovanni pressed, and pushed, and shifted aim,
And played his weapon like a tongue of flame;
Paulo retired, and warded, turned on heel,
And led him, step by step, round like a wheel.
Sometimes indeed he feigned an angrier start,
But still relapsed, and played his former part.
"What!" cried Giovanni, who grew still more fierce,
"Fighting in sport? Playing your cart and tierce?"
"Not so, my prince," said Paulo; "have a care
How you think so, or I shall wound you there."
He stamped, and watching as he spoke the word,
Drove, with his breast, full on his brother's sword.
'Twas done. He staggered, and in falling prest
Giovanni's foot with his right hand and breast:
Then on his elbow turned, and raising t'other,
He smiled, and said, "No fault of yours, my brother;
An accident—a slip—the finishing one
To errors by that poor old man begun.
You'll not—you'll not"—his heart leaped on before,
And choked his utterance; but he smiled once more.
For, as his hand grew lax, he felt it prest;—
And so, his dim eyes sliding into rest,
He turned him round, and dropt with hiding head
And, in that loosening drop, his spirit fled.

But noble passion touched Giovanni's soul;
He seemed to feel the clouds of habit roll
Away from him at once, with all their scorn;
And out he spoke, in the clear air of morn:—
"By heaven, by heaven, and all the better part
Of us poor creatures with a human heart,
I trust we reap at last, as well as plough;—
But there, meantime, my brother, liest thou;
And, Paulo, thou wert the completest knight,
That ever rode with banner to the fight;
And thou wert the most beautiful to see,
That ever came in press of chivalry;
And of a sinful man, thou wert the best,
That ever for his friend put spear in rest;
And thou wert the most meek and cordial,
That ever among ladies eat in hall;
And thou wert still, for all that bosom gored,
The kindest man, that ever struck with sword."

At this the words forsook his tongue; and he,
Who scarcely had shed tears since infancy,
Felt his stern visage thrill, and meekly bowed
His head, and for his brother wept aloud.
The squires with glimmering tears,—Tristan, indeed
Heart-struck, and hardly able to proceed,—
Double their scarfs about the fatal wound,
And raise the body up to quit the ground.
Giovanni starts; and motioning to take
The way they came, follows his brother back,
And having seen him laid upon the bed,
No further look he gave him, nor tear shed,
But went away, such as he used to be,
With looks of stately will, and calm austerity.

Tristan, who, when he was to make the best
Of something sad and not to be redressed,
Could show a heart as firm as it was kind,
Now locked his tears up, and seemed all resigned,
And to Francesca's chamber took his way,
To tell the message of that mortal day.
He found her ladies up and down the stairs
Moving with noiseless caution, and in tears,
And that the news, though to herself unknown,
On its old wings of vulgar haste had flown
The door, as tenderly as miser's purse,
Was opened to him by the aged nurse,
Who shaking her old head, and pressing close
Her withered lips to keep the tears that rose,
Made signs she guessed what grief he came about,
And so his arm squeezed gently, and went out.

The princess, who had passed a fearful night,
Toiling with dreams,—fright crowding upon fright,
Had missed her husband at that early hour,
And would have ris'n, but found she wanted power.
Yet as her body seemed to go, her mind
Felt, though in anguish still, strangely resigned;
And moving not, nor weeping, mute she lay,
Wasting in patient gravity away.
The nurse, sometime before, with gentle creep
Had drawn the curtains, hoping she might sleep:
But suddenly she asked, though not with fear,
"Nina, what bustle's that I seem to hear?"
And the poor creature, who the news had heard,
Pretending to be busy, had just stirred
Something about the room, and answered not a word.
"Who's there," said that sweet voice, kindly and clear,
Which in its stronger days was joy to hear:—
Its weakness now almost deprived the squire
Of his new firmness, but approaching nigher,
"Madam," said he, "'tis I; one who may say,
He loves his friends more than himself to-day;—
Tristan."—She paused a little, and then said—
"Tristan—my friend, what noise thus haunts my head?
Something I'm sure has happened—tell me what—
I can bear all, though you may fancy not."
"Madam," replied the squire, "you are, I know,
All sweetness—pardon me for saying so.
My master bade me say then," resumed he,
"That he spoke firmly, when he told it me,—
That I was also, madam, to your ear
Firmly to speak, and you firmly to hear,—

That he was forced this day, whether or no,
To combat with the prince; and that although
His noble brother was no fratricide,
Yet in that fight, and on his sword,—he died."
"I understand," with firmness answered she;
More low in voice, but still composedly.
"Now, Tristan—faithful friend—leave me; and take
This trifle here, and keep it for my sake."
So saying, from the curtains she put forth
Her thin white hand, that wore a ring of worth;
And he, with tears no longer to be kept
From quenching his heart's thirst, silently wept,
And kneeling took the ring, and touched her hand
To either streaming eye, with homage bland,
And looking on it once, gently up started,
And, in his reverent stillness, so departed.

Her favorite lady then with the old nurse
Returned, and fearing she must now be worse,
Gently withdrew the curtains, and looked in:—
O, who that feels one godlike spark within,
Shall bid not earth be just, before 'tis hard, with sin?
There lay she praying, upwardly intent,
Like a fair statue on a monument,
With her two trembling hands together prest,
Palm against palm, and pointing from her breast.
She ceased, and turning slowly towards the wall,
They saw her tremble sharply, feet and all,—
Then suddenly be still. Near and more near
They bent with pale inquiry and close ear;—
Her eyes were shut—no motion—not a breath—
The gentle sufferer was at peace in death.

I pass the grief that struck to every face,
And the mute anguish all about that place,
In which the silent people, here and there,
Went soft, as though she still could feel their care.
The gentle-tempered for a while forgot
Their own distress, or wept the common lot:
The warmer, apter now to take offence,
Yet hushed as they rebuked, and wondered whence
Others at such a time could get their want of sense

Fain would I haste indeed to finish all;
And so at once I reach the funeral.
Private 'twas fancied it must be, though some
Thought that her sire, the poor old duke, would come.
And some were wondering in their pity, whether
The lovers might not have one grave together.
Next day, however, from the palace gate
A blast of trumpets blew, like voice of fate;
And all in sable clad, forth came again
Of knights and squires the former sprightly train;
Gerard was next, and then a rank of friars;
And then, with heralds on each side, two squires,
The one of whom upon a cushion bore
The coroneted helm Prince Paulo wore,
His shield the other;—then there was a space,
And in the middle, with a doubtful pace,
His horse succeeded, plumed and trapped in black,
Bearing the sword and banner on his back:
The noble creature, as in state he trod,
Appeared as if he missed his princely load;
And with back-rolling eye and lingering pride,
To hope his master still might come to ride.
Then Tristan, heedless of what passed around,
Rode by himself, with eyes upon the ground.
Then heralds in a row: and last of all
Appeared a hearse, hung with an ermined pall,
And bearing on its top, together set,
A prince's and princess's coronet.
Mutely they issued forth, black, slow, dejected,
Nor stopped within the walls, as most expected;
But passed the gates—the bridge—the last abode,—
And towards Ravenna held their silent road.

The prince, it seems, struck, since his brother's death,
With what he hinted with his dying breath,
And told by others now of all they knew,
Had fixed at once the course he should pursue;
And from a mingled feeling, which he strove
To hide no longer from his taught self-love,
Of sorrow, shame, resentment, and a sense
Of justice owing to that first offence,
Had, on the day preceding, written word
To the old duke of all that had occurred:—
"And though I shall not," (so concluded he)
"Otherwise touch thine age's misery,
Yet as I would that both one grave should hide,
Which can, and must not be, where I reside,
'Tis fit, though all have something to deplore,
That he, who join'd them once, should keep to part no more."

The wretched father, who, when he had read
This letter, felt it wither his gray head,
And ever since had paced about his room.
Trembling, and seiz'd as with approaching doom,
Had given such orders, as he well could frame,
To meet devoutly whatsoever came;
And as the news immediately took flight,
Few in Ravenna went to sleep that night,
But talked the business over, and reviewed
All that they knew of her, the fair and good;
And so with wondering sorrow the next day,
Waited till they should see that sad array.

The days were then at close of autumn,—still,
A little rainy, and towards night-fall chill;
There was a fitful, moaning air abroad;
And ever and anon, over the road,
The last few leaves came fluttering from the trees,
Whose trunks now thronged to sight, in dark varieties.
The people, who from reverence kept at home,
Listened till afternoon to hear them come;
And hour on hour went by, and nought was heard
But some chance horseman, or the wind that stirred,
Till towards the vesper hour; and then 'twas said
Some heard a voice, which seemed as if it read·
And others said, that they could hear a sound
Of many horses trampling the moist ground
Still nothing came,—till on a sudden, just
As the wind opened in a rising gust,
A voice of chanting rose, and as it spread,
They plainly heard the anthem for the dead
It was the choristers, who went to meet
The train, and now were entering the first street.
Then turned aside that city, young and old,
And in their lifted hands the gushing sorrow rolled.

But of the older people, few could bear
To keep the window, when the train drew near;
And all felt double tenderness to see
The bier approaching, slow and steadily,
On which those two in senseless coldness lay,
Who but a few short months—it seemed a day,
Had left their walls, lovely in form and mind,
In sunny manhood he,—she first of womankind.

They say that when Duke Guido saw them come,
He clasped his hands, and looking round the room,
Lost his old wits for ever. From the morrow
None saw him after. But no more of sorrow:—
On that same night, those lovers silently
Were buried in one grave, under a tree.
There side by side, and hand in hand, they lay
In the green ground:—and on fine nights in May
Young hearts betrothed used to come there to pray

THE NILE.

A SONNET. BY LEIGH HUNT.

It flows through old hushed Ægypt, and its sands
Like some grave mighty thought threading a dream,
And times and things, as in that vision, seem
Keeping along it their eternal stands,—
Caves, pillars, pyramids, the shepherd bands
That roamed through the young world, the glory extreme
Of high Sesostris, and that Southern beam,
The laughing queen that caught the world's great hands
Then comes a mightier silence, stern and strong,
As of a world left empty of its throng,
And the void weighs on us; and then we wake,
And hear the fruitful stream lapsing along
'Twixt villages, and think how we shall take
Our own calm journey on for human sake

NOTES.

THE ANGEL OF THE WORLD, by the Rev. George Croly, is a paraphrase of one of the most graceful fictions of the Koran. The angels HARUTH and MARUTH had, it seems, spoken uncharitably, concerning mankind, and had expressed, in the regions above, great contempt for those temptations which are and have been long found, most efficacious for overthrowing the resolutions of terrestrial virtue. That they might have their purity put to the proof, the two proud angels were sent down to dwell for a season on the earth. A *woman* was sent to tempt them—*and they fell.* Her charms won them first to drink of the forbidden fruit of the grape; and, after that fall, all others were easy. They stained their essence with the corruptions of sense, and betrayed to mortal ears "the words that raise men to angels."

Croly writes, (for our relishing, at least,) with a better conception than Moore, for this particular style of poem, and with a far more soaring and ennobling flow of melody. The Loves of the Angels, to this poem, are as the hop of the sparrow to the long swoop of the eagle. Unparalleled splendor of language and imagery is Croly's great gift, and in reading his poem, the imagination sails easily and toweringly away and lies dreamily in the clouds, listening to him. It is marvellous that this most glorious poem should ever have been forgotten as it is—for it will be, to most readers, a work entirely new.

"The STORY of RIMINI is founded on the beautiful episode of Paulo and Francesca in the fifth book of the INFERNO, where it stands like a lily in the mouth of Tartarus. The substance of what Dante tells us of the history of the two lovers is to be found at the end of the third Canto. The rest has been gathered from the commentators. They differ in their accounts of it, but all agree that the lady was, in some measure, beguiled into the match with the elder and less attractive Malatesta,—Boccaccio says, by having the younger brother pointed out to her as her destined husband, as he was passing over a square.

Francesca of Ravenna was the daughter of Guido Novello da Polenta, lord of that city, and was married to Giovanni, or, as others call him, Launcelot Malatesta, Lord of Rimini, under circumstances that had given her an innocent predilection for Paulo, his younger brother. The falsehood thus practised upon her had fatal consequences. In the Poem before the reader, the Duke her father, a weak, though not ill-disposed man, desirous, on a political account, of marrying her to the Prince of Rimini, and dreading her objections in case she sees him, and becomes acquainted with his unamiable manners, contrives that he shall send his brother as his proxy, and that the poor girl shall believe the one prince to be the sample of the other. Experience undeceives her; Paulo has been told the perilous secret of her preference for him; and in both of them a struggle with their sense of duty takes place, for which the insincere and selfish morals of others had not prepared them. Giovanni discovers the secret, from words uttered by his wife in her sleep: he forces Paulo to meet him in single combat, and slays him, not without sorrow for both, and great indignation against the father; Francesca dies of a broken heart; and the two lovers, who had come to Ravenna in the midst of a gay cavalcade, are sent back to Ravenna, dead, in order that he who first helped to unite them with his falsehood, should bury them in one grave for his repentance. The poor old man loses his wits; and the burial takes place.

Leigh Hunt (James Henry Leigh Hunt) is of American parentage, by both father's and mother's side. He is the son of a royalist who fled to England at the commencement of the Revolution. The mother of the poet was a sister of Benj. West, the painter. Hunt was born 1784, and educated at Christ's Hospital, on leaving which he was for some time in the office of an attorney. He next obtained a situation under government, which he was obliged to quit on establishing the paper called the Examiner, in 1809, before which he was the editor of the News. His last speculation was successful, owing to the virulence of its politics, which brought upon him a prosecution for a libel against the Prince Regent, and he was kept for some time in confinement.

Personal intimacy (says Hazlitt, who gives the following interesting sketch of him) might be supposed to render us partial to Mr. Leigh Hunt. It is well when personal intimacy produces this effect; and when the light, that dazzles us at a distance, does not on a closer inspection turn out an opaque substance. This is a charge that none of his friends will bring against Mr. Leigh Hunt. He improves upon acquaintance. The author translates admirably into the man. Indeed the very faults of his style are virtues in the individual. His natural gaiety and sprightliness of manner, his high animal spirits, and the *vinous* quality of his mind produce an immediate fascination and intoxication in those who come in contact with him, and carry off in society whatever in his writings may to some seem flat and impertinent. From great sanguineness of temper, from great quickness and unsuspecting simplicity, he runs on to the public as he does at his own fire-side, and talks about himself, forgetting that he is not always among friends. His look, his tone are required to point many things that he says: his frank, cordial manner reconciles you instantly to a little over-bearing, over-weening self-complacency. "To be admired, he needs but to be seen:" but perhaps he ought to be seen to be fully appreciated. No one ever sought his society who did not come away with a more favourable opinion of him: no one was ever disappointed, except those who had entertained idle prejudices against him. He sometimes trifles with his readers, or tires of a subject (from not being urged on by the stimulus of immediate sympathy)—but in conversation he is all life and animation, combining the vivacity of the school-boy with the resources of the wit and the taste of the scholar. The personal character, the spontaneous impulses, do not appear to excuse the author, unless you are acquainted with his situation and habits—like some proud beauty who gives herself what we think strange airs and graces under a mask, but who is instantly forgiven when she shows her face. We have said that Lord Byron is a sublime coxcomb: why should we not say that Mr. Hunt is a delightful one? There is certainly an exuberance of satisfaction in his manner which is more than the strict logical premises warrant, and which dull and phlegmatic constitutions know nothing of, and cannot understand till they see it. He is the only poet or literary man we ever knew who put us in mind of Sir John Suckling or Killigrew or Carew; or who united rare intellectual acquirements with outward grace and natural gentility. Mr. Hunt ought to have been a gentleman born, and to have patronised men of letters. He might then have played, and sung, and laughed, and talked his life away; have written manly prose, elegant verse; and his *Story of Rimini* would have been praised by the Blackwood Magazine. As it is, there is no man now living who at the same time writes prose and verse so well, with the exception of Mr. Southey (an exception, we fear, that will be little palatable to either of these gentlemen.) His prose writings, however, display more consistency of principle than the laureate's: his verses more taste. We will venture to oppose his Third Canto of the *Story of Rimini*, for classic elegance and natural feeling to any equal number of lines from Mr. Southey's Epics, or even from Mr. Moore's Lalla Rookh. In a more gay and conversational style of writing, we think his *Epistle to Lord Byron* on his going abroad, is a masterpiece;—and the *Feast of the Poets* has run through several editions A light, familiar grace, and mild unpretending pathos are the characteristics of his more sportive or serious writings whether in poetry or prose. A smile plays round the features of the one; a tear is ready to start from the thoughtful gaze of the other. He perhaps takes too little pains, and indulges in too much wayward caprice in both. A wit and a poet, Mr. Hunt is also distinguished by fineness of tact and sterling sense: he has only been a visionary in humanity, the fool of virtue. It was said by a friend and contemporary, that Hunt was born with the disposition of a lord.

Leigh Hunt is the founder of a school, ridiculed in *Blackwood's Magazine* under the name of the *Cockney School.* There is much boldness in the political principles of Leigh Hunt; but his poetry is characterised by gentleness. A luxury of images in Moore's style may be discerned in it, and a degree of harmony unrestrained by rules and ordinary language: but above all an affected negligence. Mr. Hunt rhymes like a noble *bel esprit:* and thinks like a demagogue. His enthusiasm for nature has more the air of a pretence than a real emotion; for his descriptions are neither pastoral nor unartificial.

THE WORLD BEFORE THE FLOOD.

THERE is no authentic history of the world from the creation to the deluge, besides that which is found in the first chapters of Genesis. He, therefore, who fixes the date of a fictitious narrative within that period, is under obligation to no other authority whatever, for conformity of manners, events, or even localities: he has full power to accommodate these to his peculiar purposes, observing only such analogy as shall consist with the brief information, contained in the sacred records, concerning mankind in the earliest ages. The present writer acknowledges, that he has exercised this undoubted right with great freedom. Success alone sanctions bold innovation; if he has succeeded in what he has attempted, he will need no arguments to justify it; if he has miscarried, none will avail him. Those who imagine that he has exhibited the antediluvians, as more skilful in arts and arms than can be supposed, in their stage of society, may read the *Eleventh* book of PARADISE LOST: and those, who think he has made the religion of the patriarchs too evangelical, may read the *Twelfth.*

With respect to the personages and incidents of his story, the author having deliberately adopted them, under the conviction, that in the characters of the one he was not stepping out of human nature, and in the construction of the other not exceeding the limits of poetical probability—he asks no favor, he deprecates no censure, on behalf of either; nor shall the facility, with which "much malice and little wit" might turn into ridicule every line that he has written, deter him from leaving the whole to the mercy of general readers.

But, here is a large web of fiction involving a small fact of Scripture! Nothing could justify a work of this kind, if it were, in any way, calculated to impose on the credulity, pervert the principles, or corrupt the affections of its approvers. Here, then, the appeal lies to conscience rather than to taste, and the decision on this point is of infinitely more importance to the poet than his name among men or his interests on earth. It was his design, in this composition, to present a similitude of events, that might be imagined to have happened in the first age of the world, in which such Scripture characters as are introduced would probably have acted and spoken, as they are made to act and speak. The story is told as a parable only, and its value, in this view, must be determined by its moral or rather by its religious influence on the mind and on the heart. Fiction though it be, it is the fiction that represents truth, and that *is* truth—truth in the essence, though not in the name; truth in the spirit, though not in the letter.

CANTO FIRST.

THE invasion of Eden by the descendants of Cain.—The flight of Javan from the camp of the invaders to the valley where the patriarchs dwelt.—The story of Javan's former life.

EASTWARD of Eden's early-peopled plain,
When Abel perished by the hand of Cain,
The murderer from his judge's presence fled:
Thence to the rising sun his offspring spread;
But he, the fugitive of care and guilt,
Forsook the haunts he chose, the homes he built;
While filial nations hailed him sire and chief,
Empire nor honor brought his soul relief:
He found, where'er he roamed uncheered, unblest,
No pause from suffering, and from toil no rest.

Ages meanwhile, as ages now are told,
O'er the young world in long succession rolled;
For such the vigor of primeval man,
Through numbered centuries his period ran,
And the first parents saw their hardy race,
O'er the green wilds of habitable space,
By tribes and kindreds, scattered wide and far,
Beneath the track of every varying star.
But as they multiplied from clime to clime,
Emboldened by their elder brother's crime,
They spurned obedience to the patriarch's yoke,
The bonds of nature's fellowship they broke;
The weak became the victims of the strong,
And earth was filled with violence and wrong.

Yet long on Eden's fair and fertile plain,
A righteous nation dwelt, that knew not Cain:
There fruits and flowers, in genial light and dew,
Luxuriant vines, and golden harvests grew;
By freshening waters, flocks and cattle strayed,
While youth and childhood watched them from the shade;
Age, at his fig-tree, rested from his toil,
And manly vigor tilled the unfailing soil;
Green sprang the turf, by holy footsteps trod,
Round the pure altars of the living God;
Till foul idolatry those altars stained,
And lust and revelry through Eden reigned.
Then fled the people's glory and defence,
The joys of home, the peace of innocence;
Sin brought forth sorrows in perpetual birth,
And the last light from heaven forsook the earth,
Save in one forest glen, remote and wild,
Where yet a ray of lingering mercy smiled,
Their quiet course where Seth and Enoch ran,
And God and Angels deigned to walk with man.

Now from the east, supreme in arts and arms,
The tribes of Cain, awakening war-alarms,
Full in the spirit of their father, came
To waste their brethren's land with sword and flame
In vain the younger race of Adam rose,
With force unequal to repel their foes;
Their fields in blood, their homes in ruin lay,
Their whole inheritance became a prey;
The stars, to whom as Gods they raised their cry,
Rolled, heedless of their offerings through the sky;
Till urged on Eden's utmost bounds at length,
In fierce despair they rallied all their strength.
They fought, but they were vanquished in the fight,
Captured, or slain, or scattered in the flight:
The morning battle-scene at eve was spread
With ghastly heaps, the dying and the dead;
The dead unmourned, unburied left to lie,
By friends and foes, the dying left to die.

The victim, while he groaned his soul away,
Heard the gaunt vulture hurrying to his prey,
Then strengthless felt the ravening beak, that tore
His widened wounds and drank the living gore.

One sole surviving remnant, void of fear,
Woods in their front, Euphrates in their rear,
Were sworn to perish at a glorious cost,
For all they once had known, and loved, and lost,
A small, a brave, a melancholy band,
The orphans and the childless of the land.
The hordes of Cain, by giant-chieftains led,
Wide o'er the north their vast encampment spread:
A broad and sunny champaign stretched between;
Westward a maze of waters girt the scene;
There on Euphrates, in its ancient course,
Three beauteous rivers rolled their confluent force,
Whose streams, while man the blissful garden trod,
Adorned the earthly paradise of God;
But since he fell, within their triple bound,
Fenced a lone region of forbidden ground;
Meeting at once, where high athwart their bed
Repulsive rocks a curving barrier spread,
The embattled floods, by mutual whirlpools crost,
In hoary foam and surging mist were lost;
Thence, like an Alpine cataract of snow,
White down the precipice they dashed below;
There in tumultuous billows broken wide,
They spent their rage, and yoked their fourfold tide;
Through one majestic channel, calm and free,
The sister-rivers sought the parent-sea.

The midnight watch was ended; down the west
The glowing moon declined toward her rest;
Through either host the voice of war was dumb;
In dreams the hero won the fight to come;
No sound was stirring, save the breeze that bore
The distant cataract's everlasting roar,
When from the tents of Cain, a youth withdrew;
Secret and swift from post to post he flew,
And passed the camp of Eden, while the dawn
Gleamed faintly o'er the interjacent lawn;
Skirting the forest, cautiously and slow,
He feared at every step to start a foe;
Oft leaped the hare across his path, upsprung
The lark beneath his feet, and soaring sung;
What time, o'er eastern mountains seen afar,
With golden splendor rose the morning star,
As if an angel-sentinel of night,
From earth to heaven, had winged his homeward flight,
Glorious at first, but lessening by the way,
And lost insensibly in higher day.

From track of man and herd his path he chose,
Where high the grass, and thick the copsewood rose;
Thence by Euphrates' banks his course inclined,
Where the gray willows trembled to the wind;
With toil and pain their humid shade he cleared,
When at the porch of heaven the sun appeared,
Through gorgeous clouds that streaked the orient sky,
And kindled into glory at his eye;
While dark amid the dews that glittered round
From rock and tree, long shadows traced the ground.
Then climbed the fugitive an airy height,
And resting, back o'er Eden cast his sight.

Far on the left, to man for ever closed,
The Mount of Paradise in clouds reposed:
The gradual landscape opened to his view;
From Nature's face the veil of mist withdrew,
And left, in clear and purple light revealed,
The radiant river, and the tented field;
The black pine-forest, in whose girdle lay,
The patriot phalanx, hemmed in close array;
The verdant champaign narrowing to the north,
Whence from their dusky quarters sallied forth
The proud invaders, early roused to fight,
Tribe after tribe emerging into light;
Whose shields and lances, in the golden beams,
Flashed o'er the restless scene their flickering gleams,
As when the breakers catch the morning glow,
And ocean rolls in living fire below;
So round the unbroken border of the wood,
The giants poured their army like a flood,
Eager to force the covert of their foe,
And lay the last defence of Eden low.

From the safe eminence, absorbed in thought,
Even till the wind the shout of legions brought,
He gazed—his heart recoiled—he turned his head,
And o'er the southern hills his journey sped.

Who was the fugitive? in infancy
A youthful mother's only hope was he.
Whose spouse and kindred, on a festal day,
Precipitate destruction swept away:
Earth trembled, opened, and entombed them all;
She saw them sinking, heard their voices call.
Beneath the gulf—and agonized, aghast,
On the wild verge of eddying ruin cast,
Felt in one pang at that convulsive close,
A widow's anguish and a mother's throes;
A babe sprang forth, and inauspicious birth,
Where all had perished that she loved on earth.
Forlorn and helpless, on the upriven ground,
The parent, with her offspring, Enoch found;
And thence with tender care and timely aid,
Home to the patriarchs' glen his charge conveyed.

Restored to life, one pledge of former joy,
One source of bliss to come, remained—her boy!
Sweet in her eye the cherished infant rose,
At once the seal and solace of her woes;
When the pale widow clasped him to her breast,
Warm gushed the tears, and would not be represt;
In lonely anguish, when the truant child
Leaped o'er the threshold, all the mother smiled.
In him while fond imagination viewed
Husband and parents, brethren, friends renewed,
Each vanished look, each well remembered grace,
That pleased in them, she sought in Javan's face;
For quick his eye and changeable its ray,
As the sun glancing through a vernal day;
And like the lake, by storm or moonlight seen,
With darkening furrows or cerulean mien,
His countenance the mirror of his breast,
The calm or trouble of his soul expressed.

As years enlarged his form, in moody hours,
His mind betrayed its weakness with its powers:
Alike his fairest hopes and strangest fears
Were nursed in silence, or divulged with tears;
The fulness of his heart, repressed his tongue,
Though none might rival Javan when he sung.
He loved, in lonely indolence reclined,
To watch the clouds and listen to the wind;
But from the north, when snow and tempest came,
His nobler spirit mounted into flame;
With stern delight he roamed the howling woods,
Or hung in ecstacy o'er headlong floods.
Meanwhile excursive fancy longed to view
The world, which yet by fame alone he knew:
The joys of freedom were his daily theme,
Glory the secret of his midnight dream;
That dream he told not; though his heart would ache,
His home was precious for his mother's sake.
With her the lowly paths of peace he ran,
His guardian angel, till he verged to man;
But when her weary eye could watch no more,
When to the grave her timeless corse he bore,
Not Enoch's counsels could his steps restrain;
He fled, and sojourned in the land of Cain.
There, when he heard the voice of Jubal's lyre,
Instructive genius, caught the ethereal fire;
And soon, with sweetly modulating skill,
He learned to wind the passions at his will,
To rule the chords with such mysterious art,
They seemed the life-strings of the hearer's heart.
Then glory's opening field he proudly trod,
Forsook the worship and the ways of God,
Round the vain world pursued the phantom fame,
And cast away his birthright for a name.

Yet no delight the minstrel's bosom knew,
None save the tones that from his harp he drew,

And the warm visions of a wayward mind,
Whose transient splendor left a gloom behind,
Frail as the clouds of sunset, and as fair,
Pageants of light resolving into air,
The world, whose charms his young affections stole,
He found too mean for an immortal soul;
Wound with his life, through all his feelings wrought,
Death and eternity possessed his thought;
Remorse impelled him, unremitting care
Harassed his path, and stung him to despair,
Still was the secret of his griefs unknown,
Amid the universe he sighed alone;
The fame he followed, and the fame he found,
Healed not his heart's immedicable wound;
Admired, applauded, crowned, where'er he roved,
The bard was homeless, friendless, unbeloved.
All else that breathed below the circling sky,
Were linked to earth by some endearing tie;
He only, like the ocean-weed uptorn,
And loose along the world of waters borne,
Was cast companionless, from wave to wave,
On life's rough sea—and there was none to save.

The giant-king, who led the host of Cain,
Delighted in the minstrel and his vein;
No hand, no voice, like Javan's could control,
With soothing concords, his tempestuous soul.
With him the wandering Bard, who found no rest
Through ten years' exile, sought his native west;
There from the camp retiring, he pursued
His journey to the patriarchs' solitude.
This son of peace no martial armor wore,
A scrip for food, a staff in hand he bore;
Flaxen his robe; and o'er his shoulder hung,
Broad as a warrior's shield, his harp unstrung,
A shell of tortoise exquisitely wrought
With hieroglyphics of embodied thought,
Jubal himself enchased the polished frame;
And Javan won it in the strife for fame,
Among the sons of music when their sire
To his victorious skill adjudged the lyre.

'Twas noon, when Javan climbed the bordering hill,
By many an old remembrance hallowed still,
Whence he beheld, by sloping woods enclosed,
The hamlet where his parent's dust reposed,
His home of happiness in early years,
And still the home of all his hopes and fears,
When from ambition struggling to break free,
He mused on joys and sorrows yet to be.
Awhile he stood, with rumination pale,
Casting an eye of sadness o'er the vale.
When, suddenly abrupt, spontaneous prayer
Burst from his lips for one who sojourned there;
For one, whose cottage, far appearing, drew,
Even from his mother's grave, his transient view;
One, whose unconscious smiles were wont to dart
Ineffable emotion through his heart:
A nameless sympathy, more sweet, more dear
Than friendship, solaced him when she was near,
And well he guessed, while yet a timorous boy,
That Javan's artless songs were Zillah's joy.
But when ambition, with a fiercer flame
Than untold love, had fired his soul for fame,
This infant passion, cherished yet represt,
Lived in his pulse, but died within his breast;
For oft in distant lands, when hope beat high,
Westward he turned his eager glistening eye,
And gazed in spirit on her absent form,
Fair as the moon emerging through the storm,
Till sudden, strange bewildering horrors crossed
His thought, and every glimpse of joy was lost.
Even then, when melancholy numbed his brain,
And life itself stood still in every vein,
While his cold, quivering lips sent vows above,
—Never to curse her with his bitter love!
His heart, espoused with hers, in secret sware
To hold its truth unshaken by despair:
The vows dispersed that from those lips were borne,
But never, never was that heart forsworn;
Throughout the world, the charm of Zillah's name
Repelled the touch of every meaner flame.
Jealous and watchful of the sex's wiles,
He trembled at the light of woman's smiles!
So turns the mariner's mistrusting eye
From proud Orion bending through the sky,
Beauteous and terrible, who shides afar,
At once the brightest and most baneful star.*

Where Javan from that Eastern hill surveyed
The circling forest and embosomed glade,
Earth wore one summer robe of living green,
In heaven's blue arch the sun alone was seen;
Creation slumbered in the cloudless light,
And noon was silent as the depth of night.
O what a throng of rushing thoughts oppressed,
In that vast solitude, his anxious breast!
—To wither in the blossom of renown,
And unrecorded to the dust go down,
Or for a name on earth to quit the prize
Of immortality beyond the skies.
Perplexed his wavering choice: when conscience failed,
Love rose against the world, and love prevailed;
Passion, in aid of virtue, conquered pride,
And woman won the heart to heaven denied

CANTO SECOND.

Javan, descending through the Forest, arrives at the place where he had formerly parted with Zillah, when he withdrew from the Patriarchs' Glen.—There he again discovers her in a bower formed on the spot.—Their strange interview and abrupt separation.

Steep the descent, and wearisome the way;
The twisted boughs forbade the light of day;
No breath from heaven refreshed the sultry gloom,
The arching forest seemed one pillared tomb,
Upright and tall the trees of ages grow,
While all is loneliness and waste below;
There, as the massy foliage, far aloof
Displayed a dark impenetrable roof,
So, gnarled and rigid, clasped and interwound,
An uncouth maze of roots embossed the ground:
Midway beneath, the sylvan wild assumed
A milder aspect, shrubs and flowerets bloomed:
Openings of sky, and little spots of green,
And showers of sun-beams through the eaves were seen.

Awhile the traveller halted at the place,
Where last he caught a glimpse of Zillah's face,
One lonely eve, when in that calm retreat,
They met, as they were often wont to meet,
And parted, not as they were wont to part,
With gay regret, but heaviness of heart;
Though Javan named for his return the night,
When the new moon had rolled to full-orbed light.
She stood, and gazed through tears, that forced their way,
Oft as from steep to steep, with fond delay,
Lessening at every view, he turned his head,
Hailed her with weaker voice, then forward sped.
From that sad hour, she saw his face no more
In Eden's woods, or on Euphrates' shore:
Moons waxed and waned; to *her* no hope appeared,
Who much his death, but more his falsehood feared.

Now, while he paused, the lapse of years forgot,
Remembrance eyed her lingering near the spot.
Onward he hastened; all his bosom burned,
As if that eve of parting were returned;
And she, with silent tenderness of wo,
Clung to his heart, and would not let him go.
Sweet was the scene! apart the cedars stood,
A sunny islet opened in the wood;
With vernal teints the wild-brier thicket glows,
For here the desert flourished as the rose;
From sapling trees, with lucid foliage crowned,
Gay lights and shadows twinkled on the ground;
Up the tall stems luxuriant creepers run
To hang their silver blossoms in the sun;

* Cosi l'infausti rai
Spande Orione e i naviganti attrista,
Orion, chi tra gli astri in ciel risplende
Vie piu d'ogni altro, e piu d'ogni altro offende.
FILICAJA

Deep velvet verdure clad the turf beneath,
Where trodden flowers their richest odors breathe;
O'er all, the Bees, with murmuring music, flew
From bell to bell, to sip the treasured dew;
While insect myriads in the solar gleams,
Glanced to and fro, like intermingling beams;
So fresh, so pure, the woods, the sky, the air,
It seemed a place where angels might repair,
And tune their harps beneath those tranquil shades,
To morning songs, or moonlight serenades.

He paused again with memory's dream entranced;
Again his foot uncautiously advanced,
For now the laurel thicket caught his view,
Where he and Zillah wept their last adieu.
Some curious hand, since that bereaving hour,
Had twined the copse into a covert bower,
With many a light and fragrant shrub between,
Flowering aloft amidst perennial green,
As Javan searched this blossom-woven shade,
He spied the semblance of a sleeping maid;
'Tis she; 'tis Zillah, in her leafy shrine;
O'erwatched in slumber by a power divine,
In cool retirement from the heat of day,
Alone, unfearing, on the moss she lay,
Fair as the rainbow shines thro' darkening showers,
Pure as a wreath of snow on April flowers.

O Youth! in later times, whose gentle ear
This tale of ancient constancy shall hear;
If thou hast known the sweetness and the pain,
To love with secret hope, yet love in vain;
If months and years in pining silence worn,
Till doubt and fear might be no longer borne,
In evening shades thy faltering tongue confessed
The last dear wish that trembled in thy breast,
While at each pause the streamlet purled along,
And rival woodlands echoed song for song;
Recall the maiden's look;—the eye, the cheek,
The blush that spoke what language could not speak;
Recall her look, when at the altar's side
She sealed her promise, and became thy bride;
Such were to Javan Zillah's form and face,
The flower of meekness on a stem of grace;
O she was all that youth of beauty deems,
All that to love the loveliest object seems!

Moments there are, that, in their sudden flight,
Bring the slow mysteries of years to light;
Javan, in one transporting instant, knew,
That all he wished, and all he feared was true;
For while the harlot-world his soul possessed,
Love seemed a crime in his apostate breast;
How could he tempt her innocence to share
His poor ambition and his fixed despair!
But now the phantoms of a wandering brain,
And wounded spirit, crossed his thoughts in vain;
Past sins and follies, cares and woes forgot,
Peace, virtue, Zillah, seemed his present lot;
Where'er he looked around him or above,
All was the pledge of truth, the work of love,
At whose transforming hand, where last they stood,
Had sprung that lone memorial in the wood.

Thus on the slumbering maid while Javan gazed
With quicker swell her hidden bosom raised
The shadowy tresses, that profusely shed
Their golden wreaths from her reclining head;
A deeper crimson mantled o'er her cheek,
Her close lip quivered as in act to speak,
While broken sobs, and tremors of unrest,
The inward trouble of a dream expressed:
At length, amidst imperfect murmurs fell
The name of "Javan!" and a low "farewell!"
Tranquil again, her cheek resumed its hue,
And soft as infancy her breath she drew.

When Javan's ear those startling accents thrilled,
Wonder and ecstacy his bosom filled;
But quick compunction humbler feelings wrought,
He blushed to be a spy on Zillah's thought;
He turned aside; within the neighboring brake,
Resolved to tarry till the nymph awake.
There, as in luxury of thought reclined,
A calm of tenderness composed his mind;
His stringless harp upon the turf was thrown,
And on a pipe of most mellifluous tone,
Framed by himself, the musing minstrel played,
To charm the slumberer, cloistered in the shade.
Jubal had taught the lyre's responsive string,
Beneath the rapture of his touch to sing;
And bade the trumpet wake with bolder breath,
The joy of battle in the field of death;
But Javan first, whom pure affection fired,
With Love's clear eloquence the flute inspired;
At once obedient to the lip and hand,
It uttered every feeling at command.
Light o'er the stops his airy fingers flew,
A spirit spoke in every tone they drew;
'Twas now the sky-lark on the wings of morn,
Now the night-warbler leaning on her thorn;
Anon through every pulse the music stole,
And held sublime communion with the soul,
Wrung from the coyest breast the unprisoned sigh,
And kindled rapture in the coldest eye.

Thus on his dulcet pipe while Javan played,
Within her bower awoke the conscious maid;
She, in her dream, by varying fancies crost,
Had hailed her wanderer found, and mourned him lost:
In one wild vision, 'midst a land unknown,
By a dark river, as she sat alone,
Javan beyond the stream dejected stood;
He spied her soon and leapt into the flood;
The thwarting current urged him down its course,
But Love repelled it with victorious force;
She ran to help him landing, where at length
He struggled up the bank with failing strength;
She caught his hand;—when, downward from the day,
A water-monster dragged the youth away;
She followed headlong, but her garments bore
Her form, light-floating, till she saw no more:
For suddenly the dream's delusion changed,
And through a blooming wilderness she ranged:
Alone she seemed, but not alone she walked,
Javan, invisible, beside her talked.
He told, how he had journeyed many a year
With changing seasons in their swift career,
Danced with the breezes in the bowers of morn,
Slept in the valley where new moons are born,
Rode with the planets, on their golden cars,
Round the blue world inhabited by stars,
And, bathing in the sun's crystalline streams,
Became ethereal spirit in the beams,
Whence were his lineaments, from mortal sight,
Absorbed in pure transparency of light;
But now, his pilgrimage of glory past,
In Eden's vale he sought repose at last.
—The voice was mystery to Zillah's ear,
Not speech, nor song, yet full, melodious, clear;
No sounds of winds or waters, birds or bees,
Were e'er so exquisitely tuned to please.
Then while she sought him with desiring eyes,
The airy Javan darted from disguise,
Full on her view a stranger's visage broke;
She fled, she fell, he caught her,—she awoke.

Awoke from sleep,—but in her solitude
Found the enchantment of her dream renewed;
That living voice, so full, melodious, clear,
That voice of mystery warbled in her ear.
Yet words no longer wing the trembling notes,
Unearthly, inexpressive music floats,
In liquid tones so voluble and wild,
Her senses seem by slumber still beguiled:
Alarmed she started from her lonely den,
But, blushing, instantly retired again:
The viewless phantom came in sound so near,
The stranger of her dream might next appear.
Javan, concealed behind the verdant brake,
Felt his lip fail, and strength his hand forsake;
Then dropped his flute, and while he lay at rest
Heard every pulse that travelled through his breast.
Zillah, who deemed the strange illusion fled,
Now from the laurel-arbor showed her head,
Her eye quick-glancing round, as if in thought,

Recoiling from the object that she sought:
By slow degrees, to Javan in the shade,
The emerging nymph her perfect shape displayed.
Time had but touched her form to finer grace,
Years had but shed their favors on her face,
While secret Love, and unrewarded Truth,
Like cold clear dew upon the rose of youth,
Gave to the springing flower a chastened bloom,
And shut from rifling winds its coy perfume.

Words can not paint the wonder of her look,
When once again his pipe the minstrel took,
And soft in under-tones began to play,
Like the caged woodlark's low lamenting lay;
Then loud and shrill, by stronger breath impelled,
To higher strains the undaunted music swelled,
Till new born echoes through the forest rang,
And birds, at noon, in broken slumbers sang.
Bewildering transport, infantine surprise,
Throbbed in her bosom, sparkled in her eyes,
O'er every feature, every feeling shone,
Her color changed as Javan changed his tone;
While she between the bower and brake entranced,
Alternately retreated or advanced;
Sometimes the lessening cadence seemed to fly
Then the full melody came rolling nigh;
She shrunk, or followed still, with eye and feet,
Afraid to lose it, more afraid to meet;
For yet through Eden's land, by fame alone,
Jubal's harmonious minstrelsey was known,
Though nobler songs than cheered the Patriarchs' glen
Never resounded from the lips of men.

Silence, at length, the listening maiden broke;
The heart of Javan checked him while she spoke;
Though sweeter than his pipe her accents stole,
He durst not learn the tumult of her soul,
But, closely cowering in his ambuscade,
With sprightlier breath and nimbler finger played
—"'Tis not the nightingale that sang so well,
When Javan left me near this lonely cell;
'Tis not indeed the nightingale;—her voice
Could never since that hour my soul rejoice:
Some bird from Paradise hath lost her way,
And carols here a long forbidden lay;
For ne'er since Eve's transgression, mortal ear
Was privileged such heavenly sounds to hear;
Perhaps an Angel, while he rests his wings,
On earth alighting, here his descant sings;
Methinks those tones, so full of joy and love,
Must be the language of the world above!
Within this brake he rests:" with curious ken,
As if she feared to stir a lion's den,
Breathless, on tiptoe, round the copse she crept;
Her heart beat quicker, louder, as she stepped,
Till Javan rose, and fixed on her his eyes,
In dumb embarrassment, and feigned surprise;
Upright she started, at the sudden view,
Back from her brow the scattered ringlets flew,
Paleness a moment overspread her face;
But fear to frank astonishment gave place,
And, with the virgin blush of innocence,
She asked—"Who art thou, Stranger, and from whence?"

With mild demeanor, and with downcast eye,
Javan, advancing, humbly made reply;
—"A wretch, escaping from the tribes of men,
Seeks an asylum in the Patriarchs' glen;
As through the forest's breathless gloom I strayed,
Up sprang the breeze in this delicious shade;
Then, while I sate beneath the rustling tree,
I waked this pipe to wildest minstrelsey,
Child of my fancy, framed with Jubal's art,
To breathe at will the fulness of my heart;
Fairest of women! if the clamor rude
Hath scared the quiet of the solitude,
Forgive the innocent offence, and tell,
How far beyond these woods the righteous dwell."—

Though changed his voice, his look and stature changed,
In air and garb, in all but love estranged,
Still in the youthful exile Zillah sought
A dear lost friend, for ever near her thought!
Yet answered coldly,—jealous and afraid
Her heart might be mistaken, or betrayed.
—"Not far from hence the faithful race reside;
Pilgrim! to whom shall I thy footsteps guide?
Alike to all, if thou an alien be,
My father's home invites thee: follow me."

She spoke with such a thought divining look,
Color his lip, and power his tongue forsook;
At length, in hesitating tone, and low,
—"Enoch," said he, "the friend of God, I know.
To him I bear a message full of fear;
I may not rest till he vouchsafe to hear."

He paused; his cheek with red confusion burned;
Kindness through her relenting breast returned:
—"Behold the path," she cried, and led the way;
Ere long the vale unbosomed to the day:
—"Yonder, where two embracing oaks are seen,
Arched o'er a cottage roof, that peeps between,
Dwells Enoch; Stranger! peace attend thee there,
My father's sheep demand his daughter's care."

Javan was so rebuked beneath her eye,
She vanished ere he faltered a reply
And sped, while he in cold amazement stood,
Along the winding border of the wood;
Now lost, now reappearing, as the glade
Shone to the sun, or darkened in the shade.
He saw, but might not follow, where her flock
Were wont to rest at noon, beneath a rock.
He knew the willowy champaign, and the stream,
Of many an early lay the simple theme,
Chanted in boyhood's unsuspecting hours,
When Zillah joined the song, or praised his powers.
Thither he watched her, while her course she bore,
Nor ceased to gaze, when she was seen no more.

CANTO THIRD.

Javan's Soliloquy on Zillah's desertion of him.—He reaches the ruins of his Mother's Cottage.—Thence he proceeds to Enoch's dwelling.—His reception there.—Enoch and Javan proceed together toward the place of Sacrifice.—Description of the Patriarchs' Glen.—Occasion of the family of Seth retiring thither at first.

"Am I so changed by suffering, so forgot,
That Love disowns me, Zillah knows me not?
Ah! no; she shrinks from my disastrous fate,
She dare not love me, and she can not hate:
'Tis just; I merit this:—When Nature's womb
Engulphed my kindred in one common tomb,
Why was I spared?—A reprobate by birth,
To heaven rebellious, unallied on earth,
Whither, O whither shall the outcast flee?
There is no home, no peace, no hope for me.
I hate the worldling's vanity and noise,
I have no fellow-feeling in his joys;
The saint's serener bliss I can not share,
My soul, alas! hath no communion there.
This is the portion of my cup below,
Silent, unmingled, solitary wo;
To bear from clime to clime, the curse of Cain,
Sin with remorse, yet find repentance vain;
And cling, in blank despair, from breath to breath
To naught in life, except the fear of death."—

While Javan gave his bitter passion vent,
And wandered on unheeded where he went,
His feet, instinctive, led him to the spot,
Where rose the ruins of his childhood's cot:
Here, as he halted in abrupt surprise,
His mother seemed to vanish from his eyes,
As if her gentle form, unmarked before,
Had stood to greet him at the wonted door.
Yet did the pale retiring spirit dart
A look of tenderness that broke his heart:
'Twas but a thought, arrested on its flight,
And bodied forth, with visionary light.
But chill the lifeblood ran through every vein,
The fire of phrensy faded from his brain,
He cast himself in terror on the ground:
—Slowly recovering strength, he gazed around,

In wistful silence, eyed those walls decayed,
Between whose chinks the lively lizzard played;
The moss clad timbers, loose and lapsed awry,
Threatening ere long in wider wreck to lie;
The fractured roof, through which the sun-beams shone,
With rank, unflowering verdure overgrown;
The prostrate fragments of the wicker door,
And reptile traces on the damp green floor.
This mournful spectacle while Javan viewed,
Life's earliest scenes and trials were renewed?
O'er his dark mind, the light of years gone by
Gleamed like the meteors of a northern sky.
He moved his lips, but strove in vain to speak,
A few slow tears strayed down his cold wan cheek,
Till from his breast a sigh convulsive sprung,
And "O my Mother!" trembled from his tongue.
That name, though but a murmur, that dear name
Touched every kind affection into flame;
Despondency assumed a milder form,
A ray of comfort darted through the storm;
"O God! be merciful to me!" he said,
Arose, and straight to Enoch's dwelling sped.

Enoch, who sate, to taste the freshening breeze,
Beneath the shadow of his cottage trees,
Beheld the youth approaching; and his eye,
Instructed by the light of prophecy,
Knew from afar, beneath the stranger's air,
The orphan object of his tenderest care;
Forth, with a father's joy, the holy man
To meet the poor returning pilgrim ran,
Fell on his neck, and kissed him, wept and cried,
"My son! my son!"—but Javan shrunk aside;
The patriarch raised, embraced him, oft withdrew
His head to gaze, then wept and clasped anew.
The mourner bowed with agony of shame
Clung round his knees, and called upon his name.
—"Father! behold a supplicant in me,
A sinner in the sight of Heaven and thee;
Yet for thy former love, may Javan live;
O, for the mother's sake, the son forgive!—
The meanest office and the lowest seat,
In Enoch's house be mine, at Enoch's feet."

"Come to my home, my bosom, and my rest,
Not as a stranger, and wayfaring guest;
My bread of peace, my cup of blessings share,
Child of my faith! and answer to my prayer!
O I have wept through many a night for thee,
And watched through many a day, *this* day to see.
Crowned is the hope of my desiring heart,
I am resigned, and ready to depart:
With joy I hail my course of nature run,
Since I have seen thy face, my son! my son!"

So saying, Enoch led to his abode
The trembling penitent along the road
That through the garden's gay enclosure wound;
'Midst fruits and flowers the patriarch's spouse they found,
Plucking the purple clusters from the vine,
To crown the cup of unfermented wine.
She came to meet them;—but in strange surmise
Stopped, and on Javan fixed her earnest eyes;
He kneeled to greet her hand with wonted grace
Ah! then she knew him!—as he bowed his face,
His mother's features in a glimpse she caught,
And the son's image rushed upon her thought;
Pale she recoiled with momentary fright,
As if a spirit had risen before her sight;
Returning, with a heart too full to speak
She poured a flood of tears upon his cheek,
Then laughed for gladness—but her laugh was wild;
—"Where hast thou been, my own, my orphan child?
Child of my soul! bequeathed in death to me,
By her who had no other wealth than thee!"
She cried, and with a mother's love caressed
The youth who wept in silence on her breast.

This hasty tumult of affection o'er,
They passed within the hospitable door;
There on a grassy couch, with joy o'ercome,
Pensive with awe, with veneration dumb.
Javan reclined, while kneeling at his seat,
The humble patriarch washed the traveller's feet.
Quickly the spouse her plenteous table spread
With homely viands, milk and fruits and bread.
Ere long the guest grown innocently bold,
With simple eloquence his story told;
His sins, his follies, frankly were revealed,
And nothing but his nameless love concealed.
—"While thus," he cried, "I proved the world a snare,
Pleasure a serpent, fame a cloud in air;
While with the sons of men my footsteps trod,
My home, my heart was with the sons of God."

"Went not my spirit with thee," Enoch said,
"When from the mother's grave the orphan fled?
Others believed thee slain by beasts of blood,
Or self-devoted to the strangling flood,
(Too plainly in thy grief-bewildered mien,
By every eye, a breaking heart was seen;)
I mourned in secret thine apostacy,
Nor ceased to intercede, with Heaven for thee.
Strong was my faith, in dreams or waking thought,
Oft as thine image o'er my mind was brought,
I deemed thee living by this conscious sign,
The deep communion of my soul with thine.
This day a voice, that thrilled my breast with fear,
(Methought 'twas Adam's) whispered in mine ear,
—'Enoch! ere thrice the morning meet the sun,
Thy joy shall be fulfilled, thy rest begun.'—
While yet those tones were murmuring in air,
I turned to look,—but saw no speaker there:
Thought I not then of thee, my long-lost joy?
Leaped not my heart abroad to meet my boy?
Yes! and while still I sate beneath the tree,
Resolving what the signal meant to me,
I spied thee coming, and with eager feet
Ran, the returning fugitive to greet:
Nor less the welcome art thou, since I know
By this high warning, that from earth I go;
My days are numbered; peace on thine attend!
The trial comes—be faithful to the end."

"O live the years of Adam!" cried the youth;
"Yet seem thy words to breathe prophetic truth:
Sire! while I roamed the world, a transient guest,
From sunrise to the ocean of the west,
I found that sin, where'er the foot of man
Nature's primeval wilderness o'er ran,
Had tracked his steps, and through advancing time
Urged the deluded race from crime to crime,
Till wrath and strife in fratricidal war,
Gathered the force of nations from afar,
To deal and suffer death's unheeded blow,
As if the curse on Adam were too slow.
Even now a host, like locusts on their way,
That desolate the earth and dim the day,
Led by a giant-king, whose arm hath broke
Remotest realms to wear his iron yoke,
Hover o'er Eden, resolute to close
His final triumph o'er his latest foes;
A feeble band, that in their covert lie,
Like cowering doves beneath his falcon's eye.
That easy and ignoble conquest won,
There yet remains one fouler deed undone.
Oft have I heard the tyrant, in his ire,
Devote this glen to massacre and fire,
And swear to root, from earth's dishonored face,
The last least relic of the faithful race;
Thenceforth he hopes, on God's terrestrial throne
To rule the nether universe alone.
Wherefore, O sire! when evening shuts the sky,
Fly with thy kindred, from destruction fly:
Far to the south, unpeopled wilds of wood
Skirt the dark borders of Euphrates' flood;
There shall the patriarchs find secure repose,
Till Eden rest, forsaken of her foes."

At Javan's speech the matron's cheek grew pale,
Her courage, not her faith, began to fail;
Eve's youngest daughter she; the silent tear
Witnessed her patience, but betrayed her fear.
Then answered Enoch, with a smile serene,
That shed celestial beauty o'er his mien:

Here is mine earthly habitation; here
I wait till my Redeemer shall appear;
Death and the face of man I dare not shun,
God is my refuge, and his will be done."

The matron checked her unbecoming sigh,
And wiped the drop that trembled in her eye.

Javan, with shame and self-abasement blushed,
But every care at Enoch's smile was hushed:
He felt the power of truth; his heart o'erflowed,
And in his look sublime devotion glowed.
Westward the patriarch turned his tranquil face;
"The Sun," said he, "hath well nigh run his race;
I to the yearly sacrifice repair,
Our brethren meet me at the place of prayer."

"I follow; O my father! I am thine
Thy God, thy people, and thine altar mine!"
Exclaimed the youth, on highest thoughts intent,
And forth with Enoch through the valley went.

Deep was that valley, girt with rock and wood;
In rural groups the scattered hamlet stood;
Tents, arbors, cottages, adorned the scene,
Gardens and fields, and shepherds' walks between;
Through all, a streamlet, from its mountain-source,
Seen but by stealth, pursued its willowy course.

When first the mingling sons of God and man
The demon sacrifice of war began,
Self-exiled here, the family of Seth
Renounced a world of violence and death
Faithful alone amidst the faithless found,*
And innocent while murder cursed the ground.
Here, in retirement from profane mankind,
They worshipped God with purity of mind,
Fed their small flocks, and tilled their narrow soil,
Like parent Adam, with submissive toil,
–Adam whose eyes their pious hands had closed,
Whose bones beneath their quiet turf reposed.
No glen like this unstained with human blood,
Could youthful nature boast before the flood;
Far less shall earth, now hastening to decay,
A scene of sweeter loneliness display,
Where naught was heard but sounds of peace and love,
Nor seen but woods around, and heaven above.

Yet not in cold and unconcerned content,
Their years in that delicious range were spent;
Oft from their haunts the fervent patriarchs broke,
In strong affection to their kindred spoke,
With tears and prayers reproved their growing crimes,
Or told the impending judgments of the times.
In vain; the world despised the warning word,
With scorn belied it, or with mockery heard,
Forbade the zealous monitors to roam,
And stoned, or chased them to their forest home.
There, from the depth of solitude, their sighs
Pleaded with Heaven in ceaseless sacrifice,
And long did righteous Heaven the guilty spare,
Won by the holy violence of prayer.

Yet sharper pangs of unavailing wo
Those sires in secrecy were doomed to know;
Oft by the world's alluring snares misled,
Their youth from that sequestered valley fled,
Joined the wild herd, increased the godless crew,
And left the virtuous remnant weak and few.

CANTO FOURTH.

Enoch relates to Javan the Circumstances of the Death of Adam, including his appointment of an annual Sacrifice, on the Day of his Transgression and Fall in Paradise.

Thus through the valley while they held their walk,
Enoch of former days began to talk.

* "So spake the Seraph Abdiel, faithful found
Among the faithless, faithful only he."
PARADISE LOST, Book V.

—"Thou knowest our place of sacrifice and prayer,
Javan! for thou wert wont to worship there:
Built by our father's venerable hands,
On the same spot our ancient altar stands,
Where, driven from Eden's hallowed groves, he found
A home on earth's unconsecrated ground;
Whence too, his pilgrimage of trial o'er,
He reached the rest which sin can break no more.
Oft hast thou heard our elder patriarchs tell
How Adam once by disobedience fell;
Would that my tongue were gifted to display
The terror and the glory of that day,
When seized and stricken by the hand of Death,
The first transgressor yielded up his breath!
Nigh threescore years with interchanging light,
The host of heaven have measured day and night.
Since we beheld the ground from which he rose,
On his returning dust in silence close.

"With him his noblest sons might not compare,
In godlike feature and majestic air;
Not out of weakness rose his gradual frame,
Perfect from his Creator's hand he came;
And as in form excelling, so in mind
The Sire of man transcended all mankind:
A soul was in his eye, and in his speech
A dialect of heaven no art could reach;
For oft of old to him, the evening breeze
Had born the voice of God among the trees;
Angels were wont their songs with his to blend,
And talk with him as their familiar friend.
But deep remorse for that mysterious crime,
Whose dire contagion through elapsing time,
Diffused the curse of death beyond control,
Had wrought such self abasement in his soul,
That he, whose honors were approached by none,
Was yet the meekest man beneath the sun.
From sin, as from the serpent that betrayed
Eve's early innocence, he shrunk afraid;
Vice he rebuked with so austere a frown,
He seemed to bring an instant judgment down;
Yet while he chid, compunctious tears would start,
And yearning tenderness dissolve his heart;
The guilt of all his race became his own,
He suffered as if *he* had sinned alone.
Within our glen to filial love endeared,
Abroad for wisdom, truth and justice feared,
He walked so humbly in the sight of all,
The vilest ne'er reproached him with his fall.
Children were his delight;—they ran to meet
His soothing hand, and clasp his honored feet;
While 'midst their fearless sports supremely blest,
He grew in heart a child among the rest:
Yet as a Parent, naught beneath the sky
Touched him so quickly as an infant's eye;
Joy from its smile of happiness he caught,
Its flash of rage sent horror through his thought,
His smitten conscience felt as fierce a pain,
As if he fell from innocence again.

"One morn I tracked him on his lonely way,
Pale as the gleam of slow-awakening day;
With feeble step he climbed von craggy height,
Thence fixed on distant Paradise his sight;
He gazed awhile in silent thought profound,
Then falling prostrate on the dewy ground,
He poured his spirit in a flood of prayer,
Bewailed his ancient crime with self-despair,
And claimed the pledge of reconciling grace,
The promised Seed, the Savior of his race.
Wrestling with God, as Nature's vigor failed,
His faith grew stronger and his plea prevailed;
The prayer from agony to rapture rose,
And sweet as angel accents fell the close,
I stood to greet him; when he raised his head,
Divine expression o'er his visage spread,
His presence was so saintly to behold,
He seemed in sinless Paradise grown old.

"—'This day,' said he, 'in Time's star-lighted round,
Renews the anguish of that mortal wound
On me inflicted, when the serpent's tongue
My spouse with his beguiling falsehood stung.

Though years of grace through centuries have passed,
Since my transgression, this may be my last;
Infirmities without, and fears within,
Foretell the consummating stroke of sin;
The hour, the place, the form to me unknown,
But God, who lent me life, *will* claim his own:
Then, lest I sink as suddenly in death,
As quickened into being by his breath,
Once more I climbed these rocks with weary pace,
And but once more, to view my native place,
To bid yon garden of delight farewell,
The earthly Paradise from which I fell.
This mantle, Enoch! which I yearly wear
To mark the day of penitence and prayer,
These skins, the covering of my first offence,
When conscious of departed innocence,
Naked and trembling from my Judge I fled,
A hand of mercy o'er my vileness spread;—
Enoch! this mantle thus vouchsafed to me,
At my dismission I bequeath to thee;
Wear it in sad memorial on this day,
And yearly at mine earliest altar slay
A lamb immaculate, whose blood be spilt
In sign of wrath removed and cancelled guilt;
So be the sins of all my race confest,
So on their heads may peace and pardon rest.'
—Thus spake our Sire, and down the steep descent
With strengthened heart, and fearless footstep went:
O Javan! when we parted at his door,
I loved him as I never loved before.

"Ere noon, returning to his bower, I found
Our father laboring in his harvest ground,
(For yet he tilled a little plot of soil,
Patient and pleased with voluntary toil);
But O how changed from him, whose morning eye
Outshone the star, that told the sun was nigh!
Loose in his feeble grasp the sickle shook;
I marked the ghastly dolour of his look,
And ran to help him; but his latest strength
Failed;—prone upon his sheaves he fell at length:
I strove to raise him; sight and sense were fled,
Nerveless his limbs, and backward swayed his head.
Seth passed; I called him, and we bore our Sire
To neighboring shades from noon's afflictive fire:
Ere long he 'woke to feeling, with a sigh,
And half unclosed his hesitating eye;
Strangely and timidly he peered around,
Like men in dreams whom sudden lights confound:
—'Is this a new Creation?—Have I passed
The bitterness of death?'—He looked aghast
Then sorrowful;—No: men and trees appear;
'Tis not a new Creation,—pain is here:
From Sin's dominion is there no release?
Lord! let thy servant *now* depart in peace.'
—Hurried remembrance crowding o'er his soul,
He knew us; tears of consternation stole
Down his pale cheeks:—'Seth!—Enoch! Where is Eve?
How could the spouse her dying consort leave?'

"Eve looked that moment from their cottage-door
In quest of Adam, where he toiled before;
He was not there; she called him by his name;
Sweet to his ear the well-known accents came;
—'Here am I,' answered he in tone so weak,
That we who held him scarcely heard him speak;
But, resolutely bent to rise, in vain
He struggled till he swooned away with pain.
Eve called again, and turning tow'rd the shade,
Helpless as infancy, beheld him laid.

"She sprang, as smitten with a mortal wound,
Forward, and cast herself upon the ground
At Adam's feet; half-rising in despair,
Him from our arms she wildly strove to tear;
Repelled by gentle violence, she pressed
His powerless hand to her convulsive breast,
And kneeling, bending o'er him, full of fears,
Warm on his bosom showered her silent tears,
Light to his eyes at that refreshment came,
They opened on her in a transient flame;
—'And art thou here my Life! my Love!' he cried,
'Faithful in death to this congenial side?
Thus let me bind thee to my breaking heart,
One dear, one bitter moment, ere we part.
—'Leave me not, Adam! leave me not below;
With thee I tarry, or with thee I go.'
She said, and yielding to his faint embrace,
Clung round his neck, and wept upon his face.
Alarming recollection soon returned,
His fevered frame with growing anguish burned:
Ah! then, as nature's tenderest impulse wrought,
With fond solicitude of love she sought
To sooth his limbs upon their grassy bed,
And make the pillow easy to his head;
She wiped his reeking temples with her hair;
She shook the leaves to stir the sleeping air;
Moistened his lips with kisses: with her breath
Vainly essayed to quell the fire of death,
That ran and revelled through his swollen veins
With quicker pulses, and severer pains.

"The sun, in summer majesty on high,
Darted his fierce effulgence down the sky;
Yet dimmed and blunted were the dazzling rays,
His orb expanded through a dreary haze,
And, circled with a red portentous zone,
He looked in sickly horror from his throne;
The vital air was still; the torrid heat
Oppressed our hearts, that labored hard to beat.
When higher noon had shrunk the lessening shade,
Thence to his home our father we conveyed,
And stretched him, pillowed with his latest sheaves,
On a fresh couch of green and fragrant leaves.
Here, though his sufferings through the glen were known
We chose to watch his dying bed alone,
Eve, Seth, and I.——In vain he sighed for rest,
And oft his meek complainings thus expressed:
—'Blow on me, Wind! I faint with heat! O bring
Delicious water from the deepest spring;
Your sunless shadow o'er my limbs diffuse,
Ye cedars! wash me cold with midnight dews.
—Cheer me, my friends! with looks of kindness cheer:
Whisper a word of comfort in mine ear;
Those sorrowing faces fill my soul with gloom;
This silence is the silence of the tomb.
Thither I hasten; help me on my way;
O sing to sooth me, and to strengthen, pray!'
We sang to sooth him—hopeless was the song;
We prayed to strengthen him—he grew not strong.
In vain from every herb, and fruit, and flower,
Of cordial sweetness, or of healing power,
We pressed the virtue; no terrestrial balm
Nature's dissolving agony could calm.
Thus as the day declined, the fell disease
Eclipsed the light of life by slow degrees:
Yet while his pangs grew sharper, more resigned,
More self-collected, grew the sufferer's mind;
Patient of heart, though racked at every pore,
The righteous penalty of sin he bore;
Not his the fortitude that mocks at pains,
But that which feels them most, and yet sustains.
—''Tis just, 'tis merciful,' we heard him say;
'Yet wherefore hath he turned his face away?
I see him not; I hear him not; I call;
My God! my God! support me, or I fall.'

"The sun went down, amid an angry glare
Of flushing clouds, that crimsoned all the air;
The winds brake loose; the forest boughs were torn,
And dark aloof the eddying foliage borne;
Cattle to shelter scudded in affright;
The florid evening vanished into night:
Then burst the hurricane upon the vale,
In peals of thunder, and thick-volleyed hail;
Prone rushing rain with torrents whelmed the land,
Our cot amid a river seemed to stand;
Around its base, the foamy-crested streams
Flashed through the darkness to the lightning's gleams,
With monstrous throes an earthquake heaved the ground
The rocks were rent, the mountains trembled round;
Never since nature into being came,
Had such mysterious motion shook her frame,

We thought, engulfed in floods, or wrapt in fire,
The world itself would perish with our sire.

"Amid this war of elements, within
More dreadful grew the sacrifice of sin,
Whose victim on his bed of torture lay,
Breathing the slow remains of life away.
Erewhile, victorious faith sublimer rose
Beneath the pressure of collected woes:
But now his spirit wavered, went and came,
Like the loose vapor of departing flame,
Till at the point, when comfort seemed to die
For ever in his fixed unclosing eye,
Bright through the smouldering ashes of the man,
The saint brake forth, and Adam thus began:—

"'O ye, that shudder at this awful strife,
This wrestling agony of death and life,
Think not that He, on whom my soul is cast,
Will leave me thus forsaken to the last;
Nature's infirmity alone you see;
My chains are breaking, I shall soon be free;
Though firm in God the spirit holds her trust,
The flesh is frail, and trembles into dust.
Horror and anguish seize me; 'tis the hour
Of darkness, and I mourn beneath its power;
The tempter plies me with his direst art,
I feel the serpent coiling round my heart;
He stirs the wound he once inflicted there,
Instils the deadening poison of despair,
Belies the truth of God's delaying grace,
And bids me curse my Maker to his face.
—I will not curse him though his grace delay;
I will not cease to trust him, though he slay;
Full on his promised mercy I rely,
For God hath spoken—God, who can not lie.
—Thou, of my faith the author and the end!
Mine early, late, and everlasting friend!
The joy, that once thy presence gave, restore
Ere I am summoned hence, and seen no more:
Down to the dust returns this earthly frame,
Receive my spirit, Lord! from whom it came;
Rebuke the tempter, show thy power to save,
O let thy glory light me to the grave,
That these, who witness my departing breath,
May learn to triumph in the grasp of death.'

"He closed his eyelids with a tranquil smile,
And seemed to rest in silent prayer awhile:
Around his couch with filial awe we kneeled,
When suddenly a light from heaven revealed
A spirit, that stood within the unopened door;
The sword of God in his right hand he bore;
His countenance was lightning, and his vest
Like snow at sunrise on the mountain's crest,
Yet so benignly beautiful his form,
His presence stilled the fury of the storm;
At once the winds retire, the waters cease;
His look was love, his salutation 'Peace!'

"Our mother first beheld him, sore amazed,
But terror grew to transport, while she gazed:
—''Tis he, the Prince of Seraphim, who drove
Our banished feet from Eden's happy grove;*
Adam, my life, my spouse, awake!' she cried!
'Return to Paradise; behold thy guide;
O let me follow in this dear embrace!'
She sunk, and on his bosom hid her face.
Adam looked up, his visage changed its hue,
Transformed into an angel's at to view:
'I come!' he cried, with faith's full triumph fired,
And in a sigh of ecstacy expired.
The light was vanished, and the vision fled;
We stood alone, the living with the dead;
The ruddy embers, glimmering round the room,
Displayed the corse amid the solemn gloom;
But o'er the scene a holy calm reposed,
The gate of heaven had opened there, and closed.

"Eve's faithful arm still clasped her lifeless spouse:
Gently I shook it, from her trance to rouse;

* Paradise Lost, Book XI. v. 238.

She gave no answer; motionless and cold,
It fell like clay from my relaxing hold;
Alarmed, I lifted up the locks of gray
That hid her cheek; her soul had passed away;
A beauteous corse she graced her partner's side,
Love bound their lives, and death could not divide.

"Trembling astonishment of grief we felt,
Till nature's sympathies began to melt;
We wept in stillness through the long dark night:
—And O, how welcome was the morning light!"

CANTO FIFTH.

The burying-place of the patriarchs.—The sacrifice on the anniversary of the fall of Adam.—Enoch's prophecy.

"And here," said Enoch, with dejected eye,
"Behold the grave, in which our parents lie."
They stopped, and o'er the turf-enclosure wept,
Where, side by side, the first-created slept:
It seemed as if a voice, with still small sound,
Heard in their bosoms, issued from that mound:—
"From earth we came, and we returned to earth;
Descendants! spare the dust that gave you birth;
Though death, the pain for our transgression due,
By sad inheritance we left to you,
O let our children bless us in our grave,
And man forgive the wrong that God forgave!"

Thence to the altar Enoch turned his face,
But Javan lingered in that burying-place,
A scene sequestered from the haunts of men,
The loveliest nook of all that lovely glen,
Where weary pilgrims found their last repose:
The little heaps were ranged in comely rows,
With walks between, by friends and kindred trod.
Who dressed with duteous hands each hallowed so[illegible]:
No sculptured monument was taught to breathe
His praises, whom the worm devoured beneath;
The high, the low, the mighty, and the fair,
Equal in death, were undistinguished there;
Yet not a hillock mouldered near that spot,
By one dishonored or by all forgot;
To some warm heart the poorest dust was dear,
From some kind eye the meanest claimed a tear.
And oft the living by affection led,
Were wont to walk in spirit with their dead,
Where no dark cypress cast a doleful gloom,
No blighting yew shed poison o'er the tomb,
But, white and red with intermingling flowers,
The graves looked beautiful in sun and showers.
Green myrtles fenced it, and beyond their bound,
Ran the clear rill with ever-murmuring sound;
'Twas not a scene for grief to nourish care,
It breathed of hope, and moved the heart to prayer.

Why lingered Javan in that lone retreat?
The shrine of her that bare him drew his feet;
Trembling he sought it, fearing to behold
A bed of thistles, or unsightly mould;
But lo! the turf, which his own hands had piled,
With choicest flowers, and richest verdure smiled;
By all the glen, his mother's couch of rest,
In his default was visited and blest.
He kneeled, he kissed it, full of love and wo;
His heart was where his treasure lay, below;
And long he tarried, ere, with heavenward eyes,
He rose and hastened to the sacrifice.

Already on a neighboring mount, that stood
Apart amid the valley, girt with wood,
Whose open summit, rising o'er the trees,
Caught the cool fragrance of the evening-breeze,
The patriarchal worshippers were met;
The lamb was brought, the wood in order set
On Adam's rustic altar, moss-o'ergrown,
An unwrought mass of earth-embedded stone,
Long known and hallowed, where, for man's offence,
The earth first drank the blood of innocence,
When God himself ordained the typic rite
To Eden's exiles, resting on their flight,

Foremost, amid the group, was Enoch seen,
Known by his humble port and heavenly mien;
On him the priest's mysterious office lay,
For 'twas the eve of man's transgression-day.
And him had Adam, with expiring breath,
Ordained to offer yearly, from his death,
A victim on that mountain, whence the skies
Had first inhaled the fumes of sacrifice.
In Adam's coat of skins arrayed he stands,
Spreading to heaven his supplicating hands,
Ere from his robe the deadly steel he drew
To smite the victim sporting in his view
Behind him Seth, in majesty confest,
The world's great elder, towered above the rest.
Serenely shone his sweet and solemn eye,
Like the sun reigning in the western sky;
Though nine slow centuries by stealth had shed
Gray hairs, the crown of glory, on his head,
In hardy health he reared his front sublime,
Like the green aloe in perennial prime,
When full of years it shoots forth all its bloom,
And glads the forest through the inmost gloom;
So, in the blossom of a good old age,
Flourished amid his sons that peerless sage.

Around him, in august succession, stood
The fathers of the world before the flood:—
Enos; who taught mankind, on solemn days,
In sacred groves, to meet for prayer and praise,
And warned idolaters to lift their eye,
From sun and stars, to Him who made the sky:—
Canaan and Malaliel; of whom alone,
Their age, of all that once they were, is known:—
Jared; who full of hope beyond the tomb,
Hallowed his offspring from the mother's womb,*
And heaven received *the son* that parent gave,
He walked with God, and overstept the grave,
—A mighty pilgrim in the vale of tears,
Born to the troubles of a thousand years,
Methuselah, whose feet unhalting ran
To the last circle of the life of man:—
Lamech; from infancy inured to toil,
To wring slow blessings from the accursed soil,
Ere yet to dress his vineyards, reap his corn,
And comfort him in care, was Noah born,†
Who in a later age, by signal grace,
Survived to renovate the human race;
Both worlds, by sad reversion, were his due,
The orphan of the old, the father of the new.

These, with their families, on either hand,
Aliens and exiles in their native land,
The few, who loved their Maker from their youth,
And worshipped God in spirit and in truth;
These stood with Enoch: All had fixed their eyes
On him, and on the lamb of sacrifice.
For now with trembling hand he shed the blood,
And placed the slaughtered victim on the wood;
Then kneeling, as the sun went down, he laid
His hand upon the hallowed pyre and prayed.
"Maker of heaven and earth! supreme o'er all
That live, and move, and breathe, on thee we call;
Our father sinned and suffered; we, who bear
Our father's image, his transgression share;
Humbled for his offences and our own,
Thou, who art holy, wise, and just alone,
Accept, with free confession of our guilt,
This victim slain, this blood devoutly spilt,
While through the veil of sacrifice we see
Thy mercy smiling, and look up to thee;
O grant forgiveness; power and grace are thine;
God of salvation! cause thy face to shine;
Hear us in heaven! fulfil our soul's desire,
God of our father! answer now with fire."

He rose; no light from heaven around him shone,
No fire descended from the eternal throne;
Cold on the pile the offered victim lay,
Amid the stillness of expiring day;
The eyes of all, that watched in vain to view
The wonted sign, distractedly withdrew,
Fear clipt their breath, their doubling pulses raised,
And each by stealth upon his neighbor gazed;
From heart to heart a strange contagion ran,
A shuddering instinct crowded man to man;
Even Seth with secret consternation shook,
And cast on Enoch an imploring look,
Enoch, in whose sublime, unearthly mien,
No change of hue, no cloud of care was seen,
Full on the mute assembly turned his face,
Clear as the sun prepared to run his race;
He spoke; his words, with awful warning fraught,
Rallied and fixed the scattered powers of thought.
"Men, brethren, fathers! wherefore do ye fear!
Hath God departed from us? God is here;
Present in every heart, with sovereign power,
He tries, he proves his people in this hour;
Naked as light to his all-searching eye,
The thoughts that wrong, the doubts that tempt him lie
Yet slow to anger, merciful as just,
He knows our frame, remembers we are dust,
And spares our weakness: in his truth believe,
Hope against hope, and ask till ye receive.
What, though no flame on Adam's altar burn,
No signal of acceptance yet return,
God is not man, who to our father sware,
All times, in every place, to answer prayer;
He can not change; though heaven and earth decay,
The word of God shall never pass away.

"But mark the season: from the rising sun,
Westward, the race of Cain the world o'errun;
Their monarch, mightiest of the sons of men,
Hath sworn destruction to the Patriarch's Glen;
Hither he hastens; carnage strews his path:
Who will await the giant in his wrath?
Or who will take the wings of silent night,
And seek deliverance from his sword by flight?
Thus saith the Lord: Ye weak of faith and heart!
Who dare not trust the living God, depart;
The angel of his presence leads your way,
Your lives are safe, and given you as a prey:
But ye, who, unappalled at earthly harm,
Lean on the strength of his Almighty arm,
Prepared for life or death, with firm accord,
Stand still and see the glory of the Lord."

A pause, a dreary pause ensued: then cried
The holy man—"On either hand divide;
The feeble fly; with me the valiant stay;
Choose now your portion; whom will ye obey,
God or your fears? His counsel, or your own?"
"The LORD; the LORD; for HE IS GOD ALONE!"
Exclaimed at once, with consentaneous choice,
The whole assembly, heart, and soul, and voice.
Then light from heaven with sudden beauty came,
Pure on the altar blazed the unkindled flame,
And upward to their glorious source returned,
The sacred fires in which the victim burned;
While through the evening gloom, to distant eyes,
Morn o'er the patriarchs' mountain seemed to rise.

Awe-struck the congregation kneeled ar
And worshipped with their faces to the grou
The peace of God, beyond expression sweet.
Filled every spirit humbled at his feet,
And love, joy, wonder, deeply mingling there.
Drew from the heart unutterable prayer.

They rose; as if his soul had passed away,
Prostrate before the altar Enoch lay,
Entranced so deeply, all believed him dead:
At length he breathed, he moved, he raised his head;
To heaven in ecstacy he turned his eyes;
—With such a look the dead in Christ shall rise,
When the last trumpet calls them from the dust,
To join the resurrection of the just:
Yea, and from earthly grossness so refined,
(As if the soul had left the flesh behind,

* The name of *Enoch*, the son of Jared, is derived from *chance*, to *dedicate*.

† And he called his name Noah, saying, This same shall comfort us concerning our work, and toil of our hands, because of the ground which the Lord hath cursed.—GEN. v. 29.

Yet wore a mortal semblance, upright stood
The great Evangelist before the flood;
On him the vision of the Almighty broke,
And future times were present while he spoke.*

"The Saints shall suffer; righteousness shall fail,
O'er all the world iniquity prevail;
Giants, in fierce contempt of man and God,
Shall rule the nations with an iron rod;
On every mountain idol groves shall rise,
And darken heaven with human sacrifice;
But God the Avenger comes—a judgment-day,
A flood shall sweep his enemies away.
How few, whose eyes shall then have seen the sun,
—One righteous family, and only one—
Saved from that wreck of nature, shall behold
The new creation rising from the old!

"O, that the world of wickedness, destroyed,
Might lie for ever without form and void!
Or, that the earth, to innocence restored,
Might flourish as the garden of the Lord!
It will not be: among the sons of men,
The giant-spirit shall go forth again,
From clime to clime shall kindle murderous rage,
And spread the plagues of sin from age to age;
Yet shall the God of mercy, from above,
Extend the golden sceptre of his love
And win the rebels to his righteous sway,
Till every mouth confess, and heart obey.

"Amid the visions of ascending years,
What mighty chief, what conqueror appears;†
His garments rolled in blood, his eyes of flame,
And on his thigh the unutterable name? ‡
—'Tis I, that bring deliverance; strong to save,
I plucked the prey from death, and spoiled the grave.'
—Wherefore, O warrior! are thy garments red,
Like those whose feet amid the vintage tread?
—'I trod the wine-press of the field alone;
I looked around for succor; there was none;
Therefore my wrath sustained me while I fought,
And mine own arm my saint's salvation wrought,'
—Thus may thine arm for evermore prevail;
Thus may thy foes, O Lord! for ever fail;
Captive by thee captivity be led;
Seed of the woman! bruise the serpent's head;
Redeemer! promised since the world began,
Bow the high heavens and condescend to man.

"Hail to the day-spring; dawning from afar,
Bright in the east I see his natal star:
Prisoners of hope! lift up your joyful eyes;
Welcome the king of glory from the skies:
Who is the king of glory? Mark his birth;
In deep humility he stoops to earth,
Assumes a servant's form, a pilgrim's lot,
Comes to his own, his own receive him not,
Though angel-choirs his peaceful advent greet,
And Gentile sages worship at his feet.

"Fair as that sovereign plant, whose scions shoot
With healing verdure, an immortal fruit,
The tree of life, beside the stream that laves
The fields of paradise with gladdening waves;
Behold him rise from infancy to youth,
The father's image, full of grace and truth;
Tried, tempted, proved in secret, till the hour,
When, girt with meekness, but arrayed with power,
Forth in the spirit of the Lord, at length,
Like the sun shining in meridian strength,
He goes: to preach good tidings to the poor;
To heal the wounds that nature can not cure:
To bind the broken-hearted; to control
Disease and death; to raise the sinking soul;
Unbar the dungeon, set the captive free,
Proclaim the joyous year of liberty,
And from the depth of undiscovered night,
Bring life and immortality to light.

"How beauteous on the mountains are thy feet,
Thy form how comely, and thy voice how sweet,
Son of the Highest! Who can tell thy fame?
The deaf shall hear it while the dumb proclaim;
Now bid the blind behold their Savior's light,
The lame go forth rejoicing in thy might;
Cleanse with a touch yon kneeling leper's skin;
Cheer this pale penitent, forgive her sin;
O, for that mother's faith, her daughter spare;
Restore the maniac to a father's prayer;
Pity the tears those mournful sisters shed,
And BE THE RESURRECTION OF THE DEAD!

"What scene is this? Amid involving gloom,
The moonlight lingers on a lonely tomb;
No noise disturbs the garden's hallowed bound,
But the watch walking on their midnight round:
Ah! who lies here, with marred and bloodless mien,
In whom no form or comeliness is seen;
His livid limbs with nails and scourges torn,
His side transpierced, his temples wreathed with thorn!
'Tis He, the man of sorrows! He who bore
Our sins and chastisement; his toils are o'er;
On earth erewhile a suffering life he led,
Here hath he found a place to lay his head;
Ranked with transgressors he resigned his breath,
But with the rich he made his bed in death.
Sweet is the grave where angels watch and weep,
Sweet is the grave, and sanctified his sleep;
Rest, O my spirit! by this martyred form,
This wreck, that sunk beneath the Almighty storm,
When floods of wrath, that weighed the world to hell.
On him alone, in righteous vengeance fell;
While men derided, demons urged his woes,
And God forsook him—till the awful close
Then, in triumphant agony, he cried,
—'Tis finished!'—bowed his sacred head and died.
Death, as he struck that noblest victim, found
His sting was lost for ever in the wound;
The grave, that holds his corse, her richest prize,
Shall yield him back, victorious, to the skies.
He lives: ye bars of steel! ye gates of brass!
Give way and let the king of glory pass;
He lives: ye golden portals of the spheres!
Open, the son of righteousness appears.
But, ah! my spirit faints beneath the blaze,
That breaks and brightens o'er the latter days,
When every tongue his trophies shall proclaim,
And every knee shall worship at his name;
For he shall reign with undivided power,
To earth's last bounds, to nature's final hour.

"'Tis done: again the conquering chief appears
In the dread vision of dissolving years;
His vesture dipped in blood, his eyes of flame,
The WORD OF GOD his everlasting name;*
Throned in mid-heaven, with clouds of glory spread,
He sits in judgment on the quick and dead:
Strong to deliver; saints! your songs prepare;
Rush from your tombs to meet him in the air:
But terrible in vengeance; sinners! bow†
Your haughty heads, the grave protects not now;
He, who alone in mortal conflict trod
The mighty wine-press of the wrath of God,
Shall fill the cup of trembling to his foes,
The unmingled cup of inexhausted woes;
The proud shall drink it in that dreadful day,
While earth dissolves, and heaven is rolled away."

Here ceased the prophet: From the altar broke
The last dim wreaths of fire-illumined smoke;
Darkness had fallen around; but o'er the streams
The moon, new risen, diffused her brightening beams;
Homeward, with tears, the worshippers returned,
Yet while they wept, their hearts within them burned.

CANTO SIXTH.

Javan's second Interview with Zillah. He visits the various Dwellings scattered throughout the Glen, and in the Evening sings to his Harp, amidst the assembled Inhabitants:—Address to Twilight:—Jubal's Song of the Creation: the Power of Music exemplified.

SPENT with the toils of that eventful day,
All night in dreamless slumber Javan lay;

* Numbers, xxiv. 4. † Isa. lxiii.1–6. ‡ Rev. xix. 12.

* Rev. xix. 13. † Jude, verse 14–15

But early springing from his bed of leaves,
Waked by the songs of swallows on the eaves,
From Enoch's cottage in the cool gray hour,
He wandered forth to Zillah's woodland bower;
There, in his former covert, on the ground,
The frame of his forsaken harp he found;
He smote the boss; the convex orb, unstrung,
Instant with sweet reverberation rung;
The minstrel smiled, at that sonorous stroke,
To find the spell of harmony unbroke;
Trickling with dew, he bore it to the cell;
There, as with leaves, he dried the sculptured she.
He thought of Zillah, and resolved too late
To plead his constancy, and know his fate.

She from the hour, when, in a pilgrim's guise,
Javan returned, a stranger to her eyes,
Not to her heart—from anguish knew no rest,
Love, pride, resentment, struggling in her breast.
All day she strove to hide her misery,
In vain;—a mother's eye was quick to see,
Slow to rebuke a daughter's bashful fears,
And Zillah's mother only chid with tears:
Night came, but Javan came not with the night;
Light vanished, Hope departed with the light:
Her lonely couch concealed her sleepless woes,
But with the morning star the maiden rose.
The soft refreshing breeze, the orient beams,
The dew, the mist unrolling from the streams,
The light, the joy, the music of the hour,
Stole on her spirit with resistless power,
With headlong sweetness soothed her fevered brain,
And woke the pulse of tenderness again.
Thus while she wandered with unconscious feet,
Absent in thought, she reached her sylvan seat:
The youth descried her not amidst the wood,
Till, like a vision, at his side she stood.
Their eyes encountered, both at once exclaimed,
"Javan!" and "Zillah!"—each the other named;
Those sounds were life or death to either heart;
He rose; she turned in terror to depart;
He caught her hand:—"O do not, do not flee!"
—It was a moment of eternity,
And now or never must he plight his vow,
Win or abandon her for ever now.

"Stay;—hear me, Zillah!—every power above,
Heaven, earth, thyself, bear witness to my love!
Thee have I loved from earliest infancy,
Loved with supreme affection only thee.
Long in these shades my timid passion grew,
Through every change, in every trial true;
I loved thee through the world in dumb despair,
Loved *thee*, that I might love no other fair;
Guilty, yet faithful still, to thee I fly,
Receive me, love me, Zillah! or I die."

Thus Javan's lips, so long in silence sealed,
With sudden vehemence his soul revealed;
Zillah, meanwhile, recovered power to speak,
While deadly paleness overcast her cheek:
—"Say not, 'I love thee!'—Witness every tree
Around this bower, thy cruel scorn of me!
Could Javan love me through the world, yet leave
Her whom he loved, for hopeless years, to grieve?
Returning could he find her here alone,
Yet pass her by, unknowing, as unknown?
All day was she forsaken, or forgot?
Did Javan seek her at her father's cot?
That cot of old so much his soul's delight,
His mother's seemed not fairer in his sight:
No; Javan mocks me; none could love so well,
So long, so painfully,—and never tell."

"Love owns no law," rejoined the pleading youth,
"Except obedience to eternal truth;
Deep streams are silent; from the generous breast,
The dearest feelings are the last confest:
Erewhile I strove in vain to break my peace,
Now I could talk of love, and never cease:
—Still had my trembling passion been concealed;
Still but in parables by stealth revealed,
Had not thine instantaneous presence wrung,
By swift surprise, the secret from my tongue.
Yet hath affection language of her own,
And mine in everything but words was shown
In childhood, as the bird of nature free,
My song was gladness, when I sung to thee:
In youth, whene'er I mourned a bosom flame,
And praised a maiden whom I durst not name,
Couldst thou not then my hidden thought divine?
Didst thou not feel that I was wholly thine?
When for vain glory I forsook thee here,
Dear as thou wert, unutterably dear,
From virtue, truth, and innocence, estranged,
To thee, thee only, was my heart unchanged;
And as I loved without a hope before,
Without a hope I loved thee yet the more.
At length, when, weary of the ways of men,
Refuge I sought in this maternal glen,
Thy sweet remembrance drew me from afar,
And Zillah's beauty was my leading star.
Here when I found thee, fear itself grew bold,
Methought my tale of love already told;
But soon thine eyes the dream of folly broke,
And I from bliss, as they from slumber, woke;
My heart, my tongue, were chilled to instant stone,
I durst not speak thy name, nor give my own.
When thou wert vanished, horror and affright
Seized me, my sins uprose before my sight;
Like fiends they rushed upon me; but despair
Wrung from expiring faith a broken prayer;
Strength came; the path to Enoch's bower I trod;
He saw me, met me, led me back to God.
O Zillah! while I sought my Maker's grace,
And flesh and spirit failed before his face,
The tempting image from my breast I drove,
It was no season then for earthly love."—

"For earthly love it is no season now,"
Exclaimed the maiden with reproachful brow,
And eyes through tears of tenderness that shone,
And voice, half peace, half anger in its tone;
"Freely thy past unkindness I forgive;
Content to perish here, so Javan live:
The tyrant's menace to our tribe we know;
The patriarchs never seek, nor shun a foe;
Thou, while thou may'st, from swift destruction fly;
I and my father's house resolve to die."

"With thee and with thy father's house, to bear
Death or captivity, is Javan's prayer;
Remorse for ever be the recreant's lot;
If I forsake thee now, I love thee not."

Thus while he vowed, a gentle answer sprung
To Zillah's lips, but died upon her tongue;
Trembling she turned, and hastened to the rock,
Beyond those woods, that hid her folded flock,
Whose bleatings reached her ear with loud complaint
Of her delay; she loosed them from restraint;
Then bounding headlong forth with antic glee,
They roamed in all the joy of liberty.
Javan beside her walked, as in a dream,
Nor more of love renewed the fruitless theme.

Forthwith from home, to home, throughout th[illegible]
The friends whom once he knew he sought aga[illegible]
Each hailed the stranger welcome at his board,
As lost but found, as dead to life restored.
From Eden's camp no tidings came; the day
In awful expectation passed away.
At eve his harp the fond enthusiast strung,
On Adam's mount, and to the patriarchs sung;
While youth and age, an eager throng, admire,
The mingling music of the voice and lyre.

"I love thee, Twilight! as thy shadows roll,
The calm of evening steals upon my soul,
Sublimely tender, solemnly serene,
Still as the hour, enchanting as the scene.
I love thee, Twilight! for thy gleams impart
Their dear, their dying influence to my heart,
When o'er the harp of thought thy passing wind
Awakens all the music of the mind,

And joy and sorrow, as the spirit burns,
And hope and memory sweep the chords by turns,
While contemplation, on seraphic wings,
Mounts with the flame of sacrifice, and sings.
Twilight! I love thee; let thy glooms increase
Till every feeling, every pulse is peace;
Slow from the sky the light of day declines,
Clearer within the dawn of glory shines,
Revealing, in the hour of nature's rest,
A world of wonders in the Poet's breast:
Deeper, O Twilight! then thy shadows roll,
An awful vision opens on my soul.

"On such an evening, so divinely calm,
The woods all melody, the breezes balm,
Down in a vale, where lucid waters strayed,
And mountain cedars stretched their downward shade,
Jubal, the prince of song (in youth unknown),
Retired to commune with his harp alone;
For still he nursed it, like a secret thought,
Long cherished and to late perfection wrought,—
And still with cunning hand, and curious ear,
Enriched, ennobled, and enlarged its sphere,
Till he had compassed, in that magic round,
A soul of harmony, a heaven of sound,
Then sang the minstrel, in his laurel bower,
Of nature's origin, and music's power.
—'He spake, and it was done;—eternal night,
At God's command, awakened into light;
He called the elements, Earth, Ocean, Air,
He called them when they were not, and they were:
He looked through space, and kindling o'er the sky,
Sun, moon, and stars, came forth to meet his eye:
His spirit moved upon the desert earth,
And sudden life through all things warmed to birth;
Man from the dust he raised to rule the whole;
He breathed, and man became a living soul:
Through Eden's groves the Lord of nature trod,
Upright and pure, the image of his God.
Thus were the heavens and all their host displayed,
In wisdom thus were earth's foundations laid;
The glorious scene a holy sabbath closed,
Amidst his works the omnipotent reposed:
And while he viewed and blessed them from his seat,
All worlds, all beings worshipped at his feet:
The morning stars in choral concert sang,
The rolling deep with hallelujahs rang,
Adoring angels from their orbs rejoice,
The voice of music was creation's voice.

"'Alone along the lyre of nature sighed
The master-chord, to which no chord replied;
For man, while bliss and beauty reigned around,
For man alone, no fellowship was found,
No fond companion, in whose dearer breast,
His heart, repining in his own, might rest;
For, born to love, the heart delights to roam,
A kindred bosom is its happiest home.
On earth's green lap, the father of mankind,
In mild dejection, thoughtfully reclined;
Soft o'er his eyes a sealing slumber crept,
And fancy soothed him while reflection slept.
Then God—who thus would make his counsel known,
Counsel that willed not man to dwell alone,
Created woman with a smile of grace,
And left the smile that made her on her face.
The patriarch's eyelids opened on his bride,
—The morn of beauty risen from his side!
He gazed with new-born rapture on her charms,
And love's first whispers won her to his arms.
Then, tuned through all the chords supremely sweet,
Exulting nature found her lyre complete,
And from the key of each harmonious sphere,
Struck music worthy of her Maker's ear.'

"Here Jubal paused; for grim before him lay,
Couched like a lion watching for his prey,
With blood-red eye of fascinating fire,
Fixed like the gazing serpent's on the lyre,
An awful form, that through the gloom appeared,
Half brute, half human; whose terrific beard,
And hoary flakes of long dishevelled hair,
Like eagle's plumage, ruffled by the air,
Veiled a sad wreck of grandeur and of grace,
Limbs worn and wounded, a majestic face,
Deep-ploughed by Time, and ghastly pale with woes,
That goaded till remorse to madness rose;
Haunted by phantoms, he had fled his home,
With savage beasts in solitude to roam;
Wild as the waves, and wandering as the wind,
No art could tame him, and no chains could bind:
Already seven disastrous years had shed
Mildew and blast on his unsheltered head;
His brain was smitten by the sun at noon,
His heart was withered by the cold night-moon.

"'Twas Cain, the sire of nations:—Jubal knew
His kindred looks, and tremblingly withdrew;
He, darting like the blaze of sudden fire,
Leaped o'er the space between, and grasped the lyre
Sooner with life the struggling Bard would part,
And ere the fiend could tear it from his heart,
He hurled his hand, with one tremendous stroke,
O'er all the strings; whence in a whirlwind broke
Such tones of terror, dissonance, despair,
As till that hour had never jarred in air.
Astonished into marble at the shock,
Backward stood Cain, unconscious as a rock,
Cold, breathless, motionless through all his frame;
But soon his visage quickened into flame,
When Jubal's hand the crashing jargon changed
To melting harmony, and nimbly ranged
From chord to chord, ascending sweet and clear,
Then rolling down in thunder on the ear;
With power the pulse of anguish to restrain,
And charm the evil spirit from the brain.

"Slowly recovering from that trance profound,
Bewildered, touched, transported with the sound,
Cain viewed himself, the bard, the earth, the sky,
While wonder flashed and faded in his eye,
And reason by alternate phrensy crost,
Now seemed restored, and now for ever lost.
So shines the moon, by glimpses, through her shrouds,
When windy darkness rides upon the clouds,
Till through the blue, serene, and silent night,
She reigns in full tranquillity of light.
Jubal, with eager hope, beheld the chase
Of strange emotions hurrying o'er his face,
And waked his noblest numbers, to control
The tide and tempest of the maniac's soul;
Through many a maze of melody they flew,
They rose like incense, they distilled like dew,
Poured through the sufferer's breast delicious balm,
And soothed remembrance till remorse grew calm,
Till Cain forsook the solitary wild,
Led by the minstrel like a weaned child.
O! had you seen him to his home restored,
How young and old ran forth to meet their lord;
How friends and kindred on his neck did fall,
Weeping aloud, while Cain outwept them all:
But hush!—thenceforward when recoiling care
Lowered on his brow, and saddened to despair,
The lyre of Jubal, with divinest art,
Repelled the demon, and revived his heart.
Thus song, the breath of heaven, had power to bind
In chains of harmony the mightiest mind;
Thus music's empire in the soul began,
The first-born poet ruled the first-born man."

While Javan sung, the shadows fell around,
The moving glow-worm brightened on the ground.
He ceased: the mute assembly rose in tears;
Delight and wonder were chastised with fears;
That heavenly harmony, unheard before,
Awoke the feeling,—"Who shall hear it more?"
The sun had set in glory on their sight,
For them in vain might morn restore the light;
Though self-devoted, through each mortal frame,
At thought of death, a cold, sick shuddering came,
Nature's infirmity;—but faith was given,
The flame that lifts the sacrifice to heaven:
Through doubt and darkness then, beyond the skies,
Eternal prospects opened on their eyes;
Already seemed the immortal spirit free,
And death was swallowed up in victory.

CANTO SEVENTH.

The Patriarchs and their Families carried away Captive by a Detachment from the Army of the Invaders.—The Tomb of Abel.—His Murder by Cain described.—The Origin of the Giants.—The Infancy and early Adventures of their King.—The Leader of their Host encamped in Eden.

THE flocks and herds throughout the glen reposed;
No human eyelid there in slumber closed;
None, save the infant's on the mother's breast;—
With arms of love caressing and carest,
She, while her elder offspring round her clung,
Each eye intent on hers, and mute each tongue,
The voice of death in every murmur heard,
And felt his touch in every limb that stirred.

At midnight, down the forest hills, a train
Of eager warriors, from the host of Cain,
Burst on the stillness of the scene:—they spread
In bands, to clutch the victims ere they fled;
Of flight unmindful, at their summons, rose
Those victims, meekly yielded to their foes;
Though woman wept to leave her home behind,
The weak were comforted, the strong resigned,
And ere the moon, descending o'er the vale,
Grew, at the bright approach of morning, pale,
Collected thus, the patriarchal clan,
With strengthened confidence, their march began,
Since not in ashes were their dwellings laid,
And death, though threatened still, was still delayed.
Struck with their fearless innocence, they saw
Their fierce assailants checked with sacred awe;
The foe became a phalanx of defence,
And brought them, like a guard of angels, thence.
A vista-path, that through the forest led,
(By Javan shunned when from the camp he fled,)
The pilgrims tracked, till on the mountain's height;
They met the sun, new risen in glorious light;
Empurpled mists along the landscape rolled,
And all the orient flamed with clouds of gold.

Here, while they halted, on their knees they raise
To God the sacrifice of prayer and praise;
—"Glory to thee, for every blessing shed,
In days of peace, on our protected head;
Glory to thee, for fortitude to bear
The wrath of man, rejoicing o'er despair;
Glory to thee, whatever ill befall,
For faith on thy victorious name to call;
Thine own eternal purposes fulfil;
We come, O God! to suffer all thy will."

Refreshed and rested, on their course they went
Ere the clouds melted from the firmament;
Odors abroad the winds of morning breathe,
And fresh with dew the herbage sprang beneath:
Down from the hills, that gently sloped away
To the broad river shining into day,
They passed; along the brink the path they kept,
Where high aloof o'erarching willows wept,
Whose silvery foliage glistened in the beam,
And floating shadows fringed the chequered stream.

Adjacent rose a myrtle-planted mound,
Whose spiry top, a granite fragment crowned;
Tinctured with many colored moss, the stone,
Rich as a cloud of summer evening, shone
Amidst encircling verdure, that arrayed
The beauteous hillock with a cope of shade.

"Javan!" said Enoch, "on this spot began
The fatal curse;—man perished here by man;
The earliest death a son of Adam died
Was murder, and that murder fratricide!
Here Abel fell, a corse along this shore;
Here Cain's recoiling footsteps reeked with gore:
Horror upraised his locks, unloosed his knees;
He heard a voice; he hid among the trees;
—'Where is thy brother'—From the whirlwind came
The voice of God, amidst enfolding flame:
—'Am I my brother's keeper!'—hoarse and low,
Cain muttered from the copse,—'that I should know?'
—'What hast thou done?—For vengeance to the skies,
Lo! from the dust the blood of Abel cries:
Curst from the earth that drank his blood, with toil
Thine hand shall plough in vain her barren soil:
An exile and a wanderer thou shalt be;
A brother's eye shall never look on thee.'—

"The shuddering culprit answered in despair,
—'Greater the punishment than flesh can bear.'
—'Yet shalt thou bear it; on thy brow revealed,
Thus be thy sentence and thy safeguard sealed.'
Silently, swiftly as the lightning's blast,
A hand of fire athwart his temples passed:
He ran, as in the terror of a dream,
To quench his burning anguish in the stream;
But bending o'er the brink, the swelling wave
Back to the eye his branded visage gave;
As soon on murdered Abel durst he look;
Yet power to fly his palsied limbs forsook;
There turned to stone for his presumptuous crime,
A monument of wrath to latest time,
Might Cain have stood; but mercy raised his head
In prayer for help,—his strength returned,—he fled.
That mound of myrtles, o'er their favorite child,
Eve planted, and the hand of Adam piled;
Yon mossy stone, above his ashes raised,
His altar once, with Abel's offering blazed,
When God well pleased beheld the flames arise,
And smiled acceptance on the sacrifice."

Enoch to Javan, walking at his side,
Thus held discourse apart: the youth replied:
"Relieved from toil, though Cain is gone to rest,
And the turf flowers on his disburthened breast,
Among his race the murdering spirit reigns,
But riots fiercest in the giants' veins.
—Sprung from false leagues, when monstrous love combined
The sons of God and daughters of mankind,
Selfstyled the progeny of heaven and earth,
Eden first gave the world's oppressors birth:
Thence far away, beneath the rising moon,
Or where the shadow vanishes at noon,
The adulterous mothers from the sires withdrew:
—Nurst in luxuriant climes their offspring grew:
Till, as in stature o'er mankind they towered,
And giant strength all mortal strength o'erpowered,
To heaven the proud blasphemers raised their eyes,
And scorned the tardy vengeance of the skies;
On earth invincible, they sternly broke
Love's willing bonds, and nature's kindred yoke,
Mad for dominion with remorseless sway,
Compelled their reptile brethren to obey,
And doomed their human herds, with thankless toil,
Like brutes, to grow and perish on the soil.
Their sole inheritance, through lingering years,
The bread of misery and the cup of tears,
The tasks of oxen, with the hire of slaves,
Dishonored lives, and desecrated graves.

"When war, that self inflicted scourge of man,
His boldest crime and bitterest curse,—began;
As lions fierce, as forest cedars tall,
And terrible as torrents in their fall,
Headlong from rocks, through vales and vineyards hurled,
These men of prey laid waste the eastern world.
They taught their tributary hordes to wield
The sword, red-flaming, through the death-strown field,
With strenuous arm the uprooted rock to throw,
Glance the light arrow from the bounding bow,
Whirl the broad shield to meet the darted stroke,
And stand to combat like the unyielding oak.
Then eye from eye with fell suspicion turned
In kindred breasts unnatural hatred burned
Brother met brother in the lists of strife,
The son lay lurking for the father's life;
With rapid instinct, men who never knew
Each other's face before, each other slew;
All tribes, all nations learned the fatal art,
And every hand was armed to pierce a heart.
Nor man alone the giants' might subdued;
—The Camel, weaned from quiet solitude,
Grazed round their camps, or slow along the road,
Midst marching legions, bore the servile load.

With flying forelock and dishevelled mane,
They caught the wild steed prancing o'er the plain,
For war or pastime reigned his fiery force;
Fleet as the wind he stretched along the course.
Or loudly neighing at the trumpet's sound,
With hoofs of thunder smote the indented ground.
The enormous elephant obeyed their will,
And, tamed to cruelty with direst skill,
Roared for the battle, when he felt the goad,
And his proud lord his sinewy neck bestrode,
Through crashing ranks resistless havoc bore,
And writhed his trunk, and bathed his tusks in gore.

"Thus while the giants trampled friends and foes,
Among their tribe a mighty chieftain rose;
His birth mysterious, but traditions tell
What strange events his infancy befell.

"A goatherd fed his flock on many a steep,
Where Eden's rivers swell the southern deep;
A melancholy man, who dwelt alone,
Yet far abroad his evil fame was known,
The first of woman born, that might presume
To wake the dead bones mouldering in the tomb,
And, from the gulf of uncreated night,
Call phantoms of futurity to light.
'Twas said his voice could stay the falling flood,
Eclipse the sun, and turn the moon to blood,
Roll back the planets on their golden cars,
And from the firmament unfixed the stars.
Spirits of fire and air, of sea and land,
Came at his call, and flew at his command;
His spells so potent, that his changing breath
Opened or shut the gates of life and death,
O'er nature's powers he claimed supreme control,
And held communion with all nature's soul:
The name and place of every herb he knew,
Its healing balsam, or pernicious dew:
The meanest reptile, and the noblest birth
Of ocean's caverns, or the living earth,
Obeyed his mandate:—Lord of all the rest,
Man more than all his hidden art confessed,
Cringed to his face, consulted, and revered
His oracles,—detested him and feared.

"Once by the river, in a waking dream,
He stood to watch the ever-running stream,
In which, reflected upward to his eyes,
He giddily looked down upon the skies,
For thus he feigned in his ecstatic mood,
To summon divination from the flood.
His steady view, a floating object crossed;
His eye pursued it till the sight was lost.—
An outcast infant in a fragile bark!
The river whirled the willow-woven ark
Down toward the deep; the tide returning bore
The little voyager unharmed to shore;
Him in his cradle-ship securely bound
With swathing skins at eve the goatherd found.
Nurst by that foster-sire, austere and rude,
Midst rocks and glens, in savage solitude,
Among the kids, the rescued foundling grew,
Nutrition from whose shaggy dams he drew,
Till baby-curls his broader temples crowned,
And torrid suns his flexile limbs embrowned:
Then as he sprang from green to florid age,
And rose to giant stature, stage by stage,
He roamed the valleys with his browsing flock,
And leapt in joy of youth from rock to rock,
Climbed the sharp precipice's steepest breast,
To seize the eagle brooding on her nest,
And rent his way through matted woods, to tear
The skulking panther from his hidden lair.
A trodden serpent, horrible and vast,
Sprang on the heedless rover as he passed;
Limb locked o'er limb, with many a straitening fold
Of orbs inextricably involved, he rolled
On earth in vengeance, broke the twisted toils,
Strangled the hissing fiend, and wore the spoils.
With hardy exercise, and cruel art,
To nerve the frame, and petrify the heart,
The wizard trained his pupil, from a span,
To thrice the bulk and majesty of man.
His limbs were sinewy strength; commanding grace,
And dauntless spirit sparkled in his face;
His arm could pluck the lion from his prey,
And hold the horned rhinoceros at bay,
His feet o'er highest hills pursue the hind,
Or tire the ostrich buoyant on the wind.

"Yet 'twas the stripling's chief delight to brave
The river's wrath, and wrestle with the wave;
When torrent rains had swoln the furious tide,
Light on the foamy surge he loved to ride;
When calm and clear the stream was wont to flow,
Fearless he dived to search the caves below.
His childhood's story, often told, had wrought
Sublimest hopes in his aspiring thought.
—Once on a cedar, from its mountain throne
Plucked by the tempest, forth he sailed alone,
And reached the gulf; with eye of eager fire,
And flushing cheek, he watched the shores retire,
Till sky and water wide around were spread;
—Straight to the sun he thought his voyage led,
With shouts of transport hailed its setting light,
And followed all the long and lonely night:
But ere the morning-star expired, he found
His stranded bark once more on earthly ground.
Tears, wrung from secret shame, suffused his eyes,
When in the east he saw the sun arise:
Pride quickly checked them; young ambition burned
For bolder enterprise, as he returned.
"Through snares and deaths pursuing fame and power
He scorned his flock from that adventurous hour,
And, leagued with monsters of congenial birth,
Began to scourge and subjugate the earth.
Meanwhile the sons of Cain, who tilled the soil,
By noble arts had learned to lighten toil;
Wisely their scattered knowledge he combined;
Yet had a hundred years matured his mind,
Ere with the strength that laid the forest low,
And skill that made the iron furnace glow,
His genius launched the keel, and swayed the helm
(His throne and sceptre on the watery realm),
While from the tent of his expanded sail,
He eyed the heavens and flew before the gale,
The first of men, whose courage knew to guide
The bounding vessel through the refluent tide.
Then swore the giant in his pride of soul,
To range the universe from pole to pole,
Rule the remotest nations with his nod,
To live a hero, and to die a god.

"This is the king that wars in Eden: now,
Fulfilled at length he deems his early vow;
His foot hath overrun the world—his hand
Smitten to dust the pride of every land:
The patriarch's last, beneath the impious rod,
He dooms to perish or abjure their God.
—O God of truth! rebuke the tyrant's rage,
And save the remnant of thine heritage."

When Javan ceased, they stood upon the height,
Where first he rested on his lonely flight,
Whence to the sacred mountain far away,
The land of Eden in perspective lay.
'Twas noon; they tarried there, till milder hours
Woke with light airs the breath of evening flowers.

CANTO EIGHTH.

The scene changes to a mountain, on the summit of which, beneath the shade of ancient trees, the giants are assembled round their king.—A minstrel sings the monarch's praises, and describes the destruction of the remnant of the force of his enemies, in an assault, by land and water, on their encampment, between the forest on the eastern plain of Eden and the river to the west.—The captive patriarchs are presented before the king and his chieftains.

There is a living spirit in the lyre,
A breath of music, and a soul of fire;
It speaks a language to the world unknown;
It speaks that language to the bard alone:
While warbled symphonies entrance his ears,
That spirit's voice in every tone he hears;

'Tis his the mystic meaning to rehearse,
To utter oracles in glowing verse,
Heroic themes from age to age prolong,
And make the dead in nature live in song.
Through graven rocks the warrior's deeds proclaim,
And mountains, hewn to statues, wear his name;
Though shrined in adamant, his relics lie
Beneath a pyramid, that scales the sky;
All that the hand hath fashioned shall decay;
All that the eye admires shall pass away;
The mouldering rocks, the hero's hope shall fail,
Earthquakes shall heave the mountains to the vale,
The shrine of adamant betray its trust,
And the proud pyramid resolve to dust;
The lyre alone immortal fame secures,
For song alone through nature's change endures;
Transfused like life, from breast to breast it glows,
From sire to son by sure succession flows,
Spreads its unceasing flight from clime to clime,
Outstripping death upon the wings of time.

"Soul of the lyre! whose magic power can raise
Inspiring visions of departed days;
Or, with the glimpses of mysterious rhyme,
Dawn on the dreams of unawakened time;
Soul of the lyre! instruct thy bard to sing
The latest triumph of the giant-king,
Who sees this day his orb of glory filled:
—In what creative numbers shall I build,
With what exalted strains of music crown,
His everlasting pillar of renown?
Though, like the rainbow, by a wondrous birth,
He sprang to light, the joy of heaven and earth;
Though, like the rainbow—for he can not die—
His form shall pass unseen into the sky;
Say, shall the hero share the coward's lot,
Vanish from earth, ingloriously forgot?
No! the divinity that rules the lyre,
And clothes these lips with eloquence of fire,
Commands the song to rise in quenchless flame,
And light the world for ever with his fame."

Thus on a mountain's venerable head,
Where trees, coeval with creation, spread
Their massy-twisted branches, green and gray,
Mature below, their tops in dry decay,
A bard of Jubal's lineage proudly sung,
Then stayed awhile the raptures of his tongue:
A shout of horrible applause that rent
The echoing hills, and answering firmament,
Burst from the giants—where, in barbarous state,
Flushed with new wine, around their king they sate:
A chieftain each who, on his brazen car,
Had led a host of meaner men to war;
And now from recent fight on Eden's plain,
Where fell their foes in helpless conflict slain,
Victoriously returned, beneath the trees
They rest from toil, carousing at their ease.

Adjacent, where the mountain's spacious breast,
Opened in airy grandeur to the west,
Huge piles of fragrant cedars on the ground,
As altars blazed, while victims bled around,
To gods, whose worship vanished with the flood,
—Divinities of brass, and stone, and wood,
By man himself in his own image made;
The fond creator to the creature prayed;
And he, who from the forest or the rock
Hewed the rough mass, adored the shapen block;
Then seemed his flock's ignoble in his eyes,
His choicest herds too mean for sacrifice,
He poured his brethren's blood upon the pyre,
And passed his sons to demons through the fire.

Exalted o'er the vassal chiefs, behold
Their sovereign, cast in nature's mightiest mould;
Beneath an oak, whose woven boughs displayed
A verdant canopy of light and shade,
Throned on a rock the giant-king appears,
In the full manhood of five hundred years;
His robe, the spoils of lions, by his might
Dragged from their den, or slain in chase or fight;
His raven locks unblanched by withering time,
Amply dishevelled o'er his brow sublime;
His dark eyes, flushed with restless radiance, gleam
Like broken moonlight rippling on the stream.
Grandeur of soul, which nothing might appal,
And nothing satisfy if less than all,
Had stamped upon his air, his form, his face,
The character of calm and awful grace;
But direst cruelty, by guile represt,
Lurked in the dark volcano of his breast,
In silence brooding, like the secret power,
That springs the earthquake at the midnight hour.

From Eden's summit, with obdurate pride,
Red from afar the battle-scene he eyed,
Where late he crushed, with one remorseless blow,
The remnant of his last and noblest foe;
At hand he viewed the trophies of his toils,
Herds, flocks, and steeds, the world's collected spoils;
Below, his legions marched in war array,
Unstained with blood in that unequal fray:
—A hundred tribes, whose sons their arms had borne,
Without contention, from the field at morn,
Their bands dividing, when the fight was won,
Darkened the region toward the slanting sun,
Like clouds, whose shadows o'er the landscape sail,
—While to their camp, that filled the northern vale,
A waving sea of tents immensely spread,
The trumpet summoned, and the banners led.
With these a train of captives, sad and slow,
Moved to a death of shame, or life of wo,
A death on altars hateful to the skies,
Or life in chains, a slower sacrifice.
Fair smiled the face of nature; all serene
And lovely Evening tranquillized the scene;
The furies of the fight were gone to rest,
The cloudless sun grew broader down the west,
The hills beneath him melted from the sight,
Receding through the heaven of purple light;
Along the plain the maze of rivers rolled,
And verdant shadows gleamed in waves of gold.

Thus while the tyrant cast his haughty eye
O'er the broad landscape and incumbent sky,
His heart exulting whispered—"All is mine,"
And heard a voice from all things answer "Thine."
Such was the matchless chief, whose name of yore
Filled the wide world; his name is known no more:
O that for ever from the rolls of fame,
Like his, had perished every conqueror's name!
Then had mankind been spared, in after times,
Their greatest sufferings and their greatest crimes.
The hero scourges not his age alone,
His curse to late posterity is known:
He slays his thousands with his living breath,
His tens of thousands by his fame in death.
Achilles quenched not all his wrath on Greece,
Through Homer's song its miseries never cease;
Like Phœbus' shafts the bright contagion brings
Plagues on the people for the feuds of kings.
'Twas not in vain the son of Philip sighed
For worlds to conquer—o'er the western tide,
His spirit, in the Spaniard's form, o'erthrew
Realms, that the Macedonian never knew.
The steel of Brutus struck not Cæsar dead;
Cæsar in other lands hath reared his head,
And fought, of friends and foes, on many a plain,
His millions, captured, fugitive, and slain;
Yet seldom suffered, where his country died,
A Roman vengeance for his parricide.

The sun was sunk; the sacrificial pyres
From smouldering ashes breathed their last blue fires;
The smiling star that lights the world to rest,
Walked in the rosy gardens of the west,
Like Eve erewhile, through Eden's blooming bowers,
A lovelier star amid a heaven of flowers.
Now in the freshness to the falling shade,
Again the minstrel to the monarch played.
—"Where is the youth renowned? the youth whose voice
Was wont to make the listening camp rejoice,
When to his harp in many a peerless strain,
He sang the wonders of the giant's reign;

O where is Javan?" Thus the bard renewed
His lay, and with a rival's transport viewed
The cloud of sudden anger, that o'ercame
The tyrant's countenance, at Javan's name;
Javan, whose song was once his soul's delight,
Now doomed a traitor recreant by his flight.
The envious minstrel smiled; then boldly ran
His prelude o'er the chords, and thus began.

"'Twas on the morn that faithless Javan fled,
To yonder plain the king of nations led
His countless hosts, and stretched their wide array
Along the woods, within whose shelter lay
The sons of Eden:* these, with secret pride,
In ambush thus the invincible defied:
—'Girt with the forest, wherefore should we fear?
The giant's sword shall never reach us here:
Behind, the river rolls its deep defence;
The giant's hand shall never pluck us hence.'
Vain boast of fools; who to that hand prepare
For their own lives the inevitable snare:
His legions smote the standards of the wood,
And with their prostrate strength controlled the flood;
Lopt off their boughs, and jointed beam to beam,
The pines and oaks were launched upon the stream,
A hundred rafts. Yet still within a zone
Of tangled coppices—a waste, o'ergrown
With briers and thorns—the dauntless victims lie,
Scorn to surrender, and prepare to die.
The second sun went down; the monarch's plan
Was perfected; the dire assault began.

"Marshalled by twilight, his obedient bands
Engirt the wood, with torches in their hands;
The signal given, they shoot them through the air;
The blazing brands in rapid volleys glare,
Descending through the gloom with spangled light,
As if the stars were falling through the night.
Along the withered grass the wild-fire flew,
Higher and hotter with obstruction grew:
The green wood hissed; from crackling thickets broke
Light glancing flame, and heavy rolling smoke;
Till all the breadth of forest seemed to rise
In raging conflagration to the skies.
Fresh o'er our heads the winds propitious blow,
But roll the fierce combustion on the foe.
Awhile they paused of every hope bereft,
Choice of destruction all their refuge left;
If from the flames they fled, behind them lay,
The river roaring to receive his prey;
If through the stream they sought the farther strand,
Our crafts were moored to meet them ere they land;
With triple death environed thus they stood,
Till nearer peril drove them to the flood.
Safe on a hill, where sweetest moonlight slept,
As o'er the changing scene my watch I kept,
I heard their shrieks of agony; I hear
Those shrieks still ring in my tormented ear;
I saw them leap the gulf with headlong fright;
O that mine eyes could now forget that sight!
They sank in multitude; but prompt to save,
Our warriors snatched the stragglers from the wave,
And on their rafts a noble harvest bore
Of rescued heroes, captive, to the shore

"One little troop their lessening ground maintained,
Till space to perish in alone remained;
Then with a shout that rent the echoing air,
More like the shout of victory than despair,
Wedged in a solid phalanx, man by man,
Right through the scorching wilderness they ran,
Where half-extinct the smouldering fuel glowed,
And levelled copses strewed the open road.
Unharmed as spirits while they seemed to pass,
Their lighted features flared like molten brass;
Around the flames in writhing volumes spread,
Thwarted their path, or mingled o'er their head;
Beneath their feet the fires to ashes turned,
But in their wake with mounting fury burned.
Our host recoiled from that amazing sight;
Scarcely the king himself restrained their flight;

*Vide Canto I., p. 2, and Canto III., p. 7.

He, with his chiefs, in brazen armor, stood
Unmoved, to meet the maniacs from the wood.
Dark as a thunder-cloud their phalanx came,
But spilled like lightning, into forms of flame;
Soon as in purer air their heads they raised
To taste the breath of heaven, their garments blazed;
Then blind, distracted, weaponless, yet flushed
With dreadful valor, on their foes they rushed,
The giants met them midway on the plain;
'Twas but the struggle of a moment;—slain,
They fell; their relics to the flames returned,
As offerings to the immortal gods were burned;
And never did the light of morning rise
Upon the clouds of such a sacrifice."

Abruptly here the minstrel ceased to sing,
And every face was turned upon the king;
He, while the stoutest hearts recoiled with fear,
And giants trembled their own deeds to hear,
Unmoved and unrelenting, in his mind,
Deeds of more impious enterprise designed:
A dire conception labored in his breast;
His eye was sternly pointed to the west,
Where stood the Mount of Paradise sublime,
Whose guarded top, since man's presumptuous crime,
By noon, a dusky cloud appeared to rise,
But blazed a beacon through nocturnal skies.
As Ætna, viewed from ocean far away,
Slumbers in blue revolving smoke by day,
Till darkness, with terrific splendor, shows
The eternal fires that crest the eternal snows;*
So where the cherubim in vision turned
Their flaming swords, the summit lowered or burned.
And now conspicuous through the twilight gloom,
The glancing beams the distant hills illume,
And, as the shadows deepen o'er the ground,
Scatter a red and wavering lustre round.

Awhile the monarch, fearlessly amazed,
With jealous anger on the glory gazed;
Already had his arm in battle hurled
His thunders round the subjugated world;
Lord of the nether universe, his pride
Was reined, while Paradise his power defied.
An upland isle, by meeting streams embraced,
It towered to heaven amid a sandy waste;
Below, impenetrable woods displayed
Depths of mysterious solitude and shade;
Above, with adamantine bulwarks crowned,
Primeval rocks in hoary masses frowned;
O'er all were seen the cherubim of light,
Like pillared flames amid the falling night;
So high it rose, so bright the mountain shone,
It seemed the footstool of Jehovah's throne.

The giant panted with intense desire
To scale those heights, and storm the walls of fire,
His ardent soul in ecstacy of thought,
Even now with Michael and his angels fought,
And saw the seraphim like meteors driven
Before his banners through the gates of heaven,
While he secure the glorious garden trod,
And swayed his sceptre from the Mount of God.

When suddenly the bard had ceased to sing,
While all the chieftains gazed upon their king,
Whose changing looks a rising storm bespoke,
Ere from his lips the dread explosion broke,
The trumpets sounded, and before his face
Were led the captives of the patriarch's race,
—A lovely and a venerable band
Of young and old, amid their foes they stand:
Unawed they see the fiery trial near;
The feared their God and knew no other fear.†

* Sorge nel sen de la Sicilia aprica
Monte superbo al cielo,
Che d'atro incendio incoronato ha il crine
Sparso il tergo e di neve, e fatta amica
Lambe la fiamma il gielo,
E tra discreti ardor duran le brine.—I. Testi

† Je crains Dieu, cher Abner, et n'ai point d'autre crainte.—Racine

To light the dusky scene, resplendent fires,
Of pine and cedar, blazed in lofty pyres;
While from the east the moon with doubtful gleams
Now tipped the hills, now glanced athwart the streams;
Till, darting through the clouds her beauteous eye,
She opened all the temple of the sky.
The giants, closing in a narrower ring,
By turns surveyed the prisoners and the king.
Javan stood forth; to all the youth was known,
And every eye was fixed on him alone.

CANTO NINTH.

The king's determination to sacrifice the patriarchs and their families to his demon-gods. His sentence on Javan. Zillah's distress. The sorcerer pretends to declare the secret of the birth of the king, and proposes his deification. Enoch appears.

A GLEAM of joy, at that expected sight,
Shot o'er the monarch's brow with baleful light:
"Behold," thought he, "the great decisive hour;
Ere morn, these sons of God shall prove my power:
Offered by me, their blood shall be the price
Of demon-aid to conquer Paradise."
Thus while he threatened, Javan caught his view,
And instantly his visage changed its hue;
Inflamed with rage past utterance, he frowned,
He gnashed his teeth, and wildly glared around,
As one who saw a spectre in the air,
And durst not look upon it, nor forbear;
Still on the youth, his eye wherever cast,
Abhorrently returned and fixed at last:
"Slaves smite the traitor; be his limbs consigned
To flames, his ashes scattered to the wind!"
He cried in a tone so vehement, so loud,
Instinctively recoiled the shuddering crowd;
And ere the guards to seize their victim rushed,
The youth was pleading,—every breath was hushed;
Pale, but undauntedly, he faced his foes;
Warm as he spoke his kindling spirit rose;
Well pleased, on him the patriarch-fathers smiled,
And every mother loved him as her child.

"Monarch! to thee no traitor, here I stand;
These are my brethren, this my native land;
My native land, by sword and fire consumed,
My brethren, captive, and to death foredoomed;
To these indeed a Rebel in my youth,
A fugitive apostate from the truth,
Too late repentant, I confess my crime,
And mourn o'er lost irrevocable time.
—When from thy camp by conscience urged to flee,
I planned no wrong, I laid no snare for thee:
Did I provoke these sons of innocence,
Against thine arms, to rise in vain defence?
No; I conjured them, ere this threatened hour,
In sheltering forests to escape thy power;
Firm in their rectitude, they scorned to fly;
Thy foes they were not,—they resolved to die.
Yet think not thou, amidst thy warlike bands,
They lie beyond redemption in thine hands:
The God in whom they trust may help them still,
They know he *can* deliver, and HE WILL:
Whether by life, or death, afflict them not,
On his decree, not thine, they rest their lot.
For me, unworthy with the just to share
Death or deliverance, this is Javan's prayer;
Mercy, O God! to these in life be shown,
I die rejoicing, if I die alone."

"Thou shalt not die alone;" a voice replied,
A well-known voice—'twas Zillah at his side;
She, while he spake, with eagerness to hear,
Step after step, unconsciously drew near;
Her bosom with severe compunction wrung,
Pleased or alarmed, on every word she hung.
He turned his face;—with agonizing air,
In all the desolation of despair,
She stood; her hands to heaven uplift and claspt
Then suddenly unloosed, his arm she grasped,
And thus, in wild apostrophes of wo,
Vented her grief while tears refused to flow.

"O I have wronged thee, Javan!—Let us be
Espoused in death:—No, I will die for thee.
—Tyrant! behold thy victim; on my head
Be all the bitterness of vengeance shed,
But spare the innocent; let Javan live
Whose crime was love:—Can Javan too forgive
Love's slightest, fondest weakness, maiden-shame,
—It was not pride,—that hid my bosom-flame?
And wilt thou mourn the poor transgressor's death,
Who says, 'I love thee,' with her latest breath?
And when thou thinkst of days and years gone by,
Will thoughts of Zillah sometimes swell thine eye?
If ever thou hast cherished in thine heart
Visions of hope, in which I bore a part;
If ever thou hast longed with me to share
One home-born joy, one home-endearing care;
If thou didst ever love me;—speak the word,
Which late with feigned indifferency I heard;
Tell me, thou lovest me still;—haste, Javan, mark,
How high those ruffians pile the fagots,—hark,
How the flames crackle,—see, how fierce they glare,
Like fiery serpents hissing through the air;
Farewell; I fear them not—Now seize me, bind
These willing limbs,—ye can not touch the mind;
Unawed, I stand on nature's failing brink:
—Nay look not on me, Javan, lest I shrink;
Give me thy prayers, but turn away thine eye,
That I may lift my soul to heaven, and die."

Thus Zillah raved in passionate distress,
Till phrensy softened into tenderness;
Sorrow and love, with intermingling grace,
Terror and beauty, lightened o'er her face;
Her voice, her eye, in every soul was felt,
And giant-hearts were moved, unwont to melt.
Javan, in wonder, pity, and delight,
Almost forgot his being, at the sight;
That bending form, those suppliant accents, seem,
The strange illusion of a lover's dream;
And while she clung upon his arm, he found
His limbs, his lips, as by enchantment, bound;
He dare not touch her, lest the charm should break,
He dare not move, lest he himself should wake.

But when she ceased to speak and he to hear,
The silence startled him;—cold, shivering fear
Crept o'er his nerves;—in thought he cast his eye
Back on the world, and heaved a bitter sigh,
Thus from life's sweetest pleasures to be torn,
Just when he seemed to new existence born,
And cease to feel, when feeling ceased to be
A fever of protracted misery,
And cease to love, when love no more was pain,
'Twas but a pang of transient weakness:—"Vain
Are all thy sorrows," falteringly he said;
"Already I am numbered with the dead;
But long and blissfully may Zillah live!
—And canst thou Javan's cruel scorn forgive?
And wilt thou mourn the poor transgressor's death,
Who says 'I love thee,' with his latest breath?
And when thou thinkest of days and years gone by,
Will thoughts of Javan sometimes swell thine eye?
Ah! while I withered in thy chilling frown,
'Twas easy then to lay life's burden down;
When singly sentenced to these flames, my mind
Gloried in leaving all I loved behind;
How hast thou triumphed o'er me in this hour!
One look has crushed my soul's collected power;
Thy scorn I might endure, thy pride defy,
But O thy kindness makes it hard to die!"

"Then we will die together."—"Zillah! no,
Thou shalt not perish; let me, let me go;
Behold thy parents; calm thy father's fears:
Thy mother weeps; canst thou resist her tears?"

"Away with folly!" in tremendous tone,
Exclaimed a voice, more horrid than the groan
Of famished tiger leaping on his prey;
—Crouched at the monarch's feet the speaker lay;
But starting up, in his ferocious mien
That monarch's ancient foster-sire was seen,

The goatherd—he who snatched him from the flood,
The sorcerer, who nursed him up to blood;
Who still, his evil genius felly bent
On one bold purpose, went where'er he went;
That purpose, long in his own bosom sealed,
Ripe for fulfilment now, he thus revealed.
Full in the midst he rushed; alarmed, aghast,
Giants and captives trembled as he passed,
For scarcely seemed he of the sons of earth;
Unchronicled the hour that gave him birth;
Though shrunk his cheek, his temples deeply ploughed,
Keen was his vulture-eye, his strength unbowed;
Swarthy his features; venerably gray,
His beard dishevelled o'er his bosom lay:
Bald was his front; but, white as snow behind,
His ample locks were scattered to the wind;
Naked he stood, save round his loins a zone
Of shagged fur, and o'er his shoulders thrown
A serpent's skin, that crossed his breast, and round
His body thrice in glittering volumes wound.

All gazed with horror:—deep unuttered thought
In every muscle of his visage wrought;
His eye as if his eye could see the air,
Was fixed; up-writhing rose his horrent hair;
His limbs grew dislocate, convulsed his frame;
Deep from his chest mysterious noises came,
Now purring, hissing, barking, then they swelled
To hideous dissonance; he shrieked, he yelled,
As if the legion-fiend his soul possessed,
And a whole hell were worrying in his breast,
Then down he dashed himself on earth, and rolled
In agony, till powerless, stiff, and cold,
With face upturned to heaven, and arms outspread,
A ghastly spectacle he lay as dead;
The living too stood round, like forms of death,
And every pulse was hushed, and every breath.

Meanwhile the wind arose, the clouds were driven
In watery masses through the waste of heaven,
The groaning woods foretold a tempest nigh,
And silent lightnings skirmished in the sky.

Ere long the wizard started from the ground,
Giddily reeled, and looked bewildered round,
Till on the king he fixed his hideous gaze;
Then wrapt with ecstacy and broad amaze.
He kneeled in adoration, humbly bowed
His face upon his hands, and cried aloud;
Yet so remote and strange his accents fell,
They seemed the voice of an invisible:
—"Hail! king and conqueror of the peopled earth,
And more than king and conqueror! know thy birth;
Thou art a ray of uncreated fire,
The Sun himself is thy celestial sire;
The Moon thy mother, who to me consigned,
Her babe in secrecy, to bless mankind.
These eyes have watched thee rising, year by year,
More great, more glorious in thine high career.
As the young eagle plies his growing wings
In bounded flights, and sails in wider rings,
Till to the fountain of meridian day,
Full plumed and perfected he soars away;
Thus have I marked thee, since thy course began,
Still upward tending to thy sire the sun:
Now midway meet him; form yon flaming height,
Chase the vain phantoms of cherubic light;
There build a tower; whose spiral top shall rise,
Circle o'er circle, lessening to the skies:
The stars, thy brethren, in their spheres shall stand
To hail thee welcome to thy native land;
The moon shall clasp thee in her glad embrace,
The sun behold his image in thy face,
And call thee, as his offspring and his heir,
His throne, his empire, and his orb to share."

Rising and turning his terrific head,
That chilled beholders, thus the enchanter said;
—"Prepare, prepare the piles of sacrifice,
The power that rules on earth shall rule the skies:
Hither, O chiefs! the captive patriarchs bring,
And pour their blood an offering to your king;
He, like his sire the sun, in transient clouds,
Has veiled divinity from mortals shrouds,
Too pure to shine till these his foes are slain,
And conquered paradise hath crowned his reign.
Haste, heap the fallen cedars on the pyres,
And give the victims living to the fires;
Shall he, in whom they vainly trust, withstand
Your sovereign's wrath, or pluck them from his hand?
We dare him;—if he saves his servants now,
To him let every knee in nature bow,
For HE is GOD"——at that most awful name,
A spasm of horror withered up his frame;
Even as he stood and looked,—he looks, he stands,
With heaven-defying front, and clenched hands,
And lips half-opened, eager from his breast
To blot the blasphemy, by force represt;
For not in feigned abstraction, as before,
He practised foul deceit by damned lore,
A frost was on his nerves, and in his veins
A fire consuming with infernal pains;
Conscious, though motionless his limbs were grown;
Alive to suffering, but alive in stone.

In silent expectation, sore amazed,
The king and chieftains on the sorcerer gazed;
Awhile no sound was heard, save through the woods,
The wind deep-thundering, and the dashing floods:
At length, with solemn step, amidst the scene,
Where that false prophet showed his frantic mien,
Where lurid flames from green-wood altars burned,
Enoch stood forth; on him all eyes were turned,
O'er his dim form and saintly visage fell
The light that glared upon that priest of hell.
Unutterably awful was his look;
Through every joint the giant-monarch shook;
Shook, like Belshazzer, in his festive hall,
When the hand wrote his judgment on the wall;*
Shook, like Eliphaz, with dissolving fright,†
In thoughts amidst the visions of the night,
When as the spirit passed before his face,
No limb, nor lineament his eye could trace;
A form of mystery, that chilled his blood,
Close at his couch in living terror stood,
And deathlike silence, till a voice more drear,
More dreadful than the silence, reached his ear:
Thus from surrounding darkness Enoch brake,
And thus the giant trembled while he spake.

CANTO TENTH.

The prophecy of Enoch concerning the sorcerer, the king, and the flood. His translation to heaven. The conclusion.

"The Lord is jealous:—He, who reigns on high,
Upholds the earth, and spreads abroad the sky;
His voice the moon and stars by night obey,
He sends the sun his servant forth by day:
From him all beings came, on him depend,
To him return their author, sovereign, end,
Who shall destroy when he would save? or stand,
When he destroys, the stroke of his right hand?
With none his name and power will he divide,
For HE is GOD, and there is none beside.

"The proud shall perish:—mark how wild his air
In impotence of malice and despair,
What phrensy fires the bold blasphemer's cheek!
He looks the courses which he can not speak.
A hand hath touched him that he once defied
Touched, and for ever crushed him in his pride;
Yet shall he live, despised as feared before;
The great deceiver shall deceive no more;
Children shall pluck the beard of him, whose arts
Palsied the boldest hands, the stoutest hearts;
His vaunted wisdom fools shall laugh to scorn,
When muttering spells, a spectacle forlorn,
A drivelling idiot, he shall fondly roam
From house to house, and never find a home."

The wizard heard his sentence; nor remained,
A moment longer; from his trance unchained,

* Dan. v. 1—31 † Job iv 12—21

He plunged into the woods;—the prophet then
Turned, and took up his parable again.

"The proud shall perish:—Monarch! know thy doom;
Thy bones shall lack the shelter of a tomb;
Not in the battle-field thine eyes shall close,
Slain upon thousands of thy slaughtered foes;
Not on the throne of empire, nor the bed
Of weary nature, thou shalt bow thine head:
Death lurks in ambush; death, without a name,
Shall pluck thee from thy pinnacle of fame;
At eve, rejoicing o'er thy finished toil,
Thy soul shall deem the universe her spoil;
The dawn shall see thy carcase cast away,
The wolves, at sunrise, slumber on their prey.
Cut from the living, whither dost thou go?
Hall is moved to meet thee from below:
The kings thy sword had slain, the mighty dead,
Start from their thrones at thy descending tread;
They ask in scorn,—'Destroyer! is it thus?
Art thou,—thou too,—become like one of us?
Torn from the feast of music, wine, and mirth,
The worms thy covering, and thy couch the earth:
How art thou fallen from thine ethereal height,
Son of the morning! sunk in endless night:
How art thou fallen, who saidst, in pride of soul,
I will ascend above the starry pole,
Thence rule the adoring nations with my nod,
And set my throne above the mount of God.
Spilt in the dust, thy blood pollutes the ground;
Sought by the eyes that feared thee, yet not found,
Thy chieftains pause, they turn thy relics o'er,
Then pass thee by,—for thou art known no more.
Hail to thine advent! potentate, in hell,
Unfeared, unflattered, undistinguished dwell;
On earth thy fierce ambition knew no rest,
A worm, a flame for ever in thy breast;
Here feel the rage of unconsuming fire,
Intense, eternal, impotent desire;
Here lie, the deathless worm's unwasting prey,
In chains of darkness till the judgment-day.'

"Thus while the dead thy fearful welcome sing,
Thy living slaves bewail their vanished king.
Then, though thy reign with infamy expire,
Fulfilled in death shall be thy vain desire;
The traitors, reeking with thy blood, shall swear,
They saw their sovereign ravished through the air,
And point thy star revolving o'er the night,
A baleful comet with portentous light,
'Midst clouds and storms, denouncing from afar
Famine and havoc, pestilence and war.
Temples, not tombs, thy monuments shall be,
And altars blaze on hills and groves to thee;
A pyramid shall consecrate thy crimes,
Thy name and honors to succeeding times;
There shall thine image hold the highest place
Among the gods of man's revolted race!

"That race shall perish:—men and giants, all
Thy kindred and thy worshippers shall fall.
The babe, whose life with yesterday began,
May spring to youth, and ripen into man,
But ere his locks are tinged with fading gray,
This world of sinners shall be swept away.
Jehovah lifts his standard to the skies,
Swift at the signal winds and vapors rise;
The sun in sackcloth veils his face at noon,—
The stars are quenched, and turned to blood the moon,
Heaven's fountains open, clouds dissolving roll
In mingled cataracts from pole to pole.
Earth's central sluices burst, the hills upturn,
In rapid whirlpools down the gulf are borne;
The voice, that taught the deep his bounds to know,
'Thus far, O sea! nor farther shalt thou go,'—
Sends forth the floods, commissioned to devour,
With boundless license and resistless power;
They own no impulse but the tempest's sway,
Nor find a limit but the light of day.

"The vision opens:—sunk beneath the wave,
The guilty share a universal grave;
One wilderness of waters rolls in view,
And heaven and ocean wear one turbid hue;
Still stream unbroken torrents from the skies,
Higher beneath the inundations rise;
A lurid twilight glares athwart the scene,
Now thunders peal, faint lightnings flash between.
—Methinks I see a distant vessel ride,
A lonely object on the shoreless tide;
Within whose ark the innocent have found
Safety, while stayed destruction ravens round;
Thus, in the hour of vengeance, God who knows
His servants, spares them, while he smites his foes.

"Eastward I turn;—o'er all the deluged lands,
Unshaken yet, a mighty mountain stands,
Where Seth, of old, his flock to pasture led,
And watched the stars at midnight from its head;
An island now, its dark majestic form
Scowls through the thickest ravage of the storm;
While on its top, the monument of fame,
Built by thy murderers to adorn thy name,
Defies the shock;—a thousand cubits high,
The sloping pyramid ascends the sky.
Thither, their latest refuge in distress,
Like hunted wolves, the rallying giants press;
Round the broad base of that stupendous tower,
The shuddering fugitives collect their power,
Cling to the dizzy cliff, o'er ocean bend,
And howl with terror as the deeps ascend.
The mountain's strong foundations still endure,
The heights repel the surge.—Awhile secure
And cheered with frantic hope, thy votaries climb
The fabric, rising step by step sublime.
Beyond the clouds they see the summit glow
In heaven's pure daylight o'er the gloom below;
There too thy worshipped image shines like fire,
In the full glory of thy fabled sire.
They hail the omen, and with heart and voice,
Call on thy name, and in thy smile rejoice;
False omen! on thy name in vain they call;
Fools in their joy;—a moment and they fall.
Rent by an earthquake of the buried plain,
And shaken by the whole disrupted main,
The mountain trembles on its failing base,
It slides, it stoops, it rushes from its place:
From all the giants burst one drowning cry;
Hark! 'tis thy name—they curse it as they die;
Sheer to the lowest gulf the pile is hurled,
The last sad wreck of a devoted world.

"So fall transgressors:—Tyrant! now fulfil
Thy secret purposes, thine utmost will;
Here crown thy triumphs:—life or death decree,
The weakest here disdains thy power and thee."

Thus when the patriarch ceased, and every ear
Still listened in suspense of hope and fear,
Sublime, ineffable, angelic grace
Beamed in his meek and venerable face;
And sudden glory, streaming round his head,
O'er all his robes with lambent lustre spread;
His earthly features grew divinely bright,
His essence seemed transforming into light.
Brief silence, like the pause between the flash,
At midnight, and the following thunder-crash,
Ensued:—Anon, with universal cry,
The giants rushed upon the prophet—"Die!"
The king leapt foremost from his throne;—he drew
His battle-sword, as on his mark he flew;
With aim unerring, and tempestuous sound,
The blade descended deep along the ground;
The foe was fled, and, self-o'erwhelmed, his strength
Hurled to the earth his Atlantean length;
But ere his chiefs could stretch the helping arm,
He sprang upon his feet in pale alarm;
Headlong and blind with rage he searched around,
But *Enoch walked with God and was not found.*

Yet where the captives stood, in holy awe,
Rapt on the wings of cherubim, they saw
Their sainted sire ascending through the night;
He turned his face to bless them in his flight,

Then vanished:—Javan caught the prophet's eye,
And snatched his mantle falling from the sky;
O'er him the spirit of the prophet came,
Like rushing wind awakening hidden flame:
"Where is the God of Enoch now?" he cried;*
"Captives, come forth! despisers, shrink aside."
He spake, and bursting through the giant-throng,
Smote with the mantle as he moved along;
A power invisible their rage controlled
Hither and thither as he turned they rolled;
Unawed, unharmed the ransomed prisoners passed
Through ranks of foes astonished and aghast:
Close in the youth's conducting steps they trod;
—So Israel marched when Moses raised his rod,
And led their host, enfranchised, through the wave,
The people's safeguard, the pursuers' grave.

Thus from the wolves this little flock was torn,
And sheltering in the mountain-caves till morn,
They joined to sing, in strains of full delight,
Songs of deliverance through the dreary night.

The giants' phrensy, when they lost their prey,
No tongue of man or angel might portray;
First on their idol gods their vengeance turned,
Those gods on their own altar-piles they burned;
Then, at their sovereign's mandate, sallied forth
To rouse their host to combat, from the north;
Eager to risk their uttermost emprise,
Perish ere morn, or reign in paradise.
Now the slow tempest, that so long had lowered,
Keen in their faces sleet and hailstones showered,
The winds blew loud, the waters roared around,
An earthquake rocked the agonizing ground;
Red in the west the burning mount, arrayed
With tenfold terror by incumbent shade,
(For moon and stars were rapt in dunnest gloom,)
Glared like a torch amidst creation's tomb:
So Sinai's rocks were kindled when they felt
Their Maker's footstep, and began to melt;
Darkness was his pavilion, whence he came,
High in the brightness of descending flame,
While storm, and whirlwind, and the trumpet's blast,
Proclaimed his law in thunder, as he passed.

The giants reached their camp:—the night's alarms
Meanwhile had startled all their slaves to arms;
They grasped their weapons as from sleep they sprang,
From tent to tent the brazen clangor rang;
The hail, the earthquake, the mysterious light
Unnerved their strength, o'erwhelmed them with affright.
"Warriors! to battle;—summon all your powers;
Warriors! to conquest;—paradise is ours;"
Exclaimed their monarch!—not an arm was raised,
In vacancy of thought, like men amazed,
And lost amidst confounding dreams, they stood,
With palsied eyes, and horror-frozen blood.
The giants' rage to instant madness grew;
The king and chiefs on their own legions flew,
Denouncing vengeance;—then had all the plain
Been heaped with myriads by their leaders slain,
But ere a sword could fall,—by whirlwinds driven,
In mighty volumes, through the vault of heaven,
From Eden's summit, o'er the camp accurst,
The darting fires with noon-day splendor burst;
And fearful grew the scene above, below,
With sights of mystery, and sounds of wo.
The embattled cherubim appeared on high,
And coursers, winged with lightning, swept the sky;
Chariots, whose wheels with living instinct rolled,
Spirits of unimaginable mould,
Powers, such as dwell in heaven's serenest light,
Too pure, too terrible for mortal sight,
From depth of midnight suddenly revealed,
In arms, against the giants took the field.
On such a host Elisha's servant gazed,
When all the mountain round the prophet blazed;†
With such a host, when war in heaven was wrought,
Michael against the prince of darkness fought.

* "And he (*Elisha*) took the mantle of Elijah that fell from him and smote the waters (*of Jordan*) and said,—Where is the Lord God of Elijah?—and when he also had smitten the waters, they parted hither and thither: and Elisha went over."—2 Kings ii. 14.
† 2 Kings iv. 17

Roused by the trumpet, that shall wake the dead,
The torpid foe in consternation fled;
The giants headlong in the uproar ran,
The king himself the foremost of the van,
Nor e'er his rushing squadron led to fight
With swifter onset than he led that flight.
Homeward the panic-stricken legions flew;
Their arms, their vestments, from their limbs they threw;
O'er shields and helms the reinless camel strode,
And gold and purple strewed the desert road.
When through the Assyrian army, like a blast,
At midnight the destroying angel passed,
The tyrant that defied the living God,
Precipitately thus his steps retrod;
Even by the way he came, to his own land,
Returned to perish by his offspring's hand.*
So fled the giant-monarch;—but unknown
The hand that smote his life;—he died alone;
Amidst the tumult treacherously slain;
At morn his chieftains sought their lord in vain,
Then, reckless of the harvest of their toils,
Their camp, their captives, all their treasured spoils,
Renewed their flight o'er eastern hills afar,
With life alone escaping from that war,
In which their king had hailed his realm complete,
The world's last province bowed beneath his feet.

As when the waters of the flood declined,
Rolling tumultuously before the wind,
The proud waves shrunk from low to lower beds,
And high the hills and higher raised their heads,
Till ocean lay, enchased with rock and strand,
As in the hollow of the Almighty's hand,
While earth with wrecks magnificent was strewed,
And stillness reigned o'er nature's solitude.
—Thus in a storm of horror and dismay,
All night the giant army sped away;
Thus on a lonely, sad, and silent scene,
The morning rose in majesty serene.

Early, and joyful, o'er the dewy grass,
Straight to their glen the ransomed patriarchs pass;
As doves released their parent-dwelling find,
They fly for life, nor cast a look behind;
And when they reached the dear sequestered spot,
Enoch alone of all their train "*was not.*"
With them the bard, who from the world withdrew,
Javan, from folly and ambition flew;
Though poor his lot, within that narrow bound,
Friendship and home, and faithful love he found;
There did his wanderings and afflictions cease,
His youth was penitence, his age was peace.

Meanwhile the scattered tribes of Eden's plain
Turned to their desolated fields again,
And joined their brethren, captives once in fight,
But left to freedom in that dreadful flight:
Thenceforth redeemed from war's unnumbered woes,
Rich with the spoils of their retreated foes,
By giant tyranny no more opprest,
The people flourished, and the land had rest.

* 2 Kings, xix. 33-37

NOTES.

Mr. James Montgomery is by birth a Scotchman, and was born on the 4th of November, 1771, at Irvine, a small seaport town in Ayrshire, Scotland. He was the eldest son of a Moravian minister, by whom he was removed to Gracehill, in the county of Antrim, Ireland, in the year 1776; and afterward placed at the early age of six years in the seminary of the united Moravian brethren, at Fulneck, near Leeds, in Yorkshire. It may be almost said, that at this early period of Mr Montgomery's life he was for ever separated from his parents, since, previous to their departure as missionaries for the West Indies, where his mother died in 1789, and his father in 1790, he resided with them but for three months in the year 1784.

How happy the parents of Mr. Montgomery had been in placing their son, circumstanced as they were, under the guidance and tuition of the pious and learned Moravian brethren can now be easily perceived from the result it has produced For, notwithstanding that every reader of Mr Montgomery's works may trace in them the effects of a mind naturally virtuous and religious, we can not withhold from believing that he is in a great measure indebted to the education he has received for his well-earned fame as a moral poet. He began to write sacred poetry when he was no older than ten years, and report even goes so far as to say, that he had composed at this tender age, two volumes of such poetry. On finishing his studies in the seminary of the Moravian brethren, which occupied ten years, he was placed by his friends as an apprentice with a very worthy man of his own persuasion, who kept a retail shop at Mirfield, near Wakefield. This was a calling in no manner calculated to suit the genius of Montgomery; and not being under the articles of apprenticeship, he left his master at the end of a year and a half, with only three shillings and sixpence in his pocket, but big with the expectation of reaching London, which now his youthful imagination portrayed as the patron city of learning and talent. His humble means, however, did not allow him to proceed as far as he expected, and he found himself constrained on the fifth day, to enter into an employment at Wath, near Rotherham, which was not dissimilar to that he had left behind him at Mirfield. Previous to his departure from this latter place, he had left a letter with his employer, in which, besides testifying his uneasiness of mind, he promised to be heard from again in a few days. He now fulfilled his promise, and requested at the same time a character to recommend him to the trust of his new master. His upright conduct and virtuous habits not only gained him this from his late employer and the rest of the Moravian brethren, but also the promise of an establishment more congenial to his wishes, if he would return. This, however, he declined, candidly confessing the cause of his melancholy, but concealing the ambitious motives which prompted him to withdraw from their benevolent protection. It was his present master, with whom he remained only twelve months, that many years afterward, in the most calamitous period of Montgomery's life, sought him out amidst his misfortunes, not for the purpose of offering consolation only, but to serve him substantially by every means in his power. The interview which took place between the old man and his former servant, the evening previous to his trial at Doncaster, will ever live in the memory of him who can forget an injury but not a kindness. No father could have evinced a greater affection for a darling son; the tears he shed were honorable to his feelings, and were the best testimony to the conduct and integrity of James Montgomery.

On leaving Wath, he found means to introduce himself to Mr. Harrison, a bookseller, in London, in consequence of having sent him, previous to his departure, a volume of manuscript poems. This gentleman gave Mr. Montgomery employment in his shop, but not undertaking the publication of his poems, he recommended the poet to the study of prose, as likely to be more profitable than poetry. Mr. Montgomery began now to perceive that London was not so much the land of promotion as he fancied it to be; and having had at the end of eight months a misunderstanding with Mr. Harrison, which was accompanied with the misfortune of not being able to dispose of an eastern tale in prose, he returned to his former employment in Yorkshire.

He removed in 1792 to Sheffield, and engaged himself with Mr. Gales, the publisher of a very popular newspaper, at that time known by the title of the Sheffield Register. Mr. Montgomery became a useful correspondent to this paper, and gained so far the good opinion and affection of Mr. Gales and his family, that they vied with each other in demonstrating their respect and regard for him. In 1794, when Mr. Gales left England to avoid a political prosecution, Montgomery, with the assistance of a literary gentleman, with whom he had not been even personally acquainted, became the publisher of the Register, which title he changed for that of the Iris. He was not, however, long in his new profession before he fell twice into the hands of Justice, and underwent each time the penalty of fine and imprisonment. His first crime was to have printed a song, composed by an Irish clergyman, at the entreaty of a man whom he had never seen before. He was tried for this at the Quarter Sessions of 1795, and found *guilty of publishing*; but this verdict being tantamount to an acquittal, it was refused by the court, and the jury were sent to reconsider for another hour, when they gave in a general verdict of *guilty*. The sentence, which was a fine of twenty pounds and three months imprisonment in York Castle. Our readers may think that we are forgetting ourselves in this part of Mr. Montgomery's biography, and are leading them back to some remote and barbarous age; but such a trial did take place at no earlier a period than thirty or forty years ago. During his confinement, an active friend superintended his business, and on resuming his editorial duties he commenced a series of essays, entitled *the Whisperer*, which, notwithstanding that they were written in haste for his *paper*, contained a very considerable share of genuine humor.

Though he was very anxious not to leave it in the power of the law to find him guilty of an offence a second time, it was not however long after undergoing his first penalty, that he had to experience the severity of another. He gave in his paper, as he thought, in a correct manner, the particulars of a riot that took place in the streets of Sheffield, and in which two men were shot by the military. His statement of the circumstances, however, gave offence to a magistrate in the neighborhood, who preferred a bill of indictment against Mr Montgomery; and notwithstanding that the latter had a great many witnesses who verified his account of the transaction in the Iris, he was found guilty at Doncaster Sessions, in January, 1796, and sentenced to pay a fine of thirty pounds, and suffer another imprisonment in York Castle, for the space of six months.

He found his constitution greatly impaired in consequence of these two imprisonments, and immediately after his last liberation, he repaired to Scarborough for the benefit of his health. It may be said that this was the first time for him to behold the sea as a poet, and the delight which the sight of it afforded his mind was not greater than the health restored to his body. His visits thither were consequently repeated, and it was one of these which gave birth to his poem on the Ocean, written in the summer of 1805. In 1797, he published his Prison "Amusements," and in 1806, produced the volume containing the "Wanderer of Switzerland." His time was now chiefly occupied in editing his paper, and no work of considerable magnitude appeared from his pen until the year 1809, when his West Indies was published in quarto, with superb embellishments. Three years after the appearance of this last-mentioned poem, he produced "The World before the Flood," which is to stamp his fame for ever as a superior poet.

It has been frequently, and perhaps justly, observed, that the delight which beautiful poetry affords, is obtained too often to the prejudice of moral feelings and precepts, which are better calculated to ennoble the human mind. But had we not Milton, Fenelon, Klopstock, and even the divine writers themselves, to show the fallacy of this bold accusation, brought against the most powerful language and effort of man, the poems of Montgomery alone would form a compilation of proofs so able and so manifest in themselves, as to be fully sufficient for composing a refutation at once unanswerable and undoubted. Every line of his poetry invites to a love of virtue and all that is amiable in our nature; while it fills the soul at the same time with the sweet luxury of pure, yet delightful enjoyment, and creates within us an admiration and esteem for that art under which so many great and happy powers have been put forth.

The "World before the Flood," is by far Mr. Montgomery's best poem. It is divided into ten cantos, written in the heroic couplet, and has for the foundation of its story, the invasion of Eden by the descendants of Cain. The author's introductory note says:—

No place having been found, in Asia, to correspond exactly with the Mosaic description of the site of Paradise, the Author of the following Poem has disregarded both the learned and the absurd hypotheses on the subject, and at once imagining an inaccessible tract of land, at the confluence of four rivers, which after their junction take the name of the largest, and become the Euphrates of the ancient world, he has placed "the happy garden" there. Milton's noble fiction of the Mount of Paradise being removed by the deluge, and pushed

"Down the great river to the opening gulf,"

and there converted into a barren isle, implies such a change in the water-courses as will, poetically at least, account for the difference between the scene of this story and the present face of the country, at the point where the Tigris and the Euphrates meet. On the eastern side of these waters, the Author supposes the descendants of the younger children of Adam to dwell, possessing the land of Eden: the rest of the world having been gradually colonized by emigrants from these, or peopled by the posterity of Cain. In process of time, after the sons of God had formed connexions with the daughters of men, and there were giants in the earth, the latter assumed to be lords and rulers over mankind, till among themselves arose one, excelling all his brethren in knowledge and power, who became their king, and by their aid, in the course of a long life, subdued all the inhabited earth, except the land of Eden. This land, at the head of a mighty army, principally composed of the descendants of Cain, he has invaded and conquered, even to the banks of Euphrates, at the opening of the action of the poem. It is only necessary to add, that for the sake of distinction, the invaders are frequently denominated from Cain, as "the host of Cain,"—"the force of Cain,"—"the camp of Cain,"—and the remnant of the defenders of Eden are, in like manner, denominated from Eden.—The Jews have an ancient tradition, that some of the giants, at the deluge, fled to the top of a high mountain, and escaped the ruin that involved the rest of their kindred. In the tenth Canto of the preceding poem a hint is borrowed from this tradition, but is made to yield to the superior authority of Scripture testimony.

AN EXCELLENT POEM

UPON THE

LONGING OF A BLESSED HEART,

WHICH,

LOATHING THE WORLD,

DOTH

LONG TO BE WITH CHRIST.

BY NICHOLAS BRETON, GENTLEMAN.

Printed at London, A. D. 1601.

WHAT life hath he that never thinks of love?
And what such love but hath a special liking?
And what such liking but will seek to prove
The best to find the comfort of his seeking?
But while fond thoughts in Folly's pack are peeking,
Better conceited wits may easily find,
The truest wealth that may enrich the mind.

But since the difference 'twixt the good and bad
Is easily seen in notes of their delights;
And that those notes are needful to be had,
To see whose eyes are of the clearest sights;
Whose are the days, and whose may be the nights;
From the poor crutch unto the princely crown,
I will the difference, as I find, set down.

The worldly prince longs to increase his state,
To conquer kingdoms, and to wear their crowns,
A foreign power by forces to abate,
To make but footstools of their fairest towns;
And hates the spirits of those home-made clowns,
That will not venture life for victory:
But yet forgets that God should have the glory.

The worldly counsellor doth beat his brains,
How to advise his sovereign for the best,
And in his place doth take continual pains
To keep his prince in such a pleasing rest,
That he may still be leaning on his breast,
Thinking his hap unto a heaven so wrought;
But yet perhaps God is not in his thought.

The soldier he delighteth all in arms,
To see his colors in the field displayed;
And longs to see the issue of those harms,
That may reveal an enemy dismayed,
A fort defeated, or a town betrayed;
And still to be in action day and night,
But little thinks on God in all the fight.

The worldly scholar loves a world of books,
And spends his life in many an idle line:
Meanwhile his heart to heaven but little looks,
Nor loves to think upon a thought divine;
These thoughts of ours, alas! so low incline:
We seek to know what Nature can affect;
But unto God have small or no respect.

The poet with his fictions and his fancies,
Pleaseth himself with humorous inventions;
Which well considered are a kind of phrensies,
That carry little truth in their intentions:
While Wit and Reason falling at contentions,
Make Wisdom find that Folly's strong illusion
Brings Wit and Senses wholly to confusion.

The worldly lawyer studieth right and wrong;
But how he judgeth, there the question lies:
For, if you look for what his love doth long,
It is the profit of his plea doth rise:
There is the worldly lawyer's paradise!
He neither longs the right or wrong to see,
But to be fing'ring of the golden fee.

The cosmographer doth the world survey,
The hills and dales, the nooks and little crooks,
The woods, the plains, the high, and the by-way,
The seas, the rivers, and the little brooks:
All these he finds within his compast books;
And with his needle makes his measure even;
But all this while he doth not think of heaven

Th' astronomer stands staring on the sky,
And will not have a thought beneath a star;
But by his speculation doth espy
A world of wonder, coming from afar;
And tells of times and natures, peace and war:
Of Mars his sword, and Mercury his rod;
But all this while he little thinks on God.

The worldly merchant ventureth far and near;
And shuns nor land nor sea to make a gain;
Thinks neither travel, care, nor cost too dear,
If that his profit countervail his pain,
While so his mind is on the getting vein,
That if his ship do safely come on shore,
Gold is his god, and he desires no more.

The worldly courtier learns to crouch and creep,
Speak fair, wait close, observe his time and place,
And wake and watch, and scarcely catch a sleep,
Till he have got into some favor's grace,
And will all cunning in his course embrace,
That may unto authority advance:
But if he think on God, it is a chance.

The worldly farmer fills his barns with corn,
And ploughs, and sows, and digs, and delves, and hedges
Looks to his cattle, will not lose a horn,
Fells down his woods and falls unto his wedges,
And grinds his axes, and doth mend their edges,
And dearly sells that he good cheap hath bought;
But all this while, God is not in his thought.

The sailor, he doth by his compass stand,
And weighs his anchor, and doth hoist his sails,
And longs for nothing but to get on land,
While many a storm his starting spirit quails,
And fear of pirates his poor heart assails:
But once on shore, carouse and casts off fear,
Yet scarcely thinks on God that set him there.

The worldly preacher talks of sacrifice,
Of sacraments, and holy mysteries:
Meanwhile he longs but for the benefice,
That should preserve his purse from beggaries,
Because he loves no worldly miseries:
For many a preacher that God's word hath taught,
Shows by his life, God lives not in his thought.

The worldly physician, that in sickness tries
The nature of the herbs and minerals,
And in his simples and his compounds spies,
Which way to make the patients' funerals,
Or profit by his cures in generals;
Longs but to see how long they may endure;
But scarcely thinks on God in all the cure.

The worldly musician, that doth tune his voice,
Unto such notes as music's skill hath set;
Whose heart doth in the harmony rejoice,
Where pleasing consorts are most kindly met:
But still perhaps his spirit doth forget,
In all his hymns, and songs, and sweetest lays,
To think of God, or of his worthy praise.

The politician hath a world of plots,
In which his spirit hath special spies;
Ties, and unties a thousand sundry knots,
In which the substance of his study lies;
And many tricks his close experience tries,
How to deceive the world with many a wile;
But never thinks on God in all the while.

The traveller delighteth in the view
Of change and choice of sundry kind of creatures;
To mark the habits, and to note the hue
Of far born people and their sundry natures,
Their shapes, their speech, their gaits, their looks, their features,
And longs abroad to make his life's abode:
Yet haply never longs to be with God.

The painter in his colors takes delight,
And near the life to make the livelihood;
While only shadows do deceive the sight,
That take such pleasure in a piece of wood;
But doth not long for that same living food,
Which neither eye hath seen, nor heart conceived,
The God of truth, that never soul deceived.

The lover, he, but on his lady thinketh,
And how to catch her in a kind content;
And looks, and leers, and trolls the eye, and winketh;
And seeks how thoughts in silence may be sent;
And longs to see the end of his intent:
And thinks himself a king, to get a kiss;
But where is God in all these thoughts of his?

Th' artificer that hath a work to do,
And brings his hand unto his head's device,
Longs till he see what it will come unto,
And how his pains hath profit in the price,
And having cast it over twice or thrice,
Joys in his heart: but scarcely hath a thought,
To thank his God, that him the cunning taught

The churl that sits and champs upon his chaff,
And will not stir a foot from his barn floor,
Except it be among his bags to laugh,
He can the poor so with his purse devour,
Longs but to use the poison of his power
T' enrich himself, to bring a world to naught;
Shows that God never dwells within his thought.

As for those beggarly conditions
Of basest trades, that like to miry hogs,
Do show their spirit's dispositions,
In digging with their noses under logs
For slime and worms, or like to ravening dogs,
Longs but for that which doth the belly fill,
Most of them think on God against their will.

These are the worldlings, and their world's delights,
Whose longing, God knows, is not worth the loving:
These are the objects of those evil sights,
That Virtue hath from her fair eyes removing;
These are the passions of Corruption's proving:
But they that love and long for God, his sight,
In worldly trifles never take delight.

The prince, anointed with the oil of grace,
Who sits with Mercy, in the seat of peace,
Will long to see his Savior in the face,
And all his right into his hands release;
(Whose only sight would make all sorrow cease);
And lay both crown and kingdom at his feet,
But of his presence to enjoy the sweet.

The chancellor with heavenly grace inspired,
Where wisdom guides the lineaments of wit,
Although he hath to honor's place aspired,
His heart doth show it longs not after it;
His love desires a higher mark to hit:
For while he leaneth on his prince's breast,
His longing is, but with his God to rest.

The courtier, that is once in God his grace,
Whatever countenance in the court he bears,
His heart aspireth to a better place;
Which humble love doth long for with those t[illegible]
Which all to naught the pride of pleasure wea[illegible]
And never rests until his God he sees,
With whom his soul in love doth long to b[illegible]

The soldier that hath fought the spirit's fight,
Will put off war, and long to live in peace;
And not in discord, but concord delight,
While gracious kindness makes all quarrels c[illegible]
While patience doth all passions so appease,
That he shall find that soldier only blest,
Whose faith, in God, doth set his soul at re[illegible]

The lawyer that hath read the laws of God,
And in his heart is touched with his love,
And knows the smart of the supernal rod,
Will one day work, for silly souls' behove,
Who have their comfort in the heavens above
Will leave all golden fees to see the grace,
That mercy's justice shows in Jesus' face.

The scholar that begins with Christ his cross,
And seeks good speed but in the Holy Ghost,
Finds by his book that silver is but dross,
And all his labor in his study lost;
Where faith, of mercy, can not sweetly boast
And love doth long for any other bliss,
Than what in God, and in his graces is,

And such a poet, as the psalmist was,
Who had no mind but on his master's love,
Whose muses did the world in music pass,
That only sung but of the soul's behove,
In giving glory to the God above,
Would all world's fictions wholly lay aside,
And only long but with the Lord to bide.

The cosmographer, that by rules of grace
Surveys the city of the heavenly saints,
Will never long for any earthly place,
That either pen prescribes, or painter paints;
But in the faith that never fails, nor faints,
Will long to see in heaven's Jerusalem
The gracious God of glorious diadem.

The true astronomer that sees the sun,
And knows that God from whom it takes his light,
And in the course the moon and stars do run,
Finds the true guider of the day and night,
Longs but to see his only blessed sight,
Who sun, and moon, and stars their brightness gives,
And in whose face all brightness, glory, lives.

The mariner that oft hath past the seas,
And in his perils seen the power of God,
Whose only mercy doth the storms appease,
And brings the ship unto his wished road,
Will never long on earth to make abode;
But in the heavens to see that blessed hand,
That at his beck so rules both sea and land.

The merchant that hath cast within his mind,
How much the spirit's gain the flesh surmounts,
And by his faith in mercy's love doth find
The joyful sum of such a soul's accounts,
As to salvation of the whole amounts;
Will leave the world but on Christ's face to look,
Which all the faithful make their living book.

The farmer that hath felt his neighbor's need,
And found how God and charity are one;
And knows there is a better kind of feed,
Than grass, or corn, or flesh, or blood, or bone,
Will wish himself from his world's treasure gone,
Upon those joys to feed in mercy's bliss,
Where Christ his presence is heaven's paradise.

The true physician that doth know the natures
And dispositions of each element,
And knows that God created hath all creatures
Beneath, and eke above the firmament,
And over all hath only government,
Will only long that glorious God to know,
That gives the sickness and doth cure it so.

The soul's musician that doth find the ground
Of truest music, but in God his grace,
Will think all singing but an idle sound,
Where God his praise hath not the highest place,
And only longs to see that blessed face,
Which makes the virgins, saints, and angels, sing
An hallelujah to their heavenly king.

The preacher, that doth in his soul believe
The word of God, which to the world he teacheth,
And in his spirit inwardly doth grieve,
He can not live so heavenly as he preacheth,
While faith no further than to mercy reacheth;
Would wish in soul to leave his benefice,
To make himself to Christ a sacrifice.

The politician that hath plotted much
In worldly matters, greatly to his gain;
Will find, if God do once his spirit touch,
Zaccheus' heart will have another vein
To climb aloft, and to come down again;
And leave all plots to come but to that place,
Where he might see sweet Jesus in the face.

The artificer that hath a work in hand,
And feels the grace of God within his heart;
And by the same doth surely understand,
How God alone perfecteth every part,
And only is the giver of all art,
Will gladly leave his work and long to be,
Where he might Christ his soul's work-master see.

The painter that doth paint a dainty image
So near the life, as may be to the same,
And makes an ass unto an owl do homage,
While shadows bring the senses out of frame,
If God his heart once with his love inflame,
His pictures all will under foot be trod,
And he will long but for the living God.

The traveller that walks the world about,
And sees the glorious works of God on high;
If God his grace once kindly find him out,
And unto heaven do lift his humble eye,
His soul in faith will such perfections spy,
That leaving all that he on earth can see,
His love will long but with the Lord to be.

The churl that never chaunc't upon a thought
Of charity, nor what belongs thereto;
If God his grace have once his spirit brought,
To feel what good the faithful almers do,
The love of Christ will so his spirit woo,
That he will leave barns, corn, and bags of coin,
And land and life, with Jesus' love to join.

Thus from the prince unto the poorest state,
Who seems to live as void of reason's sense,
If God once come, who never comes too late,
And touch the soul with his sweet quintessence
Of mercy's gracious glorious patience,
His soul will leave whatever it doth love,
And long to live but with the Lord above.

Now to the tenure of that longing time,
That loving spirits think too long will last;
The maid new married, in her pregnant prime,
Longs till the time of forty weeks be past,
And blameth time he makes no greater haste;
Till in her arms she sweetly have received
Her comforts fruit, within her womb conceived

Thus forty weeks she labors all in love,
And at the last doth travail all in pain:
But shortly after doth such comfort prove,
As glads her heart, and makes all whole again;
So in her infant's pretty smiling vein
Pleasing herself, that all her grief is gone,
When she may have her babe to look upon.

Penelope, at her dear love's departing,
In sober kindness did conceal her care;
Though in her heart she had that inward smarting,
That Time's continuance after did declare;
Where constant love did show, without compare,
A perfect passion of true virtues vain,
Longing but for Ulysses home again.

How many years the story doth set down,
In which she felt the gall of absence, grief:
When constant faith on foul effects did frown,
Which sought to be to charity a thief,
Of nature's beauty the true honor chief:
Long languishing in absence, cruel hell;
But when she saw his presence all is well.

But if I may in holy lines begin,
To speak of Joseph, and his longing love
Unto his brethren, but to Benjamin
To note the passion Nature did approve,
Which did such tears in his affection move,
That well from thence the proverb sweet might spring,
The love of brethren is a blessed thing.

Well may I see the notes of Nature's grief,
In absence of the object of affection;
And longing for the substance of relief,
In presence find the life of love's perfection,
While eye and heart are led by one direction;
Yet all this while I do not truly prove
The blessed longing of the spirit's love.

When Mary Magdalen, so full of sin,
As made her heart a harbor of ill thought,
Felt once the grace of God to enter in,
And drive them out that her destruction sought;
Her soul was then to Jesus' love so wrought,
As that with tears in true affect did prove
The pleasing longing of the spirit's love.

In grief she went all weeping to his grave,
Longing to see him or alive or dead;
And would not cease until her love might have
Her longed fruit, on which her spirit fed,
One blessed crumb of that sweet heavenly bread
Of angels' food, but of her Lord a sight,
Whose heavenly presence proved her soul's delight.

Midas did long for nothing else but gold,
And he was kindly choked for his choice;
Such longing love doth with too many hold,
Which only do in worldly dross rejoice.
But did they hearken to the heavenly voice,
Their diamonds should not so for dross be sold,
And they would long for God and not for gold.

Zaccheus, too long, longed for such dross,
Till Jesus came, his spirit's further joy;
And then he found his vain did yield but loss,
While sin in conscience bred the soul's annoy,
And unto heaven the world was but a toy;
He left it all and climbed up a tree,
To show his longing how but Christ to see.

And well he longed that so his love received,
Who sweetly saw, and kindly called him down:
His stature low, but his love high conceived,
Who so was graced by Mercy's glorious crown,
As having cause upon his sins to frown;
Forgave the works that did deserve damnation,
And filled his house with glory of salvation.

A blessing longing of a blessed love!
Would so all souls did love, and so did long;
And in their longing might so sweetly prove
The gracious ground of such a glorious song,
As kills all sin that doth the spirit wrong;
  And sing with Simeon at his Savior's sight,
  "On now my soul depart in peace, delight!"

Oh blessed Simeon, blessed was thy love.
And thy love's longing for thy Savior so,
Who wrought so sweetly for thy soul's behove,
As from thy prayers would not let thee go,
Till to thy love he did his presence show,
  Which made thee sing, when sorrows all did cease,
  "Lord, let thy servant now depart in peace!"

"For I, according to thy word, have seen
The glorious substance of my soul's salvation;
Thy word, in whom my trust hath ever been,
And now hath found my comfort's confirmation!"
Thus did he make a joyful declaration
  Of that sweet sight of his sweet Savior's face,
  That was the glory of his spirit's grace.

How many years he all in prayer spent,
For the beholding of his blessed love!
What was the issue of his hope's event,
And how his prayers did prevail above,
That so his God did unto mercy move,
  As to his arms to send his only Son,
  The story doth of all th' Apostles run!

He was well called, good Simeon, for that grace,
That God hath given the spirit of his love;
That love that longed but in his Savior's face,
To see the blessing of his soul's behove,
And blessed prayer, that did truly prove
  A blessed soul, that could not prayer cease,
  Till Christ his presence came to give it peace.

So should all souls their love's chief longing have,
All souls I mean of every Christian heart,
That seek or hope both heart and soul to save
From hell, damnation, and supernal smart;
This is the love that, in the living part
  Of mercy's power, shall find that blessedness,
  That is the spirit's only happiness.

Nor can love look to limit out a time,
But now and then and evermore attend;
For he shall never to that comfort climb,
That will not all his life in prayer spend,
Until he see his Savior in the end:
  In whose sweet face doth all and only rest
  The heavenly joy that makes the spirit blest.

Blest be the spirit that so longs and loves,
As did Zaccheus and good Simeon:
And from his faithful prayer never moves,
Until he find his life to look upon,
And in such love is all so over-gone,
  That in such joy his heart and spirit dwells,
  As having Christ, it cares for nothing else.

Oh blessed Christ, the essence of all bliss,
All blessed souls love's longings' chief delight!
What heart can think how that soul blessed is,
That ever hath his Savior in his sight?
The sunny day that never hath a night?
  Oh that my spirit might so ever pray,
  That I might live to see that blessed day.

The day that only springeth from on high,
That high daylight wherein the heavens do live;
The life that loves but to behold that eye,
Which doth the glory of all brightness give,
And from th' enlight'ned doth all darkness drive:
  Where saints do see, and angels know to be
  A brighter light, than saints or angels see.

In this light's love, oh, let me ever live!
And let my soul have never other love,
But all the pleasures of the world to give,
The smallest spark of such a joy to prove,
And ever pray unto my God above,
  To grant my humble soul good Simeon's grace,
  In love to see my Savior in the face.

O face more fair than fairness can contain:
O eye more bright than brightness can declare:
O light more pure than passion can explain:
O life more blest than may with bliss compare:
O heaven of heavens where such perfections are!
  Let my soul live to love, to long, to be
  Ever in prayer, but to look on thee!

But, oh unworthy eye of such a sight;
And all unworthy heart of such a love;
Unworthy love, to long for such a light;
Unworthy longing such a life to prove;
Unworthy life, so high a suit to move!
  Thus all unworthy of so high a grace,
  How shall I see my Savior in the face?

All by the prayer of true penitence,
Where faith in tears attendeth grace's time,
My soul doth hope in mercy's patience,
My heart all cleansed from my sinful crime,
To see the springing of Aurora's prime,
  In those bright beams of that sweet blessed sun
  Of my dear God, in whom all bliss begun.

And that my soul may such a blessing see,
Let my heart pray, and praying never cease,
Till heart and soul may both together be,
Blest in thy sight all sorrows doth release;
And with good Simeon then depart in peace!
  Oh then: but then, and only ever then,
  Blest be my soul, sweet Jesus say Amen.

OTHER POEMS BY VARIOUS AUTHORS

STANZAS.

What are all the charms of earth,
All its pride, its treasures, worth,
With no partner at your side,
Thoughts and feelings to divide?

Therefore God, with gracious plan,
Saw, and said, and showed that man
Ne'er was made to live alone—
Therefore marriage first was known.

But without Divine communion,
What is Nature's tenderest union;
'Tis no portion for the soul,
Joy to fix, or grief control.

Where no heavenly love is found,
There can human long abound?
Iron there, the silken chain,
'Tis mere doubleness of pain!

Still may heavenly love secure
Human ties more sweet and pure:
So these human ties shall prove
Means to aid that holier love.

Then, your trial done, from this
School and type of perfect bliss,
Ye, rejoicing, in the skies,
To the marriage-feast shall rise!

Grinfield.

HOME.

Where burns the loved hearth brightest,
  Cheering the social breast?
Where beats the fond heart lightest
  Its humble hopes possessed?
Where is the smile of sadness,
  Of meek-eyed patience born,
Worth more than those of gladness,
  Which mirth's bright cheek adorn?
Pleasure is marked by fleetness
  To those who ever roam,
While grief itself has sweetness
  At home, dear home.

There blend the ties that strengthen
Our hearts in hours of grief,
The silver links that lengthen
Joy's visits, when most brief;
These eyes in all their splendor
Are vocal to the heart,
And glances, gay and tender,
Fresh eloquence impart!
Then dost thou sigh for pleasure?
Oh do not wildly roam!
But seek that hidden treasure
At home, dear home.

Does pure religion charm thee
Far more than aught below?
Wouldst thou that she should arm thee
Against the hour of wo?
Think not she dwelleth only
In temples made for prayer;
For home itself is lonely,
Unless her smiles be there.
The devotee may falter,
The bigot blindly roam;
If worshipless her altar
At home, dear home!

Love over it presideth,
With meek and watchful awe;
Its daily service guideth,
And shows its perfect law.
If there thy faith shall fail thee—
If there no shrine be found,
What can thy prayers avail thee,
With kneeling crowds around?
Go leave thy gift unoffered
Beneath Religion's dome;
And be her first-fruits proffered
At home, dear home!

B. Barton.

WHERE ARE THEY?

Our Fathers! where are they? and where
The prophets? From this mortal scene,
Gone with the dream of things that were,
As if they ne'er had been.
Beyond the wanderings of the morn,
Beyond the portals of the day,
Unto a land whence none return,
Our Fathers—where are they?

The vanished comet, long deemed lost,
And absent for a thousand years,
Again, amid the starry host,
From darkness reappears.
Seas ebb and flow upon the shore,
Moons wax when they have waned away,
But they who go to come no more—
Our Fathers—where are they?

Thou sun that light'st the boundless skies,
Where are the earth's departed gone?
Ye stars, to your all-seeing eyes,
Is the great secret known?
Ye breathe not of their place of rest,
But roll in silence on your way,
And the lorn echoes of the breast
Still answers—"Where are they?"

John Malcolm.

THE VILLAGE FUNERAL.

It was a lonely hamlet, where the trees
Waved, in green beauty, o'er the whitewashed cot:
Deepening the shade, as the light summer breeze
Clustered the boughs, so beams of sun came not;
Beneath smiled cottage flowers—'midst all a brook;
Ran hurrying off to a sequestered nook;
Then bursting forth beside a rose-wreathed grot,
Mirrored its beauties—for to it were given,
To mix the flowers of earth, and clouds of heaven.

All seemed enchantment in the flowery dell,
Yet all was solemn silence—no glad thrill
Of children's voices, breathing forth the spell
Of hope and early life—all, all was still;
And yet 'twas summer's bright unclouded noon,
When May's pale flowers gave place to those of June;
'Midst which the roving bee ranged forth at will;
At intervals was heard the cuckoo's tone.
By mimic schoolboy gayly made his own.

Lo! on the ear pealed forth another sound,
And slow and time-paced came the funeral tread,
And one, the bier with fresh-blown roses crowned
As though pale silk waved o'er the youthful dead;
Yet ill did the dark pall accord with flowers,
And the bright sun of June's unclouded hours;
While heavy sighs proclaimed all joy was fled
From him, the childless father—who gazed on
Scenes which brought memories of the loved and gone.

There the green oak in civil triumph bore
The torn remains of the once favorite kite;
And the rose-tree displayed a beauteous store
Of rosy flowers, which, budding, joyed the sight;
And sideways spread a mound of unmown grass,
O'er which such bounding feet were used to pass;
All these seemed shrouded in eternal night,
Since from their view the father could but borrow
Thoughts of past joy, to deepen present sorrow.

The bell ceased tolling—and the solemn tread
Of slow receding footsteps died away,
Till all was gloom—for thinking on the dead,
The village children had forgot their play;
They missed their loved companion—he who'd chase
Their fleetest footsteps oft, and win the race;
Sadness and silence marked the weary day;
E'en mothers fearfully looked on the bloom
Of their loved boys—and thought upon the tomb.

THE DYING MOTHER.

"Bring me my babe," she softly cried,
"Oh! let me, ere this mortal strife
Is ended, yet again behold
The treasure I have bought with life."
'Twas brought! her heart sweet welcome gave
Unto the—almost—orphan, while
Its open eyes were turned on hers,
To hail with an unconscious smile.
Some moments in her arms she held,
Then laid it on the milkless breast,
That should have nourishment supplied,
And pillowed it to rest.

Her heart, as though the warm embrace
Had a new life imparted, heaved
With greater force; and Fancy's power,
A wreath of fond endearments weaved
To crown the hapless child; but now
The struggle shook her weakened frame,
Her limbs grew cold—pulsation stopped;
And o'er her eyes death's dimness came:
In faltering accents she exclaimed—
"My sweet one, 'tis for thee I die!"
Then some few treasured drops of life,
Shed from each smiling eye.

One long but broken sigh here loosed
Her soul; yet still the tears she shed
At parting, dwelt upon her cheek,
Like dews that bows the snow-drop's head;
And still affection's dying glance
Upon her feature's left its trace—
Fast frozen, as we sometimes see
A wavelet on a river's face.
As though, in love with that rich smile,
Death, fearful of the least delay,
Had grasped her in his mighty arms,
Before it passed away.

EVENING HYMN.

The vesper time draws nigh,
The pale moon trembles in the horizon fair,
And stars are speaking in the quiet sky;
It is hour of prayer.

Bend, bend the heart and knee,
For day's long toil and trouble now are past;
Whom should we seek at this still hour but thee,
Father! at last.

It may be, in the day,
Our hearts too busy and too worldly grown,
Sometimes forget thy love—mistrust thy sway:
This hour is all thine own.

And if some falling tears,
When pleading for the loved one far away,
And cherished in our heart's deep core for years,
Should force their way;

Thou wilt forgive, for thou
Wert one of us, and earthly grief didst share;
Pardon our sorrows, and accept our vow
Now at the time of prayer.

May holy angels keep
Watch through the dark night, while we be at rest;
Send peaceful dreamings to our quiet sleep,
Of them—the lost—the blest.

Should this night be our last
Of earthly watching, and of earthly care,
Then may we wake in heaven, all sorrow past,
And praise thee there.

STANZAS.

When on her Maker's bosom
The new-born earth was laid,
And nature's opening blossom
Its fairest bloom displayed;

When all with fruit and flowers
The laughing soil was drest,
And Eden's fragrant bowers
Received their human guest:

No sin his face defiling,
The Heir of nature stood,
And God, benignly smiling,
Beheld that all was good!

Yet, in that hour of blessing,
A single want was known—
A wish, the heart distressing,
For Adam was alone!

Oh God of pure affection!
By men and saints adored,
Who gavest thy protection
To Cana's nuptial board;

May such thy bounties ever
To wedded love be shown;
Aud no rude hand dissever
Whom Thou hast linked in one.

Bishop Heber.

A THOUGHT SUGGESTED BY THE NEW YEAR.

The more we live, more brief appear,
Our life's succeeding stages;
A day to childhood seems a year,
And years like passing ages.

The gladsome current of our youth,
Ere passion yet disorders,
Steals, lingering, like a river smooth,
Along its grassy borders.

But as the care-worn cheek grows wan,
And sorrow's shafts fly thicker,
Ye stars that measure life to man!
Why seem your courses quicker?

When joys have lost their bloom and breath,
And life itself is vapid;
Why as we reach the Falls of Death,
Feel we its tide more rapid?

It may be strange—yet who would change
Time's course to slower speeding?
When one by one our friends are gone,
And left our bosoms bleeding.

Heaven gives our years of fading strength
Indemnifying fleetness;
And these of youth, a *seeming length*,
Proportioned to their sweetness.

T. Campbell

LOVE ENDURING.

Nay, tell me not, my dearest,
That time has dimmed thine eye;
Still, still my path thou cheerest,
As in days that are gone by.
Say not thy cheek is faded,
By sorrows, cares, and fears;
That thy brow is somewhat shaded
By the clouds of other years.
If Time much more had taken,
I could forgive each theft,
While thy heart remained unshaken,
And its love for me was left.

I, too, am something older,
Than when I met with thee;
But hearts become no colder,
If they are what hearts should be.
Thy own has never altered,
As years have o'er me past;
Thy love has never faltered,
When my brow has been o'ercast.
Then tell me not of changes,
In cheek, or brow, or hair;
The love such loss estranges,
Must be lighter far than air.

Though morning's early splendor
May rapture's thrill impart,
The vesper hour, more tender,
Sinks deeper in the heart.
Though spring be gay with roses,
And summer skies are clear,
Yet autumn's hand encloses
The rich harvest of the year.
E'en age's wintry weather,
Inspires no thought of gloom,
In hearts that share together,
Hopes of bliss beyond the tomb.

B[illegible]ton

THE PASTOR'S MARRIAGE.

"A good wife is from the Lord."

Dear messenger of truth divine,
Upon whose heart impress,
Thy people like the jewels shine,
As when of old the mystic sign
Appeared on Aaron's breast.

Oft on the sacred wings of prayer,
Thy name has risen above,
That He, who made our souls his care,
Himself might heavenly influence share,
Strong in the work of love.

Though not for earthly good we sought
(Thy Lord that need would know),
Yet, that thy service for him wrought
Might be with choicest blessings fraught,
To smooth thy path below.

The gracious answer, Lord! we hail,
And mark the treasure given,
A solace through the gloomy vale,
A comforter when griefs assail,
A wife—the boon of Heaven.

O may the solemn nuptial vow
Be registered on high;
And with our joyous strains below,
May angel notes accordant flow,
To bless the sacred tie.

Now, hand in hand, a favored pair,
May they thine altar raise;
Together, Lord! thy favor share;
And that which thou hast given to prayer,
Oh may it end in praise!

CHARITY.

Meek Charity! to thee we're told is given
In ·rms of holiest proof, the countless faults
Of m ı to hide; and, in the sight of Heaven,
To ender him beloved. Then, in the assaults
Of fiercest passions, when we're urged along
With unrelenting fury to pursue
Some fallen enemy, whose wilful wrong
Hath caused our hatred, let us pause and view
HIS meek example, who the precept gave;
For think not Charity sincerely shown
By ostentatious homage at the throne
Of our own vainness! Let us humbly save
The poor from want, and secretly give rest
Unto the weary desolate:—'twill please Heaven best

THE SKY-LARK.

Ethereal minstrel! pilgrim of the sky!
Dost thou despise the earth, where cares abound;
Or, while thy wings aspire, are heart and eye
Both with thy nest, upon the dewy ground?
Thy nest which thou canst drop into at will
These quivering wings composed, and music still!

To the last point of vision, and beyond,
Mount, daring warbler! that love-prompted strain,
('Twixt thee and thine a never-failing bond),
Thrills not the less the bosom of the plain;
Yet might'st thou seem, proud privilege! to sing,
All independent of the leafy Spring.

Leave to the nightingale the shady wood;—
A privacy of glorious light is thine,
Whence thou dost pour upon the world a flood
Of harmony, with rapture more divine:
Type of the wise, who soar—but never roam,
True to the kindred points of heaven and home!

Wordsworth

LITTLE STREAMS.

Little streams, in light and shadow
Flowing through the pasture meadow;
Flowing by the green way-side;
Through the forest dim and wide;
Through the hamlet still and small;
By the cottage; by the hall;
By the ruined abbey still:
Turning, here and there, a mill;
Bearing tribute to the river;
Little streams, I love you ever!

Summer music is their flowing;
Flowering plants in them are growing
Happy life is in them all,
Creatures innocent and small;
Little birds come down to drink
Fearless on their leafy brink!
Noble trees beside them grow,
Glooming them with branches low,
And between the sunshine glancing
In their little waves are dancing.

Little streams have flowers a-many,
Beautiful and fair as any;
Typha strong, and green bur-reed;
Willow-herb, with cotton-seed;
Arrow-head, with eye of jet,
And the water-violet;
There the flowering rush you meet.
And the plumy meadow-sweet;
And in places, deep and stilly,
Marble-like, the water-lily.

Little streams, their voices cheery
Sound forth welcomes to the weary;
Flowing on from day to day,
Without stint and without stay.
Here, upon their flowery bank,
In the old times pilgrims drank;
Here have seen, as now, pass by
Kingfisher and dragon-fly;
Those bright things that have their dwelling
Where the little streams are welling.

Down in valleys green and lowly,
Murmuring not and gliding slowly;
Up in mountain hollows wild,
Fretting like a peevish child;
Through the hamlet, where all day
In their waves the children play,
Running west, or running east,
Doing good to man and beast;
Always giving, weary never,
Little streams, I love you ever!

LINES TO A FRIEND ON HIS MARRIAGF

On thee, blest youth a father's hand confers
The maid thy earliest, fondest wishes knew;
Each soft enchantment of the soul is hers—
Thine be the joys to firm attachment due.

As on she moves, with hesitating grace,
She wins assurance from thy soothing voice;
And, with a look, the pencil could not trace,
Smiles through her blushes, and confirms the choice

Spare the fine tremors of her feeling frame!
To thee she turns, forgive those falling tears!
To thee she turns, with surest, tenderest claim—
Weakness that charms, reluctance that endears

At each response the sacred rite requires,
From her full bosom bursts th' unbidden sigh;
A strange mysterious awe the scene inspires,
And on her lips the trembling accents die.

O'er her fair face what soft emotions play!
What lights and shades in sweet confusion blend!
Soon shall they fly, glad harbingers of day,
And settled sunshine on her soul descend!

Ah soon thine own confessed, ecstatic thought?
That hand shall strew thy summer path with flowers;
And those blue eyes, with modest lustre fraught,
Gild the calm current of domestic hours!

Rogers.

THE POET TO HIS WIFE.

No image of creative fancy thou,
But an imbodying of truth and love—
Fond sharer of my joys and sorrows—how
Thou art such unsubstantial forms above.
Most hollow-hearted, and most ignorant
Of gentle Love's best happiness, are they
Who rail against our state; by Heaven, and cant
Apart, 'tis one of purest joy. I pray
That we may not, through stubborn will perverse,
Changing, ourselves, God's blessing to a curse,
Divert the stream of mutual delight;
But that it flow serenely, clear and bright,
Missing foul discontent's dark, shallow wave,
And passion's whirling eddies, to the grave.

APRIL.

Capricious month of smiles and tears!
  There's beauty in thy varied reign:
Emblem of being's hopes and fears—
  Its hours of joy and days of pain.
A false inconstant scene is thine;
  Changeful with light and shadow deep—
Oft-times thy clouds with pure sunshine
  Are painted—then in gloom they sleep.

Yet is there gladness in thy hours,
  Frail courier of a brighter scene—
Thou fragrant guide to buds and flowers,
  To meadows fresh and pastures green!
For as thy days grow few and brief,
  The radiant looks of spring appear—
With swelling glow, and opening leaf,
  To deck the morning of the year.

Yes, though thy light is checkered oft
  With drifting showers of sorrowing rain—
Yet balmy airs and breezes soft
  Are lingering richly in thy train:
And for thy eddying gusts will come
  The lay of the rejoicing bird,
That tries his new and brightening plume—
  'Mid the void sky's recesses heard.

And soon the many clouds that hang
  Their solemn drapery o'er the sky,
Will pass, in shadowy folds away—
  Lo! mark them now!—they break—they fly
And over earth in one broad smile,
  Looks forth the glorious eve of day—
While hill, and vale, and ocean-isle,
  Are laughing in the breath of May.

Type of existence! mayst thou be
  The emblem of the Christian's race—
Through all whose trials we may see
  The sunshine of undying grace:
The calm and heaven-enkindled eye,
  The faith that mounts on ardent wing,
That looks beyond the o'erarching sky
  To heaven's undimmed and golden spring.

Anon.

THE RETURN OF SPRING.

Dear as the dove, whose wafting wing
  The green leaf ransomed from the main,
Thy genial glow, returning Spring,
  Comes to our shores again;
For thou hast been a wanderer long,
  On many a fair and foreign strand,
In calm and beauty, sun and song,
  Passing from land to land.

Thou bring'st the blossom to the bee,
  To earth a robe of emerald die;
The leaflet to the naked tree,
  And rainbow in the sky;
I feel thy blest, benign control
  The pulses of my youth restore;
Opening the spring of sense and soul
  To love and joy once more.

I will not people thy green bowers
  With sorrow's pale and spectre band,
Or blend with thine the faded flowers
  Of memory's distant land;
For thou wert surely never given
  To wake regret for pleasures gone;
But, like an angel sent from heaven,
  To sooth creation's groan.

Then while the groves their garlands twine,
  Thy spirit breathes in flower and tree,
My heart shall kindle at thy shrine,
  And worship God in thee:
And in some calm sequestered spot,
  While listening to thy choral strain,
Past griefs shall be a while forgot
  And pleasures bloom again.

Malcomb.

THE HURRICANE.

Lord of the winds! I feel thee nigh:
I know thy breath in the burning sky!
And I wait, with a thrill in every vein,
For the coming of the hurricane!

  And lo! on the wings of the heavy gales,
Through the boundless arch of heaven he sails;
Silent and slow, and terribly strong,
The mighty shadow is borne along,
Like the dark eternity to come;
While the world below, dismayed and dumb,
Through the calm of the thick hot atmosphere
Looks up at its gloomy folds with fear.

  They darken fast,—and the golden blaze
Of the sun is quenched in the lurid haze,
And he sends through the shade a funeral ray—
A glare that is neither night nor day,
A beam that touches with hues of death
The clouds above and the earth beneath,
To its covert flies the silent bird,
While the hurricane's distant voice is heard
Uplifted among the mountains round,
And the forests hear and answer the sound.

  He is come! he is come! do ye not behold
His ample robes on the wind unrolled?
Giant of air! we bid thee hail!—
How his gray skirts toss in the whirling gale—
How his huge and writhing arms are bent,
To clasp the zone of the firmament,
And fold, at length, in their dark embrace,
From mountain to mountain, the visible space!
Darker—still darker! the whirlwinds bear
The dust of the plains to the middle air:
And hark to the crashing, long and loud,
Of the chariot of God in the thunder-cloud!
You may trace its path by the flashes that start
From the rapid wheels where'er they dart,
As the fire-bolts leap to the worlds below,
And flood the skies with a lurid glow.

  What roar is that?—'tis the rain that breaks
In torrents away from the airy lakes,
Heavily poured on the shuddering ground,
And shedding a nameless horror round.
Ah! well-known woods, and mountains, and skies,
With the very clouds!—ye are lost to my eyes:
I seek ye vainly, and see in your place
The shadowy tempest that sweeps through space—
A whirling ocean that fills the wall
Of the crystal heaven, and buries all:
And I, cut off from the world, remain
Alone with the terrible hurricane.

Bryant.

ON A SLEEPING BOY.

Sleep—and while slumber weighs thine eyelids down,
May no foul phantoms o'er thy pillow frown;
But brightest visions deck thy tranquil bed,
And angel's wings o'ercanopy thy head.
Sleep on, sweet boy! may no dark dreams arise
To mar thy rosy rest—thou babe of Paradise!

See where the glowing hands are closely pressed,
As when from prayer he softly sunk to rest;
Mark how with half-closed lips and cherub-smile
He looks, as still he prayed, and slept the while;
Yet—yet they seem as if they whispered praise
For all the blessings of his halcyon days.

Bid, oh, Almighty Father, God, and Friend,
Religion's glories on his steps attend!
To shine through all the dreary storms of life,
A splendid beacon in the world of strife;
And when to Thee recalled he sinks in death,
May prayer and praise still bless his parting breath!

THE VOICE OF GOD.

"Speak, Lord!" the youthful prophet humbly cries;
"Thy servant hears!"
And instant, hark! the voice divine replies,
Its will declares:—
No other ear in all that temple's round
Receives the deep, impressive, solemn sound;
The sacred tribe, the aged priest passed by,
God stands revealed to youthful piety.

He comes no more to rouse the outward ear
At dead of night;
No fearful dream his purposed act makes clear
To mortal sight:—
But wheresoe'er man seeks to meet him, still
A voice is near him, whispering of his will,
And ever, as he calls on God to "speak,"
That inward voice will nature's silence break.

Yes, Christian, he whose voice then spake on earth
Still speaks to thee;
Whether in sweetest music, warbling forth
From every tree,
Or in the stillness of the evening hour,
Or when the tempest gathers all its power,
Or when the sea its awful voice uprears,
Be thine to answer, "Speak; thy servant hears."

In all thy varying portion, in the strife
'Twixt earth and heaven,
Or when sweet gleamings of a better life
To thee are given,
When hard the conflict, dim the distant end,
No light to cheer thee, at thy side no friend,
Yet, hark! e'er now, in answer to thy prayer,
The voice, the voice of Love Divine is there!

Or when the page of truth before thee spreads
Its chastened light,
And some reviving promise round thee sheds
Hopes clear and bright,
There speaks the Gospel's Author: to that word,
Favored disciple of a pitying Lord,
Bend, meekly bend, a still, attentive ear:
'Tis his to speak; with reverence thine to hear.

Thankful for this, thy destined path pursue,
Or dark, or bright;
Till faith, while glory burst upon the view,
Is lost in sight:
Till then, with ever wakeful care, abide
By the least whispers of thy heavenly guide;
For still, when followed most, that voice shall be
Strength, comfort, peace, and blessedness to thee.

Emily Taylor.

RIGHT OF THE POOR TO EDUCATION.

Oh! for the coming of that glorious time
When prizing knowledge as her noblest wealth
And best protection, this imperial realm,
While she exacts allegiance, shall admit
An obligation, on her part, to *teach*
Them who are born to serve her and obey;
Binding herself by statute to secure
For all the children whom her soil maintains
The rudiments of letters, and to inform
The mind with moral and religious truth,
Both understood, and practised,—so that none,
However destitute, be left to droop
By timely culture unsustained, or run
Into a wild disorder; or be forced
To drudge through weary life without the aid
Of intellectual implements and tools;
A savage horde among the civilized,
A servile band among the lordly free!
This right, as sacred almost as the right
To exist and be supplied with sustenance
And means of life, the lisping babe proclaims
To be inherent in him, by Heaven's will,
For the protection of his innocence;
And the rude boy—who, having overpast
The sinless age, by conscience is enrolled,
Yet mutinously knits his angry brow,
And lifts his wilful hand, on mischief bent,
Or turns the sacred faculty of speech
To impious use—by process indirect
Declares his due—while he makes known his need.
—This sacred right is fruitlessly announced,
This universal plea in vain addressed,
To eyes and ears of parents who themselves
Did, in the time of their necessity
Urge it in vain; and, therefore, like a prayer
That from the humblest floor ascends to heaven,
It mounts to reach the state's parental ear;
Who, if indeed she own a mother's heart,
And be not most unfeelingly devoid
Of gratitude to providence, will grant
The unquestionable good; which, England, safe
From interference of external force,
May grant at leisure; without risk incurred
That what in wisdom for herself she doth,
Others shall e'er be able to undo.

Look! and behold from Calpe's sun-burnt cliffs
To the flat margin of the Baltic sea,
Long-reverenced titles cast away as weeds;
Laws overturned,—and territory split;
Like fields of ice rent by the polar wind
And forced to join in less obnoxious shapes,
Which, ere they gain consistence, by a gust
Of the same breath are shattered and destroyed.
Meantime the sovereignty of these fair isles
Remains entire and indivisible;
And, if that ignorance were removed, which acts
Within the compass of their several shores
To breed commotion and disquietude,
Each might preserve the beautiful repose
Of heavenly bodies shining in their spheres.
—The discipline of slavery is unknown
Amongst us,—hence the more do we require
The discipline of virtue; order else
Can not subsist, nor confidence, nor peace.
Thus, duties rising out of good possessed,
And prudent caution needful to avert
Impending evil, do alike require
That permanent provision should be made
For the whole people to be taught and trained.
So shall licentiousness and black resolve
Be rooted out, and virtuous habits
Take their place; and genuine piety descend
Like an inheritance, from age to age.

Wordsworth.

MERCY.

Mercy is welcome news indeed,
To those that guilty stand;
Wretches, who feel the help they need.
Will bless the helping hand.

Who rightly would his alms dispense,
Must give them to the poor;
None but the wounded patient knows
The comforts of a cure.

We all have sinned against our God;
Exception none can boast;
But he that feels the heaviest load,
Will prize forgiveness most.

No reckoning can we rightly keep,
For who the sum can know?
Some souls are fifty talents deep,
And some five hundred owe.

But let our debts be what they may,
However great or small,
As soon as we have naught to pay,
Our Lord forgives us all.

'Tis perfect poverty alone,
That sets the soul at large;
While we can call one mite our own,
We have no full discharge.

Hart

INVOCATION TO NIGHT.

Come, with thy sweeping cloud and starry vest,
  Mother of counsel, and the joy which lies
  In feelings deep, and inward sympathies,
Soothing like founts of health, the wearied breast!
Lo! o'er the distant hills the day-star's crest
  Sinks redly burning; and the winds arise,
  Moving, with shadowy gusts and feeble sighs
Amid the reeds which veil the bittern's nest!
Day hath its melody and light—the sense
  Of mirth which sports round fancy's fairy mine;
But the full powers which loftier aids dispense,
  To speed the soul where scenes unearthly shine—
Silence, and peace, and stern magnificence,
  And awe, and throned solemnity, are thine!

J. F. Hollings.

A LAMENT AND A REPLY.

A LAMENT.

When shall I see a flower,
  Nor muse on its decay?
When shall I know *one* happy hour,
  Nor—ere it pass away—
O'ercloud its happiness with tears,
Because it can not last for years?

When will no dread of change
  Darken my spirit's trust?
When will the knowledge, sad and strange
  That man is of the dust,
While gazing on beloved eyes,
Instead of wretched, make me wise?

Nature, and flowers, and youth,
  Birds, and their rich, wild glee,
All pleasant things in sooth,
  Why are they sad to me?
Why in each form behold I Death?
Why seems all music but his breath?

Death is my life: Delight
  Seems of his influence born;
A meteor flashing through the night—
  A lily fenced with thorn,—
A wild and momentary gladness
That in its elements hath madness.

A troubled joy in love,
  And fears when fully blest,—
Clouds when the sky is bright above
  And sadness when at rest!
Alas! my soul has left its ark
And wanders o'er the waters dark!

THE REPLY.

Restless spirit!—wouldst thou know
When will close thy night of wo?—
Cease thy wanderings to and fro.

Long thy heavy heart will beat
With its own unholy heat,
If thy fancy, wild and fleet,

Like a homeless bird must fly,
Searching rock, and plain, and sky,—
All too low, and yet too high.

Let her choose her tree, and rest,
There renew her stolen nest,—
Be again the green leaves' guest.

Stricken spirit, there's a tree
Grows for healing, grows for thee;
Haste then,—to its covert flee!

Whispering oracles are rife
'Mid its leaves to quiet strife:
Spirit!—'tis the Tree of Life.

Mrs. Fletcher.

THE EVENING STAR.

How beautiful the twilight sky,
  Whose starry worlds now spread,
Amid the purple depths of eve,
  Their glories o'er my head!

And there is one—a radiant one—
  Amid the rest shines he,
As if just risen from his sleep,
  Within the mighty sea.

The clouds fall off in glittering flakes
  Before his shining brow;
So moves a ship that flings the waves
  In bright froam fom its prow.

I marvel not in former days
  Ere purer light were given,
That men fell down and worshipped thee
  A spirit-king in heaven.

But now that knowledge great and high
  Is kindled in man's soul,
We know thee but a glorious part
  Of a more glorious whole.

Oh, mysteries of night that fill
  The mind with awe and love,
How visibly the power of God
  Is manifest above.

Oh! might and majesty that reign
  Upon the midnight sky!—
Creed of my hope! I feel thy truth
  Whene'er I gaze on high.

Miss Landon

EVENING PRAYER.

Should some seraph wing his flight,
From the realms of cloudless light,
Earth and ocean soaring over,
Where would he delight to hover?

Not o'er halls of regal pride;
Not o'er fields with carnage dyed,
Where, mid shouts of triumph breathing,
Fame the hero's brow is wreathing;

Not o'er cells of lettered age;
Not o'er haunts of hoary sage;
Not where youthful poet stealing,
Woos the muse's warm revealing;

Not o'er wood or shadowy vale
Where the lover tells his tale,
And the blush—love's fondest token—
Speaks what words had never spoken:

Not where music's silver sound
Wakes the dormant echoes round,
And with charms as pure as tender
Holds the heart in pleased surrender.

O'er the calm sequestered spot,
O'er the lone and lowly cot,
Where, its little hands enwreathing,
Childhood's guileless prayer is breathing;

While the gentle mother nigh,
Points her daughter's prayer on high,
To the God whose goodness gave her,
To the God whose love shall save her:—

There, awhile the Son of Light
Would arrest his rapid flight,
Thence would bear, to heaven ascending,
Prayers with heartfelt praises blending.

Gladly would he soar above,
With the sacrifice of love;
And, through heaven's expanded portal,
Bear it to the throne immortal!

Rev. T Dale.

ODES OF ANACREON,

TRANSLATED INTO ENGLISH VERSE.

ODE I.

I saw the smiling bard of pleasure,
The minstrel of the Teian measure;
'Twas in a vision of the night,
He beam'd upon my wondering sight.
I heard his voice, and warmly prest
The dear enthusiast to my breast.
His tresses wore a silvery dye,
But beauty sparkled in his eye;
Sparkled in his eyes of fire,
Through the mist of soft desire.
His lip exhal'd, whene'er he sigh'd,
The fragrance of the racy tide;
And, as with weak and reeling feet
He came my cordial kiss to meet,
An infant of the Cyprian band,
Guided him on with tender hand.
Quick from his glowing brows he drew
His braid, of many a wanton hue;
I took the wreath, whose inmost twine
Breath'd of him and blush'd with wine
I hung it o'er my thoughtless brow
And ah! I feel its magic now:
I feel that even his garland's touch
Can make the bosom love too much.

II.

Give me the harp of epic song,
Which Homer's finger thrill'd along;
But tear away the sanguine string,
For war is not the theme I sing.
Proclaim the laws of festal rite,
I'm monarch of the board to-night;
And all around shall brim as high,
And quaff the tide as deep as I.
And when the cluster's mellowing dews
Their warm enchanting balm infuse,
Our feet shall catch th' elastic bound,
And reel us through the dance's round.
Great Bacchus! we shall sing to thee,
In wild but sweet ebriety;
Flashing around such sparks of thought,
As Bacchus could alone have taught.

Then, give the harp of epic song,
Which Homer's finger thrill'd along;
But tear away the sanguine string,
For war is not the theme I sing.

III.

Listen to the Muse's lyre,
Master of the pencil's fire!
Sketch'd in painting's bold display,
Many a city first portray;
Many a city, revelling free,
Full of loose festivity.
Picture then a rosy train,
Bacchants straying o'er the plain·
Piping, as they roam along,
Roundelay or shepherd song,
Paint me next, if painting may
Such a theme as this portray,
All the earthly heaven of love
These delighted mortals prove

IV.

Vulcan! hear your glorious task;
I do not from your labours ask
In gorgeous panoply to shine,
For war was ne'er a sport of mine.
No—let me have a silver bowl,
Where I may cradle all my soul;
But mind that, o'er its simple frame
No mimic constellations flame;
Nor grave upon the swelling side,
Orion, scowling o'er the tide.
I care not for the glitt'ring wain,
Nor yet the weeping sister train.
But let the vine luxuriant roll
Its blushing tendrils round the bowl,
While many a rose-lipp'd bacchant maid
Is culling clusters in their shade.
Let sylvan gods, in antic shapes,
Wildly press the gushing grapes,
And flights of Loves, in wanton play,
Wing through the air their winding way;
While Venus from her harbour green,
Looks laughing at the joyous scene,
And young Lyæus by her side
Sits, worthy of so bright a bride.

V.

Sculptor, wouldst thou glad my soul,
Grave for me an ample bowl,
Worthy to shine in hall or bower,
When spring-time brings the reveller's hour
Grave it with themes of chaste design,
Fit for a simple board like mine.
Display not there the barbarous rites
In which religious zeal delights;
Nor any tale of tragic fate
Which History shudders to relate.
No—cull thy fancies from above,
Themes of heav'n and themes of love.
Let Bacchus, Jove's ambrosial boy,
Distil the grape in drops of joy,
And while he smiles at every tear,
Let warm-ey'd Venus, dancing near,
With spirits of the genial bed,
The dewy herbage deftly tread.
Let love be there, without his arms,
In timid nakedness of charms;
And all the Graces, link'd with Love,
Stray, laughing, through the shadowy grove,
While rosy boys disporting round,
In circlets trip the velvet ground
But ah! if there Apollo toys,
I tremble for the rosy boys.

VI.

As late I sought the spangled bowers,
To cull a wreath of matin flowers,
Where many an early rose was weeping,
I found the urchin Cupid sleeping.
I caught the boy, a goblet's tide
Was richly mantling by my side,
I caught him by his downy wing,
And whelm'd him in the racy spring
Then drank I down the poison'd bowl,
And Love now nestles in my soul.
Oh yes, my soul is Cupid's nest,
I feel him fluttering in my breast.

VII.

THE women tell me every day
That all my bloom has past away.
"Behold," the pretty wanton's cry,
"Behold this mirror with a sigh;
The locks upon thy brow are few,
And, like the rest, they're withering too!"
Whether decline has thinn'd my hair,
I'm sure I neither know nor care;
But this I know, and this I feel,
As onward to the tomb I steal,
That still as death approaches nearer,
The joys of life are sweeter, dearer;
And had I but an hour to live,
That little hour to bliss I'd give.

VIII.

I CARE not for the idle state
Of Persia's king, the rich, the great:
I envy not the monarch's throne,
Nor wish the treasur'd gold my own.
But oh! be mine the rosy wreath,
Its freshness o'er my brow to breathe;
Be mine the rich perfumes that flow,
To cool and scent my locks of snow.
To-day I'll haste to quaff my wine,
As if to-morrow ne'er would shine;
But if to-morrow comes, why then—
I'll haste to quaff my wine again.
And thus while all our days are bright,
Nor time has dimm'd their bloomy light,
Let us the festal hours beguile
With mantling cup and cordial smile;
And shed from each new bowl of wine
The richest drop on Bacchus' shrine.
For death may come, with brow unpleasan.
May come, when least we wish him present,
And beckon to the sable shore,
And grimly bid us—drink no more!

IX.

. PRAY thee, by the gods above,
Give me the mighty bowl I love,
And let me sing, in wild delight,
"I will—I will be mad to-night!"
Alcmæon once, as legends tell,
Was frenzied by the fiends of hell;
Orestes too, with naked tread,
Frantic pac'd the mountain-head;
And why? a murder'd mother's shade
Haunted them still where'er they strayed.
But ne'er could I a murderer be,
The grape alone shall bleed by me;
Yet can I shout, with wild delight,
"I will—I will be mad to-night."

Alcides' self, in days of yore,
Imbru'd his hands in youthful gore,
And brandish'd, with a maniac joy,
The quiver of th' expiring boy:
And Ajax, with tremendous shield,
Infuriate scour'd the guiltless field.
But I, whose hands no weapon ask,
No armour but this joyous flask;
The trophy of whose frantic hours
Is but a scatter'd wreath of flowers,
Ev'n I can sing with wild delight,
"I will—I will be mad to-night!"

X.

How am I to punish thee,
For the wrong thou'st done to me,
Silly swallow, prating thing—
Shall I clip that wheeling wing?
Or, as Tereus did, of old,
(So the fabled tale is told,)
Shall I tear that tongue away,
Tongue that utter'd such a lay.
Ah, how thoughtless hast thou been!
Long before the dawn was seen,
When a dream came o'er my mind,
Picturing her I worship, kind,
Just when I was nearly blest,
Loud thy matins broke my rest!

XI.

"TELL me, gentle youth, I pray thee,
What in purchase shall I pay thee
For this little waxen toy,
Image of the Paphian boy?"
Thus I said, the other day,
To a youth who pass'd my way:
"Sir," (he answer'd, and the while
Answer'd all in Doric style,)
"Take it, for a trifle take it;
'Twas not I who dared to make it;
No, believe me, 'twas not I;
Oh, it has cost me many a sigh,
And I can no longer keep
Little gods, who murder sleep!"
"Here, then, here," (I said with joy,)
"Here is silver for the boy:
He shall be my bosom guest,
Idol of my pious breast!"

Now, young Love, I have thee mine,
Warm me with that torch of thine;
Make me feel as I have felt,
Or thy waxen frame shall melt:
I must burn with warm desire
Or thou, my boy—in yonder fire.

XII.

THEY tell how Atys, wild with love,
Roams the mount and haunted grove;
Cybele's name he howl's around,
The gloomy blast returns the sound!
Oft too, by Claros' hallow'd spring,
The votaries of the laurell'd king
Quaff the inspiring, magic stream,
And rave in wild, prophetic dream.
But frenzied dreams are not for me,
Great Bacchus is my deity!
Full of mirth, and full of him,
While floating odours round me swim,
While mantling bowls are full supplied,
And you sit blushing by my side,
I will be mad and raving too—
Mad, my girl, with love for you!

XIII.

I WILL, I will, the conflict's past,
And I'll consent to love at last.
Cupid has long, with smiling art,
Invited me to yield my heart;
And I have thought that peace of mind
Should not be for a smile resign'd:
And so repell'd the tender lure,
And hope my heart would sleep secure.

But, slighted in his boasted charms,
The angry infant flew to arms;
He slung his quiver's golden frame,
He took his bow, his shafts of flame,
And proudly summon'd me to yield,
Or meet him on the martial field.
And what did I unthinking do?
I took to arms, undaunted, too;
Assum'd the corslet, shield, and spear,
And, like Pelides, smil'd at fear.
Then (hear it, all ye powers above!)
I fought with Love! I fought with Love!
And now his arrows all were shed,
And I had just in terror fled—
When, heaving an indignant sigh,
To see me thus unwounded fly,

And, having now no other dart,
He shot himself into my heart!
My heart—alas the luckless day!
Receiv'd the god, and died away.
Farewell, farewell, my faithless shield!
Thy lord at length is forc'd to yield.
Vain, vain, is every outward care,
The foe's within, and triumphs there.

XIV.

COUNT me, on the summer trees,
Every leaf that courts the breeze;
Count me, on the foamy deep,
Every wave that sinks to sleep;
Then, when you have number'd these
Billowy tides and leafy trees,
Count me all the flames I prove,
All the gentle nymphs I love.
First, of pure Athenian maids
Sporting in their olive shades,
You may reckon just a score,
Nay, I'll grant you fifteen more.
In the fam'd Corinthian grove,
Where such countless wantons rove,
Chains of beauties may be found,
Chains, by which my heart is bound;
There, indeed, are nymphs divine,
Dangerous to a soul like mine.
Many bloom in Lesbos' isle;
Many in Ionia smile;
Rhodes a pretty swarm can boast;
Caria too contains a host.
Sum them all—of brown and fair
You may count two thousand there.
What, you stare? I pray you, peace!
More I'll find before I cease.
Have I told you all my flames,
'Mong the amorous Syrian dames?
Have I numbered every one,
Glowing under Egypt's sun?
Or the nymphs, who blushing sweet
Deck the shrine of Love in Crete;
Where the God, with festal play,
Holds eternal holiday?
Still in clusters, still remain
Gades' warm, desiring train;
Still there lies a myriad more
On the sable India's shore;
These, and many far remov'd,
All are loving—all are lov'd!

XV.

TELL me, why, my sweetest dove,
Thus your humid pinions move,
Shedding through the air in showers
Essence of the balmiest flowers?
Tell me whither, whence you rove,
Tell me all, my sweetest dove.

Curious stranger, I belong
To the bard of Teian song;
With his mandate now I fly
To the nymph of azure eye;—
She, whose eye has madden'd many,
But the poet more than any.
Venus, for a hymn of love,
Warbled in her votive grove,
('Twas in sooth a gentle lay,)
Gave me to the bard away.
See me now his faithful minion.—
Thus with softly-gliding pinion,
To his lovely girl I bear
Songs of passion through the air
Oft he blandly whispers me,
Soon, my bird, I'll set you free."
But in vain he'll bid me fly,
I shall serve him till I die.
Never could my plumes sustain
Ruffling winds and chilling rain,
O'er the plains, or in the dell,
On the mountain's savage swell,
Seeking in the desert wood
Gloomy shelter, rustic food.
Now I lead a life of ease,
Far from rugged haunts like these.
From Anacreon's hand I eat
Food delicious, viands sweet;
Flutter o'er his goblet's brim,
Sip the foamy wine with him.
Then, when I have wanton'd round
To his lyre's beguiling sound;
Or with gently-moving wings
Fann'd the minstrel while he sings.
On his harp I sink in slumbers,
Dreaming still of dulcet numbers

This is all—away—away—
You have made me waste the day
How I've chatter'd! prating crow
Never yet did chatter so.

XVI.

THOU whose soft and rosy hues
Mimic form and soul infuse,
Best of painters, come, portray
The lovely maid that's far away.
Far away, my soul! thou art,
But I've thy beauties all by heart.
Paint her jetty ringlets playing,
Silky locks, like tendrils straying;
And, if painting hath the skill
To make the spicy balm distil,
Let every little lock exhale
A sigh of perfume on the gale.
Where her tresses' curly flow
Darkles o'er the brow of snow,
Let her forehead beam to light,
Burnish'd as the ivory bright.
Let her eyebrows smoothly rise
Its jetty arches o'er her eyes,
Each, a crescent gently gliding,
Just commingling, just dividing,

But, hast thou any sparkles warm,
The lightning of her eyes to form?
Let them effuse the azure rays
That in Minerva's glances blaze,
Mix'd with the liquid light that lies
In Cytherea's languid eyes.
O'er her nose and cheek be shed
Flushing white and soften'd red;
Mingling tints, as when there glows
In snowy milk the bashful rose.
Then her lip, so rich in blisses,
Sweet petitioner for kisses,
Rosy nest, where lurks Persuasion,
Mutely courting Love's invasion
Next, beneath the velvet chin,
Whose dimple hides a Love within,
Mould her neck with grace descending
In a heaven of beauty ending;
While countless charms, above, below,
Sport and flutter round its snow.
Now let a floating, lucid veil,
Shadow her form, but not conceal,
A charm may peep, a hue may beam,
And leave the rest to Fancy's dream.
Enough—'tis she! 'tis all I seek;
It glows, it lives, it soon will speak!

XVII

AND now with all thy pencil's truth
Portray Bathyllus, lovely youth!
Let his hair, in masses bright,
Fall like floating rays of light;
And there the raven's die confuse
With the golden sunbeam's hues.

Let no wreath, with artful twine,
The flowing of his locks confine;
But leave them loose to every breeze,
To take what shape and course they please.
Beneath the forehead, fair as snow,
But flush'd with manhood's early glow,
And guileless as the dews of dawn,
Let the majestic brows be drawn,
Of ebon hue, enrich'd by gold,
Such as dark, shining snakes unfold
Mix in his eyes the power alike,
With love to win, with awe to strike
Borrow from Mars his look of ire,
From Venus her soft glance of fire;
Blend them in such expression here,
That we by turns may hope and fear!

Now from the sunny apple seek
The velvet down that spreads his cheek;
And there, if art so far can go,
Th' ingenuous blush of boyhood show.
While, for his mouth—but no,—in vain
Would worlds its witching charm explain.
Make it the very seat, the throne,
That Eloquence would claim her own;
And let the lips, though silent, wear
A life-look, as if words were there.

Next thou his ivory neck must trace,
Moulded with soft but manly grace;
Fair as the neck of Paphia's boy,
Where Paphia's arms have hung in joy.
Give him the winged Hermes' hand,
With which he waves his snaky wand;
Let Bacchus the broad chest supply,
And Leda's sons the sinewy thigh;
While, through his whole transparent frame,
Thou show'st the stirrings of that flame,
Which kindles, when the first love-sigh
Steals from the heart, unconscious why.

But sure thy pencil, though so bright,
Is envious of the eye's delight,
Or its enamour'd touch would show
The shoulder, fair as sunless snow,
Which now in veiling shadow lies,
Remov'd from all but Fancy's eyes.
Now, for his feet—but hold—forbear—
I see the sun-god's portrait there;
Why paint Bathyllus? when, in truth,
There, in that god, thou'st sketch'd the youth.
Enough—let this bright form be mine,
And send the boy to Samos' shrine;
Phœbus shall then Bathyllus be,
Bathyllus then, the deity!

XVIII.

Now the star of day is high,
Fly, my girls, in pity fly,
Bring me wine in brimming urns,
Cool my lip, it burns, it burns!
Sunn'd by the meridian fire,
Panting, languid I expire.
Give me all those humid flowers,
Drop them o'er my brow in showers.
Scarce a breathing chaplet now
Lives upon my feverish brow;
Every dewy rose I wear
Sheds its tears, and withers there.
But to you, my burning heart,
What can now relief impart?
Can brimming bowl, or flowret's dew,
Cool the flame that scorches you?

XIX.

Here recline you, gentle maid,
Sweet is this embowering shade;
Sweet the young, the modest trees,
Ruffled by the kissing breeze;
Sweet the little founts that weep,
Lulling soft the mind to sleep;
Hark! they whisper as they roll,
Calm persuasion to the soul;
Tell me, tell me, is not this
All a stilly scene of bliss?
Who, my girl, would pass it by?
Surely neither you nor I.

XX.

One day the Muses twin'd the hands
Of infant Love with flow'ry bands;
And to celestial Beauty gave
The captive infant for her slave.
His mother comes, with many a toy,
To ransom her beloved boy;
His mother sues, but all in vain,-
He ne'er will leave his chains again.
Even should they take his chains away,
The little captive still would stay.
"If this," he cries, "a bondage be
Oh, who could wish for liberty?"

XXI.

Observe when mother earth is dry,
She drinks the droppings of the sky,
And then the dewy cordial gives
To every thirsty plant that lives.
The vapours, which at evening weep,
Are beverage to the swelling deep;
And when the rosy sun appears,
He drinks the ocean's misty tears.
The moon too quaffs her paly stream
Of lustre, from the solar beam.
Then hence with all your sober thinking.
Since Nature's holy law is drinking;
I'll make the laws of nature mine,
And pledge the universe in wine.

XXII.

The Phrygian rock, that braves the storm,
Was once a weeping matron's form;
And Progue, hapless, frantic maid,
Is now a swallow in the shade.
Oh! that a mirror's form were mine,
That I might catch that smile divine
And like my own fond fancy be,
Reflecting thee, and only thee;
Or could I be the robe which holds
That graceful form within its folds;
Or, turn'd into a fountain, lave
Thy beauties in my circling wave.
Would I were perfume for thy hair,
To breathe my soul in fragrance there,
Or, better still, the zone, that lies
Close to thy breast, and feels its sighs!
Or ev'n those envious pearls that show
So faintly round that neck of snow—
Yes, I would be a happy gem,
Like them to hang, to fade like them
What more would thy Anacreon be?
Oh, any thing that touches thee;
Nay, sandals for those airy feet—
Ev'n to be trod by them were sweet!

XXIII.

I often wish this languid lyre,
This warbler of my soul's desire,
Could raise the breath of song sublime,
To men of fame in former time.
But when the soaring theme I try,
Along the chords my numbers die,
And whisper, with dissolving tone,
"Our sighs are given to love alone
Indignant at the feeble lay,
I tore the panting chords away,

Attun'd them to a nobler swell,
And struck again the breathing shell;
In all the glow of epic fire,
To Hercules I wake the lyre.
But still its fainting sighs repeat,
"The tale of love alone is sweet!"
Then fare thee well, seductive dream,
That mad'st me follow Glory's theme;
For thou my lyre, and thou my heart,
Shall never more in spirit part;
And all that one has felt so well
The other shall as sweetly tell!

XXIV.

To all that breathe the air of heaven,
Some boon of strength has Nature given.
In forming the majestic bull,
She fenced with wreathed horns his skull;
A hoof of strength she lent the steed,
And wing'd the timorous hare with speed.
She gave the lion fangs of terror,
And o'er the ocean's crystal mirror,
Taught the unnumber'd scaly throng
To trace their liquid path along;
While for the umbrage of the grove,
She plum'd the warbling world of love.

To man she gave, in that proud hour,
The boon of intellectual power.
Then, what, oh woman, what, for thee,
Was left in Nature's treasury?
She gave thee beauty—mightier far
Than all the pomp and power of war.
Nor steel, nor fire itself hath power
Like woman in her conquering hour.
Be thou but fair, mankind adore thee,
Smile, and a world is weak before thee!

XXV.

Once in each revolving year,
Gentle bird! we find thee here.
When Nature wears her summer vest,
Thou com'st to weave thy simple nest;
But when the chilling winter lowers,
Again thou seek'st the genial bowers
Of Memphis, or the shores of Nile,
Where sunny hours for ever smile.
And thus thy pinion rests and roves,—
Alas! unlike the swarm of Loves,
That brood within this hapless breast,
And never, never change their nest!
Still every year, and all the year,
They fix their fated dwelling here;
And some their infant plumage try,
And on a tender winglet fly;
While in the shell, impregn'd with fires,
Still lurk a thousand more desires;
Some from their tiny prisons peeping,
And some in formless embryo sleeping.
Thus peopled, like the vernal groves,
My breast resounds with warbling Loves;
One urchin imps the other's feather,
Then twin-desires they wing together,
And fast as they thus take their flight,
Still other urchins spring to light.
But is there then no kindly art,
To chase these Cupids from my heart;
Ah, no! I fear, in sadness fear,
They will for ever nestle here!

XXVI.

Thy harp may sing of Troy's alarms,
Or tell the tale of Theban arms;
With other wars my song shall burn,
For other wounds my harp shall mourn,
'Twas not the crested warrior's dart,
That drank the current of my heart;
Nor naval arms, nor mailed steed,
Have made this vanquish'd bosom bleed;
No—'twas from eyes of liquid blue,
A host of quiver'd Cupids flew:
And now my heart all bleeding lies
Beneath that army of the eyes!

XXVII

We read the flying courser's name
Upon his side, in marks of flame;
And, by their turban'd brows alone,
The warriors of the East are known
But in the lover's glowing eyes,
The inlet to his bosom lies;
Through them we see the small faint mark
Where Love has dropp'd his burning spark!

XXVIII.

As, by his Lemnian forge's flame.
The husband of the Paphian dame
Moulded the glowing steel, to form
Arrows for Cupid, thrilling warm;
And Venus, as he plied his art,
Shed honey round each new made dart
While Love, at hand, to finish all,
Tipp'd every arrow's point with gall,
It chanc'd the Lord of Battles came
To visit that deep cave of flame.
'Twas from the ranks of war he rush'd
His spear with many a life-drop blush'd;
He saw the fiery darts, and smil'd
Contemptuous at the archer-child.
"What!" said the urchin, "Dost thou smile
Here, hold this little dart awhile,
And thou wilt find, though swift of flight,
My bolts are not so feathery light."

Mars took the shaft—and, oh, thy look,
Sweet Venus, when the shaft he took!—
Sighing, he felt the urchin's art,
And cried, in agony of heart,
"It is not light—I sink with pain!
Take—take thy arrow back again."
"No," said the child, "it must not be;
That little dart was made for thee!"

XXIX.

Yes—loving is a painful thrill,
And not to love more painful still;
But oh, it is the worst of pain,
To love and not be lov'd again!
Affection now has fled from earth,
For fire of genius, noble birth,
Nor heavenly virtue, can beguile
From beauty's cheek one favouring smile
Gold is the woman's only theme,
Gold is the woman's only dream.
Oh! never be that wretch forgiven—
Forgive him not, indignant heaven!
Whose grovelling eyes could first adore,
Whose heart could pant for sordid ore.
Since that devoted thirst began,
Man has forgot to feel for man;
The pulse of social life is dead,
And all its fonder feelings fled!
War too has sullied Nature's charms,
For gold provokes the world to arms:
And oh! the worst of all its arts,
It rends asunder loving hearts.

XXX.

'Twas in mocking dream of night—
I fancied I had wings as light
As a young bird's, and flew as fleet;
While Love, around whose beauteous feet,
I knew not why, hung chains of lead,
Pursued me, as I trembling fled;
And, strange to say, as swift as thought
Spite of my pinions, I was caught!

What does the wanton Fancy mean
By such a strange, illusive scene?
I fear she whispers to my breast,
That you, sweet maid, have stol'n its rest;
That though my fancy, for a while,
Hath hung on many a woman's smile,
I soon dissolv'd each passing vow,
And ne'er was caught by love till now!

XXXI.

Arm'd with hyacinthine rod,
(Arms enough for such a god,)
Cupid bade me wing my pace
And try with him the rapid race.
O'er many a torrent, wild and deep,
By tangled brake and pendent steep,
With weary foot I panting flew,
Till my brow dropp'd with chilly dew.
And now my soul, exhausted, dying,
To my lip was faintly flying;
And now I thought the spark had fled,
When Cupid hover'd o'er my head,
And fanning light his breezy pinion,
Rescued my soul from death's dominion;
Then said, in accents half-reproving,
"Why hast thou been a foe to loving?"

XXXII.

Strew me a fragrant bed of leaves,
Where lotus with the myrtle weaves;
And while in luxury's dream I sink,
Let me the balm of Bacchus drink!
In this sweet hour of revelry
Young Love shall my attendant be—
Drest for the task, with tunic round
His snowy neck and shoulders bound,
Himself shall hover by my side,
And minister the racy tide!

Oh, swift as wheels that kindling roll,
Our life is hurrying to the goal:
A scanty dust, to feed the wind,
Is all the trace 'twill leave behind.
Then wherefore waste the rose's bloom
Upon the cold, insensate tomb?
Can flowery breeze, or odour's breath,
Affect the still, cold sense of death?
Oh no; I ask no balm to steep
With fragrant tears my bed of sleep:
But now, while every pulse is glowing,
Now let me breathe the balsam flowing,
Now let the rose, with blush of fire,
Upon my brow in sweets expire;
And bring the nymph whose eye hath power
To brighten even death's cold hour.
Yes, Cupid! ere my shade retire,
To join the blest elysian choir,
With wine, and love, and social cheer,
I'll make my own elysium here!

XXXIII.

'Twas noon of night, when round the pole
The sullen Bear is seen to roll;
And mortals, wearied with the day,
Are slumbering all their cares away:
An infant, at that dreary hour,
Came weeping to my silent bower,
And wak'd me with a piteous prayer,
To shield him from the midnight air.
"And who art thou," I waking cry,
"That bid'st my blissful visions fly!"
"Ah, gentle sire!" the infant said,
"In pity take me to thy shed;
Nor fear deceit: a lonely child
I wander o'er the gloomy wild.
Chill drops the rain, and not a ray
Illumes the drear and misty way!"

I heard the baby's tale of woe;
I heard the bitter night winds blow;
And sighing for his piteous fate,
I trimm'd my lamp and op'd the gate.
'Twas Love! the little wand'ring sprite,
His pinion sparkled through the night.
I knew him by his bow and dart;
I knew him by my fluttering heart.
Fondly I take him in, and raise
The dying embers' cheering blaze;
Press from his dank and clinging hair
The crystals of the freezing air,
And in my hand and bosom hold
His little fingers thrilling cold.

And now the embers' genial ray
Had warm'd his anxious fears away;
"I pray thee," said the wanton child,
(My bosom trembled as he smil'd,)
"I pray thee let me try my bow,
For through the rain I've wander'd so,
That much I fear, the midnight shower
Has injured its elastic power."
The fatal bow the urchin drew;
Swift from the string the arrow flew;
As swiftly flew as glancing flame,
And to my inmost spirit came!
"Fare thee well," I heard him say,
As laughing wild he wing'd away;
"Fare thee well, for now I know
The rain has not relax'd my bow;
It still can send a thrilling dart,
As thou shalt own with all thy heart!"

XXXIV.

Oh thou, of all creation blest,
Sweet insect, that delight'st to rest
Upon the wild wood's leafy tops,
To drink the dew that morning drops,
And chirp thy song with such a glee,
That happiest kings may envy thee.
Whatever decks the velvet field,
Whate'er the circling seasons yield,
Whatever buds, whatever blows,
For thee it buds, for thee it grows.
Nor yet art thou the peasant's fear.
To him thy friendly notes are dear,
For thou art mild as matin dew;
And still, when summer's flowery hue
Begins to paint the bloomy plain,
We hear thy sweet prophetic strain;
Thy sweet prophetic strain we hear,
And bless the notes and thee revere!
The Muses love thy shrilly tone;
Apollo calls thee all his own;
'Twas he who gave that voice to thee,
'Tis he who tunes thy minstrelsy.

Unworn by age's dim decline,
The fadeless blooms of youth are thine.
Melodious insect, child of earth,
In wisdom mirthful, wise in mirth;
Exempt from every weak decay,
That withers vulgar frames away;
With not a drop of blood to stain
The current of thy purer vein;
So blest an age is pass'd by thee,
Thou seem'st—a little deity!

XXXV.

Cupid once upon a bed
Of roses laid his weary head;
Luckless urchin, not to see
Within the leaves a slumbering bee;
The bee awak'd—with anger wild
The bee awak'd, and stung the child.
Loud and piteous are his cries;
To Venus quick he runs, he flies;
"Oh mother!—I am wounded through—
I die with pain—in sooth I do!

Stung by some little angry thing,
Some serpent on a tiny wing—
A bee it was—for once, I know,
I heard a rustic call it so."
Thus he spoke, and she the while
Heard him with a soothing smile;
Then said, "My infant, if so much
Thou feel the little wild-bee's touch,
How must the heart, ah, Cupid! be,
The hapless heart that's stung by thee!"

XXXVI

If hoarded gold possess'd the pow'r
To lengthen life's too fleeting hour,
And purchase from the hand of death
A little span, a moment's breath,
How I would love the precious ore!
And every hour should swell my store;
That when death came, with shadowy pinion,
To waft me to his bleak dominion,
I might, by bribes, my doom delay,
And bid him call some distant day.
But, since, not all earth's golden store
Can buy for us one bright hour more,
Why should we vainly mourn our fate
Or sigh at life's uncertain date?
Nor wealth nor grandeur can illume
The silent midnight of the tomb.
No—give to others hoarded treasures—
Mine be the brilliant round of pleasures;
The goblet rich, the board of friends,
Whose social souls the goblet blends;
And mine, while yet I've life to live,
Those joys that love alone can give.

XXXVII.

'Twas night, and many a circling bowl
Had deeply warm'd my thirsty soul;
As lull'd in slumber I was laid,
Bright visions o'er my fancy play'd.
With maidens, blooming as the dawn,
I seem'd to skim the opening lawn;
Light, on tiptoe bath'd in dew,
We flew, and sported as we flew!

Some ruddy striplings who look'd on—
With cheeks, that like the wine-god's shone,
Saw me chasing, free and wild,
These blooming maids, and slyly smil'd;
Smil'd indeed with wanton glee,
Though none could doubt they envied me.
And still I flew—and now had caught
The panting nymphs, and fondly thought
To gather from each rosy lip
A kiss that Jove himself might sip—
When sudden all my dream of joys,
Blushing nymphs and laughing boys,
All were gone!—"Alas!" I said,
Sighing for th' illusion fled,
"Again, sweet sleep, that scene restore,
Oh! let me dream it o'er and o'er!"

XXXVIII.

Let us drain the nectar'd bowl,
Let us raise the song of soul
To him, the god who loves so well
The nectar'd bowl, the choral swell;
The god who taught the sons of earth
To thrid the tangled dance of mirth;
Him, who was nurs'd with infant Love,
And cradled in the Paphian grove;
Him, that the snowy Queen of Charms
So oft has fondled in her arms.
Oh 'tis from him the transport flows,
Which sweet intoxication knows;
With him the brow forgets its gloom,
And brilliant graces learn to bloom.

Behold!—my boys a goblet bear,
Whose sparkling foam lights up the air
Where are now the tear, the sigh?
To the winds they fly, they fly!
Grasp the bowl; in nectar sinking!
Man of sorrow, drown thy thinking!
Say, can the tears we lend to thought
In life's account avail us aught?
Can we discern with all our lore,
The path we've yet to journey o'er?
Alas, alas, in ways so dark,
'Tis only wine can strike a spark!
Then let me quaff the foamy tide,
And through the dance meandering glide;
Let me imbibe the spicy breath
Of odours chaf'd to fragrant death;
Or from the lips of love inhale
A more ambrosial, richer gale!
To hearts that court the phantom Care,
Let him retire and shroud him there;
While we exhaust the nectar'd bowl,
And swell the choral song of soul
To him, the god who loves so well
The nectar'd bowl, the choral swell!

XXXIX

How I love the festive boy,
Tripping through the dance of joy!
How I love the mellow sage,
Smiling through the veil of age!
And whene'er this man of years
In the dance of joy appears,
Snows may o'er his head be flung,
But his heart—his heart is young.

XL.

I know that Heaven hath sent me here
To run this mortal life's career;
The scenes which I have journey'd o'er,
Return no more—alas! no more;
And all the path I've yet to go,
I neither know nor ask to know
Away, then, wizard Care, nor think
Thy fetters round this soul to link;
Never can heart that feels with me
Descend to be a slave to thee!
And oh! before the vital thrill,
Which trembles at my heart, is still,
I'll gather Joy's luxuriant flowers,
And gild with bliss my fading hours;
Bacchus shall bid my winter bloom,
And Venus dance me to the tomb!

XLI.

When Spring adorns the dewy scene,
How sweet to walk the velvet green,
And hear the west wind's gentle sighs,
As o'er the scented mead it flies!
How sweet to mark the pouting vine,
Ready to burst in tears of wine;
And with some maid, who breathes but love,
To walk, at noontide, through the grove,
Or sit in some cool, green recess—
Oh, is not this true happiness?

XLII.

Yes, be the glorious revel mine,
Where humour sparkles from the wine
Around me, let the youthful choir
Respond to my enlivening lyre;
And while the red cup foams along,
Mingle in soul as well as song.
Then, while I sit, with flowret's crown'd,
To regulate the goblet's round,
Let but the nymph, our banquet's pride,
Be seated smiling by my side,

And earth has not a gift or power
That I would envy, in that hour.
Envy !—oh never let its blight
Touch the gay hearts met here to-night.
Far hence be slander's sidelong wounds,
Nor harsh dispute, nor discord's sounds
Disturb a scene, where all should be
Attuned to peace and harmony.

Come, let us hear the harp's gay note
Upon the breeze inspiring float,
While round us, kindling into love,
Young maidens through the light dance move.
Thus blest with mirth, and love, and peace,
Sure such a life should never cease !

XLIII.

While our rosy fillets shed
Freshness o'er each fervid head,
With many a cup and many a smile
The festal moments we beguile.
And while the harp, impassion'd, flings
Tuneful raptures from its strings,
Some airy nymph, with graceful bound,
Keeps measure to the music sound ;
Waving, in her snowy hand,
The leafy Bacchanalian wand,
Which, as the tripping wanton flies,
Trembles all over to her sighs.
A youth the while, with loosen'd hair,
Floating on the listless air,
Sings, to the wild harp's tender tone,
A tale of woes, alas, his own ;
And oh, the sadness in his sigh,
As o'er his lip the accents die !
Never sure on earth has been
Half so bright, so blest a scene.
It seems as Love himself had come
To make this spot his chosen home ;—
And Venus, too, with all her wiles,
And Bacchus, shedding rosy smiles,
All, all are here, to hail with me
The Genius of Festivity !

XLIV.

Buds of roses, virgin flowers,
Cull'd from Cupid's balmy bowers,
In the bowl of Bacchus steep,
Till with crimson drops they weep.
Twine the rose, the garland twine,
Every leaf distilling wine ;
Drink and smile, and learn to think
That we were born to smile and drink.
Rose, thou art the sweetest flower
That ever drank the amber shower ;
Rose, thou art the fondest child
Of dimpled Spring, the wood-nymph wild
Even the Gods, who walk the sky,
Are amorous of thy scented sigh.
Cupid, too, in Paphian shades,
His hair with rosy fillet braids,
When with the blushing, sister Graces,
The wanton winding dance he traces.
Then bring me, showers of roses bring,
And shed them o'er me while I sing,
Or while, great Bacchus, round thy shrine,
Wreathing my brow with rose and vine,
I lead some bright nymph through the dance,
Commingling soul with every glance.

XLV.

Within this goblet, rich and deep,
I cradle all my woes to sleep.
Why should we breathe the sigh of fear,
Or pour the unavailing tear ?
For death will never heed the sig
Nor soften at the tearful eye ;
And eyes that sparkle, eyes that weep,
Must all alike be seal'd in sleep.
Then let us never vainly stray,
In search of thorns, from pleasure's way ,
But wisely quaff the rosy wave,
Which Bacchus loves, which Bacchus gave ·
And in the goblet, rich and deep,
Cradle our crying woes to sleep

XLVI.

Behold, the young, the rosy Spring,
Gives to the breeze her scented wing ;
While virgin Graces, warm with May,
Fling roses o'er her dewy way.
The murmuring billows of the deep
Have languish'd into silent sleep ;
And mark ! the flitting sea-birds lave
Their plumes in the reflecting wave ;
While cranes from hoary winter fly
To flutter in a kinder sky.
Now the genial star of day
Dissolves the murky clouds away ;
And cultur'd field, and winding stream,
Are freshly glittering in his beam.

Now the earth prolific swells
With leafy buds and flowery bells ;
Gemming shoots the olive twine,
Clusters ripe festoon the vine ;
All along the branches creeping,
Through the velvet foliage peeping,
Little infant fruits we see,
Nursing into luxury.

XLVII.

'Tis true, my fading years decline,
Yet can I quaff the brimming wine,
As deep as any stripling fair,
Whose cheeks the flush of morning wear ;
And if, amidst the wanton crew,
I'm call'd to wind the dance's clue,
Then shalt thou see this vigorous hand,
Not faltering on the Bacchant's wand,
But brandishing a rosy flask,
The only thyrsus e'er I'll ask !

Let those, who pant for Glory's charms,
Embrace her in the field of arms ;
While my inglorious, placid soul
Breathes not a wish beyond this bowl.
Then fill it high, my ruddy slave,
And bathe me in its brimming wave.
For though my fading years decay,
Though manhood's prime hath pass'd away
Like old Silenus, sire divine,
With blushes borrow'd from my wine,
I'll wanton 'mid the dancing train,
And live my follies o'er again !

XLVIII.

When my thirsty soul I steep,
Every sorrow's lull'd to sleep.
Talk of monarchs ! I am then
Richest, happiest, first of men ;
Careless o'er my cup I sing,
Fancy makes me more than king ;
Gives me wealthy Crœsus' store,
Can I, can I wish for more ?
On my velvet couch reclining,
Ivy leaves my brow entwining,
While my soul expands with glee,
What are kings and crowns to me ?
If before my feet they lay,
I would spurn them all away.
Arm ye, arm ye, men of might,
Hasten to the sanguine fight ;
But let *me*, my budding vine !
Spill no other blood than thine

Yonder brimming goblet see,
That alone shall vanquish me—
Who think it better, wiser far
To fall in banquet than in war.

XLIX.

When Bacchus, Jove's immortal boy,
The rosy harbinger of joy,
Who, with the sunshine of the bowl,
Thaws the winter of our soul—
When to my inmost core he glides,
And bathes it with his ruby tides,
A flow of joy, a lively heat,
Fires my brain, and wings my feet,
Calling up round me visions known
To lovers of the bowl alone.

Sing, sing of love, let music's sound
In melting cadence float around,
While, my young Venus, thou and I
Responsive to its murmurs sigh.
Then, waking from our blissful trance,
Again we'll sport, again we'll dance.

L.

When wine I quaff, before my eyes
Dreams of poetic glory rise;
And freshen'd by the goblet's dews,
My soul invokes the heavenly Muse.
When wine I drink, all sorrow's o'er;
I think of doubts and fears no more;
But scatter to the railing wind
Each gloomy phantom of the mind.
When I drink wine, th' ethereal boy,
Bacchus himself, partakes my joy;
And while we dance through vernal bowers,
Whose ev'ry breath comes fresh from flowers,
In wine he makes my senses swim,
Till the gale breathes of nought but him!

Again I drink,—and, lo, there seems
A calmer light to fill my dreams;
The lately ruffled wreath I spread
With steadier hand around my head;
Then take the lyre, and sing "how blest
The life of him who lives at rest!"
But then comes witching wine again,
With glorious woman in its train;
And, while rich perfumes round me rise,
That seem the breath of woman's sighs,
Bright shapes, of every hue and form,
Upon my kindling fancy swarm,
Till the whole world of beauty seems
To crowd into my dazzled dreams!
When thus I drink, my heart refines,
And rises as the cup declines;
Rises in the genial flow,
That none but social spirits know,
When, with young revellers, round the bowl,
The old themselves grow young in soul
Oh, when I drink, true joy is mine,
There's bliss in every drop of wine.
All other blessings I have known,
I scarcely dar'd to call my own;
But this the Fates can ne'er destroy,
Till death o'ershadows all my joy.

LI.

Fly not thus my brow of snow,
Lovely wanton! fly not so.
Though the wane of age is mine,
Though youth's brilliant flush be thine,
Still I'm doom'd to sigh for thee,
Blest, if thou couldst sigh for me!
See, in yonder flowery braid,
Cull'd for thee, my blushing maid,
How the rose, of orient glow,
Mingles with the lily's snow;
Mark, how sweet their tints agree,
Just, my girl, like thee and me!

LII.

Away, away, ye men of rules,
What have I to do with schools?
They'd make me learn, they'd make me think,
But would they make me love and drink?
Teach me this, and let me swim
My soul upon the goblet's brim;
Teach me this, and let me twine
Some fond, responsive heart to mine,
For, age begins to blanch my brow,
I've time for nought but pleasure now.

Fly, and cool my goblet's glow
At yonder fountain's gelid flow;
I'll quaff, my boy, and calmly sink
This soul to slumber as I drink.
Soon, too soon, my jocund slave,
You'll deck your master's grassy grave,
And there's an end—for ah, you know
They drink but little wine below!

LIII

When I behold the festive train
Of dancing youth, I'm young again!
Memory wakes her magic trance,
And wings me lightly through the dance.
Come, Cybeba, smiling maid!
Cull the flower and twine the braid;
Bid the blush of summer's rose
Burn upon my forehead's snows;
And let me, while the wild and young
Trip the mazy dance along,
Fling my heap of years away,
And be as wild, as young, as they.
Hither haste, some cordial soul!
Help to my lips the brimming bowl;
And you shall see this hoary sage
Forget at once his locks and age.
He still can chant the festive hymn,
He still can kiss the goblet's brim;
As deeply quaff, as largely fill,
And play the fool right nobly still.

LIV.

Methinks, the pictur'd bull we see
Is amorous Jove—it must be he!
How fondly blest he seems to bear
That fairest of Phœnician fair!
How proud he breasts the foamy tide,
And spurns the billowy surge aside!
Could any beast of vulgar vein
Undaunted thus defy the main?
No: he descends from climes above,
He looks the God, he breathes of Jove!

LV.

While we invoke the wreathed spring,
Resplendent rose! to thee we'll sing:
Whose breath perfumes th' Olympian bowers;
Whose virgin blush, of chasten'd dye,
Enchants so much our mortal eye.
When pleasure's spring-tide season glows,
The Graces love to wreathe the rose;
And Venus, in its fresh-blown leaves,
An emblem of herself perceives.
Oft hath the poet's magic tongue
The rose's fair luxuriance sung;
And long the Muses, heavenly maids,
Have rear'd it in their tuneful shades.
When, at the early glance of morn,
It sleeps upon the glittering thorn,

'Tis sweet to dare the tangled fence,
To cull the timid flow'ret thence,
And wipe with tender hand away
The tear that on its blushes lay!
'Tis sweet to hold the infant stems,
Yet dropping with Aurora's gems,
And fresh inhale the spicy sighs
That from the weeping buds arise.

When revel reigns, when mirth is high,
And Bacchus beams in every eye,
Our rosy fillets scent exhale,
And fill with balm the fainting gale.
There's nought in nature bright or gay,
Where roses do not shed their ray.
When morning paints the orient skies,
Her fingers burn with roseate dyes;
Young nymphs betray the rose's hue,
O'er whitest arms it kindles through.
In Cytherea's form it glows,
And mingles with the living snows.

The rose distils a healing balm,
The beating pulse of pain to calm;
Preserves the cold inurned clay,
And mocks the vestige of decay:
And when at length, in pale decline,
Its florid beauties fade and pine,
Sweet as in youth, its balmy breath
Diffuses odour even in death!
Oh! whence could such a plant have sprung?
Listen,—for thus the tale is sung.
When, humid, from the silvery stream,
Effusing beauty's warmest beam,
Venus appeared, in flushing hues,
Mellow'd by ocean's briny dews;
When, in the starry courts above,
The pregnant brain of mighty Jove
Disclos'd the nymph of azure glance,
The nymph who shakes the martial lance;—
Then, then, in strange eventful hour,
The earth produc'd an infant flower,
Which sprung, in blushing glories drest,
And wanton'd o'er its parent breast.
The gods beheld this brilliant birth,
And hail'd the Rose, the boon of earth!
With nectar drops, a ruby tide,
The sweetly orient buds they died,
And bade them bloom, the flowers divine
Of him who gave the glorious vine;
And bade them on the spangled thorn
Expand their bosoms to the morn.

LVI.

He who instructs the youthful crew
To bathe them in the brimmer's dew,
And taste, uncloy'd by rich excesses,
All the bliss that wine possesses,
He, who inspires the youth to bound
Elastic through the dance's round,
Bacchus, the god again is here,
And leads along the blushing year;
The blushing year with vintage teems,
Ready to shed those cordial streams,
Which, sparkling in the cup of mirth,
Illuminate the sons of earth!

Then, when the ripe and vermil wine,-
Blest infant of the pregnant vine,
Which now in mellow clusters swells,—
Oh! when it bursts its roseate cells,
Brightly the joyous stream shall flow,
To balsam every mortal woe!
None shall be then cast down or weak,
For health and joy shall light each cheek;
No heart will then desponding sigh,
For wine shall bid despondence fly.
Thus—till another autumn's glow
Shall bid another vintage flow.

LVII.

Whose was the artist hand that spread
Upon this disk the ocean's bed?
And, in a flight of fancy, high
As aught on earthly wing can fly.
Depicted thus, in semblance warm,
The Queen of Love's voluptuous form
Floating along the silv'ry sea
In beauty's naked majesty!
Oh! he hath given th' enamour'd sight
A witching banquet of delight,
Where, gleaming through the waters clear,
Glimpses of undreamt charms appear,
And all that mystery loves to screen,
Fancy, like Faith, adores unseen.

Light as the leaf, that on the breeze,
Of summer skims the glassy seas,
She floats along the ocean's breast,
Which undulates in sleepy rest;
While stealing on, she gently pillows
Her bosom on the heaving billows.
Her bosom, like the dew-wash'd rose,
Her neck, like April's sparkling snows.
Illume the liquid path she traces,
And burn within the stream's embraces.
Thus on she moves, in languid pride,
Encircled by the azure tide,
As some fair lily o'er a bed
Of violets bends its graceful head.
Beneath their queen's inspiring glance,
The dolphins o'er the green sea dance,
Bearing in triumph young Desire,
And infant Love with smiles of fire!
While, glittering through the silver waves,
The tenants of the briny caves
Around the pomp their gambols play,
And gleam along the watery way.

LVIII.

When Gold, as fleet as zephyr's pinion
Escapes like any faithless minion,
And flies me (as he flies me ever,)
Do I pursue him? never, never!
No, let the false deserter go,
For who could court his direst foe?
But, when I feel my lighten'd mind
No more by grovelling gold confin'd,
Then loose I all such clinging cares,
And cast them to the vagrant airs.
Then feel I, too, the Muse's spell,
And wake to life the dulcet shell,
Which, rous'd once more, to beauty sings,
While love dissolves along the strings!

But scarcely has my heart been taught
How little Gold deserves a thought,
When, lo! the slave returns once more
And with him wafts delicious store
Of racy wine, whose genial art
In slumber seals the anxious heart.
Again he tries my soul to sever
From love and song, perhaps for ever.

Away, deceiver! why pursuing
Ceaseless thus my heart's undoing?
Sweet is the song of amorous fire,
Sweet the sighs that thrill the lyre;
Oh! sweeter far than all the gold
Thy wings can waft, thy mines can hold
Well do I know thy arts, thy wiles—
They wither'd Love's young wreathed smiles;
And o'er his lyre such darkness shed,
I thought its soul of song was fled!
They dash'd the wine-cup, that, by him,
Was fill'd with kisses to the brim
Go—fly to haunts of sordid men.
But come not near the bard again.

Thy glitter in the Muse's shade,
Scares from her bower the tuneful maid;
And not for worlds would I forego
That moment of poetic glow,
When my full soul, in Fancy's stream,
Pours o'er the lyre its swelling theme.
Away, away! to worldlings hence,
Who feel not this diviner sense;
Give gold to those who love that pest,—
But leave the poet poor and blest.

LIX.

Ripen'd by the solar beam,
Now the ruddy clusters teem,
In osier baskets borne along
By all the festal vintage throng
Of rosy youths and virgins fair,
Ripe as the melting fruits they bear.
Now, now they press the pregnant grapes,
And now the captive stream escapes,
In fervid tide of nectar gushing,
And for its bondage proudly blushing!
While, round the vat's impurpled brim,
The choral song, the vintage hymn
Of rosy youths and virgins fair,
Steals on the charm'd and echoing air.
Mark, how they drink, with all their eyes,
The orient tide that sparkling flies,
The infant Bacchus, born in mirth,
While Love stands by, to hail the birth.

When he, whose verging years decline
As deep into the vale as mine,
When he inhales the vintage-cup,
His feet, new-wing'd from earth spring up,
And as he dances, the fresh air
Plays whispering through his silvery hair.
Meanwhile young groups whom love invites,
To joys ev'n rivalling wine's delights,
Seek, arm in arm, the shadowy grove,
And there, in words and looks of love,
Such as fond lovers look and say,
Pass the sweet moonlight hours away.

LX.

Awake to life, my sleeping shell
To Phœbus let thy numbers swell,
And though no glorious prize be thine,
No Pythian wreath around thee twine,
Yet every hour is glory's hour
To him who gathers wisdom's flower.
Then wake thee from thy voiceless slumbers,
And to the soft and Phrygian numbers,
Which, tremblingly, my lips repeat,
Send echoes from thy chord as sweet.
'Tis thus the swan, with fading notes,
Down the Cayster's current floats,
While amorous breezes linger round,
And sigh responsive sound for sound,

Muse of the Lyre! illume my dream,
Thy Phœbus is my fancy's theme;
And hallow'd is the harp I bear,
And hallow'd is the wreath I wear,
Hallow'd by him, the god of lays,
Who modulates the choral maze.
I sing the love which Daphne twin'd
Around the godhead's yielding mind;
I sing the blushing Daphne's flight
From this ethereal son of Light;
And how the tender, timid maid
Flew trembling to the kindly shade,
Resign'd a form, alas, too fair,
And grew a verdant laurel there;
Whose leaves, with sympathetic thrill,
In terror seem'd to tremble still!
The god pursu'd, with wing'd desire;
And when his hopes were all on fire,
And when to clasp the nymph he thought,
A lifeless tree was all he caught;
And, stead of sighs that pleasure heaves,
Heard but the west-wind in the leaves!

But, pause, my soul, no more, no more—
Enthusiast, whither do I soar?
This sweetly-mad'ning dream of soul
Hath hurried me beyond the goal.
Why should I sing the mighty darts
Which fly to wound celestial hearts,
When ah, the song, with sweeter tone,
Can tell the darts that wound my own?
Still be Anacreon, still inspire
The descant of the Teian lyre:
Still let the nectar'd numbers float,
Distilling love in every note!
And when some youth, whose glowing soul
Has felt the Paphian star's control,
When he the liquid lays shall hear,
His heart will flutter to his ear,
And drinking there of song divine,
Banquet on intellectual wine!

LXI.

Youth's endearing charms are fled;
Hoary locks deform my head;
Bloomy graces, dalliance gay,
All the flowers of life decay.
Withering age begins to trace
Sad memorials o'er my face;
Time has shed its sweetest bloom,
All the future must be gloom.
This it is that sets me sighing;
Dreary is the thought of dying!
Lone and dismal is the road,
Down to Pluto's dark abode;
And, when once the journey's o'er,
Ah! we can return no more!

LXII.

Fill me, boy, as deep a draught,
As e'er was fill'd, as e'er was quaff'd;
But let the water amply flow,
To cool the grape's intemperate glow;
Let not the fiery god be single,
But with the nymphs in union mingle.
For though the bowl's the grave of sadness,
Ne'er let it be the birth of madness
No, banish from our board to-night
The revelries of rude delight;
To Scythians leave these wild excesses,
Ours be the joy that soothes and blesses!
And while the temperate bowl we wreathe,
In concert let our voices breathe,
Beguiling every hour along
With harmony of soul and song.

LXIII.

To Love, the soft and blooming child,
I touch the harp in descant wild;
To Love, the babe of Cyprian bowers,
The boy, who breathes and blushes flowers,
To Love, for heaven and earth adore him,
And gods and mortals bow before him!

LXIV

Haste thee, nymph, whose well aim'd spear
Wounds the fleeting mountain deer!
Dian, Jove's immortal child,
Huntress of the savage wild!
Goddess with the sun-bright hair!
Listen to a people's prayer.
Turn, to Lethe's river turn,
There thy vanquish'd people mourn!

Come to Lethe's wavy shore,
Tell them they shall mourn no more.
Thine their hearts, their altars thine;
Must they, Dian—must they pine?

LXV.

Like some wanton filly sporting,
Maid of Thrace, thou fly'st my courting.
Wanton filly! tell me why
Thou trip'st away, with scornful eye,
And seem'st to think my doating heart
Is novice in the bridling art?
Believe me, girl, it is not so;
Thou'lt find this skilful hand can throw
The reins around that tender form,
However wild, however warm.
Yes—trust me I can tame thy force,
And turn and wind thee in the course.
Though, wasting now thy careless hours,
Thou sport amid the herbs and flowers,
Soon shalt thou feel the rein's control,
And tremble at the wish'd-for goal!

LXVI.

To thee, the Queen of nymphs divine,
Fairest of all that fairest shine;
To thee, who rul'st with darts of fire
This world of mortals, young Desire!
And oh! thou nuptial Power, to thee
Who bear'st of life the guardian key,
Breathing my soul in fervent praise,
And weaving wild my votive lays,
For thee, O Queen! I wake the lyre,
For thee, thou blushing young Desire,
And oh! for thee, thou nuptial Power,
Come, and illume this genial hour.

Look on thy bride, too happy boy,
And while thy lambent glance of joy
Plays over all her blushing charms,
Delay not, snatch her to thine arms,
Before the lovely, trembling prey,
Like a young birdling, wing away!
Turn, Stratocles, too happy youth,
Dear to the queen of amorous truth,
And dear to her, whose yielding zone
Will soon resign her all thine own.
Turn to Myrilla, turn thine eye,
Breathe to Myrilla, breathe thy sigh.
To those bewitching beauties turn;
For thee they blush, for thee they burn.

Not more the rose, the queen of flowers,
Outblushes all the bloom of bowers,
Than she unrivall'd grace discloses,
The sweetest rose, where all are roses.
Oh! may the sun, benignant, shed
His blandest influence o'er thy bed;
And foster there an infant tree,
To bloom like her, and tower like thee!

LXVII.

Rich in bliss, I proudly scorn
The wealth of Amalthea's horn;
Nor should I ask to call the throne
Of the Tartessian prince my own;
To totter through his train of years,
The victim of declining fears.
One little hour of joy to me
Is worth a dull eternity!

LXVIII.

Now Neptune's month our sky deforms,
The angry night-cloud teems with storms;
And savage winds, infuriate driven
Fly howling in the face of heaven
Now, now, my friends, the gathering gloom
With roseate rays of wine illume:
And while our wreaths of parsley spread
Their fadeless foliage round our head,
Let's hymn th' almighty power of wine,
And shed libations on his shrine!

LXIX.

They wove the lotus band to deck
And fan with pensile wreath each neck;
And every guest, to shade his head,
Three little fragrant chaplets spread;
And one was of th' Egyptian leaf,
The rest were roses, fair and brief:
While from a golden vase profound,
To all on flowery beds around,
A Hebe, of celestial shape,
Pour'd the rich droppings of the grape!

LXX.

A broken cake, with honey sweet,
Is all my spare and simple treat:
And while a generous bowl I crown
To float my little banquet down,
I take the soft, the amorous lyre,
And sing of love's delicious fire:
In mirthful measures warm and free,
I sing, dear maid, and sing for thee!

LXXI.

With twenty chords my lyre is hung,
  And while I wake them all for thee,
Thou, O maiden, wild and young,
  Disport'st in airy levity.

The nursling fawn, that in some shade
  It's antler'd mother leaves behind,
Is not more wantonly afraid,
  More timid of the rustling wind!

LXXII.

Fare thee well, perfidious maid,
My soul, too long on earth delay'd,
Delay'd, perfidious girl, by thee,
Is on the wing for liberty.
I fly to seek a kindlier sphere,
Since thou hast ceas'd to love me here

LXXIII.

Awhile I bloom'd, a happy flower,
Till Love approach'd one fatal hour
And made my tender branches feel
The wounds of his avenging steel.
Then lost I fell, like some poor willow
That falls across the wintry billow!

LXXIV.

Monarch Love, resistless boy,
With whom the rosy Queen of Joy,
And nymphs, whose eyes have Heaven's hue,
Disporting tread the mountain-dew;
Propitious, oh! receive my sighs,
Which, glowing with entreaty, rise,
That thou wilt whisper to the breast
Of her I love thy soft behest;
And counsel her to learn from thee,
That lesson thou hast taught to me.
Ah! if my heart no flattery tell,
Thou'lt own I've learn'd that lesson well!

LXXV.

Spirit of Love, whose locks unroll'd,
Stream on the breeze like floating gold;

Come within a fragrant cloud
Blushing with light, thy votary shroud;
And, on those wings that sparkling play,
Waft, oh, waft me hence away!
Love! my soul is full of thee,
Alive to all thy luxury.
But she, the nymph for whom I glow,
The lovely Lesbian mocks my woe;
Smiles at the chill and hoary hues,
That time upon my forehead strews.
Alas! I fear she keeps her charms,
In store for younger, happier arms!

LXXVI.

Hither, gentle muse of mine,
Come and teach thy votary old
Many a golden hymn divine,
For the nymph with vest of gold.

Pretty nymyh, of tender age,
Fair thy silky locks unfold;
Listen to a hoary sage,
Sweetest maid with vest of gold!

LXXVII.

Would that I were a tuneful lyre,
Of burnish'd ivory fair,
Which, in thy Dionysian choir,
Some blooming boy should bear!

Would that I were a golden vase,
That some bright nymph might hold
My spotless frame, with blushing grace,
Herself as pure as gold!

LXXVIII.

When Cupid sees how thickly now,
The snows of Time fall o'er my brow,
Upon his wing of golden light,
He passes with an eaglet's flight,
And flitting onward seems to say,
"Fare thee well, thou'st had thy day!"

Cupid, whose lamp has lent the ray,
That lights our life's meandering way,
That God, within this bosom stealing,
Hath waken'd a strange, mingled feeling,
Which pleases, though so sadly teasing,
And teases, though so sweetly pleasing!

I know thou lov'st a brimming measure,
And art a kindly, cordial host;
But let me fill and drink at pleasure—
Thus I enjoy the goblet most.

I fear that love disturbs my rest,
Yet feel not love's impassion'd care,
I think there's madness in my breast,
Yet cannot find that madness there!

From dread Leucadia's frowning steep,
I'll plunge into the whitening deep:
And there lie cold, to death resign'd,
Since Love intoxicates my mind!

Mix me, child, a cup divine,
Crystal water, ruby wine:
Weave the frontlet, richly flushing,
O'er my wintry temples blushing.
Mix the brimmer—Love and I
Shall no more the contest try.
Here—upon this holy bowl,
I surrender all my soul!

Among the Epigrams of the Anthologia, are found some panegyrics on Anacreon, which I had translated, and originally intended as a sort of Coronis to this work. But I found upon consideration, that they wanted variety; and that a frequent recurrence, in them, of the same thought, would render a collection of such poems uninteresting. I shall take the liberty, however, of subjoining a few, selected from the number, that I may not appear to have totally neglected those ancient tributes to the fame of Anacreon. The four epigrams which I give are imputed to Antipater Sidonius. They are rendered, perhaps, with too much freedom; but designing originally a translation of all that are extant on the subject, I endeavoured to enliven their uniformity by sometimes indulging in the liberties of paraphrase.

Around the tomb, oh, bard divine!
Where soft thy hallow'd brow reposes,
Long may the deathless ivy twine,
And summer spread her waste of roses!

And there shall many a fount distil,
And many a rill refresh the flowers;
But wine shall be each purple rill,
And every fount be milky showers.

Thus, shade of him, whom nature taught
To tune his lyre and soul to pleasure,
Who gave to love his tenderest thought,
Who gave to love his fondest measure,—

Thus, after death, if shades can feel,
Thou may'st, from odours round thee streaming,
A pulse of past enjoyment steal,
And live again in blissful dreaming!

Here sleeps Anacreon, in this ivied shade;
Here mute in death the Teian swan is laid.
Cold, cold that heart, which while on earth it dwelt
All the sweet frenzy of love's passion felt.
And yet, oh Bard! thou art not mute in death,
Still do we catch thy lyre's luxurious breath;
And still thy songs of soft Bathylla bloom,
Green as the ivy round thy mould'ring tomb.
Nor yet has death obscur'd thy fire of love,
For still it lights thee through the Elysian grove;
Where dreams are thine, that bless th' elect alone,
And Venus calls thee even in death her own!

Oh stranger! if Anacreon's shell
Has ever taught thy heart to swell
With passion's throb or pleasure's sigh
In pity turn, as wand'ring nigh,
And drop thy goblet's richest tear
In tenderest libation here!
So shall my sleeping ashes thrill
With visions of enjoyment still.
Not even in death can I resign
The festal joys that once were mine,
When Harmony pursu'd my ways,
And Bacchus wanton'd to my lays.
Oh! if delight could charm no more,
If all the goblet's bliss were o'er,
When fate had once our doom decreed,
Then dying would be death indeed;
Nor could I think, unblest by wine,
Divinity itself divine!

At length thy golden hours have wing'd their flight,
And drowsy death that eyelid steepeth;
Thy harp, that whisper'd through each lingering night,
Now mutely in oblivion sleepeth!

She too, for whom that harp profusely shed
The purest nectar of its numbers,
She, the young spring of thy desires, hath fled,
And with her blest Anacreon slumbers!

Farewell! thou had'st a pulse for every dart
That mighty Love could scatter from his quiver,
And each new beauty found in thee a heart,
Which thou, with all thy heart and soul, didst give her

REMARKS ON ANACREON.

There is but little known with certainty of the life of Anacreon. Chamæleon Heracleotes, who wrote upon the subject, has been lost in the general wreck of ancient literature. The editors of the poet have collected the few trifling anecdotes which are scattered through the extant authors of antiquity, and, supplying the deficiency of materials by fictions of their own imagination, have arranged, what they call, a life of Anacreon. These specious fabrications are intended to indulge that interest which we naturally feel in the biography of illustrious men; but it is rather a dangerous kind of illusion, as it confounds the limits of history and romance, and is too often supported by unfaithful citation.

Our poet was born in the city of Téos, in the delicious region of Ionia, and the time of his birth appears to have been in the sixth century before Christ. He flourished at that remarkable period, when, under the polished tyrants Hipparchus and Polycrates, Athens and Samos were become the rival asylums of genius. There is nothing certain known about his family, and those who pretend to discover in Plato that he was a descendant of the monarch Codrus, show much more of zeal than of either accuracy or judgment.

The disposition and talents of Anacreon recommended him to the monarch of Samos, and he was formed to be the friend of such a prince as Polycrates. Susceptible only to the pleasures, he felt not the corruptions of the court; and, while Pythagoras fled from the tyrant, Anacreon was celebrating his praises on the lyre. We are told too by Maximus Tyrius, that, by the influence of his amatory songs, he softened the mind of Polycrates into a spirit of benevolence towards his subjects.

The amours of the poet, and the rivalship of the tyrant, I shall pass over in silence; and there are are few, I presume, who will regret the omission of most of those anecdotes, which the industry of some editors has not only promulged, but discussed. Whatever is repugnant to modesty and virtue is considered in ethical science, by a supposition very favourable to humanity, as impossible; and this amiable persuasion should be much more strongly entertained, where the transgression wars with nature as well as virtue. But why are we not allowed to indulge in the presumption? Why are we officiously reminded that there have been really such instances of depravity?

Hipparchus, who now maintained at Athens the power which his father Pisistratus had usurped, was one of those princes who may be said to have polished the fetters of their subjects. He was the first, according to Plato, who edited the poems of Homer, and commanded them to be sung by the rhapsodists at the celebration of the Panathenæa. From his court, which was a sort of galaxy of genius, Anacreon could not long be absent. Hipparchus sent a barge for him; the poet readily embraced the invitation, and the Muses and the Loves were wafted with him to Athens.

The manner of Anacreon's death was singular. We are told that in the eighty-fifth year of his age he was choked by a grape-stone; and, however we may smile at their enthusiastic partiality, who see in this easy and characteristic death a peculiar indulgence of Heaven, we cannot help admiring that his fate should have been so emblematic of his disposition. Cælius Calcagninus alludes to this catastrophe in the following epitaph on our poet:—

> Those lips, then, hallow'd sage, which pour'd along
> A music sweet as any cygnet's song,
> The grape hath clos'd for ever!
> Here let the ivy kiss the poet's tomb,
> Here let the rose he lov'd with laurels bloom,
> In bands that ne'er shall sever.
>
> But far be thou, oh! far, unholy vine,
> By whom the favourite minstrel of the Nine
> Lost his sweet vital breath;
> Thy God himself now blushes to confess,
> Once hallow'd vine! he feels he loves the less,
> Since poor Anacreon's death.

It has been supposed by some writers that Anacreon and Sappho were contemporaries; and the very thought of an intercourse between persons so congenial, both in warmth of passion and delicacy of genius, gives such play to the imagination, that the mind loves to indulge in it. But the vision dissolves before historical truth; and Chamæleon and Hermesianax, who are the source of the supposition, are considered as having merely indulged in a poetical anachronism.

To infer the moral dispositions of a poet from the tone of sentiment which pervades his works, is sometimes a very fallacious analogy; but the soul of Anacreon speaks so unequivocally through his odes, that we may safely consult them as the faithful mirrors of his heart. We find him there the elegant voluptuary, diffusing the seductive charm of sentiment over passions and propensities at which rigid morality must frown. His heart, devoted to indolence, seems to have thought that there was wealth enough in happiness, but seldom happiness in mere wealth. The cheerfulness, indeed, with which he brightens his old age is interesting and endearing: like his own rose, he is fragrant even in decay. But the most peculiar feature of his mind is that love of simplicity, which he attributes to himself so feelingly, and which breathes characteristically throughout all that he has sung. In truth, if we omit those few vices in our estimate which religion, at that time, not only connived at, but consecrated, we shall be inclined to say that the disposition of our poet was amiable; that his morality was relaxed, but not abandoned; and that Virtue with her zone loosened, may be an apt emblem of the character of Anacreon.

Of his person and physiognomy time has preserved such uncertain memorials, that it were better, perhaps, to leave the pencil to fancy; and few can read the Odes of Anacreon without imagining to themselves the form of the animated old bard, crowned with roses, and singing cheerfully to his lyre.

After the very enthusiastic eulogiums bestowed both by ancients and moderns upon the poems of Anacreon, we need not be diffident in expressing our raptures at their beauty, nor hesitate to pronounce them the most polished remains of antiquity. They are, indeed, all beauty, all enchantment. He steals us so insensibly along with him, that we sympathise even in his excesses. In his amatory odes there is a delicacy of compliment not to be found in any other ancient poet. Love at that period was rather an unrefined emotion; and the intercourse of the sexes was animated more by passion than by sentiment. They knew not those little tendernesses which form the spiritual part of affection; their expression of feeling was therefore rude and unvaried, and the poetry of love deprived it of its most captivating graces. Anacreon, however, attained some ideas of this purer gallantry; and the same delicacy of mind which led him to this refinement, prevented him also from yielding to the freedom of language, which has sullied the pages of all the other poets. His descriptions are warm; but the warmth is in the ideas, not the words. He is sportive without being wanton, and ardent without being licentious. His poetic invention is always most brilliantly displayed in those allegorical fictions which so many have endeavoured to imitate, though all have confessed them to be inimitable. Simplicity is the distinguishing feature of these odes, and they interest by their innocence, as much as they fascinate by their beauty. They may be said, indeed, to be the very infants of the Muses, and to lisp in numbers.

I shall not be accused of enthusiastic partiality by those who have read and felt the original; but to others, I am conscious, this should not be the language of a translator, whose faint reflection of such beauties can but ill justify his admiration of them.

In the age of Anacreon music and poetry were inseparable. These kindred talents were for a long time associated, and the poet always sung his own compositions to the lyre. It is probable that they were not set to any regular air, but rather a kind of musical recitation, which was varied according to the fancy and feelings of the moment. The poems of Anacreon were sung at banquets as late as the time of Aulus Gellius, who tells us that he heard one of the odes performed at a birth-day entertainment.

The singular beauty of our poet's style, and the apparent facility perhaps, of his metre have attracted, as I have already remarked, a crowd of imitators. Some of these have succeeded with wonderful felicity, as may be discerned in the few odes which are attributed to writers of a later period. But none of his imitators have been half so dangerous to his fame as those Greek ecclesiastics of the early ages, who, being conscious of their own inferiority to their great prototypes, determined on removing all possibility of comparison, and, under a semblance of moral zeal, deprived the world of some of the most exquisite treasures of ancient times. The works of Sappho and Alcæus were among those flowers of Grecian literature which thus fell beneath the rude hand of ecclesiastical presumption. It is true they pretended that this sacrifice of genius was hallowed by the interests of religion; but I have already assigned the most probable motive: and if Gregorius Nazianzenus had not written Anacreontics, we might now perhaps have the works of the Teian unmutilated, and be empowered to say exultingly with Horace,

> Nec si quid olim lusit Anacreon
> Delevit ætas.

The zeal by which these bishops professed to be actuated, gave birth more innocently indeed, to an absurd species of parody, as repugnant to piety as it is to taste, where the poet of voluptuousness was made a preacher of the gospel, and his muse, like the Venus in armour at Lacedæmon, was arrayed in all the severities of priestly instruction. Such was the "Anacreon Recantatus," by Carolus de Aquino, a Jesuit, published 1701, which consisted of a series of palinodes to the several songs of our poet. Such, too, was the Christian Anacreon of Patrignanus, another Jesuit, who preposterously transferred to a most sacred subject all that the Grecian poet had dedicated to festivity and love. His metre has frequently been adopted by the modern Latin poets; and Scaliger, Taubman, Barthius, and others, have shown that it is by no means uncongenial with that language. The Anacreontics of Scaliger, however, scarcely deserve the name; as they glitter all over with conceits, and though often elegant, are always laboured. The beautiful fictions of Angerianus preserve more happily than any others the delicate turn of those allegorical fables, which, passing so frequently through the mediums of version and imitation, have generally lost their finest rays in the transmission. Many of the Italian poets have indulged their fancies upon the subjects, and in the manner of Anacreon. Bernardo Tasso first introduced the metre, which was afterwards polished and enriched by Chabriera and others.

To judge by the references of Degen, the German language abounds in Anacreontic imitations; and Hagedorn is one among many who have assumed him as a model. La Farre, Chaulieu, and the other light poets of France, have also professed to cultivate the muse of Téos; but they have attained all her negligence with little of the simple grace that embellishes it. In the delicate bard of Schiras we find the kindred spirit of Anacreon: some of his gazelles or songs possess all the character of our poet.

We come now to a retrospect of the editions of Anacreon. To Henry Stephens we are indebted for having first recovered his remains from the obscurity in which, so singularly, they had for many ages reposed. He found the seventh ode, as we are told, on the cover of an old book, and communicated it to Victorius, who mentions the circumstance in his "Various Readings." Stephen was then very young; and this discovery was considered by some critics of that day as a literary imposition. In 1554, however, he gave Anacreon to the world, accompanied with annotations and a Latin version of the greater part of the odes. The learned still hesitated to receive them as the relics of the Teian bard, and suspected them to be the fabrication of some monks of the sixteenth century. This was an idea from which the classic muse recoiled; and the Vatican manuscript, consulted by Scaliger and Salmasius, confirmed the antiquity of the poems. A very inaccurate copy of this MS. was taken by Isaac Vossius, and this is the authority which Barnes has followed in his collation. Accordingly he misrepresents almost as often as he quotes; and the subsequent editors, relying upon his authority, have spoken of the manuscript with not less confidence than ignorance. The literary world, however, has at length been gratified with this curious memorial of the poet, by the industry of the Abbé Spaletti, who published at Rome, in 1781, a facsimile of those pages of the Vatican manuscript which contained the odes of Anacreon.

RHYMES ON THE ROAD,

EXTRACTED FROM THE JOURNAL OF A TRAVELLING MEMBER OF

THE POCO-CURANTE SOCIETY.

THE greater part of the following Rhymes were written or composed in an old *caleche*, for the purpose of beguiling the *ennui* of solitary travelling; and as verses, made by a gentleman in his sleep, have been lately called "a *psychological* curiosity," it is to be hoped that verses, composed by a gentleman to keep himself awake, may be honoured with some appellation equally Greek.

INTRODUCTORY RHYMES.

Different Attitudes in which Authors compose.—Bayes, Henry Stephens, Herodotus, &c.—Writing in Bed—in the Fields.—Plato and Sir Richard Blackmore.—Fiddling with Gloves and Twigs.—Madame de Stael—Rhyming on the Road, in an old Caleche.

WHAT various attitudes, and ways,
And tricks, we authors have in writing!
While some write sitting, some, like BAYES,
Usually stand, while they're inditing.
Poets there are, who wear the floor out,
Measuring a line at every stride;
While some, like HENRY STEPHENS, pour out
Rhymes by the dozen, while they ride.
HERODOTUS wrote most in bed;
And RICHERAND, a French physician,
Declares the clock-work of the head
Goes best in that reclin'd position.
If you consult MONTAIGNE and PLINY on
The subject, 'tis their joint opinion
That Thought its richest harvest yields
Abroad, among the woods and fields;
That Bards, who deal in small retail,
At home may, at their counters, stop;
But that the grove, the hill, the vale,
Are Poesy's true wholesale shop.
And, verily, I think they're right—
For, many a time, on summer eves,
Just at that closing hour of light,
When, like an Eastern Prince, who leaves
For distant war his Haram bow'rs,
The Sun bids farewell to the flow'rs,
Whose heads are sunk, whose tears are flowing
Mid all the glory of his going!—
Ev'n *I* have felt, beneath those beams,
When wand'ring through the fields alone,
Thoughts, fancies, intellectual gleams,
Which, far too bright to be my own,
Seem'd lent me by the Sunny Pow'r,
That was abroad at that still hour.

If thus I've felt, how must *they* feel,
The few, whom genuine Genius warms;
Upon whose souls he stamps his seal,
Graven with Beauty's countless forms;—
The few upon this earth, who seem
Born to give truth to PLATO's dream,
Since in their thoughts, as in a glass,
Shadows of heavenly things appear,
Reflections of bright shapes that pass
Through other worlds, above our sphere!

But this reminds me I digress;—
For PLATO, too, produc'd, 'tis said,
(As one, indeed, might almost guess,)
His glorious visions all in bed.
'Twas in his carriage the sublime
Sir RICHARD BLACKMORE used to rhyme;
And (if the wits don't do him wrong)
'Twixt death* and epics pass'd his time,
Scribbling and killing all day long—
Like Phœbus in his car, at ease,
Now warbling forth a lofty song,
Now murd'ring the young Niobes.

There was a hero 'mong the Danes,
Who wrote, we're told, 'mid all the pains
And horrors of exenteration,
Nine charming odes, which, if you'll look,
You'll find preserv'd, with a translation,
By BARTHOLINUS in his book.
In short, 'twere endless to recite
The various modes in which men write.
Some wits are only in the mind,
When beaux and belles are round them prating,
Some, when they dress for dinner, find
Their muse and valet both in waiting;
And manage, at the self-same time,
To adjust a neckcloth and a rhyme.

Some bards there are who cannot scribble
Without a glove, to tear or nibble;
Or a small twig to whisk about—
As if the hidden founts of Fancy,
Like wells of old, were thus found out
By mystic tricks of rhabdomancy.
Such was the little feathery wand,†
That, held for ever in the hand
Of her,‡ who won and wore the crown
Of female genius in this age,
Seem'd the conductor, that drew down
Those words of lightning to her page.
As for myself—to come, at last,
To the odd way in which *I* write—
Having employ'd these few months past
Chiefly in travelling, day and night,
I've got into the easy mode,
Of rhyming thus along the road—
Making a way-bill of my pages,
Counting my stanzas by my stages—
'Twixt lays and *re*-lays no time lost—
In short, in two words, *writing post.*

EXTRACT I.

Geneva.

View of the Lake of Geneva from the Jura.§—Anxious to reach it before the Sun went down.—Obliged to proceed on Foot.—Alps—Mont Blanc.—Effect of the Scene.

'TWAS late—the sun had almost shone
His last and best, when I ran on,

* Sir Richard Blackmore was a physician, as well as a bad poet.
† Made of paper, twisted up like a fan or feather.
‡ Madame de Stael,
§ Between Vattay and Gex

Anxious to reach that splendid view,
Before the day-beams quite withdrew;
And feeling as all feel, on first
Approaching scenes, where, they are told,
Such glories on their eyes will burst,
As youthful bards in dreams behold.

'Twas distant yet, and, as I ran,
Full often was my wistful gaze
Turn'd to the sun, who now began
To call in all his out-post rays,
And form a denser march of light,
Such as beseems a hero's flight.
Oh, how I wish'd for JOSHUA's pow'r,
To stay the brightness of that hour!
But no—the sun still less became,
Diminish'd to a speck, as splendid
And small as were those tongues of flame,
That on the Apostles' heads descended!

'Twas at this instant—while there glow'd
This last, intensest gleam of light—
Suddenly, through the opening road,
The valley burst upon my sight!
That glorious valley, with its Lake,
And Alps on Alps in clusters swelling,
Mighty, and pure, and fit to make
The ramparts of a Godhead's dwelling.

I stood entranc'd—as Rabbins say
This whole assembled, gazing world
Will stand, upon that awful day,
When the Ark's Light, aloft unfurl'd,
Among the opening clouds shall shine,
Divinity's own radiant sign!

Mighty MONT BLANC, thou wert to me,
That minute, with thy brow in heaven,
As sure a sign of Deity
As e'er to mortal gaze was given.
Nor ever, were I destin'd yet
To live my life twice o'er again,
Can I the deep-felt awe forget,
The dream, the trance that rapt me then!

'Twas all that consciousness of pow'r
And life, beyond this mortal hour;—
Those mountings of the soul within
At thoughts of Heav'n—as birds begin
By instinct in the cage to rise,
When near their time for change of skies;—
That proud assurance of our claim
To rank among the Sons of Light,
Mingled with shame—oh bitter shame!—
At having risk'd that splendid right,
For aught that earth through all its range
Of glories, offers in exchange!
'Twas all this, at that instant brought,
Like breaking sunshine, o'er my thought—
'Twas all this, kindled to a glow
Of sacred zeal, which, could it shine
Thus purely ever, man might grow,
Ev'n upon earth a thing divine,
And be, once more, the creature made
To walk unstain'd the Elysian shade!
No, never shall I lose the trace
Of what I've felt in this bright place,
And, should my spirit's hope grow weak,
Should I, oh God, e'er doubt thy pow'r,
This mighty scene again I'll seek,
At the same calm and glowing hour,
And here, at the sublimest shrine
That Nature ever rear'd to Thee,
Rekindle all that hope divine,
And *feel* my immortality!

EXTRACT II

Geneva

FATE OF GENEVA IN THE YEAR 1782.

A FRAGMENT.

YES—if there yet live some of those,
Who, when this small Republic rose,
Quick as a startled hive of bees,
Against her leaguering enemies—*
When, as the Royal Satrap shook
His well-known fetters at her gates,
Ev'n wives and mothers arm'd, and took
Their stations by their sons and mates;
And on these walls there stood—yet, no,
Shame to the traitors—*would* have stood
As firm a band as e'er let flow
At Freedom's base their sacred blood;
If those yet live, who, on that night,
When all were watching, girt for fight,
Stole, like the creeping of a pest,
From rank to rank, from breast to breast,
Filling the weak, the old with fears,
Turning the heroine's zeal to tears,—
Betraying Honour to that brink,
Where, one step more, and he must sink—
And quenching hopes, which, though the last,
Like meteors on a drowning mast,
Would yet have led to death more bright,
Than life e'er look'd in all its light!
Till soon, too soon, distrust, alarms
Throughout the embattled thousands ran,
And the high spirit, late in arms,
The zeal, that might have work'd such charms,
Fell, like a broken talisman—
Their gates, that they had sworn should be
The gates of Death, that very dawn,
Gave passage widely, bloodlessly,
To the proud foe—nor sword was drawn,
Nor ev'n one martyr'd body cast
To stain their footsteps, as they pass'd;
But, of the many sworn at night
To do or die, some fled the sight,
Some stood to look, with sullen frown,
While some, in impotent despair,
Broke their bright armour and lay down,
Weeping, upon the fragments there!—
If those, I say, who brought that shame,
That blast upon GENEVA's name,
Be living still—though crime so dark
Shall hang up, fix'd and unforgiv'n,
In History's page, the eternal mark
For Scorn to pierce—so help me, Heav'n,
I wish the traitorous slaves no worse,
No deeper, deadlier disaster,
From all earth's ills no fouler curse
Than to have *********** their master!

EXTRACT III.

Geneva.

Fancy and Truth.—Hippomenes and Atalanta.—Mont Blanc.—Clouds

EVEN here, in this region of wonders, I find
That light-footed Fancy leaves truth far behind;
Or, at least, like Hippomenes, turns her astray
By the golden illusions he flings in her way.

What a glory it seem'd the first ev'ning I gaz'd
MONT BLANC, like a vision, then suddenly rais'd
On the wreck of the sunset—and all his array
Of high-towering Alps, touch'd still with a light
Far holier, purer than that of the Day,
As if nearness to Heaven had made them so bright!
Then the dying, at last, of these splendours away
From peak after peak, till they left but a ray,
One roseate ray, that, too precious to fly,
O'er the Mighty of Mountains still glowingly hung,

* In the year 1782, when the forces of Berne, Sardinia, and France laid siege to Geneva, and when, after a demonstration of heroism and self-devotion, which promised to rival the feats of their ancestors in 1602 against Savoy, the Genevans, either panic struck or betrayed, to the surprise of all Europe, opened their gates to the besiegers, and submitted without a struggle to the extinction of their liberties.—See an account of this Revolution in Coxe's Switzerland.

Like the last sunny step of ASTRÆA, when high
From the summit of earth to Elysium she sprung!
And those infinite Alps, stretching out from the sight
Till they mingled with Heaven, now shorn of their light,
Stood lofty, and lifeless, and pale in the sky,
Like the ghosts of a Giant Creation gone by!

That scene—I have view'd it this evening again,
By the same brilliant light that hung over it then—
The valley, the lake in their tenderest charms—
MONT BLANC in his awfullest pomp—and the whole
A bright picture of Beauty, reclin'd in the arms
Of Sublimity, bridegroom elect of her soul!
But where are the mountains, that round me at first,
One dazzling horizon of miracles, burst?
Those Alps beyond Alps, without end swelling on
Like the waves of eternity—where are *they* gone?
Clouds—clouds—they were nothing but clouds, after all!*
That chain of MONT BLANCS, which my fancy flew o'er,
With a wonder that nought on this earth can recall,
Were but clouds of the evening, and now are no more.
What a picture of Life's young illusions! Oh, Night,
Drop thy curtain, at once, and hide *all* from my sight.

EXTRACT IV.

Milan.

The Picture Gallery.—Albano's Rape of Proserpine.—Reflections.—Universal Salvation.—Abraham sending away Agar, by Guercino.—Genius.

WENT to the *Brera*—saw a Dance of Loves
By smooth ALBANO;† him, whose pencil teems
With Cupids, numerous as in summer groves
The leaflets are, or motes in summer beams.

'Tis for the theft of Enna's flow'r‡ from earth,
These urchins celebrate their dance of mirth
Round the green tree, like fays upon a heath—
Those, that are nearest, link'd in order bright,
Cheek after cheek, like rose-buds in a wreath;
And those, more distant, showing from beneath
The others' wings their little eyes of light.
While see, among the clouds, their eldest brother,
But just flown up, tells with a smile of bliss
This prank of Pluto to his charmed mother
Who turns to greet the tidings with a kiss!

Well might the Loves rejoice—and well did they,
Who wove these fables, picture, in their weaving,
That blessed truth, (which, in a darker day,
ORIGEN lost his saintship for believing,)—§
That Love, eternal Love, whose fadeless ray
Nor time, nor death, nor sin can overcast,
Ev'n to the depths of hell will find his way,
And soothe, and heal, and triumph there at last!

GUERCINO'S Agar—where the bond-maid hears
From Abram's lips that he and she must part;
And looks at him with eyes half full of tears,
That seem the very last drops from her heart.
Exquisite picture!—let me not be told
Of minor faults, of colouring tame and cold—
If thus to conjure up a face so fair,||
So full of sorrow; with the story there
Of all that woman suffers, when the stay
Her trusting heart hath lean'd on falls away—
If thus to touch the bosom's tend'rest spring,
By calling into life such eyes, as bring
Back to our sad remembrance some of those
We've smil'd and wept with, in their joys and woes,
Thus filling them with tears, like tears we've known,
Till all the pictur'd grief becomes our own—
If *this* be deem'd the victory of Art—
If thus, by pen or pencil, to lay bare
The deep, fresh, living fountains of the heart
Before all eyes, be Genius—it is *there!*

EXTRACT V.

Padua

Fancy and Reality.—Rain-drops and Lakes.—Plan of a Story.—Where to place the Scene of it.—In some unknown Region.—Psalmanazar's Imposture with respect to the Island of Formosa.

THE more I've view'd this world, the more I've found,
That, fill'd as 'tis with scenes and creatures rare,
Fancy commands, within her own bright round,
A world of scenes and creatures far more fair.
Nor is it that her power can call up there
A single charm, that's not from Nature won,
No more than rainbows, in their pride, can wear
A single hue unborrow'd from the sun—
But 'tis the mental medium it shines through,
That lends to Beauty all its charm and hue;
As the same light, that o'er the level lake
One dull monotony of lustre flings,
Will, entering in the rounded rain-drop, make
Colours as gay as those on Peris' wings!

And such, I deem, the diff'rence between real,
Existing Beauty and that form ideal,
Which she assumes, when seen by poets' eyes,
Like sunshine in the drop—with all those dyes,
Which Fancy's variegating prism supplies.

I have a story of two lovers, fill'd
With all the pure romance, the blissful sadness,
And the sad, doubtful bliss, that ever thrill'd
Two young and longing hearts in that sweet madness.
But where to choose the region of my vision
In this wide, vulgar world—what real spot
Can be found out sufficiently Elysian
For two such perfect lovers, I know not.
Oh for some fair FORMOSA, such as he,
The young Jew fabled of, in the Indian Sea,
By nothing, but its name of Beauty, known,
And which Queen Fancy might make all her own,
Her fairy kingdom—take its people, lands,
And tenements into her own bright hands,
And make, at least, one earthly corner fit
For Love to live in, pure and exquisite!

EXTRACT VI.

Venice.

The Fall of Venice not to be lamented.—Former Glory.—Expedition against Constantinople.—Giustinianis.—Republic.—Characteristics of the old Government.—Golden Book.—Brazen Mouths.—Spies.—Dungeons.—Present Desolation.

MOURN not for VENICE—let her rest
In ruin, 'mong those States unblest,
Beneath whose gilded hoofs of pride,
Where'er they trampled, Freedom died.
No—let us keep our tears for them,
Where'er they pine, whose fall hath been
Not from a blood-stain'd diadem,
Like that which deck'd this ocean-queen,
But from high daring in the cause
Of human Rights—the only good
And blessed strife, in which man draws
His mighty sword on land or flood.

Mourn not for VENICE; though her fall
Be awful, as if Ocean's wave
Swept o'er her, she deserves it all,
And justice triumphs o'er her grave.
Thus perish ev'ry King and State,
That run the guilty race she ran,
Strong but in ill, and only great
By outrage against God and man!

True, her high spirit is at rest,
And all those days of glory gone,
When the world's waters, east and west,
Beneath her white-wing'd commerce shone;

* It is often very difficult to distinguish between clouds and Alps; and on the evening when I first saw this magnificent scene, the clouds were so disposed along the whole horizon as to deceive me into an idea of the stupendous extent of these mountains, which my subsequent observation was very far, of course, from confirming.

† This picture, the Agar of Guercino, and the Apostles of Guido, (the two latter of which are now the chief ornaments of the Brera,) were formerly in the Palazzo Zampieri, at Bologna.

‡ —— that fair field
Of Enna, where Proserpine, gathering flowers,
Herself a fairer flower, by gloomy Dis was gather'd

§ The extension of the Divine Love ultimately even to the regions of the damned.

|| It is probable that this fine head is a portrait, as we find it repeated in a picture by Guercino, which is in the possession of Signor Camuccini, the brother of the celebrated painter at Rome.

When, with her countless barks she went
  To meet the Orient Empire's might,*
And her Giustinianis sent
  Their hundred heroes to that fight.

Vanish'd are all her pomps, 'tis true,
But mourn them not—for vanish'd, too,
(Thanks to that Pow'r, who, soon or late,
Hurls to the dust the guilty Great,)
Are all the outrage, falsehood, fraud,
  The chains, the rapine, and the blood,
That fill'd each spot, at home, abroad,
  Where the Republic's standard stood.
Desolate VENICE! when I track
Thy haughty course through cent'ries back;
Thy ruthless pow'r, obey'd but curst—
  The stern machinery of thy State,
Which hatred would, like steam, have burst,
  Had stronger fear not chill'd ev'n hate;
Thy perfidy, still worse than aught
Thy own unblushing SARPI taught;—
Thy friendship, which, o'er all beneath
Its shadow, rain'd down dews of death;—
Thy Oligarchy's Book of Gold,
  Clos'd against humble Virtue's name,
But open'd wide for slaves who sold
  Their native land to thee and shame;—
Thy all-pervading host of spies,
  Watching o'er every glance and breath,
Till men look'd in each others' eyes,
  To read their chance of life or death;—
Thy laws, that made a mart of blood,
  And legaliz'd the assassin's knife;†
Thy sunless cells beneath the flood,
  And racks, and Leads, that burnt out life;

When I review all this, and see
The doom that now hath fall'n on thee;
Thy nobles, tow'ring once so proud,
Themselves beneath the yoke now bow'd,—
A yoke, by no one grace redeem'd,
Such as, of old, around thee beam'd,
But mean and base as e'er yet gall'd,
Earth's tyrants, when, themselves, enthrall'd,
I feel the moral vengeance sweet,
And, smiling o'er the wreck, repeat,
"Thus perish ev'ry King and State,
  "That tread the steps which VENICE trod,
"Strong but in ill, and only great,
  "By outrage against man and God!"

EXTRACT VII.

Venice.

Lord Byron's Memoirs, written by himself.—Reflections, when about to read them.

LET me, a moment,—ere with fear and hope
Of gloomy, glorious things, these leaves I ope—
As one, in fairy tale, to whom the key
  Of some enchanter's secret halls is giv'n,
Doubts, while he enters, slowly, tremblingly,
  If he shall meet with shapes from hell or heav'n—
Let me, a moment, think what thousands live
O'er the wide earth this instant, who would give,
Gladly, whole sleepless nights to bend the brow
Over these precious leaves, as I do now.
How all who know—and where is he unknown?
To what far region have his songs not flown,
Like PSAPHON's birds, speaking their master's name,
In ev'ry language, syllabled by Fame?—
How all, who've felt the various spells combin'd
Within the circle of that master-mind,—
Like spells, deriv'd from many a star, and met
Together in some wond'rous amulet,—
Would burn to know when first the Light awoke
In his young soul,—and if the gleams that broke
From that Aurora of his genius, rais'd
Most pain or bliss in those on whom they blaz'd;
Would love to trace the unfolding of that pow'r,
Which hath grown ampler, grander, ev'ry hour;
And feel, in watching o'er his first advance,
  As did the Egyptian traveller,‡ when he stood
By the young Nile, and fathom'd with his lance
  The fast small fountains of that mighty flood.

They, too, who, 'mid the scornful thoughts that dwell
  In his rich fancy, tinging all its streams,—
As if the Star of Bitterness, which fell
  On earth of old,§ had touch'd them with its beams,—
Can track a spirit, which, though driven to hate,
From Nature's hands came kind, affectionate;
And which, ev'n now, struck as it is with blight,
Comes out, at times, in love's own native light;—
How gladly all, who've watch'd these struggling rays
Of a bright, ruin'd spirit through his lays,
Would here inquire, as from his own frank lips,
  What desolating grief, what wrongs had driven
That noble nature into cold eclipse;
  Like some fair orb that, once a sun in heaven,
And born, not only to surprise, but cheer
With warmth and lustre all within its sphere,
Is now so quench'd, that of its grandeur lasts
Nought, but the wide, cold shadow which it casts.

Eventful volume! whatsoe'er the change
Of scene and clime—the adventures, bold and strange—
The griefs—the frailties, but too frankly told—
The loves, the feuds thy pages may unfold,
If Truth with half so prompt a hand unlocks
  His virtues as his failings, we shall find
The record there of friendships, held like rocks,
  And enmities, like sun-touch'd snow, resign'd;
Of fealty, cherish'd without change or chill,
In those who serv'd him, young, and serve him still;
Of gen'rous aid, giv'n with that noiseless art
Which wakes not pride, to many a wounded heart,
Of acts—but, no—*not* from himself must aught
Of the bright features of his life be sought.
While they, who court the world, like MILTON's cloud,‖
"Turn forth their silver lining" on the crowd,
This gifted Being wraps himself in night,
  And, keeping all that softens, and adorns,
And gilds his social nature hid from sight,
  Turns but its darkness on a world he scorns.

EXTRACT VIII.

Venice.

Female Beauty at Venice.—No longer what it was in the Time of Titian.—His Mistress.—Various Forms in which he has painted her.—Venus.—Divine and profane Love.—La Fragilita d'Amore.—Paul Veronese.—His Women.—Marriage of Cana.—Character of Italian Beauty.—Raphael Fornarina.—Modesty.

THY brave, thy learn'd have pass'd away:
Thy beautiful!—ah, where are they?
The forms, the faces, that once shone,
  Models of grace in Titian's eye,
Where are they now? while flowers live on
  In ruin'd places, why, oh why
  Must Beauty thus with Glory die?
That maid, whose lips would still have mov'd,
  Could art have breath'd a spirit through them;
Whose varying charms her artist lov'd
  More fondly ev'ry time he drew them,
(So oft beneath his touch they pass'd,
Each semblance fairer than the last;)
Wearing each shape that Fancy's range
  Offers to Love—yet still the one
Fair idol, seen through every change,

---

* Under the Doge Michaeli, in 1171.

† By the infamous statutes of the State Inquisition, not only was assassination recognised as a regular mode of punishment, but this secret power over life was delegated to their minions at a distance, with nearly as much facility as a licence is given under the game laws of England. The only restriction seems to have been the necessity of applying for a new certificate, after every individual exercise of the power.

‡ Bruce.

§ "And the name of the star is called wormwood, and the third part of the waters became wormwood."—*Rev.* viii.

‖ "Did a sable cloud
Turn forth her silver lining on the night?" *Comus.*

Like facets of some orient stone,—
  In each the same bright image shown.
Sometimes a Venus, unarray'd
  But in her beauty*—sometimes deck'd
In costly raiment, as a maid
  That kings might for a throne select.†
Now high and proud, like one who thought
The world should at her feet be brought;
Now, with a look reproachful, sad,—‡
Unwonted look from brow so glad;—
And telling of a pain too deep
For tongue to speak or eyes to weep.
Sometimes, through allegory's veil,
  In double semblance seem to shine,
Telling a strange and mystic tale
  Of Love Profane and Love Divine—§
Akin in features, but in heart
As far as earth and heaven apart.
Or else (by quaint device to prove
The frailty of all worldly love)
Holding a globe of glass, as thin
  As air-blown bubbles, in her hand,
With a young Love confin'd therein,
  Whose wings seem waiting to expand—
And telling, by her anxious eyes,
That, if that frail orb breaks, he flies! ‖

Thou, too, with touch magnificent,
  PAUL of VERONA!—where are they,
The oriental forms,¶ that lent
  Thy canvass such a bright array?
Noble and gorgeous dames, whose dress
Seems part of their own loveliness;
Like the sun's drapery, which, at eve,
The floating clouds around him weave
Of light they from himself receive!
Where is there now the living face
  Like those that, in thy nuptial throng,**
By their superb, voluptuous grace,
Make us forget the time, the place,
  The holy guests they smile among,—
Till, in that feast of heaven-sent wine,
We see no miracles but thine.

If e'er, except in Painting's dream,
  There bloom'd such beauty here, 'tis gone,—
Gone, like the face that in the stream
  Of Ocean for an instant shone,
When Venus at that mirror gave
A last look, ere she left the wave.
And though, among the crowded ways,
We oft are startled by the blaze
Of eyes that pass, with fitful light,
Like fire-flies on the wing at night,††
'Tis not that nobler beauty, giv'n
To show how angels look in heav'n.
Ev'n in its shape most pure and fair,
  'Tis Beauty, with but half her zone,
All that can warm the Sense is there,
  But the Soul's deeper charm is flown:—
'Tis RAPHAEL'S Fornarina,—warm,
  Luxuriant, arch, but unrefin'd;
A flower, round which the noontide swarm
  Of young Desires may buzz and wind,
But where true Love no treasure meets,
Worth hoarding in his hive of sweets.

Ah, no,—for this, and for the hue
  Upon the rounded cheek, which tells
How fresh, within the heart, this dew
  Of Love's unrifled sweetness dwells,
We must go back to our own Isles,
  Where Modesty, which here but gives
A rare and transient grace to smiles,
  In the heart's holy centre lives;
And thence, as from her throne diffuses
  O'er thoughts and looks so bland a reign,
That not a thought or feeling loses
  Its freshness in that gentle chain.

EXTRACT IX.

Venice.

The English to be met with every where.—Alps and Threadneedle Street.—The Simplon and the Stocks.—Rage for travelling.—Blue Stockings among the Wahabees.—Parasols and Pyramids.—Mrs. Hopkins and the Wall of China.

AND is there then no earthly place,
  Where we can rest, in dream Elysian,
Without some curst, round English face,
  Popping up near, to break the vision?
'Mid northern lakes, 'mid southern vines,
  Unholy cits we're doom'd to meet;
Nor highest Alps nor Apennines
  Are sacred from Threadneedle Street!

If up the Simplon's path we wind,
Fancying we leave this world behind,
Such pleasant sounds salute one's ear
As—"Baddish news from 'Change, my dear—
"The Funds—(phew, curse this ugly hill)—
"Are low'ring fast—(what, higher still?)—
"And—(zooks, we're mounting up to heaven!)—
"Will soon be down to sixty-seven."

Go where we may—rest where we will,
Eternal London haunts us still.
The trash of Almack's or Fleet Ditch—
And scarce a pin's head difference *which*—
Mixes, though ev'n to Greece we run,
With every rill from Helicon!
And, if this rage for travelling lasts,
If Cockney's, of all sects and castes,
Old maidens, aldermen, and squires,
Will leave their puddings and coal fires,
To gape at things in foreign lands,
No soul among them understands;
If Blues desert their coteries,
To show off 'mong the Wahabees·
If neither sex nor age controls,
  Nor fear of Mamelukes forbids
Young ladies, with pink parasols,
  To glide among the pyramids—‡‡
Why, then, farewell all hope to find
A spot, that's free from London-kind!
Who knows, if to the West we roam,
But we may find some *Blue* "at home"
  Among the *Blacks* of Carolina
Or, flying to the Eastward, see
Some Mrs. HOPKINS, taking tea
  And toast upon the Wall of China!

EXTRACT X.

Mantua.

Verses of Hippolyta to her Husband.

THEY tell me thou'rt the favour'd guest
  Of every fair and brilliant throng;
No wit, like thine, to wake the jest,
  No voice like thine to breathe the song.
And none could guess, so gay thou art,
That thou and I are far apart.

---

* In the Tribune at Florence.

† In the Palazzo Pitti.

‡ Alludes particularly to the portrait of her in the Sciarra collection at Rome, where the look of mournful reproach in those full, shadowy eyes, as if she had been unjustly accused of something wrong, is exquisite.

§ The fine picture in the Palazzo Borghese, called (it is not easy to say why) "Sacred and Profane Love," in which the two figures, sitting on the edge of the fountain, are evidently portraits of the same person.

‖ This fanciful allegory is the subject of a picture by Titian in the possession of the Marquis Cambian at Turin, whose collection, though small, contains some beautiful specimens of all the great masters.

¶ As Paul Veronese gave but little into the *beau ideal*, his women may be regarded as pretty close imitations of the living models which Venice afforded in his time.

** The Marriage of Cana.

†† "Certain it is (as Arthur Young truly and feelingly says) one now and then meets with terrible eyes in Italy."

‡‡ It was pink *spencers*, I believe, that the imagination of the French traveller conjured up.

Alas, alas, how diff'rent flows,
  With thee and me the time away.
Not that I wish thee sad, heaven knows—
  Still, if thou canst, be light and gay;
I only know that without thee
The sun himself is dark for me.

Do I put on the jewels rare
Thou'st always lov'd to see me wear?
Do I perfume the locks that thou
So oft hast braided o'er my brow,
Thus deck'd, through festive crowds to run,
  And all the assembled world to see,—
All but the one, the absent one,
  Worth more than present worlds to me.
No, nothing cheers this widow'd heart—
My only joy, from thee apart,
From thee thyself, is sitting hours
  And days, before thy pictur'd form—
That dream of thee, which Raphael's pow'rs
  Have made with all but life-breath warm!
And as I smile to it, and say
The words I speak to thee in play,
I fancy from their silent frame,
Those eyes and lips give back the same;
And still I gaze, and still they keep
Smiling thus on me—till I weep!
Our little boy, too, knows it well,
  For there I lead him every day,
And teach his lisping lips to tell
  The name of one that's far away.
Forgive me, love, but thus alone
My time is cheer'd, while thou art gone.

EXTRACT XI.

Florence.

No—'tis not the region where Love's to be found—
  They have bosoms that sigh, they have glances that rove,
They have language a Sappho's own lip might resound,
  When she warbled her best—but they've nothing like Love.

Nor is't that pure *sentiment* only they want,
  Which Heav'n for the mild and the tranquil hath made—
Calm, wedded affection, that home-rooted plant,
  Which sweetens seclusion, and smiles in the shade;

That feeling, which, after long years have gone by,
  Remains, like a portrait we've sat for in youth,
Where, ev'n though the flush of the colours may fly,
  The features still live, in their first smiling truth;

That union, where all that in Woman is kind,
  With all that in Man most ennoblingly tow'rs,
Grow wreath'd into one—like the column, combin'd
  Of the *strength* of the shaft and the capital's *flow'rs*

Of this—bear ye witness, ye wives, ev'ry where,
  By the Arno, the Po, by all Italy's streams—
Of this heart-wedded love, so delicious to share,
  Not a husband hath ev'n one glimpse in his dreams.

But it *is* not this, only;—born full of the light
  Of a sun, from whose fount the luxuriant festoons
Of these beautiful valleys drink lustre so bright,
  That, beside him, our suns of the north are but moons,—

We might fancy, at least, like their climate they burn'd;
  And that Love, though unus'd, in this region of spring,
To be thus to a tame Household Deity turn'd,
  Would yet be all soul, when abroad on the wing.

And there *may* be, there *are*, those explosions of heart,
  Which burst when the senses have first caught the flame:
Such fits of the blood as those climates impart,
  Where Love is a sun-stroke, that maddens the frame.

But that Passion, which springs in the depth of the soul;
  Whose beginnings are virginly pure as the source
Of some small mountain rivulet, destin'd to roll
  As a torrrent, ere long, losing peace in its course—

A course, to which Modesty's struggle but lends
  A more headlong descent, without chance of recall;
But which Modesty ev'n to the last edge attends,
  And, then, throws a halo of tears round its fall!

This exquisite Passion—ay, exquisite, even
  Mid the ruin its madness too often hath made,
As it keeps, even then, a bright trace of the heaven,
  That heaven of Virtue from which it has stray'd—

This entireness of love, which can only be found,
  Where Woman, like something that's holy, watch'd over,
And fenc'd, from her childhood, with purity round,
  Comes, body and soul, fresh as Spring, to a lover!

Where not an eye answers, where not a hand presses,
  Till spirit with spirit in sympathy move;
And the Senses, asleep in their sacred recesses,
  Can only be reach'd through the temple of Love!—

This perfection of Passion—how *can* it be found,
  Where the mystery nature hath hung round the tie
By which souls are together attracted and bound,
  Is laid open, for ever, to heart, ear, and eye;—

Where nought of that innocent doubt can exist,
  That ignorance, even than knowledge more bright,
Which circles the young, like the morn's sunny mist,
  And curtains them round in their own native light;—

Where Experience leave's nothing for Love to reveal,
  Or for Fancy, in visions, to gleam o'er the thought;
But the truths which, alone, we would die to conceal
  From the maiden's young heart, are the *only* ones taught

No, no, 'tis not here, howsoever we sigh,
  Whether purely to Hymen's *one* planet we pray,
Or adore, like Sabæans, each light of Love's sky,
  Here *is* not the region, to fix or to stray

For faithless in wedlock, in gallantry gross,
  Without honour to guard, or reserve to restrain,
What have they, a husband can mourn as a loss?
  What have they, a lover can prize as a gain?

EXTRACT XII.

Florence.

Music in Italy.—Disappointed by it.—Recollections of other Times and Friends.—Dalton.—Sir John Stevenson.—His Daughter.—Musical Evenings together.

* * * * *

If it *be* true that Music reigns,
  Supreme, in Italy's soft shades,
'Tis like that Harmony, so famous,
Among the spheres, which, He of Samos
Declar'd had such transcendent merit,
That not a soul on earth could hear it;
For, far as I have come—from Lakes,
Whose sleep the Tramontana breaks,
Through Milan, and that land, which gave
  The Hero of the rainbow vest—*
By Mincio's banks, and by that wave,†
  Which made Verona's bard so blest—
Places, that (like the Attic shore,
  Which rung back music, when the sea
Struck on its marge) should be, all o'er,
  Thrilling alive with melody—
I've heard no music—not a note
Of such sweet native airs as float,
In my own land, among the throng,
And speak our nation's soul for song.

Nay, ev'n in higher walks, where Art
Performs, as 'twere, the gardener's part,
And richer, if not sweeter, makes
The flow'rs she from the wild-hedge takes—
Ev'n there, no voice hath charm'd my ear,
  No taste hath won my perfect praise,
Like thine, dear friend ‡—long, truly dear—
  Thine, and thy lov'd Olivia's lays.

---

* Bergamo—the birth-place, it is said, of Harlequin.
† The Lago di Garda.

‡ Edward Tuite Dalton, the first husband of Sir John Stevenson's daughter, the late Marchioness of Headfort.

She, always beautiful, and growing
 Still more so ev'ry note she sings—
Like an inspir'd young Sybil,* glowing
 With her own bright imaginings!
And thou, most worthy to be tied
 In music to her, as in love,
Breathing that language by her side,
 All other language far above,
Eloquent Song—whose tones and words
In ev'ry heart find answering chords!

How happy once the hours we past,
 Singing or list'ning all day long,
Till time itself seem'd chang'd, at last,
 To music, and we liv'd in song!
Turning the leaves of HAYDN o'er,
 As quick, beneath her master hand,
They open'd all their brilliant store,
 Like chambers, touch'd by fairy wand;
Or o'er the page of MOZART bending,
 Now by his airy warblings cheer'd,
Now in his mournful *Requiem* blending
 Voices, through which the heart was heard.

And still, to lead our ev'ning choir,
Was He invok'd, thy lov'd-one's Sire—†
He, who, if aught of grace there be
 In the wild notes I write or sing,
First smooth'd their links of harmony,
 And lent them charms they did not bring;—
He, of the gentlest, simplest heart,
With whom, employ'd in his sweet art,
(That art, which gives this world of ours
 A notion how they speak in heaven,)
I've pass'd more bright and charmed hours
 Than all earth's wisdom could have giv'n.
Oh happy days, oh early friends,
 How Life, since then, hath lost its flow'rs!
But yet—though Time *some* foliage rends,
 The stem, the Friendship, still is ours;
And long may it endure, as green,
And fresh as it hath always been!

How I have wander'd from my theme!
 But where is he, that could return
To such cold subjects from a dream,
 Through which these best of feelings burn?—
Not all the works of Science, Art,
 Or Genius in this world are worth
One genuine sigh, that from the heart
 Friendship or Love draws freshly forth.

EXTRACT XIII.

Rome.

Reflections on reading Du Cerceau's Account of the Conspiracy of Rienzi in 1347.‡—The meeting of the Conspirators on the Night of the 19th of May.—Their Procession in the Morning to the Capitol.—Rienzi's Speech.

'TWAS a proud moment—ev'n to hear the words
 Of Truth and Freedom 'mid these temples breath'd,
And see, once more, the Forum shine with swords,
 In the Republic's sacred name unsheath'd—
That glimpse, that vision of a brighter day,
 For his dear ROME, must to a Roman be,
Short as it was, worth ages pass'd away
 In the dull lapse of hopeless slavery.

'Twas on a night of May, beneath that moon,
Which had, through many an age, seem Time untune
The strings of this Great Empire, till it fell
From his rude hands, a broken, silent shell—
The sound of the church clock, near ADRIAN'S Tomb,
Summon'd the warriors, who had risen for ROME,
To meet unarm'd,—with none to watch them there,
But God's own eye,—and pass the night in pray'r.
Holy beginning of a holy cause,
When heroes, girt for Freedom's combat, pause
Before high Heav'n, and, humble in their might,
Call down its blessing on that coming fight.
At dawn, in arms, went forth the patriot band;
And, as the breeze, fresh from the TIBER, fann'd
Their gilded gonfalons, all eyes could see
 The palm-tree there, the sword, the keys of Heav'n·
Types of the justice, peace, and liberty,
 That were to bless them, when their chains were riv'n
On to the Capitol the pageant mov'd,
 While many a Shade of other times, that still
Around that grave of grandeur sighing rov'd,
 Hung o'er their footsteps up the Sacred Hill,
And heard its mournful echoes, as the last
High-minded heirs of the Republic pass'd.
'Twas then that thou, their Tribune,§ (name, which brought
Dreams of lost glory to each patriot's thought,)
Didst, with a spirit Rome in vain shall seek
To wake up in her sons again, thus speak:—
"ROMANS, look round you—on this sacred place
 "There once stood shrines, and gods, and godlike men.
"What see you now? what solitary trace
 "Is left of all, that made ROME'S glory then?
"The shrines are sunk, the Sacred Mount bereft
 "Ev'n of its name—and nothing now remains
"But the deep mem'ry of that glory, left
 "To whet our pangs and aggravate our chains!
"But *shall* this be?—our sun and sky the same,—
 "Treading the very soil our fathers trode,—
"What with'ring curse hath fall'n on soul and frame,
 "What visitation hath there come from God,
"To blast our strength, and rot us into slaves,
 "*Here*, on our great forefathers' glorious graves?
"It cannot be—rise up, ye Mighty Dead,—
 "If we, the living, are too weak to crush
"These tyrant priests, that o'er your empire tread,
 "Till all but Romans at Rome's tameness blush!

"Happy, PALMYRA, in thy desert domes,
 "Where only date-trees sigh and serpents hiss;
"And thou, whose pillars are but silent homes
 "For the stork's brood, superb PERSEPOLIS!
"Thrice happy both, that your extinguish'd race
"Have left no embers—no half-living trace—
"No slaves, to crawl around the once proud spot,
"Till past renown in present shame's forgot.
"While ROME, the Queen of all, whose very wrecks,
 "If lone and lifeless through a desert hurl'd,
"Would wear more true magnificence than decks
 "The assembled thrones of all the existing world—
"ROME, ROME alone, is haunted, stain'd and curst,
 "Through every spot her princely TIBER laves,
"By living human things—the deadliest, worst,
 "This earth engenders—tyrants and their slaves!
"And we—oh shame!—we, who have ponder'd o'er
 "The patriot's lesson and the poet's lay;||
"Have mounted up the streams of ancient lore,
 "Tracking our country's glories all the way—
"Ev'n *we* have tamely, basely kiss'd the ground
 "Before that Papal Power,—that Ghost of Her,
"The World's Imperial mistress—sitting, crown'd
 "And ghastly, on her mould'ring sepulchre!¶

"But this is past:—too long have lordly priests
 "And priestly lords led us, with all our pride
"With'ring about us—like devoted beasts,
 "Dragg'd to the shrine, with faded garlands tied.

---

* Such as those of Domenichino in the Palazzo Borghese at the Capitol, &c.

† Sir John Stevenson.

‡ The "Conjuration de Nicolas Gabrini, dit de Rienzi," by the Jesuit Du Cerceau, is chiefly taken from the much more authentic work of Fortifiocca on the same subject. Rienzi was the son of a laundress

§ Rienzi.

|| The fine Canzone of Petrarch, beginning "Spirto gentil," is supposed, by Voltaire and others, to have been addressed to Reinzi; but there is much more evidence of its having been written, as Ginguene asserts, to the young Stephen Colonna, on his being created a Senator of Rome. That Petrarch, however, was filled with high and patriotic hopes by the first measures of this extraordinary man, appears from one of his letters, quoted by Du Cerceau, where he says,—"Pour tout dire, en un mot, l'atteste, non comme lecteur, mais comme temoin oculaire, qu'il nous a ramene la justice, la paix, la bonne foi, la securite, et tous les autres vestiges de l'age d'or."

¶ This image is borrowed from Hobbes, whose words are, as near as I can recollect:—"For what is the Papacy, but the Ghost of the old Roman Empire, sitting crowned on the grave thereof?"

"'Tis o'er—the dawn of our deliverance breaks!
"Up from his sleep of centuries awakes
"The Genius of the Old Republic, free
"As first he stood in chainless majesty,
And sends his voice through ages yet to come,
Proclaiming Rome, Rome, Rome, Eternal Rome!"

EXTRACT XIV

Rome

Fragment of a Dream.—The great Painters supposed to be Magicians.—The Beginnings of the Art.—Gildings on the Glories and Draperies.—Improvements under Giotto, &c.—The first Dawn of the true Style in Masaccio.—Studied by all the great Artists who followed him.—Leonardo da Vinci, with whom commenced the Golden Age of Painting.—His Knowledge of Mathematics and of Music.—His female Heads all like each other.—Triangular Faces.—Portraits of Mona Lisa, &c.—Picture of Vanity and Modesty.—His chef-d'œuvre, the Last Supper.—Faded and almost effaced.

Fill'd with the wonders I had seen,
In Rome's stupendous shrines and halls,
I felt the veil of sleep, serene,
Come o'er the mem'ry of each scene,
As twilight o'er the landscape falls.
Nor was it slumber, sound and deep,
But such as suits a poet's rest—
That sort of thin, transparent sleep,
Through which his day-dreams shine the best
Methought upon a plain I stood,
Where certain wondrous men, 'twas said,
With strange, mirac'lous power endu'd,
Were coming, each in turn, to shed
His arts' illusions o'er the sight,
And call up miracles of light.
The sky above this lonely place,
Was of that cold, uncertain hue,
The canvass wears, ere, warm'd apace,
Its bright creation dawns to view

But soon a glimmer from the east
Proclaim'd the first enchantments nigh;*
And as the feeble light increas'd,
Strange figures mov'd across the sky,
With golden glories deck'd, and streaks
Of gold among their garments' dyes;†
And life's resemblance ting'd their cheeks,
But nought of life was in their eyes;—
Like the fresh-painted Dead one meets,
Borne slow along Rome's mournful streets
But soon these figures pass'd away;
And forms succeeded to their place,
With less of gold in their array,
But shining with more natural grace,
And all could see the charming wands
Had pass'd into more gifted hands.‡

Among these visions there was one,§
Surpassing fair, on which the sun,
That instant ris'n, a beam let fall,
Which through the dusky twilight trembled,
And reach'd at length, the spot where all
Those great magicians stood assembled
And as they turn'd their heads, to view
The shining lustre, I could trace
The bright varieties it threw
On each uplifted studying face;‖
While many a voice with loud acclaim,
Call'd forth, "Masaccio" as the name
Of him, the Enchanter, who had rais'd
This miracle, on which all gaz'd.

'Twas daylight now—the sun had ris'n,
From out the dungeon of old Night,-
Like the Apostle, from his prison
Led by the Angel's hand of light;
And—as the fetters, when that ray
Of glory reach'd them, dropp'd away,¶
So fled the clouds at touch of day!
Just then, a bearded sage** came forth,
Who oft in thoughtful dream would stand
To trace upon the dusky earth
Strange learned figures with his wand;††
And oft he took the silver lute
His little page behind him bore,
And wak'd such music as, when mute,
Left in the soul a thirst for more!

Meanwhile, his potent spells went on,
And forms and faces, that from out
A depth of shadow mildly shone,
Were in the soft air seen about.
Though thick as midnight stars they beam'd,
Yet all like living sisters seem'd,
So close, in every point, resembling
Each other's beauties—from the eyes
Lucid as if through crystal trembling,
Yet soft as if suffus'd with sighs,
To the long, fawn-like mouth, and chin,
Lovely tapering, less and less,
Till, by this very charm's excess,
Like virtue on the verge of sin,
It touch'd the bounds of ugliness.
Here look'd as when they liv'd the shades
Of some of Arno's dark-ey'd maids—
Such maids as should alone live on,
In dreams thus, when their charms are gone:
Some Mona Lisa, on whose eyes
A painter for whole years might gaze,‡‡
Nor find in all his pallet's dyes,
One that could even approach their blaze

Here float two spirit shapes,§§ the one,
With her white fingers to the sun
Outspread, as if to ask his ray
Whether it e'er had chanc'd to play
On lilies half so fair as they!
This self-pleas'd nymph, was Vanity—
And by her side another smil'd,
In form as beautiful as she,
But with that air, subdu'd and mild,
That still reserve of purity,
Which is to beauty like the haze
Of ev'ning to some sunny view,
Soft'ning such charms as it displays,
And veiling others in that hue,
Which fancy only can see through!
This phantom nymph, who could she be,
But the bright Spirit, Modesty?

Long did the learn'd enchanter stay
To weave his spells, and still there pass'd,
As in the lantern's shifting play.
Group after group in close array,
Each fairer, grander, than the last
But the great triumph of his pow'r
Was yet to come:—gradual and slow,
(As all that is ordain'd to tow'r,
Among the works of man must grow,)
The sacred vision stole to view,
In that half light, half shadow shown,

* The paintings of those artists who were introduced into Venice and Florence from Greece.

† Margaritone of Orezzo, who was a pupil and imitator of the Greeks, is said to have invented this art of gilding the ornaments of pictures, a practice which, though it gave way to a purer taste at the beginning of the 16th century, was still occasionally used by many of the great masters: as by Raphael in the ornaments of the Fornarina, and by Rubens not unfrequently in glories and flames.

‡ Cimabue, Giotto, &c.

§ The works of Masaccio.—For the character of this powerful and original genius, see Sir Joshua Reynold's twelfth discourse. His celebrated frescoes are in the church of St. Pietro del Carmine, at Florence.

‖ All the great artists studied and many of them borrowed from Masaccio. Several figures in the Cartoons of Raphael are taken, with but little alteration, from his frescoes.

¶ "And a light shined in the prison . . . and his chains fell off from his hands."—*Acts.*

** Leonardo da Vinci.

†† His treatise on Mechanics, Optics, &c. preserved in the Ambrosian library at Milan.

‡‡ He is said to have been four years employed upon the portrait of this fair Florentine, without being able, after all, to come up to his idea of her beauty.

§§ Vanity and Modesty in the collection of Cardinal Fesch, at Rome. The composition of the four hands here is rather awkward, but the picture, altogether, is very delighful. There is a repetition of the subject in the possession of Lucien Bonaparte.

Which gives to ev'n the gayest hue,
  A sober'd, melancholy tone.
It was a vision of that last,*
Sorrowful night which Jesus pass'd
With his disciples, when he said
  Mournfully to them—"I shall be
"Betray'd by one, who here hath fed
  "This night at the same board with me."
And though the Saviour, in the dream
Spoke not these words, we saw them beam
Legibly in his eyes (so well
The great magician work'd his spell,)
And read in every thoughtful line
Imprinted on that brow divine,
The meek, the tender nature, griev'd,
Not anger'd, to be thus deceived—
Celestial love requited ill
For all its care, yet loving still—
Deep, deep regret that there should fall
  From man's deceit so foul a blight
Upon that parting hour—and all
  His Spirit must have felt that night,
Who, soon to die for human-kind,
  Thought only, 'mid his mortal pain,
How many a soul was left behind
  For whom he died that death in vain!

Such was the heavenly scene—alas,
That scene so bright so soon should pass!
But pictur'd on the humid air,
Its tints, ere long, grew languid there;†
And storms came on, that, cold and rough,
  Scatter'd its gentlest glories all—
As when the baffling winds blow off
  The hues that hang o'er Terni's fall,—
Till, one by one, the vision's beams
  Faded away, and soon it fled,
To join those other vanish'd dreams
That now flit palely 'mong the dead,—
The shadows of those shades, that go,
Around Oblivion's lake, below!

EXTRACT XV.

Rome.

Mary Magdalen.—Her Story.—Numerous Pictures of her.—Correggio.—Guido.—Raphael, &c.—Canova's two exquisite Statues.—The Somariva Magdalen.—Chantrey's Admiration of Canova's Works

No wonder, MARY, that thy story
  Touches all hearts—for there we see
The soul's corruption, and its glory,
  Its death and life combin'd in thee

From the first moment, when we find
  Thy spirit haunted by a swarm
Of dark desires,—like demons shrin'd
  Unholily in that fair form,—
Till when, by touch of Heav'n set free,
  Thou cam'st, with those bright locks of gold
(So oft the gaze of BETHANY,)
  And, cov'ring in their precious fold
Thy Saviour's feet, didst shed such tears
As paid, each drop, the sins of years!
Thence on, through all thy course of love
  To Him, thy Heavenly Master,—Him,
Whose bitter death-cup from above
  Had yet this cordial round the brim,
That woman's faith and love stood fast
And fearless by Him to the last:—
Till, oh, blest boon for truth like thine!
  Thou wert, of all, the chosen one,
Before whose eyes that Face Divine,
  When risen from the dead, first shone;
That thou might'st see how, like a cloud,
Had pass'd away its mortal shroud,
And make that bright revealment known
To hearts, less trusting than thy own.
All is affecting, cheering, grand;
  The kindliest record ever giv'n,
Ev'n under God's own kindly hand,
  Of what Repentance wins from Heav'n.

No wonder, MARY, that thy face,
  In all its touching light of tears,
Should meet us in each holy place,
  Where Man before his God appears,
Hopeless—were he not taught to see
All hope in Him, who pardon'd thee!
No wonder that the painter's skill
  Should oft have triumph'd in the pow'r
Of keeping thee all lovely still
  Ev'n in thy sorrow's bitt'rest hour;
That soft CORREGGIO should diffuse
  His melting shadows round thy form;
That GUIDO's pale, unearthly hues
  Should, in portraying thee, grow warm;
That all—from the ideal, grand,
Inimitable Roman hand,
Down to the small, enamelling touch
  Of smooth CARLINO—should delight
In pict'ring her, who "lov'd so much,"
  And was, in spite of sin, so bright!

But, MARY, 'mong these bold essays
Of Genius and of Art to raise
A semblance of those weeping eyes—
  A vision, worthy of the sphere
Thy faith has earn'd thee in the skies,
  And in the hearts of all men here,—
None e'er hath match'd, in grief or grace,
CANOVA's day-dream of thy face,
In those bright sculptur'd forms, more bright
With true expression's breathing light,
Than ever yet, beneath the stroke
Of chisel, into life awoke.
The one,‡ portraying what thou wert
  In thy first grief,—while yet the flow'r
Of those young beauties was unhurt
  By sorrow's slow, consuming pow'r;
And mingling earth's seductive grace
  With heav'n's subliming thoughts so well,
We doubt, while gazing, in *which* place
  Such beauty was most form'd to dwell!
The other, as thou look'dst, when years
Of fasting, penitence, and tears
Had worn thy frame;—and ne'er did Art
  With half such speaking pow'r express
The ruin which a breaking heart
  Spreads, by degrees, o'er loveliness.
Those wasting arms, that keep the trace,
Ev'n still, of all their youthful grace,
That loosen'd hair, of which thy brow
Was once so proud,—neglected now!—
Those features, ev'n in fading worth
  The freshest bloom to others giv'n,
And those sunk eyes, now lost to earth,
  But, to the last, still full of heav'n!

Wonderful artist! praise, like mine—
  Though springing from a soul that feels
Deep worship of those works divine,
  Where Genius all his light reveals—
How weak 'tis to the words that came
From him, thy peer in art and fame,§
Whom I have known, by day, by night,
Hang o'er thy marble with delight;
And, while his ling'ring hand would steal

---

* The Last Supper of Leonardo da Vinci, which is in the Refectory of the Convent delle Grazie at Milan. See L'Histoire de la Peinture in Italie, liv. iii. chap. 45. The writer of that interesting work (to whom I take this opportunity of offering my acknowledgments, for the copy he sent me a year since from Rome,) will see I have profited by some of his observations on this celebrated picture.

† Leonardo appears to have used a mixture of oil and varnish for this picture, which alone, without the various other causes of its ruin, would have prevented any long duration of its beauties. It is now almost entirely effaced.

‡ This statue is one of the last works of Canova, and was not yet in marble when I left Rome. The other, which seems to prove, in contradiction to very high authority, that expression, of the intensest kind, is fully within the sphere of sculpture, was executed many years ago, and is in the possession of the Count Somariva, at Paris.

§ Chantrey.

O'er every gra . .ne taper's rays,*
Give thee, with all the gen'rous zeal
Such master-spirits only feel,
That best of fame, a rival's praise!

EXTRACT XVI.

Les Charmettes.

A visit to the House where Rousseau lived with Madame de Warrens.—Their Menage.—Its Grossness.—Claude Anet.—Reverence with which the Spot is now visited.—Absurdity of this blind Devotion to Fame.—Feelings excited by the Beauty and Seclusion of the Scene.—Disturbed by its Associations with Rousseau's History.—Impostures of men of Genius.—Their power of mimicking all the best Feelings, Love, Independence, &c.

STRANGE power of Genius, that can throw
Round all that's vicious, weak, and low,
Such magic lights, such rainbow dyes
As dazzle ev'n the steadiest eyes
*   *   *   *   *   *
*   *   *   *   *   *

'Tis worse than weak—'tis wrong, 'tis shame,
This mean prostration before Fame;
This casting down, beneath the car
Of Idols, whatsoe'er they are,
Life's purest, holiest decencies,
To be career'd o'er, as they please.
No—give triumphant Genius all
For which his loftiest wish can call:
If he be worshipp'd let it be
For attributes, his noblest, first;
Not with that base idolatry,
Which sanctifies his last and worst.

I may be cold;—may want that glow
Of high romance, which bards should know;
That holy homage, which is felt
In treading where the great have dwelt;
This rev'rence, whatsoe'er it be,
I fear, I feel, I have it *not*:—
For here, at this still hour, to me
The charms of this delightful spot;
Its calm seclusion from the throng,
From all the heart would fain forget;
This narrow valley, and the song
Of its small murm'ring rivulet;
The flitting, to and fro, of birds,
Tranquil and tame as they were once
In Eden, ere the startling words
Of Man disturb'd their orisons;
Those little, shadowy paths, that wind
Up the hill-side, with fruit-tree's lin'd,
And lighted only by the breaks
The gay wind in the foliage makes,
Or vistas, here and there, that ope
Through weeping willows, like the snatches
Of far-off scenes of light, which Hope
Even through the shade of sadness catches!—
All this, which—could I once but lose
The memory of those vulgar ties,
Whose grossness all the heavenliest hues
Of Genius can no more disguise,
Than the sun's beams can do away
The filth of fens o'er which they play—
This scene, which would have fill'd my heart
With thoughts of all that happiest is;
Of Love, where self hath only part,
As echoing back another bliss;
Of solitude, secure and sweet,
Beneath whose shade the virtues meet;
Which, while it shelters, never chills
Our sympathies with human woe,
But keeps them, like sequester'd rills,
Purer and fresher in their flow;
Of happy days, that share their beams
'Twixt quiet mirth and wise employ;
Of tranquil nights, that give, in dreams,
The moonlight of the morning's joy!—
All this my heart could dwell on here,
But for those gross memento's near;
Those sullying truths, that cross the track
Of each sweet thought, and drive them back
Full into all the mire, and strife,
And vanities of that man's life,
Who, more than all that e'er have glow'd
With Fancy's flame (and it was *his*,
In fullest warmth and radiance) show'd
What an impostor Genius is;
How, with that strong, mimetic art,
Which forms its life and soul, it takes
All shapes of thought, all hues of heart,
Nor feels, itself, one throb it wakes;
How like a gem its light may smile
O'er the dark path, by mortals trod,
Itself as mean a worm, the while,
As crawls at midnight o'er the sod,
What gentle words and thoughts may fall
From its false lip, what zeal to bless,
While home, friends, kindred, country, all,
Lie waste beneath its selfishness;
How, with the pencil hardly dry
From colouring up such scenes of love
And beauty, as make young hearts sigh,
And dream, and think through heav'n they rove,
They, who can thus describe and move,
The very workers of these charms,
Nor seek, nor know a joy, above
Some Maman's or Theresa's arms!

How all, in short, that makes the boast
Of their false tongues, they want the most,
And, while with freedom on their lips,
Sounding their trimbrels, to set free
This bright world, labouring in the eclipse
Of priestcraft, and of slavery,—
They may, themselves, be slaves as low
As ever Lord or Patron made
To blossom in his smile, or grow,
Like stunted brushwood, in his shade.
Out on the craft!—I'd rather be
One of those hinds, that round me tread,
With just enough of sense to see
The noonday sun that's o'er his head,
Than thus, with high-built genius curst,
That hath no heart for its foundation,
Be all, at once, that's brightest, worst,
Sublimest, meanest in creation!

* Canova always shows his fine statue, the Venere Vincitrice, by the light of a small candle.

ALCIPHRON:

A FRAGMENT.

LETTER I.

FROM ALCIPHRON AT ALEXANDRIA TO CLEON AT ATHENS.

WELL may you wonder at my flight
From those fair Gardens, in whose bowers
Lingers whate'er of wise and bright,
Of Beauty's smile or Wisdom's light,
Is left to grace this world of ours.
Well may my comrades, as they roam,
On such sweet eves as this, inquire
Why I have left that happy home
Where all is found that all desire,
And Time hath wings that never tire;
Where bliss, in all the countless shapes,
That Fancy's self to bliss hath given,
Comes clustering round like road-side grapes
That woo the traveller's lip, at even;

Where Wisdom flings not joy away—
As Pallas in the stream, they say,
Once flung her flute—but smiling owns
That woman's lip can send forth tones
Worth all the music of those spheres
So many dream of, but none hears;
Where Virtue's self puts on so well
Her sister Pleasure's smile, that, loth
From either nymph apart to dwell,
We finish by embracing both.

Yes, such the place of bliss, I own,
From all whose charms I just have flown;
And even while thus to thee I write,
And by the Nile's dark flood recline,
Fondly, in thought, I wing my flight
Back to those groves and gardens bright,
And often think, by this sweet light,
How lovelily they all must shine;
Can see that graceful temple throw
Down the green slope its lengthened shade,
While, on the marble steps below,
There sits some fair Athenian maid,
Over some favourite volume bending;
And, by her side, a youthful sage
Holds back the ringlets that, descending,
Would else o'ershadow all the page.
But hence such thoughts!—nor let me grieve
O'er scenes of joy that I but leave,
As the bird quits awhile its nest
To come again with livelier zest.

And now to tell thee—what I fear
Thou'lt gravely smile at—*why* I'm here.
Though through my life's short, sunny dream,
I've floated without pain or care,
Like a light leaf, down pleasure's stream,
Caught in each sparkling eddy there;
Though never Mirth awaked a strain
That my heart echoed not again;
Yet have I felt, when even most gay,
Sad thoughts—I knew not whence or why—
Suddenly o'er my spirit fly,
Like clouds, that, ere we've time to say
"How bright the sky is!" shade the sky.
Sometimes so vague, so undefin'd,
Were these strange dark'nings of my mind—
While nought but joy around me beam'd—
So causelessly they've come and flown,
That not of life or earth they seem'd,
But shadows from some world unknown.
More oft, however, 'twas the thought
How soon that scene, with all its play
Of life and gladness, must decay—
Those lips I prest, the hands I caught—
Myself—the crowd that mirth had brought
Around me—swept like weeds away!

This thought it was that came to shed
O'er rapture's hour its worst alloys;
And, close as shade with sunshine, wed
Its sadness with my happiest joys.
Oh, but for this disheart'ning voice,
Stealing amid our mirth to say
That all, in which we most rejoice,
Ere night may be the earth-worm's prey;
But for this bitter—only this—
Full as the world is brimm'd with bliss,
And capable as feels my soul
Of draining to its dregs the whole,
I should turn earth to heav'n, and be,
If bliss made Gods, a Deity!

Thou know'st that night—the very last
That 'mong my Garden friends I pass'd—
When the School held its feast of mirth
To celebrate our founder's birth,
And all that He in dreams but saw
When he set Pleasure on the throne
Of this bright world, and wrote her law
In human hearts, was felt and known—
Not in unreal dreams, but true
Substantial joy as pulse e'er knew—
By hearts and bosoms, that each felt
Itself the realm where Pleasure dwelt.

That night, when all our mirth was o'er,
The minstrels silent, and the feet
Of the young maidens heard no more—
So stilly was the time, so sweet,
And such a calm came o'er that scene,
Where life and revel late had been—
Lone as the quiet of some bay,
From which the sea hath ebb'd away—
That still I linger'd, lost in thought,
Gazing upon the stars of night,
Sad and intent, as if I sought
Some mournful secret in their light;
And ask'd them, 'mid that silence, why
Man, glorious man, alone must die,
While they, less wonderful than he,
Shine on through all eternity.

That night—thou haply may'st forget
Its loveliness—but 'twas a night
To make earth's meanest slave regret
Leaving a world so soft and bright.
On one side, in the dark blue sky,
Lonely and radiant, was the eye
Of Jove himself, while, on the other,
'Mong stars that came out one by one,
The young moon—like the Roman mother
Among her living jewels—shone.
"Oh that from yonder orbs," I thought,
"Pure and eternal as they are,
"There could to earth some power be brought,
"Some charm, with their own essence fraught,
"To make man deathless as a star;
"And open to his vast desires
"A course, as boundless and sublime
"As that which waits those comet-fires,
"That burn and roam throughout all time!"

While thoughts like these absorb'd my mind,
That weariness which earthly bliss,
However sweet, still leaves behind,
As if to show how earthly 'tis,
Came lulling o'er me, and I laid
My limbs at that fair statue's base—
That miracle, which Art hath made
Of all the choice of Nature's grace—
To which so oft I've knelt and sworn,
That, could a living maid like her
Unto this wondering world be born,
I would, myself, turn worshipper.

Sleep came then o'er me—and I seem'd
To be transported far away
To a bleak desert plain, where gleam'd
One single, melancholy ray,
Throughout that darkness dimly shed
From a small taper in the hand
Of one, who, pale as are the dead,
Before me took his spectral stand,
And said, while, awfully, a smile
Came o'er the wanness of his cheek—
"Go, and beside the sacred Nile
"You'll find the Eternal Life you seek."

Soon as he spoke these words, the hue
Of death o'er all his features grew,
Like the pale morning, when o'er night
She gains the victory, full of light;
While the small torch he held became
A glory in his hand, whose flame
Brighten'd the desert suddenly,
Even to the far horizon's line—
Along whose level I could see
Gardens and groves, that seem'd to shine,
As if then o'er them freshly play'd
A vernal rainbow's rich cascade;
And music floated every where,
Circling, as 'twere itself the air,

And spirits, on whose wings the hue
Of heaven still linger'd, round me flew,
Till from all sides such splendours broke,
That, with the excess of light, I woke!

Such was my dream;—and, I confess,
  Though none of all our creedless School
E'er conn'd, believ'd, or reverenc'd less
  The fables of the priest-led fool,
Who tells us of a soul, a mind,
Separate and pure, within us shrin'd,
Which is to live—ah, hope too bright!
For ever in yon fields of light;
Who fondly thinks the guardian eyes
  Of Gods are on him—as if, blest
And blooming in their own blue skies,
The eternal Gods were not too wise
  To let weak man disturb their rest!—
Though thinking of such creeds as thou
  And all our Garden sages think,
Yet is there something, I allow,
  In dreams like this—a sort of link
With worlds unseen, which, from the hour
  I first could lisp my thoughts till now,
Hath master'd me with spell-like power.

And who can tell, as we're combin'd
Of various atoms—some refin'd,
Like those that scintillate and play
In the fix'd stars—some, gross as they
That frown in clouds or sleep in clay—
Who can be sure, but 'tis the best
  And brightest atoms of our frame,
  Those most akin to stellar flame,
That shine out thus, when we're at rest
Ev'n as the stars themselves, whose lig[illegible]
Comes out but in the silent night.
Or is it that there lurks, indeed,
Some truth in Man's prevailing cree[illegible]
And that our Guardians, from on hi[illegible]
  Come, in that pause from toil an[illegible],
To put the senses' curtain by,
  And on the wakeful soul look i[illegible]

Vain thought!—but yet, howe'[illegible] be,
Dreams, more than once, hath prov'd to me
Oracles, truer far than Oak,
Or Dove, or Tripod, ever s[illegible]ke.
And 'twas the words—thou'lt hear and smile—
  The words that phantom seem'd to speak—
"Go, and beside the sacred Nile
  "You'll find the Eternal Life you seek—"
That, haunting me by night, by day,
  At length, as with the unseen hand
Of Fate itself, urg'd me away
  From Athens to this Holy Land;
Where, 'mong the secrets, still untaught,
  The myst'ries that, as yet, nor sun
Nor eye hath reach'd—oh, blessed thought!—
  May sleep this everlasting one.

Farewell—when to our Garden friends
Thou talk'st of the wild dream that sends
The gayest of their school thus far,
Wandering beneath Canopus' star,
Tell them that, wander where he will,
  Or, howsoe'er they now condemn
His vague and vain pursuit, he still
  Is worthy of the School and them;—
Still, all their own—nor e'er forgets,
  Ev'n while his heart and soul pursue
Th' Eternal Light which never sets,
  The many meteor joys that *do*,
But seeks them, hails them with delight,
Where'er they meet his longing sight.
And, if his life *must* wane away,
Like other lives, at least the day,
The hour it lasts shall, like a fire
With incense fed, in sweets expire.

LETTER II.

FROM THE SAME TO THE SAME.

Memphis.

'Tis true, alas—the myst'ries and the lore
I came to study on this wondrous shore,
Are all forgotten in the new delights,
The strange, wild joys that fill my days and nights.
Instead of dark, dull oracles that speak
From subterranean temples, those *I* seek
Come from the breathing shrines where Beauty lives
And Love, her priest, the soft responses gives
Instead of honouring Isis in those rites
At Coptos held, I hail her, when she lights
Her first young crescent on the holy stream—
When wandering youths and maidens watch her beam,
And number o'er the nights she hath to run,
Ere she again embrace her bridegroom sun.
While o'er some mystic leaf, that dimly lends
A clue into past times, the student bends,
And by its glimmering guidance learns to tread
Back through the shadowy knowledge of the dead—
The only skill, alas, *I* yet can claim
Lies in deciphering some new lov'd-one's name—
Some gentle missive, hinting time and place,
In language, soft as Memphian reed can trace.

And where—oh where's the heart that could withstand
The unnumber'd witcheries of this sun-born land,
Where first young Pleasure's banner was unfurl'd,
And Love hath temples ancient as the world!
Where mystery, like the veil by Beauty worn,
Hides but to win, and shades but to adorn;
Where that luxurious melancholy, born
Of passion and of genius, sheds a gloom
Making joy holy;—where the bower and tomb
Stand side by side, and Pleasure learns from Death
The instant value of each moment's breath

Couldst thou but see how like a poet's dream
This lovely land now looks!—the glorious stream,
That late, between its banks, was seen to glide
'Mong shrines and marble cities, on each side
Glitt'ring like jewels strung along a chain,
Hath now sent forth its waters, and o'er plain
And valley, like a giant from his bed
Rising with outstretch'd limbs, hath grandly spread;
While far as sight can reach, beneath as clear
And blue a heaven as ever bless'd our sphere,
Gardens, and pillar'd streets, and porphyry domes,
And high-built temples, fit to be the homes
Of mighty Gods, and pyramids, whose hour
Outlasts all time, above the waters tower!

Then, too, the scenes of pomp and joy, that make
One theatre of this vast, peopled lake,
Where all that Love, Religion, Commerce gives
Of life and motion, ever moves and lives.
Here, up the steps of temples from the wave
Ascending, in procession slow and grave,
Priests in white garments go, with sacred wands
And silver cymbals gleaming in their hands;
While there, rich barks—fresh from those sunny tracts
Far off, beyond the sounding cataracts—
Glide, with their precious lading to the sea,
Plumes of bright birds, rhinoceros ivory,
Gems from the Isle of Meroe, and those grains
Of gold, wash'd down by Abyssinian rains.
Here, where the waters wind into a bay
Shadowy and cool, some pilgrims, on their way
To Saïs or Bubastus, among beds
Of lotus flowers, that close above their heads,
Push their light barks, and there, as in a bower,
Sing, talk, or sleep away the sultry hour;
Oft dipping in the Nile, when faint with heat,
That leaf, from which its waters drink most sweet—
While haply, not far off, beneath a bank
Of blossoming acacias, many a prank
Is played in the cool current by a train
Of laughing nymphs, lovely as she,* whose chain

* Cleopatra.

Around two conquerors of the world was cast,
But, for a third too feeble, broke at last.

For oh, believe not them, who dare to brand,
As poor in charms, the women of this land.
Though darkened by that sun, whose spirit flows
Through every vein, and tinges as it goes,
'Tis but the embrowning of the fruit that tells
How rich within the soul of ripeness dwells—
The hue their own dark sanctuaries wear,
Announcing heaven in half-caught glimpses there.
And never yet did tell-tale looks set free
The secret of young hearts more tenderly.
Such eyes!—long, shadowy, with that languid fall
Of the fring'd lids, which may be seen in all
Who live beneath the sun's too ardent rays—
Lending such looks as, on their marriage days,
Young maids cast down before a bridegroom's gaze!
Then for their grace—mark but the nymph-like shapes
Of the young village girls, when carrying grapes
From green Anthylla, or light urns of flowers—
Not our own Sculpture, in her happiest hours,
E'er imag'd forth, even at the touch of him *
Whose touch was life, more luxury of limb;
Then, canst thou wonder if, 'mid scenes like these,
I should forget all graver mysteries,
All lore but Love's, all secrets but that best
In heaven or earth, the art of being blest!
Yet are there times—though brief, I own, their stay,
Like Summer clouds that shine themselves away—
Moments of gloom, when even these pleasures pall
Upon my sadd'ning heart, and I recall
That Garden dream—that promise of a power—
Oh, were there such!—to lengthen out life's hour,
On, on, as through a vista, far away
Opening before us into endless day!
And chiefly o'er my spirit did this thought
Come on that evening—bright as ever brought
Light's golden farewell to the world—when first
The eternal pyramids of Memphis burst
Awfully on my sight—standing sublime
'Twixt earth and heaven, the watch-towers of Time,
From whose lone summit, when his reign hath past
From earth for ever, he will look his last!

There hung a calm and solemn sunshine round
Those mighty monuments, a hushing sound
In the still air that circled them, which stole
Like music of past times into my soul.
I thought what myriads of the wise, and brave,
And beautiful, had sunk into the grave,
Since earth first saw these wonders—and I said,
" Are things eternal only for the Dead?
" Hath man no loftier hope than this, which dooms
" His only lasting trophies to be tombs?
" But '*tis* not so—earth, heaven, all nature shows
" He *may* become immortal—*may* unclose
" The wings within him wrapt, and proudly rise,
" Redeem'd from earth, a creature of the skies!

" And who can say, among the written spells
" From Hermes' hand, that, in these shrines and cells
" Have, from the Flood, lay hid, there may not be
" Some secret clue to immortality,—
" Some amulet, whose spell can keep life's fire
" Awake within us, never to expire!
" 'Tis known that, on the Emerald Table,† hid
" For ages in yon loftiest pyramid,
" The Thrice-Great‡ did himself, engrave, of old,
" The chymic mystery that gives endless gold.
" And why may not this mightier secret dwell
" Within the same dark chambers? who can tell
" But that those kings, who, by the written skill
" Of the Emerald Table, call'd forth gold at will,
" And quarries upon quarries heap'd and hurl'd,
" To build them domes that might outstand the world—
" Who knows but that the heavenlier art, which shares
" The life of Gods with man, was also theirs—

* Apelles.
† See Notes on the Epicurean.
‡ The Hermes Trismegistus

" That they themselves, triumphant o'er the power
" Of fate and death, are living at this hour;
" And these, the giant homes they still possess,
" Not tombs, but everlasting palaces,
" Within whose depths, hid from the world above,
" Even now they wander, with the few they love,
" Through subterranean gardens, by a light
" Unknown on earth, which hath nor dawn nor night!
" Else, why those deathless structures? why the grand
" And hidden halls, that undermine this land?
" Why else hath none of earth e'er dared to go
" Through the dark windings of that realm below,
" Nor aught from heav'n itself, except the God
" Of Silence, through those endless labyrinths trod?"
Thus did I dream—wild, wandering dreams, I own,
But such as haunt me ever, if alone,
Or in that pause, 'twixt joy and joy I be,
Like a ship hush'd between two waves at sea.
Then do these spirit whisperings, like the sound
Of the Dark Future, come appalling round;
Nor can I break the trance that holds me then,
Till high o'er Pleasure's surge I mount again!

Even now for new adventure, new delight,
My heart is on the wing;—this very night,
The Temple on that Island, half-way o'er
From Memphis' gardens to the eastern shore,
Sends up its annual rite § to her, whose beams
Bring the sweet time of night-flowers and dreams,
The nymph, who dips her urn in silent lakes,
And turns to silvery dew each drop it takes;
Oh, not our Dian of the North, who chains
In vestal ice the current of young veins,
But she who haunts the gay Bubastian ‖ grove,
And owns she sees, from her bright heaven above,
Nothing on earth to match that heaven but Love.
Think, then, what bliss will be abroad to-night!—
Besides those sparkling nymphs, who meet the sight
Day after day, familiar as the sun,
Coy buds of beauty, yet unbreath'd upon,
And all the hidden loveliness, that lies,
Shut up, as are the beams of sleeping eyes,
Within these twilight shrines—to-night shall be
Let loose, like birds, for this festivity!

And mark, 'tis nigh; already the sun bids
His evening farewell to the Pyramids,
As he hath done, age after age, till they
Alone on earth seem ancient as his ray;
While their great shadows, stretching from the light,
Look light the first colossal steps of Night,
Stretching across the valley, to invade
The distant hills of porphyry with their shade
Around, as signals of the setting beam,
Gay, gilded flags on every house-top gleam:
While, hark!—from all the temples a rich swell
Of music to the Moon—farewell—farewell.

LETTER III

FROM THE SAME TO THE SAME.

Memphis

There is some star—or it may be
That moon we saw so near last night—
Which comes athwart my destiny
For ever, with misleading light.
If for a moment, pure and wise
And calm I feel, there quick doth fall
A spark from some disturbing eyes,
That through my heart, soul, being flies,
And makes a wildfire of it all.
I've seen—oh, Cleon, that this earth
Should e'er have given such beauty birth!—
That man—but, hold—hear all that pass'd
Since yester-night, from first to last.

The rising of the Moon, calm, slow,
And beautiful, as if she came

§ The great Festival of the Moon.
‖ Bubastis, or Isis, was the Diana of the Egyptian mythology

Fresh from the Elysian bowers below,
  Was, with a loud and sweet acclaim,
Welcom'd from every breezy height,
  Where crowds stood waiting for her light.
And well might they who view'd the scene
  Then lit up all around them, say,
That never yet had Nature been
  Caught sleeping in a lovelier ray,
Or rivall'd her own noon-tide face,
With purer show of moonlight grace.

Memphis—still grand, though not the same
  Unrivall'd Memphis, that could seize
From ancient Thebes the crown of Fame,
  And wear it bright through centuries—
Now, in the moonshine, that came down
Like a last smile upon that crown,—
Memphis, still grand, among her lakes,
  Her pyramids and shrines of fire,
Rose, like a vision, that half breaks
On one who, dreaming still, awakes,
  To music from some midnight choir:
While to the west—where gradual sinks
  In the red sands, from Libya roll'd,
Some mighty column, or fair sphynx,
  That stood in kingly courts, of old—
It seem'd as, 'mid the pomp that shone
Thus gaily round him, Time look'd on,
Waiting till all, now bright and blest,
Should sink beneath him like the rest.

No sooner had the setting sun
Proclaim'd the festal rite begun,
And, 'mid their idol's fullest beams,
  The Egyptian world was all afloat,
Than I, who live upon these streams,
  Like a young Nile-bird, turn'd my boat
To the fair island, on whose shores,
Through leafy palms and sycamores,
Already shone the moving lights
Of pilgrims hastening to the rites.
While far around, like ruby sparks
Upon the water, lighted barks,
Of every form and kind—from those
  That down Syene's cataract shoots,
To the grand, gilded barge, that rows
  To tambour's beat and breath of flutes,
And wears at night, in words of flame,
On the rich prow, its master's name;
All were alive, and made this sea
  Of cities busy as a hill
Of summer ants, caught suddenly
  In the overflowing of a rill.

Landed upon the isle, I soon
  Through marble alleys and small groves
  Of that mysterious palm she loves,
Reach'd the fair Temple of the Moon;
And there—as slowly through the last
Dim-lighted vestibule I pass'd—
Between the porphyry pillars, twin'd
  With palm and ivy, I could see
A band of youthful maidens wind,
  In measur'd walk, half dancingly,
Round a small shrine, on which was plac'd
  That bird,* whose plumes of black and white
Wear in their hue, by Nature trac'd
  A type of the moon's shadow'd light.

In drapery, like woven snow,
These nymphs were clad; and each, below
The rounded bosom, loosely wore
  A dark blue zone, or bandelet,
With little silver stars all o'er,
  As are the skies at midnight, set,
While in their tresses, braided through,
  Sparkled that flower of Egypt's lakes,
The silvery lotus, in whose hue
  As much delight the young Moon takes,
As doth the Day-God to behold
  The lofty bean-flower's buds of gold.
And, as they gracefully went round
  The worshipp'd bird, some to the beat
Of castanets, some to the sound
  Of the shrill sistrum tim'd their feet:
While others, at each step they took,
A tinkling chain of silver shook.

They seem'd all fair—but there was one
On whom the light had not yet shone,
Or shone but partly—so downcast
She held her brow as slow she past.
And yet to me, there seem'd to dwell
  A charm about that unseen face—
A something in the shade that fell
  Over that brow's imagin'd grace,
Which won me more than all the best
Outshining beauties of the rest.
And *her* alone my eyes could see,
Enchain'd by this sweet mystery;
And her alone I watch'd, as round
She glided o'er that marble ground,
Stirring not more the unconscious air
Than if a Spirit were moving there.
Till suddenly, wide open flew
The temple's folding gates, and threw
A splendour from within, a flood
Of glory, where these maiden's stood,
While, with that light—as if the same
Rich source gave birth to both—there came
A swell of harmony, as grand
As e'er was born of voice and hand,
Filling the gorgeous aisles around
With luxury of light and sound.

Then was it, by the flash that blaz'd
  Full o'er her features—oh 'twas then,
As startingly her eyes she rais'd,
  But quick let fall their lids again,
I saw—Not Psyche's self, when first
  Upon the threshold of the skies
She paus'd, while heaven's glory burst
  Newly upon her downcast eyes,
Could look more beautiful, or blush
  With holier shame, than did this maid,
Whom now I saw, in all that gush
  Of splendour from the aisles, display'd,
Never—though well thou knowst how much
  I've felt the sway of Beauty's star—
Never did her bright influence touch
  My soul into its depths so far;
And had that vision linger'd there
  One minute more, I should have flown,
Forgetful *who* I was and where,
  And, at her feet in worship thrown,
Proffer'd my soul through life her own.

But, scarcely had that burst of light
And music broke on ear and sight,
Than up the aisle the bird took wing,
  As if on heavenly mission sent,
While after him, with graceful spring,
  Like some unearthly creatures, meant
  To live in that mix'd element
  Of light and song, the young maids went,
And she, who in my heart had thrown
A spark to burn for life, was flown.

In vain I tried to follow;—bands
  Of reverend chanters fill'd the aisle:
Where'er I sought to pass, their wands
  Motion'd me back, while many a file
Of sacred nymphs—but ah, not they
Whom my eyes look'd for—throng'd the way.
Perplex'd, impatient, 'mid this crowd
Of faces, lights—the o'erwhelming cloud
Of incense round me, and my blood
Full of its new born fire—I stood,
Nor mov'd, nor breath'd, but when I caught
  A glimpse of some blue, spangled zone,

* The Ibis.

Or wreath of lotus, which, I thought,
Like those she wore at distance shone.

But no, 'twas vain—hour after hour,
Till my heart's throbbing turn'd to pain,
And my strain'd eyesight lost its power,
I sought her thus, but all in vain.
At length, hot—wilder'd—in despair,
I rush'd into the cool night-air,
And, hurrying (though with many a look
Back to the busy Temple,) took
My way along the moonlight shore,
And sprung into my boat once more.

There is a Lake, that to the north
Of Memphis stretches grandly forth,
Upon whose silent shore the Dead
Have a proud City of their own,*
With shrines and pyramids o'erspread—
Where many an ancient kingly head
Slumbers, immortalis'd in stone;
And where, through marble grots beneath,
The lifeless, rang'd like sacred things,
Nor wanting aught of life but breath,
Lie in their painted coverings,
And on each new successive race,
That visit their dim haunts below,
Look with the same unwithering face,
They wore three thousand years ago.
There, Silence, thoughtful God, who loves
The neighbourhood of death, in groves
Of asphodel lies hid, and weaves
His hushing spell among the leaves—
Nor ever noise disturbs the air,
Save the low, humming, mournful sound
Of priests, within their shrines, at prayer
For the fresh Dead entomb'd around

'Twas tow'rd this place of death—in mood
Made up of thoughts, half bright, half dark—
I now across the shining flood
Unconscious turn'd my light wing'd bark.
The form of that young maid, in all
Its beauty, was before me still;
And oft I thought, if thus to call
Her image to my mind at will,
If but the memory of that one
Bright look of hers, for ever gone,
Was to my heart worth all the rest
Of woman-kind, beheld, possest—
What would it be, if wholly mine,
Within these arms, as in a shrine,
Hallow'd by Love, I saw her shine—
An idol, worshipp'd by the light
Of her own beauties, day and night—
If 'twas a blessing but to see
And lose again, what would *this* be?

In thoughts like these—but often crost
By darker threads—my mind was lost,
Till, near that City of the Dead,
Wak'd from my trance, I saw o'erhead—
As if by some enchanter bid
Suddenly from the wave to rise—
Pyramid over pyramid
Tower in succession to the skies;
While one, aspiring, as if soon
'Twould touch the heavens, rose o'er all;
And, on its summit, the white moon
Rested, as on a pedestal!

The silence of the lonely tombs
And temples round, where nought was heard
But the high palm-trees' tufted plumes,
Shaken, at times, by breeze or bird,
Form'd a deep contrast to the scene
Of revel, where I late had been;
To those gay sounds, that still came o'er,
Faintly, from many a distant shore,
And the unnumber'd lights, that shone
Far o'er the flood, from Memphis on
To the Moon's Isle and Babylon.

My oars were lifted, and my boat
Lay rock'd upon the rippling stream;
While my vague thoughts, alike afloat,
Drifted through many an idle dream,
With all of which, wild and unfix'd
As was their aim, that vision mix'd,
That bright nymph of the Temple—now,
With the same innocence of brow
She wore within the lighted fane—
Now kindling, through each pulse and vein,
With passion of such deep-felt fire
As Gods might glory to inspire;—
And now—oh Darkness of the tomb,
That must eclipse even light like hers!
Cold, dead, and blackening, 'mid the gloom
Of those eternal sepulchres.

Scarce had I turn'd my eyes away
From that dark death-place, at the thought,
When by the sound of dashing spray
From a light oar my ear was caught,
While past me, through the moonlight, sail'd
A little gilded bark that bore
Two female figures, closely veil'd
And mantled, towards that funeral shore
They landed—and the boat again
Put off across the watery plain.

Shall I confess—to *thee* I may—
That never yet hath come the chance
Of a new music, a new ray
From woman's voice, from woman's glance,
Which—let it find me how it might,
In joy or grief—I did not bless,
And wander after, as a light
Leading to undreamt happiness.
And chiefly now, when hopes so vain
Were stirring in my heart and brain,
When fancy had allur'd my soul
Into a chase, as vague and far
As would be his, who fix'd his goal
In the horizon, or some star—
Any bewilderment, that brought
More near to earth my high-flown thought
The faintest glimpse of joy, less pure,
Less high and heavenly, but more sure,
Came welcome—and was then to me
What the first flowery isle must be
To vagrant birds blown out to sea.

Quick to the shore I urg'd my bark,
And, by the bursts of moonlight, shed
Between the lofty tombs, could mark
Those figures, as with hasty tread
They glided on—till in the shade
Of a small pyramid, which through
Some boughs of palm its peak display'd,
They vanish'd instant from my view.

I hurried to the spot—no trace
Of life was in that lonely place;
And, had the creed I hold by taught
Of other worlds, I might have thought
Some mocking spirits had from thence
Come in this guise to cheat my sense.

At length exploring darkly round
The Pyramid's smooth sides, I found
An iron portal—opening high
'Twixt peak and base—and, with a prayer
To the bliss-loving Moon, whose eye
Alone beheld me, sprung in there.
Downward the narrow stairway led
Through many a duct obscure and dread,
A labyrinth for mystery made,
With wanderings onward, backward, round,
And gathering still, where'er it wound,
But deeper density of shade.

* Necropolis, or the City of the Dead, to the south of Memphis.

Scarce had I ask'd myself, "Can aught
"That man delights in sojourn here?"—
When, suddenly, far off, I caught
A glimpse of light, remote, but clear—
Whose welcome glimmer seem'd to pour
From some alcove or cell, that ended
The long, steep, marble corridor,
Through which I now, all hope, descended.
Never did Spartan to his bride
With warier foot at midnight glide.
It seem'd as echo's self were dead
In this dark place, so mute my tread.
Reaching, at length, that light, I saw—
Oh listen to the scene, now rais'd
Before my eyes—then guess the awe,
The still, rapt awe with which I gaz'd.
'Twas a small chapel, lin'd around
With the fair, spangling marble found
In many a ruin'd shrine that stands
Half seen above the Libyan sands
The walls were richly sculptur'd o'er,
And character'd with that dark lore,
Of times before the Flood, whose key
Was lost in the "Universal Sea."—
While on the roof was pictur'd bright
The Theban beetle, as he shines,
When the Nile's mighty flow declines,
And forth the creature springs to light,
With life regenerate in his wings:—
Emblem of vain imaginings!
Of a new world, when this is gone,
In which the spirit still lives on!

Direct beneath this type, reclin'd
On a black granite altar, lay
A female form, in crystal shrin'd,
And looking fresh as if the ray
Of soul had fled but yesterday.
While in relief, of silv'ry hue,
Grav'd on the altar's front were seen
A branch of lotus, broken in two,
As that fair creature's life had been,
And a small bird that from its spray
Was winging, like her soul, away.

But brief the glimpse I now could spare,
To the wild, mystic wonders round;
For there was yet *one* wonder there,
That held me as by witch'ry bound.
The lamp, that through the chamber shed
Its vivid beam, was at the head
Of her who on that altar slept;
And near it stood, when first I came—
Bending her brow, as if she kept
Sad watch upon its silent flame—
A female form, as yet so plac'd
Between the lamp's strong glow and me,
That I but saw, in outline trac'd,
The shadow of her symmetry.
Yet did my heart—I scarce knew why—
Even at that shadow'd shape beat high.
Nor was it long, ere full in sight
The figure turn'd; and by the light
That touch'd her features, as she bent
Over the crystal monument,
I saw 'twas she—the same—the same—
That lately stood before me, bright'ning
The holy spot, where she but came
And went again, like summer lightning

Upon the crystal, o'er the breast
Of her who took that silent rest,
There was a cross of silver lying—
Another type of that blest home,
Which hope, and pride, and fear of dying
Build for us in a world to come:—
This silver cross the maiden rais'd
To her pure lips:—then, having gaz'd
Some minutes on that tranquil face,
Sleeping in all death's mournful grace,
Upward she turn'd her brow serene,
As if, intent on heaven, those eyes
Saw then nor roof nor cloud between
Their own pure orbits and the skies·
And, though her lips no motion made,
And that fix'd look was all her speech,
I saw that the rapt spirit pray'd
Deeper within than words could reach

Strange power of Innocence, to turn
To its own hue whate'er comes near,
And make even vagrant passion burn
With purer warmth within its sphere!
She who, but one short hour before,
Had come, like sudden wild-fire, o'er
My heart and brain—whom gladly, even
From that bright Temple, in the face
Of those proud ministers of heaven,
I would have borne, in wild embrace,
And risk'd all punishment, divine
And human, but to make her mine;—
She, she was now before me, thrown
By fate itself into my arms—
There standing, beautiful, alone,
With nought to guard her, but her charms
Yet did I, then—did even a breath
From my parch'd lips, too parch'd to move,
Disturb a scene where thus, beneath
Earth's silent covering, Youth and Death
Held converse through undying love?
No—smile and taunt me as thou wilt—
Though but to gaze thus was delight,
Yet seem'd it like a wrong, a guilt,
To win by stealth so pure a sight:
And rather than a look profane
Should then have met those thoughtful eyes,
Or voice or whisper broke the chain
That link'd her spirit with the skies,
I would have gladly, in that place,
From which I watch'd her heavenward face,
Let my heart break, without one beat
That could disturb a prayer so sweet.
Gently, as if on every tread,
My life, my more than life, depended,
Back through the corridor that led
To this blest scene I now ascended,
And with slow seeking, and some pain,
And many a winding tried in vain,
Emerg'd to upper air again.

The sun had freshly risen, and down
The marble hills of Araby,
Scatter'd, as from a conqueror's crown,
His beams into that living sea.
There seem'd a glory in his light,
Newly put on—as if for pride
Of the high homage paid this night
To his own Isis, his young bride,
Now fading feminine away
In her proud Lord's superior ray.

My mind's first impulse was to fly
At once from this entangling net—
New scenes to range, new loves to try,
Or, in mirth, wine, and luxury
Of every sense, that night forget.
But vain the effort—spell-bound still,
I linger'd, without power or will
To turn my eyes from that dark door,
Which now enclos'd her 'mong the dead;
Oft fancying, through the boughs, that o'er
The sunny pile their flickering shed,
'Twas her light form again I saw
Starting to earth—still pure and bright,
But wakening, as I hop'd, less awe,
Thus seen by morning's natural light,
Than in that strange, dim cell at night

But no, alas—she ne'er return'd:
Nor yet—though still I watch—nor yet,
Though the red sun for hours hath burn'd,
And now, in his mid course hath met

The peak of that eternal pile
  He pauses still at noon to bless,
Standing beneath his downward smile,
  Like a great Spirit, shadowless!—
Nor yet she comes—while here, alone,
  Saunt'ring through this death-peopled place,
Where no heart beats except my own,
Or 'neath a palm-tree's shelter thrown,
  By turns I watch, and rest, and trace
These lines, that are to waft to thee
My last night's wondrous history.

Dost thou remember, in that Isle
  Of our own Sea, where thou and I
Linger'd so long, so happy a while,
  'Till all the summer flowers went by—
How gay it was, when sunset brought
  To the cool Well our favourite maids—
Some we had won, and some we sought—
  To dance within the fragrant shades,
And, till the stars went down attune
Their Fountain Hymns* to the young moon?

That time, too—oh, 'tis like a dream—
  When from Scamander's holy tide
I sprung as Genius of the Stream,
  And bore away that blooming bride,
Who thither came, to yield her charms
  (As Phrygian maids are wont, ere wed)
Into the cold Scamander's arms,
  But met, and welcom'd mine, instead—
Wondering, as on my neck she fell,
How river-gods could love so well!
Who would have thought that he, who rov'd
  Like the first bees of summer then,
Rifling each sweet, nor ever lov'd
  But the free hearts, that lov'd again,
Readily as the reed replies
To the least breath that round it sighs—
Is the same dreamer who, last night,
Stood aw'd and breathless at the sight
Of one Egyptian girl; and now
Wanders among these tombs, with brow
Pale, watchful, sad, as though he just,
Himself, had risen from out their dust!

Yet so it is—and the same thirst
  For something high and pure, above
This withering world, which, from the first,
  Made me drink deep of woman's love—
As the one joy, to heaven most near
Of all our hearts can meet with here—
Still burns me up, still keeps awake
A fever nought but death can slake.

Farewell; Whatever may befall—
Or bright, or dark—thoul't know it all.

LETTER IV.

FROM ORCUS, HIGH PRIEST OF MEMPHIS, TO DECIUS,
THE PRÆTORIAN PREFECT.

Rejoice, my friend, rejoice:—the youthful Chief
Of that light Sect which mocks at all belief,
And, gay and godless, makes the present hour
Its only heaven, is now within our power.
Smooth, impious school!—not all the weapons aim'd
At priestly creeds, since first a creed was fram'd,
E'er struck so deep as that sly dart they wield,
The Bacchant's pointed spear in laughing flowers conceal'd.
And oh, 'twere victory to this heart, as sweet
As any *thou* can'st boast—even when the feet
Of thy proud war-steed wade through Christian blood.
To wrap this scoffer in Faith's blinding hood,
And bring him, tam'd and prostrate, to implore
The vilest gods even Egypt's saints adore.
What!—do these sages think, to *them* alone
The key of this world's happiness is known?
That none but they, who make such proud parade
Of Pleasure's smiling favours, win the maid,
Or that Religion keeps no secret place,
No niche, in her dark fanes, for Love to grace?
Fools!—did they know how keen the zest that's given
To earthly joy, when season'd well with heaven;
How Piety's grave mask improves the hue
Of Pleasure's laughing features, half seen through,
And how the Priest, set aptly within reach
Of two rich worlds, traffics for bliss with each,
Would they not, Decius—thou, whom the ancient tie
'Twixt Sword and Altar makes our best ally—
Would they not change their creed, their craft, for ours?
Leave the gross daylight joys that, in their bowers,
Languish with too much sun, like o'erblown flowers,
For the veil'd loves, the blisses undisplay'd
That slily lurk within the Temple's shade?
And, 'stead of haunting the trim Garden's school—
Where cold Philosophy usurps a rule,
Like the pale moon's, o'er passion's heaving tide,
Till Pleasure's self is chill'd by Wisdom's pride—
Be taught by *us*, quit shadows for the true,
Substantial joys we sager Priests pursue,
Who far too wise to theorise on bliss,
Or Pleasure's substance for its shade to miss,
Preach *other* worlds, but live for only *this*:
Thanks to the well-paid Mystery round us flung,
Which, like its type, the golden cloud that hung
O'er Jupiter's love-couch its shade benign,
Round human frailty wraps a veil divine.

Still less should they presume, weak wits, that they
Alone despise the craft of us who pray;—
Still less their creedless vanity deceive
With the fond thought, that we who pray believe.
Believe!—Apis forbid—forbid it, all
Ye monster Gods, before whose shrines we fall—
Deities, fram'd in jest, as if to try
How far gross Man can vulgarise the sky;
How far the same low fancy that combines
Into a drove of brutes yon zodiac's signs,
And turns that Heaven itself into a place
Of sainted sin and deified disgrace,
Can bring Olympus even to shame more deep,
Stock it with things that earth itself holds cheap,
Fish, flesh, and fowl, the kitchen's sacred brood,
Which Egypt keeps for worship, not for food—
All, worthy idols of a Faith that sees
In dogs, cats, owls, and apes, divinities!

Believe!—oh, Decius, thou, who feel'st no care
For things divine, beyond the soldier's share,
Who takes on trust the faith for which he bleeds,
A good, fierce God to swear by, all he needs—
Little canst thou, whose creed around thee hangs
Loose as thy summer war-cloak, guess the pangs
Of loathing and self-scorn with which a heart,
Stubborn as mine is, acts the zealot's part—
The deep and dire disgust with which I wade
Through the foul juggling of this holy trade—
This mud profound of mystery, where the feet,
At every step, sinks deeper in deceit.
Oh! many a time, when 'mid the Temple's blaze,
O'er prostrate fools the sacred cist I raise,
Did I not keep still proudly in my mind
The power this priestcraft gives me o'er mankind—
A lever, of more might, in skilful hand,
To move this world, than Archimede e'er plann'd—
I should, in vengeance of the shame I feel
At my own mockery, crush the slaves that kneel
Besotted round; and—like that kindred breed
Of reverend, wolf-drest crocodiles they feed,
At fam'd Arsinoë†—make my keepers bless,
With their last throb, my sharp-fang'd Holiness.

Say, *is* it to be borne, that scoffers, vain
Of their own freedom from the altar's chain,

* These songs of the Well, as they were called by the ancients, are still common in the Greek isles.

† For the trinkets with which the sacred Crocodiles were ornamented, see the Epicurean, chap. x

Should mock thus all that thou thy blood hast sold,
And I my truth, pride, freedom, to uphold?
It must not be:—think'st thou that Christian sect,
Whose followers, quick as broken waves, erect
Their crests anew and swell into a tide,
That threats to sweep away our shrines of pride—
Think'st thou, with all their wondrous spells, even they
Would triumph thus, had not the constant play
Of Wit's resistless archery clear'd their way?—
That mocking spirit, worst of all the foes,
Our solemn fraud, our mystic mummery knows,
Whose wounding flash thus ever 'mong the signs
Of a fast-falling creed, prelusive shines,
Threat'ning such change as do the awful freaks
Of summer lightning, ere the tempest breaks.

But, to my point—a youth of this vain school,
But one, whom Doubt itself hath fail'd to cool
Down to that freezing point where Priest's despair
Of any spark from the altar catching there—
Hath, some nights since—it was, methinks, the night
That follow'd the full Moon's great annual rite—
Through the dark, winding ducts, that downward stray
To these earth-hidden temples, track'd his way,
Just at that hour when, round the Shrine, and me,
The choir of blooming nymphs thou long'st to see,
Sing their last night-hymn in the Sanctuary.
The clangour of the marvellous Gate, that stands
At the Well's lowest depth—which none but hands
Of new, untaught adventurers, from above,
Who know not the safe path, e'er dare to move—
Gave signal that a foot profane was nigh:—
'Twas the Greek youth, who, by that morning's sky,
Had been observ'd, curiously wand'ring round
The mighty fanes of our sepulchral ground.

Instant, the Initiate's Trials were prepar'd,—
The Fire, Air, Water; all that Orpheus dar'd,
That Plato, that the bright-hair'd Samian* pass'd,
With trembling hope, to come to—*what*, at last?
Go, ask the dupes of Priestcraft! question him
Who, mid terrific sounds and spectres dim,
Walks at Eleusis; ask of those, who brave
The dazzling miracles of Mithra's Cave,
With its seven starry gates; ask all who keep
Those terrible night-mysteries, where they weep
And howl sad dirges to the answering breeze,
O'er their dead Gods, their mortal Deities—
Amphibious, hybrid things, that died as men,
Drown'd, hang'd, empal'd, to rise, as gods, again;—
Ask *them*, what mighty secret lurks below
This seven-fold mystery—can they tell thee? No;
Gravely they keep that only secret, well
And fairly kept—that they have none to tell;
And, dup'd themselves, console their humbled pride
By duping thenceforth all mankind beside.

And such the advance in fraud since Orpheus' time—
That earliest master of our craft sublime—
So many minor Mysteries, imps of fraud,
From the great Orphic Egg have wing'd abroad,
That, still to uphold our Temple's ancient boast,
And seem most holy, we must cheat the most;
Work the best miracles, wrap nonsense round
In pomp and darkness, till it seems profound;
Play on the hopes, the terrors of mankind,
With changeful skill; and make the human mind
Like our own Sanctuary, where no ray,
But by the Priest's permission, wins its ray—
Where through the gloom as wave our wizard-rods,
Monsters, at will, are conjur'd into Gods;
While Reason, like a grave-fac'd mummy, stands,
With her arms swath'd in hieroglyphic bands.
But chiefly in that skill with which we use
Man's wildest passions for Religion's views,
Yoking them to her car like fiery steeds,
Lies the main art in which our craft succeeds.
And oh! be blest, ye men of yore, whose toil
Hath, for her use, scoop'd out from Egypt's soil
This hidden Paradise, this mine of fanes,
Gardens, and palaces, where Pleasure reigns

* Pythagoras.

In a rich, sunless empire of her own,
With all earth's luxuries lighting up her throne;—
A realm for mystery made, which undermines
The Nile itself, and, 'neath the Twelve Great Shrines
That keep Initiation's holy rite,
Spreads its long labyrinths of unearthly light,
A light that knows no change—its brooks that run
Too deep for day, its gardens without sun,
Where soul and sense, by turns, are charm'd, surpris'd
And all that bard or prophet e'er devis'd
For man's Elysium, priests have realis'd

Here, at this moment—all his trials past,
And heart and nerve unshrinking to the last—
Our new Initiate roves—as yet left free
To wander through this realm of mystery;
Feeding on such illusions as prepare
The soul, like mist o'er waterfalls, to wear
All shapes and hues, at Fancy's varying will,
Through every shifting aspect, vapour still;—
Vague glimpses of the Future, vistas shown,
By scenic skill, into that world unknown,
Which saints and sinners claim alike their own;
And all those other witching, wildering arts,
Illusions, terrors, that make human hearts,
Aye, even the wisest and the hardiest, quail
To *any* goblin thron'd behind a veil.

Yes—such the spells shall haunt his eye, his ear,
Mix with his night-dreams, form his atmosphere;
Till, if our Sage be not tam'd down, at length,
His wit, his wisdom, shorn of all their strength,
Like Phrygian priests, in honour of the shrine—
If he become not absolutely mine,
Body and soul, and, like the tame decoy
Which wary hunters of wild doves employ,
Draw converts also, lure his brother wits
To the dark cage where his own spirit flits,
And give us, if not saints, good hypocrites—
If I effect not this, then be it said
The ancient spirit of our craft hath fled,
Gone with that serpent-god the Cross hath chas'd
To hiss its soul out in the Theban waste.
* * * * * * *

A WARNING.—TO ——

Oh fair as heaven and chaste as light!
Did nature mould thee all so bright,
That thou shouldst e'er be brought to weep
O'er languid virtue's fatal sleep,
O'er shame extinguish'd, honour fled,
Peace lost, heart wither'd, feeling dead?

No, no! a star was born with thee,
Which sheds eternal purity.
Thou hast, within those sainted eyes,
So fair a transcript of the skies,
In lines of light such heavenly lore,
That man should read them and adore.
Yet have I known a gentle maid
Whose mind and form were both array'd
In nature's purest light, like thine;—
Who wore that clear, celestial sign,
Which seems to mark the brow that's fair
For destiny's peculiar care:
Whose bosom too, like Dian's own,
Was guarded by a sacred zone,
Where the bright gem of virtue shone,
Whose eyes had, in their light, a charm
Against all wrong, and guile, and harm.
Yet, hapless maid, in one sad hour,
These spells have lost their guardian power,
The gem has been beguil'd away;
Her eyes have lost their chast'ning ray;
The modest pride, the guiltless shame,
The smiles that from reflection came,
All, all have fled, and left her mind
A faded monument behind;
The ruins of a once pure shrine,
No longer fit for guest divine.
Oh! 'twas a sight I wept to see—
Heaven keep the lost one's fate from thee!

THE

PASSION FLOWER.

THE IMPROVISATRICE.

I AM a daughter of that land
Where the poet's lip and the painter's hand
Are most divine,—where the earth and sky,
Are picture both and poetry—
I am of Florence. 'Mid the chill
Of hope and feeling, oh! I still
Am proud to think to where I owe
My birth, though but the dawn of wo!

My childhood passed 'mid radiant things,
Glorious as Hope's imaginings;
Statues but known from shapes of the earth
By being too lovely for mortal birth;
Paintings whose colors of life were caught
From the fairy teints in the rainbow wrought;
Music whose sighs had a spell like those
That float on the sea at the evening's close;
Language so silvery, that every word
Was like the lute's awakening chord;
Skies half sunshine, and half starlight;
Flowers whose lives were a breath of delight;
Leaves whose green pomp knew no withering;
Fountains bright as the skies of our spring;
And songs whose wild and passionate line
Suited a soul of romance like mine.

My power was but a woman's power;
Yet, in that great and glorious dower
Which Genius gives, I had my part:
I poured my full and burning heart
In song, and on the canvass made
My dreams of beauty visible;
I knew not which I loved the most—
Pencil or lute,—both loved so well.

Oh, yet my pulse throbs to recall,
When first upon the gallery's wall
Picture of mine was placed, to share
Wonder and praise from each one there!
Sad were my shades; methinks they had
Almost a tone of prophecy—
I ever had, from earliest youth,
A feeling what my fate would be.

My first was of a gorgeous hall,
Lighted up for festival;
Braided tresses, and cheeks of bloom,
Diamond agraff, and foam-white plume;
Censers of roses, vases of light,
Like what the moon sheds on a summer night.
Youths and maidens with linked hands
Joined in the graceful sarabands,
Smiled on the canvass; but apart
Was one who leant in silent mood,
As revelry to his sick heart
Were worse than veriest solitude.
Pale, dark-eyed, beautiful, and young,
Such as he had shone o'er my slumbers,
When I had only slept to dream
Over again his magic numbers.

Divinest Petrarch! he whose lyre,
Like morning light, half dew, half fire,
To Laura and to love was vowed—
He looked on one, who with the crowd
Mingled, but mixed not; on whose cheek
There was a blush, as if she knew
Whose look was fixed on hers. Her eye,
Of a spring sky's delicious blue,
Had not the language of that bloom,
But mingling tears, and light, and gloom,
Was raised abstractedly to Heaven:—
No sign was to her lover given.
I painted her with golden tresses,
Such as float on the wind's caresses,
When the laburnums wildly fling
Their sunny blossoms to the spring,
A cheek which had the crimson hue
Upon the sun-touched nectarine;
A lip of perfume and of dew;
A brow like twilight's darkened line.
I strove to catch each charm that long
Has lived,—thanks to her lover's song!
Each grace he numbered one by one,
That shone in her of Avignon.

I ever thought that poet's fate
Utterly lone and desolate.
It is the spirit's bitterest pain
To love, to be beloved again;
And yet between a gulf which ever
The hearts that burn to meet must sever.
And he was vowed to one sweet star,
Bright yet to him, but bright afar.

O'er some Love's shadow may but pass
As passes the breathstain o'er glass;
And pleasures, cares, and pride, combined
Fill up the blank Love leaves behind.
But there are some whose love is high,
Entire—and sole idolatry;
Who, turning from a heartless world,
Ask some dear thing which may renew
Affection's several links, and be
As true as they themselves are true.
But love's bright fount is never pure,
And all his pilgrims must endure
All passion's mighty suffering
Ere they may reach the blessed spring.
And some who waste their lives to find
A prize which they may never win:
Like those who search for Irem's groves,
Which found, they may not enter in.
Where is the sorrow but appears
In Love's long catalogue of tears?
And some there are who leave the path
In agony and fierce disdain,
But bear upon each cankered breast
The scar that never heals again.

My next was of a minstrel too,
Who proved that woman's hand might do,
When, true to the heart pulse, it woke
The harp. Her head was bending down,
As if in weariness, and near,
But unworn, was a laurel crown.
She was not beautiful, if bloom
And smiles form beauty; for, like death,
Her brow was ghastly; and her lip
Was parched, as fever were its breath.
There was a shade upon her dark,
Large, floating eyes, as if each spark

Of minstrel ecstasy was fled,
Yet leaving them no tears to shed;
Fixed in their hopelessness of care,
And reckless in their great despair.
She sat beneath a cypress tree,
  A little fountain ran beside,
And, in the distance, one dark rock
  Threw its long shadow o'er the tide;
And to the west, where the nightfall
Was darkening day's gemmed coronal,
Its white shafts crimsoning in the sky,
Arose the sun-god's sanctuary.
I deemed, that of lyre, life, and love
  She was a long, last farewell taking;—
That from her pale and parched lips,
  Her latest, wildest song was breaking.

SAPPHO'S SONG.

FAREWELL, my lute!—and would that I
  Had never waked thy burning chords!
Poison has been upon thy sigh,
  And fever has breathed in thy words.

Yet wherefore, wherefore should I blame
  Thy power, thy spell, my gentlest lute?
I should have been the wretch I am,
  Had every chord of thine been mute.

It was my evil star above,
  Not my sweet lute, that wrought me wrong;
It was not song that taught me love,
  But it was love that taught me song.

If song be past, and hope undone,
  And pulse, and head, and heart, are flame;
It is thy work, thou faithless one!
  But, no!—I will not name thy name!

Sun-god! lute, wreath, are vowed to thee!
  Long be their light upon my grave—
My glorious grave—yon deep blue sea:
  I shall sleep calm—beneath its wave!

FLORENCE! with what idolatry
  I've lingered in thy radiant halls,
Worshipping, till my dizzy eye
  Grew dim with gazing on those walls,
Where Time had spared each glorious gift
By Genius unto Memory left!
And when seen by the pale moonlight,
More pure, more perfect, though less bright,
What dreams of song flashed on my brain,
Till each shade seemed to live again;
And then the beautiful, the grand,
The glorious of my native land,
In every flower that threw its veil
Aside, when wooed by the spring gale;
In every vineyard, where the sun,
His task of summer ripening done,
Shone on their clusters, and a song
Came lightly from the peasant throng;
In the dim loveliness of night,
In fountains with their diamond light,
In aged temple, ruined shrine,
And its green wreath of ivy twine;
In every change of earth and sky,
Breathed the deep soul of poesy.

  As yet I loved not; but each wild
High thought I nourished raised a pyre
For love to light; and lighted once
By love, it would be like the fire
The burning lava floods that dwell
In Etna's cave unquenchable.

One evening in the lovely June,
  Over the Arno's waters gliding,
I had been watching the fair moon
  Amid her court of white clouds riding:
I had been listening to the gale,
  Which wafted music from around,
(For scarce a lover, at that hour,
  But waked his mandolin's light sound).
And odor was upon the breeze,
Sweet thefts from rose and lemon trees.
They stole me from my lulling dream,
  And said they knew that such an hour
Had ever influence on my soul,
  And raised my sweetest minstrel power.
I took my lute,—my eye had been
Wandering round the lovely scene,
Filled with those melancholy tears,
Which come when all most bright appears,
And hold their strange and secret power,
Even on pleasure's golden hour.
I had been looking on the river,
Half-marvelling to think that ever
Wind, wave, or sky, could darken where
All seemed so gentle and so fair;
And mingled with these thoughts there came
  A tale, just one that memory keeps—
Forgotten music, till some chance
  Vibrate the chord whereon it sleeps!

A MOORISH ROMANCE.

SOFTLY through the pomegranate groves
Came the gentle song of the doves;
Shone the fruit in the evening light,
Like Indian rubies, blood-red and bright;
Shook the date-trees each tufted head,
As the passing wind their green nuts shed;
And, like dark columns, amid the sky
The giant palms ascended on high:
And the mosque's gilded minaret
Glistened and glanced as the daylight set.
Over the town a crimson haze
Gathered and hung of the evening's rays;
And far beyond, like molten gold,
The burning sands of the desert rolled.
Far to the left, the sky and sea
Mingled their gray immensity;
And with flapping sail and idle prow
The vessels threw their shades below
Far down the beach, where a cypress grove
Cast its shade round a little cove,
Darkling and green, with just a space
For the stars to shine on the water's face,
A small bark lay, waiting for night
And its breeze to waft and hide its flight.
Sweet is the burden, and lovely the freight,
For which those furled-up sails await
To a garden, fair as those
Where the glory of the rose
Blushes, charmed from the decay
That wastes other blooms away;
Gardens of the fairy tale
Told, till the wood fire grows pale,
By the Arab tribes, when night
With its dim and lovely light,
And its silence, suiteth well
With the magic tales they tell.
Through that cypress avenue,
Such a garden meets the view,
Filled with flowers—flowers that seem
Lighted up by the sunbeam;
Fruits of gold and gems, and leaves
Green as hope before its grieves
O'er the false and brokenhearted,
All with which its youth has parted,
Never to return again,
Save in memories of pain!

  There is a white rose in yon bower,
But holds it yet a fairer flower:
And music from that cage is breathing,
Round which a jasmine braid is wreathing,
A low song from a lonely dove,
A song such exiles sing and love,
Breathing of fresh fields, summer skies,—
Not to be breathed of but in sighs!
But fairer smile and sweeter sigh
Are near when LEILA'S step is nigh!
With eyes dark as the midnight time,
Yet lighted like a summer clime

With sun-rays from within; yet now
Lingers a cloud upon that brow,—
Though never lovelier brow was give
To Houri of an Eastern heaven!
Her eye is dwelling on that bower,
As every leaf and every flower
Were being numbered in her heart;
There are no looks like those which dwell
On long-remembered things, which soon
Must take our first and last farewell.

Day fades apace: another day,
That maiden will be far away,
A wanderer o'er the dark-blue sea,
And bound for lovely Italy,
Her mother's land! Hence, on her breast
The cross beneath a Moorish vest;
And hence those sweetest sounds, that seem
Like music murmuring in a dream,
When in our sleeping ear is ringing
The song the nightingale is singing;
When by that white and funeral stone,
Half hidden by the cypress gloom,
The hymn the mother taught her child
Is sung each evening at her tomb.
But quick the twilight time has past
Like one of those sweet calms that last
A moment and no more to cheer,
The turmoil of our pathway here.
The bark is waiting in the bay,
Night darkens round:—LEILA, away!
Far, ere to-morrow, o'er the tide,
Or wait and be—ABDALLA's bride?

She touched her lute—never again
Her ear will listen to its strain!
She took her cage, first kissed the breast—
Then freed the white dove prisoned there:
It paused one moment on her hand,
Then spread its glad wings to the air.
She drank the breath, as it were health,
That sighed from every scented blossom;
And taking from each one a leaf,
Hid them, like spells, upon her bosom.
Then sought the sacred path again
She once before had traced, when lay
A Christian in her father's chain;
And gave him gold, and taught the way
To fly. She thought upon the night,
When, like an angel of the light,
She stood before the prisoner's sight,
And led him to the cypress grove,
And showed the bark and hidden cove;
And bade the wandering captive flee,
In words he knew from infancy!
And when she thought how for her love
He had braved slavery and death,
That he might only breathe the air
Made sweet and sacred by her breath.
She reached the grove of cypresses—
Another step is by her side:
Another moment, and the bark
Bears the fair Moor across the tide!

'Twas beautiful, by the pale moonlight,
To mark her eyes—now dark, now bright,
As now they met, now shrank away,
From the gaze that watched and worshipped their day.
They stood on the deck, and the midnight gale
Just waved the maiden's silver veil—
Just lifted a curl, as if to show
The cheek of rose that was burning below:
And never spread a sky of blue
More clear for the stars to wander through!
And never could their mirror be
A calmer or a lovelier sea!
For every wave was a diamond gleam:
And that light vessel well may seem
A fairy ship, and that graceful pair
Young Genii, whose home was of light and air!

Another evening came, but dark;
The storm clouds hovered round the bark
Of misery:—they just could see
The distant shore of Italy,
As the dim moon through vapors shone—
A few short rays, her light was gone.
O'er head a sullen scream was heard,
As sought the land the white sea bird,
Her pale wings like a meteor streaming
Upon the waves a light is gleaming—
Ill-omened brightness, sent by Death
To light the night-black depths beneath.
The vessel rolled amid the surge;
The winds howled round it, like a dirge
Sung by some savage race. Then came
The rush of thunder and of flame:
It showed two forms upon the deck,—
One clasped around the other's neck,
As there she could not dream of fear—
In her lover's arms could danger be near?
He stood and watched her with the eye
Of fixed and silent agony.
The waves swept on: he felt her heart
Beat close and closer yet to his!
They burst upon the ship!—the sea
Has closed upon their dream of bliss!

Surely theirs is a pleasant sleep
Beneath that ancient cedar tree,
Whose solitary stem has stood
For years alone beside the sea!
The last of a most noble race,
That once had there their dwelling-place,
Long past away! Beneath its shade,
A soft green couch the turf has made:
And glad the morning sun is shining
On those beneath the boughs reclining.
Nearer the fisher drew. He saw
The dark hair of the Moorish maid,
Like a veil, floating o'er the breast
Where tenderly her head was laid;
And yet her lover's arm was placed
Clasping around the graceful waist;
But then he marked the youth's black curls
Were dripping wet with foam and blood;
And that the maiden's tresses dark
Were heavy with the briny flood!
Wo for the wind!—wo for the wave!
They sleep the slumber of the grave!
They buried them beneath that tree;
It long had been a sacred spot.
Soon it was planted round with flowers
By many who had not forgot;
Or yet lived in those dreams of truth
The Eden birds of early youth,
That make the loveliness of love:
And called the place "THE MAIDEN'S COVE.
That she who perished in the sea
Might thus be kept in memory.

FROM many a lip came sounds of praise
Like music from sweet voices ringing;
For many a boat had gathered round,
To list the song I had been singing.
There are some moments in our fate
That stamp the color of our days;
As, till then, life had not been felt,—
And mine was sealed in the slight gaze
Which fixed my eye, and fired my brain,
And bowed my heart beneath the chain.
'Twas a dark and flashing eye,
Shadows, too, that tenderly,
With almost female softness, came
O'er its mingled gloom and flame,
His cheek was pale; or toil, or care,
Or midnight study, had been there,
Making its young colors dull,
Yet leaving it most beautiful.
Raven curls their shadow threw,
Like the twilight's darkening hue,
O'er the pure and mountain snow
Of his high and haughty brow:
Lighted by a smile, whose spell
Words are powerless to tell.

Such a lip!—oh, poured from thence
Lava floods of eloquence
Would come with fiery energy,
Like those words that can not die.
Words the Grecian warrior spoke
When the Persian's chain he broke,
Or that low and honey tone,
Making woman's heart his own;
Such as should be heard at night,
In the dim and sweet starlight;
Sounds that haunts a beauty's sleep,
Treasures for her heart to keep.
Like the pine of summer tall;
Apollo, on his pedestal
In our own gallery, never bent
More graceful, more magnificent;
Ne'er looked the hero, or the king,
  More nobly than the youth who now,
As if soul-centred in my song,
  Was leaning on a galley's prow.
He spoke not when the others spoke,
  His heart was all too full for praise;
But his dark eyes kept fixed on mine,
  Which sank beneath their burning gaze.
Mine sank—but yet I felt the thrill
Of that look burning on me still.
I heard no word that others said—
  Heard nothing, save one low-breathed sigh.
My hand kept wandering on my lute,
  In music, but unconsciously
My pulses throbbed, my heart beat high,
A flush of dizzy ecstasy
  Crimsoned my cheek; I felt warm tears
Dimming my sight, yet was it sweet,
My wild heart's most bewildering beat,
  Consciousness, without hopes or fears,
Of a new power within me waking,
Like light before the morn's full breaking.
I left the boat—the crowd: my mood
Made my soul pant for solitude.

Amid my palace halls was one,
The most peculiarly my own:
The roof was blue and fretted gold,
The floor was of the Parian stone,
Shining like snow, as only meet
For the light tread of fairy feet;
And in the midst, beneath a shade
Of clustered rose, a fountain played,
Sprinkling its scented waters round,
With a sweet and lulling sound,—
O'er oranges, like Eastern gold,
Half hidden by the dark green fold
Of their large leaves;—o'er hyacinth bells,
Where every summer odor dwells,
And, nestled in the midst, a pair
Of white wood doves, whose home was there;
And like an echo to their song,
At times a murmur passed along;
A dying tone, a plaining fall,
So sad, so wild, so musical—
As the wind swept across the wire,
And waked my lone Æolian lyre,
Which lay upon the casement, where
The lattice wooed the cold night air,
Half hidden by a bridal twine
Of jasmine with the emerald vine.
And ever as the curtains made
A varying light, a changeful shade,
As the breeze waved them to and fro,
Came on the eye the glorious show
Of pictured walls where landscape wild
Of wood, and stream, or mountain piled,
Or sunny vale, or twilight grove,
Or shapes whose every look was love;
Saints, whose diviner glance seemed caught
From Heaven,—some whose earthlier thought
Was yet more lovely,—shone like gleams
Of Beauty's spirit seen in dreams.
I threw me on a couch to rest,
  Loosely I flung my long black hair;
It seemed to soothe my troubled breast
  To drink the quiet evening air.
I looked upon the deep-blue sky,
And it was all hope and harmony.
Afar I could see the Arno's stream
Glorying in the clear moonbeam;
And the shadowy city met my gaze,
Like the dim memory of other days;
And the distant wood's black coronal
Was like oblivion that covereth all.
I know not why my soul felt sad;
  I touched my lute, it would not waken,
Save to old songs of sorrowing—
  Of hope betrayed—of hearts forsaken—
Each lay of lighter feeling slept,
I sang, but, as I sang, I wept.

THE CHARMED CUP.

And fondly round his neck she clung;
Her long black tresses round him flung,—
Love chains, which would not let him part·
And he could feel her beating heart,
The pulses of her small white hand,
The tears she could no more command,
The lip which trembled, though near his,
The sigh that mingled with her kiss;—
Yet parted he from that embrace.
He cast one glance upon her face:
His very soul felt sick to see
Its look of utter misery;
Yet turned he not; one moment's grief,
One pang, like lightning, fierce and brief,
One thought, half pity, half remorse,
Passed o'er him. On he urged his horse;
Hill, ford, and valley spurred he by,
And when his castle-gate was nigh,
White foam was on his 'broidered rein,
And each spur had a blood-red stain.
But soon he entered that fair hall:
His laugh was loudest there of all;
And the cup that wont one name to bless,
Was drained for his forgetfulness.
The ring, once next his heart, was broken;
The gold chain kept another token.
Where is the curl he used to wear—
The raven tress of silken hair?
The winds have scattered it. A braid
Of the first spring day's golden shade,
Waves with the dark plumes on his crest.
Fresh colors are upon his breast:
The slight blue scarf, of simplest fold,
Is changed for one of woven gold.
And he is by a maiden's side,
Whose gems of price, and robes of pride,
Would suit the daughter of a king;
And diamonds are glistening
Upon her arm. There's not one curl
Unfastened by a loop of pearl.
And he is whispering in her ear
Soft words that ladies love to hear.

Alas!—the tale is quickly told—
His love hath felt the curse of gold!
And he is bartering his heart
For that in which it hath no part.
There's many an ill that clings to love;
But this is one all else above;—
For love to bow before the name
Of this world's treasure: shame! oh, shame!
Love, be thy wings as light as those
That waft the zephyr from the rose,—
This may be pardoned—something rare
In loveliness has been thy snare!
But how, fair love, canst thou become
A thing of mines—a sordid gnome?

  And she whom Julian left—she stood
A cold white statue; as the blood
Had, when in vain her last wild prayer,
Flown to her heart, and frozen there.
Upon her temple, each dark vein
Swelled in its agony of pain.
Chill, heavy damps were on her brow;
Her arms were stretched at length, though now

Their clasp was on the empty air:
A funeral pall—her long black hair;
Fell over her: herself the tomb
Of her own youth, and breath, and bloom.

Alas! that man should ever win
So sweet a shrine to shame and sin
As woman's heart!—and deeper wo
For her fond weakness, not to know
That yielding all but breaks the chain
That never reunites again!

It was a dark and tempest night—
No pleasant moon, no blest starlight;
But meteors glancing o'er the way,
Only to dazzle and betray.
And who is she that, 'mid the storm,
Wraps her slight mantle round her form?
Her hair is wet with rain and sleet,
And blood is on her small snow feet.
She has been forced a way to make
Through prickly weed and thorned brake,
Up rousing from its coil the snake;
And stirring from their damp abode
The slimy worm and loathsome toad:
And shuddered as she heard the gale
Shriek like an evil spirit's wail;
When followed, like a curse, the crash
Of the pines in the lightning flash:—
A place of evil and of fear—
Oh! what can JULIAN's love do here?

On, on the pale girl went. At last
The gloomy forest depths are past,
And she has reached the wizard's den,
Accursed by God and shunned by men.
And never had a ban been laid
Upon a more unwholesome shade.
There grew dank elders, and the yew
Its thick sepulchral shadow threw;
And brooded there each bird most foul,
The gloomy bat and sullen owl.
But IDA entered in the cell,
Where dwelt the wizard of the dell.
Her heart lay dead, her life-blood froze
To look upon the shape which rose
To bar her entrance. On that face
Was scarcely left a single trace
Of human likeness: the parched skin
Showed each discolored bone within;
And, but for the most evil stare
Of the wild eyes' unearthly glare,
It was a corpse, you would have said,
From which life's freshness long had fled.
Yet IDA knelt her down and prayed
To that dark sorcerer for his aid.
He heard her prayer with withering look;
Then from unholy herbs he took
A drug, and said it would recover
The lost heart of her faithless lover.
She trembled as she turned to see
His demon sneer's malignity;
And every step was winged with dread,
To hear the curse howled as she fled.

It is the purple twilight hour,
And JULIAN is in IDA's bower.
He has brought gold, as gold could bless
His work of utter desolateness!
He has brought gems, as if Despair
Had any pride in being fair!
But IDA only wept, and wreathed
Her white arms round his neck; then breathed
Those passionate complaints that ring
A woman's heart, yet never bring
Redress. She called upon each tree
To witness her lone constancy!
She called upon the silent boughs,
The temple of her JULIAN's vows
Of happiness too dearly bought!
Then wept again. At length she thought
Upon the forest sorcerer's gift—
The last, lone hope that love had left!

She took the cup, and kissed the brim,
Mixed the dark spell, and gave it him
To pledge his once dear IDA's name!
He drank it. Instantly the flame
Ran through his veins; one fiery throb
Of bitter pain—one gasping sob
Of agony—the cold death-sweat
Is on his face—his teeth are set—
His bursting eyes are glazed and still;
The drug has done its work of ill.
Alas! for her who watched each breath,
The cup her love had mixed bore—death.

LORENZO!—when next morning came
For the first time I heard thy name!
LORENZO!—how each ear-pulse drank
The more than music of that tone!
LORENZO!—how I sighed that name,
As breathing it, made it mine own!
I sought the gallery: I was wont
To pass the noontide there, and trace
Some statue's shape of loveliness—
Some saint, some nymph, or muse's face.
There, in my rapture, I could throw
My pencil in its hues aside,
And, as the vision passed me, pour
My song of passion, joy, and pride.
And he was there,—LORENZO there!
How soon the morning passed away,
With finding beauties in each thing
Neither had seen before that day!
Spirit of Love! soon thy rose-plumes wear
The weight and the sully of canker and care;
Falsehood is round thee; Hope leads thee on,
Till every hue from thy pinion is gone.
But the bright moment is all thine own,
The one ere thy visible presence is known;
When, like the wind of the south, thy power,
Sunning the heavens, sweetening the flower,
Is felt but not seen. Thou art sweet and calm
As the sleep of a child, as the dew full of balm.
Fear has not darkened thee; Hope has not made
The blossoms expand, it but opens to fade.
Nothing is known of those wearing fears
Which will shadow the light of thy after years.
Then art thou bliss:—but once throw by
The veil which shrouds thy divinity;
Stand confessed,—and thy quiet is fled!
Wild flashes of rapture may come instead,
But pain will be with them. What may restore
The gentle happiness known before?
I owned not to myself I loved,—
No word of love LORENZO breathed;
But I lived in a magic ring,
Of every pleasant flower wreathed.
A brighter blue was on the sky,
A sweeter breath in music's sigh;
The orange shrubs all seemed to bear
Fruit more rich, and buds more fair.
There was a glory on the noon,
A beauty in the crescent moon,
A lulling stillness in the night,
A feeling in the pale starlight.
There was a charmed note on the wind,
A spell in Poetry's deep store—
Heart-uttered words, passionate thoughts,
Which I had never marked before.
'Twas as my heart's full happiness
Poured over all its own excess.

One night there was a gorgeous feast
For maskers in COUNT LEON's hall;
And all of gallant, fair, and young,
Were bidden to the festival.
I went, garbed as a Hindoo girl;
Upon each arm an amulet,
And by my side a little lute
Of sandal wood with gold beset.
And shall I own that I was proud
To hear, amid the gazing crowd,
A murmur of delight, when first
My mask and veil I threw aside?

For well my conscious cheek betrayed
Whose eye was gazing on me too!
And never yet had praise been dear,
As on that evening, to mine ear,
LORENZO! I was proud to be
Worshipped and flattered but for thee!

THE HINDOO GIRL'S SONG.

PLAYFUL and wild as the fire-flies light,
This moment hidden, and next moment bright,
Like the foam on the dark-green sea,
Is the spell that is laid on my lover by me.
Were your sigh as sweet as the sumbal's sigh
When the wind of the evening is nigh;
Were your smile like that glorious light,
Seen when the stars gem the deep midnight;
Were that sigh and that smile for ever the same—
They were shadows, not fuel, to love's dulled flame

Love once formed an amulet,
With pearls, and a rainbow, and rose-leaves set.
The pearls were pure as pearls could be,
And white as maiden purity;
The rose had the beauty and breath of soul,
And the rainbow-changes crowned the whole.
Frown on your lover one little while,
Dearer will be the light of your smile;
Let your blush, laugh, and sigh ever mingle together,
Like the bloom, sun, and clouds of the sweet spring weather.
Love never must sleep in security,
Or most calm and cold will his waking be.

And as that light strain died away,
Again I swept the breathing strings:
But now the notes I waked were sad
As those the pining wood-dove sings.

THE INDIAN BRIDE.

SHE has lighted her lamp, and crowned it with flowers,
The sweetest that breathed of the summer hours;
Red and white roses linked in a band,
Like a maiden's blush, or a maiden's hand;
Jasmines—some like silvery spray,
Some like gold in the morning ray;
Fragrant stars,—and favorites they,
When Indian girls on a festival day,
Braid their dark tresses: and over all weaves
The rosy-bower of lotus leaves—
Canopy suiting the lamp-lighted bark,
Love's own flowers, and Love's own ark.

She watched the sky, the sunset grew dim;
She raised to CAMDEO her evening hymn.
The scent of the night-flowers came on the air;
And then, like a bird escaped from the snare,
She flew to the river—(no moon was bright,
But the stars and the fire-flies gave her their light);
She stood beneath the mangoes' shade,
Half delighted and half afraid;
She trimmed the lamp, and breathed on each bloom,
(Oh, that breath was sweeter than all their perfume!)
Threw spices and oil on the spire of flame,
Called thrice on her absent lover's name;
And every pulse throbbed as she gave
Her little boat to the Ganges wave.

There are a thousand fanciful things
Linked round the young heart's imaginings.
In its first love-dream, a leaf, or a flower
Is gifted then with a spell and a power;
A shade is an omen, a dream is a sign,
From which the maiden can well divine
Passion's whole history. Those only can
Who have loved as young hearts can love so well,
How the pulses will beat, and the cheek will be died,
When they have some love-augury tried
Oh, it is not for those whose feelings are cold,
Withered by care, or blunted by gold;
Whose brows have darkened with many years,
To feel again youth's hopes and fears—
What they might blush now to confess,
Yet what made their spring-day's happiness!

ZAIDE watched her flower-built vessel glide,
Mirrored beneath on the deep-blue tide;
Lovely and lonely, scented and bright,
Like Hope's own bark, all bloom and light.
There's not one breath of wind on the air,
The heavens are cloudless, the waters are fair,
No dew is falling: yet wo to that shade!
The maiden is weeping—her lamp has decayed.

Hark to the ring of the cimeter!
It tells that the soldier returns from afar.
Down from the mountains the warriors come:
Hark to the thunder-roll of the drum!—
To the startling voice of the trumpet's call!—
To the cymbal's clash!—to the atabal!
The banners of crimson float in the sun,
The warfare is ended, the battle is won.
The mother hath taken the child from her breast,
And raised it to look on its father's crest.
The pathway is lined, as the bands pass along,
With maidens, who meet them with flowers and song.
And ZAIDE hath forgotten in AZIM's arms
All her so false lamp's falser alarms.

This looks not a bridal,—the singers are mute,
Still is the mandore, and breathless the lute;
Yet there the bride sits. Her dark hair is bound,
And the robe of her marriage floats white on the ground.
Oh! where is the lover, the bridegroom?—oh! where?
Look under yon black pall—the bridegroom is there!
Yet the guests are all bidden, the feast is the same,
And the bride plights her troth amid smoke and 'mid flame!
They have raised the death-pyre of sweet-scented wood,
And sprinkled it o'er with the sacred flood
Of the Ganges. The priests are assembled:—their song
Sinks deep on the ear as they bear her along,
That bride of the dead. Ay, is not this love?—
That one pure, wild feeling all others above:
Vowed to the living, and kept to the tomb!—
The same in its blight as it was in its bloom.
With no tear in her eye, and no change in her smile
Young ZAIDE had come nigh to the funeral pile.
The bells of the dancing-girls ceased from their sound;
Silent they stood by that holiest mound.
From a crowd like the sea-waves there came not a breath
When the maiden stood by the place of death!
One moment was given—the last she might spare!
To the mother, who stood in her weeping there.
She took the jewels that shone on her hand;
She took from her dark hair its flowery band,
And scattered them round. At once they raise
The hymn of rejoicing and love in her praise.
A prayer is muttered, a blessing said,—
Her torch is raised!—she is by the dead.
She has fired the pile! At once there came
A mingled rush of smoke and of flame:
The wind swept it off. They saw the bride,
Laid by her AZIM, side by side.
The breeze had spread the long curls of her hair:
Like a banner of fire they played on the air.
The smoke and the flame gathered round as before,
Then cleared; but the bride was seen no more.

I heard the words of praise, but not
The one voice that I paused to hear;
And other sounds to me were like
A tale poured in a sleeper's ear.
Where was LORENZO?—He had stood
Spell-bound; but when I closed the lay,
As if the charm ceased with the song,
He darted hurriedly away.
I masqued again, and wandered on
Through many a gay and gorgeous room
What with sweet waters, sweeter flowers,
The air was heavy with perfume,
The harp was echoing the lute,
Soft voices answered to the flute,
And, like rills in the noontide clear,
Beneath the flame-hung gondolier,

Shone mirrors peopled with the shades
Of stately youths and radiant maids;
And on the ear in whispers came
Those winged words of soul and flame,
Breathed in the dark-eyed beauty's ear
By some young love-touched cavalier;
Or mixed at times some sound more gay,
Of dance, or laugh, or roundelay.
O, it is sickness at the heart
To bear in revelry its part,
And yet feel bursting:—not one thing
Which has part in its suffering,—
The laugh as glad, the step as light,
The song as sweet, the glance as bright;
As the laugh, step, and glance, and song,
Did to young happiness belong.

I turned me from the crowd, and reached
A spot which seemed unsought by all—
An alcove filled with shrubs and flowers,
But lighted by the distant hall,
With one or two fair statues placed,
Like deities of the sweet shrine.
That human art should ever frame
Such shapes so utterly divine!
A deep sigh breathed,—I knew the tone;
My cheek blushed warm, my heart beat high,
One moment more I too was known,
I shrank before LORENZO's eye.
He leant beside a pedestal,
The glorious brow, of Parian stone,
Of the Antinous, by his side,
Was not more noble than his own!
They were alike: he had the same
Thick-clustering curls the Roman wore—
The fixed and melancholy eye—
The smile which passed like lightning o'er
The curved lip. We did not speak,
But the heart breathed upon each cheek,
We looked round with those wondering looks,
Which seek some object for their gaze,
As if each other's glance was like
The too much light of morning's rays.
I saw a youth beside me kneel;
I heard my name in music steal;
I felt my hand trembling in his;—
Another moment, and his kiss
Had burnt upon it; when, like thought,
So swift it passed, my hand was thrown
Away, as if in sudden pain.
LORENZO like a dream had flown!
We did not meet again:—he seemed
To shun each spot where I might be:
And, it was said, another claimed
The heart—more than the world to me!

I loved him as young Genius loves,
When its own wild and radiant heaven
Of starry thought burns with the light,
The love, the life, by passion given.
I loved him, too, as woman loves—
Reckless of sorrow, sin, or scorn:
Life had no evil destiny
That, with him, I could not have borne!
I had been nursed in palaces;
Yet earth had not a spot so drear,
That I should not have thought a home,
In paradise, had he been near!
How sweet it would have been to dwell,
Apart from all, in some green dell
Of sunny beauty, leaves, and flowers;
And nestling birds to sing the hours!
Our home, beneath some chestnut's shade,
But of the woven branches made;
Our vesper hymn, the low, lone wail
The rose hears from the nightingale;
And waked at morning by the call
Of music from a waterfall.
But not alone in dreams like this,
Breathed in the very hope of bliss,
I loved: my love had been the same
In hushed despair, in open shame.

I would have rather been a slave,
In tears, in bondage, by his side,
Than shared in all, if wanting him,
This world had power to give beside!
My heart was withered,—and my heart
Had ever been the world to me:
And love had been the first fond dream,
Whose life was in reality.
I had sprung from my solitude
Like a young bird upon the wing
To meet the arrow; so I met
My poisoned shaft of suffering.
And as that bird with drooping crest
And broken wing, will seek his nest,
But seek in vain; so vain I sought
My pleasant home of song and thought.
There was one spell upon my brain,
Upon my pencil, on my strain;
But one face to my colors came;
My chords replied but to one name—
LORENZO!—all seemed vowed to thee,
To passion, and to misery!
I had no interest in the things
That once had been like life, or light;
No tale was pleasant to mine ear,
No song so sweet, no picture bright.
I was wild with my great distress.
My lone, my utter hopelessness!
I would sit hours by the side
Of some clear rill, and mark it glide,
Bearing my tears along, till night
Came with dark hours; and soft starlight
Watch o'er its shadowy beauty keeping,
Till I grew calm:—then I would take
The lute, which had all day been sleeping
Upon a cypress tree, and wake
The echoes of the midnight air
With words that love wrung from despair.

SONG.

FAREWELL!—we shall not meet again
As we are parting now!
I must my beating heart restrain—
Must veil my burning brow!
O, I must coldly learn to hide
One thought all else above—
Must call upon my woman's pride
To hide my woman's love!
Check dreams I never may avow;
Be free, be careless, cold as thou!
O! those are tears of bitterness,
Wrung from the breaking heart,
When two, blest in their tenderness,
Must learn to live—apart!
But what are they to that long sigh,
That cold and fixed despair,
That weight of wasting agony
It must be mine to bear?
Methinks I should not thus repine,
If I had but one vow of thine.
I could forgive inconstancy
To be one moment loved by thee!
With me the hope of life is gone
The sun of joy is set;
One wish my soul still dwells upon—
The wish it could forget.
I would forget that look, that tone,
My heart hath all too dearly known.
But who could ever yet efface
From memory love's enduring trace?
All may revolt, all may complain—
But who is there may break the chain?
Farewell!—I shall not be to thee
More than a passing thought;
But every time and place will be
With thy remembrance fraught!
Farewell! we have not often met—
We may not meet again?
But on my heart the seal is set,
Love never sets in vain!
Fruitless as constancy may be,
No chance, no change, may turn from thee

One who has loved thee wildly, well—
But whose first love-vow breathed—farewell?

And lays which only told of love
In all its varied sorrowing,
The echoes of the broken heart,
Were all the songs I now could sing.
Legends of olden times in Greece,
When not a flower but had its tale;
When spirits haunted each green oak;
When voices spoke in every gale;
When not a star shone in the sky
Without its own love history.
Amid its many songs was one
That suited well with my sick mind.
I sang it when the breath of flowers
Came sweet upon the midnight wind.

LEADES AND CYDIPPE.

She sat her in her twilight bower,
A temple formed of leaf and flower;
Rose and myrtle framed the roof,
To a shower of April proof;
And primroses, pale gems of spring,
Lay on the green turf glistening,
Close by the violet, whose breath
Is so sweet in a dewy wreath.
And O, that myrtle! how green it grew!
With flowers as white as the pearls of dew
That shone beside: and the glorious rose
Lay like a beauty in warm repose,
Blushing in slumber. The air was bright
With the spirit and glow of its crimson light.

Cydippe had turned from her columned hall,
Where the queen of the feast, she was worshipped by all:
Where the vases were burning with spices and flowers,
And the odorous waters were playing in showers;
And lamps were blazing—those lamps of perfume
Which shed such a charm of light over the bloom
Of woman, when Pleasure a spell has thrown
Over one night hour and made it her own.
And the ruby wine-cup shone with a ray,
As the gems of the East had there melted away;
And the bards were singing those songs of fire,
That bright eyes and the goblet so well inspire;
While she, the glory and pride of the hour,
Sat silent and sad in her secret bower!

There is a grief that wastes the heart,
Like mildew on a tulip's dies,—
When hope, deferred but to depart,
Loses its smiles, but keeps its sighs:
When love's bark, with its anchor gone,
Clings to a straw, and still trusts on.
O, more than all!—methinks that love
Should pray that it might ever be
Beside the burning shrine which had
Its young heart's fond idolatry.
O, absence is the night of love!
Lovers are very children then!
Fancying ten thousand feverish shapes,
Until their light returns again.
A look, a word, is then recalled,
And thought upon until it wears
What is, perhaps, a very shade,
The tone and aspect of our fears.
And this is what was withering now
The radiance of Cydippe's brow.
She watched until her cheek grew pale;
The green wave bore no bounding sail:
Her sight grew dim; 'mid the blue air
No snowy dove came floating there,
The dear scroll hid beneath his wing,
With plume and soft eye glistening,
To seek again, in leafy dome,
The nest of its accustomed home!
Still far away, o'er land and seas,
Lingered the faithless Leades.

She thought on the spring days when she had been
Lonely and lovely, a maiden queen
When passion to her was a storm at sea,
Heard 'mid the green land's tranquillity.
But a stately warrior came from afar;
He bore on his bosom the glorious scar
So worshipped by woman—the death-seal of wa
And the maiden's heart was an easy prize,
When valor and faith were her sacrifice.

Methinks, might that sweet season last,
In which our first love-dream is past,
Ere doubts and cares, and jealous pain,
Are flaws in the heart's diamond-chain
Men might forget to think on heaven,
And yet have the sweet sin forgiven.

But ere the marriage-feast was spread,
Leades said that he must brook
To part awhile from that best light,
Those eyes which fixed his every look
Just press again his native shore,
And then he would that shore resign
For her dear sake, who was to him
His household god!—his spirit's shrine!

He came not! Then the heart's decay
Wasted her silently away:—
A sweet fount, which the mid-day sun
Has all too hotly looked upon!

It is most sad to watch the fall
Of autumn leaves!—but worst of all
It is to watch the flower of spring
Faded in its fresh blossoming!
To see the once so clear blue orb
Its summer light and warmth forget;
Darkening beneath its tearful lid,
Like a rain-beaten violet!
To watch the banner-rose of health
Pass from the cheek!—to mark how plain
Upon the wan and sunken brow,
Become the wanderings of each vein!
The shadowy hand so thin, so pale!
The languid step!—the drooping head!
The long wreaths of neglected hair!
The lip whence red and smile are fled!
And having watched thus, day by day,
Light, life, and color, pass away!
To see, at length, the glassy eye
Fix dull in dread mortality;
Mark the last ray, catch the last breath,
Till the grave sets its sign of death!

This was Cydippe's fate!—They laid
The maiden underneath the shade
Of a green cypress,—and that hour
The tree was withered, and stood bare!
The spring brought leaves to other trees,
But never other leaf grew there!
It stood, 'mid others flourishing,
A blighted, solitary thing.

The summer sun shone on that tree
When shot a vessel o'er the sea—
When sprang a warrior from the prow—
Leades! by the stately brow.
Forgotten toil, forgotten care,
All his warm heart has had to bear.
That heart is full! He hears the sigh
That breathed "Farewell!" so tenderly.
If even then it was most sweet,
What will it be that now they meet?
Alas! alas! Hope's fair deceit!
He spurred o'er land, has cut the wave,
To look but on Cydippe's grave.

It has blossomed in beauty, that lone tree,
Leades' kiss restored its bloom;
For wild he kissed the withered stem—
It grew upon Cydippe's tomb!
And there he dwelt. The hottest ray,
Still dew upon the branches lay
Like constant tears. The winter came;
But still the green tree stood the same.
And it was said at evening's close,
A sound of whispered music rose;

That 'twas the trace of viewless feet
Made the flowers more than flowers sweet.
At length LEADES died. That day,
Bark and green foliage past away
From the lone tree,—again a thing
Of wonder and of perishing!

ONE evening I had roamed beside
The winding of the Arno's tidé;
The sky was flooded with moonlight:
Below the waters azure bright,
Palazzos with their marble halls,
Green gardens, silver waterfalls,
And orange groves and citron shades,
And cavaliers and dark-eyed maids;
Sweet voices singing, echoes sent
From many a rich-toned instrument.
I could not bear this loveliness!
It was on such a night as this
That love had lighted up my dream
Of long despair and short-lived bliss.
I sought the city; wandering on,
Unconscious where my steps might be:
My heart was deep in other thoughts;
All places were alike to me:—
At length I stopped beneath the walls
Of San Mark's old cathedral halls.
I entered;—and, beneath the roof,
Ten thousand wax-lights burnt on high,
And incense on the censers fumed
As for some great solemnity.
The white-robed choristers were singing,
Their cheerful peals the bells were ringing:
Then deep-voiced music floated round,
As the far arches sent forth sound—
The stately organ:—and fair bands
Of young girls strewed, with lavish hands,
Violets o'er the mosaic floor;
And sang while scattering the sweet store.

I turned me to a distant aisle
Where but a feeble glimmering came
(Itself in darkness) of the smile
Sent from the tapers' perfumed flame
And colored as each pictured pane
Shed o'er the blaze its crimson stain:—
While, from the window o'er my head,
A dim and sickly gleam was shed
From the young moon,—enough to show
That tomb and tablet lay below.
I leant upon one monument,—
'Twas sacred to unhappy love:
On it were carved a blighted pine—
A broken ring—a wounded dove.
And two or three brief words told all
Her history who lay beneath:—
"The flowers—at morn her bridal flowers,—
Formed, e'er the eve, her funeral wreath."

I could but envy her. I thought,
How sweet it must be thus to die!
Your last looks watched—your last sigh caught,
As life or heaven were in that sigh!
Passing in loveliness and light;
Your heart as pure,—your cheek as bright
As the spring-rose, whose petals shut
By sun unscorched, by shower unwet;
Leaving behind a memory
Shrined in love's fond eternity.

But I was wakened from this dream
By a burst of light—a gush of song—
A welcome, as the stately doors
Poured in a gay and gorgeous throng.
I could see all from where I stood.
And first I looked upon the bride;
She was a pale and lovely girl;
But, O God! who was by her side?—
LORENZO!—No, I did not speak;
My heart beat high, but could not break.
I shrieked not, wept not; but stood there
Motionless in my still despair;
As I were forced by some strange thrall,
To bear with and to look on all,—
I heard the hymn, I heard the vow:
(Mine ear throbs with them even now!)
I saw the young bride's timid cheek
Blushing beneath her silver veil.
I saw LORENZO kneel! Methought
('Twas but a thought!) he too was pale.
But when it ended, and his lip
Was pressed to hers—I saw no more!
My heart grew cold,—my brain swam round,—
I sank upon the cloister floor!
I lived,—if that may be called life,
From which each charm of life has fled—
Happiness gone, with hope and love,—
In all but breath already dead.

Rust gathered on the silent chords
Of my neglected lyre,—the breeze
Was now its mistress: music brought
For me to bitter memories!
The ivy darkened o'er my bower;
Around, the weeds choked every flower.
I pleased me in this desolateness,
As each thing bore my fate's impress.

At length I made myself a task—
To paint that Cretan maiden's fate,
Whom Love taught such deep happiness,
And whom Love left so desolate.
I drew her on a rocky shore:—
Her black hair loose, and sprinkled o'er
With white sea-foam;—her arms were bare,
Flung upward in their last despair.
Her naked feet the pebbles prest;
The tempest-wind sang in her vest:
A wild stare in her glassy eyes;
White lips, as parched by their hot sighs;
And cheek more pallid than the spray,
Which, cold and colorless, on it lay:—
Just such a statue as should be
Placed ever, Love! beside thy shrine;
Warning thy victims of what ills—
What burning tears, false god! are thine.
Before her was the darkling sea:
Behind the barren mountains rose—
A fit home for the broken heart
To weep away life, wrongs, and woes!

I had now but one hope:—that when
The hand that traced these teints was cold—
Its pulse but in their passion seen—
LORENZO might these teints behold,
And find my grief;—think—see—feel all
I felt in this memorial!

It was one evening,—the rose-light
Was o'er each green verandah shining;
Spring was just breaking, and white buds
Were 'mid the darker ivy twining.
My hall was filled with the perfume
Sent from the early orange bloom:
The fountain, in the midst, was fraught
With rich hues from the sunset caught;—
And the first song came from the dove,
Nestling in the shrub alcove.
But why pause on my happiness?—
Another step was with mine there
Another sigh than mine made sweet
With its dear breath the scented air!
LORENZO! could it be my hand,
That now was trembling in thine own?
LORENZO! could it be mine ear
That drank the music of thy tone?

We sat us by a lattice, where
Came in the soothing evening breeze,
Rich with the gifts of early flowers,
And the soft wind-lute's symphonies.
And in the twilight's vesper-hour,
Beneath the hanging jasmine-flower,
I heard a tale,—as fond, as dear
As e'er was poured in woman's ear!

LORENZO'S HISTORY.

I was betrothed from earliest youth
  To a fair orphan, who was left
Beneath my father's roof and care,—
  Of every other friend bereft:
An heiress, with her fertile vales,
  Caskets of Indian gold and pearl;
Yet meek as poverty itself,
  And timid as a peasant girl:
A delicate, frail thing, but made
For spring sunshine, or summer shade;—
A slender flower, unmeet to bear
One April shower,—so slight, so fair.

I loved her as a brother loves
  His favorite sister:—and when war
First called me from our long-shared home
  To bear my father's sword afar,
I parted from her,—not as one
  Whose life and soul are wrung by parting:
With death-cold brow and throbbing pulse,
  And burning tears like lifeblood starting.
Lost in war dreams, I scarcely heard
  The prayer that bore my name above:
The "Farewell!" that kissed off her tears,
  Had more of pity than of love!
I thought of her not with that deep,
Intensest memory love will keep
More tenderly than life. To me
  She was but as a dream of home,—
One of those calm and pleasant thoughts
  That o'er the soldier's spirit come;
Remembering him, when battle lowers,
Of twilight walks and fireside hours.

I came to thy bright Florence when
  The task of blood was done:
I saw thee! Had I lived before?
  O, no! my life but then begun.
Ay, by that blush! the summer rose
  Has not more luxury of light!
Ay, by those eyes! whose language is
  Like what the clear stars speak at night,
Thy first look was a fever spell!—
Thy first word was an oracle
Which sealed my fate! I worshipped thee,
My beautiful, bright deity!
Worshipped thee as a sacred thing
Of Genius' high imagining;
But loved thee for thy sweet revealing
Of woman's own most gentle feeling,
I might have broken from the chain
  Thy power, thy glory round me flung!
But never might forget thy blush—
  The smile which on thy sweet lips hung!
I lived but in thy sight! One night
  From thy hair fell a myrtle blossom;
It was a relic that breathed of thee:
  Look! it has withered in my bosom!
Yet I was wretched, though I dwelt
  In the sweet sight of Paradise:
A curse lay on me. But now now,
  Thus smiled upon by those dear eyes,
Will I think over thoughts of pain.
  I'll only tell thee that the line
That ever told Love's misery,
  Ne'er told of misery like mine!
I wedded. I could not have borne
  To see the young Ianthe blighted
By that worst light the spring can know—
  Trusting affection ill requited!
O, was it that she was too fair,
  Too innocent for this damp earth;
And that her native star above
  Reclaimed again its gentle birth?
She faded. O, my peerless queen,
  I need not pray thee pardon me
For owning that my heart then felt
  For any other than for thee!
I bore her to those azure isles
  Where health dwells by the side of spring;
And deemed their green and sunny vales,
  And calm and fragrant airs, might bring
Warmth to the cheek, light to the eye,
Of her who was too young to die.
It was in vain!—and, day by day,
The gentle creature died away.
As parts the odor from the rose—
As fades the sky at twilight's close—
She passed so tender and so fair;
  So patient, though she knew each breath
Might be her last; her own mild smile
  Parted her placid lips in death.
Her grave is under southern skies;
Green turf and flowers o'er it rise.
O! nothing but a pale spring wreath
Would fade o'er her who lies beneath!
I gave her prayers—I gave her tears—
  I staid awhile beside her grave;
Then led by Hope, and led by Love,
  Again I cut the azure wave.
What have I more to say, my life!
  But just to pray one smile of thine,
Telling I have not loved in vain—
  That thou dost join these hopes of mine?
Yes, smile, sweet love! our life will be
  As radiant as a fairy tale!
Glad as the sky-lark's earliest song—
  Sweet as the sigh of the spring gale!
All, all that life will ever be,
Shone o'er divinest love! by thee.

O, mockery of happiness
  Love now was all too late to save.
False Love! O what had you to do
  With one you had led to the grave?
A little time I had been glad
To mark the paleness on my cheek;
To feel how, day by day, my step
  Grew fainter, and my hand more weak
To know the fever of my soul
  Was also preying on my frame:
But now I would have given worlds
  To change the crimson's hectic's flame
For the pure rose of health; to live
For the dear life that Love could give.
—O, youth may sicken at its bloom,
And wealth and fame pray for the tomb;—
But can love bear from love to part,
And not cling to that one dear heart?
I shrank away from death,—my tears
Had been unwept in other years:—
But thus, in love's first ecstasy.
Was it not worse than death to die?
Lorenzo! I would live for thee!
But thou wilt have to weep for me!
That sun has kissed the morning dews,—
  I shall not see its twilight close!
That rose is fading in the noon,
  And I shall not outlive that rose!
Come, let me lean upon thy breast,
My last, best place of happiest rest!
Once more let me breathe thy sighs—
Look once more in those watching eye
O! but for thee, and grief of thine,
And parting, I should not repine!
It is deep happiness to die,
Yet live in Love's dear memory.
Thou wilt remember me,—my name
Is linked with beauty and with fame.
The summer airs, the summer sky,
The soothing spell of Music's sigh,—
Stars in their poetry of night,
The silver silence of moonlight,—
The dim blush of the twilight hours,
The fragrance of the bee-kissed flowers:—
But, more than all, sweet songs will be
Thrice sacred unto Love and me.
Lorenzo! be this kiss a spell!
My first!—my last! Farewell! Farewell!

There is a lone and stately hall,
Its master dwells apart from all.

A wanderer through Italia's land,
One night a refuge there I found.
The lightning flash rolled o'er the sky,
The torrent rain was sweeping round:
These won me entrance. He was young,
The castle's lord, but pale like age;
His brow, as sculpture beautiful,
Was wan as grief's corroded page,
He had no words, he had no smiles,
No hopes: his sole employ to brood
Silently over his sick heart
In sorrow and in solitude.
I saw the hall where, day by day,
He mused his weary life away;
It scarcely seemed a place for wo,
But rather like a genie's home.
Around were graceful statues ranged,
And pictures shone around the dome
But there was one—a loveliest one!—
One picture brightest of all there!
O! never did the painter's dream
Shape anything so gloriously fair!
It was a face!—the summer day
Is not more radiant in its light!
Dark flashing eyes, like the deep stars
Lighting the azure brow of night;
A blush like sunrise o'er the rose;
A cloud of raven hair, whose shade
Was sweet as evening's, and whose curls
Clustered beneath a laurel braid.
She leant upon a harp:—one hand
Wandered, like snow, amid the chords;
The lips were opening with such life,
You almost heard the silvery words.
She looked a form of life and light,—
All soul, all passion, and all fire;
A priestess of Apollo's, when
The morning beams fall on her lyre;
A Sappho, or ere love had turned
The heart to stone where once it burned.
But by the picture's side was placed
A funeral urn, on which was traced
The heart's recorded wretchedness;—
And on a tablet hung above,
Was 'graved one tribute of sad words—
"Lorenzo to his Minstrel love!"

THE VENETIAN BRACELET.

Those subtle poisons which made science crime,
And knowledge a temptation: could we doubt
One moment the great curse upon our world,
We must believe, to find that even good
May thus be turned to evil.

Another tale of thine! fair Italie—
What makes my lute, my heart, aye turn to thee?
I do not know thy language,—that is still
Like the mysterious music of the rill;—
And neither have I seen thy cloudless sky,
Where the sun hath his immortality;
Thy cities crowned with palaces, thy halls
Where art's great wonders light the storied walls;
Thy fountain's silver sweep, thy groves, where dwell
The rose and orange, summer's citadel;
Thy songs that rise at twilight on the air,
Wedding the breath thy thousand flowers sigh there;
Thy tales of other times, thy marble shrines,
Lovely, though fallen,—for the ivy twines
Its graceful wreath around each ruined fane,
As still in some shape beauty would remain.
I know them not, yet Italie, thou art
The promised land that haunts my dreaming heart.
Perchance it is as well thou art unknown:
I could not bear to lose what I have thrown
Of magic round thee,—but to find in thee
What hitherto I still have found in all—
Thou art not stamped with that reality
Which makes our being's sadness, and its thrall'
But now, whenever I am mixed too much
With worldly natures till I feel as such;—
(For these are as the waves that turn to stone,
Till feelings keep their outward show alone)—
When wearied by the vain, chilled by the cold,
Impatient of society's set mould—
The many meannesses, the petty cares,
The long avoidance of a thousand snares,
The lip that must be chained, the eye so taught
To image all but its own actual thought;
(Deceit is this world's passport: who would dare
However pure the breast, to lay it bare?)—
When worn, my nature struggling with my fate,
Checking, my love, but, O, still more my hate;—
(Why should I love? flinging down pearl and gem
To those who scorn, at least care not for them:
Why should I hate? as blades in scabbards melt,
I have no power to make my hatred felt;
Or, I should say, my sorrow:—I have borne
So much unkindness, felt so lone, so lorn,
I could but weep, and tears may not redress,
They only fill the cup of bitterness)—
Wearied of this, upon what eager winds
My spirit turns to thee, and birdlike flings
Its best, its breath, its spring, and song o'er thee,
My lute's enchanted world, fair Italie.
To me thou art a vision half divine,
Of myriad flowers lit up with summer shine:
The passionate rose, the violet's Tyrian die,
The wild bee loves them not more tenderly;
Of vineyards like Aladdin's gem-set hall,
Fountains like fairy ones with music's fall;
Of sorrows, too; for e'en on this bright soil
Grief has its shadow, and care has its coil,
But e'en amid its darkness and its crime,
Touched with the native beauty of such clime,
Till wonder rises with each gushing tear:—
And hath the serpent brought his curse even here?
Such is the tale that haunts me: I would fain
Wake into pictured life the heart's worst pain;
And seek I if pale cheek and tearful eye
Answer the notes that wander sadly by.
And say not this is vain, in our cold world,
Where feelings sleep like withered leaves unfurled.
'Tis much to wash them with such gentle rain,
Calling their earlier freshness back again.
The heart of vanity, the head of pride,
Touched by such sorrow, are half purified;
And we rise up less selfish, having known
Part in deep grief, yet that grief not our own.

I.

They stood beside the river, that young pair—
She with her eyes cast down, for tears were there,
Glittering upon the eyelash, though unshed;
He murmuring those sweet words so often said
By parting lover, still as fondly spoken
As his could be, the only ones not broken.
The girl was beautiful; her forehead high
Was white as are the marble fanes that lie
On Grecian lands, making a fitting shrine
Where the mind spoke; the arched and raven line
Was very proud, but that was softened now,
Only sad tenderness was on her brow.
She wore the peasant dress,—the snowy lawn
Closely around her whiter throat was drawn,
A crimson boddice, and the skirt of blue
So short, the fairy ankle was in view;
The arm was hidden by the long loose sleeves,
But the small hand was snow; around her hair
A crimson net, such as the peasants weave,
Bound the rich curls, and left the temples bare.
She wore the rustic dress, but there was not
Aught else in her that marked the rustic's lot:
Her bearing seemed too stately, though subdued
By all that makes a woman's gentlest mood—
The parting hour of love. And there they leant,
Mirrored below in the clear element
That rolled along, with wild shrubs overhung,
And colored blossoms that together clung—
That peasant girl, that high-born cavalier,
Whispering those gentle words so sweet to hear,
And answered by flushed cheek, and downcast eye,
And roselip parted, with half smile, half sigh.

Young, loving, and beloved,—these are brief words,
And yet they touch on all the finer chords,
Whose music is our happiness: the tone
May die away and be no longer known
In the harsh wisdom brought by after years,
Lost in that worldliness which sears and sears,
And makes the misery of life's troubled scene;—
Still it is much to think that it has been.
They loved with such deep tenderness and truth,—
Feelings forsaking us as does our youth,—
They did not dream that love like theirs could die,
And such belief half makes eternity.
Yes, they were parting; still the fairy hope
Had in their clear horizon ample scope
For her sweet promises without the showers
That are their comrades in life's after hours.
They parted trustingly; they did not know
The vanity of youthful trust and vow;
And each believed the other,—for each read
In their own hearts the truth of what each said.
The dews are drying rapidly:—away,
Young warrior! those far banners chide thy stay.
Hark! the proud trumpet swells upon the wind,—
His first of fields, he must not be behind.
The maiden's cheek flushed crimson, and her eye
Flashed as the martial music floated by.
She saw him spring upon his snow-white steed,—
It dashed across the plain with arrowy speed.
The beat of heart, the flush of cheek are gone,
AMENAÏDE but felt she was alone.
The vow which soothed her, and the hope which cheered,
The pride which nerved, with him had disappeared.
"LEONI, dear LEONI!"—'twas in vain:—
The mocking echo answered her again.
—It is deep wretchedness, this passionate burst
Of parting's earlier grief, but not the worst;
It is the lingering days of after care,
That try the wasted spirit most to bear.
Now listless, languid, as the world had left
Nothing to interest, of him bereft;
Now lulled by opiate thoughts that but restore
The mind its tone, to make it sink the more;
Now fevered by anxiety, for rife
Are fears when fancy calls them into life;
And then that nameless dread of coming wo,
Which only those who've felt it ere can know;
These still have been in absence, still will be,
And these, AMENAÏDE, were all for thee.
The valley in a summer twilight lay—
That fairy confine of the night and day—
When leant AMENAÏDE behind the shade
The fragrant shrubs around her lattice made,
'Scaped from her nurse and each consoling phrase
Sinking the spirit that it fain would raise.
The room was small and dark; but when the wind
Moved the green branches of the myrtle-blind,
A crimson beauty wooed the maiden's eye:
She looked and saw, where, dark against the sky,
His father's battlements rose on the air;—
Alas, how haughty and how high they were!
An orphan she, a rustic's nursling child,
O, how could hope have ever so beguiled!
"AMENAÏDE!" her kind old nurse's voice;
"Nay, come to me, dear child, come and rejoice."
Wondering, she enters,—strangers round her stand,
And kindly takes her lordly chief her hand.
"So fair a peasant, sooth, but it is shame
To tell thee, maiden of another name.
In the wild troubles which have rent our state
Thy noble father met an exile's fate:—
Nay, not that anxious look; he is no more,
And sorrowing Genoa can but restore
His honors to his child: I was aware,
Thanks to that faithful creature's parent care,
His daughter lived; and dear the task to me
To bring these words, and let AREZZI be
The first to greet and honor, countess, mine,
Loveliest, and last of ALFIORI's line.

II.

Fit for a palace was that lovely room,
Hung with the azure of an eastern loom,
And carpeted with velvet, where the flowers
Companioned those whereon the April hours
Had shed their beauty; numbers stood around
Of vases where each varying hue was found,
From the white myrtle-bud and lily-bell,
Like pearls that in the ocean waters dwell,
To those rich teints which on the tulip lie,
Telling their southern birth and sunny sky
The wine-cups of the sun:—each silken blind
Waved to and fro upon the scented wind,
Now closing till the twilight-haunted room
Was in an atmosphere of purple gloom,
First scarcely letting steal one crimson ray,
Then flung all open to the glowing day.
Pictures were hung above; how more than fair!
The changing light made almost life seem there
A faint rose-color wandered o'er the cheek,
Seemed the chance beams from each dark eye to break;
And you could deem each braided auburn wave
Moved, as its gold the glancing sunlight gave.
And fitting mistress had the charmed scene:
Leant, like a beautiful and eastern queen,
Upon a purple couch—how soft and warm
Clung the rich color to her ivory arm!—
AMENAÏDE reclined. Awhile she lay,—
Then, as if movement hurried time away,
She paced the room, gazed on each pictured face,—
Then wreathed the flowers, then watched, as if to trace
The evening close: again the couch was pressed,
But feverish, restless, more for change than rest:
And yet all this was only the excess
Of overmuch impatient happiness.
Many a weary hour and day had past
For that young countess,—this day was the last.
He was returned, with all war could confer
Of honorable name, to home and her.
LEONI would to-night be in the hall
Where Count AREZZI held his festival,
Would hear her history; how there was now
Nothing to chain the heart or check the vow.
—And must they meet first in a careless crowd?
This was a moment's grief; though she felt proud
That he should see how well she could beseem
Her present rank, yet keep her early dream;
See her the worshipped of the courtly throng,
Sigh of each lip, and idol of each song;
Hear the fair flatteries offered, yet behold
Her courtesy so graceful, but so cold;
And know it was for him her heart's young throne
Was ever kept, the lovely and the lone.

III.

O pleasant was that night the toilet's care—
What broidered robe to don, what gems to wear!
Her hair was parted on her brow, each braid
Black as the dark-winged raven's darkest shade,
And gathered up with diamonds,—few there were—
Just stars to light the midnight of her hair.
Well did the sweeping robe of emerald green,
Wrought in rich gold, suit with her stately mien.
"How beautiful she looks this evening!" burst
From every lip, when that fair countess first
Entered AREZZI's hall: her heart's content
To every lighted look its lustre lent.
Her beauty's fault had been, it was too cold;
Features too tranquil in their perfect mould,
A cheek somewhat too pale; but not to-night—
The eye was sparkling, and the cheek was bright.
Gently she glided to a balustrade,
Where jessamine a pleasant shadow made;
It raised no marvel; never had her hand
With its white beauty linked the saraband;
And seldom did she join the converse gay,
Where the light flattery gains its gilded way;
They seldom won more than a few cold words,
As when unskilful hands awake the chords
Of some lorn lute, the music of whose tone
Lives for one touch, and only for that one.
She dwelt within the circle of her heart,
A charmed world, lovely, lonely, and apart;
Where it had seemed to her as sin and shame
Aught there had entered, not in his dear name.

—It was a spell-touched hour. That gorgeous hall
With perfumes floating and with music's fall,
Light steps, and gentle laugh, and whispers bland,—
Was in their words or the sweet airs that fanned
The beauty's cheek into a redder rose?—
And starry eyes, like what the clear night shows,
But wandering ones; and there were golden curls
Like sudden sunshine; and dark braids, whose pearls
Were lost on the white neck when there they fell;
And there were shapes, such as in pictures dwell;
It looked like fairy land. With eager glance
She watched the door, and counted every dance;
Then time grew long, hope caught a shade of fear—
"LEONI—but they said he would be here!"
When sudden came AREZZI to her side,—
"Look there, the Count LEONI and his bride!
She with the violet wreath in her bright hair;
Sooth but to say, that English bride is fair!
But I must go and have my welcome paid."
Alone AMENAÏDE stood in the shade,—
Alone! ay, utterly. A couch was nigh,
And there she sank—O, had it been to die!

IV.

Alas for the young heart thus early thrown
Back on itself, the unloved and the lone!
For this should be the lesson of long years,
The weary knowledge taught and traced by tears,
Till even those are frozen, and we grow
Cold as the grave that yawns for us below:
But this was like those sudden blasts that fling
Unlooked-for winter on the face of spring,—
And worst wo for the heart, whose early fate
Leaves it so young, and, O, so desolate.
She had one feeling left—it was of pride—
O, misery, how much she had to hide!
And steps were now approaching her: she sprung
From off the couch, and every nerve was strung
For that worst rack, the rack of outward show,
Still haunts such vanity the deepest wo.
The heart may swell to bursting, but the while
The features wear the seeming of a smile:
The eye be lessened, and the lip be sealed,
And wretchedness be, like the plague, concealed.
—It was the Count AREZZI: "What still here!—
Come, thou wild dreamer of another sphere,
I must shut out the sky, if thus it share
My stars, thine eyes, which should be shining there,
Making yon hall its equal; but to-night
You have, AMENAÏDE, a rival light.
The English bride,—see round they crowd to gaze
On the new loveliness her form displays.
Why, she should bear the name which once you bore,
—The peasant countess,—it would suit her more."
A moment, and the group were pressed aside,
She stood before LEONI and his bride.
He knew her history, and each met prepared;
Cold looks were given, careless converse shared;
At first LEONI shunned to meet her eye,—
A moment's awkwardness,—but that passed by.
How much we give to other hearts our tone,
And judge of others' feelings by our own!
Himself has altered: all he sought to do
Was to believe that she was altered too.
Her cheek was paler than 'twas wont to be,—
That was its round of midnight gayety:
Her smile less frequent, and her brow more grave,—
'Twas her new rank its stateliness that gave:
New friends pressed round,—their interview is o'er,—
And he passed on, to think of it no more;
And she to seem as thoughtless. Till to-night,
Like some fair planet in its own far light,
She shone apart; to-night she sought the crowd,
Joined in their mirthfulness, and laughed aloud;
Was ready with gay converse,—that light mirth
Which like the meteor has from darkness birth:
She watched her circle,—ready smile or sneer,—
Sneers for the absent ones, smiles for the near,
Till every other hall sent forth its tide,
And half the guests were gathered at her side.
It was an evil feeling that which now
Flushed on her cheek, and lighted up her brow—
Part bitterness, part vanity, part wo—
The passionate strife which pride and misery know:
A burning wish to make a vain regret
In that false one, who now had best forget;
To show LEONI how that she, the queen,
Made his fair EDITH nothing on the scene;
Her rival—hers—language has not a word
By woman's ear so utterly abhorred.
No marvel, for it robs her only part
Of sweet dominion—empire o'er the heart.

V.

LEONI and his bride have left the hall.
Why does that cheek grow pale, that dark eye fall?
Why does that lip its wit, its smiling cease?
It only passed for beauty's gay caprice.
She left the feast—but O, not yet alone;
Many a cavalier has eager flown
Upon her gondola's home course to wait,
And sigh farewell at her own palace gate.
Her maidens gathered round. What more, yet more
To read the breast now throbbing to the core?
She hurried not their task,—each silken braid
Of raven hair was in set order laid:
But once she showed her weakness,—when her hand
Strove vainly to unloose a glittering band,
It trembled like a leaf:—but that passed by;
Struggle she might, but no one heard her sigh;
And when her last good night was courteous said
Never more queenlike seemed that lofty head.
The last step died upon the marble stair,—
She sprang toward the door,—the bolt is there:—
She tried the spring, gave one keen look around,
Muttered "alone!" and dashed her on the ground.
Corpselike she lay,—her dark hair wildly thrown
Far on the floor before her; white as stone,
As rigid stretched each hand, her face was pressed
Close to the earth; and but the heaving vest
Told of some pang the shuddering frame confessed,
She seemed as stricken down by instant death.—
Sudden she raised her head, and gasped for breath;
And nature mastered misery. She sought,
Panting, the air from yonder lattice brought.
Ah, there is blood on that white lip and brow!—
She struggles still—in vain—she must weep now.
She wept, childlike, till sleep began to press
Upon her eyes, for very weariness.
She sleeps!—so sleeps the wretch beside the stake:
She sleeps!—how dreadful from such sleep to wake!

VI.

She was both proud and cold: not hers the heart
Easy to lure, and ready to depart—
A trifle, toy—but that fair countess gave
No common gift when she became a slave;
And only did she hold her gift redeemed,
By that high worthiness she had but dreamed.
A peasant, yet she felt his equal still;
And when her lofty state beseemed her will,
It was such pride, such pleasure, to have known
LEONI's love was for herself alone.
And in her young romances loftier view,
One touch of vanity might mingle too.
It was the triumph of her lowlier state,
She had been even then a noble's mate.
AMENAÏDE had many faults; her youth
Had seen too soon life's bitterness and truth:
The cutting word, the cold or scornful look,
All that her earlier days had had to brook—
The many slights the humble one receives—
Lay on her memory like withered leaves;
And homage from the crowd, and lovers' praise,
Were all too apt disgust and doubt to raise.
There was a something wayward in her mood;
She left her heart too much to solitude:
For kindly thoughts are social; but she held
A scornful creed, and sympathy repelled.
That sullen barrier had one gentle break—
She loved,—she loved,—and for LEONI's sake
Believed there were some angel steps on earth:—
As truth that keeps the promise of its birth;

As faith that will not change, that will not tire,
And deems its gold the purer for the fire.
Her love was all her nature's better part,
The confidence, the kindness of her heart,
The source of all the sweet or gentle there:
But this was past—what had it left!—despair!

VII.

The wind threw back the curtain fraught with rose —
Can sorrow be upon such gales as those?
Yes, for it waked the countess. Up she sprung,
Startled, surprised, to see how she was flung
By the verandah, and that open, too;
Her hair was heavy with the weight of dew;
Scarcely aroused, painful and slow she raised
Her weary head, and round in wonder gazed.
It was her own fair room,—some frightful dream,
But indistinct,—she struggled with a scream:
Her eye has caught a mirror,—that pale face,—
Why lip and brow are sullied by the trace
Of blood; its stain is on her tangled hair,
Which shroudlike hides the neck that else were bare.
Around that neck there is a fragile chain,
And memory's flood comes rushing o'er her brain:
LEONI's gift,—its slight gold links are broken,—
So are the vows of which it was the token.
Who has not loathed that worst,—that waking hour,
When grief and consciousness assert their power;
When misery has morn's freshness, yet we fain
Would hold it as a dream, and sleep again;
Then know 'tis not illusion of the night
And sicken at the cold and early light?
How ever shall we pass the weary day,
When thus we shudder at its opening ray?
She gazed upon the glass, then glanced around,
In wonder at the contrast which she found.
The walls were faintly covered with the bloom
Which comes when morn has struggled through the gloom,
And blushes for success; the silken veil
Of the blue hangings seemed to catch the gale,
Then keep its sweetness prisoner: on the floor
The Persian loom had spread its velvet store:
Vases stood round, each carved with such fine art,
The flowers that filled seemed of themselves a part:
A sandal lute lay on an inlaid stand,
Whose rich wrought ivory spoke its Indian land;
Shells of bright colors, foreign toys of gold,
And crystals wrought in many a curious mould:
Pictures, a prince's ransom in their worth;
Small alabaster statues—all that earth
Has rich or varied, all that wealth could buy,
Loathing she turned. "Yet what a wretch am I?
This must not be!—stained cheek and fevered brow
Too much the secret of my soul avow.
Aye deep as is the grave my heart shall keep
What burning tears AMENAÏDE could weep.
O, never let LEONI know the worst;
'Tis well if he believe I changed the first.
Too much e'en to myself has been revealed,
—And thus be every trace of tears concealed."
She sought the alcove where the fountain played,
And washed from lip and cheek their crimson shade,
And bathed her long hair, till its glossy curls
Wore not a trace but of the dewy pearls
The waters left, as if in pity shed;
She loosed the bolt, and sought her silken bed;
But easier far had been the rack, the wheel:—
When hath the body felt what mind can feel!

VIII.

The weary day passed on—night came again:—
AMENAÏDE has joined the glittering train;
Self-torturer—self-deceiver—cold and high,
She said it was to mock the curious eye.
Such strength is weakness. Was it not to be
Where still, LEONI, she might gaze on thee
—She heard the history of his English bride
A patient nurse at her pale mother's side,
LEONI saw her first:—that mother's hand
(A stranger she and wanderer in the land)
Gave the sweet orphan to his care,—and here
Was all to soften, all that could endear.
Together wept they o'er the funeral stone,
His the sole heart she had to lean upon.
Now months had passed away, and he was come
To bring his beautiful, his dear one home.
Her beauty was like morning's, breathing, bright,
Eyes glittering first with tears, and then with light,
And blue, too glad to be the violet's blue,
But that which hangs upon it, lucid dew,—
Its first clear moment, ere the sun has burst
The azure radiance which it kindled first;—
A cheek of thousand blushes; golden hair,
As if the summer sunshine made it fair:
A voice of music, and such touching smile,
AMENAÏDE sighed, "Well might they beguile!"
Love, what a mystery thou art!—how strange
Thy constancy, yet still more so thy change!
How the same love, born in the self-same hour,
Holds over different hearts such different power;
How the same feeling lighted in the breast
Makes one so wretched, and makes one so blest;
How one will keep the dream of passion born
In youth with all the freshness of its morn;
How from another will thine image fade!
Far deeper records on the sand are made.
—Why hast thou separate being? why not die
At once in both, and not leave one to sigh,
To weep, to rave, to struggle with the chains
Pride would fling off, but memory retains?
There are remembrances that will not vanish,—
Thoughts of the past we would but can not banish.
As if to show how impotent mere will:
We loathe the pang and yet must suffer still:
For who is there can say they will forget?
—It is a power no science teaches yet.
O love, how sacred thy least words should be,
When on them hangs such abject misery!

IX.

The fountain's music murmured through the grove,
Like the first plaint that sorrow teaches love;
The orange boughs shut out the sultry sky,
While their rich scent, as passed the countess by,
Came homagelike. For hours that chestnut tree—
The only one that grew there—wont to be
Her favorite summer seat; but now she paced
Hurriedly, though 'twas noon; her memory traced
Her galling wrongs, and many an evil thought
Envy and hatred in her bosom wrought.
She felt LEONI had not loved till now;
Hers was but youthful phantasy's light vow.
Had he not trifled with her?—She, the proud,
The cold, had of such mocking suit allowed.
Her heart was wrung, and worse, her pride was bowed
She hears a step: who is it dares intrude
On this her known and guarded solitude?
She sees an aged Jew; a box he bore
Filled with gay merchandise and jewelled store.
Ere she could speak, he spread before her eyes
Those glittering toys that loveliest ladies prize:—
"Fair dame, in sooth so fair thou seemest to be,
That almost it is vain to offer thee
The many helps for meaner beauty made;
But yet these gems would light that dark hair's shade;
Well would these pearls around that white throat show
Each purple vein that wanders through its snow."
Angrily turned the countess,—"Fool, away!"—
"So young, so fair, has vanity no sway?
But I have things most curious, and 'mid these
Somewhat may chance your wayward fancy please."
He took a bracelet,—'twas of fine wrought gold,
And twisted as a serpent, whose lithe fold
Curled round the arm:—he spoke in whispering tone—
"Here, lady, look at this, I have but one:
Here, press this secret spring; it lifts a lid,—
Beneath there is the subtlest poison hid:
I come from Venice; of the wonders there,
There is no wonder like this bracelet rare."
She started—evil thoughts, at first repressed,
Now struggled like a storm within her breast.

Alas! alas! how plague-spot like will sin
Spread over the wrung heart it enters in!
Her brow grew dark:—"Amid thy baubles shine
This ruby cross,—but be the bracelet mine."
Around her arm the fatal band is fast,
Away its seller, like a vision, passed.

X.

That night she joined the revel; but not long
AMENAÏDE was seen amid the throng.
No eye beheld her pace her lonely room:
Fearing the light, yet trembling in the gloom;
The ghastly cheek, as marble cold and white;
The wild eye flashing with unholy light;
The quivering lip, the forehead's dew-moist pore,
The sudden start, the rapid step once more,—
As if it would annihilate the time:—
But who may paint the solitude of crime?

XI.

That night there was another saddest scene:
Halls where mirth, music, festival had been
Were as the house of mourning; crowds stood nigh,
Horror and pity marked in every eye.
Upon a crimson couch—a contrast strange
To those pale features in that ghastly change—
The young, the beautiful, the happy lay,
Life passing in convulsive sobs away.
Still mid her hair the red rose wreath was hung,
Mocking her cheek with the rich die it flung;
The festal robe still sparkled as it flowed;
Still on her neck a few fresh flowers glowed:
The warmth her sandalled foot hath scarcely left,
Light from the dance, though now of motion reft!
The agony is over,—and she raised
Her feeble head, and round her faintly gazed:
She saw, she leant upon LEONI's breast,
Murmured his name, and sank as if to rest.
"EDITH, sweet EDITH, speak to me again!"
Thou fond one—even thou must ask in vain:
Ay, kiss those lips, and fancy they have breath,
Till they chill even thee: they're damp with death.

XII.

The night is over,—night which seemed to be
Endless, O lost AMENAÏDE! to thee:
Yet what has daylight brought?—a haunting dread.
Hark! the hall echoes to a stranger's tread—
It is the Count AREZZI:—"My fair child,
How now!—thy cheek is wan, thine eyes are wild.
Ah, well the rose is brightening on thy cheek:
I was too hasty with my sudden break
Upon thy solitude; scarce may I tell
The crime and horror which last night befell.
I have no time. The Count LEONI's bride—
You saw her—by some sudden poison died;
And strange suspicions on her husband fall:
There were so many present who recall
He gave her the sherbet:—'twas not all drained;
Part of the venom in the cup remained.
Some say 'twas jealousy:—I'm on my way
To the tribunal that will sit to-day.
—AMENAÏDE, dear, thou art very pale:
I would I had not told thee of this tale.—
Ha! 'tis the summons of the council bell,—
I loathe my task,—sweet, hastily farewell."
She strove to speak,—to only wave her hand,—
To rise,—her trembling limbs refused to stand:
She sought her cross, she strove to think a prayer,—
She gasped for breath,—no ruby cross is there;
But full in view the fatal bracelet shone:
"LEONI, this is what my love has done;
I who would willingly have died for thee,
The fiend has triumphed in my misery.
I'll rush before the judges,—is there time?—
But no, I can not bear to own the crime!
And there is naught of proof,—there can be none,—
And then his known love for that happier one;
His noble house,—his brave and stainless name:—
He must escape his doom,—and I my shame."
Long hours passed by, she stirred not from her place,
A very statue, with that cold set face,
Save that red flushes came at each light sound,
While the wild eyes glanced fearfully around;
But still she moved not, spoke not,—such distress
Seeks no distraction from its wretchedness.
There rose loud voices in the outer hall:—
She nerves her with despair, she will know all;
Her ear, acute with agony, can hear
A name at once so dreaded and so dear:—
"Yes, Lady, he is guilty!"—but no more:—
They raise her senseless from the marble floor.
Long did it last, that stony trance like death;
She roused, but scarce it seemed with mortal breath.
She showed no weakness, rose from off the bed
Distinct, though low and few, the words she said,
She took a scroll and wrote,—the phrase was brief
But a life's sorrow was upon that leaf.
"To Count AREZZI this, with all thy speed;
And here, my page, is gold for present meed.
Now all away,—my spirit is opprest:"
She flung her on the couch as if for rest:
They deemed she slept: at length her maidens came
To ask her will, to light the lamp's sweet flame,
Where is the countess? why, the couch is bare,—
They search the halls in vain,—she is not there.

XIII.

"Gold, O! take double, so my prayer I win."
When hath such offer failed?—She entered in:
Heavily iron chain and barrier fell,
Ere she could reach the prisoner's midnight cell.
They grated on her very heart. At last
She saw LEONI in his misery cast
Abject upon the ground:—not her strange tread
Brought aught to make him raise his bowed down head.
She gazed upon him:—has it come to this,
Her passionate love, her youth's long dream of bliss?
She felt her frame convulsed, her pulse grow weak—
"LEONI, O LEONI! hear me speak."
He started at her voice: "AMENAÏDE!
I did not merit this from thee indeed;
And yet thy name was heavy on my heart:
I pray thee pardon me before we part."
He sought to take her hand; but back she flung
The shrouding mantle that around her clung.
"Ah! start you at my livid lip and brow?
You are familiar with such signs ere now!
O for a few short words! I've owned the whole:
Ere this the Count AREZZI has my scroll.—
The darkness gathers on my failing eye,—
LEONI, let me gaze on thee and die!
O God, unloose this bracelet's fiery clasp!"—
Her spirit passed in that convulsive gasp.
The struggle's o'er,—that wild heart does not beat;
She lies a ghastly corpse before his feet.

XIV.

They show the traveller still a lonely tomb,
Hid in the darkness of a cloister's gloom;
As scarcely worthy of such holy ground,
No other monument is near it found.
A figure closely veiled bends o'er the stone,
Only the arm with its strange bracelet shown—
A serpent twining round: beneath are graved
A few brief words, that passing pity craved—
"Pray for the wounded heart, the sinful deed;"
And, half effaced, a name—"AMENAÏDE."

LOVE, HOPE, AND BEAUTY.

LOVE may be increased by fears,
May be fanned with sighs,
Nurst by fancies, fed by doubts;
But without Hope it dies!
As in the far Indian isles
Dies the young cocoa tree,
Unless within the pleasant shade
Of the parent plant it be:
So Love may spring up at first
Lighted at Beauty's eyes;—
But Beauty is not all its life,
For without Hope it dies.

THE LOST PLEIAD.

A story from the stars; or rather one
Of starry fable from the olden time,
When young Imagination was as fresh
As the fair world it peopled with itself.
The Poet's spirit does so love to link
Its feelings, thoughts, with nature's loveliness:
And hence the twilight grove, the lonely spring,
The ocean-caves, the distant planets, all
Were filled with radiant creatures; and the heart
Became interpreter, and language made
From its own warm sad sympathies, for those
Of whom the dream was beauty. mm

He was weary of flinging the feathered reed,
He was weary of curbing his raven steed;
He heard the gay din from the palace hall,
But he was not in mood for the festival.
There was that crimson, the last on the sky,
Blushes that fade in the moon's cold eye;
The sigh of the flowers arose sweet on the air,
For the breath of the twilight was wandering there.
He looked to the west, and the tranquil main
Was branched with many a lifelike vein;
Hues of the rosebud the clouds had cast,
Like a cheek on its mirror in gliding past.
It tempted him forth,—to the lulling gale
Prince Cyris has opened his silken sail,
And the little boat went over the sea
Like foam, for it was of ivorie,
And carved and shaped like a wreathed shell,
And it was lined with the rose as well;
For the couch was made of those plumes that fling
The one warm teint neath the wood-dove's wing.
O'er the purple sail the golden flowers run,
For it was wrought for a monarch's son;
And as it passed on, the air was filled
With odors, for only waters distilled
From clove, and sandal, and cinnamon,
E'er washed that boat when its task was done:
'Twas left in the care of maidens three,
Lovely they were as maidens should be;
And in the soft airs that around it flew,
Perhaps their own breath left a perfume too.
—There lay Prince Cyris, and his mood
Made harmony with the solitude.
—O pleasant is it for the heart
To gather up itself apart;
To think its own thoughts, and to be
Free, as none ever yet were free,
When, prisoners to their gilded thrall,
Vain crowd meets crowd in lighted hall;
With frozen feelings, tutored eye,
And smile which is itself a lie.
—O but for lonely hours like these,
Would every finer current freeze;
Those kindlier impulses that glow,
Those clear and diamond streams that flow
Only in crystal, while their birth,
Is all unsoiled with stain of earth.
Ever the lover hath gainsayed
The creed his once religion made,—
That pure, that high, that holy creed,
Without which love is vain indeed;
While that which was a veiled shrine,
Whose faith was only not divine,
Becomes a vague, forgotten dream,—
A thing of scorn—an idle theme.
Denied, degraded, and represt,
Love dies beneath the heartless jest.
O vain! for not with such can be
One trace of his divinity.
Ever from poet's lute hath flown
The sweetness of its early tone,
When from its wild flight it hath bowed.
To seek for homage 'mid the crowd;
Be the one wonder of the night,
As if the soul could be a sight;
As all his burning numbers speak,
Were written upon brow and cheek;
And he forsooth must learn his part,
Must choose his words, and school his heart
To one set mould, and pay again
Flattery with flattery as vain;
Till, mixing with the throng too much,
The cold, the vain, he feels as such;
Then marvels that his silent lute
Beneath that worldly hand is mute.
—Away! these scenes are not for thee:
Go dream beneath some lonely tree;
Away to some far woodland spring,
Dash down thy tinsel crown, and wring
The scented unguents from thine hair
If thou dost hope that crown to share
The laurelled bards immortal wear:
Muse thou o'er leaf and drooping flower,
Wander at evening's haunted hour;
Listen to stockdove's plaining song
Until it bear thy soul along;
Then call upon thy freed lute's strain,
And it will answer thee again.
O mine own song, did I not hold
Such faith as held the bards of old,—
That one eternal hope of fame
Which sanctifies the poet's name,—
I'd break my lyre in high disdain,
And hold my gift of song as vain
As those forced flowers which only bloom
One hot night for a banquet-room.
—But I have wandered from my tale,—
The ivory bark, the purple sail,
That bore Prince Cyris o'er the sea,—
Content with that slow ebb to be
Danced on the wave. By nightfall shaded,
The red lights from the clouds are faded;
Leaving one palest amber line
To mark the last of day's decline;
And all o'er heaven is that clear blue
The stars so love to wander through.
They're rising from the silent deep,
Like bright eyes opening after sleep.
Young Cyris watched them till their ray
Grew sad—so far they were away.
He felt so earthly, thus to see
What he might never hope to be.
He thought upon earth's loveliest eyes;
What were they to those shining there?
He thought upon earth's sweetest sighs:
What were they to the lulling air?
"O no, my heart," he mournful sighed,
"To thee is that dear boon denied;
That wildering dream whose fair deceit
Makes languid earth a temple meet
For light, such light as dwells above,—
I have no faith in thee, false love!
I've knelt at many a beauteous shrine,
And called, but thought them not, divine.
I've dived in many a beating heart,
But searched them only to depart;
For selfish care, or heartless pride,
Were all they ever had to hide.
I'm weary, weary: one by one,
The life charms of my youth are gone.
I had a dream of stirring fame—
It was a promise, and a name,
Thrice glorious, shining from afar,
But nearer earth had touched the star;
With toil and trouble won from many,
Yet trembling on the breath of any.
The bard, the warrior, and the sage,
What win they but one lying page,
Where deeds and words, at hazard thrown,
May be or may not be their own?
And pleasure, lighted halls, red wine,
Bright smiles, gay words, have all been mine
They only left what haunts me now,—
A wasted heart, a weary brow.
Ye distant stars, so calm, so bright,
Would I had portion in your light,
Could read the secrets of your birth,—
Aught, anything but this dull earth!"
—It was not long, ere, still and deep,
Those restless eyes were closed in sleep.
There lay he like a statue pale,
His canopy that silken sail.

There lay he as Endymion slept
When Dian came to him, and wept
Beside the sleep she might not break,
Love, thus we sorrow for thy sake.
There lay he:—well might Cyris seem
The being of a poet's dream.
Ay, beautiful as a star in the sky,
When the clouds are gloom, and the storm is high,
But still in defiance keeps shining on,
Till the shades are past, and the wind is done.
His hair was gold, like the pheasant's wing,
And curled like the hyacinth flower in spring
And his eye was that blue so clear, so dark,
Like the falcon's when flying his highest mark.
And telling a tale of gallant war,
On his brow was a slight but glorious scar.
His voice had that low and lutelike sound,
Whose echo within the heart is found.
His very faults were those that win
Too dazzling and ready an entrance in.
Daring, and fiery, wild to range,
Reckless of what might ensue from the change;
Too eager for pleasure to fill up the void,
Till the very impatience their nature destroyed;
Restless, inconstant, he sought to possess,—
The danger was dared, and the charm grew less.
But, O! these were only youth's meteor fires,
The ignis blaze that with youth expires.
No never!—the heart should childlike be trained,
And its wilful waywardness somewhat enchained.
—Was it the spell of morning dew
That o'er his lips its influence threw,
Clearing those earthly mists away,
That erst like veils before them lay?
Whether fair dream, or actual sight,
It was a vision of delight:
For free to his charmed eyes were given
The spirits of the starry heaven.
It was that hour, when each faint die
Of rose upon the morning's cheek
Warns the bright watchers of the sky
Their other ocean home to seek.
He saw the Archer with his bow,
Guide now his radiant car below;
He saw the shining Serpent fold
Beneath the wave his scales of gold.
But of all the pageants nigh,
Only one fixed Cyris' eye:
Borne by music on their way,
Every chord a living ray,
Sinking on a songlike breeze,
The lyre of the Pleiades,
With its seven fair sisters bent
O'er their starry instrument;
Each a star upon her brow,
Somewhat dim in daylight's glow,
That clasped the flashing coronet
On their midnight tresses set.
—All were young, all were fair—
But one—O! Cyris gazed but there.
Each other lip wore sterner mould,—
Fair, but so proud,—bright, but so cold;
And clear pale cheek, and radiant eye,
Wore neither blush, nor smile, nor sigh,
Those sweet signs of humanity.
But o'er Cyrene's cheek the rose
Like moon-touched water, ebbs [illegible] flows;
And eyes that droop like summ[illegible] flowers
Told they could change with shine and showers.
The starry lyre has reached the sea,—
Started young Cyris to his knee:
Surely her dark eyes met his own;
But, ah! the lovely dream is flown.
I need not tell how long the day
Passed in its weariness away;
I need not say how Cyris' sight
Pined for the darkness of the night.
But darkness came, and with it brought
The vision which the watcher sought.
He saw the starry lyre arise—
The seven fair sisters' glittering car—
Till lost amid the distant skies,
Each only looked a burning star.
Again, at morning's dewy hour,
He saw them seek their ocean bower;
Again those dark eyes met his own—
Again the lovely dream is flown.
Night after night thus passed; but now
The young Moon wears less vestal brow.
Her silver veil is lined with gold;
Like a crowned queen, she comes to hold
Her empire in the sky alone—
No rival near her midnight throne.
Sometimes he fancied o'er the tide
He saw pale phantoms dimly glide:
The moonbeams fell o'er sea and sky,
No other light met Cyris' eye.
The night—the moon—he watched in vain,
No starry lyre rose from the main.
—And who were they the lovely seven,
With shape of earth, and home in heaven?
Daughters of King Atlas they—
He of the enchanted sway;
He who read the mystic lines
Of the planets' wondrous signs:
He the sovereign of the air—
They were his, these daughters fair.
Six were brides, in sky and sea,
To some crowned divinity;
But his youngest, loveliest one,
Was as yet unwooed, unwon.
She's kneeling at her father's side:—
What the boon could be denied
To that fair but tear-washed cheek,
That looked so earnest, yet so meek;
To that mouth whose gentle words
Murmur like the wind-lute's chords;
To that soft and pleasing eye
Who is there could suit deny?
Bent the king, with look of care,
O'er the dear one kneeling there;
Bent and kissed his pleading one,—
Ah, that smile! her suit is won.
—It was a little fountain made
A perfect sanctuary of shade;
The pine boughs like a roof, beneath
The tapestry of the acacia wreath.
The air was haunted, sounds, and sighs,
The falling waters' melodies;
The breath of flowers, the faint perfume
Of the green pineleaf's early bloom;
And murmurs from the music hung
Ever the woodland boughs among;
His couch of moss, his pillow flowers,
Dreaming away the listless hours—
Those dreams so vague, those dreams so vain,
Yet iron links in lover's chain—
Prince Cyris leant: the solitude
Suited such visionary mood;
For love hath delicate delights,—
The silence of the summer nights;
The leaves and buds, whose languid sighs
Seem like the echo of his own;
The wind which like a lute note dies;
The shadow by the branches thrown,
Although a sweet uncertain smile
Wanders through those boughs the while,
As if the young Moon liked to know
Her fountain mirror bright below;
Linking his thoughts with all of these,
For love is full of phantasies.
—Why starts young Cyris from his dream?
There is a shadow on the stream,
There is an odor on the air;—
What shape of beauty fronts him there!
He knows her by her clear dark eye,
Touched with the light that rules the sky;
The star upon her forehead set,
Her wild hair's sparkling coronet;
Her white arms, and her silvery vest,—
The lovely Pleiad stands confest.
—I can not sing as I have sung;
My hearts is changed, my lute unstrung;
Once said I that my early chords

Were vowed to love or sorrow's words;
But love has like an odor past,
Or echo, all too sweet to last:
And sorrow now holds lonely sway
O'er my young heart, and lute, and lay.
Be it for those whose unwaked youth
Believes that hope and love are sooth—
The loved, the happy—let them dream
This meeting by the forest stream.
No more they parted till the night
Called on her starry host for light,
And that bright lyre arose on high
With its fair watchers to their sky.
Then came the wanderings long and lonely,
As if the world held them, them only;
The gathered flower which is to bear
Some gentle secret whispered there;
The seat beneath the forest tree;
The breathless silence, which to love
Is all that eloquence can be;
The looks ten thousand words above;
The fond deep gaze, till the fixed eye
Casts each on each a mingled die;
The interest round each little word,
Though scarcely said, and scarcely heard.
Little love asks of language aid,
For never yet hath vow been made
In that young hour when love is new:
He feels at first so deep, so true,
A promise is a useless token,
When neither dream it can be broken.
Alas! vows are his after sign!—
We prop the tree in its decline—
The ghosts that haunt a parting hour,
With all of grief, and naught of power;
A chain half sundered in the making,—
The plighted vows already breaking.
From such dreams all too soon we wake;
For like the moonlight on the lake,
One passing cloud, one waving bough—
The silver light, what is it now?
Said I not, that young prince was one
Who wearied when the goal was won:
To whom the charm of change was all
That bound his heart in woman's thrall?
And she now lingering at his side,
His bright, his half-immortal bride,
Though she had come with him to die,
Share earthly tear, and earthly sigh;
Left for his sake her glorious sphere,—
What mattered that?—she now was here.
At first 'twas like a frightful dream:
Why should such terror even seem?
Again—again—it can not be!
Wo for such wasting misery!—
This watching love's o'erclouding sky,
Though still believing it must clear;
This closing of the trusting eye;
The hope that darkens into fear;
The lingering change of doubt and dread;
All in the one dear presence fled.
Till days of anguish passed alone,
Till careless look, and altered tone,
Relieve us from the rack, to know
Our last of fate, our worst of wo.
And she, the guileless, pure, and bright,
Whose nature was her morning's light:
Who deemed of love as it is given
The sunniest element to heaven;
Whose sweet belief in it was caught
Only from what her own heart taught—
Her woman's heart, that dreamy shrine,
Of what itself made half divine,—
CYRENE, when thy shadow came
With thy first step that touched the earth,
It was an omen how the same
Doth sorrow haunt all mortal birth.
Thou hast but left those starry spheres
For woman's destiny of tears.
—They parted as all lovers part,—
She with her wronged and breaking heart;
But he, rejoicing he is free,
Bounds like the captive from his chain,
And wilfully believing she
Hath found her liberty again:
Or if dark thoughts will cross his mind,
They are but clouds before the wind.
—Thou false one, go!—but deep and dread
Be minstrel curse upon thy head!
—Go, be the first in battle line,
Where banners sweep, and falchions shine;
Go thou to lighted festival,
Be there the peerless one of all;
Let bright cheeks wear yet brighter rays
If they can catch Prince CYRIS' gaze;
Be thine in all that honored name,
Men hold to emulate is fame;
Yet not the less my curse shall rest,
A serpent coiling in thy breast.
Weariness, like a weed, shall spring
Wherever is thy wandering.
Thy heart a lonely shrine shall be,
Guarded by no divinity.
Thou shalt be lonely, and shalt know
It is thyself has made thee so.
Thou hast been faithless, and shalt dread
Deceit in aught of fondness said.
Go, with the doom thou'st made thine own!
Go, false one! to thy grave—alone.
'Twas the red hue of twilight's hour
That lighted up the forest bower;
Where that sad Pleiad looked her last.
The white wave of his plume is past;
She raised her listening head in vain,
To catch his echoing step again;
Then bowed her face upon her hand,
And once or twice a burning tear
Wandered beyond their white command,
And mingled with the waters clear.
'Tis said that ever from that day
Those waters caught their diamond ray.
The evening shades closed o'er the sky,
The night winds sang their melody:
They seemed to rouse her from the dream
That chained her by that lonely stream.
She came when first the starry lyre
Tinged the green wave with kindling fire;
"Come, sister," sang they, "to thy place."
The Pleiad gazed, then hid her face.
Slowly that lyre rose while they sung,—
Alas! there is one chord unstrung.
It rose, until CYRENE's ear
No longer could its music hear.
She sought the fountain, and flung there
The crown that bound her raven hair;
The starry crown, the sparkles died,
Darkening within its fated tide.
She sinks by that lone wave:—'tis past;
There the lost Pleiad breathed her last.
No mortal hand e'er made her grave;
But one pale rose was seen to wave,
Guarding a sudden growth of flowers,
Not like those sprung in summer hours,
But pale and drooping; each appears
As if their only due were tears.
On that sky lyre a chord is mute:
Haply one echo yet remains,
To linger on the poet's lute,
And tell in his most mournful strains,
—A star hath left its native sky,
To touch our cold earth, and to die;
To warn the young heart how it trust
To mortal vows, whose faith is dust;
To bid the young cheek guard its bloom
From wasting by such early doom;
Warn by the histories linked with all
That ever bowed to passion's thrall;
Warn by all—above—below,
By that lost Pleiad's depth of wo,—
Warn them, Love is of heavenly birth,
But turns to death on touching earth.

INEZ.

Alas! that clouds should ever steal
O'er Love's delicious sky;
That ever Love's sweet lip should feel
Aught but the gentlest sigh!

Love is a pearl of purest hue,
But stormy waves are round it;
And dearly may a woman rue
The hour that first she found it.

The lips that breathed this song were fair
As those the rose-touched Houries wear,
And dimpled by a smile, whose spell
Not even sighs could quite dispel;
And eyes of that dark azure light
Seen only at the deep midnight:
A cheek, whose crimson hues seemed caught
From the first teint by April brought
To the peach bud; and clouds of curl
Over a brow of blue-veined pearl,
Falling like sunlight, just one shade
Of chestnut on its golden braid.
Is she not all too fair to weep?
Those young eyes should be closed in sleep,
Dreaming those dreams the moonlight brings,
When the dew falls and the nightingale sings;
Dreams of a word, of a look, of a sigh,
Till the cheek burns and the heart beats high.
But Inez sits and weeps in her bower,
Pale as the gleam on the white orange-flower,
And counting the wearying moments o'er
For his return, who returns no more!

There was a time—a time of bliss,—
When to have met his Inez' kiss,
To but look in her deep-blue eye,
To breathe the air sweet with her sigh,
Young Juan would have urged his steed
With the lightning of a lover's speed,—
Ere she should have shed one single tear,
He had courted danger, and smiled at fear;
But he had parted in high disdain,
And sworn to dash from his heart the chain
Of one who, he said, was too light to be
Holy and pure in her constancy.
Alas! that woman, not content
With her peculiar element
Of gentle love, should ever try
The meteor spells of vanity!
Her world should be of love alone,
Of one fond heart and only one.
For heartless flattery, and sighs
And looks false as the rainbow's dies,
Are very worthless. And that morn
Had Juan from his Inez borne
All woman's pettiness of scorn;
Had watched for her averted eye
In vain,—had seen a rival nigh
And smiled upon: he wildly swore
To look on the false one no more.
Who thus could trifle, thus could break
A fond heart for the triumph's sake.
And yet she loved him,—O! how well,
Let woman's own fond spirit tell.
When the warriors met in their high career,
Went not her heart along with his spear?
The dance seemed sad, and the festival dim,
If her hand was unclaimed by him;
Waked she her lute, if it breathed not his name?
Lay she in dreams, but some thought of him came?
No flowers, no smiles, were on life's dull tide,
When Juan was not by his Inez' side.
And yet they parted! Still there clings
An earth-stain to the fairest things;
And love, that most delicious gift
Upon life's shrine of sorrow left,
Has its own share of suffering:
A shade falls from its radiant wing,
A spot steals o'er its sunny brow,
Fades the rose-lip's witching glow.
'Tis well,—for earth were too like heaven,
If length of life to love were given.

He has left the land of the chestnut and lime
For the cedar and rose of a southern clime,
With a pilgrim's vow and a soldier's brand,
To fight in the wars of the Holy Land.
No colors are placed on his helm beside,
No lady's scarf o'er his neck is tied,
A dark plume alone does young Juan wear:—
Look where warriors are thickest, that plume wi[ll]
be there.
But what has fame to do with one
Whose light and hope of fame are gone?
O, fame is as the moon above,
Whose sun of light and life is love.
There is more in the smile of one gentle eye
Than the thousand pages of history;
There is more in the spell of one slight gaze,
Than the loudest plaudits the crowd can raise.
Take the gems in glory's coronal,
And one smile of beauty is worth them all.

He was not lonely quite,—a shade,
A dream, a fancy, round him played;
Sometimes low, at the twilight hour,
He heard a voice like that whose power
Was on his heart: it sang a strain
Of those whose love was fond, yet vain:
Sweet like a dream,—yet none might say
Whose was the voice, or whose the lay.
And once, when worn with toil and care,
All that the soldier has to bear,
With none to sooth and none to bless
His hour of sickly loneliness,
When, waked to consciousness again,
The fire gone from his heart and brain,
He could remember some fair thing
Around his pillow hovering;
Of white arms in whose clasp he slept;
Of young blue eyes that o'er him wept;
How, when on the parched lip and brow
Burnt the red fever's hottest glow,
Some one had brought dew of the spring,
With woman's own kind solacing.
And he had heard a voice, whose thrill
Was echoed by his bosom still.
It was not hers—it could but be
A dream, the fever's phantasie. . . .

Deadly has been the fight to-day;
But now the infidels give way,
And cimeter and turbaned band
Scatter before the foeman's hand;
And in the rear, with sword and spur
Follows the Christian conqueror.
And one dark chief rides first of all—
A warrior at his festival—
Chasing his prey, till none are near
To aid the single soldier's spear,
Save one slight boy. Of those who flew
Three turn, the combat to renew;
They fly, but death is on the field—
That page's breast was Juan's shield.
He bore the boy where, in the shade
Of the green palm, a fountain made
Its pleasant music; tenderly
He laid his head upon his knee,
And from the dented helm unrolled
The blood-stained curls of summer gold
Knew he not then those deep-blue eyes
That lip of rose, and smiles, and sighs!
His Inez!—his!—could this be her,—
Thus for his sake a wanderer!
He spoke not, moved not, but sate there
A statue in his cold despair,
Watching the lip and cheek decay,
As faded life's last hue away,
While she lay sweet and motionless,
As only faint with happiness.
At length she spoke, in that sweet tone
Women and love have for their own
"This is what I have prayed might be
Has death not sealed my truth to thee!

A cypress springs by yonder grave,
And music from the fountain wave
Sings its low dirge to the pale rose
That, near, in lonely beauty blows.
Two lovers sleep beneath. O, sweet,
Even in the grave, it is to meet;
Sweet even the death-couch of stone,
When shared with some beloved one;
And sweeter than life the silent rest
Of INEZ on her JUAN's breast.

A SUMMER EVENING'S TALE.

COME, let thy careless sail float on the wind;
Come, lean by me, and let thy little boat
Follow like thee its will; come, lean by me.
Freighted with roses which the west has flung,
Over its waters on the vessel glides,
Save where the shadowy boughs shut out the sky,
And make a lovely darkness, while the wind
Stirs the sad music of their plaining leaves.
The sky grows paler, as it burnt away
Its crimson passion; and the falling dew
Seems like the tears that follow such an hour.
I'll tell thee, love, a tale,—just such a tale
As you once said my lips could breathe so well;
Speaking as poetry should speak of love,
And asking from the depths of mine own heart
The truth that touches, and by what I feel
For thee, believe what others' feelings are.
There, leave the sail, and look with earnest eyes;
Seem not as if the worldly element
In which thou movest were of thy nature part,
But yield thee to the influence of those thoughts
That haunt thy solitude;—ah, but for those
I never could have loved thee; I, who now
Live only in my other life with thee;
Out on our beings' falsehood!—studied, cold,
Are we not like that actor of old time,
Who wore his mask so long, his features took
Its likeness?—thus we feign we do not feel,
Until our feelings are forgotten things,
Their nature warped in one base selfishness;
And generous impulses, and lofty thoughts,
Are counted folly, or are not believed:
And he who doubts or mocks at excellence
(Good that refines our nature, and subdues),
Is riveted to earth by sevenfold chains.
O, never had the poet's lute a hope,
An aim so glorious as it now may have,
In this our social state, where petty cares
And mercenary interests only look
Upon the present's littleness, and shrink
From the bold future, and the stately past,—
Where the smooth surface of society
Is polished by deceit, and the warm heart
With all its kind affections' early flow,
Flung back upon itself, forgets to beat,
At least for others;—'tis the poet's gift
To melt these frozen waters into tears,
By sympathy with sorrows not our own,
By wakening memory with those mournful notes,
Whose music is the thoughts of earlier years,
When truth was on the lip, and feelings wore
The sweetness and the freshness of their morn.
Young poet, if thy dreams have not such hope
To purify, refine, exalt, subdue,
To touch the selfish, and to shame the vain
Out of themselves, by gentle mournfulness,
Or chords that rouse some aim of enterprise,
Lofty and pure, and meant for general good;
If thou hast not some power that may direct
The mind from the mean round of daily life,
Waking affections that might else have slept,
Or high resolves, the petrified before,
Or rousing in that mind a finer sense
Of inward and external loveliness,
Making imagination serve as guide
To all of heaven that yet remains on earth,—
Thine is a useless lute: break it, and die.
Love mine, I know my weakness, and I know
How far I fall short of the glorious goal
I purpose to myself; yet if one line
Has stolen from the eye unconscious tears,
Recalled one lover to fidelity,
Which is the holiness of love, or bade
One maiden sicken at cold vanity,
When dreaming o'er affection's tenderness,
The deep, the true, the honored of my song,
If but one worldly soil has been effaced,
That song has not been utterly in vain.
All true deep feeling purifies the heart.
Am I not better by my love for you?
At least, I am less selfish; I would give
My life to buy you happiness:—Hush, hush!
I must not let you know how much I love,—
So to my tale. 'Twas on an eve like this,
When purple shadows floated round, and light,
Crimson and passionate, o'er the statues fell.
Like life, for that fair gallery was filled
With statues, each one an eternity
Of thought and beauty: there were lovely shapes,
And noble ones; some which the poet's song
Had touched with its own immortality;
Others whose glory flung o'er history's page
Imperishable lustre. There she stood,
Forsaken ARIADNE; round her brow
Wreathed the glad vine leaves; but it wore a shade
Of early wretchedness, that which once flung
May never be effaced; and near her leant
ENDYMION, and his spiritual beauty wore
The likeness of divinity; for love
Doth elevate to itself, and she who watched
Over his sleeping face, upon it left
The brightness of herself. Around the walls
Hung pictures, some which gave the summer all
Summer can wish, a more eternal bloom;
And others in some young and lovely face
Imbodied dreams into reality.
There hung a portrait of St. ROSALIE,
She who renounced the world in youth, and made
Her heart an altar but for heavenly hopes—
Thrice blessed in such sacrifice. Alas!
The weakness, yet the strength of earthly ties!
Who hath not in the weariness of life
Wished for the wings of morning or the dove,
To bear them heavenward, and have wished in vain?
For wishes are effectual but by will,
And that too much is impotent and void
In frail humanity; and times steal by,
Sinful and wavering, and unredeemed.
Bent by a casement, whence her eye could dwell
Or on the countenance of that sweet saint,
Or the fair valley, where the river wound
Like to a fairy thing, now light, now shade,
Which the eye watches in its wandering,
A maiden passed each summer eve away.
Life's closing color was upon her cheek,
Crimson as that which marks the closing day.
And her large eyes, the radiant and the clear,
Wore all the ethereal beauty of that heaven
Where she was hastening. Still her rosebud mouth
Wore the voluptuous sweetness of a spring
Haunted by fragrance and by melody.
Her hair was gathered in a silken net,
As if its luxury of auburn curls
Oppressed the feverish temples all too much;
For you might see the azure pulses beat
In the clear forehead painfully; and oft
Would her small hands be pressed upon her brow,
As if to still its throbbing. Days passed by,
And thus beside that casement would she spend
The summer evenings. Well she knew her doom,
And sought to linger with such loveliness:
Surely it soothed her passage to the grave.
One gazed upon her, till his very life
Was dedicate to that idolatry
With which young Love makes offering of itself.
In the vast world he only saw her face.
The morning blush was lighted up by hope,—
The hope of meeting her; the noontide hours
Were counted for her sake; in the soft wind,
When it had passed o'er early flowers, he caught

The odor of her sigh; upon the rose
He only saw the color of her cheek.
He watched the midnight stars until they wore
Her beauty's likeness—love's astrology.
His was the gifted eye, which grace still touched
As if with second nature; and his dreams,
His childish dreams, were lit by hues from heaven—
Those which make genius. Now his visions wore
A grace more actual, and one worshipped face
Inspired the young sculptor, till like life
His spirit warmed the marble. Who shall say
The love of genius is a common thing,
Such as the many feel—half selfishness,
Half vanity?—for genius is divine,
And, like a god, doth turn its dwelling-place
Into a temple; and the heart redeemed
By its fine influence is immortal shrine
For love's divinity. In common homes
He dies, as he was born, in nothingness,
But love, inspiring genius, makes the world
Its glorious witness; hence the poet's page
Wakens its haunting sympathy of pain;
And hence the painter with a touch creates
Feelings imperishable. 'Twas from that hour
Canova took his inspiration: love
Made him the sculptor of all loveliness;
The overflowing of a soul imbued
By most ideal grace, the memory
Which lingers round first passion's sepulchre.
—Why do I say first love?—there is no second.
Who asks in the same year a second growth
Of spring leaves from the tree, corn from the field?—
They are exhausted. Thus 'tis with the heart;
'Tis not so rich in feeling or in hope
To bear that one be crushed, the other faded,
Yet find them ready to put forth again.
It does not always last; man's temper is
Often forgetful, fickle, and throws down
The temple he can never build again;
But when it does last, and that asks for much,—
A fixed yet passionate spirit, and a mind
Master of its resolves,—when that love lasts,
It is in noblest natures. After years
Tell how Canova felt the influence.
They never spoke: she looked too spiritual,
Too pure for human passion; and her face
Seemed hallowed by the heaven it was so near.
And days passed on: is was an eve in June—
How ever could it be so fair a one?
And she came not: hue after hue forsook
The clouds, like Hope, which died with them, and night
Came all too soon and shadowy. He rose,
And wandered through the city, o'er which hung
The darkness of his thoughts. At length a strain
Of ominous music wailed along the streets:
It was the mournful chanting for the dead,
And the long tapers flung upon the air
A wild red light, and showed the funeral train:
Wreaths—O what mockeries!—hung from th[illegible];
And there, pale, beautiful, as if in sleep.
Her dark hair braided graceful with white flowers,
She lay,—his own beloved one!
No more, no more!—love, turn thy boat to land,—
I am so sorrowful at my own words.
Affection is an awful thing! Alas!
We give our destiny from our own hands,
And trust to those most frail of all frail things,
The chances of humanity.
The wind hath a deep sound, more stern than sweet;
And the dark sky is clouded; tremulous,
A few far stars—how pale they look to-night!—
Touch the still waters with a fitful light.
There is strange sympathy between all things,
Though in the hurrying weariness of life
We do not pause to note it: the glad day,
Like a young king surrounded by the pomp
Of gold and purple, sinks but to the shade
Of the black night:—the chronicle I told
Began with hope, fair skies, and lovely shapes,
And ended in despair. Even thus our life
In these has likeness; with its many joys,
Its fears, its eagerness, its varying page,
Marked with its thousand colors, only tends
To darkness, and to silence, and the grave!

THE PAINTER'S LOVE.

Your skies are blue, your sun is bright;
But sky nor sun has that sweet light
Which gleamed upon the summer sky
Of my own lovely Italy!
'Tis long since I have breathed the air,
Which, filled with odors, floated there,—
Sometimes in sleep a gale sweeps by,
Rich with the rose and myrtle's sigh;
'Tis long since I have seen the vine
With Autumn's topaz clusters shine;
And watched the laden branches bending
And heard the vintage songs ascending,
'Tis very long since I have seen
The ivy's death wreath, cold and green,
Hung round the old and broken stone
Raised by the hands now dead and gone!
I do remember one lone spot,
By most unnoticed or forgot—
Would that I too recalled it not!
It was a little temple, gray—
With half its pillars worn away,
No roof left,—but one cypress tree
Flinging its branches mournfully:
In ancient days this was a shrine
For goddess or for nymph divine.
And sometimes I have dreamed I heard
A step soft as a lover's word,
And caught a perfume on the air,
And saw a shadow gliding fair,
Dim, sad as if it came to sigh
O'er thoughts, and things, and time passed by
On one side of the temple stood
A deep and solitary wood,
Where chestnuts reared their giant length,
And mocked the fallen columns strength;
It was the lone wood-pigeon's home,
And flocks of them would ofttimes come
And, lighting on the temple, pour
A cooing dirge to days no more!
And by its side there was a lake
With only snow-white swans to break,
With ebon feet and silver wing,
The quiet waters' glittering.
And when sometimes, as eve closed in,
I waked my lonely mandolin,
The gentle birds came gliding near,
As if they loved that song to hear.

'Tis past, 'tis past, my happiness
Was all too pure and passionless!
I waked from calm and pleasant dreams
To watch the morning's earliest gleams,
Wandering with light feet 'mid the dew,
Till my cheek caught its rosy hue;
And when uprose the bright-eyed moon,
I sorrowed day was done so soon;
Save that I loved the sweet starlight,
The soft, the happy sleep of night!

Time has changed since, and I have wept
The day away; and when I slept,
My sleeping eyes ceased not their tears;
And jealousies, griefs, hopes, and fears,
Even in slumber held their reign,
And gnawed my heart, and racked my brain
O much,—most withering 'tis to feel
The hours like guilty creatures steal,
To wish the weary day was past,
And yet to have no hope at last!
All's in that curse, aught else above,
That fell on me—betrayed love!

There was a stranger sought our land,
A youth, who with a painter's hand
Traced our sweet valleys and our vines,
The moonlight on the ruined shrines.

And now and then the brow of pearl
And black eyes of the peasant girl:
We met and loved—ah! even now
My pulse throbs to recall that vow
Our first kiss sealed, we stood beneath
The cypress tree's funereal wreath,
That temple's roof. But what thought I
Of aught like evil augury!
I only felt his burning sighs,
I only looked within his eyes,
I saw no dooming star above,
There is such happiness in love!
I left, with him, my native shore,
Not as a bride who passes o'er
Her father's threshold with his blessing,
With flowers strewn and friends caressing,
Kind words, and purest hopes to cheer
The bashfulness of maiden fear;
But I—I fled as culprits fly,
By night, watched only by one eye,
Whose look was all the world to me,
And it met mine so tenderly,
I thought not of the days to come,
I thought not of my own sweet home,
Nor of mine aged father's sorrow,—
Wild love takes no thought for to-morrow.
I left my home, and I was left
A stranger in his land, bereft
Of even hope; there was not one
Familiar face to look upon.—
Their speech was strange. This penalty
Was meet; but surely not from thee,
False love!—'twas not for thee to break
The heart but sullied for thy sake!

I could have wished once more to see
Thy [illegible] hills, loveliest ITALY!
I coul[illegible] wished yet to have hung
Upon the music of thy tongue;
I could have wished thy flowers to bloom—
Thy cypress planted by the tomb!
This wish is vain,—my grave must be
Far distant from my own country!
I must rest here. O lay me then
By the white church in yonder glen,
Amid the darkening elms, it seems,
Thus silvered over by the beams
Of the pale moon, a very shrine
For wounded hearts—it shall be mine!
There is one corner, green and lone,
A dark yew over it has thrown
Long, nightlike boughs; 'tis thickly set
With primrose and with violet.
Their bloom's now past; but in the spring
They will be sweet and glistening.
There is a bird, too, of your clime,
That sings there in the winter time;
My funeral hymn his song will be,
Which there are none to chant, save he;
And let there be memorial none,
No name upon the cold white stone:
The only heart where I would be
Remembered, is now dead to me!
I would not even have him weep
O'er his Italian's love last sleep.
O, tears are a most worthless token
When hearts they would have soothed are broken!

LOVE'S LAST LESSON.

TEACH it me, if you can,—forgetfulness
I surely shall forget, if you can bid me;
I who have worshipped thee, my god on earth,
I who have bowed me at thy lightest word.
Your last command, "Forget me," will it not
Sink deeply down within my inmost soul?
Forget thee!—ay, forgetfulness will be
A mercy to me. By the many nights
When I have wept for that I dared not sleep,—
A dream had made me live my woes again,
Acting my wretchedness, without the hope
My foolish heart still clings to, though that hope
Is like the opiate which may lull a while,
Then wake to double torture; by the days
Passed in lone watching and in anxious fears,
When a breath sent the crimson to my cheek,
Like the red gushing of a sudden wound;
By all the careless looks and careless words
Which have to me been like the scorpion's stinging;
By happiness blighted, and by thee, for ever;
By the eternal work of wretchedness;
By all my withered feelings, ruined health,
Crushed hopes, and rifled heart, I will forget thee!
Alas! my words are vanity. Forget thee!
Thy work of wasting is too surely done.
The April shower may pass and be forgotten,
The rose fall and one fresh spring in its place,
And thus it may be with light summer love.
It was not thus with mine: it did not spring,
Like the bright color on an evening cloud,
Into a moment's life, brief, beautiful;
Not amid lighted halls, when flatteries
Steal on the ear like dew upon the rose,
As soft, as soon dispersed, as quickly passed;
But you first called my woman's feelings forth,
And taught me love ere I had dreamed love's name.
I loved unconsciously; your name was all
That seemed in language, and to me the world
Was only made for you; in solitude,
When passions hold their interchange together,
Your image was the shadow of my thought;
Never did slave, before his Eastern lord,
Tremble as I did when I met your eye,
And yet each look was counted as a prize;
I laid your words up in my heart like pearls
Hid in the ocean's treasure cave. At last
I learned my heart's deep secret: for I hoped,
I dreamed you loved me; wonder, fear, delight,
Swept my heart like a storm; my soul, my life,
Seemed all too little for your happiness;
Had I been mistress of the starry worlds
That light the midnight, they had all been yours,
And I had deemed such boon but poverty.
As it was, I gave all I could—my love,
My deep, my true, my fervent, faithful love;
And now you bid me learn forgetfulness:
It is a lesson that I soon shall learn.
There is a home of quiet for the wretched,
A somewhat dark, and cold, and silent rest,
But still it is rest,—for it is the grave.

She flung aside the scroll, as it had part
In her great misery. Why should she write?
What could she write? Her woman's pride forbad
To let him look upon her heart, and see
It was an utter ruin;—and cold words,
And scorn and slight, that may repay his own,
Were as a foreign language, to whose sound
She might not frame her utterance. Down she bent
Her head upon an arm so white that tears
Seemed but the natural melting of its snow,
Touched by the flushed cheek's crimson; yet life-blood
Less wrings in shedding than such tears as those.

And this then is love's ending! It is like
The history of some fair southern clime.
Hot fires are in the bosom of the earth,
And the warmed soil puts forth its thousand flowers,
Its fruits of gold, summer's regality,
And sleep and odors float upon the air:
At length the subterranean element
Breaks from its secret dwelling-place, and lays
All waste before it; the red lava stream
Sweeps like the pestilence; and that which was
A garden in its colors and its breath,
Fit for the princes of a fairy tale,
Is as a desert, in whose burning sands,
And ashy waters, who is there can trace
A sign, a memory of its former beauty?
It is thus with the heart; love lights it up
With hopes like young companions, and w[illegible]
Dreaming deliciously of their sweet selves.

This is at first; but what is the result?
Hopes that lie mute in their own sullenness,

For they have quarrelled even with themselves;
And joys indeed like birds of Paradise:*
And in their stead despair coils scorpionlike
Stinging itself; and the heart, burnt and crushed
With passion's earthquake, scorched and withered up,
Lies in its desolation,—this is love.

What is the tale that I would tell? Not one
Of strange adventure, but a common tale
Of woman's wretchedness; one to be read
Daily in many a young and blighted heart.
The lady whom I spake of rose again
From the red fever's couch, to careless eyes
Perchance the same as she had ever been.
But O, how altered to herself! She felt
That birdlike pining for some gentle home
To which affection might attach itself.
That weariness which hath but outward part
In what the world calls pleasure, and that chill
Which makes life taste the bitterness of death.

And he she loved so well,—what opiate
Lulled consciousness into its selfish sleep?—
He said he loved her not; that never vow
Or passionate pleading won her soul for him;
And that he guessed not her deep tenderness.

Are words, then, only false? are there no looks,
Mute but most eloquent; no gentle cares
That win so much upon the fair weak things
They seem to guard? And had he not long read
Her heart's hushed secret in the soft dark eye
Lighted at his approach, and on the cheek
Coloring all crimson at his lightest look?
This is the truth; his spirit wholly turned
To stem ambition's dream, to that fierce strife
Which leads to life's high places, and recked not
What lovely flowers might perish in his path.

And here at length is somewhat of revenge:
For man's most golden dreams of pride and power
Are vain as any woman-dreams of love;
Both end in weary brow and withered heart,
And the grave closes over those whose hopes
Have lain there long before.

A VILLAGE TALE.

. . . . How the spirit clings
To that which once it loved, with the same feeling
That makes the traveller turn from his way
To look upon some boyish haunt, though dark
And very desolate grown, no longer like
That which was dear to him.

It was a low white church: the elm which grew
Beside it shadowed half the roof; the clock
Was placed where full the sunbeams fell;—what deep,
Simple morality spoke in those hands,
Going their way in silence, till a sound,
Solemn and sweet, made their appeal to Time,
And the hour spoke its only warning!—Strange
To note how mute the soft song of the wren,
Whose nest was in that old elm tree, became
When the clock struck: and when it ceased again,
Its music like a natural anthem breathed.
Lowly the osiered graves around, wild flowers
Their epitaph, and not one monument
Was there rich with the sculptor's graceful art.
There sat one, by a grave whose weeded turf
Showed more than common care, his face bent down,
A fine and manly brow, though sun and wind
Had darkened it, and that a shade of grief
Seemed natural from long habit; by his side
A little laughing child, with clear blue eyes,
Cheek like a dimpled rose, and sunny curls,
Was gathering blossoms, gathering but to crush,
Till the sod was all colors with the leaves.
Even in childhood's innocence of pleasure
Lives that destroying spirit which in time
Will waste, then want, the best of happiness.
I marked the boy's companion: he was yet
In life's first summer; and he seemed to watch
With such sad tenderness the child, which came
When tired to nestle in his bosom, sure
That it was welcome,—and the grave was kept
So fresh, so green, so covered with sweet flowers,
I deemed 'twas some young widower, whose love
Had passed away, or ever it had known
One sting of sorrow or one cloud of care,—
Passed in its first delicious confidence
Of vow'd affection;—'twas the grave, I thought,
Of his young wife, and that the child was left
A dear memorial of that cherished one.
I read his history wrong. In early youth,
When hopes and pleasures flit like butterflies
Around our pleasant spring, had Edward loved,
And sought in Marion's deep blue eyes his world,—
Loved with the truth, the fervor of first love,
That delicate bloom which can come o'er the soul
But only once. All other thoughts and feelings
The heart may know again, but first love never!
Its hopes, bright as the azure flower that springs
Where'er the radiance of the rainbow falls;
Its fears, soft as the leaves that shade the lily;
Its fairyland romance, its tenderness,
Its timid, and yet passionate devotion—
These are not annual blooms, that die, then rise
Again into another summer world.
They may live long, and be the life of life,
But, like the rose, when they are once destroyed
They perish utterly. And, like that tree,
How sweet a memory, too, remains! though dead
The green leaves, and decayed the stem, yet still
The spirit of fragrance lingers, loath to leave
Its dear abode. Just so love haunts the heart,
Though withered, and to be revived no more.
O, nothing has the memory of love!
It was a summer twilight; crimson lights
Played o'er the bridal bowers of the west,
And in the gray horizon the white moon
Was faintly visible, just where the sky
Met the green rolling of the shadowy sea.
Upon a little hill, whose broken ridge
Was covered with the golden furze and heath
Gay with its small pink blossoms, in a shade
Formed of thick hazels and the graceful sweep
Of the ash-boughs, an old beach-trunk the seat,
With a sweet canopy of honeysuckle
Mixed with the wild brier-roses, Edward sat,
Happy, for Marion leaned upon his bosom
In the deep fondness of the parting hour;
One of those partings memory will keep
Among its precious things. The setting sun
Shed such rich color o'er the cheek, which pressed
Closer and closer, like a rose, that sought
A shelter next his heart; the radiant eyes,
Glorious as though the sky's own light were there,
Yet timid, blue, and tender as the dove's;
The soft arm thrown around his neck; the hair
Falling in such profusion o'er a face
That nestled like a bird upon his breast.
Murmurs, the very breath of happiness;
Low and delighted sighs, and lengthened looks,
As life were looking words inaudible,
Yet full of music; whispers such as are
What love should ever speak in, soft yet deep,
As jealous even that the air should share
In the delicious feeling. And around,
All seemed the home and atmosphere of love:
The air sweet with the woodbine and the rose;
The rich red light of evening; the far sea,
So still, so calm; the vale, with its cornfields
Shooting their green spears 'mid the scarlet banners
Of the wild poppies; meadows with the hay
Scattered in fragrance, clover yet uncut.
And in the distance a small wood, where oaks
And elms threw giant shadows; and a river
Winding, now hidden and now visible,
Till close beside their bower it held its course,
And fed a little waterfall, the harp
That answered to the woodlark's twilight hymn
Their last, last evening! Ah, the many vows
That Edward and his Marion pledged! She took
A golden ring and broke it, hid one half

* In Eastern tales, the bird of Paradise never rests on earth.

Next her own heart, then cut a shining curl,
As bright as the bright gift, and round his neck
Fastened the silken braid, and bade him keep
The ring and hair for Marion's sake. They talked
Of pleasant hopes, of Edward's quick return
With treasure gathered on the stormy deep,
And how they then would build a little cot;
They choose the very place; and the bright moon
Shone in her midnight, ere their schemes
Were half complete. They parted. The next morn
With the day-blush had Marion sought the bower
Alone, and watched upon the distant sea
A ship just visible to those long looks
With which love gazes. . . . How most sweet it is
To have one lonely treasure, which the heart
Can feed upon in secret, which can be
A star in sorrow, and a flower in joy;
A thought to which all other thoughts refer;
A hope, from whence all other hopes arise,
Nursed in the solitude of happiness!
Love, passionate young Love, how sweet it is
To have the bosom made a Paradise
By thee—life lighted by thy rainbow smile!
Edward lived in one feeling, one that made
Care, toil, and suffering pleasant; and he hailed
England, dear England, happy in success,
In hope, and love. It was a summer morn—
The very season he had left that vale—
When he returned. How cheerfully the fields,
Spread in their green luxuriance of corn,
The purple clover, and the newcut hay,
Loading the air with fragrance! the soft river
Winding so gently! there seemed nothing changed,
And Edward's heart was filled with gladness: all
He fancied, looked as if they welcomed him.
His eyes filled with sweet tears, and hasty words
Of love and thankfulness came to his lips.
His path lay through the churchyard, and the bells
Were ringing for a wedding. What fond thoughts
They wakened, of how merrily their round
Would peal for him and Marion! He kissed
The broken ring, the braid of golden hair,
And bounded, with light step and lighter heart,
Across the churchyard; from it he could see
The cottage where his own true maiden dwelt.
Just then the bridal party left the church,
And, half unconsciously, young Edward looked
Upon the bride—that bride was Marion!
He stopped not in the village,—spoke to none,—
But went again to sea; and never smile
Lighted the settled darkness in his eyes:
His cheek grew pale, his hair turned gray, his voice
Became so sad and low. He once had loved
To look upon the sunset, as that hour
Brought pleasant memories, such as feed sweet hopes;
Now ever gazed he on it with the look
Of the young widow over her fair child,
Her only child, in the death agony.
His heart was withered. Yet, although so false,
He never parted with his Marion's gift:
Still the soft curl and the bright ring were kept,
Like treasures, in his bosom. Years passed by,
And he grew tired of wandering; back he came
To his own village, as a place of rest.
'Twas a drear autumn morning, and the trees
Were bare, or covered but with yellow leaves;
The fields lay fallow, and a drizzling rain
Fell gloomily: it seemed as all was changed,
Even as he himself was changed; the bell
Of the old church was tolling dolefully
The farewell of the living to the dead.
The grave was scant, the holy words were said
Hurriedly, coldly; but for a poor child,
That begged the pit to give him back his mother,
There had not been one single tear. The boy
Kept on his wail; but all his prayers were made
To the dark tomb, as conscious those around
Would chide if he asked them; and when they threw
The last earth on the coffin, down he laid
His little head, and sobbed most bitterly.
And Edward took him in his arms, and kissed
His wet pale cheeks; while the child clung to him,
Not with the shyness of one petted, loved,
And careless of a stranger's fond caress,
But like one knowing well what kindness was
But knew not where to seek it, as he pined
Beneath neglect and harshness, fear and want.
'Twas strange, this mingling of their destinies:
That boy was Marion's—it was Marion's grave!
She had died young, and poor, and broken-hearted.
Her husband had deserted her: one child
Was buried with its mother, one was left
An orphan unto chance; but Edward took
The boy unto him even as his own.
He buried the remembrance of his wrongs,
Only recalling that he once had loved,
And that his love was dead.

THE INDIAN GIRL.

She sat alone beside her hearth—
  For many nights alone;
She slept not on the pleasant couch
  Where fragrant herbs were strown.

At first she bound her raven hair
  With feather and with shell;
But then she hoped; at length, like night,
  Around her neck it fell.

They saw her wandering 'mid the woods,
  Lone, with the cheerless dawn,
And then they said, "Can this be her
  We called 'The Startled Fawn.'"

Her heart was in her large sad eyes,
  Half sunshine and half shade;
And love, as love first springs to life,
  Of everything afraid.

The red leaf far more heavily
  Fell down to autumn earth,
Than her light feet, which seemed to move
  To music and to mirth.

With the light feet of early youth,
  What hopes and joys depart!
Ah! nothing like the heavy step
  Betrays the heavy heart.

It is a usual history
  That Indian girl could tell;
Fate sets apart one common doom
  For all who love too well.

The proud—the shy—the sensitive,—
  Life has not many such;
They dearly buy their happiness,
  By feeling it too much.

A stranger to her forest home,
  That fair young stranger came
They raised for him the funeral song—
  For him the funeral flame.

Love sprang from pity,—and her arms
  Around his arms she threw;
She told her father, "If he dies,
  Your daughter dieth too."

For her sweet sake they set him free—
  He lingered at her side;
And many a native song yet tells
  Of that pale stranger's bride.

Two years have passed—how much two years
  Have taken in their flight!
They've taken from the lip its smile,
  And from the eye its light.

Poor child! she was a child in years—
  So timid and so young;
With what a fond and earnest faith
  To desperate hope she clung!

His eyes grew cold—his voice grew strange—
They only grew more dear.
She served him meekly, anxiously,
With love—half faith, half fear.

And can a fond and faithful heart
Be worthless in those eyes
For which it beats?—Ah! wo to those
Who such a heart despise.

Poor child! what lonely days she passed.
With nothing to recall
But bitter taunts, and careless words,
And looks more cold than all.

Alas! for love, that sits at home,
Forsaken, and yet fond;
The grief that sits beside the hearth,
Life hast no grief beyond.

He left her, but she followed him—
She thought he could not bear
When she had left her home for him
To look on her despair.

Adown the strange and mighty stream
She took her lonely way!
The stars at night her pilots were,
As was the sun by day.

Yet mournfully—how mournfully;—
The Indian looked behind,
When the last sound of voice or step
Died on the midnight wind.

Yet still adown the gloomy stream
She plied her weary oar;
Her husband—he had left their home,
And it was home no more.

She found him—but she found in vain—
He spurned her from his side;
He said, her brow was all too dark,
For her to be his bride.

She grasped his hands,—her own were cold,—
And silent turned away,
As she had not a tear to shed,
And not a word to say.

And pale as death she reached her boat,
And guided it along;
With broken voice she strove to raise
A melancholy song.

None watched the lonely Indian girl,—
She passed unmarked of all,
Until they saw her slight canoe
Approach the mighty Fall!*

Upright, within that slender boat
They saw the pale girl stand,
Her dark hair streaming far behind—
Upraised her desperate hand.

The air is filled with shriek and shout—
They call, but call in vain;
The boat amid the waters dashed—
'Twas never seen again!

THE LILY OF THE VALLEY.

" A fair young face—yet mournful in its youth—
Brooding above sad thoughts."

It is the last token of love and of thee!
Thy once faith is broken, thou false one to me.
I think on the letters with which I must part;
Too dear are the fetters which wind round my heart.

Thy words were enchanted—and ruled me at will;
My spirit is haunted, remembering them still.
So earnest, so tender—the full heart was there;
Ah! song might surrender its lute in despair.

* Niagara.

I deemed that I knew thee as none ever knew;
That 'twas mine to subdue thee, and thine to be true.
I deemed to my keeping thy memory had brought
The depths that were sleeping of innermost thought.

The bitter concealings life's treacheries teach,
The long-subdued feelings the world can not reach—
Thy mask to the many was worn not for me;
I saw thee—can any seem like unto thee?

No other can know thee as I, love, have known,
No future will show thee a love like mine own.
That love was no passion that walketh by day,
A fancy—a fashion that flitteth away.

'Twas life's whole emotion—a storm in its might—
'Twas deep as the ocean, and silent as night.
It swept down life's flowers, the fragile and fair,
The heart had no powers from passion to spare.

Thy faults but endeared thee, so stormy and wild
My lover! I feared thee as feareth a child.
They seemed but the shrouding of spirit too high,
As vapors come crowding the sunniest sky.

I worshipped in terror a comet above;
Ah! fatal the error—ah! fatal the love!
For thy sake life never will charm me again;
Its beauty for ever is vanished and vain.

Thou canst not restore me the depth and the truth
Of the hopes that come o'er me in earliest youth.
Their gloss is departed—their magic is flown,
And sad and faint-hearted I wander alone.

'Tis vain to regret me—you will not regret;
You will try to forget me—you can not forget.
We shall hear of each other—O! misery to hear
Those names from another that once were so dear!

What slight words will sting us that breathe of the past
And slight things will bring us thoughts fated to last.
The fond hopes that centred in thee are all dead,
But the iron has entered the soul where they fed.

Like others in seeming, we'll walk through life's part,
Cold, careless, and dreaming—with death in the heart,
No hope—no repentance; the spring of life o'er;
All died with that sentence——I love thee no more!

CAN YOU FORGET ME?

Can you forget me?—I who have so cherished
The veriest trifle that was memory's link;
The roses that you gave me, although perished,
Were precious in my sight; they made me think
You took them in their scentless beauty stooping
From the warm shelter of the garden wall;
Autumn, while into languid winter drooping,
Gave its last blossoms, opening but to fall.
Can you forget them?

Can you forget me? I am not relying
On plighted vows—alas! I know their worth.
Man's faith to woman is a trifle, dying
Upon the very breath that gave it birth
But I remember hours of quiet gladness,
When, if the heart had truth, it spoke it then,
When thoughts would sometimes take a tone of sadness
And then unconsciously grow glad again.
Can you forget them?

Can you forget me? My whole soul was blended:
At least it sought to blend itself with thine;
My life's whole purpose, winning thee, seemed ended;
Thou wert my heart's sweet home—my spirit's shrine.
Can you forget me?—when the firelight burning,
Flung sudden gleams around the quiet room,
How would thy words, to long past moments turning,
Trust me with thoughts soft as the shadowy gloom!
Can you forget them?

There is no truth in love, whate'er its seeming,
And heaven itself could scarcely seem more true—
Sadly have I awakened from the dreaming,
Whose charmed slumber—false one!—was of you.
I gave mine inmost being to thy keeping—
I had no thought I did not seek to share;
Feelings that hushed within my soul were sleeping,
Waked into voice, to trust them to thy care.
Can you forget them?

Can you forget me? This is vainly tasking
The faithless heart where I, alas! am not.
Too well I know the idleness of asking—
The misery—of why am I forgot?
The happy hours that I have passed while kneeling
Half slave, half child, to gaze upon thy face.
—But what to thee this passionate appealing—
Let my heart break—it is a common case.
You have forgotten me.

DISENCHANTMENT.

Do not ask me why I loved him,
Love's cause is to love unknown;
Faithless as the past has proved him,
Once his heart appeared mine own.
Do not say he did not merit
All my fondness, all my truth;
Those in whom love dwells inherit
Every dream that haunted youth.

He might not be all I dreamed him,
Noble, generous, gifted, true,
Not the less I fondly deemed him,
All those flattering visions drew.
All the hues of old romances
By his actual self grew dim;
Bitterly I mock the fancies
That once found their life in him.

From the hour by him enchanted,
From the moment when we met,
Henceforth with one image haunted,
Life may never more forget.
All my nature changed—his being
Seemed the only source of mine.
Fond heart, hadst thou no foreseeing
Thy sad future to divine?

Once, upon myself relying,
All I asked were words and thought;
Many hearts to mine replying,
Owned the music that I brought.
Eager, spiritual, and lonely,
Visions filled the fairy hour,
Deep with love—though love was only
Not a presence, but a power.

But from that first hour I met thee,
All caught actual life from you.
Alas! how can I forget thee,
Thou who madest the fancied true?
Once my wide world was ideal,
Fair it was—ah! very fair;
Wherefore hast thou made it real?
Wherefore is thy image there?

Ah! no more to me is given
Fancy's far and fairy birth;
Chords upon my lute are riven,
Never more to sound on earth.
Once, sweet music could it borrow
From a look, a word, a tone;
I could paint another's sorrow—
Now I think but of mine own.

Life's dark waves have lost the glitter
Which at morning-tide they wore,
And the well within is bitter;
Naught its sweetness may restore:
For I know how vainly given
Life's most precious things may be,
Love that might have looked on heaven,
Even as it looked on thee.

Ah, farewell!—with that word dying,
Hope and love must perish too:
For thy sake themselves denying,
What is truth with thee untrue?
Farewell!—'tis a dreary sentence,
Like the death-doom of the grave,
May it wake in thee repentance,
Stinging when too late to save!

THE CHANGE.

Thy features do not wear the light
They wore in happier days;
Though still there may be much to love,
There's little left to praise.

The rose has faded from thy cheek—
There's scarce a blush left now;
And there's a dark and weary sign
Upon thine altered brow.

Thy raven hair is dashed with gray,
Thine eyes are dim with tears;
And care, before thy youth is past,
Has done the work of years.

Beautiful wreck! for still thy face,
Though changed, is very fair:
Like beauty's moonlight, left to show
Her morning sun was there.

Come, here are friends and festival,
Recall thine early smile;
And wear yon wreath, whose glad red rose
Will lend its bloom awhile.

Come, take thy lute, and sing again
The song you used to sing—
The birdlike song:—See, though unused,
The lute has every string,

What, doth thy hand forget the lute?
Thy brow reject the wreath?
Alas! whate'er the change above,
There's more of change beneath!

The smile may come, the smile may go,
The blush shine and depart;
But farewell when their sense is quenched
Within the breaking heart.

And such is thine: 'tis vain to seek
The shades of past delight:
Fling down the wreath, and break the lute;
They mock our souls to-night.

LOVE.

She prest her slight hand to her brow, or pain
Or bitter thoughts were passing there. The room
Had no light but that from the fireside,
Which showed, then hid her face. How very pale
It looked when over it the glimmer shone!
Is not the rose companion of the spring?
Then wherefore has the red-leaved flower forgotten
Her cheek? The tears stood in her large dark eyes—
Her beautiful dark eyes—like hyacinth stars,
When shines their shadowy glory through the dew
That summer nights have wept;—she felt them not,
Her heart was far away! Her fragile form,
Like the young willow when from the first time
The wind sweeps o'er it rudely, had not lost
Its own peculiar grace; but it was bowed
By sickness, or by worse than sickness—sorrow!
And thus is Love!—O! why should woman love;
Wasting her dearest feelings, till health, hope,
Happiness, are but things of which henceforth
She'll only know the name? Her heart is seared.
A sweet light has been thrown upon its life,
To make its darkness the more terrible.
And this is Love!

JULIET AFTER THE MASQUERADE.

She left the festival, for it seemed dim
Now that her eye no longer dwelt on him,
And sought her chamber,—gazed (then turned away)
Upon a mirror that before her lay,
Half fearing, half believing her sweet face
Would surely claim within his memory place.
The hour was late, and that night her light foot
Had been the constant echo of the lute;
Yet sought she not her pillow, the cool air
Came from the casement, and it lured her there.
The terrace was beneath, and the pale moon
Shone o'er the couch which she had pressed at noon,
Soft-lingering o'er some minstrel's lovelorn page,—
Alas, tears are the poet's heritage!

She flung her on that couch, but not for sleep;
No, it was only that the wind might steep
Her fevered lip in its delicious dew:
Her brow was burning, and aside she threw
Her cap and plume, and, loosened from its fold,
Came o'er her neck and face a shower of gold,
A thousand curls. It was a solitude
Made for young hearts in love's first dreaming mood:—
Beneath the garden lay, filled with rose trees
Whose sighings came like passion on the breeze.
Two graceful statues of the Parian stone
So finely shaped, that as the moonlight shone
The breath of life seemed to their beauty given,
But less the life of earth than that of heaven.
'Twas Psyche and her boy-god, so divine
They turned the terrace to an idol shrine,
With its white vases and their summer share
Of flowers, like altars raised to that sweet pair.

And there the maiden leant, still in her ear
The whisper dwelt of that young cavalier;
It was no fancy, he had named the name
Of love, and at that thought her cheek grew flame:
It was the first time her young ear had heard
A lover's burning sigh, or silver word;
Her thoughts were all confusion, but most sweet,—
Her heart beat high, but pleasant was its beat.
She murmured over many a snatch of song
That might to her own feelings now belong;
She thought upon old histories she had read,
And placed herself in each high heroine's stead,
Then woke her lute,—O! there is little known
Of music's power till aided by love's own.
And this is happiness: O! love will last
When all that made it happiness is past,—
When all its hopes are as the glittering toys
Time present offers, time to come destroys,—
When they have been too often crushed to earth,
For further blindness to their little worth,—
When fond illusions have dropt one by one,
Like pearls from a rich carkanet, till none
Are left upon life's soiled and naked string,—
And this is all what time will ever bring.
—And that fair girl,—what can the heart foresee
Of her young love, and of its destiny?
There is a white cloud o'er the moon, its form
Is very light, and yet there sleeps the storm:
It is an omen, it may tell the fate
Of love known all too soon, repented all too late.

THE FAIRY QUEEN SLEEPING.

She lay upon a bank, the favorite haunt
Of the spring wind in its first sunshine hour,
For the luxuriant strawberry blossoms spread
Like a snow-shower there, and violets
Bowed down their purple vases of perfume
About her pillow,—linked in a gay band
Floated fantastic shapes, these were her guards,
Her lithe and rainbow elves.

We have been o'er land and sea
Seeking lovely dreams for thee,—
Where is there we have not been
Gathering gifts for our sweet queen?
We are come with sound and sight
Fit for fairy's sleep to-night,—
First around thy couch shall sweep
Odors, such as roses weep
When the earliest spring rain
Calls them into life again;
Next upon thine ear shall float
Many a low and silver note,
Stolen from a darkeyed maid
When her lover's serenade,
Rising as the stars grew dim,
Wakened from her thoughts of him.
There shall steal o'er lip and cheek
Gales, but all too light to break
Thy soft rest,—such gales as hide
All day orange-flowers inside,
Or that, while hot noontide, dwell
In the purple hyacinth bell;
And before thy sleeping eyes
Shall come glorious pageantries,
Palaces of gems and gold,
Such as dazzle to behold.—
Gardens, in which every tree
Seems a world of bloom to be,—
Fountains, whose clear waters show
The white pearls that lie below.—
During slumber's magic reign
Other times shall live again;
First thou shalt be young and free
In thy days of liberty,—
Then again be wooed and won
By the stately Oberon.
Or thou shalt descend to earth,
And see all of mortal birth.
No, that world's too full of care
For e'en dreams to linger there.
But, behold, the sun is set,
And the diamond coronet
Of the young moon is on high
Waiting for our revelry;
And the dew is on the flower,
And the stars proclaim our hour;
Long enough thy rest has been,
Wake, Titania, wake our queen!

A CHILD SCREENING A DOVE FROM A HAWK.

Ay, screen thy favorite dove, fair child,
Ay, screen it if you may,—
Yet I misdoubt thy trembling hand
Will scare the hawk away.

That dove will die, that child will weep,—
Is this their destinie?
Ever amid the sweets of life
Some evil thing must be.

Ay, moralize,—is it not thus
We've mourned our hope and love?
Alas! there's tears for every eye,
A hawk for every dove.

LINES

WRITTEN UNDER A PICTURE OF A GIRL BURNING A LOVE LETTER.

The lines were filled with many a tender thing,
All the impassioned heart's fond communing

I took the scroll: I could not brook,
An eye to gaze on it save mine;
I could not bear another look
Should dwell upon one thought of thine.
My lamp was burning by my side,
I held thy letter to the flame,
I marked the blaze swift o'er it glide,
It did not even spare thy name.
Soon the light from the embers past,
I felt so sad to see it die,
So bright at first, so dark at last,
I feared it was love's history.

CUPID AND SWALLOWS FLYING FROM WINTER.

"We fly from the cold."

Away, away, o'er land and sea,
This is now no home for me;
My light wings may never bear
Northern cloud or winter air.
Murky shades are gathering fast,
Sleet and snow are on the blast,
Trees from which the leaves are fled,
Flowers whose very roots are dead,
Grass of its green blade bereft,
These are all that now are left.
—Linger here another day,
I shall be as sad as they;
My companions fly with spring,
I too must be on the wing.

Where are the sweet gales whose song
Wont to waft my darts along?
Scented airs! O, not like these,
Rough as they which sweep the seas;
But those sighs of rose which bring
Incense from their wandering.
Where are the bright flowers that kept
Guard around me while I slept?
Where the sunny eyes whose beams
Wakened me from my soft dreams?
These are with the swallows gone,—
Beauty's heart is chilled to stone.

O! for some sweet southern clime,
Where 'tis ever summer time.—
Where, if blossoms fall, their tomb
Is amid new birth of bloom,—
Where green leaves are ever springing,
Where the lark is always singing,—
One of those bright isles which lie
Fair beneath an azure sky,
Isles of cinnamon and spice,
Shadow each of Paradise,—
Where the flowers shine with dies,
Teinted bright from the sunrise,—
Where the birds which drink their dew,
Wave wings of yet brighter hue,
And each river's course is rolled
Over bed of pearl and gold!

O! for those lime-scented groves
Where the Spanish lover roves,
Tuning to the western star,
His soft song and light guitar,—
Where the dark-haired girls are dancing
Fairies in the moonlight glancing,
With pencilled brows, and radiant eyes,
Like their planet-lighted skies!
Or those clear Italian lakes
Where the silver cygnet makes
Its soft nest of leaf and flower,
A white lily for its bower!
Each of these a home would be,
Fit for beauty and for me:
I must seek their happier sphere
While the Winter lords it here.

LOVE NURSED BY SOLITUDE.

Ay, surely, it is here that Love should come,
And find (if he may find on earth) a home;
Here cast off all the sorrow and the shame
That cling like shadows to his very name.

Young Love, thou art belied: they speak of thee,
And couple with thy mention misery;
Talk of the broken heart, the wasted bloom,
The spirit blighted, and the early tomb;
As if these waited on thy golden lot,—
They blame thee for the faults which thou hast not.
Art thou to blame for that they bring on thee
The soil and weight of their mortality?
How can they hope that ever links with hold
Formed, as they form them now, of the harsh gold?
Or worse than even this, how can they think
That vanity will bind the failing link?
How can they dream that thy sweet life will bear
Crowds', palaces', and cities' heartless air?
Where the lip smiles while the heart's desolate,
And courtesy lends its deep mask to hate;
Where looks and thoughts alike must feel the chain,
And naught of life is real but its pain;
Where the young spirit's high imaginings
Are scorned and cast away as idle things;
Where, think or feel, you are foredoomed to be
A marvel and a sign for mockery;
Where none must wander from the beaten road,—
All alike champ the bit, and feel the goad.
It is not made for thee, young Love! away
To where the green earth laughs to the clear day.
To the deep valley, where a thousand trees
Keep a green court for fairy revelries,—
To some small island on a lonely lake,
Where only swans the diamond waters break—
Where the pines hang in silence o'er the tide,
And the stream gushes from the mountain side;
These, Love, are haunts for thee; where canst thou brood
With thy sweet wings furled but in Solitude.

A GIRL AT HER DEVOTIONS.

She was just risen from her bended knee,
But yet peace seemed not with her piety;
For there was paleness upon her young cheek,
And thoughts upon the lips which never speak,
But wring the heart that at the last they break.
Alas! how much of misery may be read
In that wan forehead, and that bowed down head:—
Her eye is on a picture, wo that ever
Love should thus struggle with a vain endeavor
Against itself: it is a common tale,
And ever will be while earth soils prevail
Over earth's happiness; it tells she strove
With silent, secret, unrequited love.

It matters not its history; love has wings
Like lightning, swift and fatal, and it springs
Like a wild flower where it is least expected,
Existing whether cherished or rejected;
Living with only but to be content,
Hopeless, for love is its own element,—
Requiring nothing so that it may be
The martyr of its fond fidelity.
A mystery thou art, thou mighty one!
We speak thy name in beauty, yet we shun
To own thee, Love, a guest; the poet's songs
Are sweetest when their voice to thee belongs,
And hope, sweet opiate, tenderness, delight,
Are terms which are thy own peculiar right;
Yet all deny their master,—who will own
His breast thy footstool, and his heart thy throne!

'Tis strange to think if we could fling aside
The masque and mantle that love wears from pride,
How much would be, we now so little guess,
Deep in each heart's undreamed, unsought recess.
The careless smile, like a gay banner borne,
The laugh of merriment, the lip of scorn,—
And for a cloak what is there that can be
So difficult to pierce as gayety?
Too dazzling to be scanned, the haughty brow
Seems to hide something it would not avow;
But rainbow words, light laugh, and thoughtless jest,
These are the bars, the curtain to the breast,
That shuns a scrutiny: and she, whose form
Now bends in grief beneath the bosom's storm,
Has hidden well her wound,—now none are nigh
To mock with curious or with careless eye,
(For love seeks sympathy, a chilling yes,
Strikes at the root of its best happiness,
And mockery is wormwood,) she may dwell
On feelings which that picture may not tell.

THE NEGLECTED ONE.

And there is silence in that lonely hall,
Save where the waters of the fountain fall.
And the wind's distant murmuring, which takes
Sweet messages from every bud it wakes.
'Tis more than midnight; all the lamps are gone,
Their fragrant oils exhausted,—all but one,
A little silver lamp beside a scroll,
Where a young maiden leant, and poured her soul,
In those last words, the bitter and the brief.
How can they say confiding is relief?
Light are the woes that to the eyelids spring,
Subdued and softened by the tears they bring;
But there are some too long, too well concealed,
Too deeply felt,—that are but once revealed:
Like the withdrawing of the mortal dart,
And then the lifeblood follows from the heart;
Sorrow, before unspoken by a sigh,
But which, once spoken, only hath to die.

Young, very young, the lady was, who now
Bowed on her slender hand her weary brow:
Not beautiful, save when the eager thought
In the soft eyes a sudden beauty wrought:
Not beautiful, save when the cheek's warm blush
Grew eloquent with momentary flush
Of feeling, that made beauty, not to last,
And scarcely caught, so quickly is it past.
—Alas! she knew it well; too early thrown
Mid a cold world, the unloved and the lone,
With no near kindred ties on whom could dwell
Love that so sought to be beloved as well.
Too sensitive for flattery, and too kind
To bear the loneliness by fate assigned,
Her life had been a struggle: long she strove
To fix on things inanimate her love;
On pity, kindness, music, gentle lore,
All that romance could yield of fairy store.
In vain! she loved:—she loved and from that hour
Gone were the quiet loves of bird or flower;
The unread book dropped listless on her knee,
The untouched lute hung on the bending tree
Whose unwreathed boughs no more a pleasant shade
For the lone dreamings of her twilight made.
—Well might she love him: every eye was turned
On that young knight, and bright cheeks brighter burned,
Save one, that grew the paler for his sake:
Alas! for her, whose heart but beat to break;
Who knew too well, not hers the lip or eye
For which the youthful lover swears to die.
How deep, how merciless, the love represt,
That robs the silent midnight of its rest;
That sees in gathered crowds but one alone;
That hears in mingled footsteps only one;
That turns the poet's page, to only find
Some mournful image for itself designed;
That seeks in music, but the plaining tone
Which secret sorrow whispers is its own!
Alas for the young heart, when love is there,
Its comrade and its confidant, despair!

How often leant in some unnoticed spot,
Her very being by the throng forgot,
Shrunk back to shun the glad lamp's mocking ray,
Passed many a dark and weary hour away,
Watching the young, the beautiful, the bright,
Seeming more lovely in that lonely light;
And as each fair face glided through the dance,
Stealing at some near mirror one swift glance,
Then, starting at the contrast, seek her room,
To weep, at least in solitude and gloom!
And he, her stately idol, he, with eye
Dark as the eagle's in a summer sky,
And darker curls, amid whose raven shade
The very wild wind amorously delayed,
With that bright smile, which makes all others dim,
So proud, so sweet,—what part had she in him?
And yet she loved him: who may say, be still,
To the fond heart that beats not at our will?

'Twas too much wretchedness:—the convent cell,
There might the maiden with her misery dwell.
And that, to-morrow was her chosen doom:
There might her hopes, her feelings, find a tomb.
Her feelings!—no: pray, struggle, weep, condemn,—
Her feelings,—there was but one grave for them.
'Twas her last night, and she had looked her last,
And she must live henceforward in the past.
She lingered in the hall,—he had been there;
Her pale lips grew yet paler with the prayer
That only asked his happiness. She took
A blank leaf from an old emblazoned book,
Which told love's chronicles; a faint hope stole,—
A sweet light o'er the darkness of her soul—
Might she not leave remembrance, like the wreath,
Whose dying flowers their scents on twilight breathe
Just one faint tone of music, low and clear,
Coming when other songs have left the ear?
Might she not tell him how she loved, and pray
A mournful memory for some distant day?
She took the scroll:—what! bare perhaps to scorn
The timid sorrow she so long had borne!
Silent as death, she hid her face, for shame
In rushing crimson to her forehead came;
Through the small fingers fell the bitter rain,
And tremblingly she closed the leaves again.
—The hall is lit with rose, that morning hour,
Whose lights are colored by each opening flower:
A sweet bird by the casement sat and sang
A song so glad, that like a laugh it rang,
While its wings shook the jessamine, till the bloom
Floated like incense round that joyous room.
—They found the maiden: still her face was bowed,
As with some shame that might not be avowed;
They raised the long hair which her face concealed,—
And she is dead,—her secret unrevealed.

WHEN SHOULD LOVERS BREATHE THEIR VOWS?

When should lovers breathe their vows?
  When should ladies hear them?
When the dew is on the boughs,
  When none else are near them;
When the moon shines cold and pale,
  When the birds are sleeping,
When no voice is on the gale,
  When the rose is weeping;
When the stars are bright on high,
  Like hopes in young Love's dreaming,
And glancing round the light clouds fly,
  Like soft fears to shade their beaming.
The fairest smiles are those that live
  On the brow by starlight wreathing;
And the lips their richest incense give
  When the sigh is at midnight breathing.
O, softest is the cheek's love-ray
  When seen by moonlight hours,
Other roses seek the day,
  But blushes are night flowers.
O, when the moon and stars are bright,
  When the dew-drops glisten,
Then their vows should lovers plight,
  Then should ladies listen!

THE EMERALD RING.

A SUPERSTITION.

It is a gem which hath the power to show
If plighted lovers keep their faith or no:
If faithful, it is like the leaves of spring;
If faithless like those leaves when withering.
  Take back again your emerald gem,
    There is no color in the stone;
  It might have graced a diadem,
    But now its hue and light are gone!
Take back your gift, and give me mine—
  The kiss that sealed our last love-vow;
Ah, other lips have been on thine,—
  My kiss is lost and sullied now!
The gem is pale, the kiss forgot,
  And, more than either, you are changed;
But *my* true love has altered not,
  My heart is broken—not estranged!

A NIGHT IN MAY.

A night not sacred to Spring's opening leaves,
But one of crowded festival.

LIGHT and glad through the rooms the gay music is waking,
Where the young and the lovely are gathered to-night;
And the soft cloudless lamps, with their lustre, are making
A midnight hour only than morning less bright.

There are vases,—the flowers within them are breathing
Sighs almost as sweet as the lips that are near;
Light feet are glancing, white arms are wreathing,—
O temple of pleasure! thou surely art here.

I gazed on the scene; 'twas the dream of a minute;
But it seemed to me even as fairy land fair;
Twas the cup's bright inside; and on glancing within it,
What but the dregs and the darkness were there?

—False wave of the desert, thou art less beguiling
Than false beauty over the lighted hall shed:
What but the smiles that have practised their smiling,
Or honey words measured, and reckoned as said?

O, heart of mine! turn from the revellers before thee;
What part hast thou in them, or have they in thee?
What was the feeling that too soon came o'er thee?—
Weariness ever that feeling must be.

Praise—flattery—opiates the meanest, yet sweetest,
Are ye the fame that my spirit hath dreamed?
Lute, when in such scenes, if homage thou meetest,
Say, if like glory such vanity seemed?

O for some island far off in the ocean,
Where never a footstep has pressed but mine own:
With one hope, one feeling, one utter devotion
To my gift of song, once more, the lovely, the lone!

My heart is too much in the things which profane it,
The cold, and the worldly, why am I like them?
Vanity! with my lute chords I must chain it,
Nor thus let it sully the minstrel's best gem.

It rises before me, that island, where blooming,
The flowers in their thousands are comrades for me·
And where if one perish, so sweet its entombing,
The welcome it seems of fresh leaves to the tree.

I'll wander among them when morning is weeping
Her earliest tears, if such pearls can be tears;
When the birds and the roses together are sleeping,
Till the mist of the daybreak, like hope fulfilled, clears.

Grove of dark cypress, when noontide is flinging
Its radiance of light, thou shalt then be my shrine;
I'll listen the song which the wild dove is singing,
And catch from its sweetness a lesson for mine.

And when the red sunset at even is dying,
I'll watch the last blush as it fades on the wave;
While the wind, through the shells in its low music sighing,
Will seem like the anthem pearled over its grave.

And when the bright stars which I worship are beaming,
And writing in beauty and fate on the sky,
Then, mine own lute, be the hour of thy dreaming,
And the night-flowers will open and echo thy sigh.

Alas! but my dream has like sleep's visions vanished;
The hall and the crowd are before me again:
Sternly my sweet thoughts like fairies are banished;
Nay, the faith which believed in them now seems but vain.

I left the gay circle:—if I found it dreary,
Were all others there, then, the thoughtless and glad?
Methinks that fair cheek in its paleness looked weary,
Methinks that dark eye in its drooping was sad.

—I went to my chamber,—I sought to be lonely,—
I leant by the casement to catch the sweet air;
The thick tears fell blinding; and am I then only
Sad, weary, although without actual care?

The heart hath its mystery, and who may reveal it;
Or who ever read in the depths of their own?—
How much, we never may speak of, yet feel it,
But, even in feeling it, know it unknown!

Sky of wild beauty, in those distant ages
Of which time hath left scarce a wreck or a name,
Say were thy secrets laid bare to the sages,
Who held that the stars were life's annals of flame?

Spirit, that ruleth man's life to its ending,
Chance, Fortune, Fate, answer my summoning now;
The storm o'er the face of the night is descending,—
Fair moon, the dark clouds hide thy silvery brow.

Let these bring thy answer, and tell me if sadness
For ever man's penance and portion must be;
Doth the morning come forth from a birthplace of gladness?
Is there peace, is there rest, in thine empire or thee?

Spirit of fate, from yon troubled west leaning,
As its meteor-piled rack were thy home and thy shrine,
Grief is our knowledge, 'twill teach me thy meaning,
Although thou but speakest it in silence and sign.

I marked a soft arch sweep its way over heaven;
It spanned as it ruled the fierce storm which it bound;
The moonshine, the shower, to its influence seemed given,
And the black clouds grew bright in the beautiful round.

I looked out again, but few hues were remaining
On the side nearest earth; while I gazed, they were past:
As a steed for a time with its curb proudly straining,
Then freed in its strength, came the tempest at last.

And this was the sign of thy answer, dark spirit!
Alas! and such ever our pathway appears;
Tempest and change still our earth must inherit,
Its glory a shade, and its loveliness tears.

THE SULTANA'S REMONSTRANCE

IT suits thee well to weep,
As thou lookest on the fair land,
Whose sceptre thou hast held
With less than woman's hand.

On yon bright city gaze,
With its white and marble halls,
The glory of its lofty towers,
The strength of its proud walls.

And look to yonder palace,
With its garden of the rose,
With its groves and silver fountains,
Fit for a king's repose.

There is weeping in that city,
And a cry of wo and shame,
There's a whisper of dishonor,
And that whisper is thy name.

And the stranger's feast is spread,
But it is no feast of thine;
In thine own halls accursed lips
Drain the forbidden wine.

And aged men are in the streets,
Who mourn their length of days,
And young knights stand with folded arms,
And eyes they dare not raise.

There is not one whose blood was not
As the waves of ocean free,—
Their fathers died for thy fathers,
They would have died for thee.

Weep not, 'tis mine to weep
That ever thou wert born;
Alas, that all a mother's love
Is lost in a queen's scorn!

Yet weep, thou less than woman, weep,
Those tears become thine eye,—
It suits thee well to weep the land
For which thou darest not die.*

* these lines allude to the flight of the last king of Grenada

WARNING.

Pray thee, maiden, hear him not!
Take thou warning by my lot;
Read my scroll, and mark thou all
I can tell thee of thy thrall.
Thou hast owned that youthful breast
Treasures its most dangerous guest;
Thou hast owned that Love is there:
Though now features he may wear,
Such as would a saint deceive,
Win a skeptic to believe,
Only for a time that brow,
Will seem what 'tis seeming now.
I have said, heart, be content!
For Love's power o'er thee is spent.
That I love not now, O true!—
I have bade such dreams adieu:
Therefore deemest thou my heart
Saw them tranquilly depart;
That they past, nor left behind
Wreck and ruin in my mind.
Thou art in the summer hour
Of first passion's early power;
I am in the autumn day,
Of its darkness, and decay.
—Seems thine idol now to thee
Even as a divinity?
Such the faith that I too held;
Not the less am I compelled
All my heart-creed to gainsay,
Own my idol gilded clay,
And yet pine to dream again
What I know is worse than vain.
Ay, I did love, and how well,
Let thine own fond weakness tell:
Still upon the softened mood
Of my twilight solitude,
Still upon my midnight tear,
Rises image all too dear;
Dark and starry eyes, whose light
Make the glory of the night;
Brow like ocean's morning foam,
For each noble thought a home.
Well such temple's fair outline
Seemed the spirit's fitting shrine.
—Is he hero, who hath won
Fields we shrink to think upon?
Patriot, on whose gifted tongue
Senates in their wonder hung?
Sage, before whose gifted eyes
Nature spreads her mysteries?
Bard, to whose charmed lute is given
All that earth can breathe of heaven?
Seems thy lover these to thee?
Even more mine seemed to me.
Now, my fond belief is past;
Strange, methinks, if thine should last.
"Be content, thou lovest not now:"
Free, thou sayest,—dreamest thou how?
Loathing wouldst thou shun dismayed
Freedom by such ransom paid.
—Girl, for thee I'll lay aside
Veil of smiles and mask of pride;
Shrouds that only ask of Fate
Not to seem so desolate.
—I am young,—but age's snow
Hides not colder depths below;
I am gay—but such a light
Shines upon the grave by night.
—Yet mine is a common tale;
Hearts soon changed, and vows were frail
Each one blamed the other's deed,
Yet both felt they were agreed;
Ne'er again might either prove
Those sweet fallacies of love.
—Still for what so vain I hold
Is my waisted heart grown cold.
Can hopes be again believed,
When their sweetest have deceived?
Can affection's chain be trusted,
When its dearest links have rusted?
Can life's dreams again be cherished,
When its dearest one have perished.
I know Love will not endure;—
Nothing now to me seems sure.
—Maiden, by the thousand tears
Lava floods on my first years;
By the nights, when burning pain
Fed upon my heart and brain;
By the wretched days now past,
By the weary days to last;
Be thou warned, for still the same
Is Love, beneath whatever name.
Keep thy fond faith like a thing
Where Time never change may bring.
Vow thee to thy idol's shrine,—
Then, maiden! read thy fate in mine.

THE NAMELESS GRAVE.

A nameless grave,—there is no stone
To sanctify the dead:
O'er it the willow droops alone,
With only wild flowers spread.

"O, there is naught to interest here,
No record of a name,
A trumpet call upon the ear,
High on the roll of fame.

"I will not pause beside a tomb
Where nothing calls to mind
Aught that can brighten mortal gloom,
Or elevate mankind;—

"No glorious memory to efface
The stay of meaner clay;
No intellect whose heavenly trace
Redeemed our earth:—away!"

Ah, these are thoughts that well may rise
On youth's ambitious pride;
But I will sit and moralize
This lowly stone beside.

Here thousands might have slept, whose name
Had been to thee a spell,
To light thy flashing eyes with flame,—
To bid thy young heart swell.

Here might have been a warrior's rest,
Some chief who bravely bled,
With waving banner, sculptured crest,
And laurel on his head.

That laurel must have had its blood,
That blood have caused its tear,—
Look on the lovely solitude—
What! wish for warfare here!

A poet might have slept,—what! he
Whose restless heart first wakes
Its lifepulse into melody,
Then o'er it pines and breaks?—

He who hath song of passionate love,
His life a feverish tale:—
O! not the nightingale, the dove
Would suit its quiet vale.

See, I have named your favorite two,—
Each had been glad to crave
Rest 'neath this turf's unbroken dew,
And such a nameless grave!

THINK OF ME.

Farewell!—and never think of me
In lighted hall or lady's bower!
Farewell!—and never think of me
In spring sunshine or summer hour!
But when you see a lonely grave,
Just where a broken heart might be,
With not one mourner by its sod,
Then—and then only—THINK OF ME!

SONG OF THE HUNTER'S BRIDE.

Another day—another day
 And yet he comes not nigh;
I look amid the dim blue hills,
 Yet nothing meets mine eye.

I hear the rush of mountain streams
 Upon the echoes borne;
I hear the singing of the birds,
 But not my hunter's horn.

The eagle sails in darkness past,
 The watchful chamois bounds;
But what I look for comes not near,—
 My Ulric's hawk and hounds.

Three times I thus have watched the snow
 Grow crimson with the stain,
The setting sun threw o'er the rock,
 And I have watched in vain.

I love to see the graceful bow
 Across his shoulder slung,—
I love to see the golden horn
 Beside his baldric hung.

I love his dark hounds, and I love
 His falcon's sweeping flight;
I love to see his manly cheek
 With mountain colors bright.

I've waited patiently, but now
 Would that the chase were o'er:
Well may he love the hunter's toil,
 But he should love me more.

Why stays he thus?—he would be here
 If his love equalled mine—
Methinks had I one fond caged dove,
 I would not let it pine.

But, hark! what are those ringing steps
 That up the valley come?
I see his hounds,—I see himself,—
 My Ulric, welcome home!

THE WOODLAND BROOK.

Thou art flowing, thou art flowing,
 O, small and silvery brook;
The rushes by thee growing,
 And with a patient look
The pale narcissus o'er thee bends
Like one who asks in vain for friends.

I bring not back my childhood,
 Sweet comrade of its hours;
The music of the wild wood,
 The color of the flowers;
They do not bring again the dream
That haunted me beside thy stream.

When black-lettered old romances
 Made a world for me alone;
O, days of lovely fancies,
 Are ye for ever flown?
Ye are fled, sweet, vague, and vain,
So I can not dream again.

I have left a feverish pillow
 For thy soothing song;
Alas, each fairy billow
 An image bears along,
Look where I will, I only see
One face too much beloved by me.

In vain my heart remembers
 What pleasure used to be,
My past thoughts are but embers
 Consumed by love for thee.
I wish to love thee less—and feel
A deeper fondness o'er me steal.

I PRAY THEE LET ME WEEP TO-NIGHT.

I pray thee let me weep to-night,
 'Tis rarely I am weeping;
My tears are buried in my heart,
 Like cave-locked fountains sleeping.

But O, to-night, those words of thine,
 Have brought the past before me;
And shadows of long-vanished years
 Are passing sadly o'er me.

The friends I loved in early youth,
 The faithless and forgetting,
Whom, though they were not worth my love,
 I can not help regretting;—

My feelings, once the kind, the warm,
 But now the hard, the frozen;
The errors I've too long pursued,
 The path I should have chosen;—

The hopes that are like falling lights
 Around my pathway dying;
The consciousness none others rise,
 Their vacant place supplying;—

The knowledge by experience taught,
 The useless, the repelling;
For what avails to know how false
 Is all the charmer's telling?

I would give worlds, could I believe
 One half that is professed me;
Affection! could I think it thee,
 When Flattery has caressed me?

I can not bear to think of this,—
 O, leave me to my weeping;
A few tears for that grave my heart,
 Where hope in death is sleeping.

THE WREATH.

Nay, fling not down those faded flowers,
 Too late they're scattered round;
And violet and rose-leaf lie
 Together on the ground.

How carefully this very morn
 Those buds were culled and wreathed;
And 'mid the cloud of that dark hair,
 How sweet a sigh they breathed!

And many a gentle word was said
 Above their morning die,
How that the rose had touched thy cheek,
 The violet thine eye.

Methinks, if but for memory,
 I should have kept these flowers;
Ah! all too lightly does thy heart
 Dwell upon vanished hours.

Already has thine eager hand
 Stripped yonder rose-hung bough;
The wreath that bound thy raven curls
 Thy feet are on it now.

That glancing smile, it seems to say
 "Thou art too fanciful:
What matters it what roses fade,
 While there are no more to cull?"

Ay, I was wrong to ask of thee
 Such gloomy thoughts as mine:
Thou in thy Spring, how shouldst thou dream
 Of Autumn's pale decline?

Young, lovely, loved,—O! far from thee
 Life's after-death and doom;
Long ere thou learn how memory clings
 To even faded bloom!

THE PLEA

OF

THE MIDSUMMER FAIRIES.

BY THOMAS HOOD.

It is my design, in the following Poem, to celebrate, by an allegory, that immortality, which Shakspere has conferred on the Fairy mythology by his Midsummer Night's Dream. But for him, those pretty children of our childhood would leave barely their names to our maturer years; they belong, as the mites upon the plum, to the bloom of fancy, a thing generally too frail and beautiful to withstand the rude handling of time: but the Poet has made this most perishable part of the mind's creation equal to the most enduring; he has so intertwined the Elfins with human sympathies, and linked them by so many delightful associations with the productions of nature, that they are as real to the mind's eye as their green magical circles to the outer sense.

It would have been a pity for such a race to go extinct, even though they were but as the butterflies that hover about the leaves and blossoms of the visible world.

I.

'Twas in that mellow season of the year,
When the hot Sun singes the yellow leaves
Till they be gold,—and with a broader sphere
The Moon looks down on Ceres and her sheaves;
When more abundantly the spider weaves,
And the cold wind breathes from a chillier clime;
That forth I fared, on one of those still eves,
Touched with the dewy sadness of the time,
To think how the bright months had spent their prime.

II.

So that, wherever I addressed my way,
I seemed to track the melancholy feet
Of him that is the Father of Decay,
And spoils at once the sour weed and the sweet;
Wherefore regretfully I made retreat
To some unwasted regions of my brain,
Charmed with the light of summer and the heat,
And bade that bounteous season bloom again,
And sprout fresh flowers in mine own domain.

III.

It was a shady and sequestered scene,
Like those famed gardens of Boccaccio,
Planted with his own laurels evergreen,
And roses that for endless summer blow;
And there were fount springs to overflow
Their marble basins,—and cool green arcades
Of tall o'erarching sycamores, to throw
Athwart the dappled path their dancing shades,—
With timid conies cropping the green blades.

IV.

And there were crystal pools, peopled with fish,
Argent and gold; and some of Tyrian skin,
Some crimson-barred;—and ever at a wish
They rose obsequious till the wave grew thin
As glass upon their backs, and then dived in,
Quenching their ardent scales in watery gloom;
Whilst others with fresh hues rowed forth to win
My changeable regard,—for so we doom
Things born of thought to vanish or to bloom.

V.

And there were many birds of many dies,
From tree to tree still faring to and fro,
And stately peacocks with their splendid eyes,
And gorgeous pheasants with their golden glow
Like Iris just bedabbled in her bow,
Besides some vocalists, without a name,
That oft on fairy errands come and go,
With accents magical; and all were tame,
And peckled at my hand where'er I came.

VI.

And for my sylvan company, in lieu
Of Pampinea with her lively peers,
Sat Queen Titania with her pretty crew,
All in their liveries quaint, with elfin gears,
For she was gracious to my childish years,
And made me free of her enchanted round;
Wherefore this dreamy scene she still endears,
And plants her court upon a verdant mound,
Fenced with umbrageous woods and groves profound.

VII.

"Ah me," she cries, "was ever moonlight seen,
So clear and tender for our midnight trips?
Go some one forth, and with a trump convene
My lieges all!" Away the goblin skips
A pace or two apart, and deftly strips
The ruddy skin from a sweet rose's cheek,
Then blows the shuddering leaf between his lips,
Making it utter forth a shrill small shriek,
Like a frayed bird in the gray owlet's beak.

VIII.

And lo! upon my fixed delighted ken
Appeared the loyal Fays. Some by degrees
Crept from the primrose buds that opened then,
And some from bell-shaped blossoms like the bees,
Some from the dewy meads, and rushy leas,
Flew up like chafers when the rustics pass;
Some from the rivers, others from tall trees
Dropped, like shed blossoms, silent to the grass,
Spirits and elfins small, of every class.

IX.

Peri and Pixy, and quaint Puck the Antic,
Brought Robin Goodfellow, that merry swain;
And stealthy Mab, queen of old realms romantic,
Came too, from distance, in her tiny wain,
Fresh dripping from a cloud—some bloomy rain,
Then circling the bright Moon, had washed her car,
And still bedewed it with a various stain:
Lastly came Ariel, shooting from a star,
Who bears all fairy embassies afar.

X.

But Oberon, that night elsewhere exiled,
Was absent, whether some distempered spleen
Kept him and his fair mate unreconciled,
Or warfare with the Gnome (whose race had been
Sometime obnoxious), kept him from his queen,
And made her now peruse the starry skies
Prophetical with such an absent mien;
Howbeit, the tears stole often to her eyes,
And oft the Moon was incensed with her sighs—

XI.

Which made the elves sport drearily, and soon
Their hushing dances languished to a stand,
Like midnight leaves when, as the Zephyrs swoon,
All on their drooping stems they sink unfanned,—
So into silence drooped the fairy band,
To see their empress dear so pale and still,
Crowding her softly round on either hand,
As pale as frosty snow-drops, and as chill,
To whom the sceptred dame reveals her ill.

XII.

"Alas," quoth she, "ye know our fairy lives
Are leased upon the fickle faith of men;
Not measured out against fate's mortal knives,
Like human gossamers, we perish when
We fade, and are forgot in worldly ken,—
Though poesy has thus prolonged our date,
Thanks be to the sweet Bard's auspicious pen
That rescued us so long!—howbeit of late
I feel some dark misgivings of our fate.

XIII.

"And this dull day my melancholy sleep
Hath been so thronged with images of wo,
That even now I can not choose but weep
To think this was some sad prophetic show
Of future horror to befall us so,—
Of mortal wreck and uttermost distress,—
Yea, our poor empire's fall and overthrow,—
For this was my long vision's dreadful stress,
And when I waked my trouble was not less.

XIV.

"Whenever to the clouds I tried to seek,
Such leaden weight dragged these Icarian wings,
My faithless wand was wavering and weak,
And slimy toads had trespassed in our rings—
The birds refused to sing for me—all things
Disowned their old allegiance to our spells;
The rude bees pricked me with their rebel stings;
And, when I passed, the valley-lily's bells
Rang out, methought, most melancholy knells.

XV.

"And even on the faint and flagging air
A doleful spirit with a dreary note
Cried in my fearful ear, 'Prepare! prepare!'
Which soon I knew came from a raven's throat,
Perched on a cypress bough not far remote,
A cursed bird, too crafty to be shot,
That alway cometh with his soot-black coat
To make hearts dreary:—for he is a blot
Upon the book of life, as well ye wot!

XVI.

"Wherefore some while I bribed him to be mute,
With bitter acorns stuffing his foul maw,
Which barely I appeased, when some fresh bruit
Startled me all aheap!—and soon I saw
The horridest shape that ever raised my awe,
A monstrous giant, very huge and tall,
Such as in elder times, devoid of law
With wicked might grieved the primeval ball,
And this was sure the deadliest of them all!

XVII.

"Gaunt was he as a wolf of Languedoc,
With bloody jaws, and frost upon his crown;
So from his barren poll one hoary lock
Over his wrinkled front fell far adown,
Well nigh to where his frosty brows did frown
Like jagged icicles at cottage eaves;
And for his coronal he wore some brown
And bristled ears gathered from Ceres' sheaves,
Entwined with certain sere and russet leaves.

XVIII.

"And lo! upon a mast reared far aloft,
He bore a very bright and crescent blade,
The which he waved so dreadfully, and oft,
In meditative spite, that, sore dismayed,
I crept into an acorn-cup for shade;
Meanwhile the horrid effigy went by:
I trow his look was dreadful, for it made
The trembling birds betake them to the sky,
For every leaf was lifted by his sigh.

XIX.

"And ever as he sighed, his foggy breath
Blurred out the landscape like a flight of smoke:
Thence knew I this was either dreary Death
Or Time, who leads all creatures to his stroke.
Ah wretched me!" Here, even as she spoke,
The melancholy Shape came gliding in,
And leaned his back against an antique oak,
Folding his wings, that were so fine and thin,
They scarce were seen against the Dryad's skin.

XX.

Then what a fear seized all the little rout!
Look how a flock of panicked sheep will stare
And huddle close—and start—and wheel about,
Watching the roaming mongrel here and there,
So did that sudden Apparition scare
All close aheap those small affrighted things;
Nor sought they now the safety of the air,
As if some leaden spell withheld their wings;
But who can fly that ancientest of Kings?

XXI.

Whom now the Queen, with a forestalling tear
And previous sigh, beginneth to entreat,
Bidding him spare, for love, her lieges dear:
"Alas!" quoth she, "is there no nodding wheat
Ripe for thy crooked weapon, and more meet,
Or withered leaves to ravish from the tree,
Or crumbling battlements for thy defeat?
Think but what vaunting monuments there be
Builded in spite and mockery of thee.

XXII.

"O fret away the fabric walls of Fame,
And grind down marble Cæsars with the dust:
Make tombs inscriptionless—raze each high name
And waste old armors of renown with rust:
Do all of this, and thy revenge is just:
Make such decays the trophies of thy prime,
And check Ambition's overweening lust,
That dares exterminating war with Time,—
But we are guiltless of that lofty crime.

XXIII.

"Frail feeble sprites! the children of a dream!
Leased on the sufferance of fickle men,
Likes motes dependant on the sunny beam,
Living but in the sun's indulgent ken,
And when that light withdraws, withdrawing then,
So do we flutter in the glance of youth
And fervid fancy, and so perish when
The eye of faith grows aged;—in sad truth,
Feeling thy sway, O Time! though not thy tooth!

XXIV.

"Where be those old divinities forlorn,
That dwelt in trees, or haunted in a stream?
Alas! their memories are dimmed and torn,
Like the remainder tatters of a dream:
So will it fare with our poor thrones, I deem;
For us the same dark trench Oblivion delves,
That holds the wastes of every human scheme.
O spare us then, and these our pretty elves,
We soon, alas! shall perish of ourselves!"

XXV.

Now as she ended, with a sigh, to name
Those old Olympians, scattered by the whirl
Of fortune's giddy wheel and brought to shame,
Methought a scornful and malignant curl
Showed on the lips of that malicious churl,
To think what noble havocks he had made;
So that I feared he all at once would hurl
The harmless fairies into endless shade.—
Howbeit he stopped awhile to whet his blade.

XXVI.

Pity it was to hear the elfins' wail
Rise up in concert from their mingled dread;
Pity it was to see them, all so pale,
Gaze on the grass as for a dying bed;
But Puck was seated on a spider's thread,
That hung between two branches of a brier,
And 'gan to swing and gambol heels o'er head,
Like any Southwark tumbler on a wire,
For him no present grief could long inspire.

XXVII.

Meanwhile the queen with many piteous drops,
Falling like tiny sparks full fast and free,
Bedews a pathway from her throne; and stops
Before the foot of her arch enemy,
And with her little arms enfolds his knee,
That shows more gristly from that fair embrace;
But she will ne'er depart. "Alas!" quoth she,
"My painful fingers I will here enlace
Till I have gained your pity for our race.

XXVIII.

"What have we ever done to earn this grudge,
And hate—(if not too humble for thy hating?)—
Look o'er our labors and our lives, and judge
If there be any ills of our creating;
For we are very kindly creatures, dating
With nature's charities still sweet and bland:
O think this murder worthy of debating!"
Herewith she makes a signal with her hand,
To beckon some one from the Fairy band.

XXIX.

Anon I saw one of those elfin things,
Clad all in white like any chorister,
Come fluttering forth on his melodious wings,
That made soft music at each little stir,
But something louder than a bee's demur
Before he lights upon a bunch of broom,
And thus 'gan he with Saturn to confer,—
And O his voice was sweet, touched with the gloom
Of that sad theme that argued of his doom!

XXX.

Quoth he, "We make all melodies our care,
That no false discords may offend the Sun,
Music's great master—tuning everywhere
All pastoral sounds and melodies, each one
Duly to place and season, so that none
May harshly interfere. We rouse at morn
The shrill sweet lark; and when the day is done,
Hush silent pauses for the bird forlorn,
That singeth with her breast against a thorn.

XXXI.

"We gather in loud choirs the twittering race,
That make a chorus with their single note;
And tend on new-fledged birds in every place,
That duly they may get their tunes by rote;
And oft, like echoes, answering remote,
We hide in thickets from the feathered throng,
And strain in rivalship each throbbing throat,
Singing in shrill responses all day long,
Whilst the glad truant listens to our song.

XXXII.

"Wherefore, great King of Years, as thou dost love
The raining music from a morning cloud,
When vanished larks are carolling above,
To wake Apollo with their pipings loud;
If ever thou hast heard in leafy shroud
The sweet and plaintive Sappho of the dell,
Show thy sweet mercy on this little crowd,
And we will muffle up the sheepfold bell
Whene'er thou listenest to Philomel."

XXXIII.

Then Saturn thus: "Sweet is the merry lark,
That carols in man's ear so clear and strong;
And youth must love to listen in the dark
That tuneful elegy of Tereus' wrong;
But I have heard that ancient strain too long,
For sweet is sweet but when a little strange,
And I grow weary for some newer song;
For wherefore had I wings, unless to range
Through all things mutable from change to change?

XXXIV.

"But would thou hear the melodies of Time,
Listen when sleep and drowsy darkness roll
Over hushed cities, and the midnight chime
Sounds from their hundred clocks, and deep bells toll
Like a last knell over the dead world's soul,
Saying, Time shall be final of all things,
Whose late, last voice must elegize the whole,—
O then I clap aloft my brave broad wings,
And make the wide air tremble while it rings!"

XXXV.

Then next a fair Eve-Fay made meek address,
Saying, "We be the handmaids of the Spring,
In sign whereof, May, the quaint broideress,
Hath wrought her samplers on our gauzy wing.
We tend upon buds' birth and blossoming,
And count the leafy tributes that they owe—
As, so much to the earth—so much to fling
In showers to the brook—so much to go
In whirlwinds to the clouds that made them grow.

XXXVI.

"The pastoral cowslips are our little pets,
And daisy stars, whose firmament is green;
Pansies, and those veiled nuns, meek violets,
Sighing to that warm world from which they screen;
And golden daffodils, plucked for May's Queen;
And lonely harebells, quaking on the heath;
And Hyacinth, long since a fair youth seen,
Whose tuneful voice, turned fragrance in his breath,
Kissed by sad Zephyr, guilty of his death.

XXXVII.

"The widowed primrose weeping to the moon,
And saffron crocus in whose chalice bright
A cool libation hoarded for the noon
Is kept—and she that purifies the light,
The virgin-lily, faithful to her white,
Whereon Eve wept in Eden for her shame;
And the most dainty rose, Aurora's spright,
Our every godchild, by whatever name—
Spare us our lives, for we did nurse the same!"

XXXVIII.

Then that old Mower stamped his heel, and struck
His hurtful scythe against the harmless ground,
Saying, "Ye foolish imps, when am I stuck
With gaudy buds, or like a wooer crowned
With flowery chaplets, save when they are found
Withered? Whenever have I plucked a rose,
Except to scatter its vain leaves around?
For so all gloss of beauty I oppose,
And bring decay on every flower that blows.

XXXIX.

"Or when am I so wroth as when I view
The wanton pride of Summer; how she decks
The birth-day world with blossoms ever new,
As if time had not lived, and heaped great wrecks
Of years on years? O then I bravely vex
And catch the gay months in their gaudy plight,
And slay them with the wreaths about their necks,
Like foolish heifers in the holy rite,
And raise great trophies to my ancient might."

XL.

Then saith another, "We are kindly things,
And like her offspring nestle with the dove,—
Witness these hearts embroidered on our wings,
To show our constant patronage of love:
We sit at even, in sweet bowers above
Lovers, and shake rich odors on the air,
To mingle with their sighs; and still remove
The startling owl, and bid the bat forbear
Their privacy, and haunt some other where.

XLI.

"And we are near the mother when she sits
Beside her infant in its wicker bed;
And we are in the fairy scene that flits
Across its tender brain; sweet dreams we shed,
And while the tender little soul is fled
Away, to sport with our young elves, the while
We touch the dimpled cheek with roses red,
And tickle the soft lips until they smile,
So that their careful parents they beguile.

XLII.

"O then, if ever thou hast breathed a vow
At Love's dear portal, or at pale moon-rise
Crushed the dear curl on a regardful brow
That did not frown thee from thy honey prize—
If ever thy sweet son sat on thy thighs,
And wooed thee from thy careful thoughts within
To watch the harmless beauty of his eyes,
Or glad thy fingers on his smooth soft skin,
For Love's dear sake, let us thy pity win!"

XLIII.

Then Saturn fiercely thus: "What joy have I
In tender babes, that have devoured mine own,
Whenever to the light I heard them cry,
Till foolish Rhea cheated me with stone?
Whereon, till now, is my great hunger shown,
In monstrous dints of my enormous tooth;
And,—but the peopled world is too full grown
For hunger's edge,—I would consume all youth
At one great meal, without delay or ruth!

XLIV.

"For I am well nigh crazed and wild to hear
How boastful fathers taunt me with their breed,
Saying, We shall not die nor disappear,
But in these other selves, ourselves succeed,
Even as ripe flowers pass into their seed
Only to be renewed from prime to prime,
All of which boastings I am forced to read,
Beside a thousand challenges to Time
Which bragging lovers have compiled in rhyme.

XLV.

"Wherefore, when they are sweetly met o' nights,
There will I steal, and with my hurried hand
Startle them suddenly from their delights
Before the next encounter hath been planned,
Ravishing hours in little minutes spanned;
But when they say farewell, and grieve apart,
Then like a leaden statue I will stand,
Meanwhile their many tears encrust my dart,
And with a ragged edge cut heart from heart."

XLVI.

Then next a merry Woodsman, clad in green,
Stept vanward from his mates, that idly stood
Each at his proper ease, as they had been
Nursed in the liberty of old Sherwood,
And wore the livery of Robin Hood,
Who wont in forest shades to dine and sup,—
So came this chief right frankly, and made good
His haunch against his axe, and thus spoke up,
Doffing his cap, which was an acorn's cup:

XLVII.

"We be small foresters and gay, who tend
On trees, and all their furniture of green,
Training the young boughs airily to bend,
And show blue snatches of the sky between:
Or knit more close intricacies, to screen
Birds' crafty dwellings as may hide them best
But most the timid blackbird's—she, that seen,
Will bear black poisonous berries to her nest,
Lest man should cage the darlings of her breast.

XLVIII.

"We bend each tree in proper attitude,
And founting willows train in silvery falls;
We frame all shady roofs and arches rude,
And verdant aisles leading to Dryad's halls,
Or deep recesses where the Echo calls;
We shape all plumy trees against the sky,
And carve tall elms' Corinthian capitals,—
When sometimes, as our tiny hacthets ply,
Men say, the tapping woodpecker is nigh.

XLIX.

"Sometimes we scoop the squirrel's hollow cell,
And sometimes carve quaint letters on trees' rind,
That haply some lone musing wight may spell
Dainty Aminta,—Gentle Rosalind,—
Or chastest Laura,—sweetly called to mind
In sylvan solitudes, ere he lies down;
And sometimes we enrich gray stems, with twined
And fragrant ivy, or rich moss, whose brown
Burns into gold as the warm sun goes down.

L.

"And, lastly, for mirth's sake and Christmas cheer,
We bear the seedling berries, for increase,
To graft the Druid oaks, from year to year,
Careful that mistletoe may never cease;
Wherefore, if thou dost prize the shady peace
Of sombre forests, or to see light break
Through sylvan cloisters, and in spring release
Thy spirit among leaves from careful ake,
Spare us our lives for the Green Dryad's sake."

LI.

Then Saturn, with a frown: "Go forth, and fell
Oak for your coffins, and thenceforth lay by
Your axes for the rust, and bid farewell
To all sweet birds, and the blue peeps of sky
Through tangled branches, for ye shall not spy
The next green generation of the tree;
But hence with the dead leaves, whene'er they fly,—
Which in the bleak air I would rather see,
Than flights of the most tuneful birds that be.

LII.

"For I dislike all prime, and verdant pets,
Ivy except, that on the aged wall
Preys with its worm-like roots, and daily frets
The crumbled tower it seems to league withal,
King-like, worn down by its own coronal:
Neither in forest haunts love I to won,
Before the golden plumage 'gins to fall,
And leaves the brown bleak limbs with few leaves on,
Or bare—like Nature in her skeleton.

LIII.

"For then sit I among the crooked boughs,
Wooing dull Memory, with kindred sighs;
And there in rustling nuptials we espouse,
Smit by the sadness in each other's eyes;
But Hope must have green bowers and blue skies,
And must be courted with the gauds of spring;
While Youth leans god-like on her lap, and cries,
What shall we always do, but love and sing?—
And Time is reckoned a discarded thing."

LIV.

Here in my dream it made me fret to see
How Puck, the antic, all this dreary while
Had blithely jested with calamity,
With mistimed mirth mocking the doleful style
Of his sad comrades, till it raised my bile
To see him so reflect their grief aside,
Turning their solemn looks to half a smile—
Like a straight stick shown crooked in the tide:
But soon a novel advocate I spied.

LV.

Quoth he—"We teach all natures to fulfil
Their fore-appointed crafts, and instincts meet,—
The bee's sweet alchymy,—the spider's skill,—
The pismire's care to garner up his wheat,—
And rustic masonry to swallows fleet,—
The lapwing's cunning to preserve her nest,—
But most, that lesser pelican, the sweet
And shrilly ruddock, with its bleeding breast,
Its tender pity of poor babes distrest.

LVI.

"Sometimes we cast our shapes, and in sleek skins
Delve with the timid mole, that aptly delves
From our example; so the spider spins,
And eke the silk-worm, patterned by ourselves:
Sometimes we travail on the summer shelves
Of early bees, and busy toils commence,
Watched of wise men, that know not we are elves,
But gaze and marvel at our stretch of sense,
And praise our human-like intelligence.

LVII.

"Wherefore, by thy delight in that old tale,
And plaintive dirges the late robins sing,
What time the leaves are scattered by the gale,
Mindful of that old forest burying;
As thou dost love to watch each tiny thing,
For whom our craft most curiously contrives,
If thou hast caught a bee upon the wing,
To take his honey-bag,—spare us our lives,
And we will pay the ransom in full hives."

LVIII.

"Now by my glass," quoth Time, "ye do offend
In teaching the brown bees that careful lore,
And frugal ants, whose millions would have end,
But they lay up for need a timely store,
And travail with the seasons evermore;
Whereas Great Mammoth long hath passed away,
And none but I can tell what hide he wore;
Whilst purblind men, the creatures of a day,
In riddling wonder his great bones survey."

LIX.

Then came an elf, right beauteous to behold,
Whose coat was like a brooklet that the sun
Hath all embroidered with its crooked gold,
It was so quaintly wrought, and overrun
With spangled traceries,—most meet for one
That was a warden of the pearly streams;
And as he stept out of the shadow's dun,
His jewels sparkled in the pale moon's gleams,
And shot into the air their pointed beams.

LX.

Quoth he, "We bear the cold and silver keys
Of bubbling springs and fountains, that below
Course through the veiny earth, which when they freeze
Into hard crysolites, we bid to flow,
Creeping like subtle snakes, when, as they go,
We guide their windings to melodious falls,
At whose soft murmurings, so sweet and low,
Poets have tuned their smoothest madrigals,
To sing to ladies in their banquet halls.

LXI.

"And when the hot sun with his steadfast heat
Parches the river god,—whose dusty urn
Drips miserly, till soon his crystal feet
Against his pebbly floor wax faint and burn,
And languid fish, unpoised, grow sick and yearn,—
Then scoop we hollows in some sandy nook,
And little channels dig, wherein we turn
The thread-worn rivulet, that all forsook
The Naiad-lily, pining for her brook.

LXII.

"Wherefore, by thy delight in cool green meads,
With living sapphires daintily inlaid,—
In all soft songs of waters and their reeds,—
And all reflections in a streamlet made,
Haply of thy own love, that, disarrayed,
Kills the fair lily with a livelier white,—
By silver trouts unspringing from green shade,
And winking stars reduplicate at night,
Spare us, poor ministers to such delight."

LXIII.

Howbeit his pleading and his gentle looks
Moved not the spiteful Shade: Quoth he, "Your taste
Shoots wide of mine, for I despise the brooks
And slavish rivulets that run to waste
In noontide sweats, or, like poor vassals, haste
To swell the vast dominion of the sea,
In whose great presence I am held disgraced,
And neighbored with a king that rivals me
In ancient might and hoary majesty.

LXIV.

"Whereas I ruled in Chaos, and still keep
The awful secrets of that ancient dearth,
Before the briny fountains of the deep
Brimmed up the hollow cavities of earth;
I saw each trickling Sea-God at his birth,
Each pearly Naiad with her oozy locks,
And infant Titans of enormous girth,
Whose huge young feet yet stumbled on the rocks,
Stunning the early world with frequent shocks.

LXV.

"Where now is Titan, with his cumbrous brood,
That scared the world? By this sharp scythe they fell,
And half the sky was curdled with their blood:
So have all primal giants sighed farewell.
No Wardens now by sedgy fountains dwell,
Nor pearly Naiads. All their days are done
That strove with Time, untimely, to excel;
Wherefore I razed their progenies, and none
But my great shadow intercepts the sun!"

LXVI.

Then said the timid Fay, "Oh, mighty Time!
Well hast thou wrought the cruel Titans' fall,
For they were stained with many a bloody crime:
Great giants work great wrongs,—but we are small,
For love goes lowly; but Oppression's tall,
And with surpassing strides goes foremost still
Where love indeed can hardly reach at all;
Like a poor dwarf o'erburthened with good will,
That labors to efface the tracks of ill.

LXVII.

"Man even strives with Man, but we eschew
The guilty feud, and all fierce strifes abhor;
Nay, we are gentle as sweet heaven's dew,
Beside the red and horrid drops of war,
Weeping the cruel hates men battle for,
Which worldly bosoms nourish in our spite:
For in the gentle breast we ne'er withdraw,
But only when all love hath taken flight,
And youth's warm gracious heart is hardened quite.

LXVIII.

"So are our gentle natures intertwined
With sweet humanities, and closely knit
In kindly sympathy with human kind.
Witness how we befriend, with elfin wit,
All hopeless maids and lovers, nor omit
Magical succors unto hearts forlorn:
We charm man's life, and do not perish it;
So judge us by the helps we showed this morn,
To one who held his wretched days in scorn.

LXIX.

"'Twas nigh sweet Amwell; for the queen had tasked
Our skill to-day amid the silver Lea,
Whereon the noontide sun had not yet basked;
Wherefore some patient man we thought to see,
Planted in moss-grown rushes to the knee,
Beside the cloudy margin cold and dim;
Howbeit no patient fisherman was he
That cast his sudden shadow from the brim,
Making us leave our toils to gaze on him.

LXX.

"His face was ashy pale, and leaden care
Had sunk the levelled arches of his brow,
Once bridges for his joyous thoughts to fare
Over those melancholy springs and slow,
That from his piteous eyes began to flow,
And fell anon into the chilly stream;
Which as his mimicked image showed below,
Wrinkled his face with many a needless seam
Making grief sadder in its own esteem.

LXXI.

"And lo! upon the air we saw him stretch
His passionate arms; and, in a wayward strain,
He 'gan to elegize that fellow wretch
That with mute gestures answered him again,
Saying, 'Poor slave, how long wilt thou remain
Life's sad weak captive in a prison strong,
Hoping with tears to rust away thy chain,
In bitter servitude to worldly wrong?
Thou wearest that mortal livery too long!

LXXII.

"This, with more spleenful speeches and some tears,
When he had spent upon the imaged wave,
Speedily I convened my elfin peers
Under the lily-cups, that we might save
This woful mortal from a wilful grave
By shrewd diversions of his mind's regret,
Seeing he was mere melancholy's slave,
That sank wherever a dark cloud he met,
And straight was tangled in her secret net.

LXXIII.

"Therefore, as still he watched the water's flow,
Daintily we transformed, and with bright fins
Came glancing through the gloom; some from below
Rose like dim fancies when a dream begins,
Snatching the light upon their purple skins;
Then under the broad leaves made slow retire;
One like a golden galley bravely wins
Its radiant course,—another glows like fire,—
Making that wayward man our pranks admire.

LXXIV.

"And so he banished thought, and quite forgot
All contemplation of that wretched face;
And so we wiled him from that lonely spot
Along the river's brink; till, by heaven's grace,
He met a gentle haunter of the place,
Full of sweet wisdom gathered from the brooks,
Who there discussed his melancholy case
With wholesome texts learned from kind nature's books,
Meanwhile he newly trimmed his lines and hooks."

LXXV.

Herewith the Fairy ceased. Quoth Ariel now—
"Let me remember how I saved a man,
Whose fatal noose was fastened on a bough,
Intended to abridge his sad life's span;
For haply I was by when he began
His stern soliloquy in life's dispraise,
And overheard his melancholy plan,
How he had made a vow to end his days,
And therefore followed him in all his ways.

LXXVI.

"Through brake and tangled copse, for much he loathed
All populous haunts, and roamed in forests rude
To hide himself from man. But I had clothed
My delicate limbs with plumes, and still pursued,
Where only foxes and wild cats intrude,
Till we were come beside an ancient tree
Late blasted by a storm. Here he renewed
His loud complaints,—choosing that spot to be
The scene of his last horrid tragedy.

LXXVII.

"It was a wild and melancholy glen,
Made gloomy by tall firs and cypress dark,
Whose roots, like any bones of buried men,
Pushed through the rotten sod for fear's remark;
A hundred horrid stems, jagged and stark,
Wrestled with crooked arms in hideous fray,
Beside sleek ashes with their dappled bark,
Like crafty serpents climbing for a prey,
With many blasted oaks moss-grown and gray.

LXXVIII.

"But here upon his final desperate clause
Suddenly I pronounced so sweet a strain,
Like a panged nightingale, it made him pause,
Till half the phrensy of his grief was slain,
The sad remainder oozing from his brain
In timely ecstasies of healing tears,
Which through his ardent eyes began to drain;—
Meanwhile the deadly Fates unclosed their shears:—
So pity me and all my fated peers."

LXXIX.

Thus Ariel ended, and was sometime hushed:
When with the hoary shape a fresh tongue pleads,
And red as rose the gentle Fairy blushed
To read the record of her own good deeds:
"It chanced," quoth she, "in seeking through the meads
For honeyed cowslips, sweetest in the morn,
While yet the buds were hung with dewy beads,
And echo answered to the huntsman's horn,
We found a babe left in the swarths forlorn.

LXXX.

"A little, sorrowful, deserted thing,
Begot of love, and yet no love begetting;
Guiltless of shame, and yet for shame to wring;
And too soon banished from a mother's petting,
To churlish nurture and the wide world's fretting,
For alien pity and unnatural care;
Alas! to see how the cold dew kept wetting
His childish coats, and dabbled all his hair,
Like gossamers across his forehead fair.

LXXXI.

"His pretty pouting mouth, witless of speech,
Lay half-way open like a rose-lipped shell;
And his young cheek was softer than a peach,
Whereon his tears, for roundness, could not dwell,
But quickly rolled themselves to pearls, and fell,
Some on the grass, and some against his hand,
Or haply wandered to the dimpled well,
Which love beside his mouth had sweetly planned,
Yet not for tears, but mirth and smilings bland.

LXXXII.

"Pity it was to see those frequent tears
Falling regardless from his friendless eyes;
There was such beauty in those twin-blue spheres,
As any mother's heart might leap to prize;
Blue were they, like the zenith of the skies
Softened betwixt two clouds, both clear and mild;—
Just touched with thought, and yet not over wise
They showed the gentle spirit of a child,
Nor yet by care or any craft defiled.

LXXXIII.

"Pity it was to see the ardent sun
Scorching his helpless limbs—it shone so warm;
For kindly shade or shelter he had none,
Nor mother's gentle breast, come fair or storm.
Meanwhile I bade my pitying mates transform
Like grasshoppers, and then with shrilly cries,
All round the infant noisily we swarm,
Haply some passing rustic to advise—
While providential Heaven our care espies,

LXXXIV.

"And sends full soon a tender-hearted hind,
Who, wondering at our loud unusual note,
Strays curiously aside, and so doth find
The orphan child laid in the grass remote,
And laps the foundling in his russet coat,
Who thence was nurtured in his kindly cot:
But how he prospered let proud London quote,
How wise, how rich, and how renowned he got,
And chief of all her citizens I wot.

LXXXV.

"Witness his goodly vessels on the Thames,
Whose holds were fraught with costly merchandise,—
Jewels from Ind, and pearls for courtly dames,
And gorgeous silks that Samarcand supplies:
Witness the Royal Bourse he bade arise,
The mart of merchants from the East and West;
Whose slender summit pointing to the skies,
Still bears, in token of his grateful breast,
The tender grasshopper, his chosen crest—

LXXXVI.

"The tender grasshopper, his chosen crest,
That all the summer, with a tuneful wing,
Makes merry chirpings in its grassy nest,
Inspirited with dew to leap and sing:
So let us also live, eternal King!
Partakers of the green and pleasant earth:—
Pity it is to slay the meanest thing,
That, like a mote, shines in the smile of mirth—
Enough there is of joy's decrease and dearth!

LXXXVII.

"Enough of pleasure, and delight, and beauty,
Perished and gone, and hasting to decay;
Enough to sadden even thee, whose duty
Or spite it is to havoc and to slay:
Too many a lovely race razed quite away,
Hath left large gaps in life and human loving:—
Here then begin thy cruel war to stay,
And spare fresh sighs, and tears, and groans, reproving
Thy desolating hand for our removing."

LXXXVIII.

Now here I heard a shrill and sudden cry,
And, looking up, I saw the antic Puck
Grappling with Time, who clutched him like a fly,
Victim of his own sport,—the jester's luck!
He, while his fellows grieved, poor wight, had stuck
His freakish gauds upon the Ancient's brow,
And now his ear, and now his beard, would pluck;
Whereas the angry churl had snatched him now,
Crying, "Thou impish mischief, who art thou?"

LXXXIX.

"Alas!" quoth Puck, "a little random elf,
Born in the sport of nature, like a weed,
For simple sweet enjoyment of myself,
But for no other purpose, worth, or need;
And yet withal of a most happy breed;—
And there is Robin Goodfellow besides,
My partner dear in many a prankish deed
To make dame Laughter hold her jolly sides,
Like merry mummers twain on holy tides.

XC.

"'Tis we that bob the angler's idle cork,
Till e'en the patient man breathes half a curse;
We steal the morsel from the gossip's fork,
And curdling looks with secret straws disperse,
Or stop the sneezing chanter at mid verse:
And when an infant's beauty prospers ill,
We change, some mothers say, the child at nurse;
But any graver purpose to fulfil,
We have not wit enough, and scarce the will.

XCI.

"We never let the canker melancholy
To gather on our faces like a rust,
But gloss our features with some change of folly,
Taking life's fabled miseries on trust,
But only sorrowing when sorrow must:
We ruminate no sage's solemn cud,
But own ourselves a pinch of lively dust
To frisk upon a wind,—whereas the flood
Of tears would turn us into heavy mud.

XCII.

"Beshrew those sad interpreters of nature,
Who gloze her lively universal law,
As if she had not formed our cheerful feature
To be so tickled with the slightest straw!
So let them vex their mumping mouths, and draw
The corners downward, like a watery moon,
And deal in gusty sighs and rainy flaw—
We will not woo foul weather all too soon,
Or nurse November on the lap of June.

XCIII.

"For ours are winging sprites, like any bird,
That shun all stagnant settlements of grief;
And even in our rest our hearts are stirred,
Like insects settled on a dancing leaf:
This is our small philosophy in brief,
Which thus to teach has set me agape:
But dost thou relish it? O hoary chief!
Unclasp thy crooked fingers from my nape,
And I will show thee many a pleasant scrape.

XCIV.

Then Saturn thus:—shaking his crooked blade
O'erhead, which made aloft a lightning flash
In all the fairies' eyes, dismally frayed!
His ensuing voice came like the thunder crash—
Meanwhile the bolt shatters some pine or ash—
"Thou feeble, wanton, foolish, fickle thing!
Whom naught can frighten, sadden, or abash,—
To hope my solemn countenance to wring
To idiot smiles!—but I will prune thy wing!

XCV.

"Lo! this most awful handle of my scythe
Stood once a May-pole, with a flowery crown,
Which rustics danced around, and maidens blithe,
To wanton pipings; but I plucked it down,
And robed the May Queen in a churchyard gown,
Turning her buds to rosemary and rue;
And all their merry minstrelsey did drown,
And laid each lusty leaper in the dew;—
So thou shalt fare—and every jovial crew!"

XCVI.

Here he lets go the struggling imp, to clutch
His mortal engine with each grisly hand,
Which frights the elfin progeny so much,
They huddle in a heap, and trembling stand
All round Titania, like the queen bee's band,
With sighs and tears and very shrieks of wo!
Meanwhile, some moving argument I planned,
To make the stern shade merciful, when lo!
He drops his fatal scythe without a blow!

XCVII.

For just at need, a timely Apparition
Steps in between to bear the awful brunt;
Making him change his horrible position,
To marvel at this comer, brave and blunt,
That dares Time's irresistible affront,
Whose strokes have scarred even the gods of old
Whereas this seemed a mortal, at mere hunt
For conies, lighted by the moonshine cold,
Or stalker of stray deer, stealthy and bold.

XCVIII.

Who, turning to the small assembled fays,
Doffs to the lily queen his courteous cap,
And holds her beauty for a while in gaze,
With bright eyes kindling at this pleasant hap;
And thence upon the fair moon's silver map,
As if in question of this magic chance,
Laid like a dream upon the green earth's lap;
And then upon old Saturn turns askance,
Exclaiming, with a glad and kindly glance:—

XCIX.

"Oh, these be Fancy's revellers by night!
Stealthy companions of the downy moth—
Diana's motes, that flit in her pale light,
Shunners of sunbeams in diurnal sloth;
These be the feasters on night's silver cloth—
The gnat with shrilly trump is their convener,
Forth from their flowery chambers, nothing loath,
With lulling tunes to charm the air serener,
Or dance upon the grass to make it greener.

C.

"These be the pretty genii of the flowers,
Daintily fed with honey and pure dew—
Midsummer's phantoms in her dreaming hours,
King Oberon, and all his merry crew,
The darling puppets of romance's view;
Fairies, and sprites, and goblin elves we call them,
Famous for patronage of lovers true;
No harm they act, neither shall harm befall them,
So do not thus with rapid frowns appal them."

CI.

O what a cry was Saturn's then! it made
The fairies quake. "What care I for their pranks,
However they may lovers choose to aid,
Or dance their roundelays on flowery banks?
Long must they dance before they earn my thanks,
So step aside, to some far safer spot,
While with my hungry scythe I mow their ranks,
And leave them in the sun, like weeds, to rot,
And with the next day's sun to be forgot."

CII.

Anon, he raised afresh his weapon keen;
But still the gracious Shade disarmed his aim,
Stepping with brave alacrity between,
And made his sere arm powerless and tame.
His be perpetual glory, for the shame
Of hoary Saturn in that grand defeat!
But I must tell how here Titania came
With all her kneeling lieges, to entreat
His kindly succor, in sad tones, but sweet.

CIII.

Saying, "Thou seest a wretched queen before thee,
The fading power of a failing land,
Who for her kingdom kneeleth to implore thee
Now menaced by this tyrant's spoiling hand;
No one but thee can hopefully withstand
That crooked blade, he longeth so to lift.
I pray thee blind him with his own vile sand,
Which only times all ruins by its drift,
Or prune his eagle wings that are so swift.

CIV.

"Or take him by that sole and grizzled tuft,
That hangs upon his bald and barren crown;
And we will sing to see him so rebuffed,
And lend our little mights to pull him down,
And make brave sport of his malicious frown,
For all his boastful mockery o'er men.
For thou wast born I know for this renown,
By my most magical and inward ken,
That readeth even at Fate's forestalling pen.

CV.

"Nay by the golden lustre of thine eye,
And by thy brow's most fair and ample span,
Thought's glorious palace, framed for fancies high,
And by thy cheek thus passionately wan,
I know the signs of an immortal man—
Nature's chief darling, and illustrious mate,
Destined to foil old Death's oblivious plan,
And shine untarnished by the fogs of Fate,
Time's famous rival till the final date!

CVI.

"O shield us then from this usurping Time,
And we will visit thee in moonlight dreams;
And teach thee tunes, to wed unto thy rhyme,
And dance about thee in all midnight gleams,
Giving thee glimpses of our magic schemes,
Such as no mortal's eye hath ever seen;
And for thy love to us in our extremes,
Will ever keep thy chaplet fresh and green,
Such as no poet's wreath hath ever been!

CVII.

"And we'll distil the aromatic dews,
To charm thy sense, when there shall be no flowers
And flavored sirups in thy drinks infuse,
And teach the nightingale to haunt thy bowers,
And with our games divert thy weariest hours,
With all that elfin wits can e'er devise.
And, this churl dead, there'll be no hasting hours
To rob thee of thy joys, as now joy flies:"
Here she was stopped by Saturn's furious cries.

CVIII.

Whom, therefore, the kind Shade rebukes anew,
Saying, "Thou haggard Sin, go forth, and scoop
Thy hollow coffin in some churchyard yew,
Or make th' autumnal flowers turn pale and droop;
Or fell the bearded corn, till gleaners stoop
Under fat sheaves—or blast the piny grove;
But here thou shalt not harm this pretty group,
Whose lives are not so frail and feebly wove,
But leased on Nature's loveliness and love.

CIX.

"'Tis these that free the small entangled fly,
Caught in the venomed spider's crafty snare;
These be the petty surgeons that apply
The healing balsams to the wounded hare,
Bedded in bloody fern, no creature's care!
These be providers for the orphan brood,
Whose tender mother hath been slain in air
Quitting with gaping bill her darling's food,
Hard by the verge of her domestic wood.

CX.

"'Tis these befriend the timid trembling stag,
When with a bursting heart beset with fears.
He feels his saving speed begin to flag;
For then they quench the fatal taint with tears,
And prompt fresh shifts in his alarumed ears,
So piteously they view all bloody morts;
Or if the gunner, with his arm, appears,
Like noisy pyes and jays, with harsh reports,
They warn the wild fowl of his deadly sports.

CXI.

"For these are kindly ministers of nature,
To sooth all covert hurts and dumb distress;
Pretty they be, and very small of stature—
For mercy still consorts with littleness;
Wherefore the sum of good is still the less,
And mischief grossest in this world of wrong;
So do these charitable dwarfs redress
The tenfold ravages of giants strong,
To whom great malice and great might belong.

CXII.

"Likewise to them are poets much beholden
For secret favors in the midnight glooms;
Brave Spenser quaffed out of their goblets golden,
And saw their tables spread of prompt mushrooms
And heard their horns of honeysuckle blooms
Sounding upon the air most soothing soft,
Like humming bees busy about the brooms,
And glanced this fair queen's witchery full oft,
And in her magic wain soared far aloft.

CXIII.

"Nay I myself, though mortal, once was nursed
By fairy gossips, friendly at my birth,
And in my childish ear glib Mab rehearsed
Her breezy travels round our planet's girth,
Telling me wonders of the moon and earth:
My gramarye at her grave lap I conned,
Where Puck hath been convened to make me mirth;
I have had from Queen Titania tokens fond,
And toyed with Oberon's permitted wand.

CXIV.

"With figs, and plums, and Persian dates they fed me,
And delicate cates after my sunset meal,
And took me by my childish hand, and led me
By craggy rocks crested with keeps of steel,
Whose awful bases deep dark woods conceal,
Staining some dead lake with their verdant dies:
And when the West sparkled at Phœbus' wheel,
With fairy euphrasy they purged mine eyes,
To let me see their cities in the skies.

CXV.

"'Twas they first schooled my young imagination
To take its flights like any new-fledged bird,
And showed the span of winged meditation
Stretched wider than things grossly seen or heard.
With sweet swift Ariel how I soared and stirred
The fragrant blooms of spiritual bowers!
'Twas they endeared what I have still preferred,
Nature's blest attributes and balmy powers,
Her hills and vales and brooks, sweet birds and flowers!

CXVI.

"Wherefore with all true loyalty and duty
Will I regard them in my honoring rhyme,
With love for love, and homages to beauty,
And magic thoughts gathered in night's cool clime,
With studious verse trancing the dragon Time,
Strong as old Merlin's necromantic spells;
So these dear monarchs of the summer's prime
Shall live unstartled by his dreadful yells,
Till shrill larks warn them to their flowery cells."

CXVII.

Look how a poisoned man turns livid black,
Drugged with a cup of deadly hellebore,
That sets his horrid features all at rack,—
So seemed these words into the ear to pour
Of ghastly Saturn, answering with a roar
Of mortal pain and spite and utmost rage,
Wherewith his grisly arm he raised once more,
And bade the clustered sinews all engage,
As if at one fell stroke to wreck an age.

CXVIII.

Whereas the blade flashed on the dinted ground,
Down through his steadfast foe, yet made no scar
On that immortal Shade, or death-like wound;
But Time was long benumbed, and stood ajar,
And then with baffled rage took flight afar,
To weep his hurt in some Cimmerian gloom,
Or meaner fames (like mine) to mock and mar,
Or sharp his scythe for royal strokes of doom,
Whetting its edge on some Old Cæsar's tomb.

CXIX.

Howbeit he vanished in the forest shade,
Distantly heard as if some grumbling pard,
And, like Narcissus, to a sound decayed;
Meanwhile the fays clustered the gracious Bard,
The darling centre of their dear regard:
Besides of sundry dances on the green,
Never was mortal man so brightly starred,
Or won such pretty homages, I ween.
"Nod to him, Elves!" cries the melodious queen.

CXX.

"Nod to him, Elves, and flutter round about him,
And quite enclose him with your pretty crowd,
And touch him lovingly, for that, without him,
The silk-worm now had spun our dreary shroud;
But he hath all dispersed death's tearful cloud,
And Time's dread effigy scared quite away:
Bow to him then, as though to me ye bowed,
And his dear wishes prosper and obey
Wherever love and wit can find a way!

CXXI.

"'Noint him with fairy dews of magic savors,
Shaken from orient buds still pearly wet,
Roses and spicy pinks,—and, of all favors,
Plant in his walks the purple violet,
And meadow-sweet, under the hedges set,
To mingle breaths with dainty eglantine
And honeysuckles sweet, nor yet forget
Some pastoral flowery chaplets to entwine,
To vie the thoughts about his brow benign!

CXXII.

"Let no wild things astonish him or fear him,
But tell them all how mild he is of heart,
Till e'en the timid hares go frankly near him,
And eke the dappled does, yet never start;
Nor shall their fawns into the thickets dart,
Nor wrens forsake their nests among the leaves,
Nor speckled thrushes flutter far apart;
But bid the sacred swallow haunt his eaves,
To guard his roof from lightning and from thieves.

CXXIII.

"Or when he goes the nimble squirrel's visiter,
Let the brown hermit bring his hoarded nuts,
For, tell him, this is Nature's kind inquisitor,—
Though man keeps cautious doors that conscience shuts
For conscious wrong all curious quest rebuts,—
Nor yet shall bees uncase their jealous stings,
However he may watch their straw-built huts;
So let him learn the crafts of all small things,
Which he will hint most aptly when he sings."

CXXIV.

Here she leaves off, and with a graceful hand
Waves thrice three splendid circles round his head;
Which, though deserted by the radiant wand,
Wears still the glory which her waving shed,
Such as erst crowned the old Apostle's head,
To show the thoughts there harbored were divine
And on immortal contemplations fed:
Goodly it was to see that glory shine
Around a brow so lofty and benign!

CXXV.

Goodly it was to see the elfin brood
Contend for kisses of his gentle hand,
That had their mortal enemy withstood,
And stayed their lives, fast ebbing with the sand.
Long while this strife engaged the pretty band;
But now bold Chanticleer, from farm to farm,
Challenged the dawn creeping o'er eastern land,
And well the fairies knew that shrill alarm,
Which sounds the knell of every elfish charm.

CXXVI.

And soon the rolling mist, that 'gan arise
From plashy mead and undiscovered stream,
Earth's morning incense to the early skies,
Crept o'er the failing landscape of my dream.
Soon faded then the Phantom of my theme—
A shapeless shade, that fancy disavowed,
And shrank to nothing in the mist extreme.
Then flew Titania,—and her little crowd,
Like flocking linnets, vanished in a cloud.

THE DREAM OF EUGENE ARAM.

'Twas in the prime of summer time,
  An evening calm and cool,
And four-and-twenty happy boys,
  Came bounding out of school:
There were some that ran, and some that leapt
  Like troutlets in a pool.

Away they sped with gamesome minds,
  And souls untouched by sin;
To a level mead they came, and there
  They drave the wickets in:
Pleasantly shone the setting sun
  Over the town of Lynn.

Like sportive deer they coursed about,
  And shouted as they ran;
Turning to mirth all things of earth,
  As only boyhood can;
But the Usher sat remote from all,
  A melancholy man!

His hat was off, his vest apart,
  To catch heaven's blessed breeze;
For a burning thought was in his brow,
  And his bosom ill at ease:
So he leaned his head on his hands, and rea..
  The book between his knees!

Leaf after leaf, he turned it o'er,
  Nor ever glanced aside;
For the peace of his soul he read that book
  In the golden eventide.
Much study had made him very lean,
  And pale, and leaden-eyed.

At last he shut the ponderous tome,
  With a fast and fervent grasp
He strained the dusky covers close,
  And fixed the brazen hasp:
'O God! could I so close my mind,
  And clasp it with a clasp!"

Then leaping on his feet upright,
  Some moody turns he took;
Now up the mead, now down the mead,
  And past a shady nook;
And lo! he saw a little boy
  That pored upon a book!

"My gentle lad, what is't you read—
  Romance or fairy fable?
Or is it some historic page,
  Of kings and crowns unstable?"
The young boy gave an upward glance;
  "It is 'The Death of Abel.'"

The Usher took six hasty strides,
  As smit with sudden pain;
Six hasty strides beyond the place,
  Then slowly back again;
And then he sat beside the lad,
  And talked with him of Cain:

And, long since then, of bloody men
  Whose deeds tradition saves;
Of lonely folk cut off unseen,
  And hid in sudden graves;
Of horrid stabs, in groves forlorn,
  And murders done in caves;

And how the sprites of injured men
  Shriek upward from the sod;
Ay, how the ghostly hand will point
  To show the burial clod;
And unknown facts of guilty acts
  Are seen in dreams from God!

He told how murderers walk the earth
  Beneath the curse of Cain;
With crimson clouds before their eyes,
  And flames about their brain:
For blood has left upon their souls
  Its everlasting stain!

"And well," quoth he, "I know for truth,
  Their pangs must be extreme;—
Wo, wo, unutterable wo—
  Who spill life's sacred stream!
For why? Methought last night, I wrought
  A murder in a dream!

"One that had never done me wrong—
  A feeble man, and old:
I led him to a lonely field,
  The moon shone clear and cold.
'Now here,' said I, 'this man shall die,
  And I will have his gold!'

"Two sudden blows with a ragged stick,
  And one with a heavy stone;
One hurried gash with a hasty knife,
  And then the deed was done.
There was nothing lying at my foot,
  But lifeless flesh and bone;

"Nothing but lifeless flesh and bone,
  That could not do me ill;
And yet I feared him all the more,
  For lying there so still:
There was a manhood in his look,
  That murder could not kill!

"And, lo! the universal air
  Seemed lit with ghastly flame;
Ten thousand thousand dreadful eyes
  Were looking down in blame:
I took the dead man by the hand,
  And called upon his name!

"O God! it made me quake to see
  Such sense within the slain!
But when I touched the lifeless clay,
  The blood gushed out amain;
For every clot, a burning spot
  Was scorching in my brain!

"My head was like an ardent coal;
  My heart as solid ice;
My wretched, wretched soul, I knew,
  Was at the devil's price.
A dozen times I groaned; the dead
  Had never groaned but twice!

"And now, from forth the frowning sky
  From the heaven's topmost height,
I heard a voice—the awful voice
  Of the blood-avenging Sprite:—
'Thou guilty man! take up thy dead,
  And hide it from my sight!'

"I took the dreary body up,
  And cast it in a stream;
A sluggish water, black as ink,
  The depth was so extreme.—
My gentle boy, remember this
  Is nothing but a dream!

"Down went the corse, with a hollow plunge,
  And vanished in the pool:
Anon I cleansed my bloody hands,
  And washed my forehead cool;
And sat among the urchins young
  That evening in the school!

"Oh heaven, to think of their white souls,
  And mine so black and grim!
I could not share in childish prayer,
  Nor join in evening hymn:
Like a devil of the pit, I seemed,
  Mid holy cherubim!

"And peace went with them, one and all,
  And each calm pillow spread;
But Guilt was my grim chamberlain
  That lighted me to bed,
And drew my midnight curtains round,
  With fingers bloody red!

"All night I lay in agony,
  In anguish dark and deep;
My fevered eyes I dared not close,
  But stared aghast at sleep;
For sin had rendered unto her
  The keys of hell to keep!

"All night I lay in agony,
  From weary chime to chime,
With one besetting horrid hint,
  That racked me all the time;
A mighty yearning, like the first
  Fierce impulse unto crime!

"One stern tyrannic thought that made
  All other thoughts its slave;
Stronger and stronger every pulse,
  Did that temptation crave:
Still urging me to go and see
  The dead man in his grave!

"Heavily I rose up, as soon
  As light was in the sky,
And sought the black accursed pool
  With a wild misgiving eye;
And I saw the dead in the river bed,
  For the faithless stream was dry!

"Merrily rose the lark, and shook
  The dewdrop from its wing;
But I never marked its morning flight,
  I never heard it sing:
For I was stooping once again
  Under the horrid thing.

"With breathless speed, like a soul in chase,
  I took him up and ran;
There was no time to dig a grave
  Before the day began:
In a lonesome wood, with heaps of leaves,
  I hid the murdered man!

"And all that day I read in school,
  But my thought was other where;
As soon as the mid-day task was done,
  In secret I was there:
And a mighty wind had swept the leaves,
  And still the corse was bare!

"Then down I cast me on my face,
  And first began to weep;
For I knew my secret then was one
  That earth refused to keep:
Or land, or sea, though he should be
  Ten thousand fathoms deep!

"So wills the fierce avenging Sprite,
  Till blood for blood atones!
Ay, though he's buried in a cave,
  And trodden down with stones,
And years have rotted off his flesh—
  The world shall see his bones!

"O God! that horrid, horrid dream
  Besets me now awake!
Again—again, with a dizzy brain,
  The human life I take;
And my red right hand grows raging hot,
  Like Cranmer's at the stake.

"And still no peace for the restless clay
  Will wave or mould allow;
The horrid thing pursues my soul—
  It stands before me now!"
The fearful boy looked up and saw
  Huge drops upon his brow!

That very night, while gentle sleep
  The urchin eyelids kissed,
Two stern-faced men set out from Lynn,
  Through the cold and heavy mist;
And Eugene Aram walked between,
  With gyves upon his wrist.*

A RETROSPECTIVE REVIEW.

Oh, when I was a tiny boy
My days and nights were full of joy,
  My mates were blithe and kind!
No wonder that I sometimes sigh,
And dash the tear-drop from my eye,
  To cast a look behind!

A hoop was an eternal round
Of pleasure. In those days I found
  A top a joyous thing;
But now those past delights I drop;
My head, alas! is all my top,
  And careful thoughts the string!

My marbles—once my bag was stored—
Now I must play with Elgin's lord,
  With Theseus for a taw!
My playful horse has slipt his string,
Forgotten all his capering,
  And harnessed to the law!

My kite—how fast and far it flew!
Whilst I, a sort of Franklin, drew
  My pleasure from the sky!
'Twas papered o'er with studious themes—
The tasks I wrote—my present dreams
  Will never soar so high!

My joys are wingless all and dead;
My dumps are made of more than lead;
  My flights soon find a fall.
My fears prevail, my fancies droop,
Joy never cometh with a hoop,
  And seldom with a call!

My football's laid upon the shelf;
I am a shuttlecock myself
  The world knocks to and fro;
My archery is all unlearned,
And grief against myself has turned
  My arrows and my bow!

No more in noontide sun I bask;
My authorship's an endless task;
  My head's ne'er out of school.
My heart is pained with scorn and slight,
I have too many foes to fight,
  And friends grow strangely cool!

The very chum that shared my cake
Holds out so cold a hand to shake
  It makes me shrink and sigh;
On this I will not dwell and hang,
The changeling would not feel a pang
  Though these should meet his eye!

No skies so blue or so serene
As then;—no leaves look half so green
  As clothed the playground tree!
All things I loved are altered so,
Nor does it ease my heart to know
  That change resides in me!

O, for the garb that marked the boy,
The trowsers made of corduroy,
  Well inked with black and red;
The crownless hat, ne'er deemed an ill—
It only let the sunshine still
  Repose upon my head!

O, for the riband round the neck!
The careless dog's ears apt to deck
  My book and collar both!
How can this formal man be styled
Merely an Alexandrine child,
  A boy of larger growth?

O for that small, small beer anew!
And (heaven's own type) that mild sky-blue
  That washed my sweet meals down;
The master even!—and that small Turk
That fagged me!—worse is now my work—
  A fag for all the town!

O for the lessons learned by heart!
Ay, though the very birch's smart
  Should mark those hours again;
I'd "kiss the rod," and be resigned
Beneath the stroke, and even find
  Some sugar in the cane!

The Arabian Nights rehearsed in bed!
The Fairy Tales in school-time read,
  By stealth, 'twixt verb and noun!
The angel form that always walked
In all my dreams, and looked and talked
  Exactly like Miss Brown!

* The late Admiral Burney went to school at an establishment where the unhappy Eugene Aram was usher subsequent to his crime. The admiral stated, that Aram was generally liked by the boys: and that he used to discourse to them about murder, in somewhat of the spirit which is attributed to him in this poem.

The *omne bene*—Christmas come!
The prize of merit, won for home—
  Merit had prizes then!
But now I write for days and days
For fame—a deal of empty praise,
  Without the silver pen!

Then home, sweet home! the crowded coach—
The joyous shout—the loud approach—
  The winding horns like rams'!
The meeting sweet that made me thrill,
The sweetmeats almost sweeter still,
  No "satis" to the "jams."

When that I was a tiny boy
My days and nights were full of joy,
  My mates were blithe and kind!
No wonder that I sometimes sigh,
And dash the tear-drop from my eye,
  To cast a look behind!

FAIR INES.

O saw ye not fair Ines?
She's gone into the west,
To dazzle when the sun is down,
And rob the world of rest.
She took our daylight with her,
The smiles that we love best,
With morning blushes on her cheek,
And pearls upon her breast.

O turn again, fair Ines,
Before the fall of night,
For fear the moon should shine alone,
And stars unrivalled bright;
And blessed will the lover be
That walks beneath their light,
And breathes the love against thy cheek
I dare not even write!

Would I had been, fair Ines,
That gallant cavalier,
Who rode so gayly by thy side,
And whispered thee so near!—
Were there no bonny dames at home,
Or no true lovers here,
That he should cross the seas to win
The dearest of the dear?

I saw thee, lovely Ines,
Descend along the shore,
With bands of noble gentlemen,
And banners waved before;
And gentle youth and maidens gay,
And snowy plumes they wore:
It would have been a beauteous dream,
If it had been no more!

Alas, alas, fair Ines!
She went away with song,
With Music waiting on her steps,
And shoutings of the throng;
But some were sad and felt no mirth,
But only Music's wrong,
In sounds that sang, Farewell, farewell,
To her you've loved so long.

Farewell, farewell, fair Ines,
That vessel never bore
So fair a lady on its deck,
Nor danced so light before
Alas for pleasure on the sea,
And sorrow on the shore!
The smile that blest one lover's heart
Has broken many more!

WHAT CAN AN OLD MAN DO BUT DIE?

    Spring, it is cheery,
    Winter is dreary,
Green leaves hang, but the brown must fly;
    When he's forsaken,
    Withered and shaken,
What can an old man do but die?

    Love will not clip him,
    Maids will not lip him,
Maud and Marian pass him by;
    Youth it is sunny,
    Age has no honey,—
What can an old man do but die?

    June it was jolly;
    O for its folly!
A dancing leg and a laughing eye;
    Youth may be silly,
    Wisdom is chilly,—
What can an old man do but die?

    Friends they are scanty,
    Beggars are plenty,
If he has followers, I know why;
    Gold's in his clutches,
    (Buying him crutches!)—
What can an old man do but die?

HYMN TO THE SUN.

Giver of glowing light!
Though but a god of other days,
    The kings and sages
    Of wiser ages
Still live and gladden in thy genial rays!

King of the tuneful lyre,
Still poet's hymns to thee belong;
    Though lips are cold
    Whereon of old
Thy beams all turned to worshipping and song!

Lord of the dreadful bow,
None triumph now for Python's death;
    But thou dost save
    From hungry grave
The life that hangs upon a summer breath.

Father of rosy day,
No more thy clouds of incense rise;
    But waking flowers
    At morning hours,
Give out their sweets to meet thee in the skies.

God of the Delphic fane,
No more thou listenest to hymns sublime;
    But they will leave
    On winds at eve,
A solemn echo to the end of time.

TO A COLD BEAUTY.

Lady, wouldst thou heiress be,
  To Winter's cold and cruel part?
When he sets the rivers free,
  Thou dost still lock up thy heart;—
That thou shouldst outlast the snow,
But in the whiteness of thy brow?

Scorn and cold neglect are made
  For winter gloom and winter wind;
But thou wilt wrong the summer air,
  Breathing it to words unkind;
Breath which only should belong
To love, to sunlight, and to song!

When the little buds unclose,
  Red and white and pied and blue,
And that virgin flower, the rose,
  Opes her heart to hold the dew,
Wilt thou lock thy bosom up,
With no jewel in its cup?

Let not cold December sit
  Thus in Love's peculiar throne;—
Brooklets are not prisoned now,
  But crystal frosts are all agone,
And that which hangs upon the spray
  It is no snow, but flower of May!

A LAKE AND A FAIRY BOAT.

A LAKE and a fairy boat
To sail in the moonlight clear;
And merrily we would float
From the dragons that watch us here!

Thy gown should be snow-white silk,
And strings of orient pearls,
Like gossamers dipped in milk,
Should twine with thy raven curls!

Red rubies should deck thy hands,
And diamonds should be thy dower;
But fairies have broke their wands
And wishing has lost its power!

THE THANKLESS GIRL

SHE's up and gone, the graceless girl!
And robbed my failing years;
My blood before was thin and cold,
But now 'tis turned to tears.
My shadow falls upon my grave,
So near the brink I stand;
She might have stayed a little yet,
And led me by the hand!

Ay, call her on the barren moor,
And call her on the hill;
'Tis nothing but the heron's cry,
And plover's answer shrill.
My child is flown on wilder wings
Than they have ever spread;
And I may even walk a waste
That widened when she fled.

Full many a thankless child has been,
But never one like mine;
Her meat was served on plates of gold,
Her drink was rosy wine;
But now she'll share the robin's food,
And sup the common rill,
Before her feet will turn again
To meet her father's will!

RUTH.

SHE stood breast high amid the corn,
Clasped by the golden light of morn,
Like the sweetheart of the sun,
Who many a glowing kiss had won.

On her cheek an autumn flush
Deeply ripened;—such a blush
In the midst of brown was born,
Like red poppies grown with corn.

Round her eyes her tresses fell,
Which were blackest none could tell;
But long lashes veiled a light,
That had else been all too bright.

And her hat, with shady brim,
Made her tressy forehead dim;
Thus she stood amid the stooks,
Praising God with sweetest looks.

"Sure," I said, "heaven did not mean,
Where I reap thou shouldst but glean:
Lay thy sheaf adown, and come
Share my harvest and my home."

THE SEA OF DEATH.

A FRAGMENT.

———— Methought I saw
Life swiftly treading over endless space;
And, at her foot-print, but a by-gone pace,
The ocean-past, which, with increasing wave,
Swallowed her steps like a pursuing grave.

Sad were my thoughts that anchored silently
On the dead waters of that passionless sea,
Unstirred by any touch of living breath:
Silence hung over it, and drowsy Death
Like a gorged sea-bird, slept with folded wings
On crowded carcasses—sad passive things
That wore the thin gray surface, like a veil
Over the calmness of their features pale.

And there were spring-faced cherubs, that did sleep
Like water-lilies on that motionless deep—
How beautiful! with bright unruffled hair
On sleek unfretted brows, and eyes that were
Buried in marble tombs, a pale eclipse!
And smile-bedimpled cheeks, and pleasant lips,
Meekly apart, as if the soul intense
Spake out in dreams of its own innocence.

And so they lay in loveliness, and kept
The birth-night of their peace, that Life e'en wept
With very envy of their happy fronts;
For there were neighbor brows, scarred by the brunts
Of strife and sorrowing—where Care had set
His crooked autograph, and marred the jet
Of glossy locks, with hollow eyes forlorn,
And lips that curled in bitterness and scorn—
Wretched—as they had breathed of this world's pain,
And so bequeathed it to the world again,
Through the beholder's heart in heavy sighs.

So lay they garmented in torpid light,
Under the pall of a transparent night,
Like solemn apparitions lulled sublime
To everlasting rest; and with them Time
Slept, as he sleeps upon the silent face
Of a dark dial in a sunless place.

THE EXILE.

THE Swallow with summer
Will wing o'er the seas,
The wind that I sigh to
Will visit thy trees,
The ship that it hastens
Thy ports will contain,
But me—I must never
See England again!

There's many that weep there,
But one weeps alone,
For the tears that are falling
So far from her own;
So far from thy own, love.
We know not our pain;
If death is between us,
Or only the main.

When the white cloud reclines
On the verge of the sea,
I fancy the white cliffs,
And dream upon thee;
But the cloud spreads its wings
To the blue heaven and flies.
We shall never meet, love,
Except in the skies!

TO AN ABSENTEE.

O'ER hill, and dale, and distant sea,
Through all the miles that stretch between,
My thought must fly to rest on thee,
And would, though worlds should intervene.

Nay, thou art now so dear, methinks
The farther we are forced apart,
Affection's firm elastic links
But bind the closer round the heart.

For now we sever each from each,
I learn what I have lost in thee;
Alas, that nothing less could teach,
How great indeed my love should be!

Farewell! I did not know thy worth,
But thou art gone, and now 'tis prized:
So angels walked unknown on earth,
But when they flew were recognised!

THE DEMON-SHIP.

'Twas off the Wash—the sun went down—the sea looked black and grim,
For stormy clouds, with murky fleece were mustering at the brim;
Titanic shades! enormous gloom! as if the solid night
Of Erebus rose suddenly to seize upon the light!
It was a time for mariners to bear a wary eye,
With such a dark conspiracy between the sea and sky!

Down went my helm—close reefed—the tack held freely in my hand—
With ballast snug—I put about, and scudded for the land.
Loud hissed the sea beneath her lee—my little boat flew fast,
But faster still the rushing storm came borne upon the blast.
Lord! what a roaring hurricane beset the straining sail!
What furious sleet, with level drift, and fierce assaults of hail!
What darksome caverns yawned before! what jagged steeps behind!
Like battle-steeds, with foamy manes, wild tossing in the wind.
Each after each sank down astern, exhausted in the chase,
But where it sank another rose and galloped in its place;
As black as night—they turned to white, and cast against the cloud
A snowy sheet, as if each surge upturned a sailor's shroud—
Still flew my boat; alas! alas! her course was nearly run;
Behold yon fatal billow rise—ten billows heaped in one!
With fearful speed the dreary mass came rolling, rolling fast,
As if the scooping sea contained one only wave at last!
Still on it came, with horrid roar, a swift pursuing grave;
It seemed as though some cloud had turned its hugeness to a wave!
Its briny sleet began to beat beforehand in my face—
I felt the rearward keel begin to climb its swelling base!
I saw its alpine hoary head impending over mine!
Another pulse—and down it rushed—an avalanche of brine;
Brief pause had I, on God to cry, or think of wife and home;
The waters closed—and when I shrieked, I shrieked below the foam!
Beyond that rush I have no hint of any after deed—
For I was tossing on the waste, as senseless as a weed.

* * * * *

"Where am I? in the breathing world, or in the world of death?
With sharp and sudden pang I drew another birth of breath;
My eyes drank in a doubtful light, my ears a doubtful sound—
And was that ship a *real* ship, whose tackle seemed around?
A moon, as if the earthly moon, was shining up aloft;
But were those beams, the very beams that I had seen so oft;
A face, that mocked the human face, before me watched alone;
But were those eyes the eyes of man, that looked against my own?

Oh! never may the moon again disclose me such a sight
As met my gaze, when first I looked, on that accursed night!
I've seen a thousand horrid shapes begot of fierce extremes
Of fever; and most frightful things have haunted in my dreams—
Hyenas—cats—blood-loving bats—and apes with hateful stare—
Pernicious snakes, and shaggy bulls—the lion and she-bear—
Strong enemies, with Judas looks, of treachery and spite—
Detested features, hardly dimmed and banished by the light!
Pale-sheeted ghosts, with gory locks, upstarting from their tombs—
All phantasies and images that flit in midnight glooms—
Hags, goblins, demons, lemures, have made me all aghast,—
But nothing like that Grimly One who stood beside the mast!

His cheek was black—his brow was black—his eyes and hair as dark:
His hand was black, and where it touched, it left a sable mark;
His throat was black, his vest the same, and when I looked beneath,
His breast was black—all, all was black except his grinning teeth.
His sooty crew were like in hue, as black as Afric slaves!
Oh, horror! e'en the ship was black that ploughed the inky waves!

"Alas!" I cried, "for love of truth and blessed mercy's sake,
Where am I? in what dreadful ship? upon what dreadful lake?
What shape is that, so very grim, and black as any coal?
It is Mahound, the Evil One, and he has won my soul!
Oh, mother dear! my tender nurse! dear meadows that beguiled
My happy days, when I was yet a little sinless child:
My mother dear—my native fields, I never more shall see!
I'm sailing in the Devil's Ship, upon the Devil's Sea!"

Loud laughed that Sable Mariner, and loudly in return
His sooty crew sent forth a laugh that rang from stem to stern—
A dozen pair of grimly cheeks were crumpled on the nonce—
As many sets of grinning teeth came shining out at once:
A dozen gloomy shapes at once enjoyed the merry fit,
With shriek and yell, and oaths as well, like Demons of the Pit.
They crowed their fill, and then the Chief made answer for the whole:—
"Our skins," said he, "are black ye see, because we carry coal;
You'll find your mother sure enough, and see your native fields—
For this here ship has picked you up—the Mary Ann of Shields!"

THE FORSAKEN.

The dead are in their silent graves,
And the dew is cold above,
And the living weep and sigh,
Over dust that once was love.

Once I only wept the dead,
But now the living cause my pain:
How couldst thou steal me from my tears,
To leave me to my tears again?

My mother rests beneath the sod,—
Her rest is calm and very deep:
I wished that she could see our loves,—
But now I gladden in her sleep.

Last night unbound my raven locks,
The morning saw them turned to gray,
Once they were black and well-beloved,
But thou art changed—and so are they!

The useless lock I gave thee once,
To gaze upon and think of me,
Was ta'en with smiles,—but this was torn
In sorrow that I send to thee!

THE STARS ARE WITH THE VOYAGER

The stars are with the voyager
Wherever he may sail;
The moon is constant to her time;
The sun will never fail;
But follow, follow round the world,
The green earth and the sea;
So love is with the lover's heart,
Wherever he may be.

Wherever he may be, the stars
Must daily lose their light;
The moon will veil her in the shade;
The sun will set at night.
The sun may set but constant love
Will shine when he's away;
So that dull night is never night,
And day is brighter day.

ODE TO MELANCHOLY.

Come, let us set our careful breasts,
Like Philomel, against the thorn,
To aggravate the inward grief,
That makes her accents so forlorn;
The world has many cruel points,
Whereby our bosoms have been torn,
And there are dainty themes of grief,
In sadness to outlast the morn,—
True honor's dearth, affection's death,
Neglectful pride, and cankering scorn,
With all the piteous tales that tears
Have watered since the world was born.

The world!—it is a wilderness,
Where tears are hung on every tree;
For thus my gloomy phantasy
Makes all things weep with me!
Come, let us sit and watch the sky,
And fancy clouds, where no clouds be;
Grief is enough to blot the eye,
And make heaven black with misery.
Why should birds sing such merry notes,
Unless they were more blest than we?
No sorrow ever chokes their throats,
Except sweet nightingale; for she
Was born to pain our hearts the more
With her sad melody.
Why shines the sun, except that he
Makes gloomy nooks for Grief to hide,
And pensive shades for Melancholy,
When all the earth is bright beside?
Let clay wear smiles, and green grass wave,
Mirth shall not win us back again,
While man is made of his own grave,
And fairest clouds but gilded rain!

I saw my mother in her shroud,
Her cheek was cold and very pale;
And ever since I've looked on all
As creatures doomed to fail!
Why do buds ope, except to die?
Ay, let us watch the roses wither,
And think of our loves' cheeks;
And oh, how quickly time doth fly
To bring death's winter hither!
Minutes, hours, days, and weeks,
Months, years, and ages, shrink to naught;
An age past is but a thought!

Ay, let us think of him a while,
That, with a coffin for a boat,
Rows daily o'er the Stygian moat,
And for our table choose a tomb:
There's dark enough in any skull
To charge with black a raven plume;
And for the saddest funeral thoughts
A winding sheet hath ample room,
Where Death, with his keen-pointed style,
Hath writ the common doom.
How wide the yew-tree spreads its gloom,
And o'er the dead lets fall its dew,
As if in tears it wept for them,
The many human families
That sleep around its stem!

How cold the dead have made these stones,
With natural drops kept ever wet!
Lo! here the best, the worst, the world
Doth now remember or forget,
Are in one common ruin hurled,
And love and hate are calmly met;
The loveliest eyes that ever shone,
The fairest hands, and locks of jet.
Is 't not enough to vex our souls,
And fill our eyes, that we have set
Our love upon a rose's leaf,
Our hearts upon a violet?
Blue eyes, red cheeks, are frailer yet;
And sometimes at their swift decay
Beforehand we must fret.
The roses bud and bloom again;
But love may haunt the grave of love,
And watch the mould in vain.
O clasp me, sweet, while thou art mine,
And do not take my tears amiss;
For tears must flow to wash away
A thought that shows so stern as this:
Forgive, if somewhat I forget,
In wo to come, the present bliss,
As frighted Proserpine let fall
Her flowers at the sight of Dis,
E'en so the dark and bright will kiss.
The sunniest things throw sternest shade,
And there is e'en a happiness
That makes the heart afraid!

Now let us with a spell invoke
The full-orbed moon to grieve our eyes;
Not bright, not bright, but, with a cloud
Lapped all about her, let her rise
All pale and dim, as if from rest
The ghost of the late-buried sun
Had crept into the skies.
The Moon! she is the source of sighs,
The very face to make us sad;
If but to think in other times
The same calm quiet look she had,
As if the world held nothing base,
Of vile and mean, of fierce and bad;
The same fair light that shone in streams,
The fairy lamp that charmed the lad;
For so it is, with spent delights
She taunts men's brains, and makes them mad.

All things are touched with melancholy,
Born of the secret soul's mistrust,
To feel her fair ethereal wings
Weighed down with vile degraded dust;
Even the bright extremes of joy
Bring on conclusions of disgust,
Like the sweet blossoms of the May,
Whose fragrance ends in must.
O give her, then, her tribute just,
Her sighs and tears, and musings holy!
There is no music in the life
That sounds with idiot laughter solely;
There's not a string attuned to mirth,
But has its chord in melancholy.

TO ——.

Welcome, dear Heart, and a most kind good morrow;
The day is gloomy, but our looks shall shine:—
Flowers I have none to give thee, but I borrow
Their sweetness in a verse to speak for thine.

Here are red roses, gathered at thy cheeks,—
The white were all too happy to look white:
For love the rose, for faith the lily speaks;
It withers in false hands, but here 'tis bright!

Dost love sweet Hyacinth? Its scented leaf
Curls manifold,—all love's delights blow double:
'Tis said this floweret is inscribed with grief,—
But let that hint of a forgotten trouble.

I plucked the Primrose at night dewy noon;
Like Hope, it showed its blossoms in the night;
'Twas, like Endymion, watching for the Moon!
And here are Sun-flowers, amorous of light!

These golden Buttercups are April's seal,—
The Daisy stars her constellations be:
These grew so lowly, I was forced to kneel,
Therefore I pluck no Daisies but for thee!

Here's Daisies for the morn, Primrose for gloom,
Pansies and Roses for the noontide hours:
A wight once made a dial of their bloom,—
So may thy life be measured out by flowers!

SIGH ON, SAD HEART.

SIGH on, sad heart, for Love's eclipse,
And Beauty's fairest queen,
Though 'tis not for my peasant lips
To soil her name between:
A king might lay his sceptre down,
But I am poor and nought,
The brow should wear a golden crown,
That wears her in its thought.

The diamonds glancing in her hair,
Whose sudden beams surprise,
Might bid such humble hopes beware
The glancing of her eyes;
Yet looking once, I looked too long,
And if my love is sin,
Death follows on the heels of wrong,
And kills the crime within.

Her dress seemed wove of lily leaves,
It was so pure and fine,
O lofty wears, and lowly weaves,
But hoddan gray is mine;
And homely hose must step apart,
Where gartered princes stand,
But may he wear my love at heart
That wins her lily hand!

Alas! there's far from russet frieze
To silks and satin gowns,
But I doubt if God made like degrees,
In courtly hearts and clowns.
My father wronged a maiden's mirth,
And brought her cheeks to blame,
And all that's lordly of my birth,
Is my reproach and shame!

'Tis vain to weep, 'tis vain to sigh,
'Tis vain this idle speech,
For where her happy pearls do lie,
My tears may never reach;
Yet when I'm gone, e'en lofty pride
May say of what has been,
His love was nobly born and died,
Though all the rest was mean!

My speech is rude—but speech is weak
Such love as mine to tell,
Yet had I words, I dare not speak,
So Lady, fare thee well;
I will not wish thy better state
Was one of low degree,
But I must weep that partial fate
Made such a churl of me.

THE WATER LADY.

ALAS, the moon should ever beam
To show what man should never see!
I saw a maiden on a stream,
And fair was she!

I stayed awhile to see her throw
Her tresses back, that all beset
The fair horizon of her brow
With clouds of jet.

I stayed a little while to view
Her cheek, that wore in place of red
The bloom of water, tender blue,
Daintily spread.

I stayed to watch a little space,
Her parted lips if she would sing;
The waters closed above her face
With many a ring.

And still I stayed a little more,
Alas! she never comes again;
I throw my flowers from the shore,
And watch in vain.

I know my life will fade away,
I know that I must vainly pine,
For I am made of mortal clay,
But she's divine!

I REMEMBER, I REMEMBER.

I remember, I remember,
The house where I was born,
The little window where the sun
Came peeping in at morn;
He never came a wink too soon,
Nor brought too long a day,
But now I often wish the night
Had borne my breath away!

I remember, I remember,
The roses, red and white,
The violets, and the lily-cups,
Those flowers made of light!
The lilacs where the robin built,
And where my brother set
The liburnam on his birth-day—
The tree is living yet!

I remember, I remember,
Where I was used to swing,
And thought the air must rush as fresh
To swallows on the wing;
My spirit flew in feathers then,
That is so heavy now,
And summer pools could hardly cool
The fever on my brow!

I remember, I remember,
The fir-trees dark and high;
I used to think their slender tops
Were close against the sky:
It was a childish ignorance,
But now 'tis little joy
To know I'm farther off from heaven
Than when I was a boy.

SILENCE.

THERE is a silence where hath been no sound,
There is a silence where no sound may be,
In the cold grave—under the deep, deep sea,
Or in wide desert, where no life is found,
Which hath been mute, and still must sleep profound;
No voice is hushed—no life treads silently,
But clouds and cloudy shadows wander free,
That never spoke, over the idle ground;
But in green ruins, in the desolate walls
Of antique palaces, where man hath been,
Though the dun fox, or wild hyena calls,
And owls, that flit continually between,
Shriek to the echo, and the low winds moan,
There the true silence is, self-conscious and alone.

TO AN ENTHUSIAST.

YOUNG ardent soul, graced with fair Nature's truth,
Spring warmth of heart, and fervency of mind,
And still a large late love of all thy kind,
Spite of the world's cold practice, and Time's tooth;
For all these gifts, I know not, in fair sooth,
Whether to give thee joy, or bid thee blind
Thine eyes with tears—that thou hast not resigned
The passionate fire and freshness of thy youth:
For as the current of thy life shall flow,
Gilded by shine of sun or shadow-stained,
Through flowery valley or unwholesome fen,
Thrice blessed in thy joy, or in thy wo
Thrice cursed of thy race—thou art ordained
To share beyond the lot of common men.

THE

BEAUTIES OF GOLDSMITH.

THE DESERTED VILLAGE.*

TO SIR JOSHUA REYNOLDS.

DEAR SIR: I can have no expectations, in an address of this kind, either to add to your reputation, or to establish my own. You can gain nothing from my admiration, as I am ignorant of that art in which you are said to excel; and I may lose much by the severity of your judgment, as few have a juster taste in poetry than you. Setting interest, therefore, aside, to which I never paid much attention, I must be indulged at present in following my affections. The only dedication I ever made was to my brother, because I loved him better than most other men. He is since dead. Permit me to inscribe this Poem to you.

How far you may be pleased with the versification and mere mechanical parts of this attempt, I do not pretend to inquire: but I know you will object (and indeed several of our best and wisest friends concur in the opinion) that the depopulation it deplores is nowhere to be seen, and the disorders it laments are only to be found in the poet's own imagination. To this I can scarcely make any other answer, than that I sincerely believe what I have written; that I have taken all possible pains, in my country excursions, for these four or five years past, to be certain of what I allege; and that all my views and inquiries have led me to believe those miseries real, which I here attempt to display. But this is not the place to enter into an inquiry whether the country be depopulating or not: the discussion would take up much room, and I should prove myself, at best, an indifferent politician, to tire the reader with a long preface, when I want his unfatigued attention to a long poem.

In regretting the depopulation of the country, I inveigh against the increase of our luxuries; and here also I expect the shout of modern politicians against me. For twenty or thirty years past, it has been the fashion to consider luxury as one of the greatest national advantages; and all the wisdom of antiquity in that particular as erroneous. Still, however, I must remain a professed ancient on that head, and continue to think those luxuries prejudicial to states by which so many vices are introduced, and so many kingdoms have been undone. Indeed, so much has been poured out of late on the other side of the question, that merely for the sake of novelty and variety, one would sometimes wish to be in the right.

I am, dear sir,
Your sincere friend, and ardent admirer,
OLIVER GOLDSMITH.

SWEET Auburn! loveliest village of the plain,
Where health and plenty cheered the laboring swain,
Where smiling spring its earliest visit paid,
And parting summer's lingering blooms delayed:
Dear lovely bowers of innocence and ease,
Seats of my youth, when every sport could please,
How often have I loitered o'er thy green,
Where humble happiness endeared each scene!
How often have I paused on every charm,
The sheltered cot, the cultivated farm,
The never-failing brook, the busy mill,
The decent church that topt the neighboring hill,
The hawthorn bush, with seats beneath the shade,
For talking age and whispering lovers made!
How often have I blest the coming day,
When toil remitting lent its turn to play,
And all the village train, from labor free,
Led up their sports beneath the spreading tree;
While many a pastime circled in the shade,
The young contending as the old surveyed;
And many a gambol frolicked o'er the ground,
And sleights of art and feats of strength went round;
And still as each repeated pleasure tired,
Succeeding sports the mirthful band inspired;
The dancing pair that simply sought renown,
By holding out to tire each other down;
The swain mistrustless of his smutted face,
While secret laughter tittered round the place;
The bashful virgin's sidelong looks of love,
The matron's glance that would those looks reprove:
These were thy charms, sweet village! sports like these,
With sweet succession, taught e'en toil to please;
These round thy bowers their cheerful influence shed,
These were thy charms—but all these charms are fled.
Sweet smiling village, loveliest of the lawn,
Thy sports are fled, and all thy charms withdrawn!
Amid thy bowers the tyrant's hand is seen
And Desolation saddens all thy green:
One only master grasps the whole domain,
And half a tillage stints thy smiling plain.
No more thy grassy brook reflects the day,
But, choked with sedges, works its weedy way;
Along thy glades, a solitary guest,
The hollow-sounding bittern guards its nest;
Amid thy desert walks the lapwing flies,
And tires their echoes with unvaried cries;
Sunk are thy bowers in shapeless ruin all,
And the long grass o'ertops the mouldering wall;
And, trembling, shrinking from the spoiler's hand,
Far, far away thy children leave the land.
Ill fares the land, to hastening ills a prey,
Where wealth accumulates, and men decay:
Princes and lords may flourish, or may fade;
A breath can make them, as a breath has made;
But a bold peasantry, their country's pride,
When once destroyed, can never be supplied.
A time there was, ere England's griefs began,
When every rood of ground maintained its man:
For him light Labor spread her wholesome store,
Just gave what life required, but gave no more;
His best companions, innocence and health,
And his best riches, ignorance of wealth.
But times are altered: trade's unfeeling train
Usurp the land, and dispossess the swain;
Along the lawn, where scattered hamlets rose,
Unwieldy wealth and cumbrous pomp repose,
And every want to luxury allied,
And every pang that folly pays to pride.
Those gentle hours that plenty bade to bloom,
Those calm desires that asked but little room,
Those healthful sports that graced the peaceful scene,
Lived in each look, and brightened all the green,—
These, far departing, seek a kinder shore,
And rural mirth and manners are no more

* The locality of this poem is supposed to be Lissoy, near Ballymahon, where the poet's brother Henry had his living. As usual in such cases, the place afterward became the fashionable resort of poetical pilgrims, and paid the customary penalty of furnishing relics for the curious. The *hawthorn bush* has been converted into snuff-boxes, and now adorns the cabinets of poetical virtuosi.

Sweet Auburn! parent of the blissful hour,
Thy glades forlorn confess the tyrant's power.
Here as I take my solitary rounds,
Amid thy tangling walks and ruined grounds,
And, many a year elapsed, return to view
Where once the cottage stood, the hawthorn grew,
Remembrance wakes with all her busy train,
Swells at my breast, and turns the past to pain.
In all my wanderings round this world of care,
In all my griefs—and God has given my share—
I still had hopes, my latest hours to crown,
Amid these humble bowers to lay me down;
To husband out life's taper at the close,
And keep the flame from wasting, by repose:
I still had hopes—for pride attends us still—
Amid the swains to show my book-learned skill,
Around my fire an evening group to draw,
And tell of all I felt and all I saw;
And, as a hare, whom hounds and horns pursue,
Pants to the place from whence at first she flew,
I still had hopes, my long vexations past,
Here to return, and die at home at last.
O blest retirement, friend to life's decline,
Retreat from cares, that never must be mine!
How blest is he who crowns, in shades like these,
A youth of labor with an age of ease;
Who quits a world where strong temptations try,
And, since 't is hard to combat, learns to fly!
For him no wretches, born to work and weep,
Explore the mine, or tempt the dangerous deep;
No surly porter stands in guilty state,
To spurn imploring famine from the gate;
But on he moves to meet his latter end,
Angels around befriending virtue's friend;
Sinks to the grave with unperceived decay,
While resignation gently slopes the way;
And, all his prospects brightening to the last,
His heaven commences ere the world be past.
Sweet was the sound, when oft, at evening's close,
Up yonder hill the village murmur rose;
There, as I passed with careless steps and slow,
The mingling notes came softened from below;
The swain responsive as the milk-maid sung,
The sober herd that lowed to meet their young;
The noisy geese that gabbled o'er the pool,
The playful children just let loose from school;
The watch-dog's voice that bayed the whispering wind,
And the loud laugh that spoke the vacant mind,—
These all in sweet confusion sought the shade,
And filled each pause the nightingale had made.
But now the sounds of population fail,
No cheerful murmurs fluctuate in the gale,
No busy steps the grass-grown footway tread,
But all the bloomy flush of life is fled:
All but yon widowed, solitary thing,
That feebly bends beside the plashy spring;
She, wretched matron, forced in age, for bread,
To strip the brook with mantling cresses spread,
To pick her wintry fagot from the thorn,
To seek her nightly shed, and weep till morn;
She only left of all the harmless train,
The sad historian of the pensive plain.
Near yonder copse, where once the garden smiled,
And still where many a garden-flower grows wild,
There, where a few torn shrubs the place disclose,
The village preacher's modest mansion rose.
A man he was to all the country dear,
And passing rich with forty pounds a-year:
Remote from towns he ran his godly race,
Nor e'er had changed, nor wished to change, his place,
Unskilful he to fawn, or seek for power,
By doctrines fashioned to the varying hour
Far other aims his heart had learned to prize,
More bent to raise the wretched than to rise.
His house was known to all the vagrant train,
He chid their wanderings, but relieved their pain:
The long-remembered beggar was his guest,
Whose beard descending swept his aged breast;
The ruined spendthrift, now no longer proud,
Claimed kindred there, and had his claims allowed;
The broken soldier, kindly bade to stay,
Sat by his fire, and talked the night away,
Wept o'er his wounds, or, tales of sorrow done,
Shouldered his crutch, and showed how fields were won
Pleased with his guests, the good man learned to glow,
And quite forgot their vices in their wo:
Careless their merits or their faults to scan,
His pity gave ere charity began.
Thus to relieve the wretched was his pride,
And e'en his failings leaned to virtue's side;
But in his duty prompt at every call,
He watched and wept, he prayed and felt, for all·
And, as a bird each fond endearment tries
To tempt its new-fledged offspring to the skies,
He tried each art, reproved each dull delay,
Allured to brighter worlds, and led the way.
Beside the bed where parting life was laid,
And sorrow, guilt, and pain, by turns dismayed,
The reverend champion stood. At his control,
Despair and anguish fled the struggling soul;
Comfort came down the trembling wretch to raise,
And his last faltering accents whispered praise.
At church, with meek and unaffected grace,
His looks adorned the venerable place;
Truth from his lips prevailed with double sway,
And fools, who came to scoff, remained to pray.
The service past, around the pious man,
With ready zeal, each honest rustic ran;
E'en children followed, with endearing wile,
And plucked his gown, to share the good man's smile;
His ready smile a parent's warmth expressed;
Their welfare pleased him, and their cares distressed;
To them his heart, his love, his griefs, were given,
But all his serious thoughts had rest in heaven.
As some tall cliff that lifts its awful form,
Swells from the vale, and midway leaves the storm,
Though round its breast the rolling clouds are spread,
Eternal sunshine settles on its head.
Beside yon straggling fence that skirts the way,
With blossomed furze unprofitably gay,
There in his noisy mansion, skilled to rule,
The village master taught his little school.
A man severe he was, and stern to view;
I knew him well, and every truant knew:
Well had the boding tremblers learned to trace
The day's disasters in his morning face;
Full well they laughed, with counterfeited glee,
At all his jokes, for many a joke had he;
Full well the busy whisper, circling round,
Conveyed the dismal tidings when he frowned:
Yet he was kind, or, if severe in aught,
The love he bore to learning was in fault,
The village all declared how much he knew,
'Twas certain he could write and cipher too;
Lands he could measure, terms and tides presage,
And e'en the story ran—that he could gauge:
In arguing, too, the parson owned his skill,
For e'en though vanquished he could argue still;
While words of learned length, and thundering sound,
Amazed the gazing rustics ranged around;
And still they gazed, and still the wonder grew,
That one small head could carry all he knew.
But past is all his fame. The very spot
Where many a time he triumphed is forgot.
Near yonder thorn, that lifts its head on high,
Where once the sign-post caught the passing eye,
Low lies that house where nut-brown draughts inspired,
Where graybeard mirth, and smiling toil, retired,
Where village statesmen talked with looks profound,
And news much older than their ale went round
Imagination fondly stoops to trace
The parlor splendors of that festive place:
The white-washed wall, the nicely-sanded floor,
The varnished clock that clicked behind the door;
The chest, contrived a double debt to pay,
A bed by night, a chest of drawers by day;
The pictures placed for ornament and use,
The twelve good rules, the royal game of goose;
The hearth, except when winter chilled the day,
With aspen boughs, and flowers, and fennel gay,
While broken teacups, wisely kept for show,
Ranged o'er the chimney, glistened in a row.
Vain transitory splendors! Could not all
Reprieve the tottering mansion from its fall?

Obscure it sinks, nor shall it more impart
An hour's importance to the poor man's heart:
Thither no more the peasant shall repair,
To sweet oblivion of his daily care;
No more the farmer's news, the barber's tale,
No more the woodman's ballad shall prevail;
No more the smith his dusky brow shall clear,
Relax his ponderous strength, and lean to hear;
The host himself no longer shall be found
Careful to see the mantling bliss go round;
Nor the coy maid, half willing to be prest,
Shall kiss the cup to pass it to the rest.
  Yes! let the rich deride, the proud disdain,
These simple blessings of the lowly train;
To me more dear, congenial to my heart,
One native charm, than all the gloss of art.
Spontaneous joys, where nature has its play,
The soul adopts, and owns their first-born sway;
Lightly they frolic o'er the vacant mind,
Unenvied, unmolested, unconfined:
But the long pomp, the midnight masquerade,
With all the freaks of wanton wealth arrayed,—
In these, ere triflers half their wish obtain,
The toiling pleasure sickens into pain;
And, e'en while fashion's brightest arts decoy,
The heart, distrusting, asks if this be joy?
  Ye friends to truth, ye statesmen, who survey
The rich man's joys increase, the poor's decay,
'Tis yours to judge how wide the limits stand
Between a splendid and a happy land.
Proud swells the tide with loads of freighted ore,
And shouting Folly hails them from her shore;
Hoards, e'en beyond the miser's wish, abound,
And rich men flock from all the world around.
Yet count our gains: this wealth is but a name
That leaves our useful products still the same.
Not so the loss: the man of wealth and pride
Takes up a space that many poor supplied;
Space for his lake, his park's extended bounds,
Space for his horses, equipage, and hounds:
The robe that wraps his limbs in silken sloth,
Has robbed the neighboring fields of half their growth;
His seat, where solitary sports are seen,
Indignant spurns the cottage from the green;
Around the world each needful product flies,
For all the luxuries the world supplies:—
While thus the land, adorned for pleasure all,
In barren splendor feebly waits its fall.
  As some fair female, unadorned and plain,
Secure to please while youth confirms her reign,
Slights every borrowed charm that dress supplies,
Nor shares with art the triumph of her eyes;
But when those charms are past—for charms are frail—
When time advances, and when lovers fail,
She then shines forth, solicitous to bless,
In all the glaring impotence of dress:
Thus fares the land, by luxury betrayed;
In Nature's simplest charms at first arrayed;
But verging to decline, its splendors rise,
Its vistas strike, its palaces surprise;
While, scourged by famine from the smiling land,
The mournful peasant leads his humble band;
And while he sinks, without one arm to save,
The country blooms—a garden and a grave.
  Where, then, ah! where shall poverty reside,
To 'scape the pressure of contiguous pride?
If to some common's fenceless limits strayed,
He drives his flock to pick the scanty blade,
Those fenceless fields the sons of wealth divide,
And even the bare-worn common is denied.
  If to the city sped, what waits him there?
To see profusion that he must not share:
To see ten thousand baneful arts combined
To pamper luxury, and thin mankind;
To see each joy the sons of pleasure know
Extorted from his fellow-creatures' wo.
Here while the courtier glitters in brocade,
There the pale artist plies his sickly trade;
Here while the proud their long-drawn pomps display,
There the black gibbet glooms beside the way.
The dome where Pleasure holds her midnight reign,
Here richly decked, admits the gorgeous train;
Tumultuous grandeur crowds the blazing square,
The rattling chariots clash, the torches glare.
Sure scenes like these no troubles e'er annoy!
Sure these denote one universal joy!
Are these thy serious thoughts?—Ah, turn thine eyes
Where the poor houseless shivering female lies:
She once, perhaps, in village plenty blest,
Has wept at tales of innocence distrest:
Her modest looks the cottage might adorn,
Sweet as the primrose peeps beneath the thorn;
Now lost to all—her friends, her virtue fled,
Near her betrayer's door she lays her head,
And, pinched with cold, and shrinking from the shower,
With heavy heart deplores that luckless hour,
When idly first, ambitious of the town,
She left her wheel, and robes of country brown.
  Do thine, sweet Auburn, thine, the loveliest train,
Do thy fair tribes participate her pain?
Even now, perhaps, by cold and hunger led,
At proud men's doors they ask a little bread!
  Ah, no. To distant climes, a dreary scene,
Where half the convex world intrudes between,
Through torrid tracts with fainting steps they go,
Where wild Altama* murmurs to their wo.
Far different there from all that charmed before,
The various terrors of that horrid shore;
Those blazing suns that dart a downward ray,
And fiercely shed intolerable day;
Those matted woods where birds forget to sing,
But silent bats in drowsy clusters cling;
Those poisonous fields with rank luxuriance crowned,
Where the dark scorpion gathers death around;
Where at each step the stranger fears to wake
The rattling terrors of the vengeful snake;
Where crouching tigers wait their hapless prey,
And savage men, more murderous still than they;
While oft in whirls the mad tornado flies,
Mingling the ravaged landscape with the skies.
Far different these from every former scene,
The cooling brook, the grassy-vested green,
The breezy covert of the warbling grove,
That only sheltered thefts of harmless love.
  Good Heaven! what sorrows gloomed that parting day
That called them from their native walks away;
When the poor exiles, every pleasure past,
Hung round the bowers, and fondly looked their last,
And took a long farewell, and wished in vain
For seats like these beyond the western main;
And, shuddering still to face the distant deep,
Returned and wept, and still returned to weep!
The good old sire the first prepared to go
To new-found worlds, and wept for others' wo;
But for himself, in conscious virtue brave,
He only wished for worlds beyond the grave;
His lovely daughter, lovelier in her tears,
The fond companion of his helpless years,
Silent went next, neglectful of her charms,
And left a lover's for her father's arms:
With louder plaints the mother spoke her woes,
And blest the cot where every pleasure rose,
And kissed her thoughtless babes with many a tear,
And clasped them close, in sorrow doubly dear;
Whilst her fond husband strove to lend relief
In all the silent manliness of grief.
  O luxury! thou curst by Heaven's decree,
How ill exchanged are things like these for thee.
How do thy potions, with insidious joy,
Diffuse their pleasures only to destroy!
Kingdoms by thee, to sickly greatness grown,
Boast of a florid vigor not their own;
At every draught more large and large they grow,
A bloated mass of rank unwieldy wo;
Till, sapped their strength, and every part unsound,
Down, down they sink, and spread a ruin round.
  E'en now the devastation is begun,
And half the business of destruction done;
E'en now, methinks, as pondering here I stand,
I see the rural Virtues leave the land.
Down where yon anchoring vessel spreads the sail
That idly waiting flaps with every gale,

* The Altama (or Altamaha) is a river in Georgia, United States.

Downward they move, a melancholy band,
Pass from the shore, and darken all the strand,
Contented Toil, and hospitable Care,
And kind connubial Tenderness, are there;
And Piety with wishes placed above,
And steady Loyalty, and faithful Love.
And thou, sweet Poetry, thou loveliest maid,
Still first to fly where sensual joys invade;
Unfit, in these degenerate times of shame,
To catch the heart, or strike for honest fame;
Dear charming nymph, neglected and decried,
My shame in crowds, my solitary pride;
Thou source of all my bliss, and all my wo,
That foundst me poor at first, and keepst me so;
Thou guide, by which the nobler arts excel,
Thou nurse of every virtue, fare thee well!
Farewell; and oh! where'er thy voice be tried,
On Torno's cliffs, or Pambamarca's side,
Whether where equinoctial fervors glow,
Or winter wraps the polar world in snow,
Still let thy voice, prevailing over time,
Redress the rigors of the inclement clime;
Aid slighted truth with thy persuasive strain;
Teach erring man to spurn the rage of gain;
Teach him, that states of native strength possest,
Though very poor, may still be very blest;
That trade's proud empire hastes to swift decay,
As ocean sweeps the labored mole away;
While self-dependant power can time defy,
As rocks resist the billows and the sky.

THE TRAVELLER;
OR
A PROSPECT OF SOCIETY.

TO THE REV. HENRY GOLDSMITH.

DEAR SIR,—I am sensible that the friendship between us can acquire no new force from the ceremonies of a dedication; and perhaps it demands an excuse thus to prefix your name to my attempts, which you decline giving with your own. But as a part of this poem was formerly written to you from Switzerland, the whole can now, with propriety, be only inscribed to you. It will also throw a light upon many parts of it, when the reader understands, that it is addressed to a man who, despising fame and fortune, has retired early to happiness and obscurity, with an income of forty pounds a-year.

I now perceive, my dear brother, the wisdom of your humble choice. You have entered upon a sacred office, where the harvest is great, and the laborers are but few; while you have left the field of ambition, where the laborers are many, and the harvest not worth carrying away. But of all kinds of ambition—what from the refinement of the times, from different systems of criticism, and from the divisions of party—that which pursues poetical fame is the wildest.

Poetry makes a principal amusement among unpolished nations; but in a country verging to the extremes of refinement, painting and music come in for a share. As these offer the feeble mind a less laborious entertainment, they at first rival poetry, and at length supplant her; they engross all that favor once shown to her, and though but younger sisters, seize upon the elder's birthright.

Yet, however this art may be neglected by the powerful, it is still in greater danger from the mistaken efforts of the learned to improve it. What criticisms have we not heard of late in favor of blank verse and Pindaric odes, choruses, anapests and iambics, alliterative care and happy negligence! Every absurdity has now a champion to defend it; and as he is generally much in the wrong, so he has always much to say; for error is ever talkative.

But there is an enemy to this art still more dangerous—I mean party. Party entirely distorts the judgment, and destroys the taste. When the mind is once infected with this disease, it can only find pleasure in what contributes to increase the distemper. Like the tiger, that seldom desists from pursuing man after having once preyed upon human flesh, the reader, who has once gratified his appetite with calumny, makes ever after the most agreeable feast upon murdered reputation. Such readers generally admire some half-witted thing, who wants to be thought a bold man, having lost the character of a wise one. Him they dignify with the name of poet: his tawdry lampoons are called satires; his turbulence is said to be force, and his phrensy fire.

What reception a poem may find, which has neither abuse, party, nor blank verse to support it, I can not tell, nor am I solicitous to know. My aims are right. Without espousing the cause of any party, I have attempted to moderate the rage of all. I have endeavored to show, that there may be equal happiness in states that are differently governed from our own; that every state has a particular principle of happiness, and that this principle in each may be carried to a mischievous excess. There are few can judge better than yourself how far these positions are illustrated in this poem.

I am, dear sir, your most affectionate brother,
OLIVER GOLDSMITH.

REMOTE, unfriended, melancholy, slow,
Or by the lazy Scheld, or wandering Po;
Or onward, where the rude Carinthian boor
Against the houseless stranger shuts the door;
Or where Campania's plain forsaken lies,
A weary waste expanding to the skies:
Where'er I roam, whatever realms to see,
My heart untravelled fondly turns to thee;
Still to my brother turns, with ceaseless pain,
And drags at each remove a lengthening chain.
Eternal blessings crown my earliest friend,
And round his dwelling guardian saints attend!
Blest be that spot, where cheerful guests retire
To pause from toil, and trim their evening fire!
Blest that abode, where want and pain repair,
And every stranger finds a ready chair.
Blest be those feasts with simple plenty crowned,
Where all the ruddy family around
Laugh at the jests or pranks that never fail
Or sigh with pity at some mournful tale;
Or press the bashful stranger to his food,
And learn the luxury of doing good!
But me, not destined such delights to share,
My prime of life in wandering spent, and care;
Impelled, with steps unceasing, to pursue
Some fleeting good, that mocks me with the view,
That, like the circle bounding earth and skies,
Allures from far, yet, as I follow, flies:
My fortune leads to traverse realms alone,
And find no spot of all the world my own.
E'en now, where Alpine solitudes ascend,
I sit me down a pensive hour to spend;
And, placed on high above the storm's career,
Look downward where a hundred realms appear:
Lakes, forests, cities, plains extending wide,
The pomp of kings, the shepherd's humbler pride.
When thus Creation's charms around combine,
Amid the store should thankless pride repine?
Say, should the philosophic mind disdain
That good which makes each humbler bosom vain?
Let school-taught pride dissemble all it can,
These little things are great to little man;
And wiser he, whose sympathetic mind
Exults in all the good of all mankind.
Ye glittering towns, with wealth and splendor crowned
Ye fields, where summer spreads profusion round;
Ye lakes, whose vessels catch the busy gale;
Ye bending swains, that dress the flowery vale;
For me your tributary stores combine,
Creation's heir, the world—the world is mine
As some lone miser, visiting his store,
Bends at his treasure, counts, recounts it o'er,
Hoards after hoards, his rising raptures fill,
Yet still he sighs, for hoards are wanting still:
Thus to my breast alternate passions rise,
Pleased with each good that Heaven to man supplies;
Yet oft a sigh prevails, and sorrows fall,
To see the sum of human bliss so small:
And oft I wish, amid the scene to find
Some spot to real happiness consigned,
Where my worn soul, each wandering hope at rest,
May gather bliss to see my fellows blest.
But where to find that happiest spot below
Who can direct, when all pretend to know?

The shuddering tenant of the frigid zone
Boldly proclaims that happiest spot his own;
Extols the treasures of his stormy seas,
And his long nights of revelry and ease:
The naked negro, panting at the Line,
Boasts of his golden sands and palmy wine,
Basks in the glare, or stems the tepid wave,
And thanks his gods for all the good they gave.
Such is the patriot's boast where'er we roam,
His first, best country, ever is at home.
And yet, perhaps, if countries we compare,
And estimate the blessings which they share,
Though patriots flatter, still shall wisdom find
An equal portion dealt to all mankind;
As different good, by art or nature given,
To different nations makes their blessings even.
Nature, a mother kind alike to all,
Still grants her bliss at labor's earnest call;
With food as well the peasant is supplied
On Idra's cliffs as Arno's shelvy side;
And though the rocky crested summits frown,
These rocks by custom turn to beds of down.
From art more various are the blessings sent—
Wealth, commerce, honor, liberty, content.
Yet these each other's power so strong contest,
That either seems destructive of the rest.
Where wealth and freedom reign, contentment fails,
And honor sinks where commerce long prevails.
Hence every state, to one loved blessing prone,
Conforms and models life to that alone.
Each to the favorite happiness attends,
And spurns the plan that aims at other ends;
Till carried to excess in each domain
This favorite good begets peculiar pain.
But let us try these truths with closer eyes,
And trace them through the prospect as it lies;
Here, for a while, my proper cares resigned,
Here let me sit in sorrow for mankind;
Like yon neglected shrub at random cast,
That shades the steep and sighs at every blast.
Far to the right, where Apennine ascends,
Bright as the summer, Italy extends;
Its uplands sloping deck the mountains side,
Woods over woods in gay theatric pride;
While oft some temple's mouldering tops between
With venerable grandeur mark the scene.
Could Nature's bounty satisfy the breast,
The sons of Italy were surely blest;
Whatever fruits in different climes are found,
That proudly rise, or humbly court the ground;
Whatever blooms in torrid tracts appear,
Whose bright succession decks the varied year;
Whatever sweets salute the northern sky
With vernal lives that blossom but to die;
These here disporting own the kindred soil,
Nor ask luxuriance from the planter's toil;
While sea-born gales their gelid wings expand,
To winnow fragrance round the smiling land.
But small the bliss that sense alone bestows,
And sensual bliss is all this nation knows.
In florid beauty groves and fields appear,
Man seems the only growth that dwindles here.
Contrasted faults through all his manners reign:
Though poor, luxurious; though submissive, vain;
Though grave, yet trifling; zealous, yet untrue!
And e'en in penance planning sins anew.
All evils here contaminate the mind,
That opulence departed leaves behind:
For wealth was theirs; not far removed the date,
When Commerce proudly flourished through the state;
At her command the palace learned to rise,
Again the long-fallen column sought the skies;
The canvass glowed beyond e'en nature warm,
The pregnant quarry teemed with human form:
Till, more unsteady than the southern gale,
Commerce on other shores displayed her sail;
While naught remained, of all that riches gave,
But towns unmanned, and lords without a slave:
And late the nation found, with fruitless skill,
Its former strength was but plethoric ill.
Yet, still the loss of wealth is here supplied
By arts, the splendid wrecks of former pride:
From these the feeble heart and long-fallen mind
An easy compensation seem to find.
Here may be seen in bloodless pomp arrayed,
The pasteboard triumph and the cavalcade;
Processions formed for piety and love,
A mistress or a saint in every grove.
By sports like these are all their cares beguiled;
The sports of children satisfy the child:
Each nobler aim, repressed by long control,
Now sinks at last or feebly mans the soul;
While low delights succeeding fast behind,
In happier meanness occupy the mind:
As in those domes where Cesars once bore sway,
Defaced by time, and tottering in decay,
There in the ruin, heedless of the dead,
The shelter-seeking peasant builds his shed;
And, wondering man could want the larger pile,
Exults, and owns his cottage with a smile.
My soul, turn from them! turn we to survey
Where rougher climes a nobler race display,
Where the bleak Swiss their stormy mansion tread,
And force a churlish soil for scanty bread:
No product here the barren hills afford,
But man and steel, the soldier and his sword;
No vernal blooms their torpid rocks array,
But winter lingering chills the lap of May;
No zephyr fondly sues the mountain's breast,
But meteors glare, and stormy glooms invest.
Yet still, even here, content can spread a charm,
Redress the clime and all its rage disarm.
Though poor the peasant's hut, his feast though small,
He sees his little lot the lot of all;
Sees no contiguous palace rear its head
To shame the meanness of his humble shed;
No costly lord the sumptuous banquet deal
To make him loathe his vegetable meal;
But calm, and bred in ignorance and toil,
Each wish contracting, fits him to the soil.
Cheerful, at morn, he wakes from short repose,
Breathes the keen air, and carols as he goes;
With patient angle trolls the finny deep,
Or drives his venturous ploughshare to the steep;
Or seeks the den where snow-tracks mark the way
And drags the struggling savage into day.
At night returning, every labor sped,
He sits him down the monarch of a shed;
Smiles by a cheerful fire, and round surveys
His children's looks that brighten at the blaze,
While his loved partner, boastful of her hoard,
Displays her cleanly platter on the board;
And haply too some pilgrim, thither led,
With many a tale repays the nightly bed.
Thus every good his native wilds impart,
Imprints the patriot passion on his heart;
And e'en those ills that round his mansion rise,
Enhance the bliss his scanty fund supplies.
Dear is that shed to which his soul conforms,
And dear that hill which lifts him to the storms;
And as a child, when scaring sounds molest,
Clings close and closer to the mother's breast,
So the loud torrent, and the whirlwind's roar,
But bind him to his native mountains more.
Such are the charms to barren states assigned:
Their wants but few, their wishes all confined:
Yet let them only share the praises due—
If few their wants, their pleasures are but few;
For every want that stimulates the breast,
Becomes a source of pleasure when redrest.
Hence from such lands each pleasing science flies,
That first excites desire, and then supplies;
Unknown to them, when sensual pleasures cloy,
To fill the languid pause with finer joy;
Unknown those powers that raise the soul to flame,
Catch every nerve, and vibrate through the frame.
Their level life is but a smouldering fire,
Nor quenched by want, nor fanned by strong desire
Unfit for raptures, or, if raptures cheer
On some high festival of once a-year,
In wild excess the vulgar breast takes fire,
Till, buried in debauch, the bliss expire.
But not their joys alone thus coarsely flow—
Their morals, like their pleasures, are but low:

For, as refinement stops, from sire to son
Unaltered, unimproved the manners run;
And love's and friendship's finely pointed dart
Fall blunted from each indurated heart.
Some sterner virtues o'er the mountain's breast,
May sit like falcons cowering on the nest;
But all the gentler morals,—such as play
Through life's more cultured walks, and charm the way,—
These, far dispersed, on timorous pinions fly,
To sport and flutter in a kinder sky.
  To kinder skies, where gentler manners reign,
I turn; and France displays her bright domain.
Gay, sprightly land of mirth and social ease,
Pleased with thyself, whom all the world can please,
How often have I led thy sportive choir,
With tuneless pipe beside the murmuring Loire!
Where shading elms along the margin grew,
And, freshened from the wave, the zephyr flew;
And haply, though my harsh touch faltering still,
But mocked all tune, and marred the dancer's skill;
Yet would the village praise my wondrous power,
And dance, forgetful of the noontide hour.
Alike all ages: dames of ancient days
Have led their children through the mirthful maze;
And the gay grandsire, skilled in gestic lore,
Has frisked beneath the burden of threescore.
  So blest a life these thoughtless realms display;
Thus idly busy rolls their world away:
Theirs are those arts that mind to mind endear,
For honor forms the social temper here:
Honor, that praise which real merit gains,
Or e'en imaginary worth obtains,
Here passes current; paid from hand to hand,
It shifts in splendid traffic round the land;
From courts to camps, to cottages it strays,
And all are taught an avarice of praise:
They please, are pleased; they give to get esteem;
Till, seeming blest, they grow to what they seem.
  But while this softer art their bliss supplies.
It gives their follies also room to rise;
For praise too dearly loved, or warmly sought,
Enfeebles all internal strength of thought:
And the weak soul, within itself unblest,
Leans for all pleasure on another's breast.
Hence Ostentation here, with tawdry art,
Pants for the vulgar praise which fools impart;
Here Vanity assumes her pert grimace,
And trims her robes of frieze with copper lace;
Here beggar Pride defrauds her daily cheer,
To boast one splendid banquet once a-year:
The mind still turns where shifting fashion draws,
Nor weighs the solid worth of self-applause.
  To men of other minds my fancy flies,
Embosomed in the deep where Holland lies.
Methinks her patient sons before me stand,
Where the broad ocean leans against the land,
And, sedulous to stop the coming tide,
Lift the tall rampire's artificial pride.
Onward, methinks, and diligently slow,
The firm connected bulwark seems to grow,
Spreads its long arms amid the watery roar,
Scoops out an empire, and usurps the shore;
While the pent ocean, rising o'er the pile,
Sees an amphibious world beneath him smile;
The slow canal, the yellow-blossomed vale,
The willow-tufted bank, the gliding sail,
The crowded mart, the cultivated plain,
A new creation rescued from his reign.
  Thus, while around the wave-subjected soil
Impels the native to repeated toil,
Industrious habits in each bosom reign,
And industry begets a love of gain.
Hence all the good from opulence that springs,
With all those ills superfluous treasure brings,
Are here displayed. Their much-loved wealth imparts
Convenience, plenty, elegance, and arts;
But view them closer, craft and fraud appear;
Even liberty itself is bartered here:
At gold's superior charms all freedom flies,
The needy sell it, and the rich man buys.
A land of tyrants, and a den of slaves,
Here wretches seek dishonorable graves,
And, calmly bent, to servitude conform,
Dull as their lakes that slumber in the storm.
  Heavens! how unlike their Belgic sires of old!
Rough, poor, content, ungovernably bold,
War in each breast, and freedom on each brow;
How much unlike the sons of Britain now!
  Fired at the sound, my genius spreads her wing,
And flies where Britain courts the western spring;
Where lawns extend that scorn Arcadian pride,
And brighter streams than famed Hydaspes glide.
There all around the gentlest breezes stray,
There gentle music melts on every spray;
Creation's mildest charms are there combined,
Extremes are only in the master's mind!
Stern o'er each bosom Reason holds her state,
With daring aims irregularly great,
Pride in their port, defiance in their eye,
I see the lords of human kind pass by;
Intent on high designs, a thoughtful band,
By forms unfashioned, fresh from nature's hand,
Fierce in their native hardiness of soul,
True to imagined right above control,—
While e'en the peasant boasts these rights to scan,
And learns to venerate himself as man.
  Thine, Freedom, thine the blessings pictured here,
Thine are those charms that dazzle and endear!
Too blest indeed were such without alloy;
But, fostered e'en by freedom, ills annoy:
That independence Britons prize too high,
Keeps man from man, and breaks the social tie;
The self-dependant lordlings stand alone,
All claims that bind and sweeten life unknown;
Here, by the bonds of nature feebly held,
Minds combat minds, repelling and repelled;
Ferments arise, imprisoned factions roar,
Represt ambition struggles round her shore;
Till, overwrought, the general system feels
Its motion stop, or phrensy fire the wheels.
  Nor this the worst. As nature's ties decay,
As duty, love, and honor fail to sway,
Fictitious bonds, the bonds of wealth and law,
Still gather strength, and force unwilling awe.
Hence all obedience bows to these alone,
And talent sinks, and merit weeps unknown:
Till time may come, when stript of all her charms,
The land of scholars, and the nurse of arms,
Where noble stems transmit the patriot flame,
Where kings have toiled, and poets wrote for fame,
One sink of level avarice shall lie,
And scholars, soldiers, kings, unhonored die.
  Yet think not, thus when Freedom's ills I state,
I mean to flatter kings, or court the great:
Ye powers of truth, that bid my soul aspire,
Far from my bosom drive the low desire!
And thou, fair Freedom, taught alike to feel
The rabble's rage, and tyrant's angry steel;
Thou transitory flower, alike undone
By proud contempt, or favor's fostering sun—
Still may thy blooms the changeful clime endure!
I only would repress them to secure:
For just experience tells, in every soil,
That those that think must govern those that toil;
And all that Freedom's highest aims can reach,
Is but to lay proportioned loads on each.
Hence, should one order disproportioned grow,
Its double weight must ruin all below.
  Oh, then how blind to all that truth requires,
Who think it freedom when a part aspires!
Calm is my soul, nor apt to rise in arms,
Except when fast approaching danger warms:
But when contending chiefs blockade the throne,
Contracting regal power to stretch their own;
When I behold a factious band agree
To call it freedom when themselves are free;
Each wanton judge new penal statutes draw,
Laws grind the poor, and rich men rule the law;
The wealth of climes, where savage nations roam,
Pillaged from slaves to purchase slaves at home,—
Fear, pity, justice, indignation, start,
Tear off reserve, and bear my swelling heart;
Till, half a patriot, half a coward grown,
I fly from petty tyrants to the throne.

Yes, brother, curse me with that baleful hour,
When first ambition struck at regal power;
And thus, polluting honor in its source,
Gave wealth to sway the mind with double force.
Have we not seen, round Britain's peopled shore,
Her useful sons exchanged for useless ore?
Seen all her triumphs but destruction haste,
Like flaring tapers brightening as they waste?
Seen Opulence, her grandeur to maintain,
Lead stern Depopulation in her train,
And over fields, where scattered hamlets rose,
In barren, solitary pomp repose?
Have we not seen, at Pleasure's lordly call,
The smiling, long-frequented village fall?
Beheld the duteous son, the sire decayed,
The modest matron, and the blushing maid,
Forced from their homes, a melancholy train,
To traverse climes beyond the western main,
Where wild Oswego spreads her swamps around,
And Niagara stuns with thundering sound?
E'en now, perhaps, as there some pilgrim strays
Through tangled forests, and through dangerous ways,
Where beasts with man divided empire claim,
And the brown Indian marks with murderous aim;
There, while above the giddy tempest flies,
And all around distressful yell arise,
The pensive exile, bending with his wo,
To stop too fearful, and too faint to go,
Casts a long look where England's glories shine,
And bids his bosom sympathize with mine.
Vain, very vain, my weary search to find
That bliss which only centres in the mind:
Why have I stayed from pleasure and repose,
To seek a good each government bestows?
In every government, though terrors reign,
Though tyrant kings, or tyrant laws restrain,
How small, of all that human hearts endure,
That part which laws or kings can cause or cure!
Still to ourselves in every place consigned,
Our own felicity we make or find:
With secret course which no loud storms annoy,
Glides the smooth current of domestic joy.
The lifted axe, the agonizing wheel,
Luke's iron crown, and Damien's bed of steel,
To men remote from power but rarely known,
Leave reason, faith, and conscience, all our own.

THE HERMIT.

A BALLAD.

"Turn, gentle Hermit of the dale,
And guide my lonely way,
To where yon taper cheers the vale
With hospitable ray.

"For here forlorn and lost I tread,
With fainting steps and slow,
Where wilds, immeasurably spread,
Seem length'ning as I go."

"Forbear, my son," the Hermit cries,
"To tempt the dangerous gloom;
For yonder faithless phantom flies
To lure thee to thy doom.

"Here to the houseless child of want
My door is open still;
And though my portion is but scant,
I give it with good will.

"Then turn to-night, and freely share
Whate'er my cell bestows;
My rushy couch and frugal fare,
My blessing and repose.

"No flocks that range the valley free
To slaughter I condemn;
Taught by that Power that pities me,
I learn to pity them:

"But from the mountain's grassy side
A guiltless feast I bring;
A scrip with herbs and fruits supplied,
And water from the spring.

"Then, pilgrim, turn, thy cares forego,
All earth-born cares are wrong;
Man wants but little here below,
Nor wants that little long."

Soft as the dew from heaven descends,
His gentle accents fall:
The modest stranger lowly bends,
And follows to the cell.

Far in the wilderness obscure
The lonely mansion lay,
A refuge to the neighb'ring poor,
And strangers led astray.

No stores beneath its humble thatch,
Required a master's care;
The wicket, opening with a latch,
Received the harmless pair.

And now, when busy crowds retire
To take their evening rest,
The Hermit trimmed his little fire,
And cheered his pensive guest;

And spread his vegetable store,
And gayly pressed and smiled;
And, skilled in legendary lore,
The lingering hours beguiled.

Around in sympathetic mirth,
Its tricks the kitten tries,
The cricket chirrups on the hearth,
The crackling fagot flies.

But nothing could a charm impart
To sooth the stranger's wo;
For grief was heavy at his heart,
And tears began to flow.

His rising cares the Hermit spied,
With answering care oppressed:
And, "Whence, unhappy youth," he cried
"The sorrows of thy breast?

"From better habitations spurned,
Reluctant dost thou rove?
Or grieve for friendship unreturned,
Or unregarded love?

"Alas! the joys that fortune brings
Are trifling, and decay;
And those who prize the paltry things,
More trifling still than they.

"And what is friendship but a name,
A charm that lulls to sleep;
A shade that follows wealth or fame,
But leaves the wretch to weep?

"And love is still an emptier sound,
The modern fair one's jest;
On earth unseen, or only found
To warm the turtle's nest.

"For shame, fond youth, thy sorrows hush
And spurn the sex," he said;
But while he spoke, a rising blush
His love-lorn guest betrayed.

Surprised he sees new beauties rise,
Swift mantling to the view;
Like colors o'er the morning skies,
As bright as transient too.

The bashful look, the rising breast,
Alternate spread alarms:
The lovely stranger stands confessed
A maid in all her charms.

And, "Ah! forgive a stranger rude—
A wretch forlorn," she cried;
"Whose feet unhallowed thus intrude
Where Heaven and you reside.

"But let a maid thy pity share,
Whom love has taught to stray;
Who seeks for rest, but finds despair
Companion of her way.

"My father lived beside the Tyne,
A wealthy lord was he:
And all his wealth was marked as mine,
He had but only me.

"To win me from his tender arms,
Unnumbered suiters came,
Who praised me for imputed charms,
And felt, or feigned a flame.

"Each hour a mercenary crowd
With richest proffers strove;
Among the rest young Edwin bowed.
But never talked of love.

"In humble, simplest habit clad,
No wealth nor power had he;
Wisdom and worth were all he had,
But these were all to me.

"And when beside me in the dale,
He carolled lays of love,
His breath lent fragrance to the gale,
And music to the grove.*

"The blossom opening to the day,
The dews of heaven refined,
Could naught of purity display
To emulate his mind.

"The dew, the blossom on the tree,
With charms inconstant shine:
Their charms were his, but wo to me,
Their constancy was mine.

"For still I tried each fickle art,
Importunate and vain;
And while his passion touched my heart,
I triumphed in his pain:

"Till, quite dejected with my scorn,
He left me to my pride;
And sought a solitude forlorn,
In secret, where he died.

"But mine the sorrow, mine the fault,
And well my life shall pay;
I'll seek the solitude he sought,
And stretch me where he lay.

"And there forlorn, despairing, hid,
I'll lay me down and die;
'Twas so for me that Edwin did,
And so for him will I."

"Forbid it, Heaven!" the Hermit cried,
And clasped her to his breast:
The wondering fair one turned to chide—
'Twas Edwin's self that pressed!

"Turn, Angelina, ever dear,
My charmer, turn to see
Thy own, thy long-lost Edwin here,
Restored to love and thee.

"Thus let me hold thee to my heart,
And every care resign:
And shall we never, never part,
My life—my all that's mine.

"No, never from this hour to part,
We'll live and love so true,
The sigh that rends thy constant heart
Shall break thy Edwin's too.

* This stanza was preserved by Richard Archdale, Esq., a member of the Irish Parliament, to whom it was given by Goldsmith, and was first inserted after the author's death.

THE CAPTIVITY: AN ORATORIO.*

THE PERSONS.

First Jewish Prophet.	*First Chaldean Priest.*
Second Jewish Prophet.	*Second Chaldean Priest.*
Israelitish Woman.	*Chaldean Woman.*

Chorus of Youths and Virgins.

SCENE.—*The Banks of the River Euphrates near Babylon.*

ACT THE FIRST.

FIRST PROPHET.

Ye captive tribes that hourly work and weep
Where flows Euphrates murmuring to the deep,
Suspend your woes a while, the task suspend,
And turn to God, your father and your friend;
Insulted, chained, and all the world our foe,
Our God alone is all we boast below.

Air.

FIRST PROPHET.

Our God is all we boast below,
To him we turn our eyes;
And every added weight of wo
Shall make our homage rise.

SECOND PROPHET.

And though no temple richly dressed,
Nor sacrifice is here,
We'll make his temple in our breast,
And offer up a tear.
[*The first stanza repeated by the* CHORUS.

ISRAELITISH WOMAN.

That strain once more! it bids remembrance rise,
And brings my long-lost country to mine eyes;
Ye fields of Sharon, dressed in flowery pride,
Ye plains where Kedron rolls its glassy tide,
Ye hills of Lebanon, with cedars crowned,
Ye Gilead groves, that fling perfumes around,—
How sweet those groves! that plain how wondrous fair!
How doubly sweet when Heaven was with us there!

Air.

O Memory! thou fond deceiver,
Still importunate and vain!
To former joys recurring ever,
And turning all the past to pain:

Hence, intruder most distressing!
Seek the happy and the free:
The wretch who wants each other blessing
Ever wants a friend in thee.

SECOND PROPHET.

Yet why complain? What though by bonds confined,
Should bonds repress the vigor of the mind?
Have we not cause for triumph, when we see
Ourselves alone from idol-worship free?
Are not, this very morn, those feasts begun
Where prostrate error hails the rising sun?
Do not our tyrant lords this day ordain
For superstitious rites and mirth profane?
And should we mourn? Should coward virtue fly,
When vaunting folly lifts her head on high?
No! rather let us triumph still the more,
And as our fortunes sinks, our spirits soar.

Air.

The triumphs that on vice attend
Shall ever in confusion end;
The good man suffers but to gain,
And every virtue springs from pain:
As aromatic plants bestow
No spicy fragrance while they grow;
But crushed, or trodden to the ground,
Diffuse their balmy sweets around.

FIRST PROPHET.

But hush, my sons, our tyrant lords are near,
The sounds of barbarous pleasure strike mine ear;

* This was first printed from the original, in Doctor Goldsmith's own hand writing, in the 8vo. edition of his *Miscellaneous Works,* published in 1820.

Triumphant music floats along the vale,
Near, nearer still, it gathers on the gale:
The growing sound their swift approach declares—
Desist, my sons, nor mix the strain with theirs.

Enter CHALDEAN PRIESTS *attended.*

Air.

FIRST PRIEST.

Come on, my companions, the triumph display,
Let rapture the minutes employ;
The sun calls us out on this festival day,
And our monarch partakes in the joy.

SECOND PRIEST.

Like the sun, our great monarch all rapture supplies,
Both similar blessings bestow:
The sun with his splendor illumines the skies,
And our monarch enlivens below.

Air.

CHALDEAN WOMAN.

Haste, ye sprightly sons of pleasure,
Love presents the fairest treasure,
Leave all other joys for me.

A CHALDEAN ATTENDANT.

Or rather, love's delights despising,
Haste to raptures ever rising,
Wine shall bless the brave and free.

FIRST PRIEST.

Wine and beauty thus inviting,
Each to different joys exciting,
Whither shall my choice incline?

SECOND PRIEST.

I'll waste no longer thought in choosing,
But, neither this nor that refusing,
I'll make them both together mine.

FIRST PRIEST.

But whence, when joy should brighten over the land,
This sullen gloom in Judah's captive band?
Ye sons of Judah, why the lute unstrung?
Or why those harps on yonder willows hung?
Come, take the lyre, and pour the strain along,
The day demands it: sing us Sion's song,
Dismiss your griefs, and join our warbling choir,
For who like you can wake the sleeping lyre?

Air.

Every moment as it flows
Some peculiar pleasure owes:
Come, then, providently wise,
Seize the debtor ere it flies.

SECOND PRIEST.

Think not to-morrow can repay
The debt of pleasure lost to-day:
Alas! to-morrow's richest store
Can but pay its proper score.

SECOND PROPHET.

Chained as we are, the scorn of all mankind,
To want, to toil, and every ill consigned,
Is this a time to bid us raise the strain,
Or mix in rites that Heaven regards with pain?
No, never! may this hand forget each art
That wakes to finest joys the human heart,
Ere I forget the land that gave me birth,
Or join to sounds profane its sacred mirth!

SECOND PRIEST.

Rebellious slaves! if soft persuasion fail,
More formidable terrors shall prevail.

FIRST PROPHET.

Why, let them come, one good remains to cheer—
We fear the Lord, and scorn all other fear.
[*Exeunt* CHALDEANS.

CHORUS OF ISRAELITES.

Can chains or tortures bend the mind
On God's supporting breast reclined?
Stand fast, and let our tyrants see
That fortitude is victory. *Exeunt.*

ACT THE SECOND.

ISRAELITES *and* CHALDEANS, *as before.*

Air.

FIRST PROPHET.

O peace of mind, angelic guest,
Thou soft companion of the breast,
Dispense thy balmy store!
Wing all our thoughts to reach the skies,
Till earth, receding from our eyes,
Shall vanish as we soar!

FIRST PRIEST.

No more. Too long has justice been delayed,
The king's commands must fully be obeyed;
Compliance with his will your peace secures,
Praise but our gods, and every good is yours:
But if, rebellious to his high command,
You spurn the favors offered from his hand,
Think, timely think, what terrors are behind,
Reflect, nor tempt to rage the royal mind.

Air.

Fierce is the tempest howling
Along the furrowed main,
And fierce the whirlwind rolling
Over Afric's sandy plain:

But storms that fly
To rend the sky,
Every ill presaging,
Less dreadful show
To worlds below
Than angry monarchs raging.

ISRAELITISH WOMAN.

Ah me! what angry terrors round us grow!
How shrinks my soul to meet the threatened blow
Ye prophets, skilled in Heaven's eternal truth,
Forgive my sex's fears, forgive my youth!
Ah! let us one, one little hour obey;
To-morrow's tears may wash the stain away,

Air.

Fatigued with life, yet loath to part,
On hope the wretch relies;
And every blow that sinks the heart
Bids the deluder rise.

Hope, like the taper's gleamy light,
Adorns the wretch's way;
And still, as darker grows the night,
Emits a brighter ray.

SECOND PRIEST.

Why this delay? At length for joy prepare:
I read your looks, and see compliance there.
Come on, and bid the warbling rapture rise,
Our monarch's fame the noblest theme supplies.
Begin, ye captive bands, and strike the lyre,
The time, the theme, the place, and all conspire.

Air.

CHALDEAN WOMAN.

See the ruddy morning smiling,
Hear the grove to bliss beguiling;
Zephyrs through the woodland playing,
Streams along the valley straying.

FIRST PRIEST.

While these a constant revel keep,
Shall reason only teach to weep?
Hence, intruder! we'll pursue
Nature, a better guide than you.

SECOND PRIEST.

But hold! see, foremost of the captive choir,
The master prophet grasps his full-toned lyre.
Mark where he sits, with executing art,
Feels for each tone, and speeds it to the heart!
See, how prophetic rapture fills his form,
Awful as clouds that nurse the growing storm!
And now his voice, accordant to the string,
Prepares our monarch's victories to sing.

Air.

FIRST PROPHET.

From north, from south, from east, from west,
Conspiring nations come:
Tremble, thou vice-polluted breast!
Blasphemers, all be dumb.

The tempest gathers all around,
On Babylon it lies;
Down with her! down, down to the ground
She sinks, she groans, she dies.

SECOND PROPHET.

Down with her, Lord, to lick the dust,
Before yon setting sun;
Serve her as she hath served the just!
'Tis fixed—it shall be done.

FIRST PRIEST.

No more! when slaves thus insolent presume,
The king himself shall judge and fix their doom.
Unthinking wretches! have not you and all
Beheld our power in Zedekiah's fall?
To yonder gloomy dungeon turn your eyes:
See where dethroned your captive monarch lies,
Deprived of sight, and rankling in his chain;
See where he mourns his friends and children slain.
Yet know, ye slaves, that still remain behind
More ponderous chains, and dungeons more confined.

CHORUS OF ALL.

Arise, all potent ruler, rise,
And vindicate thy people's cause,
Till every tongue in every land
Shall offer up unfeigned applause.

[*Exeunt.*

ACT THE THIRD.

FIRST PRIEST.

Yes, my companions, Heaven's decrees are passed,
And our fixed empire shall for ever last;
In vain the maddening prophet threatens wo,
In vain rebellion aims her secret blow;
Still shall our name and growing power be spread,
And still our justice crush the traitor's head.

Air.

Coeval with man
Our empire began,
And never shall fall
Till ruin shakes all.
When ruin shakes all,
Then shall Babylon fall.

SECOND PROPHET.

'Tis thus the proud triumphant rear the head,—
A little while, and all their power is fled.
But, ha! what means yon sadly plaintive train,
That onward slowly bends along the plain?
And now, behold, to yonder bank they bear
A pallid corse, and rest the body there.
Alas! too well mine eyes indignant trace
The last remains of Judah's royal race:
Fallen is our king, and all our fears are o'er,
Unhappy Zedekiah is no more.

Air.

Ye wretches, who by fortune's hate
In want and sorrow groan,
Come, ponder his severer fate,
And learn to bless your own.

FIRST PROPHET.

Ye vain, whom youth and pleasure guide,
A while the bliss suspend;
Like yours, his life began in pride,
Like his, your lives shall end.

SECOND PROPHET.

Behold his wretched corse with sorrow worn,
His squalid limbs by ponderous fetters torn;
Those eyeless orbs that shook with ghastly glare,
Those unbecoming rags, that matted hair!
And shall not Heaven for this avenge the foe,
Grasp the red bolt, and lay the guilty low?
How long, how long, Almighty God of all,
Shall wrath vindictive threaten ere it fall?

Air.

ISRAELITISH WOMAN.

As panting flies the hunted hind
Where brooks refreshing stray;
And rivers through the valley wind,
That stop the hunter's way:

Thus, we, O Lord, alike distressed,
For streams of mercy long;
Streams which cheer the sore oppressed,
And overwhelm the strong.

FIRST PROPHET.

But whence that shout? Good heavens! Amazement all!
See yonder tower just nodding to the fall:
Behold, an army covers all the ground,
'Tis Cyrus here that pours destruction round,
And now, behold, the battlements recline—
O God of hosts, the victory is thine!

CHORUS OF CAPTIVES.

Down with them, Lord, to lick the dust,
Thy vengeance be begun;
Serve them as they have served the just,
And let thy will be done.

FIRST PRIEST.

All, all is lost! The Syrian army fails,
Cyrus, the conqueror of the world, prevails.
The ruin smokes, the torrent pours along—
How low the proud, how feeble are the strong!
Save us, O Lord! to Thee, though late, we pray,
And give repentance but an hour's delay.

Air.

FIRST AND SECOND PRIEST.

O happy, who in happy hour
To God their praise bestow,
And own his all-consuming power
Before they feel the blow!

SECOND PROPHET.

Now, now's our time! ye wretches bold and blind,
Brave but to God, and cowards to mankind,
Ye seek in vain the Lord unsought before,
Your wealth, your lives, your kingdom, are no more.

Air.

O Lucifer, thou son of morn,
Of Heaven alike and man the foe,—
Heaven, men, and all,
Now press thy fall,
And sink thee lowest of the low.

FIRST PROPHET.

O Babylon, how art thou fallen!
Thy fall more dreadful from delay!
Thy streets forlorn
To wilds shall turn,
Where toads shall pant and vultures prey.

SECOND PROPHET.

Such be her fate. But hark! how from afar
The clarion's note proclaims the finished war!
Our great restorer, Cyrus, is at hand,
And this way leads his formidable band.
Give, give your songs of Sion to the wind,
And hail the benefactor of mankind:
He comes, pursuant to divine decree,
To chain the strong, and set the captive free.

CHORUS OF YOUTHS.

Rise to transports past expressing,
Sweeter by remembered woes;
Cyrus comes, our wrongs redressing,
Comes to give the world repose.

CHORUS OF VIRGINS.

Cyrus comes, the world redressing,
Love and pleasure in his train;
Comes to heighten every blessing,
Comes to soften every pain.

SEMI-CHORUS.

Hail to him with mercy reigning,
Skilled in every peaceful art;
Who, from bonds our limbs unchaining,
Only binds the willing heart.

THE LAST CHORUS.

But chief to thee, our God, defender, friend,
Let praise be given to all eternity;
O Thou, without beginning, without end,
Let us all begin and end in Thee!

THRENODIA AUGUSTALIS.*

SACRED TO THE MEMORY OF HER LATE ROYAL HIGHNESS THE PRINCESS DOWAGER OF WALES

AIR—TRIO.

Arise, ye sons of earth, arise,
And waken every note of wo!
When truth and virtue reach the skies
'Tis ours to weep the want below.

CHORUS.

When truth and virtue, &c.

MAN SPEAKER.

The praise attending pomp and power,
The incense given to kings,
Are but the trappings of an hour,
Mere transitory things.
The base bestow them; but the good agree
To spurn the venal gifts as flattery.
But when to pomp and power are joined
An equal dignity of the mind;
When titles are the smallest claim;
When wealth, and rank, and noble blood,
But aid the power of doing good;
Then all their trophies last—and flattery turns to fame.
Blest spirit thou, whose fame, just born to bloom,
Shall spread and flourish from the tomb,
How hast thou left mankind for Heaven!
Even now reproach and faction mourn,
And, wondering how their rage was born,
Request to be forgiven!
Alas! they never had thy hate;
Unmoved, in conscious rectitude,
Thy towering mind self-centred stood,
Nor wanted man's opinion to be great.
In vain, to charm the ravished sight,
A thousand gifts would fortune send;
In vain, to drive thee from the right,
A thousand sorrows urged thy end:
Like some well-fashioned arch thy patience stood,
And purchased strength from its increasing load.
Pain met thee like a friend to set thee free,
Affliction still is virtue's opportunity!
Virtue, on herself relying,
Every passion hushed to rest,
Loses every pain of dying
In the hopes of being blest.
Every added pang she suffers
Some increasing good bestows,
And every shock that malice offers,
Only rocks her to repose.

WOMAN SPEAKER.

Yet ah! what terrors frowned upon her fate,
Death, with his formidable band,
Fever, and pain, and pale consumptive care,
Determined took their stand.

* This poem was prepared in little more than two days, and spoken and sung in the great room in Soho-square, Thursday, the 20th of February, 1772.

Nor did the cruel ravagers design
To finish all their efforts at a blow:
But, mischievously slow,
They robbed the relic and defaced the shrine.
With unavailing grief,
Despairing of relief,
Her weeping children round
Beheld each hour
Death's growing power,
And trembled as he frowned.
As helpless friends who view from shore
The laboring ship, and hear the tempest roar,
While winds and waves their wishes cross,—
They stood, while hope and comfort fail,
Not to assist, but to bewail
The inevitable loss.
Relentless tyrant, at thy call
How do the good, the virtuous fall!
Truth, beauty, worth, and all that most engage,
But wake thy vengeance and provoke thy rage.

SONG. BY A MAN—BASSO, STACCATO, SPIRITUOSO.

When vice my dart and scythe supply,
How great a King of Terrors I!
If folly, frauds, your hearts engage,
Tremble, ye mortals, at my rage!
Fall, round me fall, ye little things,
Ye statesmen, warriors, poets, kings,
If virtue fail her counsel sage,
Tremble, ye mortals, at my rage!

MAN SPEAKER.

Yet let that wisdom, urged by her example,
Teach us to estimate what all must suffer:
Let us prize death as the best gift of nature,
As a safe inn where weary travellers,
When they have journeyed through a world of cares,
May put off life, and be at rest for ever.
Groans, weeping friends, indeed, and gloomy sables
May oft distract us with their sad solemnity:
The preparation is the executioner.
Death, when unmasked, shows me a friendly face,
And is a terror only at a distance:
For as the line of life conducts me on
To Death's great court, the prospect seems more fair,
'Tis Nature's kind retreat, that's always open
To take us in when we have drained the cup
Of life, or worn our days to wretchedness.
In that secure, serene retreat,
Where all the humble, all the great,
Promiscuously recline;
Where, wildly huddled to the eye,
The beggar's pouch and prince's purple lie:
May every bliss be thine!
And, ah! blest spirit, wheresoe'er thy flight,
Through rolling worlds, or fields of liquid light,
May cherubs welcome their expected guest!
May saints with songs receive thee to their rest!
May peace, that claimed, while here, thy warmest love,
May blissful, endless peace be thine above!

SONG. BY A WOMAN—AMOROSO.

Lovely, lasting Peace, below,
Comforter of every wo,
Heavenly born, and bred on high,
To crown the favorites of the sky!
Lovely, lasting Peace, appear!
This world itself, if thou art here,
's once again with Eden blest,
And man contains it in his breast.

WOMAN SPEAKER.

Our vows are heard! Long, long to mortal eyes,
Her soul was fitting to its kindred skies:
Celestial-like her bounty fell,
Where modest Want and patient Sorrow dwell;
Want passed for Merit at her door,
Unseen the modest were supplied,
Her constant pity fed the poor,—
Then only poor, indeed, the day she died.
And, oh! for this, while sculpture decks thy shrine,
And art exhausts profusion round,
The tribute of a tear be mine.

A simple song, a sigh profound.
There Faith shall come—a pilgrim gray,
To bless the tomb that wraps thy clay!
And calm Religion shall repair
To dwell a weeping hermit there.
Truth, Fortitude, and Friendship, shall agree
To blend their virtues while they think of thee.

AIR—CHORUS POMPOSO.

Let us—let all the world agree,
To profit by resembling thee.

PART II.

MAN SPEAKER.

Fast by that shore where Thames' translucent stream
Reflects new glories on his breast,
Where, splendid as the youthful poet's dream,
He forms a scene beyond Elysium blest;
Where sculptured elegance and native grace
Unite to stamp the beauties of the place;
While, sweetly blending, still are seen
The wavy lawn, the sloping green;
While novelty, with cautious cunning,
Through every maze of fancy running,
From China borrows aid to deck the scene:
There, sorrowing by the river's glassy bed,
Forlorn, a rural band complained,
All whom Augusta's bounty fed,
All whom her clemency sustained;
The good old sire, unconscious of decay,
The modest matron, clad in home-spun gray,
The military boy, the orphaned maid,
The shattered veteran now first dismayed,—
These sadly join beside the murmuring deep,
And, as they view the towers of Kew,
Call on their mistress—now no more—and weep.

CHORUS—AFFETUOSO, LARGO.

Ye shady walks, ye waving greens,
Ye nodding towers, ye fairy scenes,
Let all your echoes now deplore,
That she who formed your beauties is no more.

MAN SPEAKER.

First of the train the patient rustic came,
Whose callous hand had formed the scene,
Bending at once with sorrow and with age,
With many a tear, and many a sigh between:
"And where," he cried, "shall now my babes have bread,
Or how shall age support its feeble fire?
No lord will take me now, my vigor fled,
Nor can my strength perform what they require:
Each grudging master keeps the laborer bare,
A sleek and idle race is all their care.
My noble mistress thought not so:
Her bounty, like the morning dew,
Unseen, though constant, used to flow,
And as my strength decayed, her bounty grew."

WOMAN SPEAKER.

In decent dress, and coarsely clean,
The pious matron next was seen,
Clasped in her hand a godly book was borne,
By use and daily meditation worn;
That decent dress, this holy guide,
Augusta's cares had well supplied.
"And, ah!" she cries, all wobegone,
"What now remains for me?
Oh! where shall weeping want repair
To ask for charity?
Too late in life for me to ask,
And shame prevents the deed,
And tardy, tardy are the times
To succor should I need.
But all my wants, before I spoke,
Were to my mistress known;
She still relieved, nor sought my praise,
Contented with her own.
But every day her name I'll bless,
My morning prayer, my evening song,
I'll praise her while my life shall last,
A life that can not last me long."

SONG.—BY A WOMAN.

Each day, each hour, her name I'll bless,
My morning and my evening song,
And when in death my vows shall cease,
My children shall the note prolong.

MAN SPEAKER.

The hardy veteran after struck the sight,
Scarred, mangled, maimed in every part,
Lopped of his limbs in many a gallant fight,
In naught entire—except his heart:
Mute for a while, and sullenly distrest,
At last th' impetuous sorrow fired his breast:
"Wild is the whirlwind rolling
O'er Afric's sandy plain,
And wide the tempest howling
Along the billowed main:
But every danger felt before,
The raging deep, the whirlwind's roar,
Less dreadful struck me with dismay
Than what I feel this fatal day.
Oh, let me fly a land that spurns the brave,
Oswego's dreary shores shall be my grave;
I'll seek that less inhospitable coast,
And lay my body where my limbs were lost."

SONG.—BY A MAN.—BASSO SPIRITUOSO.

Old Edward's sons, unknown to yield,
Shall crowd from Cressy's laurelled field,
To do thy memory right:
For thine and Britain's wrongs they feel,
Again they snatch the gleamy steel,
And wish th' avenging fight.

WOMAN SPEAKER.

In innocence and youth complaining,
Next appeared a lovely maid;
Affliction, o'er each feature reigning,
Kindly came in beauty's aid:
Every grace that grief dispenses,
Every glance that warms the soul,
In sweet succession charms the senses,
While Pity harmonized the whole.
"The garland of beauty," 'tis thus she would say,
"No more shall my crook or my temples adorn;
I'll not wear a garland—Augusta's away—
I'll not wear a garland until she return.
But, alas! that return I never shall see:
The echoes of Thames shall my sorrows proclaim,
There promised a lover to come—but, ah me!
'Twas death—'twas the death of my mistress that came
But ever, for ever, her image shall last,
I'll strip all the Spring of its earliest bloom;
On her grave shall the cowslip and primrose be cast,
And the new-blossomed thorn shall whiten her tomb.'

SONG.—BY A WOMAN.—PASTORALE.

With garlands of beauty the Queen of the May
No more will her crook or her temples adorn;
For who'd wear a garland when she is away,
When she is removed and shall never return?

On the grave of Augusta these garlands be placed,
We'll rifle the Spring of its earliest bloom,
And there shall the cowslip and primrose be cast,
And the new-blossomed thorn shall whiten her tomb

CHORUS.—ALTRO MODO.

On the grave of Augusta this garland be placed,
We'll rifle the Spring of its earliest bloom,
And there shall the cowslip and primrose be cast,
And the tears of her country shall water her tomb.

WEEPING.

Weeping, murmuring, complaining,
Lost to every gay delight,
Myra too sincere for feigning,
Fears the approaching bridal night.

Yet why impair thy bright perfection,
Or dim thy beauty with a tear?
Had Myra followed my direction,
She long had wanted cause of fear

THE HAUNCH OF VENISON.*

A POETICAL EPISTLE TO LORD CLARE.

Thanks, my lord, for your venison, for finer or fatter
Ne'er ranged in a forest, or smoked in a platter.
The haunch was a picture for painters to study,
The fat was so white, and the lean was so ruddy;
Though my stomach was sharp, I could scarce help regret-
ting
To spoil such a delicate picture by eating:
I had thoughts, in my chamber to place it in view,
To be shown to my friends as a piece of virtû;
As in some Irish houses, where things are so so,
One gammon of bacon hangs up for a show;
But for eating a rasher of what they take pride in,
They 'd as soon think of eating the pan it is fried in.
But hold—let me pause—do n't I hear you pronounce,
This tale of the bacon's a damnable bounce?
Well, suppose it a bounce—sure a poet may try,
By a bounce now and then, to get courage to fly.
But, my lord, it 's no bounce: I protest, in my turn,
It 's a truth, and your lordship may ask Mr. Burn.†
To go on with my tale: as I gazed on the haunch,
I thought of a friend that was trusty and staunch,
So I cut it, and sent it to Reynolds undrest,
To paint it, or eat it, just as he liked best.
Of the neck and the breast I had next to dispose—
'T was a neck and a breast that might rival Monroe's:
But in parting with these I was puzzed again,
With the how, and the who, and the where, and the when.
There 's H—d, and C—y, and H—rth, and H—ff,
I think they love venison—I know they love beef;
There 's my countryman, Higgins—oh, let him alone
For making a blunder, or picking a bone:
But, hang it, to poets who seldom can eat,
Your very good mutton 's a very good treat;
Such dainties to them their health it might hurt,
It's like sending them ruffles, when wanting a shirt.
While thus I debated, in revery centred,
An acquaintance—a friend, as he called himself—entered;
An under-bred, fine-spoken fellow was he,
And he smiled as he looked at the venison and me,—
"What have we got here?—Why, this is good eating!
Your own, I suppose—or is it in waiting?"
"Why, whose should it be?" cried I, with a flounce,
"I get these things often"—but that was a bounce:
"Some lords, my acquaintance, that settle the nation,
Are pleased to be kind—but I hate ostentation."
"If that be the case, then," cried he, very gay,
I am glad I have taken this house in my way:
To-morrow you take a poor dinner with me;
No words—I insist on 't—precisely at three;
We 'll have Johnson, and Burke, all the wits will be there:
My acquaintance is slight, or I 'd ask my lord Clare.
And, now that I think on 't, as I am a sinner,
We wanted this venison to make out a dinner.
What say you—a pasty? it shall, and it must,
And my wife, little Kitty, is famous for crust.
Here, porter—this venison with me to Mile-end:
No stirring, I beg—my dear friend—my dear friend!"
Thus, snatching his hat, he brushed off like the wind,
And the porter and eatables followed behind.
Left alone to reflect, having emptied my shelf,
And "nobody with me at sea but myself!"‡
Though I could not help thinking my gentleman hasty,
Yet Johnson, and Burke, and a good venison pasty,
Were things that I never disliked in my life,
Though clogged with a coxcomb, and Kitty his wife.
So next day, in due splendor to make my approach,
I drove to his door in my own hackney-coach.
When come to the place where we all were to dine,
(A chair-lumbered closet, just twelve feet by nine,)
My friend bade me welcome, but struck me quite dumb
With tidings that Johnson and Burke would not come;
"For I knew it," he cried, "both eternally fail,
The one with his speeches, and t' other with Thrale:§
But no matter, I 'll warrant we 'll make up the party
With two full as clever, and ten times as hearty.
The one is a Scotchman, the other a Jew:
They 're both of them merry, and authors like you:
The one writes the Snarler, the other the Scourge;
Some think he writes Cinna—he owns to Panurge."
While thus he described them, by trade and by name,
They entered, and dinner was served as they came.
At the top a fried liver and bacon were seen;
At the bottom, was tripe in a swinging tureen;
At the sides, there was spinach, and pudding made hot;
In the middle, a place where the pasty—was not.
Now, my lord, as for tripe, it 's my utter aversion,
And your bacon I hate like a Turk or a Persian;
So there I sat stuck like a horse in a pound,
While the bacon and liver went merrily round:
But what vexed me most was that d——d Scottish rogue,
With his long-winded speeches, his smiles, and his brogue;
And, "Madam," quoth he, "may this bit be my poison,
A prettier dinner I never set eyes on:
Pray, a slice of your liver, though, may I be curst,
But I 've eat of your tripe till I 'm ready to burst."
"The tripe!" quoth the Jew with his chocolate cheek,
"I could dine on this tripe seven days in a week:
I like these here dinners, so pretty and small;
But your friend there, the Doctor, eats nothing at all."
"O ho!" quoth my friend, "he 'll come on in a trice,
He 's keeping a corner for something that 's nice:
There 's a pasty."—"A pasty!" repeated the Jew,
"I do n't care if I keep a corner for 't too."
"What the deil mon, a pasty!" re-echoed the Scot,
"Though splitting, I 'll still keep a corner for that."
"We 'll all keep a corner," the lady cried out;
"We 'll all keep a corner," was echoed about.
While thus we resolved, and the pasty delayed,
With looks that quite petrified, entered the maid:
A visage so sad, and so pale with affright,
Waked Priam, in drawing his curtains by night.
But we quickly found out—for who could mistake her?—
That she came with some terrible news from the baker;
And so it fell out; for that negligent sloven
Had shut out the pasty on shutting his oven.
Sad Philomel thus—but let similes drop—
And now that I think on 't, the story may stop.
To be plain, my good lord, it 's but labor misplaced,
To send such good verses to one of your taste:
You 've got an odd something—a kind of discerning,
A relish—a taste—sickened over by learning;
At least it 's your temper, as very well known,
That you think very slightly of all that 's your own:
So, perhaps, in your habits of thinking amiss,
You may make a mistake, and think slightly of this.

* The description of the dinner party in this poem is imitated from Boileau's fourth Satire. Boileau himself took the hint from Horace, Lib. ii., Sat. 8, which has also been imitated by Regnier, Sat. 10.

† Lord Clare's nephew.

‡ See the letters that passed between his Royal Highness Henry Duke of Cumberland, and Lady Grosvenor. 12mo. 1769.

§ An eminent London brewer, M. P. for the borough of Southwark at whose table Dr. Johnson was a frequent guest.

THE DOUBLE TRANSFORMATION.

A TALE.

Secluded from domestic strife,
Jack Book-worm led a college life;
A fellowship at twenty-five
Made him the happiest man alive;
He drank his glass, and cracked his joke,
And freshmen wondered as he spoke.

Such pleasures, unalloyed with care,
Could any accident impair?
Could Cupid's shaft at length transfix
Our swain, arrived at thirty-six?

Oh, had the archer ne'er come down
To ravage in a country town!
Or Flavia been content to stop
At triumphs in a Fleet street shop!
Oh, had her eyes forgot to blaze!
Or Jack had wanted eyes to gaze!
Oh! but let exclamation cease,
Her presence banished all his peace;
So with decorum all things carried,
Miss frowned, and blushed, and then was—married.

Need we expose to vulgar sight
The raptures of the bridal night?
Need we intrude on hallowed ground,
Or draw the curtains closed around?

Let it suffice that each had charms:
He clasped a goddess in his arms;
And though she felt his usage rough,
Yet in a man 'twas well enough.

The honeymoon like lightning flew,
The second brought its transports too;
A third, a fourth, were not amiss,
The fifth was friendship mixed with bliss:
But, when a twelvemonth passed away,
Jack found his goddess made of clay;
Found half the charms that decked her face
Arose from powder, shreds, or lace;
But still the worst remained behind—
That very face had robbed her mind.

Skilled in no other arts was she,
But dressing, patching, repartee;
And, just as humor rose or fell,
By turns a slattern or a belle.
'Tis true she dressed with modern grace,
Half-naked, at a ball or race;
But when at home, at board or bed,
Five greasy nightcaps wrapped her head.
Could so much beauty condescend
To be a dull domestic friend?
Could any curtain-lectures bring
To decency so fine a thing!
In short, by night, 'twas fits or fretting;
By day, 'twas gadding or coquetting.
Fond to be seen, she kept a bevy
Of powdered coxcombs at her levee;
The squire and captain took their stations,
And twenty other near relations:
Jack sucked his pipe, and often broke
A sigh in suffocating smoke;
While all their hours were passed between
Insulting repartee and spleen.

Thus, as her faults each day were known,
He thinks her features coarser grown;
He fancies every vice she shows,
Or thins her lip, or points her nose:
Whenever rage or envy rise,
How wide her mouth, how wild her eyes!
He knows not how, but so it is,
Her face is grown a knowing phiz;
And, though her fops are wondrous civil,
He thinks her ugly as the devil.

Now, to perplex the ravelled noose,
As each a different way pursues,
While sullen or loquacious strife
Promised to hold them on for life,
That dire disease, whose ruthless power
Withers the beauty's transient flower—
Lo! the small-pox with horrid glare,
Levelled its terrors at the fair;
And, rifling every youthful grace,
Left but the remnant of a face.

The glass grown hateful to her sight,
Reflected now a perfect fright:
Each former art she vainly tries
To bring back lustre to her eyes;
In vain she tries her paste and creams
To smooth her skin or hide its seams;
Her country beaux and city cousins,
Lovers no more, flew off by dozens;
The squire himself was seen to yield,
And e'en the captain quit the field.

Poor madam, now condemned to hack
The rest of life with anxious Jack,
Perceiving others fairly flown,
Attempted pleasing him alone.
Jack soon was dazzled to behold
Her present face surpass the old:
With modesty her cheeks are died,
Humility displaces pride;
For tawdry finery is seen
A person ever neatly clean;
No more presuming on her sway,
She learns good nature every day:
Serenely gay, and strict in duty,
Jack finds his wife a perfect beauty

THE LOGICIANS REFUTED.*

IN IMITATION OF DEAN SWIFT.

LOGICIANS have but ill defined
As rational the human mind:
Reason, they say, belongs to man,
But let them prove it if they can.
Wise Aristotle and Smiglesius,
By ratiocinations specious,
Have strove to prove with great precision,
With definition and division,
Homo est ratione preditum;
But for my soul I can not credit them;
And must in spite of them maintain,
That man and all his ways are vain;
And that this boasted lord of nature
Is both a weak and erring creature;
That instinct is a surer guide
Than reason, boasting mortals' pride;
And that brute beasts are far before 'em—
Deus est anima bru orum.
Who ever knew an honest brute
At law his neighbor prosecute,
Bring action for assault and battery?
Or friend beguile with lies and flattery?
O'er plains they ramble unconfined,
No politics disturb their mind;
They eat their meals, and take their sport,
Nor know who's in or out at court:
They never to the levee go
To treat as dearest friend a foe;
They never importune his grace,
Nor ever cringe to men in place;
Nor undertake a dirty job,
Nor draw the quill to write for Bob,†
Fraught with invective they ne'er go
To folks at Paternoster Row:
No judges, fiddlers, dancing-masters,
No pickpockets, or poetasters,
Are known to honest quadrupeds;
No single brute his fellows leads.
Brutes never meet in bloody fray,
Nor cut each other's throats for pay.
Of beasts, it is confessed, the ape
Comes nearest us in human shade;
Like man, he imitates each fashion,
And malice is his ruling passion:
But both in malice and grimaces,
A courtier any ape surpasses.
Behold humbly cringing wait
Upon the minister of state;
View him soon after to inferiors
Aping the conduct of superiors:
He promises with equal air,
And to perform takes equal care.
He in his turn finds imitators:
At court the porters, lacqueys, waiters,
Their masters' manners still contract,
And footmen, lords and dukes can act,
Thus at the court, both great and small
Behave alike, for all ape all.

A NEW SIMILE.

IN THE MANNER OF SWIFT.

LONG had I sought in vain to find
A likeness for the scribbling kind—
The modern scribbling kind, who write
In wit, and sense, and nature's spite—
Till reading—I forget what day on—
A chapter out of Tooke's Pantheon,
I think I met with something there
To suit my purpose to a hair.
But let us not proceed too furious,—
First please to turn to god Mercurius;
You'll find him pictured at full length,
In book the second, page the tenth:

* This happy imitation was adopted by his Dublin publisher, as genuine poem of Swift, and as such it has been reprinted in almost every edition of the Dean's works. Even Sir Walter Scott has inserted it without any remark in his edition of Swift's Works.

† Sir Robert Walpole.

The stress of all my proofs on him I lay,
And now proceed we to our simile.

'Imprimis, pray observe his hat,
Wings upon either side—mark that.
Well! what is it from thence we gather?
Why, these denote a brain of feather.
A brain of feather! very right,
With wit that's flighty, learning light;
Such as to modern bard's decreed:
A just comparison—proceed.

In the next place, his feet peruse,
Wings grow again from both his shoes;
Designed, no doubt their part to bear,
And waft his godship through the air:
And here my simile unites;
For in a modern poet's flights,
I'm sure it may be justly said,
His feet are useful as his head.

Lastly, vouchsafe to observe his hand,
Filled with a snake-encircled wand,
By classic authors termed caduceus,
And highly famed for several uses:
To wit,—most wondrously endued,
No poppy water half so good;
For let folks only get a touch,
Its soporific virtue's such,
Though ne'er so much awake before,
That quickly they begin to snore;
Add, too, what certain writers tell,
With this he drives men's souls to hell.

Now, to apply, begin we then:—
His wand's a modern author's pen;
The serpents round about it twined
Denote him of the reptile kind,
Denote the rage with which he writes,
His frothy slaver, venomed bites;
An equal semblance still to keep,
Alike, too, both conduce to sleep;
This difference only, as the god
Drove souls to Tartarus with his rod,
With his goose-quill the scribbling elf,
Instead of others, damns himself.

And here my simile almost tript,
Yet grant a word by way of postscript.
Moreover, Mercury had a failing;
Well! what of that? out with it—stealing;
In which all modern bards agree,
Being each as great a thief as he.
But e'en this deity's existence
Shall lend my simile assistance:
Our modern bards! why, what a pox,
Are they but senseless stones and blocks?

A PROLOGUE,

WRITTEN AND SPOKEN BY THE POET LABERIUS, A ROMAN KNIGHT, WHOM CESAR FORCED UPON THE STAGE.

What! no way left to shun the inglorious stage,
And save from infamy my sinking age!
Scarce half alive, oppressed with many a year,
What in the name of dotage drives me here?
A time there was, when glory was my guide,
Nor force nor fraud could turn my steps aside;
Unawed by power, and unappalled by fear,
With honest thrift I held my honor dear:
But this vile hour disperses all my store,
And all my hoard of honor is no more;
For, ah! too partial to my life's decline,
Cesar persuades, submission must be mine;
Him I obey, whom Heaven itself obeys,
Hopeless of pleasing, yet inclined to please.
Here then at once I welcome every shame,
And cancel, at threescore, a life of fame:
No more my titles shall my children tell,
The old buffoon will fit my name as well:
This day beyond its term my fate extends,
For life is ended when our honor ends.

ON A BEAUTIFUL YOUTH,

STRUCK BLIND BY LIGHTNING.

Sure 'twas by Providence designed,
Rather in pity than in hate,
That he should be, like Cupid, blind,
To save him from Narcissus' fate.

THE CLOWN'S REPLY.

John Trott was desired by two witty peers
To tell them the reason why asses had ears;
"An't please you," quoth John, "I'm not given to letters,
Nor dare I pretend to know more than my betters:
Howe'er, from this time, I shall ne'er see your graces—
As I hope to be saved!—without thinking on asses."

EPITAPH ON DR. PARNELL.

This tomb, inscribed to gentle Parnell's name,
May speak our gratitude, but not his fame.
What heart but feels his sweetly moral lay,
That leads to truth through pleasure's flowery way?
Celestial themes confessed his tuneful aid;
And Heaven, that lent him genius, was repaid.
Needless to him the tribute we bestow,
The transitory breath of fame below:
More lasting rapture from his works shall rise,
While converts thank their poets in the skies.

LINES.

E'en have you seen, bathed in the morning dew,
The budding rose its infant bloom display;
When first its virgin teints unfold to view,
It shrinks and scarcely trusts the blaze of day:

So soft, so delicate, so sweet she came,
Youth's damask glow just dawning on her cheek;
I gazed, I sighed, I caught the tender flame,
Felt the fond pang, and drooped with passion weak.

PROLOGUE TO ZOBEIDE.*

In these bold times, when Learning's sons explore
The distant climates and the savage shore;
When wise astronomers to India steer,
And quit for Venus many a brighter here;
While botanists, all cold to smiles and dimpling,
Forsake the fair, and patiently—go simpling:
Our bard into the general spirit enters,
And fits his little frigate for adventures.
With Scythian stores, and trinkets deeply laden,
He this way steers his course, in hopes of trading;
Yet ere he lands he's ordered me before,
To make an observation on the shore.
Where are we driven? our reckoning sure is lost!
This seems a rocky and a dangerous coast.
Lord, what a sultry climate am I under!
Yon ill-foreboding cloud seems big with thunder:
There mangroves spread, and larger than I've seen 'em—
Here trees of stately size—and billing turtles in 'em.
Here ill-conditioned oranges abound—
And apples, bitter apples, strew the ground:
The inhabitants are cannibals, I fear:
I heard a hissing—there are serpents here!
Oh, there the people are—best keep my distance:
Our Captain, gentle natives, craves assistance;
Our ship's well stored—in yonder creek we've laid her
His honor is no mercenary trader.
This is his first adventure: lend him aid,
And we may chance to drive a thriving trade.
His goods, he hopes, are prime, and brought from far,
Equally fit for gallantry and war.
What! no reply to promises so ample?
I'd best step back and order up a sample.

* A tragedy, written by Joseph Cradock, Esq., and acted at the Theatre Royal, Covent Garden, 1772.

THE GIFT.

TO IRIS, IN BOW STREET COVENT GARDEN.

Say, cruel Iris, pretty rake,
Dear mercenary beauty,
What annual offering shall I make
Expressive of my duty?

My heart, a victim to thine eyes,
Should I at once deliver,
Say, would the angry fair one prize
The gift, who slights the giver?

A bill, a jewel, watch, or toy,
My rivals give—and let 'em:
If gems, or gold, impart a joy,
I'll give them—when I get 'em.

I'll give—but not the full-blown rose,
Or rose-bud more in fashion;
Such short-lived offerings but disclose
A transitory passion—

I'll give thee something yet unpaid,
Not less sincere than civil,—
I'll give thee—ah! too charming maid!—
I'll give thee—to the Devil!

AN ELEGY ON THE DEATH OF A MAD DOG.

Good people all, of every sort,
Give ear unto my song,
And if you find it wondrous short,
It can not hold you long.

In Islington there was a man,
Of whom the world might say,
That still a godly race he ran,
When'er he went to pray.

A kind and gentle heart he had,
To comfort friends and foes:
The naked every day he clad,
When he put on his clothes.

And in that town a dog was found,
As many dogs there be,
Both mongrel, puppy, whelp, and hound,
And curs of low degree.

This dog and man at first were friends;
But when a pique began,
The dog to gain his private ends,
Went mad, and bit the man.

Around from all the neighboring streets
The wondering neighbors ran,
And swore the dog had lost its wits,
To bite so good a man.

The wound it seemed both sore and sad
To every Christian eye;
And while they swore the dog was mad,
They swore the man would die.

But soon a wonder came to light,
That showed the rogues they lied:
The man recovered of the bite—
The dog it was that died.

ON THE DEATH OF WOLFE.

Amidst the clamor of exulting joys,
Which triumph forces from the patriot heart,
Grief dares to mingle her soul-piercing voice,
And quells the raptures which from pleasure start.

O Wolfe! to thee a streaming flood of wo
Sighing we pay, and think e'en conquest dear;
Quebec in vain shall teach our breast to glow,
While thy sad fate extorts the heart-wrung tear.

Alive, the foe thy dreadful vigor fled,
And saw thee fall with joy-pronouncing eyes;
Yet they shall know thou conquerest, though dead!
Since from thy tomb a thousand heroes rise.

DESCRIPTION OF AN AUTHOR'S BED-CHAMBER

Where the Red Lion, staring o'er the way,
Invites each passing stranger that can pay;
Where Calvert's butt, and Parson's black champagne,
Regale the drabs and bloods of Drury-lane:
There, in a lonely room, from bailiffs snug,
The Muse found Scroggen stretched beneath a rug;
A window, patched with paper, lent a ray,
That dimly showed the state in which he lay;
The sanded floor that grits beneath the tread;
The humid wall with paltry pictures spread;
The royal game of goose was there in view,
And the twelve rules the Royal Martyr drew;
The Seasons, framed with listing, found a place,
And brave Prince William showed his lamp-black face
The morn was cold; he views with keen desire
The rusty grate unconscious of a fire:
With beer and milk arrears the frieze was scored,
And five cracked tea-cups dressed the chimney-board;
A night cap decked his brows instead of bay,
A cap by night—a stocking all the day!

AN ELEGY ON THE GLORY OF HER SEX, MRS. MARY BLAIZE.

Good people all, with one accord
Lament for Madam Blaize,
Who never wanted a good word—
From those who spoke her praise.

The needy seldom passed her door,
And always found her kind;
She freely lent to all the poor—
Who left a pledge behind.

She strove the neighborhood to please
With manners wondrous winning;
And never followed wicked ways—
Unless when she was sinning.

At church in silks and satins new,
With hoop of monstrous size,
She never slumbered in her pew—
But when she shut her eyes.

Her love was sought, I do aver
By twenty beaux and more;
The king himself has followed her—
When she has walked before.

But now, her wealth and finery fled,
Her hangers-on cut short all;
The doctors found, when she was dead—
Her last disorder mortal.

Let us lament in sorrow sore,
For Kent street well may say,
That had she lived a twelvemonth more—
She had not died to-day.

STANZAS ON WOMAN.

When lovely woman stoops to folly,
And finds too late that men betray,
What charm can sooth her melancholy?
What art can wash her guilt away?

The only art her guilt to cover,
To hide her shame from every eye,
To give repentance to her lover,
And wring his bosom, is—to die.

WHEN SHALL I MARRY ME?

Ah me! when shall I marry me?
Lovers are plenty, but fail to relieve me.
He, fond youth, that could carry me,
Offers to love, but means to deceive me.

But I will rally, and combat the ruiner:
Not a look, nor a smile, shall my passion discover
She that gives all to the false one pursuing her,
Makes but a penitent, and loses a lover.

THE ALBUM OF LOVE.

"Love rules the court, the camp, the grove,
And men below and saints above."

DEDICATION.

To those who *have already learned to love*, and, to those who have *yet to love*, these pages are alike dedicated ; and thus the Dedication becomes of universal application ; for—

"It is decreed by Heaven above,
That soon or late we *all* must love."

That the love of all, who may find an echo to their own thoughts within this little volume, may be pure and prosperous, is the sincere desire of their well-wisher,

THE EDITOR

INVITATION.

COME, thou lover, on whose eyes
Dreams of absent beauty rise,
In my little page thou'lt find
Balmy medicine for the mind:
Love still living in its prime,
Tried by sorrow, tried by time.
O'er the clouds of human ill
Soaring angel-pinioned still.

Come, thou maiden, sweet and young,
Like a lyre with silver strung,
Like the breathing violet,
Still with morning's kisses wet;
Like a sweet bird in its nest,
Stranger to the world's unrest,
Ere upon the breeze it flings
The rich painting of its wings:
Thou shalt find a wondrous spell
In my little oracle.
Visions bright of happy youth,
Thoughts of tenderness and truth,
Blooms that, borrowed from the skies,
Tell on earth of paradise!

Αριαδνη.

LOVE.

I'LL sing of heroes and of kings,
In mighty numbers, mighty things.
Begin, my Muse! but, lo! the strings
To my great song rebellious prove;
The strings *will* sound of naught but love.
I broke them all, and put on new;
'Tis this or nothing sure will do.
These sure, said I, will me obey;
These sure heroic notes will play.
Straight I began with "Thundering Jove,
And all the immortal powers;" but Love,
Love smiled, and from my enfeebled lyre
Came gentle airs, such as inspire
Melting love and tender fire.
Farewell, then, heroes! farewell kings!
And mighty numbers, mighty things!
Love tunes my heart just to my strings.

COWLEY.

YET marked I where the bolt of Cupid fell:
It fell upon a little western flower,
Before milk-white, now purpled with love's wound,
And maidens call it "Love in idleness."

SHAKSPERE.

TO LOVE.

O SACRED fire that burnest mightily
In living breasts, ykindled first above
Emongst th' eternal spheres and lamping sky,
And thence poured into men, which men call love.

• • • • • •

'Tis that sweet fit, that does true beauty love,
And choseth virtue for his dearest dame,
Whence spring all noble deeds, and never-dying fame.

Well did antiquitie a god thee deeme
That over mortal minds has so great might,
To order them as best to thee doth seeme,
And all their actions to direct aright;
The fatal purpose of divine foresight
Thou dost effect in destined descents,
Through deep impression of thy secret might;
And stirrest up the hero's high intents,
Which the late world admires for wondrous monuments

• • • • • •

Ne suffereth uncomely idleness
In his free thought to build her sluggish nest.
Ne suffereth it thought of ungentleness
Ever to creep into his noble breast;
But to the highest and the worthiest
Lifteth it up that else would lowly fall;
It lets not fall—it lets it not to rest:
It lets not scare the prince to breathe at all,
But to his first pursuit him forward still doth call.

SPENSER.

LOVE? I will tell thee what it is to love.
It is to build with human thoughts a shrine,
Where Hope sits brooding like a beauteous dove;
Where Time seems young, and Life a thing divine.
All tastes, all pleasures, all desires combine
To consecrate this sanctuary of bliss.
Above, the stars in shroudless beauty shine;
Around the streams their flowery margin kiss;
And if there's heaven on earth, that heaven is surely this.

Yes, this is Love, the steadfast and the true,
The immortal glory which hath never set;
The best, the brightest boon the heart e'er knew:
Of all life's sweets the very sweetest yet!
Oh! who but can recall the eve they met
To breathe in some green walk their first young vow,
While summer flowers with moonlight dews were wet,
And winds sighed soft around the mountain's brow,
And all was rapture then which is but memory now!

CHARLES SWAIN

Dans un délire extrême
On veut fuir ce qu'on aime;
On veut se venger;
On jure de changer;
On devient infidèle;
On court de belle en belle;
Mais on revient toujours
A ses premiers amours.

Love should be like that bird of light
Which floateth still on radiant wings,
A creature glorious, soft, and bright,
Beyond young Thought's imaginings;
A spirit of the bowers of air,
Which dwells in silent beauty there;
A delicate fair thing; too pure
This world's cold vapors to endure;
Which far away from shade and gloom
In sun-bright regions fearless flies!
But if on earth-stain soil, its plume
Of paradise declines and dies.

ELIZA ACTON.

Love is like the glass
That throws its own rich color over all,
And makes all beautiful. The morning looks
Its very loveliest when the fresh air
Has tinged the cheek we love with its glad red;
And the hot noon flits by most rapidly
When dearest eyes gaze with us on the page
Bearing the poet's words of love: and then
The twilight walk when the linked arms can feel
The beating of the heart: upon the air
There is a music never heard but once,
A light the eyes can never see again;
Each star has its own prophecy of hope,
And every song and tale that breathe of love
Seem echoes of the heart.

LANDON.

WOMAN'S LOVE.

O, the voice of woman's love!
What a bosom-stirring word!
Was a sweeter ever uttered,
Was a dearer ever heard,
Than woman's love?

How it melts upon the ear!
How it nourishes the heart!
Cold, ah! cold must his appear
That has never shared a part
Of woman's love.

'Tis pleasure to the mourner,
'Tis freedom to the thrall;
The pilgrimage of many,
And the resting-place of all,
Is woman's love.

'Tis the gem of beauty's birth;
It competes with joys above;
What were angels upon earth,
If without woman's love—
Sweet woman's love?

JOHN CLARE.

Oh! man may bear with suffering: his heart
Is a strong thing, and godlike in the grasp
Of pain that wrings mortality; but tear
One chord affection clings to, part one tie
That binds him unto woman's delicate love,
And his great spirit yieldeth like a reed.

N. P. WILLIS.

Amour! toi seul remplis notre ame, toi seul es la source de tous les biens, tant que la *vertu* s'accorde avec toi. Ah! qu'elle soit toujours ton guide, et que tu sois son consolateur! Ne vous quittez jamais, enfans du ciel; marchez ensemble, en vous tenant la main. Si vous rencontrez dans votre route ou les chagrins, ou les malheurs, soutenez-vous mutuellement. Ils passeront, ces malheurs; et la félicité dont vous jouirez en aura cent fois plus de charmes: le souvenir des peines passées rendra plus touchants vos plaisirs. C'est ainsi qu'après un orage on trouve plus verd le gazon, plus riante la campagne couverte de perles liquides, plus belles les fleurs des champs relevant leurs têtes penchées; et l'on écoute avec plus de délices l'alouette ou le rossignol qui chantent en secouant leurs ailes.

FLORIAN.

A LOVER TO HIS MISTRESS.

Sing, siren, for thyself, and I will dote;
Spread o'er the silver waves thy golden hairs;
And—as a bed I'll take them and there lie;
And in that glorious supposition think
He gains by death that hath such means to die.

SHAKSPERE.

No telling how love thrives! to what it comes!
Whence grows! 'Tis e'en of as mysterious root
As the pine that makes its lodging of the rock,
Where you would think a blade of grass would die!
What is love's poison if it be not hate?
Yet in that poison oft is found love's food.
Frowns, that are clouds to us, are suns to him!
He finds a music in a scornful tongue,
That melts him more than softest melody—
Passion perverting all things to its mood,
And, spite of nature, matching opposites!

SHERIDAN KNOWLES.

LOVE THE VICTOR.

"De tout ce qui t'aimait, n'est il plus rien qui t'aime?"

Mighty ones, Love and Death!
Ye are strong in this world of ours,
Ye meet at the banquets, ye dwell midst the flowers,
Which hath the conqueror's wreath?

Thou art the victor, Love!
Thou art the fearless, the crowned, the free,
The strength of the battle is given to thee,
The spirit from above!

Thou hast looked on Death and smiled!
Thou hast borne up the reed-like and fragile form
Through the waves of the fight, through the rush of the storm,
On field, and flood, and wild!

No! thou art the victor, Death!
Thou comest, and where is that which spoke
From the depth of the eye, when the spirit woke?
Gone with the fleeting breath!

Thou comest, and what is left
Of all that loved us, to say if aught
Yet loves—yet answers the burning thought
Of the spirit lone and reft?

Silence is where thou art!
Silently there must kindred meet,
No smile to cheer, and no voice to greet,
No bounding of heart to heart!

Boast not thy victory, Death!
It is but as the clouds o'er the sunbeam's power,
It is but as the winters o'er leaf and flower,
That slumber the snow beneath.

It is but a tyrant's reign
O'er the voice and the lip which he bids be still;
But the fiery thought and the lofty will
Are not for him to chain!

They shall soar his might above!
And thus with the root whence affection springs,
Though buried, it is not of mortal things—
Thou art the victor, Love!

HEMANS

THE RETURN.

OH! have I lived to see thee once again?
Breathe the same air? my own, my blessed one!
Look up—look up—these are the arms which sheltered
When the storm howled around; and these the lips
Where, till this hour, the sad and holy kiss
Of parting lingered—as the fragrance left
By angels when they touch the earth and vanish.
Look up.—Night never panted for the sun,
As for thine eyes, my soul!

SIR E. L. BULWER.

How silver-sweet sound lovers' tongues by night,
Like softest music to attending ears!

SHAKSPERE.

THE FIRST AVOWAL.

IT was no fancy, he had named the name
Of love, and at the thought her cheek grew flame:
It was the first time her young ear had heard
A lover's burning sigh, or silver word:
Her thoughts were all confusion, but most sweet;
Her heart beat high, but pleasant was its beat.
She murmured over many a snatch of song
That might to her own feelings now belong;
She thought upon old histories she had read,
And placed herself in each high heroine's stead;
Then woke her lute,—oh! there is little known
Of music's power till aided by love's own.
And this is happiness: Oh! love will last
When all that made it happiness is past,—
When all its hopes are as the glittering toys
Time present offers, time to come destroys,—
When they have been too often crushed to earth,
For further blindness to their little worth,
When fond illusions have dropt one by one,
Like pearls from a rich carcanet, till none,
Are left upon life's soiled and naked string,—
And this is all what time will ever bring!

LANDON.

Lo t, passionate young Love, how sweet it is
To have the bosom made a paradise
By thee, life-lighted with thy rainbow smile!

LANDON.

ALAS! how light a cause may move
Dissension between hearts that love!
Hearts that the world in vain had tried
And sorrow but more closely tied;
That stood the storm when waves were rough,
Yet in a sunny hour fall off,
Like ships that have gone down at sea
When heaven was all tranquillity!
A something light as air—a look,
A word unkind, or wrongly taken,—
Oh! Love that tempests never shook,
A breath, a touch like this hath shaken.
And ruder words will soon rush in
To spread the breach that words begin;
And eyes forget the gentle ray
They wore in courtship's smiling day;
And voices lose the tone that shed
A tenderness round all they said;
Till fast declining, one by one,
The sweetnesses of love are gone;
And hearts so lately mingled seem
Like broken clouds,—or like the stream
That smiling left the mountain's brow
As though its waters ne'er could sever;
Yet e'er it reach the plain below,
Breaks into floods that part for ever.

* * * * * * *

Oh! you who have the charge of Love,
Keep him in rosy bondage bound;
As in the fields of bliss above
He sits with flowerets fettered round.
Loose not a tie that round him clings;
Nor ever let him use his wings;
For even an hour, a minute's flight,
Will rob the plumes of half their light.
Like that celestial bird whose nest
Is found beneath far Eastern skies,--
Whose wings, though radiant when at rest,
Lose all their glory when he flies.

T. MOORE

WOMAN'S CONSTANCY.

OH! woman, what bliss, what enchantment we owe
To the spell of thy heart, to thy solace below,
To thy truth so enduring, thy kindness and care
In the morning of joy, in the night of despair!

To thy soul's chosen love thou unchanged wilt remain
In health and in sickness, in pleasure and pain;
And when closed are his lips in Death's mortal eclipse,
Even then, still is his the last kiss of thy lips!

And over his grave thou wilt mournfully keep
Thy lone vigil of sorrow, to pray and to weep:
Yes! to pray, that his errors of heart be forgiven,
And that *thou* may'st yet meet him unsullied in heaven.

JAMES BIRD.

EASTERN LOVE-LETTER.

IN Eastern lands they talk in flowers,
And they tell in a garland their loves and cares;
Each blossom that blooms in their garden bowers.
On its leaves a mystic language bears.

The rose is the sign of joy and love,
Young blushing love in its earliest dawn;
And the mildness that suits the gentle dove,
From the myrtle's snowy flower is drawn.

Innocence shines in the lily's bell,
Pure as a heart in its native heaven;
Fame's bright star, and glory's swell,
By the glossy leaf of the bay is given.

The silent, soft, and humble heart
In the violet's hidden sweetness breathes;
And the tender soul that can not part,
A twine of evergreen fondly wreathes.

The cypress that darkly shadows the grave,
Is sorrow that mourns its bitter lot;
And faith that a thousand ills can brave,
Speaks in thy blue leaves, forget-me-not.

Then gather a wreath from thy garden bowers,
And tell the wish of thy heart in flowers.

PERCIVAL.

——— STILL there clings
An earth-stain to the fairest things;
And love, that most delicious gift
Upon life's shrine of sorrow left,
Has its own share of suffering.
A shade falls from its radiant wing,
A spot steals o'er its sunny brow,
Fades the rose-lip's witching glow.
'T is well—for earth were too like heaven
If length of life to love were given.

LANDON

TO THE ALTAR.

OH! there are hearts that well may date
The era of their joy from thee,
The birthplace of the brightest fate
That wedded life and love may be;
Hearts that have blessed, that bless thee now,
In memory of their plighted vow.

How long, how fondly, memory dwells
On moments past that led to bliss!
Not Time, which breaks all other spells,
E'er broke the heavenly charm of this,
Which falls upon the heart like dew
That decks the faded flower anew.

JAMES BIRD.

WHAT is Love? Ask him who lives, *what* is life? ask him who adores, *what* is God?—*Thou* demandest, what is Love? It is that powerful attraction toward all we conceive, or fear, or hope, beyond ourselves, when we find within our own thoughts the chasm of an insufficient void, and seek to awaken in all things that are, a community with what we experience within ourselves. If we reason, we would be understood; if we imagine, we would that the airy children of our own brain were born anew within another's; if we feel, we would that another's nerves should vibrate to our own; that the beams of their eyes should kindle at once and melt into our own; that lips of motionless ice should not reply to lips quivering and burning with the heart's best blood. This is Love. This is the bond and the sanction which connects not only man with man, but with everything that exists. We are born into the world, and there is something within us which, from the instant that we live, more and more thirsts after its likeness. This propensity develops itself with the development of our nature. We dimly see within our intellectual nature a miniature, as it were, of our entire self, yet deprived of all that we condemn or despise: the ideal prototype of everything excellent and lovely that we are capable of conceiving as belonging to the nature of man. Not only the portrait of our external being, but an assemblage of the minutest particles of which our nature is composed: a mirror whose surface reflects only the forms of purity and brightness: a soul within our own soul that describes a circle around its proper paradise, which pain, and sorrow, and evil, dare not overleap. To this we eagerly refer all sensations, thirsting that they should resemble and correspond with it. The discovery of its antitype; the meeting with an understanding capable of clearly estimating our own; an imagination which should enter into and seize upon the subtle and delicate peculiarities which we have delighted to cherish and unfold in secret; with a frame whose nerves, like the chords of two exquisite lyres strung to the accompaniment of one delightful voice, vibrate with the vibrations of our own; and a combination of all these in such proportion as the type within demands: this is the invisible and unattainable point to which Love tends, and to attain which it urges forth the powers of men to arrest the faintest shadow of that without the possession of which there is no rest nor respite to the heart over which it rules. Hence in solitude, or that deserted state when we are surrounded by human beings, and yet they sympathise not with us,—we love the flowers, the grass, the waters, and the sky. In the motion of the very leaves of spring, in the blue air, there is then found a secret correspondence with our heart. There is eloquence in the tongueless wind, and a melody in the flowing brooks and the rustling of the reeds beside them, which, by their inconceivable relation to something within the soul, awakens the spirit to breathless rapture, and brings tears of mysterious tenderness to the eyes, like the enthusiasm of patriotic success, or the voice of one beloved singing to you alone. Sterne says that if he were in a desert, he would love some cypress. So soon as this want or power is dead, man becomes a living sepulchre of himself, and what yet survives is the mere husk of what once he was.

SHELLEY.

LOVE UNCHERISHED—DIES.

LOVE can not bear rude passion's blast;
  Neglect pales all its fires.
When once its brilliancy is past,
Its struggles, but it can not last;
  It flickers and expires.

And who that radiant light can blame
  If quickly it depart?
So delicate, so pure a flame,
Which from ethereal regions came,
  Must live in kindred heart.

Is it a crime in yon sweet flower,
  The child of lovelier skies,
Because exposed in killing hour
To blighting winds, to tempest's power,
  It sickens, fades, and dies?

Ah! had it grown beneath the ray
  Of genial native sun,
Whose beams had cherished it by day,
And zephyrs fanned it as they play,
  Its life had not been done.

Then ye selected, sacred few,
  Whose bosoms are Love's shrine,
Preserve a flame, so bright, so true,
Glowing with each celestial hue,
  And fed from source divine!

MRS. DOWNING.

I LOVE THEE.

I LOVE thee, as I love the calm
  Of sweet, star-lighted hours!
I love thee, as I love the balm
  Of early jasmine flowers.

I love thee, as I love the last
  Rich smile of fading day,
Which lingereth, like the look we cast
  On rapture past away.

I love thee, as I love the tone
  Of soul soft-breathing flute,
Whose soul is waked for me alone
  When all beside is mute.

I love thee, as I love the first
  Young violet of the spring;
Or the pale lily, April nursed,
  To scented blossoming.

I love thee, as I love the full
  Clear gushings of the song,
Which lonely, sad, and beautiful,
  At night-fall floats along;

Poured by the bul-bul forth to greet
  The hours of rest and dew,
When melody and moonlight meet
  To blend their charm and hue.

I love thee, as the glad bird loves
  The freedom of its wing,
On which delightedly it moves
  In wildest wandering.

I love thee, as I love the swell
  And hush of some low strain,
Which bringeth, by its gentle spell,
  The past to life again.

Such is the feeling which from thee
  Naught earthly can allure;
'Tis ever linked to all I see
  Of gifted—high—and pure.

ELIZA ACTON.

WOMAN'S LOVE.

ERE the tongue
Can utter, or the eye a wo reveal,
Her smile is round us, like a guardian spell
Which nothing scatters, save the tyrant gloom
Of death: and *then*, whose unforsaken glance
Till the last hue of being fade, from dawn
To midnight keeps angelic watch beside
The ebbing spirit, lighting it to heaven.
'Tis action makes the world of man: but life
Is feeling, such as gentle woman bears:
The fairy people of her inward world
Are *true affections*; when the blight hath touched
Or wronged their beauty, darkly cold this earth
Becomes; the elements of being fade,
And silence is the sepulchre of thought,
Wherein the anguish of her spirit dwells.

R. MONTGOMERY.

IF music be the food of love, play on!
Give me excess of it; that, surfeiting,
The appetite may sicken, and so die.—
That strain again!—it had a dying fall:

Oh, it came o'er my ear like the sweet south,
That breathes upon a bank of violets,
Stealing, and giving odor. — Enough; no more;
'Tis not so sweet now as it was before.
O spirit of love, how quick and fresh art thou!
That, notwithstanding thy capacity
Receiveth as the sea,—naught enters there
Of what validity and pitch soever,
But falls into abatement and low price
Even in a minute! So full of shapes is fancy,
That it alone is high-fantastical.

SHAKSPERE.

TO LOVE.

THOU blushing thing of pain and bliss!
Child of a happier sphere than this!
Wert thou a nursling of the sky,
Fostered in paradise on high,
To thrill the radiant breasts above?
No; angels feel not youthful love:
Theirs is a flame we can not know,
A holy ardor free from wo;
But ours a joy supreme, intense,
A short and splendid recompense
For an esteem unbroke, unmoved,
Which man immortal might have proved.
Art thou not then, O virtuous Love,
The dearest gift of Heaven above?

HOGG.

A LOVER'S PRAISE.

——————WHAT you do
Still betters what is done. When you speak, sweet
I'd have you do it ever; when you sing,
I'd have you buy and sell so; so give alms;
Pray so; and for the ord'ring your affairs
To sing them too. When you do dance, I wish you
A wave o' the sea, that you might ever do
Nothing but that; move still, still so,
And own no other function: each your doing,
So singular in each particular,
Crowns what you're doing in the present deeds,
That all your acts are queens.

SHAKSPERE.

LOVE'S EMPIRE.

HOLD there a moment, Love replied,
Nor boast dominion quite so wide.
Is there no province to invade
But that by Love and meekness swayed?
All other empire I resign;
But be the sphere of beauty mine.
For in the downy lawn of rest
That opens on a woman's breast,
Attended by my peaceful train,
I choose to love, and choose to reign.
Far-sighted Faith I bring along,
And Truth, above an army strong.
And Chastity, of icy mould,
Within the burning tropics cold:
And Lowliness, to whose mild brow
The power and pride of nations bow;
And Modesty, with downcast eye,
That lends the morn her virgin die;
And Innocence, arrayed in light,
And Honor, as a tower upright;
With sweetly winning graces, more
Than poets ever dreamt of yore;
In unaffected conduct free,
All smiling sisters, three times three;
And rosy Peace, the cherub blest,
That nightly sings us all to rest.
Hence, from the bud of nature's prime,
From the first step of infant time,
Woman, the world's appointed light,
Has skirted every shade with white;
Has stood for imitation high,
To every heart and every eye;
From ancient deeds of fair renown
Has brought her bright memorials down,
To time affixed perpetual youth,
And formed each tale of love and truth,
Upon a new Promethean plan
She moulds the essence of a man,
Tempers his mass, his genius fires,
And, as a better soul, inspires.
The rude she softens, warms the cold,
Exalts the meek, and checks the bold,
Calls Sloth from his supine repose,
Within the coward's bosom glows,
Of pride unplumes the lofty crest,
Bids bashful merit stand confest,
And, like coarse metal from the mines,
Collects, irradiates, and refines.
The gentle science she imparts,
All manners smooths, informs all hearts,
From her sweet influence are felt
Passions that please and thoughts that melt;
To stormy rage she bids control,
And sinks serenely on the soul,
Softens Deucalion's flinty race,
And tunes the warring world to peace.
Thus armed 'gainst all that's light and vain,
And freed from thy fantastic chain,
She fills the sphere by Heaven assigned,
And ruled by me, o'errules mankind!

MOORE.

LOVE SECRETS.

LOVE's eye should but answer the beam that invites it,
The glance that tells secrets true heart never won,
The delicate mind veils the hope that requites it,
Lest it die, like the fire when exposed to the sun.

Dear woman's the exquisite magnet of nature,
And love is the heart-thrilling homage we pay;
But Beauty has not a more delicate feature,
Than the caution that Love should, if grateful display

That name to the heart which sweet transport discloses
Too sacred should be for a toast or a tale;
And the breathings of Love, like the perfumes of roses,
Are exquisite death when surcharging the gale.

C. DIBDIN.

THE SUPPLICATION.

LEAVE me not yet! through rosy skies from far,
But now the song-birds to their nests return;
The quivering image of the first pale star
On the dim lake scarce yet begins to burn:
Leave me not yet!

Not yet! Oh, hark! low tones from hidden streams
Piercing the shivery leaves e'en now arise;
Their voices mingle not with day-light dreams—
They are of vesper's hymns and harmonies:
Leave me not yet!

My thoughts are like those gentle sounds, dear love,
By day shut up in their own still recess;
They wait for dews on earth, for stars above,
Then to breathe out their soul of tenderness.
Leave me not yet!

HEMANS.

'TIS something if in absence we can trace
The footsteps of the past: it sooths the heart
To breathe the air scented in other years
By lips beloved, to wander through the groves
Where once we were not lonely; where the rose
Reminds us of the hair we used to wreath
With its fresh buds—where every hill and vale,
And wood and fountain, speak of time gone by,
And Hope springs up in joy from Memory's ashes.

LANDON.

SONNET.

Perhaps the lady of my love is now
Looking upon the skies. A single star
Is rising in the east, and from afar
Sheds a most tremulous lustre: silent night
Doth wear it like a jewel on her brow:
But see! it motions with its lovely light
Onward and onward through those depths of blue
To its appointed course, steadfast and true.
So, dearest, would I fain be unto thee
Steadfast for ever—like yon planet fair;
And yet more like art thou a jewel rare,
Oh! brighter than the brightest star to me.
Come hither, my young love, and I will wear
Thy beauty on my breast delightedly.

Barry Cornwall.

THE DIFFIDENCE OF LOVE.

Why should I blush to own I love?
'Tis love that rules the realms above.
Why should I blush to say to all
That virtue holds my heart in thrall?

Why should I seek the thickest shade,
Lest Love's dear secret be betrayed?
Why the stern brow deceitful move,
When I am languishing with love?

Is it a weakness thus to dwell
On passion that I dare not tell?
Such weakness I would ever prove:
'Tis painful, but 'tis sweet to love!

Henry Kirk White.

THE PRIDE OF LOVE.

'Tis strange with how much power and pride
The softness is of love allied;
How much of power to force the breast
To be in outward show at rest.
How much of pride that never eye
May look upon its agony!
Ah! little will the lip reveal
Of all the burning heart can feel.
Oh! why should woman ever love
Trusting to one sole star above;
And fling her little chance away
Of sunshine, for its doubtful ray!

Landon.

THE PROPOSAL.

Ay, they are Love's own words! his breath of flame
Hath sighed upon the fair unconscious page,
And thy cheek kindles at the "one loved name,"
Whose every thought doth thy young heart engage;
Fondly as pilgrims greet some hallowed shrine,
Thy lips would greet the words, "Thine, dearest, ever thine."

Ay, it is Love's own tracing! every word
Of eloquence is written by his pen!
'Tis the heart's language—all thine ear hath heard
(Like music from his tongue) is told again!
Each fondly-murmured sigh, each half-breathed vow
From his soul's depths are drawn, unsealed, acknowledged now!

With all a lover's tenderness, he lays
His heart, his hopes, his fortunes, at thy feet;
Implores thee, by those well-remembered days
That ye have passed so oft in "converse sweet,"
By many a whispered word in wood or grove,
Not to reject his suit, or scorn his proffered love.

What does thy young heart prompt thee to reply?
By the carnation heightening on thy cheeks,
And the bright crystal in thy downcast eye—
More eloquent than words—'tis *thus* it speaks:
"Beloved one! each sigh thy breast hath known,
Found, though unheard by thee, an echo in my own."

Thou fair and lovely creature! Who may tell
All the fond thoughts that crowd upon thy soul?
Who analyse the varied hopes that swell
Thy young untutored heart? or who control
The brilliant visions floating o'er thy brain,
That like spring flowers, once crushed, can never bloom again?

Ah! through life's chequered range, but *one* such hour
Of cloudless radiance shines upon the breast;
'Tis that when Love comes with a conqueror's power,
And reigns sole monarch of the heart confessed;
When (like the Indian wood of sacred fame)
The bosom's lord pours forth its sweetness to the flame.

In after years a thousand passions take
Possession of the soul; with cunning art
They win its fond idolatry, and make
Themselves a shrine to rest in! To the heart
Love comes but once, like blossom to the rose,
The deep soul-searching flame our first affection knows.

Ay, ye may smile, ye stoics! but 'tis true,
And not the fiction of a poet's brain;
The heart's first bloom of love, like morning dew,
Once brushed, ne'er sparkles on the flower again,
Till the long day is closed in evening skies,
And on the drooping plant another morn arise!

Mrs. C. B. Wilson

UNREQUITED LOVE.

Sister! since I met thee last,
O'er thy brow a change hath past.
In the softness of thine eyes
Deep and still a shadow lies;
From thy voice there thrills a tone
Never to thy childhood known;
Through thy soul a storm hath moved
—Gentle sister, thou hast loved!

Yes! thy varying cheek hath caught
Hues too bright from troubled thought
Far along the wandering stream,
Thou art followed by a dream;
In the woods and valleys lone
Music haunts thee not thine own:
Wherefore fall thy tears like rain?
—Sister, thou hast loved in vain!

Tell me not the tale, my flower!
On my bosom pour that shower!
Tell me not of kind thoughts wasted;
Tell me not of young hopes blasted;
Wring not forth one burning word,
Let thy heart no more be stirred!
Home alone can give thee rest.
—Weep, sweet sister, on my breast!

Hemans.

LOVE SYMPATHIES.

There are ten thousand tones and signs
We hear and see, but none defines—
Involuntary sparks of thought
Which strike from out the heart o'erwrought,
And form a strange intelligence
Alike mysterious and intense;
Which link the burning chain that binds,
Without their will, young hearts and minds,
Conveying, as the electric wire,
We know not how, the absorbing fire.

Byron.

LOVE'S HERALD'S.

Love's herald's should be thoughts
Which ten times faster glide than the sunbeams
Driving back shadows over lowering hills:
Therefore do nimble-pinioned doves draw Love,
And therefore hath the wind-swift Cupid wings.

Shakspere.

LOVE'S WISHES.

I wish that I were
A voiceless sigh,
Floating through air,
When thy beauty draws nigh:
Unperceived I would steal o'er thy cheek of down,
And kiss thy soft lips unchecked by a frown.

I would that I were
A dying tone,
To dwell on thine ear
Though the music were gone:
I would charm thy heart with my latest breath,
And yield thee pleasure e'en in my death.
I would I might pass from this living tomb,
Into the violet's sweetest perfume;
On the wings of the morning to thee I would fly,
And mingle my soul with thy sweeter sigh.

My heart is bound
With a viewless chain,—
I see no wound,—
But I feel its pain.
Break my prison, and set me free!
Bondage, though sweet, hath no charms for me.
Yet no!—e'en in fetters my fond heart will dwell,
Since thy shadow floats o'er it, and hallows its cell!

Oh! for some fairy talisman to conjure
Up to these longing eyes the form they pine for!
And yet in love there's no such word as absence!
The loved one, like our guardian spirit, walks
Beside us ever,—shines upon the beam—
Perfumes the flower—and sighs in every breeze!
Its presence gives such beauty to the world
That all things beautiful its likeness are;
And aught in sound most sweet, to sight most fair,
Breathes with its voice, or like its aspect smiles.

Sir E. L. Bulwer.

THE TRYSTING HOUR.

The night-wind's Eolian breezes,
Chase melody o'er the grove,
The fleecy clouds wreathing in tresses,
Float rosy the woodlands above;
Then tarry no longer, my true love,
The stars hang their lamps in the sky,
'T is lovely the landscape to view, love,
When each bloom has a tear in its eye.

So stilly the evening is closing
Bright dew-drops are heard as they fall,
Eolian whispers reposing,
Breathe softly, I hear my love call;
Yes! the light fairy step of my true love,
The night-breeze is wafting to me;
Over heath-bell and violet blue, love,
Perfuming the shadowy lea.

Thomas Lyle.

LOVE.

There is a love so fond, so true,
No art the magic tie can sever;
'T is ever beauteous, ever new;—
Its chain once linked is linked for ever.

There is a love, but passion's beam,—
Too fond, too warm, too bright to last,—
The phrensy of a fevered dream,
That burns a moment, then is past.

'T is like the lightning's lurid glare,
That streams its blaze of fatal light,
Flames for an instant through the air,
Then sinks away in deepest night.

There is a love whose feeling rolls
In pure unruffled calmness on,—
The meeting of congenial souls,
Of hearts whose currents flow in one.

It is a blessing that is felt
But by united minds that flow,
As sunbeams into sunbeams melt,
To light a frozen world below.

There is a love that o'er the war
Of jarring passion pours its light,
And sheds its influence like a star
That brightest burns in darkest night.

It is a love best known to those
Who hand in hand, amidst the strife
Together have withstood their foes,
Together shared the storms of life.

It is so true, so fixed, so strong,
It parts not with the parting breath;
In the soul's flight 't is borne along,
And hold's the heart's strings e'en in death

'T is never quenched by sorrow's tide;—
No, 't is a flame caught from above,—
A tie that death can not divide;—
'T is the bright torch of wedded love.

But there is one love, not of earth,
Though sullied by the streaming tear
It is a star of heavenly birth,
And only shines unshaken there.

'T is when this clay resigns its breath,
And the soul quits its frail abode,
That rising from the bed of death,
This love is pure—the love of God.

M. A. Browne.

Oh! there are looks and tones that dart
An instant sunshine to the heart;
As if the soul that moment caught
Some treasure, it through life had sought—

As if the very lips and eyes,
Predestined to have all our sighs,
And never be forgot again,
Sparkled and spoke before us then.

So beamed on me thy speech and tone
When first on me they breathed and shone;
New, as if brought from other spheres,
Yet welcome as if loved for years.

Then come with me, if thou hast known
No other flame, nor rudely thrown
A gem away, which thou hadst sworn
Should ever in thy breast be worn.

Come! if the love thou bear'st for me
Is pure and fresh as mine for thee;
Fresh as the fountain under ground
When first 't is by the lapwing found.

But if for me thou dost forsake
Some other maid, and rudely break
Her worshipped image from its base,
To give to *me* the ruined place—

Then, fare thee well!—I'd rather make
My bower upon some icy lake
Where thawing suns begin to shine,
Than trust to love so false as thine!

T. Moore.

LOVE NURSED BY SOLITUDE.

Young Love, thou art belied: they speak of thee,
And couple with thy mention misery;
Talk of the broken heart, the wasted bloom,
The spirit blighted, and the early tomb;
As if these waited on thy golden lot,—
They blame thee for the faults that thou hast not.
Art thou to blame for that they bring to thee,
The soil and weight of their mortality?
How can they hope that ever links will hold
Formed, as they form them now, of the harsh gold?
Or worse than even this, how can they think
That vanity will bind the failing link?

How can they dream that thy sweet life will bear
Crowds', palaces', and cities' heartless air?
When looks and thoughts alike must feel the chain,
And naught of life is real but its pain;
Where the young spirit's high imaginings
Are scorned and cast away as idle things;
Where, think or feel, you are foredoomed to be
A marvel, and a sign for mockery;
Where none must wander from the beaten road,—
All alike champ the bit and feel the goad.
It is not made for thee, young Love!—away!
To where the green earth laughs to the clear day;
To the deep valley, where a thousand trees
Keep a green court for fairy revelries;—
To some small island in a lonely lake,
Where only swans the diamond waters break;
Where the pine hangs in silence o'er the tide,
And the stream gushes from the mountain side;
These, Love, are haunts for thee: where canst thou brood
With thy sweet wings furled—but in solitude!

LANDON.

GENIUS SINGING TO LOVE.

"*Leave me not!*" was still
The burden of their music; and I knew
The lay which Genius, in its loneliness,
Its own still world amid the o'erpeopled world,
Hath ever breathed to Love.

They crown me with the glistening crown
Borne from a deathless tree;
I hear the pealing music of renown—
Oh, Love! forsake me not!
Mine were a lone dark lot,
Bereft of thee!

They tell me that my soul can throw
A glory o'er the earth;
From thee, from *thee* is caught that golden glow,
Shed by thy gentle eyes,
It gives to flower and skies
A bright new birth!

Thence gleams the path of morning
Over the kindling hills a sunny zone!
Thence to its heart of hearts the rose is burning
With lustre not its own!
Thence every wood-recess
Is filled with loveliness,
Each bower to ring-doves and dim violets known.

I see all beauty by the ray
That streameth from thy smile:
Oh! bear it, bear it not away!
Can that sweet light beguile?
Too pure, too spirit-like it seems,
To linger long by earthly streams;
I clasp it with the alloy
Of fear midst quivering joy,
Yet must I perish if the gift depart—
Leave me not, Love! to mine own beating heart!

The music from my lyre
With thy swift step would flee;
The world's cold breath would quench the starry fire
In my deep soul—a temple filled with thee!
Sealed would the fountains lie,
The waves of harmony,
Which thou alone canst free!

Like a shrine 'mid rocks forsaken,
Whence the oracle hath fled;
Like a harp which none might waken
But a mighty master dead;
Like the vase of a perfume scattered,
Such would my spirit be,
So mute, so void, so shattered,
Bereft of thee!

Leave me not, Love! or, if this earth
Yield not for thee a home,
If the bright summer-land of thy June birth
Send thee a silvery voice that whispers "*Come!*"
Then, with the glory from the rose,
With the sparkle from the stream,
With the light thy rainbow-presence throws
Over the poet's dream;
With all the Elysian hues
Thy pathway that suffuse,
With joy, with music, from the fading grove,
Take *me*, too, heavenward, on thy wing, sweet Love

HEMANS.

It is the soft and silent hour
When mighty Love hath mightiest power
To bind the heart, subdue the will,
Bid Reason's cold stern voice be still.
Oh! never sounds in Beauty's ear
The whispered word so sweet and dear,
As when the gathering shadows hide
The tell-tale cheek, which Feeling's tide,
In one full, happy, joyous gush,
Hath teinted with a crimson blush!
So calm, so still, the scene around,
Almost the heart's own echoes sound!
How many a breast, on eve like this,
Is steeped in rapture—filled with bliss!

MRS. WALKER

SLIGHTED LOVE.

May slighted woman turn,
And as a vine the oak hath shaken off,
Bend lightly to her tendencies again?
Oh, no! by all her loveliness, by all
That makes life poetry and beauty, no!
Make her a slave, steal from her rosy cheek
By needless jealousies; let the last star
Leave her a watcher by your couch of pain;
Wrong her by petulance, suspicion, all
That makes her cup a bitterness—yet give
One evidence of love, and earth has not
An emblem of devotedness like hers.
But, oh! estrange her once, it boots not how,
By wrong or silence, any thing that tells
A change has come upon your tenderness,
And there is not a high thing out of heaven
Her pride o'ermastereth not!

N. P. WILLIS.

THE MINSTREL'S LOVE.

He loved,—as minstrel-elf must prove,—
For song itself is born of love.
So the young glow and melting shower
Of April animate the flower—
Perfume and suppliance of an hour;—
Too exquisitely loved to last,
Such curse upon the lyre is cast:
Brief must they feel who feel the spell
Of love too sensitively well,
As fires of sudden vividness
Exhausted by their own excess.
And such the wreath his passion braided
For thousand bosoms, bright but vain,
Like cistus-bloom scarce blown till faded,
Scarce faded till full blown again;
Short-lived alike the bliss and pain.
Thus still adored he, still endured,
Wandering for ever, never cured.

ISHMAEL FITZADAM

Yes! so it is—and the same thirst
For something high and pure, above
This withering world, which, from the first,
Made me drink deep of woman's love,—
As the one joy, to heaven most near
Of all our hearts can meet with here,—
Still burns me up, still keeps awake
A fever naught but death can slake.

T. MOORE.

LOVERS PARTING.

SWEET, good night!
This bud of love, by summer's ripening breath,
May prove a beauteous flower when next we meet.
Good night, good night!—as sweet repose and rest
Come to thy heart, as that within my breast!

SHAKSPERE.

HARD is the heart, and unsubdued by love,
That feels no pain, nor ever heaves a sigh,
Such hearts the fiercest passions only prove,
Or freeze in cold insensibility.
Oh! then indulge thy grief, nor fear to tell
The gentle source from whence thy sorrows flow!
Nor think it weakness when we love, to feel;
Nor think it weakness what we feel to show.

COWPER.

LOVE'S ECHOES.

How sweet the answer Echo makes
To music at night,
When, roused by lute or horn, she wakes,
And far away, o'er lawns and lakes,
Goes answering light!

Yet Love hath echoes truer far,
And far more sweet,
Than e'er beneath the moonlight's star,
Of horn, or lute, or soft guitar,
The songs repeat.

'Tis when the sigh, in youth sincere
And only then,—
The sigh that's breathed for one to hear,
Is by that one, that only dear,
Breathed back again!

T. MOORE.

SONG OF THE ABSENT.

LADY! when the moonlight hour
Sheds its soft lustre o'er thy bower,
When the rich key of memory
Unlocks its golden treasury,
And visions sweet of bygone hours
Float round thee with the breath of flowers,
Oh! give one vesper sigh to me!
Remembering I am still to thee
Faithful, though far away!

Lady! when the deep midnight
Veils nature's loveliness and light,
When thy sweet lips in secret bless
The objects of thy tenderness,
And thy pure orisons arise
Wafting their names beyond the skies,
Oh! breathe one fervent prayer for me!
Remembering I am still to thee
Faithful, though far away!

KAPPA.

WITH thee for ever I in woods could rest,
Where never human foot the ground hath pressed.
Thou from all shades the darkness canst exclude,
And from a desert banish solitude.

COWLEY.

LOVE.

WHEN Virtue dies in pallid Want's embrace
Not friendless, though abandoned by the base
Then o'er the grave, from which all flatterers fly,
Love sheds a tear which kingdoms could not buy.
And, as the April sunbeams melt the snow,
Till peeps the golden flower that slept below,—
Thy look can charm the fiend beneath whose eye
All joys but thine and blest Religion's die,
The king of woes, pride-humbling poverty!

E. ELLIOTT.

THEY sin, who tell us Love can die:
With life all other passions fly;
All others are but vanity.
In heaven Ambition can not dwell,
Nor Avarice in the vaults of hell.
Earthly these passions of the earth,
They perish where they had their birth.
But Love is indestructible!
Its holy flame for ever burneth.
From heaven it came, to heaven returneth.

SOUTHEY

AMOUR, l'on doit bénir tes chaînes:
Si deux amans ont à souffrir,
Ils n'ont que la moitié des peines,
Et tu sais doubler leur plaisir.

WOMAN IS THE LIGHT OF LOVE.

O WOMAN! Woman! thou art formed to bless
The heart of restless man, to chase his care,
And charm existence by thy loveliness:
Bright as the sunbeam, as the morning fair.
If but thy foot fall on a wilderness,
Flowers spring, and shed their roseate blossoms there,
Shrouding the thorns that on thy pathway rise,
And scattering o'er it hues of Paradise.

Thy voice of love is music to the ear,
Soothing and soft, and gentle as the stream
That strays 'mid summer flowers; thy glittering tear
Is mutely eloquent; thy smile a beam
Of light ineffable, so sweet, so dear,
It wakes the heart from sorrow's darkest dream,
Shedding a hallowed lustre o'er our fate,
And when it beams we are not desolate.

No! no! when woman smiles we feel a charm
Thrown bright around us, binding us to earth;
Her tender accents breathing forth the balm
Of pure affection, give to transport birth;
Then life's wide sea is billowless and calm:
O lovely woman! thy consummate worth
Is far above thy frailty—far above
All earthly praise—Thou art the Light of Love.

J. BIRD.

SONG OF THE FORSAKEN.

AND will she love thee as well as I?
Will she do for thee what I have done?
See all the pomps of the world pass by,
And look only for thee—beloved one?

Will she feel when another pronounces thy name
All the thrilling sensations that I have done?
Pride when they praise thee, regret when they blame,
And tenderness always—beloved one?

Will she watch when a cloud passes over thy brow,
And strive to chase it—as I have done?
Forgetting all but the thought that now
It is hers to console thee—beloved one?

Will she, undoubting, consent to resign
Friends long cherished—as I have done?
Renounce them, forget them, nor ever repine,
Since thou art with her—beloved one?

And *thou*—wilt not thou feel a pang of regret,
Thus remembering all that I have done?
Have done! though forsaken would do so yet,
And am thine, and *thine* only—beloved one!

HON. MRS. NORTON.

THE HOUR OF LOVE.

IT is the hour when from the boughs
The nightingale's high notes are heard;
It is the hour when lovers' vows
Seem sweet in every whispered word;
And gentle winds and waters near
Make music to the listening ear.

Each flower the dews have lightly wet,
And in the sky the stars are met,
And on the wave is deeper blue,
And on the leaf a browner hue,
And in the heaven the clear obscure
So softly dark, and darkly pure,
Which follows the decline of day
When twilight melts beneath the moon away.

Byron.

SONNET.

Sweet as the cry of joy, or as the song
Of tender birds—like the beloved tone
Of one who loves us, loved by us alone—
Such are the honeyed accents of thy tongue;
Like Orpheus' lyre, so eloquent, so strong:
Such sounds the muse herself might not disown,
So speaks harmonious, her most favored son,
And pours the rapturous tide of verse along.
Oh! if fond love should once that voice inspire,
And breathe the mingling harmony of sighs,
The soul of such rare music ne'er could tire;
It speaks the ecstacy of Paradise.
Sure then, thy sweetness might a mortal move,
And win at once to more than mortal love.

THE LOVE BORN OF SORROW.

Our love has been no summer-flower,
For joy's bright chaplet braided;
Drooping when tempests darkly lower,
By grief's bleak winter faded.

We have not loved as those who plight
Their troth in sunny weather,
While leaves are green, and skies are bright,
To tread life's path together.

But we have loved as those who tread
The thorny path of sorrow,
With clouds o'ercast—and cause to dread
Yet deeper gloom to-morrow.

That thorny path, those cloudy skies,
Have drawn our spirits nearer.
And rendered us, by holiest ties,
Each to the other dearer!

Love born in hours of joy and mirth,
With mirth and joy may perish;
That to which darker days gave birth
Still more and more we cherish.

It looks beyond the clouds of time,
Through Death's dim shadowy portal;
Made by adversity sublime,
By faith and hope immortal!

B. Barton.

PERHAPS I LOVE.

Perhaps I love
To visit my heart's treasure by that light
When misers seek their buried hoards; to steal
Upon the loved one, like a mermaid's song,
Unseen and floating between sea and sky;
To creep upon her in love's loveliest hour,
Not in her daylight beauty with the glare
Of the bright sun around her; but thus pure,
And white, and delicate, under the cool moon
Or lamp of alabaster. Thus I love
To think of thee, thou dear one! thus with flowers
About thee, and fresh air, and such a light,
And such a stillness; thus I dream of thee!

Miss Mitford.

He who would stem a stream with sand,
And fetter flame with flaxen band,
Hath yet a harder task to prove—
By firm resolve to conquer love!

Sir W. Scott.

FRAGMENT.

I'll lay me on the wintry lea
And sleep amid the cauld and weet,
And ere another's bride I be
Oh! bring to me my winding sheet!

What can a helpless lassie do,
When ilka friend would prove her foe,
Would gar her break her dearest vow,
And wed with ane she canna loe?

Robert Tannahill.

Where is the heart that hath not bowed,
A slave, eternal love, to thee?
Look on the cold, the gay, the proud,
And is there one among them free?
The cold, the proud—oh! Love has turned
The marble till with fire it burned;
The gay, the young—alas! that they
Should ever bend beneath thy sway!
Look on the cheek the rose might own,
The smile around like sunshine thrown;
The rose, the smile alike are thine,
To fade and darken at thy shrine.
And what must love be in a heart
All passion's fiery depths concealing,
Which has in its minutest part,
More than another's depth of feeling?

Landon.

God gives us Love. Something to love,
He lends us; but when love is grown
To ripeness, that on which it throve
Falls off and love is left alone!

Tennyson.

L'ABSENCE ET LE RETOUR.

Il faut l'avoir connu l'affreux malheur de vivre loin de ce qu'on aime, pour pouvoir se faire une idée des ravissemens qu'éprouve notre ame, lorsqu'on lui rend le bien qu'elle avoit perdu. Il faut avoir répandu les larmes amères de l'absence pour sentir toute la volupté des douces larmes du retour. Je te plains, malheureux amant, qu'un sort cruel a forcé de quitter l'objet de tes vœux. Chaque pas que tu fais ajoute à tes maux; chaque heure te rappelle un plaisir perdu: tu calcules avec désespoir tous les instans qui s'écouleront avant la fin de ton exil; tu crois les abréger en les recomptant. Tu portes sans cesse les yeux sur le chemin qui conduit aux lieux où tu laissas ton cœur; tu le mesure avec effroi; et le voyageur que tu découvres sur cette route te semble jouir d'un destin plus heureux que celui des rois. Je te plains: mais que tu seras digne d'envie le jour où tu revoleras vers elle! le jour où, reconnaissant de loin sa maison, tu la verras attendre l'heureux instant qui doit payer tant de chagrins! Ah! cet instant —— s'il se prolongeoit, tu ne pourrois le supporter; ton ame, qui trouva de la force contre les maux, serait accablée de tant de bonheur.

Florian.

TRUE LOVE DIFFIDENT.

If long I lingered to avow
The latent flame my bosom proved,
Yet, fairest, dearest, deem not thou
I feebly felt, or lightly loved;
I came not with the wealthier throng
Who breathed their heartless vows to thee;
Yet, maiden! I have loved thee long,
And not the less though hopelessly.
For, oh! I deemed not it could be
That thou shouldst deign to smile on me;
For how should friendless misery gain
The prize by monarchs sought in vain?
How should the falcon meet that sun
Which eagles dare not gaze upon?

Dale.

POWER OF LOVE.

One after one the joys of youth
Had died away,
And visions of unfading truth,
As false as they;

Then came a dark and dreary chill,
More sad than grief;
The very pang that bade me feel
Had seemed relief.

I saw thee smile; the icy chain
Began to melt;
I heard thee speak; and once again
I lived, I felt!

Thy gentle care once more for me
Hope's garland wove;
And all my soul's dark apathy,
Touched by thy love,

Grew rapture—as the languid mist
Of sullen hue,
By morning's summer radiance kissed,
Melts in bright dew.

And thou hast given me light and life,
Fond hopes, sweet fears;
The varying passions' pleasing strife,
And smiles and tears.

H. Townsend.

I fain would sing, but will be silent now,
For pain is sitting on my lover's brow;
And he would hear me--and, though silent, deem
I pleased myself, but little thought of him,
While of naught else I think; to him I give
My spirit, and for him alone I live:
Bear him within my heart, as mothers bear
The last and youngest object of their care.

Servian Poetry.—Bowring.

THE VOW.

That is the hour, beloved of Heaven,
When plighted faith is purely given;
When lovers blending heart with heart,
And, silent, mingling hand with hand,
Before God's sacred altar stand,
No more in life to part;
Then lowly kneel them down to pray,
That youth's devoted fire
Should ever burn with equal sway,
Till love with life expire.
That, when fast gathering storms prevail,
And sorrow dims the tearful eye,
And those we once deemed faithful, fly
Before the changing gale,
Those vows might not be given in vain:
That summer hours of cloudless joy,
That years of sickness, grief, and pain,
Might ne'er that silver link destroy.
And oh! in man's most dreary hour,
Has woman's voice the magic power
That tames the haughty heart, and glads the aching sight,
And gilds with brighter gleam the deep'ning nig[illegible]

Lord Porchester.

SONG.

Deck not with gems that lovely form for me,
They in my eyes can add no charm to thee.
Braid not for me the tresses of thy hair;
I must have loved thee hadst thou not been fair.

How oft, when half in tears, hast thou beguiled
The sorrow from my heart, and I have smiled.
Oh! formed alike my tears and smiles to share,
I must have loved thee hadst thou [illegible]en fair.

Time on that cheek his withering hand may press,
He may do all but make me love thee less;
The mind defies him, and thy charm lies there,
I must have loved thee hadst thou not been fair.

Bayley.

THE PRAYER OF EARTHLY LOVE.

——— Unseen she prayed,
With all the still, small whispers of the night,
And with the searching glances of the stars,
And with her God alone! She lifted up
Her sad, sweet voice, while trembling o'er her head
The dark leaves thrilled with prayer—the tearful prayer
Of woman's quenchless yet repentant love.

"Father of spirits, hear!
Look on the inmost soul, to thee revealed:
Look on the fountain of the burning tear,
Before thy sight in solitude unsealed!

"Hear, Father! hear and aid!
If I have loved too well, if I have shed,
In my vain fondness, o'er a mortal head,
Gifts, on thy shrine, my God, more fitly laid;

"If I have sought to live
But in one light, and made a mortal eye
The lonely star of my idolatry,
Thou, that art Love, oh! pity and forgive!

"Chastened and schooled at last,
No more my struggling spirit burns,
But fixed on thee, from that vain worship turns!
What have I said? the deep dream is not past.

"Yet hear! If still I love,
Oh! still too fondly—if, for ever seen,
An earthly image comes my soul between,
And thy calm glory, Father, throned above;

"If still a voice is near,
(Even while I strive these wanderings to control)
An earthly voice, disquieting my soul,
With its deep music, too intensely dear;

"O, Father, draw to thee
My lost affections back!—the dreaming eyes
Clear from the mist—sustain the heart that dies;
Give the worn soul once more its pinions free!

"I must love on, O God!
This bosom must love on! but let thy breath
Touch and make pure the flame that knows not death,
Bearing it up to Heaven, Love's own abode!"

Hemans.

——— I do love violets!
They tell the history of woman's love;
They open with the earliest breath of spring;
Lead a sweet life of perfume, dew and light,
And, if they perish, perish with a sigh
Delicious as that life. On the hot June
They shed no perfume: the flowers may remain,
But the rich breathing of their leaves is past.—
The violet breath of love is purity.

Landon.

WEDDED LOVE.

In joyous youth what soul hath never known
Thought, feeling, taste, harmonious to his own?
Who hath not paused while Beauty's pensive eye
Asked from his heart the homage of a sigh?
Who hath not owned, with rapture-smitten frame,
The power of grace, the magic of a name?

Who that would ask a heart to dulness wed,
The waveless calm, the slumber of the dead?
No; the wild bliss of Nature needs alloy,
And fear and sorrow fan the fire of joy!
And say, without our hopes, without our fears,
Without the home that plighted love endears,

Without the smile from partial beauty won,
Oh! what were man?—a world without a sun!
Till Hymen brought his love-delighted hour,
There dwelt no joy in Eden's rosy bower!
In vain the viewless seraph lingering there,
At starry midnight charmed the silent air;
In vain the wild-bird carolled on the steep,
To hail the sun, slow wheeling from the deep;
In vain, to sooth the solitary shade,
Aërial notes in mingling pleasure played;
The summer wind that shook the spangled tree,
The whispering wave, the murmur of the bee;—
Still slowly passed the melancholy day,
And still the stranger wist not where to stray;—
The world was sad!—the garden was a wild!
And Man, the hermit, sighed—till Woman smiled!

CAMPBELL.

O LOVE, first learned in a lady's eyes,
Lives not alone immurèd in the brain;
But, with the motion of all elements,
Courses as swift as thought in every power;
And gives to every power a double power.
Above their functions and their offices.
It adds a precious feeling to the eye;—
A lover's eyes will gaze an eagle blind:
A lover's ears will hear the lowest sound,
When the suspicious head of theft is stopt.—
For valor, is not love a Hercules,
Still climbing trees in the Hesperides?
Subtle as Shpinx; as sweet and musical
As bright Apollo's lute, strung with his hair:
And when Love speaks, the voice of all the gods
Makes heaven drowsy with the harmony.
Never durst poet touch a pen to write,
Until his ink were tempered with Love's sighs:
O! then his lines would ravage savage ears,
And plant in tyrants mild humility.
From women's eyes this doctrine I derive:
They sparkle still the right Promethean fire;
They are the books, the arts, the academes,
That show, contain, and nourish all the world;
Else, none at all in aught proves excellent.

SHAKSPERE.

THE CONFESSION.

THERE is a language by the virgin made,
Not read but felt, not uttered but betrayed,
A mute communion, yet so wondrous sweet,
Eyes must impart what tongue can ne'er repeat.
'Tis written on her cheeks and meaning brows;
In one short glance whole volumes it avows;
In one short moment tells of many days,
In one short speaking silence all conveys.
Joy, sorrow, love, recounts,—hope, pity, fear,
And looks a sigh, and weeps without a tear.
Oh! 'tis so chaste, so touching, so refined,
So soft, so wistful, so sincere, so kind!
Were eyes melodious, and could music shower
From orient rays new striking on a flower,
Such heavenly music from that glance might rise,
And angels own the music of the skies.

E. S. BARRET.

A ROYAL BRIDE.

——————— Too proud
For less than absolute command, too soft
For aught but gentle tender thought; her hair
Clustered as from an orb of gold, cast out
A dazzling and overpowering radiance, save
Here and there on her white neck reposed,
In a soothed brilliance, some thin wandering tress.
The azure flashing of her eye was fringed
With virgin meekness, and her tread that seemed
Earth to disdain, as softly fell on it
As the light dew shower on a tuft of flowers.

MILMAN.

THE TWO FOUNTAINS.

I SAW, from yonder silent cave,
  Two fountains running side by side;
The one was Memory's limpid wave,
  The other cold Oblivion's tide.
"Oh! Love," said I, in thoughtless dream,
  As o'er my lips the Lethe passed,
Here, in this dark and chilly stream,
  Be all my pains forgot at last."

But who could bear that gloomy blank,
  Where joy was lost as well as pain?
Quickly of Memory's fount I drank,
  And brought the past all back again,
And said, "Oh! Love, whate'er my lot,
  Still let this soul to thee be true:
Rather than have one bliss forgot,
  Be all my pains remembered too!"

T. MOORE

OH! if thou lovest,
And art a woman, hide thy love from him
Whom thou dost worship; never let him know
How dear he is; flit like a bird before him,—
Lead him from tree to tree, from flower to flower;
But be not won, or thou mayest like that bird,
When caught and caged, be left to pine neglected,
And perish in forgetfulness.

LANDON.

LOVE'S BONDAGE.

MYSTERIOUS Love!
Thy presence is around me, and I feel
All its o'ermastering influence. A chain—
A viewless chain—binds my stern spirit down
To more than woman's gentleness. A spell,
As 'twere of voiceless music, through my soul
Steals with a soft delight unfelt before.
I strive to break this thraldom, and arouse
The vigor of my mind;—but Love's own breath,
Like the sweet south upon the Eolian lyre,
Sweeps o'er my heartstrings. I'm again subdued,
And all my efforts sink into—a sigh!

LOVE'S YOUNG DREAM.

OH! the days are gone when Beauty bright
    My heart's chain wove;
When my dream of life from morn till night
    Was love, still love!
    New hope may bloom,
    And days may come,
  Of milder, calmer beam;
But there's nothing half so sweet in life
  As Love's young dream.
No! there's nothing half so sweet in life
  As Love's young dream!

Though the bard to purer fame may soar,
    When wild youth's past;
Though he win the wise, who frowned before,
    To smile at last;
    He 'll never meet
    A joy so sweet
  In all his noon of fame,
As when first he sung to woman's ear
  His soul-felt flame,
And at every close she blushed to hear
  The one loved name.

Oh! that hallowed form is ne'er forgot
    Which first love traced;
Still it lingering haunts the greenest spot
    On Memory's waste!
    'Twas odor fled
    As soon as shed,
  'Twas morning's winged dream,
'Twas a light that ne'er can shine again
  On life's dull stream!
Oh! 'twas light that ne'er can shine again
  On life's dull stream!

T. MOORE.

SONNET.

Let me not to the marriage of true minds
Admit impediments. Love is not love
Which alters when it alteration finds,
Or bends with the remover to remove:
Oh no! it is an ever-fixed mark,
That looks on tempests and is never shaken;
It is the star to every wandering bark,
Whose worth's unknown, although his height be taken.
Love's not Time's fool, though rosy lips and cheeks
Within his bending sickle's compass come;
Love alters not with his brief hours and weeks,
But bears it out e'en to the edge of doom.
If this be error, and upon me proved,
I never writ, nor no man ever loved.

Shakspere.

Look through mine eyes with thine. True wife,
Round my true heart thine arms entwine,
My other dearer life in life,
Look through my very soul with thine.
Untouched with any shade of years,
May those kind eyes for ever dwell!
They have not shed a many tears,
Dear eyes! since first I knew them well.

Tennyson.

WOMAN'S LOVE.

Oh! woman's love is a holy light,
Which when once kindled can not die;
Though time, and treachery, and slight,
To quench the deathless flame may try.
Like ivy, when it grows 'tis seen
To wear an everlasting green;
Like ivy, too, 'tis found to cling
Too often round a worthless thing.
O woman's love! at times it may
Seem cold and clouded; but it burns
With an undeviating ray,
And never from its idol turns.
Its sunshine is a smile; a frown
The heavy cloud that weighs it down;
A tear its weapon is—(beware
Of woman's tears, there's danger there):—
Its sweetest place on which to rest,
A constant and confiding breast;—
Its joy—to meet;—its death—to part;—
Its sepulchre—a broken heart!

HER NAME.

With more than Jewish reverence as yet
Do I the sacred name conceal;
When, ye kind stars, ah! when will it be fit
This gentle mystery to reveal!
When will our love be named, and we possess
That christening as a badge of happiness?

So bold as yet no verse of mine has been,
To wear that gem on any line;
Nor, till the happy nuptial muse be seen,
Shall any stanza with it shine.
Rest, mighty name! till then; for thou must be
Laid down by her, ere taken up by me.

Then all the fields and woods shall with it ring;
Then Echo's burden it shall be;
Then all the birds in several notes shall sing,
And all the rivers murmur,—*thee;*
Then every wind the sound shall upward bear,
And softly whisper 't to some angel's ear.

Cowley.

THE BRIDE.

Nay, 'tis not
The grace of her meek, bending, snowy neck
The flowing outline of proportioned limbs
Moving with health's elastic lightness, blent
With all that nameless suavity of air
That marks high birth; 'tis not, alone, a face
Whose features are all symmetry; an eye
In whose ethereal blue Love sits enshrined,
A spirit in a star; cheeks eloquent
In changeful blushes, as her sweetest lips
In the harmonious utterance of pure thoughts:
'Tis not all these—the palpable ornaments
Of the material mould,—Love's pageantry
Floating o'er beauty's surface.—
No, no! it is not these that win my heart;
But 'tis the pure intelligence of mind
That, like some inborn light, beams from her soul;
The virtuous thoughts that clothe her like a garment;
The chastity, the candor, and the meekness,
That, through her parted hair, look from a brow
And features, where the seal of heaven is set!

J. Bird.

THE HOME OF LOVE.

Thou movest in visions, of Love! Around thy way
E'en through this world's rough path and changeful day
For ever floats a gleam,—
Not from the realms of moonlight or the morn,
But thine own soul's illumined chambers born,—
The coloring of a dream!

Love, shall I read thy dream?—oh! is it not
All of some sheltering wood-embosomed spot—
A bower for thee and thine?
Yes! lone and lowly is that home; yet there
Something of heaven in the transparent air
Makes every flower divine.

Something that mellows and that glorifies
Breathes o'er it ever from the tender skies,
As o'er some blessed isle;
E'en like the soft and spiritual glow
Kindling rich woods whereon the ethereal bow
Sleeps lovingly awhile.

The very whispers of the wind have there
A flute-like harmony, that seems to bear
Greeting from some bright shore,
Where none have said *Farewell!*—where no decay
Lends the faint crimson to the dying day;
Where the storm's might is o'er,

And there thou dreamest of Elysian rest,
In the deep sanctuary of one true breast
Hidden from earthly ill:
There wouldst thou watch the homeward step whose sound
Wakening all Nature to sweet echoes round,
Thine inmost soul can thrill.

There by the hearth should many a glorious page,
From mind to mind the immortal heritage,
For thee its treasures pour;
Or music's voice at vesper hours be heard,
Or dearer interchange of playful word,
Affection's household lore.

And the rich unison of mingled prayer,
The melody of hearts in heavenly air,
Thence duly should arise;
Lifting the eternal hope, the adoring breath,
Of spirits, not to be disjoined by death,
Up to the starry skies.

There dost thou well believe, no storm should come
To mar the stillness of that angel home;-
There should thy slumbers be
Weighed down with honey-dew, serenely blest,
Like theirs who first in Eden's grove took rest
Under some balmy tree.

Love! Love! thou passionate in joy and wo!
And canst *thou* hope for cloudless peace below—
Here, where bright things must die?
Oh! thou, that, wildly worshipping, dost shed
On the frail altar of a mortal head
Gifts of infinity!

Thou must be still a trembler, fearful Love!
Danger seems gathering from beneath, above,
Still round thy precious things;

Thy stately pine-tree, or thy gracious rose,
In their sweet shade can yield thee no repose,
Here, where the blight hath wings.

And, as a flower with some fine sense imbued,
To shrink before the wind's vicissitude,
So in thy prescient breast
Are lyre-strings quivering with prophetic thrill
To the low footstep of each coming ill;
—Oh! canst *thou* dream of rest?

Bear up thy dream! thou mighty and thou weak!
Heart strong as death, yet as a reed to break;
As a flame, tempest-swayed!
He that sits calm on high is yet the source
Whence thy soul's current hath its troubled course,
He that great deep hath made!

Will He not pity? He, whose searching eye
Reads all the secrets of thine agony?—
Oh! pray to be forgiven
Thy fond idolatry, thy blind excess,
And seek with *Him* that bower of blessedness:—
Love! *thy* sole home is heaven!

HEMANS.

LOVE.

A MYSTERY thou art, thou mighty one!
We speak thy name in beauty, yet we shun
To own thee, Love, a guest; the poet's songs
Are sweetest when their voice to thee belongs,
And hope, sweet opiate, tenderness, delight,
Are terms which are thy own peculiar right;
Yet all deny their master; who will own
His breast thy footstool, and his heart thy throne?

LANDON.

WAKE, oh, wake! the morning star
Hath ceased to grace his glittering car:
Slowly the redd'ning clouds enfold,
And frequent streaks of living gold
Announce the lord of day.
The light breeze wafts perfume on high,
Less sweet alone than thy sweet sigh!
The flower with fresher teints is glowing,
The fount with clearer crystal flowing.
Oh come! oh come!
Hours like this a charm impart,
That wins the eye but not the heart,
While Love is still away!

Wake, oh, wake! through every grove
Is heard the matin round of love;
—And shall a *dearer* love be vain
To bid thee burst dull slumber's chain,
And spurn at slow delay?
Though morning glow with teints divine
I'd change her brightest blush for thine,
And deem thine eye from sleep awaking,
Outshone the sun through darkness breaking.
Oh come! oh come!
Hours like this are quickly fled,
But thy fond smile a joy can shed
Which melts not thus away!

T. DALE.

AH, me! for aught that ever I could read,
Could ever hear by tale or history,
The course of true love never did run smooth:
But either it was different in blood,
Or else misgrafted in respect of years;
Or else it stood upon the choice of friends:
Or, if there were a sympathy in choice,
War, death, or sickness, did lay siege to it;
Making it momentary as a sound,
Swift as a shadow, short as any dream;
Brief as the lightning in the colled night,
That in a spleen, unfolds both heaven and earth;
And, ere a man hath power to say, Behold!
The jaws of darkness do devour it up:
So quick bright things come to confusion!

SHAKSPERE.

LOVE'S LAST EVENING.

Oh! that word *was*, how sad a word it is!—SHAKSPERE

DOST *thou* recal it? *'twas* a glorious eve!
The air was precious with the breath of flowers
That had been weeping—and the harps of eve
Played vespers to the stars! and in the blue,
The deep blue sky, (how beautiful she looked!)
Stood the young moon! * * * * * * *

Thou dost know how many years,
How long and well my soul has worshipped thee,
Till my mind made itself a solitude
For only thee to dwell in—and thou wert
The spirit of all fountains in my breast!
—We will not speak of that; but oh! that eve
Amid the pines, our fondest and our last!
(Ere it had crossed my heart, or thine, to think
That *we could part*—and *one* could change so soon)
How it has haunted me, with all the sounds
That made it silent—and the starry eyes
And flitting shapes that made it solitude!
Did I not love thee! oh! but for one throb,
One pulse of all the pulses beating then;
One feeling—though the feeling were a pang!
One passion—though the passion spoke in tears!
I deemed thy love was boundless; oh! the queen,
The eastern queen, who melted down her pearl,
And drank the treasure in a single draught,
Was wiser far than hearts that love too well,
If love be finite! In that last adieu
Our young and ardent spirits burnt away,
And flung their *ashes* on the winds of heaven!
Our love has perished like the sound that dies,
And *leaves no echo*—like the eastern day
That *has no twilight*—like the lonely flower
Flung forth to wither on the wind, that wastes
Even its perfume: dead, thou false one! dead,
With all the precious thoughts on which it fed,
And all the hopes which made it beautiful—
Sound, light, and perfume, gone—and gone for ever!

J. K. HERVEY.

LE véritable amour ne peut exister sans l'estime; mais l'estime la plus parfaite ne suffit pas pour l'amour. Cette passion si douce et si violente, source de plaisirs et de peines, de tourmens et de délices, cette flamme qui consume, et fait vivre, ne s'allume jamais qu'une fois. Les ames pures savent l'immoler à la vertu, et donner ensuite au devoir tout ce qui dépend encore d'elles: mais cet attrait, ce charme irrésistible, cet élan rapide de toutes les pensées, de tous les sentimens vers un seul objet, ces craintes terribles, ces vives espérances, et ces profondes douleurs pour un regard de colère, et ces ravissemens inexprimables pour un serrement de main, on ne les éprouve plus; ils sont passés avec le premier amour. Le cœur n'en est plus susceptible. C'est le lis coupé sur sa tige; la plante vit encore, mais ne produit plus de fleurs.

FLORIAN.

LOVE'S DARING.

OH, never did achievement rival Love's,
For daring enterprise and execution!
It will do miracles: attempt such things
As make ambition, fiery as it is,
Dull plodding tameness in comparison.
Talk of the miser's passion for his store—
'Tis milk and water to the lover's, which
Defies the mines of earth and caves of ocean
To match its treasure! Talk of height, breadth, depth,
There is no measure for the lover's passion,
No bounds to what 'twill do!

SHERIDAN KNOWLES.

LOVE is a gift which God hath given
To man alone beneath the heaven.
It is the secret sympathy,
The silver link, the silken tie,
Which heart to heart, and mind to mind
In body and in soul can bind.

SCOTT.

THE FAREWELL.

FAREWELL, fair Rosebud of the isles!
  Yet one farewell to thee;
Brief was the blessing of thy smiles
  Like all of bliss for me.
Deputed dreams! sent down to bless
  The sleep of beauty, tell
With what impassioned tenderness
  The minstrel breathes farewell!

Oh! tell her she's my sheltering tree,
  My love-star o'er the waves,
The camel's treasured draught to me,
  That midst the desert saves.
This heart itself a desert bare
  As that my footstep knows;
One only rose left blooming there,
  And she that virgin rose.

ISHMAEL FITZADAM.

MERCENARY LOVE DESPISED.

——————— LADY,
Ye who have dwelt upon the sordid land,
Amid the everlasting gloomy war
Of Poverty with Wealth—ye can not know
How we, the wild sons of the ocean, mock
At men who fret out life with care for gold.
Oh! the fierce sickness of the soul—to see
Love bought and sold, and all the heaven-roofed temple
Of God's great globe, the money-change of Mammon!
I dream of love, enduring faith, a heart
Mingled with mine—a deathless heritage
Which I can take unsullied to the stars,
When the Great Father calls his children home;
And in the midst of this Elysian dream,
Lo, Gold—the demon Gold! alas! the creeds
Of the false land!

SIR E. L. BULWER.

THE SAILOR LOVER.

MY bark shall be our home;
The gale shall chant our bridal melodies;
The stars that light the angel palaces
Of air, our lamps; our floor, the crystal deep
Studded with sapphires sparkling as we pass;
Our roof, all Heaven! my beautiful, my own!
Never did sail more gladly glide to port
Than I to thee! my anchor in thy faith,
And in thine eyes my haven!

SIR E. L. BULWER.

DOMESTIC LOVE.

OH! happy they, the happiest of their kind!
Whom gentler stars unite, and in one fate
Their hearts, their fortunes, and their beings blend
'Tis not the coarser ties of human laws,
Unnatural oft, and foreign to the mind,
That binds their peace, but harmony itself,
Attuning all their passions into love:
Where friendship full exerts her softest power,
Perfect esteem, enlivened by desire
Ineffable, and sympathy of soul;
Thought meeting thought, and will preventing will,
With boundless confidence; for naught but love
Can answer love, and render bliss secure.

THOMSON.

FLOWERS LOVE'S LANGUAGE.

BEAUTIFUL language! Love's peculiar own,
But only to the spring and summer known.
Ah! little marvel in such clime and age
As that of our too earth-born pilgrimage,
That we should daily hear that Love is fled,
And Hope grown pale, and lighted feelings dead.
Not for the cold, the careless to impart,
By such sweet signs, the silence of the heart;
But surely in the countries where the sun
Lights loveliness in all he shines upon—
Where Love is as a mystery and a dream,
One single flower upon life's troubled stream;
There, there, perchance, may the young bosom thrill,
Feeling and Fancy linger with Love still.

LANDON.

LOVE'S REMEMBRANCE.

I WILL remember thee,—in that still hour
  When, like a dream of beauty, from the west,
Heaven's sweetest star sheds down her golden dower
  Of light upon the waters,—whose unrest
And moodiness might well be charmed away,
By the pure loveliness of that soft ray!

I will remember thee,—when night hath thrown
  Its dreams around the sleeper, and repose
Hath calmed the worn and aching spirit down
  To brief oblivion of its waking woes;
Then,—when deep silence reigneth over all,
My lonely thoughts thine image shall recal.

I will remember thee,—when morn hath hung
  Her banner on the hills,—and kindling gleams
Of sunlight, in warm diamond showers are flung
  Upon the surface of the bounding streams,
Which move in their exulting course along,
Free as the murmurs of their own wild song.

I will remember thee,—when summer's sigh
  Breathes o'er the mountains, and the laughing earth
Is zoned with roses,—while deep melody
  Hath in the woods, with the wild flowers its birth
From joyous birds, who mid their green homes there
Pour forth their music on the clear blue air

I will remember thee,—through many a scene
  Of pleasantness and solitude;—for thou
Upon my dark and troubled path hast been
  A vision blest and cheering,—as the bow
That spans the thunder-cloud: a thing of light,
As early hope's first dreamings pure and bright.

ELIZA ACTON.

LOVE.

OH! Love hath wings on which we fly,
To breathe in joy's unclouded sky!
And Love hath wings, on which we go
Down to the hopeless depths of wo!
Love is a light in sorrow's night,
  It shines with pure and gladdening ray,
And Love is a flame which from heaven came,
  A beacon that shines o'er our earthly way,

When kindred hearts in rapture meet,
When e'en their plaintive sighs are sweet,
Then dwells celestial bliss below,
Then flies all thought of care or wo!
Then trip the hours o'er summer flowers;
  Then life glides like a gentle stream:
Earth yields no bliss so sweet as this,
  Though it sometimes fade like an earthly dream.

The pair inspired by rosy love,
Foretaste the joys of heaven above!
Their hearts are blessed, and what to them
Is glittering pomp or costly gem?
They rapture breathe! on earth beneath
  They tread a soft enchanted path.
If o'er the hour the tempest lower,
  They reck not the fate of its bursting wrath.

Alas! if Love do not reveal
His warmth to stamp the marriage seal,
Then grief and bitter wo betide
The wedded lord and hapless bride:
Then hope will die, and true Love fly
  Far off upon his trembling wing;
The withered breast shall know no rest
  From the scorpion care, and his poisoned sting.

J. BIRD.

'Tis sweet to hear
At midnight, o'er the blue and moonlit deep,
The song and oar of Adria's gondolier,
By distance mellowed, o'er the waters sweep:
'Tis sweet to see the evening star appear;
'Tis sweet to listen as the night-winds creep
From leaf to leaf; 'tis sweet to view on high
The rainbow, based on ocean, span the sky.

'Tis sweet to hear the watchdog's honest bark
Bay deep-mouthed welcome as we draw near home;
'Tis sweet to know there is an eye will mark
Our coming, and look brighter when we come.
'Tis sweet to be awakened by the lark,
Or lulled with falling waters; sweet the hum
Of bees, the voice of girls, the song of birds,
The lisp of children, and their earliest words.

But sweeter far than this, than these, than all,
Is first and passionate love: It stands *alone*,
Like Adam's recollection of his fall.

BYRON.

THE SAILOR'S FAREWELL.

FAREWELL! Farewell! the voice you hear,
Has left its last soft tone with you,—
Its next must join the seaward cheer,
And shout among the shouting crew.

The accents which I scarce could form
Beneath your frown's controlling check,
Must give the word, above the storm,
To cut the mast and clear the wreck.

The timid eye I dared not raise,—
The hand that shook when pressed to thine,
Must point the guns upon the chase,
Must bid the deadly cutlass shine.

To all I love, or hope, or fear,
Honor, or own, a long adieu!
To all that life has soft and dear,
Farewell! save memory of you!

SCOTT.

LOVE, like the grave, levels earth's vain distinctions,
Hearts blend beneath his influence, as the colors
Blend in the rainbow, where each separate hue
Grows faint and fainter, till its varied teints
Fade on our wandering eyes, and we behold
Nothing but heaven.

NEELE.

THE RETREAT OF LOVE.

—— BY heavenly feet thy paths are trod,—
Undying Love's, who here ascends a throne
To which the steps are mountains; where the god
Is a pervading life and light,—so shown
Not on those summits solely, nor alone
In the still cave and forest; o'er the flower
His eye is sparkling, and his breath hath blown,
His soft and summer breath, whose tender power
Passes the strength of storms in their most desolate hour

All things are here of *him;* from the black pines
That are his shade on high, and the loud roar
Of torrents, where he listeneth; to the vines
Which slope his green path downward to the shore,
Where the bowed waters meet him, and adore,
Kissing his feet with murmurs; and the wood,
The covert of old trees, with trunks all hoar,
But light leaves, young as joy, stands where it stood,
Offering to him and his a populous solitude.

A populous solitude of bees and birds,
And fairy-formed and many-colored things,
Who worship him with notes more sweet than words.
And innocently open their glad wings,
Fearless and full of life: the gush of springs,
And fall of lofty fountains, and the bend
Of stirring branches, and the bud which brings
The swiftest thought of beauty, here extend,
Mingling, and made by Love, unto one mighty end.

He who hath loved not, here would learn that lore,
And make his heart a spirit; he who knows
That tender mystery will love the more,
For this is Love's recess, where vain men's woes,
And the world's waste, have driven him far from those,
For 'tis his nature to advance or die;
He stands not still, but or decays, or grows
Into a boundless blessing, which may vie
With the immortal lights, in its eternity.

BYRON

THE LOVE OF LATER YEARS.

THEY err who deem Love's brightest hour in blooming youth is known:
Its purest, tenderest, holiest power in after life is shown,
When passions chastened and subdued to riper years are given,
And earth and earthly things are viewed in light that breaks from Heaven.

It is not in the flush of youth, or days of cloudless mirth,
We feel the tenderness and truth of Love's devoted worth;
Life then is like a tranquil stream which flows in sunshine bright,
And objects mirrored in it seem to share its sparkling light.

'Tis when the howling winds arise, and life is like the ocean,
Whose mountain billows brave the skies, lashed by the storm's commotion,
When lightning cleaves the murky cloud, and thunderbolts astound us,
'Tis then we feel our spirits bowed by loneliness around us.

Oh! then, as to the seaman's sight the beacon's twinkling ray
Surpasses far the lustre bright of summer's cloudless day,
E'en such, to tried and wounded hearts in manhood's darker years,
The gentle light true love imparts, mid sorrows, cares, and fears.

Its beams on minds of joy bereft their freshening brightness fling,
And show that life has somewhat left to which their hopes may cling;
It steals upon the sick at heart, the desolate in soul,
To bid their doubts and fears depart, and point a brighter goal.

If such be Love's triumphant power o'er spirits touched by time,
Oh! who shall doubt its loveliest hour of happiness sublime?
In youth, 'tis like the meteor's gleam which dazzles and sweeps by,
In after life, its splendors seem linked with eternity!

B. BARTON.

THE BRIDAL.

OH! they are blest indeed, and swift the hours
Till her young sisters wreath her hair in flowers.
Then before *all* they stand; the holy vow,
And ring of gold—no fond illusions now—
Bind her as his. Across the threshold led,
And every tear kissed off as soon as shed,
His house she enters, there to be a light,
Shining within when all without is night;
A guardian angel o'er his life presiding,
Doubling his pleasure, and his cares dividing!
How oft her eyes read his; her gentle mind
To all his wishes, all his thoughts inclined,
Still subject—ever on the watch to borrow
Mirth of his mirth, and sorrow of his sorrow—
The soul of music slumbers in the shell
Till waked to rapture by the master's spell;
And feeling hearts—touch them but rightly, pour
A thousand melodies unheard before.

ROGERS.

THE ECHO.

FOR EVER thine! when hills and seas divide,
When storms combine;
When west winds sigh, or deserts part us wide—
For ever thine!

In the gay circle of the proud saloon,
Whose splendors shine;
In the lone stillness of the evening moon—
For ever thine!

And when the light of song, that fires me now,
Shall life resign,
My breaking heart shall breathe its latest vow,
For ever thine!

From the German.

THY life was all one oath of love to me!
Sworn to me daily, hourly, by thine eyes,
Which, when they saw me, lightened up as though
An angel's presence did enhance their sense,
That I have seen their very color change,
Subliming into lines past earthliness.
Talk of the adjuration of the tongue—
Compare Love's name—a sound which any life
May pipe! a breath! with holy love itself!
Thou'rt not forsworn, because thou tookst no oath?
What were thy accents, then? thy accents? tell me!
Oh! they did turn thy lightest words to oaths,
Vouching the burden of a love-fraught soul!
Telling a tale which my young nature caught
With interest so deep, 'twas conned by heart
Before I knew the fatal argument!

SHERIDAN KNOWLES.

SONG OF THE AGED MINSTREL.

AND said I that my limbs were old,
And said I that my blood was cold,
And that my kindly fire was fled,
And my poor withered heart was dead,
And that I might not sing of love?
How could I to the dearest theme
That ever warmed a minstrel's dream,
So foul, so false a recreant prove?
How could I name Love's very name,
Nor wake my heart to notes of flame!

In peace Love tunes the shepherd's reed;
In war, he mounts the warrior's steed;
In halls, in gay attire is seen;
In hamlets dances on the green.
Love rules the court, the camp, the grove,
And men below, and saints above,
For love is heaven and heaven is love!

SCOTT.

WILT THOU BE MINE.

IF thou'lt be mine, the treasures of air,
Of earth and sea, shall lie at thy feet;
Whatever in Fancy's eye looks fair,
Or in Hope's sweet music is *most* sweet,
Shall be ours, if thou wilt be mine, love!

Bright flowers shall bloom wherever we rove,
A voice divine shall talk in each stream,
The stars shall look like worlds of love,
And this earth be all one beautiful dream
In our eyes, if thou wilt be mine, love!

And thoughts, whose source is hidden and high,
Like streams that come from heavenward hills,
Shall keep our hearts—like meads that lie
To be bathed by those eternal rills—
Ever green, if thou wilt be mine, love!

All this and more the Spirit of Love
Can breathe o'er them who feel his spells!
The heaven which forms his home above,
He can make on earth, where'er he dwells,
And he *will*, if thou wilt be mine, love!

T. MOORE.

2

BRIDAL GREETINGS.

OCEAN and land the globe divide;
Summer and winter share the year;
Darkness and light walk side by side;
And earth and heaven are always near

Though each be good and fair alone,
And glorious in its time and place,
In all, when fitly paired, is shown
More of their Maker's power and grace.

Then may the union of young hearts
So early and so well begun,
Like sea and shore, in all their parts
Appear as twain, but be as one.

Be it like summer—may they find
Bliss, beauty, hope, where'er they roam;
Be it like winter—when confined,
Peace, comfort, happiness, at home.

Like day and night, sweet interchange
Of care, enjoyment, action, rest;
Absence nor coldness e'er estrange
Hearts by unfailing love possest.

Like earth's horizon be their scene
Of life, a rich and various ground;
And, whether lowering or serene,
Heaven all above it and around.

When land and ocean, day and night,
When years and nature cease to be,
May their inheritance be light,
Their union one eternity!

J. MONTGOMERY.

I LOVED thee once!
Oh! tell me when was it I loved thee not?
Was't in my childhood, boyhood, manhood? Oh!
In all of them I loved thee! And, were I now
To live the span of my first life twice told,
And then to wither, thou surviving me,
And yet I lived in thy sweet memory,
Then might'st thou say of me, "He loved me once,
But that was all his life!"

SHERIDAN KNOWLES.

IT is the spirit's bitterest pain
To love and be beloved again,
And yet between a gulf which ever
The hearts that burn to meet must sever.
O'er some Love's shadow may but pass
As passes the breath-stain o'er glass;
And pleasures, cares, and pride, combined
Fill up the blank Love leaves behind.
But there are some whose love is high,
Entire—almost idolatry;
Who, turning from a heartless world,
Ask some dear thing which may renew
Affection's severed links, and be
As true as they themselves are true.
But love's bright fount is never pure,
And all his pilgrims must endure
All passion's mighty suffering
Ere they may reach the blessed spring.
And some who waste their lives to find
A prize which they may never win;
Like those who seek for Irem's groves,
Which found, they may not enter in.
And some there are who leave the path
In agony and fierce disdain,
And bear upon each wounded heart
The scar that never heals again.

LANDON.

A SILVER lute, a minstrel hand,
To youth and love belong,
For is not Love's own magic wand
The melody of song

H. B.

THE ABSENT LOVER TO HIS BETROTHED.

Summer was on the hills when last we parted,
  Flowers in the vale, and beauty on the sky,
Our hearts were true, although our hopes were thwarted;
  Forward, with wistful eye,
Scarce half-resigned we looked, yet thought how sweet
'Twould be again in after months to meet.
And months have passed: now the bright moon is shining
  O'er the gray mountains and the stilly sea,
As, by the streamlet's willowy bend reclining,
  I pause, remembering thee,
Who to the moonlight lent a softer charm,
As through these wilds we wandered arm in arm!

Yes! as we roamed, the sylvan earth seemed glowing
  With many a beauty unremarked before:
The soul was like a deep urn overflowing
  With thoughts a treasured store;
The very flowers seemed born but to exhale,
As breathed the West, their fragrance to the gale.
Methinks I see thee yet—thy form of lightness,
  An angel phantom gliding through the trees,
Thine alabaster brow, thy cheek of brightness,
  Thy tresses in the breeze
Floating their auburn, and thine eyes that made,
So rich their blue, heaven's azure like a shade.

Methinks even yet I feel thy timid fingers,
  With their bland pressure thrilling bliss to mine.
Methinks yet on my cheek thy breathing lingers
  As, fondly leant to thine,
I told how life all pleasureless would be,
Green palm-tree of earth's desert, wanting thee.
Not yet, not yet, had disappointment shrouded
  Youth's summer calms with storms of wintry strife;
The star of Hope shone o'er our path unclouded,
  And Fancy colored life
With those elysian rainbow-hues, which Truth
Melts with his rod, when disenchanting youth.

Where art thou now? I look around, but see not
  The features and the form that haunt my dreams!
Where art thou now? I listen, but for me not
  The deep, rich music streams
Of that entrancing voice, which could bestow
A zest to pleasure, and a balm to wo:—
I miss thy smile, when morn's first light is bursting
  Through the green branches of the casement tree;
To list thy voice my lonely ear is thirsting,
  Beside the moonlight sea:
Vain are my longings, my repinings vain;
Sleep only gives thee to my arms again.

Yet should it cheer me, that nor wo hath shattered
  The ties that link our hearts, nor Hate, nor Wrath,
And soon the day may dawn, when shall be scattered
  All shadows from our path;
And visions be fulfilled, by Hope adored,
In thee, the long-lost, to mine arms restored.
Ah! could I see thee!—see thee, were it only
  But for a moment looking bliss to me!
Ah! could I hear thee!—desolate and lonely
  Is life deprived of thee:
I start from out my revery, to know
That hills between us rise, and rivers flow!

Let Fortune change—be fickle Fate preparing
  To shower her arrows, or to shed her balm,
All that I ask for, pray for, is the sharing
  With thee life's storm or calm:
For, ah! with others' Wealth and Mirth would be
Less sweet by far than Sorrow shared with thee!
Yes! vainly, foolishly, the vulgar reckon
  That Happiness resides in outward shows:
Contentment from the lowliest cot may beckon
  True Love to sweet repose:
For genuine bliss can ne'er be far apart,
When soul meets soul, and heart responds to heart.

Farewell! let tyrannous Time roll on, estranging
  The eye and heart from each familiar spot:
Be fickle friendships with the seasons changing,
  So that thou changest not!
I would not that the love, which owes its birth
To heaven, should perish like the things of earth!—
Adieu! as falls the flooding moonlight round me,
  Fall Heaven's best joys on thy beloved head!
May cares that harass, and may griefs that wound me,
  Flee from thy path and bed!
Be every thought that stirs, and hour that flies,
Sweet as thy smile, and radiant as thine eyes!

Delta.

AMBITIOUS LOVE.

I am undone; there is no living, none,
If —— be away. It were all one
That I should love a bright particular star,
And think to wed it, he is so above me!
In his bright radiance and collateral light
Must I be comforted, not in his sphere;
The ambition in my love thus plagues itself:
The hind that would be mated by the lion
Must die for love. 'Twas pretty, though a plague,
To see him every hour, to sit and draw
His arched brows, his hawking eye, his curls,
In our heart's table; heart too capable
Of every line and trick of his sweet favor!
But now he's gone, and my idolatrous fancy
Must sanctify his relics!

Shakspere.

UNCHANGEABLE LOVE.

Believe me, if all those endearing young charms,
  Which I gaze on so fondly to-day,
Were to change by to-morrow, and fleet in my arms
  Like fairy-gifts fading away;
Thou wouldst still be adorned, as this moment thou art,
  Let thy loveliness fade as it will;
And around the dear ruin each wish of my heart
  Would entwine itself verdantly still.

It is not while beauty and youth are thine own,
  And thy cheeks unprofaned by a tear,
That the fervor and faith of a soul can be known,
  To which time will but make thee more dear!
Oh! the heart that has truly loved never forgets,
  But as truly loves on to the close;
As the sunflower turns to her god when he sets,
  The same look which she turned when he rose!

T. Moore

LOVE AUGURIES.

There are a thousand fanciful things
Linked round the young heart's imaginings.
In its first love-dream, a leaf or a flower,
Is gifted then with a spell and a power;
A shade is an omen, a dream is a sign,
From which the maiden can well divine
Passion's whole history. Those only can tell
Who have loved as young hearts can love so well,
How the pulses will beat, and the cheek will be died,
When they have some love augury tried.
Oh! it is not for those whose feelings are cold,
Withered by care, or blunted by gold;
Whose brows have darkened with many years,
To feel again youth's hopes and fears—
What they now might blush to confess,
Yet what made their spring-day's happiness!

Landon.

THE WEALTH OF LOVE.

Here, in our souls, we treasure up the wealth
Fraud can not filch, nor waste destroy;—the more
'Tis spent, the more we have;—the sweet affections—
The heart's religion—the diviner instincts
Of what we shall be when the world is dust!

Sir E. L. Bulwer.

ON PARTING.

THE kiss, dear maid! thy lip hath left
Shall never part from mine,
Till happier hours restore the gift
Untainted back to thine.

Thy parting glance, which fondly beams,
An equal love may see:
The tear that from thine eyelid streams,
Can weep no change in me.

I ask no pledge to make me blest
In gazing when alone;
Nor one memorial for a breast
Whose thoughts are all thine own.

Nor need I write—to tell the tale
My pen were doubly weak:
Oh! what can idle words avail,
Unless the heart could speak?

By day or night, in weal or wo,
That heart, no longer free,
Must bear the love it can not show,
And silent ache for thee.

BYRON.

JAMAIS nous ne verrions briller un jour serein,
Toujours par la douleur l'âme seroit flétrie,
Si l'amour ne venoit consoler notre vie,
Et semer quelques fleurs sur ce triste chemin.

THE REPROACH.

WHY art thou silent? Is thy love a plant
Of such weak fibre that the treacherous air
Of absence withers what was once so fair?
Is there no debt to pay, no boon to grant?
Yet have my thoughts for thee been vigilant
(As would my deeds have been) with hourly care,
The mind's least generous wish a mendicant
For naught but what thy happiness could spare.
Speak, though this soft warm heart, once free to hold
A thousand tender pleasures, thine and mine,
Be left more desolate, more dreary cold
Than a forsaken bird's-nest filled with snow
'Mid its own bush of leafless eglantine;
Speak, that my torturing doubts their end may know!

WORDSWORTH.

LOVE'S ARTIFICE.

I SAID it was a wilful, wayward thing,
And so it is, fantastic and perverse!
Which makes its sport of persons and of seasons,
Takes its own way, no matter right or wrong.
It is the bee that finds the honey out,
Where least you dream 'twould seek the nectarous store.
And 'tis an errant masquer—this same love—
That most outlandish, freakish faces wears
To hide his own! Looks a proud Spaniard now;
Now a grave Turk; hot Ethiopian next;
And then phlegmatic Englishman; and then
Gay Frenchman; by-and-by Italian, at
All things a song; and in another skip,
Gruff Dutchman; still is Love behind the masque!
It is a hypocrite! looks every way
But that where lie its thoughts! will openly
Frown at the thing it smiles in secret on;
Shows most like hate, e'en when it most is love;
Would fain convince you it is very rock
When it is water! ice when it is fire!
Is oft its own dupe, like a thorough cheat;
Persuades itself 'tis not the thing it is;
Holds up its head, purses its brows, and looks
Askant, with scornful lip, hugging itself
That it is high disdain—till suddenly
It falls on its knees, making most piteous suit
With hail of tears and hurricane of sighs,
Calling on heaven and earth for witnesses
That it is love, true love—nothing but love!

SHERIDAN KNOWLES.

A WIFE TO HER HUSBAND.

WITH thee conversing I forget all time;
All seasons and their change, all please alike;
Sweet is the breath of morn, her rising sweet,
With charm of earliest birds; pleasant the sun,
When first on this delightful land he spreads
His orient beams on herb, tree, fruit, and flower,
Glistering with dew; fragrant the fertile earth
After soft showers; and sweet the coming on
Of grateful evening mild; then silent night,
With this her solemn bird, and this fair moon,
And these the gems of heaven, her starry train:—
But neither breath of morn, when she ascends
With charm of earliest birds; nor rising sun
On this delightful land; nor herb, fruit, flower,
Glistering with dew; nor fragrance after showers;
Nor grateful evening mild; nor silent night
With this her solemn bird, nor walk by moon,
Or glittering starlight,—without thee is sweet.

MILTON

THE TRANCE OF LOVE.

LOVE in a drowsy mood one day
Reclined with all his nymphs around him,
His feathered darts neglected lay,
And faded were the flowers that crowned him.
Young Hope, with eye of light, in vain
Led smiling Beauty to implore him,
While Genius poured his sweetest strain,
And Pleasure shook his roses o'er him.

At length a stranger sought the grove,
And fiery Vengeance seemed to guide him,
He rudely tore the wreaths of Love,
And broke the darts that lay beside him.
The little god now wakeful grew,
And, angry at the bold endeavor,
He rose, and wove his wreaths anew,
And strung his bow more firm than ever.

When, lo! the invader cried, "Farewell!
My skill, bright nymphs, this lesson teaches—
While Love is sprightly bind him well
With smiles, and songs, and honeyed speeches;
But should dull languor seize the god,
Recall me on my friendly mission;
For know when Love begins to nod,
His surest spur is opposition."

From the Italian.

SONNET.

OH! were I loved as I desire to be,
What is there in the great sphere of the earth,
And range of evil between death and birth,
That I should fear—if I were loved by thee?
All the inner, all the outer world of pain
Clear Love would pierce and cleave, if thou wert mine;
As I have heard that, somewhere in the main
Fresh water springs come up through bitter brine.
'Twere joy, not fear, clasped hand in hand with thee,
To wait for death—mute—careless of all ills,
Apart upon a mountain, through the surge
Of some new deluge from a thousand hills
Flung leagues of roaring foam into the gorge
Below us, as far on as eye could see.

A. TENNYSON.

LOVE is a thing of frail and delicate growth;
Soon checked, soon fostered; feeble and yet strong,
It will endure much, suffer long, and bear
What would weigh down an angel's wing to earth,
And yet mount heavenward; but not the less
It dieth of a word, a look, a thought;
And when it dies, it dies without a sign
To tell how fair it was in happier hours:
It leaves behind reproaches and regrets,
And bitterness within affection's well.
For which there is no healing.

THE FAITH OF LOVE.

Thou hast watched beside the bed of death,
 O fearless human love!
Thy lip received the last faint breath,
 Ere the spirit fled above.

Thy prayer was heard by the parting bier,
 In a low and farewell tone,
Thou hast given the grave both flower and tear.
 —O Love! thy task is done.

Then turn thee from each pleasant spot,
 Where thou wert wont to rove;
For there the friend of thy soul is not,
 Nor the joy of thy youth, O Love!

Thou wilt meet but mournful Memory there,
 Her dreams in the grove she weaves,
With echoes filling the summer air,
 With sighs the trembling leaves.

Then turn thee to the world again,
 From these dim haunted bowers,
And shut thine ear to the wild sweet strain
 That tells of vanished hours.

And wear not on thine aching heart
 The image of the dead,
For the tie is rent that gave thee part
 In the gladness its beauty shed:

And gaze on the pictured smile no more
 That thus can life outlast,
All between parted souls is o'er;
 —Love! Love! forget the past!

"Voice of vain boding! away, be still!
 Strive not against the faith
That yet my bosom with light can fill,
 Unquenched and undimmed by death:

"From the pictured smile I will not turn,
 Though sadly now it shine;
Nor quit the shades that in whispers mourn
 For the step once linked with mine:

"Nor shut mine ear to the song of old,
 Though its notes the pang renew,
—Such memories deep in my heart I hold,
 To keep it pure and true.

"By the holy instinct of my heart,
 By the hope that bears me on,
I have still my own undying part
 In the deep affection gone.

"By the presence that about me seems
 Through night and day to dwell,
Voice of vain bodings and fearful dreams!
 —I have breathed no *last* farewell!"

Hemans

THE BETROTHED.

Betrothed to one long worshipped and enshrined
In the veiled altars of that vestal mind,
Dreaming of years unwrecked and fate defied,
With one dear treasure ever by her side—
Pure—gentle—tender as the evening air,
When something holy blends with beauty there—
While vague and voiceless, through the light above
Moves the impassioned spirit of deep love,
The noble maiden sat! and in her ear
Came those low tones which maidens deem most dear,
And o'er her young cheeks softest beauty stole
And went, the blushes speeding from the soul;
And oft from earth all guilelessly she raised
The eye e'en Love had ne'er too wildly praised;
The eye which wooed you like a star to gaze,
And dream that worlds lay couched beneath its rays;
And as you gazed, your softening spirit drew,
As from some holy fount, *a virtue* from its hue.
Sad scenes had tempered with a pensive grace
The maiden lustre of that faultless face,
Had hung a sweet and dreamlike spell upon
The gliding music of her silver tone;
And shaded the soft soul which loved to lie
In the deep pathos of that volumed eye.
Lone—thoughtful—tender—ever from her birth,
Her heart had been too gentle for light mirth.
Such are the thrones where love too surely reigns,
And turns his slightest chaplets into chains:
To them the world of others is as naught;
They shrink from earth and banquet on sweet thought,
And passion grows their life; alas! for those
Whom rapture leaves too restless for repose,
Who bind on reeds their hopes—their joys—their all,
And idly chide the wild winds when they fall!

Oh! cast thou not
Affection from thee! In this bitter world
Hold to thy heart that only treasure fast;
Watch—guard it—suffer not a breath to dim
The bright gem's purity!

Hemans.

A WOMAN'S HEART.

That hallowed sphere, a woman's heart, contains
Empires of feeling, and the rich domains
Where Love, disporting in his sunniest hours,
Breathes his sweet incense o'er ambrosial flowers;
A woman's heart!—that gem, divinely set
In native gold—that peerless amulet,
Which firmly linked to Love's electric chain,
Connects the worlds of transport and of pain!

J. Bird.

GIVE ME BUT THY LOVE.

Give me but thy love, and I
Envy none beneath the sky;
Pains and perils I defy
 If thy presence cheer me.
Give me but thy love, my sweet!
Joy shall bless us when we meet;
Pleasures come, and cares retreat,
 When thou smilest near me.

Happy 'twere, beloved one,
When the toils of day are done,
Ever with the set of sun
 To thy fond arms retiring;—
There to feel, and there to know
A balm that baffles every wo,
While hearts that beat and eyes that glow
 Are sweetest thoughts inspiring.

What are all the joys of earth?
What are revelry and mirth?
Vacant blessings—nothing worth
 To hearts that ever knew love.
What is all the pomp of state,
What the grandeur of the great,
To the raptures that await
 On the path of true love?

Should joy our days and years illume,
How sweet with thee to share such doom!
Nor, oh! less sweet, should sorrows come,
 To cherish and caress thee;
Then, while I live, then till I die,
Oh! be thou only smiling by,
And, while I breathe, I'll fondly try
 With all my heart to bless thee!

Delta.

When the heart is full, the overflow
Of bliss, by being shared, is sweeter still.
The very flowers that in the May breeze shake,
Bloom out together; and the blessed stars
Of night, walk not the pathless heavens alone,
But twinkle, though unseen, in blissful trines
Of sympathetic light. All beauteous things
Hold mystic fellowship!

R. Montgomery.

MEET ME AT SUNSET.

Meet me at sunset, the hour we love best,
Ere day's last crimson blushes have died in the west,
When the shadowless ether is blue as thine eye,
And the breeze is as balmy and soft as thy sigh;
When giant-like forms lengthen fast o'er the ground
From the motionless mill and the linden trees round;
When the stillness below, the mild radiance above,
Softly sink on the heart and attune it to love.

Meet me at sunset—oh! meet me once more,
'Neath the wide-spreading thorn where you met me of yore,
When our hearts were as calm as the broad summer sea
That lay gleaming before us, bright, boundless, and free;
And with hand clasped in hand, we sat trance-bound, and deemed
That life would be ever the thing it then seemed.
The tree we then planted, green record! lives on,
But the hopes that grew with it are faded and gone.

Meet me at sunset, beloved! as of old,—
When the boughs of the chestnut are waving in gold;
When the pure starry clematis bends with its bloom,
And the jasmine exhales a more witching perfume.
That sweet hour shall atone for the anguish of years,
And though fortune still frown, bid us smile through our tears;
Through the storms of the future shall sooth and sustain;
Then meet me at sunset—oh! meet me again!

A. A. Watts.

LOVE'S MINSTREL LUTE.

Love's minstrel lute was once so dear
To every youthful breast,
Each maiden thronged its notes to hear,
Each swain its spells confessed!
Love rambled oft in hours of joy,
Through Pleasure's flowery way,
A gay light-hearted minstrel boy
Chanting his merry lay!

Love's minstrel lute has lost its tune,
Its sweetest lay is sung!
And passion's fervid breath hath flown,
That sighed those chords among!
A blighted flower, a broken toy,
Love's lute must now remain,
No pulse of hope, no thrill of joy,
Shall rouse its fire again!

For Reason came amid the throng
To hear the god one day
Like a chill blight the flowers among
And checked his merry lay!
His icy fingers round the boy
Threw Wealth's enslaving chain,
And Love's soft lute, that soul of joy,
Ne'er sang of bliss again!

Mrs. C. B. Wilson.

What spirit e'er so gentle shall be found.
So softly reared in humble privacy!
What form so fragile on wide earth's vast bound,
Shrinking from every blast beneath the sky,
That will not brave severest destiny,
Bear, uncomplaining, want and cruel wrong,
And look on danger with unblenching eye,
If Love hath made that gentle spirit strong?
Love, pure, approved by Heaven, leads that frail form along!

Lady Dacre.

LOVE.

Love in the soul, not bold and confident,
But like Aurora, trembles into being;
And with faint flickering, and uncertain beams,
Gives notice to the awakening world within us
Of the full blazing orb, that soon shall rise,
And kindle all its passions. Then begin
Sorrow and joy.—unutterable joy,
And rapturous sorrow. Then the world is nothing;
Pleasure is nothing; suffering is nothing;
Ambition, riches, praise, power, all are nothing;
Love rules and reigns despotic and alone!
Then, oh! the shape of magic loveliness
He conjures up before us. In her form
Is perfect symmetry. Her swan-like gait,
As she glides by us, like a lovely dream,
Seems not of earth. From her bright eye the soul
Looks out, and, like the topmost gem o' the heap,
Shows the mine's wealth within. Upon her face,
As on a lovely landscape, shade and sunlight,
Play as strong feeling sways; now her eye flashes
A beam of rapture; now lets drop a tear;
And now upon her brow, as when the rainbow
Rears its fair arch in heaven, Peace sits and gilds
The sweet drops as they fall. The soul of mind
Dwells in her voice, and her soft spiritual tones
Sink in the heart, soothing its cares away;
As Halcyon's brood upon the troubled wave
And charm it into calmness. When she weeps,
Her tears are like the waters upon which
Love's mother rose to Heaven. E'en her sighs,
Although they speak the troubles of her soul,
Breathe of its sweetness, as the wind that shakes
The cedar's boughs, becomes impregnated
With its celestial odors.

Neele

A HUSBAND TO HIS WIFE.

There is a mystic thread of life,
So dearly wreathed with mine alone,
That destiny's relentless knife
At once must sever *both* or *none*.

There is a *form* on which these eyes
Have often gazed with fond delight;
By day that form their joy supplies,
And dreams restore it through the night.

There is a *voice* whose tones inspire
Such thrills of rapture through my breast,
I would not hear a seraph choir
Unless that voice could join the rest.

There is a *face* whose blushes tell
Affection's tale upon the cheek;
But pallid at one fond farewell,
Proclaims more love than words can speak.

There is a *lip* which mine hath pressed,
And none had ever pressed before;
It vowed to make me sweetly blest,
And mine—mine only—pressed it more

There is a *bosom*—all my own—
Hath pillowed oft this aching head;
A *mouth* which smiles on me alone,
An *eye* whose tears with mine are shed.

There are two *hearts* whose movements thrill
In unison so closely sweet;
That pulse to pulse responsive still,
They both must heave—or cease to beat.

There are two *souls* whose equal flow,
In gentle streams so calmly run,
That when they part—*they part!*—ah, no!
They can not part—*those souls are one!*

Byron.

LOVE IN ABSENCE.

Oh! my dear peerless wife!
By the blue sky and all its crowding stars
I love you better—oh! far better than
Woman was ever loved. There's not an hour
Of day or dreaming night but I am with thee:
There's not a wind but whispers of thy name,
And not a flower that sleeps beneath the moon,
But in its hues or fragrance tells a tale
Of thee, my love, to my fond anxious heart!

Barry Cornwall.

—— Love's sooner felt than seen:
Oft in a voice he creeps down through the ear;
Oft from a blushing cheek he lights his fire;
Oft shrouds his golden flame in likest hair;
Oft in a soft, smooth cheek doth close retire;
Oft in a smile, oft in a silent tear;
And if all fail, yet Virtue's self will lure!

Phineas Fletcher.

BEAUTY, WEALTH, AND LOVE.

Wealth, with golden key, once sought
To win the way to Beauty's shrine;
Many a sparkling gem he brought,
And many a diamond from the mine;
But Love, veiled in slight disguise,
Hovered round near Beauty's bower,
Lest the gems of Eastern skies
Should weigh against his power.

Wealth displayed his dazzling store,
Pearly wreaths and ruby crowns;
Beauty ran the treasures o'er,
And smiles succeeded frowns.
What could Love oppose to this?
He had but his crown of simple flowers,
That were bathed in the honeyed dew of bliss,
Culled fresh from his roseate bowers.

Then Wealth laughed out triumphantly,
As he led young Beauty's steps along,
Who turned on Love a scornful eye,
And a cold ear to his song.
Away they went—and their path was strewn
With many a rare and precious gem,
That springs up at Wealth's command alone;
All—all shone brightly for them!

But Beauty, at last, found out her mistake,
When time had broken the charm;
As the moonbeam shines on the frozen lake,
Wealth may glitter—but can not warm!
Then—too late—she remembered Love's rosy bowers,
When the spell that beguiled was o'er;
And she sighed for the fresh unfading flowers
That could blossom for *her*—no more!

Mrs. C. B. Wilson.

Oh! where is there the heart but knows
Love's first steps are upon the rose?
The first, the very first; oh! none
Can feel again as they have done;
In love, in war, in pride, in all
The planets of life's coronal,
However beautiful and bright,
What can be like their first sweet light?

Landon.

Oh! Love hath spoken to thy heart.
(That Love should *ever* speak in vain,
When, like the aloe that has bloomed,
It never blooms again!)
Love, covered all with rose-like flowers,
A fragrant, but an *early* thing,
The spirit's almond-tree that buds
And blossoms in its spring.

J. K. Hervey.

Lady! sweet maid, with flowing auburn hair,
Lips like twin cherries, eyes of heavenly blue,
And blooming cheek, tinctured with Health's own hue,
Such as in Spring the apple-blossoms wear;
Cheerful as Morn, and innocent as fair!
Accept this Garland, for it is thy due:
Thou didst direct me oft where hidden grew
Love's fairest plants, of scent and beauty rare,
And warn me oft against a noxious flower,
Of color bright, and tempting to the eye,
But all unfit in Beauty's breast to lie,
To wreath her brow, or deck her latticed bower:
Uncropped I passed such canker-blossoms by,
Wandering with thee through meads in summer hour.

A SOLEMN CONCEIT.

Doth Love live in Beauty's eyes?
Why, then, are they so unloving?
Patience in her passion proving
There his sorrow chiefly lies.

Lives belief in lovers' hearts?
Why, then, are they unbelieving?
Hourly so the spirit grieving
With a thousand jealous smarts.

Is there pleasure in love's passion?
Why, then, is it so unpleasing,
Heart and spirit both diseasing,
Where the wits are out of fashion?

No: Love sees in Beauty's eyes
He hath only lost his seeing,
Where, in Sorrow's only being
All his comfort wholly dies:

Fain within the heart of love,
Fearful of the thing it hath,
Treading of a trembling path,
Doth but jealousy approve.

In Love's passion, then, what pleasure,
Which is but a lunacy,
Where grief, fear, and jealousy,
Plague the senses out of measure?

Farewell, then, unkindly fancy,
In thy courses all too cruel:
Wo the price of such a jewel
As turns reason to a phrensy!

N. Breton

AN ODE.

Now each creature joys the other,
Passing happy days and hours;
One bird reports unto another,
In the fall of silver showers;
Whilst the Earth, our common mother,
Hath her bosom decked with flowers.

Whilst the greatest torch of heaven
With bright ray warms Flora's lap,
Making nights and days both even,
Cheering plants with fresher sap;
My field of flowers, quite bereaven,
Wants refresh of better hap.

Echo, daughter of the air,
Babbling guest of rocks and hills,
Knows the name of my fierce fair,
And sounds the accents of my ills:
Each thing pities my despair,
Whilst that she her lover kills.

Whilst that she, O cruel maid!
Doth me and my love despise,
My life's flourish is decayed,
That depended on her eyes;
But her will must be obeyed,
And well he ends for love who dies.

Samuel Daniel.

SONNET.

I must not grieve my love, whose eyes would read
Lines of delight whereon her youth might smile;
Flowers have a time before they come to seed,
And she is young, and now must sport the while.
And sport, sweet maid, in season of these years,
And learn to gather flowers before they wither,
And where the sweetest blossom first appears,
Let love and youth conduct thy pleasures thither.
Lighten forth smiles to clear the clouded air,
And calm the tempest which my sighs do raise;
Pity and smiles do best become the fair;
Pity and smiles must only yield thee praise.
Make me to say, when all my griefs are gone,
Happy the heart that sighed for such a one!

Samuel Daniel.

OF LINGERINGE LOVE.

In lingeringe love mislikinge growes,
Wherby our fancies ebbs and flowes;
We love to day, and hate to morne,
And dayly when we list to scorne.
Take heed, therefore,
If she mislike, then love no more:
Quick speed makes waste;
Love is not gotten in such haste.

The suit is colde that soone is done;
The fort is feeble, easily wonne;
The hawk that soon comes by her prey,
May take a toy and soar away.
Mark what means this;
Some thinke to hit, and yet they miss:
First creepe, then goe;
Me thinke our love is handled soe.

For lacke of bellowes the fire goes out;
Some say the nighest way is about:
Few things are had without some suit;
The tree at first will bear no fruit.
Serve long, hope well,
Loe here is all that I can tell:
Time tries out troth,
And troth is liked wherere it go'th.

Some thinke all theirs that they do seeke;
Some wantons woo but for a weeke;
Some woo to shew their subtle wits,
Such palfreys play upon their bits.
Fine heads, God knows,
That plucke a nettle for a rose!
They meet their match,
And fare the worse because they snatch.

We silly women can not rest
For men that love to woo in jest;
Some lay their baite in ev'ry nooke,
And ev'ry fish doth spie their hooke.
Ill ware, good cheape,*
Which makes us looke before we leape;
Craft can cloke much;
God save all simple souls from such!

Though lingeringe love be lost some while,
Yet lingeringe lovers laugh and smile;
Who will not linger for a day,
To banish hope, and hop away?
Love must be plied;
Who thinkes to sayle must wait the tide.
Thus ends his dance:
God send all lingerers happie chance!

ANONYMOUS.

MY MISTRESS' FACE.

And would you see my mistress' face?
It is a flow'ry garden place,
Where knots of beauty have such grace,
That all is work, and no where space.

It is a sweet delicious morn,
Where day is breeding never born;
It is a meadow yet unshorn,
Which thousand flowers do adorn.

It is the heaven's bright reflex,
Weak to dazzle and to vex;
It is the Idæa of her sex,
Envy of whom doth world perplex.

It is a face of death that smiles,
Pleasing, though it kills the whiles;
Where Death and Love, in pretty wiles,
Each other mutually beguiles.

It is fair Beauty's freshest youth;
It is the feigned Elysium's truth;
The spring that wintered hearts renew'th,
And this is that my soul pursu'th.

THOMAS CAMPION.

* Bargain.

SIGH NO MORE.

Sigh no more, ladies, sigh no more;
Men were deceivers ever;
One foot in sea, and one on shore,
To one thing constant never:
Then sigh not so,
But let them go,
And be you blithe and bonny:
Converting all your sounds of wo
Into, hey! nonny, nonny.

Sing no more ditties, sing no mo
Of dumps so dull and heavy;
The fraud of men was ever so,
Since summer first was leavy:
Then sigh not so,
But let them go,
And be you blithe and bonny;
Converting all your sounds of wo
Into, hey! nonny, nonny.

SHAKSPERE.

CONQUEST BY FLIGHT.

Ladies, fly from Love's smooth tale!
Oaths steeped in tears do oft prevail;
Grief is infectious, and the air
Inflamed with sighs will blast the fair!
Then stop your ears when lovers cry,
Lest yourself weep, when no soft eye
Shall with a sorrowing tear repay
That pity which you cast away.

Young men, fly, when Beauty darts
Amorous glances at your hearts!
The fixed mark gives the shooter aim,
And ladies' looks have power to maim;
Now 'twixt their lips, now in their eyes,
Wrapped in a smile, or kiss, Love lies.
Then fly betimes; for only they
Conquer Love that run away.

THOMAS CAREW

THE PRIMROSE.

Ask me why I send you here,
This firstling of the infant year;
Ask me why I send to you
This primrose all bepearled with dew;
I straight will whisper in your ears,
The sweets of love are washed with tears:
Ask me why this flower doth show
So yellow, green, and sickly too;
Ask me why the stalk is weak,
And bending, yet it doth not break;
I must tell you, these discover
What doubts and fears are in a lover.

THOMAS CAREW.

LOVE IS A SICKNESS.

Love is a sickness full of woes,
All remedies refusing;
A plant that with most cutting grows;
Most barren with best using:
Why so?
More we enjoy it, more it dies;
If not enjoyed, it sighing cries,
Hey, ho!

Love is a torment of the mind,
A tempest everlasting;
And Jove hath made it of a kind
Not well, nor full, nor fasting:
Why so?
More we enjoy it, more it dies
If not enjoyed, it sighing cries,
Hey, ho!

SAMUEL DANIEL.

DRINK TO ME ONLY WITH THINE EYES.

DRINK to me only with thine eyes,
And I will pledge with mine;
Or leave a kiss but in the cup,
And I'll not look for wine.
The thirst that from the soul doth rise
Doth ask a drink divine;
But might I of Jove's nectar sup,
I would not change for thine.

I sent thee late a rosy wreath,
Not so much honoring thee,
As giving it a hope that there
It could not withered be;
But thou thereon didst only breathe,
And sent'st it back to me;
Since when it grows and smells, I swear,
Not of itself, but thee.

BEN JONSON.

POWER OF LOVE.

LET those complain that feel Love's cruelty,
And in sad legends write their woes:
With roses gently he has corrected me;
My war is without rage or blows;
My mistress' eyes shine fair on my desires,
A hope springs up inflamed with her new fires.

No more an exile will I dwell,
With folded arms and sighs all day,
Reckoning the torments of my hell,
And flinging my sweet joys away.
I am called home again to quiet peace;
My mistress smiles, and all my sorrows cease.

Yet what is living in her eye,
Or being blessed with her sweet tongue,
If these no other joys imply?
A golden gyve,* a pleasing wrong.
To be your own but one poor month, I'd give
My youth, my fortune, and then leave to live.

BEAUMONT AND FLETCHER.

LOVE HATH NO PHYSICIAN.

A RESTLESS lover I espied,
That went from place to place;
Lay down and turned from side to side,
And sometimes on his face;
And when that med'cines were applied,
In hope of intermission,
As one that felt no ease, he cried,
"Hath Cupid no physician?"

What do the ladies with their looks,
Their kisses, and their smiles?
Can no receipts in those fair books
Repair their former spoils?
But they complain as well as we,
Their pains have no remission;
And when both sexes wounded be,
"Hath Cupid no physician?"

Have we such palsies and such pains,
Such fevers and such fits,
No quintessential chymic grains,
No Æsculapian wits,
No creature can beneath the sun
Prevail in opposition?
And when all wonders can be done,
"Hath Cupid no physician?"

Into what poison do they dip
Their arrows and their darts,
That, touching but an eye or lip,
The pain goes to our hearts?
But now I see, before I get
Into their inquisition,
That Death had never surgeon yet,
Nor Cupid a physician.

EARL OF PEMBROKE.

* A fetter.

LOVE IN THE COUNTRY.

DEAR, leave thy home and come with me
That scorn the world for love of thee:
Here we will live, within this park,
A court of joy and pleasure's ark.

Here we will hunt, here we will range;
Constant in love, our sports we'll change;
Of hearts, if any change we make,
I will have thine, thou mine shalt take.

Here we will walk upon the lawns,
And see the tripping of the fawns;
And all the deer shall wait on thee,
Thou shalt command both them and me.

The leaves a whisp'ring noise shall make,
Their music-notes the birds shall wake;
And while thou art in quiet sleep,
Through the green wood shall silence keep.

And while my herds about thee feed,
Love's lessons in thy face I'll read,
And feed upon thy lovely look,
For beauty hath no fairer book.

It's not the weather, nor the air.
It is thyself, that is so fair;
Nor doth it rain when heaven lowers,
But when you frown, then fall the showers.

One sun alone moves in the sky—
Two suns thou hast, one in each eye;
Only by day that sun gives light—
Where thine doth rise there is no night.

Fair starry twins scorn not to shine
Upon my lambs, upon my kine;
My grass doth grow, my corn and wheat,
My fruit, my vines, thrive by their heat.

Thou shalt have wool, thou shalt have silk,
Thou shalt have honey, wine, and milk;
Thou shalt have all, for all is due
Where thoughts are free and love is true.

EARL OF PEMBROKE.

INCONSTANCY OF LOVE.

So glides along a wanton brook
With gentle pace into the main;
Courting the banks with amorous look
He never means to see again:
And so does Fortune use to smile
Upon the short-lived fav'rite's face,
Whose swelling hopes she does beguile,
And always casts him in the race:
And so doth the fantastic boy,
The god of the ill-managed flames,
Who ne'er kept word in promised joy
To lover nor to loving dames:
So all alike will constant prove,
Both Fortune, running streams, and Love.

EARL OF PEMBROKE.

STILL TO BE NEAT, STILL TO BE DREST.

STILL to be neat, still be drest
As you were going to a feast;
Still to be powdered, still perfumed:
Lady, it is to be presumed,
Though art's hid causes are not found,
All is not sweet, all is not sound.

Give me a look, give me a face,
That makes simplicity a grace;
Robes loosely flowing, hair as free;
Such sweet neglect more taketh me
Than all th' adulteries of art:
They strike mine eyes, but not my heart.

BEN JONSON.

TELL ME, DEAREST, WHAT IS LOVE?

Tell me dearest, what is love?
"'Tis a lightning from above;
'Tis an arrow, 'tis a fire;
'Tis a boy they call Desire;
'Tis a grave
Gapes to have
Those poor fools that long to prove."

Tell me more, are women true?
"Yes, some are, and some as you.
Some are willing, some are strange,
Since you men first taught to change;
And till troth
Be in both,
All shall love, to love anew."

Tell me more yet, can they grieve?
"Yes, and sicken sore, but live,
And be wise, and delay,
When you men are as wise as they."
Then I see
Faith will be
Never, till they both believe.

Beaumont and Fletcher.

TO THE VIRGINS, TO MAKE MUCH OF TIME.

Gather ye rose-buds while ye may,
Old Time is still a flying;
And this same flower that smiles to-day,
To-morrow will be dying.

The glorious lamp of heaven, the Sun,
The higher he's a getting,
The sooner will his race be run,
And nearer he's to setting.

That age is best, which is the first,
When youth and blood are warmer;
But being spent, the worse and worst
Times still succeed the former.

Then be not coy, but use your time,
And while ye may, go marry;
For having lost but once your prime,
You may for ever tarry.

Robert Herrick.

THE BLEEDING HAND.

From this bleeding hand of mine,
Take this sprig of Eglantine,
Which, though sweet unto your smell,
Yet the fretful brier will tell,
He who plucks the sweets, shall prove
Many thorns to be in love.

Robert Herrick.

TO THE WILLOW-TREE.

Thou art to all lost love the best,
The only true plant found,
Wherewith young men and maids distrest,
And left off love, are crowned.

When once the lover's rose is dead,
Or laid aside forlorn,
Then willow-garlands, 'bout the head,
Bedewed with tears are worn.

When with neglect, the lover's bane,
Poor maids rewarded be,
For their lost love, their only gain
Is but a wreath from thee.

And underneath thy cooling shade,
When weary of the light,
The love-spent youth, and love-sick maid,
Come to weep out the night.

Robert Herrick.

THE ROSE.

Go, lovely rose!
Tell her that wastes her time and me,
That now she knows,
When I resemble her to thee,
How sweet and fair she seems to be.

Tell her that 's young,
And shuns to have her graces spied,
That, hadst thou sprung
In deserts where no men abide,
Thou must have uncommended died.

Small is the worth
Of beauty from the light retired;
Bid her come forth,
Suffer herself to be desired,
And not blush so to be admired.

Then, die; that she
The common fate of all things rare
May read in thee;
How small a part of time they share,
That are so wondrous sweet and fair.

Edmund Waller.

A DIALOGUE BETWEEN A NYMPH AND A SHEPHERD.

Why sigh you, swain? this passion is not common;
Is 't for your kids or lambkins?—"For a woman."
How fair is she that on so sage a brow
Prints lowering looks?—"Just such a toy as thou."
Is she a maid?—"What man can answer that?"
Or widow?—"No."—What then?—"I know not what.
Saint-like she looks; a siren if she sing;
Her eyes are stars; her mind is everything."
If she be fickle, shepherd, leave to woo,
Or fancy me.—"No: thou art woman too."
But I am constant.—"Then thou art not fair."
Bright as the morning!—"Wavering as air!"
What grows upon this cheek?—"A pure carnation."
Come taste a kiss.—"O sweet, O sweet temptation!'

BOTH.

Ah, Love, and canst thou never lose the field?
Where Cupid lays the siege, the town must yield;
He warms the chilly blood with glowing fire,
And thaws the icy frost of cold desire.

Thomas Randolph.

THE KISS.—A DIALOGUE.

1. Among thy fancies tell me this,
What is the thing we call a kiss?
2. I shall resolve ye what it is.

It is a creature born and bred
Between the lips, all cherry-red,
By love and warm desires fed
Chor. And makes more soft the bridal bed.

2. It is an active flame, that flies,
First to the babies of the eyes,
And charms them there with lullabies,
Chor. And stills the bride too when she cries.

2. Then to the chin, the cheek, the ear,
It frisks and flies, now here, now there;
'Tis now far off, and then 'tis near,
Chor. And here, and there, and everywhere.

1. Has it a speaking virtue? 2. Yes.
1. How speaks it, say? 2. Do you but this,
Part your joined lips, then speaks your kiss;
Chor. And this Love's sweetest language is.

1. Has it a body? 2. Ay, and wings,
With thousand rare encolorings;
And as it flies, it gently sings,
Chor. Love honey yields, but never stings.

Robert Herrick.

A WEDDING.

I TELL thee, Dick, where I have been,
Where I the rarest things have seen;
Oh! things without compare!
Such sights again can not be found
In any place on English ground,
Be it at wake or fair.

At Charing-cross, hard by the way
Where we (thou knowest) do sell our hay,
There is a house with stairs;
And there did I see coming down
Such folk as are not in our town,
Forty at least, in pairs.

Amongst the rest, one pestilent fine
(His beard no bigger, though, than thine)
Walked on before the rest:
Our landlord looks like nothing to him;
The king, (God bless him!) 'twould undo him,
Should he go still so drest.

At course-a-park, without all doubt,
He should have first been taken out
By all the maids i'th' town;
Though lusto Roger there had been,
Or little George upon the green,
Or Vincent of the Crown.

But, wot you what? the youth was going
To make an end of all his wooing;
The parson for him staid;
Yet, by his leave, for all his haste.
He did not so much wish all past,
Perchance, as did the maid.

The maid (and thereby hangs a tale;
For such a maid no Whitsun ale
Could ever yet produce)—
No grape that's kindly ripe could be
So round, so plump, so soft as she,
Nor half so full of juice.

Her finger was so small, the ring
Would not stay on which they did bring,
It was too wide a peck:
And to say truth, for out it must,
It looked like the great collar, just,
About our young colt's neck.

Her feet beneath her petticoat,
Like little mice, stole in and out,
As if they feared the light:
But, oh! she dances such a way—
No sun upon an Easter day
Is half so fine a sight!

• • • • • •

Her cheeks so rare a white was on,
No daisy makes comparison,
(Who sees them is undone;)
For streaks of red were mingled there,
Such as are on a Catherine pear,
(The side that 's next the sun.)

Her lips were red, and one was thin,
Compared to that was next her chin,
(Some bee had stung it newly);
But, Dick, her eyes so guard her face,
I durst no more upon them gaze
Than on the sun in July.

Her mouth so small when she does speak,
Thou 'dst swear her teeth her words did break,
That they might passage get;
But she so handled still the matter,
They came as good as ours, or better,
And are not spent a whit.

• • • • • •

Passion o' me! how I run on!
There's that that would be thought upon,
I trow, besides the bride;
The business of the kitchen's great,
For it is fit that men should eat
Nor was it there denied.

Just in the nick, the cook knocked thrice,
And all the waiters in a trice
His summons did obey:
Each serving man, with dish in hand,
Marched boldly up, like our trained band,
Presented, and away.

When all the meat was on the table,
What man of knife or teeth was able
To stay to be entreated?
And this the very reason was,
Before the parson could say grace,
The company was seated.

Now hats fly off, and youths carouse,
Healths first go round, and then the house.
The bride's came thick and thick;
And when 'twas named another's health,
Perhaps he made it hers by stealth;
(And who could help it, Dick?)

O' th' sudden up they rise and dance;
Then sit again, and sigh, and glance;
Then dance again and kiss:
Thus several ways the time did pass,
Till every woman wished her place,
And every man wished his.

By this time all were stolen aside
To counsel and undress the bride;—
But that he must not know:—
But yet 'twas thought he guessed her mind,
And did not mean to stay behind
Above an hour or so.

When in he came, Dick, there she lay,
Like new-fallen snow melting away:
('Twas time, I trow, to part.)
Kisses were now the only stay,
Which soon she gave, as who would say,
"Good-by! with all my heart."

But just as heavens would have, to cross it,
In came the bride-maids with the posset;
The bridegroom ate in spite;
For had he left the women to 't,
It would have cost two hours to do 't,
Which were too much that night.

• • • • • •

SIR JOHN SUCKLING.

THE CHANGE.

LOVE in her sunny eyes does basking play;
Love walks the pleasant mazes of her hair;
Love does on both her lips for ever stay,
And sows and reaps a thousand kisses there:
In all her outward parts Love's always seen;
But, oh! he never went within.

Within, Love's foes, his greatest foes, abide,
Malice, Inconstancy, and Pride:
So the earth's face, trees, herbs, and flowers, do dress,
With other beauties numberless;
But at the centre darkness is, and hell;
There wicked spirits, and there the damned, dwell.

With me, alas! quite contrary it fares;
Darkness and death lie in my weeping eyes,
Despair, and paleness, in my face appears,
And grief, and fear, Love's greatest enemies;
But, like the Persian tyrant, Love within
Keeps his proud court, and ne'er is seen.

Oh! take my heart, and by that means you'll prove
Within too stored enough of love:
Give me but yours, I'll by that change so thrive,
That love in all my parts shall live.
So powerful is this change, it render can
My outside Woman, and your inside Man.

ABRAHAM COWLEY

TO. B. R., IN RETURN FOR HER BRACELET.

'Tis not, dear love, that amber twist,
Which circles round my captive wrist,
Can have the power to make me more
Your prisoner than I was before;
Though I that bracelet dearer hold
Than misers would a chain of gold;
Yet this but ties my outward part,—
Heart-strings alone can tie my heart.

'Tis not that soft and silken wreath.
Your hands did unto mine bequeath,
Can bind with half so powerful charms
As the embraces of your arms;
Although not iron bands, my fair,
Can bind more fiercely than your hair:
Yet what will chain me most will be,
Your heart in true-love's knot to me.

'Tis not those beams, your hairs, nor all
Your glorious outside doth me thrall,—
Although your looks have force enow,
To make the stateliest tyrants bow,
Nor any angel could deny
Your person his idolatry,—
Yet I do not so much adore
The temple, but the goddess more.

If, then, my soul you would confine
To prison, tie your heart to mine;
Your noble virtues, constant love,
The only powerful chains will prove
To bind me ever: such as those
The hands of death shall ne'er unloose.
Until I such a prisoner be,
No liberty can make me free.

From "Wit Restored."

TO ALTHEA, FROM PRISON.

When Love, with unconfined wings,
 Hovers within my gates,
And my divine Althea brings
 To whisper at the grates;
When I lie tangled in her hair,
 And fettered to her eye,—
The birds, that wanton in the air,
 Know no such liberty.

When flowing cups run swiftly round,
 With no allaying Thames,
Our careless heads with roses bound,
 Our hearts with loyal flames;
When thirsty grief in wine we steep,
 When healths and draughts go free,—
Fishes, that tipple in the deep,
 Know no such liberty.

When, like committed linnets, I
 With shriller throat shall sing
The sweetness, mercy, majesty,
 And glories of my king;
When I shall voice aloud how good
 He is, how great should be,—
Enlarged winds, that curl the flood,
 Know no such liberty.

Stone walls do not a prison make,
 Nor iron bars a cage;
Minds innocent and quiet take
 That for an hermitage.
If I have freedom in my love,
 And in my soul am free,—
Angels alone, that soar above,
 Enjoy such liberty.

Richard Lovelace.

ON A GIRDLE.

That which her slender waist confined
Shall now my joyful temples bind:
No monarch but would give his crown,
His arms might do what this has done.

It was my heaven's extremest sphere,
The pale that held that lovely deer:
My joy, my grief, my hope, my love,
Did all within this circle move.

A narrow compass! and yet there
Dwelt all that 's good, and all that 's fair:
Give me but what this riband bound,
Take all the rest the sun goes round.

Edmund Waller.

FOND LOVER.

Why so pale and wan, fond lover?
 Prithee, why so pale?
Will, when looking well can't move her,
 Looking ill prevail?
 Prithee, why so pale?

Why so dull and mute, young sinner?
 Prithee, why so mute?
Will, when speaking well can't win her,
 Saying nothing do't?
 Prithee, why so mute?

Quit, quit for shame; this will not move
 This can not take her:
If of herself she will not love,
 Nothing can make her.
 The devil take her?

Sir John Suckling.

TO AMORET.

Amoret, the milky way,
 Framed of many nameless stars!
The smooth stream, where none can say
 He this drop to that prefers!

Amoret, my lovely foe!
 Tell me where thy strength does lie?
Where the power that charms us so?
 In thy soul, or in thy eye?

By that snowy neck alone,
 Or thy grace in motion seen,
No such wonders could be done;
 Yet thy waist is straight and clean
As Cupid's shaft, or Hermes' rod,
And powerful too as either god.

Edmund Waller.

TO A FAIR YOUNG LADY GOING OUT OF THE TOWN IN THE SPRING.

Ask not the cause why sullen spring
 So long delays her flowers to bear;
Why warbling birds forget to sing,
 And winter-storms invert the year:
Chloris is gone, and Fate provides
To make it spring where she resides.

Chloris is gone, the cruel fair!
 She cast not back a pitying eye;
But left her lover in despair,
 To sigh, to languish, and to die:
Ah, how, can those fair eyes endure
To give the wounds they will not cure!

Great God of Love! why hast thou made
 A face that can all hearts command,
That all religions can invade,
 And change the laws of every land?
Where thou hadst placed such power before,
Thou shouldst have made her mercy more.

When Chloris to the temple comes,
 Adoring crowds before her fall;
She can restore the dead from tombs,
 And every life but mine recall.
I only am by love designed
To be the victim of mankind.

John Dryden.

THE ENRAPTURED LOVER.

When I lie burning in thine eye,
Or freezing in thy breast,
What martyrs in wished flames that die,
Are half so pleased or blest?

When thy soft accents through mine ear
Into my soul do fly,
What angel would not quit his sphere
To hear such harmony?

Or when the kiss thou gavest me last,
My soul stole in its breath.
What life would sooner be embraced,
Than so desired a death?

Then think no freedom I desire,
Or would my fetters leave;
Since, Phœnix-like, I from this fire
Both life and youth receive.

THOMAS STANLEY.

SPEAKING AND KISSING.

The air which thy smooth voice doth break,
Into my soul like lightning flies;
My life retires while thou dost speak,
And thy soft breath its room supplies.

Lost in this pleasing ecstacy,
I join my trembling lips to thine,
And back receive that life from thee
Which I so gladly did resign.

Forbear, Platonic fools, t' inquire
What numbers do the soul compose;
No harmony can life inspire,
But that which from these accents flows.

THOMAS STANLEY.

THE RESOLVE.

I pray thee let my heart alone,
Since now 'tis raised above thee;
Not all the beauty thou didst own,
Again can make me love thee.

He that was shipwrecked once before
By such a siren's call,
And yet neglects to shun that shore,
Deserves his second fall.

Each fluttering kiss, each tempting smile,
Which thou in vain bestows,
Some other lover might beguile,
Who not thy falsehood knows.

But I am proof against all art;
No vows shall e'er persuade me
Twice to present a wounded heart
To her that hath betrayed me.

Could I again be brought to love
Thy form, though more divine,
I might thy scorn as justly move,
As now thou sufferest mine.

THOMAS STANLEY.

THE SUPERANNUATED LOVER.

Dead to the soft delights of love,
Spare me! O spare me, cruel boy!
Nor seek in vain that heart to move,
Which pants no more with amorous joy.

Of old, thy faithful, hardy swain,
(When smit with fair Pastora's charms),
I served thee many a long campaign,
And wide I spread thy conquering arms.

Now, mighty god! dismiss thy slave,
To feeble age let youth succeed;
Recruit among the strong and brave,
And kindly spare an invalid.

Adieu, fond hopes, fantastic cares!
Ye killing joys, ye pleasing pains!
My soul for better guests prepares;
Reason restored, and Virtue reigns.

But why, my Chloe! tell me why,
Why trickles down this silent tear?
Why do those blushes rise and die?
Why stand I mute when thou art here?

E'en sleep affords my soul no rest,
Thee bathing in the stream I view;
With thee I dance, with thee I feast,
Thee through the gloomy grove pursue.

Triumphant god of gay desires!
Thy vassal's raging pains remove;
I burn, I burn, with fiercer fires,
Oh! take my life, or crown my love!

WILLIAM SOMERVILLE.

THE RELAPSE.

Oh, turn away those cruel eyes,
The stars of my undoing!
Or death in such a bright disguise,
May tempt a second wooing.

Punish their blindly impious pride
Who dare contemn thy glory:
It was my fall that deified
Thy name, and sealed thy story.

Yet no new sufferings can prepare
A higher praise to crown thee;
Though my first death proclaim thee fair,
My second will unthrone thee.

Lovers will doubt thou canst entice
No other for thy fuel;
And, if thou burn one victim twice,
Both think thee poor and cruel.

THOMAS STANLEY.

FAIR, SWEET, AND YOUNG, RECEIVE A PRIZE.

Fair, sweet, and young, receive a prize
Reserved for your victorious eyes:
From crowds, whom at your feet you see,
O pity and distinguish me!
As I, from thousand beauties more,
Distinguish you, and only you adore.

Your face for conquest was designed;
Your every motion charms my mind;
Angels, when you your silence break,
Forget their hymns to hear you speak;
But when, at once, they hear and view,
Are loath to mount, and long to stay with you.

No graces can your form improve,
But all are lost unless you love;
While that sweet passion you disdain,
Your veil and beauty are in vain:
In pity then prevent my fate,
For after dying all reprieve's too late.

JOHN DRYDEN.

AMATORY LINES.

With beauty, with pleasure surrounded, to languish—
To weep, without knowing the cause of his anguish:
To start from short slumbers, and wish for the morning;
To close my dull eyes when I see it returning;
Sighs sudden and frequent, looks ever dejected,
Words that steal from my tongue, but no meaning connected!
Ah, say, fellow swains, how these symptoms befell me?
They smile, but reply not—sure Delia can tell me!

THOMAS GRAY

HOW SWEET IT IS TO LOVE.

Ah, how sweet it is to love!
Ah, how gay is young Desire!
And what pleasing pains we prove
When we first approach Love's fire!
Pains of love be sweeter far
Than all other pleasures are.

Sighs which are from lovers blown
Do but gently heave the heart:
E'en the tears they shed alone
Cure like trickling balm their smart.
Lovers, when they lose their breath,
Bleed away in easy death.

Love and Time with reverence use!
Treat them like a parting friend:
Nor the golden gifts refuse
Which in youth sincere they send:
For each year their price is more,
And they less simple than before.

Love, like spring-tides full and high,
Swells in every youthful vein:
But each tide does less supply,
Till they quite shrink in again;
If a flow in age appear,
'Tis but rain, and runs not clear.

John Dryden.

INDIFFERENCE EXCUSED.

Love, when 'tis true, needs not the aid
Of sigh, nor oaths, to make it known:
And to convince the cruel'st maid,
Lovers should use their love alone.

Into their very looks 'twill steal,
And he that most would hide his flame
Does in that case his pain reveal:
Silence itself can love proclaim.

This, my Aurelia, made me shun
The paths that common lovers tread,
Whose guilty passions are begun,
Not in their heart, but in their head.

I could not sigh, and with crossed arms
Accuse your rigor, and my fate;
Nor tax your beauty with such charms
As men adore, and women hate;

But careless loved, and without art,
Knowing my love you must have spied;
And thinking it a foolish part
To set to show what none can hide.

Sir Charles Sedley.

EVENING ODE.—TO STELLA.

Evening now from purple wings
Sheds the grateful gifts she brings;
Brilliant drops bedeck the mead.
Cooling breezes shake the reed;
Shake the reed, and curl the stream
Silvered o'er with Cynthia's beam;
Near the chequered, lonely grove,
Hears and keeps thy secrets, Love!
Stella, thither let us stray,
Lightly o'er the dewy way.
Phœbus drives his burning car,
Hence, my lovely Stella, far;
In his stead the queen of night
Round us pours a lambent light:
Light that seems but just to show
Breasts that beat, and cheeks that glow;
Let us now, in whispered joy,
Evening's silent hours employ;
Silence best, the conscious shades,
Please the hearts that love invades;
Other pleasures give them pain,
Lovers all but love disdain.

Samuel Johnson.

I SAID TO MY HEART.

I said to my heart, between sleeping and waking,
"Thou wild thing, that always art leaping or aching,
What black, brown, or fair, in what clime, in what nation,
By turns has not taught thee a pit-a-patation?"

Thus accused, the wild thing gave this sober reply:—
"See, the heart without motion, though Celia pass by!
Not the beauty she has, not the wit that she borrows,
Give the eye any joys, or the heart any sorrows.

"When our Sappho appears—she, whose wit so refined,
I am forced to applaud with the rest of mankind—
Whatever she says is with spirit and fire;
Every word I attend, but I only admire.

"Prudentia as vainly would put in her claim,
Ever gazing on heaven, though man is her aim:
'Tis love, not devotion, that turns up her eyes—
Those stars of this world are too good for the skies.

"But Chloe so lively, so easy, so fair,
Her wit so genteel, without art, without care
When she comes in my way—the motion, the pain,
The leapings, the achings, return all again."

O wonderful creature! a woman of reason!
Never grave out of pride, never gay out of season;
When so easy to guess who this angel should be,
Would one think Mrs. Howard ne'er dreamt it was she?

Earl of Peterborough.

THE DISSEMBLERS.

The merchant, to secure his treasure,
Conveys it in a borrowed name;
Euphelia serves to grace my measure,
But Chloe is my real flame.

My softest verse, my darling lyre,
Upon Euphelia's toilet lay,
When Chloe noted her desire
That I should sing, that I should play.

My lyre I tune, my voice I raise,
But with my numbers mix my sighs;
And while I sing Euphelia's praise,
I fix my soul on Chloe's eyes.

Fair Chloe blushed; Euphelia frowned:
I sung and gazed; I played and trembled:
And Venus, to the Loves around,
Remarked how ill we all dissembled.

Matthew Prior

'TWAS WHEN THE SEAS WERE ROARING.

'Twas when the seas were roaring
With hollow blasts of wind,
A damsel lay deploring,
All on a rock reclined:
Wide o'er the foaming billows
She cast a wistful look;
Her head was crowned with willows,
That trembled o'er the brook.

"Twelve months are gone and over,
And nine long tedious days;
Why didst thou, venturous lover,
Why didst thou trust the seas?
Cease, cease, thou cruel ocean,
And let a lover rest:
Ah! what's thy troubled motion
To that within my breast?

"The merchant, robbed of pleasure,
Views tempests in despair;
But what's the loss of treasure
To losing of my dear?
Should you some coast be laid on,
Where gold and diamonds grow,
You may find some richer maiden,
But none that loves you so.

"How can they say that Nature
Has nothing made in vain?
Why, then, beneath the water
Do hideous rocks remain?
No eyes those rocks discover,
That lurk beneath the deep,
To wreck the wandering lover,
And leave the maid to weep."

All melancholy lying,
Thus wailed she for her dear,
Repaid each blast with sighing,
Each billow with a tear;
When o'er the white waves stooping,
His floating corpse she spied;
Then, like a lily drooping,
She bowed her head, and died.

JOHN GAY.

CHLOE HUNTING.

WHILE thousands court fair Chloe's love,
She fears the dangerous joy,
But Cynthia-like, frequents the grove,
As lovely and as coy.

With the same speed she seeks the hind,
Or hunts the flying hare;
She leaves pursuing swains behind,
To languish and despair.

Oh, strange caprice in thy dear breast,
Whence first this whim began;
To follow thus each worthless beast,
And shun their sovereign, man!

Consider, fair, what 'tis you do,
How thus they both must die;
Not surer they, when you pursue,
Than we, whene'er you fly.

SOAME JENYNS.

ON PLATONIC LOVE.

PLATONIC Love! a pretty name
For that romantic fire,
When souls confess a mutual flame
Devoid of loose desire.

If this new doctrine once prove true,
I own it something odd is,
That lovers should each other view
As if they wanted bodies.

If spirits thus can live embraced,
The union may be lasting:
But, faith! 'tis hard the mind should feast,
And keep its partner fasting.

"Nature," says Horace, "is in tears,
When her just claim's denied her;"
And this Platonic love appears,
To be a scrimp provider.

• • • • • •

SAMUEL BOYSE.

UNLESS WITH MY AMANDA BLESSED.

UNLESS with my Amanda blessed,
In vain I twine the woodbine bower;
Unless to deck her sweeter breast,
In vain I rear the breathing flower.

Awakened by the genial year,
In vain the birds around me sing;
In vain the freshening fields appear:
Without my love there is no spring.

JAMES THOMSON.

THE SHAPE ALONE LET OTHERS PRIZE.

THE shape alone let others prize,
The features of the fair;
I look for spirit in her eyes,
And meaning in her air.

A damask cheek, an ivory arm,
Shall ne'er my wishes win;
Give me an animated form
That speaks a mind within.

A face where lawful honor shines,
Where sense and sweetness move,
And angel innocence refines
The tenderness of love.

These are the soul of Beauty's frame,
Without whose vital aid,
Unfinished all her features seem,
And all her roses dead.

But, ah! where both their charms unite,
How perfect is the view;
With every image of delight,
With graces ever new.

Of power to charm the greatest wo,
The wildest rage control,
Diffusing mildness o'er the brow,
And rapture through the soul.

Their power but faintly to express
All language must despair;
But go, behold Arpasia's face,
And read it perfect there.

MARK AKENSIDE.

FOR EVER, FORTUNE, WILT THOU PROVE.

FOR ever, Fortune, wilt thou prove
An unrelenting foe to Love,
And when we meet a mutual heart,
Come in between, and bid us part?

Bid us sigh on from day to day,
And wish, and wish the soul away;
Till youth and genial years are flown,
And all the love of life is gone?

But busy, busy still art thou,
To bind the loveless, joyless vow,
The heart from pleasure to delude,
To join the gentle to the rude.

For once, O Fortune! hear my prayer,
And I absolve thy future care;
All other blessings I resign,
Make but the dear Amanda mine.

JAMES THOMSON.

THE SCHOLAR'S RELAPSE.

By the side of a grove, at the foot of a hill,
Where whispered the beech, and where murmured the rill
I vowed to the Muses my time and my care,
Since neither could win me the smiles of my fair.

Free I ranged like the birds, like the birds free I sung,
And Delia's loved name scarce escaped from my tongue:
But if once a smooth accent delighted my ear,
I should wish, unawares, that my Delia might hear.

With fairest ideas my bosom I stored,
Allusive to none but the nymph I adored;
And the more I with study my fancy refined,
The deeper impression she made on my mind.

So long as of Nature the charms I pursue,
I still must my Delia's dear image renew;
The Graces have yielded with Delia to rove,
And the Muses are all in alliance with Love.

WILLIAM SHENSTONE.

WHEN FIRST I DARED.

When first I dared, by soft surprise,
To breathe my love in Flavia's ear
I saw the mixed sensations rise
Of trembling joy and pleasing fear;
Her cheek forgot its rosy hue,
For what has art with love to do?

But soon the crimson glow returned,
Ere half my passion was expressed
The eye that closed, the cheek that burned,
The quivering lip, the panting breast,
Showed that she wished or thought me true;
For what has art with love to do?

Ah! speak, I cried, thy soft assent:
She strove to speak, she could but sigh;
A glance, more heavenly eloquent,
Left language nothing to supply.
She pressed my hand with fervor new;
For what has art with love to do?

Ye practised nymphs, who from your charms,
By Fashion's rules, enjoy your skill;
Torment your swains with false alarms,
And, ere you cure, pretend to kill:
Still, still your sex's wiles pursue,
Such tricks she leaves to art and you.

Secure of native powers to please,
My Flavia scorns all mean pretence;
Her form is elegance and ease,
Her soul is truth and innocence;
And these, O heartfelt ecstasy!
She gives to honor, love, and me.

William Mason.

HOLYDAY GOWN.

In holyday gown, and my new-fangled hat,
Last Monday I tripped to the fair;
I held up my head, and I'll tell you for what,—
Brisk Roger I guessed would be there:
He woos me to marry whenever we meet,
There's honey sure dwells on his tongue!
He hugs me so close, and he kisses so sweet—
I'd wed—if I were not too young.

Fond Sue, I'll assure you, laid hold on the boy,
(The vixen would fain be his bride,)
Some token she claimed, either riband or toy,
And swore that she 'd not be denied:
A top-knot he bought her, and garters of green,—
Pert Susan was cruelly stung;
I hate her so much that, to kill her with spleen,
I'd wed—if I were not too young.

He whispered such soft pretty things in mine ear!
He flattered, he promised, and swore!
Such trinkets he gave me, such laces and geer,
That, trust me,—my pockets ran o'er:
Some ballads he bought me, the best he could find,
And sweetly their burden he sung;
Good faith! he's so handsome, so witty, and kind,
I'd wed—if I were not too young.

The sun was just setting, 'twas time to retire,
(Our cottage was distant a mile);
I rose to be gone—Roger bowed like a squire,
And handed me over the stile:
His arms he threw round me—love laughed in his eye;
He led me the meadows among,
There pressed me so close, I agreed, with a sigh,
To wed—for I was not too young.

John Cunningham

ADDRESS TO THE WOOD-LARK.

O, stay, sweet warbling wood-lark, stay,
Nor quit for me the trembling spray;
A hapless lover courts thy lay,
Thy soothing fond complaining.

Again, again that tender part,
That I may catch thy melting art;
For surely that wad touch her heart,
Wha kills me wi' disdaining.

Say, was thy little mate unkind,
And heard thee as the careless wind?
Oh, notch but love and sorrow joined,
Sic notes o' wae could wauken!

Thou tells o' never-ending care;
O' speechless grief, and dark despair;
For pity's sake, sweet bird, nae mair!
Or my poor heart is broken!

Robert Burns.

WHERE SHALL THE LOVER REST.

Where shall the lover rest,
Whom the fates sever
From his true maiden's breast,
Parted for ever?—
Where, through groves deep and high,
Sounds the far billow,
Where early violets die,
Under the willow.

CHORUS.

Soft shall be his pillow.

There, through the summer day,
Cool streams are laving;
There, while the tempests sway,
Scarce are boughs waving;
There, thy rest shalt thou take,
Parted for ever,
Never again to wake,
Never, O never!

CHORUS.

Never, O never!

Where shall the traitor rest,
He, the deceiver,
Who could win maiden's breast,
Ruin and leave her?—
In the lost battle,
Borne down by the flying,
Where mingles war's rattle
With groans of the dying.

CHORUS.

There shall he be lying.

Her wing shall the eagle flap
O'er the false-hearted,
His warm blood the wolf shall lap,
Ere life be parted,
Shame and dishonor sit
By his grave ever;
Blessing shall hallow it,—
Never, O never!

CHORUS.

Never, O never!

Sir Walter Scott

ON A FADED VIOLET.

The odor from the flower is gone,
Which, like thy kisses, breathed on me;
The color from the flower is flown,
Which glowed of thee, and only thee!

A shrivelled, lifeless, vacant form,
It lies on my abandoned breast,
And mocks the heart, which yet is warm,
With cold and silent rest.

I weep—my tears revive it not!
I sigh—it breathes no more on me;
Its mute and uncomplaining lot
Is such as mine should be.

Percy Bysshe Shelley

LOVE'S PHILOSOPHY.

* * * * *

See the mountains kiss high heaven,
And the waves class one another;
No sister flower would be forgiven,
If it disdained its brother:
And the sunlight clasps the earth,
And the moonbeams kiss the sea,
What are all these kissings worth,
If thou kiss not me?

Percy Bysshe Shelley.

MOURN NOT, SWEET MAID.

Mourn not, sweet maid, nor fondly try
To rob me of my sorrow;
It is the only friend that I
Have left in my captivity,
To bid my heart good-morrow.

I would not chase him from my heart,
For he is Love's own brother;
And each has learned his brother's part
So aptly, that 'tis no mean art
To know one from the other.

Thus Love will fold his arms and moan,
And sigh, and weep, like Sorrow;
And Sorrow has caught Love's soft tone,
And mixed his arrows with his own,
And learned his smile to borrow.

Only one mark of difference they
Preserve, which leaves them never;
Young Love has wings, and flies away,
While Sorrow, once received, will stay
The soul's sad guest for ever!

Henry Neele.

GO, FORGET ME.

Go, forget me—why should sorrow
O'er that brow a shadow fling?
Go, forget me—and to-morrow
Brightly smile and sweetly sing.
Smile—though I shall not be near thee:
Sing—though I shall never hear thee:
May thy soul with pleasure shine,
Lasting as the gloom of mine.

Like the sun, thy presence glowing,
Clothes the meanest things in light;
And when thou, like him, art going,
Loveliest objects fade in night.
All things looked so bright about thee,
That they nothing seem without thee;
By that pure and lucid mind
Earthly things were too refined.

Go, thou vision, wildly gleaming,
Softly on my soul that fell;
Go, for me no longer beaming—
Hope and Beauty! fare ye well!
Go, and all that once delighted
Take, and leave me all benighted—
Glory's burning generous swell,
Fancy, and the Poet's shell.

Rev. Charles Wolfe.

LOVE.

Oh, Love! what is it in this world of ours
Which makes it fatal to be loved? Ah why
With cypress branches hast thou wreathed thy bowers,
And made thy best interpreter a sigh?
As those who doat on odors pluck the flowers,
And place them on their breast—but place to die—
Thus the frail beings we would fondly cherish,
Are laid within our bosoms but to perish.

Lord Byron.

LINES TO AN INDIAN AIR.

I arise from dreams of thee
In the first sweet sleep of night,
When the winds are breathing low,
And the stars are shining bright:
I arise from dreams of thee,
And a spirit in my feet
Has led me—who knows how?
To thy chamber-window, sweet!

The wandering airs they faint
On the dark, the silent stream—
The champak odors fail
Like sweet thoughts in a dream;
The nightingale's complaint,
It dies upon her heart,
As I must on thine,
Beloved as thou art!

O lift me from the grass!
I die, I faint, I fail!
Let thy love in kisses rain
On my lips and eyelids pale.
My cheek is cold and white, alas!
My heart beats loud and fast,
Oh! press it close to thine again,
Where it will break at last.

Percy Bysshe S[illegible]ey.

STANZAS FOR MUSIC.

There be none of Beauty's daughters
With a magic like thee:
And like music on the waters
Is thy sweet voice to me:
When, as if its sound were causing
The charmed ocean's pausing,
The waves lie still and gleaming,
And the lulled winds seem dreaming.

And the midnight moon is weaving
Her bright chain o'er the deep;
Whose breast is gently heaving,
As an infant's asleep:
So the spirit bows before thee,
To listen and adore thee;
With a full but soft emotion,
Like the swell of summer's ocean.

Lo[illegible]

THE FAREWELL.

Lady! whose soft and dove-like eye,
Beaming with Love's own witchery,
Hath from our Album's pages caught
Feelings responsive to thy thought;
Sweet lady! twine no sacred ties
With Pleasure's heartless votaries!
Hide thy soul's richness! like that flower
Whose sweet aroma to no power
But the pure sunshine is revealed—
Long, long, midst leaves and moss concealed;
But, when *secure* of well-tried worth,
Then pour its hidden treasure forth:
And blend thy trusting tenderness
With man's strong, deep devotedness;
Nor turn thee with "a scornful eye,"
From faith a kingdom could not buy!
And thou, fond Lover! to whose truth
Woman intrusts her hopes, her youth,
Her very life—oh! guard and cherish
Feelings which once neglected—perish!
Keep her fair form, and spotless mind,
Within thy heart of hearts enshrined:
Be thou the oak, round which may twine
The graceful foliage of the vine:
And ask, to bless thee, from above
The precious boon of woman's love!
"Now, farewell, lords and ladies bright!
To each and all we wish good night!
And rosy dreams and slumbers light."
"Good night, good night! parting is such sweet sorrow,
That we shall say good night till it be morrow."

EVENINGS IN GREECE.

BY THOMAS MOORE.

In thus connecting together a series of Songs by a thread of poetical narrative, my chief object has been to combine Recitation with Music, so as to enable a greater mumber of persons to join in the performance, by enlisting, as readers, those who may not feel willing or competent to take a part as singers.

The Island of Zea, where the scene is laid, was called by the ancients Ceos, and was the birthplace of Simonides, Bacchylides, and other eminent persons. An account of its present state may be found in the Travels of Dr. Clarke, who says, that "it appeared to him to be the best cultivated of any of the Grecian Isles."—Thomas Moore.

FIRST EVENING.

"The sky is bright—the breeze is fair,
"And the mainsail flowing, full and free—
"Our farewell word is woman's pray'r,
"And the hope before us—Liberty!
"Farewell, farewell.
"To Greece we give our shining blades,
"And our hearts to you, young Zean Maids!

"The moon is in the heavens above,
"And the wind is on the foaming sea—
"Thus shines the star of woman's love
"On the glorious strife of Liberty!
"Farewell, farewell.
"To Greece we give our shining blades,
"And our hearts to you, young Zean Maids!"

Thus sung they from the bark, that now
Turn'd to the sea its gallant prow,
Bearing within it hearts as brave,
As e'er sought Freedom o'er the wave;
And leaving on that islet's shore,
Where still the farewell beacons burn,
Friends, that shall many a day look o'er
The long, dim sea for their return.

Virgin of Heaven! speed their way—
Oh, speed their way,—the chosen flow'r,
Of Zea's youth, the hope and stay
Of parents in their wintry hour,
The love of maidens, and the pride
Of the young, happy, blushing bride,
Whose nuptial wreath has not yet died—
All, all are in that precious bark,
Which now, alas, no more is seen—
Though every eye still turns to mark
The moonlight spot where it had been.
Vainly you look, ye maidens, sires,
And mothers, your belov'd are gone!—
Now may you quench those signal fires,
Whose light they long look'd back upon
From their dark deck—watching the flame
As fast it faded from their view,
With thoughts, that, but for manly shame,
Had made them droop and weep like you.

Home to your chambers! home, and pray
For the bright coming of that day,
When, bless'd by heaven, the Cross shall sweep
The Crescent from the Ægean deep,
And your brave warriors, hast'ning back,
Will bring such glories in their track,
As shall, for many an age to come,
Shed light around their name and home.

There is a Fount on Zea's isle,
Round which, in soft luxuriance, smile
All the sweet flowers, of every kind,
On which the sun of Greece looks down,
Pleas'd as a lover on the crown
His mistress for her brow hath twin'd,
When he beholds each flow'ret there,
Himself had wish'd her most to wear;
Here bloom'd the laurel-rose,* whose wreath
Hangs radiant round the Cypriot shrines,
And here those bramble-flowers, that breathe
Their odour into Zante's wines:—†
The splendid woodbine, that, at eve,
To grace their floral diadems,
The lovely maids of Patmos weave:—‡.
And that fair plant, whose tangled stems
Shine like a Nereid's hair, § when spread,
Dishevell'd, o'er her azure bed;—
All these bright children of the clime,
(Each at his own most genial time,
The summer, or the year's sweet prime,)
Like beautiful earth-stars, adorn
The Valley, where that Fount is born:
While round, to grace its cradle green,
Groups of Velani oaks are seen,
Tow'ring on every verdant height—
Tall, shadowy, in the evening light,
Like Genii, set to watch the birth
Of some enchanted child of earth—
Fair oaks, that over Zea's vales,
Stand with their leafy pride unfurl'd;
While Commerce, from her thousand sails,
Scatters their fruit throughout the world! ‖

'Twas here—as soon as prayer and sleep
(Those truest friends to all who weep)
Had lighten'd every heart, and made
Ev'n sorrow wear a softer shade—

* "Nerium Oleander. In Cyprus it retains its ancient name, Rhododaphne, and the Cypriots adorn their churches with the flowers on feast-days."—*Journal of Dr. Sibthorpe, Walpole's Turkey.*

† Id

‡ Lonicera Caprifolium, used by the girls of Patmos for garlands

§ Cuscuta europæa. "From the twisting and twining of the stems, it is compared by the Greeks to the dishevelled hair of the Nereids."—*Walpole's Turkey.*

‖ "The produce of the island in these acorns alone amounts annually to fifteen thousand quintals."—*Clarke's Travels.*

'Twas here, in this secluded spot,
Amid whose breathings calm and sweet
Grief might be sooth'd, if not forgot,
The Zean nymphs resolv'd to meet
Each evening now, by the same light
That saw their farewell tears that night;
And try, if sound of lute and song,
If wand'ring 'mid the moonlight flowers
In various talk, could charm along
With lighter step, the ling'ring hours,
Till tidings of that Bark should come,
Or Victory waft their warriors home!

When first they met—the wonted smile
Of greeting having gleam'd awhile—
'Twould touch ev'n Moslem heart to see
The sadness that came suddenly
O'er their young brows, when they look'd round
Upon that bright, enchanted ground;
And thought, how many a time, with those
Who now were gone to the rude wars,
They there had met, at evening's close,
And danc'd till morn outshone the stars!

But seldom long doth hang th' eclipse
Of sorrow o'er such youthful breasts—
The breath from her own blushing lips,
That on the maiden's mirror rests,
Not swifter, lighter from the glass,
Than sadness from her brow doth pass.
Soon did they now, as round the Well
They sat, beneath the rising moon—
And some, with voice of awe, would tell
Of midnight fays, and nymphs who dwell
In holy founts—while some would tune
Their idle lutes, that now had lain,
For days, without a single strain;—
And others, from the rest apart,
With laugh that told the lighten'd heart,
Sat, whisp'ring in each other's ear
Secrets, that all in turn would hear;—
Soon did they find this thoughtless play
So swiftly steal their griefs away,
That many a nymph, though pleas'd the while,
Reproach'd her own forgetful smile,
And sigh'd to think she *could* be gay

Among these maidens there was one,
Who to Leucadia* late had been—
Had stood, beneath the evening sun,
On its white tow'ring cliffs, and seen
The very spot where Sappho sung
Her swan-like music, ere she sprung
(Still holding, in that fearful leap,
By her lov'd lyre,) into the deep,
And dying quench'd the fatal fire,
At once, of both her heart and lyre.

Mutely they listen'd all—and well
Did the young travell'd maiden tell
Of the dread height to which that steep
Beetles above the eddying deep—†
Of the lone sea-birds, wheeling round
The dizzy edge with mournful sound—
And of those scented lilies‡ found
Still blooming on that fearful place—
As if call'd up by Love, to grace
Th' immortal spot, o'er which the last
Bright footsteps of his martyr pass'd!

While fresh to ev'ry listener's thought
These legends of Leucadia brought
All that of Sappho's hapless flame
Is kept alive, still watch'd by Fame—
The maiden, tuning her soft lute,
While all the rest stood round her, mute,
Thus sketch'd the languishment of soul,
That o'er the tender Lesbian stole;
And, in a voice, whose thrilling tone
Fancy might deem the Lesbian's own,
One of those fervid fragments gave,
Which still,—like sparkles of Greek Fire,
Undying, ev'n beneath the wave,—
Burn on through Time, and ne'er expire

SONG.

As o'er her loom the Lesbian Maid
In love-sick languor hung her head,
Unknowing where her finger's stray'd,
She weeping turn'd away, and said,
"Oh, my sweet Mother—'tis in vain—
"I cannot weave, as once I wove—
"So wilder'd is my heart and brain
"With thinking of that youth I love!"§

Again the web she tried to trace,
But tears fell o'er each tangled thread;
While, looking in her mother's face,
Who watchful o'er her lean'd, she said,
"Oh, my sweet Mother—'tis in vain
"I cannot weave, as once I wove—
"So wilder'd is my heart and brain
"With thinking of that youth I love!"

A silence follow'd this sweet air,
As each in tender musing stood,
Thinking, with lips that mov'd in pray'r,
Of Sappho and that fearful flood:
While some, who ne'er till now had known
How much their hearts resembled hers,
Felt as they made her griefs their own,
That *they*, too, were Love's worshippers

At length a murmur, all but mute,
So faint it was, came from the lute
Of a young melancholy maid,
Whose fingers, all uncertain play'd
From chord to chord, as if in chase
Of some lost melody, some strain
Of other times, whose faded trace
She sought among those chords again.
Slowly the half-forgotten theme
(Though born in feelings ne'er forgot)
Came to her memory—as a beam
Falls broken o'er some shaded spot.
And while her lute's sad symphony
Fill'd up each sighing pause between;
And Love himself might weep to see
What ruin comes where he hath been—
As wither'd still the grass is found
Where fays have danc'd their merry round—
Thus simply to the list'ning throng
She breath'd her melancholy song:—

SONG

Weeping for thee, my love, through the long day,
Lonely and wearily life wears away.
Weeping for thee, my love, through the long night—
No rest in darkness, no joy in light!
Nought left but Memory, whose dreary tread
Sounds through this ruin'd heart, where all lies dead-
Wakening the echo's of joy long fled!

Of many a stanza, this alone
Had scaped oblivion—like the one
Stray fragment of a wreck, which thrown,
With the lost vessel's name, ashore,
Tells who they were that live no more.

When thus the heart is in a vein
Of tender thought, the simplest strain

* Now Santa Maura—the island, from whose cliffs Sappho leaped into the sea.

† "The precipice, which is fearfully dizzy, is about one hundred and fourteen feet from the water, which is of a profound depth, as appears from the dark-blue colour and the eddy that plays round the pointed and projecting rocks."—*Goodisson's Ionian Isles.*

‡ See Mr. Goodisson's very interesting description of all these circumstances.

§ I have attempted, in these four lines, to give some idea of that beautiful fragment of Sappho, beginning Γλυκεῖα μᾶτερ, which represents, so truly (as Warton remarks) "the languor and listlessness of a person deeply in love."

Can touch it with peculiar power
  As when the air is warm, the scent
Of the most wild and rustic flower
  Can fill the whole rich element—
And, in such moods, the homeliest tone
That's link'd with feelings, once our own—
With friends or joys gone by—will be
Worth choirs of loftiest harmony!

But some there were, among the group
  Of damsels there, too light of heart
To let their spirits longer droop,
  Ev'n under music's melting art;
And one upspringing, with a bound,
From a low bank of flowers, look'd round
With eyes that, though so full of light,
  Had still a trembling tear within;
And, while her fingers, in swift flight,
  Flew o'er a fairy mandolin,
Thus sung the song her lover late
  Had sung to her—the eve before
  That joyous night, when, as of yore,
All Zea met, to celebrate
  The Feast of May, on the sea-shore.

SONG.

When the Balaika*
  Is heard o'er the sea,
I'll dance the Romaika
  By moonlight with thee.
If waves then, advancing,
  Should steal on our play,
Thy white feet in dancing,
  Shall chase them away.†
When the Balaika
  Is heard o'er the sea,
Thou'lt dance the Romaika,
  My own love, with me.

Then, at the closing
  Of each merry lay,
How sweet 'tis, reposing,
  Beneath the night ray!
Or if, declining,
  The moon leave the skies,
We'll talk by the shining
  Of each other's eyes.

Oh then, how featly
  The dance we'll renew,
Treading so fleetly
  Its light mazes through:‡
Till stars, looking o'er us
  From heaven's high bow'rs,
Would change their bright chorus
  For one dance of ours!
When the Balaika
  Is heard o'er the sea,
Thou'lt dance the Romaika,
  My own love, with me.

How changingly for ever veers
The heart of youth, 'twixt smiles and tears.
Ev'n as in April, the light vane
Now points to sunshine, now to rain.
Instant this lively lay dispell'd
  The shadow from each blooming brow,
And Dancing, joyous Dancing, held
  Full empire o'er each fancy now.

But say—*what* shall the measure be?
  "Shall we the old Romaika tread,
(Some eager ask'd) "as anciently
  "'Twas by the maids of Delos led,
"When, slow at first, then circling fast,
"As the gay spirits rose—at last,
"With hand in hand, like links, enlock'd,
  "Through the light air they seem'd to flit
"In labyrinthine maze, that mock'd
  "The dazzled eye that follow'd it?"
Some call'd aloud "the Fountain Dance!"—
  While one young, dark-ey'd Amazon,
Whose step was air-like, and whose glance
  Flash'd, like a sabre in the sun,
Sportively said, "Shame on these soft
"And languid strains we hear so oft.
"Daughters of Freedom! have not we
  "Learn'd from our lovers and our sires
"The Dance of Greece, while Greece was free—
  "That Dance, where neither flutes nor lyres,
"But sword and shield clash on the ear
"A music tyrants quake to hear?§
"Heroines of Zea, arm with me,
"And dance the dance of Victory!"

Thus saying, she, with playful grace,
Loos'd the wide hat, that o'er her face
(From Anatolia|| came the maid)
  Hung, shadowing each sunny charm;
And, with a fair young armourer's aid,
  Fixing it on her rounded arm,
A mimic shield with pride display'd;
Then, springing tow'rds a grove that spread
  Its canopy of foliage near,
Pluck'd off a lance-like twig, and said,
"To arms, to arms!" while o'er her head
  She wav'd the light branch, as a spear.

Promptly the laughing maidens all
Obey'd their Chief's heroic call;—
Round the shield-arm of each was tied
  Hat, turban, shawl, as chance might be,
  The grove, their verdant armoury,
Falchion and lance¶ alike supplied;
  And as their glossy locks, let free,
  Fell down their shoulders carelessly,
You might have dream'd you saw a throng
  Of youthful Thyads, by the beam
Of a May moon, bounding along
  Peneus' silver-eddied** stream!

And now they stepp'd, with measur'd tread,
  Martially, o'er the shining field;
Now, to the mimic combat led
(A heroine at each squadron's head,)
  Struck lance to lance and sword to shield
While still, through every varying feat,
Their voices, heard in contrast sweet
With some, of deep but soften'd sound,
From lips of aged sires around,
Who smiling watch'd their children's play
Thus sung the ancient Pyrrhic lay:—

SONG.

"Raise the buckler—poise the lance—
"Now here—now there—retreat—advance!"

Such were the sounds, to which the warrior boy
  Danc'd in those happy days, when Greece was free
When Sparta's youth, ev'n in the hour of joy,
  Thus train'd their steps to war and victory.
"Raise the buckler—poise the lance—
"Now here—now there—retreat—advance!"
Such was the Spartan warriors' dance.
"Grasp the falchion—gird the shield—
"Attack—defend—do all, but yield."

---

* This word is defrauded here, I suspect, of a syllable; Dr. Clarke, if I recollect right, makes it "Balalaika."

† "I saw above thirty parties engaged in dancing the Romaika upon the sand; in some of those groups, the girl who led them chased the retreating wave."—*Douglas on the Modern Greeks.*

‡ "In dancing the Romaika (says Mr. Douglas) they begin in slow and solemn step till they have gained the time, but by degrees the air becomes more sprightly; the conductress of the dance sometimes setting to her partner, sometimes darting before the rest, and leading them through the most rapid revolutions; sometimes crossing under the hands, which are held up to let her pass, and giving as much liveliness and intricacy as she can to the figures, into which she conducts her companions, while their business is to follow her in all her movements, without breaking the chain, or losing the measure."

§ For a description of the Pyrrhic Dance, see De Guys, &c.—It appears from Apuleius (lib. x.) that this war-dance was, among the ancients, sometimes performed by females.

|| See the *costume* of the Greek women of Natolia in *Castellan's Mœurs des Othomans.*

¶ The sword was the weapon chiefly used in this dance

** Homer, Il. ii. 753.

Thus did thy sons, oh Greece, one glorious night,
Dance by a moon like this, till o'er the sea
That morning dawn'd by whose immortal light
They nobly died for thee and liberty! *
"Raise the buckler—poise the lance—
"Now here—now there—retreat—advance!'
Such was the Spartan heroes' dance.

Scarce had they clos'd this martial lay
When, flinging their light spears away,
The combatants, in broken ranks,
All breathless from the war-field fly;
And down, upon the velvet banks
And flow'ry slopes, exhausted lie,
Like rosy huntresses of Thrace,
Resting at sunset from the chase.

"Fond girls!" an aged Zean said—
One who, himself, had fought and bled,
And now, with feelings, half delight,
Half sadness, watch'd their mimic fight—
"Fond maids! who thus with War can jest—
"Like Love, in Mars's helmet drest,
"When, in his childish innocence,
"Pleas'd with the shade that helmet flings,
"He thinks not of the blood, that thence
"Is dropping o'er his snowy wings.
"Ay—true it is, young patriot maids,
"If Honour's arm still won the fray,
"If luck but shone on righteous blades,
"War were a game for gods to play!
"But, no, alas!—hear one, who well
"Hath track'd the fortunes of the brave—
"Hear *me*, in mournful ditty, tell
"What glory waits the patriot's grave:"—

SONG.

As by the shore, at break of day,
A vanquish'd Chief expiring lay,
Upon the sands, with broken sword,
He trac'd his farewell to the Free;
And, there, the last unfinish'd word
He dying wrote was "Liberty!"

At night a Sea-bird shriek'd the knell
Of him who thus for Freedom fell;
The words he wrote, ere evening came,
Were cover'd by the sounding sea;—
So pass away the cause and name
Of him who dies for Liberty!

That tribute of subdued applause
A charm'd, but timid, audience pays,
That murmur, which a minstrel draws
From hearts, that feel, but fear to praise,
Follow'd this song, and left a pause
Of silence after it, that hung
Like a fix'd spell on every tongue.

At length, a low and tremulous sound
Was heard from midst a group, that round
A bashful maiden stood, to hide
Her blushes, while the lute she tried—
Like roses, gath'ring round to veil
The song of some young nightingale,
Whose trembling notes steal out between
The cluster'd leaves, herself unseen.
And, while that voice, in tones that more
Through feeling than through weakness err'd,
Came, with a stronger sweetness, o'er
Th' attentive ear, this strain was heard:—

SONG.

I SAW, from yonder silent cave,
Two Fountains running, side by side,
The one was Mem'ry's limpid wave,†
The other cold Oblivion's tide.
"Oh Love!" said I, in thoughtless mood,
As deep I drank of Lethe's stream,
"Be all my sorrows in this flood,
"Forgotten like a vanish'd dream!"

But who could bear that gloomy blank,
Where joy was lost as well as pain?
Quickly of Mem'ry's fount I drank,
And brought the past all back again;
And said, "Oh Love! whate'er my lot,
"Still let this soul to thee be true—
"Rather than have one bliss forgot,
"Be all my pains remember'd too!"

SONG.

The group that stood around, to shade
The blushes of that bashful maid,
Had, by degrees, as came the lay
More strongly forth, retir'd away,
Like a fair shell, whose valves divide,
To show the fairer pearl inside:
For such she was—a creature, bright
And delicate as those day-flow'rs,
Which, while they last, make up, in light
And sweetness, what they want in hours

So rich upon the ear had grown
Her voice's melody its tone
Gath'ring new courage, as it found
An echo in each bosom round—
That, ere the nymph, with downcast eye
Still on the chords, her lute laid by,
"Another Song," all lips exclaim'd,
And each some matchless fav'rite nam'd
While blushing, as her fingers ran
O'er the sweet chords, she thus began

SONG.

OH, Memory, how coldly
Thou paintest joy gone by:
Like rainbows, thy pictures
But mournfully shine and die
Or, if some tints thou keepest,
That former days recall,
As o'er each line thou weepest,
Thy tears efface them all.

But, Memory, too truly
Thou paintest grief that's past;
Joy's colour's are fleeting,
But those of Sorrow last.
And, while thou bring'st before us
Dark pictures of past ill,
Life's evening, closing o'er us,
But makes them darker still

So went the moonlight hours along,
In this sweet glade; and so, with song
And witching sounds—not such as they,
The cymbalists of Ossa, play'd,
To chase the moon's eclipse away,‡
But soft and holy—did each maid
Lighten her heart's eclipse awhile,
And win back Sorrow to a smile.

Not far from this secluded place,
On the sea-shore a ruin stood;-
A relic of th' extinguish'd race,
Who once look'd o'er that foamy flood,
When fair Ioulis,§ by the light
Of golden sunset, on the sight
Of mariners who sail'd that sea,
Rose, like a city of chrysolite,
Call'd from the wave by witchery.

---

* It is said that Leonidas and his companions employed themselves, on the eve of the battle, in music and the gymnastic exercises of their country.

† "This morning we paid our visit to the Cave of Trophonius, and the Fountains of Memory and Oblivion, just upon the water of Hercyna, which flows through stupendous rocks."—*Williams's Travels in Greece*

‡ This superstitious custom of the Thessalians exists also, as Pietro della Valle tells us, among the Persians.

§ An ancient city of Zea, the walls of which were of marble. Its remains (says Clarke) "extend from the shore, quite into a valley watered by the streams of a fountain, whence Ioulis received its name"

This ruin—now by barb'rous hands
  Debas'd into a motley shed,
Where the once splendid column stands
  Inverted on its leafy head—
Form'd, as they tell, in times of old,
  The dwelling of that bard, whose lay
Could melt to tears the stern and cold,
  And sadden, mid their mirth, the gay—
Simonides,* whose fame, through years
And ages past, still bright appears—
Like Hesperus, a star of tears!

'Twas hither now—to catch a view
  Of the white waters, as they play'd
Silently in the light—a few
  Of the more restless damsels stray'd,
And some would linger 'mid the scent
  Of hanging foliage, that perfum'd
The ruin'd walls; while others went,
  Culling whatever flowret bloom'd
In the lone leafy space between,
Where gilded chambers once had been;
Or, turning sadly to the sea,
  Sent o'er the wave a sigh unblest
To some brave champion of the Free—
Thinking, alas, how cold might be,
  At that still hour, his place of rest!

Meanwhile there came a sound of song
  From the dark ruins—a faint strain,
As if some echo, that among
Those minstrel halls had slumber'd long,
  Were murm'ring into life again.

But, no—the nymphs knew well the tone—
  A maiden of their train, who lov'd,
Like the night-bird, to sing alone,
  Had deep into those ruins rov'd,
And there, all other thoughts forgot,
  Was warbling o'er, in lone delight,
A lay that, on that very spot,
  Her lover sung one moonlight night:—

SONG.

Ah! where are they, who heard, in former hours,
The voice of Song in these neglected bow'rs?
  They are gone—all gone!

The youth, who told his pain in such sweet tone,
That all, who heard him, wish'd his pain their own—
  He is gone—he is gone!

And she, who, while he sung, sat list'ning by,
And thought, to strains like these 'twere sweet to die—
  She is gone—she too is gone!

'Tis thus, in future hours, some bard will say
Of her, who hears, and him, who sings this lay—
  They are gone—They both are gone!

The moon was now, from Heaven's steep,
  Bending to dip her silv'ry urn
Into the bright and silent deep—
  And the young nymphs, on their return
From those romantic ruins, found
Their other playmates, rang'd around
The sacred Spring, prepar'd to tune
Their parting hymn,† ere sunk the moon,
To that fair Fountain, by whose stream
Their hearts had form'd so many a dream.

Who has not read the tales, that tell
Of old Eleusis' sacred Well,
Or heard what legend-songs recount
Of Syra, and its holy Fount,‡
Gushing, at once, from the hard rock
  Into the laps of living flowers—
Where village maidens lov'd to flock,
  On summer-nights, and, like the hours,
Link'd in harmonious dance and song,
Charm'd the unconscious night along;
While holy pilgrims, on their way
  To Delos' isle, stood looking on,
Enchanted with a scene so gay,
  Nor sought their boats, till morning shone!

Such was the scene this lovely glade
And its fair inmates now display'd,
As round the Fount, in linked ring,
  They went, in cadence slow and light,
And thus to that enchanted Spring
  Warbled their Farewell for the night:—

SONG.

Here, while the moonlight dim
Falls on that mossy brim,
Sing we our Fountain Hymn,
  Maidens of Zea!
Nothing but Music's strain,
When Lovers part in pain,
Soothes, till they meet again,
  Oh, Maids of Zea!

Bright Fount, so clear and cold,
Round which the nymphs of old
Stood, with their locks of gold,
  Fountain of Zea!
Not even Castaly,
Fam'd though its streamlet be,
Murmurs or shines like thee,
  Oh, Fount of Zea!

Thou, while our hymn we sing,
Thy silver voice shall bring,
Answering, answering,
  Sweet Fount of Zea!
For, of all rills that run,
Sparkling by moon or sun,
Thou art the fairest one,
  Bright Fount of Zea!

Now, by those stars that glance
Over heaven's still expanse,
Weave we our mirthful dance,
  Daughters of Zea!
Such as, in former days,
Danc'd they, by Dian's rays,
Where the Eurotas strays,§
  Oh, Maids of Zea!

But when to merry feet
Hearts with no echo beat,
Say, can the dance be sweet?
  Maidens of Zea!
No, nought but Music's strain,
When lovers part in pain,
Soothes, till they meet again,
  Oh, Maids of Zea!

SECOND EVENING.

SONG.

When evening shades are falling
  O'er Ocean's sunny sleep,
To pilgrim hearts recalling
  Their home beyond the deep;

* Zea was the birthplace of this poet, whose verses are by Catullus called "tears."

† These "Songs of the Well," as they were called among the ancients, still exist in Greece. *De Guys* tells us that he has seen "the young women in Prince's Island assembled in the evening at a public well, suddenly strike up a dance, while others sung in concert to them."

‡ "The inhabitants of Syra, both ancient and modern, may be considered as the worshippers of water. The old fountain, at which the nymphs of the island assembled in the earliest ages, exists in its original state; the same rendezvous as it was formerly, whether of love and gallantry, or of gossiping and tale-telling. It is near to the town, and the most limpid water gushes continually from the solid rock. It is regarded by the inhabitants with a degree of religious veneration; and they preserve a tradition, that the pilgrims of old time, in their way to Delos, resorted hither for purification."—*Clarke.*

§ "Qualis in Eurotæ ripis, aut per juga Cynthi
  Exercet Diana choros."—

When, rest o'er all descending,
The shores with gladness smile,
And lutes, their echoes blending,
Are heard from isle to isle,
Then, Mary, Star of the Sea,*
We pray, we pray, to thee!

The noon-day tempest over,
Now Ocean toils no more,
And wings of halcyons hover,
Where all was strife before.
Oh thus may life, in closing
Its short tempestuous day,
Beneath heaven's smile reposing,
Shine all its storms away:
Thus, Mary, Star of the Sea,
We pray, we pray, to thee!

On Helle's sea the light grew dim,
As the last sounds of that sweet hymn
Floated along its azure tide—
Floated in light, as if the lay
Had mix'd with sunset's fading ray,
And light and song together died.
So soft through evening's air had breath'd
That choir of youthful voices, wreath'd
In many-linked harmony,
That boats, then hurrying o'er the sea,
Paus'd, when they reach'd this fairy shore,
And linger'd till the strain was o'er.

Of those young maids who've met to fleet
In song and dance this evening's hours,
Far happier now the bosoms beat,
Than when they last adorn'd these bowers;
For tidings of glad sound had come,
At break of day, from the fair isles—
Tidings like breath of life to some—
That Zea's sons would soon wing home,
Crown'd with the light of Vict'ry's smiles
To meet that brightest of all meeds
That wait on high, heroic deeds,
When gentle eyes that scarce, for tears,
Could trace the warrior's parting track,
Shall, like a misty morn that clears,
When the long-absent sun appears,
Shine out, all bliss, to hail him back.

How fickle still the youthful breast!—
More fond of change than a young moon,
No joy so new was e'er possess'd
But Youth would leave for newer soon.
These Zean nymphs, though bright the spot,
Where first they held their evening play,
As ever fell to fairy's lot
To wanton o'er by midnight's ray,
Had now exchang'd that shelter'd scene
For a wide glade beside the sea—
A lawn, whose soft expanse of green
Turn'd to the west sun smilingly,
As though, in conscious beauty bright,
It joy'd to give him light for light.

And ne'er did evening more serene
Look down from heaven on lovelier scene.
Calm lay the flood around, while fleet,
O'er the blue shining element,
Light barks, as if with fairy feet
That stirr'd not the hush'd waters, went;
Some that, ere rosy eve fell o'er
The blushing wave, with mainsail free,
Had put forth from the Attic shore,
Or the near Isle of Ebony;—
Some, Hydriot barks, that deep in caves
Beneath Colonna's pillar'd cliffs,
Had all day lurk'd, and o'er the waves
Now shot their long and dart-like skiffs.
Woe to the craft, however fleet,
These sea-hawks in their course shall meet,
Laden with juice of Lesbian vines,
Or rich from Naxos' emery mines;
For not more sure, when owlets flee
O'er the dark crags of Pendelee,
Doth the night-falcon mark his prey,
Or pounce on it more fleet than they.

And what a moon now lights the glade
Where these young island nymphs are met!
Full-orb'd, yet pure, as if no shade
Had touch'd it's virgin lustre yet;
And freshly bright, as if just made
By Love's own hands, of new-born light
Stol'n from his mother's star to-night.

On a bold rock, that o'er the flood
Jutted from that soft glade, there stood
A Chapel, fronting tow'rds the sea,—
Built in some by-gone century,—
Where, nightly, as the seaman's mark,
When waves rose high or clouds were dark,
A lamp, bequeath'd by some kind Saint,
Shed o'er the wave its glimmer faint,
Waking in way-worn men a sigh
And pray'r to heav'n, as they went by.
'Twas there, around that rock-built shrine,
A group of maidens and their sires
Had stood to watch the day's decline,
And, as the light fell o'er their lyres,
Sung to the Queen-Star of the Sea
That soft and holy melody.

But lighter thoughts and lighter song
Now woo the coming hours along:
For, mark, where smooth the herbage lies,
Yon gay pavilion, curtain'd deep
With silken folds, through which, bright eyes,
From time to time, are seen to peep;
While twinkling lights that, to and fro,
Beneath those veils, like meteors, go,
Tell of some spells at work, and keep
Young fancies chain'd in mute suspense,
Watching what next may shine from thence.
Nor long the pause, ere hands unseen
That mystic curtain backward drew
And all, that late but shown between,
In half-caught gleams, now burst to view
A picture 'twas of the early days
Of glorious Greece, ere yet those rays
Of rich, immortal Mind were hers
That made mankind her worshippers:
While, yet unsung, her landscapes shone
With glory lent by Heaven alone;
Nor temples crown'd her nameless hills,
Nor Muse immortalis'd her rills;
Nor aught but the mute poesy
Of sun, and stars, and shining sea
Illum'd that land of bards to be.
While, prescient of the gifted race
That yet would realm so blest adorn,
Nature took pains to deck the place
Where glorious Art was to be born.

Such was the scene that mimic stage
Of Athens and her hills portray'd;
Athens, in her first, youthful age,
Ere yet the simple violet braid,†
Which then adorn'd her, had shone down
The glory of earth's loftiest crown.
While yet undream'd, her seeds of Art
Lay sleeping in the marble mine—
Sleeping till Genius bade them start
To all but life, in shapes divine;
Till deified the quarry shone
And all Olympus stood in stone!

There, in the foreground of that scene,
On a soft bank of living green,
Sat a young nymph, with her lap full
Of newly gather'd flowers, o'er which

---

* One of the titles of the Virgin:—"Maria illuminatrix sive Stella Maris."—*Isidor.*

† "Violet-crowned Athens."—*Pindar*

She graceful lean'd, intent to cull
  All that was there of hue most rich,
To form a wreath, such as the eye
Of her young lover, who stood by,
With pallet mingled fresh, might choose
To fix by Painting's rainbow hues.

The wreath was form'd; the maiden rais'd
  Her speaking eyes to his, while he—
Oh *not* upon the flowers now gaz'd,
  But on that bright look's witchery.
While, quick as if but then the thought,
Like light, had reach'd his soul, he caught
His pencil up, and warm and true
As life itself, that love-look drew:
And, as his raptur'd task went on,
And forth each kindling feature shone,
Sweet voices, through the moonlight air,
  From lips as moonlight fresh and pure,
Thus hail'd the bright dream passing there,
  And sung the Birth of Portraiture.*

SONG.

As once a Grecian maiden wove
  Her garland mid the summer bow'rs,
There stood a youth, with eyes of love,
  To watch her while she wreath'd the flow'rs.
The youth was skill'd in Painting's art,
  But ne'er had studied woman's brow,
Nor knew what magic hues the heart
  Can shed o'er Nature's charms, till now.

CHORUS.

Blest be Love, to whom we owe
All that's fair and bright below.

His hand had pictured many a rose,
  And sketch'd the rays that light the brook;
But what were these, or what were those,
  To woman's blush, to woman's look?
"Oh, if such magic pow'r there be,
  "This, this," he cried, "is all my prayer,
"To paint that living light I see,
  "And fix the soul that sparkles there."
His prayer, as soon as breath'd, was heard;
  His pallet, touch'd by Love, grew warm,
And Painting saw her hues transferr'd
  From lifeless flow'rs to woman's form.
Still as from tint to tint he stole,
  The fair design shone out the more,
And there was now a life, a soul,
  Where only colours glow'd before.

Then first carnations learn'd to speak,
  And lilies unto life were brought;
While, mantling on the maiden's cheek,
  Young roses kindled into thought.
Then hyacinths their darkest dyes
  Upon the locks of Beauty threw;
And violets, transform'd to eyes,
  Inshrin'd a soul within their blue.

CHORUS.

Blest be Love, to whom we owe
All that's fair and bright below.
Song was cold and Painting dim
Till Song and Painting learn'd from him

Soon as the scene had clos'd, a cheer
  Of gentle voices, old and young,
Rose from the groups that stood to hear
  This tale of yore so aptly sung;
And while some nymphs, in haste to tell
The workers of that fairy spell
How crown'd with praise their task had been,
Stole in behind the curtain'd scene,
The rest, in happy converse stray'd—
  Talking that ancient love-tale o'er—
Some, to the groves that skirt the glade,
  Some, to the chapel by the shore,
To look what lights were on the sea,
And think of th' absent silently.

But soon that summons, known so well
  Through bow'r and hall, in Eastern lands,
Whose sound, more sure than gong or bell,
  Lovers and slaves alike commands,—
  The clapping of young female hands,
Calls back the groups from rock and field
To see some new-form'd scene reveal'd;—
And fleet and eager, down the slopes
Of the green glade, like antelopes,
When, in their thirst, they hear the sound
Of distant rills, the light nymphs bound.

Far different now the scene—a waste
  Of Lybian sands, by moonlight's ray;
An ancient well, whereon were trac'd
  The warning words, for such as stray
  Unarmed there, "Drink and away!"†
While, near it, from the night-ray screen'd,
  And like his bells, in hush'd repose,
A camel slept—young as if wean'd
When last the star, Canopus, rose.‡

Such was the back-ground's silent scene;—
  While nearer lay, fast slumb'ring too,
In a rude tent, with brow serene,
  A youth whose cheeks of way-worn hue
And pilgrim-bonnet, told the tale
That he had been to Mecca's Vale:
Happly in pleasant dreams, ev'n now
  Thinking the long wish'd hour is come
  When, o'er the well-known porch at home,
His hand shall hang the aloe bough—
Trophy of his accomplish'd vow.§
But brief his dream—for now the call
  Of the camp-chiefs from rear to van,
"Bind on your burdens,||" wakes up all
  The widely slumb'ring caravan;
And thus meanwhile, to greet the ear
  Of the young pilgrim as he wakes,
The song of one who, ling'ring near,
  Had watch'd his slumber, cheerly breaks

SONG.

Up and march! the timbrel's sound
Wakes the slumb'ring camp around
Fleet thy hour of rest hath gone,
Armed sleeper, up, and on!
Long and weary is our way
O'er the burning sands to-day;
But to pilgrim's homeward feet
Ev'n the desert's path is sweet.

When we lie at dead of night,
Looking up to heaven's light,
Hearing but the watchman's tone
Faintly chaunting "God is one,"¶
Oh what thoughts then o'er us come
Of our distant village home,
Where that chaunt, when ev'ning sets
Sounds from all the minarets.

Cheer thee!—soon shall signal lights,
Kindling o'er the Red Sea heights,

* The whole of this scene was suggested by Pliny's account of the artist Pausias and his mistress Glycera, lib. xxxv. c. 40.

† The traveller Shaw mentions a beautful rill in Barbary, which is received into a large bason called *Shrub wee krub*, "Drink and away,"—there being great danger of meeting with thieves and assassins in such places.

‡ The Arabian shepherd has a peculiar ceremony in weaning the young camel: when the proper time arrives, he turns the camel towards the rising star, Canopus, and says, "Do you see Canopus? from this moment you taste not another drop of milk."—*Richardson.*

§ "Whoever returns from a pilgrimage to Mecca hangs this plant (the mitre-shaped Aloe) over his street door, as a token of his having performed this holy journey."—*Hasselquist.*

|| This form of notice to the caravans to prepare for marching was applied by Hafiz to the necessity of relinquishing the pleasures of this world, and preparing for death:—"For me what room is there for pleasure in the bower of Beauty, when every moment the bell makes proclamation, 'Bind on your burdens?'"

¶ The watchmen, in the camp of the caravans go their rounds crying one after another "God is one," &c. &c.

Kindling quick fro1 1 man to man,
Hail our coming ca.avan:*
Think what bliss that hour will be
Looks of home again to see,
And our names again to hear
Murmur'd out by voices dear.

So pass'd the desert dream away,
Fleeting as his who heard this lay.
Nor long the pause between, nor mov'd
The spell-bound audience from that spot;
While still, as usual, Fancy rov'd
On to the joy that yet was not;—
Fancy, who hath no present home,
But builds her bower in scenes to come,
Walking for ever in a light
That flows from regions out of sight.

But see, by gradual dawn descried,
A mountain realm—rugged as e'er
Uprais'd to heav'n its summits bare,
Or told to earth, with frown of pride,
That Freedom's falcon rest was there,
Too high for hand of lord or king
To hood her brow, or chain her wing.

'Tis Maina's land—her ancient hills,
The abode of nymphs †—her countless rills
And torrents, in their downward dash,
Shining, like silver, through the shade
Of the sea-pine and flow'ring ash—
All with a truth so fresh portray'd
As wants but touch of life to be
A world of warm reality.

And now, light bounding forth, a band
Of mountaineers, all smiles, advance—
Nymphs with their lovers, hand in hand,
Link'd in the Ariadne dance; ‡
And while, apart from that gay throng,
A minstrel youth, in varied song,
Tells of the loves, the joys, the ills
Of these wild children of the hills,
The rest by turns, or fierce or gay,
As war or sport inspires the lay,
Follow each change that wakes the strings,
And act what thus the lyrist sings:—

SONG.

No life is like the mountaineer's,
His home is near the sky,
Where, thron'd above this world, he hears
Its strife at distance die.
Or, should the sound of hostile drum
Proclaim below, "We come—we come,"
Each crag that tow'rs in air
Gives answer, "Come who dare!"
While, like bees, from dell and dingle,
Swift the swarming warriors mingle,
And their cry "Hurra!" will be,
"Hurra, to victory!"

Then, when battle's hour is over,
See the happy mountain lover,
With the nymph, who'll soon be bride,
Seated blushing by his side,—
Every shadow of his lot
In her sunny smile forgot.
Oh, no life is like the mountaineer's,
His home is near the sky,
Where, thron'd above this world, he hears
Its strife at distance die.
Nor only thus through summer suns
His blithe existence cheerly runs—
Ev'n winter, bleak and dim,
Brings joyous hours to him;
When, his rifle behind him flinging,
He watches the roe-buck springing,
And away, o'er the hills away
Re-echoes his glad "Hurra."

Then how blest, when night is closing,
By the kindled hearth reposing,
To his rebeck's drowsy song,
He beguiles the hour along;
Or, provok'd by merry glances,
To a brisker movement dances,
Till, weary at last, in slumber's chain,
He dreams o'er chase and dance again,
Dreams, dreams them o'er again.

As slow that minstrel, at the close,
Sunk, while he sung, to feign'd repose,
Aptly did they, whose mimic art
Follow'd the changes of his lay,
Portray the lull, the nod, the start,
Through which, as faintly died away
His lute and voice, the minstrel pass'd,
Till voice and lute lay hush'd at last.

But now far other song came o'er
Their startled ears—song that, at first,
As solemnly the night wind bore
Across the wave its mournful burst,
Seem'd to the fancy, like a dirge
Of some lone Spirit of the Sea,
Singing o'er Helle's ancient surge
The requiem of her Brave and Free.

Sudden, amid their pastime, pause
The wond'ring nymphs; and, as the sound
Of that strange music nearer draws,
With mute inquiring eye look round,
Asking each other what can be
The source of this sad minstrelsy?
Nor longer can they doubt, the song
Comes from some island-ba.k, which now
Courses the bright wave swift along,
And soon, perhaps, beneath the brow
Of the Saint's Rock will shoot its prow.

Instantly all, with hearts that sigh'd
'Twixt fear's and fancy's influence,
Flew to the rock, and saw from thence
A red-sail'd pinnace tow'rds them glide,
Whose shadow, as it swept the spray,
Scatter'd the moonlight's smiles away.
Soon as the mariners saw that throng
From the cliff gazing, young and old,
Sudden they slack'd their sail and song,
And while their pinnace idly roll'd
On the light surge, these tidings told:—

'Twas from an isle of mournful name,
From Missolonghi, last they came—
Sad Missolonghi, sorrowing yet
O'er him, the noblest Star of Fame
That e'er in life's young glory set!—
And now were on their mournful way,
Wafting the news through Helle's isles;—
News that would cloud ev'n Freedom's ray,
And sadden Vict'ry 'mid her smiles.
Their tale thus told, and heard, with pain,
Out spread the galliot's wings again;
And, as she sped her swift career,
Again that Hymn rose on the ear—
"Thou art not dead—thou art not dead!"
As oft 'twas sung, in ages flown,
Of him, the Athenian, who, to shed
A tyrant's blood, pour'd out his own

SONG.

Thou art not dead—thou art not dead!" §
No, dearest Harmodius, no.
Thy soul, to realms above us fled,
Though, like a star, it dwells o'er head,

---

* "It was customary," says Irwin, to light up fires on the mountains, within view of Cosseir, to give notice of the approach of the caravans that came from the Nile."

† ——— virginibus bacchata Laconis
Taygeta. Virg.

‡ See, for an account of this dance, De Guy's Travels.

§ Φίλταθ' Ἁρμόδι' οὔπω τέθνηκας

Still lights this world below.
Thou art not dead—thou art not dead!
No, dearest Harmodius, no.

Through isles of light, where heroes tread
And flow'rs ethereal blow.
Thy god-like Spirit now is led,
Thy lip, with life ambrosial fed,
Forgets all taste of woe.
Thou art not dead—thou art not dead!
No, dearest Harmodius, no.

The myrtle, round that falchion spread
Which struck the immortal blow,
Throughout all time, with leaves unshed—
The patriot's hope, the tyrant's dread—
Round Freedom's shrine shall grow.
Thou art not dead—thou art not dead!
No, dearest Harmodius, no.

Where hearts like thine have broke or bled,
Though quench'd the vital glow,
Their mem'ry lights a flame, instead,
Which, ev'n from out the narrow bed
Of death its beams shall throw.
Thou art not dead—thou art not dead!
No, dearest Harmodius, no,

Thy name, by myriads sung and said,
From age to age shall go,
Long as the oak and ivy wed,
As bees shall haunt Hymettus' head,
Or Helle's waters flow.
Thou art not dead—thou art not dead!
No, dearest Harmodius, no.

'Mong those who linger'd list'ning there,—
List'ning, with ear and eye, as long
As breath of night could tow'rds them bear
A murmur of that mournful song,—
A few there were, in whom the lay
Had call'd up feelings far too sad
To pass with the brief strain away,
Or turn at once to theme more glad;
And who, in mood untun'd to meet
The light laugh of the happier train,
Wander'd to seek some moonlight seat
Where they might rest, in converse sweet,
Till vanish'd smiles should come again.

And seldom e'er hath noon or night
To sadness lent more soothing light.
On one side, in the dark blue sky,
Lonely and radiant, was the eye
Of Jove himself, while, on the other,
'Mong tiny stars that round her gleam'd,
The young moon, like the Roman mother
Among her living "jewels," beam'd.

Touch'd by the lovely scenes around,
A pensive maid—one who, though young,
Had known what 'twas to see unwound
The ties by which her heart had clung—
Waken'd her soft tamboura's sound,
And to its faint accords thus sung·—

SONG.

Calm as, beneath its mother's eyes,
In sleep the smiling infant lies,
So, watch'd by all the stars of night,
Yon landscape sleeps in light.
And, while the night-breeze dies away,
Like relics of some faded strain,
Lov'd voices, lost for many a day,
Seem whisp'ring round again.
Oh youth! oh Love! ye dreams, that shed
Such glory once—where are ye fled?

Pure ray of light that, down the sky,
Art pointing, like an angel's wand,
As if to guide to realms that lie
In that bright sea beyond:
Who knows but, in some brighter deep
Than ev'n that tranquil, moon-lit main,
Some land may lie, where those who weep
Shall wake to smile again!

With cheeks that had regain'd their power
And play of smiles,—and each bright eye,
Like violets after morning's shower,
The brighter for the tears gone by,
Back to the scene such smiles should grace
These wand'ring nymphs their path retrace,
And reach the spot, with rapture new,
Just as the veils asunder flew,
And a fresh vision burst to view.

There, by her own bright Attic flood,
The blue-ey'd Queen of Wisdom stood;—
Not as she haunts the sage's dreams,
With brow unveil'd, divine, severe;
But soften'd, as on bards she beams,
When fresh from Poesy's high sphere,
A music, not her own, she brings,
And, through the veil which Fancy flings
O'er her stern features, gently sings.

But who is he—that urchin nigh,
With quiver on the rose-trees hung,
Who seems just dropp'd from yonder sky,
And stands to watch that maid, with eye
So full of thought, for one so young?—
That child—but, silence! lend thine ear,
And thus in song the tale thou'lt hear.—

SONG.

As Love, one summer eve, was straying,
Who should he see, at that soft hour,
But young Minerva, gravely playing
Her flute within an olive bow'r.
I need not say, 'tis Love's opinion
That, grave or merry, good or ill,
The sex all bow to his dominion,
As woman will be woman still.

Though seldom yet the boy hath giv'n
To learned dames his smiles or sighs,
So handsome Pallas look'd, that ev'n,
Love quite forgot the maid was wise.
Besides, a youth of his discerning
Knew well that, by a shady rill,
At sunset hour, whate'er her learning,
A woman will be woman still.

Her flute he prais'd in terms extatic,—
Wishing it dumb nor car'd how soon;—
For Wisdom's notes, howe'er chromatic,
To Love seem always out of tune.
But long as he found face to flatter,
The nymph found breath to shake and thrill;
As, weak or wise—it doesn't matter—
Woman, at heart, is woman still.

Love chang'd his plan, with warmth exclaiming,
"How rosy was her lip's soft dye!"
And much that flute, the flatt'rer blaming,
For twisting lips so sweet awry.
The nymph look'd down, beheld her features
Reflected in the passing rill,
And started, shock'd—for, ah, ye creatures!
Ev'n when divine, you're women still.

Quick from the lips it made so odious,
That graceless flute the Goddess took,
And, while yet fill'd with breath melodious,
Flung it into the glassy brook;
Where, as its vocal life was fleeting
Adown the current, faint and shrill,
'Twas heard in plaintive tone repeating,
"Woman, alas, vain woman still!"

An interval of dark repose—
Such as the summer lightning knows,
'Twixt flash and flash, as still more bright
The quick revealment comes and goes,
Op'ning each time the veils of night,
To show, within, a world of light—
Such pause, so brief, now pass'd between
This last gay vision and the scene,
Which now its depth of light disclos'd.
A bow'r it seem'd, an Indian bow'r,
Within whose shade a nymph repos'd,
Sleeping away noon's sunny hour—
Lovely as she, the Sprite, who weaves
Her mansion of sweet Durva leaves,
And there, as Indian legends say,
Dreams the long summer hours away.
And mark, how charm'd this sleeper seems
With some hid fancy—she, too, dreams!
Oh for a wizard's art to tell
The wonders that now bless her sight!
'Tis done—a truer, holier spell
Than e'er from wizard's lip yet fell
Thus brings her vision all to light:—

SONG.

"Who comes so gracefully
"Gliding along,
"While the blue rivulet
"Sleeps to her song;
"Song, richly vying
"With the faint sighing
"Which swans, in dying,
"Sweetly prolong?"

So sung the shepherd-boy
By the stream's side,
Watching that fairy boat
Down the flood glide,
Like a bird winging,
Through the waves bringing
That Syren, singing
To the hush'd tide.

"Stay," said the shepherd-boy,
"Fairy-boat, stay,
"Linger, sweet minstrelsy,
"Linger, a day."
But vain his pleading,
Past him, unheeding,
Song and boat, speeding,
Glided away.

So to our youthful eyes
Joy and hope shone;
So, while we gaz'd on them
Fast they flew on;—
Like flow'rs, declining
Ev'n in the twining,
One moment shining,
And, the next, gone!

Soon as the imagin'd dream went by,
Up rose the nymph, with anxious eye
Turn'd to the clouds, as though some boon
She waited from the sun-bright dome,
And marvell'd that it came not soon
As her young thoughts would have it come

But joy is in her glance!—the wing
Of a white bird is seen above;
And oh, if round his neck he bring
The long-wish'd tidings from her love,
Not half so precious in her eyes
Ev'n that high-omen'd bird* would be,
Who dooms the brow o'er which he flies
To wear a crown of Royalty.

She had, herself, last evening, sent
A winged messenger, whose flight
Through the clear, roseate element,
She watch'd till, less'ning out of sight,
Far to the golden West it went,
Wafting to him, her distant love,
A missive in that language wrought
Which flow'rs can speak, when aptly wove,
Each hue a word, each leaf a thought.

And now—oh speed of pinion, known
To Love's light messengers alone!—
Ere yet another ev'ning takes
Its farewell of the golden lakes,
She sees another envoy fly,
With the wish'd answer, through the sky.

SONG.

Welcome, sweet bird, through the sunny air winging,
Swift hast thou come o'er the far-shining sea,
Like Seba's dove, on thy snowy neck bringing
Love's written vows from my lover to me.
Oh, in thy absence, what hours did I number!—
Saying oft, "Idle bird, how could he rest?"
But thou art come at last, take now thy slumber,
And lull thee in dreams of all thou lov'st best

Yet dost thou droop—even now while I utter
Love's happy welcome, thy pulse dies away;
Cheer thee, my bird—were it life's ebbing flutter,
This fondling bosom should woo it to stay.
But no—thou'rt dying—thy last task is over—
Farewell, sweet martyr to Love and to me!
The smiles thou hast waken'd by news from my lover,
Will now all be turn'd into weeping for thee.

While thus the scene of song (their last
For the sweet summer season) pass'd,
A few presiding nymphs, whose care
Watch'd over all, invisibly,
As do those guardian sprites of air,
Whose watch we feel, but cannot see,
Had from the circle—scarcely miss'd,
Ere they were sparkling there again—
Glided, like fairies, to assist
Their handmaids on the moonlight plain,
Where, hid by intercepting shade
From the stray glance of curious eyes,
A feast of fruits and wines was laid—
Soon to shine out, a glad surprise!

And now the moon, her ark of light
Steering through Heav'n, as though she bore
In safety through that deep of night,
Spirits of earth, the good, the bright,
To some remote immortal shore,
Had half-way sped her glorious way,
When, round reclin'd on hillocks green,
In groups, beneath that tranquil ray,
The Zeans at their feast were seen,
Gay was the picture—every maid
Whom late the lighted scene display'd,
Still in her fancy garb array'd;—
The Arabian pilgrim, smiling here
Beside the nymph of India's sky;
While there the Mainote mountaineer
Whisper'd in young Minerva's ear,
And urchin Love stood laughing by.

Meantime the elders round the board,
By mirth and wit themselves made young
High cups of juice Zacynthian pour'd,
And, while the flask went round, thus sung —

SONG.

Up with the sparkling brimmer,
Up to the crystal rim;
Let not a moon-beam glimmer
'Twixt the flood and brim.
When hath the world set eyes on
Aught to match this light,
Which, o'er our cup's horizon,
Dawns in bumpers bright?

* The Huma.

Truth in a deep well lieth—
So the wise aver:
But Truth the fact denieth—
Water suits not her.
No, her abode's in brimmers,
Like this mighty cup—
Waiting till we, good swimmers,
Dive to bring her up.

Thus circled round the song of glee,
And all was tuneful mirth the while,
Save on the cheeks of some, whose smile,
As fix'd they gaze upon the sea,
Turns into paleness suddenly!
What see they there? a bright blue light
That, like a meteor, gliding o'er
The distant wave, grows on the sight,
As though 'twere wing'd to Zea's shore

To some, 'mong those who came to gaze,
It seem'd the night-light, far away,
Of some lone fisher, by the blaze
Of pine torch, luring on his prey;
While others, as, 'twixt awe and mirth,
They breath'd the bless'd Panaya's* name,
Vow'd that such light was not of earth,
But of that drear, ill-omen'd flame,
Which mariners see on sail or mast,
When Death is coming in the blast.
While marv'lling thus they stood, a maid,
Who sat apart, with downcast eye,
Nor yet had, like the rest, survey'd
That coming light which now was nigh,
Soon as it met her sight, with cry
Of pain-like joy, "Tis he! 'tis he!"
Loud she exclaim'd, and hurrying by
The assembled throng, rush'd tow'rds the sea.

At burst so wild, alarm'd, amaz'd,
All stood, like statues, mute, and gaz'd
Into each other's eyes, to seek
What meant such mood, in maid so meek?

Till now, the tale was known to few,
But now from lip to lip it flew:—
A youth, the flower of all the band,
Who late had left this sunny shore,
When last he kiss'd that maiden's hand,
Ling'ring, to kiss it o'er and o'er,
By his sad brow too plainly told
Th' ill-omen'd thought which cross'd him then,
That once those hands should lose their hold,
They ne'er would meet on earth again!
In vain his mistress, sad as he,
But with a heart from Self as free
As gen'rous woman's only is,
Veil'd her own fears to banish his:—
With frank rebuke, but still more vain,
Did a rough warrior, who stood by,
Call to his mind this martial strain,
His favourite once, ere Beauty's eye
Had taught his soldier-heart to sigh:—

SONG.

March! nor heed those arms that hold thee,
Though so fondly close they come;
Closer still will they enfold thee,
When thou bring'st fresh laurels home.
Dost thou dote on woman's brow?
Dost thou live but in her breath?
March!—one hour of victory now
Wins thee woman's smile till death.

Oh what bliss, when war is over,
Beauty's long-miss'd smile to meet
And, when wreaths our temples cover,
Lay them shining at her feet!

Who would not, that hour to reach,
Breathe out life's expiring sigh,—
Proud as waves that on the beach
Lay their war-crests down, and die?

There! I see thy soul is burning
She herself, who clasps thee so,
Paints, ev'n now, thy glad returning,
And, while clasping, bids thee go.
One deep sigh, to passion given,
One last glowing tear and then—
March!—nor rest thy sword, till Heaven
Brings thee to those arms again.

Even then, e'er loth their hands could part,
A promise the youth gave, which bore
Some balm unto the maiden's heart,
That soon as the fierce fight was o'er,
To home he'd speed, if safe and free—
Nay, ev'n if dying, still would come,
So the blest word of "Victory!"
Might be the last he'd breathe at home.
"By day," he cried, "thoul't know my bark;
"But, should I come through midnight dark,
"A blue light on the prow shall tell
"That Greece hath won, and all is well!"

Fondly the maiden, every night,
Had stolen to seek that promis'd light;
Nor long her eyes had now been turn'd
From watching, when the signal burn'd
Signal of joy—for her, for all—
Fleetly the boat now nears the land,
While voices, from the shore-edge, call
For tidings of the long-wish'd band.

Oh the blest hour, when those who've been
Through peril's paths by land or sea,
Lock'd in our arms again are seen
Smiling in glad security;
When heart to heart we fondly strain,
Questioning quickly o'er and o'er—
Then hold them off, to gaze again,
And ask, though answer'd oft before,
If they, *indeed*, are ours once more?

Such is the scene, so full of joy,
Which welcomes now this warrior-boy,
As fathers, sisters, friends all run
Bounding to meet him—all but one,
Who, slowest on his neck to fall,
Is yet the happiest of them all.

And now behold him, circled round
With beaming faces, at that board,
While cups, with laurel foliage crown'd,
Are to the coming warriors pour'd,—
Coming, as he, their herald, told,
With blades from vict'ry scarce yet cold,
With hearts untouch'd by Moslem steel,
And wounds that home's sweet breath will heal

"Ere morn," said he,—and, while he spoke,
Turn'd to the east, where, clear, and pale,
The star of dawn already broke—
"We'll greet, on yonder wave, their sail."
Then, wherefore part? all, all agree
To wait them here, beneath this bower;
And thus, while ev'n amidst their glee,
Each eye is turn'd to watch the sea,
With song they cheer the anxious hour

SONG

"'Tis the Vine! 'tis the Vine!" said the cup loving boy,
As he saw it spring bright from the earth
And call'd the young Genii of Wit, Love, and Joy,
To witness and hallow its birth.
The fruit was full grown, like a ruby it flam'd
Till the sun-beam that kiss'd it look'd pale·
"'Tis the Vine! 'tis the Vine!" ev'ry Spirit exclaim'd
"Hail, hail to the Wine-tree, all hail!"

* The name which the Greeks give to the Virgin Mary.

First, fleet as a bird, to the summons Wit flew,
While a light on the vine-leaves there broke,
In flashes so quick and so brilliant, all knew
'Twas the light from his lips as he spoke.
"Bright tree! let thy nectar but cheer me," he cried,
"And the fount of Wit never can fail:"
"'Tis the Vine! 'tis the Vine!" hills and valleys reply,
"Hail, hail to the Wine-tree, all hail!"

Next, Love, as he lean'd o'er the plant to admire
Each tendril and cluster it wore,
From his rosy mouth sent such a breath of desire,
As made the tree tremble all o'er.
Oh, never did flow'r of the earth, sea, or sky,
Such a soul-giving odour inhale:
"'Tis the Vine! 'tis the Vine!" all re-echo the cry,
"Hail, hail to the Wine-tree, all hail!"

Last, Joy, without whom even Love and Wit die,
Came to crown the bright hour with his ray;
And scarce had that mirth-waking tree met his eye,
When a laugh spoke what Joy could not say;—
A laugh of the heart, which was echoed around
Till, like music, it swell'd on the gale;
"'Tis the Vine! 'tis the Vine!" laughing myriads resound,
"Hail, hail to the Wine-tree, all hail!"

THE SUMMER FÊTE.

TO

THE HONOURABLE MRS. NORTON.

For the groundwork of the following Poem I am indebted to a memorable Fête, given some years since, at Boyle Farm, the seat of the late Lord Henry Fitzgerald. In commemoration of that evening—of which the lady to whom these pages are inscribed was, I well recollect, one of the most distinguished ornaments—I was induced at the time to write some verses, which were afterwards, however, thrown aside unfinished, on my discovering that the same task had been undertaken by a noble poet,* whose playful and happy *jeu-d'esprit* on the subject has since been published. It was but lately, that, on finding the fragments of my own sketch among my papers, I thought of founding on them such a description of an imaginary Fête as might furnish me with situations for the introduction of music.

Such is the origin and object of the following Poem, and to Mrs. Norton it is, with every feeling of admiration and regard, inscribed by her father's warmly attached friend,

THOMAS MOORE.

Sloperton Cottage, November, 1831.

THE SUMMER FÊTE.

"Where are ye now, ye summer days,
"That once inspir'd the poet's lays?
"Blest time! ere England's nymphs and swains,
"For lack of sunbeams, took to coals—
"Summers of light, undimm'd by rains,
"Whose only mocking trace remains
"In watering pots and parasols."

Thus spoke a young Patrician maid,
As, on the morning of that Fête
Which bards unborn shall celebrate,
She backward drew her curtain's shade,
And, closing one half-dazzled eye,
Peep'd with the other at the sky—
Th' important sky, whose light or gloom
Was to decide, this day, the doom
Of some few hundred beauties, wits,
Blues, Dandies, Swains, and Exquisites.

Faint were her hopes; for June had now
Set in with all his usual rigour!
Young Zephyr yet scarce knowing how
To nurse a bud, or fan a bough,
But Eurus in perpetual vigour;
And, such the biting summer air,
That she, the nymph now nestling there—
Snug as her own bright gems recline,
At night within their cotton shrine—
Had, more than once, been caught of late
Kneeling before her blazing grate,
Like a young worshipper of fire,
With hands uplifted to the flame,
Whose glow as if to woo them nigher,
Through the white fingers flushing came.

But oh! the light, th' unhop'd-for light,
That now illum'd this morning's heaven!
Up sprung Ïanthe at the sight,
Though—hark!—the clocks but strike eleven,
And rarely did the nymph surprise
Mankind so early with her eyes.

Who now will say that England's sun
(Like England's self, these spendthrift days)
His stock of wealth hath near outrun,
And must retrench his golden rays—
Pay for the pride of sunbeams past,
And to mere moonshine come at last?

"Calumnious thought!" Ïanthe cries,
While coming mirth lit up each glance,
And, prescient of the ball, her eyes
Already had begun to dance:
For brighter sun than that which now
Sparkled o'er London's spires and towers,
Had never bent from heaven his brow
To kiss Firenze's City of Flowers.
What must it be—if thus so fair
Mid the smok'd groves of Grosvenor Square—
What must it be where Thames is seen
Gliding between his banks of green,
While rival villas, on each side,
Peep from their bowers to woo his tide,
And, like a Turk between two rows
Of Harem beauties, on he goes—
A lover, lov'd for ev'n the grace
With which he slides from their embrace

In one of those enchanted domes,
One, the most flow'ry, cool, and bright
Of all by which that river roams,
The Fête is to be held to night—
That Fête already link'd to fame,
Whose cards, in many a fair one's sight
(When look'd for long, at last they came,)
Seem'd circled with a fairy light;—
That Fête to which the cull, the flower
Of England's beauty, rank and power,
From the young spinster just come *out*,
To the old Premier, too long *in*—
From legs of far descended gout,
To the last new-mustachio'd chin-
All were convoked by Fashion's spells
To the small circle where she dwells,
Collecting nightly, to allure us,
Live atoms, which, together hurl'd,
She, like another Epicurus,
Sets dancing thus, and calls "the World"

Behold how busy in those bowers
(Like May-flies in a [illegible] out of flowers,)

* Lord Francis Egerton.

The countless menials swarming run,
To furnish forth, ere set of sun,
The banquet-table, richly laid
Beneath yon awning's lengthen'd shade,
Where fruits shall tempt, and wines entice,
And Luxury's self, at Gunter's call,
Breathe from her summer-throne of ice
A spirit of coolness over all.

And now th' important hour drew nigh,
When, 'neath the flush of evening's sky,
The west end "world" for mirth let loose,
And mov'd, as he of Syracuse*
Ne'er dreamt of moving worlds, by force
Of four-horse power, had all combin'd
Through Grosvenor Gate to speed their course,
Leaving that portion of mankind,
Whom they call "Nobody," behind;—
No star for London feasts to-day,
No moon of beauty, new this May,
To lend the night her crescent ray;—
Nothing, in short, for ear or eye,
But veteran belles, and wits gone by,
The relics of a past beau-monde,
A world, like Cuvier's, long dethron'd!
Ev'n Parliament this evening nods
Beneath th' harangues of minor gods,
On half its usual opiate's share;
The great dispensers of repose,
The first-rate furnishers of prose
Being all call'd to—prose elsewhere.

Soon as through Grosvenor's lordly square—†
That last impregnable redoubt,
Where, guarded with Patrician care,
Primeval Error still holds out—
Where never gleam of gas must dare
'Gainst ancient Darkness to revolt,
Nor smooth Macadam hope to spare
The dowagers one single jolt;—
Where, far too stately and sublime
To profit by the lights of time,
Let Intellect march how it will,
They stick to oil and watchmen still:—
Soon as through that illustrious square
The first epistolary bell,
Sounding by fits upon the air,
Of parting pennies rung the knell;
Warn'd by that telltale of the hours,
And by the daylight's westering beam,
The young Ïanthe, who, with flowers
Half-crown'd, had sat in idle dream
Before her glass, scarce knowing where
Her fingers rov'd through that bright hair,
While, all capriciously, she now
Dislodg'd some curl from her white brow,
And now again replac'd it there;—
As though her task was meant to be
One endless change of ministry—
A routing-up of Loves and Graces,
But to plant others in their places.

Meanwhile—what strain is that which floats
Through the small boudoir near—like notes
Of some young bird, its task repeating
For the next linnet music-meeting?
A voice it was, whose gentle sounds
Still kept a modest octave's bounds,
Nor yet had ventur'd to exalt
Its rash ambition to *B alt*,
That point towards which when ladies rise,
The wise man takes his hat and—flies.
Tones of a harp, too, gently play'd,
Came with this youthful voice communing,
Tones true, for once, without the aid
Of that inflictive process, tuning—
A process which must oft have given
Poor Milton's ears a deadly wound;
So pleas'd, among the joys of Heav'n,
He specifies "harps *ever* tun'd."‡
She who now sung this gentle strain
Was our young nymph's still younger sister—
Scarce ready yet for Fashion's train
In their light legions to enlist her,
But counted on, as sure to bring
Her force into the field next spring.

The song she thus, like Jubal's shell,
Gave forth "so sweetly and so well,"
Was one in Morning Post much fam'd,
From a *divine* collection, nam'd,
"Songs of the toilet"—every Lay
Taking for subject of its Muse,
Some branch of feminine array,
Some item, with full scope, to choose,
From diamonds down to dancing shoes;
From the last hat that Herbault's hands
Bequeath'd to an admiring world,
Down to'the latest flounce that stands
Like Jacob's Ladder—or expands
Far forth, tempestuously unfurl'd.

Speaking of one of these new Lays,
The Morning Post thus sweetly says:—
"Not all that breathes from Bishop's lyre,
"That Barnett dreams, or Cooke conceives,
"Can match for sweetness, strength, or fire,
"This fine Cantata upon Sleeves.
"The very notes themselves reveal
"The cut of each new sleeve so well;
"A *flat* betrays the *Imbécilles*,§
"Light fugues the flying lappets tell;
"While rich cathedral cords awake
"Our homage for the *Manches d'Evêque*."

'Twas the first op'ning song—the Lay
Of all least deep in toilet-lore,
That the young nymph, to while away
The tiring-hour, thus warbled o'er:—

SONG.

Array thee, love, array thee, love,
In all thy best array thee;
The sun's below—the moon's above—
And Night and Bliss obey thee.
Put on thee all that's bright and rare,
The zone, the wreath, the gem,
Not so much gracing charms so fair,
As borrowing grace from them.
Array thee, love, array thee, love,
In all that's bright array thee;
The sun's below—the moon's above—
And Night and Bliss obey thee.

Put on the plumes thy lover gave,
The plumes, that, proudly dancing,
Proclaim to all, where'er they wave,
Victorious eyes advancing.
Bring forth the robe, whose hue of heaven
From thee derives such light,
That Iris would give all her seven
To boast but *one* so bright.
Array thee, love, array thee, love, &c &c.

Now hie thee, love, now hie thee, love,
Through Pleasure's circles hie thee,
And hearts, where'er thy footsteps move,
Will beat, when they come nigh thee.
Thy every word shall be a spell,
Thy every look a ray,
And tracks of wond'ring eyes shall tell
The glory of thy way!
Now hie thee, love, now hie thee, love,
Through Pleasure's circles hie thee.

* Archimedes.

† I am not certain whether the Dowagers of this Square have yet yielded to the innovations of Gas and Police, but, at the time when the above lines were written, they still obstinately persevered in their old *regime*; and would not suffer themselves to be either well guarded or well lighted.

‡ ——— "their golden harps they took—
Harps ever tun'd." *Paradise Lost*, book iii.

§ The name given to those large sleeves that hang loosely.

And hearts, where'er thy footsteps move,
Shall beat when they come nigh thee.

Now in his Palace of the West,
Sinking to slumber, the bright Day,
Like a tir'd monarch fann'd to rest,
Mid the cool airs of Evening lay;
While round his couch's golden rim
The gaudy clouds, like courtiers, crept—
Struggling each other's light to dim,
And catch his last smile e'er he slept.
How gay, as o'er the gliding Thames
The golden eve its lustre pour'd,
Shone out the high-born knights and dames
Now group'd around that festal board;
A living mass of plumes and flowers,
As though they'd robb'd both birds and bowers—
A peopled rainbow, swarming through
With habitants of every hue;
While, as the sparkling juice of France
High in the crystal brimmers flow'd,
Each sunset ray that mix'd by chance
With the wine's sparkles, show'd
How sunbeams may be taught to dance.

If not in written form exprest,
'Twas known, at least, to every guest,
That, though not bidden to parade
Their scenic powers in masquerade,
(A pastime little found to thrive
In the bleak fog of England's skies,
Where wit's the thing we best contrive,
As masquerader's to *disguise*,)
It yet was hop'd—and well that hope
Was answer'd by the young and gay—
That, in the toilet's task to-day,
Fancy should take her wildest scope;—
That the rapt milliner should be
Let loose through fields of poesy,
The tailor, in inventive trance,
Up to the heights of Epic clamber,
And all the regions of Romance
Be ransack'd by the *femme de chambre*.

Accordingly, with gay Sultanas,
Rebeccas, Sapphos, Roxalanas—
Circassian slaves whom Love would pay
Half his maternal realms to ransom;—
Young nuns, whose chief religion lay
In looking most profanely handsome;—
Muses in muslin—pastoral maids
With hats from the *Arcade-ian* shades,
And fortune-tellers, rich, 'twas plain,
As fortune-*hunters* form'd their train.

With these, and more such female groups,
Were mix'd no less fantastic troops
Of male exhibitors—all willing
To look, ev'n more than usual, killing;—
Beau tyrants, smock-fac'd braggadocios,
And brigands, charmingly ferocious;—
M. P.'s turn'd Turks, good Moslems then,
Who, last night, voted for the Greeks;
And Friars, staunch No-Popery men,
In close confab with Whig Caciques.

But where is she—the nymph, whom late
We left before her glass delaying,
Like Eve, when by the lake she sate,
In the clear wave her charms surveying,
And saw in that first glassy mirror
The first fair face that lur'd to error.
"Where is she," ask'st thou?—watch all looks
As cent'ring to one point they bear,
Like sun-flowers by the sides of brooks,
Turn'd to the sun—and she is there.
Ev'n in disguise, Oh never doubt
By her own light you'd track her out:
As when the moon, close shawl'd in fog,
Steals as she thinks through heaven *incog*,
Though hid herself, some sidelong ray,
At every step, detects her way.

But not in dark disguise to-night
Hath our young heroine veil'd her light:
For see, she walks the earth, Love's own,
His wedded bride, by holiest vow
Pledg'd in Olympus, and made known
To mortals by the type which now
Hangs glitt'ring on her snowy brow,
That butterfly, mysterious trinket,
Which means the Soul (tho' few would think it,)
And sparkling thus on brow so white,
Tells us we've Psyche here to-night

But hark! some song hath caught her ears—
And, lo, how pleas'd, as though she'd ne'er
Heard the Grand Opera of the Spheres,
Her goddess-ship approves the air;
And to a mere terrestrial strain,
Inspir'd by nought but pink champagne.
Her butterfly as gaily nods
As though she sat with all her train
At some great Concert of the Gods,
With Phœbus, leader—Jove director
And half the audience drunk with nectar.

From a male group the carol came—
A few gay youths, whom round the board
The last-tried flask's superior fame
Had lur'd to taste the tide it pour'd;
And one, who, from his youth and lyre,
Seem'd grandson to the Teian sire,
Thus gaily sung, while, to his song,
Replied in chorus the gay throng:—

SONG.

Some mortals there may be, so wise, or so fine
As in evenings like this no enjoyment to see:
But, as *I'm* not particular—wit, love, and wine,
Are for one night's amusement sufficient for me.
Nay—humble and strange as my tastes may appear—
If driv'n to the worst, I could manage, thank Heaven,
To put up with eyes such as beam round me here,
And such wine as we're sipping, six days out of seven
So pledge me a bumper—your sages profound
May be blest, if they will, on their own patent plan
But as we are *not* sages, why—send the cup round—
We must only be happy the best way we can.

A reward by some king was once offer'd, we're told,
To whoe'er could invent a new bliss for mankind;
But talk of *new* pleasures!—give me but the old,
And I'll leave your inventors all new ones they find
Or should I, in quest of fresh realms of bliss,
Set sail in the pinnace of Fancy some day,
Let the rich rosy sea I embark on be this,
And such eyes as we've here be the stars of my way!
In the meantime, a bumper—your Angels, on high,
May have pleasures unknown to life's limited span;
But, as we are *not* Angels, why—let the flask fly—
We must only be happy *all* ways that we can

Now nearly fled was sunset's light,
Leaving but so much of its beam
As gave to objects, late so bright,
The colouring of a shadowy dream;
And there was still where Day had set
A flush that spoke him loth to die—
A last link of his glory yet,
Binding together earth and sky.
Say, why is it that twilight best
Becomes even brows the loveliest?
That dimness, with its soft'ning touch,
Can bring out grace, unfelt before,
And charms we ne'er can see too much,
When seen but half enchant the more?
Alas, it is that every joy
In fulness finds its worst alloy,
And half a bliss, but hop'd or guess'd,
Is sweeter than the whole possess'd;—
That Beauty, when least shown upon,
A creature most ideal grows;
And there's no light from moon or sun
Like that Imagination throws;—

It is, alas, that Fancy shrinks
 Ev'n from a bright reality,
And turning inly, feels and thinks
 Far heav'nlier things than e'er will *be*.

Such was th' effect of twilight's hour
 On the fair groups that, round and round,
From glade to grot, from bank to bow'r,
 Now wander'd through this fairy ground;
And thus did Fancy—and champagne—
 Work on the sight their dazzling spells,
Till nymphs that look'd, at noon-day, plain,
 Now brighten'd, in the gloom, to belles;
And the brief interval of time,
 'Twixt after dinner and before,
T. dowagers brought back their prime,
 And shed a halo round two-score.

Meanwhile, new pastimes for the eye,
 The ear, the fancy, quick succeed;
And now along the waters fly
 Light gondoles, of Venetian breed,
With knights and dames, who calm reclin'd
 Lisp out love-sonnets as they glide—
Astonishing old Thames to find
 Such doings on his moral tide.

So bright was still that tranquil river,
With the last shaft from Daylight's quiver,
That many a group, in turn were seen
Embarking on its wave serene;
And, 'mong the rest, in chorus gay,
 A band of mariners, from th' isles
 Of sunny Greece, all song and smiles,
As smooth they floated, to the play
Of their oar's cadence, sung this lay:—

TRIO.

Our home is on the sea, boy,
 Our home is on the sea;
  When Nature gave
  The ocean-wave,
 She mark'd it for the Free.
Whatever storms befall, boy,
 Whatever storms befall,
  The island bark
  Is Freedom's ark,
And floats her safe through all.

Behold yon sea of isles, boy,
 Behold yon sea of isles,
  Where ev'ry shore
  Is sparkling o'er
 With Beauty's richest smiles.
For us hath Freedom claim'd, boy,
 For us hath Freedom claim'd
  Those ocean-nests
  Where valour rests
 His eagle wing untam'd.

And shall the Moslem dare, boy,
 And shall the Moslem dare,
  While Grecian hand
  Can wield a brand,
 To plant his Crescent there?
No—by our fathers, no, boy,
 No, by the Cross we show—
  From Maina's rills
  To Thracia's hills
 All Greece re-echoes "No!"

Like pleasant thoughts that o'er the mind
 A minute come, and go again,
Ev'n so, by snatches, in the wind,
 Was caught and lost that choral strain,
Now full, now faint upon the ear,
As the bark floated far or near.

At length, when, lost, the closing note
 Had down the waters died along,
Forth from another fairy boat,
 Freighted with music, came this song:-

SONG.

Smoothly flowing through verdant vales,
 Gentle river, thy current runs,
Shelter'd safe from winter gales,
 Shaded cool from summer suns.
Thus our Youth's sweet moments glide,
 Fenc'd with flow'ry shelter round;
No rude tempest wakes the tide,
 All its path is fairy ground.

But, fair river, the day will come,
 When, woo'd by whisp'ring groves in vain,
Thou'lt leave those banks, thy shaded home,
 To mingle with the stormy main.
And thou, sweet Youth, too soon wilt pass
 Into the world's unshelter'd sea,
Where, once thy wave hath mix'd, alas,
 All hope of peace is lost for thee

Next turn we to the gay saloon
Resplendent as a summer noon,
 Where, 'neath a pendent wreath of lights,
A Zodiac of flowers and tapers—
(Such as in Russian ball-rooms sheds
Its glory o'er young dancers' heads)—
 Quadrille performs her mazy rites,
And reigns supreme o'er slides and capers;—
Working to death each opera strain,
 As, with a foot that ne'er reposes,
She jigs through sacred and profane,
 From "Maid and Magpie" up to "Moses;"—*
Wearing out tunes as fast as shoes,
 Till fagg'd Rossini scarce respires;
Till Mayerbeer for mercy sues,
 And Weber at her foot expires.

And now the set hath ceas'd—the bows
Of fiddlers taste a brief repose,
While light along the painted floor,
 Arm within arm, the couples stray,
Talking their stock of nothings o'er,
 Till—nothing's left, at last, to say.
When, lo!—most opportunely sent—
 Two Exquisites, a he and she,
Just brought from Dandyland, and meant
 For Fashion's grand Menagerie,
Enter'd the room—and scarce were there
When all flock'd round them, glad to stare
At *any* monsters, *any* where.

Some thought them perfect, to their tastes
While others hinted that the waists
(That in particular of the *he* thing)
Left far too ample room for breathing:
Whereas, to meet these critics' wishes,
 The isthmus there should be so small,
That Exquisites, at last, like fishes,
 Must manage not to breathe at all.
The female (these same critics said,)
 Though orthodox from toe to chin,
Yet lack'd that spacious width of head
 To hat of toadstool much akin—
That build of bonnet, whose extent
Should, like a doctrine of dissent,
 Puzzle church-doors to let it in.

However—sad as 'twas, no doubt,
That nymph so smart should go about,
With head unconscious of the place
It *ought* to fill in Infinite Space—
Yet all allow'd that, of *her kind*,
 A prettier show 'twas hard to find;

* In England the *partition* of this opera of Rossini was transferred to the story of Peter the Hermit; by which means the indecorum of giving such names as "Moise," "Pharaon," &c. to the dances selected from it (as was done in Paris) has been avoided.

While of that doubtful genus, "dressy men,"
The male was thought a first-rate specimen.
Such *Savans*, too, as wish'd to trace
The manners, habits, of this race—
To know what rank (if rank at all)
'Mong reas'ning things to them should fall—
What sort of notions heaven imparts
To high-built heads and tight-lac'd hearts,
And how far Soul, which Plato says,
Abhors restraint, can act in stays—
Might now, if gifted with discerning,
Find opportunities of learning:
As these two creatures—from their pout
And frown, 'twas plain—had just fall'n out;
And all their little thoughts, of course,
Were stirring in full fret and force:—
Like mites, through microscope espied,
A world of nothings magnified.

But mild the vent such beings seek,
The tempest of their souls to speak:
As Opera swains to fiddles sigh,
To fiddles fight, to fiddles die,
Even so this tender couple set
Their well-bred woes to a Duet.

WALTZ DUET.*

HE.

Long as I waltz'd with only thee,
Each blissful Wednesday that went by,
Nor stylish Stultz, nor neat Nugee
Adorn'd a youth so blest as I.
Oh! ah! ah! oh!
Those happy days are gone—heigho!

SHE.

Long as with thee I skimm'd the ground,
Nor yet was scorn'd for Lady Jane,
No blither nymph tetotum'd round
To Collinet's immortal strain.
Oh! ah! &c.
Those happy days are gone—heigho!

HE.

With Lady Jane now whirl'd about,
I know no bounds of time or breath;
And, should the charmer's head hold out,
My heart and heels are hers till death.
Oh! ah! &c.
Still round and round through life we'll go.

SHE.

To Lord Fitznoodle's eldest son,
A youth renown'd for waistcoats smart,
I now have given (excuse the pun)
A vested interest in my heart.
Oh! ah! &c.
Still round and round with him I'll go.

HE.

What if, by fond remembrance l[illegible]
Again to wear our mutual c[illegible]ain,
For me thou cut'st Fitznoodle dead,
And I *levant* from Lady Jane.
Oh! ah! &c.
Still round and round again we'll go.

SHE.

Though he the Noodle honours give,
And thine, dear youth, are not so high,
With thee in endless waltz I'd live,
With thee, to Weber's Stop-Waltz, die!
Oh! ah! &c.
Thus round and round through life we'll go.
[*Exeunt waltzing.*

While thus, like motes that dance away
Existence in a summer ray,
These gay things, born but to quadrille,
The circle of their doom fulfil—
(That dancing doom, whose law decrees
That they should live, on the alert toe,
A life of ups-and-downs, like keys
Of Broadwood's in a long concerto:—)
While thus the fiddle's spell, *within*,
Calls up its realm of restless sprites,
Without, as if some Mandarin
Were holding there his Feast of Lights,
Lamps of all hues, from walks and bowers
Broke on the eye, like kindling flowers,
Till, budding into light, each tree
Bore its fu[illegible] fruit of brilliancy.

Here shone a garden—lamps all o'er
As though the Spirits of the Air
Had tak'n it in their heads to pour
A shower of summer meteors there;—
While here a lighted shrubb'ry led
To a small lake that sleeping lay,
Cradled in foliage, but, o'er-head,
Open to heaven's sweet breath and ray;
While round its rim there burning stood
Lamps, with young flowers beside them bedded,
That shrunk from such warm neighbourhood;
And, looking bashful in the flood,
Blush'd to behold themselves so wedded

Hither, to this embower'd retreat,
Fit but for nights so still and sweet,
Nights, such as Eden's calm recall
In its first lonely hour, when all
So silent is, below, on high,
That if a star falls down the sky,
You almost think you hear it fall—
Hither, to this recess, a few,
To shun the dancers' wild'ring noise,
And give an hour, ere night-time flew,
To Music's more ethereal joys,
Came with their voices—ready all
As Echo, waiting for a call—
In hymn or ballad, dirge or glee,
To weave their mingling minstrelsy.

And, first, a dark-ey'd nymph, array'd—
Like her, whom Art hath deathless made,
Bright Mona Lisa†—with that braid
Of hair across the brow, and one
Small gem that in the centre shone—
With face, too, in its form resembling
Da Vinci's Beauties—the dark eyes,
Now lucid, as through crystal trembling,
Now soft, as if suffus'd with sighs—
Her lute, that hung beside her, took,
And, bending o'er it with shy look,
More beautiful, in shadow thus,
Than when with life most luminous,
Pass'd her light finger o'er the chords,
And sung to them these mournful words.

SONG.

Bring hither, bring thy lute, while day is dying
Here will I lay me, and list to thy song;
Should tones of other days mix with its sighing,
Tones of a light heart, now banish'd so long,
Chase them away—they bring but pain,
And let thy theme be woe again.

Sing on, thou mournful lute—day is fast going,
Soon will its light from thy chords die away;
One little gleam in the west is still glowing,
When that hath vanish'd, farewell to thy lay
Mark, how it fades!—see, it is fled!
Now, sweet lute, be thou, too, dead.

The group, that late, in garb of Greeks,
Sung their light chorus o'er the tide—
Forms, such as up the wooded creeks

* It is hardly necessary to remind the reader that this Duet is a parody of the often-translated and parodied ode of Horace, "Donec gratus eram tibi," &c.

† The celebrated portrait by Leonardo da Vinci, which he is said to have occupied four years in painting.—*Vasari*, vol. vii

Of Helle's shore at noon-day glide,
Or, nightly, on her glist'ning sea,
Woo the bright waves with melody—
Now link'd their triple league again
Of voices sweet, and sung a strain,
Such as, had Sappho's tuneful ear
But caught it, on the fatal steep,
She would have paus'd, entranc'd, to hear,
And, for that day, deferr'd her leap.

SONG AND TRIO.

On one of those sweet nights that oft
Their lustre o'er the Ægean fling,
Beneath my casement, low and soft,
I heard a Lesbian lover sing;
And, list'ning both with ear and thought,
These sounds upon the night-breeze caught—
"Oh, happy as the gods is he,
"Who gazes at this hour on thee!"

The song was one by Sappho sung,
In the first love-dreams of her lyre,
When words of passion from her tongue
Fell like a shower of living fire.
And still, at close of ev'ry strain,
I heard these burning words again—
"Oh, happy as the gods is he,
"Who listens at this hour to thee!"

Once more to Mona Lisa turn'd
Each asking eye—nor turn'd in vain;
Though the quick, transient blush that burn'd
Bright o'er her cheek, and died again,
Show'd with what inly shame and fear
Was utter'd what all lov'd to hear.
Yet not to sorrow's languid lay
Did she her lute-song now devote;
But thus, with voice that, like a ray
Of southern sunshine, seem'd to float—
So rich with climate was each note—
Call'd up in every heart a dream
Of Italy, with this soft theme:—

SONG.

Oh, where art thou dreaming,
On land, or on sea?
In my lattice is gleaming
The watch-light for thee;
And this fond heart is glowing
To welcome thee home,
And the night is fast going,
But thou art not come:
No, thou com'st not!

'Tis the time when night-flowers
Should wake from their rest;
'Tis the hour of all hours,
When the lute singeth best.
But the flowers are half sleeping
Till *thy* glance they see!
And the hush'd lute is keeping
Its music for thee.
Yet, thou com'st not!

Scarce had the last word left her lip,
When a light, boyish form, with trip
Fantastic, up the green walk came,
Prank'd in gay vest, to which the flame
Of every lamp he pass'd, or blue,
Or green, or crimson, lent its hue;
As though a live cameleon's skin
He had despoil'd to robe him in.
A zone he wore of clatt'ring shells,
And from his lofty cap, where shone
A peacock's plume, there dangled bells
That rung as he came dancing on.

Close after him, a page—in dress
And shape, his miniature express—
An ample basket, fill'd with store
Of toys and trinkets, laughing bore;
Till, having reach'd this verdant seat,
He laid it at his master's feet,
Who, half in speech and half in song,
Chaunted this invoice to the throng:—

SONG.

Who'll buy?—'tis Folly's shop, who'll buy?—
We've toys to suit all ranks and ages;
Besides our usual fools' supply,
We've lots of playthings, too, for sages.
For reasoners, here's a juggler's cup,
That fullest seems when nothing's in it;
And nine-pins set, like systems, up,
To be knock'd down the following minute.
Who'll buy?—'tis folly's shop, who'll buy?

Gay caps we've here of foolscap make,
For bards to wear in dog-day weather;
Or bards the bells alone may take,
And leave to wits the cap and feather.
Tetotums we've for patriots got,
Who court the mob with antics humble;
Like theirs the patriot's dizzy lot,
A glorious spin, and then—a tumble.
Who'll buy, &c. &c.

Here, wealthy misers to inter,
We've shrouds of neat post-obit paper;
While, for their heirs, we've *quick*silver,
That, fast as they can wish, will caper
For aldermen we've dials true,
That tell no hour but that of dinner:
For courtly parsons sermons new,
That suit alike both saint and sinner.
Who'll buy, &c. &c.

No time we've now to name our terms,
But, whatsoe'er the whims that seize you,
This oldest of all mortal firms,
Folly & Co., will try to please you.
Or, should you wish a darker hue
Of goods than *we* can recommend you,
Why then (as we with lawyers do)
To Knavery's shop next door we'll send you.
Who'll buy, &c. &c.

While thus the blissful moments roll'd,
Moments of rare and fleeting light,
That show themselves, like grains of gold
In the mine's refuse, few and bright;
Behold where, opening far away,
The long Conservatory's range,
Stripp'd of the flowers it wore all day,
But gaining lovelier in exchange,
Presents, on Dresden's costliest ware,
A supper such as Gods might share.

Ah much-lov'd Supper!—blithe repast
Of other times, now dwindling fast,
Since Dinner far into the night
Advanc'd the march of appetite;
Deploy'd his never-ending forces
Of various vintage and three courses,
And, like those Goths who play'd the dickens
With Rome and all her sacred chickens,
Put Supper and her fowls so white,
Legs, wings, and drumsticks, all to flight

Now wak'd once more by wine—whose tide
Is the true Hippocrene, where glide
The muse's swans with happiest wing,
Dipping their bills, before they sing—
The minstrels of the table greet
The list'ning ear with descant sweet:—

SONG AND TRIO.

THE LEVEE AND COUCHEE.

Call the Loves around,
Let the whisp'ring sound
Of their wings be heard alone,
Till soft to rest
My Lady blest
At this bright hour hath gone.
Let Fancy's beams
Play o'er her dreams,
Till, touch'd with light all through,
Her spirit be
Like a summer sea,
Shining and slumb'ring too.
And, while thus hush'd she lies,
Let the whisper'd chorus rise—
"Good evening, good evening, to our Lady's bright eyes."

But the day-beam breaks,
See, our Lady wakes!
Call the Loves around once more,
Like stars that wait
At Morning's gate,
Her first steps to adore.
Let the veil of night
From her dawning sight
All gently pass away,
Like mists that flee
From a summer sea,
Leaving it full of day.
And, while her last dream flies.
Let the whisper'd chorus rise—
"Good morning, good morning, to our Lady's bright eyes."

SONG.

If to see thee be to love thee,
If to love thee be to prize
Nought of earth or heav'n above thee,
Nor to live but for those eyes:
If such love to mortal given,
Be wrong to earth, be wrong to heav'n,
'Tis not for thee the fault to blame,
For from those eyes the madness came.
Forgive but thou the crime of loving,
In this heart more pride 'twill raise
To be thus wrong, with thee approving,
Than right, with all a world to praise

But say, while light these songs resound,
What means that buz of whisp'ring round,
From lip to lip—as if the Power
Of Mystery, in this gay hour,
Had thrown some secret (as we fling
Nuts among children) to that ring
Of rosy, restless lips, to be
Thus scrambled for so wantonly?
And, mark ye, still as each reveals
The mystic news, her hearer steals
A look tow'rds yon enchanted chair,
Where, like the Lady of the Masque,
A nymph, as exquisitely fair
As Love himself for bride could ask,
Sits blushing deep, as if aware
Of the wing'd secret circling there.
Who is this nymph? and what, oh Muse,
What, in the name of all odd things
That woman's restless brain pursues,
What mean these mystic whisperings.

Thus runs the tale:—yon blushing maid,
Who sits in beauty's light array'd,
While o'er her leans a tall young Dervise,
(Who from her eyes, as all observe, is
Learning by heart the Marriage Service,)
Is the bright heroine of our song,—
The Love-wed Psyche, whom so long
We've miss'd among this mortal train,
We thought her wing'd to heaven again.
But no—earth still demands her smile;
Her friends, the Gods, must wait awhile.
And if, for maid of heavenly birth,
A young Duke's proffer'd heart and hand
Be things worth waiting for on earth,
Both are, this hour, at her command
To-night, in yonder half-lit shade,
For love concerns expressly meant,
The fond proposa' first was made,
And love and silence blush'd consent
Parents and friends (all here, as Jews,
Enchanters, housemaids, Turks, Hindoos,)
Have heard, approv'd, and blest the tie;
And now, hadst thou a poet's eye,
Thou might'st behold in th' air, above
That brilliant brow, triumphant Love,
Holding, as if to drop it down
Gently upon her curls, a crown
Of Ducal shape—but, oh, such gems
Pilfer'd from Peri diadems,
And set in gold like that which shines
To deck the Fairy of the Mines:
In short, a crown all glorious—such as
Love orders when he makes a Duchess.

But see, 'tis morn in heaven; the Sun
Up the bright orient hath begun
To canter his immortal team;
And, though not yet arriv'd in sight,
His leader's nostrils send a steam
Of radiance forth, so rosy bright
As makes their onward path all light
What's to be done? if Sol will be
So deuced early, so must we;
And when the day thus shines outright,
Ev'n dearest friends must bid good night.
So, farewell, scene of mirth and masking,
Now almost a by-gone tale;
Beauties, late in lamp-light basking,
Now, by daylight, dim and pale;
Harpers, yawning o'er your harps,
Scarcely knowing flats from sharps;
Mothers who, while bor'd you keep
Time by nodding, nod to sleep;
Heads of air, that stood last night
Crêpé, crispy, and upright,
But have now, alas, one sees, a
Leaning like the tower of Pisa;
Fare ye well—thus sinks away
All that's mighty, all that's bright;
Tyre and Sidon had their day,
And ev'n a Ball—has but its night!

MISCELLANEOUS POEMS.

VARIETY.

Ask what prevailing, pleasing power
Allures the sportive, wandering bee
To roam, untired, from flower to flower,
He'll tell you, 'tis variety.

Look Nature round, her features trace,
Her seasons, all her changes see;
And own, upon Creation's face,
The greatest charm's variety

For me, ye gracious powers above
Still let me roam, unfix'd and free;
In all things,—but the nymph I love,
I'll change, and taste variety.

But, Patty, not a world of charms
Could e'er estrange my heart from thee;—
No, Let me ever seek those arms,
There still I'll find variety.

IF I SWEAR BY THAT EYE

If I swear by that eye, you'll allow,
Its look is so shifting and new,
That the oath I might take on it now
The very next glance would undo.

Those balmy lips that nestle so sly
  Such thousands of arrows have got,
That an oath, on the glance of an eye
  Such as yours, may be off in a shot.

Should I swear by the dew on your lip,
  Though each moment the treasure renews,
If my constancy wishes to trip,
  I may kiss off the oath when I choose.

Or a sigh may disperse from that flow'r
  Both the dew and the oath that are there
And I'll make a new vow every hour,
  To lose them so sweetly in air.

But clear up the heav'n of your brow,
  Nor fancy my faith is a feather;
On my heart I will pledge you my vow,
  And they both must be broken together!

WHEN TIME, WHO STEALS OUR YEARS AWAY.

When Time, who steals our years away,
  Shall steal our pleasures too,
The mem'ry of the past will stay,
  And half our joys renew.
Then, Julia, when thy beauty's flow'r
  Shall feel the wintry air,
Remembrance will recall the hour
  When thou alone wert fair.
Then talk no more of future gloom;
  Our joys shall always last;
For Hope shall brighten days to come,
  And Mem'ry gild the past.

Come, Chloe, fill the genial bowl,
  I drink to Love and thee:
Thou never canst decay in soul,
  Thou'lt still be young for me.
And as thy lips the tear-drop chase,
  Which on my cheek they find,
So hope shall steal away the trace
  That sorrow leaves behind.
Then fill the bowl!—away with gloom!
  Our joys shall always last;
For Hope shall brighten days to come,
  And Mem'ry gild the past.

But mark, at thought of future years
  When love shall lose its soul,
My Chloe drops her timid tears,
  They mingle with my bowl.
How like this bowl of wine, my fair,
  Our loving life shall fleet;
Though tears may sometimes mingle there,
  The draught will still be sweet.
Then fill the cup—away with gloom!
  Our joys shall always last;
For Hope will brighten days to come,
  And Mem'ry gild the past.

HAVE YOU NOT SEEN THE TIMID TEAR.

Have you not seen the timid tear,
  Steal trembling from mine eye?
Have you not mark'd the flush of fear,
  Or caught the murmur'd sigh?
And can you think my love is chill,
  Nor fix'd on you alone?
And can you rend, by doubting still,
  A heart so much your own?

To you my soul's affections move,
  Devoutly, warmly true;
My life has been a task of love,
  One long, long thought of you.
If all your tender faith be o'er,
  If still my truth you'll try;
Alas, I know but *one* proof more—
  I'll bless your name, and die!

DID NOT.

'Twas a new feeling—something more
Than we had dar'd to own before,
    Which then we hid not;
We saw it in each other's eye,
And wish'd, in every half-breath'd sigh,
    To speak, but did not.

She felt my lips' impassion'd touch—
'Twas the first time I dared so much,
    And yet she chid not;
But whisper'd o'er my burning brow,
"Oh! do you doubt I love you now?"
    Sweet soul! I did not.

Warmly I felt her bosom thrill,
I press'd it closer, closer still,
    Though gently bid not;
Till—oh! the world hath seldom heard
Of lovers, who so nearly err'd,
    And yet, who did not.

FRIEND OF MY SOUL.

Friend of my soul, this goblet sip,
  'Twill chase that pensive tear;
'Tis not so sweet as woman's lip,
  But, oh! 'tis more sincere.
    Like her delusive beam,
      'Twill steal away thy mind:
    But, truer than love's dream,
      It leaves no sting behind.

Come, twine the wreath, thy brows to shade;
  These flow'rs were cull'd at noon;—
Like woman's love the rose will fade,
  But, ah! not half so soon.
    For though the flower's decay'd,
      Its fragrance is not o'er;
    But once when love's betray'd,
      Its sweet life blooms no more.

"GOOD NIGHT! GOOD NIGHT!"

"Good night! good night!"—And is it so?
And must I from my Rosa go?
Oh Rosa, say "Good night!" once more,
And I'll repeat it o'er and o'er,
Till the first glance of dawning light
Shall find us saying, still, "Good night."

And still "Good night," my Rosa, say—
But whisper still, "A minute stay;"
And I will stay, and every minute
Shall have an age of transport in it;
Till Time himself shall stay his flight,
To listen to our sweet "Good night."

"Good night!" you'll murmur with a sigh,
And tell me it is time to fly:
And I will vow, will swear to go,
While still that sweet voice murmurs "No!"
Till slumber seal our weary sight—
And then, my Love, my soul, "Good night!"

WHY DOES AZURE DECK THE SKY?

Why does azure deck the sky?
  'Tis to be like thy looks of blue;
Why is red the rose's dye?
  Because it is thy blushes' hue.
All that's fair, by Love's decree,
Has been made resembling thee!

Why is falling snow so white,
  But to be like thy bosom fair?
Why are solar beams so bright?
  That they may seem thy golden hair!
All that's bright, by Love's decree,
Has been made resembling thee!

Why are nature's beauties felt?
  Oh! 'tis thine in her we see!
Why has music power to melt?
  Oh! because it speaks like thee
All that's sweet, by Love's decree
Has been made resembling thee!

TO ROSA.

Say, why should the girl of my soul be in tears
  At a meeting of rapture like this,
When the glooms of the past and the sorrow of years
  Have been paid by one moment of bliss?

Are they shed for that moment of blissful delight,
  Which dwells on her memory yet?
Do they flow, like the dews of the love-breathing night,
  From the warmth of the sun that has set?

Oh! sweet is the tear on that languishing smile,
  That smile, which is loveliest then;
And if such are the drops that delight can beguile,
  Thou shalt weep them again and again.

FLY FROM THE WORLD.

Fly from the world, O Bessy! to me,
  Thou wilt never find any sincerer;
I'll give up the world, O Bessy! for thee,
  I can never meet any that's dearer.
Then tell me no more, with a tear and a sigh,
  That our loves will be censured by many;
All, all have their follies, and who will deny
  That ours is the sweetest of any?

When your lip has met mine, in communion so sweet,
  Have we felt as if virtue forbid it?—
Have we felt as if heav'n denied them to meet?
  No, rather 'twas heav'n that did it.
So innocent, love, is the joy we then sip,
  So little of wrong is there in it,
That I wish all my errors were lodg'd on your lip,
  And I'd kiss them away in a minute.

Then come to your lover, Oh! fly to his shed,
  From a world which I know thou despisest;
And slumber will hover as light o'er our bed
  As e'er on the couch of the wisest.
And when o'er our pillow the tempest is driven,
  And thou, pretty innocent, fearest,
I'll tell thee, it is not the chiding of heav'n,
  'Tis only our lullaby, dearest.

And, oh! while we lay on our deathbed, my love,
  Looking back on the scene of our errors,
A sigh from my Bessy shall plead then above,
  And Death be disarm'd of his terrors.
And each to the other embracing will say,
  "Farewell! let us hope we're forgiven."
Thy last fading glance will illumine the way,
  And a kiss be our passport to heaven!

FANNY, DEAREST.

Yes! had I leisure to sigh and mourn,
  Fanny, dearest, for thee I'd sigh;
And every smile on my cheek should turn
  To tears when thou art nigh.
But, between love, and wine, and sleep,
  So busy a life I live,
That even the time it would take to weep
  Is more than my heart can give.
Then bid me not to despair and pine,
  Fanny, dearest of all the dears!
The Love that's order'd to bathe in wine,
  Would be sure to take cold in tears.

Reflected bright in this heart of mine,
  Fanny, dearest, thy image lies;
But, ah, the mirror would cease to shine,
  If dimm'd too often with sighs
They lose the half of beauty's light,
  Who view it through sorrow's tear;
And 'tis but to see thee truly bright
  That I keep my eye-beam clear.
Then wait no longer till tears shall flow,
  Fanny, dearest—the hope is vain;
If sunshine cannot dissolve thy snow,
  I shall never attempt it with rain

THINK ON THAT LOOK.

Think on that look whose melting ray
  For one sweet moment mix'd with mine
And for that moment seem'd to say,
  "I dare not, or I would be thine!"

Think on thy ev'ry smile and glance,
  On all thou hast to charm and move;
And then forgive my bosom's trance,
  Nor tell me it is sin to love.

Oh, *not* to love thee were th sin;
  For sure, if Fate's decrees be done,
Thou, thou art destin'd still to win,
  As I am destin'd to be won!

THE CATALOGUE.

"Come, tell me," says Rosa, as kissing and kist,
  One day she reclin'd on my breast;
"Come, tell me the number, repeat me the list
  "Of the nymphs you have lov'd and carest"—
Oh Rosa! 'twas only my fancy that roved,
  My heart at the moment was free;
But I'll tell thee, my girl, how many I've loved
  And the number shall finish with thee

My tutor was Kitty; In infancy wild
  She taught me the way to be blest;
She taught me to love her, I lov'd like a child,
  But Kitty could fancy the rest.
This lesson of dear and enrapturing lore
  I have never forgot, I allow.
I have had it *by rote* very often before,
  But never *by heart* until now.

Pretty Martha was next, and my soul was all flame,
  But my head was so full of romance
That I fancied her into some chivalry dame,
  And I was her knight of the lance.
But Martha was not of this fanciful school,
  And she laugh'd at her poor little knight;
While I thought her a goddess, she thought me a fool,
  And I'll swear *she* was most in the right.

My soul was now calm, till, by Cloris's looks,
  Again I was tempted to rove;
But Cloris, I found, was so learned in books
  That she gave me more logic than love.
So I left this young Sappho, and hasten'd to fly
  To those sweeter logicians in bliss,
Who argue the point with a soul-telling eye,
  And convince us at once with a kiss.

Oh! Susan was then all the world unto me,
  But Susan was piously given;
And the worst of it was, we could never agree
  On the road that was shortest to Heaven
"Oh, Susan!" I've said, in the moments of mirth,
  "What's devotion to thee or to me?
"I devoutly believe there's a heaven on earth,
  "And believe that that heaven's in *thee*!"

MARY, I BELIEV'D THEE TRUE.

Mary, I believ'd thee true,
  And I was blest in thus believing;
But now I mourn that e'er I knew
  A girl so fair and so deceiving.
    Fare thee well.

Few have ever lov'd like me,—
  Yes, I have lov'd thee too sincerely!
And few have e'er deceiv'd like thee,—
  Alas! deceiv'd me too severely.

Fare thee well!—yet think awhile
  On one whose bosom bleeds to doubt thee;
Who now would rather trust that smile,
  And die with thee than live without thee.

Fare thee well! I'll think of thee,
  Thou leav'st me many a bitter token;
For see, distracting woman, see,
  My peace is gone, my heart is broken!—
    Fare thee well!

TAKE BACK THE SIGH.

Take back the sigh, thy lips of art
  In passion's moment breath'd to me;
Yet no—it must not, will not part,
'Tis now the life-breath of my heart,
  And has become too pure for thee.

Take back the kiss, that faithless sigh
  With all the warmth of truth imprest;
Yet, no—the fatal kiss may lie,
Upon *thy* lip its sweets would die,
  Or bloom to make a rival blest.

Take back the vows that, night and day,
  My heart receiv'd, I thought, from thine;
Yet, no—allow them still to stay,
They might some other heart betray,
  As sweetly as they've ruin'd mine.

TO CLOE.—IMITATED FROM MARTIAL.

I could resign that eye of blue
  Howe'er its splendour used to thrill me;
And ev'n that cheek of roseate hue,—
  To lose it, Cloe, scarce would kill me.

That snowy neck I ne'er should miss,
  However much I've rav'd about it;
And sweetly as that lip can kiss,
  I *think* I could exist without it.

In short, so well I've learnt to fast,
  That, sooth my love, I know not whether
I might not bring myself at last,
  To—do without you altogether.

THE WREATH AND THE CHAIN.

I bring thee, love, a golden chain,
  I bring thee too a flowery wreath;
The gold shall never wear a stain,
  The flow'rets long shall sweetly breathe.
Come, tell me which the tie shall be,
To bind thy gentle heart to me.

The chain is form'd of golden threads,
  Bright as Minerva's yellow hair,
When the last beam of evening sheds
  Its calm and sober lustre there.
The Wreath's of brightest myrtle wove,
  With sun-lit drops of bliss among it,
And many a rose-leaf, cull'd by Love,
  To heal his lip when bees have stung it.
Come, tell me which the tie shall be,
To bind thy gentle heart to me.

Yes, yes, I read that ready eye,
  Which answers when the tongue is loath,
Thou lik'st the form of either tie,
  And spread'st thy playful hands for both.
Ah!—if there were not something wrong,
  The world would see them blended oft;
The Chain would make the Wreath so strong!
  The Wreath would make the Chain so soft!
Then might the gold, the flow'rets be
Sweet fetters for my love and me.

But, Fanny, so unblest they twine,
  That (Heaven alone can tell the reason)
When mingled thus they cease to shine,
  Or shine but for a transient season.
Whether the Chain may press too much,
  Or that the Wreath is slightly braided,
Let but the gold the flow'rets touch,
  And all their bloom, their glow is faded!
Oh! better to be always free,
Than thus to bind my love to me.

The timid girl now hung her head,
  And, as she turn'd an upward glance,
I saw a doubt its twilight spread
  Across her brows divine expanse.
Just then, the garland's brightest rose
  Gave one of its love-breathing sighs—
Oh! who can ask how Fanny chose,
  That ever look'd in Fanny's eyes?
"The Wreath, my life, the Wreath shall be
"The tie to bind my soul to thee."

THE SALE OF LOVES.

I dreamt that, in the Paphian groves,
  My nets by moonlight laying,
I caught a flight of wanton Loves,
  Among the rose-beds playing.
Some just had left their silv'ry shell,
  While some were full in feather;
So pretty a lot of Loves to sell,
  Were never yet strung together.
    Come buy my Loves,
    Come buy my Loves,
Ye dames and rose-lipp'd misses!—
    They're new and bright,
    The cost is light,
For the coin of this isle is kisses.

First Cloris came, with looks sedate,
  Their coin on her lips was ready;
"I buy," quoth she, "my Love by weight,
  "Full grown, if you please, and steady."
"Let mine be light," said Fanny, "pray—
  "Such lasting toys undo one;
"A light little Love that will last to-day,—
  "To-morrow I'll sport a new one."
    Come buy my Loves,
    Come buy my Loves,
Ye dames and rose-lipp'd misses!—
    There's some will keep,
    Some light and cheap,
At from ten to twenty kisses.

The learned Prue took a pert young thing,
  To divert her virgin Muse with,
And pluck sometimes a quill from his wing,
  To indite her billet-doux with.
Poor Cloe would give for a well-fledg'd pair
  Her only eye, if you'd ask it;
And Tabitha begg'd, old toothless fair,
  For the youngest Love in the basket.
  Come buy my Loves, &c. &c.

But *one* was left, when Susan came,
  One worth them all together;
At sight of her dear looks of shame,
  He smil'd, and prun'd his feather.
She wish'd the boy—'twas more than whim—
  Her looks, her sighs betray'd it;
But kisses were not enough for him,
  I ask'd a heart, and she paid it!
    Good-by, my Loves,
    Good-by, my Loves,
'Twould make you smile to've seen us
    First trade for this
    Sweet child of bliss,
And then nurse the boy between us.

TO A BOY WITH A WATCH

Is it not sweet, beloved youth,
  To rove through Erudition's bowers,
And cull the golden fruits of truth,
  And gather Fancy's brilliant flowers?

And is it not more sweet than this,
To feel thy parents' hearts approving,
And pay them back in sums of bliss
The dear, the endless debt of loving?

It must be so to thee, my youth;
With this idea toil is lighter;
This sweetens all the fruits of truth,
And makes the flower of fancy brighter.

The little gift we send thee, boy,
May sometimes teach thy soul to ponder,
If indolence or siren joy
Should ever tempt that soul to wander.

'Twill tell thee that the winged day
Can ne'er be chain'd by man's endeavour
That life and time shall fade away,
While heav'n and virtue bloom forever!

To . . . .

Remember him thou leav'st behind,
Whose heart is warmly bound to thee,
Close as the tend'rest links can bind
A heart as warm as heart can be.

Oh! I had long in freedom rov'd,
Though many seem'd my soul to share;
'Twas passion when I thought I lov'd,
'Twas fancy when I thought them fair.

Ev'n she, my muse's early theme,
Beguil'd me only while she warm'd;
'Twas young desire that fed the dream,
And reason broke what passion form'd.

But thou—ah! better had it been
If I had still in freedom rov'd,
If I had ne'er thy beauties seen,
For then I never should have lov'd.

Then all the pain which lovers feel
Had never to this heart been known;
But then, the joys that lovers steal,
Should *they* have ever been my own?

Oh! trust me when I swear thee this,
Dearest! the pain of lov[illegible]g thee,
The very pain is sweeter bliss
Than passion's wildest ecstasy.

That little cage I would not part,
In which my soul is prison'd now,
For the most light and winged heart
That wantons on the passing vow.

Still, my belov'd! still keep in mind,
However far remov'd from me,
That there is one thou leav'st behind
Whose heart respires for only thee!

And though ungenial ties have bound
Thy fate unto another's care,
That arm, which clasps thy bosom round,
Cannot confine the heart that's there.

No, no! That heart is only mine
By ties all other ties above,
For I have wed it at a shrine
Where we have had no priest but Love.

REUBEN AND ROSE

A TALE OF ROMANCE.

The darkness that hung upon Willumberg's walls
Had long been remember'd with awe and dismay;
For years not a sunbeam had play'd in its halls,
And it seem'd as shut out from the regions of day.

Though the valleys were brighten'd by many a beam,
Yet none could the woods of that castle illume;
And the lightning, which flash'd on the neighbouring stream,
Flew back, as if fearing to enter the gloom!

"Oh! when shall this horrible darkness disperse!"
Said Willumberg's lord to the Seer of the Cave;—
"It can never dispel," said the wizard of verse,
"Till the bright star of chivalry sinks in the wave!"

And who was the bright star of chivalry then?
Who *could* be but Reuben, the flow'r of the age?
For Reuben was first in the combat of men,
Though Youth had scarce written his name on her page.

For Willumberg's daughter his young heart had beat,—
For Rose, who was bright as the spirit of dawn,
When with wand dropping diamonds, and silvery feet,
It walks o'er the flow'rs of the mountain and lawn.

Must Rose, then, from Reuben so fatally sever.
Sad, sad were the words of the Seer of the Cave,
That darkness should cover that castle for ever,
Or Reuben be sunk in the merciless wave!

To the wizard she flew, saying, "Tell me, oh, tell!
Shall my Reuben no more be restor'd to my eyes?"
"Yes, yes—when a spirit shall toll the great bell
Of the mould'ring abbey, your Reuben shall rise!"

Twice, thrice he repeated "Your Reuben shall rise!"
And Rose felt a moment's release from her pain;
And wip'd, while she listen'd, the tears from her eyes,
And hop'd she might yet see her hero again.

That hero could smile at the terrors of death,
When he felt that he died for the sire of his Rose,
To the Oder he flew, and there, plunging beneath,
In the depth of the billows soon found his repose

How strangely the order of destiny falls!—
Not long in the waters the warrior lay,
When a sunbeam was seen to glance over the walls,
And the castle of Willumberg bask'd in the ray

All, all but the soul of the maid was in light,
There sorrow and terror lay gloomy and blank
Two days did she wander, and all the long night,
In quest of her love, on the wide river's bank

Oft, oft did she pause for the toll of the bell,
And heard but the breathings of night in the air;
Long, long did she gaze on the watery swell,
And saw but the foam of the white billow there

And often as midnight its veil would undraw,
As she look'd at the light of the moon in the stream,
She thought 'twas his helmet of silver she saw,
As the curl of the surge glitter'd high in the beam.

And now the third night was begemming the sky;
Poor Rose, on the cold dewy margent reclin'd,
There wept till the tear almost froze in her eye,
When—hark!—'twas the bell that came deep in the wind!

She startled, and saw, through the glimmering shade,
A form o'er the waters in majesty glide;
She knew 'twas her love, though his cheek was decay'd,
And his helmet of silver was wash'd by the tide

Was this what the Seer of the Cave had foretold?—
Dim, dim, through the phantom the moon shot a gleam
'Twas Reuben, but, ah! he was deathly and cold,
And flected away like the spell of a dream!

Twice, thrice did he rise, and as often she thought
From the bank to embrace him, but vain her endeavour
Then, plunging beneath, at a billow she caught,
And sunk to repose on its bosom for ever!

ANACREONTIC

Press the grape, and let it pour
Around the board its purple show'r,
And, while the drops my goblet steep,
I'll think in woe the clusters weep.

Weep on, weep on, my pouting vine!
Heav'n grant no tears, but tears of wine.
Weep on; and, as thy sorrows flow,
I'll taste the luxury of woe.

To . . . .

THAT wrinkle, when first I espied it
  At once put my heart out of pain;
Till the eye, that was glowing beside it,
  Disturb'd my ideas again.

Thou art just in the twilight at present,
  When woman's declension begins;
When, fading from all that is pleasant,
  She bids a good night to her sins.

Yet thou still art so lovely to me,
  I would sooner, my exquisite mother!
Repose in the sunset of thee,
  Than bask in the noon of another.

TO MRS. . . . .

ON SOME CALUMNIES AGAINST HER CHARACTER

Is not thy mind a gentle mind?
Is not that heart a heart refin'd?
Hast thou not every gentle grace,
We love in woman's mind and face?
And, oh! art *thou* a shrine for Sin
To hold her hateful worship in?

No, no, be happy—dry that tear—
Though some thy heart hath harbour'd near,
May now repay its love with blame;
Though man, who ought to shield thy fame,
Ungenerous man, be first to shun thee;
Though all the world look cold upon thee,
Yet shall thy pureness keep thee still
Unharm'd by that surrounding chill;
Like the fam'd drop, in crystal found,
Floating, while all was froz'n round,—
Unchill'd, unchanging shalt thou be,
Safe in thy own sweet purity.

To . . . .

WHEN I lov'd you, I can't but allow
  I had many an exquisite minute;
But the scorn that I feel for you now
  Hath even more luxury in it.

Thus, whether we're on or we're off,
  Some witchery seems to await you;
To love you was pleasant enough,
  And, oh! 'tis delicious to hate you!

TO JULIA.

IN ALLUSION TO SOME ILLIBERAL CRITICISMS.

WHY, let the stingless critic chide
With all that fume of vacant pride
Which mantles o'er the pedant fool,
Like vapour on a stagnant pool.
Oh! if the song, to feeling true,
Can please th' elect, the sacred few,
Whose souls, by Taste and Nature taught,
Thrill with the genuine pulse of thought—
If some fond feeling maid like thee,
The warm-ey'd child of Sympathy,
Shall say, while o'er my simple theme
She languishes in Passion's dream,
"He was, indeed, a tender soul—
"No critic law, no chill control,
"Should ever freeze, by timid art,
"The flowings of so fond a heart!"
Yes, soul of Nature! soul of Love!
That, hov'ring like a snow-wing'd dove,
Breath'd o'er my cradle warblings wild,
And hail'd me Passion's warmest child,—
Grant me the tear from Beauty's eye,
From Feeling's breast the votive sigh;
Oh! let my song, my mem'ry, find
A shrine within the tender mind;
And I will smile when critic's chide,
And I will scorn the fume of pride
Which mantles o'er the pedant fool,
Like vapour round some stagnant pool!

TO JULIA.

MOCK me no more with Love's beguiling dream,
  A dream, I find, illusory as sweet:
One smile of friendship, nay, of cold esteem,
  Far dearer were than passion's bland deceit!

I've heard you oft eternal truth declare;
  Your heart was only mine, I once believ'd.
Ah! shall I say that all your vows were air?
  And *must* I say, my hopes were all deceiv'd?

Vow, then, no longer that our souls are twin'd,
  That all our joys are felt with mutual zeal;
Julia!—'tis pity, pity makes you kind;
  You know I love, and you would *seem* to feel.

But shall I still go seek within those arms
  A joy in which affection takes no part?
No, no, farewell! you give me but your charms,
  When I had fondly thought you gave your hear

THE SHRINE

MY fates had destin'd me to rove
A long, long pilgrimage of love;
And many an altar on my way
Has lur'd my pious steps to stay;
For, if the saint was young and fair,
I turn'd and sung my vespers there.
This, from a youthful pilgrim's fire,
Is what your pretty saints require:
To pass, nor tell a single bead,
With them would be profane indeed!
But, trust me, all this young devotion
Was but to keep my zeal in motion;
And, ev'ry humbler altar past,
I now have reach'd THE SHRINE at last!

TO A LADY,

WITH SOME MANUSCRIPT POEMS, ON LEAVING THE COUNTRY.

WHEN, casting many a look behind,
  I leave the friends I cherish here—
Perchance some other friends to find,
  But surely finding none so dear—

Haply the little simple page,
  Which votive thus I've trac'd for thee,
May now and then a look engage,
  And steal one moment's thought for me.

But, oh! in pity let not those
  Whose hearts are not of gentle mould,
Let not the eye that seldom flows
  With feeling's tear, my song behold.

For, trust me, they who never melt
  With pity, never melt with love;
And such will frown at all I've felt,
  And all my loving lays reprove.

But if, perhaps, some gentler mind,
  Which rather loves to praise than blame,
Should in my page an interest find,
  And linger kindly on my name;

Tell him—or, oh! if, gentler still,
  By female lips my name be blest:
For where do all affections thrill
  So sweetly as in woman's breast?—

Tell her, that he whose loving themes
  Her eye indulgent wanders o'er,
Could sometimes wake from idle dreams,
  And bolder flights of fancy soar;

That Glory oft would claim the lay,
  And Friendship oft his numbers move;
But whisper then, that, "sooth to say,
  "His sweetest song was given to Love!"

TO JULIA.

THOUGH Fate, my girl, may bid us part,
  Our souls it cannot, shall not sever;
The heart will seek its kindred heart,
  And cling to it as close as ever.

But must we, must we part indeed?
  Is all our dream of rapture over?
And does not Julia's bosom bleed
  To leave so dear, so fond a lover?

Does *she* too mourn?—Perhaps she may;
  Perhaps she mourns our bliss so fleeting·
But why is Julia's eye so gay,
  If Julia's heart like mine is beating?

I oft have lov'd that sunny glow
  Of gladness in her blue eye gleaming—
But can the bosom bleed with woe,
  While joy is in the glances beaming?

No, no!—Yet, love, I will not chide;
  Although your heart *were* fond of roving,
Nor that, nor all the world beside
  Could keep your faithful boy from loving

You'll soon be distant from his eye,
  And, with you, all that's worth possessing
Oh! then it will be sweet to die,
  When life has lost its only blessing!

To . . . . .

SWEET lady, look not thus again:
  Those bright deluding smiles recall
A maid remember'd now with pain,
  Who was my love, my life, my all!

Oh! while this heart bewilder'd took
  Sweet poison from her thrilling eye,
Thus would she smile, and lisp, and look,
  And I would hear, and gaze, and sigh!

Yes, I did love her—wildly love—
  She was her sex's best deceiver!
And oft she swore she'd never rove—
  And I was destin'd to believe her!

Then, lady, do not wear the smile
  Of one whose smile could thus betray;
Alas! I think the lovely wile
Again could steal my heart away.

For, when those spells that charm'd my mind,
  On lips so pure as thine I see,
I fear the heart which she resign'd
  Will err again, and fly to thee!

NATURE'S LABELS.

A FRAGMENT.

IN vain we fondly strive to trace
The soul's reflection in the face;
In vain we dwell on lines and crosses,
Crooked mouth, or short proboscis;
Boobies have look'd as wise and bright
As Plato or the Stagirite:
And many a sage and learned skull
Has peep'd through windows dark and dull
Since then, though art do all it can,
We ne'er can reach the inward man,
Nor (howsoe'er "learn'd Thebans" doubt)
The inward woman, from without,
Methinks 'twere well if Nature could
(And Nature could, if Nature would)
Some pithy, short descriptions write,
On tablets large, in black and white,
Which she might hang about our throttles,
Like labels upon physic-bottles;
And where all men might read—but stay—
As dialectic sages say,
The argument most apt and ample
For common use is the example.
For instance, then, if Nature's care
Had not portray'd, in lines so fair,
The inward soul of Lucy L–nd–n,
This is the label she'd have pinn'd on.

LABEL FIRST.

Within this form there lies enshrin'd
The purest, brightest gem of mind.
Though Feeling's hand may sometimes throw
Upon its charms the shade of woe,
The lustre of the gem, when veil'd,
Shall be but mellow'd, not conceal'd.

Now, sirs, imagine, if you're able,
That Nature wrote a second label,
They're her own words,—at least suppose so—
And boldly pin it on Pomposo.

LABEL SECOND.

When I compos'd the fustian brain
Of this redoubted Captain Vain,
I had at hand but few ingredients,
And so was forc'd to use expedients
I put therein some small discerning,
A grain of sense, a grain of learning;
And when I saw the void behind.
I fill'd it up with—froth and wind!
*   *   *   *   *

TO JULIA.

ON HER BIRTHDAY

WHEN Time was entwining the garland of years,
  Which to crown my beloved was given,
Though some of the leaves might be sullied with tears,
  Yet the flow'rs were all gather'd in heaven.

And long may this garland be sweet to the eye,
  May its verdure for ever be new;
Young Love shall enrich it with many a sigh,
  And Sympathy nurse it with dew.

A REFLECTION AT SEA.

SEE how, beneath the moonbeam's smile,
  Yon little billow heaves its breast,
And foams and sparkles for awhile,—
  Then murmuring subsides to rest.

Thus man, the sport of bliss and care,
  Rises on time's eventful sea;
And, having swell'd a moment there,
  Thus melts into eternity!

CLORIS AND FANNY.

CLORIS! if I were Persia's king,
  I'd make my graceful queen of thee;
While FANNY, wild and artless thing,
  Should but thy humble handmaid be.

There is but *one* objection in it—
  That, verily, I'm much afraid
I should, in some unlucky minute,
  Forsake the mistress for the maid.

THE SHIELD.

SAY, did you not hear a voice of death!
  And did you not mark the paly form
Which rode on the silvery mist of the heath,
  And sung a ghostly dirge in the storm?

Was it the wailing bird of the gloom,
  That shrieks on the house of woe all night?
Or a shiv'ring fiend that flew to a tomb,
  To howl and to feed till the glance of light?

'Twas *not* the death-bird's cry from the wood,
  For shiv'ring fiend that hung on the blast;
'Twas the shade of Helderic—man of blood—
  It screams for the guilt of days that are past.

See, how the red, red lightning strays,
  And scares the gliding ghosts of the heath!
Now on the leafless yew it plays,
  Where hangs the shield of this son of death.

That shield is blushing with murd'rous stains;
  Long has it hung from the cold yew's spray;
It is blown by storms and wash'd by rains,
  But neither can take the blood away!

Oft by that yew, on the blasted field,
  Demons dance to the red moon's light;
While the damp boughs creak, and the swinging shield
  Sings to the raving spirit of night!

DREAMS.

To . . . .

In slumber, I prithee how is it
  That souls are oft taking the air,
And paying each other a visit,
  While bodies are heaven knows where?

Last night, 'tis in vain to deny it,
  Your Soul took a fancy to roam,
For I heard her, on tiptoe so quiet,
  Come ask, whether *mine* was at home.

And mine let her in with delight,
  And they talk'd and they laugh'd the time through;
For, when souls come together at night,
  There is no saying what they mayn't do!

And *your* little Soul, heaven bless her!
  Had much to complain and to say,
Of how sadly you wrong and oppress her
  By keeping her prison'd all day.

"If I happen," said she, "but to steal
  "For a peep now and then to her eye,
"Or, to quiet the fever I feel,
  "Just venture abroad on a sigh;

"In an instant she frightens me in
  "With some phantom of prudence or terror,
"For fear I should stray into sin,
  "Or, what is still worse, into error!

So, instead of displaying my graces,
  "By daylight, in language and mien,
"I am shut up in corners and places,
  "Where truly I blush to be seen!"

Upon hearing this piteous confession,
  My Soul, looking tenderly at her,
Declar'd, as for grace and discretion,
  He did not know much of the matter;

"But, to-morrow, sweet Spirit!" he said,
  "Be at home after midnight, and then
"I will come when your lady's in bed,
  "And we'll talk o'er the subject again."

So she whisper'd a word in his ear,
  I suppose to her door to direct him,
And, just after midnight, my dear,
  Your polite little soul may expect him.

TO ROSA.

WRITTEN DURING ILLNESS.

The wisest soul, by anguish torn,
  Will soon unlearn the lore it knew;
And when the shrining casket's worn,
  The gem within will tarnish too.

But love's an essence of the soul,
  Which sinks not with this chain of clay;
Which throbs beyond the chill control
  Of with'ring pain or pale decay.

And surely, when the touch of Death
  Dissolves the spirit's earthly ties,
Love still attends th' immortal breath,
  And makes it purer for the skies!

Oh Rosa, when, to seek its sphere,
  My soul shall leave this orb of men,
That love which form'd its treasure here,
  Shall be its *best* of treasures then!

And as, in fabled dreams of old,
  Some air-born genius, child of time,
Presided o'er each star that roll'd,
  And track'd it through its path sublime;

So thou, fair planet, not unled,
  Shalt through thy mortal orbit stray,
Thy lover's shade, to thee still wed,
  Shall linger round thy earthly way.

Let other spirits range the sky,
  And play around each starry gem;
I'll bask beneath that lucid eye,
  Nor envy worlds of suns to them.

And when that heart shall cease to beat,
  And when that breath at length is free,
Then, Rosa, soul to soul we'll meet,
  And mingle to eternity!

TO JULIA, WEEPING.

Oh! if your tears are giv'n to care,
  If real woe disturbs your peace,
Come to my bosom, weeping fair!
  And I will bid your weeping cease.

But if with Fancy's vision'd fears,
  With dreams of woe your bosom thrill,
You look so lovely in your tears,
  That I must bid you drop them still.

THE WREATH YOU WOVE.

The wreath you wove, the wreath you wove
  Is fair—but oh, how fair,
If Pity's hand had stol'n from Love
  One leaf to mingle there!

If every rose with gold were tied,
  Did gems for dewdrops fall,
One faded leaf where Love had sigh'd
  Were sweetly worth them all.

The wreath you wove, the wreath you wove
  Our emblem well may be,
Its bloom is yours, but hopeless Love
  Must keep its tears for me.

To . . . .

The world had just begun to steal
  Each hope that led me lightly on;
I felt not, as I us'd to feel,
  And life grew dark and love was gone

No eye to mingle sorrow's tear,
  No lip to mingle pleasure's breath,
No circling arms to draw me near—
  'Twas gloomy, and I wish'd for death

But when I saw that gentle eye,
  Oh! something seem'd to tell me then,
That I was yet too young to die.
  And hope and bliss might bloom again

With every gentle smile that crost
  Your kindling cheek, you lighted home
Some feeling, which my heart had lost,
  And peace, which far had learn'd to roam.

'Twas then indeed so sweet to live,
  Hope look'd so new and Love so kind,
That, though I mourn, I yet forgive
  The ruin they have left behind

I could have lov'd you—oh, so well!—
The dream, that wishing boyhood knows,
Is but a bright, beguiling spell,
That only lives while passion glows:

But when this early flush declines,
When the heart's sunny morning fleets,
You know not then how close it twines
Round the first kindred soul it meets.

Yes, yes, I could have lov'd, as one
Who, while his youth's enchantments fall,
Finds something dear to rest upon,
Which pays him for the loss of all.

TO . . . .

NEVER mind how the pedagogue proses,
You want not antiquity's stamp;
A lip, that such fragrance discloses,
Oh! never should smell of the lamp.

Old Cloe, whose withering kiss
Hath long set the Loves at defiance,
Now, done with the science of bliss,
May take to the blisses of science.

But for *you* to be buried in books—
Ah, Fanny, they're pitiful sages,
Who could not in *one* of your looks
Read more than in millions of pages.

Astronomy finds in those eyes
Better light than she studies above;
And Music would borrow your sighs
As the melody fittest for Love.

Your Arithmetic only can trip
If to count your own charms you endeavour;
And eloquence glows on your lip
When you swear, that you'll love me for ever.

Thus you see, what a brilliant alliance
Of arts is assembled in you;—
A course of more exquisite science
Man never need wish to pursue.

And, oh!—if a Fellow like me
May confer a diploma of hearts,
With my lip thus I seal your degree,
My divine little Mistress of Arts!

ON THE DEATH OF A LADY.

SWEET spirit! if thy airy sleep
Nor sees my tears nor hears my sighs,
Then will I weep, in anguish weep,
Till the last heart's drop fills mine eyes.

But if thy sainted soul can feel,
And mingles in our misery;
Then, then my breaking heart I'll seal—
Thou shalt not hear one sigh from me.

The beam of morn was on the stream,
But sullen clouds the day deform:
Like thee was that young, orient beam,
Like death, alas, that sullen storm!

Thou wert not form'd for living here,
So link'd thy soul was with the sky;
Yet, ah, we held thee all so dear,
We thought thou wert not form'd to die.

TO . . . .

THE MORNING OF HER BIRTHDAY.

IN witching slumbers of the night,
I dreamt I was the airy sprite
That on thy natal moment smil'd;
And thought I wafted on my wing
Those flow'rs which in Elysium spring,
To crown my lovely mortal child.

With olive-branch I bound thy head,
Heart's ease along thy path I shed,
Which was to bloom through all thy years
Nor yet did I forget to bind
Love's roses, with his myrtle twin'd,
And dew'd by sympathetic tears.

Such was the wild but precious boon
Which Fancy, at her magic noon,
Bade me to Nona's image pay;
And where it thus my fate to be
Thy little guardian deity,
How blest around thy steps I'd play.

Thy life in peace should glide along,
Calm as some lonely shepherd's song
That's heard at distance in the grove;
No cloud should ever dim thy sky,
No thorns along thy pathway lie,
But all be beauty, peace, and love.

Indulgent Time should never bring
To thee one blight upon his wing,
So gently o'er thy brow he'd fly;
And death itself should but be felt
Like that of daybeams, when they melt,
Bright to the last, in evening's sky!

INCONSTANCY.

AND do I then wonder that Julia deceives me,
When surely there's nothing in nature more common
She vows to be true, and while vowing she leaves me—
And could I expect any more from a woman?

Oh, woman! your heart is a pitiful treasure;
And Mahomet's doctrine was not too severe,
When he held that you were but materials of pleasure,
And reason and thinking were out of your sphere

By your heart, when the fond sighing lover can win it,
He thinks that an age of anxiety's paid;
But, oh, while he's blest, let him die at the minute—
If he live but a *day*, he'll be surely betray'd.

ELEGIAC STANZAS,

SUPPOSED TO BE WRITTEN BY JULIA, ON THE DEATH OF HER BROTHER.

THOUGH sorrow long has worn my heart;
Though every day I've counted o'er
Hath brought a new and quick'ning smart
To wounds that rankled fresh before;

Though in my earliest life bereft
Of tender links by nature tied;
Though hope deceiv'd, and pleasure left,
Though friends betray'd and foes belied;

I still had hopes—for hope will stay
After the sunset of delight;
So like the star which ushers day,
We scarce can think it heralds night!—

I hop'd that, after all its strife,
My weary heart at length should rest,
And, fainting from the waves of life,
Find harbour in a brother's breast.

That brother's breast was warm with truth,
Was bright with honour's purest ray;
He was the dearest, gentlest youth—
Ah, why then was he torn away?

He should have stay'd, have linger'd here
To soothe his Julia's every woe;
He should have chas'd each bitter tear,
And not have caus'd those tears to flow

We saw within his soul expand
The fruits of genius, nurs'd by taste;
While Science, with a fost'ring hand,
Upon his brow her chaplet plac'd

We saw, by bright degrees, his mind
Grow rich in all that makes men dear;—
Enlighten'd, social, and refin'd,
In friendship firm, in love sincere.

Such was the youth we lov'd so well,
And such the hopes that fate denied;—
We lov'd, but ah! could scarcely tell
How deep, how dearly, till he died!

Close as the fondest links could strain,
Twin'd with my very heart he grew;
And by that fate which breaks the chain,
The heart is almost broken too.

TO THE LARGE AND BEAUTIFUL MISS . . . .

IN ALLUSION TO SOME PARTNERSHIP IN A LOTTERY SHARE.

In wedlock a species of lottery lies,
Where in blanks and in prizes we deal;
But how comes it that you, such a capital prize,
Should so long have remain'd in the wheel?

If ever, by Fortune's indulgent decree,
To me such a ticket should roll,
A sixteenth, Heav'n knows! were sufficient for me;
For what could *I* do with the whole?

A DREAM.

I thought this heart enkindled lay
On Cupid's burning shrine:
I thought he stole thy heart away,
And plac'd it near to mine.

I saw thy heart begin to melt,
Like ice before the sun;
Till both a glow congenial felt,
And mingled into one!

TO . . . . . .

With all my soul, then, let us part,
Since both are anxious to be free;
And I will send you home your heart,
If you will send back mine to me.

We've had some happy hours together,
But joy must often change its wing;
And spring would be but gloomy weather,
If we had nothing else but spring.

'Tis not that I expect to find
A more devoted, fond and true one,
With rosier cheek or sweeter mind—
Enough for me that she's a new one.

Thus let us leave the bower of love,
Where we have loiter'd long in bliss;
And you may down *that* pathway rove,
While I shall take my way through *this*

ANACREONTIC.

"She never look'd so kind before—
"Yet why the wanton's smile recall?
"I've seen this witchery o'er and o'er,
"'Tis hollow, vain, and heartless all!"

Thus I said and, sighing, drain'd
The cup which she so late had tasted;
Upon whose rim still fresh remain'd
The breath, so oft in falsehood wasted.

I took the harp, and would have sung
As if 'twere not of her I sang;
But still the notes on Lamia hung—
On whom but Lamia *could* they hang?

Those eyes of hers, that floating shine,
Like diamonds in some Eastern river;
That kiss, for which, if worlds were mine,
A world for every kiss I'd give her.

That frame so delicate, yet warm'd
With flushes of love's genial hue;
A mould transparent, as if form'd
To let the spirit's light shine through

Of these I sung, and notes and words
Were sweet, as if the very air
From Lamia's lip hung o'er the chords,
And Lamia's voice still warbled there!

But when, alas, I turn'd the theme,
And when of vows and oaths I spoke,
Of truth and hope's seducing dream—
The chord beneath my finger broke.

False harp! false woman!—such, oh, such
Are lutes too frail and hearts too willing;
Any hand, whate'er its touch,
Can set their chords or pulses thrilling.

And when that thrill is most awake,
And when you think Heaven's joys await you,
The nymph will change, the chord will break—
Oh Love, oh Music, how I hate you!

TO JULIA.

I saw the peasant's hand unkind
From yonder oak the ivy sever;
They seem'd in very being twin'd;
Yet now the oak is fresh as ever!

Not so the widow'd ivy shines:
Torn from its dear and only stay,
In drooping widowhood it pines,
And scatters all its bloom away.

Thus, Julia, did our hearts entwine,
Till fate disturb'd their tender ties:
Thus gay indifference blooms in thine,
While mine, deserted, droops and dies!

HYMN OF A VIRGIN OF DELPHI,

AT THE TOMB OF HER MOTHER

Oh, lost, for ever lost—no more
Shall Vesper light our dewy way
Along the rocks of Crissa's shore,
To hymn the fading fires of day;
No more to Tempè's distant vale
In holy musings shall we roam,
Through summer's glow and winter's gale,
To bear the mystic chaplets home.
'Twas then my soul's expanding zeal,
By nature warm'd and led by thee,
In every breeze was taught to feel
The breathings of a Deity.
Guide of my heart! still hovering round,
Thy looks, thy words are still my own—
I see thee raising from the ground
Some laurel, by the winds o'erthrown,
And hear thee say, "This humble bough
"Was planted for a doom divine;
"And, though it droop in languor now,
"Shall flourish on the Delphic shrine!
"Thus, in the vale of earthly sense,
"Though sunk awhile the spirit lies,
"A viewless hand shall cull it thence,
"To bloom immortal in the skies!"

All that the young should feel and know,
By thee was taught so sweetly well,
Thy words fell soft as vernal snow,
And all was brightness where they fell!
Fond soother of my infant tear,
Fond sharer of my infant joy,
Is not thy shade still ling'ring here?
Am I not still thy soul's employ?
Oh yes—and, as in former days,
When, meeting on the sacred mount,
Our nymphs awak'd their choral lays,
And danc'd around Cassotis' fount;

As then, 'twas all thy wish and care,
That mine should be the simplest mien,
My lyre and voice the sweetest there,
My foot the lightest o'er the green:
So still, each look and step to mould,
Thy guardian care is round me spread,
Arranging every snowy fold,
And guiding every mazy tread.
And, when I lead the hymning choir,
Thy spirit still, unseen and free,
Hovers between my lip and lyre,
And weds them into harmony.
Flow, Plistus, flow, thy murmuring wave
Shall never drop its silv'ry tear
Upon so pure, so blest a grave,
To memory so entirely dear!

LOVE AND MARRIAGE

STILL the question I must parry,
Still a wayward truant prove:
Where I love, I must not marry;
Where I marry, cannot love.

Were she fairest of creation,
With the least presuming mind;
Learned without affectation;
Not deceitful, yet refin'd;

Wise enough, but never rigid;
Gay, but not too lightly free;
Chaste as snow, and yet not frigid;
Fond, yet satisfied with me:

Were she all this ten times over,
All that heav'n to earth allows,
I should be too much her lover
Ever to become her spouse—

Love will never bear enslaving;
Summer garments suit him best;
Bliss itself is not worth having,
If we're by compulsion blest.

TO JULIA.

OUR hearts, my love, were form'd to be
The genuine twins of Sympathy,
They live with one sensation:
In joy or grief, but most in love,
Like chords in unison they move,
And thrill with like vibration.

How oft I've heard thee fondly say,
Thy vital pulse shall cease to play
When mine no more is moving;
Since, now, to feel a joy *alone*
Were worse to thee than feeling none
So twinn'd are we in loving!

THE SNAKE.

MY Love and I, the other day,
Within a myrtle arbour lay,
When near us, from a rosy bed,
A little Snake put forth its head.

"See," said the maid with thoughtful eyes—
"Yonder the fatal emblem lies!
"Who could expect such hidden harm
"Beneath the rose's smiling charm?"
Never did grave remark occur
Less *à-propos* than this from her

I rose to kill the snake, but she,
Half-smiling, pray'd it might not be.
"No," said the maiden—And, alas,
Her eyes spoke volumes while she said it—
"Long as the snake is in the grass,
"One *may*, perhaps, have cause to dread i:
"But, when its wicked eyes appear,
"And when we know for what they wink so,
"One must be *very* simple, dear,
"To let it wound one—don't you think so?"

TO ROSA.

Is the song of Rosa mute?
Once more such lays inspir'd her lute!
Never doth a sweeter song
Steal the breezy lyre along,
When the wind, in odours dying,
Wooes it with enamour'd sighing

Is my Rosa's lute unstrung?
Once a tale of peace it sung
To her lover's throbbing breast—
Then was he divinely blest!
Ah! but Rosa loves no more,
Therefore Rosa's song is o'er;
And her lute neglected lies;
And her boy forgotten sighs.
Silent lute—forgotten lover—
Rosa's love and song are over!

ELEGIAC STANZAS.

WHEN wearied wretches sink to sleep,
How heavenly soft their slumbers lie!
How sweet is death to those who weep,
To those who weep and long to die!

Saw you the soft and grassy bed,
Where flow'rets deck the green earth's breast!
'Tis there I wish to lay my head,
'Tis there I wish to sleep at rest.

Oh, let not tears embalm my tomb,—
None but the dews at twilight given!
Oh, let not sighs disturb the gloom,—
None but the whisp'ring winds of heaven

THE TEAR.

ON beds of snow the moonbeam slept,
And chilly was the midnight gloom,
When by the damp grave Ellen wept—
Fond maid! it was her Lindor's tomb!

A warm tear gush'd, the wintry air
Congeal'd it as it flow'd away:
All night it lay an ice-drop there,
At morn it glitter'd in the ray.

An angel, wand'ring from her sphere,
Who saw this bright, this frozen gem,
To dew-ey'd Pity brought the tear,
And hung it on her diadem?

ANACREONTIC.

I FILL'D to thee, to thee I drank,
I nothing did but drink and fill;
The bowl by turns was bright and blank,
'Twas drinking, filling, drinking still.

At length I bid an artist paint
Thy image in this ample cup,
That I might see the dimpled saint
To whom I quaff'd my nectar up.

Behold, how bright that purple lip
Now blushes through the wave at me
Every roseate drop I sip
Is just like kissing wine from thee

And still I drink the more for this:
For, ever when the draught I drain,
Thy lip invites another kiss,
And—in the nectar flows again.

So, here's to thee, my gentle dear,
And may that eyelid never shine
Beneath a darker, bitterer tear
Than bathes it in this bowl of mine!

THE SURPRISE.

Chloris, I swear, by all I ever swore,
That from this hour I shall not love thee more.—
"What! love no more? Oh! why this alter'd vow?"
Because I *cannot* love thee *more*—than *now!*

To MISS . . . . . .

ON HER ASKING THE AUTHOR WHY SHE HAD SLEEPLESS NIGHTS.

I'll ask the sylph who round thee flies,
 And in thy breath his pinion dips,
Who suns him in thy radiant eyes,
 And faints upon thy sighing lips:

I'll ask him where's the veil of sleep
 That us'd to shade thy looks of light;
And why those eyes their vigil keep,
 When other suns are sunk in night?

And I will say—her angel breast
 Has never throbb'd with guilty sting;
Her bosom is the sweetest nest
 Where Slumber could repose his wing!

And I will say—her cheeks that flush,
 Like vernal roses in the sun,
Have ne'er by shame been taught to blush,
 Except for what her eyes have done!

Then tell me, why, thou child of air!
 Does slumber from her eyelids rove?
What is her heart's impassion'd care?
 Perhaps, oh sylph! perhaps, 'tis *love.*

THE WONDER.

Come, tell me where the maid is found,
 Whose heart can love without deceit,
And I will range the world around,
 To sigh one moment at her feet.

Oh! tell me where's her sainted home,
 What air receives her blessed sigh,
A pilgrimage of years I'll roam
 To catch one sparkle of her eye!

And if her cheek be smooth and bright,
 While truth within her bosom lies,
I'll gaze upon her morn and night,
 Till my heart leave me through my eyes.

Show me on earth a thing so rare,
 I'll own all miracles are true;
To make one maid sincere and fair,
 Oh, 'tis the utmost Heaven can do!

LYING.

I do confess, in many a sigh,
My lips have breath'd you many a lie;
And who, with such delights in view,
Would lose them, for a lie or two?

 Nay, look not thus, with brow reproving;
Lies are, my dear, the soul of loving.
If half we tell the girls were true,
If half we swear to think and do,
Were aught but lying's bright illusion,
This world would be in strange confusion
If ladies' eyes were, every one,
As lovers swear, a radiant sun,
Astronomy must leave the skies,
To learn her lore in ladies' eyes
Oh, no—believe me, lovely girl,
When nature turns your teeth to pearl,
Your neck to snow, your eyes to fire,
Your amber locks to golden wire,
Then, only then can Heaven decree,
That you should live for only me,
Or I for you, as night and morn,
We've swearing kist, and kissing sworn

 And now, my gentle hints to clear,
For once I'll tell you truth, my dear.
Whenever you may chance to meet
Some loving youth, whose love is sweet,
Long as you're false and he believes you,
Long as you trust and he deceives you,
So long the blissful bond endures,
And while he lies, his heart is yours:
But, oh! you've wholly lost the youth
The instant that he tells you truth.

THE PHILOSOPHER ARISTIPPUS

TO A LAMP WHICH HAD BEEN GIVEN HIM BY LAIS

"Oh! love the Lamp" (my Mistress said,)
 "The faithful Lamp that, many a night,
"Beside thy Lais' lonely bed
 "Has kept its little watch of light.

"Full often has it seen her weep,
 "And fix her eye upon its flame,
"Till, weary, she has sunk to sleep,
 "Repeating her beloved's name.

"Then love the Lamp—'twill often lead
 "Thy step through learning's sacred way
"And when those studious eyes shall read,
 "At midnight, by its lonely ray,
 "Of things sublime, of nature's birth,
 "Of all that's bright in heaven or earth,
"Oh, think that she, by whom 'twas given,
"Adores thee more than earth or heaven!"

Yes—dearest Lamp, by every charm
 On which thy midnight beam has hung;
The head reclin'd, the graceful arm
 Across the brow of ivory flung;

The heaving bosom, partly hid,
 The sever'd lip's unconscious sighs,
The fringe that from the half-shut lid
 Adown the cheek of roses lies:

By these, by all that bloom untold,
 And long as all shall charm my heart,
I'll love my little Lamp of gold—
 My Lamp and I shall never part.
And often, as she smiling said,
 In fancy's hour, thy gentle rays
Shall guide my visionary tread
 Through poesy's enchanting maze.
Thy flame shall light the page refin'd,
 Where still we catch the Chian's breath,
 Where still the bard, though cold in death,
Has left his soul unquench'd behind.
Or, o'er thy humbler legend shine,
 Oh man of Ascra's dreary glades!
To whom the nightly warbling Nine
 A wand of inspiration gave,
Pluck'd from the greenest tree, that shades
 The crystal of Castalia's wave.

Then, turning to a purer lore,
We'll cull the sages' deep-hid store;
From Science steal her golden clue,
And every mystic path pursue,
Where Nature, far from vulgar eyes,
Through labyrinths of wonder flies.
'Tis thus my heart shall learn to know
How fleeting is this world below,
Where all that meets the morning light,
Is chang'd before the fall of night!

I'll tell thee, as I trim thy fire,
 "Swift, swift the tide of being runs,
"And Time, who bids thy flame expire,
 "Will also quench yon heaven of suns."

Oh, then if earth's united power
Can never chain one feathery hour;
If every print we leave to-day
To-morrow's wave will sweep away;

Who pauses to inquire of heaven
Why were the fleeting treasures given,
The sunny days, the shady nights,
And all their brief but dear delights,
Which heaven has made for man to use,
And man should think it crime to lose?
Who that has cull'd a fresh-blown rose
Will ask it why it breathes and glows,
Unmindful of the blushing ray,
In which it shines its soul away;
Unmindful of the scented sigh,
With which it dies and loves to die.

Pleasure, thou only good on earth!
One precious moment giv'n to thee—
Oh! by my Lais' lip, 'tis worth
The sage's immortality.

Then far be all the wisdom hence,
That would our joys one hour delay!
Alas, the feast of soul and sense
Love calls us to in youth's bright day,
If not soon tasted, fleets away.

Ne'er wert thou form'd, my Lamp, to shed
Thy splendour on a lifeless page;—
Whate'er my blushing Lais said
Of thoughtful lore and studies sage,
'Twas mockery all—her glance of joy
Told me thy dearest, best employ.

And, soon as night shall close the eye
Of heaven's young wanderer in the west;
When seers are gazing on the sky,
To find their future orbs of rest;
Then shall I take my trembling way,
Unseen but to those worlds above,
And, led by thy mysterious ray,
Steal to the night-bower of my love.

TO ROSA.

Like one who trusts to summer skies,
And puts his little bark to sea,
Is he who, lur'd by smiling eyes,
Consigns his simple heart to thee.

For fickle is the summer wind,
And sadly may the bark be tost;
For thou art sure to change thy mind,
And then the wretched heart is lost!

WRITTEN IN A COMMONPLACE BOOK.

This tribute's from a wretched elf,
Who hails thee, emblem of himself.
The book of life, which I have trac'd,
Has been, like thee, a motley waste
Of follies scribbled o'er and o'er,
One folly bringing hundreds more.
Some have indeed been writ so neat,
In characters so fair, so sweet,
That those who judge not too severely,
Have said they lov'd such follies dearly:
Yet, still, O book! the illusion stands;
For these were penn'd by *female* hands:
The rest—alas! I own the truth—
Have all been scribbled so uncouth
Th. Prudence, with a with'ring look,
Disdainful, flings away the book.
Like thine, its pages here and there
Have oft been stain'd with blots of care;
And sometimes hours of peace, I own,
Upon some fairer leaves have shown,
White as the snowings of that heav'n
By which those hours of peace were given.
But now no longer—such, oh, such
The blast of Disappointment's touch!—
No longer now those hours appear;
Each leaf is sullied by a tear:
Blank, blank is every page with care,
Not ev'n a folly brightens there.
Will they yet brighten?—never, never!
Then *shut the book*, O God, for ever!

LIGHT SOUNDS THE HARP.

Light sounds the harp when the combat is over,
When heroes are resting, and joy is in bloom;
When laurels hang loose from the brow of the lover,
And Cupid makes wings of the warrior's plume.
But, when the foe returns,
Again the hero burns;
High flames the sword in his hand once more:
The clang of mingling arms
Is then the sound that charms,
And brazen notes of war, that stirring trumpets pour;—
Then, again comes the Harp, when the combat is over—
When heroes are resting, and Joy is in bloom—
When laurels hang loose from the brow of the lover,
And Cupid makes wings of the warrior's plume.

Light went the harp when the War-God, reclining,
Lay lull'd on the white arm of Beauty to rest,
When round his rich armour the myrtle hung twining,
And flights of young doves made his helmet their nest
But, when the battle came,
The hero's eye breath'd flame:
Soon from his neck the white arm was flung;
While, to his wak'ning ear,
No other sounds were dear
But brazen notes of war, by thousand trumpets sung.
But then came the light harp, when danger was ended,
And Beauty once more lull'd the War-God to rest;
When tresses of gold with his laurels lay blended,
And flights of young doves made his helmet their nest

FROM THE GREEK OF MELEAGER

Fill high the cup with liquid flame,
And speak my Heliodora's name
Repeat its magic o'er and o'er,
And let the sound my lips adore,
Live in the breeze, till every tone,
And word, and breath, speaks her alone.

Give me the wreath that withers there,
It was but last delicious night,
It circled her luxuriant hair,
And caught her eyes' reflected light.
Oh! haste, and twine it round my brow:
'Tis all of her that's left me now.
And see—each rosebud drops a tear,
To find the nymph no longer here—
No longer, where such heavenly charms
As hers *should* be—within these arms.

THE RING.

No—Lady! Lady! keep the ring:
Oh! think, how many a future year,
Of placid smile and downy wing,
May sleep within its holy sphere.

Do not disturb their tranquil dream,
Though love hath ne'er the myst'ry warm'd;
Yet heav'n will shed a soothing beam,
To bless the bond itself hath form'd.

But then, that eye that burning eye,—
Oh! it doth ask, with witching power,
If heaven can ever bless the tie
Where love inwreaths no genial flower

Away, away, bewildering look,
Or all the boast of virtue's o'er;
Go—hie thee to the sage's book,
And learn from him to feel no more

I cannot warn thee; every touch,
That brings my pulses close to thine,
Tells me I want thy aid as much—
Ev'n more, alas, than thou dost mine.

Yet, stay,—one hope, one effort yet—
A moment turn those eyes away,
And let me, if I can, forget
The light that leads my soul astray

Thou say'st, that we were born to meet,
That our hearts bear one common seal;—
Think, Lady, think, how man's deceit
Can seem to sigh and feign to feel.

When, o'er thy face some gleam of thought,
Like daybeams through the morning air,
Hath gradual stole, and I have caught
The feeling ere it kindled there.

The sympathy I then betray'd,
Perhaps was but the child of art,
The guile of one, who long hath play'd
With all these wily nets of heart.

Oh! thine is not my earliest vow;
Though few the years I yet have told,
Canst thou believe I've liv'd till now,
With loveless heart or senses cold?

No—other nymphs to joy and pain
This wild and wandering heart hath mov'd;
With some it sported, wild and vain,
While some it dearly, truly, lov'd.

The cheek to thine I fondly lay,
To theirs hath been as fondly laid;
The words to thee I warmly say,
To them have been as warmly said.

Then, scorn at once a worthless heart,
Worthless alike, or fix'd or free;
Think of the pure, bright soul thou art,
And—love not me, oh love not me.

Enough—now, turn thine eyes again;
What, still that look and still that sigh!
Dost thou not feel my counsel then?
Oh! no, beloved,—nor do I.

THE RESEMBLANCE.

Yes, if 'twere my common love,
That led my pliant heart astray,
I grant, there's not a power above,
Could wipe the faithless crime away.

But, 'twas my doom to err with one
In every look so like to thee
That, underneath yon blessed sun,
So fair there are but thou and she.

Both born of beauty, at a birth,
She held with thine a kindred sway,
And wore the only shape on earth
That could have lur'd my soul to stray,

Then blame me not, if false I be,
'Twas love that wak'd the fond excess;
My heart had been more true to thee,
Had mine eye priz'd thy beauty less.

TO THE INVISIBLE GIRL.

They try to persuade me, my dear little sprite,
That your'e *not* a true daughter of ether and light,
Nor have any concern with those fanciful forms
That dance upon rainbows and ride upon storms;
That, in short, you're a woman; your lip and your eye
As mortal as ever drew gods from the sky.
But I *will* not believe them—no, Science, to you
I have long bid a last and a careless adieu:
Still flying from Nature to study her laws,
And dulling delight by exploring its cause,
You forget how superior, for mortals below,
Is the fiction they dream to the truth that they know
Oh! who, that has e'er enjoyed rapture complete,
Would ask *how* we feel it, or *why* it is sweet;
How rays are confus'd, or how particles fly
Through the medium refin'd of a glance or a sigh;
Is there one, who but once would not rather have known it,
Than written, with Harvey, whole volumes upon it?

As for you my sweet-voiced and invisible love,
You must surely be one of those spirits that rove
By the bank where, at twilight, the poet reclines,
When the star of the west on his solitude shines,
And the magical fingers of fancy have hung
Every breeze with a sigh, every leaf with a tongue.
Oh! hint to him then, 'tis retirement alone
Can hallow his harp or ennoble its tone;
Like you, with a veil of seclusion between,
His song to the world let him utter unseen,
And like you, a legitimate child of the spheres,
Escape from the eye to enrapture the ears.

Sweet spirit of mystery! how I should love,
In the wearisome ways I am fated to rove,
To have you thus ever invisibly nigh,
Inhaling for ever your song and your sigh!
Mid the crowds of the world and the murmurs of care,
I might sometimes converse with my nymph of the air,
And turn with distaste from the clamorous crew,
To steal in the pauses one whisper from you.

Then come and be near me, for ever be mine,
We shall hold in the air a communion divine,
As sweet as, of old, was imagin'd to dwell
In the grotto of Numa, or Socrates' cell.
And oft, at those lingering moments of night,
When the heart's busy thoughts have put slumber to flight,
You shall come to my pillow and tell me of love,
Such as angel to angel might whisper above.
Sweet spirit!—and then, could you borrow the tone
Of that voice, to my ear like some fairy-song known,
The voice of the one upon earth, who has twin'd
With her being for ever my heart and my mind,
Though lonely and far from the light of her smile,
An exile, and weary and hopeless the while,
Could you shed for a moment her voice on my ear,
I will think, for that moment, that Cara is near;
That she comes with consoling enchantment to speak,
And kisses my eyelid and breathes on my cheek,
And tells me, the night shall go rapidly by,
For the dawn of our hope, of our heaven is nigh

Fair spirit! if such be your magical power,
It will lighten the lapse of full many an hour;
And, let fortune's realities frown as they will,
Hope, fancy, and Cara may smile for me still.

TO MRS. BL——.

WRITTEN IN HER ALBUM.

They say that Love had once a book
(The urchin likes to copy you,)
Where, all who came, the pencil took,
And wrote, like us, a line or two.

'Twas Innocence, the maid divine,
Who kept this volume bright and fair,
And saw that no unhallow'd line
Or thought profane should enter there;

And daily did the pages fill
With fond device and loving lore,
And every leaf she turn'd was still
More bright than that she turn'd before

Beneath the touch of Hope, how soft,
How light the magic pencil ran!
Till Fear would come, alas, as oft,
And trembling close what Hope began

A tear or two had dropp'd from Grief,
And Jealousy would, now and then,
Ruffle in haste some snow-white leaf,
Which Love had still to smooth again

But, ah! there came a blooming boy,
Who often turn'd the pages o'er,
And wrote therein such words of joy,
That all who read them sigh'd for more

And Pleasure was this spirit's name,
And though so soft his voice and look,
Yet Innocence, whene'er he came,
Would tremble for her spotless book.

For, oft a Bacchant cup he bore,
With earth's sweet nectar sparkling bright;
And much she fear'd lest, mantling o'er,
Some drops should on the pages light.

And so it chanc'd, one luckless night,
The urchin let that goolet fall
O'er the fair book, so pure, so white,
And sullied lines and marge and all!

In vain now, touch'd with shame, he tried
To wash those fatal stains away;
Deep, deep had sunk the sullying tide,
The leaves grew darker every day.

And Fancy's sketches lost their hue,
And Hope's sweet lines were all effac'd,
And Love himself now scarcely knew
What love himself so lately trac'd.

At length the urchin Pleasure fled,
(For how, alas! could Pleasure stay?)
And Love, while many a tear he shed,
Reluctant flung the book away.

The index now alone remains,
Of all the pages spoil'd by Pleasure,
And though it bears some earthly stains,
Yet Memory counts the leaf a treasure.

And oft, they say, she scans it o'er,
And oft, by this memorial aided,
Brings back the pages now no more,
And thinks of lines that long have faded.

I know not if this tale be true,
But thus the simple facts are stated;
And I refer their truth to you,
Since Love and you are near related.

WRITTEN IN A LADY'S COMMONPLACE BOOK.

Here is one leaf reserv'd for me,
From all thy sweet memorials free;
And here my simple song might tell
The feelings thou must guess so well.
But could I thus, within thy mind,
One little vacant corner find,
Where no impression yet is seen,
Where no memorial yet hath been,
Oh! it should be my sweetest care
To *write my name* for ever *there!*

To . . . .

ON SEEING HER WITH A WHITE VEIL AND A RICH GIRDLE

Put off the vestal veil, nor oh!
Let weeping angels view it;
Your cheeks belie its virgin snow,
And blush repenting through it.

Put off the fatal zone you wear;
The shining pearls around it
Are tears, that fell from Virtue there,
The hour when Love unbound it.

A NIGHT THOUGHT.

How oft a cloud, with envious veil,
Obscures yon bashful light,
Which seems so modestly to steal
Along the waste of night!

'Tis thus the world's obtrusive wrongs
Obscure with malice keen
Some timid heart, which only longs
To live and die unseen.

PEACE AND GLORY.

Where is now the smile, that lighten'd
Every hero's couch of rest?
Where is now the hope, that brighten'd
Honour's eye and Pity's breast?
Have we lost the wreath we braided
For our weary warrior men?
Is the faithless olive faded?
Must the bay be pluck'd again?

Passing hour of sunny weather
Lovely, in your light awile,
Peace and Glory, wed together,
Wander'd through our blessed isle.
And the eyes of Peace would glisten,
Dewy as a morning sun,
When the timid maid would listen
To the deeds her chief had done

Is their hour of dallianse over?
Must the maiden's trembling feet
Waft her from her warlike lover
To the desert's still retreat?
Fare you well! with sighs we banish
Nymph so fair and guests so bright;
Yet the smile, with which you vanish,
Leaves behind a soothing light;—

Soothing light, that long shall sparkle
O'er your warrior's sanguin'd way,
Through the field where horrors darkle,
Shedding hope's consoling ray.
Long the smile his heart will cherish,
To its absent idol true;
While around him myriads perish,
Glory still will sigh for you!

THE KISS.

Grow to my lip, thou sacred kiss,
On which my soul's beloved swore
That there should come a time of bliss,
When she would mock my hopes no more
And fancy shall thy glow renew,
In sighs at morn, and dreams at night.
And none shall steal thy holy dew
Till thou'rt absolv'd by rapture's rite.
Sweet hours that are to make me blest,
Fly, swift as breezes, to the goal,
And let my love, my more than soul
Come blushing to this ardent breast.
Then, while in every glance I drink
The rich o'erflowings of her mind,
Oh! let her all enamour'd sink
In sweet abandonment resign'd,
Blushing for all our struggles past,
And murmuring, "I am thine at last!"

TO A LADY, ON HER SINGING.

Thy song has taught my heart to feel
Those soothing thoughts of heav'nly love,
Which o'er the sainted spirits steal
When list'ning to the spheres above!

When, tir'd of life and misery,
I wish to sigh my latest breath,
Oh, Emma! I will fly to thee,
And thou shalt sing me into death.

And if along thy lip and cheek
That smile of heav'nly softness play,
Which,—ah! forgive a mind that's weak,—
So oft has stol'n my mind away;

Thou'lt seem an angel of the sky,
That comes to charm me into bliss:
I'll gaze and die—Who would not die,
If death were half so sweet as this?

NATIONAL AIRS,

BY

THOMAS MOORE.

A TEMPLE TO FRIENDSHIP.*

"A Temple to Friendship," said Laura, enchanted,
"I'll build in this garden—the thought is divine!"
Her temple was built, and she now only wanted
An image of Friendship to place on the shrine.
She flew to a sculptor, who set down before her
A Friendship, the fairest his art could invent;
But so cold and so dull, that the youthful adorer
Saw plainly this was not the idol she meant.

"Oh! never," she cried, "could I think of enshrining
An image, whose looks are so joyless and dim;—
But yon little god, upon roses reclining,
We'll make, if you please, sir, a Friendship of him."
So the bargain was struck; with the little god laden
She joyfully flew to her shrine in the grove;
"Farewell," said the sculptor, "you're not the first maiden
Who came but for Friendship and took away Love."

FLOW ON, THOU SHINING RIVER.

Flow on, thou shining river;
But, ere thou reach the sea,
Seek Ella's bower, and give her
The wreaths I fling o'er thee.
And tell her thus, if she'll be mine,
The current of our lives shall be,
With joys along their course to shine,
Like those sweet flowers on thee.

But if, in wand'ring thither,
Thou find'st she mocks my prayer,
Then leave those wreaths to wither
Upon the cold bank there;
And tell her thus, when youth is o'er,
Her lone and loveless charms shall be
Thrown by upon life's weedy shore,
Like those sweet flowers from thee.

ALL THAT'S BRIGHT MUST FADE.

All that's bright must fade—
The brightest still the fleetest;
All that's sweet was made
But to be lost when sweetest.
Stars that shine and fall;—
The flower that drops in springing;—
These, alas! are types of all
To which our hearts are clinging

All that's bright must fade—
The brightest still the fleetest;
All that's sweet was made
But to be lost when sweetest!

Who would seek or prize
Delights that end in aching?
Who would trust to ties
That every hour are breaking?
Better far to be
In utter darkness lying,
Than to be blessed with light and see
That light for ever flying.
All that's bright must fade—
The brightest still the fleetest;
All that's sweet was made
But to be lost when sweetest!

SO WARMLY WE MET.

So warmly we met and so fondly we parted,
That which was the sweeter even I could not tell—
That first look of welcome her sunny eyes darted,
Or that tear of passion, which blessed our farewell.
To meet was a heaven, and to part thus another—
Our joy and our sorrow seemed rivals in bliss;
Oh! Cupid's two eyes are not liker each other
In smiles and in tears, than that moment to this.

The first was like daybreak, new, sudden, delicious—
The dawn of a pleasure scarce kindled up yet;
The last like the farewell of daylight, more precious,
More glowing and deep, as 'tis nearer its set.
Our meeting, though happy, was tinged by a sorrow
To think that such happiness could not remain;
While our parting, though sad, gave a hope that to-morrow
Would bring back the blest hour of meeting again.

THOSE EVENING BELLS.

Those evening bells! those evening bells!
How many a tale their music tells,
Of youth, and home, and that sweet time,
When last I heard their soothing chime.

Those joyous hours are passed away;
And many a heart that then was gay,
Within the tomb now darkly dwells,
And hears no more those evening bells.

And so 'twill be when I am gone;
That tuneful peal will still ring on,
While other bards shall walk these dells,
And sing your praise, sweet evening bells!

* The thought is taken from a song by Le Prieur, called "La Statue de l'Amitie."

SHOULD THOSE FOND HOPES.

Should those fond hopes e'er forsake thee,*
Which now so sweetly thy heart employ;
Should the cold world come to wake thee
From all thy visions of youth and joy;
Should the gay friends, for whom thou wouldst banish
Him who once thought thy young heart his own,
All, like spring birds, falsely vanish,
And leave thy winter unheeded and lone;—

Oh! 'tis then that he thou hast slighted
Would come to cheer thee, when all seemed o'er;
Then the truant, lost and blighted,
Would to his bosom be taken once more.
Like that dear bird we both can remember,
Who left us while summer shone round,
But, when chilled by bleak December,
On our threshold a welcome still found.

REASON, FOLLY, AND BEAUTY.

Reason, and Folly, and Beauty, they say,
Went on a party of pleasure one day;
Folly played
Around the maid,
The bells of his cap rung merrily out;
While Reason took
To his sermon-book—
Oh! which was the pleasanter no one need doubt,
Which was the pleasanter no one need doubt.

Beauty, who likes to be thought very sage,
Turned for a moment to Reason's dull page,
Till Folly said,
"Look here, sweet maid!"
The sight of his cap brought her back to herself;
While Reason read
His leaves of lead,
With no one to mind him, poor sensible elf!
No—no one to mind him, poor sensible elf!

Then Reason grew jealous of Folly's gay cap;
Had he that on, he her heart might entrap—
"There it is,"
Quoth Folly, "old quiz!"
(Folly was always good-natured, 'tis said),
"Under the sun
There's no such fun,
As Reason with my cap and bells on his head,
Reason with my cap and bells on his head!"

But Reason the head-dress so awkwardly wore,
That Beauty now liked him still less than before;
While Folly took
Old Reason's book,
And twisted the leaves in a cap of such *ton*,
That Beauty vowed
(Though not aloud),
She liked him still better in that than his own,
Yes—liked him still better in that than his own.

FARE THEE WELL, THOU LOVELY ONE!

Fare thee well, thou lovely one!
Lovely still, but dear no more;
Once his soul of truth is gone,
Love's sweet life is o'er.
Thy words, whate'er their flattering spell,
Could scarce have thus deceived;
But eyes that acted truth so well
Were sure to be believed.
Then, fare thee well, thou lovely one!
Lovely still, but dear no more;
Once his soul of truth is gone,
Love's sweet life is o'er.

Yet those eyes look constant still,
True as stars they keep their light;
Still those cheeks their pledge fulfil
Of blushing always bright.
'Tis only on thy changeful heart
The blame of falsehood lies;
Love lives in every other part,
But there, alas! he dies.
Then, fare thee well, thou lovely one!
Lovely still, but dear no more;
Once his soul of truth is gone,
Love's sweet life is o'er.

DOST THOU REMEMBER.

Dost thou remember that place so lonely,
A place for lovers, and lovers only,
Where first I told thee all my secret sighs?
When, as the moonbeam, that trembled o'er thee,
Illum'd thy blushes, I knelt before thee,
And read my hope's sweet triumph in those eyes?
Then, then, while closely heart was drawn to heart,
Love bound us—never, never more to part!

And when I called thee by names the dearest*
That love could fancy, the fondest, nearest—
"My life, my only life!" among the rest;
In those sweet accents that still enthral me,
Thou saidst, "Ah! wherefore thy life thus call me?
Thy soul, thy soul's the name that I love best;
For life soon passes—but how blessed to be
That soul which never, never parts from thee!"

OH, COME TO ME WHEN DAYLIGHT SETS.

Oh, come to me when daylight sets;
Sweet! then come to me,
When smoothly go our gondolets
O'er the moonlight sea.
When Mirth's awake, and Love begins,
Beneath that glancing ray,
With sound of lutes and mandolins,
To steal young hearts away.
Then, come to me when daylight sets;
Sweet! then come to me,
When smoothly go our gondolets
O'er the moonlight sea.

Oh, then's the hour for those who love,
Sweet! like thee and me;
When all's so calm below, above,
In heaven and o'er the sea.
When maiden's sing sweet barcarolles†
And echo sings again
So sweet, that all with ears and souls
Should love and listen then.
So, come to me when daylight sets,
Sweet! then come to me,
When smoothly go our gondolets
O'er the moonlight sea.

OFT, IN THE STILLY NIGHT.

Oft, in the stilly night,
Ere slumber's chain has bound me,
Fond Memory brings the light
Of other days around me;
The smiles, the tears,
Of boyhood's years,
The words of love then spoken;
The eyes that shone,
Now dimmed and gone,
The cheerful hearts now broken!
Thus, in the stilly night,
Ere Slumber's chain hath bound me,
Sad Memory brings the light
Of other days around me.

When I remember all
The friends, so linked together,
I've seen around me fall,
Like leaves in wintry weather;

* This is one of the many instances among my lyrical poems—though the above, it must be owned, is an extreme case—where the metre has been necessarily sacrificed to the structure of the air

* The thought in this verse is borrowed from the original Portuguese words.

† Barcarolles, sorte de chansons en langue Venitienne, que chantent les gondoliers a Venise.—*Rousseau, Dictionnaire de Musique.*

I feel like one,
Who treads alone
Some banquet-hall deserted,
Whose lights are fled,
Whose garlands dead,
And all but he departed!
Thus, in the stilly night,
Ere Slumber's chain has bound me,
Sad Memory brings the light
Of other days around me.

HARK! THE VESPER HYMN IS STEALING.

Hark! the vesper hymn is stealing
O'er the waters soft and clear;
Nearer yet and nearer pealing,
And now bursts upon the ear;
Jubilate, Amen.
Farther, now, now farther stealing,
Soft it fades upon the ear;
Jubilate, Amen.

Now, like moonlight waves retreating
To the shore, it dies along;
Now, like angry surges meeting,
Breaks the mingled tide of song;
Jubilate, Amen.
Hush! again, like waves, retreating
To the shore, it dies along;
Jubilate, Amen.

THERE COMES A TIME.

There comes a time, a dreary time,
To him whose heart hath flown
O'er all the fields of youth's sweet prime,
And made each flower its own.
'Tis when his soul must first renounce
Those dreams so bright, so fond;
Oh! then's the time to die at once,
For life has naught beyond.

When sets the sun on Afric's shore,
That instant all is night;
And so should life at once be o'er,
When Love withdraws his light;
Nor, like our northern day, gleam on
Through twilight's dim delay,
The cold remains of lustre gone,
Of fire long passed away.

LOVE AND HOPE.

At morn, beside yon summer sea,
Young Hope and Love reclined;
But scarce had noon-tide come, when he
Into his bark leaped smilingly,
And left poor Hope behind.

"I go," said Love, "to sail awhile
Across this sunny main;"
And then so sweet his parting smile,
That Hope, who never dreame of guile
Believed he'd come again.

She lingered there till evening's beam
Along the waters lay;
And o'er the sands, in thoughtful dream,
Oft traced his name, which still the stream,
As often washed away.

At length a sail appears in sight,
And toward the maiden moves!
'Tis Wealth that comes, and gay and bright,
His golden bark reflects the light,
But ah! it is not Love's.

Another sail—'twas Friendship showed
Her night-lamp o'er the sea;
And calm the light that lamp bestowed;
But Love had lights that warmer glowed,
And where, alas? was he?

Now fast around the sea and shore
Night threw her darkling chain;
The sunny sails were seen no more,
Hope's morning dreams of bliss were o'er,—
Love never came again.

MY HARP HAS ONE UNCHANGING THEME.

My harp has one unchanging theme,
One strain that still comes o'er
Its languid chord, as 'twere a dream
Of joy that's now no more.
In vain I try, with livelier air,
To wake the breathing string;
That voice of other times is there,
And saddens all I sing.

Breath on, breathe on, thou languid strain,
Henceforth be all my own;
Though thou art oft so full of pain
Few hearts can bear thy tone.
Yet oft thou'rt sweet, as if the sigh,
The breath that Pleasure's wings
Gave out, when last they wantoned by,
Were still upon thy strings.

OH, NO—NOT EVEN WHEN FIRST WE LOVED.

Oh, no—not even when first we loved,
Wert thou as dear as now thou art;
Thy beauty then my senses moved,
But now thy virtues bind my heart.
What was but Passion's sigh before,
Has since been turned to Reason's vow
And, though I then might love thee *more*,
Trust me, I love thee *better* now.

Although my heart in earlier youth
Might kindle with more wild desire,
Believe me, it has gained in truth
Much more than it has lost in fire.
The flame now warms my inmost core,
That then but sparkled o'er my brow,
And, though I seemed to love thee more
Yet, oh, I love thee better now

WHEN LOVE WAS A CHILD.

When Love was a child, and went idling round,
'Mong flowers, the whole summer's day,
One morn in the valley a bower he found,
So sweet, it allured him to stay.

O'erhead, from the trees, hung a garland fair,
A fountain ran darkly beneath;—
'Twas Pleasure had hung up the flow'rets there;
Love knew it, and jumped at the wreath.

But Love didn't know—and, at *his* weak years,
What urchin was likely to know?—
That Sorrow had made of her own salt tears
The fountain that murmured below.

He caught at the wreath—but with too much haste,
As boys when impatient will do—
It fell in those waters of briny taste,
And the flowers were all wet through.

This garland he now wears night and day;
And, though it all sunny appears
With Pleasure's own light, each leaf they say,
Still tastes of the fountain of tears.

HEAR ME BUT ONCE.

Hear me but once, while o'er the grave,
In which our Love lies cold and dead,
I count each flattering hope he gave
Of joys, now lost, and charms now fled.

Who could have thought the smile he wore,
When first we met, would fade away?
Or that a chill would e'er come o'er
Those eyes so bright through many a day?
Hear me but once, &c.

COMMON SENSE AND GENIUS.

WHILE I touch the string,
  Wreath my brows with laurel,
For the tale I sing
  Has, for once, a moral.
Common Sense, one night,
  Though not used to gambols,
Went out by moonlight,
  With Genius, on his rambles,
    While I touch the string, &c.

Common Sense went on,
  Many wise things saying;
While the light that shone
  Soon set Genius straying.
One his eye ne'er raised
  From the path before him;
T'other idly gazed
  On each night-cloud o'er him.
    While I touch the string, &c.

So they came, at last,
  To a shady river;
Common Sense soon passed,
  Safe, as he doth ever;
While the boy, whose look
  Was in heaven that minute,
Never saw the brook
  But tumbled headlong in it!
    While I touch the string, &c.

How the Wise One smiled,
  When safe o'er the torrent,
At that youth so wild,
  Dripping from the current!
Sense went home to bed;
  Genius, left to shiver
On the bank, 'tis said,
  Died of that cold river!
    While I touch the string, &c.

JOYS OF YOUTH, HOW FLEETING!

WHISP'RINGS, heard by wakeful maids,
  To whom the night-stars guide us;
Stolen walks through moonlight shades,
  With those we love beside us,
      Hearts beating,
      At meeting;
      Tears starting,
      At parting;
Oh, sweet youth, how soon it fades!
  Sweet joys of youth, how fleeting!

Wand'rings far away from home,
  With life all new before us;
Greetings warm, when home we come,
  From hearts whose prayers watched o'er us.
      Tears starting,
      At parting;
      Hearts beating,
      At meeting;
Oh, sweet youth, how lost on some!
  To some, how bright and fleeting!

GAYLY SOUNDS THE CASTANET.

GAYLY sounds the castanet,
  Beating time to bounding feet,
When, after daylight's golden set,
  Maids and youths by moonlight meet.
Oh, then, how sweet to move
  Through all that maze of mirth,
Led by light from eyes we love
  Beyond all eyes on earth.

Then, the joyous banquet spread
  On the cool and fragrant ground,
With heaven's bright sparklers overhead,
  And still brighter sparkling round.
Oh, then, how sweet to say
  Into some loved one's ear,
Thoughts reserved through many a day
  To be thus whispered here.

When the dance and feast are done,
  Arm in arm as home we stray,
How sweet to see the dawning sun
  O'er her cheek's warm blushes play!
Then, too, the farewell kiss—
  The words, whose parting tone
Lingers still in dreams of bliss,
  That haunt young hearts alone.

THEN, FARE THEE WELL.

THEN, fare thee well, my own dear love,
  This world has now for us
No greater grief, no pain above
  The pain of parting thus,
    Dear love!
  The pain of parting thus.

Had we but known, since first we met,
  Some few short hours of bliss,
We might, in numbering them, forget
  The deep, deep pain of this,
    Dear love!
  The deep, deep pain of this.

But no, alas, we've never seen
  One glimpse of pleasure's ray,
But still there came some cloud between,
  And chased it all away,
    Dear love!
  And chased it all away.

Yet even could those sad moments last,
  Far dearer to my heart
Were hours of grief, together past,
  Than years of mirth apart,
    Dear love!
  Than years of mirth apart.

Farewell! our hope was born in fears,
  And nursed 'mid vain regrets;
Like winter suns, it rose in tears,
  Like them in tears it sets,
    Dear love!
  Like them in tears it sets.

PEACE BE AROUND THEE.

PEACE be around thee, wherever thou rovest;
  May life be for thee one summer's day,
And all that thou wishest, and all that thou lovest,
  Come smiling around thy sunny way!
If sorrow e'er this calm should break,
  May even thy tears pass off so lightly,
Like spring-showers, they'll only make
  The smiles that follow shine more brightly.

May Time, who sheds his blight o'er all,
  And daily dooms some joy to death,
O'er thee let years so gently fall,
  They shall not crush one flower beneath.
As half in shade and half in sun
  This world along its path advances,
May that side the sun's upon
  Be all that e'er shall meet thy glances!

LOVE IS A HUNTER-BOY.

LOVE is a hunter-boy,
  Who makes young hearts his prey;
And, in his nets of joy,
  Ensnares them night and day.
In vain concealed they lie—
  Love tracks them everywhere;
In vain aloft they fly—
  Love shoots them flying there.

But 'tis his joy most sweet,
  At early dawn to trace
The print of Beauty's feet,
  And give the trembler chase.
And if, through virgin snow,
  He tracks her footsteps fair,
How sweet for Love to know
  None went before him there.

OH, DAYS OF YOUTH.

Oh, days of youth and joy, long clouded,
  Why thus for ever haunt my view?
When in the grave your light lay shrouded,
  Why did not Memory die there too?
Vainly doth Hope her strain now sing me,
  Telling of joys that yet remain—
No, never more can this life bring me
  One joy that equals youth's sweet pain.

Dim lies the way to death before me,
  Cold winds of Time blow round my brow;
Sunshine of youth! that once fell o'er me,
  Where is your warmth, your glory now?
'*Tis* not that then no pain could sting me;
  'Tis not that now no joys remain;
Oh, 'tis that life no more can bring me
  One joy so sweet as that worst pain.

WHEN FIRST THAT SMILE.

When first that smile, like sunshine, blessed my sight,
  Oh what a vision then came o'er me!
Long years of love, of calm and pure delight,
  Seemed in that smile to pass before me.
Ne'er did the peasant dream of summer skies,
  Of golden fruit, and harvests springing,
With fonder hope than I of those sweet eyes,
  And of the joy their light was bringing.

Where now are all those fondly promised hours?
  Ah! woman's faith is like her brightness—
Fading as fast as rainbows, or day-flowers,
  Or aught that's known for grace and lightness.
Short as the Persian's prayer, at close of day,
  Should be each vow of Love's repeating;
Quick let him worship Beauty's precious ray—
  Even while he kneels, that ray is fleeting!

PEACE TO THE SLUMBERERS!

Peace to the slumb'rers!
  They lie on the battle-plain,
With no shroud to cover them;
  The dew and the summer rain
Are all that weep over them.
    Peace to the slumb'rers!

Vain was their bravery!—
  The fallen oak lies where it lay
Across the wintry river;
  But brave hearts, once swept away,
Are gone, alas! for ever.
    Vain was their bravery!

Wo to the conqu'ror!
  Our limbs shall lie as cold as theirs
Of whom his sword bereft us,
  Ere we forget the deep arrears
Of vengeance they have left us!
    Wo to the conqu'ror!

COME, CHASE THAT STARTING TEAR AWAY.

Come, chase that starting tear away,
  Ere mine to meet it springs;
To-nigh, at least, to-night be gay,
  Whate'er to-morrow brings.
Like sun-set gleams, that linger late
  When all is darkening fast,
Are hours like these we snatch from Fate—
  The brightest, and the last.
    Then, chase that starting tear, &c.

To gild the deepening gloom of heaven
  But one bright hour allow,
Oh, think that one bright hour is given,
  In all its splendor, now.
Let's live it out—then sink in night,
  Like waves that from the shore
One minute swell, are touched with light,
  Then lost for evermore?
    Come, chase that starting tear, &c.

WHO'LL BUY MY LOVE-KNOTS?

Hymen, late, his love-knots selling,
Called at many a maiden's dwelling,
None could doubt, who saw or knew them,
Hymen's call was welcome to them.
    "Who'll buy my love-knots?
    Who'll buy my love-knots?"
Soon as that sweet cry resounded
How his baskets were surrounded!

Maids, who now first dreamt of trying
These gay knots of Hymen's tying;
Dames, who long had sat to watch him
Passing by, but ne'er could catch him;—
    "Who'll buy my love-knots?
    Who'll buy my love-knots?"
All at that sweet cry assembled;
Some laughed, some blushed, and some trembled.

"Here are knots," said Hymen, taking
Some loose flowers, "of Love's own making;
"Here are gold ones—you may trust 'em"—
(These, of course, found ready custom).
    "Come, buy my love-knots!
    Come, buy my love-knots!
Some are labelled 'Knots to tie men—
Love the maker—bought of Hymen.'"

Scarce their bargains were completed,
When the nymphs all cried, "We're cheated!
See these flowers—they're drooping sadly;
This gold-knot, too, ties but badly—
    Who'd buy such love-knots?
    Who'd buy such love-knots?
Even this tie, with Love's name round it—
All a sham—he never bound it."

Love, who saw the whole proceeding,
Would have laughed, but for good-breeding;
While Old Hymen, who was used to
Cries like that these dames gave loose to—
    "Take back our love-knots!
    Take back our love-knots!"
Coolly said, "There's no returning
Wares on Hymen's hands—good morning!"

HOW OFT, WHEN WATCHING STARS.

Oft, when the watching stars grow pale,
  And round me sleeps the moonlight scene,
To hear a flute through yonder vale
  I from my casement lean.
"Come, come, my love!" each note then seems to say,
"Oh, come, my love! the night wears fast away!"
    Never to mortal ear
      Could words, though warm they be,
    Speak Passion's language half so clear
      As do those notes to me!

Then quick my own light lute I seek,
  And strike the chords with loudest swell;
And, though they naught to others speak,
  He knows their language well.
"I come, my love!" each note then seems to say,
"I come, my love!—thine, thine till break of day."
    Oh, weak the power of words,
      The hues of painting dim,
    Compared to what those simple chords
      Then say and paint to him!

WHEN THOU SHALT WANDER.

When thou shalt wander by that sweet light
  We used to gaze on so many an eve,
When love was new and hope was bright,
  Ere I could doubt or thou deceive—
Oh, then, rememb'ring how swift went by
Those hours of transport, even *thou* mayst sigh.

Yes, proud one! even thy heart may own
  That love like ours was far too sweet
To be, like summer garments, thrown
  Aside, when passed the summer's heat;
And wish in vain to know again
Such days, such nights, as blest thee then.

SAY, WHAT SHALL BE OUR SPORT TO-DAY?

Say, what shall be our sport to-day?
  There's nothing on earth, in sea, or air,
Too bright, too high, too wild, too gay,
  For spirits like mine to dare!
'Tis like the returning bloom
  Of those days, alas, gone by,
When I loved, each hour—I scarce knew whom—
  And was blessed—I scarce knew why.

Ay—those were days when life had wings,
  And flew, oh, flew so wild a height,
That, like the lark which sunward springs,
  'Twas giddy with too much light.
And though of some plumes bereft,
  With that sun, too nearly set,
I've enough of light and wing still left,
  For a few gay soarings yet.

FAREWELL, THERESA!

Farewell, Theresa! yon cloud that over
  Heaven's pale night-star gathering we see,
Will scarce from that pure orb have passed, ere thy lover
  Swift o'er the wide wave shall wander from thee.

Long, like that dim cloud, I've hung around thee,
  Darkening thy prospects, saddening thy brow;
With gay heart, Theresa, and bright cheek I found thee;
  Oh, think how changed love, how changed art thou now!

But here I free thee; like one awaking
  From fearful slumber, thou breakst the spell;
'Tis over—the moon, too, her bondage is breaking—
  Past are the dark clouds; Theresa, farewell!

SEE, THE DAWN FROM HEAVEN.

See, the dawn from heaven is breaking
    O'er our sight,
And Earth, from sin awaking,
    Hails the light!
See those groups of angels, winging
    From the realms above,
On their brows, from Eden, bringing
    Wreaths of Hope and Love.

Hark, their hymns of glory pealing
    Through the air,
To mortal ears revealing
    Who lies there!
In that dwelling, dark and lowly,
    Sleeps the Heavenly Son,
He, whose home's above—the Holy
    Ever Holy One!

NETS AND CAGES.*

Come, listen to my story, while
  Your needle's task you ply;
At what I sing some maids will smile,
  While some, perhaps, may sigh.
Though Love's the theme, and Wisdom blames
  Such florid songs as ours,
Yet Truth sometimes, like eastern dames,
  Can [illegible]er thoughts by flowers.
    Then listen, maids, come listen, while
      Your needle's task you ply;
    At what I sing there's some may smile,
      While some, perhaps, will sigh.

Young Cloe, bent on catching Loves,
  Such nets had learned to frame,
That none, in all our vales and groves,
  E'er caught so much small game:
But gentle Sue, less given to roam,
  While Cloe's nets were taking
Such lots of Loves, sat still at home,
  One little love-cage making.
    Come, listen, maids, &c.

Much Cloe laughed at Susan's task;
  But mark how things went on;
These light-caught Loves, ere you could ask
  Their name and age, were gone!
So weak poor Cloe's nets were wove,
  That, though she charmed into them
New game each hour, the youngest Love
  Was able to break through them.
    Come, listen, maids, &c.

Meanwhile, young Sue, whose cage was wrought
  Of bars too strong to sever,
One Love with golden pinions caught,
  And caged him there for ever;
Instructing, thereby, all coquettes,
  Whate'er their looks or ages,
That, though 'tis pleasant weaving nets,
  'Tis wiser to make cages.
    Thus, maidens, thus do I beguile
      The task your fingers ply.—
    May all who hear like Susan smile,
      And not, like Cloe, sigh!

* Suggested by the following remark of Swift: "The reason why so few marriages are happy, is, because young ladies spend their time in making nets, not in making cages."

THE CRYSTAL-HUNTERS.

      O'er mountains bright
      With snow and light,
  We Crystal Hunters speed along;
      While rocks and caves,
      And icy waves,
  Each instant echo to our song;
  And, when we meet with store of gems,
  We grudge not kings their diadems.
      O'er mountains bright
      With snow and light,
  We Crystal-Hunters speed along;
      While grots and caves,
      And icy waves,
  Each instant echo to our song.

Not half so oft the lover dreams
  Of sparkles from his lady's eyes,
As we of those refreshing gleams
  That tell where deep the crystal lies;
Though, next to crystal, we too grant,
That ladies' eyes may most enchant.
    O'er mountains bright, &c.

Sometimes, when on the Alpine rose
  The golden sunset leaves its ray,
So like a gem the floweret glows,
  We thither bend our headlong way;
And, though we find no treasure there,
We bless the rose that shines so fair,
      O'er mountains bright
      With snow and light,
  We Crystal-Hunters speed along;
      While rocks and caves,
      And icy waves,
  Each instant echo to our song,

ROW GENTLY HERE.

    Row gently here,
    My gondolier,
  So softly wake the tide,
    That not an ear,
    On earth, may here,
  But hers to whom we glide.
Iad heaven but tongues to speak, as well
  As starry eyes to see,
Oh, think what tales 'twould have to tell
  Of wandering youths like me!

    Now rest thee here,
    My gondolier;
  Hush, hush, for up I go,
    To climb yon light
    Balcony's height,
  While thou keepst watch below.
Ah! did we take for heaven above
  But half such pains as we
Take, day and night, for woman's love,
  What angels we should be!

BRIGHT BE THY DREAMS.

Bright be thy dreams—may all thy weeping
Turn into smiles while thou art sleeping.
May those by death or seas removed,
The friends, who in thy spring-time knew thee,
All, thou hast ever prized or loved,
In dreams come smiling to thee!

There may the child, whose love lay deepest,
Dearest of all, come while thou sleepest;
Still as she was—no charm forgot—
No lustre lost that life had given;
Or, if changed, but changed to what
Thou'lt find her yet in Heaven!

GO, THEN—'TIS VAIN.

Go, then—'tis vain to hover
Thus round a hope that's dead;
At length my dream is over;
'Twas sweet—'twas false—'tis fled!
Farewell! since naught it moves thee,
Such truth as mine to see—
Some one, who far less loves thee,
Perhaps more blest will be.

Farewell, sweet eyes, whose brightness
New life around me shed;
Farewell, false heart, whose lightness
Now leaves me death instead.
Go, now, those charms surrender
To some new lover's sigh—
One who, though far less tender,
May be more blest than I.

WHEN THROUGH THE PIAZETTA.

When through the Piazetta
Night breathes her cool air,
Then, dearest Ninetta,
I'll come to thee there.
Beneath thy mask shrouded,
I'll know thee afar,
As Love knows, though clouded,
His own Evening Star.

In garb, then, resembling
Some gay gondolier,
I'll whisper thee, trembling,
"Our bark, love, is near;
Now, now, while there hover
Those clouds o'er the moon,
'Twill waft thee safe over
Yon silent Lagoon."

GO, NOW, AND DREAM.

Go, now, and dream o'er that joy in thy slumber—
Moments so sweet again ne'er shalt thou number.
Of Pain's bitter draught the flavor ne'er flies,
While Pleasure's scarce touches the lip ere it dies.
Go, then, and dream, &c.

That moon, which hung o'er your parting, so splendid,
Often will shine again, bright as she then did—
But, never more will the beam she saw burn
In those happy eyes, at your meeting, return.
Go, then, and dream, &c.

TAKE HENCE THE BOWL.

Take hence the bowl; though beaming
Brightly as bowl ere shone,
Oh, it but sets me dreaming
Of happy days now gone.
There, in its clear reflection,
As in a wizard's glass,
Lost hopes and dead affection,
Like shades, before me pass.

Each cup I drain brings hither
Some scene of bliss gone by;
Bright lips, too bright to wither,
Warm hearts, too warm to die.
Till, as the dream comes o'er me
Of those long vanished years,
Alas, the wine before me
Seems turning all to tears!

WHEN THE FIRST SUMMER BEE.

When the first summer bee
O'er the young rose shall hover,
Then, like that gay rover,
I'll come to thee.
He to flowers, I to lips, full of sweets to the brim—
What a meeting, what a meeting for me and for him!
When the first summer bee, &c.

Then, to every bright tree
In the garden he'll wander;
While I, oh, much fonder,
Will stay with thee.
In search of new sweetness through thousands he'll run,
While I find the sweetness of thousands in one
Then, to every bright tree, &c.

THOUGH 'TIS ALL BUT A DREAM.

Though 'tis all but a dream at the best,
And still, when happiest, soonest o'er,
Yet, even in a dream, to be blessed
Is so sweet, that I ask for no more.
The bosom that opes
With earliest hopes,
The soonest finds those hopes untrue;
As flowers that first
In spring-time burst
The earliest wither too!
Ay—'tis all but a dream, &c.

Though by Friendship we oft are deceived,
And find Love's sunshine soon o'ercast,
Yet Friendship will still be believed,
And Love trusted on to the last.
The web 'mong the leaves
The spider weaves
Is like the charm Hope hangs o'er men;
Though often she sees
'Tis broke by the breeze,
She spins the bright tissue again.
Ay—'tis all but a dream, &c.

WHERE ARE THE VISIONS.

"Where are the visions that round me once hovered,
Forms that shed grace from their shadows alone;
Looks fresh as light from a star just discovered,
And voices that Music might take for her own?"

Time, while I spoke, with his wings resting o'er me,
Heard me say, "Where are those visions, oh where?"
And pointing his wand to the sunset before me,
Said, with a voice like the hollow wind, "There."

Fondly I looked, when the wizard had spoken,
And there, 'mid the dim shining ruins of day,
Saw, by their light, like a talisman broken,
The last golden fragments of hope melt away.

WIND THY HORN, MY HUNTER BOY.

Wind thy horn, my hunter boy,
And leave thy lute's inglorious sighs;
Hunting is the hero's joy,
Till war his nobler game supplies.
Hark! the hound-bells ringing sweet,
While hunters shout, and the woods repeat,
Hilli-ho! Hilli-ho!

Wind again thy cheerful horn,
Till echo, faint with answ'ring, dies:
Burn, bright torches, burn till morn,
And lead us where the wild boar lies.
Hark! the cry, "He's found, he's found,"
While hill and valley our shouts resound,
Hilli-ho! Hilli-ho!

WHEN THE WINE-CUP IS SMILING.

When the wine-cup is smiling before us,
And we pledge round to hearts that are true, boy, true,
Then the sky of this life opens o'er us,
And Heaven gives a glimpse of its blue.
Talk of Adam in Eden reclining,
We are better, far better off thus, boy, thus;
For *him* but *two* bright eyes were shining—
See, what numbers are sparkling for us!

When on *one* side the grape-juice is dancing,
While on t'other a blue eye beams, boy, beams,
'Tis enough, 'twixt the wine and the glancing,
To disturb even a saint from his dreams.
Yet, though life like a river is flowing,
I care not how fast it goes on, boy, on,
So the grape on its bank is still growing,
And love lights the waves as they run.

WHERE SHALL WE BURY OUR SHAME?

Where shall we bury our shame?
Where, in what desolate place,
Hide the last wreck of a name
Broken and stained by disgrace?
Death may dissever the chain,
Oppression will cease when we're gone;
But the dishonor, the stain,
Die as we may, will live on.

Was it for this we sent out
Liberty's cry from our shore?
Was it for this that her shout
Thrilled to the world's very core?
Thus to live cowards and slaves!—
Oh, ye free hearts that lie dead,
Do you not, e'en in your graves,
Shudder, as o'er you we tread?

NE'ER TALK OF WISDOM'S GLOOMY SCHOOLS.

Ne'er talk of Wisdom's gloomy schools;
Give me the sage who's able
To draw his moral thoughts and rules
From the study of the table;—
Who learns how lightly, fleetly pass
This world and all that's in it,
From the bumper that but crowns his glass,
And is gone again next minute!

The diamond sleeps within the mine,
The pearl beneath the water;
While Truth, more precious, dwells in wine,
The grape's own rosy daughter.
And none can prize her charms like him,
Oh, none like him obtain her,
Who thus can, like Leander, swim
Through sparkling floods to gain her!

HERE SLEEPS THE BARD.

Here sleeps the Bard who knew so well
All the sweet windings of Apollo's shell;
Whether its music rolled like torrents near,
Or died, like distant streamlets, on the ear.
Sleep, sleep, mute bard: alike unheeded now
The storm and zephyr sweep thy lifeless brow;—
That storm, whose rush is like thy martial lay;
That breeze which, like thy love-song, dies away!

DO NOT SAY THAT LIFE IS WANING.

Do not say that life is waning,
Or that Hope's sweet day is set;
While I've thee and love remaining,
Life is in th' horizon yet.

Do not think those charms are flying,
Though thy roses fade and fall;
Beauty hath a grace undying,
Which in thee survives them all.

Not for charms, the newest, brightest,
That on other cheeks may shine,
Would I change the least, the slightest,
That is ling'ring now o'er thine.

THE GAZELLE.

Dost thou not hear the silver bell,
Through yonder lime-trees ringing?
'Tis my lady's light gazelle,
To me her love-thoughts bringing—
All the while that silver bell
Around his dark neck ringing.

See, in his mouth he bears a wreath,
My love hath kissed in tying;
Oh, what tender thoughts beneath
Those silent flowers are lying—
Hid within the mystic wreath
My love hath kissed in tying!

Welcome, dear gazelle, to thee,
And joy to her, the fairest,
Who thus hath breathed her soul to me,
In every leaf thou bearest;
Welcome, dear gazelle, to thee,
And joy to her, the fairest!

Hail, ye living, speaking flowers,
That breathe of her who bound ye;
Oh, 'twas not in fields, or bowers,
'Twas on her lips she found ye;—
Yes, ye blushing, speaking flowers,
'Twas on her lips she found ye.

NO—LEAVE MY HEART TO REST.

No—leave my heart to rest, if rest it may,
When youth, and love, and hope, have passed away.
Couldst thou, when summer hours are fled,
To some poor leaf that's fallen and dead,
Bring back the hue it wore, the scent it shed?
No—leave this heart to rest, if rest it may,
When youth, and love, and hope, have passed away.

Oh, had I met thee then, when life was bright,
Thy smile might still have fed its tranquil light;
But now thou com'st like sunny skies,
Too late to cheer the seaman's eyes,
When wrecked and lost his bark before him lies!
No—leave this heart to rest, if rest it may,
Since youth, and love, and hope, have passed away.

OH, GUARD OUR AFFECTION.

Oh guard our affection, nor e'er let it feel
The blight that this world o'er the warmest will steal:
While the faith of all round us is fading or past,
Let ours, ever green, keep its bloom to the last.

Far safer for Love 'tis to wake and to weep,
As he used in his prime, than go smiling to sleep;
For death on his slumber, cold death follows fast,
While the love that is wakeful lives on to the last.

And though, as Time gathers his clouds o'er our head,
A shade somewhat darker o'er life they may spread,
Transparent, at least, be the shadow they cast,
So that Love's softened light may shine through to the last.

IF IN LOVING, SINGING.

If in loving, singing, night and day
We could trifle merrily life away,
Like atoms dancing in the beam,
Like day-flies skimming o'er the stream,
Or summer blossoms, born to sigh
Their sweetness out, and die—
How brilliant, thoughtless, side by side,
Thou and I could make our minutes glide!
No atoms ever glanced so bright,
No day-flies ever danced so light,
Nor summer blossoms mixed their sigh
So close, as thou and I!

SLUMBER, OH SLUMBER.

"Slumber, oh slumber; if sleeping thou mak'st
My heart beat so wildly, I'm lost if thou wak'st."
Thus sung I to a maiden,
Who slept one summer's day,
And, like a flower o'erladen
With too much sunshine, lay.
Slumber, oh slumber, &c.

'Breathe not, oh breathe not, ye winds, o'er her cheeks;
If mute thus she charm me, I'm lost when she speaks."
Thus sing I, while, awaking,
She murmurs words that seem
As if her lips were taking
Farewell of some sweet dream.
Breathe not, oh breathe not, &c.

BRING THE BRIGHT GARLANDS HITHER.

Bring the bright garlands hither,
Ere yet a leaf is dying;
If so soon they must wither,
Ours be their last sweet sighing.
Hark, that low dismal chime!
'Tis the dreary voice of Time.
Oh, bring beauty, bring roses,
Bring all that yet is ours;
Let life's day, as it closes,
Shine to the last through flowers.

Haste, ere the bowl's declining,
Drink of it now or never;
Now, while Beauty is shining,
Love, or she's lost for ever.
Hark! again that dull chime,
'Tis the dreary voice of Time.
Oh, if life be a torrent,
Down to oblivion going,
Like this cup be its current,
Bright to the last drop flowing!

THOU LOV'ST NO MORE.

Too plain, alas! my doom is spoken,
Nor canst thou veil the sad truth o'er;
Thy heart is changed, thy vow is broken,
Thou lov'st no more—thou lov'st no more.

Though kindly still those eyes behold me,
The smile is gone, which once they wore;
Though fondly still those arms enfold me,
'Tis not the same—thou lov'st no more.

Too long my dream of bliss believing,
I've thought thee all thou wert before;
But now—alas! there's no deceiving,
'Tis all too plain, thou lov'st no more.

Oh, thou as soon the dead couldst waken,
As lost affection's life restore,
Give peace to her that is forsaken,
Or bring back him who loves no more.

LIKE ONE WHO, DOOMED.

Like one who, doomed o'er distant seas
His weary path to measure,
When home at length, with fav'ring breeze,
He brings the far-sought treasure;

His ship, in sight of shore, goes down,
That shore to which he hasted;
And all the wealth he thought his own,
Is o'er the waters wasted.

Like him, this heart, through many a track
Of toil and sorrow straying,
One hope alone brought fondly back,
Its toil and grief repaying.

Like him, alas! I see that ray
Of hope before me perish,
And one dark minute sweep away
What years were given to cherish.

WHEN ABROAD IN THE WORLD.

When abroad in the world thou appearest,
And the young and the lovely are there,
To my heart while of all thou'rt the dearest,
To my eyes thou'rt of all the most fair.
They pass, one by one,
Like waves of the sea.
That say to the Sun,
"See, how fair we can be."
But where's the light like thine,
In sun or shade to shine?
No—no, 'mong them all, there is nothing like thee,
Nothing like thee.

Oft, of old, without farewell or warning,
Beauty's self used to steal from the skies;
Fling a mist round her head, some fine morning,
And post down to earth in disguise;
But, no matter what shroud
Around her might be,
Men peeped through the cloud,
And whispered, "'Tis She."
So thou, where thousands are,
Shin'st forth the only star—
Yes, yes, 'mong them all, there is nothing like thee,
Nothing like thee.

O SAY, THOU BEST AND BRIGHTEST.

O say, thou best and brightest,
My first love and my last,
When he, whom now thou slightest,
From life's dark scene hath past,
Will kinder thoughts then move thee?
Will pity wake one thrill
For him who lived to love thee,
And dying, loved thee still?

If when, that hour recalling
From which he dates his woes.
Thou feel'st a tear-drop falling,
Ah! blush not while it flows:
But, all the past forgiving,
Bend gently o'er his shrine,
And say, "This heart, when living,
With all its faults, was mine."

WHEN NIGHT BRINGS THE HOUR.

When night brings the hour,
Of starlight and joy,
There comes to my bower
A fairy-winged boy;
With eyes so bright,
So full of wild arts,
Like nets of light,
To tangle young hearts;
With lips, in whose keeping
Love's secret may dwell,
Like Zephyr asleep in
Some rosy sea-shell.
Guess who he is,
Name but his name,
And his best kiss,
For reward, you may claim.

Where'er o'er the ground
He prints his light feet,
The flowers there are found
Most shining and sweet:
His looks, as soft
As lightning in May,
Though dangerous oft,
Ne'er wound but in play:
And oh, when his wings
Have brushed o'er my lyre,
You'd fancy its strings
Were turning to fire.
Guess who he is,
Name but his name,
And his best kiss,
For reward, you may claim.

KEEP THOSE EYES STILL PURELY MINE.

KEEP those eyes still purely mine,
Though far off I be:
When on others most they shine,
Then think they're turned on me.

Should those lips as now respond
To sweet minstrelsey,
When their accents seem most fond,
Then think they're breathed for me.

Make what hearts thou wilt thy own,
If when all on thee
Fix their charmed thoughts alone,
Thou thinkst the while on me.

HOPE COMES AGAIN.

HOPE comes again, to this heart long a stranger,
Once more she sings me her flattering strain;
But hush, gentle syren—for, ah! there's less danger
In still suff'ring on, than in hoping again.

Long, long, in sorrow, too deep for repining,
Gloomy, but tranquil, this bosom hath lain;
And joy coming now, like a sudden light shining
O'er eyelids long darkened, would bring me but pain.

Fly then, ye visions, that Hope would shed o'er me;
Lost to the future, my sole chance of rest
Now lies not in dreaming of bliss that's before me,
But, ah—in forgetting how once I was blest.

FEAR NOT THAT, WHILE AROUND THEE.

FEAR not that, while around thee
Life's varied blessings pour,
One sigh of hers shall wound thee,
Whose smile thou seekst no more.
No, dead and cold for ever
Let our past love remain;
Once gone, its spirit never
Shall haunt thy rest again.

May the new ties that bind thee
Far sweeter, happier prove,
Nor e'er of me remind thee,
But by their truth and love.
Think how, asleep or waking,
Thy image haunts me yet;
But, how this heart is breaking
For thy own peace, forget.

WHEN LOVE IS KIND.

WHEN Love is kind,
Cheerful and free,
Love's sure to find
Welcome from me.

But when Love brings
Heartache or pang,
Tears, and such things,
Love may go hang!

If Love can sigh
For one alone,
Well pleased am I
To be that one.

But should I see
Love given to rove
To two or three,
Then—good-by, Love!

Love must, in short,
Keep fond and true,
Through good report,
And evil too.

Else, here I swear,
Young Love may go,
For aught I care—
To Jericho.

THE GARLAND I SEND THEE.

THE Garland I send thee was culled from those bowers
Where thou and I wandered in long vanished hours;
Not a leaf or a blossom its bloom here displays,
But bears some remembrance of those happy days.

The roses were gathered by that garden gate,
Where our meetings, though early, seemed always too late;
Where ling'ring full oft through a summer-night's moon,
Our partings, though late, appeared always too soon.

The rest were all culled from the banks of that glade,
Where, watching the sunset, so often we strayed,
And mourned, as the time went, that Love had no power
To bind in his chain even one happy hour.

SPRING AND AUTUMN.

EV'RY season hath its pleasures!
Spring may boast her flow'ry prime,
Yet the vineyard's ruby treasures
Brighten Autumn's sob'rer time.
So Life's year begins and closes;
Days, though short'ning, still can shine;
What though youth gave love and roses,
Age still leaves us friends and wine.

Phillis, when she might have caught me,
All the Spring looked coy and shy,
Yet herself in Autumn sought me,
When the flowers were all gone by.
Ah, too late;—she found her lover
Calm and free beneath his vine,
Drinking to the Spring-time over
In his best autumnal wine.

Thus may we, as years are flying,
To their flight our pleasures suit,
Nor regret the blossoms dying,
While we still may taste the fruit.
Oh, while days like this are ours,
Where's the lip that dares repine?
Spring may take our loves and flowers,
So Autumn leaves us friends and wine.

LOVE ALONE.

IF thou wouldst have thy charms enchant our eyes,
First win our hearts, for there thy empire lies:
Beauty in vain would mount a heartless throne,
Her Right Divine is given by Love alone.

What would the rose with all her pride be worth,
Were there no sun to call her brightness forth?
Maidens, unloved, like flowers in darkness thrown,
Wait but that light, which comes from Love alone.

Fair as thy charms in yonder glass appear,
Trust not their bloom, they'll fade from year to year:
Wouldst thou they still should shine as first they shone,
Go, fix thy mirror in Love's eyes alone.

HOW SHALL I WOO?

IF I speak to thee in Friendship's name,
Thou thinkst I speak too coldly;
If I mention Love's devoted flame,
Thou say'st I speak too boldly.
Between these two unequal fires,
Why doom me thus to hover?
I'm a friend, if such thy heart requires,
If more thou seekst, a lover.
Which shall it be? How shall I woo?
Fair one, choose between the two.

Though the wings of Love will brightly play,
When first he comes to woo thee,
There's a chance that he may fly away
As fast as he flies *to* thee.
While Friendship, though on foot she come,
No flights of fancy trying,
Will, therefore, oft be found at home,
When Love abroad is flying.
Which shall it be? How shall I woo?
Dear one, choose between the two.

If neither feeling suits thy heart,
Let's see, to please thee, whether
We may not learn some precious art
To mix their charms together;
One feeling, still more sweet, to form
From two so sweet already—
A friendship that like love is warm,
A love like friendship steady.
Thus let it be, thus let me woo,
Dearest, thus we'll join the two.

LEGENDARY BALLADS.

THE VOICE.

It came o'er her sleep, like a voice of those days,
When love, only love, was the light of her ways;
And, soft as in moments of bliss long ago,
It whispered her name from the garden below.

"Alas!" sighed the maiden, "how fancy can cheat!
The world once had lips that could whisper thus sweet;
But cold now they slumber in yon fatal deep,
Where, oh that beside them this heart too could sleep!"

She sunk on her pillow—but no, 'twas in vain
To chase the illusion, that Voice came again!
She flew to the casement—but, hushed as the grave,
In moonlight lay slumbering woodland and wave.

"Oh sleep, come and shield me," in anguish she said,
"From that call of the buried, that cry of the Dead!"
And sleep came around her—but, starting, she woke,
For still from the garden that spirit-Voice spoke!

"I come," she exclaimed, "be thy home where it may,
On earth or in heaven, that call I obey;"
Then forth through the moonlight, with heart beating fast
And loud as a death-watch, the pale maiden past.

Still round her the scene all in loneliness shone;
And still, in the distance, that Voice led her on;
But whither she wandered, by wave or by shore,
None ever could tell, for she came back no more.

No, ne'er came she back—but the watchman who stood
That night in the tower which o'ershadows the flood,
Saw dimly, 'tis said, o'er the moon-lighted spray,
A youth on a steed bear the maiden away.

CUPID AND PSYCHE.

They told her that he, to whose vows she had listened
Through night's fleeting hours, was a spirit unblest;—
Unholy the eyes, that beside her had glistened,
And evil the lips she in darkness had prest.

"When next in thy chamber the bridegroom reclineth,
Bring near him thy lamp, when in slumber he lies;
And there, as the light o'er his dark features shineth,
Thou'lt see what a demon hath won all thy sighs!"

Too fond to believe them, yet doubting, yet fearing,
When calm lay the sleeper she stole with her light;
And saw—such a vision!—no image, appearing
To bards in their day-dreams, was ever so bright.

A youth, but just passing from childhood's sweet morning,
While round him still lingered its innocent ray;
Though gleams, from beneath his shut eyelids, gave warning
Of summer-noon lightnings that under them lay.

His brow had a grace more than mortal around it,
While, glossy as gold from a fairy-land mine,
His sunny hair hung, and the flowers that crowned it
Seemed fresh from the breeze of some garden divine.

Entranced stood the bride, on that miracle gazing,
What late was but love is idolatry now;
But, ah—in her tremor the fatal lamp raising—
A sparkle flew from it and dropped on his brow.

All's lost—with a start from his rosy sleep waking,
The Spirit flashed o'er her his glances of fire;
Then, slow from the clasp of her snowy arms breaking,
Thus said, in a voice more of sorrow than ire:—

"Farewell—what a dream thy suspicion hath broken!
Thus ever Affection's fond vision is crost;
Dissolved are her spells when a doubt is but spoken,
And love, once distrusted, for ever is lost!"

THE HIGH-BORN LADYE.

In vain all the Knights of the Underwald wooed her,
Though brightest of maidens, the proudest was she;
Brave chieftains they sought, and young minstrels they sued her,
But worthy were none of the high-born Ladye.

"Whomsoever I wed," said this maid, so excelling,
"That Knight must the conqu'ror of conquerors be;
He must place me in halls fit for monarchs to dwell in;—
None else shall be Lord of the high-born Ladye!"

Thus spoke the proud damsel, with scorn looking round her
On Knights and on Nobles of highest degree;
Who humbly and hopelessly left as they found her,
And worshipped at distance the high-born Ladye.

At length came a Knight, from a far land to woo her,
With plumes on his helm like the foam of the sea;
His vizor was down—but, with voice that thrilled through her,
He whispered his vows to the high-born Ladye.

"Proud maiden! I come with high spousals to grace thee,
In me the great conqu'ror of conquerors see;
Enthroned in a hall fit for monarchs I'll place thee,
And mine thou'rt for ever, thou high-born Ladye!"

The maiden she smiled, and in jewels arrayed her,
Of thrones and tiaras already dreamt she;
And proud was the step, as her bridegroom conveyed her
In pomp to his home, of that high-born Ladye.

"But whither," she, starting, exclaims, "have you led me?
Here's naught but a tomb and a dark cypress-tree;
Is *this* the bright palace in which thou wouldst wed me?"
With scorn in her glance, said the high-born Ladye.

"'Tis the home," he replied, "of earth's loftiest creatures"—
Then lifted his helm for the fair one to see;
But she sunk on the ground—'twas a skeleton's features,
And Death was the Lord of the high-born Ladye!

HERO AND LEANDER.

"The night-wind is moaning with mournful sigh,
There gleameth no moon in the misty sky,
No star over Helle's sea;
Yet, yet, there is shining one holy light,
One love-kindled star through the deep of night,
To lead me, sweet Hero, to thee!"

Thus saying, he plunged in the foamy stream,
Still fixing his gaze on that distant beam
No eye but a lover's could see;
And still, as the surge swept over his head,
"To-night," he said tenderly, "living or dead,
Sweet Hero, I'll rest with thee!"

But fiercer around him the wild waves speed;
Oh, Love! in that hour of thy votary's need,
Where, where could thy Spirit be?
He struggles—he sinks—while the hurricane's breath
Bears rudely away his last farewell in death—
"Sweet Hero, I die for thee!"

THE LEAF AND THE FOUNTAIN.

"Tell me, kind Seer, I pray thee,
So may the stars obey thee,
So may each airy
Moon-elf and fairy
Nightly their homage pay thee!
Say, by what spell, above, below,
In stars that wink or flowers that blow,
I may discover,
Ere night is over,
Whether my love loves me or no,
Whether my love loves me."

"Maiden, the dark tree nigh thee
Hath charms no gold could buy thee:
Its stem enchanted,
By moon-elves planted,
Will all thou seekst supply thee.
Climb to yon boughs that highest grow,
Bring thence their fairest leaf below;
And thou'lt discover,
Ere night is over,
Whether thy love loves thee or no,
Whether thy love loves thee."

"See, up the dark tree going,
With blossoms round me blowing,
From thence, oh Father,
This leaf I gather,
Fairest that there is growing.
Say, by what sign I now shall know
If in this leaf lie bliss or wo;
And thus discover,
Ere night is over,
Whether my love loves me or no,
Whether my love loves me."

"Fly to yon fount that's welling,
Where moonbeam ne'er had dwelling,
Dip in its water
That leaf, oh Daughter,
And mark the tale 'tis telling;*
Watch thou if pale or bright it grow,
List thou, the while, that fountain's flow,
And thou'lt discover
Whether thy lover,
Loved as he is, loves thee or no,
Loved as he is, loves thee."

Forth flew the nymph, delighted,
To seek that fount benighted;
But, scarce a minute
The leaf lay in it,
When, lo, its bloom was blighted!
And as she asked, with voice of wo—
List'ning, the while, that fountain's flow—
"Shall I recover
My truant lover?"
The fountain seemed to answer, "No;"
The fountain answered, "No."

* The ancients had a mode of divination somewhat similar to this; and we find the Emperor Adrian, when he went to consult the Fountain of Castalia, plucking a bay-leaf and dipping it into the sacred water.

YOUTH AND AGE.*

"Tell me, what's Love?" said Youth, one day,
To drooping Age, who crossed his way.—
"It's a sunny hour of play,
For which repentance dear doth pay;
Repentance! Repentance!
And this is Love, as wise men say."

"Tell me, what's Love?" said Youth once more,
Fearful, yet fond, of Age's lore.—
"Soft as a passing summer's wind:
Wouldst know the blight it leaves behind?
Repentance! Repentance!
And this is Love—when love is o'er."

"Tell me, what's Love?" said Youth again,
Trusting the bliss, but not the pain.
"Sweet as a May tree's scented air—
Mark ye what bitter fruit 'twill bear,
Repentance! Repentance!
This, this is Love—sweet Youth, beware."

Just then, young Love himself came by,
And cast on Youth a smiling eye;
Who could resist that glance's ray?
In vain did Age his warning say,
"Repentance! Repentance!"
Youth laughing went with Love away.

CEPHALUS AND PROCRIS.

A hunter once in that grove reclined,
To shun the noon's bright eye,
And oft he wooed the wandering wind,
To cool his brow with its sigh.
While mute lay even the wild bee's hum,
Nor breath could stir the aspen's hair,
His song was still, "Sweet Air, oh come!"
While Echo answered, "Come, sweet Air!"

But, hark, what sounds from the thicket rise?
What meaneth that rustling spray?
"'Tis the white-horned doe," the Hunter cries,
"I have sought since break of day,"
Quick o'er the sunny glade he springs,
The arrow flies from his sounding bow,
"Hilliho—hilliho!" he gayly sings,
While Echo sighs forth "Hilliho!"

Alas! 'twas not the white-horned doe
He saw in the rustling grove,
But the bridal veil, as pure as snow,
Of his own young wedded love.
And, ah! too sure that arrow sped,
For pale at his feet he sees her lie;—
"I die, I die," was all she said,
While Echo murmured, "I die, I die!"

THE DYING WARRIOR.

A wounded Chieftain, lying
By the Danube's leafy side,
Thus faintly said, in dying,
"Oh! bear, thou foaming tide,
This gift to my lady-bride."

'Twas then, in life's last quiver,
He flung the scarf he wore
Into the foaming river,
Which, ah too quickly, bore
That pledge of one no more!

With fond impatience burning,
The Chieftain's lady stood,
To watch her love returning
In triumph down the flood,
From that day's field of blood.

* The air, to which I have adapted these words, was composed by Mrs. Arkwright to some old verses, "Tell me what's love, kind shepherd, pray?" and it has been my object to retain as much of the structure and phraseology of the original words as possible

But, field, alas! ill-fated,
The lady saw, instead
Of the bark whose speed she waited,
Her hero's scarf, all red
With the drops his heart ad shed.

One shriek—and all was over—
Her life-pulse ceased to beat;
The gloomy waves now cover
That bridal-flower so sweet,
And the scarf is her winding-sheet!

THE MAGIC MIRROR.

"Come, if thy magic Glass have power
To call up forms we sigh to see;
Show me my love, in that rosy bower,
Where last she pledged her truth to me."

The Wizard showed him his Lady bright,
Where lone and pale in her bower she lay;
"True-hearted maid," said the happy Knight,
"She's thinking of one, who is far away."

But, lo! a page, with looks of joy,
Brings tidings to the Lady's ear;
"'Tis," said the Knight, "the same bright boy,
Who used to guide me to my dear."

The Lady now, from her fav'rite tree,
Hath, smiling, plucked a rosy flower;
"Such," he exclaimed, "was the gift that she
Each morning sent me from that bower!"

She gives her page the blooming rose,
With looks that say, "Like lightning, fly!"
"Thus," thought the Knight, "she sooths her woes,
By fancying, still, her true-love nigh."

But the page returns—and—oh, what a sight,
For trusting lover's eyes to see!—
Leads to that bower another Knight,
As young and, alas! as loved as he!"

"Such," quoth the Youth, "is Woman's love!"
Then, darting forth, with furious bound,
Dashed at the Mirror his iron glove,
And strewed it all in fragments round.

MORAL.

Such ills would never have come to pass,
Had he ne'er sought that fatal view:
The Wizard would still have kept his Glass,
And the Knight still thought his Lady true.

THE STRANGER.

Come list, while I tell of the heart-wounded Stranger
Who sleeps her last slumber in this haunted ground;
Where often, at midnight, the lonely wood-ranger
Hears soft fairy music re-echo around.

None e'er knew the name of that heart-stricken lady,
Her language, though sweet, none could e'er understand;
But her features so sunned, and her eyelash so shady,
Bespoke her a child of some far Eastern land.

'Twas one summer night, when the village lay sleeping,
A soft strain of melody came o'er our ears;
So sweet, but so mournful, half song and half weeping,
Like music that Sorrow had steeped in her tears.

We thought 'twas an anthem some angel had sung us;—
But, soon as the day-beams had gushed from on high,
With wonder we saw this bright stranger among us,
All lovely and lone, as if strayed from the sky.

Nor long did her life for this sphere seem intended,
For pale was her cheek, with that spirit-like hue,
Which comes when the day of this world is nigh ended,
And light from another already shines through.

Then her eyes when she sung—oh, but once to have seen them—
Left thoughts in the soul that can never depart;
While her looks and her voice made a language between them,
That spoke more than holiest words to the heart.

But she passed like a day-dream—no skill could restore her—
Whate'er was her sorrow, its ruin came fast;
She died with the same spell of mystery o'er her,
That song of past days on her lips to the last.

Nor even in the grave is her sad heart reposing—
Still hovers the spirit of grief round her tomb;
For oft, when the shadows of midnight are closing,
The same strain of music is heard through the gloom

THE INDIAN BOAT.

'Twas midnight dark,
The seaman's bark
Swift o'er the waters bore him,
When, through the night,
He spied a light
Shoot o'er the wave before him.
"A sail! a sail!" he cries;
"She comes from the Indian shore,
And to-night shall be our prize,
With her freight of golden ore:
Sail on! sail on!"
When morning shone,
He saw the gold still clearer;
But, though so fast
The waves he passed,
That boat seemed never the nearer.

Bright daylight came,
And still the same
Rich bark before him floated;
While on the prize
His wishful eyes
Like any young lover's doated:
"More sail! more sail!" he cries,
While the waves o'ertop the mast;
And his bounding galley flies,
Like an arrow before the blast.
Thus on, and on,
Till day was gone,
And the moon through heaven did hie her,
He swept the main,
But all in vain,
That boat seemed never the nigher.

And many a day
To night gave way,
And many a morn succeeded:
While still his flight,
Through day and night,
That restless mariner speeded.
Who knows—who knows what seas
He is now careering o'er?
Behind, the eternal breeze,
And that mocking bark, before!
For, oh till sky
And earth shall die,
And their death leave none to rue it,
That boat must flee
O'er the boundless sea,
And that ship in vain pursue it.

THE PILGRIM.

Still thus, when twilight gleamed,
Far off his Castle seemed,
Traced on the sky;
And still, as fancy bore him
To those dim towers before him,
He gazed with wishful eye,
And thought his home was nigh.

"Hall of my Sires!" he said,
"How long, with weary tread,
Must I toil on?
Each eve, as thus, I wander,
Thy towers seem rising yonder,
But, scarce hath daylight shone,
When, like a dream, thou'rt gone!"

So went the Pilgrim still,
Down dale and over hill,
Day after day;
That glimpse of home, so cheering,
At twilight still appearing,
But still, with morning's ray,
Melting, like mist, away!

Where rests the Pilgrim now?
Here, by this cypress bough,
Closed his career;
That dream, of Fancy's weaving,
No more his steps deceiving,
Alike past hope and fear,
The Pilgrim's home is here.

SET OF GLEES

MUSIC BY MOORE.

THE MEETING OF THE SHIPS.

When o'er the silent seas alone,
For days and nights we've cheerless gone,
Oh they who've felt it know how sweet,
Some sunny morn a sail to meet.

Sparkling at once is every eye,
"Ship ahoy! ship ahoy!" our joyful cry;
While answering back the sounds we hear
"Ship ahoy! ship ahoy! what cheer? what cheer?"

Then sails are backed, we nearer come,
Kind words are said of friends and home;
And soon, too soon, we part with pain,
To sail o'er silent seas again.

SAY, WHAT SHALL WE DANCE?

Say, what shall we dance?
Shall we bound along the moonlight plain,
To music of Italy, Greece, or Spain?
Say, what shall we dance?
Shall we, like those who rove
Through bright Grenada's grove,
To the light Bolero's measures move?
Or choose the Guaracia's languishing lay,
And thus to its sound die away?

Strike the gay chords,
Let us hear each strain from ev'ry shore
That music haunts, or young feet wander o'er.
Hark! 'tis the light march, to whose measured time,
The Polish lady, by her lover led,
Delights through gay saloons with step untired to tread,
Or sweeter still, through moonlight walks,
Whose shadows serve to hide
The blush that's raised by him who talks
Of love the while by her side;
Then comes the smooth waltz, to whose floating sound
Like dreams we go gliding around—
Say, which shall we dance? which shall we dance?

HUSH, HUSH!

"Hush, hush!"—how well
That sweet word sounds,
When Love, the little sentinel,
Walks his night-rounds;
Then, if a foot but dare
One rose-leaf crush,
Myriads of voices in the air
Whisper, "Hush, hush!"

"Hark, hark, 'tis he!"
The night-elves cry,
And hush their fairy harmony,
While he steals by;
But if his silv'ry feet
One dewdrop brush,
Voices are heard in chorus sweet,
Whisp'ring, "Hush, hush!"

THE EVENING GUN.

Rememb'rest thou that setting sun,
The last I saw with thee,
When loud we heard the evening gun
Peal o'er the twilight sea?
Boom!—the sounds appeared to sweep
Far o'er the verge of day,
Till, into realms beyond the deep,
They seemed to die away.

Oft, when the toils of day are done,
In pensive dreams of thee,
I sit to hear that evening gun
Peal o'er the stormy sea.
Boom!—and while, o'er billows curled,
The distant sounds decay,
I weep and wish, from this rough world,
Like them to die away.

THE WATCHMAN.

A TRIO.

WATCHMAN.

Past twelve o'clock—past twelve.

Good-night, good-night, my dearest—
How fast the moments fly!
'Tis time to part, thou hearest
That hateful watchman's cry.

WATCHMAN.

Past one o'clock—past one.

Yet stay a moment longer—
Alas! why is it so,
The wish to stay grows stronger,
The more 'tis time to go?

WATCHMAN.

Past two o'clock—past two.

Now wrap thy cloak about thee—
The hours must sure go wrong,
For when they're passed without thee,
They're, oh, ten times as long.

WATCHMAN.

Past three o'clock—past three.

Again that dreadful warning!
Had ever time such flight?
And see the sky, 'tis morning—
So now, *indeed*, good-night.

WATCHMAN.

Past three o'clock—past three.

Good-night, good-night.

THE PARTING BEFORE THE BATTLE.

HE.

On to the field, our doom is sealed,
To conquer or be slaves:
This sun shall see our nation free,
Or set upon our graves.

SHE.

Farewell, oh farewell, my love,
May Heaven thy guardian be,
And send bright angels from above
To bring thee back to me.

HE.

On to the field, the battle-field,
Where Freedom's standard waves,
This sun shall see our tyrant yield,
Or shine upon our graves.

HIP, HIP, HURRA!

Come, fill round a bumper, fill up to the brim,
He who shrinks from a bumper, I pledge not to him;
"Here's the girl that each loves, be her eye of what hue,
Or lustre, it may, so her heart is but true."
Charge! (drinks) hip, hip, hurra, hurra!

Come, charge high again, boys, nor let the full wine
Leave a space in the brimmer, where daylight may shine;
"Here's the friends of our youth—though of some we're bereft,
May the links that are lost but endear what are left!"
Charge! (drinks) hip, hip, hurra, hurra!

Once more fill a bumper—ne'er talk of the hour;
On hearts thus united old Time has no power.
"May our lives, though, alas! like the wine of to-night,
They must soon have an end, to the last flow as bright."
Charge! (drinks) hip, hip, hurra, hurra!

Quick, quick, now, I'll give you, since Time's glass will run
Even faster than ours doth, three bumpers in one;
"Here's the poet who sings—here's the warrior who fights—
Here's the statesman who speaks in the cause of men's rights!"
Charge! (drinks) hip, hip, hurra, hurra!

Come, once more, a bumper!—then drink as you please,
Though, *who* could fill half-way to toast such as these?
"Here's our next joyous meeting—and oh! when we meet,
May our wine be as bright, and our union as sweet!"
Charge! (drinks) hip, hip, hurra, hurra!

BALLADS, SONGS, MISCELLANEOUS POEMS, ETC.

TO-DAY, DEAREST! IS OURS.

To-day, dearest! is ours;
Why should Love carelessly lose it?
This life shines or lowers
Just as we, weak mortals, use it.
'Tis time enough, when its flowers decay,
To think of the thorns of Sorrow;
And Joy, if left on the stem to-day,
May wither before to-morrow.

Then why, dearest! so long
Let the sweet moments fly over?
Though now, blooming and young,
Thou hast me devoutly thy lover;
Yet Time from both in his silent lapse,
Some treasure may steal or borrow;
Thy charms may be less in bloom, perhaps,
Or I less in love to-morrow.

DEAR FANNY.

"She has beauty, but still you must keep your heart cool;
She has wit but you musn't be caught so;"
Thus Reason advises, but Reason's a fool,
And 'tis not the first time I have thought so,
Dear Fanny,
'Tis not the first time I have thought so.

"She is lovely; then love her, nor let the bliss fly;
'Tis the charm of youth's vanishing season;"
Thus Love has advised me, and who will deny
That Love reasons much better than Reason,
Dear Fanny?
Love reasons much better than Reason.

POOR BROKEN FLOWER.

Poor broken flower! what art can now recover thee?
Torn from the stem that fed thy rosy breath—
In vain the sun-beams seek
To warm that faded cheek;
The dews of heaven, that once like balm fell over thee,
Now are but tears, to weep thy early death.

So droops the maid whose lover hath forsaken her,—
Thrown from his arms, as lone and lost as thou;
In vain the smiles of all
Like sun-beams round her fall;
The only smile that could from death awaken her,
That smile, alas! is gone to others now.

TELL HER, OH, TELL HER.

Tell her, oh, tell her, the lute she left lying
Beneath the green arbor, is still lying there;
And breezes, like lovers, around it are sighing,
But not a soft whisper replies to their prayer.

Tell her, oh, tell her, the tree that, in going,
Beside the green arbor she playfully set,
As lovely as ever is blushing and blowing,
And not a bright leaflet has fallen from it yet.

So while away from that arbor forsaken,
The maiden is wandering, still let her be
As true as the lute, that no sighing can waken,
And blooming for ever, unchanged as the tree!

POOR WOUNDED HEART.

Poor wounded heart, farewell!
Thy hour of rest is come;
Thou soon wilt reach thy home,
Poor wounded heart, farewell!
The pain thou'lt feel in breaking
Less bitter far will be,
Than that long, deadly aching,
This life has been to thee.

There—broken heart, farewell!
The pang is o'er—
The parting pang is o'er;
Thou now wilt bleed no more,
Poor broken heart, farewell!
No rest for thee but dying—
Like waves, whose strife is past,
On death's cold shore thus lying,
Thou sleepst in peace at last—
Poor broken heart, farewell!

WHEN ON THE LIP THE SIGH DELAYS.

When on the lip the sigh delays,
As if 'twould linger there for ever;
When eyes would give the world to gaze,
Yet still look down, and venture never;
When, though with fairest nymphs we rove,
There's one we dream of more than any—
If all this is not real love,
'Tis something wondrous like it, Fanny!

To think and ponder, when apart,
On all we've got to say at meeting;
And yet when near, with heart to heart,
Sit mute, and listen to their beating;
To see but one bright object move,
The only moon, where stars are many—
If all this is not downright love,
I prithee say what *is*, my Fanny!

When Hope foretells the brightest, best,
Though Reason on the darkest reckons;
When Passion drives us to the west,
Though Prudence to the eastward beckons;
When all turns round, below, above,
And our own heads the most of any—
If this is not stark, staring love,
Then you and I are sages, Fanny.

THE EAST INDIAN.

Come, May, with all thy flowers,
Thy sweetly-scented thorn,
Thy cooling evening showers,
Thy fragrant breath at morn;
When May-flies haunt the willow,
When May-buds tempt the bee,
Then o'er the shining billow
My love will come to me.

From Eastern Isles she's winging
Through wat'ry wilds her way,
And on her cheek is bringing
The bright sun's orient ray;
Oh, come and court her hither,
Ye breezes mild and warm—
One winter's gale would wither
So soft, so pure a form.

The fields where she was straying
Are blest with endless light,
With zephyrs always playing
Through gardens always bright.
Then now, sweet May! be sweeter
Than e'er thou'st been before;
Let sighs from roses meet her
When she comes near our shore.

OH CALL IT BY SOME BETTER NAME.

Oh, call it by some better name,
For Friendship sounds too cold,
While Love is now a worldly flame,
Whose shrine must be of gold;
And Passion, like the sun at noon,
That burns o'er all he sees,
Awhile as warm, will set as soon—
Then, call it none of these.

Imagine something purer far,
More free from stain of clay
Than Friendship, Love, or Passion, are,
Yet human still as they;
And if thy lip, for love like this,
No mortal word can frame,
Go, ask of angels what it is,
And call it by that name!

HERE, TAKE MY HEART.

Here, take my heart—'twill be safe in thy keeping,
While I go wand'ring o'er land and o'er sea;
Smiling or sorrowing, waking or sleeping,
What need I care, so my heart is with thee?

If, in the race we are destined to run, love,
They who have light hearts the happiest be,
Then, happier still must be they who have none, love,
And that will be *my* case when mine is with thee.

It matters not where I may now be a rover,
I care not how many bright eyes I may see;
Should Venus herself come and ask me to love her,
I'd tell her I couldn't—my heart is with thee.

And there let it lie, growing fonder and fonder—
For, even should Fortune turn truant to me,
Why, let her go—I've a treasure beyond her,
As long as my heart's out at int'rest with thee!

BLACK AND BLUE EYES.

The brilliant black eye
May in triumph let fly
All its darts without caring who feels 'em;
But the soft eye of blue,
Though it scatter wounds too,
Is much better pleased when it heals 'em—
Dear Fanny!
But the soft eye of blue,
Though it scatter wounds too,
Is much better pleased when it heals 'em.

The black eye may say,
"Come and worship my ray—
By adoring, perhaps, you may move me!"
But the blue eye, half hid,
Says, from under its lid,
"I love, and am yours, if you love me!"
Yes, Fanny!
The blue eye, half hid,
Says, from under its lid,
"I love, and am yours, if you love me!"

Come tell me, then, why,
In that lovely blue eye,
Not a charm of its teint I discover;
Oh why should you wear
The only blue pair
That ever said "No" to a lover?
Dear Fanny!
Oh, why should you wear
The only blue pair
That ever said "No" to a lover?

THE YOUNG MULETEERS OF GRENADA.

Oh, the joys of our evening posada,
Where, resting at close of day,
We young Muleteers of Grenada,
Sit and sing the sunshine away;
So merry, that even the slumbers,
That round us hung, seem gone;
Till the lute's soft drowsy numbers
Again beguile them on.
Oh the joys, &c.

Then as each to his loved sultana
In sleep still breathes the sigh,
The name of some black-eyed Tirana
Escapes our lips as we lie.
Till, with morning's rosy twinkle,
Again we're up and gone—
While the mule-bell's drowsy tinkle
Beguiles the rough way on.
Oh the joys of our merry posada,
Where, resting at close of day,
We, young Muleteers of Grenada,
Thus sing the gay moments away.

OUR FIRST YOUNG LOVE.

Our first young love resembles
That short but brilliant ray,
Which smiles, and weeps, and trembles
Through April's earliest day.
And not all life before us,
However its lights may play,
Can shed a lustre o'er us
Like that first April ray.

Our summer sun may squander
A blaze serener, grander;
Our autumn beam
May, like a dream
Of heaven, die calm away;
But, no—let life before us
Bring all the light it may,
'Twill ne'er shed lustre o'er us
Like that first youthful ray.

THE PRETTY ROSE-TREE.

Being weary of love,
I flew to the grove,
And chose me a tree of the fairest;
Saying, "Pretty Rose-tree
Thou my mistress shalt be,
And I'll worship each bud thou bearest.
For the hearts of this world are hollow,
And fickle the smiles we follow;
And 'tis sweet when all
Their witch'ries pall,
To have a pure love to fly to;
So, my pretty Rose-tree,
Thou my mistress shalt be,
And the only one now I shall sigh to."

When the beautiful hue
Of thy cheek through the dew
Of morning is bashfully peeping,
"Sweet tears," I shall say
(As I brush them away),
"At least there's no art in this weeping."
Although thou shouldst die to-morrow,
'Twill not be from pain or sorrow;
And the thorns of thy stem
Are not like them
With which men wound each other;
So my pretty Rose-tree,
Thou my mistress shalt be,
And I'll ne'er again sigh to another.

NIGHTS OF MUSIC.

Nights of music, nights of loving,
Lost too soon, remembered long,
When we went by moonlight roving,
Hearts all love and lips all song.
When this faithful lute recorded
All my spirit felt to thee;
And that smile the song rewarded—
Worth whole years of fame to me!

Nights of song, and nights of splendor,
Filled with joys too sweet to last—
Joys that, like the star-light, tender,
While they shone, no shadow cast.
Though all other happy hours
From my fading memory fly,
Of that star-light, of those bowers,
Not a beam, a leaf shall die!

SHINE OUT, STARS!

Shine out, Stars! let Heaven assemble
Round us every festal ray,
Lights that move not, lights that tremble,
All to grace this Eve of May.
Let the flower-beds all lie waking,
And the odors shut up there,
From their downy prisons breaking,
Fly abroad through sea and air.

And would Love, too, bring his sweetness,
With our other joys to weave,
Oh, what glory, what completeness,
Then would crown this bright May eve!
Shine out, Stars! let night assemble
Round us every festal ray,
Lights that move not, lights that tremble,
To adorn this Eve of May.

FROM LIFE WITHOUT FREEDOM.

From life without freedom, say, who would not fly?
For one day of freedom, oh! who would not die?
Hark!—hark! 'tis the trumpet! the call of the brave,
The death-song of tyrants, the dirge of the slave.
Our country lies bleeding—haste, haste to her aid;
One arm that defends is worth hosts that invade.

In death's kindly bosom our last hope remains—
The dead fear no tyrants, the grave has no chains.
On, on to the combat; the heroes that bleed
For virtue and mankind are heroes indeed.
And oh, even if Freedom from *this* world be driven,
Despair not—at least we shall find her in heaven.

HERE'S THE BOWER.

Here's the bower she loved so much,
And the tree she planted;
Here's the harp she used to touch—
Oh, how that touch enchanted!
Roses now unheeded sigh;
Where's the hand to wreath them?
Songs around neglected lie;
Where's the lip to breathe them?
Here's the bower, &c.

Spring may bloom, but she we loved
Ne'er shall feel its sweetness;
Time, that once so fleetly moved,
Now hath lost its fleetness.
Years were days, when here she strayed,
Days were moments near her;
Heaven ne'er formed a brighter maid,
Nor Pity wept a dearer!
Here's the bower, &c.

I SEE THE MOON RISE CLEAR.

A FINLAND LOVE-SONG.

I saw the moon rise clear
O'er hills and vales of snow,
Nor told my fleet reindeer
The track I wished to go.
Yet quick he bounded forth;
For well my reindeer knew
I've but one path on earth—
The path which leads to you.

The gloom that winter cast
How soon the heart forgets,
When summer brings, at last,
Her sun that never sets!
So dawned my love for you;
So, fixed through joy and pain,
Than summer sun more true,
'Twill never set again.

LOVE AND THE SUN-DIAL.

Young Love found a Dial once, in a dark shade,
Where man ne'er had wandered nor sunbeam played
"Why thus in darkness lie," whispered young Love;
"Thou, whose gay hours in sunshine should move?"
"I ne'er," said the Dial, "have seen the warm sun,
So noonday and midnight to me, Love, are one."

Then Love took the Dial away from the shade,
And placed her where Heaven's beam warmly played
There she reclined, beneath Love's gazing eye,
While, marked all with sunshine, her hours flew by.
"Oh, how," said the Dial, "can any fair maid,
That's born to be shone upon, rest in the shade?"

But night now comes on, and the sunbeam's o'er,
And Love stops to gaze on the Dial no more.
Alone and neglected, while bleak rain and winds
Are storming around her, with sorrow she finds
That Love had but numbered a few sunny hours—
Then left the remainder to darkness and showers!

LOVE AND TIME.

'Tis said—but whether true or not
Let bards declare who've seen 'em—
That Love and Time have only got
One pair of wings between 'em.
In courtship's first delicious hour,
The boy full oft can spare 'em;
So, loit'ring in his lady's bower,
He lets the gray-beard wear 'em.
Then is Time's hour of play;
Oh, how he flies, flies away!

But short the moments, short as bright,
When he the wings can borrow;
If Time to-day has had his flight,
Love takes his turn to-morrow.
Ah! Time and Love, your change is then
The saddest and most trying,
When one begins to limp again,
And t'other takes to flying.
Then is Love's hour to stray;
Oh, how he flies, flies away!

But there's a nymph whose chains I feel,
And bless the silken fetter,
Who knows, the dear one, how to deal
With Love and Time much better.
So well she checks their wanderings,
So peacefully she pairs 'em,
That Love with her ne'er thinks of wings,
And Time for ever wears 'em.
This is Time's holyday;
Oh, how he flies, flies sway!

LOVE, WANDERING THROUGH THE GOLDEN MAZE.

Love, wand'ring through the golden maze
Of my beloved's hair,
Traced every lock with fond delays,
And, doting, lingered there.
And soon he found 'twere vain to fly;
His heart was close confined,
For, every ringlet was a tie—
A chain by beauty twined.

MERRILY EVERY BOSOM BOUNDETH.

THE TYROLESE SONG OF LIBERTY.

Merrily every bosom boundeth,
Merrily, oh!
Where the song of Freedom soundeth,
Merrily, oh!
There the warrior's arms
Shed more splendor;
There the maiden's charms
Shine more tender;
Ev'ry joy the land surroundeth,
Merrily, oh! merrily, oh!

Wearily every bosom pineth,
Wearily, oh!
Where the bond of slavery twineth
Wearily, oh!
There the warrior's dart
Hath no fleetness;
There the maiden's heart
Hath no sweetness—
Ev'ry flower of life declineth,
Wearily, oh! wearily, oh!

Cheerily then from hill and valley,
Cheerily, oh!
Like your native fountains sally,
Cheerily, oh!
If a glorious death,
Won by bravery,
Sweeter be than breath
Sighed in slavery,
Round the flag of Freedom rally
Cheerily, oh! cheerily, oh!

LOVE'S LIGHT SUMMER-CLOUD.

Pain and sorrow shall vanish before us—
Youth may wither, but feeling will last;
All the shadow that e'er shall fall o'er us,
Love's light summer-cloud only shall cast.
Oh, if to love thee more
Each hour I number o'er,
If this a passion be
Worthy of thee,
Then be happy, for thus I adore thee.
Charms may wither, but feeling shall last:
All the shadow that e'er shall fall o'er thee,
Love's light summer-cloud sweetly shall cast.

Rest, dear bosom, no sorrows shall pain thee,
Sighs of pleasure alone shalt thou steal;
Beam, bright eyelid, no weeping shall stain thee
Tears of rapture alone shalt thou feel.
Oh, if there be a charm
In love, to banish harm—
If pleasure's truest spell
Be to love well,
Then be happy, for thus I adore thee.
Charms may wither, but feeling shall last:
All the shadow that e'er shall fall o'er thee,
Love's light summer-cloud sweetly shall cast.

REMEMBER THE TIME.

THE CASTILIAN MAID.

Remember the time, in La Mancha's shades,
When our moments so blissfully flew;
When you called me the flower of Castilian maids,
And I blushed to be called so by you;
When I taught you to warble the gay seguadille,
And to dance to the light castanet;
Oh, never, dear youth, let you roam where you will,
The delight of those moments forget.

They tell me, you lovers from Erin's green isle,
Every hour a new passion can feel;
And that soon, in the light of some lovelier smile,
You'll forget the poor maid of Castile.
But they know not how brave in the battle you are,
Or they never could think you would rove;
For 'tis always the spirit most gallant in war
That is fondest and truest in love.

LOVE THEE?

Love thee?—so well, so tenderly
Thou'rt loved, adored by me,
Fame, fortune, wealth, and liberty,
Were worthless without thee.
Though brimmed with blessings, pure and rare,
Life's cup before me lay,
Unless thy love were mingled there,
I'd spurn the draught away.
Love thee?—so well, so tenderly
Thou'rt loved, adored by me,
Fame, fortune, wealth, and liberty,
Are worthless without thee.

Without thy smile, the monarch's lot
To me were dark and lone,
While, *with* it, even the humblest cot,
Were brighter than his throne.
Those worlds, for which the conqu'ror sighs,
For me would have no charms;
My only world thy gentle eyes—
My throne thy circling arms!
Oh, yes, so well, so tenderly
Thou'rt loved, adored by me,
Whole realms of light and liberty
Were worthless without thee.

OH, SOON RETURN.

Our white sail caught the evening ray,
The wave beneath us seemed to burn,
When all the weeping maid could say
Was, "Oh, soon return!"

Through many a clime our ship was driven,
O'er many a billow rudely thrown;
Now chilled beneath a northern heaven,
Now sunned in summer's zone:
And still, where'er we bent our way,
When evening bid the west wave burn,
I fancied still I heard her say,
"Oh, soon return!"

If ever yet my bosom found
Its thoughts one moment turned from thee,
'Twas when the combat raged around,
And brave men looked to me.
But though the war-field's wild alarm
For gentle Love was all unmeet,
He lent to Glory's brow the charm,
Which made even danger sweet.
And still, when vict'ry's calm came o'er
The hearts where rage had ceased to burn,
Those parting words I heard once more,
"Oh, soon return!—Oh, soon return!"

ONE DEAR SMILE.

Couldst thou look as dear as when
First I sighed for thee;
Couldst thou make me feel again
Every wish I breathed thee then,
Oh, how blissful life would be!
Hopes, that now beguiling leave me,
Joys, that lie in slumber cold—
All would wake, couldst thou but give me
One dear smile like those of old.

No—there's nothing left us now,
But to mourn the past;
Vain was every ardent vow—
Never yet did Heaven allow
Love so warm, so wild, to last.
Not even hope could now deceive me—
Life itself looks dark and cold:
Oh, thou never more canst give me
One dear smile like those of old.

THE DAY OF LOVE.

The beam of morning trembling
Stole o'er the mountain brook,
With timid ray resembling
Affection's early look.
Thus love begins—sweet morn of love!

The noontide ray ascended,
And o'er the valley's stream
Diffused a glow as splendid
As passion's riper dream.
Thus love expands—warm noon of love!

But evening came, o'ershading
The glories of the sky,
Like faith and fondness fading
From passion's altered eye.
Thus love declines—cold eve of love!

WHEN TWILIGHT DEWS.

When twilight dews are falling soft
Upon the rosy sea, love,
I watch the star, whose beam so oft
Has lighted me to thee, love.
And thou too, on that orb so dear,
Dost often gaze at even,
And think, though lost for ever here,
Thou'lt yet be mine in heaven.

There's not a garden walk I tread,
There's not a flower I see, love,
But brings to mind some hope that's fled,
Some joy that's gone with thee, love.
And still I wish that hour was near,
When, friends and foes forgiven,
The pains, the ills we've wept through here,
May turn to smiles in heaven

LUSITANIAN WAR-SONG.

The song of war shall echo through our mountains,
Till not one hateful link remains
Of slavery's lingering chains;
Till not one tyrant tread our plains,
Nor traitor lip pollute our fountains.
No! never till that glorious day
Shall Lusitania's sons be gay,
Or hear, oh Peace, thy welcome lay
Resounding through her sunny mountains.

The song of war shall echo through our mountains,
Till Victory's self shall, smiling, say,
"Your cloud of foes hath passed away,
And Freedom comes, with newborn ray,
To gild your vines and light your fountains."
Oh, never till that glorious day
Shall Lusitania's sons be gay,
Or hear, sweet Peace, thy welcome lay
Resounding through her sunny mountains.

THE YOUNG ROSE.

The young rose I give thee, so dewy and bright,
Was the flow'ret most dear to the sweet bird of night,
Who oft, by the moon, o'er her blushes hath hung,
And thrilled every leaf with the wild lay he sung.

Oh, take thou this young rose, and let her life be
Prolonged by the breath she will borrow from thee;
For, while o'er her bosom thy soft notes shall thrill,
She'll think the sweet night-bird is courting her still.

HOW HAPPY, ONCE.

How happy once, though winged with sighs,
My moments flew along,
While looking on those smiling eyes,
And list'ning to thy magic song!
But vanished now, like summer dreams,
Those moments smile no more;
For me that eye no longer beams,
That song for me is o'er.
Mine the cold brow,
That speaks thy altered vow,
While others feel thy sunshine now,

Oh, could I change my love like thee,
One hope might yet be mine—
Some other eyes as bright to see,
And hear a voice as sweet as thine:
But never, never can this heart
Be waked to life again;
With thee it lost its vital part,
And withered then!
Cold its pulse lies,
And mute are even its sighs,
All other grief it now defies.

I LOVE BUT THEE.

If, after all, you still will doubt and fear me,
And think this heart to other loves will stray,
If I must swear, then, lovely doubter, hear me;
By ev'ry dream I have when thou'rt away,
By ev'ry throb I feel when thou art near me,
I love but thee—I love but thee!

By those dark eyes, where light is ever playing,
Where Love, in depth of shadow, holds his throne,
And by those lips, which give whate'er thou'rt saying,
Or grave or gay, a music of its own,
A music far beyond all minstrel's playing,
I love but thee—I love but thee!

By that fair brow, where Innocence reposes,
As pure as moonlight sleeping upon snow,
And by that cheek, whose fleeting blush discloses
A hue too bright to bless this world below,
And only fit to dwell on Eden's roses,
I love but thee—I love but thee!

YES, YES, WHEN THE BLOOM.

Yes, yes, when the bloom of Love's boyhood is o'er,
He'll turn into friendship that feels no decay;
And though Time may take from him the wings he once wore,
The charms that remain will be bright as before,
And he'll lose but his young trick of flying away.

Then let it console thee, if Love should not stay,
That Friendship our last happy moments will crown:
Like the shadows of morning, Love lessens away,
While Friendship, like those at the closing of day,
Will linger and lengthen as life's sun goes down.

WHEN MIDST THE GAY I MEET.

When midst the gay I meet
That gentle smile of thine,
Though still on me it turns most sweet,
I scarce can call it mine:
But when to me alone
Your secret tears you show,
Oh, then I feel those tears my own,
And claim them while they flow.
Then still with bright looks bless
The gay, the cold, the free;
Give smiles to those who love you less,
But keep your tears for me.

The snow on Jura's steep
Can smile in many a beam,
Yet still in chains of coldness sleep,
How bright soe'er it seem.
But, when some deep-felt ray,
Whose touch is fire, appears,
Oh, then the smile is warmed away,
And, melting, turns to tears.
Then still with bright looks bless
The gay, the cold, the free;
Give smiles to those who love you less,
But keep your tears for me.

YOUNG JESSICA.

Young Jessica sat all the day,
With heart o'er idle love-thoughts pining;
Her needle bright beside her lay,
So active once!—now idly shining.
Ah! Jessy, 'tis in idle hearts
That love and mischief are most nimble;
The safest shield against the darts
Of Cupid, is Minerva's thimble.

The child, who with a magnet plays,
Well knowing all its arts, so wily,
The tempter near a needle lays,
And laughing, says, "We'll steal it slyly."
The needle, having naught to do,
Is pleased to let the magnet wheedle;
Till closer, closer come the two,
And—off, at length, elopes the needle.

Now, had this needle turned its eye
To some gay reticule's construction,
It ne'er had strayed from duty's tie,
Nor felt the magnet's sly seduction.
Thus, girls, would you keep quiet hearts,
Your snowy fingers must be nimble;
The safest shield against the darts
Of Cupid, is Minerva's thimble.

LET JOY ALONE BE REMEMBERED NOW.

Let thy joys alone be remembered now,
Let thy sorrows go sleep awhile;
Or if thought's dark cloud come o'er thy brow,
Let Love light it up with his smile.
For thus to meet, and thus to find,
That Time, whose touch can chill
Each flower of form, each grace of mind,
Hath left thee blooming still—
Oh, joy alone should be thought of now,
Let our sorrows go sleep awhile;
Or, should thought's dark cloud come o'er thy brow
Let Love light it up with his smile.

When the flowers of life's sweet garden fade,
If but *one* bright leaf remain,
Of the many that once its glory made,
It is not for us to complain.
But thus to meet and thus to wake
In all Love's early bliss;
Oh, Time all other gifts may take,
So he but leaves us this!
Then let joy alone be remembered now,
Let our sorrows go sleep awhile;
Or if thought's dark cloud come o'er thy brow,
Let Love light it up with his smile!

LOVE THEE, DEAREST? LOVE THEE?

Love thee, dearest? love thee?
Yes, by yonder star I swear,
Which through tears above thee
Shines so sadly fair;
Though often dim,
With tears, like him,
Like him thy truth will shine,
And—love thee, dearest? love thee?
Yes, till death I'm thine.

Leave thee, dearest? leave thee?
No, that star is not more true;
When my vows deceive thee,
He will wander too.
A cloud of night
May veil his light,
And death shall darken mine—
But—leave thee, dearest? leave thee?
No, till death I'm thine.

MY HEART AND LUTE.

I give thee all—I can no more—
Though poor the off'ring be;
My heart and lute are all the store
That I can bring to thee.
A lute whose gentle song reveals
The soul of love full well;
And, better far, a heart that feels
Much more than lute could tell.

Though love and song may fail, alas!
To keep life's clouds away,
At least 'twill make them lighter pass,
Or gild them if they stay.
And even if Care, at moments, flings
A discord o'er life's happy strain,
Let love but gently touch the strings,
'Twill all be sweet again!

PEACE, PEACE TO HIM THAT'S GONE.

When I am dead,
Then lay my head
In some lone, distant dell,
Where voices ne'er
Shall stir the air,
Or break its silent spell

If any sound
Be heard around,
Let the sweet bird alone,
That weeps in song
Sing all night long,
"Peace, peace to him that's gone!"

Yet, oh, were mine
One sigh of thine,
One pitying word from thee,
Like gleams of heaven,
To sinners given,
Would be that word to me.

Howe'er unblest,
My shade would rest
While list'ning to that tone;—
Enough 'twould be
To hear from thee,
"Peace, peace to him that's gone!"

'TIS ALL FOR THEE.

If life for me hath joy or light,
'Tis all from thee,
My thoughts by day, my dreams by night,
Are but of thee, of only thee.
Whate'er of hope or peace I know,
My zest in joy, my balm in wo,
To those dear eyes of thine I owe,
'Tis all from thee.

My heart, even ere I saw those eyes,
Seemed doomed to thee;
Kept pure till then from other ties,
'Twas all for thee, for only thee.
Like plants that sleep, till sunny May
Calls forth their life, my spirit lay,
Till touched by Love's awak'ning ray,
It lived for thee, it lived for thee.

When Fame would call me to her heights,
She speaks by thee;
And dim would shine her proudest lights,
Unshared by thee, unshared by thee.
Whene'er I seek the Muse's shrine,
Where bards have hung their wreathes divine,
And wish those wreaths of glory mine,
'Tis all for thee, for only thee.

THE SONG OF THE OLDEN TIME.*

There's a song of the olden time,
Falling sad o'er the ear,
Like the dream of some village chime,
Which in youth we loved to hear.
And even amid the grand and gay,
When Music tries her gentlest art,
I never hear so sweet a lay,
Or one that hangs so round my heart,
As that song of the olden time,
Falling sad o'er the ear,
Like the dream of some village chime,
Which in youth we loved to hear.

And when all of this life is gone,—
Even the hope, lingering now,
Like the last of the leaves left on
Autumn's sere and faded bough,—
'Twill seem as still those friends were near,
Who loved me in youth's early day,
If in that parting hour I hear
The same sweet notes, and die away,—
To that song of the olden time,
Breathed like Hope's farewell strain,
To say, in some brighter clime,
Life and youth will shine again!

ROSE OF THE DESERT.

Rose of the Desert! thou, whose blushing ray,
Lonely and lovely, fleets unseen away;
No hand to cull thee, none to woo thy sigh,—
In vestal silence left to live and die,—
Rose of the Desert! thus should woman be,
Shining uncourted, lone and safe, like thee.

Rose of the Garden, how unlike thy doom!
Destined for others, not thyself, to bloom;
Culled ere thy beauty lives through half its day;
A moment cherished, and then cast away;
Rose of the Garden! such is woman's lot,—
Worshipped, while blooming—when she fades, forgot.

* In this song, which is one of the many set to music by myself, the occasional lawlessness of the metre arises, I need hardly say, from the peculiar structure of the air.

WAKE THEE, MY DEAR.

Wake thee, my dear—thy dreaming
Till darker hours will keep;
While such a moon is beaming,
'Tis wrong tow'rd Heaven to sleep.

Moments there are we number,
Moments of pain and care,
Which to oblivion's slumber
Gladly the wretch would spare.
But now—who'd think of dreaming
When Love his watch should keep?
While such a moon is beaming,
'Tis wrong tow'rd Heaven to sleep.

If e'er the Fates should sever
My life and hopes from thee, love,
The sleep that lasts for ever
Would then be sweet to me, love;
But now,—away with dreaming!
Till darker hours 'twill keep;
While such a moon is beaming,
'Tis wrong tow'rd Heaven to sleep.

THE BOY OF THE ALPS.

Lightly, Alpine rover,
Tread the mountains over;
Rude is the path thou'st yet to go;
Snow cliffs hanging o'er thee,
Fields of ice before thee,
While the hid torrent moans below.
Hark, the deep thunder,
Through the vales yonder!
'Tis the huge av'lanche downward cast;
From rock to rock
Rebounds the shock.
But courage, boy! the danger's past.
Onward, youthful rover,
Tread the glacier over,
Safe shalt thou reach thy home at last.
On, ere light forsake thee,
Soon will dusk o'ertake thee;
O'er yon ice-bridge lies the way!
Now, for the risk prepare thee;
Safe it yet may bear thee,
Though 'twill melt in morning's ray.

Hark, that dread howling!
'Tis the wolf prowling,—
Scent of thy track the foe hath got;
And cliff and shore
Resound his roar.
But courage, boy,—the danger's past!
Watching eyes have found thee,
Loving arms are round thee.
Safe hast thou reached thy father's cot.

THE YOUNG INDIAN MAID.

There came a nymph dancing
Gracefully, gracefully,
Her eye a light glancing
Like the blue sea;
And while all this gladness
Around her steps hung,
Such sweet notes of sadness
Her gentle lips sung,
That ne'er while I live from my mem'ry shall fade
The song, or the look, of that young Indian maid.

Her zone of bells ringing
Cheerily, cheerily,
Chimed to her singing
Light echos of glee;
But in vain did she borrow
Of mirth the gay tone,
Her voice spoke of sorrow,
And sorrow alone.
Nor e'er while I live from my mem'ry shall fade
The song, or the look, of that young Indian maid

FOR THEE ALONE.

For thee alone I brave the boundless deep,
Those eyes my light through ev'ry distant sea;
My waking thoughts, the dream that gilds my sleep,
The noontide rev'ry, all are given to thee,
To thee alone, to thee alone.

Though future scenes present to Fancy's eye
Fair forms of light that crowd the distant air,
When nearer viewed, the fairy phantoms fly,
The crowds dissolve, and thou alone art there,
Thou, thou alone.

To win thy smile, I speed from shore to shore,
While Hope's sweet voice is heard in every blast,
Still whisp'ring on, that when some years are o'er,
One bright reward shall crown my toil at last,
Thy smile alone, thy smile alone

Oh place beside the transport of that hour
All earth can boast of fair, of rich, and bright,
Wealth's radiant mines, the lofty thrones of power—
Then ask where first thy lover's choice would light?
On thee alone, on thee alone.

HER LAST WORDS, AT PARTING.

Her last words, at parting, how can I forget?
Deep treasured through life, in my heart they shall stay;
Like music, whose charm in the soul lingers yet,
When its sounds from the ear have long melted away.
Let Fortune assail me, her threat'nings are vain;
Those still-breathing words shall my talisman be—
"Remember, in absence, in sorrow, and pain,
There's one heart, unchanging, that beats but for thee."

From the desert's sweet well though the pilgrim must hie,
Never more of that fresh-springing fountain to taste,
He hath still of its bright drops a treasured supply,
Whose sweetness lends life to his lips through the waste.
So, dark as my fate is still doomed to remain,
These words shall my well in the wilderness be—
"Remember, in absence, in sorrow, and pain,
There's one heart, unchanging, that beats but for thee."

SONG OF HERCULES TO HIS DAUGHTER.*

"I've been, oh, sweet daughter,
To fountain and sea,
To seek in their water
Some bright gem for thee,
Where diamonds were sleeping,
Their sparkle I sought,
Where crystal was weeping,
Its tears I have caught.

The sea-nymph I've courted
In rich coral halls;
With Naiads have sported
By bright waterfalls.
But sportive or tender,
Still sought I, around,
That gem, with whose splendor
Thou yet shalt be crowned.

And see, while I'm speaking,
Yon soft light afar;—
The pearl I've been seeking
There floats like a star!
In the deep Indian Ocean
I see the gem shine,
And quick as light's motion
Its wealth shall be thine."

Then eastward, like lightning,
The hero-god flew,
His sunny looks bright'ning
The air he went through.
And sweet was the duty,
And hallowed the hour,
Which saw thus young Beauty
Embellished by Power.

* Founded on the fable reported by Arrian (in Indicis) of Hercules having searched the Indian Ocean, to find the pearl with which he adorned his daughter Pandæa.

LOVE'S VICTORY.

Sing to Love—for, oh, 'twas he
Who won the glorious day;
Strew the wreaths of victory
Along the conqu'ror's way.
Yoke the Muses to his car,
Let them sing each trophy won;
While his mother's joyous star
Shall light the triumph on.

Hail to Love, to mighty Love,
Let spirits sing around;
While the hill, the dale, and grove,
With "mighty Love" resound;
Or, should a sigh of sorrow steal
Amid the sounds thus echoed o'er,
'Twill but teach the god to feel
His victories the more.

See his wings, like amethyst
Of sunny Ind their hue;
Bright as when, by Psyche kist,
They trembled through and through.
Flowers spring beneath his feet;
Angel forms beside him run;
While unnumbered lips repeat
"Love's victory is won!"
Hail to Love, to mighty Love, &c.

LET'S TAKE THIS WORLD AS SOME WIDE SCENE.

Let's take this world as some wide scene,
Through which, in frail, but buoyant boat,
With skies now dark and now serene,
Together thou and I must float;
Beholding oft, on either shore,
Bright spots where we should love to stay;
But Time plies swift his flying oar,
And away we speed, away, away.

Should chilling winds and rains come on,
We'll raise our awning 'gainst the shower;
Sit closer till the storm is gone,
And, smiling, wait a sunnier hour.
And if that sunnier hour should shine,
We'll know its brightness can not stay,
But happy, while 'tis thine and mine,
Complain not when it fades away.

So shall we reach at last that Fall
Down which life's currents all must go,
The dark, the brilliant, destined all
To sink into the void below.
Nor even that hour shall want its charms,
If, side by side, still fond we keep,
And calmly, in each other's arms
Together linked, go down the steep.

THE HOMEWARD MARCH.

Be still, my heart: I hear them come:
Those sounds announce my lover near:
The march that brings our warriors home
Proclaims he'll soon be here.

Hark, the distant tread,
O'er the mountain's head,
While hills and dales repeat the sound;
And the forest deer
Stand still to hear,
As those echoing steps ring round.

Be still, my heart, I hear them come,
Those sounds that speak my soldier near;
Those joyous steps seem winged for home—
Rest, rest, he'll soon be here.

But hark, more faint the footsteps grow,
And now they wind the distant glades·
Not here their home—alas! they go
To gladden happier maids!

Like sounds in a dream,
The footsteps seem,
As down the hills they die away;
And the march, whose song
So pealed along,
Now fades like a funeral lay.

'Tis past, 'tis o'er—hush, heart, thy pain!
And though not here, alas! they come,
Rejoice for those, to whom that strain
Brings sons and lovers home.

THE DREAM OF HOME.

Who has not felt how sadly sweet
The dream of home, the dream of home,
Steals o'er the heart too soon to fleet,
When far o'er sea or land we roam?
Sunlight more soft may o'er us fall,
To greener shores our bark may come;
But far more bright, more dear than all,
That dream of home, that dream of home.

Ask of the sailor youth when far
His light bark bounds o'er ocean's foam,
What charms him most, when evening's star
Smiles o'er the wave? to dream of home.
Fond thoughts of absent friends and loves
At that sweet hour around him come;
His heart's best joy, where'er he roves,
That dream of home, that dream of home.

THEY TELL ME THOU'RT THE FAVORED GUEST.*

They tell me thou'rt the favored guest,
Of every fair and brilliant throng;
No wit like thine to wake the jest,
No voice like thine to breathe the song;
And none could guess, so gay thou art,
That thou and I are far apart.

Alas! alas! how diff'rent flows
With thee and me the time away!
Not that I wish thee sad—Heaven knows—
Still, if thou canst, be light and gay;
I only know, that without thee
The sun himself is dark to me.

Do I thus haste to hall and bower,
Among the proud and gay to shine?
Or deck my hair with gem and flower,
To flatter other eyes than thine?
Ah! no, with me love's smiles are past,
Thou hadst the first, thou hadst the last.

WAKE UP, SWEET MELODY.

Wake up, sweet melody!
Now is the hour
When young and loving hearts
Feel most thy power.
One note of music, by moonlight's soft ray—
Oh, 'tis worth thousands heard coldly by day.
Then wake up, sweet melody!
Now is the hour
When young and loving hearts
Feel most thy power.

Ask the fond nightingale,
When his sweet flower
Loves most to hear his song,
In her green bower?
Oh, he will tell thee, through summer-nights long,
Fondest she lends her whole soul to his song.
Then wake up, sweet melody!
Now is the hour
When young and loving hearts
Feel most thy power.

* Part of a translation of some Latin verses, supposed to have been addressed by Hippolyta Taurella to her husband, during his absence at the gay court of Leo X. The verses may be found in the appendix to Roscoe's work.

CALM BE THY SLEEP.

Calm be thy sleep as infants' slumbers!
Pure as angel thoughts thy dreams!
May ev'ry joy this bright world numbers
Shed o'er thee their mingled beams!
Or if, where Pleasure's wing hath glided,
There ever must some pang remain,
Still be thy lot with me divided—
Thine all the bliss, and mine the pain!

Day and night my thoughts shall hover
Round thy steps where'er they stray;
As, even when clouds his idol cover,
Fondly the Persian tracks its ray.
If this be wrong, if Heaven offended
By worship to its creature be,
Then let my vows to both be blended,
Half breathed to Heaven and half to thee

THE EXILE.

Night waneth fast, the morning star
Saddens with light the glimm'ring sea,
Whose waves shall soon to realms afar
Waft me from hope, from love, and thee.
Coldly the beam from yonder sky
Looks o'er the waves that onward stray;
But colder still the stranger's eye
To him whose home is far away.

Oh, not at hour so chill and bleak,
Let thoughts of me come o'er thy breast;
But of the lost one think and speak,
When summer suns sink calm to rest.
So, as I wander, Fancy's dream
Shall bring me o'er the sunset seas,
Thy look, in ev'ry melting beam,
Thy whisper, in each dying breeze.

STILL WHEN DAYLIGHT.

Still when daylight o'er the wave
Bright and soft its farewell gave,
I used to hear, while light was falling,
O'er the wave a sweet voice calling,
Mournfully at distance calling.

Ah! once how blest that maid would come,
To meet her sea-boy hast'ning home;
And through the night those sounds repeating,
Hail his bark with joyous greeting,
Joyously his light bark greeting.

But, one sad night, when winds were high,
Nor earth, nor heaven, could hear her cry,
She saw his boat come tossing over
Midnight's wave—but not her lover!
No, never more her lover.

And still that sad dream loath to leave,
She comes with wand'ring mind at eve,
And oft we hear, when night is falling,
Faint her voice through twilight calling,
Mournfully at twilight calling.

THE SUMMER WEBS.

The summer webs that float and shine,
The summer dews that fall,
Though light they be, this heart of mine
Is lighter still than all.
It tells me every cloud is past
Which lately seemed to lour;
That Hope hath wed young Joy at last,
And now's their nuptial hour!

With light thus round, within, above,
With naught to wake one sigh,
Except the wish, that all we love
Were at this moment nigh—
It seems as if life's brilliant sun
Had stopped in full career,
To make this hour its brightest one,
And rest in radiance here.

THE FANCY FAIR.

Come, maids and youths, for here we sell
All wondrous things of earth and air;
Whatever wild romancers tell,
Or poets sing, or lovers swear,
You'll find at this our Fancy Fair.

Here eyes are made like stars to shine,
And kept, for years, in such repair,
That even when turned of thirty-nine,
They'll hardly look the worse for wear,
If bought at this our Fancy Fair.

We've lots of tears for bards to shower,
And hearts that such ill usage bear,
That, though they're broken ev'ry hour,
They'll still in rhyme fresh breaking bear,
If purchased at our Fancy Fair.

As fashions change in everything,
We've goods to suit each season's air,
Eternal friendships for the spring,
And endless loves for summer wear—
All sold at this our Fancy Fair.

We've reputations white as snow,
That long will last, if used with care,
Nay, safe through all life's journey go,
If packed and marked as "brittle ware"—
Just purchased at the Fancy Fair.

IF THOU WOULDST HAVE ME SING AND PLAY.

If thou wouldst have me sing and play,
As once I played and sung,
First take this time-worn lute away,
And bring one freshly strung.
Call back the time when pleasure's sigh
First breathed among the strings;
And Time himself, in flitting by,
Made music with his wings.

But how is this? though new the lute,
And shining fresh the chords,
Beneath this hand they slumber mute,
Or speak but dreamy words.
In vain I seek the soul that dwelt
Within that once sweet shell,
Which told so warmly what it felt,
And felt what naught could tell.

Oh, ask not then for passion's lay,
From lyre so coldly strung;
With this I ne'er can sing or play,
As once I played and sung.
No, bring that long-loved lute again—
Though chilled by years it be,
If *thou* wilt call the slumb'ring strain,
'Twill wake again for thee.

Though time have frozen the tuneful stream
Of thoughts that gushed along,
One look from thee, like summer's beam,
Will thaw them into song.
Then give, oh give, that wak'ning ray,
And once more blithe and young,
Thy bard again will sing and play,
As once he played and sung.

MIND NOT THOUGH DAYLIGHT.

Mind not though daylight around us is breaking—
Who'd think now of sleeping when morn's but just waking?
Sound the merry viol, and daylight or not,
Be all for one hour in the gay dance forgot.

See young Aurora, up heaven's hill advancing,
Though fresh from her pillow, even she too is dancing:
While thus all creation, earth, heaven, and sea,
Are dancing around us, oh, why should not we?

Who'll say that moments we use thus are wasted?
Such sweet drops of time only flow to be tasted;
While hearts are high beating, and harps full in tune,
The fault is all morning's for coming so soon.

THEY MET BUT ONCE.

They met but once, in youth's sweet hour,
And never since that day
Hath absence, time, or grief had power
To chase that dream away.
They've seen the suns of other skies,
On other shores have sought delight;
But never more, to bless their eyes,
Can come a dream so bright!
They met but once—a day was all
Of Love's young hopes they knew;
And still their hearts that day recall
As fresh as then it flew.

Sweet dream of youth! oh, ne'er again
Let either meet the brow
They left so smooth and smiling then,
Or see what it is now.
For, Youth, the spell was only thine;
From thee alone the enchantment flows,
That makes the world around thee shine
With light thyself bestows.
They met but once—oh, ne'er again
Let either meet the brow
They left so smooth and smiling then,
Or see what it is now.

WITH MOONLIGHT BEAMING.

With moonlight beaming
Thus o'er the deep,
Who'd linger dreaming
In idle sleep?
Leave joyless souls to live by day—
Our life begins with yonder ray;
And while thus brightly
The moments flee,
Our barks skim lightly
The shining sea.

To halls of splendor
Let great ones hie;
Through light more tender
Our pathways lie.
While round, from banks of brook or lake,
Our company blithe echoes make;
And, as we lend 'em
Sweet word or strain,
Still back they send 'em,
More sweet, again.

BEAUTY AND SONG.

Down in yon summer vale,
Where the rill flows,
Thus said a Nightingale
To his loved Rose:—
"Though rich the pleasures
Of song's sweet measures,
Vain were its melody,
Rose, without thee."

Then from the green recess
Of her night-bower,
Beaming with bashfulness,
Spoke the bright flower:—
"Though morn should lend her
Its sunniest splendor,
What would the Rose be,
Unsung by thee?"

Thus still let Song attend
Woman's bright way:
Thus still let woman lend
Light to the ray.
Like stars, through heaven's sea,
Floating in harmony,
Beauty shall glide along,
Circled by Song.

CHILD'S SONG. FROM A MASQUE.

I have a garden of my own,
  Shining with flowers of every hue;
I loved it dearly while alone,
  But I shall love it more with you:
And there the golden bees shall come,
  In summer-time at break of morn,
And wake us with their busy hum
  Around the Siha's fragrant thorn.

I have a fawn from Aden's land,
  On leafy buds and berries nurst;
And you shall feed him from your hand
  Though he may start with fear at first.
And I will lead you where he lies
  For shelter in the noontide heat;
And you may touch his sleeping eyes,
  And feel his little silv'ry feet.

THE HALCYON HANGS O'ER OCEAN.

The halcyon hangs o'er ocean,
  The sea-lark skims the brine;
This bright world's all in motion,
  No heart seems sad but mine.

To walk through sunbright places,
  With heart all cold the while;
To look in smiling faces,
  When we no more can smile;

To feel, while earth and heaven
  Around thee shine with bliss,
To thee no light is given—
  Oh, what a doom is this!

THE WORLD WAS HUSHED.

The world was hushed, the moon above
  Sailed through ether slowly;
When, near the casement of my love,
  Thus I whispered lowly:
"Awake, awake, how canst thou sleep?
  The field I seek to-morrow
Is one where man hath fame to reap,
  And woman gleans but sorrow."

"Let battle's field be what it may,"
  Thus spoke a voice replying,
"Think not thy love, while thou'rt away,
  Will here sit idly sighing.
No—woman's soul, if not for fame,
  For love can brave all danger!"
Then forth from out the casement came
  A plumed and armed stranger.

A stranger? No: 'twas she, the maid,
  Herself before me beaming,
With casque arrayed, and falchion blade
  Beneath her girdle gleaming!
Close side by side, in freedom's fight,
  That blessed morning found us;
In Vict'ry's light we stood ere night,
  And Love, the morrow, crowned us!

THE TWO LOVES.

There are two loves, the poet sings,
  Both born of Beauty at a birth:
The one, akin to heaven, hath wings,
  The other, earthly, walks on earth.
With *this* through bowers below we play,
  With *that* through clouds above we soar;
With both, perchance, may lose our way:—
    Then, tell me which,
  Tell me which shall we adore?

The one, when tempted down from air,
  At Pleasure's fount to lave his lip,
Nor lingers long, nor oft will dare
  His wing within the wave to dip.
While, plunging deep and long beneath,
  The other bathes him o'er and o'er
In that sweet current, even to death:—
    Then, tell me which,
  Tell me which shall we adore?

The boy of heaven, even while he lies
  In Beauty's lap, recalls his home;
And when most happy, inly sighs
  For something happier still to come.
While he of earth, too fully blest
  With this bright world to dream of more,
Sees all his heaven on Beauty's breast:—
    Then, tell me which,
  Tell me which shall we adore?

The maid who heard the poet sing
  These twin-desires of earth and sky,
And saw, while one inspired his string,
  The other glistened in his eye—
To name the earthlier boy ashamed,
  To choose the other fondly loath,
At length, all blushing, she exclaimed—
    "Ask not which,
  Oh, ask not which—we'll worship both.

Th' extremes of each thus taught to shun,
  With hearts and souls between them given,
When weary of this earth with one,
  We'll with the other wing to heaven."
Thus pledged the maid her vow of bliss;
  And while *one* Love wrote down the oath,
The other sealed it with a kiss;
    And Heaven looked on,
  Heaven looked on, and hallowed both.

THE LEGEND OF PUCK THE FAIRY.

Wouldst know what tricks, by the pale moonlight,
Are played by me, the merry little Sprite,
Who wing through air from the camp to the court,
From king to clown, and of all make sport;
    Singing, I am the Sprite
    Of the merry midnight,
Who laugh at weak mortals, and love the moonlight.

To a miser's bed, where he snoring slept,
And dreamt of his cash, I slyly crept;
Chink, chink o'er his pillow like money I rang,
And he waked to catch—but away I sprang,
    Singing, I am the Sprite, &c.

I saw through the leaves, in a damsel's bower:
She was waiting her love at that starlight hour:
"Hist—hist!" quoth I, with an amorous sigh,
And she flew to the door, but away flew I,
    Singing, I am the Sprite, &c.

While a bard sat inditing an ode to his love,
Like a pair of blue meteors I stared from above,
And he swooned—for he thought 'twas the ghost, poor man!
Of his lady's eyes, while away I ran,
    Singing, I am the Sprite, &c.

WHEN THOU ART NIGH.

When thou art nigh, it seems
  A new creation round;
The sun hath fairer beams,
  The lute a softer sound.
Though thee alone I see,
  And hear alone thy sigh,
'Tis light, 'tis song to me,
  'Tis all—when thou art nigh.

When thou art nigh, no thought
  Of grief comes o'er my heart;
I only think—could aught
  But joy be where thou art?
Life seems a waste of breath,
  When far from thee I sigh;
And death—ay, even death
  Were sweet, if thou wert nigh.

SONG OF A HYPERBOREAN.

I come from a land in the sun-bright deep,
Where golden gardens grow;
Where the winds of the north, becalmed in sleep,
Their conch-shells never blow.*
Haste to that holy Isle with me,
Haste—haste!

So near the track of the stars are we,†
That oft, on night's pale beams,
The distant sounds of their harmony
Come to our ears, like dreams.
Then, haste to that holy Isle with me, &c., &c.

The Moon, too, brings her world so nigh,‡
That when the night-seer looks
To that shadowless orb, in a vernal sky,
He can number its hills and brooks.
Then, haste, &c., &c.

To the Sun-god all our hearts and lyres‖
By day, by night, belong;
And the breath we draw from his living fires,
We give him back in song.
Then, haste, &c., &c.

From us descends the maid who brings
To Delos gifts divine;
And our wild bees lend their rainbow wings
To glitter on Delphi's shrine.§
Then, haste to that holy Isle with me,
Haste—haste!

THOU BIDST ME SING.

Thou bidst me sing the lay I sung to thee
In other days, ere joy had left this brow;
But think though still unchanged the notes may be,
How diff'rent feels the heart that breathes them now!
The rose thou wear'st to-night is still the same
We saw this morning on its stem so gay;
But, ah! that dew of dawn, that breath which came
Like life o'er all its leaves, hath passed away.

Since first that music touched thy heart and mine,
How many a joy and pain o'er both have past—
The joy, a light too precious long to shine,
The pain, a cloud whose shadows always last.
And though that lay would like the voice of home
Breathe o'er our ear, 'twould waken now a sigh—
Ah! not, as then, for fancied woes to come,
But, sadder far, for real bliss gone by.

CUPID ARMED.

Place the helm on thy brow,
In thy hand take the spear;
Thou art armed, Cupid, now,
And thy battle-hour is near.
March on! march on! thy shaft and bow
Were weak against such charms;
March on! march on! so proud a foe
Scorns all but martial arms.

See the darts in her eyes,
Tipt with scorn, how they shine!
Ev'ry shaft, as it flies,
Mocking proudly at thine.
March on! march on! thy feathered darts
Soft bosoms soon might move;
But ruder arms to ruder hearts
Must teach what 'tis to love.
Place the helm on thy brow;
In thy hand take the spear—
Thou art armed, Cupid, now,
And thy battle-hour is near.

* In the Tower of the Winds, at Athens, there is a conch-shell placed in the hands of Boreas.—See "Stuart's Antiquities."
"The north wind," says Herodotus, in speaking of the Hyperboreans, "never blows with them."
† "Sub ipso siderum cardine jacent."—Pompon. Mela.
‡ "They can show the moon very near."—Diodorus Siculus.
‖ Hecatæus tells us that this Hyperborean island was dedicated to Apollo; and most of the inhabitants were either priests or songsters.
§ Pausan.

ROUND THE WORLD GOES.

Round the world goes, by day and night,
While with it also round go we;
And in the flight of one day's light
An image of all life's course we see.
Round, round, while thus we go round,
The best thing a man can do,
Is to make it, at least, a *merry*-go-round,
By—sending the wine round too.

Our first gay stage of life is when
Youth, in its dawn, salutes the eye—
Season of bliss! Oh, who wouldn't then
Wish to cry, "Stop!" to earth and sky?
But, round, round, both boy and girl
Are whisked through that sky of blue;
And much would their hearts enjoy the whirl,
If—their heads didn't whirl round too.

Next, we enjoy our glorious noon,
Thinking all life a life of light;
But shadows come on, 'tis evening soon,
And, ere we can say, "How short!"—'tis night.
Round, round, still all goes round,
Even while I'm thus singing to you;
And the best way to make it a *merry*-go-round,
Is to—chorus my song round too.

OH, DO NOT LOOK SO BRIGHT AND BLEST.

Oh, do not look so bright and blest,
For still there comes a fear,
When brow like thine looks happiest,
That grief is then most near.
There lurks a dread in all delight,
A shadow near each ray,
That warns us then to fear their flight,
When most we wish their stay.
Then look not thou so bright and blest,
For ah! there comes a fear,
When brow like thine looks happiest,
That grief is then most near.

Why is it thus that fairest things
The soonest fleet and die?—
That when most light is on their wings,
They're then but spread to fly!
And, sadder still, the pain will stay—
The bliss no more appears;
As rainbows take their light away,
And leave us but the tears!
Then look not thou so bright and blest,
For ah! there comes a fear,
When brow like thine looks happiest,
That grief is then most near.

THE LANGUAGE OF FLOWERS.

Fly swift, my light gazelle,
To her who now lies waking,
To hear thy silver bell
The midnight silence breaking.
And, when thou comest, with gladsome feet,
Beneath her lattice springing,
Ah, well she'll know how sweet
The words of love thou'rt bringing.

Yet, no—not words, for they
But half can tell love's feeling;
Sweet flowers alone can say
What passion fears revealing,
A once bright rose's withered leaf,
A tow'ring lily broken—
Oh these may paint a grief
No words could e'er have spoken.

Not such, my gay gazelle,
The wreath thou speedest over
Yon moonlight dale, to tell
My lady how I love her.
And, what to her will sweeter be
Than gems the richest, rarest,
From Truth's immortal tree*
One fadeless leaf thou bearest.

* The tree, called in the East, Amrita or the Immortal

THE MUSICAL BOX.

"Look here," said Rose, with laughing eyes,
"Within this box, by magic hid,
A tuneful Sprite imprisoned lies,
Who sings to me whene'er he's bid.
Though roving once his voice and wing,
He'll now lie still the whole day long;
Till thus I touch the magic spring—
Then hark, how sweet and blithe his song!"
(*A symphony.*)

"Ah, Rose," I cried, "the poet's lay
Must ne'er e'en Beauty's slave become;
Through earth and air his song may stray,
If all the while his heart's at home.
And though in Freedom's air he dwell,
Nor bond nor chain his spirit knows,
Touch but the spring thou know'st so well,
And—hark, how sweet the love-song flows!"
(*A symphony.*)

Thus pleaded I for Freedom's right;
But when young Beauty takes the field,
And wise men seek defence in flight,
The doom of poets is to yield.
No more my heart the enchantress braves,
I'm now in Beauty's prison hid;
The Sprite and I are fellow-slaves,
And I, too, sing whene'er I'm bid.

WHEN TO SAD MUSIC SILENT YOU LISTEN.

When to sad music silent you listen,
And tears on those eyelids tremble like dew,
Oh, then there dwells in those eyes as they glisten
A sweet holy charm that mirth never knew.
But when some lively strain resounding
Lights up the sunshine of joy on that brow,
Then the young reindeer o'er the hills bounding
Was ne'er in its mirth so graceful as thou.

When on the skies at midnight thou gazest,
A lustre so pure thy features then wear,
That, when to some star that bright eye thou raisest,
We feel 'tis thy home thou'rt looking for there.
But, when the word for the gay dance is given,
So buoyant thy spirit, so heartfelt thy mirth,
Oh then we exclaim, "Ne'er leave earth for heaven,
But linger still here, to make heaven of earth."

THE DAWN IS BREAKING O'ER US.

The dawn is breaking o'er us,
See, heaven hath caught its hue!
We've day's long light before us,
What sport shall we pursue?
The hunt o'er hill and lee?
The sail o'er summer sea?
Oh let not hour so sweet
Unwinged by pleasure fleet.
The dawn is breaking o'er us,
See, heaven hath caught its hue;
We've day's long light before us,
What sport shall we pursue?

But see, while we're deciding,
What morning sport to play,
The dial's hand is gliding,
And morn hath passed away!
Ah, who'd have thought that noon
Would o'er us steal so soon—
That morn's sweet hour of prime
Would last so short a time?
But come, we've day before us,
Still heaven looks bright and blue
Quick, quick, ere eve come o'er us,
What sport shall we pursue?

Alas! why thus delaying?
We're now at evening's hour;
Its farewell beam is playing
O'er hill and wave and bower.
That light we thought would last,
Behold, e'en now, 'tis past;
And all our morning dreams
Have vanished with its beams!
But come! 'twere vain to borrow
Sad lessons from this lay,
For man will be to-morrow—
Just what he's been to-day.

YOUNG LOVE.

Young Love lived once in an humble shed,
Where roses breathing,
And woodbines wreathing
Around the lattice their tendrils spread,
As wild and sweet as the life he led.
His garden flourished,
For young Hope nourished
The infant buds with beams and showers;
But lips, though blooming, must still be fed,
And not even Love can live on flowers.

Alas! that Poverty's evil eye
Should e'er come hither,
Such sweets to wither!
The flowers laid down their heads to die,
And Hope fell sick as the witch drew nigh.
She came one morning,
Ere Love had warning,
And raised the latch, where the young god lay;
"Oh ho!" said Love—"is it you? good-by;"
So he he ope'd the window, and flew away!

TO SIGH, YET FEEL NO PAIN.

To sigh, yet feel no pain,
To weep, yet scarce know why;
To sport an hour with Beauty's chain,
Then throw it idly by.
To kneel at many a shrine,
Yet lay the heart on none;
To think all other charms divine,
But those we just have won.
This is love, faithless love,
Such as kindleth hearts that rove.

To keep one sacred flame,
Through life unchilled, unmoved,
To love, in wintry age, the same
As first in youth we loved;
To feel that we adore,
Even to such fond excess,
That, though the heart would break with *more*,
It could not live with *less*.
This is love, faithful love,
Such as saints might feel above.

SPIRIT OF JOY.

Spirit of Joy, thy altar lies
In youthful hearts that hope like mine;
And 'tis the light of laughing eyes,
That leads us to thy fairy shrine.
There if we find the sigh, the tear,
They are not those to Sorrow known;
But breath so soft, and drops so clear,
That Bliss may claim them for her own.
Then give me, give me, while I weep,
The sanguine hope that brightens wo,
And teaches even our tears to keep
The tinge of pleasure as they flow.

The child, who sees the dew of night
Upon the spangled hedge at morn,
Attempts to catch the drops of light,
But wounds his finger with the thorn.
Thus oft the brightest joys we seek,
Are lost, when touched, and turned to pain;
The flush they kindled leaves the cheek,
The tears they wakenlong remain.
But give me, give me, &c., &c.

WHEN LEILA TOUCHED THE LUTE.

When Leila touched the lute,
Not *then* alone 'twas felt,
But, when the sounds were mute,
In memory still they dwelt.
Sweet lute! in nightly slumbers
Still we heard thy morning numbers.

Ah! how could she, who stole
Such breath from simple wire,
Be led, in pride of soul,
To string with gold her lyre?
Sweet lute! thy chords she breaketh;
Golden now the strings she waketh?

But where are all the tales
Her lute so sweetly told?
In lofty themes she fails,
And soft ones suit not gold.
Rich lute! we see thee glisten,
But, alas! no more we listen!

BOAT GLEE.

The song that lightens our languid way
When brows are glowing,
And faint with rowing,
Is like the spell of Hope's airy lay,
To whose sound through life we stray.
The beams that flash on the oar awhile,
As we row along through waves so clear,
Illume its spray, like the fleeting smile
That shines o'er Sorrow's tear.

Nothing is lost on him who sees
With an eye that feeling gave;
For him there's a story in every breeze,
And a picture in every wave.
Then sing to lighten the languid way;—
When brows are glowing,
And faint with rowing:
'Tis like the spell of Hope's airy lay,
To whose sound through life we stray.

OH THINK, WHEN A HERO IS SIGHING.

Oh think, when a hero is sighing,
What danger in such an adorer!
What woman could dream of denying
The hand that lays laurels before her?
No heart is so guarded around,
But the smile of a victor would take it;
No bosom can slumber so sound,
But the trumpet of Glory will wake it.

Love sometimes is given to sleeping,
And wo to the heart that allows him;
For soon neither smiling nor weeping
Will e'er from such slumber arouse him.
B t though he were sleeping so fast,
That the life almost seemed to forsake him,
Even then, one soul-thrilling blast
From the trumpet of Glory would wake him.

SONG.*

Though sacred the tie that our country entwineth,
And dear to the heart her remembrance remains,
Yet dark are the ties where no liberty shineth,
And sad the remembrance that slavery stains.
Oh Liberty, born in the cot of the peasant,
But dying of languor in luxury's dome,
Our vision, when absent—our glory, when present—
Where thou art, O Liberty! there is my home.

Farewell to the land where in childhood I wandered!
In vain is she mighty, in vain is she brave;
Unblessed is the blood that for tyrants is squandered,
And Fame has no wreaths for the brow of the slave.
But hail to thee, Albion! who meet'st the commotion
Of Europe, as calm as thy cliffs meet the foam;
With no bonds but the law, and no slave but the ocean,
Hail, Temple of Liberty! thou art my home.

* Sung in the character of a Frenchman.

CUPID'S LOTTERY.

A Lottery, a lottery,
In Cupid's Court there used to be;
Two roguish eyes
The highest prize
In Cupid's scheming Lottery;
And kisses, too,
As good as new,
Which weren't very hard to win,
For he, who won
The eyes of fun,
Was sure to have the kisses in.
A Lottery, a Lottery, &c.

This Lottery, this Lottery,
In Cupid's Court went merrily,
And Cupid played
A Jewish trade
In this his scheming Lottery;
For hearts, we're told,
In *shares* he sold
To many a fond believing drone,
And cut the hearts
So well in parts,
That each believed the whole his own.
Chorus.—A Lottery, a Lottery,
In Cupid's Court there used to be;
Two roguish eyes
The highest prize
In Cupid's scheming Lottery.

GAZEL.

Halte, Maami, the spring is nigh;
Already, in th' unopened flowers
That sleep around us, Fancy's eye
Can see the blush of future bowers;
And joy it brings to thee and me,
My own beloved Maami!

The streamlet frozen on its way,
To feed the marble Founts of Kings,
Now, loosened by the vernal ray,
Upon its path exulting springs—
As doth this bounding heart to thee,
My ever blissful Maami!

Such bright hours were not made to stay;
Enough if they a while remain,
Like Irem's bowers, that fade away,
From time to time, and come again.
And life shall all one Irem be
For us, my gentle Maami!

Oh haste, for this impatient heart
Is like the rose in Yemen's vale,
That rends its inmost leaves apart
With passion for the nightingale;
So languishes this soul for thee,
My bright and blushing Maami!

LOVE AND HYMEN.

Love had a fever—ne'er could close
His little eyes till day was breaking;
And wild and strange enough, Heaven knows,
The things he raved about while waking.

To let him pine so were a sin;—
One, to whom all the world's a debtor—
So Doctor Hymen was called in,
And Love that night slept rather better.

Next day the case gave further hope yet,
Though still some ugly fever latent;—
"Dose, as before"—a gentle opiate,
For which old Hymen has a patent.

After a month of daily call,
So fast the dose went on restoring,
That Love, who first ne'er slept at all,
Now took, the rogue! to downright snoring.

SONGS FROM THE GREEK ANTHOLOGY.

HERE AT THY TOMB.*

BY MELEAGER.

Here, at thy tomb, these tears I shed,
Tears, which though vainly now they roll,
Are all love hath to give the dead,
And wept o'er thee with all love's soul;—

Wept in remembrance of that light,
Which naught on earth, without thee, gives,
Hope of my heart! now quenched in night,
But dearer, dead, than aught that lives.

Where is she? where the blooming bough
That once my life's sole lustre made?
Torn off by death, 'tis withering now,
And all its flowers in dust are laid.

Oh earth! that to thy matron breast
Hast taken all those angel charms,
Gently, I pray thee, let her rest—
Gently, as in a mother's arms.

MY MOPSA IS LITTLE.†

BY PHILODEMUS.

My Mopsa is little, my Mopsa is brown,
But her cheek is as smooth as the peach's soft down,
And, for blushing, no rose can come near her;
In short she has woven such nets round my heart,
That I ne'er from my dear little Mopsa can part,—
Unless I can find one that's dearer.

Her voice hath a music that dwells on the ear,
And her eye from its orb gives a daylight so clear,
That I'm dazzled whenever I meet her;
Her ringlets, so curly, are Cupid's own net,
And her lips, oh their sweetness I ne'er shall forget—
Till I light upon lips that are sweeter.

But 'tis not hêr beauty that charms me alone
'Tis her mind, 'tis that language whose eloquent tone
From the depths of the grave could revive one;
In short, here I swear, that if death were her doom,
I would instantly join my dead love in the tomb—
Unless I could meet with a live one.

TO WEAVE A GARLAND FOR THE ROSE.‡

BY PAUL, THE SILENTIARY.

To weave a garland for the rose,
And think thus crowned 'twould lovelier be,
Were far less vain than to suppose
That silks and gems add grace to thee.
Where is the pearl whose orient lustre
Would not, beside thee, look less bright?
What gold could match the glossy cluster
Of those young ringlets full of light?

Bring from the land, where fresh it gleams,
The bright blue gem of India's mine,
And see how soon, though bright its beams,
'Twill pale before one glance of thine;
Those lips, too, when their sounds have blest us
With some divine, mellifluous air,
Who would not say that Beauty's cestus
Had let loose all its witch'ries there?‖

*Δακρυα σοι και νερθε δια χθονος, Ηλιοδωρα.
Ap. Brunck.

† Μικκη και μελανευσα Φιλιννιον.
Ap. Brunck. x.

‡ Ουτε ῥοδων στεφανων επιδευεται, ουτε ου πεπλων.
Ap. Brunck. xvii.

‖ ——και ἡ μελιφυρτος εκεινη
Ηθεος ἁρμονιη, κεστος εφυ Παφιης.

Here, to this conquering host of charms
I now give up my spell-bound heart,
Nor blush to yield e'en Reason's arms,
When thou her bright-eyed conqueror art.
Thus to the wind all fears are given;
Henceforth those eyes alone I see,
Where Hope, as in her own blue heaven,
Sits beck'ning me to bliss and thee!

SALE OF CUPID.*

BY MELEAGER.

Who'll buy a little boy? Look, yonder is he,
Fast asleep, sly rogue, on his mother's knee;
So bold a young imp 'tisn't safe to keep,
So I'll part with him now, while he's sound asleep.
See his arch little nose, how sharp 'tis curled,
His wings, too, even in sleep unfurled;
And those fingers, which still ever ready are found
For mirth or for mischief, to tickle, or wound.

He'll try with his tears your heart to beguile,
But never you mind—he's laughing all the while,
For little he cares, so he has his own whim,
And weeping or laughing are all one to him.
His eye is as keen as the lightning's flash,
His tongue like the red bolt quick and rash;
And so savage is he, that his own dear mother,
Is scarce more safe in his hands than another.

In short, to sum up this darling's praise,
He's a downright pest in all sorts of ways;
And if any one wants such an imp to employ,
He shall have a dead bargain of this little boy.
But see, the boy wakes—his bright tears flow—
His eyes seem to ask could I sell him? oh no,
Sweet child no, no—though so naughty you be,
You shall live evermore with my Lesbia and me.

TWINEST THOU WITH LOFTY WREATH THY BROW?†

BY PAUL, THE SILENTIARY.

Twin'st thou with lofty wreath thy brow?
Such glory then thy beauty sheds,
I almost think, while awed I bow,
'Tis Rhea's self before me treads.
Be what thou wilt—this heart
Adores whate'er thou art!

Dost thou thy loosened ringlets leave,
Like sunny waves to wander free?
Then, such a chain of charms they weave,
As draws my inmost soul from me.
Do what thou wilt—I must
Be charmed by all thou dost!

E'en when, enwrapped in silv'ry veils,‡
Those sunny locks elude the sight—
Oh, not e'en then their glory fails
To haunt me with its unseen light.
Change as thy beauty may,
It charms in every way.

For, thee the Graces still attend,
Presiding o'er each new attire,
And lending every dart they send
Some new, peculiar touch of fire.
Be what thou wilt—this heart
Adores whate'er thou art!

* Πωλεισθω, και ματρος ετ' εν κολποισι καθευδων.
Ap. Brunck. *Analect.* xcv.

† Κεκρυφαλοι σφιγγουσι τεην τριχα;
Ap. Brunck. xxxiv.

‡ Αργενναις οθονησι κατηορα βοστρυχα κευθεις

WHEN THE SAD WORD.*

BY PAUL, THE SILENTIARY.

When the sad word, "Adieu," from my lip is nigh falling,
  And with it Hope passes away,
Ere the tongue hath half breathed it, my fond heart recalling
  That fatal farewell, bids me stay.
For oh! 'tis a penance so weary
  One hour from thy presence to be,
That death to this soul were less dreary,
  Less dark than long absence from thee.

Thy beauty, like Day, o'er the dull world breaking,
  Brings life to the heart it shines o'er,
And, in mine, a new feeling of happiness waking
  Made light what was darkness before.
But mute is the Day's sunny glory,
  While thine hath a voice,† on whose breath,
More sweet than than the Syren's sweet story,‡
  My hopes hang, through life and through death!

STILL, LIKE DEW IN SILENCE FALLING.||

BY MELEAGER.

Still, like dew in silence falling,
  Drops for thee the nightly tear;
Still that voice the past recalling,
  Dwells, like echo, on my ear,
    Still, still!

Day and night the spell hangs o'er me,
  Here for ever fixed thou art;
As thy form first shone before me,
  So 'tis graven on this heart,
    Deep, deep!

Love, oh Love, whose bitter sweetness,
  Dooms me to this lasting pain,
Thou who cam'st with so much fleetness,
  Why so slow to go again?§
    Why? why?

UP, SAILOR BOY, 'TIS DAY.

Up, sailor boy, 'tis day!
  The west wind blowing,
  The spring tide flowing,
Summon thee hence away.
Didst thou not hear yon soaring swallow sing?
Chirp, chirp,—in every note he seemed to say
'Tis Spring, 'tis Spring.
Up, boy, away,—
Who'd stay on land to-day?
  The very flowers
  Would from their bowers
Delight to wing away!

Leave languid youths to pine
  On silken pillows,
  But be the billows
Of the great deep thine.
Hark, to the sail the breese sings, "Let us fly;"
While soft the sail, replying to the breeze,
Says, with a yielding sigh,
"Yes, where you please."
Up, boy! the wind, the ray,
  The blue sky o'er thee,
  The deep before thee,
Al. [illegible] aloud, "Away!"

* Σωζεο σοι μελλων ενεπειν.
Ap. Brunck. xxxix.

† Ημαρι γαρ σεο φεγγος δμοιιν. αλλα το μεν που
Αφθογγον.

‡ Συ δ' εμοι και το λαλημα φερεις
Κεινο, το Σειρηνων γλυκυερωτερον.

|| Αιει μοι δυνει μεν εν ουασιν ηχος Ερωτος.
Ap. Brunck. liii.

§ Ω πτανοι, μη καί ποτ' εφιπτασθαι μεν, Ερωτες
Οιδατ', αποπτηναι δ' ουδ' δσον ισχυετε.

IN MYRTLE WREATHS.

BY ALCÆUS.

In myrtle wreaths my votive sword I'll cover,
  Like them of old whose one immortal blow
Struck off the galling fetters that hung over
  Their own bright land, and laid her tyrant low.
Yes, loved Harmodius, thou'rt undying;
  Still midst the brave and free,
In isles, o'er ocean lying,
  Thy home shall ever be.

In myrtle leaves my sword shall hide its lightning,
  Like his, the youth, whose ever-glorious blade
Leaped forth like flame, the midnight banquet bright'ning,
  And in the dust a despot victim laid.
Blest youths, how bright in Freedom's story
  Your wedded names shall be;
A tyrant's death your glory,
  Your meed, a nation free!

WHY DOES SHE SO LONG DELAY?*

BY PAUL, THE SILENTIARY.

Why does she so long delay?
Night is waning fast away;
Thrice have I my lamp renewed,
Watching here in solitude.
Where can she so long delay?
  Where, so long delay?

Vainly now have two lamps shone;
See the third is nearly gone;†
Oh that Love would, like the ray
Of that weary lamp, decay!
But no, alas, it burns still on,
  Still, still, burns on.

Gods, how oft the traitress dear
Swore, by Venus, she'd be here!
But to one so false as she
What is man or deity?
Neither doth this proud one fear,—
  No, neither doth she fear.

* Δηθυνει Κλεοφαντις.
Ap. Brunck. xxviii.

† ὁ δε τριτος αρχεται ηδε
Λυχνος ὑποκλαζειν.

UNPUBLISHED SONGS, ETC.

NOT FROM THEE.

Not from thee the wound should come,
  No, not from thee.
I care not what, or whence, my doom,
  So not from thee!
Cold triumph! first to make
  This heart thy own;
And then the mirror break
Where fixed thou shinest alone.

Not from thee the wound should come,
  Oh, not from thee.
I care not what, or whence, my doom,
  So not from thee.

Yet no—my lips that wish recall;
  From thee, from thee—
If ruin o'er this head must fall,
  'Twill welcome be.

Here to the blade I bare
This faithful heart;
Wound deep—thou'lt find that there,
In every pulse thou art.
Yes from thee I'll bear it all;
If ruin be
The doom that o'er this heart must fall,
'Twere sweet from thee.

GUESS, GUESS.

I LOVE a maid, a mystic maid,
Whose form no eyes but mine can see;
She comes in light, she comes in shade,
And beautiful in both is she.
Her shape in dreams I oft behold,
And oft she whispers in my ear
Such words as when to others told,
Awake the sigh, or wring the tear;—
Then guess, guess, who she,
The lady of my love, may be.

I find the lustre of her brow,
Come o'er me in my darkest ways;
And feel as if her voice, even now,
Were echoing far off my lays.
There is no scene of joy or wo
But she doth gild with influence bright;
And shed o'er all so rich a glow,
As makes even tears seem full of light;
Then guess, guess, who she,
The lady of my love, may be.

ASK NOT IF STILL I LOVE.

ASK not if still I love,
Too plain these eyes have told thee;
Too well their tears must prove
How near and dear I hold thee.
If, where the brightest shine,
To see no form but thine,
To feel that earth can show
No bliss above thee,—
If this be love, then know
That thus, that thus, I love thee.

'Tis not in pleasure's idle hour
That thou canst know affection's power.
No, try its strength in grief or pain;
Attempt, as now, its bonds to sever,
Thou'lt find true love's a chain
That binds for ever!

DEAR? YES.

DEAR? yes, though mine no more,
Even this but makes thee dearer;
And love, since hope is o'er,
But draws thee nearer.

Change as thou wilt to me,
The same thy charm must be;
New loves may come to weave
Their witchery o'er thee,
Yet still, though false, believe
That I adore thee, yes, still adore thee.
Thinkst thou that aught but death could end
A tie not falsehood's self can rend?
No, when alone, far off I die,
No more to see, no more caress thee,
Even then, my life's last sigh
Shall be to bless thee, yes, still to bless thee.

UNBIND THEE, LOVE.

UNBIND thee, love, unbind thee, love,
From those dark ties unbind thee;
Though fairest hand the chain hath wove
Too long its links have twined thee.
Away from earth!—thy wings were made
In yon mid sky to hover,
With earth beneath their dove-like shade,
And heaven all radiant over.

Awake thee, boy, awake thee, boy,
Too long thy soul is sleeping;
And thou mayest from this minute's joy
Wake to eternal weeping.
Oh, think, this world is not for thee;
Though hard its links to sever;
Though sweet and bright and dear they be,
Break, or thou'rt lost for ever.

THE RUSSIAN LOVER.

FLEETLY o'er the moonlight snows
Speed we to my lady's bower;
Swift our sledge as lightning goes,
Nor shall stop till morning's hour.
Bright, my steed, the northern star
Lights us from yon jewelled skies;
But, to greet us, brighter far,
Morn shall bring my lady's eyes.

Lovers, lulled in sunny bowers,
Sleeping out their dream of time,
Know not half the bliss that's ours,
In this snowy, icy clime.
Like yon star that livelier gleams
From the frosty heavens around,
Love himself the keener beams
When with snows of coyness crowned.

Fleet then on, my merry steed,
Bound, my sledge, o'er hill and dale;—
What can match a lover's speed?
See, 'tis daylight, breaking pale!
Brightly hath the northern star
Lit us from yon radiant skies;
But, behold, how brighter far
Yonder shine my lady's eyes!

BRIGHT MOON.

BRIGHT moon, that high in heaven art shining,
All smiles, as if within thy bower to-night
Thy own Endymion lay reclining,
And thou wouldst wake him with a kiss of light.—
By all the bliss thy beam discovers,
By all those visions far too bright for day,
Which dreaming bards and waking lovers
Behold, this night, beneath thy ling'ring ray—

I pray thee, queen of that bright heaven,
Quench not to-night thy love-lamp in the sea,
Till Anthe, in this bower, hath given
Beneath thy beam, her long-vowed kiss to me.
Guide hither, guide her steps benighted,
Ere thou, sweet moon, thy bashful crescent hide;
Let Love but in this bower be lighted,
Then shroud in darkness all the world beside.

LONG YEARS HAVE PASSED.

LONG years have passed, old friend, since we
First met in life's young day;
And friends long loved by thee and me,
Since then have dropped away;—
But enough remain to cheer us on,
And sweeten, when thus we're met,
The glass we fill to the many gone,
And the few who're left us yet.

Our locks, old friend, now thinly grow,
And some hang white and chill;
While some, like flowers 'mid Autumn's snow,
Retain youth's color still.
And so, in our hearts, though one by one,
Youth's sunny hopes have set,
Thank Heaven, not all their light is gone—
We've some to cheer us yet.

Then here's to thee, old friend, and long
May thou and I thus meet,
To brighten still with wine and song
This short life, ere it fleet.
And still as death comes stealing on,
Let's never, old friend, forget,
Even while we sigh o'er blessings gone,
How many are left us yet

WHEN LOVE, WHO RULED.

When Love, who ruled as Admiral o'er
His rosy mother's isles of light,
Was cruising off the Paphian shore,
A sail at sunset hove in sight.
"A chase, a chase! my Cupids all,"
Said Love, the little Admiral.

Aloft the winged sailors sprung,
And, swarming up the mast like bees.
The snow-white sails expanding flung,
Like broad magnolias to the breeze.
"Yo ho, yo ho, my Cupids all!"
Said Love, the little Admiral.

The chase was o'er—the bark was caught,
The winged crew her freight explored;
And found 'twas just as Love had thought,
For all was contraband aboard.
"A prize! a prize! my Cupids all!"
Said Love, the little Admiral.

Safe stowed in many a package there,
And labelled slyly o'er, as "Glass,"
Were lots of all th' illegal ware,
Love's Custom-House forbids to pass.
"O'erhaul, o'erhaul, my Cupids all,"
Said Love, the little Admiral.

False curls they found, of every hue,
With rosy blushes, ready made;
And teeth of ivory, good as new,
For veterans in the smiling trade.
"Ho, ho, ho, ho, my Cupids all,"
Said Love, the little Admiral.

Mock sighs, too—kept in bags for use,
Like breezes bought of Lapland seers—
Lay ready here to be let loose,
When wanted, in young spinsters' ears.
"Ha, ha, ha, ha, my Cupids all,"
Said Love, the little Admiral.

False papers next on board were found,
Sham invoices of flames and darts,
Professedly for Paphos bound,
But meant for Hymen's golden marts.
"For shame, for shame, my Cupids all!"
Said Love, the little Admiral.

Nay, still to every fraud awake,
Those pirates all Love's signals knew,
And hoisted oft his flag, to make
Rich wards and heiresses *bring-to.**
"A foe, a foe, my Cupids all!"
Cried Love, the little Admiral.

"This must not be," the boy exclaims,
"In vain I rule the Paphian seas,
If Love's and Beauty's sovereign names
Are lent to cover frauds like these.
Prepare, prepare, my Cupids all!"
Said Love, the little Admiral.

Each Cupid stood with lighted match—
A broadside struck the smuggling foe,
And swept the whole unhallowed batch
Of falsehood to the depths below.
"Huzza! huzza! my Cupids all!"
Said Love, the little Admiral.

STILL THOU FLIEST.

Still thou fliest, and still I woo thee,
Lovely phantom—all in vain;
Restless ever, my thoughts pursue thee,
Fleeting ever, thou mockst their pain.
Such doom, of old, that youth betided,
Who wooed, he thought, some angel's charms,
But found a cloud that from him glided—
As thou dost from these outstretched arms.

Scarce I've said, "How fair thou shinest,"
Ere thy light hath vanished by;
And 'tis when thou lookst divinest
Thou art still more sure to fly.
Even as the lightning, that, dividing
The clouds of night, saith, "Look on me,"
Then flits again, its splendor hiding—
Even such the glimpse I catch of thee.

* To Bring-to, to check the course of a ship."—Falconer.

THEN FIRST FROM LOVE.

Then first from Love, in Nature's bowers,
Did Painting learn her fairy skill,
And cull the hues of loveliest flowers,
To picture woman lovelier still.
For vain was every radiant hue,
Till Passion lent a soul to art,
And taught the painter, ere he drew,
To fix the model in his heart.

Thus smooth his toil awhile went on,
Till, lo, one touch his art defies;
The brow, the lip, the blushes shone,
But who could dare to paint those eyes?
'Twas all in vain the painter strove;
So turning to that boy divine,
"Here take," he said, "the pencil, Love,
No hand should paint such eyes, but thine."

HUSH, SWEET LUTE.

Hush, sweet Lute, thy songs remind me
Of past joys, now turned to pain;
Of ties that long have ceased to bind me,
But whose burning marks remain.
In each tone, some echo falleth
On my ear of joys gone by;
Ev'ry note some dream recalleth
Of bright hopes but born to die.

Yet, sweet Lute, though pain it bring me,
Once more let thy numbers thrill;
Though death were in the strain they sing me,
I must woo its anguish still.
Since no time can e'er recover
Love's sweet light when once 'tis set—
Better to weep such pleasures over,
Than smile o'er any left us yet.

DREAMING FOR EVER.

Dreaming for ever, vainly dreaming,
Life to the last pursues its flight;
Day hath its visions fairly beaming,
But false as those of night.
The one illusion, the other real,
But both the same brief dreams at last;
And when we grasp the bliss ideal,
Soon as it shines, 'tis past.

Here, then, by this dim lake reposing,
Calmly I'll watch, while light and gloom
Flit o'er its face till night is closing—
Emblem of life's short doom!
But though, by turns, thus dark and shining,
'Tis still unlike man's changeful day,
Whose light returns not, once declining,
Whose cloud, once come, will stay.

THOUGH LIGHTLY SOUNDS THE SONG I SING

A SONG OF THE ALPS.

Though lightly sounds the song I sing to thee,
Though like the lark's its soaring music be,
Thou'lt find even here some mournful note that tells
How near such April joy to weeping dwells.
'Tis 'mong the gayest scenes that oft'nest steal
Those sadd'ning thoughts we fear, yet love to feel;
And music never half so sweet appears,
As when her mirth forgets itself in tears.

Then say not thou this Alpine song is gay—
It comes from hearts that, like their mountain-lay,
Mix joy with pain, and oft when pleasure's breath
Most warms the surface, feel most sad beneath.
The very beam in which the snow-wreath wears
Its gayest smile is that which wins its tears—
And passion's power can never lend the glow
Which wakens bliss, without some touch of wo

IRISH MELODIES,

BY

THOMAS MOORE.

GO WHERE GLORY WAITS THEE.

Go where glory waits thee,
But, while fame elates thee,
Oh! still remember me.
When the praise thou meetest
To thine ear is sweetest,
Oh! then remember me.
Other arms may press thee,
Dearer friends caress thee,
All the joys that bless thee,
Sweeter far may be;
But when friends are nearest,
And when joys are dearest,
Oh! then remember me!

When, at eve, thou rovest
By the star thou lovest,
Oh! then remember me.
Think, when home returning,
Bright we've seen it burning,
Oh! thus remember me.
Oft as summer closes,
When thine eye reposes
On its ling'ring roses,
Once so loved by thee,
Think of her who wove them,
Her who made thee love them,
Oh! then remember me.

When, around thee dying,
Autumn leaves are lying,
Oh! then remember me.
And at night, when gazing
On the gay hearth blazing,
Oh! still remember me.
Then should music, stealing
All the soul of feeling,
To thy heart appealing,
Draw one tear from thee;
Then let memory bring thee
Strains I used to sing thee—
Oh! then remember me.

OH! BREATHE NOT HIS NAME.

Oh! breathe not his name, let it sleep in the shade,
Where cold and unhonored his relics are laid:
Sad, silent, and dark, be the tears that we shed,
As the night-dew that falls on the grass o'er his head.

But the night-dew that falls, though in silence it weeps,
Shall brighten with verdure the grave where he sleeps;
And the tear that we shed, though in secret it rolls,
Shall long keep his memory green in our souls.

ERIN! THE TEAR AND THE SMILE IN THINE EYES.

Erin, the tear and the smile in thine eyes,
Blend like the rainbow that hangs in thy skies!
Shining through sorrow's stream,
Saddening through pleasure's beam,
Thy suns with doubtful gleam,
Weep while they rise.

Erin, thy silent tear never shall cease,
Erin, thy languid smile ne'er shall increase,
Till, like the rainbow's light,
Thy various teints unite,
And form in heaven's sight
One arch of peace!

REMEMBER THE GLORIES OF BRIEN THE BRAVE.*

WAR-SONG.

Remember the glories of Brien the brave,
Though the days of the hero are o'er;
Though lost to Mononia,† and cold in the grave,
He returns to Kinkora‡ no more.
That star of the field, which so often hath poured
Its beam on the battle, is set;
But enough of its glory remains on each sword,
To light us to victory yet.

Mononia! when Nature embellished the teint
Of thy fields, and thy mountains so fair,
Did she ever intend that a tyrant should print
The footsteps of slavery there?
No! Freedom, whose smile we shall never resign,
Go, tell, our invaders, the Danes,
That 'tis sweeter to bleed for an age at thy shrine,
Than to sleep but a moment in chains.

Forget not our wounded companions, who stood‖
In the day of distress by our side;
While the moss of the valley grew red with their blood,
They stirred not, but conquered and died.

* Brien Borombe, the great monarch of Ireland, who was killed at the battle of Clontarf, in the beginning of the eleventh century, after having defeated the Danes in twenty-five engagements.

† Munster.

‡ The palace of Brien.

‖ This alludes to an interesting circumstance related of the Dalgais, the favorite troops of Brien, when they were interrupted in their return from the battle of Clontarf, by Fitzpatrick, prince of Ossory. The wounded men entreated that they might be allowed to fight with the rest: "*Let stakes*," they said, "*be stuck in the ground, and suffer each of us, tied to and supported by one of these stakes, to be placed in his rank by the side of a sound man.*"—"Between seven and eight hundred wounded men (adds O'Halloran), pale, emaciated, and supported in this manner, appeared mixed with the foremost of the troops; never was such another sight exhibited."—*History of Ireland*, book xii., chap. 1.

That sun which now blesses our arms with his light,
Saw them fall upon Ossory's plain;—
Oh! let him not blush, when he leaves us to-night,
To find that they fell there in vain.

WHEN HE WHO ADORES THEE.

When he who adores thee has left but the name
Of his fault and his sorrows behind,
Oh! say wilt thou weep, when they darken the fame
Of a life that for thee was resigned?
Yes, weep, and however my foes may condemn,
Thy tears shall efface their decree;
For Heaven can witness, though guilty to them,
I have been but too faithful to thee.

With thee were the dreams of my earliest love
Every thought of my reason was thine;
In my last humble prayer to the Spirit above,
Thy name shall be mingled with mine.
Oh! blest are the lovers and friends who shall live
The days of thy glory to see;
But the next dearest blessing that Heaven can give,
Is the pride of thus dying for thee.

THE HARP THAT ONCE THROUGH TARA'S HALLS.

The harp that once through Tara's halls
The soul of music shed,
Now hangs as mute on Tara's walls,
As if that soul were fled.
So sleeps the pride of former days,
So glory's thrill is o'er,
And hearts, that once beat high for praise,
Now feel that pulse no more.

No more to chiefs and ladies bright
The harp of Tara swells;
The chord alone, that breaks at night,
Its tale of ruin tells.
Thus Freedom now so seldom wakes,
The only throb she gives,
Is when some heart indignant breaks,
To show that still she lives.

FLY NOT YET.

Fly not yet, 'tis just the hour
When pleasure, like the midnight flower
That scorns the eye of vulgar light,
Begins to bloom for sons of night,
And maids who love the moon.
'Twas but to bless these hours of shade
That beauty and the moon were made;
'Tis then their soft attractions glowing
Set the tides and goblets flowing.
Oh! stay Oh! stay—
Joy so seldom weaves a chain
Like this to-night, that oh! 'tis pain
To break its links so soon.

Fly not yet, the fount that played
In times of old through Ammon's shade,*
Though icy cold by day it ran,
Yet still, like souls of mirth, began
To burn when night was near.
And thus, should woman's heart and looks
At noon be cold as winter brooks,
Nor kindle till the night, returning,
Brings their genial hour for burning.
Oh! stay—Oh! stay—
When did morning ever break,
And find such beaming eyes awake
As those that sparkle here?

OH THINK NOT MY SPIRITS ARE ALWAYS AS LIGHT.

Oh! think not my spirits are always as light,
And as free from a pang as they seem to you now;
Nor expect that the heart beaming smile of to-night
Will return with to-morrow to brighten my brow.

* Solis Fons, near the Temple of Ammon.

No: life is a waste of wearisome hours,
Which seldom the rose of enjoyment adorns;
And the heart that is soonest awake to the flowers,
Is always the first to be touched by the thorns.
But send round the bowl, and be happy awhile—
May we never meet worse, in our pilgrimage here,
Than the tear that enjoyment may gild with a smile,
And the smile that compassion can turn to a tear.

The thread of our life would be dark, Heaven knows!
If it were not with friendship and love intertwined;
And I care not how soon I may sink to repose,
When these blessings shall cease to be dear to my mind.
But they who have loved the fondest, the purest,
Too often have wept o'er the dream they believed;
And the heart that has slumbered in friendship securest,
Is happy indeed if 'twas never deceived.
But send round the bowl; while a relic of truth
Is in man or in woman, this prayer shall be mine—
That the sunshine of love may illumine our youth,
And the moonlight of friendship console our decline.

THOUGH THE LAST GLIMPSE OF ERIN WITH SORROW I SEE.

Though the last glimpse of Erin with sorrow I see,
Yet wherever thou art shall seem Erin to me;
In exile thy bosom shall still be my home,
And thine eyes make my climate wherever we roam.

To the gloom of some desert, or cold rocky shore,
Where the eye of the stranger can haunt us no more,
I will fly with my Coulin, and think the rough wind
Less rude than the foes we leave frowning behind.

And I'll gaze on thy gold hair, as graceful it wreathes,
And hang o'er thy soft harp, as wildly it breathes;
Nor dread that the cold-hearted Saxon will tear
One chord from that harp, or one lock from that hair.*

AS A BEAM O'ER THE FACE OF THE WATERS MAY GLOW.

As a beam o'er the face of the waters may glow
While the tide runs in darkness and coldness below,
So the cheek may be tinged with a warm sunny smile,
Though the cold heart to ruin runs darkly the while.

One fatal remembrance, one sorrow that throws
Its bleak shade alike o'er our joys and our woes,
To which life nothing darker or brighter can bring,
For which joy has no balm, and affliction no sting—

Oh! this thought in the midst of enjoyment will stay,
Like a dead, leafless branch in the summer's bright ray
The beams of the warm sun play round it in vain,
It may smile in his light, but it blooms not again.

THE MEETING OF THE WATERS.†

There is not in the wide world a valley so sweet
As that vale in whose bosom the bright waters meet;‡
Oh! the last rays of feeling and life must depart,
Ere the bloom of that valley shall fade from my heart.

Yet it *was* not that Nature had shed o'er the scene
Her purest of crystal and brightest of green;
'Twas *not* her soft magic of streamlet or hill,
Oh! no—it was something more exquisite still.

* "In the twenty-eighth year of the reign of Henry VIII. an act was made respecting the habits, and dress in general, of the Irish, whereby all persons were restrained from being shorn or shaven above the ears, or from wearing Glibbes, or *Coulins* (long locks), on their heads, or hair on their upper lip, called Crommeal. On this occasion a song was written by one of our bards, in which an Irish virgin is made to give the preference to her dear *Coulin* (or the youth with the flowing locks) to all strangers (by which the English were meant), or those who wore their habits. Of this song, the air alone has reached us, and is universally admired."—*Walker's Historical Memoirs of Irish Bards*. p. 134. Mr. Walker informs us also, that, about the same period, there were some harsh measures taken against the Irish Minstrels.

† "The Meeting of the Waters" forms a part of that beautiful scenery which lies between Rathdrum and Arklow, in the county of Wicklow, and these lines were suggested by a visit to this romantic spot, in the summer of the year 1807.

‡ The rivers Avon and Avoca

'Twas that friends, the beloved of my bosom, were near,
Who made every dear scene of enchantment more dear,
And who felt how the best charms of nature improve,
When we see them reflected from looks that we love.

Sweet vale of Avoca! how calm could I rest
In thy bosom of shade, with the friends I love best,
Where the storms that we feel in this cold world should cease,
And our hearts, like thy waters, be mingled in peace.

RICH AND RARE WERE THE GEMS SHE WORE.*

Rich and rare were the gems she wore,
And a bright gold ring on her wand she bore;
But oh! her beauty was far beyond
Her sparkling gems, or snow-white wand.

"Lady! dost thou not fear to stray,
So lone and lovely through this bleak way?
Are Erin's sons so good or so cold,
As not to be tempted by woman or gold?"

"Sir Knight! I feel not the least alarm,
No son of Erin will offer me harm:
For though they love woman and golden store,
Sir Knight! they love honor and virtue more!"

On she went, and her maiden smile
In safety lighted her round the Green Isle;
And blest for ever is she who relied
Upon Erin's honor and Erin's pride.

HOW DEAR TO ME THE HOUR.

How dear to me the hour when daylight dies,
And sunbeams melt along the silent sea;
For then sweet dreams of other days arise,
And memory breathes her vesper sigh to thee.

And, as I watch the line of light, that plays
Along the smooth wave tow'rd the burning west,
I long to tread that golden path of rays,
And think 'twould lead to some bright isle of rest.

TAKE BACK THE VIRGIN PAGE.

WRITTEN ON RETURNING A BLANK BOOK.

Take back the virgin page,
White and unwritten still;
Some hand, more calm and sage,
The leaf must fill.
Thoughts come, as pure as light,
Pure as even *you* require:
But, oh! each word I write
Love turns to fire.

Yet let me keep the book:
Oft shall my heart renew,
When on its leaves I look,
Dear thoughts of you.
Like you, 'tis fair and bright;
Like you, too bright and fair
To let wild passion write
One wrong wish there.

Haply, when from those eyes
Far, far away I roam,
Should calmer thoughts arise
Tow'rd you and home;
Fancy may trace some line,
Worthy those eyes to meet,
Thoughts that not burn, but shine,
Pure, calm, and sweet.

* This ballad is founded upon the following anecdote: "The people were inspired with such a spirit of honor, virtue, and religion, by the great example of Brien, and by his excellent administration, that, as a proof of it, we are informed that a young lady of great beauty, adorned with jewels and a costly dress, undertook a journey alone, from one end of the kingdom to the other, with a wand only in her hand, at the top of which was a ring of exceeding great value; and such an impression had the laws and government of this monarch made on the minds of all the people, that no attempt was made upon her honor, nor was she robbed of her clothes or jewels."—*Warner's History of Ireland*, vol. i., book x.

And as, o'er ocean far,
Seamen their records keep,
Led by some hidden star
Through the cold deep;
So may the words I write
Tell through what storms I stray—
You still the unseen light,
Guiding my way.

THE LEGACY.

When in death I shall calmly recline,
O bear my heart to my mistress dear;
Tell her it lived upon smiles and wine
Of the brightest hue, while it lingered here.
Bid her not shed one tear of sorrow
To sully a heart so brilliant and light;
But balmy drops of the red grape borrow,
To bathe the relic from morn till night.

When the light of my song is o'er,
Then take my harp to your ancient hall;
Hang it up at that friendly door,
Where weary travellers love to call.*
Then, if some bard, who roams forsaken,
Revive its soft note in passing along,
Oh! let one thought of its master waken
Your warmest smile for the child of song

Keep this cup, which is now o'erflowing,
To grace your revel, when I'm at rest;
Never—oh! never its balm bestowing
On lips that beauty hath seldom blest.
But when some warm devoted lover
To her he adores shall bathe its brim,
Then, then my spirit around shall hover,
And hallow each drop that foams for him.

WE MAY ROAM THROUGH THIS WORLD.

We may roam through this world, like a child at a feast,
Who but sips of a sweet, and then flies to the rest;
And, when pleasure begins to grow dull in the east,
We may order our wings, and be off to the west;
But if hearts that feel, and eyes that smile,
Are the dearest gifts that Heaven supplies,
We never need leave our own green isle,
For sensitive hearts, and for sun-bright eyes.
Then remember, wherever your goblet is crowned,
Through this world, whether eastward or westward you roam,
When a cup to the smile of dear woman goes round,
Oh! remember the smile which adorns her at home

In England, the garden of Beauty is kept
By a dragon of prudery placed within call;
But so oft this unamiable dragon has slept,
That the garden's but carelessly watched after all.
Oh! they want the wild sweet-briery fence,
Which round the flowers of Erin dwells;
Which warns the touch, while winning the sense,
Nor charms us least when it most repels.
Then remember, wherever your goblet is crowned,
Through this world, whether eastward or westward you roam,
When a cup to the smile of dear woman goes round,
Oh! remember the smile that adorns her at home.

In France, when the heart of a woman sets sail,
On the ocean of wedlock its fortune to try,
Love seldom goes far in a vessel so frail,
But just pilots her off, and then bids her good-by
While the daughters of Erin keep the boy,
Ever smiling beside his faithful oar,
Through billows of wo, and beams of joy.
The same as he looked when he left the shore.
Then remember, wherever your goblet is crowned,
Through this world, whether eastward or westward you roam,
When a cup to the smile of dear woman goes round,
Oh! remember the smile that adorns her at home.

* "In every house was one or two harps, free to all travellers, who were the more caressed, the more they excelled in music."—*O'Halloran.*

HOW OFT HAS THE BENSHEE CRIED.

How oft has the Benshee cried,
How oft has death untied
Bright links that Glory wove,
Sweet bonds entwined by Love!
Peace to each manly soul that sleepeth;
Rest to each faithful eye that weepeth;
Long may the fair and brave
Sigh o'er the hero's grave.

We're fallen upon gloomy days!*
Star after star decays,
Every bright name, that shed
Light o'er the land, is fled.
Dark falls the tear of him who mourneth
Lost joy, or hope that ne'er returneth;
But brightly flows the tear,
Wept o'er a hero's bier.

Quenched are our beacon lights—
Thou, of the Hundred Fights!†
Thou, on whose burning tongue
Truth, peace, and freedom hung!‡
Both mute—but long as valor shineth,
Or mercy's soul at war repineth,
So long shall Erin's pride
Tell how they lived and died.

EVELEEN'S BOWER.

Oh! weep for the hour,
When to Eveleen's bower
The Lord of the Valley with false vows came;
The moon hid her light
From the heavens that night,
And wept behind her clouds o'er the maiden' shame.

The clouds passed soon
From the chaste cold moon,
And heaven smiled again with her vestal flame;
But none will see the day,
When the clouds shall pass away,
Which that dark hour left upon Eveleen's fame.

The white snow lay
On the narrow pathway,
When the Lord of the Valley crossed over the moor;
And many a deep print
On the white snow's teint
Showed the track of his footstep to Eveleen's door.

The next sun's ray
Soon melted away
Every trace on the path where the false Lord came;
But there's a light above,
Where alone can remove
That stain upon the snow of fair Eveleen's fame.

COME, SEND ROUND THE WINE.

Come, send round the wine, and leave points of belief
To simpleton sages, and reasoning fools;
This moment's a flower too fair and brief,
To be withered and stained by the dust of the schools.
Your glass may be purple, and mine may be blue,
But, while they are filled from the same bright bowl,
The fool, who would quarrel for difference of hue,
Deserves not the comfort they shed o'er the soul.

Shall I ask the brave soldier, who fights by my side
In the cause of mankind, if our creeds agree?
Shall I give up the friend I have valued and tried,
If he kneel not before the same altar with me?
From the heretic girl of my soul should I fly,
To seek somewhere else a more orthodox kiss?
No: perish the hearts, and the laws that try
Truth, valor, or love, by a standard like this!

* I have endeavored here, without losing that Irish character, which it is my object to preserve throughout this work, to allude to the sad and ominous fatality, by which England has been deprived of so many great and good men, at a moment when she most requires all the aids of talent and integrity.

† This designation, which has been before applied to Lord Nelson, is the title given to a celebrated Irish hero, in a poem by O'Guive, the bard of O'Niel, which is quoted in the "Philosophical Survey of the South of Ireland," page 433. "Con, of the Hundred Fights, sleep in thy grass-grown tomb, and upbraid not our defeats with thy victories."

‡ Fox, "Romanorum ultimus."

THE SONG OF FIONNUALA.*

Silent, O Moyle, be the roar of thy water,
Break not, ye breezes, your chain of repose,
While, murmuring mournfully, Lir's lonely daughter
Tells to the night-star her tale of woes.
When shall the swan, her death-note singing,
Sleep, with wings in darkness furled?
When will Heaven, its sweet bell ringing,
Call my spirit from this stormy world?

Sadly, O Moyle, to thy winter-wave weeping,
Fate bids me languish long ages away;
Yet still in her darkness doth Erin lie sleeping,
Still doth the pure light its dawning delay.
When will that day-star, mildly springing,
Warm our isle with peace and love?
When will Heaven, its sweet bell ring,
Call my spirit to the fields above?

LET ERIN REMEMBER THE DAYS OF OLD.

Let Erin remember the days of old,
Ere her faithless sons betrayed her;
When Malachi wore the collar of gold,†
Which he won from her proud invader,
When her kings, with standard of green unfurled,
Led the Red-Branch Knights to danger;‡
Ere the emerald gem of the western world
Was set in the crown of a stranger.

On Lough Neagh's bank, as the fisherman strays,
When the clear cold eve's declining,
He sees the round towers of other days
In the wave beneath him shining;
Thus shall memory often, in dreams sublime,
Catch a glimpse of the days that are over;
Thus, sighing, look through the waves of time
For the long-faded glories they cover.‖

BELIEVE ME, IF ALL THOSE ENDEARING YOUNG CHARMS.

Believe me, if all those endearing young charms,
Which I gaze on so fondly to-day,
Were to change by to-morrow, and fleet in my arms,
Like fairy-gifts fading away,

* To make this story intelligible in a song would require a much greater number of verses than any one is authorized to inflict upon an audience at once: the reader must therefore be content to learn, in a note, that Fionnuala, the daughter of Lir, was, by some supernatural power, transformed into a swan, and condemned to wander, for many hundred years, over certain lakes and rivers in Ireland, till the coming of Christianity, when the first sound of the mass-bell was to be the signal of her release. I found this fanciful fiction among some manuscript translations from the Irish, which were begun under the direction of that enlightened friend of Ireland, the late Countess of Moira.

† "This brought on an encounter between Malachi (the monarch of Ireland in the tenth century) and the Danes, in which Malachi defeated two of their champions, whom he encountered successively, hand to hand, taking a collar of gold from the neck of one, and carrying off the sword of the other, as trophies of his victory."—*Warner's History of Ireland*, vol. i., book ix.

‡ "Military orders of knights were very early established in Ireland; long before the birth of Christ we find an hereditary order of Chivalry in Ulster, called *Curaidhe na Craiobhe ruadh*, or the Knights of the Red Branch, from their chief seat in Emania, adjoining to the palace of the Ulster kings, called *Teagh na Craiobhe ruadh*, or the Academy of the Red Branch; and contiguous to which was a large hospital, founded for the sick knights and soldiers, called *Bronbhearg*, or the House of the Sorrowful Soldier."—*O'Halloran's Introduction, &c.*, part i., chap. 5.

‖ It was an old tradition, in the time of Giraldus, that Lough Neagh had been originally a fountain, by whose sudden overflowing the country was inundated, and a whole region, like the Atlantis of Plato, overwhelmed. He says that the fishermen, in clear weather, used to point out to strangers the tall ecclesiastical towers under the water. *Piscatores aquæ illius turres ecclesiasticas, quæ more patriæ arctæ sunt et altæ, necnon et rotundæ, sub undis manifeste sereno tempore conspiciunt, et extraneis transeuntibus, reique causas admirantibus, frequenter ostendunt.*—Topogr. Hib. dist. 2., c. 9

Thou wouldst still be adored, as this moment thou art,
Let thy loveliness fade as it will,
And around the dear ruin each wish of my heart
Would entwine itself verdantly still.

It is not while beauty and youth are thine own,
And thy cheeks unprofaned by a tear,
That the fervor and faith of a soul can be known,
To which time will but make thee more dear;
No, the heart that has truly loved never forgets,
But as truly loves on to the close,
As the sun-flower turns on her god, when he sets,
The same look which she turned when he rose.

SUBLIME WAS THE WARNING.

Sublime was the warning that Liberty spoke,
And grand was the moment when Spaniards awoke
Into life and revenge from the conqueror's chain.
Oh, Liberty! let not this spirit have rest,
Till it move, like a breeze, o'er the waves of the west—
Give the light of your look to each sorrowing spot,
Nor, oh, be the Shamrock of Erin forgot
While you add to your garland the Olive of Spain!

If the fame of our fathers, bequeathed with their rights,
Give to country its charm, and to home its delights,
If deceit be a wound, and suspicion a stain,
Then, ye men of Iberia, our cause is the same!
And oh! may his tomb want a tier and a name,
Who would ask for a nobler, a holier death,
Than to turn his last sigh into victory's breath,
For the Shamrock of Erin and Olive of Spain!

Ye Blakes and O'Donnels, whose fathers resigned
The green hills of their youth, among strangers to find
That repose which at home they had sighed for in vain,
Join, join in our hope that the flame, which you light,
May be felt yet in Erin, as calm, and as bright,
And forgive even Albion while blushing she draws,
Like a truant, her sword, in the long-slighted cause
Of the Shamrock of Erin and Olive of Spain!

God prosper the cause!—oh, it can not but thrive,
While the pulse of one patriot heart is alive,
Its devotion to feel, and its rights to maintain;
Then, how sainted by sorrow, its martyrs will die!
The finger of glory shall point where they lie;
While, far from the footstep of coward or slave,
The young spirit of Freedom shall shelter their grave
Beneath Shamrocks of Erin and Olives of Spain!

ERIN, OH ERIN.

Like the bright lamp, that shone in Kildare's holy fane,*
And burned through long ages of darkness and storm,
Is the heart that sorrows have frowned on in vain,
Whose spirit outlives them, unfading and warm.
Erin, oh Erin, thus bright through the tears
Of a long night of bondage, thy spirit appears.

The nations have fallen, and thou still art young,
Thy sun is but rising, when others are set;
And though slavery's cloud o'er thy morning hath hung,
The full noon of freedom shall beam round thee yet.
Erin, oh Erin, though long in the shade,
Thy star will shine out when the proudest shall fade.

Unchilled by the rain, and unwaked by the wind,
The lily lies sleeping through winter's cold hour,
Till Spring's light touch her fetters unbind,
And daylight and liberty bless the young flower.†
Thus Erin, oh Erin, *thy* winter is past,
And the hope that lived through it shall blossom at last.

* The inextinguishable fire of St. Bridget, at Kildare, which Giraldus mentions: "Apud Kildariam occurrit ignis Sanctæ Brigidæ, quem inextinguibilem vocant; non quod extingui non possit, sed quod tam solicite moniales et sanctæ mulieres ignem, suppetente materia, fovent et nutriunt, ut a tempore virginis per tot annorum curricula semper mansit inextinctus."—*Girald. Camb de Mirabil. Hibern.*, dist. 2. c. 34.

† Mrs. H. Tighe, in her exquisite lines on the Lily, has applied this image to a still more important object.

OH! BLAME NOT THE BARD.*

Oh! blame not the bard, if he fly to the bowers,
Where Pleasure lies, carelessly smiling at Fame,
He was born for much more, and in happier hours
His soul might have burned with a holier flame.
The string, that now languishes loose o'er the lyre,
Might have bent a proud bow to the warrior's dart;†
And the lip, which now breathes but the song of desire,
Might have poured the full tide of a patriot's heart.

But alas for his country!—her pride is gone by,
And that spirit is broken, which never would bend;
O'er the ruin her children in secret must sigh,
For 'tis treason to love her, and death to defend.
Unprized are her sons, till they've learned to betray;
Undistinguished they live, if they shame not their sires,
And the torch, that would light them through dignity's way,
Must be caught from the pile, where their country expires.

Then blame not the bard, if in pleasure's soft dream,
He should try to forget, what he never can heal:
Oh! give but a hope—let a vista but gleam
Through the gloom of his country, and mark how he'll feel!
That instant, his heart at her shrine would lay down
Every passion it nursed, every bliss it adored;
While the myrtle, now idly entwined with his crown,
Like the wreath of Harmodius, should cover his sword.‡

But though glory be gone, and though hope fade away,
Thy name, loved Erin, shall live in his songs;
Not e'en in the hour, when his heart is most gay,
Will he lose the remembrance of thee and thy wrongs.
The stranger shall hear thy lament on his plains;
The sigh of thy harp shall be sent o'er the deep,
Till thy masters themselves, as they rivet thy chains,
Shall pause at the song of their captive, and weep.

ILL OMENS.

When daylight was yet sleeping under the billow,
And stars in the heavens still lingering shone,
Young Kitty, all blushing, rose up from her pillow,
The last time she e'er was to press it alone.
For the youth whom she treasured her heart and her soul in,
Had promised to link the last tie before noon;
And, when once the young heart of a maiden is stolen,
The maiden herself will steal after it soon.

As she looked in the glass, which a woman ne'er misses,
Nor ever wants time for a sly glance or two,
A butterfly,‖ fresh from the night-flower's kisses,
Flew over the mirror, and shaded her view.
Enraged with the insect for hiding her graces,
She brushed him—he fell, alas! never to rise.
"Ah! such," said the girl, "is the pride of our faces,
For which the soul's innocence too often dies."

While she stole through the garden, where heart's-ease was growing,
She culled some, and kissed off its night-fallen dew;
And a rose, further on, looked so tempting and glowing,
That, spite of her haste, she must gather it too:
But while o'er the roses too carelessly leaning,
Her zone flew in two, and the heart's-ease was lost:
"Ah! this means," said the girl (and she sighed at its meaning),
"That love is scarce worth the repose it will cost!"

* We may suppose this apology to have been uttered by one of those wandering bards, whom Spenser so severely and perhaps truly describes in his "State of Ireland," and whose poems, he tells us, "were sprinkled with some pretty flowers of their natural device, which have good grace and comeliness unto them, the which it is great pity to see abused to the gracing of wickedness and vice, which, with good usage, would serve to adorn and beautify virtue."

† It is conjectured by Wormius, that the name of Ireland is derived from *Yr*, the Runic for a *bow*, in the use of which weapon the Irish were once very expert. This derivation is certainly more creditable to us than the following: "So that Ireland, called the land of *Ire*, from the constant broils therein for four hundred years, was now become the land of concord."—*Lloyd's State Worthies*, art. *The Lord Grandison.*

‡ See the Hymn, attributed to Alcæus, Εν μυρτου κλαδι το ξιφος φορησω—"I will carry my sword, hidden in myrtles, like Harmodius, and Aristogiton," &c.

‖ An emblem of the soul.

DRINK TO HER.

Drink to her, who long
Hath waked the poet's sigh,
The girl, who gave to song
What gold could never buy.
Oh! woman's heart was made
For minstrel hands alone;
By other fingers played,
It yields not half the tone.
Then here's to her, who long
Hath waked the poet's sigh,
The girl who gave to song
What gold could never buy.

At Beauty's door of glass,
When Wealth and Wit once stood,
They asked her, "*Which* might pass?"
She answered, "He, who could."
With golden key Wealth thought
To pass—but 'twould not do;
While Wit a diamond brought,
Which cut his bright way through.
So here's to her, who long
Hath waked the poet's sigh,
The girl, who gave to song
What gold could never buy.

The love that seeks a home
Where wealth or grandeur shines,
Is like the gloomy gnome,
That dwells in dark gold mines.
But oh! the poet's love
Can boast a brighter sphere;
Its native home's above,
Though woman keeps it here.
Then drink to her, who long
Hath waked the poet's sigh,
The girl, who gave to song
What gold could never buy.

WHILE GAZING ON THE MOON'S LIGHT.

While gazing on the moon's light,
A moment from her smile I turned,
To look at orbs, that, more bright,
In lone and distant glory burned.
But *too* far
Each proud star,
For me to feel its warming flame;
Much more dear
That mild sphere,
Which near our planet smiling came;—*
Thus, Mary, be but thou my own;
While brighter eyes unheeded play,
I'll love those moonlight looks alone,
That bless my home and guide my way.

The day had sunk in dim showers,
But midnight now, with lustre meet,
Illumined all the pale flowers,
Like hope upon a mourner's cheek.
I said (while
The moon's smile
Played o'er a stream, in dimpling bliss),
"The moon looks
On many brooks—
The brook can see no moon but this;"†
And thus, I thought, our fortunes run,
For many a lover looks to thee,
While, oh! I feel there is but *one*,
One Mary in the world for me.

* "Of such celestial bodies as are visible, the sun excepted, the single moon, as despicable as it is in comparison to most of the others, is much more benefical than they all put together."—*Whiston's Theory, &c.*

In the *Entretiens d'Ariste*, among other ingenious emblems, we find a starry sky without a moon, with these words, "*Non mille, quod absens.*"

† This image was suggested by the following thought, which occurs somewhere in Sir William Jones's works: "The moon looks upon many night flowers—the night-flower sees but one moon."

BEFORE THE BATTLE.

By the hope within us springing,
Herald of to-morrow's strife;
By that sun, whose light is bringing
Chains or freedom, death or life—
Oh! remember life can be
No charm for him, who lives not free!
Like the day-star in the wave,
Sinks a hero in his grave,
Midst the dew-fall of a nation's tears.

Happy is he o'er whose decline
The smiles of home may soothing shine,
And light him down the steep of years:
But oh, how blest they sink to rest,
Who close their eyes on Victory's breast!

O'er his watch-fire's fading embers
Now the foeman's cheek turns white,
When his heart that field remembers,
Where we tamed his tyrant might.
Never let him bind again
A chain, like that we broke from then.
Hark! the horn of combat calls—
Ere the golden evening falls,
May we pledge that horn in triumph round!*

Many a heart that now beats high,
In slumber cold at night shall lie,
Nor waken even at victory's sound.—
But oh, how blest that hero's sleep,
O'er whom a wond'ring world shall weep!

AFTER THE BATTLE.

Night closed around the conqueror's way,
And lightnings showed the distant hill,
Where those who lost that dreadful day,
Stood few and faint, but fearless still.
The soldier's hope, the patriot's zeal,
For ever dimmed, for ever crost—
Oh! who shall say what heroes feel,
When all but life and honor's lost?

The last sad hour of freedom's dream,
And valor's task, moved slowly by,
While mute they watched, till morning's beam
Should rise and give them light to die.
There's yet a world, where souls are free,
Where tyrants taint not nature's bliss;—
If death that world's bright opening be,
Oh! who would live a slave in this?

THE IRISH PEASANT TO HIS MISTRESS.†

Through grief and through danger thy smile hath cheered my way,
Till hope seemed to bud from each thorn that round me lay;
The darker our fortune, the brighter our pure love burned,
Till shame into glory, till fear into zeal was turned;
Yes, slave as I was, in thy arms my spirit felt free,
And blessed even the sorrows that made me more dear to thee.

Thy rival was honored, while thou wert wronged and scorned,
Thy crown was of briers, while gold her brows adorned;
She wooed me to temples, while thou layst hid in caves,
Her friends were all masters, while thine, alas! were slaves,
Yet cold in the earth, at thy feet, I would rather be,
Than wed what I loved not, or turn one thought from thee.

They slander thee sorely, who say thy vows are frail—
Hadst thou been a false one, thy cheek had looked less pale.
They say, too, so long thou hast worn those lingering chains,
That deep in thy heart they have printed their servile stains—
Oh! foul is the slander—no chain could that soul subdue—
Where shineth *thy* spirit, there liberty shineth too!‡

* "The Irish Corna was not entirely devoted to martial purposes. In the heroic ages, our ancestors quaffed Meadh out of them, as the Danish hunters do their beverage at this day."—*Walker.*

† Meaning, allegorically, the ancient Church of Ireland.

‡ "Where the Spirit of the Lord is, there is liberty."—*St. Paul*, 2 Cor., iii. 17.

'TIS SWEET TO THINK.

'Tis sweet to think, that, where'er we rove,
We are sure to find something blissful and dear,
And that, when we're far from the lips we love,
We've but to make love to the lips we are near.*
The heart, like a tendril, accustomed to cling,
Let it grow where it will, can not flourish alone,
But will lean to the nearest, and loveliest thing,
It can twine with itself, and make closely its own.
Then oh! what pleasure, where'er we rove,
To be sure to find something, still, that is dear,
And to know, when far from the lips we love,
We've but to make love to the lips we are near.

'Twere a shame, when flowers around us rise,
To make light of the rest, if the rose isn't there;
And the world's so rich in resplendent eyes,
'Twere a pity to limit one's love to a pair.
Love's wing and the peacock's are nearly alike,
They are both of them bright, but they're changeable too,
And, wherever a new beam of beauty can strike,
It will tincture Love's plume with a different hue.
Then oh! what pleasure, where'er we rove,
To be sure to find something, still, that is dear,
And to know, when far from the lips we love,
We've but to make love to the lips we are near.

ON MUSIC.

When through life unblest we rove,
Losing all that made life dear,
Should some notes we used to love,
In days of boyhood, meet our ear,
Oh! how welcome breathes the strain!
Wakening thoughts that long have slept;
Kindling former smiles again
In faded eyes that long have wept.

Like the gale, that sighs along
Beds of oriental flowers,
Is the grateful breath of song,
That once was heard in happier hours;
Filled with balm, the gale sighs on,
Though the flowers have sunk in death;
So, when pleasure's dream is gone,
Its memory lives in Music's breath.

Music, oh how faint, how weak,
Language fades before thy spell!
Why should Feeling ever speak,
When thou canst breathe her soul so well?
Friendship's balmy words may feign,
Love's are even more false than they;
Oh! 'tis only music's strain
Can sweetly sooth and not betray.

WEEP ON, WEEP ON.

Weep on, weep on, your hour is past;
Your dreams of pride are o'er;
The fatal chain is round you cast,
And you are men no more.
In vain the hero's heart hath bled;
The sage's tongue hath warned in vain;
Oh, Freedom! once thy flame hath fled,
It never lights again.

Weep on—perhaps in after days,
They'll learn to love your name;
When many a deed may wake in praise
That long hath slept in blame.
And when they tread the ruined Isle,
Where rest, at length, the lord and slave,
They'll wond'ring ask, how hands so vile
Could conquer hearts so brave?

"'Twas fate," they'll say, "a wayward fate
Your web of discord wove;
And while your tyrants joined in hate,
You never joined in love.
But hearts fell off, that ought to twine,
And man profaned what God had given;
Till some were heard to curse the shrine,
Where others knelt to heaven!"

IT IS NOT THE TEAR AT THIS MOMENT SHED.*

It is not the tear at this moment shed,
When the cold turf has just been laid o'er him,
That can tell how beloved was the friend that's fled,
Or how deep in our hearts we deplore him.
'Tis the tear, through many a long day wept,
'Tis life's whole path o'ershaded;
'Tis the one remembrance, fondly kept,
When all lighter griefs have faded.

Thus his memory, like some holy light,
Kept alive in our hearts, will improve them,
For worth shall look fairer, and truth more bright,
When we think how he lived but to love them.
And, as fresher flowers the sod perfume
Where buried saints are lying,
So our hearts shall borrow a sweetening bloom
From the image he left there in dying!

THE ORIGIN OF THE HARP.

'Tis believed that this Harp, which I wake now for thee,
Was a Syren of old, who sung under the sea;
And who often, at eve, through the bright waters roved,
To meet, on the green shore, a youth whom she loved.

But she loved him in vain, for he left her to weep,
And in tears, all the night, her gold tresses to steep;
Till Heaven looked with pity on true love so warm,
And changed to this soft Harp the sea-maiden's form.

Still her bosom rose fair—still her cheeks smiled the same,
While her sea-beauties gracefully formed the light frame;
And her hair, as, let loose, o'er her white arm it fell,
Was changed to bright chords utt'ring melody's spell.

Hence it came, that this soft Harp so long hath been known
To mingle love's language with sorrow's sad tone;
Till *thou* didst divide them, and teach the fond lay
To speak love when I'm near thee, and grief when away.

I SAW THY FORM IN YOUTHFUL PRIME.

I saw thy form in youthful prime,
Nor thought that pale decay
Would steal before the steps of Time,
And waste its bloom away, Mary!
Yet still thy features wore that light,
Which fleets not with the breath;
And life ne'er looked more truly bright
Than in thy smile of death, Mary!

As streams that run o'er golden mines,
Yet humbly, calmly glide,
Nor seem to know the wealth that shines
Within their gentle tide, Mary!
So veiled beneath the simplest guise,
Thy radiant genius shone,
And that, which charmed all other eyes,
Seemed worthless in thy own, Mary!

If souls could always dwell above,
Thou ne'er hadst left that sphere;
Or could we keep the souls we love,
We ne'er had lost thee here, Mary!
Though many a gifted mind we meet,
Though fairest forms we see,
To live with them is far less sweet,
Than to remember thee, Mary!†

* I believe it is Marmontel who says, "*Quand on n'a pas ce que l'on aime, il faut aimer ce que l'on a.*" There are so many matter-of-fact people, who take such *jeux d'esprit* as this defence of inconstancy, to be the actual and genuine sentiments of him who writes them, that they compel one, in self-defence, to be as matter-of-fact as themselves, and to remind them that Democritus was not the worse physiologist, for having playfully contended that snow was black; nor Erasmus, in any degree, the less wise, for having written an ingenious encomium of folly

* These lines were occasioned by the loss of a very near and dear relative, who had died lately at Madeira.

† I have here made a feeble effort to imitate that exquisite inscription of Shenstone, "Heu! quanto minus est cum reliquis versari quam meminisse!"

WHAT THE BEE IS TO THE FLOWERET.

He.—What the bee is to the flow'ret,
When he looks for honey-dew,
Through the leaves that close embower it,
That, my love, I'll be to you.

She.—What the bank, with verdure glowing,
Is to waves that wander near,
Whisp'ring kisses, while they're going,
That I'll be to you, my dear.

She.—But they say, the bee's a rover,
Who will fly, when sweets are gone;
And, when once the kiss is over,
Faithless brooks will wander on.

He.—Nay, if flowers *will* lose their looks,
If sunny banks *will* wear away,
'Tis but right, that bees and brooks
Should sip and kiss them while they may.

'TIS THE LAST ROSE OF SUMMER.

'Tis the last rose of summer
Left blooming alone;
All her lovely companions
Are faded and gone;
No flower of her kindred,
No rose-bud is nigh,
To reflect back her blushes,
Or give sigh for sigh.

I'll not leave thee, thou lone one!
To pine on the stem;
Since the lovely are sleeping,
Go, sleep thou with them.
Thus kindly I scatter
Thy leaves o'er the bed,
Where thy mates of the garden
Lie scentless and dead.

So soon may *I* follow,
When friendships decay,
And from Love's shining circle
The gems drop away.
When true hearts lie withered,
And fond ones are flown,
Oh! who would inhabit
This bleak world alone?

AT THE MID HOUR OF NIGHT.

At the mid hour of night, when stars are weeping, I fly
To the lone vale we loved, when life shone warm in thine eye;
And I think oft, if spirits can steal from the regions of air,
To revisit past scenes of delight, thou wilt come to me there,
And tell me our love is remembered, even in the sky.

Then I sing the wild song 'twas once such pleasure to hear!
When our voices commingling breathed, like one, on the ear;
And, as Echo far off through the vale my sad orison rolls,
I think, oh my love! 'tis thy voice from the Kingdom of Souls,*
Faintly answering still the notes that once were so dear.

LOVE AND THE NOVICE.

"Here we dwell, in holiest bowers,
Where angels of light o'er our orisons bend;
Where sighs of devotion and breathings of flowers
To heaven in mingled odor ascend.
Do not disturb our calm, oh Love!
So like is thy form to the cherubs above,
It well might deceive such hearts as ours."

Love stood near the Novice and listened,
And Love is no novice in taking a hint;
His laughing blue eyes soon with piety glistened;
His rosy wing turned to heaven's own teint.
"Who would have thought," the urchin cries,
"That Love could so well, so gravely disguise
His wandering wings and wounding eyes?"

Love now warms thee, waking and sleeping,
Young Novice, to him all thy orisons rise.
He tinges the heavenly fount with his weeping,
He brightens the censer's flame with his sighs.
Love is the Saint enshrined in thy breast,
And angels themselves would admit such a guest,
If he came to them clothed in Piety's vest.

* "There are countries," says Montaigne, "where they believe the souls of the happy live in all manner of liberty, in delightful fields; and that it is those souls, repeating the words we utter, which we call Echo."

THIS LIFE IS ALL CHEQUERED WITH PLEASURES AND WOES.

This life is all chequered with pleasures and woes,
That chase one another like waves of the deep—
Each brightly or darkly, as onward it flows,
Reflecting our eyes, as they sparkle or weep.
So closely our whims on our miseries tread,
That the laugh is awaked ere the tear can be dried;
And, as fast as the rain-drop of Pity is shed,
The goose-plumage of Folly can turn it aside.
But pledge me the cup—if existence would cloy,
With hearts ever happy, and heads ever wise,
Be ours the light Sorrow, half-sister to Joy,
And the light, brilliant Folly, that flashes and dies.

When Hylas was sent with his urn to the fount,
Through fields full of light, and with heart full of play,
Light rambled the boy, over meadow and mount,
And neglected his task for the flowers on the way.*
Thus many, like me, who in youth should have tasted
The fountain that runs by Philosophy's shrine,
Their time with the flowers on the margin have wasted,
And left their light urns all as empty as mine.
But pledge me the goblet—while Idleness weaves
These flow'rets together, should Wisdom but see
One bright drop or two that has fallen on the leaves,
From her fountain Divine, 'tis sufficient for me.

OH THE SHAMROCK.

Through Erin's Isle,
To sport awhile,
As Love and Valor wandered,
With Wit, the sprite,
Whose quiver bright
A thousand arrows squandered.
Where'er they pass,
A triple grass†
Shoots up, with dewdrops streaming,
As softly green
As emeralds seen
Through purest crystal gleaming.
Oh the Shamrock, the green, immortal Shamrock
Chosen leaf,
Of Bard and Chief,
Old Erin's native Shamrock!

Says Valor, "See,
They spring for me,
Those leafy gems of morning!"—
Says Love, "No, no,
For *me* they grow,
My fragrant path adorning."
But Wit perceives
The triple leaves,
And cries, "Oh! do not sever
A type, that blends
Three godlike friends,
Love, Valor, Wit, for ever!"

* "Proposito florem prætulit officio."—Propert., lib. i., eleg. 20.

† It is said that St. Patrick, when preaching the Trinity to the Pagan Irish, used to illustrate his subject by reference to that species of trefoil called in Ireland by the name of the Shamrock; and hence, perhaps, the Island of Saints adopted this plant as her national emblem. Hope, among the ancients, was sometimes represented as a beautiful child, standing upon tiptoes, and a trefoil of three-colored grass in her hand.

Oh the Shamrock, the green, immortal Shamrock!
Chosen leaf
Of Bard and Chief,
Old Erin's native Shamrock!

So firmly fond
May last the bond
They wove that morn together,
And ne'er may fall
One drop of gall
On Wit's celestial feather.
May Love, as twine
His flowers divine,
Of thorny falsehood weed 'em;
May Valor ne'er
His standard rear,
Against the cause of Freedom!
Oh the Shamrock, the green, immortal Shamrock!
Chosen leaf
Of Bard and Chief,
Old Erin's native Shamrock!

OH! HAD WE SOME BRIGHT LITTLE ISLE OF OUR OWN.

Oh! had we some bright little isle of our own,
In a blue summer ocean, far off and alone,
Where a leaf never dies in the still blooming bowers,
And the bee banquets on through a whole year of flowers;
Where the son loves to pause
With so fond a delay,
That the night only draws
A thin veil o'er the day;
Where simply to feel that we breathe, that we live,
Is worth the best joy that life elsewhere can give.

There, with souls ever ardent, and pure as the clime,
We should love, as they loved in the first golden time;
The glow of the sunshine, the balm of the air,
Would steal to our hearts, and make all summer there.
With affection as free
From decline as the bowers,
And, with hope, like the bee,
Living always on flowers,
Our life should resemble a long day of light,
And our death come on, holy and calm as the night.

THE SONG OF O'RUARK,

PRINCE OF BREFFNI.*

The valley lay smiling before me,
Where lately I left her behind;
Yet I trembled, and something hung o'er me,
That saddened the joy of my mind.
I looked for the lamp which, she told me,
Should shine, when her Pilgrim returned;
But, though darkness began to infold me,
No lamp from the battlements burned!

I flew to her chamber—'twas lonely,
As if the loved tenant lay dead;—
Ah, would it were death, and death only!
But no, the young false one had fled.
And there hung the lute that could soften
My very worst pains into bliss;
While the hand, that had waked it so often,
Now throbbed to a proud rival's kiss.

There *was* a time, falsest of women,
When Breffni's good sword would have sought
That man, through a million of foemen,
Who dared but to wrong thee *in thought!*
While now—oh degenerate daughter
Of Erin, how fallen is thy fame!
And through ages of bondage and slaughter,
Our country shall bleed for thy shame.

Already, the curse is upon her,
And strangers her valleys profane;
They come to divide, to dishonor,
And tyrants they long will remain.
But onward!—the green banner rearing,
Go, flesh every sword to the hilt;
On *our* side is Virtue and Erin,
On *theirs* is the Saxon and guilt.

THE YOUNG MAY MOON.

The young May moon is beaming, love,
The glow-worm's lamp is gleaming, love,
How sweet to rove
Through Morna's grove,*
When the drowsy world is dreaming, love!
Then awake!—the heavens look bright, my dear,
'Tis never too late for delight, my dear,
And the best of all ways
To lengthen our days,
Is to steal a few hours from the night, my dear!

Now all the world is sleeping, love,
But the Sage, his star-watch keeping, love
And I, whose star,
More glorious far,
Is the eye from that casement peeping, love.
Then awake!—till rise of sun, my dear,
The Sage's glass we'll shun, my dear,
Or, in watching the flight
Of bodies of light,
He might happen to take thee for one, my dear.

I'D MOURN THE HOPES.

I'd mourn the hopes that leave me,
If thy smiles had left me too;
I'd weep when friends deceive me,
If thou wert, like them, untrue.
But while I've thee before me,
With heart so warm and eyes so bright,
No clouds can linger o'er me,
That smile turns them all to light.

'Tis not in fate to harm me,
While fate leaves thy love to me;
'Tis not in joy to charm me,
Unless joy be shared with thee.
One minute's dream about thee
Were worth a long, an endless year
Of waking bliss without thee,
My only love, my only dear!

And though the hope be gone, love,
That long sparkled o'er our way,
Oh! we shall journey on, love,
More safely, without its ray.
Far better lights shall win me
Along the path I've yet to roam:—
The mind that burns within me,
And pure smiles from thee at home.

Thus when the lamp that lighted
The traveller at first goes out,
He feels awhile benighted,
And looks round in fear and doubt.
But soon, the prospect clearing,
By cloudless starlight on he treads,
And thinks no lamp so cheering
As that light which Heaven sheds.

* These stanzas are founded upon an event of most melancholy importance to Ireland: if, as we are told by our Irish historians, it gave England the first opportunity of profiting by our divisions and subduing us. The following are the circumstances, as related by O'Halloran: "The king of Leinster had long conceived a violent affection for Dearbhorgil, daughter to the king of Meath, and though she had been for some time married to O'Ruark, prince of Breffni, yet it could not restrain his passion. They carried on a private correspondence, and she informed him that O'Ruark intended soon to go on a pilgrimage (an act of piety frequent in those days), and conjured him to embrace that opportunity of conveying her from a husband she detested to a lover she adored. Mac Murchad too punctually obeyed the summons, and had the lady conveyed to his capital of Ferns." The monarch Roderick espoused the cause of O'Ruark, while Mac Murchard fled to England, and obtained the assistance of Henry II.

"Such," adds Giraldus Cambrensis (as I find him in an old translation), "is the variable and fickle nature of woman, by whom all mischief in the world (for the most part) do happen and come, as may appear by Marcus Antonius, and by the destruction of Troy."

* "Steals silently to Morna's grove."—See, in Mr. Bunting's collection, a poem translated from the Irish, by the late John Brown, one of my earliest college companions and friends, whose death was as singularly melancholy and unfortunate as his life had been amiable, honorable, and exemplary.

SHE IS FAR FROM THE LAND.

She is far from the land where her young hero sleeps,
And lovers are round her, sighing:
But coldly she turns from their gaze, and weeps,
For her heart in his grave is lying.

She sings the wild song of her dear native plains,
Every note which he loved awaking;—
Ah! little they think who delight in her strains,
How the heart of the Minstrel is breaking.

He had lived for his love, for his country he died,
They were all that to life had entwined him;
Nor soon shall the tears of his country be dried,
Nor long will his love stay behind him.

Oh! make her a grave where the sunbeams rest,
When they promise a glorious morrow;
They'll shine o'er her sleep, like a smile from the West,
From her own loved island of sorrow.

THE PRINCE'S DAY.*

Though dark are our sorrows, to-day we'll forget them,
And smile through our tears, like a sunbeam in showers:
There never were hearts, if our rulers would let them,
More formed to be grateful and blest than ours.
But just when the chain
Has ceased to pain,
And hope has enwreathed it round with flowers,
There comes a new link
Our spirits to sink—
Oh! the joy that we taste, like the light of the poles,
Is a flash amid darkness, too brilliant to stay;
But, though 'twere the last little spark in our souls,
We must light it up now, on our Prince's Day.

Contempt on the minion, who calls you disloyal!
Though fierce to your foe, to your friends you are true;
And the tribute most high to a head that is royal,
Is love from a heart that loves liberty too.
While cowards, who blight
Your fame, your right,
Would shrink from the blaze of the battle array,
The Standard of Green
In front would be seen—
Oh, my life on your faith! were you summoned this minute,
You'd cast every bitter remembrance away,
And show what the arm of old Erin has in it,
When roused by the foe, on her Prince's Day.

He loves the Green Isle, and his love is recorded
In hearts, which have suffered too much to forget;
And hope shall be crowned, and attachment rewarded,
And Erin's gay jubilee shine out yet.
The gem may be broke
By many a stroke,
But nothing can cloud its native ray;
Each fragment will cast
A light, to the last—
And thus, Erin, my country, though broken thou art,
There's a lustre within thee, that ne'er will decay;
A spirit, which beams through each suffering part,
And now smiles at all pain on the Prince's Day.

LOVE'S YOUNG DREAM.

Oh! the days are gone, when Beauty bright
My heart's chain wove;
When my dream of life, from morn till night,
Was love, still love.
New hope may bloom,
And days may come,
Of milder, calmer beam,
But there's nothing half so sweet in life
As love's young dream:
', there's nothing half so sweet in life
As love's young dream.

Though the bard to purer fame may soar,
When wild youth's past;
Though he win the wise, who frowned before
To smile at last;
He'll never meet
A joy so sweet,
In all his noon of fame,
As when first he sung to woman's ear,
His soul-felt flame,
And at every close, she blushed to hear
The one loved name.

No—that hallowed form is ne'er forgot
Which first love traced;
Still it lingering haunts the greenest spot
On memory's waste.
'Twas odor fled
As soon as shed;
'Twas morning's winged dream:
'Twas a light, that ne'er can shine again
On life's dull stream:
Oh! 'twas light that ne'er can shine again
On life's dull stream.

NAY, TELL ME NOT, DEAR.

Nay, tell me not, dear, that the goblet drowns
One charm of feeling, one fond regret;
Believe me, a few of thy angry frowns
Are all I've sunk in its bright wave yet.
Ne'er hath a beam
Been lost in the stream
That ever was shed from thy form or soul;
The spell of those eyes,
The balm of thy sighs,
Still float on the surface, and hallow my bowl.
Then fancy not, dearest, that wine can steal
One blissful dream of the heart from me;
Like founts that awaken the pilgrim's zeal,
The bowl but brightens my love for thee.

They tell us that Love in his fairy bower
Had two blush-roses, of birth divine;
He sprinkled the one with a rainbow's shower,
But bathed the other with mantling wine.
Soon did the buds
That drank of the floods
Distilled by the rainbow, decline and fade;
While those which the tide
Of ruby had died
All blushed into beauty, like thee, sweet maid
Then fancy not, dearest, that wine can steal
One blissful dream of the heart from me;
Like founts, that awaken the pilgrim's zeal,
The bowl but brightens my love for thee.

BY THAT LAKE, WHOSE GLOOMY SHORE.*

By that Lake, whose gloomy shore
Sky-lark never warbles o'er,†
Where the cliff hangs high and steep
Young Saint Kevin stole to sleep.
"Here, at least," he calmly said,
"Woman ne'er shall find my bed."
Ah! the good Saint little knew
What that wily sex can do.

'Twas from Kathleen's eyes he flew—
Eyes of most unholy blue!
She had loved him well and long,
Wished him hers, nor thought it wrong.
Wheresoe'er the Saint would fly,
Still he heard her light foot nigh;
East or west, where'er he turned,
Still her eyes before him burned.

On the bold cliff's bosom cast,
Tranquil now he sleeps at last;

* This song was written for a fête in honor of the Prince of Wales's birthday, given by my friend Major Bryan, at his seat in the county of Kilkenny.

* This ballad is founded upon one of the many stories related of St. Kevin, whose bed in the rock is to be seen at Glendalough, a most gloomy and romantic spot in the county of Wicklow.

† There are many other curious traditions concerning this Lake, which may be found in Giraldus, Colgan, etc.

Dreams of heaven, nor thinks that e'er
Woman's smile can haunt him there.
But nor earth nor heaven is free
From her power, if fond she be:
Even-now, while calm he sleeps,
Kathleen o'er him leans and weeps.

Fearless she had tracked his feet
To this rocky, wild retreat;
And when morning met his view,
Her mild glances met it too.
Ah, your Saints have cruel hearts!
Sternly from his bed he starts,
And with rude repulsive shock,
Hurls her from the beetling rock.

Glendalough, thy gloomy wave
Soon was gentle Kathleen's grave!
Soon the Saint (yet ah! too late)
Felt her love, and mourned her fate.
When he said, "Heaven rest her soul!"
Round the Lake light music stole;
And her ghost was seen to glide,
Smiling o'er the fatal tide.

AVENGING AND BRIGHT.

Avenging and bright fall the swift sword of Erin*
On him who the brave sons of Usna betrayed!—
For every fond eye he hath wakened a tear in,
A drop from his heart-wounds shall weep o'er her blade.

By the red cloud that hung over Conor's dark dwelling,†
When Ulad's‡ three champions lay sleeping in gore—
By the billows of war, which so often, high swelling,
Have wafted these heroes to victory's shore—

We swear to revenge them!—no joy shall be tasted,
The harp shall be silent, the maiden unwed,
Our halls shall be mute, and our fields shall lie wasted,
Till vengeance is wreaked on the murderer's head.

Yes, monarch! though sweet are our home recollections,
Though sweet are the tears that from tenderness fall;
Though sweet are our friendships, our hopes, our affections,
Revenge on a tyrant is sweetest of all!

THE MINSTREL BOY.

The Minstrel Boy to the war is gone,
In the ranks of death you'll find him;
His father's sword he has girded on,
And his wild harp slung behind him.—
"Land of song!" said the warrior-bard,
"Though all the world betrays thee,
One sword, at least, thy rights shall guard,
One faithful harp shall praise thee!"

The Minstrel fell!—but the foeman's chain
Could not bring his proud soul under!
The harp he loved ne'er spoke again,
For he tore its chords asunder;
And said, "No chains shall sully thee,
Thou soul of love and bravery!
Thy songs were made for the pure and free,
They shall never sound in slavery!"

* The words of this song were suggested by the very ancient ish story called "Deirdri, or the Lamentable Fate of the sons of snach," which has been translated literally from the Gaelic, by r. O'Flanagan (see vol. i. of "Transactions of the Gaelic Society Dublin"), and upon which it appears that the "Darthula of Macherson" is founded. The treachery of Conor, king of Ulster, in utting to death the three sons of Usna, was the cause of a desoting war against Ulster, which terminated in the destruction of man. "This story," says Mr. O'Flanagan, "has been, from time immemorial, held in high repute as one of the three tragic stories the Irish. These are, 'The death of the children of Touran;' the death of the children of Lear' (both regarding Tuatha de Danans); and this, 'The death of the children of Usnach,' which is a ilesian story." It will be recollected that, in the second number these Melodies, there is a ballad upon the story of the children Lear or Lir: "Silent, oh Moyle!" &c.
Whatever may be thought of those sanguine claims to antiquity hich Mr. O'Flanagan and others advance for the literature of Ireland, it would be a lasting reproach upon our nationality if the aelic researches of this gentleman did not meet with all the libal encouragement they so well merit.

† "Oh Nasi! view that cloud that I here see in the sky! I see er Eman-green a chilling cloud of blood-tinged red."—*Deirdri's* ?w

‡ Ulster.

LESBIA HATH A BEAMING EYE.

Lesbia hath a beaming eye,
But no-one knows for whom it beameth;
Right and left its arrows fly,
But what they aim at no one dreameth.
Sweeter 'tis to gaze upon
My Nora's lid that seldom rises;
Few its looks, but every one,
Like unexpected light, surprises!
Oh, my Nora Creina, dear,
My gentle, bashful Nora Creina,
Beauty lies
In many eyes,
But Love in yours, my Nora Creina.

Lesbia wears a robe of gold,
But all so close the nymph hath laced it,
Not a charm of beauty's mould
Presumes to stay where nature placed it.
Oh! my Nora's gown for me,
That floats as wild as mountain breezes,
Leaving every beauty free
To sink or swell as Heaven pleases.
Yes, my Nora Creina, dear,
My simple, graceful Nora Creina,
Nature's dress
Is loveliness—
The dress *you* wear, my Nora Creina.

Lesbia hath a wit refined,
But, when its points are gleaming round us
Who can tell if they're designed
To dazzle merely, or to wound us?
Pillowed on my Nora's heart,
In safer slumber Love reposes—
Bed of peace! whose roughest part
Is but the crumpling of the roses.
Oh! my Nora Creina, dear,
My mild, my artless Nora Creina!
Wit, though bright,
Hath no such light,
As warms your eyes, my Nora Creina.

ONE BUMPER AT PARTING.

One bumber at parting!—though many
Have circled the board since we met,
The fullest, the saddest of any,
Remains to be crowned by us yet.
The sweetness that pleasure hath in it,
Is always so slow to come forth,
That seldom, alas! till the minute
It dies, do we know half its worth.
But come—may our life's happy measure
Be all of such moments made up;
They're born on the bosom of Pleasure,
They die 'midst the tears of the cup.

As onward we journey, how pleasant
To pause and inhabit awhile
Those few sunny spots, like the present,
That 'mid the dull wilderness smile!
But Time, like a pitiless master,
Cries "Onward!" and spurs the gay hours
Ah, never doth Time travel faster,
Than when his way lies among flowers
But come—may our life's happy measure
Be all of such moments made up:
They're born on the bosom of Pleasure,
They die 'midst the tears of the cup.

We saw how the sun looked in sinking,
The waters beneath him how bright;
And now, let our farewell of drinking
Resemble that farewell of light.
You saw how he finished, by darting
His beam o'er a deep billow's brim—
So fill up, let's shine at our parting,
In full liquid glory, like him.
And oh! may our life's happy measure
Of moments like this be made up,
'Twas born on the bosom of Pleasure,
It dies 'mid the tears of the cup.

FAREWELL!—BUT WHENEVER YOU WELCOME THE HOUR.

Farewell!—but whenever you welcome the hour,
That awakens the night-song of mirth in your bower,
Then think of the friend who once welcomed it too,
And forgot his own griefs to be happy with you.
His griefs may return, not a hope may remain
Of the few that have brightened his pathway of pain,
But he ne'er will forget the short vision, that threw
Its enchantment around him, while lingering with you.

And still on that evening, when pleasure fills up
To the highest top sparkle each heart and each cup,
Where'er my path lies, be it gloomy or bright,
My soul, happy friends, shall be with you that night;
Shall join in your revels, your sports, and your wiles,
And return to me, beaming all o'er with your smiles—
Too blest, if it tells me that, 'mid the gay cheer,
Some kind voice had murmured, "I wish he were here!"

Let Fate do her worst, there are relics of joy,
Bright dreams of the past, which she can not destroy;
Which come in the night-time of sorrow and care,
And bring back the features that joy used to wear,
Long, long be my heart with such memories fill'd!
Like the vase, in which roses have once been distilled—
You may break, you may shatter the vase, if you will,
But the scent of the roses will hang round it still.

HAS SORROW THY YOUNG DAYS SHADED.

Has sorrow thy young days shaded,
As clouds o'er the morning fleet?
Too fast have those young days faded,
That, even in sorrow, were sweet!
Does Time with his cold wing wither
Each feeling that once was dear?—
Then, child of misfortune, come hither,
I'll weep with thee, tear for tear.

Has love to that soul, so tender,
Been like our Lagenian mine,*
Where sparkles of golden splendor
All over the surface shine—
But, if in pursuit we go deeper,
Allured by the gleam that shone,
Ah! false as the dream of the sleeper,
Like Love, the bright ore is gone.

Has Hope, like the bird in the story,†
That flitted from tree to tree
With the talisman's glittering glory—
Has Hope been that bird to thee?
On branch after branch alighting,
The gem did she still display,
And, when nearest and most inviting,
Then waft the fair gem away?

If thus the young hours have fleeted,
When sorrow itself looked bright;
If thus the fair hope hath cheated,
That led thee along so light;
If thus the cold world now wither
Each feeling that once was dear:—
Come, child of misfortune, come hither,
I'll weep with thee, tear for tear.

NO, NOT MORE WELCOME.

No, not more welcome the fairy numbers
Of music fall on the sleeper's ear,
When half-awaking from fearful slumbers,
He thinks the full choir of heaven is near—
Than came that voice, when, all forsaken,
This heart long had sleeping lain,
Nor thought its cold pulse would ever waken
To such benign, blessed sounds again.

* Our Wicklow Gold Mines, to which this verse alludes, deserves, I fear, but too well the character here given of them.

† "The bird, having got its prize, settled not far off, with the talisman in his mouth. The prince drew near it, hoping it would drop it; but, as he approached, the bird took wing, and settled again."
— *Arabian Nights.*

Sweet voice of comfort! 'twas like the stealing
Of summer wind through some wreathed shell—
Each secret winding, each inmost feeling
Of all my soul echoed to its spell.
'Twas whispered balm—'twas sunshine spoken!—
I'd live years of grief and pain
To have my long sleep of sorrow broken
By such benign, blessed sounds again.

OH! DOUBT ME NOT.

Oh! doubt me not—the season
Is o'er, when Folly made me rove,
And now the vestal, Reason,
Shall watch the fire awaked by Love.
Although this heart was early blown,
And fairest hands disturbed the tree,
They only shook some blossoms down,
Its fruit has all been kept for thee
Then doubt me not—the season
Is o'er, when Folly made me rove,
And now the vestal, Reason,
Shall watch the fire awaked by Love.

And though my lute no longer
May sing of Passion's ardent spell,
Yet, trust me, all the stronger
I feel the bliss I do not tell.
The bee through many a garden roves,
And hums his lay of courtship o'er,
But when he finds the flower he loves,
He settles there, and hums no more.
Then doubt me not—the season
Is o'er, when Folly kept me free,
And now the vestal, Reason,
Shall guard the flame awaked by thee.

YOU REMEMBER ELLEN.*

You remember Ellen, our hamlet's pride,
How meekly she blessed her humble lot,
When the stranger, William, had made her his bride,
And love was the light of their lowly cot.
Together they toiled through winds and rains,
Till William, at length, in sadness said,
"We must seek our fortune on other plains;"—
Then, sighing, she left her lowly shed.

They roamed a long and a weary way,
Nor much was the maiden's heart at ease,
When now, at close of one stormy day,
They see a proud castle among the trees.
"To-night," said the youth, "we'll shelter there;
The wind blows cold, the hour is late:"
So he blew the horn with a chieftain's air,
And the porter bowed, as they passed the gate.

"Now, welcome, Lady!" exclaimed the youth—
"This castle is thine, and these dark woods all!"
She believed him crazed, but his words were truth,
For Ellen is Lady of Rosna Hall!
And dearly the Lord of Rosna loves
What William, the stranger, wooed and wed,
And the light of bliss, in these lordly groves,
Shines pure as it did in the lowly shed.

WHEN FIRST I MET THEE.

When first I met thee, warm and young,
There shone such truth about thee,
And on thy lip such promise hung,
I did not dare to doubt thee.
I saw thee change, yet still relied,
Still clung with hope the fonder,
And thought, though false to all beside,
From me thou couldst not wander.
But go, deceiver! go,
The heart, whose hopes could make it
Trust one so false, so low,
Deserves that thou shouldst break it.

* This ballad was suggested by a well-known and interesting story told of a certain noble family in England.

When every tongue thy follies named,
I fled the unwelcome story;
Or found, in even the faults they blamed,
Some gleams of future glory.
I still was true, when nearer friends
Conspired to wrong, to slight thee;
The heart that now thy falsehood rends
Would then have bled to right thee.
But go, deceiver! go—
Some day, perhaps, thou'lt waken
From pleasure's dream, to know
The grief of hearts forsaken.

Even now, though youth its bloom has shed,
No lights of age adorn thee:
The few, who loved thee once, have fled,
And they, who flatter, scorn thee.
Thy midnight cup is pledged to slaves,
No genial ties enwreath it;
The smiling there, like light on graves,
Has rank cold hearts beneath it.
Go—go—though worlds were thine,
I would not now surrender
One taintless tear of mine
For all thy guilty splendor!

And days may come, thou false one! yet,
When even those ties shall sever;
When thou wilt call, with vain regret,
On her thou'st lost for ever;
On her who, in thy fortune's fall,
With smiles had still received thee,
And gladly died to prove thee all
Her fancy first believed thee.
Go—go—'tis vain to curse,
'Tis weakness to upbraid thee;
Hate can not wish thee worse
Than guilt and shame have made thee.

COME O'ER THE SEA.

COME o'er the sea,
Maiden, with me,
Mine through sunshine, storm, and snows;
Seasons may roll,
But the true soul
Burns the same, where'er it goes.
Let fate frown on, so we love and part not;
'Tis life where *thou* art, 'tis death where thou'rt not.
Then come o'er the sea,
Maiden, with me,
Come wherever the wild wind blows;
Seasons may roll,
But the true soul
Burns the same, where'er it goes.

Was not the sea
Made for the Free,
Land for courts and chains alone?
Here we are slaves,
But, on the waves,
Love and Liberty's all our own.
No eye to watch, and no tongue to wound us,
All earth forgot, and all heaven around us—
Then come o'er the sea,
Maiden, with me,
Mine through sunshine, storm, and snows;
Seasons may roll,
But the true soul
Burns the same, where'er it goes.

WHILE HISTORY'S MUSE.

HILE History's Muse the memorial was keeping
Of all that the dark hand of Destiny weaves,
side her the Genius of Erin stood weeping,
For hers was the story that blotted the leaves.
t oh! how the tear in her eyelids grew bright,
hen, after whole pages of sorrow and shame,
She saw History write,
With a pencil of light
at illumined the whole volume, her Wellington's name.

"Hail Star of my Isle!" said the Spirit, all sparkling
With beams, such as break from her own dewy skies—
"Through ages of sorrow, deserted and darkling,
I've watched for some glory like thine to arise.
For, though Heroes I've numbered, unblest was their lot,
And unhallowed they sleep in the crossways of Fame;—
But oh! there is not
One dishonoring blot
On the wreath that encircles my Wellington's name.

Yet still the last crown of thy toils is remaining,
The grandest, the purest, even *thou* hast yet known;
Though proud was thy task, other nations unchaining,
Far prouder to heal the deep wounds of thy own.
At the foot of that throne for whose weal thou hast stood,
Go, plead for the land that first cradled thy fame,
And, bright o'er the flood
Of her tears and her blood,
Let the rainbow of Hope be her Wellington's name!"

THE TIME I'VE LOST IN WOOING.

THE time I've lost in wooing,
In watching and pursuing
The light, that lies
In woman's eyes,
Has been my heart's undoing.
Though Wisdom oft has sought me,
I scorned the lore she brought me,
My only books
Were woman's looks,
And folly's all they've taught me.

Her smile when Beauty granted,
I hung with gaze enchanted,
Like him the sprite,*
Whom maids by night
Oft meet in glen that's haunted.
Like him, too, Beauty won me,
But while her eyes were on me,
If once their ray
Was turned away,
O! winds could not outrun me.

And are those follies going?
And is my proud heart growing
Too cold or wise
For brilliant eyes
Again to set it glowing?
No, vain, alas! th' endeavor
From bonds so sweet to sever;
Poor Wisdom's chance
Against a glance
Is now as weak as ever.

I SAW FROM THE BEACH.

I SAW from the beach, when the morning was shining,
A bark o'er the waters move gloriously on;
I came when the sun o'er that beach was declining,
The bark was still there, but the waters were gone.

And such is the fate of our life's early promise,
So passing the spring-tide of joy we have known;
Each wave, that we danced on at morning, ebbs from us,
And leaves us, at eve, on the bleak shore alone.

Ne'er tell me of glories, serenely adorning
The close of our day, the calm eve of our night;—
Give me back, give me back the wild freshness of Morning,
Her clouds and her tears are worth Evening's best light.

Oh, who would not welcome that moment's returning,
When passion first waked a new life through his frame,
And his soul, like the wood, that grows precious in burning,
Gave out all its sweets to love's exquisite flame?

* This alludes to a kind of Irish fairy, which is to be met with, they say, in the fields at dusk. As long as you keep your eyes upon him, he is fixed, and in your power; but the moment you look away (and he is ingenious in furnishing some inducement), he vanishes. I had thought that this was the sprite which we call the Leprechaun; but a high authority upon such subjects, Lady Morgan (in a note upon her national and interesting novel, "O'Donnel"), has given a very different account of that goblin.

WHERE IS THE SLAVE?

Oh, where's the slave so lowly,
Condemned to chains unholy,
Who, could he burst
His bonds at first,
Would pine beneath them slowly?
What soul, whose wrongs degrade it,
Would wait till time decayed it,
When thus its wing
At once may spring
To the throne of Him who made it?

Farewell, Erin—farewell, all,
Who live to weep our fall!

Less dear the laurel growing,
Alive, untouched and blowing,
Than that, whose braid
Is plucked to shade
The brows with victory glowing.
We tread the land that bore us,
Her green flag glitters o'er us,
The friends we've tried
Are by our side,
And the foe we hate before us.

Farewell, Erin—farewell, all,
Who live to weep our fall!

COME, REST IN THIS BOSOM.

Come, rest in this bosom, my own stricken deer,
Though the herd have fled from thee, thy home is still here;
Here still is the smile, that no cloud can o'ercast,
And a heart and a hand all thy own to the last.

Oh! what was love made for, if 'tis not the same
Through joy and through torment, through glory and shame?
I know not, I ask not, if guilt's in that heart,
I but know that I love thee, whatever thou art.

Thou hast called me thy Angel in moments of bliss,
And thy Angel I'll be, 'mid the horrors of this—
Through the furnace, unshrinking, thy steps to pursue,
And shield thee, and save thee—or perish there too!

FILL THE BUMPER FAIR.

Fill the bumper fair!
Every drop we sprinkle
O'er the brow of Care
Smooths away a wrinkle.
Wit's electric flame
Ne'er so swiftly passes,
As when through the frame
It shoots from brimming glasses
Fill the bumper fair!
Every drop we sprinkle
O'er the brow of Care
Smooths away a wrinkle.

Sages can, they say,
Grasp the lightning's pinions,
And bring down its ray
From the starred dominions:
So we, Sages, sit,
And, 'mid bumpers bright'ning,
From the Heaven of Wit
Draw down all its lightning.

Wouldst thou know what first
Made our souls inherit
This ennobling thirst
For wine's celestial spirit?
It chanced upon that day,
When, as bards inform us,
Prometheus stole away
The living fires that warm us:

The careless Youth, when up
To Glory's fount aspiring,
Took nor urn nor cup
To hide the pilfered fire in.—
But oh his joy, when, round
The halls of Heaven spying,
Among the stars he found
A bowl of Bacchus lying!

Some drops were in that bowl,
Remains of last night's pleasure,
With which the Sparks of Soul
Mixed their burning treasure.
Hence the goblet's shower
Hath such spells to win us;
Hence its mighty power
O'er that flame within us.
Fill the bumper fair!
Every drop we sprinkle
O'er the brow of Care
Smooths away a wrinkle.

'TIS GONE, AND FOR EVER.

'Tis gone, and for ever, the light we saw breaking,
Like Heaven's first dawn o'er the sleep of the dead—
When Man, from the slumber of ages awaking,
Looked upward, and blessed the pure ray, ere it fled.
'Tis gone, and the gleams it has left of its burning
But deepen the long night of bondage and mourning,
That dark o'er the kingdoms of earth is returning,
And darkest of all, hapless Erin, o'er thee.

For high was thy hope, when those glories were darting
Around thee, through all the gross clouds of the world
When Truth, from her fetters indignantly starting,
At once, like a Sun-burst, her banner unfurled.*
Oh! never shall earth see a moment so splendid!
Then, then—had one Hymn of Deliverance blended
The tongues of all nations—how sweet had ascended
The first note of liberty, Erin, from thee!

But, shame on those tyrants, who envied the blessing!
And shame on the light race, unworthy its good,
Who, at Death's reeking altar, like furies, caressing
The young hope of Freedom, baptized it in blood.
Then vanished for ever that fair, sunny vision,
Which, spite of the slavish, the cold heart's derision,
Shall long be remembered, pure, bright, and elysian,
As first it arose, my lost Erin, on thee!

MY GENTLE HARP.

My gentle Harp, once more I waken
The sweetness of thy slumb'ring strain;
In tears our last farewell was taken,
And now in tears we meet again.
No light of joy hath o'er thee broken,
But, like those Harps whose heavenly skill
Of slavery, dark as thine, hath spoken,
Thou hang'st upon the willows still.

And yet, since last thy chord resounded,
An hour of peace and triumph came,
And many an ardent bosom bounded
With hopes—that now are turned to shame.
Yet even then, while Peace was singing
Her halcyon song o'er land and sea,
Though joy and hope to others bringing,
She only brought new tears to thee.

Then, who can ask for notes of pleasure,
My drooping Harp, from chords like thine?
Alas! the lark's gay morning measure
As ill would suit the swan's decline!
Or how shall I, who love, who bless thee,
Invoke thy breath for Freedom's strains,
When even the wreaths in which I dress thee,
Are sadly mixed—half flowers, half chains?

But come—if yet thy frame can borrow
One breath of joy, oh, breathe for me,
And show the world, in chains and sorrow,
How sweet thy music still can be;

* "The Sun-burst" was the fanciful name given by the ancient Irish to the royal banner

How gayly, even 'mid gloom surrounding,
Thou yet canst wake at pleasure's thrill—
Like Memnon's broken image sounding,
'Mid desolation tuneful still!*

DEAR HARP OF MY COUNTRY.

Dear Harp of my Country! in darkness I found thee,
The cold chain of silence had hung o'er thee long,†
When proudly, my own Island Harp, I unbound thee,
And gave all thy chords to light, freedom, and song!
The warm lay of love and the light note of gladness
Have wakened thy fondest, thy liveliest thrill;
But, so oft hast thou echoed the deep sigh of sadness,
That even in thy mirth it will steal from thee still.

Dear Harp of my Country! farewell to thy numbers,
This sweet wreath of song is the last we shall twine!
Go, sleep with the sunshine of Fame on thy slumbers,
Till touched by some hand less unworthy than mine;
If the pulse of the patriot, soldier, or lover,
Have throbbed at our lay, 'tis thy glory alone;
I was *but* as the wind, passing heedlessly over,
And all the wild sweetness I waked was thy own.

IN THE MORNING OF LIFE.

In the morning of life, when its cares are unknown,
And its pleasures in all their new lustre begin,
When we live in a bright-beaming world of our own,
And the light that surrounds us is all from within;
Oh 'tis not, believe me, in that happy time
We can love, as in hours of less transport we may;—
Of our smiles, of our hopes, 'tis the gay sunny prime,
But affection is truest when these fade away.

When we see the first glory of youth pass us by,
Like a leaf on the stream that will never return;
When our cup, which had sparkled with pleasure so high,
First tastes of the *other*, the dark-flowing urn;
Then, then is the time when affection holds sway
With a depth and a tenderness joy never knew;
Love, nursed among pleasures, is faithless as they,
But the love born of Sorrow, like Sorrow, is true.

In climes full of sunshine, though splendid the flowers,
Their sighs have no freshness, their odor no worth;
'Tis the cloud and the mist of our own Isle of Showers,
That call the rich spirit of fragrancy forth.
So it is not 'mid splendor, prosperity, mirth,
That the depth of Love's generous spirit appears;
To the sunshine of smiles it may first owe its birth,
But the soul of its sweetness is drawn out by tears.

AS SLOW OUR SHIP.

As slow our ship her foamy track
Against the wind was cleaving,
Her trembling pennant still looked back
To that dear Isle 'twas leaving.
So loath we part from all we love,
From all the links that bind us;
So turn our hearts as on we rove,
To those we've left behind us.

When, round the bowl, of vanished years
We talk, with joyous seeming—
With smiles that might as well be tears,
So faint, so sad their beaming;
While mem'ry brings us back again
Each early tie that twined us,
Oh, sweet's the cup that circles then
To those we've left behind us.

And when, in other climes, we meet
Some isle, or vale enchanting,
Where all looks flow'ry, wild, and sweet,
And naught but love is wanting;
We think how great had been our bliss,
If Heaven had but assigned us
To live and die in scenes like this,
With some we've left behind us!

As trav'llers oft look back at eve,
When eastward darkly going,
To gaze upon that light they leave
Still faint behind them glowing—
So, when the close of pleasure's day
To gloom hath near consigned us,
We turn to catch one fading ray
Of joy that's left behind us.

WHEN COLD IN THE EARTH.

When cold in the earth lies the friend thou hast loved,
Be his faults and his follies forgot by thee then;
Or, if from their slumber the veil be removed,
Weep o'er them in silence, and close it again.
And oh! if 'tis pain to remember how far
From the pathways of light he was tempted to roam,
Be it bliss to remember that thou wert the star
That arose on his darkness, and guided him home.

From thee and thy innocent beauty first came
The revealings, that taught him true love to adore,
To feel the bright presence, and turn him with shame
From the idols he blindly had knelt to before.
O'er the waves of a life, long benighted and wild,
Thou camest, like a soft golden calm o'er the sea;
And if happiness purely and glowingly smiled
On his evening horizon, the light was from thee.

And though, sometimes, the shades of past folly might rise,
And though falsehood again would allure him to stray,
He but turned to the glory that dwelt in those eyes,
And the folly, the falsehood, soon vanished away.
As the Priests of the Sun, when their altar grew dim,
At the day-beam alone could its lustre repair,
So, if virtue a moment grew languid in him,
He but flew to that smile, and rekindled it there.

REMEMBER THEE.

Remember thee? yes, while there's life in this heart,
It shall never forget thee, all lorn as thou art;
More dear in thy sorrow, thy gloom, and thy showers,
Than the rest of the world in their sunniest hours.

Wert thou all that I wish thee, great, glorious, and free,
First flower of the earth, and first gem of the sea,
I might hail thee with prouder, with happier brow,
But oh! could I love thee more deeply than now?

No, thy chains as they rankle, thy blood as it runs,
But make thee more painfully dear to thy sons—
Whose hearts, like the young of the desert-bird's nest,
Drink love in each life-drop that flows from thy breast.

WHENE'ER I SEE THOSE SMILING EYES.

Whene'er I see those smiling eyes,
So full of hope, and joy, and light,
As if no cloud could ever rise,
To dim a heaven so purely bright—
I sigh to think how soon that brow
In grief may lose its every ray,
And that light heart, so joyous now,
Almost forget it once was gay.

For time will come with all its blights,
The ruined hope, the friend unkind,
And love, that leaves, where'er it lights,
A chilled or burning heart behind:—
While youth, that now like snow appears,
Ere sullied by the dark'ning rain,
When once 'tis touched by sorrow's tears
Can never shine so bright again.

* "Dimidio magicæ resonant ubi Memnone chordæ."—Juvenal.

† In that rebellious but beautiful song, "When Erin first rose," there is, if I recollect right, the following line:—

"The dark chain of Silence was thrown o'er the deep."

The chain of Silence was a sort of practical figure of rhetoric among the ancient Irish. Walker tells us of "a celebrated contention for precedence between Finn and Gaul, near Finn's palace at Almhaim, where the attending Bards, anxious, if possible, to produce a cessation of hostilities, shook the chain of Silence, and flung themselves among the ranks." See also the "Ode to Gaul, the Son of Morni," in Miss Brooke's "Reliques of Irish Poetry."

WREATH THE BOWL.

Wreath the bowl
With flowers of soul,
The brightest Wit can find us
We'll take a flight
Toward heaven to-night,
And leave dull earth behind us.
Should Love amid
The wreaths be hid,
That Joy, th' enchanter, brings us,
No danger fear,
While wine is near,
We'll drown him if he stings us;
Then, wreath the bowl
With flowers of soul,
The brightest Wit can find us;
We'll take a flight
Toward heaven to-night,
And leave dull earth behind us.

'Twas nectar fed
Of old, 'tis said,
Their Junos, Joves, Apollos;
And man may brew
His nectar too,
The rich receipt's as follows:
Take wine like this,
Let looks of bliss
Around it well be blended,
Then bring Wit's beam
To warm the stream,
And there's your nectar, splendid!
So wreath the bowl
With flowers of soul,
The brightest Wit can find us,
We'll take a flight
Toward heaven to-night,
And leave dull earth behind us.

Say, why did Time,
His glass sublime,
Fill up with sands unsightly,
When wine, he knew,
Runs brisker through,
And sparkles far more brightly?
Oh, lend it us,
And, smiling thus,
The glass in two we'll sever,
Make pleasure glide
In double tide,
And fill both ends for ever!
Then wreath the bowl
With flowers of soul,
The brightest Wit can find us;
We'll take a flight
Toward heaven to-night,
And leave dull earth behind us,

IF THOU'LT BE MINE.

If thou'lt be mine, the treasures of air,
Of earth, and sea, shall lie at thy feet,
Whatever in Fancy's eye looks fair,
Or in Hope's sweet music sounds *most* sweet,
Shall be ours—if thou wilt be mine, love!

Bright flowers shall bloom wherever we rove,
A voice divine shall talk in each stream;
The stars shall look like worlds of love,
And this earth be all one beautiful dream
In our eyes—if thou wilt be mine, love!

And thoughts, whose source is hidden and high,
Like streams, that come from heavenward hills,
Shall keep our hearts, like meads, that lie
To be bathed by those eternal rills,
Ever green, if thou wilt be mine, love

All this and more the Spirit of Love
Can breathe o'er them who feel his spells
That heaven, which forms his home above,
He can make on earth, wherever he dwells,
As thou'lt own—if thou wilt be mine, love!

TO LADIES' EYES.

To ladies' eyes around, boy,
We can't refuse, we can't refuse,
Though bright eyes so abound, boy,
'Tis hard to choose, 'tis hard to choose.
For thick as stars that lighten
Yon airy bowers, yon airy bowers,
The countless eyes that brighten
This earth of ours, this earth of ours.
But fill the cup—where'er, boy,
Our choice may fall, our choice may fall,
We're sure to find Love there, boy,
So drink them all! so drink them all!

Some looks there are so holy,
They seem but given, they seem but given,
As shining beacons solely,
To light to heaven, to light to heaven.
While some—oh! ne'er believe them—
With tempting ray, with tempting ray,
Would lead us (God forgive them!)
The other way, the other way.
But fill the cup—where'er, boy,
Our choice may fall, our choice may fall,
We're sure to find Love there, boy,
So drink them all! so drink them all!

In some, as in a mirror,
Love seems portrayed, Love seems portrayed,
But shun the flatt'ring error,
'Tis but his shade, 'tis but his shade.
Himself has fixed his dwelling
In eyes we know, in eyes we know,
And lips—but this is telling—
So here they go! so here they go!
Fill up, fill up—where'er, boy,
Our choice may fall, our choice may fall,
We're sure to find Love there, boy,
So drink them all! so drink them all!

THEY MAY RAIL AT THIS LIFE.

They may rail at this life—from the hour I began it,
I found it a life full of kindness and bliss;
And, until they can show me some happier planet,
More social and bright, I'll content me with this.
As long as the world has such lips and such eyes,
As before me this moment enraptured I see,
They may say what they will of their orbs in the skies,
But this earth is the planet for you, love, and me.

In Mercury's star, where each moment can bring them
New sunshine and wit from the fountain on high,
Though the nymphs may have livelier poets to sing them,*
They've none, even there, more enamored than I.
And, as long as this harp can be wakened to love,
And that eye its divine inspiration shall be,
They may talk as they will of their Edens above,
But this earth is the planet for you, love, and me.

In that star of the west, by whose shadowy splendor,
At twilight so often we've roamed through the dew,
There are maidens, perhaps, who have bosoms as tender
And look, in their twilights, as lovely as you.†
But though they were even more bright than the queen
Of that isle they inhabit in heaven's blue sea,
As I never those fair young celestials have seen,
Why—this earth is the planet for you, love, and me.

As for those chilly orbs on the verge of creation,
Where sunshine and smiles must be equally rare,
Did they want a supply of cold hearts for that station,
Heaven knows we have plenty on earth we could spare.
Oh! think what a world we should have of it here,
If the haters of peace, of affection, and glee,
Were to fly up to Saturn's comfortless sphere,
And leave earth to such spirits as you, love, and me!

* Tous les habitans de Mercure sont vifs.—*Pluralite des Mondes.*

† La terre pourra être pour Vénus l'étoile du berger et la mère des amours, comme Venus l'est pour nous.—*Pluralite des Mondes*

FORGET NOT THE FIELD.

Forget not the field where they perished,
  The truest, the last of the brave,
All gone—and the bright hope we cherished
  Gone with them, and quenched in their grave!

Oh! could we from death but recover
  Those hearts as they bounded before,
In the face of high heaven, to fight over
  That combat for freedom once more;—

Could the chain for an instant be riven
  Which Tyranny flung round us then,
No, 'tis not in Man, nor in Heaven,
  To let Tyranny bind it again!

But 'tis past—and, though blazoned in story
  The name of our Victor may be,
Accursed is the march of that glory
  Which treads o'er the hearts of the free.

Far dearer the grave or the prison,
  Illumed by one patriot name,
Than the trophies of all, who have risen
  On Liberty's ruins to fame.

SAIL ON, SAIL ON.

Sail on, sail on, thou fearless bark—
  Wherever blows the welcome wind,
It can not lead to scenes more dark,
  More sad than those we leave behind.
Each wave that passes seems to say,
  "Though death beneath our smile may be,
Less cold we are, less false than they,
  Whose smiling wrecked thy hopes and thee."

Sail on, sail on—through endless space—
  Through calm—through tempest—stop no more:
The stormiest sea's a resting place
  To him who leaves such hearts on shore.
Or—if some desert land we meet,
  Where never yet false-hearted men
Profaned a world, that else were sweet—
  Then rest thee, bark, but not till then.

ST. SENANUS AND THE LADY.

ST. SENANUS.*

"Oh! haste and leave this sacred isle,
Unholy bark, ere morning smile;
For on thy deck, though dark it be,
  A female form I see;
And I have sworn this sainted sod
Shall ne'er by woman's feet be trod."

THE LADY.

"Oh! Father, send not hence my bark,
Through wintry winds and billows dark:
I come with humble heart to share
  Thy morn and evening prayer:
Nor mine the feet, oh! holy Saint,
The brightness of thy sod to taint."

The Lady's prayer Senanus spurned;
The winds blew fresh, the bark returned;
But legends hint, that had the maid
  Till morning's light delayed;
And given the saint one rosy smile,
She ne'er had left his lonely isle.

* In a metrical life of St. Senanus, which is taken from an old ...lkenny MS., and may be found among the *Acta Sanctorum Hi-...ernicæ*, we are told of his flight to the island of Scattery, and his ...esolution not to admit any woman of the party; and that he re-...used to receive even a sister saint, St. Cannera, whom an angel ...ad taken to the island for the express purpose of introducing her ...o him. The following was the ungracious answer of St. Senanus, ...ccording to his poetical biographer:—

"*Cui Præsul, quid fœminis*
Commune est cum monachis?
Nec te nec ullam aliam
Admittemus in insulam."

See the *Acta Sanct. Hib.*, page 610.

According to Dr. Ledwich, St. Senanus was no less a personage ...an the river Shannon; but O'Connor and other antiquarians deny ...e metamorphose indignantly.

THE PARALLEL.

Yes, sad one of Sion,* if closely resembling,
  In shame and in sorrow, thy withered-up heart—
If drinking deep, deep, of the same "cup of trembling,"—
  Could make us thy children, our parent thou art.

Like thee doth our nation lie conquered and broken,
  And fallen from her head is the once royal crown;
In her streets, in her halls, Desolation hath spoken,
  And "while it is day yet, her sun hath gone down."†

Like thine doth her exile, 'mid dreams of returning,
  Die far from the home it were life to behold;
Like thine do her sons, in the day of their mourning,
  Remember the bright things that blessed them of old.

Ah, well may we call her, like thee, "the Forsaken,"‡
  Her boldest are vanquished, her proudest are slaves;
And the harps of her minstrels, when gayest they waken,
  Have tones 'mid their mirth like the wind over graves!

Yet hadst thou thy vengeance—yet came there the morrow
  That shines out, at last, on the longest dark night,
When the sceptre that smote thee with slavery and sorrow,
  Was shivered at once, like a reed, in thy sight.

When that cup, which for others the proud Golden City‖
  Had brimmed full of bitterness, drenched her own lips;
And the world she had trampled on heard, without pity,
  The howl in her halls, and the cry from her ships.

When the curse Heaven keeps for the haughty came over
  Her merchants rapacious, her rulers unjust,
And a ruin, at last, for the earthworm to cover,§
  The Lady of Kingdoms¶ lay low in the dust.

DRINK OF THIS CUP.

Drink of this cup; you'll find there's a spell in
  Its every drop 'gainst the ills of mortality.
Talk of the cordial that sparkled for Helen!
  Her cup was a fiction, but this is reality.
Would you forget the dark world we are in,
  Just taste of the bubble that gleams on the top of it;
But would you rise above earth, till akin
  To Immortals themselves, you must drain every drop of it,
Send round the cup—for oh, there's a spell in
  Its every drop 'gainst the ills of mortality:
Talk of the cordial that sparkled for Helen!
  Her cup was a fiction, but this is reality.

Never was philter formed with such power
  To charm and bewilder as this we are quaffing;
Its magic began when, in Autumn's rich hour,
  A harvest of gold in the fields it stood laughing.
There having, by Nature's enchantment, been filled
  With the balm and the bloom of her kindliest weather,
This wonderful juice from its core was distilled
  To enliven such hearts as are here brought together.
Then drink of the cup—you'll find there's a spell in
  Its every drop 'gainst the ills of mortality:
Talk of the cordial that sparkled for Helen!
  Her cup was a fiction, but this is reality.

And though, perhaps—but breathe it to no one—
  Like liquor the witch brew sat midnight so awful,
This philter in secret was first taught to flow on,
  Yet 'ts n't less potent for being unlawful.
And, ev'n though it taste of the smoke of that flame,
  Which in silence extracted its virtue forbidden—
Fill up—there's a fire in some hearts I could name,
  Which may work to its charm, though as lawless and hidden.
So drink of the cup—for oh there's a spell in
  Its every drop 'gainst the ills of mortality:
Talk of the cordial that sparkled for Helen!
  Her cup was a fiction, but this is reality.

* These verses were written after the perusal of a treatise by Mr. Hamilton, professing to prove that the Irish were originally Jews.

† "Her sun is gone down while it was yet day."—*Jer.* xv. 9.

‡ "Thou shalt no more be termed Forsaken."—*Isaiah*, lxii. 4.

‖ "How hath the oppressor ceased! the golden city ceased!"—*Isaiah*, xiv. 4.

§ "Thy pomp is brought down to the grave . . . . . . and the worms cover thee."—*Isaiah* xiv. 11.

¶ "Thou shalt no more be called the Lady of Kingdoms."—*Isaiah*, xlvii. 5.

OH FOR THE SWORDS OF FORMER TIME!

Oh for the swords of former time!
  Oh for the men who bore them,
When armed, for Right they stood sublime,
  And tyrant's crouched before them:
When free yet, ere courts began
  With honors to enslave him,
The best honors worn by Man
  Were those which virtue gave him.
Oh for the swords, &c., &c.

Oh for the Kings who flourished then!
  Oh for the pomp that crowned them,
When hearts and hands of freeborn men
  Were all the ramparts round them:
When, safe built on bosoms true,
  The throne was but the centre,
Round which Love a circle drew,
  That Treason durst not enter.
Oh for the Kings who flourished then!
  Oh for the pomp that crowned them,
When hearts and hands of freeborn men
  Were all the ramparts round them!

NE'ER ASK THE HOUR.

Ne'er ask the hour—what is it to us
  How Time deals out his treasures?
The golden moments lent us thus
  Are not *his* coin, but Pleasure's.
If counting them o'er could add to their blisses,
  I'd number each glorious second:
But moments of joy are, like Lesbia's kisses,
  Too quick and sweet to be reckoned.
Then fill the cup—what is it to us
  How Time his circle measures?
The fairy hours we call up thus,
  Obey no wand but Pleasure's.

Young Joy ne'er thought of counting hours,
  Till Care, one summer's morning,
Set up, among his smiling flowers,
  A dial, by way of warning.
But Joy loved better to gaze on the sun,
  As long as its light was glowing,
Than to watch with old Care how the shadow stole on,
  And how fast that light was going.
So fill the cup—what is it to us
  How Time his circle measures?
The fairy hours we call up thus,
  Obey no wand, but Pleasure's.

THE FORTUNE-TELLER.

Down in the valley come meet me to-night,
  And I'll tell you your fortune truly
As ever was told, by the new moon's light,
  To a young maiden, shining as newly.

But, for the world, let no one be nigh,
  Lest haply the stars should deceive me;
Such secrets between you and me and the sky
  Should never go farther, believe me.

If at that hour the heavens be not dim,
  My science shall call up before you
A male apparition—the image of him
  Whose destiny 'tis to adore you.

And if to that phantom you'll be kind,
  So fondly around you he'll hover,
You'll hardly, my dear, any difference find
  'Twixt him and a true living lover.

Down at your feet, in the pale moonlight,
  He'll kneel, with a warmth of devotion—
An ardor, of which such an innocent sprite
  You'd scarcely believe had a notion.

What other thoughts and events may arise,
  As in destiny's book I've not seen them,
Must only be left to the stars and your eyes
  To settle, ere morning, between them.

OH, YE DEAD!

Oh, ye Dead! oh, ye Dead!* whom we know by the light
    you give
From your cold gleaming eyes, though you move like men
    who live,
      Why leave you thus your graves,
      In far-off fields and waves,
Where the worm and the sea-bird only know your bed,
      To haunt this spot where all
      Those eyes that wept your fall,
And the hearts that wailed you, like your own, lie dead?

It is true, it is true, we are shadows cold and wan;
And the fair and the brave whom we loved on earth are gone.
      But still thus even in death,
      So sweet the living breath
Of the fields and the flowers in our youth we wandered o'er,
      That ere, condemned, we go
      To freeze 'mid Hecla's snow,
We would taste it awhile, and think we live once more!

O'DONOHUE'S MISTRESS.

Of all the fair months that round the sun
In light-linked dance their circles run,
  Sweet May, shine thou for me:
For still, when thy earliest beams arise,
That youth, who beneath the blue lake lies,
  Sweet May, returns to me.

Of all the bright haunts where daylight leaves
Its lingering smile on golden eves,
  Fair Lake, thou'rt dearest to me:
For when the last April sun grows dim,
Thy Naïads prepare his steed† for him
  Who dwells, bright Lake, in thee.

Of all the proud steeds that ever bore
Young plumed Chiefs on sea or shore,
  White Steed, most joy to thee;
Who still, with the first young glance of spring,
From under that glorious lake dost bring
  My love, my chief, to me.

While, white as the sail some bark unfurls,
When newly launched, thy long mane‡ curls,
  Fair Steed, as white and free;
And spirits, from all the lake's deep bowers,
Glide o'er the blue wave scattering flowers,
  Around my love and thee.

Of all the sweet deaths that maidens die,
Whose lovers beneath the cold wave lie,
  Most sweet that death will be,
Which, under the next May evening's light,
When thou and thy steed are lost to sight,
  Dear love, I'll die for thee.

THEE, THEE, ONLY THEE.

The dawning of morn, the daylight's sinking,
The night's long hours still find me thinking
    Of thee, thee, only thee.
When friends are met, and goblets crowned,
  And smiles are near, that once enchanted,
Unreached by all that sunshine round,
  My soul, like some dark spot is haunted
    By thee, thee, only thee.

* Paul Zealand mentions that there is a mountain in some part of Ireland, where the ghosts of persons who have died in foreign lands walk about and converse with those they meet, like living people. If asked why they do not return to their homes, they say they are obliged to go to Mount Hecla, and disappear immediately.

† The particulars of the tradition respecting O'Donohue and his White Horse, may be found in Mr. Weld's Account of Killarney, or more fully detailed in Derrick's Letters. For many years after his death, the spirit of this hero is supposed to have been seen on the morning of May-day, gliding over the lake on his favorite white horse, to the sound of sweet unearthly music, and preceded by groups of youths and maidens, who flung wreaths of delicate spring flowers in his path.

Among other stories connected with this Legend of the Lakes, it is said that there was a young and beautiful girl whose imagination was so impressed with the idea of this visionary chieftain, that she fancied herself in love with him, and at last, in a fit of insanity, on a May-morning, threw herself into the lake.

‡ The boatmen at Killarney call those waves which come on a windy day, crested with foam, "O'Donohue's white horses."

Whatever in fame's high path could waken
My spirit once, is now forsaken
For thee, thee, only thee.
Like shores, by which some headlong bark
To the ocean hurries, resting never,
Life's scenes go by me, bright or dark,
I know not, heed not, hastening ever
To thee, thee, only thee.

I have not a joy but of thy bringing,
And pain itself seems sweet when springing
From thee, thee, only thee.
Like spells that naught on earth can break,
Till lips, that know the charm, have spoken,
This heart, howe'er the world may wake
Its grief, its scorn, can but be broken
By thee, thee, only thee.

ECHO.

How sweet the answer Echo makes
To music at night,
When, roused by lute or horn, she wakes,
And far away, o'er lawns and lakes,
Goes answering light.

Yet Love hath echoes truer far,
And far more sweet,
Than e'er beneath the moonlight's star,
Of horn, or lute, or soft guitar,
The songs repeat.

'Tis when the sigh, in youth sincere,
And only then—
The sigh that's breathed for one to hear,
Is by that one, that only dear,
Breathed back again!

OH BANQUET NOT.

Oh banquet not in those shining bowers,
Where Youth resorts, but come to me:
For mine's a garden of faded flowers,
More fit for sorrow, for age, and thee.
And there we shall have our feast of tears,
And many a cup in silence pour;
Our guests, the shades of former years,
Our toasts, to lips that bloom no more.

There, while the myrtle's withering boughs
Their lifeless leaves around us shed,
We'll brim the bowl to broken vows,
To friends long lost, the changed, the dead.
Or, while some blighted laurel waves
Its branches o'er the dreary spot,
We'll drink to those neglected graves,
Where valor sleeps, unnamed, forgot.

THE MOUNTAIN SPRITE.

In yonder valley there dwelt, alone,
A youth, whose moments had calmly flown,
Till spells came o'er him, and, day and night,
He was haunted and watched by a Mountain Sprite.

As once, by moonlight, he wandered o'er
The golden sands of that island shore,
A foot-print sparkled before his sight—
'Twas the fairy foot of the Mountain Sprite!

Beside a fountain, one sunny day,
As bending over the stream he lay,
There peeped down o'er him two eyes of light,
And he saw in that mirror the Mountain Sprite.

He turned, but, lo, like a startled bird,
That spirit fled!—and the youth but heard
Sweet music, such as marks the flight
Of some bird of song, from the Mountain Sprite.

One night, still haunted by that bright look,
The boy, bewildered, his pencil took,
And, guided only by memory's light,
Drew the once-seen form of the Mountain Sprite.

"Oh thou, who lovest the shadow," cried
A voice, low whispering by his side,
"Now turn and see,"—here the youth's delight
Sealed the rosy lips of the Mountain Sprite.

"Of all the Spirits of land and sea,"
Then rapt he murmured, "there's none like thee,
"And oft, oh oft, may thy foot thus light
In this lonely bower, sweet Mountain Sprite!"

SWEET INNISFALLEN.

Sweet Innisfallen, fare thee well,
May calm and sunshine long be thine!
How fair thou art let others tell—
To *feel* how fair shall long be mine.

Sweet Innisfallen, long shall dwell
In memory's dream that sunny smile,
Which o'er thee on that evening fell,
When first I saw thy fairy isle.

'Twas light, indeed, too blest for one,
Who had to turn to paths of care—
Through crowded haunts again to run,
And leave thee bright and silent there;

No more unto thy shores to come,
But, on the world's rude ocean tost,
Dream of thee sometimes, as a home
Of sunshine he had seen and lost.

Far better in thy weeping hours
To part from thee, as I do now,
When mist is o'er thy blooming bowers,
Like sorrow's veil on beauty's brow.

For, though unrivalled still thy grace,
Thou dost not look, as then, *too* blest,
But thus in shadow, seem'st a place
Where erring man might hope to rest—

Might hope to rest, and find in thee
A gloom like Eden's, on the day
He left its shade, when every tree,
Like thine, hung weeping o'er his way.

Weeping or smiling, lovely isle!
And all the lovelier for thy tears—
For though but rare thy sunny smile,
'Tis heaven's own glance when it appears.

Like feeling hearts, whose joys are few,
But, when *indeed* they come, divine—
The brightest light the sun e'er threw
Is lifeless to one gleam of thine!

QUICK! WE HAVE BUT A SECOND.

Quick! we have but a second,
Fill round the cup, while you may;
For Time, the churl, hath beckoned,
And we must away, away!
Grasp the pleasure that's flying,
For oh, not Orpheus' strain
Could keep sweet hours from dying,
Or charm them to life again.
Then, quick! we have but a second,
Fill round the cup, while you may;
For Time, the churl, hath beckoned,
And we must away, away!

See the glass, how it flushes,
Like some young Hebe's lip,
And half meets thine, and blushes
That thou shouldst delay to sip.
Shame, oh shame unto thee,
If ever thou seest that day,
When a cup or lip shall woo thee,
And turn untouched away!
Then, quick! we have but a second,
Fill round, fill round, while you may
For Time, the churl, hath beckoned,
And we must away, away!

FAIREST! PUT ON AWHILE.

Fairest! put on awhile
These pinions of light I bring thee,
And o'er thine own Green Isle
In fancy let me wing thee.
Never did Ariel's plume,
At golden sunset hover
O'er scenes so full of bloom,
As I shall waft thee over.

Fields, where the Spring delays,
And fearlessly meets the ardor
Of the warm Summer's gaze,
With only her tears to guard her.
Rocks, through myrtle boughs
In grace majestic frowning;
Like some bold warrior's brows
That Love hath just been crowning.

Islets, so freshly fair,
That never hath bird come nigh them,
But from his course through air
He hath been won down by them;—*
Types, sweet maid of thee,
Whose look, whose blush inviting,
Never did Love yet see
From Heaven, without alighting.

Lakes, where the pearl lies hid,†
And caves, where the gem is sleeping,
Bright as the tears thy lid
Lets fall in lonely weeping.
Glens,‡ where Ocean comes,
To 'scape the wild wind's rancor,
And Harbors, worthiest homes
Where Freedom's fleet can anchor.

Then, if, while scenes so grand,
So beautiful, shine before thee,
Pride for thy own dear land
Should haply be stealing o'er thee,
Oh, let grief come first,
O'er pride itself victorious—
Thinking how man hath curst
What Heaven had made so glorious!

OH, THE SIGHT ENTRANCING.

Oh, the sight entrancing,
When morning's beam is glancing
O'er files arrayed
With helm and blade,
And plumes, in the gay wind dancing!
When hearts are all high beating,
And the trumpet's voice repeating
That song, whose breath
May lead to death,
But never to retreating.
Oh the sight entrancing,
When morning's beam is glancing
O'er files arrayed,
With helm and blade,
And plumes, in the gay wind dancing.

Yet, 'tis not helm or feather—
For ask yon despot, whether
His plumed bands
Could bring such hands
And hearts as ours together.
Leave pomps to those who need 'em—
Give man but heart and freedom,
And proud he braves
The gaudiest slaves
That crawl where monarchs lead 'em.

The sword may pierce the beaver,
Stone walls in time may sever,
'Tis mind alone,
Worth steel and stone,
That keeps men free for ever.
Oh that sight entrancing,
When the morning's beam is glancing,
O'er files arrayed
With helm and blade,
And in Freedom's cause advancing!

AND DOTH NOT A MEETING LIKE THIS.

And doth not a meeting like this make amends,
For all the long years I've been wandering away—
To see thus around me my youth's early friends,
As smiling and kind as in that happy day?
Though haply o'er some of your brows, as o'er mine,
The snow-fall of time may be stealing—what then?
Like Alps in the sunset, thus lighted by wine,
We'll wear the gay tinge of youth's roses again.

What softened remembrances come o'er the heart,
In gazing on those we've been lost to so long!
The sorrows, the joys, of which once they were part,
Still round them, like visions of yesterday, throng,
As letters some hand hath invisible traced,
When held to the flame will steal out on the sight,
So many a feeling, that long seemed effaced,
The warmth of a moment like this brings to light.

And thus, as in memory's bark we shall glide,
To visit the scenes of our boyhood anew,
Though oft we may see, looking down on the tide,
The wreck of full many a hope shining through;
Yet still, as in fancy we point to the flowers,
That once made a garden of all the gay shore,
Deceived for a moment, we'll think them still ours,
And breathe the fresh air of life's morning once more.*

So brief our existence, a glimpse, at the most,
Is all we can have of the few we hold dear;
And oft even joy is unheeded and lost,
For want of some heart, that could echo it, near.
Ah, well may we hope, when this short life is gone,
To meet in some world of more permanent bliss,
For a smile, or a grasp of the hand, hastening on,
Is all we enjoy of each other in this.†

But, come, the more rare such delights to the heart,
The more we should welcome and bless them the more;
They're ours, when we meet—they are lost when we part,
Like birds that bring summer, and fly when 'tis o'er.
Thus circling the cup, hand in hand, ere we drink,
Let Sympathy pledge us, through pleasure, through pain.
Then, fast as a feeling but touches one link,
Her magic shall send it direct through the chain.

'TWAS ONE OF THOSE DREAMS.‡

'Twas one of those dreams, that by music are brought,
Like a bright summer haze, o'er the poet's warm thought—
When, lost in the future, his soul wanders on,
And all of this life, but its sweetness, is gone.

The wild notes he heard o'er the water were those
He had taught to sing Erin's dark bondage and woes,
And the breath of the bugle now wafted them o'er
From Dinis' green isle, to Glenà's wooded shore.

He listened—while, high o'er the eagle's rude nest,
The lingering sounds on their way loved to rest;
And the echoes sung back from their full mountain choir,
As if loth to let song so enchanting expire.

* In describing the Skeligs (islands of the Barony of Forth), Dr. Keating says, "There is a certain attractive virtue in the soil, which draws down all the birds that attempt to fly over it, and obliges them to light upon the rock."

† "Nennius, a British writer of the ninth century, mentions the abundance of pearls in Ireland. *Their* princes, he says, hung them behind their ears: and this we find confirmed by a present made A. C. 1094, by Gilbert, Bishop of Limerick, to Anselm, Archbishop of Canterbury, of a considerable quantity of Irish pearls."—*O'Halloran.*

‡ Glengariff.

* "Jours charmans, quand je songe a vos heureux instans,
Je pense remonter le fleuve de mes ans;
Et mon cœur, enchante sur sa rive fleurie,
Respire encore l'air pur du matin de la vie."

† The same thought has been happily expressed by my friend Mr. Washington Irving, in his *Bracebridge Hall*, vol. i., p. 213. The sincere pleasure which I feel in calling this gentleman my friend, is much enhanced by the reflection that he is too good an American to have admitted me so readily to such a distinction, if he had not known that my feelings toward the great and free country that gave him birth, have been long such as every real lover of the liberty and happiness of the human race must entertain.

‡ Written during a visit to Lord Kenmare, at Killarney.

It seemed as if every sweet note, that died here,
Was again brought to life in some airier sphere,
Some heaven in those hills, where the soul of the strain
That had ceased upon earth was awaking again!

Oh forgive, if, while listening to music, whose breath
Seemed to circle his name with a charm against death,
He should feel a proud Spirit within him proclaim,
"Even so shalt thou live in the echoes of Fame:

Even so, though thy memory should now die away,
'Twill be caught up again in some happier day,
And the hearts and the voices of Erin prolong,
Through the answering Future, thy name and thy song."

AS VANQUISHED ERIN.

As vanquished Erin wept beside
The Boyne's ill-fated river,
She saw where Discord, in the tide,
Had dropped his loaded quiver.
"Lie hid," she cried, "ye venomed darts,
Where mortal eye may shun you;
Lie hid—the stain of manly hearts,
That bled for me, is on you."

But vain her wish, her weeping vain—
As Time too well hath taught her—
Each year the Fiend returns again,
And dives into that water;
And brings, triumphant, from beneath
His shafts of desolation,
And sends them, winged with worse than death,
Through all her maddening nation.

Alas for her who sits and mourns,
Even now, beside that river—
Unwearied still the Fiend returns,
And stored is still his quiver.
"When will this end, ye Powers of Good?"
She weeping asks for ever;
But only hears, from out that flood,
The Demon answer, "Never!"

SHALL THE HARP, THEN, BE SILENT.

SHALL the Harp, then, be silent, when he who first gave
To our country a name, is withdrawn from all eyes?
Shall a Minstrel of Erin stand mute by the grave,
Where the first—where the last of her Patriots lies?

No—faint though the death-song may fall from his lips,
Though his Harp, like his soul, may with shadows be crost,
Yet, yet shall it sound, 'mid a nation's eclipse,
And proclaim to the world what a star hath been lost;—*

What a union of all the affections and powers
By which life is exalted, embellished, refined,
Was embraced in that spirit—whose centre was ours,
While its mighty circumference circled mankind.

Oh, who that loves Erin, or who that can see,
Through the waste of her annals, that epoch sublime—
Like a pyramid raised in the desert—where he
And his glory stand out to the eyes of all time;

That *one* lucid interval, snatched from the gloom
And the madness of ages, when filled with his soul,
A Nation o'erleaped the dark bounds of her doom,
And for *one* sacred instant, touched Liberty's goal?

Who, that ever hath heard him—hath drank at the source
Of that wonderful eloquence, all Erin's own,
In whose high-thoughted daring, the fire, and the force,
And the yet untamed spring of her spirit are shown?

An eloquence rich, wheresoever its wave
Wandered free and triumphant, with thoughts that shone through,
As clear as the brook's "stone of lustre," and gave,
With the flash of the gem, its solidity too.

Who, that ever approached him, when free from the crowd,
In a home full of love, he delighted to tread
'Mong the trees which a nation had given, and which bowed,
As if each brought a new civic crown for his head—

Is there one, who hath thus, through his orbit of life
But at distance observed him—through glory, through blame,
In the calm of retreat, in the grandeur of strife,
Whether shining or clouded, still high and the same—

Oh no, not a heart, that e'er knew him, but mourns
Deep, deep o'er the grave, where such glory is shrined—
O'er a monument Fame will preserve, 'mong the urns
Of the wisest, the bravest, the best of mankind!

* These lines were written on the death of our great patriot, Grattan, in the year 1820. It is only the first two verses that are either intended or fitted to be sung.

DESMOND'S SONG.*

BY the Feal's wave benighted,
No star in the skies,
To thy door by Love lighted,
I first saw those eyes.
Some voice whispered o'er me,
As the threshold I crost,
There was ruin before me,
If I loved, I was lost.

Love came, and brought sorrow
Too soon in his train;
Yet so sweet, that to-morrow
'Twere welcome again.
Though misery's full measure
My portion should be,
I would drain it with pleasure,
If poured out by thee.

You, who call it dishonor
To bow to this flame,
If you've eyes, look but on her,
And blush while you blame.
Hath the pearl less whiteness
Because of its birth?
Hath the violet less brightness
For growing near earth?

No—Man for his glory
To ancestry flies;
But Woman's bright story
Is told in her eyes.
While the Monarch but traces
Through mortals his line,
Beauty, born of the Graces,
Ranks next to Divine!

THOUGH HUMBLE THE BANQUET.

THOUGH humble the banquet to which I invite thee,
Thou'lt find there the best a poor bard can command:
Eyes, beaming with welcome, shall throng round, to light thee,
And Love serve the feast with his own willing hand.

And though Fortune may seem to have turned from the dwelling
Of him thou regardest her favoring ray,
Thou wilt find there a gift, all her treasures excelling,
Which, proudly he feels, hath ennobled his way.

'Tis that freedom of mind, which no vulgar dominion
Can turn from the path a pure conscience approves;
Which, with hope in the heart, and no chain on the pinion,
Holds upward its course to the light which it loves.

'Tis this makes the pride of his humble retreat,
And, with this, though of all other treasures bereaved,
The breeze of his garden to him is more sweet
Than the costliest incense that Pomp e'er received.

* "Thomas, the heir of the Desmond family, had accidentally been so engaged in the chase, that he was benighted near Tralee, and obliged to take shelter at the Abbey of Feal, in the house of one of his dependants, called Mac Cormac. Catherine, a beautiful daughter of his host, instantly inspired the earl with a violent passion, which he could not subdue. He married her, and by this inferior alliance alienated his followers, whose brutal pride regarded this indulgence of his love as an unpardonable degradation of his family."—*Leland*, vol. ii.

Then, come—if a board so untempting hath power
  To win thee from grandeur, its best shall be thine;
And there's one, long the light of the bard's happy bower,
  Who, smiling, will blend her bright welcome with mine.

THEY KNOW NOT MY HEART.

They know not my heart, who believe there can be
One stain of this earth in its feelings for thee;
Who think, while I see thee in beauty's young hour,
As pure as the morning's first dew on the flower,
I could harm what I love—as the sun's wanton ray
But smiles on the dewdrop to waste it away.

No—beaming with light as those young features are,
There's a light round thy heart which is lovelier far;
It *is* not that cheek—'tis the soul dawning clear
Through its innocent blush makes thy beauty so dear;
As the sky we look up to, though glorious and fair,
Is looked up to the more, because Heaven lies there!

I WISH I WAS BY THAT DIM LAKE.

I wish I was by that dim Lake,*
Where sinful souls their farewell take
Of this vain world, and half-way lie
In death's cold shadow, ere they die.
There, there, far from thee,
Deceitful world, my home should be;
Where, come what might of gloom and pain,
False hope should ne'er deceive again.

The lifeless sky, the mournful sound
Of unseen waters falling round;
The dry leaves, quiv'ring o'er my head,
Like man, unquiet even when dead!
These, ay, these shall wean
My soul from life's deluding scene,
And turn each thought, o'ercharged with gloom,
Like willows, downward toward the tomb.

As they, who to their couch at night
Would win repose, first quench the light,
So must the hopes, that keep this breast
Awake, be quenched, ere it can rest.
Cold, cold, this heart must grow,
Unmoved by either joy or wo,
Like freezing founts, where all that's thrown
Within their current turns to stone.

SING—SING—MUSIC WAS GIVEN.

Sing—sing—Music was given,
  To brighten the gay, and kindle the loving;
Souls here, like planets in heaven,
  By harmony's laws alone are kept moving.
Beauty may boast of her eyes and her cheeks,
  But Love from the lips his true archery wings;
And she, who but feathers the dart when she speaks,
  At once sends it home to the heart when she sings.
    Then sing—sing—Music was given,
      To brighten the gay, and kindle the loving;
    Souls here, like planets in heaven,
      By harmony's laws alone are kept moving.

When Love, rocked by his mother,
  Lay sleeping as calm as slumber could make him,
"Hush, hush," said Venus, "no other
  Sweet voice but his own is worthy to wake him."

Dreaming of music, he slumbered the while,
  Till faint from his lips a soft melody broke,
And Venus, enchanted, looked on with a smile,
  While Love to his own sweet singing awoke.
    Then sing—sing—Music was given,
      To brighten the gay and kindle the loving;
    Souls here, like planets in heaven,
      By harmony's laws alone are kept moving.

SHE SUNG OF LOVE.

She sung of Love, while o'er her lyre
  The rosy rays of evening fell,
As if to feed, with their soft fire,
  The soul within that trembling shell.
The same rich light hung o'er her cheek,
  And played around those lips that sung
And spoke, as flowers would sing and speak,
  If Love could lend their leaves a tongue.

But soon the West no longer burned,
  Each rosy ray from heaven withdrew;
And, when to gaze again I turned,
  The minstrel's form seemed fading too.
As if *her* light and heaven's were one,
  The glory all had left that frame;
And from her glimmering lips the tone,
  As from a parting spirit, came.*

Who ever loved, but had the thought
  That he and all he loved must part?
Filled with this fear, I flew and caught
  The fading image to my heart—
And cried, "Oh Love! is this thy doom?
  Oh light of youth's resplendent day!
Must ye then lose your golden bloom,
  And thus, like sunshine, die away?"

SING, SWEET HARP.

Sing, sweet Harp, oh sing to me
  Some song of ancient days,
Whose sounds, in this sad memory,
  Long-buried dreams shall raise:—
Some lay that tells of vanished fame,
  Whose light once round us shone;
Of noble pride, now turned to shame,
  And hopes for ever gone.—
Sing, sad Harp, thus sing to me;
  Alike our doom is cast,
Both lost to all but memory,
  We live but in the past.

How mournfully the midnight air
  Among thy chords doth sigh,
As if it sought some echo there
  Of voices long gone by;—
Of Chieftains, now forgot, who seemed
  The foremost then in fame;
Of Bards who, once immortal deemed,
  Now sleep without a name.—
In vain, sad Harp, the midnight air
  Among thy chords doth sigh;
In vain it seeks an echo there
  Of voices long gone by.

Couldst thou but call those spirits round,
  Who once, in bower and hall,
Sat listening to thy magic sound,
  Now mute and mould'ring all;—
But, no; they would but wake to weep
  Their children's slavery;
Then leave them in their dreamless sleep,
  The dead, at least, are free!—
Hush, hush, sad Harp, that dreary tone,
  That knell of Freedom's day;
Or, listening to its deathlike moan,
  Let me, too, die away.

* These verses are meant to allude to that ancient haunt of superstition, called Patrick's Purgatory. "In the midst of these gloomy regions of Donegall (says Dr. Campbell), lay a lake, which was to become the mystic theatre of this fabled and intermediate state. In the lake were several islands; but one of them was dignified with that called the Mouth of Purgatory, which, during the dark ages, attracted the notice of all Christendom, and was the resort of penitents and pilgrims from almost every country in Europe."

"It was," as the same writer tells us, "one of the most dismal and dreary spots in the North almost inaccessible, through deep glens and rugged mountains, frightful with impending rocks, and the hollow murmurs of the western winds in dark caverns, peopled only with such fantastic beings as the mind, however gay, is, from strange association, wont to appropriate to such gloomy scenes."—*Strictures on the Ecclesiastical and Literary History of Ireland.*

* The thought here was suggested by some beautiful lines in Mr Rogers's Poem of *Human Life*, beginning—

"Now in the glimmering, dying light she grows
  Less and less earthly."

I would quote the entire passage, did I not fear to put my own humble imitation of it out of countenance.

SONG OF THE BATTLE EVE.

TIME—THE NINTH CENTURY.

To-morrow, comrade, we
On the battle-plain must be,
There to conquer, or both lie low!
The morning star is up—
But there's wine still in the cup,
And we'll take another quaff, ere we go, boy, go;
We'll take another quaff, ere we go.

'Tis true, in manliest eyes
A passing tear will rise,
When we think of the friends we leave lone;
But what can wailing do?
See, our goblet's weeping too!
With its tears we'll chase away our own, boy, our own;
With its tears we'll chase away our own.

But daylight's stealing on;—
The last that o'er us shone
Saw our children around us play;
The next—ah! where shall we
And those rosy urchins be?
But—no matter—grasp thy sword and away, boy, away;
No matter—grasp thy sword and away!

Let those, who brook the chain
Of Saxon or of Dane,
Ignobly by their firesides stay;
One sigh to home be given,
One heartfelt prayer to heaven,
Then, for Erin and her cause, boy, hurra! hurra! hurra!
Then, for Erin and her cause, hurra!

THE WANDERING BARD.

What life like that of the bard can be—
The wandering bard, who roams as free
As the mountain lark that o'er him sings,
And, like that lark, a music brings
Within him, where'er he comes or goes—
A fount that for ever flows!
The world's to him like some play-ground,
Where fairies dance their moonlight round;—
If dimmed the turf where late they trod,
The elves but seek some greener sod;
So, when less bright his scene of glee,
To another away flies he!

Oh, what would have been young Beauty's doom,
Without a bard to fix her bloom?
They tell us, in the moon's bright round,
Things lost in this dark world are found;
So charms, on earth long passed and gone,
In the poet's lay live on.—
Would ye have smiles that ne'er grow dim?
You've only to give them all to him,
Who, with but a touch of Fancy's wand,
Can lend them life, this life beyond,
And fix them high, in Poesy's sky—
Young stars that never die!

Then, welcome the bard where'er he comes—
For, though he hath countless airy homes,
To which his wing excursive roves,
Yet still, from time to time, he loves
To light upon earth and find such cheer
As brightens our banquet here.
No matter how far, how fleet he flies,
You've only to light up kind young eyes,
Such signal-fires as here are given—
And down he'll drop from Fancy's heaven,
The minute such call to love or mirth
Proclaims he's wanting on earth!

ALONE IN CROWDS TO WANDER ON.

Alone in crowds to wander on,
And feel that all the charm is gone
Which voices dear and eyes beloved
Shed round us once, where'er we roved—
This, this the doom must be
Of all who've loved, and lived to see
The few bright things they thought would stay
For ever near them, die away.

Though fairer forms around us throng,
Their smiles to others all belong,
And want that charm which dwells alone
Round those the fond heart calls its own.
Where, where the sunny brow?
The long-known voice—where are they now?
Thus ask I still, nor ask in vain,
The silence answers all too plain.

Oh, what is Fancy's magic worth,
If all her art can not call forth
One bliss like those we felt of old
From lips now mute, and eyes now cold?
No, no—her spell is vain—
As soon could she bring back again
Those eyes themselves from out the grave,
As wake again one bliss they gave

SONG OF INNISFAIL.

They came from a land beyond the sea,
And now o'er the western main
Set sail, in their good ships, gallantly,
From the sunny land of Spain.
"Oh, where's the Isle we've seen in dreams,
Our destined home or grave?"*
Thus sung they, as, by the morning's beams,
They swept the Atlantic wave.

And, lo, where afar o'er ocean shines
A sparkle of radiant green,
As though in that deep lay emerald mines,
Whose light through the wave was seen.
"'Tis Innisfail†—'tis Innisfail!"
Rings o'er the echoing sea;
While, bending to heaven, the warriors hail
That home of the brave and free.

Then turned they unto the eastern wave,
Where now their Day-God's eye
A look of such sunny omen gave
As lighted up sea and sky.
Nor frown was seen through sky or sea,
Nor tear o'er leaf or sod,
When first on their Isle of Destiny
Our great forefathers trod.

THE NIGHT DANCE.

Strike the gay harp! see the moon is on high,
And, as true to her beam as the tides of the ocean,
Young hearts, when they feel the soft light of her eye,
Obey the mute call, and heave into motion.
Then, sound notes—the gayest, the lightest,
That ever took wing, when heaven looked brightest!
Again! Again!
Oh! could such heart-stirring music be heard
In that City of Statues described by romancers,
So wakening its spell, even stone would be stirred,
And statues themselves all start into dancers!

Why then delay, with such sounds in our ears,
And the flower of Beauty's own garden before us—
While stars overhead leave the song of their spheres,
And listening to ours, hang wondering o'er us?
Again, that strain!—to hear it thus sounding
Might set even Death's cold pulses bounding—
Again! Again!
Oh, what delight when the youthful and gay,
Each with eye like a sunbeam and foot like a feather,
Thus dance, like the Hours to the music of May,
And mingle sweet song and sunshine together!

* "Milesius remembered the remarkable prediction of the principal Druid, who foretold that the posterity of Gadelus should obtain the possession of a Western Island (which was Ireland), and there inhabit.—*Keating*.

† The Island of Destiny, one of the ancient names of Ireland.

I'VE A SECRET TO TELL THEE.

I'VE a secret to tell thee, but hush! not here—
  Oh! not where the world its vigils keeps;
I'll seek, to whisper it in thine ear,
  Some shore where the Spirit of Silence sleeps;
Where summer's wave unmurm'ring dies,
  Nor fay can hear the fountain's gush;
Where, if but a note her night-bird sighs,
  The rose saith, chidingly, "Hush, sweet, hush!"

There, amid the deep silence of that hour,
  When stars can be heard in ocean dip,
Thyself shall, under some rosy bower,
  Sit mute, with thy finger on thy lip:
Like him, the boy,* who born among
  The flowers that on the Nile-stream blush,
Sits ever thus—his only song
  To earth and heaven, "Hush, all, hush!"

THERE ARE SOUNDS OF MIRTH.

THERE are sounds of mirth in the night-air ringing,
  And lamps from every casement shown;
While voices blithe within are singing,
  That seem to say "Come," in every tone.
Ah! once how light, in Life's young season,
  My heart had leaped at that sweet lay;
Nor paused to ask of graybeard Reason
  Should I the syren call obey.

And, see—the lamps still livelier glitter,
  The syren lips more fondly sound;
No, seek, ye nymphs, some victim fitter
  To sink in your rosy bondage bound.
Shall a bard, whom not the world in arms
  Could bend to tyranny's rude control,
Thus quail, at sight of woman's charms,
  And yield to a smile his freeborn soul?

Thus sung the sage, while, slyly stealing,
  The nymphs their fetters around him cast,
And—their laughing eyes, the while, concealing—
  Led Freedom's Bard their slave at last.
For the Poet's heart, still prone to loving,
  Was like that rock of the Druid race,†
Which the gentlest touch at once set moving,
  But all earth's power couldn't cast from its base.

OH! ARRANMORE, LOVED ARRANMORE.

OH! Arranmore, loved Arranmore,
  How oft I dream of thee,
And of those days when, by thy shore,
  I wandered young and free.
Full many a path I've tried, since then,
  Through pleasure's flowery maze,
But ne'er could find the bliss again
  I felt in those sweet days.

How blithe upon thy breezy cliffs
  At sunny morn I've stood,
With heart as bounding as the skiffs
  That danced along thy flood;
Or, when the western wave grew bright
  With daylight's parting wing,
Have sought that Eden in its light
  Which dreaming poets sing;—‡

That Eden where th' immortal brave
  Dwell in a land serene—
Whose bowers beyond the shining wave,
  At sunset, oft are seen.
Ah dream too full of saddening truth!
  Those mansions o'er the main
Are like the hopes I built in youth—
  As sunny and as vain!

* The God of Silence, thus pictured by the Egyptians.

† The Rocking Stones of the Druids, some of which no force is able to dislodge from their stations.

‡ "The inhabitants of Arranmore are still persuaded that, in a clear day, they can see from this coast Hy Brysail, or the Enchanted Island, the Paradise of the Pagan Irish, and concerning which they relate a number of romantic stories."—*Beaufort's Ancient Topography of Ireland.*

LAY HIS SWORD BY HIS SIDE.

LAY his sword by his side,* it hath served him too well
  Not to rest near his pillow below;
To the last moment true, from his hand ere it fell,
  Its point was still turned to a flying foe.
Fellow-laborers in life, let them slumber in death,
  Side by side, as becomes the reposing brave—
That sword which he loved still unbroke in its sheath
  And himself unsubdued in his grave.

Yet pause—for, in fancy, a still voice I hear
  As if breathed from his brave heart's remains;—
Faint echo of that which, in Slavery's ear,
  Once sounded the war-word, "Burst your chains!"
And it cries, from the grave where the hero lies deep,
  "Though the day of your Chieftain for ever hath set,
O leave not his sword thus inglorious to sleep—
  It hath victory's life in it yet!

Should some alien, unworthy such weapon to wield,
  Dare to touch thee, my own gallant sword,
Then rest in thy sheath, like a talisman sealed,
  Or return to the grave of thy chainless lord.
But, if grasped by a hand that hath learned the proud use
  Of a falchion, like thee, on the battle-plain—
Then, at Liberty's summons, like lightning let loose,
  Leap forth from thy dark sheath again!"

OH, COULD WE DO WITH THIS WORLD OF OURS.

OH, could we do with this world of ours
As thou dost with thy garden bowers,
Reject the weeds and keep the flowers,
  What a heaven on earth we'd make it!
So bright a dwelling should be our own,
So warranted free from sigh or frown,
That angels soon would be coming down,
  By the week or month to take it.

Like those gay flies that wing through air,
And in themselves a lustre bear,
A stock of light, still ready there,
  Whenever they wish to use it;
So, in this world I'd make for thee,
Our hearts should all like fire-flies be,
And the flash of wit or poesy
  Break forth whenever we choose it.

While every joy that glads our sphere
Hath still some shadow hovering near,
In this new world of ours, my dear,
  Such shadows will all be omitted:—
Unless they're like that graceful one,
Which, when thou'rt dancing in the sun,
Still near thee, leaves a charm upon
  Each spot where it hath flitted!

FROM THIS HOUR THE PLEDGE IS GIVEN.

FROM this hour the pledge is given,
  From this hour my soul is thine:
Come what will, from earth or heaven,
  Weal or wo, thy fate be mine.
When the proud and great stood by thee,
  None dared thy rights to spurn;
And if now they're false and fly thee,
  Shall I, too, basely turn?
No;—whate'er the fires that try thee,
  In the same this heart shall burn.

Though the sea, where thou embarkest,
  Offers now a friendly shore,
Light may come where all looks darkest,
  Hope hath life, when life seems o'er.
And, of those past ages dreaming,
  When glory decked thy brow,
Oft I fondly think, though seeming
  So fallen and clouded now,
Thou'lt again break forth, all beaming—
  None so bright, so blest as thou!

* It was the custom of the ancient Irish, in the manner of the Scythians, to bury the favorite sword of their heroes along with them.

THE WINE-CUP IS CIRCLING.

THE wine-cup is circling in Almhin's hall,*
And its Chief, mid his heroes reclining,
Looks up, with a sigh, to the trophied wall,
Where his sword hangs idly shining.
When, hark! that shout
From the vale without—
"Arm ye quick! the Dane—the Dane is nigh!"
Every Chief starts up
From his foaming cup,
And "To battle, to battle!" is the Finian's cry.

The minstrels have seized their harps of gold,
And they sing such thrilling numbers—
'Tis like the voice of the Brave, of old,
Breaking forth from their place of slumbers!
Spear to buckler rang,
As the minstrels sang,
And the Sun-burst† o'er them floated wide;
While remembering the yoke
Which their fathers broke,
"On for liberty, for liberty!" the Finians cried.

Like clouds of the night the Northmen came,
O'er the valley of Almhin lowering;
While onward moved, in the light of its fame,
That banner of Erin, towering.
With the mingling shock
Rung cliff and rock,
While, rank on rank, the invaders die:
And the shout, that last
O'er the dying passed,
Was "Victory! victory!"—the Finian's cry.

THE DREAM OF THOSE DAYS.

THE dream of those days when first I sung thee is o'er,
Thy triumph hath stained the charm thy sorrows then wore;
And even of the light which Hope once shed o'er thy chains,
Alas, not a gleam to grace thy freedom remains.

Say, is it that slavery sunk so deep in thy heart,
That still the dark brand is there, though chainless thou art;
And Freedom's sweet fruit, for which thy spirit long burned,
Now, reaching at last thy lip, to ashes hath turned?
Up Liberty's steep by Truth and Eloquence led,
With eyes on her temple fixed, how proud was thy tread!
Ah, better thou ne'er hadst lived that summit to gain,
Or died in the porch, than thus dishonor the fane.

* The Palace of Fin Mac-Cumhal (the Fingal of Macpherson), in Leinster. It was built on the top of the hill, which has retained from thence the name of the Hill of Allen, in the county of Kildare. The Finians, or Fenni, were the celebrated National Militia of Ireland, which this chief commanded. The introduction of the Danes in the above song is an anachronism common to most of the Finian and Ossianic legends.

† The name given to the banner of the Irish.

SILENCE IS IN OUR FESTAL HALLS.*

SILENCE is in our festal halls—
Sweet Son of Song! thy course is o'er;
In vain on thee sad Erin calls,
Her minstrel's voice responds no more;—
All silent as th' Eolian shell
Sleeps at the close of some bright day,
When the sweet breeze, that waked its swell
At sunny morn, hath died away.

Yet, at our feasts, thy spirit long,
Awaked by music's spell shall rise;
For, name so linked with deathless song
Partakes its charm and never dies:
And even within the holy fane,
When music wafts the soul to heaven,
One thought to him, whose earliest strain
Was echoed there, shall long be given.

But, where is now the cheerful day,
The social night, when, by thy side,
He, who now weaves this parting lay,
His skilless voice with thine allied;
And sung those songs whose every tone,
When bard and minstrel long have past,
Shall still, in sweetness all their own,
Embalmed by fame, undying last.

Yes, Erin, thine alone the fame—
Or, if thy bard have shared the crown,
From thee the borrowed glory came,
And at thy feet is now laid down.
Enough, if Freedom still inspire
His latest song, and still there be,
As evening closes round his lyre,
One ray upon its chords from thee.

* It is hardly necessary, perhaps, to inform the reader that these lines are meant as a tribute of sincere friendship to the memory of an old and valued colleague in this work, Sir John Stevenson.

SACRED SONGS.

THOU ART, OH GOD.

"The day is thine, the night also is thine: thou hast prepared the light and the sun.
"Thou hast set all the borders of the earth: thou hast made summer and winter."—*Psalm* lxxiv. 16, 17.

THOU art, O GOD, the life and light
Of all this wondrous world we see;
Its glow by day, its smile by night,
Are but reflections caught from Thee.
Where'er we turn, thy glories shine,
And all things fair and bright are Thine!

When Day, with farewell beam, delays
Among the opening clouds of Even,
And we can almost think we gaze
Through golden vistas into Heaven—
Those hues that make the Sun's decline
So soft, so radiant, LORD! are Thine.

When Night, with wings of starry gloom,
O'ershadows all the earth and skies,
Like some dark, beauteous bird, whose plume
Is sparkling with unnumbered eyes—
That sacred gloom, those fires divine,
So grand, so countless, LORD! are Thine.

When youthful Spring around us breathes,
Thy spirit warms her fragrant sigh;
And every flower the Summer wreathes
Is born beneath that kindling eye.
Where'er we turn, thy glories shine,
And all things fair and bright are Thine!

THIS WORLD IS ALL A FLEETING SHOW

THIS world is all a fleeting show,
For man's illusion given;
The smiles of Joy, the tears of Wo,
Deceitful shine, deceitful flow—
There's nothing true, but Heaven!

And false the light on Glory's plume,
As fading hues of Even;
And Love, and Hope, and Beauty's bloom,
Are blossoms gathered for the tomb—
There's nothing bright, but Heaven!

Poor wanderers of a stormy day!
From wave to wave we're driven,
And Fancy's flash, and Reason's ray,
Serves but to light the troubled way—
There's nothing calm, but Heaven!

THE BIRD LET LOOSE.

The bird, let loose in eastern skies,*
When hastening fondly home,
Ne'er stoops to earth her wing, nor flies
Where idle warblers roam.
But high she shoots through air and light,
Above all low delay,
Where nothing earthly bounds her flight,
Nor shadow dims her way.

So grant me, God, from every care
And stain of passion free,
Aloft, through Virtue's purer air,
To hold my course to Thee!
No sin to cloud, no lure to stay
My soul, as home she springs;—
Thy Sunshine on her joyful way,
Thy Freedom in her wings!

FALLEN IS THY THRONE.

Fallen is thy Throne, oh Israel!
Silence is o'er thy plains;
Thy dwellings all lie desolate,
Thy children weep in chains.
Where are the dews that fed thee
On Etham's barren shore?
That fire from Heaven which led thee,
Now lights thy path no more.

Lord! thou didst love Jerusalem—
Once she was all thy own;
Her love thy fairest heritage,†
Her power thy glory's throne.‡
Till evil came, and blighted
Thy long-loved olive-tree;—‖
And Salem's shrines were lighted
For other gods than Thee.

Then sunk the star of Solyma—
Then passed her glory's day,
Like heath that, in the wilderness,§
The wild wind whirls away.
Silent and waste her bowers,
Where once the mighty trod,
And sunk those guilty towers,
While Baal reigned as God.

"Go"—said the Lord—"Ye Conquerors!
Steep in her blood your swords,
And raze to earth her battlements,¶
For they are not the Lord's.
Till Zion's mournful daughter
O'er kindred bones shall tread,
And Hinnom's vale of slaughter**
Shall hide but half her dead!"

THE TURF SHALL BE MY FRAGRANT SHRINE.

The turf shall be my fragrant shrine;
My temple, Lord! that Arch of thine;
My censer's breath the mountain airs,
And silent thoughts my only prayers.††

* The carrier-pigeon, it is well known, flies at an elevated pitch, in order to surmount every obstacle between her and the place to which she is destined.

† "I have left mine heritage; I have given the dearly beloved of my soul into the hands of her enemies."—*Jeremiah*, xii. 7.

‡ "Do not disgrace the throne of thy glory."—*Jeremiah*, xiv. 21.

‖ "The Lord called thy name a green olive-tree; fair, and of goodly fruit," &c.—*Jeremiah*, xi. 16.

§ "For he shall be like the heath in the desert."—*Jeremiah*, xvii. 6.

¶ "Take away her battlements; for they are not the Lord's."—*Jeremiah*, v. 10.

** "Therefore, behold, the days come, saith the Lord, that it shall no more be called Tophet, nor the Valley of the Son of Hinnom, but the Valley of Slaughter: for they shall bury in Tophet till there be no place."—*Jeremiah*, vii. 32.

†† Pii orant tacitè.

My choir shall be the moonlight waves,
When murmuring homeward to their caves,
Or when the stillness of the sea,
Even more than music, breathes of Thee!

I'll seek, by day, some glade unknown,
All light and silence, like thy throne;
And the pale stars shall be, at night,
The only eyes that watch my rite.

Thy heaven, on which 'tis bliss to look,
Shall be my pure and shining book,
Where I shall read, in words of flame,
The glories of thy wondrous name.

I'll read thy anger in the rack
That clouds awhile the day-beam's track;
Thy mercy in the azure hue
Of sunny brightness, breaking through.

There's nothing bright, above, below,
From flowers that bloom to stars that glow,
But in its light my soul can see
Some feature of thy Deity.

There's nothing dark, below, above,
But in its gloom I trace thy Love,
And meekly wait that moment, when
Thy touch shall turn all bright again!

WHO IS THE MAID?

ST. JEROME'S LOVE.*

Who is the Maid my spirit seeks,
Through cold reproof and slander's blight?
Has *she* Love's roses on her cheeks?
Is *hers* an eye of this world's light?
No—wan and sunk with midnight prayer
Are the pale looks of her I love;
Or if, at times, a light be there,
Its beam is kindled from above.

I chose not her, my heart's elect,
From those who seek their Maker's shrine
In gems and garlands proudly decked,
As if themselves were things divine.
No—Heaven but faintly warms the breast
That beats beneath a broidered veil;
And she who comes in glitt'ring vest
To mourn her frailty, still is frail.†

Not so the faded form I prize
And love, because its bloom is gone;
The glory in those sainted eyes
Is all the grace *her* brow puts on.
And ne'er was Beauty's dawn so bright,
So touching as that form's decay,
Which, like the altar's trembling light,
In holy lustre wastes away.

OH, THOU! WHO DRYEST THE MOURNER'S TEAR.

"He healeth the broken in heart, and bindeth up their wounds."—*Psalm* cxlvii. 3.

Oh, Thou! who dry'st the mourner's tear,
How dark this world would be,
If, when deceived and wounded here,
We could not fly to Thee!
The friends, who in our sunshine live,
When winter comes, are flown;
And he who has but tears to give,
Must weep those tears alone.
But thou wilt heal that broken heart,
Which, like the plants that throw
Their fragrance from the wounded part,
Breathes sweetness out of wo.

* These lines were suggested by a passage in one of St. Jerome' letters, replying to some calumnious remarks that had been circu lated respecting his intimacy with the matron Paula: "Numqui me vestes sericæ, nitentes gemmæ, picta facies, aut auri rapu ambitio? Nulla fuit alia Romæ matronarum, quæ meam poss edomare mentem, nisi lugens atque jejunans, fletu pene cæcata. —*Epist.* "*Si tibi putem.*"

† Ου γαρ χρυσοφορειν την δακρυουσαν δει. *Chrysost. Homil.* 8 *Epist. ad Tim.*

When joy no longer sooths or cheers,
  And even the hope that threw
A moment's sparkle o'er our tears,
  Is dimmed and vanished too,
Oh, who would bear life's stormy doom,
  Did not thy Wing of Love
Come brightly wafting through the gloom
  Our Peace-branch from above?
Then sorrow, touched by Thee, grows bright
  With more than rapture's ray;
As darkness shows us worlds of light
  We never saw by day!

WEEP NOT FOR THOSE.

Weep not for those whom the veil of the tomb,
  In life's happy morning, hath hid from our eyes,
Ere sin threw a blight o'er the spirit's young bloom,
  Or earth had profaned what was born for the skies.
Death chilled the fair fountain, ere sorrow had stained it;
  'Twas frozen in all the pure light of its course,
And but sleeps till the sunshine of Heaven has unchained it,
  To water that Eden where first was its source.
Weep not for those whom the veil of the tomb,
  In life's happy morning, hath hid from our eyes
Ere sin threw a blight o'er the spirit's young bloom,
  Or earth had profaned what was born for the skies.

Mourn not for her, the young Bride of the Vale,*
  Our gayest and loveliest, lost to us now,
Ere life's early lustre had time to grow pale,
  And the garland of Love was yet fresh on her brow.
Oh, then was her moment, dear spirit, for flying
  From this gloomy world, while its gloom was unknown—
And the wild hymns she warbled so sweetly, in dying,
  Were echoed in heaven by lips like her own.
Weep not for her—in her spring-time she flew
  To that land where the wings of the soul are unfurled;
And now, like a star beyond evening's cold dew,
  Looks radiantly down on the tears of this world.

SOUND THE LOUD TIMBREL.

MIRIAM'S SONG.

"And Miriam the Prophetess, the sister of Aaron, took a timbrel in her hand; and all the women went out after her with timbrels and with dances."—*Exod.* xv. 20.

Sound the loud Timbrel o'er Egypt's dark sea!
Jehovah has triumphed—his people are free.
Sing—for the pride of the tyrant is broken,
  His chariots, his horsemen, all splendid and brave—
How vain was their boast, for the Lord hath but spoken,
  And chariots and horsemen are sunk in the wave.
Sound the loud Timbrel o'er Egypt's dark sea;
Jehovah has triumphed—his people are free.

Praise to the conqueror, praise to the Lord!
His word was our arrow, his breath was our sword.—
Who shall return to tell Egypt the story
  Of those she sent forth in the hour of her pride?
For the Lord hath looked out from his pillar of glory,†
  And all her brave thousands are dashed in the tide.
Sound the loud Timbrel o'er Egypt's dark sea;
Jehovah has triumphed—his people are free!

GO, LET ME WEEP.

Go, let we weep—there's bliss in tears,
  When he who sheds them inly feels
Some lingering stain of early years
  Effaced by every drop that steals.
The fruitless showers of worldly wo
  Fall dark to earth and never rise;
While tears that from repentance flow,
  In bright exhalement reach the skies.
    Go, let me weep.

Leave me to sigh o'er hours that flew
  More idly than the summer's wind,
And, while they passed, a fragrance threw,
  But left no trace of sweets behind.—
The warmest sigh that pleasure heaves
  Is cold, is faint to those that swell
The heart, where pure repentance grieves
  O'er hours of pleasure, loved too well.
    Leave me to sigh.

COME NOT, OH LORD.

Come not, oh Lord, in the dread robe of splendor
  Thou wor'st on the Mount, in the day of thine ire:
Come veiled in those shadows, deep, awful, but tender,
  Which Mercy flings over thy features of fire!

Lord, thou rememb'rest the night, when thy Nation*
  Stood fronting her Foe by the red-rolling stream;
O'er Egypt thy pillar shed dark desolation,
  While Israel basked all the night in its beam.

So, when the dread clouds of anger enfold thee,
  From us, in thy mercy, the dark side remove;
While shrouded in terrors the guilty behold thee,
  Oh, turn upon us the mild light of thy Love!

WERE NOT THE SINFUL MARY'S TEARS.

Were not the sinful Mary's tears
  An offering worthy Heaven,
When, o'er the faults of former years,
  She wept—and was forgiven?

When, bringing every balmy sweet
  Her day of luxury stored,
She o'er her Savior's hallowed feet,
  The precious odors poured;

And wiped them with that golden hair,
  Where once the diamond shone;
Though now those gems of grief were there
  Which shine for God alone!

Were not those sweets, so humbly shed—
  That hair—those weeping eyes—
And the sunk heart, that inly bled—
  Heaven's noblest sacrifice?

Thou, that hast slept in error's sleep,
  Oh, wouldst thou wake in Heaven,
Like Mary kneel, like Mary weep,
  "Love much,"† and be forgiven!

AS DOWN IN THE SUNLESS RETREATS.

As down in the sunless retreats of the Ocean,
  Sweet flowers are springing no mortal can see,
So, deep in my soul the still prayer of devotion,
  Unheard by the world, rises silent to Thee,
    My God! silent, to thee—
    Pure, warm, silent, to thee.

As still to the star of its worship, though clouded,
  The needle points faithfully o'er the dim sea,
So, dark as I roam, in this wintry world shrouded,
  The hope of my spirit turns trembling to Thee,
    My God! trembling, to thee—
    True, fond, trembling, to thee.

ANGEL OF CHARITY.

Angel of Charity, who, from above,
  Comest to dwell a pilgrim here,
Thy voice is music, thy smile is love,
  And Pity's soul is in thy tear.

* This second verse, which I wrote long after the first, alludes to the fate of a very lovely and amiable girl, the daughter of the late Colonel Bainbrigge, who was married in Ashbourne church, October 31, 1815, and died of a fever in a few weeks after; the sound of her marriage-bells seemed scarcely out of our ears when we heard of her death. During her last delirium she sung several hymns, in a voice even clearer and sweeter than usual, and among them were some from the present collection (particularly, "There's nothing bright but Heaven"), which this very interesting girl had often heard me sing during the summer.

† "And it came to pass, that, in the morning watch, the Lord looked unto the hos of the Egyptians, through the pillar of fire and of the cloud, and troubled the host of the Egyptians."—*Exod.* xiv. 24.

* "And it came between the camp of the Egyptians and the camp of Israel; and it was a cloud and darkness to them, but it gave light by night to these."—*Exod.* xiv. 20.

† "Her sins, which are many, are forgiven: for she loved much."—*Luke*, vii 47

When on the shrine of God were laid
  First-fruits of all most good and fair,
That ever bloomed in Eden's shade,
  Thine was the holiest offering there.

Hope and her sister, Faith, were given
  But as our guides to yonder sky;
Soon as they reach the verge of heaven,
  There, lost in perfect bliss, they die.*
But, long as Love, Almighty Love,
  Shall on his throne of thrones abide,
Thou, Charity, shall dwell above,
  Smiling for ever by His side!

BUT WHO SHALL SEE.

But who shall see the glorious day
  When, throned on Zion's brow,
The Lord shall rend that veil away
  Which hides the nations now?†
When earth no more beneath the fear
  Of his rebuke shall lie;‡
When pain shall cease, and every tear
  Be wiped from ev'ry eye.||

Then, Judah, thou no more shalt mourn
  Beneath the heathen's chain;
Thy days of splendor shall return,
  And all be new again.§
The Fount of Life shall then be quaffed
  In peace, by all who come;¶
And every wind that blows shall waft
  Some long-lost exile home.

ALMIGHTY GOD!

CHORUS OF PRIESTS.

Almighty God! when round thy shrine
The palm-tree's heavenly branch we twine,**
(Emblem of Life's eternal ray,
And Love that "fadeth not away,")
We bless the flowers, expanded all,††
We bless the leaves that never fall,
And trembling say—"In Eden thus
The Tree of Life may flower for us!"

When round thy Cherubs—smiling calm,
Without their flames‡‡ we read the palm,
Oh God! we feel the emblem true—
Thy Mercy is eternal too.
Those Cherubs, with their smiling eyes,
That crown of palm which never dies,
Are but the types of thee above—
Eternal Life, and Peace, and Love!

BEHOLD THE SUN.

Behold the Sun, how bright
  From yonder East he springs,
As if the soul of life and light
  Were breathing from his wings.

So bright the Gospel broke
  Upon the souls of men;
So fresh the dreaming world awoke
  In Truth's full radiance then.

Before yon Sun arose,
  Stars clustered through the sky—
But oh, how dim! how pale were those,
  To His one burning eye!

So Truth lent many a ray,
  To bless the Pagan's night—
But, Lord, how weak, how cold were they
  To Thy One glorious Light!

OH FAIR! OH PUREST!

SAINT AUGUSTINE TO HIS SISTER.*

Oh fair! oh purest! be thou the dove
That flies alone to some sunny grove,
And lives unseen, and bathes her wing,
All vestal white, in the limpid spring.
There, if the hov'ring hawk be near,
That limpid spring, in its mirror clear,
Reflects him, ere he reach his prey,
And warns the timorous bird away.
    Be thou this dove;
Fairest, purest, be thou this dove.

The sacred pages of God's own book
Shall be the spring, the eternal brook,
In whose holy mirror, night and day,
Thou'lt study Heaven's reflected ray;—
And should the foes of virtue dare,
With gloomy wing to seek thee there,
Thou wilt see how dark their shadows lie
Between Heaven and thee, and trembling fly!
    Be thou that dove;
Fairest, purest, be thou that dove.

LORD, WHO SHALL BEAR THAT DAY?

Lord, who shall bear that day, so dread, so splendid,
  When we shall see thy Angel, hov'ring o'er
This sinful world, with hand to heaven extended,
  And hear him swear by thee that Time's no more?†
When Earth shall feel thy fast-consuming ray—
Who, Mighty God, oh who shall bear that day?

When through the world thy awful call hath sounded—
  "Wake, all ye Dead, to judgment wake, ye Dead!"‡
And from the clouds, by seraph eyes surrounded,
  The Savior shall put forth his radiant head;||
While Earth and Heaven before him pass away—§
Who, Mighty God, oh who shall bear that day?

When, with a glance, th' Eternal Judge shall sever
  Earth's evil spirits from the pure and bright,
And say to *those*, "Depart from me for ever!"
  To *these*, "Come, dwell with me in endless light!"¶
When each and all in silence take their way—
Who, Mighty God! oh who shall bear that day?

* "Then Faith shall fail, and holy Hope shall die,
One lost in certainty, and one in joy."—*Prior.*

† "And he will destroy, in this mountain, the face of the covering cast over all people, and the veil that is spread over all nations."—*Isaiah*, xxv. 7.

‡ "The rebuke of his people shall he take away from off all the earth."—*Isaiah*, xxv. 8.

|| "And God shall wipe away all tears from their eyes; . . . . neither shall there be any more pain."—*Rev.* xxi. 4.

§ "And he that sat upon the throne said, Behold, I make all things new."—*Rev.* xxi. 5.

¶ "And whosoever will, let him take the water of life freely."—*Rev.* xxii. 17.

** "The Scriptures having declared that the Temple of Jerusalem was a type of the Messiah, it is natural to conclude that the *Palms*, which made so conspicuous a figure in that structure, represented that *Life* and *Immortality* which were brought to light by the Gospel."—*Observations on the Palm, as a Sacred Emblem*, by W. Tighe.

†† "And he carved all the walls of the house round about with carved figures of cherubims, and palm-trees, and *open flowers*."—1 *Kings*, vi. 29.

‡‡ "When the passover of the tabernacles was revealed to the great lawgivor in the mount, then the cherubic images which appeared in that structure were no longer surrounded by flames; for the tabernacle was a type of the dispensation of mercy, by which Jehovah confirmed his gracious covenant to redeem mankind."—*Observations on the Palm.*

* In St. Augustine's treatise upon the advantages of a solitary life, addressed to his sister, there is the following fanciful passage, from which, the reader will perceive, the thought of this song was taken: "Te, soror, nunquam, nolo esse securam, sed timere semperque, tuam fragilitatem habere suspectam, ad instar pavidæ columbæ frequentare rivos aquarum et quasi in speculo accipitris cernere supervolantis effigiem et cavere. Rivi aquarum sententiæ sunt scripturarum, quæ de limpidissimo sapientiæ fonte profluentes," &c., &c.—*De Vit. Eremit. ad Sororem.*

† "And the angel which I saw stand upon the sea and upon the earth, lifted up his hand to heaven, and sware by Him that liveth for ever and ever, ... that there should be time no longer."—*Rev.* x. 5, 6.

‡ "Awake, ye dead, and come to judgment."

|| "They shall see the Son of Man coming in the clouds of heaven—and all the angels with him."—*Matt.* xxiv. 30, and xxv. 31.

§ "From whose face the earth and the heaven fled away."—*Rev.* xx. 11.

¶ "And before Him shall be gathered all nations, and He shall separate them one from another. . . . .

"Then shall the King say unto them on his right hand, Come, ye blessed of my Father, inherit the kingdom prepared for you, &c.

"Then shall he say also unto them on the left hand, Depart from me, ye cursed, &c.

"And these shall go away into everlasting punishment: but the righteous into life eternal."—*Matt.* xxv. 32, *et seq.*

OH, TEACH ME TO LOVE THEE.

Oh, teach me to love Thee, to feel what thou art,
Till, filled with the one sacred image, my heart
Shall all other passions disown;
Like some pure temple, that shines apart,
Reserved for thy worship alone.

In joy and in sorrow, through praise and through blame,
Thus still let me, living and dying the same,
In *thy* service bloom and decay—
Like some lone altar, whose votive flame
In holinesss wasteth away.

Though born in this desert, and doomed by my birth
To pain and affliction, to darkness and dearth,
On thee let my spirit rely—
Like some rude dial, that, fixed on earth,
Still looks for its light from the sky.

WEEP, CHILDREN OF ISRAEL.

Weep, weep for him, the Man of God—*
In yonder vale he sunk to rest;
But none of earth can point the sod†
That flowers above his sacred breast.
Weep, children of Israel, weep!

His doctrine fell like Heaven's rain,‡
His words refreshed like Heaven's dew—
Oh, ne'er shall Israel see again
A Chief, to God and her so true.
Weep, children of Israel, weep!

Remember ye his parting gaze,
His farewell song by Jordan's tide,
When, full of glory and of days,
He saw the promised land—and died.‖
Weep, children of Israel, weep!

Yet died he not as men who sink,
Before our eyes, to soulless clay;
But, changed to spirit, like a wink
Of summer lightning, passed away.§
Weep, children of Israel, weep!

LIKE MORNING, WHEN HER EARLY BREEZE.

Like morning, when her early breeze
Breaks up the surface of the seas,
That, in those furrows, dark with night,
Her hand may sow the seeds of light—

Thy Grace can send its breathings o'er
The Spirit, dark and lost before,
And, fresh'ning all its depths, prepare
For Truth divine to enter there.

Till David touched his sacred lyre,
In silence lay th' unbreathing wire;
But when he swept its chords along,
Even Angels stooped to hear that song.

So sleeps the soul, till thou, oh Lord,
Shalt deign to touch its lifeless chord—
Till, waked by thee, its breath shall rise
In music, worthy of the skies!

COME, YE DISCONSOLATE.

Come, ye disconsolate, where'er you languish,
Come, at God's altar fervently kneel;
Here bring your wounded hearts, here tell your anguish—
Earth has no sorrow that Heaven can not heal.

Joy of the desolate, Light of the straying,
Hope, when all others die, fadeless and pure,
Here speaks the Comforter, in God's name saying—
"Earth has no sorrow that Heaven can not cure."

Go, ask the infidel, what boon he brings us,
What charm for aching hearts *he* can reveal,
Sweet as that heavenly promise Hope sings us—
"Earth has no sorrow that God can not heal."

AWAKE, ARISE, THY LIGHT IS COME.

Awake, arise, thy light is come;*
The nations, that before outshone thee,
Now at thy feet lie dark and dumb—
The glory of the Lord is on thee!

Arise—the Gentiles to thy ray,
From every nook of earth shall cluster;
And kings and princes haste to pay
Their homage to thy rising lustre.†

Lift up thine eyes around, and see,
O'er foreign fields, o'er farthest waters,
Thy exiled sons return to thee,
To thee return thy homesick daughters.‡

And camels rich, from Midian's tents,
Shall lay their treasures down before thee;
And Saba bring her gold and scents,
To fill thy air and sparkle o'er thee.‖

See, who are these, that, like a cloud,§
Are gathering from all earth's dominions,
Like doves, long absent, when allowed
Homeward to shoot their trembling pinions.

Surely the isles shall wait for me,¶
The ships of Tarshish round will hover,
To bring thy sons across the sea,
And waft their gold and silver over.

And Lebanon thy pomp shall grace—**
The fir, the pine, the palm victorious,
Shall beautify our Holy Place,
And make the ground I tread on glorious.

No more shall Discord haunt thy ways,††
Nor ruin waste thy cheerless nation;
But thou shalt call thy portals, Praise,
And thou shalt name thy walls, Salvation.

The sun no more shall make thee bright,‡‡
Nor moon shall lend her lustre to thee;
But God, himself, shall be thy Light,
And flash eternal glory through thee.

Thy sun shall never more go down;
A ray, from Heaven itself descended,
Shall light thy everlasting crown—
Thy days of mourning all are ended.‖‖

My own, elect, and righteous Land!
The Branch, for ever green and vernal,
Which I have planted with this hand—
Live thou shalt in Life Eternal.§§

* "And the children of Israel wept for Moses in the plains of Moab."—*Deut.* xxxiv. 8.

† "And he buried him in a valley in the land of Moab; . . . . but no man knoweth of his sepulchre unto this day."—*Ibid*, ver. 6.

‡ "My doctrine shall drop as the rain; my speech shall distil as the dew."—*Moses' Song. Deut.* xxxii. 2.

‖ "I have caused thee to see it with thine eyes, but thou shalt not go over thither."—*Deut.* xxxiv. 4.

§ "As he was going to embrace Eleazer and Joshua, and was still discoursing with them, a cloud stood over him on the sudden, and he disappeared in a certain valley, although he wrote in the holy Books that he died, which was done out of fear, lest they should venture to say, that, because of his extraordinary virtue, he went to God."—*Josephus*, Book iv., chap. viii

* "Arise, shine! for thy light is come, and the glory of the Lord is risen upon thee."—*Isaiah*, lx.

† "And the Gentiles shall come to thy light, and kings to the brightness of thy rising."—*Ib.*

‡ "Lift up thine eyes round about, and see; all they gather themselves together, they come to thee: thy sons shall come from afar, and thy daughters shall be nursed at thy side."—*Ib.*

‖ "The multitude of camels shall cover thee; the dromedaries of Midian and Ephah; all they from Sheba shall come; they shall bring gold and incense."—*Ib.*

§ "Who are these that fly as a cloud, and as the doves to their windows?"—*Ib.*

¶ "Surely the isles shall wait for me, and the ships of Tarshish first, to bring thy sons from far, their silver and their gold with them."—*Ib.*

** "The glory of Lebanon shall come unto thee: the fir-tree, the pine-tree, and the box together, to beautify the place of my sanctuary; and I will make the place of my feet glorious."—*Ib.*

†† "Violence shall no more be heard in thy land, wasting nor destruction within thy borders; but thou shalt call thy walls Salvation, and thy gates praise."—*Ib.*

‡‡ "Thy sun shall be no more thy light by day; neither for brightness shall the moon give light unto thee; but the Lord shall be unto thee an everlasting light, and thy God thy glory."—*Ib.*

‖‖ "Thy sun shall no more go down; . . . . for the Lord shall be thine everlasting light, and the days of thy mourning shall be ended."—*Ib.*

§§ "Thy people also shall be all righteous, they shall inherit the land for ever, the branch of my planting the work of my hands."—*Ib.*

THERE IS A BLEAK DESERT.

There is a bleak Desert, where daylight grows weary
Of wasting its smile on a region so dreary—
What may that desert be?
'Tis Life, cheerless Life, where the few joys that come
Are lost like that daylight, for 'tis not their home.

There is a lone Pilgrim, before whose faint eyes
The water he pants for but sparkles and flies—
Who may that Pilgrim be?
'Tis Man, hapless Man, through this life tempted on
By fair shining hopes, that in shining are gone.

There is a bright Fountain, through that Desert stealing
To pure lips alone its refreshment revealing—
What may that Fountain be?
'Tis Truth, holy Truth, that, like springs under ground,
By the gifted of Heaven alone can be found.*

There is a fair Spirit, whose wand hath the spell
To point where those waters in secrecy dwell—
Who may that Spirit be?
'Tis Faith, humble Faith, who hath learned that, where'er
Her wand bends to worship, the Truth must be there!

SINCE FIRST THY WORD.

Since first Thy Word awaked my heart,
Like new life dawning o'er me,
Where'er I turn mine eyes, Thou art,
All light and love before me.
Naught else I feel, or hear or see—
All bonds of earth I sever—
Thee, O God, and only Thee
I live for, now and ever.

Like him whose fetters dropped away
When light shone o'er his prison,†
My spirit, touched by Mercy's ray,
Hath from her chains arisen.
And shall a soul Thou bidst be free,
Return to bondage?—Never!
Thee, O God, and only Thee
I live for, now and ever.

HARK! 'TIS THE BREEZE.

Hark! 'tis the breeze of twilight calling
Earth's weary children to repose;
While, round the couch of Nature falling,
Gently the night's soft curtains close.
Soon o'er a world, in sleep reclining,
Numberless stars, through yonder dark,
Shall look, like eyes of Cherubs shining
From out the veils that hid the Ark.

Guard us, oh Thou, who never sleepest,
Thou who, in silence throned above,
Throughout all time, unwearied, keepest
Thy watch of Glory, Power, and Love,
Grant that, beneath thine eye, securely,
Our souls, awhile from life withdrawn,
May, in their darkness, stilly, purely,
Like "sealed fountains," rest till dawn.

WHERE IS YOUR DWELLING, YE SAINTED?

Where is your dwelling, ye Sainted?
Through what Elysium more bright
Than fancy or hope ever painted,
Walk ye in glory and light?
Who the same kingdom inherits?
Breathes there a soul that may dare
Look to that world of Spirits,
Or hope to dwell with you there?

Sages! who, even in exploring
Nature through all her bright ways,
Went, like the Seraphs adoring,
And veiled your eyes in the blaze—
Martyrs! who left for our reaping
Truths you had sown in your blood—
Sinners! whom long years of weeping
Chastened from evil to good—

Maidens! who, like the young Crescent,
Turning away your pale brows
From earth, and the light of the Present,
Looked to your Heavenly Spouse—
Say, through what region enchanted,
Walk ye, in Heaven's sweet air?
Say, to what spirits 'tis granted,
Bright souls, to dwell with you there?

HOW LIGHTLY MOUNTS THE MUSE'S WING

How lightly mounts the Muse's wing,
Whose theme is in the skies—
Like morning larks, that sweeter sing
The nearer Heaven they rise.

Though Love his magic lyre may tune,
Yet ah, the flowers he round it wreathes
Were plucked beneath pale Passion's moon,
Whose madness in their odor breathes.

How purer far the sacred lute,
Round which Devotion ties
Sweet flowers that turn to heavenly fruit,
And palm that never dies.

Though War's high-sounding harp may be
Most welcome to the hero's ears.
Alas, his chords of victory
Are wet, all o'er, with human tears.

How far more sweet their numbers run,
Who hymn, like Saints above,
No victor, but th' Eternal One,
No trophies but of Love!

IS IT NOT SWEET TO THINK, HEREAFTER.

Is it not sweet to think, hereafter,
When the Spirit leaves this sphere,
Love, with deathless wing, shall waft her
To those she long hath mourned for here?

Hearts, from which 'twas death to sever
Eyes, this world can ne'er restore,
There, as warm, as bright as ever,
Shall meet us and be lost no more.

When wearily we wander, asking
Of earth and heaven, where are they,
Beneath whose smile we once lay basking,
Blest, and thinking bliss would stay?

Hope still lifts her radiant finger,
Pointing to th' eternal Home,
Upon whose portal yet they linger,
Looking back for us to come.

Alas, alas—doth Hope deceive us?
Shall friendship—love—shall all those ties
That bind a moment, and then leave us,
Be found again where nothing dies?

Oh, if no other boon were given,
To keep our hearts from wrong and stain,
Who would not try to win a Heaven
Where all we love shall live again?

WAR AGAINST BABYLON.

"War against Babylon!" shout we around,*
Be our banners through earth unfurled;
Rise up, ye nations, ye kings, at the sound—†
"War against Babylon!" shout through the world!

* In singing, the following line had better be adopted.—
"Can but by the gifted of Heaven be found."

† "And, behold, the angel of the Lord came upon him, and a light shined in the prison, ... and his chains fell off from his hands."—*Acts*, xii. 7

* "Shout against her round about."—*Jer.* l. 15.

† "Set ye up a standard in the land, blow the trumpet among the nations, prepare the nations against her, call together against her the kingdoms," &c., &c.—*Jer* li. 27

Oh thou, that dwellest on many waters,*
Thy day of pride is ended now;
And the dark curse of Israel's daughters
Breaks, like a thunder-cloud, over thy brow!
War, war, war against Babylon!

Make bright the arrows, and gather the shields,†
Set the standard of God on high;
Swarm we, like locusts, o'er all her fields,
"Zion" our watchward, and "Vengeance" our cry!
Wo! wo!—the time of thy visitation‡
Is come, proud Land, thy doom is cast—
And the black surge of desolation
Sweeps o'er thy guilty head, at last!
War, war, war against Babylon!

GO FORTH TO THE MOUNT.

Go forth to the Mount—bring the olive-branch home,‖
And rejoice, for the day of our Freedom is come!

* "Oh thou that dwellest upon many waters, ... thine end is come."—*Jer.* li. 13.
† "Make bright the arrows; gather the shields, ... set up the standard upon the walls of Babylon."—*Jer.* li. 11, 12.
‡ "Wo unto them! for their day is come, the time of their visitation!"—*Jer.* l. 27.
‖ "And that they should publish and proclaim in all their cities, and in Jerusalem, saying, Go forth unto the mount, and fetch olive-branches," &c., &c.—*Neh.* viii. 15.

From that time,* when the moon upon Ajalon's vale,
Looking motionless down,† saw the kings of the earth,
In the presence of God's mighty Champion, grow pale—
Oh, never had Judah an hour of such mirth!
Go forth to the Mount—bring the olive-branch home,
And rejoice, for the day of our Freedom is come!

Bring myrtle and palm—bring the boughs of each tree
That's worthy to wave o'er the tents of the Free.‡
From that day, when the footsteps of Israel shone,
With a light not their own, through the Jordan's deep tide,
Whose waters shrunk back as the Ark glided on—‖
Oh, never had Judah an hour of such pride!
Go forth to the Mount—bring the olive-branch home,
And rejoice, for the day of our Freedom is come!

* "For since the days of Jeshua the son of Nun unto that day, had not the children of Israel done so: and there was very great gladness."—*Neh.* viii. 17.
† "Sun, stand thou still upon Gibeon; and thou, Moon, in the valley of Ajalon."—*Josh.* x. 12.
‡ "Fetch olive-branches, and pine-branches, and myrtle-branches, and palm-branches, and branches of thick trees, to make booths."—*Neh.* viii. 15.
‖ "And the priests that bare the ark of the covenant of the Lord stood firm on dry ground in the midst of Jordan, and all the Israelites passed over on dry ground."—*Josh.* iii. 17.

NOTES.

If the two following criticisms on Moore be not *colossal*, it is from no lack in the straddle—one having been written on the other side of the Atlantic, and one on this. Together they make a free-and-easy commentary, which will let the reader down softly from the high flight of the poetry foregone:—

Moore's Muse is another Ariel—as light, as tricksy, as indefatigable, and as humane a spirit. His fancy is for ever on the wing, flutters in the gale, glitters in the sun. Everything lives, moves, and sparkles in his poetry, while over all Love waves his purple light. His thoughts are as restless, as many, and as bright, as the insects that people the sun's beam. "So work the honeybees," extracting liquid sweets from opening buds; so the butterfly expands its wings to the idle air; so the thistle's silver down is wafted over summer seas. An airy voyager on life's stream, his mind inhales the fragrance of a thousand shores, and drinks of endless pleasures under halcyon skies. Wherever his footsteps tend over the enamelled ground of fairy fiction—

> "Around him the bees in play flutter and cluster,
> And gaudy butterflies frolic around."

The fault of Mr. Moore is an exuberance of involuntary power. His facility of production lessens the effect of, and hangs as a dead weight upon, what he produces. His levity at last oppresses. The infinite delight he takes in such an infinite number of things, produces indifference in minds less susceptible of pleasure than his own. He exhausts attention by being inexhaustible. His variety cloys; his rapidity dazzles and distracts the sight. The graceful ease with which he lends himself to every subject, the genial spirit with which he indulges in every sentiment, prevents him from giving their full force to the masses of things, from connecting them into a whole. He wants intensity, strength, and grandeur. His mind does not brood over the great and permanent; it glances over the surfaces, the first impressions of things, instead of grappling with the deep-rooted prejudices of the mind, its inveterate habits, and that "perilous stuff that weighs upon the heart." His pen, as it is rapid and fanciful, wants momentum and passion. It requires the same principle to make us thoroughly like poetry, that makes us like ourselves so well, the feeling of continued identity. The impressions of Mr. Moore's poetry are detached, desultory, and physical. Its gorgeous colors brighten and fade like the rainbow's. Its sweetness evaporates like the effluvia exhaled from beds of flowers! His gay laughing style, which relates to the immediate pleasures of love or wine, is better than his sentimental and romantic vein. His "Irish Melodies" are not free from affectation and a certain sickliness of pretension. His serious descriptions are apt to run into flowery tenderness. His pathos sometimes melts into a mawkish sensibility, or crystallizes into all the prettiness of allegorical language, and glittering hardness of external imagery. But he has wit at will, and of the first quality. His "Twopenny Post-Bag" is a perfect "nest of spicery;" where the Cayenne is not spared. The politician there sharpens the poet's pen. In this too, our bard resembles the bee—he has its honey and its sting.

"Lalla Rookh" is not what people wanted to see whether Mr. Moore could do; namely, whether he could write a long epic poem. It is four short tales. The interest, however, is often high-wrought and tragic, but the execution still turns to the effeminate and voluptuous side. Fortitude of mind is the first requisite of a tragic or epic writer. Happiness of nature and felicity of genius are the pre-eminent characteristics of the bard of Erin. If he is not perfectly contented with what he is, all the world beside is. He had no temptation to risk anything in adding to the love and admiration of his age, and more than one country.

> "Therefore to be possessed with double pomp
> To guard a title that was rich before,
> To gild refined gold, to paint the lily,
> To throw a perfume on the violet,
> To smooth the ice, or add another hue
> Unto the rainbow, or with taper light
> To seek the beauteous eye of heaven to garnish,
> Is wasteful and ridiculous excess."

The same might be said of Mr. Moore's seeking to bind an epic crown, or the shadow of one, round his other laurels.

Thomas Moore has become moral and almost chaste. Let us follow him through the history of his various writings; we shall find him more superficial than profound, more tender than pathetic, more graceful than energetic; addressing the heart rather than the mind; but still on all occasions an amiable poet, sometimes a great poet, and almost always imbued with imagination, wit, and taste. Diderot affirms, that in order to write well on the subject of females, it would be requisite to dip the pen in the dies of the rainbow, and dry the paper with powder borrowed from the wings of the butterfly. It might be imagined, that Thomas Moore had employed this recipe, in order to compose his oriental imagery, and depict his Peris, or not less brilliant mortal fairies; there is so prodigious a luxury of metaphors and ornaments lavished on his verses, that they may be styled a selection of poetical arabesques.

The Grand Nazir of the Mogul Princess might have added to the above-noticed critique, that the elements of Thomas Moore's poetry consist in the ingenious distribution of divers butterfly wings, angel plumes, beams of light, pearls, precious stones, perfumes, etc. All these fictitious appendages do not always adorn perfect beauties; but, as paste and false diamonds produce enchanting metamorphoses at the opera, with the aid of singing and music, the poet operates an illusion by the magic of his pictures and the melody of his verses. He has carried this melody far ther than any English poet since Chaucer: Thomas Moore's poetry is almost Italian. This melody was already conspicuous in his first pieces, addressed to Julia, Rose, Jessy Bessy, Mary, and to thirty others, whom the discreet Mr Little designates by three asterisks.

With his charming social verses, and his amiable manners, Mr. Moore succeeded, not only in winning the ear of the ladies, but also of some influential noblemen. He was appointed to a situation in the Vice-Admiralty Court at Bermudas, and he embarked for that island, which Shakspere makes the birth-place of his sylph Ariel. During his leisure moments Mr. Moore did not neglect the muses, and the beauties of the Azores; and on his return to England published a collection of odes, epistles, and fugitive poems, in which he celebrates the enchantments of a climate well-calculated to seduce, by its various features, the poet's imagination. Of these pieces, some are rich with brilliant descriptions, while others reproduce the tender emotions with which Mr. Moore delights to inspire himself. He had, however, found the ladies of the Bermudas more fond than beautiful; he treats their husbands still less favorably, telling us that the ancient philosopher, who held that after this life, the men are changed into mules, and the women into turtles, might have seen this metamorphosis nearly accomplished at Bermudas.

There can be little doubt that the primitive songs, or lyrical compositions of the rhapsodists, were the spontaneous production of a poetical musician, who struck off the words and the air in the same heat. Subsequently, songs have generally preceded the music. But such is the triumph of music, which is the true universal language, over poetry, which only appertains to one language, that the tune still survives, when the words are lost. The Virgilian Shepherd was thence induced to exclaim, "I remember the air, but I have forgotten the words."

"Numeros meminl, si verba tenerem."

Ireland possessed an original and popular music, which supplied numerous allusions to its manners, customs, and history, and which, still more than the Scotch music, deserved that a Burns should render it popular, and consecrate it, as it were, by an alliance with the national poetry. Miss Owenson had already adapted words to some of these airs of old Erin: but to Thomas Moore belongs the merit of assembling almost all of them in one historical record.

The luxury of the *costumes*, and of the periphrasis in *Lalla Rookh*, tend to persuade us that we are reading an oriental poem; it might be almost called, according to a well-known expression, more Arabic than Arabia. But in the *Irish Melodies*, if Mr. Moore is almost always a remarkable lyrical poet, he is seldom an Irishman, while Burns always remains a Scotchman in his Caledonian melodies. We have said enough to explain the reason; Mr. Moore has composed exclusively for the pianos of pretty women. Burns has preserved his somewhat savage independence in his songs; Moore resembles a caged nightingale, who devotes his dulcet voice to an imitation of the airs of the bird-organ. There are, however, some honorable exceptions to the general tone of the melodies of the Irish Anacreon: "Rich and Rare," is a fragment rendered exquisite by its affecting simplicity; it describes the voyage of a young virgin, clothed in rich vestures, who, on the faith of the virtues of Brien and his people, travels through the entire kingdom, without fear of outrage. "O the sight-entrancing," is the almost sublime expression of a warrior's enthusiasm at the sight of arms. Divested of their rhythm and their music, these melodies would perhaps justify what Moore himself has modestly said of them in the style of Fadladeen—they resemble insects in amber, which are esteemed on account of the precious substance which embalm them.

[And now let us add an admiring sketch of the poet and his ways, written in that country which he himself describes as—

"A world so bright, but born to grace
Its own half-organized, half-minded race,"

but which is destined, notwithstanding, to be the second home of his immortality:]—

Well—how does Moore write a song?

In the twilight of a September evening he strolls through the park to dine with the marquis. As he draws on his white gloves, he sees the evening star looking at him steadily through the long vista of the avenue, and he construes its punctual dispensation of light into a reproach for having, himself a star, passed a day of poetic idleness. "Damme," soliloquizes the little fat planet, "this will never do! Here have I hammered the whole morning at a worthless idea, that, with the mere prospect of dinner, shows as trumpery as a 'penny fairing.' Labor wasted! —and at my time of life too! Faith!—it's a dining at home these two days with nobody to drink with me! It's eye-water I want! Don't trouble yourself to sit up for me, brother Hesper! I shall see clearer when I come back!

'Bad are the rhymes
That scorn old wine,'

as my friend Barry sings. Poetry? hum!—Claret? Prithee, call it claret!"

And Moore is mistaken! He draws his inspiration, it is true, with the stem of a glass between his thumb and finger, but the wine is the least stimulus to his brain. *He talks, and is listened to admiringly*, and that is his Castaly. He sits next to Lady Fanny at dinner, who thinks him "an adorable little Love," and he employs the first two courses in making her in love with herself—that is, blowing everything she says up to the red heat of poetry. Moore can do this; for the most stupid things on earth are, after all, the beginnings of ideas, and every fool is susceptible of the flattery of seeing the words go straight from his lips to the "highest heaven of invention." And Lady Fanny is not a fool, but a quick and appreciative woman, and to almost everything she says, the poet's *trump* is a germe of poetry. "Ah!" says Lady Fanny with a sigh, "this will be a memorable dinner—not to you, but to me; for you see pretty women every day, but I seldom see Tom Moore!" The poet looks into Lady Fanny's eyes, and makes no immediate answer. Presently she asks with a delicious look of simplicity, "Are you as agreeable to everybody, Mr. Moore?" "There is but one Lady Fanny," replies the poet; "or, *to use your own* beautiful simile, 'The moon sees many brooks, but the brook sees but one moon!'" (Mem. jot that down.) And so is treasured up *one* idea for the morrow, and when the marchioness rises and the ladies follow her to the drawing-room, Moore finds himself sandwiched between a couple of whig lords, and opposite a past or future premier—an audience of cultivation, talent, scholarship, and appreciation; and as the fresh pitcher of claret is passed round, all regards radiate to the Anacreon of the world, and with that suction of expectation—let alone Tom Moore—even our "Secretary of the Navy and National Songster" would "turn out his lining"—such as it is. And Moore is delightful, and with his "As you say, my lord!" he gives birth to a constellation of bright things, no one of which is dismissed with the claret. Every one at the table, except Moore, is subject to the hour—to its enthusiasm, its enjoyment—but the hour is to Moore a precious slave. So is the wine. It works for him! It brings him money from Longman! It plays his trumpet in the reviews! It is his filter among the ladies! Well may he sing its praises! Of all the poets, Moore is probably the only one who is thus *master of his wine*. The glorious *abandon* with which we fancy him, a brimming glass in his hand, singing "Fly not yet!" exists only in the fancy. He keeps a cool head and coins his conviviality; and to revert to my former figure, they who wish to know what Moore's electricity amounts to *without* the convivial friction, may read his "History of Ireland." Not a sparkle in it, from the landing of the Phenicians to the battle of Vinegar Hill! He wrote *that* as other people write—with nothing left from the day before but the habit of labor; and the travel of a collapsed balloon on a man's back, is not more unlike the same thing, inflated and soaring, than Tom Moore, historian, and Tom Moore, bard!

Somewhere in the small hours the poet walks home, and sitting down soberly in his little library, he puts on paper the half score of scintillations that collision, in one shape or another, has struck into the tinder of his fancy. If read from this paper, the world would probably think little of their prospect of ever becoming poetry. But the mysterious part is done—the life is breathed into the chrysalis—and the clothing of these naked fancies with winged words, Mr. Moore knows very well can be done in very uninspired moods by patient industry. Most people have very little idea of what that industry is—how deeply language is ransacked, how often turned over, how untiringly rejected and recalled with some new combination, how resolutely sacrificed when only tolerable enough to pass, how left untouched day after day in the hope of a fresh impulse after repose. The vexation of a Chinese puzzle is slight, probably, to that which Moore has expended on some of his most natural and flowing single verses. The exquisite nicety of his ear, though it eventually gives his poetry its honeyed fluidity, gives him no quicker choice of words, nor does more, in any way, than pass inexorable judgment on what his industry brings forward. Those who think a song dashed off like an invitation to dinner, would be edified by the progressive phases of a "Moore's Melody." Taken with all its re-writings, emendations, &c., I doubt whether, in his most industrious seclusion, Moore averages a couplet a day. Yet this persevering, resolute, unconquerable patience of labor, is the secret of his fame. Take the best thing he ever wrote, and translate its sentiment and similitudes into plain prose, and do the same thing by a song of any second-rate imitator of Moore, one abstract would read as well as the other. Yet Moore's song is immortal, and the other ephemeral as a paragraph in a newspaper, and the difference consists in the patient elaboration of language and harmony, and in that only. And even thus short, *seems* the space between the *ephemeron* and the immortal. But it is wider than they think, oh glorious Tom Moore!

THE SACRED POEMS

OF

MRS. HEMANS.

THE SUN.

THE Sun comes forth;—each mountain height
Glows with a tinge of rosy light,
And flowers that slumbered through the night,
Their dewy leaves unfold;
A flood of splendor bursts on high,
And ocean's breast reflects a sky
Of crimson and of gold.

Oh! thou art glorious, orb of day!
Exulting nations hail thy ray,
Creation swells a choral lay,
To welcome thy return;
From thee all Nature draws her hues,
Thy beams the insect's wings suffuse,
And in the diamond burn.

Yet must thou fade;—when earth and heaven
By fire and tempest shall be riven,
Thou, from thy sphere of radiance driven,
Oh Sun! must fall at last;
Another heaven, another earth,
Far other glory shall have birth,
When all we see is past.

But He, who gave the word of might,
"Let there be light"—and there *was* light,
Who bade thee chase the gloom of night,
And beam, the world to bless;—
For ever bright, for ever pure,
Alone unchanging shall endure,
The Sun of righteousness!

CHRIST STILLING THE TEMPEST

"But the ship was now in the midst of the sea, tossed with waves; for the wind was contrary."—*Matthew*, xiv. 24.

FEAR was within the tossing bark,
When stormy winds grew loud;
And waves came rolling high and dark,
And the tall mast was bowed.

And men stood breathless in their dread,
And baffled in their skill—
But One was there, who rose and said
To the wild sea, "Be still!"

And the wind ceased—it ceased!—that word
Passed through the gloomy sky;
The troubled billows knew their Lord,
And sank beneath his eye.

And slumber settled on the deep,
And silence on the blast,
As when the righteous falls asleep,
When death's fierce throes are past.

Thou that didst rule the angry hour,
And tame the tempest's mood—
Oh! send thy spirit forth in power,
O'er our dark souls to brood!

Thou that didst bow the billow's pride,
Thy mandates to fulfil—
Speak, speak, to passion's raging tide,
Speak and say—"Peace, be still!"

THE ISRAELITE'S LAMENT.

Em Babylonia sobre os rios, quando.

BESIDE the streams of Babylon, in tears
Of vain desire, we sat; remembering thee,
O hallowed Sion! and the vanished years,
When Israel's chosen sons were blest and free:

Our harps, neglected and untuned, we hung
Mute on the willows of the stranger's land;
When songs, like those that in thy fanes we sung,
Our foes demanded from their captive band.

How shall our voices, on a foreign shore,
(We answered those whose chains the exile wore,)
The songs of God, our sacred songs, renew?
If I forget, midst grief and wasting toil,
Thee, O Jerusalem! my native soil!
May my right hand forget its cunning too!

ON ASCENDING A HILL LEADING TO A CONVENT.

No baxes temeroso, o peregrino.

PAUSE not with lingering foot, O pilgrim, here;
Pierce the deep shadows of the mountain-side;
Firm be thy step, thy heart unknown to fear,
To brighter worlds this thorny path will guide

Soon shall thy feet approach the calm abode,
So near the mansions of supreme delight;
Pause not—but tread this consecrated road,
'Tis the dark basis of the heavenly height.

Behold, to cheer thee on the toilsome way,
How many a fountain glitters down the hill!
Pure gales, inviting, softly round thee play,
Bright sunshine guides—and wilt thou linger still?
Oh! enter there, where, freed from human strife,
Hope is reality, and time is life.

EVENING SONG OF THE WEARY.

FATHER of Heaven and Earth!
I bless thee for the night,
The soft, still night!
The holy pause of care and mirth,
Of sound and light!

Now far in glade and dell,
Flower-cup, and bud, and bell,
Have shut around the sleeping woodlark's nest—
The bee's long murmuring toils are done,
And I, the o'erwearied one,
O'erwearied and o'erwrought,
Bless thee, O God, O Father of the oppressed
With my last waking thought,
In the still night!

Yes, ere I sing to rest,
By the fire's dying light,
Thou Lord of Earth and Heaven!
I bless thee, who hast given
Unto life's fainting travellers, the night,
The soft, still, holy night!

PARAPHRASE OF PSALM CXLVIII.

Praise ye the Lord. Praise ye the Lord from the heavens, praise him in the heights.

PRAISE ye the Lord! on every height
Songs to his glory raise!
Ye angel-hosts, ye stars of light,
Join in immortal praise!

Oh! heaven of heavens! let praise far-swelling
From all your orbs be sent!
Join in the strain, ye waters, dwelling
Above the firmament!

For his the word which gave you birth,
And majesty and might;
Praise to the Highest from the earth,
And let the deeps unite!

Oh! fire and vapor, hail and snow,
Ye servants of his will;
Oh! stormy winds, that only blow
His mandates to fulfil;

Mountains and rocks, to heaven that rise
Fair cedars of the wood;
Creatures of life, that wing the skies,
Or track the plains for food;

Judges of nations; kings, whose hand
Waves the proud sceptre high;
Oh! youths and virgins of the land,
Oh! age and infancy;

Praise ye *His* name, to whom alone
All homage should be given;
Whose glory from the eternal throne
Spreads wide o'er earth and heaven!

THE HOUR OF PRAYER.

CHILD, amidst the flowers at play,
While the red light fades away;
Mother, with thine earnest eye
Ever following silently;
Father, by the breeze of eve
Called thy harvest-work to leave;
Pray!—ere yet the dark hours be,
Lift the heart and bend the knee!

Traveller, in the stranger's land
Far from thine own household band;
Mourner, haunted by the tone
Of a voice from this world gone;
Captive, in whose narrow cell
Sunshine hath not leave to dwell;
Sailor, on the darkening sea—
Lift the heart and bend the knee!

Warrior, that from battle won
Breathest now at set of sun!
Woman o'er the lowly slain
Weeping on his burial plain:
Ye that triumph, ye that sigh,
Kindred by one holy tie,
Heaven's first star alike ye see—
Lift the heart and bend the knee!

THE HOUR OF DEATH.

LEAVES have their time to fall,
And flowers to wither at the north wind's breath,
And stars to set—but all,
Thou hast all seasons for thine own, oh! Death.

Day is for mortal care,
Eve for glad meetings round the joyous hearth,
Night for the dreams of sleep, the voice of prayer—
But all for thee, thou Mightiest of the earth.

The banquet hath its hour,
Its feverish hour of mirth, and song, and wine;
There comes a day for griefs o'erwhelming power,
A time for softer tears—but all are thine.

Youth and the opening rose
May look like things too glorious for decay,
And smile at thee—but thou art not of those
That wait the ripened bloom to seize their prey.

Leaves have their time to fall,
And flowers to wither at the north wind's breath,
And stars to set—but all,
Thou hast all seasons for thine own, oh! Death.

We know when moons shall wane,
When summer-birds from far shall cross the sea,
When autumn's hue shall tinge the golden grain—
But who shall teach us when to look for thee?

Is it when spring's first gale
Comes forth to whisper where the violets lie?
Is it when roses in our paths grow pale?—
They have *one* season—*all* are ours to die!

Thou art where billows foam,
Thou art where music melts upon the air,
Thou art around us in our peaceful home,
And the world calls us forth—and thou art there.

Thou art where friend meets friend,
Beneath the shadow of the elm to rest—
Thou art where foe meets foe, and trumpets rend
The skies, and swords beat down the princely crest.

Leaves have their time to fall,
And flowers to wither at the north wind's breath,
And stars to set—but all,
Thou hast all seasons for thine own, oh! Death.

HYMN FOR CHRISTMAS.

OH! lovely voices of the sky
Which hymned the Savior's birth,
Are ye not singing still on high,
Ye that sang, "Peace on earth?"
To us yet speak the strains
Wherewith, in time gone by,
Ye blessed the Syrian swains,
Oh! voices of the sky!

Oh! clear and shining light, whose beams
That hour Heaven's glory shed,
Around the palms, and o'er the streams,
And on the shepherd's head.
Be near, through life and death,
As in that holiest night
Of hope, and joy, and faith—
Oh! clear and shining light!

Oh! star which led to Him, whose love
Brought down man's ransom free—
Where art thou?—'midst the host above,
May we still gaze on thee?
In Heaven thou art not set,
Thy rays earth may not dim,
Send them to guide us yet,
Oh! star which led to Him!

NIGHT HYMN AT SEA.

THE WORDS WRITTEN FOR A MELODY BY FELTON.

NIGHT sinks on the wave,
Hollow gusts are sighing,
Sea-birds to their cave
Through the gloom are flying.
Oh! should storms come sweeping
Thou, in heaven unsleeping,
O'er thy children vigil keeping,
Hear, hear, and save!

Stars look o'er the sea,
Few, and sad, and shrouded!
Faith our light must be,
When all else is clouded.
Thou, whose voice came thrilling,
Wind and billow stilling,
Speak once more! our prayer fulfilling—
Power dwells with thee!

CHRIST'S AGONY IN THE GARDEN.

He knelt—the Savior knelt and prayed,
When but his Father's eye
Looked through the lonely garden's shade,
On that dread agony!
The Lord of all, above, beneath,
Was bowed with sorrow unto death.

The sun set in a fearful hour,
The skies might well grow dim,
When this mortality had power
So to o'ershadow *him*.
That He who gave man's breath might know
The very depths of human wo.

He knew them all—the doubt, the strife,
The faint, perplexing dread,
The mists that hang o'er parting life,
All darkened round his head!
And the Deliverer knelt to pray—
Yet passed it not, that cup, away.

It passed not—though the stormy wave
Had sunk beneath his tread;
It passed not—though to him the grave
Had yielded up its dead.
But there was sent him from on high
A gift of strength, for man to die.*

And was *his* mortal hour beset
With anguish and dismay?
—How may *we* meet our conflict yet,
In the dark, narrow way?
How, but through Him, that path who trod?
Save, or we perish, Son of God!

THE MINSTER.

A fit abode, wherein appear enshrined
Our hopes of immortality.—*Byron.*

Speak low!—the place is holy to the breath
Of awful harmonies, of whispered prayer;
Tread lightly!—for the sanctity of death
Broods with a voiceless influence on the air:
Stern, yet serene!—a reconciling spell,
Each troubled billow of the soul to quell.

Leave me to linger silently awhile!
—Not for the light that pours its fervid streams
Of rainbow glory down through arch and aisle,
Kindling old banners into haughty gleams,
Flushing proud shrines, or by some warrior's tomb
Dying away in clouds of gorgeous gloom:

Not for rich music, though in triumph pealing,
Mighty as forest sounds when winds are high;
Nor yet for torch, and cross, and stole, revealing
Through incense-mists their sainted pageantry:—
Though o'er the spirit each hath charm and power
Yet not for *these* I ask one lingering hour.

But by strong sympathies, whose silver cord
Links me to mortal weal, my soul is bound;
Thoughts of the human hearts, that here have poured
Their anguish forth, are with me and around;—
I look back on the pangs, the burning tears,
Known to these altars of a thousand years.

Send up a murmur from the dust, Remorse!
That here hast bowed with ashes on thy head;
And thou still battling with the tempest's force—
Thou, whose bright spirit through all time hath bled—
Speak, wounded Love! if penance here, or prayer,
Hath laid one haunting shadow of despair?

No voice, no breath!—of conflicts past, no trace?
—Does not this hush give answer to my quest?
Surely the dread religion of the place
By every grief hath made its might confest!
—Oh! that within my heart I could but keep
Holy to Heaven, a spot thus pure, and still, and deep!

* "And there appeared an angel unto him from heaven, strengthening him."—*Luke*, xxii. 43.

HYMN OF THE MOUNTAIN CHRISTIAN.

"Thanks be to God for the mountains."
Howitt's Book of the Seasons

For the strength of the hills we bless thee,
Our God, our fathers' God!
Thou hast made thy children mighty,
By the touch of the mountain sod.
Thou hast fixed our ark of refuge
Where the spoiler's foot ne'er trod;
For the strength of the hills we bless thee,
Our God, our fathers' God!

We are watchers of a beacon
Whose lights must never die;
We are guardians of an altar
Midst the silence of the sky;
The rocks yield founts of courage
Struck forth as by thy rod—
For the strength of the hills we bless thee,
O God, our fathers' God!

For the dark, resounding heavens,
Where thy still small voice is heard,
For the strong pines of the forests,
That by thy breath are stirred;
For the storms on whose free pinions
Thy spirit walks abroad—
For the strength of the hills we bless thee,
O God, our fathers' God!

The royal eagle darteth
On his quarry from the heights,
And the stag that knows no master,
Seeks there his wild delights;
But we for *thy* communion
Have sought the mountain sod—
For the strength of the hills we bless thee,
Our God, our fathers' God!

The banner of the chieftain
Far, far below us waves;
The war-horse of the spearman
Can not reach our lofty caves;
Thy dark clouds wrap the threshold
Of freedom's last abode;
For the strength of the hills we bless thee,
Our God, our father's God!

For the shadow of thy presence
Round our camp of rock outspread;
For the stern defiles of battle,
Bearing record of our dead;
For the snows, and for the torrents,
For the free heart's burial sod,
For the strength of the hills we bless thee,
Our God, our fathers' God!

MOTHER'S LITANY BY THE SICK-BED OF A CHILD.

Savior that of woman born,
Mother-sorrow didst not scorn,
Thou with whose last anguish strove
One dear thought of earthly love;
Hear and aid!

Low he lies, my precious child,
With his spirit wandering wild
From its gladsome tasks and play,
And its bright thoughts far away:—
Savior, aid!

Pain sits heavy on his brow,
E'en though slumber seal it now;
Round his lip is quivering strife,
In his hand unquiet life;
Aid, oh! aid!

Savior! loose the burning chain
From his fevered heart and brain,
Give, oh! give his young soul back
Into its own cloudless track!
Hear and aid!

Thou that saidst, "Awake, arise!"
E'en when death had quenched the eyes,
In this hour of grief's deep sighing,
When o'erwearied hope is dying!
Hear and aid!

Yet, oh! make him thine, all thine,
Savior! whether Death's or mine!
Yet, oh! pour on human love,
Strength, trust, patience, from above!
Hear and aid!

A PRAYER OF AFFECTION.

Blessings, O Father, shower!
Father of mercies! round his precious head!
On his lone walks and on his thoughtful hour,
And the pure visions of his midnight bed,
Blessings be shed!

Father! I pray Thee not
For earthly treasure to that most beloved,
Fame, fortune, power;—oh! be his spirit proved
By these, or by their absence, at thy will!
But let thy peace be wedded to his lot,
Guarding his inner life from touch of ill,
With its dove-pinion still!

Let such a sense of Thee,
Thy watching presence, thy sustaining love,
His bosom guest inalienably be,
That wheresoe'er he move,
A heavenly light serene
Upon his heart and mein
May sit undimmed! a gladness rest his own,
Unspeakable, and to the world unknown!
Such as from childhood's morning land of dreams,
Remembered faintly, gleams,
Faintly remembered, and too swiftly flown!

So let him walk with Thee,
Made by Thy spirit free;
And when thou callest him from his mortal place
To his last hour be still that sweetness given,
That joyful trust! and brightly let him part,
With lamp clear burning, and unlingering heart,
Mature to meet in heaven
His Savior's face!

FEMALE CHARACTERS OF SCRIPTURE.

Your tents are desolate: your stately steps,
Of all their choral dances, have not left
One trace beside the fountains; your full cup
Of gladness and of trembling, each alike
Is broken: yet amidst undying things,
The mind still keeps your loveliness, and still
All the fresh glories of the early world
Hang round you in the spirit's pictured halls
Never to change!

INVOCATION.

As the tired voyager on stormy seas
Invokes the coming of bright birds from shore,
To waft him tidings with the gentler breeze,
Of dim sweet woods that hear no billows roar;
So from the depths of days, when earth yet wore
Her solemn beauty and primeval dew,
I call you gracious Forms! Oh! come, restore
Awhile that holy freshness, and renew
Life's morning dreams. Come with the voice, the lyre,
Daughters of Judah! with the timbrel rise!
Ye of the dark prophetic eastern eyes,
Imperial in their visionary fire;
Oh! steep my soul in that old glorious time,
When God's own whisper shook the cedars of your clime!

INVOCATION CONTINUED.

And come, ye faithful! round Messiah seen,
With a soft harmony of tears and light
Streaming through all your spiritual mien,
As in calm clouds of pearly stillness bright,
Showers weave with sunshine, and transpierce their slight
Ethereal cradle. From your heart subdued
All haughty dreams of power had winged their flight,
And [illegible] ace for martyr fortitude,
True faith, long suffering love. Come to me, come!
And as the seas beneath your master's tread
Fell into crystal smoothness round him spread
Like the clear pavement of his heavenly home;
So in your presence, let the soul's great deep
Sink to the gentleness of infant sleep.

THE SONG OF MIRIAM.

A song for Israel's God! Spear, crest, and helm,
Lay by the billows of the old Red sea,
When Miriam's voice o'er that sepulchral realm
Sent on the blast a hymn of jubilee;
With her lit eye, and long hair floating free,
Queen-like she stood, and glorious was the strain,
E'en as instinct with the tempestuous glee
Of the dark waters tossing o'er the slain.
A song for God's own victory! O, thy lays,
Bright Poesy! were holy in their birth:—
How hath it died, thy seraph note of praise,
In the bewildering melodies of earth!
Return from troubling bitter founts—return,
Back to the life-springs of thy native urn!

RUTH.

The plume-like swaying of the auburn corn,
By soft winds to a dreamy motion fanned,
Still brings me back mine image—Oh! forlorn,
Yet not forsaken, Ruth! I see thee stand
Lone, 'midst the gladness of the harvest band—
Lone as a wood-bird on the ocean's foam,
Fallen in its weariness. Thy father-land
Smiles far away! yet to the sense of home,
That finest, purest, which can recognise
Home in affection's glance for ever true
Beats thy calm heart; and if thy gentle eyes
Gleam tremulous through tears, 'tis not to rue
Those words, immortal in their deep love's tone,
"*Thy people and thy God shall be mine own!*"

THE VIGIL OF RIZPAH.

"And Rizpah, the daughter of Aiah, took sackcloth, and spread it for her upon the rock, from the beginning of harvest until water dropped upon them out of heaven; and suffered neither the birds of the air to rest on them, by day, nor the beasts of the field by night."—*2 Sam.* xxi. 10.

Who watches on the mountain with the dead,
Alone before the awfulness of night?—
A seer awaiting the deep spirit's might?
A warrior guarding some dark pass of dread?
No, a lorn woman! On her drooping head,
Once proudly graceful, heavy beats the rain:
She recks not—living for the unburied slain,
Only to scare the vultures from their bed.
So, night by night, her vigil hath she kept
With the pale stars, and with the dews hath wept;
Oh! surely some bright Presence from above
On those wild rocks the lonely one must aid!—
E'en so; a strengthener through all storm and shade,
The unconquerable Angel, mightiest Love!

THE REPLY OF THE SHUNAMMITE WOMAN.

"And she answered, I dwell among mine own people."—*2 Kings* iv. 13.

"I dwell among mine own."—Oh! happy thou!
Not for the sunny clusters of the vine,
Nor for the olives on the mountain's brow;
Nor the flocks wondering by the flowery line
Of streams, that make the green land where they shine
Laugh to the light of waters—not for these,
Nor the soft shadow of ancestral trees,
Whose kindly whisper floats o'er thee and thine—
Oh! not for these I call thee richly blest,
But for the meekness of thy woman's breast,
Where that sweet depth of still contentment lies;
And for thy holy household love, which clings
Unto all ancient and familiar things,
Weaving from each some link for home's dear charities.

THE ANNUNCIATION.

Lowliest of women, and most glorified !
  In thy still beauty sitting calm and lone,
A brightness round thee grew—and by thy side
  Kindling the air, a form ethereal shone,
  Solemn, yet breathing gladness. From her throne
A queen had risen with more imperial eye,
A stately prophetess of victory
  From her proud lyre had struck a tempest's tone,
For such high tidings as to thee were brought,
  Chosen of Heaven ! that hour :—but thou, O thou !
E'en as a flower with gracious rains o'erfraught
  Thy virgin head beneath its crown didst bow,
And take to thy meek breast the all holy word,
  And own thyself *the handmaid of the Lord.*

—

THE SONG OF THE VIRGIN.

Yet as a sun-burst flushing mountain snow,
  Fell the celestial touch of fire ere long
On the pale stillness of thy thoughtful brow,
  And thy calm spirit lightened into song.
  Unconsciously perchance, yet free and strong
Flowed the majestic joy of tuneful words,
  Which living hearts the choirs of Heaven among
Might well have linked with their divinest chords,
Full many a strain, borne far on glory's blast,
Shall leave, where once its haughty music passed,
  No more to memory than a reed's faint sight ;
While thine, O childlike virgin ! through all time
Shall send its fervent breath o'er every clime,
  Being of God, and therefore not to die.

—

THE PENITENT ANOINTING CHRIST'S FEET.

There was a mournfulness in angel eyes,
  That saw thee, woman ! bright in this world's train,
Moving to pleasure's airy melodies,
  Thyself the idol of the enchanted strain.
  But from thy beauty's garland, brief and vain,
When one by one the rose-leaves had been torn,
  When thy heart's core had quivered to the pain
Through every life-nerve sent by arrowy scorn;
When thou didst kneel to pour sweet odors forth
  On the Redeemer's feet with many a sigh,
And showering tear-drop, of yet richer worth
  Than all those costly balms of Araby ;
Then was their joy, a song of joy in Heaven,
For thee, the child won back, the penitent forgiven !

—

MARY AT THE FEET OF CHRIST.

Oh ! blest beyond all daughters of the earth !
  What were the Orient's thrones to that low seat
Where thy hushed spirit drew celestial birth ?
  Mary ! meek listener at the Savior's feet ?
  No feverish cares to that divine retreat
Thy woman's heart of silent worship brought,
  But a fresh childhood, heavenly truth to meet,
With love, and wonder, and submissive thought.
Oh ! for the holy quiet of thy breast,
  'Midst the world's eager tones and footsteps flying !
  Thou whose calm soul was like a well-spring lying
So deep and still in its transparent rest,
That e'en when noontide burns upon the hills,
Some one bright solemn star all its lone mirror fills.

—

THE SISTERS OF BETHANY AFTER THE DEATH OF LAZARUS.

One grief, one faith, O sisters of the dead !
  Was in your bosoms—thou, whose steps, made fleet
By keen hope fluttering in the heart which bled,
  Bore thee as wings, the Lord of Life to greet ;
  And thou, that duteous in thy still retreat
Didst wait his summons then with reverent love
  Fall weeping at the blest Deliverer's feet,
Whom e'en to heavenly tears thy wo could move,
And which to Him, the All-Seeing and All-Just,
Was loveliest, that quick zeal, or lowly trust ?
Oh ! question not, and let no law be given
  To those unveilings of its deepest shrine,
  By the wrong spirit made in outward sign :
Free service from the heart is all in all to Heaven.

THE MEMORIAL OF MARY.

"Verily I say unto you, wheresoever this gospel shall be preac[illegible] ed in the whole world, there shall also this, that this woman h[illegible] done, be told for a memorial of her."—*Matthew* xxvi. 13. See [illegible] *John* xii. 3.

Thou hast thy record in the monarch's hall ;
  And on the waters of the far mid sea ;
And where the mighty mountain-shadows fall,
  The Alpine hamlet keeps a thought of thee :
  Where'er, beneath some Oriental tree,
The Christian traveller rests—where'er the child
  Looks upward from the English mother's knee,
With earnest eyes in wondering reverence mild,
There art thou known—where'er the Book of Light
Bears hope and healing, there, beyond all blight,
  Is borne thy memory, and all praise above ;
Oh ! say what deed so lifted thy sweet name,
Mary ! to that pure silent place of fame ?
  One lowly offering of exceeding love !

—

THE WOMEN OF JERUSALEM AT THE CROSS.

Like those pale stars of tempest hours, whose gleam
  Waves calm and constant on the rocking mast,
Such by the cross doth your bright lingering seem,
  Daughters of Zion ! faithful to the last !
  Ye, through the darkness o'er the wide earth cast
By the death-cloud within the Savior's eye,
  E'en till away the heavenly spirit passed,
Stood in the shadow of his agony.
O blessed faith ! a guiding lamp, that hour,
Was lit for woman's heart ; to her, whose dower
  Is all of love and suffering from her birth ;
Still hath your act a voice—through fear, through st[illegible]e
Bidding her bind each tendril of her life,
  To that which her deep soul hath proved of ho[illegible]st worth.

—

MARY MAGDALENE AT THE SEPULCHRE.

Weeper ! to thee how bright a morn was given
  After thy long, long vigil of despair,
When that high voice which burial rocks had riven,
  Thrilled with immortal tones the silent air !
Never did clarion's royal blast declare
  Such tale of victory to a breathless crowd,
As the deep sweetness of one word could bear,
  Into thy heart of hearts, O woman ! bowed
By strong affection's anguish !—one low word—
  "*Mary !*"—and all the triumph wrung from death
Was thus revealed ! and thou, that so hadst erred,
  So wept and been forgiven, in trembling faith
Didst cast thee down before the all-conquering Son,
Awed by the mighty gift thy tears and love had won !

—

MARY MAGDALENE BEARING TIDINGS OF THE RESURRECTION

Then was a task of glory all thine own,
  Nobler than e'er the still small voice assigned
To lips in awful music making known
  The stormy splendors of some prophet's mind.
"Christ is arisen !" by thee to wake mankind,
  First from the sepulchre those words were brought !
Thou wert to send the mighty rushing wind
  First on its way, with those high tidings fraught—
"*Christ has arisen !*" Thou, *thou*, the sin enthralled
Earth's outcast, Heaven's own ransomed one, wert cal[illegible]
  In human hearts to give that rapture birth ;
Oh ! raised from shame to brightness !—there doth lie
The tenderest meaning of His ministry,
  Whose undespairing love still owned the spirit's worth

HYMNS, DEVOTIONAL AND MEMORIAL.

THE SACRED HARP.

How shall the harp of poesy regain,
  That old victorious tone of prophet-years,
  A spell divine o'er guilt's perturbing fears,
And all the hovering shadows of the brain ?

Dark evil wings took flight before the strain,
And showers of holy quiet, with its fall,
Sank on the soul:—Oh! who may now recall
The mighty music's consecrated reign?—
Spirit of God! whose glory once o'erhung
A throne, the Ark's dread cherubim between,
So let thy presence brood, though now unseen,
O'er those two powers by whom the harp is strung—
Feeling and Thought!—till the rekindled chords
Give the long-buried tone back to immortal words!

TO A FAMILY BIBLE.

What household thoughts around thee, as their shrine
Cling reverently! of anxious looks beguiled,
My mother's eyes, upon thy page divine,
Each day were bent:—her accents, gravely mild,
Breathed out thy lore: whilst I, a dreamy child,
Wandered on breeze-like fancies oft away,
To some lone tuft of gleaming spring-flowers wild,
Some fresh-discovered nook for woodland play,
Some secret nest:—yet would the solemn Word
At times, with kindlings of young wonder heard,
Fall on my wakened spirit, there to be
A seed not lost;—for which, in darker years,
O Book of Heaven! I pour, with grateful tears,
Heart blessings on the holy dead and thee!

REPOSE OF A HOLY FAMILY.

From an old Italian Picture.

Under a palm-tree, by the green old Nile,
Lulled on his mother's breast, the fair child lies,
With dove-like breathings, and a tender smile,
Brooding above the slumber of his eyes.
While, through the stillness of the burning skies,
Lo! the dread work of Egypt's buried kings
Temple and pyramid beyond him rise,
Regal and still as everlasting things!—
Vain pomps! from Him, with that pure flowery cheek,
Soft shadowed by his mother's drooping head,
A new-born spirit, mighty, and yet meek,
O'er the whole world like vernal air shall spread!
And bid all earthly grandeurs cast the crown,
Before the suffering and the lowly, down.

PICTURE OF THE INFANT CHRIST WITH FLOWERS.

All the bright hues from eastern garlands glowing,
Round the young Child luxuriantly are spread;
Gifts, fairer far than Magian kings, bestowing,
In adoration, o'er his cradle shed.
Roses, deep-filled with rich midsummer's red,
Circle his hands; but in his grave sweet eye,
Thought seems e'en now to wake and prophecy
Of ruder coronals for that meek head.
And thus it was! a diadem of thorn
Earth gave to Him who mantled her with flowers,
To Him who poured forth blessings in soft showers,
O'er all her paths, a cup of bitter scorn!
And we repine, for whom that cup He took
O'er blooms that mocked our hope, o'er idols that forsook!

ON A REMEMBERED PICTURE OF CHRIST.

An Ecce Homo, by Leonardo da Vinci.

I met that image on a mirthful day
Of youth, and sinking with a stilled surprise,
The pride of life before those holy eyes,
In my quick heart died thoughtfully away,
Abashed to mute confessions of a sway,
Awful, though meek; and now, that from the strings,
Of my soul's lyre, the tempest's mighty wings,
Have struck forth tones which then awakened lay;
Now, that around the deep life of my mind,
Affections, deathless as itself, have twined,
Oft does the pale bright vision still float by;
But more divinely sweet, and speaking now
Of One whose pity, throned on that sad brow,
Sounded all depths of love, grief, death, humanity!

THE CHILDREN WHOM JESUS BLEST.

Happy were they, the mothers, in whose sight
Ye grew, fair children! hallowed from that hour
By your Lord's blessing! surely thence a shower
Of heavenly beauty, a transmitted light,
Hung on your brows and eyelids, meekly bright,
Through all the after years, which saw ye move
Lowly, yet still majestic in the might,
The conscious glory of the Savior's love!
And honored be all childhood, for the sake
Of that high love! let reverential care
Watch to behold the mortal spirit wake,
And shield its first bloom from unholy air;
Owning, in each young suppliant glance, the sign
Of claims upon a heritage divine.

MOUNTAIN SANCTUARIES.

"He went up to a mountain apart to pray."

A child 'midst ancient mountains I have stood,
Where the wild falcons make their lordly nest
On high. The spirit of the solitude
Fell solemnly upon my infant breast,
Though that I prayed not; but deep thoughts have pressed
Into my being since it breathed that air,
Nor could I now one moment live the guest
Of such dread scenes, without the springs of prayer
O'erflowing all my soul. No minsters rise
Like them in pure communion with the skies,
Vast, silent, open unto night and day;
So might the o'erburdened Son of man have felt,
When, turning where inviolate stillness dwelt,
He sought high mountains, there apart to pray.

THE LILIES OF THE FIELD.

"Consider the lilies of the fields."

Flowers! when the Savior's calm benignant eye
Fell on your gentle beauty—when from you
That heavenly lesson from all hearts he drew,
Eternal, universal as the sky—
Then, in the bosom of your purity,
A voice He set, as in a temple-shrine,
That life's quick travellers ne'er might pass you by
Unwarned of that sweet oracle divine.
And though too oft its low, celestial sound,
By the harsh notes of work-day care is drowned,
And the loud steps of vain unlistening Haste,
Yet, the great ocean hath no tone of power
Mightier to reach the soul, in thought's hushed hour,
Than yours, ye Lilies! chosen thus and graced!

THE BIRDS OF THE AIR.

"And behold the birds of the air."

Ye too, the free and fearless birds of air,
Were charged that hour, on missionary wing,
The same bright lesson o'er the seas to bear,
Heaven-guided wanderers with the wings of spring!
Sing on, before the storm and after, sing!
And call us to your echoing woods away
From worldly cares; and bid our spirits bring
Faith to imbibe deep wisdom from your lay.
So may those blessed vernal strains renew
Childhood, a childhood yet more pure and true
E'en than the first, within the awakened mind;
While sweetly, joyously, they tell of life,
That knows no doubts, no questionings, no strife,
But hangs upon its God, unconsciously resigned.

THE RAISING OF THE WIDOW'S SON.

"And he that was dead sat up and began to speak."

He that was dead rose up and spoke—He spoke!
Was it of that majestic world unknown?
Those words, which first the bier's dread silence broke,
Came they with revelation in each tone?

Were the far cities of the nations gone,
  The solemn halls of consciousness or sleep,
For man uncurtained by that spirit lone,
  Back from their portal summoned o'er the deep?
Be hushed, my soul! the veil of darkness lay
  Still drawn:—thy Lord called back the voice departed,
  To spread his truth, to comfort his weak-hearted,
Not to reveal the mysteries of its way.
Oh! take that lesson home in silent faith,
Put on submissive strength to *meet*, not *question* death!

—

THE OLIVE TREE.

The palm—the vine—the cedar—each hath power
  To bid fair Oriental shapes glance by,
And each quick glistening of the laurel bower
  Wafts Grecian images o'er fancy's eye.
But thou, pale olive!—in thy branches lie
  Far deeper spells than prophet-grove of old
Might e'er enshrine:—I could not hear thee sigh
  To the wind's faintest whisper, nor behold
One shiver of thy leaves' dim silvery green,
Without high thoughts and solemn, of that scene
When, in the garden, the Redeemer prayed—
  When pale stars looked upon his fainting head,
  And angels, ministering in silent dread,
Trembled, perchance, within thy trembling shade.

—

THE DARKNESS OF THE CRUCIFIXION.

On Judah's hills a weight of darkness hung,
  Felt shudderingly at noon:—the land had driven
  A Guest divine back to the gates of Heaven,
A life, whence all pure founts of healing sprung,
All grace, all truth:—and, when to anguish wrung,
  From the sharp cross the enlightening spirit fled,
  O'er the forsaken earth a pall of dread
By the great shadow of that death was flung.
O Savior! O Atoner! thou that fain
  Wouldst make thy temple in each human breast,
Leave not such darkness in my soul to reign,
Ne'er may thy presence from its depths depart,
  Chased thence by guilt!—Oh! turn not thou away,
  The bright and morning star, my guide to perfect day!

—

PLACES OF WORSHIP.

"God is a spirit."

Spirit! whose life-sustaining presence fills
  Air, ocean, central depths, by man untried
  Thou for thy worshippers hast sanctified
All place, all time! The silence of the hills
  Breathes veneration: founts and choral rills
Of thee are murmuring:—to its inmost glade
  The living forest with thy whisper thrills,
And there is holiness on every shade.
Yet must the thoughtful soul of man invest
  With dearer consecration those pure fanes,
Which, severed from all sound of earth's unrest,
  Hear naught but suppliant or adoring strains
Rise heavenward. Ne'er may rock or cave possess
Their claim on human hearts to solemn tenderness.

—

OLD CHURCH IN AN ENGLISH PARK.

Crowning a flowery slope, it stood alone
  In gracious sanctity. A bright rill wound,
  Caressingly, about the holy ground;
And warbled, with a never-dying tone,
Amidst the tombs. A hue of ages gone
  Seemed, from that ivied porch, that solemn gleam
  Of tower and cross, pale quivering on the stream,
O'er all the ancestral woodlands to be thrown,
And something yet more deep. The air was fraught
With noble memories, whispering many a thought
  Of England's fathers; loftily serene,
They that had toiled, watched, struggled to secure,
Within such fabrics, worship free and pure,
  Reigned there, the o'ershadowing spirits of the scene.

A CHURCH IN NORTH WALES.

Blessings be round it still! that gleaming fane,
  Low in its mountain glen! old mossy trees
Mellow the sunshine through the unteinted pane,
  And oft, borne in upon some fitful breeze,
The deep sound of the ever-pealing seas,
  Filling the hollows with its anthem-tone,
  There meets the voice of psalms!—yet not alone.
For memories lulling to the heart as these,
I bless thee, 'midst thy rocks, gray house of prayer!
But for their sakes who unto thee repair
  From the hill-cabins and the ocean-shore.
Oh! may the fisher and the mountaineer,
Words to sustain earth's toiling children bear,
  Within thy lowly walls for evermore!

—

LOUISE SCHEPLER.

Louise Schepler was the faithful servant and friend of the pastor Oberlin. The last letter addressed by him to his children for their perusal after his decease, affectionately commemorates her unwearied zeal in visiting and instructing the children of the mountain hamlets, through all seasons, and in all circumstances of difficulty and danger.

A fearless journeyer o'er the mountain snow
  Wert thou, Louise! the sun's decaying light,
Oft, with its latest melancholy glow,
  Reddened thy steep wild way; the starry night
  Oft met thee, crossing some lone eagle's height,
Piercing some dark ravine: and many a dell
Knew, through its ancient rock-recesses, well,
  Thy gentle presence, which hath made them bright
Oft in mid-storm; oh! not with beauty's eye,
  Nor the proud glance of genius keenly burning;
No! pilgrim of unwearying charity!
Thy spell was love—the mountain deserts turning
  To blessed realms, where stream and rock rejoice,
  When the glad human soul lifts a thanksgiving voice

—

TO THE SAME.

For thou, a holy shepherdess and kind,
  Through the pine forests by the upland rills,
  Didst roam to seek the children of the hills,
A wild neglected flock! to seek, and find,
And meekly win! there feeding each young mind
  With balms of heavenly eloquence: not thine,
  Daughter of Christ! but his, whose love divine,
Its own clear spirit in thy breast had shrined,
A burning light! Oh! beautiful, in truth,
  Upon the mountains are the feet of those
Who bear his tidings! From thy morn of youth,
  For this were all thy journeyings, and the close
Of that long path, Heaven's own bright sabbath-rest,
Must wait thee, wanderer! on thy Savior's breast.

LINES TO A BUTTERFLY RESTING ON A SCULL

  Creature of air and light!
Emblem of that which will not fade or die!
    Wilt thou not speed thy flight,
To chase the south wind through the glowing sky?
    What lures thee thus to stay,
    With silence and decay,
Fixed on the wreck of cold mortality?

    The thoughts, once chambered there,
Have gathered up their treasures, and are gone;—
    Will the dust tell thee where
That which hath burst the prison-house is flown?
    Rise, nursling of the day!
    If thou wouldst trace its way—
Earth has no voice to make the secret known.

    Who seeks the vanished bird,
Near the deserted nest and broken shell?
    Far thence, by us unheard,
He sings, rejoicing in the woods to dwell;
    Thou of the sunshine born,
    Take the bright wings of morn!
Thy hope springs heavenward from yon ruined cell.

CHURCH MUSIC.

——"All the train
Sang Hallelujah as the sound of seas."—*Milton.*

Again! oh, send those anthem notes again!
Through the arched roof in triumph to the sky!
Bid the old tombs give echoes to the strain,
The banners tremble, as with victory!

Sing them once more!—they waft my soul away,
High where no shadow of the past is thrown;
No earthly passion through the exulting lay,
Breathes mournfully one haunting under tone.

All is of Heaven!—yet wherefore to mine eye,
Gush the quick tears unbidden from their source,
E'en while the waves of that strong harmony,
Sweep with my spirit on their sounding course?

Wherefore must rapture its full tide reveal,
Thus by the signs betokening sorrow's power?
-Oh! is it not that humbly we may feel
Our nature's limits in its proudest hour!

THOUGHTS FROM AN ITALIAN POET.

Where shall I find, in all this fleeting earth,
This world of changes, and farewells, a friend
That will not fail me in his love and worth,
Tender, and firm, and faithful to the end?

Far hath my spirit sought a place of rest—
Long on vain idols its devotion shed;
Some have forsaken whom I loved the best,
And some deceived, and some are with the dead.

But thou, my Savior! thou, my hope and trust,
Faithful art thou when friends and joys depart,
Teach me to lift these yearnings from the dust,
And fix on thee, the Unchanging One, my heart.

A FATHER READING THE BIBLE.

'Twas early day, and sunlight streamed
Soft through a quiet room,
That hushed, but not forsaken, seemed,
Still, but with naught of gloom.
For there, serene in happy age,
Whose hope is from above,
A father communed with the page
Of Heaven's recorded love.

Pure fell the beam, and meekly bright,
On his gray holy hair,
And touched the page with tenderest light,
As if its shrine were there!
But oh! that patriarch's aspect shone
With something lovelier far,
A radiance all the spirit's own,
Caught not from sun or star.

Some word of life e'en then had met
His calm, benignant eye,
Some ancient promise, breathing yet
Of Immortality:
Some martyr's prayer, wherein the glow
Of quenchless faith survives:
For every feature said—"I know
That my Redeemer lives!"

And silent stood his children by,
Hushing their very breath,
Before the solemn sanctity
Of thoughts o'ersweeping death.
Silent—yet did not each young breast
With love and reverence melt?
Oh! blest be those fair girls, and blest
That home where God is felt!

HYMN BY THE SICK-BED OF A MOTHER.

Father! that in the olive shade
When the dark hour came on,
Didst, with a breath of heavenly aid,
Strengthen thy Son;

Oh! by the anguish of that night,
Send us down blest relief;
Or to the chastened, let thy might
Hallow this grief;

And Thou, that when the starry sky
Saw the dead strife begun,
Didst teach adoring faith to cry,
"Thy will be done!"

By thy meek spirit, Thou, of all
That e'er have mourned the chief—
Thou Savior! if the stroke must fall,
Hallow this grief!

A DIRGE.

Calm on the bosom of thy God,
Young spirit! rest thee now!
E'en while with us thy footsteps trod,
His soul was on thy brow.

Dust, to its narrow house beneath!
Soul, to its place on high!
They that have seen thy look in death,
No more may fear to die.

Lone are the paths, and sad the bowers,
Whence thy meek smile is gone;
But oh! a brighter home than ours,
In heaven, is now thine own.

THE PENITENT'S OFFERING.

St. Luke vii. 37, 38.

Thou that with pallid cheek,
And eyes in sadness meek,
And faded locks that humbly swept the ground,
From their long wanderings won,
Before the all-healing Son,
Didst bow thee to the earth, oh, lost and found!

When thou wouldst bathe his feet,
With odors richly sweet,
And many a shower of woman's burning tear,
And dry them with that hair,
Brought low the dust to wear
From the crowded beauty of its festal year.

Did he reject thee then,
While the sharp scorn of men
On thy once bright and stately head was cast?
No, from the Savior's mien,
A solemn light serene,
Bore to thy soul the peace of God at last.

For thee, their smiles no more
Familiar faces wore,
Voices, once kind, had learned the stranger's tone,
Who raised thee up and bound
Thy silent spirit's wound?
He, from all guilt the stainless, He alone!

But which, oh, erring child!
From home so long beguiled,
Which of thine offerings won those words of Heaven
That o'er the bruised reed,
Condemned of earth to bleed,
In music passed, "Thy sins are all forgiven?"

Was it that perfume fraught
With balm and incense, brought
From the sweet woods of Araby the blest?
Or that fast flowing rain
Of tears, which not in vain
To Him who scorned not tears, thy woes confessed?

No, not by these restored
Unto thy Father's board,
Thy peace, that kindled joy in heaven, was made;
But costlier in his eyes,
By that blest sacrifice,
Thy heart, thy full deep heart, before him laid.

COME TO ME, DREAMS OF HEAVEN.

Come to me, dreams of heaven!
  My fainting spirit bear
On your bright wings, by morning given,
  Up to celestial air.
Away, far, far away,
  From bowers by tempests riven,
Fold me in blue, still, cloudless day,
  O blessed dreams of heaven!

Come but for one brief hour,
  Sweet dreams! and yet again,
O'er burning thought and memory shower
  Your soft effacing rain!
Waft me where gales divine,
  With dark clouds ne'er have striven,
Where living founts for ever shine—
  O blessed dreams of heaven!

THE ANGELS' CALL.

"Hark! they whisper! angels say,
Sister spirit come away!"

Come to the land of peace!
Come where the tempest hath no longer sway,
The shadow passes from the soul away,
  The sounds of weeping cease!

Fear hath no dwelling there!
Come to the mingling of repose and love,
Breathed by the silent spirit of the dove
  Through the celestial air!

Come to the bright and blest
And crowned for ever!—'midst that shining band,
Gathered to Heaven's own wreath from every land,
  Thy spirit shall find rest!

Thou hast been long alone:
Come to thy mother!—on the sabbath shore,
The heart that rocked thy childhood back once more
  Shall take its wearied one.

In silence wert thou left!
Come to thy sisters!—joyously again
All the home voices, blest in one sweet strain,
  Shall greet their long-bereft.

Over thine orphan head
The storm hath swept as o'er a willow's bough:
Come to thy father!—it is finished now:
  Thy tears have all been shed.

In thy divine abode
Change finds no pathway, memory no dark trace,
And, oh! bright victory—death by love no place!
  Come, spirit! to thy God!

THE FOUNTAIN OF MARAH.

"And when they came to Marah, they could not drink of the waters of Marah, for they were bitter.
"And the people murmured against Moses, saying, What shall we drink?
"And he cried unto the Lord; and the Lord showed him a tree, which when he had cast into the waters, the waters were made sweet."—*Exod.* xv. 23-25.

Where is the tree the prophet threw
  Into the bitter wave?
Left it no scion where it grew,
  The thirsting soul to save?

Hath nature lost the hidden power
  Its precious foliage shed?
Is there no distant eastern bower,
  With such sweet leaves o'erspread,

Nay, wherefore ask?—since gifts are ours,
  Which yet may well imbue
Earth's many-troubled founts with showers
  Of Heaven's own balmy dew.

Oh! mingled with the cup of grief,
  Let faith's deep spirit be;
And every prayer shall win a leaf
  From that blest healing tree!

THINGS THAT CHANGE.

Knowest thou that seas are sweeping
  Where cities once have been?
When the calm wave is sleeping,
  Their towers may yet be seen;
Far down below the glassy tide
  Man's dwelling's where his voice hath died!

Knowest thou that flocks are feeding
  Above the tombs of old,
Which kings, their armies leading,
  Have lingered to behold?
A short, smooth greensward o'er them spread
Is all that marks where heroes bled.

Knowest thou that now the token
  Of temples once renowned,
Is but a pillar, broken,
  With glass and wall-flowers crowned?
And the lone serpent rears her young
Where the triumphant lyre hath sung?

Well, well, I know the story
  Of ages passed away,
And the mournful wrecks that glory
  Has left to dull decay.
But thou hast yet a tale to learn
More full of warnings sad and stern

Thy pensive eye but ranges
  O'er ruined fane and hall,
Oh! the deep soul has changes
  More sorrowful than all.
Talk not, while these before thee throng
Of silence in the place of song.

See scorn—where love has perished;
  Distrust—where friendship grew;
Pride—where once nature cherished
  All tender thoughts and true!
And shadows of oblivion thrown
O'er every trace of idols gone.

Weep not for tombs far scattered,
  For temples prostrate laid—
In thine own heart lie shattered
  The altars it had made.
Go, sound its depths in doubt and fear!
Heap up no more its treasures here.

THE POETRY OF THE PSALMS.

Nobly thy song, O minstrel! rushed to meet
  The Eternal on the pathway of the blast,
  With darkness round him, as a mantle, cast,
And cherubim to waft his flying seat.
Amidst the hills, that smoked beneath his feet,
  With trumpet voice thy spirit called aloud,
And bade the trembling rocks his name repeat,
  And the bent cedars and the bursting cloud,
But far more gloriously to earth made known
By that high strain, than by the thunder's tone,
  Than flashing torrents or the ocean's roll;
Jehovah spoke through the inbreathing fire,
Nature's vast realms for ever to inspire
  With the deep worship of a living soul.

THE SABBATH.

How many blessed groups this hour are bending
  Through England's primrose meadow paths their way
Toward spire and tower, 'midst shadowy elms ascending,
  Whence the sweet chimes proclaim the hallowed day.
The halls, from old heroic ages gray,
  Pour their fair children forth; and hamlets low,
With whose thick orchard blooms the soft winds play,
  Send out their inmates in a happy flow,
Like a free vernal stream. I may not tread
With them those pathways—to the feverish bed
  Of sickness bound; yet, oh, my God! I bless
Thy mercy, that with sabbath peace hath filled
My chastened heart, and all its throbbings stilled
  To one deep calm of lowliest thankfulness.

THE VOICE OF GOD.

"I heard thy voice in the garden and I was afraid."

Amidst the thrilling leaves, thy voice,
  At evening's fall, drew near;
Father! and did not man rejoice
  That blessed sound to hear!

Did not his heart within him burn,
  Touched by the solemn tone?
Not so! for, never to return,
  Its purity was gone.

Therefore, 'midst holy stream and bower,
  His spirit shook with dread,
And called the cedars in that hour,
  To veil his conscious head.

Oh! in each wind, each fountain flow,
  Each whisper of the shade,
Grant me, my God, thy voice to know,
  And not to be afraid!

A PRAYER.

Father in Heaven! from whom the simplest flower
  On the high Alps or fiery desert thrown,
  Draws not sweet odor or young life alone,
But the deep virtue of an inborn power
To cheer the wanderer in his fainting hour,
  With thoughts of Thee; to strengthen, to infuse
  Faith, love, and courage, by the tender hues
That speak thy presence; oh! with such a dower
Grace thou my song!—the precious gift bestow
  From thy pure spirit's treasury divine,
To wake one tear of purifying flow,
  To soften one wrung heart for thee and thine;
So shall the life breathed through the lowly strain,
Be as the meek wild-flower's—if transient, yet not vain.

PRAYER CONTINUED.

"What in me is dark
Illumine: what is low raise and support."—*Milton.*

Far are the wings of intellect astray,
  That strive not, Father! to thy heavenly seat;
  They rove, but mount not; and the tempests beat
Still on their plumes; O source of mental day!
Chase from before my spirit's track the array
  Of mists and shadows, raised by earthly care
  In troubled hosts that cross the purer air,
And veil the opening of the starry way,
  Which brightens on to thee! Oh! guide thou right
  My thought's weak pinion, clear mine inward sight,
The eternal springs of beauty to discern,
  Welling beside thy throne; unseal mine ear,
  Nature's true oracles in joy to hear:
Keep my soul wakeful still to listen and to learn.

HE WALKED WITH GOD.

Genesis v. 24.

He walked with God, in holy joy,
  Whilst yet his days were few;
The deep glad spirit of the boy
  To love and reverence grew.
Whether, each nightly star to count
  The ancient hills he trod,
Or sought the flowers by stream and fount—
  Alike he walked with God.

The graver noon of manhood came,
  The full of cares and fears;
One voice was in his heart—the same
  It heard through child ood's years.
Amidst fair tents, and flocks, and swains,
  O'er his green pasture-sod,
A shepherd-king on eastern plains—
  The patriarch walked with God.

And calmly, brightly, that pure life
  Melted from earth away;
No cloud it knew, no parting strife,
  No sorrowful decay;
He bowed him not, like all beside,
  Unto the spoiler's rod,
But joined at once the glorified,
  Where angels walk with God!

So let us walk!—the night must come
  To us that comes to all;
We through the darkness must go home,
  Hearing the trumpet's call.
Closed is the path for evermore,
  Which without death he trod;
Not so that way, wherein of yore
  His footsteps walked with God!

THE ROD OF AARON.

(*Numbers* xvii. 8.)

Was it the sigh of the southern gale
  That flushed the almond bough?
Brightest and first the young spring to hail,
  Still its red blossoms glow.

Was it the sunshine that woke its flowers
  With a kindling look of love?
Oh, far and deep, and through hidden bowers
  That smile of Heaven can rove!

No! from the breeze and the living light
  Shut was the sapless rod;
But it felt in the stillness a secret might,
  And thrilled to the breath of God.

E'en so may that breath, like the vernal air,
  O'er our glad spirits move;
And all such things as are good and fair,
  Be the blossoms, its track that prove!

A PRAYER.

WRITTEN AT THE AGE OF NINE.

Oh! God, my Father and my Friend,
Ever thy blessings to me send;
Let me have Virtue for my guide,
And wisdom always at my side;
Thus cheerfully through life I'll go,
Nor ever feel the sting of wo;
Contented with the humblest lot,
Happy, though in the meanest cot.

THE OCEAN.

"They that go down to the sea in ships, that do business in gr[illegible] waters, these see the works of the Lord, and his wonders in t[illegible] deep."—*Psalm* cvii. 23, 24.

He that in venturous barks hath been
  A wanderer on the deep,
Can tell of many an awful scene,
  Where storms for ever sweep.

For many a fair majestic sight
  Hath met his wandering eye,
Beneath the streaming northern light,
  Or blaze of Indian sky.

Go! ask him of the whirlpool's roar,
  Whose echoing thunder peals
Loud, as if rushed along the shore
  An army's chariot-wheels;

Of icebergs, floating o'er the main,
  Or fixed upon the coast,
Like glittering citadel or fane,
  'Mid the bright realms of frost

Of coral rocks from waves below
  In steep ascent that tower,
And fraught with peril, daily grow,
  Formed by an insect's power;

Of sea-fires, which at dead of night
  Shine o'er the tides afar,
And make the expanse of ocean bright
  As heaven, with many a star.

Oh God! thy name they well may praise,
  Who to the deep go down,
And trace the wonders of thy ways,
  Where rocks and billows frown.

If glorious be that awful deep,
  No human power can bind,
What then art Thou, who bidst it keep
  Within its bounds confined!

Let heaven and earth in praise unite,
  Eternal praise to Thee,
Whose word can rouse the tempest's might,
  Or still the raging sea!

THE TRUMPET.

The trumpet's voice hath roused the land,
  Light up the beacon pyre!
—A hundred hills have seen the brand
  And waved the sign of fire.
A hundred banners to the breeze
  Their gorgeous folds have cast—
And hark!—was that the sound of seas?
  —A king to war went past.

The chief is arming in his hall,
  The peasant by his hearth;
The mourner hears the thrilling call,
  And rises from the earth.
The mother on her first-born son
  Looks with a boding eye—
They come not back, though all be won,
  Whose young hearts leap so high.

The bard hath ceased his song, and bound
  The falchion to his side;
E'en for the marriage altar crowned,
  The lover quits his bride.
And all this haste, and change, and fear,
  By earthly clarion spread!—
How will it be when kingdoms hear
The blast that wakes the dead?

THE STARS.

"The heavens declare the glory of God, and the firmament showeth his handy work."—*Psalm* xix. 1.

No cloud obscures the summer sky,
The moon in brightness walks on high,
And, set in azure, every star
Shines, like a gem of heaven, afar!

Child of the earth! oh! lift thy glance
To yon bright firmament's expanse;
The glories of its realm explore,
And gaze, and wonder, and adore!

Doth it not speak to every sense
The marvels of Omnipotence?
Seest thou not there the Almighty name,
Inscribed in characters of flame?

Count o'er those lamps of quenchless light,
That sparkle through the shades of night!
Behold them!—can a mortal boast
To number that celestial host?

Mark well each little star, whose rays
In distant splendor meet thy gaze,
Each is a world by Him sustained,
Who from eternity hath reigned.

Each, shining not for earth alone,
Hath suns and planets of its own,
And beings, whose existence springs
From Him the all-powerful King of kings.

Haply, those glorious beings know
Nor stain of guilt, nor tear of wo!
But raising still the adoring voice,
For ever in their God rejoice.

What then art thou, oh! child of clay!
Amid creation's grandeur, say?
—E'en as an insect on the breeze,
E'en as a dew-drop, lost in seas!

Yet fear thou not!—the sovereign hand,
Which spread the ocean and the land,
And hung the rolling spheres in air,
Hath, e'en for thee, a Father's care!

Be thou at peace!—the all-seeing eye,
Pervading earth, and air, and sky,
The searching glance which none may flee,
Is still, in mercy, turned on thee.

DIRGE OF A CHILD.

No bitter tears for thee be shed,
  Blossom of being! seen and gone!
With flowers alone we strew thy bed,
  O blest departed one!
Whose all of life, a rosy ray,
Blushed into dawn, and passed away.

Yes! thou art fled, ere guilt had power
  To stain thy cherub soul and form,
Closed is the soft ephemeral flower,
  That never felt a storm!
The sunbeam's smile, the zephyr's breath,
All that it knew from birth to death.

Thou wert so like a form of light,
  That Heaven benignly called thee hence,
Ere yet the world could breathe one blight
  O'er thy sweet innocence:
And thou, that brighter home to bless,
Art passed, with all thy loveliness!

Oh! hadst thou still on earth remained,
  Vision of beauty! fair as brief!
How soon thy brightness had been stained
  With passion or with grief?
Now not a sullying breath can rise,
To dim thy glory in the skies.

We rear no marble o'er thy tomb,
  No sculptured image there shall mourn;
Ah! fitter far the vernal bloom
  Such dwelling to adorn.
Fragrance, and flowers, and dews, must be
The only emblems meet for thee.

Thy grave shall be a blessed shrine,
  Adorned with Nature's brightest wreath,
Each glowing season shall combine
  Its incense there to breathe;
And oft, upon the midnight air,
Shall viewless harps be murmuring there.

And oh! sometimes in visions blest,
  Sweet spirit! visit our repose,
And bear from thine own world of rest,
  Some balm for human woes!
What form more lovely could be given
Than thine, to messenger of Heaven?

THE LANDING OF THE PILGRIM FATHERS.

The breaking waves dashed high
  On a stern and rock-bound coast,
And the woods, against a stormy sky,
  Their giant branches tossed;

And the heavy night hung dark
  The hills and waters o'er,
When a band of exiles moored their bark
  On the wild New England shore.

Not as the conqueror comes,
  They, the true-hearted came,
Not with the roll of the stirring drums,
  And the trumpet that sings of fame;

Not as the flying come,
  In silence and in fear,—
They shook the depths of the desert's gloom
  With their hymns of lofty cheer.

Amidst the storm they sang,
  And the stars heard and the sea!
And the sounding aisles of the dim woods rang
  To the anthem of the free!

The ocean-eagle soared
  From his nest by the white wave's foam,
And the rocking pines of the forest roared—
  This was their welcome home!

There were men with hoary hair,
  Amidst that pilgrim-band—
Why had they come to wither there
  Away from their childhood's land?

There was woman's fearless eye,
  Lit by her deep love's truth;
There was manhood's brow serenely high,
  And the fiery heart of youth.

What sought they thus afar?
  Bright jewels of the mine?
The wealth of seas, the spoils of war?
  —They sought a faith's pure shrine!

Ay, call it holy ground,
  The soil where first they trod!
They have left unstained what there they found—
  Freedom to worship God!

THE HEBREW MOTHER.

The rose was rich in bloom on Sharon's plain,
When a young mother with her first-born thence
Went up to Zion, for the boy was vowed
Unto the temple-service;—by the hand
She led him, and her silent soul, the while,
Oft as the dewy laughter of his eye
Met her sweet serious glance, rejoiced to think
That aught so pure, so beautiful, was hers,
To bring before her God. So passed they on,
O'er Judah's hills; and wheresoe'er the leaves
Of the broad sycamore made sounds at noon,
Like lulling rain-drops, or the olive-boughs,
With their cool dimness, crossed the sultry blue
Of Syria's heaven, she paused, that he might rest;
Yet from her own meek eyelids chased the sleep
That weighed their dark fringe down, to sit and watch
The crimson deepening o'er his cheek's repose,
As at a red flower's heart. And where a fount
Lay like a twilight star 'midst palmy shades,
Making its banks green gems along the wild,
There too she lingered from the diamond wave
Drawing bright water for his rosy lips,
And softly parting clusters of jet curls
To bathe his brow. At last the Fane was reached,
The earth's One Sanctuary—and rapture hushed
Her bosom, as before her, through the day,
It rose, a mountain of white marble, steeped
In light, like flowing gold. But when that hour
Waned to the farewell moment, when the boy
Lifted, through rainbow-gleaming tears, his eye
Beseechingly to hers, and half in fear
Turned from the white-robed priest, and round her arm
Clung as the ivy clings—the deep spring tide
Of Nature then swelled high, and o'er her child
Bending, her soul broke forth, in mingled sounds
Of weeping and sad song. "Alas," she cried,

"Alas! my boy, thy gentle grasp is on me,
The bright tears quiver in thy pleading eyes,
    And now fond thoughts arise,
And silver cords again to earth have won me;
And like a vine thou claspest my full heart—
    How shall I hence depart?

"How the lone paths retrace where thou wert playing
So late, along the mountains, at my side?
    And I, in joyous pride,
By every place of flowers my course delaying
Wove, e'en as pearls, the lilies round thy hair,
    Beholding thee so fair!

"And oh! the home whence thy bright smile hath parted,
Will it not seem as if the sunny day
    Turned from its door away?
While through its chambers wandering, weary-hearted,
I languish for thy voice, which past me still
    Went like a singing rill!

"Under the palm-trees thou no more shall meet me,
When from the fount at evening I return,
    With the full water-urn;
Nor will thy sleep's low dove-like breathings greet me,
As midst the silence of the stars I wake,
    And watch for thy dear sake.

"And thou, will slumber's dewy cloud fall round thee,
Without thy mother's hand to smooth thy bed?
    Wilt thou not vainly spread
Thine arms, when darkness as a veil hath wound thee,
To fold my neck, and lift up, in thy fear,
    A cry which none shall hear?

"What have I said, my child! Wilt He not hear thee,
Who the young ravens heareth from their nest?
    Shall He not guard thy rest,
And, in the hush of holy midnight near thee,
Breathe o'er thy soul, and fill its dreams with joy?
    Thou shalt sleep soft, my boy!

"I give thee to thy God—the God that gave thee,
A well-spring of deep gladness to my heart!
    And precious, as thou art,
And pure as dew of Hermon, He shall have thee,
My own, my beautiful, my undefiled!
    And thou shalt be his child

"Therefore, farewell! I go, my soul may fail me,
As the hart panteth for the water-brooks,
    Yearning for thy sweet looks—
But thou, my first-born, droop not, nor bewail me;
Thou in the Shadow of the Rock shalt dwell,
    The Rock of Strength. Farewell!"

SPANISH EVENING HYMN.

Ave! now let prayer and music
  Meet in love on earth and sea!
Now, sweet Mother! may the weary
  Turn from this cold world to thee!

From the wide and restless waters
  Hear the sailor's hymn arise!
From his watch-fire 'midst the mountains,
  Lo! to thee the shepherd cries!

Yet, when thus full hearts find voices
  If o'erburdened souls there be,
Dark and silent in their anguish,
  Aid those captives! set them free!

Touch them, every fount unsealing,
  Where the frozen tears lie deep;
Thou, the Mother of all Sorrows,
  Aid, oh! aid to pray and weep!

DEATH OF AN INFANT.

Death found strange beauty on that cherub brow,
And dashed it out. There was a teint of rose
On cheek and lip—he touched the veins with ice,
And the rose faded; forth from those blue eyes
There spoke a wishful tenderness—a doubt
Whether to grieve or sleep, which innocence
Alone can wear. With ruthless haste he bound
The silken fringes of their curtaining lids
For ever; there had been a murmuring sound,
With which the babe would claim its mother's ear,
Charming her even to tears. The spoiler set
His seal of silence. But there beamed a smile
So fixed and holy from that marble brow—
Death gazed, and left it there; he dared not steal
The signet-ring of Heaven.

THE HEBREW MELODIES

OF

LORD BYRON.

SHE WALKS IN BEAUTY.

She walks in beauty, like the night
Of cloudless climes and starry skies;
And all that's best of dark and bright
Meet in her aspect and her eyes:
Runs mellowed to that tender light
Which heaven to gaudy day denies.

One shade the more, one ray the less,
Had half-impaired the nameless grace,
Which waves in every raven tress,
Or softly lightens o'er her face:
Where thoughts serenely sweet express
How pure, how dear their dwelling-place.

And on that cheek, and o'er that brow,
So soft, so calm, yet eloquent,
The smiles that win, the teints that glow,
But tell of days in goodness spent,
A mind at peace with all below,
A heart whose love is innocent.

THE HARP THE MONARCH MINSTREL SWEPT.

The harp the monarch minstrel swept,
The king of men, the loved of Heaven,
Which music hallowed while she wept
O'er tones her heart of hearts had given.
Redoubled be her tears, its chords are riven!
It softened men of iron mould,
It gave them virtues not their own;
No ear so dull, no soul so cold,
That felt not, fired not to the tone,
Till David's lyre grew mightier than his throne.

It told the triumphs of our king,
It wafted glory to our God;
It made our gladdened valleys ring,
The cedars bow, the mountains nod;
Its sound aspired to Heaven, and there abode!
Since then, though heard on earth no more,
Devotion and her daughter Love
Still bid the bursting spirit soar
To sounds that seem as from above,
In dreams that day's broad light can not remove.

IF THAT HIGH WORLD.

If that high world, which lies beyond
Our own, surviving love endears;
If there the cherished heart be fond,
The eye the same, except in tears—
How welcome those untrodden spheres!
How sweet this very hour to die!
To soar from earth, and find all fears
Lost in thy light—Eternity!

It must be so: 'tis not for self
That we so tremble on the brink;
And striving to o'erleap the gulf,
Yet cling to being's severing link.
O, in that future let us think
To hold each heart the heart that shares,
With them the immortals' waters drink
And soul in soul grow deathless theirs!

THE WILD GAZELLE.

The wild gazelle on Judah's hills
Exulting yet may bound,
And drink from all the living rills
That gush on holy ground;
Its airy step and glorious eye,
May glance in tameless transport by:—

A step as fleet, an eye more bright,
Hath Judah witnessed there;
And o'er her scenes of lost delight,
Inhabitants more fair.
The cedars wave on Lebanon,
But Judah's statelier maids are gone!

More blest each palm that shades those plains
Than Israel's scattered race;
For, taking root, it there remains
In solitary grace:
It can not quit his place of birth,
It will not live in other earth.

But we must wander witheringly,
In other lands to die;
And where our fathers' ashes be
Our own may never lie:
Our temple hath not left a stone,
And mockery sits on Salem's throne.

O WEEP FOR THOSE.

O weep for those that wept by Babel's stream,
Whose shrines are desolate, whose land a dream;
Weep for the harp of Judah's broken shell:
Mourn—where their God hath dwelt the godless dwell.

And where shall Israel lave her bleeding feet?
And when shall Zion's songs again seem sweet?
And Judah's melody once more rejoice
The hearts that leaped before its heavenly voice?

Tribes of the wandering foot and weary breast,
How shall ye flee away and be at rest?
The wild-dove hath her nest, the fox his cave,
Mankind their country—Israel but the grave.

ON JORDAN'S BANKS.

On Jordan's banks the Arab's camels stray,
On Sion's hill the False One's votaries pray,
The Baal-adorer bows on Sinai's steep—
Yet there—even there—O God! thy thunders sleep.

There—where thy finger scorched the tablet stone!
There—where thy shadow to thy people shone!
Thy glory shrouded in its garb of fire:
Thyself—none living see and not expire!

O! in the lightning let thy glance appear!
Sweep from his shivered hand the oppressor's spear.
How long by tyrants shall thy land be trod?
How long thy temple worshipless, O God?

JEPHTHAH'S DAUGHTER.

SINCE our country, our God—O my sire!
Demand that thy daughter expire;
Since thy triumph was bought by thy vow—
Strike the bosom that's bared for thee now!

And the voice of my mourning is o'er,
And the mountains behold me no more:
If the hand that I love lay me low,
There can not be pain in the blow!

nd of this, O my father! be sure—
hat the blood of thy child is as pure
the blessing I beg ere it flow,
ıd the last thought that sooths me below.

ıough the virgins of Salem lament,
the judge and the hero unbent!
have won the great battle for thee
nd my father and country are free!

When this blood of thy giving hath gushed,
When the voice that thou lovest is hushed,
Let my memory still be thy pride,
And forget not I smiled as I died.

! SNATCHED AWAY IN BEAUTY'S BLOOM.

O! SNATCHED away in beauty's bloom,
On thee shall press no ponderous tomb;
But on thy turf shall roses rear
Their leaves the earliest of the year;
And the wild cypress wave in tender gloom:

And oft by yon blue gushing stream,
Shall sorrow lean her drooping head,
And feed deep thought with many a dream,
And lingering pause and lightly tread:
Fond wretch! as if her steps disturbed the dead.

Away! we know that tears are vain,
That death nor heeds nor hears distress:
Will this unteach us to complain?
Or make one mourner weep the less?
And thou—who tell'st me to forget,
Thy looks are wan, thine eyes are wet.

MY SOUL IS DARK.

MY soul is dark.—O quickly string
The harp I yet can brook to hear;
And let thy gentle fingers fling
Its melting murmurs o'er mine ear.
If in this heart a hope be dear,
That sound shall charm it forth again;
If in these eyes there lurk a tear,
'Twill flow, and cease to burn my brain.

But bid the strain be wild and deep,
Nor let thy notes of joy be first;
I tell thee, minstrel, I must weep
Or else this heavy heart will burst;
For it hath been by sorrow nurst,
And ached in sleepless silence long;
And now 'tis doomed to know the worst,
And break at once or yield to song.

›ONG OF SAUL BEFORE HIS LAST BATTLE.

WARRIORS and chiefs! should the shaft or the sword
Pierce me in leading the host of the Lord,
Heed not the corse, though a king's, in your path:
Bury your steels in the bosom of Gath!

Thou who art bearing my buckler and bow,
Should the soldiers of Saul look away from the foe,
Stretch me that moment in blood at thy feet!
Mine be the doom which they dared not to meet.

Farewell to others, but never we part,
Heir to my royalty, son of my heart!
Bright is the diadem, boundless the sway,
Or kingl· the death which awaits us to-day.

I SAW THEE WEEP.

I SAW thee weep—the big bright tear
Came o'er that eye of blue;
And then methought it did appear
A violet dropping dew;
I saw thee smile—the sapphire's blaze
Beside thee ceased to shine,
It could not match the living r[illegible]s
That filled that glance of thine.

As clouds from yonder sun receive
A deep and mellow die,
Which scarce the shade of coming eve
Can banish from the sky,
Those smiles unto the moodiest mind
Their own pure joy impart;
Their sunshine leaves a glow behind
That lightens o'er the heart.

SAUL.

THOU whose spell can raise the dead,
Bid the prophet's form appear.
"Samuel raise thy buried head!
King behold the phantom seer."
Earth yawned; he stood the centre of a cloud:
Light changed its hue, retiring from his shroud:
Death stood all glassy in his fixed eye;
His hand was withered and his veins were dry,
His foot, in bony whiteness, glittered there,
Shrunken and sinewless, and ghastly bare:
From lips that moved not and unbreathing frame,
Like caverned winds, the hollow accents came.
Saul saw, and fell to earth, as falls the oak,
At once, and blasted by the thunder-stroke.
"Why is my sleep disquieted?
Who is he that calls the dead?
Is it thou, O king? Behold,
Bloodless are these limbs, and cold:
Such are mine; and such shall be
Thine, to-morrow, when with me:
Ere the coming day is done,
Such shalt thou be, such thy son.
Fare thee well, but for a day;
Then we mix our mouldering clay.
Thou, thy race, lie pale and low,
Pierced by shafts of many a bow:
And the falchion by thy side
To thy heart, thy hand shall guide;
Crownless, breathless, headless fall,
Son and sire, the house of Saul."

"ALL IS VANITY, SAITH THE PREACHER."

FAME, wisdom, love, and power, were mine,
And health and youth possessed me;
My goblets blushed from every vine,
And lovely forms caressed me;
I sunned my heart in beauty's eyes,
And felt my soul grow tender;
All earth can give, or mortal prize,
Was mine of regal splendor.

I strive to number o'er what days
Remembrance can discover,
Which all that life or earth displays
Would lure me to live over.
There rose no day, there rolled no hour
Of pleasure unembittered;
And not a trapping decked my power
That galled not while it glittered.

The serpent of the field, by art
And spells, is won from harming;
But that which coils around the heart,
O who hath power of charming?
It will not list to wisdom's lore,
Nor music's voice can lure it;
But there it stings for evermore
The soul that must endure it.

THY DAYS ARE DONE.

Thy days are done, thy fame begun;
 Thy country's strains record
The triumphs of her chosen son,
 The slaughters of his sword!
The deeds he did, the fields he won,
 The freedom he restored!

Though thou art fallen, while we are free
 Thou shalt not taste of death!
The generous blood that flowed from thee
 Disdained to sink beneath:
Within our veins its currents be,
 Thy spirit on our breath:

Thy name, our charging hosts along,
 Shall be the battle-word!
Thy fall, the theme of choral song
 From virgin voices poured!
To weep would do thy glory wrong;
 Thou shalt not be deplored.

WHEN COLDNESS WRAPS THIS SUFFERING CLAY.

When coldness wraps this suffering clay,
 Ah, whither strays the immortal mind?
It can not die, it can not stay,
 But leaves its darkened dust behind.
Then, unembodied, doth it trace
 By steps each planet's heavenly way?
Or fill at once the realms of space,
 A thing of eyes, that all survey?

Eternal, boundless, undecayed,
 A thought unseen, but seeing all,
All, all in earth, or skies displayed,
 Shall it survey, shall it recall:
Each fainter trace that memory holds,
 So darkly of departed years,
In one broad glance the soul beholds,
 And all, that was, at once appears.

Before creation peopled earth,
 Its eye shall roll through chaos back;
And where the furthest heaven had birth,
 The spirit trace its rising track,
And where the future mars or makes,
 Its glance dilate o'er all to be,
While sun is quenched or system breaks,
 Fixed in its own eternity.

Above, or love, hope, hate, or fear,
 It lives all passionless and pure;
An age shall fleet like earthly year;
 Its years as moments shall endure.
Away, away, without a wing,
 O'er all, through all, its thoughts shall fly;
A nameless and eternal thing
 Forgetting what it was to die.

VISION OF BELSHAZZAR.

The king was on his throne,
 The satraps thronged the hall,
A thousand bright lamps shone
 O'er that high festival.
A thousand cups of gold,
 In Judah deemed divine—
Jehovah's vessels hold
 The godless heathen's wine!

In that same hour and hall,
 The fingers of a hand
Came forth against the wall,
 And wrote as if on sand:
The fingers of a man;—
 A solitary hand
Along the letters ran,
 And traced them like a wand.

The monarch saw, and shook,
 And bade no more rejoice;
All bloodless waxed his look,
 And tremulous his voice.
"Let the men of lore appear,
 The wisest of the earth,
And expound the words of fear,
 Which mar our royal mirth."

Chaldea's seers are good,
 But here they have no skill:
And the unknown letters stood,
 Untold and awful still.
And Babel's men of age
 Are wise and deep in lore;
But now they were not sage,
 They saw—but knew no more.

A captive in the land,
 A stranger and a youth,
He heard the king's command,
 He saw that writing's truth.
The lamps around were bright,
 The prophecy in view;
He read it on that night—
 The morrow proved it true.

"Belshazzar's grave is made,
 His kingdom passed away,
He in the balance weighed,
 Is light and worthless clay.
The shroud, his robe of state,
 His canopy, the stone;
The Mede is at his gate!
 The Persian on his throne."

WERE MY BOSOM AS FALSE AS THOU DEEMST IT TO BE.

Were my bosom as false as thou deemst it to be,
I need not have wandered from far Galilee;
It was but abjuring my creed to efface
The curse which, thou say'st, is the crime of my race.

If the bad never triumph, then God is with thee!
If the slave only sin, thou art spotless and free!
If the exile on earth is an outcast on high,
Live on in thy faith, but in mine I will die.

I have lost for that faith more than thou canst bestow,
As the God who permits thee to prosper doth know;
In his hand is my heart and my hope—and in thine
The land and the life which for him I resign.

HEROD'S LAMENT FOR MARIAMNE.

O Mariamne! now for thee
 The heart for which thou bled'st is bleeding:
Revenge is lost in agony,
 And wild remorse to rage succeeding.
O, Mariamne! where art thou?
 Thou canst not hear my bitter pleading:
Ah, couldst thou—thou wouldst pardon now,
 Though Heaven were to my prayer unheeding.

And is she dead?—and did they dare
 Obey my phrensy's jealous raving?
My wrath but doomed my own despair:
 The sword that smote her's o'er me waving.
But thou art cold, my murdered love!
 And this dark heart is vainly craving
For her who soars alone above,
 And leaves my soul unworthy saving.

She's gone, who shared my diadem!
 She sunk, with her my joys entombing;
I swept that flower from Judah's stem
 Whose leaves for me alone were blooming,
And mine's the guilt, and mine the hell,
 This bosom's desolation dooming;
And I have earned those tortures well,
 Which unconsumed are still consuming!

SUN OF THE SLEEPLESS.

Sun of the sleepless! melancholy star!
Whose tearful beams glows tremulously far,
That show'st the darkness thou canst not dispel,
How like art thou to joy remembered well!
So gleams the past, the light of other days,
Which shines, but warms not with its powerless rays;
A night-beam sorrow watcheth to behold,
Distinct, but distant—clear—but, O how cold!

THE DESTRUCTION OF JERUSALEM BY TITUS.

From the last hill that looks on thy once holy dome,
I beheld thee, O Sion! when rendered to Rome:
'Twas thy sun went down, and the flames of thy fall
Flashed back on the last glance I gave to thy wall.

I looked for thy temple, I looked for my home,
And forgot for a moment my bondage to come:
I beheld but the death-fire that fed on thy fane,
And the fast-fettered hands that made vengeance in vain.

On many an eve, the high spot whence I gazed
Had reflected the last beam of day as it blazed;
While I stood on the height, and beheld the decline
Of the rays from the mountain that shone on thy shrine.

And now on that mountain I stood on that day,
But I marked not the twilight beam melting away;
O, would that the lightning had glared in its stead,
And the thunderbolt burst on the conqueror's head!

But the gods of the pagan shall never profane
The shrine where Jehovah disdained not to reign:
And scattered and scorned as the people may be,
Our worship, O Father! is only for thee.

THE LAMENT BY THE RIVERS OF BABYLON.

We sat down and wept by the waters
Of Babel, and thought of the day
When our foe, in the hue of his slaughters,
Made Salem's high places his prey;
And ye, O her desolate daughters!
Were scattered all weeping away.

While sadly we gazed on the river
Which rolled on in freedom below,
They demanded the song; but, O never
That triumph the stranger shall know!
May this right hand be withered for ever,
Ere it string our high harp for the foe!

On the willow that harp is suspended—
O Salem! its sound should be free;
And the hour when thy glories were ended,
But left me that token of thee;
And ne'er shall its soft tones be blended
With the voice of the spoiler by me!

THE DESTRUCTION OF SENNACHERIB.

The Assyrian came down like the wolf on the fold,
And his cohorts were gleaming in purple and gold;
And the sheen of their spears was like stars on the sea,
When the blue wave rolls nightly on deep Galilee.

Like the leaves of the forest when summer is green,
That host with their banners at sunset were seen:
Like the leaves of the forest when autumn hath blown,
That host on the morrow lay withered and strown.

For the angel of death spread his wings on the blast,
And breathed in the face of the foe as he passed;
And the eyes of the sleepers waxed deadly and chill,
And their hearts but once heaved, and for ever grew still.

And there lay the steed with his nostril all wide,
But through it there rolled not the breath of his pride;
And the foam of his gasping lay white on the turf,
And cold as the spray of the rock-beating surf.

And there lay the rider distorted and pale,
With the dew on his brow and the rust on his mail;
And the tents were all silent, the banners alone,
The lances unlifted, the trumpet unblown.

And the widows of Ashur are loud in their wail,
And the idols are broke in the temple of Baal,
And the might of the Gentile, unsmote by the sword;
Hath melted like snow in the glance of the Lord!

FROM JOB.

A spirit passed before me: I beheld
The face of immortality unveiled—
Deep sleep came down on every eye save mine—
And there it stood—all formless—but divine:
Along my bones the creeping flesh did quake;
And as my damp hair stiffened, thus it spake:

"Is man more just than God? Is man more pure
Than he who deems even seraphs insecure?
Creatures of clay—vain dwellers in the dust!
The moth survives you, and are ye more just?
Things of a day! you wither ere the night,
Heedless and blind to wisdom's wasted light."

THE PRAYER OF NATURE.

Father of Light! great God of Heaven!
Hearest thou the accents of despair?
Can guilt like man's be e'er forgiven?
Can vice atone for crimes by prayer?
Father of light, on thee I call!
Thou seest my soul is dark within;
Thou who canst mark the sparrow's fall,
Avert from me the death of sin.
No shrine I seek to sects unknown;
Oh point to me the path of truth!
Thy dread omnipotence I own;
Spare, yet amend, the faults of youth.
Let bigots rear a gloomy fane,
Let superstition hail the pile,
Let priests, to spread their sable reign,
With tales of mystic rites beguile.
Shall man confine his Maker's sway
To Gothic domes of mouldering stone?
Thy temple is the face of day;
Earth, ocean, heaven, thy boundless throne.
Shall man condemn his race to hell
Unless they bend in pompous form;
Tell us that all, for one who fell,
Must perish in the mingling storm?
Shall each pretend to reach the skies,
Yet doom his brother to expire,
Whose soul a different hope supplies,
Or doctrines less severe inspire?
Shall these, by creeds they can't expound,
Prepare a fancied bliss or wo?
Shall reptiles, grovelling on the ground,
Their great Creator's purpose know?
Shall those, who live for self alone,
Whose years float on in daily crime—
Shall they by Faith for guilt atone,
And live beyond the bounds of time?
Father! no prophet's laws I seek—
Thy laws in Nature's works appear:—
I own myself corrupt and weak,
Yet will I pray, for thou wilt hear!
Thou, who canst guide the wandering star
Through trackless realms of ether's space;
Who calmst the elemental war,
Whose hand from pole to pole I trace;
Thou, who in wisdom placed me here,
Who, when thou wilt, can take me hence,
Ah! whilst I tread this earthly sphere,
Extend to me thy wide defence.
To thee, my God, to thee I call,
Whatever weal or wo betide,
By thy command I rise or fall,
In thy protection I confide.
If, when this dust to dust restored,
My soul shall float on airy wing,
How shall thy glorious name adored
Inspire her feeble voice to sing!
But, if this fleeting spirit share
With clay the grave's eternal bed,
While life yet throbs I raise my prayer,
Though doomed no more to quit the dead.
To thee I breathe my humble strain,
Grateful for all thy mercies past,
And hope, my God, to thee again
This erring life may fly at last.

THE SACRED ROSARY.

GOD.

O Thou eternal One! whose presence bright
  All space doth occupy, all motion guide;
Unchanged through time's all-devastating flight;
  Thou only God! there is no God beside!
Being above all beings! Mighty One!
  Whom none can comprehend and none explore;
Who fill'st existence with *thyself* alone:
  Embracing all—supporting—ruling o'er—
  Being whom we call God—and know no more!

In its sublime research, philosophy
  May measure out the ocean deep—may count
The sands or the sun's rays—but, God! for thee
  There is no weight nor measure:—none can mount
Up to thy mysteries; reason's brightest spark,
  Though kindled by thy light, in vain would try
To trace thy counsels, infinite and dark:
  And thought is lost ere thought can soar so high,
  Even like past moments in eternity.

Thou from primeval nothingness didst call
  First chaos, then existence;—Lord, on thee
Eternity had its foundation: all
  Sprung forth from thee: of light, joy, harmony,
Sole origin: all life—all beauty thine.
  Thy word created all, and doth create:
Thy splendor fills all space with rays divine.
  Thou art, and wert, and shalt be, glorious! great!
  Light-giving, life-sustaining Potentate.

Thy chains the unmeasured universe surround;
  Upheld by thee, by thee inspired with breath!
Thou the beginning with the end hast bound,
  And beautifully mingled life and death!
As sparks mount upward from the fiery blaze,
  So suns are born, so worlds spring forth from thee;
And as the spangles in the sunny rays
  Shine round the silver snow, the pageantry
Of heaven's bright army glitters in thy praise.

A million torches lighted by thy hand
  Wander unwearied through the blue abyss:
They own thy power, accomplish thy command,
  All gay with life, all eloquent with bliss.
What shall we call them? Piles of crystal light—
  A glorious company of golden streams—
Lamps of celestial ether, burning bright—
  Suns lighting systems with their joyous beams?
But thou to these art as the noon to night.

Yes! as a drop of water in the sea,
  All this magnificence in thee is lost;
What are ten thousand worlds compared to thee?
  And what am *I*, then? Heaven's unnumbered host,
Though multiplied by myriads, and arrayed
  In all the glory of sublimest thought,
Is but an atom in the balance weighed
  Against thy greatness—is a cipher brought
  Against infinity! What am I, then?—Naught!

Naught! But the effluence of thy light divine,
  Pervading worlds, hath reached my bosom too;
Yes! in my spirit doth thy Spirit shine,
  As shines the sunbeam in a drop of dew.
Naught!—but I live, and on hope's pinions fly
  Eager toward thy presence; for in thee
I live, and breathe, and dwell: aspiring high,
  Even to the throne of thy divinity.
  I am, O God, and surely *thou* must be!

Thou art! directing, guiding all.—Thou art!
  Direct my understanding then to thee;
Control my spirit, guide my wandering heart:
  Though but an atom 'mid immensity
Still I am something, fashioned by thy hand!
  I hold a middle rank 'twixt heaven and earth,
On the last verge of mortal being stand,
  Close to the realms where angels have their birth,
Just on the boundaries of the spirit-land!

The chain of being is complete in me;
  In me is matter's last gradation lost,
And the next step is spirit—deity!
  I can command the lightning, and am dust!
A monarch, and a slave! a worm, a god!
  Whence came I here, and how? so marvellously
Constructed and conceived! unknown? this clod
  Lives surely through some higher energy?
  For from itself alone it could not be!

Creator, yes! thy wisdom and thy word
  Created *me*, thou source of life and good!
Thou Spirit of my spirit, and my Lord!
  Thy light, thy love, in their bright plenitude
Filled me with an immortal soul, to spring
  Over the abyss of death, and bade it wear
The garments of eternal day, and wing
  Its heavenly flight beyond this little sphere,
  Even to its source—to thee—its Author there.

O thoughts ineffable! O visions blest!
  Though worthless our conceptions all of thee,
Yet shall thy shadowed image fill our breasts,
  And waft its homage to thy Deity.
God! thus alone my lowly thoughts can soar;
  Thus seek thy presence—Being wise and good!
'Midst thy vast works, admire, obey, adore!
And when the tongue is eloquent no more,
  The soul shall speak in tears of gratitude.

Translated from Derzhavin (*a Russian gentleman, born* 1743), by Dr. Bowring

HYMN OF PRAISE.

Sing to the Lord! let harp, and lute, and voice,
Up to the expanding gates of heaven rejoice,
While the bright martyrs to their rest are borne;
Sing to the Lord! their blood-stained course is run,
And every head its diadem hath won,
Rich as the purple of the coming morn:
Sing the triumphant champions of their God,
While burn their mounting feet along their skyward road.

Sing to the Lord! for her in beauty's prime
Snatched from the wintry earth's ungenial clime,
In the eternal spring of Paradise to bloom;
For her the world displayed its brightest treasure,
And the air panted with the songs of pleasure;
Before earth's throne she chose the lowly tomb,
The vale of tears with willing footsteps trod,
Bearing her cross with Thee, incarnate Son of God!

Sing to the Lord! it is not shed in vain,
The blood of martyrs! from its freshening rain
High springs the church, like some fount-shadowing palm;
The nations crowd beneath its branching shade,
Of its green leaves are kingly diadems made,
And wrapt within its deep embosoming calm
Earth sinks to slumber like the breezeless deep,
And war's tempestuous vultures fold their wings and sleep.

Sing to the Lord! No more the angels fly
Far in the bosom of the stainless sky
The sound of fierce licentious sacrifice.
From shrined alcove, and stately pedestal,
The marble gods in cumbrous ruin fall,
Headless in dust the awe of nations lies;
Jove's thunder crumbles in his mouldering hand,
And mute as sepulchres the hymnless temples stand.

Sing to the Lord! From damp prophetic cave
No more the loose-haired sybils burst and rave,
Nor the pale augurs watch the wandering bird:
No more on hill or in the murky wood,
'Mid frantic shout and dissonant music rude,
In human tones are wailing victims heard;
Nor fathers by the reeking altar-stone
Cowl their dark heads t' escape their children's dying groan.

Sing to the Lord! No more the dead are laid
In cold despair beneath the cypress shade,
To sleep the eternal sleep that knows no morn:
There, eager still to burst death's brazen bands,
The angel of the resurrection stands;
While, on its own immortal pinions borne,
Following the breaker of the imprisoning tomb,
Forth springs the exulting soul, and shakes away its gloom.

Sing to the Lord! The desert rocks break out,
And the thronged cities, in one gladdening shout,
The farthest shores by pilgrim step explored;
Spread all your wings, ye winds, and waft around,
Even to the starry cope's pale waning bound,
Earth's universal homage to the Lord;
Lift up thy head, imperial Capital,
Proud on thy height to see the bannered cross unroll.

Sing to the Lord! when time itself shall cease,
And final ruin's desolating peace
Enwrap this wide and restless world of man;
When the Judge rides upon the enthroning wind,
And o'er all generations of mankind
Eternal justice waves its winnowing fan;
To vast infinity's remotest space,
While ages run their everlasting race,
Shall all the beatific hosts prolong,
Wide as the glory of the Lamb, the Lamb's triumphant song!

Milman.

ON THE DEATH OF A YOUNG GIRL.

She hath gone in the spring-time of life,
Ere her sky had been dimmed by a cloud,
While her heart with the rapture of love was yet rife,
And the hopes of her youth were unbowed—
From the lovely, who loved her too well;
From the heart that had grown to her own;
From the sorrow which late o'er her young spirit fell,
Like a dream of the night she hath flown;
And the earth hath received to its bosom its trust—
Ashes to ashes, and dust unto dust.

The spring, in its loveliness dressed,
Will return with its music-winged hours,
And, kissed by the breath of the sweet southwest,
The buds shall burst out in flowers;
And the flowers her grave-sod above,
Though the sleeper beneath recks it not,
Shall thickly be strown by the hand of Love,
To cover with beauty the spot—
Meet emblems are they of the pure one and bright,
Who faded and fell with so early a blight.

Ay, the spring will return—but the blossom
That bloomed in our presence the sweetest,
By the spoiler is borne from the cherishing bosom,
The loveliest of all and the fleetest!
The music of stream and of bird,
Shall come back when the winter is o'er;
But the voice that was dearest to us shall be heard
In our desolate chambers no more!
The sunlight of May on the waters shall quiver—
The light of her eye hath departed for ever!

As the bird to its sheltering nest,
When the storm on the hills is abroad,
So her spirit hath flown from this world of unrest
To repose on the bosom of God!
Where the sorrows of earth never more
May fling o'er its brightness a stain;
Where, in rapture and love, it shall ever adore,
With a gladness unmingled with pain;
And its thirst shall be slaked by the waters which spring
Like a river of light, from the throne of the King!

There is weeping on earth for the lost!
There is bowing in grief to the ground!
But rejoicing and praise 'mid the sanctified host,
For a spirit in paradise found!
Though brightness hath passed from the earth,
Yet a star is newborn in the sky,
And a soul hath gone home to the land of its birth,
Where are pleasures and fulness of joy!
And a new harp is strung, and a new song is given
To the breezes that float o'er the gardens of heaven!

William H. Burleigh.

MY CHILD.

I can not make him dead!
His fair sunshiny head
Is ever bounding round my study-chair;
Yet, when my eyes, now dim
With tears, I turn to him,
The vision vanishes—he is not there!

I walk my parlor floor,
And, through the open door,
I hear a footfall on the chamber stair:
I'm stepping toward the hall
To give the boy a call;
And then bethink me that—he is not there!

I thrid the crowded street—
A satchelled lad I meet,
With the same beaming eyes and colored hair:
And, as he's running by,
Follow him with my eye,
Scarcely believing that—he is not there!

I know his face is hid
Under the coffin lid;
Closed are his eyes, cold is his forehead fair;
My hand that marble felt;
O'er it in prayer I knelt;
Yet my heart whispers that—he is not there!

I can not *make* him dead!
When passing by the bed,
So long watched over with parental care,
My spirit and my eye
Seek it inquiringly,
Before the thought comes that—he is not there!

When at the cool, gray break
Of day, from sleep I wake,
With my first breathing of the morning air,
My soul goes up, with joy,
To Him who gave my boy:
Then comes the sad thought that—he is not there!

When at the day's calm close,
Before we seek repose,
I'm with his mother, offering up our prayer:
Whate'er I may be *saying*,
I am, in spirit, praying
For our boy's spirit, though—he is not there!

Not there!—Where, then, is he?
The form I used to see
Was but the *raiment* that he used to wear.
The grave, that now doth press
Upon that cast-off dress,
Is but his wardrobe locked;—*he* is not there!

He lives!—In all the past,
He lives; nor, to the last,
Of seeing him again will I despair;
In dreams I see him now;
And, on his angel brow,
I see it written, "Thou shalt see me *there!*"

Yes, we all live to God!
FATHER, thy chastening rod
So help us, thine afflicted ones, to bear,
That, in the spirit-land,
Meeting at thy right hand,
'Twill be our heaven to find that—he is *there!*

REV. JOHN PIERPONT.

WEEP NOT FOR HER!

WEEP not for her! Her span was like the sky,
Whose thousand stars shine beautiful and bright,
Like flowers that know not what it is to die,
Like long linked shadeless months of polar light,
Like music floating o'er a waveless lake,
While echo answers from the flowery brake,
Weep not for her!

Weep not for her! She died in early youth,
Ere hope had lost its rich romantic hues,
When human bosoms seemed the homes of truth,
And earth still gleamed with beauty's radiant dews.
Her summer prime waned not to days that freeze,
Her *wine* of life was not run to the lees:
Weep not for her!

Weep not for her! By fleet or slow decay
It never grieved her bosom's core to mark
The playmates of her childhood wane away,
Her prospects wither, and her hopes grow dark.
Translated by her God with spirit shriven,
She passed, as 'twere on smiles, from earth to heaven:
Weep not for her!

Weep not for her! It was not hers to feel
The miseries that corrode amassing years,
'Gainst dreams of baffled bliss the heart to steel,
To wander sad down age's vale of tears,
As whirl the withered leaves from friendship's tree,
And on earth's wintry wold alone to be:
Weep not for her!

Weep not for her! She is an angel now,
And treads the sapphire floors of Paradise,
All darkness wiped from her refulgent brow,
Sin, sorrow, suffering, banished from her eyes;
Victorious over death, to her appears
The vistaed joys of heaven's eternal years:
Weep not for her!

Weep not for her! Her memory is the shrine
Of pleasant thoughts, soft as the scent of flowers,
Calm as on windless eve the sun's decline,
Sweet as the song of birds among the bowers,
Rich as a rainbow with its hues of light,
Pure as the moonshine of an autumn night:
Weep not for her!

Weep not for her! There is no cause of wo,
But rather nerve the spirit that it walk
Unshrinking o'er the thorny path below,
And from earth's low defilements keep thee back.
So, when a few fleet swerving years have flown,
She'll meet thee at heaven's gate—and lead thee on:
Weep not for her!

D. M. MOIR.

HYMN TO THE UNIVERSE.

ROLL on, thou Sun, for ever roll,
Thou giant, rushing through the heaven,
Creation's wonder, nature's soul;
Thy golden wheels by angels driven;
The planets die without thy blaze,
And cherubim with star-dropt wing
Float in thy diamond-sparkling rays,
Thou brightest emblem of their King!

Roll, lovely Earth! and still roll on,
With ocean's azure beauty bound;
While one sweet star, the pearly Moon,
Pursues thee through the blue profound;
And angels with delighted eyes
Behold thy teints of mount and stream,
From the high walls of paradise;
Swift-wheeling like a glorious dream.

Roll, Planets! on your dazzling road,
For ever sweeping round the sun;
What eye beheld when first ye glowed?
What eye shall see your courses done?
Roll in your solemn majesty,
Ye deathless splendors of the skies!
High altars, from which angels see
The incense of creation rise.

Roll, Comets! and ye million Stars!
Ye that through boundless nature roam;
Ye monarchs on your flame-winged cars;
Tell us in what more glorious dome—
What orb to which your pomps are dim,
What kingdom but by angels trod—
Tell us, where swells the eternal hymn
Around His throne—where dwells your God!

Paraphrased from GOETHE.

TYRE.

HIGH on the stately wall
The spear of Anrad hung,
Through corridor and hall
Gemadin's war-note rung.
Where are they now? the note is o'er;
Yes! for a thousand years and more
Five fathoms deep beneath the sea
Those halls have lain all silently;
Naught listing save the mermaid's song,
While rude sea-monsters roam the corridors along.

Far from the wondering East
Tubal and Javan came,
And Araby the blest,
And Kedar, mighty name—
Now on that shore, a lonely guest,
Some dripping fisherman may rest,
Watching on rock or naked stone
His dark net spread before the sun,
Unconscious of the dooming lay
That broods o'er that dull spot, and there shall brood for aye!

Lyra Apostolica.

A POET'S PRAYER.

O God! it is an awful thing indeed
For one who estimates our nature well,
Be what it may his outward sect, or creed,
To name thee, thou incomprehensible!
Hadst thou not chosen of thyself to tell,
As in thy gospel thou hast done; nor less,
By condescending in our hearts to dwell;
Could man have ever found to thee access,
Or worshipped thee aright in spiritual holiness?

No! for the utmost that we could have done,
Were to have raised, as Paul at Athens saw
Altars unto the dread and unknown One,
Bending before we knew not what with awe,
And even now, instructed by a law
Holier than that of Moses, what know we
Of thee, the Highest? Yet thou bidst us draw
Near thee in spirit; O then pardon me
If, in this closing strain, I crave a boon of thee.

It shall be this: Permit me not to place
My soul's affections on the things of earth;
But, conscious of the treasures of thy grace,
To let them, in my inmost heart, give birth
To gratitude proportioned to their worth:
Teach me to feel that all that thou hast made
Upon this mighty globe's gigantic girth,
Though meant with filial love to be surveyed,
Is nothing to thyself—the shadow of a shade.

If thou hast given me, more than unto some,
A feeling sense of nature's beauties fair,
Which sometimes renders admiration dumb,
From consciousness that words can not declare
The beauty thou hast scattered everywhere;
O grant that this may lead me still, through all
Thy works, to thee! nor prove a treach'rous snare
Adapted those affections to enthrall
Which should be thine alone, and waken at thy call.

I would not merely dream my life away
In fancied rapture, or imagined joy;
Nor that a perfumed flower, a dew-gemmed spray,
A murmuring brook, or any prouder toy,
Should, for its own sake, thought or song employ;
So far alone as nature's charms can lead
To thee who framed them all, and can destroy,
Or innocent enjoyment serve to feed,
Grant me to gaze and love, and thus thy works to read.

But while from one extreme thy power may keep
My erring frailty, O preserve me still
From dullness! nor let cold indifference steep
My senses in oblivion: if the thrill
Of early bliss must sober, as it will,
And should, when earthly things to heavenly yield,
I would have feelings left time can not chill;
That while I yet can walk through grove or field,
I may be conscious there of charms by thee revealed.

And when I shall, as soon or late I must,
Become infirm; in age, if I grow old;
Or, sooner, if my strength should fail its trust;
When I relinquish haunts where I have strolled
At morn or eve, and can no more behold
Thy glorious works: forbid me to repine;
Let memory still their loveliness unfold
Before my mortal eye, and let them shine
With borrowed light from thee, for they are thine!

Bernard Barton.

THE MOTHER AND CHILD.

What is that, mother?
The Lark, my child.—
The morn has but just looked out, and smiled,
When he starts from his humble, grassy nest,
And is up and away with the dew on his breast,
And a hymn in his heart, to yon pure, bright sphere,
To warble it out in his Maker's ear.
Ever, my child, be thy morn's first lays
Tuned, like the lark's, to thy Maker's praise.

What is that, mother?
The Dove, my son.—
And that low, sweet voice, like a widow's moan,
Is flowing out from her gentle breast,
Constant and pure by that lonely nest,
As the wave is poured from some crystal urn,
For the distant dear one's quick return.
Ever, my son, be thou, like the dove—
In friendship as faithful, as constant in love.

What is that, mother?
The Eagle, boy—
Proudly careering his course of joy,
Firm in his own mountain vigor relying,
Breasting the dark storm, the red bolt defying;
His wing on the wind, and his eye on the sun,
He swerves not a hair, but bears onward, right on.
Boy, may the eagle's flight ever be thine,
Onward and upward, true to the line.

What is that, mother?
The Swan, my love.—
He is floating down from his native grove,
No loved one now, no nestling nigh;
He is floating down by himself to die;
Death darkens his eye, it unplumes his wings,
Yet the sweetest song is the last he sings.
Live so, my son, that when death shall come,
Swan-like and sweet, it may waft thee home.

Bishop Doane.

THE MISSIONARY.

My heart goes with thee, dauntless man,
Freely as thou dost hie
To sojourn with some barbarous clan,
For them to toil or die.
Fondly our spirits to our own
Cling, nor to part allow;
Thine to some land forlorn has flown—
We turn—and where art thou?

Thou climbst the vessel's lofty side,
Numbers are gathering there;
The youthful warrior in his pride,
The merchant in his care;
Hearts which for knowledge track the seas,
Spirits which lightly move
Glad as the billows and the breeze—
And thou—the child of love.

A savage shore receives thy tread;
Companion thou hast none;
The wild boughs wave above thy head,
Yet still thou journeyest on;
Thridding the tangled wild-wood drear,
Piercing the mountain glen,
Till, wearily, thou drawest near
The haunts of lonely men.

Strange is thy aspect to their eyes,
Strange is thy foreign speech;
And wild and strong is their surprise
At marvels thou dost teach.
Thy strength alone is in thy words;
Yet armies could not bow
The spirit of those barbarous hordes
So readily as thou.

But oh! thy heart, thou home-sick man,
With saddest thoughts runs o'er,
Sitting, as fades the evening wan,
Silently at thy door.
Yet that poor hut upon the wild,
A stone beneath the tree,
And souls to heaven's love reconciled—
These are enough for thee.

William Howitt.

A PREPARATIVE TO PRAYER.

WHEN thou dost talk to God—by prayer I mean—
 Lift up pure hands, lay down all lust's desires;
Fix thoughts on heaven, present a conscience clean;
 Such holy blame to mercy's throne aspires.
Confess faults, guilt, crave pardon for thy sin,
Tread holy paths, call grace to guide therein.

It is the spirit with reverence must obey
 Our Maker's will, to practise what he taught;
Make not the flesh thy counsel when thou pray;
 'Tis enemy to every virtuous thought;
It is the foe we daily feed and clothe;
It is the prison that the soul doth loath.

Even as Elias mounting to the sky,
 Did cast his mantle to the earth behind;
So when the heart presents the prayer on high,
 Exclude the world from traffic with the mind;
Lips near to God, and ranging heart within,
Is but vain babbling, and converts to sin.

Like Abraham ascending up the hill
 To sacrifice, his servants left below,
That he might act the Great Commander's will,
 Without impeach to his obedient blow;
Even so the soul remote from earthly things,
Should mount salvation's shelter—mercy's wings.

SOUTHWELL.

CONSOLATIONS OF RELIGION TO THE POOR.

THERE is a mourner, and her heart is broken
 She is a widow; she is old and poor;
Her only hope is in that sacred token
 Of peaceful happiness when life is o'er;
She asks nor wealth nor pleasure, begs no more
 Than heaven's delightful volume, and the sight
 Of her Redeemer. Skeptics, would you pour
 Your blasting vials on her head, and blight
Sharon's sweet rose, that blooms and charms her being's night?

She lives in her affections; for the grave
 Has closed upon her husband, children; all
Her hopes are with the arm she trusts will save
 Her treasured jewels; though her views are small,
Though she has never mounted high to fall
 And writhe in her debasement, yet the spring
Of her meek, tender feelings, can not pall
 Her unperverted palate, but will bring
A joy without regret, a bliss that has no sting.

Even as a fountain, whose unsullied wave
 Wells in the pathless valley, flowing o'er
With silent waters, kissing, as they lave,
 The pebbles with light rippling, and the shore
Of matted grass and flowers—so softly pour
 The breathings of her bosom, when she prays,
Low-bowed, before her Maker; then no more
 She muses on the griefs of former days;
Her full heart melts, and flows in heaven's dissolving rays.

And faith can see a new world, and the eyes
 Of saints look pity on her; Death will come—
A few short moments over, and the prize
 Of peace eternal waits her, and the tomb
Becomes her fondest pillow; all its gloom
 Is scattered. What a meeting there will be
To her and all she loved here! and the bloom
 Of new life from those cheeks shall never flee;
Theirs is the health which lasts through all eternity.

PERCIVAL.

HYMN OF NATURE.

GOD of the earth's extended plains!
 The dark green fields contented lie;
The mountains rise like holy towers,
 Where man might commune with the sky;
The tall cliff challenges the storm
 That lowers upon the vale below,
Where shaded fountains send their streams,
 With joyous music in their flow.

God of the dark and heavy deep!
 The waves lie sleeping on the sands,
Till the fierce trumpet of the storm
 Hath summoned up their thundering bands
Then the white sails are dashed in foam,
 Or hurry, trembling, o'er the seas,
Till calmed by thee, the sinking gale
 Serenely breathes, Depart in peace.

God of the forest's solemn shade!
 The grandeur of the lonely tree,
That wrestles singly with the gale,
 Lifts up admiring eyes to Thee.
But more majestic far they stand,
 When, side by side, their ranks they form,
To wave on high their plumes of grace,
 And fight their battles with the storm.

God of the light and viewless air!
 When summer breezes sweetly flow,
Or, gathering in their angry might,
 The fierce and angry tempests blow.
All—from the evening's plaintive sigh,
 That hardly lifts the drooping flower,
To the wild whirlwind's midnight cry
 Breathe forth the language of thy power.

God of the fair and open sky!
 How gloriously above us springs,
The tented dome of heavenly blue,
 Suspended on the rainbow's wings.
Each brilliant star that sparkles through,
 Each gilded cloud that wanders free,
In evening's purple radiance gives
 The beauty of its praise to Thee.

God of the rolling orbs above!
 Thy name is written clearly bright
In the warm day's unvarying blaze,
 Or evening's golden shower of light.
For every fire that fronts the sun,
 And every spark that walks alone
Around the utmost verge of heaven,
 Were kindled at thy burning throne.

God of the world! the hour must come,
 And Nature's self to dust return;
Her crumbling altars must decay,
 Her incense fires shall cease to burn;
But still her grand and lovely scenes
 Have made man's warmest praises flow;
For hearts grow holier as they trace
 The beauty of the world below.

PEABODY.

MORTALITY OF MAN.

LIKE as the damask rose you see,
Or like the blossoms on the tree,
Or like the dainty flower of May,
Or like the morning to the day,
Or like the sun, or like the shade,
Or like the gourd which Jonas had,
E'en such is man;—whose thread is spun,
Drawn out and cut, and so is done.—
The rose withers, the blossom blasteth,
The flower fades, the morning hasteth,
The sun sets, the shadow flies,
The gourd consumes—and man he dies!
Like to the grass that's newly sprung,
Or like a tale that's new begun,
Or like the bird that's here to-day,
Or like the pearled dew of May,
Or like an hour, or like a span,
Or like the singing of a swan,
E'en such is man;—who lives by breath,
Is here, now there, in life and death.—
The grass withers, the tale is ended,
The bird is flown, the dew's ascended,
The hour is short, the span not long,
The swan's near death,—man's life is done!

WASTELL.

WHO IS MY NEIGHBOR?

Thy neighbor? It is he whom thou
  Hast power to aid and bless,
Whose aching heart or burning brow
  Thy soothing hand may press.

Thy neighbor? 'Tis the fainting poor,
  Whose eye with want is dim,
Whom hunger sends from door to door;
  Go thou, and succor him.

Thy neighbor? 'Tis that weary man,
  Whose years are at their brim,
Bent low with sickness, cares, and pain;—
  Go thou, and comfort him.

Thy neighbor? 'Tis the heart bereft
  Of every earthly gem,
Widow and orphan, helpless left;—
  Go thou, and shelter them.

Thy neighbor? Yonder toiling slave,
  Fettered in thought and limb,
Whose hopes are all beyond the grave;—
  Go thou and ransom him.

Where'er thou meetest a human form
  Less favored than thine own,
Remember 'tis thy neighbor worm,
  Thy brother, or thy son.

Oh! pass not, pass not heedless by;
  Perhaps thou canst redeem
The breaking heart from misery—
  Go, share thy lot with him.

Anonymous.

PAUL AND SILAS AT PHILIPPI.

Hearest thou that solemn symphony, that swells
And echoes through Philippi's gloomy cells?
From vault to vault the heavy notes rebound,
And granite rocks reverberate the sound.
The wretch, who long in dungeons cold and dank
Had shook his fetters, that their iron clank
Might break the grave-like silence of that prison,
On which the star of hope had never risen;
Then sunk in slumbers, by despair oppressed,
And dreamed of freedom in his broken rest;
Wakes at the music of these mellow strains,
Thinks it some spirit, and forgets his chains.
'Tis Paul and Silas; who, at midnight pay
To Him of Nazareth a grateful lay.
Soon is that anthem wafted to the skies;
An angel bears it, and a God replies.
At that reply, a pale portentous light
Plays through the air,—then leaves a gloomier night.
The darkly tottering towers,—the trembling arch,—
The rocking walls confess an earthquake's march,—
The stars look dimly through the roof:—behold,
From saffron dews and melting clouds of gold,
Brightly uncurling on the dungeon's air,
Freedom walks forth serene; from her loose hair,
And every glistening feather of her wings,
Perfumes that breathe of more than earth she flings,
And with a touch dissolves the prisoner's chains,
Whose song had charmed her from celestial plains.

Pierpont.

MISSIONS.

Light for the dreary vales
  Of ice-bound Labrador!
Where the frost-king breathes on the slippery sails,
  And the mariner wakes no more;
Lift high the lamp that never fails,
  To that dark and steril shore.

Light for the forest child!
  An outcast though he be,
From the haunts where the sun of his childhood smiled,
  And the country of the free;
Pour the hope of Heaven o'er his desert wild,
  For what home on earth has he?

Light for the hills of Greece!
  Light for that trampled clime,
Where the rage of the spoiler refused to cease
  Ere it wrecked the boast of time;
If the Moslem hath dealt the gift of peace,
  Can you grudge your boon sublime.

Light on the Hindoo shed!
  On the maddening idol-train.
The flame of the Suttee is dire and red,
  And the Fakir faints with pain;
And the dying moan on their cheerless bed,
  By the Ganges laved in vain.

Light for the Persian sky!
  The Sophi's wisdom fades,
And the pearls of Ormus are poor to buy
  Armor when death invades;
Hark! Hark!—'tis the sainted Martyn's sigh
  From Ararat's mournful shades.

Light for the Burman vales!
  For the islands of the sea!
For the coast where the slave-ship fills its sails
  With sighs of agony;
And her kidnapped babes the mother wails
  'Neath the lone banana-tree!

Light for the ancient race
  Exiled from Zion's rest!
Homeless they roam from place to place
  Benighted and oppressed;
They shudder at Sinai's fearful base:
  Guide them to Calvary's breast.

Light for the darkened earth!
  Ye blessed, its beams who shed,
Shrink not, till the day-spring hath its birth,
  Till, wherever the footstep of man doth tread,
Salvation's banner, spread broadly forth,
  Shall gild the dream of the cradle-bed,
    And clear the tomb
    From its lingering gloom,
  For the aged to rest his weary head.

Sigourney.

THE PILGRIM'S SONG.

And wilt Thou hear the fevered heart
  To Thee in silence cry?
And as the inconstant wildfires dart
  Out of the restless eye,
Wilt Thou forgive the wayward thought,
By kindly woes yet half untaught
A Savior's right, so dearly bought,
  That Hope should never die?

Thou wilt; for many a languid prayer
  Has reached Thee from the wild,
Since the lorn mother, wandering there,
  Cast down her fainting child,
Then stole apart to weep and die,
Nor knew an angel form was nigh
To show soft waters gushing by
  And dewy shadows mild.

Thou wilt—for Thou art Israel's God,
  And Thine unwearied arm
Is ready yet with Moses' rod,
  The hidden rill to charm
Out of the dry unfathomed deep
Of sands, that lie in lifeless sleep,
Save when the scorching whirlwinds heap
  Their waves in rude alarm.

These moments of wild wrath are Thine—
  Thine too the drearier hour
When o'er the horizon's silent line
  Fond hopeless fancies cower,
And on the traveller's listless way
Rises and sets the unchanging day,
No cloud in heaven to slake its ray,
  On earth no sheltering bower.

Thou wilt be there, and not forsake,
To turn the bitter pool
Into a bright and breezy lake,
The throbbing brow to cool;
Till left awhile with thee alone
The wilful heart be fain to own
That He, by whom our bright hours shone,
Our darkness best may rule.

The scent of water far away
Upon the breeze is flung;
The desert pelican to-day
Securely leaves her young
Reproving thankless man, who fears
To journey on a few lone years,
Where on the sand thy step appears,
Thy crown in sight is hung.

Thou, who didst sit on Jacob's well
The weary hour of noon,
The languid pulses Thou canst tell,
The nerveless spirit tune.
Thou from whose cross in anguish burst
The cry that owned thy dying thirst,
To thee we turn, our last and first,
Our Sun and soothing Moon.

From darkness here, and weariness,
We ask not full repose,
Only be Thou at hand to bless
Our trial hour of woes;
Is not the pilgrim's toil o'erpaid
By the clear rill and palmy shade?
And see we not, up earth's dark glade,
The gate of heaven unclose?

KEBLE.

EXCELLENCY OF CHRIST.

HE is a path, if any be misled;
He is a robe, if any naked be;
If any chance to hunger, he is bread;
If any be a bondman, he is free;
If any be but weak, how strong is he!
To dead men life he is, to sick men health;
To blind men sight, and to the needy wealth—
A pleasure without loss, a treasure without stealth.

GILES FLETCHER.

DISTANT CHURCH BELLS.

UP steeps reclining in the autumnal calm,
The woodland nook retired, and quiet field,
Upon the tranquil noon
The Sunday chime is borne;

Rising and sinking on the silent air,
With many a dying fall most musical,
And fitful bird hard by,
Blending harmoniously.

The sky is looking on the sunny earth,
The fleecy clouds stand still in heaven,
Making the blue expanse
More still and beautiful.

If aught there be upon this rude, bad earth,
Which angels, from their happy spheres above,
Could lean and listen to,
It were those peaceful sounds.

There is unearthly balm upon the air,
And holier lights which are with Sunday born,
That man may lay aside
Himself, and be at rest.

The week-day cares like shackles from us fall,
As from our Lord the clothings of the grave,
And we, too, seem with him
To walk in endless morn.

Not that these musical wings would bear us up
On buoyant thoughts too high for sinful man,
But that they speak the best
Which earth hath left to give—
Of better hopes, and prayer, and penitence,
Rising in incense on the sacred air,
From many a woodland spire,
Or hill-embosomed tower.

THE CATHEDRAL.

THE CHRISTIAN MARTYR.

THE eyes of thousands glanced on him, as 'mid the cirque he stood,
Unheeding of the shout which broke from that vast multitude.
The prison damps had paled his cheek; and on his lofty brow
Corroding care had deeply traced the furrows of his plough.
Amid the crowded cirque he stood, and raised to heaven his eye,
For well that feeble old man knew they brought him forth to die!
Yet joy was beaming in that eye—while from his lips a prayer
Passed up to heaven, and faith secured his peaceful dwelling there.
Then calmly on his foes he looked; and, as he gazed, a tear
Stole o'er his cheeks—but 'twas the birth of pity, not of fear.
He knelt down on the glory land—once more he looked toward heaven,
And to the Christian's God he prayed that they might be forgiven.
But hark! another shout, o'er which the hungry lion's roar
Is heard, like thunder, 'mid the swell on wild tempestuous shore!
And forth the Libyan savage bursts—rolls his red eyes around;
Then on his helpless victim springs, and beats him to the ground.
Short pause was left for hope or fear—the instinctive love of life
One struggle made, but vainly made, in such unequal strife,
Then with the scanty stream of life his jaws the savage dyed;
While one by one the quivering limbs his bloody feast supplied.
Rome's prince and senators partook the shouting crowd's delight;
And beauty gazed unshrinkingly on that unhallowed sight.
But say what evil had he done?—what sin of deepest hue?
A blameless faith was all the crime that Christian martyr knew:
And where his precious blood was spilt, even from that barren sand
There sprung a stem, whose vigorous boughs soon overspread the land:
O'er distant isles its shadow fell; nor knew its roots decay,
Even when the Roman Cæsar's throne and empire passed away.

REV. HAMILTON BUCHANAN.

THE CLOUD.

A CLOUD lay cradled near the setting sun,
A gleam of crimson tinged its braided snow;
Long had I watched the glory moving on,
O'er the still radiance of the lake below:
Tranquil its spirit seemed, and floated slow,
E'en in its very motion there was rest,
While every breath of eve that chanced to blow,
Wafted the traveller to the beauteous west.
Emblem, methought, of the departed soul,
To whose white robe the gleam of bliss is given,
And by the breath of mercy made to roll
Right onward to the golden gates of heaven,
While to the eye of faith it peaceful lies,
And tells to man his glorious destinies.

WILSON.

SABBATH THOUGHTS.

Welcome thou peaceful dawn!
O'er field and wooded lawn
The wonted sound of busy toil is laid.
And hark! the village bell!
Whose simple tinklings swell,
Sweet as soft music on the straw-roofed shed,
And bid the pious cottager prepare
To keep the appointed rest, and seek the house of prayer.

How goodly 'tis to see
The rustic family
Duly along the church-way path repair:
The mother trim and plain,
Leading her ruddy train,
The father pacing slow with modest air.
With honest heart and humble guise they come,
To serve Almighty God, and bear his blessing home.

At home they gayly share
Their sweet and simple fare,
And thank the Giver of the festal board:
Around the blazing hearth
They sit in harmless mirth,
Or turn with awe the volume of the Lord:
Then full of heavenly joy, retiring pay
Their sacrifice of prayer to Him who blessed the day.

O sabbath-bell, thy voice
Makes hearts like these rejoice;
Not so the child of vanity and power.
He the blest pavement treads
Perchance as custom bids,
Perchance to gaze away a listless hour;
Then crowns the bowl, or roams along the road,
Nor hides his shame from men, nor heeds the eye of God.

When the seventh morning's gleam
Purpled the lonely stream,
On its green bank of old the Christian bowed.
The hand adoring spread,
And broke the mystic bread;
And, leagued in bonds of holy concord, vowed
From the cleansed heart to wash each foul offence,
And give his days tc peace and saintly innocence.

In vain the Roman lord
Waved the relentless sword,
And spread the terrors of the circling flame;
In vain the heathen sought,
If chance some lurking spot
Might mar the lustre of the Christian name,
Th' Eternal Spirit by his fruits confessed,
In life secured from stains, and steeled in death the breast.

O would his influence bless
With faith and holiness,
The laggard people of our favored isle!
But if too deep and wide
Heaven spread corruption's tide,
O might he deign on me and mine to smile;
So shall we ne'er with due devotion fail
The consecrated day of solemn rest to hail:

So shall we still resort
To Sion's hallowed court,
And lift the heart to Him that dwells above;
Thence, home returning, muse
On sweet and solemn views,
Or fill the mind with acts of holy love;
Then lay us down in peace, to think we're given
Another precious day to fit our souls for heaven.

Mant.

A COTTAGE SCENE.

I saw a cradle at a cottage-door,
Where the fair mother, with her cheerful wheel,
Carolled so sweet a song, that the young bird
Which, timid, near the threshold sought for seed,
Paused on his lifted foot, and raised his head
As if to listen. The rejoicing bees
Nestled in throngs amid the woodbine cups
That o'er the lattice clustered. A clear stream
Came leaping from its sylvan height, and poured
Music upon the pebbles; and the winds,
Which gently 'mid the vernal branches played
Their idle freaks, brought show'ring blossoms down,
Surfeiting earth with sweetness. Sad I came
From weary commerce with the heartless world:
But, when I felt upon my withered cheek
My mother Nature's breath, and heard the tramp
Of those gay insects at their honeyed toil,
Shining like winged jewelry, and drank
The healthful odor of the flow'ring trees
And bright-eyed violets—but, most of all,
When I beheld mild slumb'ring innocence,
And on that young maternal brow the smile
Of those affections which do purify
And renovate the soul—I turned me back
In gladness, and with added strength, to run
My weary race, lifting a thankful prayer
To Him who showed me some bright teint of heaven
Here on the earth, that I might safer walk,
And firmer combat sin, and surer rise
From earth to heaven.

Sigourney

WHERE IS HE?

And where is he? Not by the side
Of her whose wants he loved to tend;
Not o'er those valleys wandering wide,
Where sweetly lost, he oft would wend!
That form beloved he marks no more;
Those scenes admired no more shall see—
Those scenes are lovely as before,
And she as fair—but where is he?

No, no, the radiance is not dim
That used to gild his favorite hill;
The pleasures that were dear to him,
Are dear to life and nature still:
But ah! his home is not so fair,
Neglected must his garden be—
The lilies droop and wither there,
And seem to whisper, where is he?

His was the pomp, the crowded hall!
But where is now the proud display?
His riches, honors, pleasures, all
Desire could frame: but where are they?
And he, as some tall rock that stands
Protected by the circling sea,
Surrounded by admiring bands,
Seemed proudly strong—and where is he?

The churchyard bears an added stone,
The fireside shows a vacant chair!
Here sadness dwells and weeps alone,
And death displays his banner there;
The life has gone, the breath has fled,
And what has been no more shall be;
The well-known form, the welcome tread,
Oh! where are they? and where is he?

Neele.

JACOB'S DREAM.

The sun was sinking on the mountain zone
That guards thy vale of beauty, Palestine!
And lovely from the desert rose the moon,
Yet lingering on the horizon's purple line,
Like a pure spirit o'er its earthly shrine.
Up Padan-aram's height abrupt and bare
A pilgrim toiled, and oft on day's decline
Looked pale, then paused for eve's delicious air;
The summit gained, he knelt, and breathed his evening prayer.

He spread his cloak and slumbered—darkness fell
Upon the twilight hills; a sudden sound
Of silver trumpets o'er him seemed to swell;
Clouds heavy with the tempest gathered round;
Yet was the whirlwind in its caverns bound;
Still deeper rolled the darkness from on high,
Gigantic volume upon volume wound;

Above, a pillar shooting to the sky;
Below, a mighty sea that spread incessantly.

Voices are heard—a choir of golden strings,
Low winds, whose breath is loaded with the rose;
Then chariot-wheels—the nearer rush of wings;
Pale lightning round the dark pavilion glows.
It thunders—the resplendent gates unclose
Far as the eye can glance; on height o'er height
Rise fiery waving wings, and star-crowned brows,
Millions on millions, brighter and more bright,
Till all is lost in one supreme unmingled light.

But two beside the sleeping pilgrim stand,
Like cherub-kings, with lifted mighty plume,
Fixed sun-bright eyes, and looks of high command:
They tell the patriarch of his glorious doom;
Father of countless myriads that shall come,
Sweeping the land like billows of the sea,
Bright as the stars of heaven from twilight's gloom,
Till he is given, whose angels long to see,
And Israel's splendid line is crowned with Deity.

CROLY.

THE MARTYRDOM OF CRANMER.

Lo! gathering round a dungeon door,
Appear the soldier's plume and lance;
And restless crowds around it pour,
With eager step and wrathful glance—
Upon their cheeks the bigot's smile—
The bondslaves dark of priestly guile.

And now the dungeon's portals ope,
Now from its archway deep and dim,
Gleam silver cross and broidered cope,
And solemn swells the priestly hymn;
Beneath the torch's ruddy glare,
Are mitred brows and tonsures bare.

But who comes forth? His step is slow,
His eye is bent upon the ground,
And when are heard the sighs of wo,
He looks as if he heard the sound—
As if no other soul was there—
With wan lips moving still in prayer:

No longer stoops that captive's brow,
His form erect in majesty,
His pale cheek lighted with the glow
Of one who sees deliverance nigh—
The entrance to the promised rest—
The welcome 'mong the Savior's blest.

The pile is lit—the flames ascend;
Yet peace is in the martyr's face;
And unseen visitants attend
That chief of England's priestly race:
Mightier in peril's darkest hour,
Than when enthroned in rank and power.

Steadfast he stood in that fierce flame,
As standing in his own high hall:
He said, as sadness o'er him came,
Remembrance of his mournful fall—
Stretching it to the burning brand—
"First perish this unworthy hand!"

Thy foul and cruel deed, O Rome!
Is vain; that blazing funeral pyre
Where Cranmer died, shall soon become
To England as a beacon-fire:
And he hath left a glorious name,
Victorious over gore and flame.

ANDREW R. BONAR.

HYMN FOR CHILDREN.

JESUS, our gentle Shepherd, see
These tender lambs of Zion's fold;
Lo! we are come to follow thee;
Gather and guard us as of old:
While through the desert world we stray,
Preserve us in the narrow way.

Where Thy refreshing pastures grow,
Where all Thy chosen flock is fed,
Where living waters gently flow,
There may our wandering feet be led;
Direct us toward the heavenly hill,
And bear us in thy bosom still.

Much do we need Thy watchful care,
Through every day and every hour;
For life is set with many a snare,
And Satan wanders to devour:
But we are safe from all alarms,
Within our heavenly Shepherd's arms.

Here in the Gospel we are told
What great compassion was in Thee,
When mothers brought their babes of old—
Poor helpless children such as we;
E'en to thy tender bosom brought—
And thou didst say—"Forbid them not."

And thus encouraged by thy grace,
To those still open arms we fly!
And though we can not see Thy face,
Yet Thou canst bless us from on high:
For still Thy gracious word, we see,
Says—"Suffer them to come to me."

JANE TAYLOR.

MORNING IN JUDEA.

THE sun is up—from Carmel's woody brow
His orient radiance rushes like a flood—
A generous stream by whose fresh influence grow
The flowers that blossom, and the trees that bud;
The moon that rose at eve as if the blood
Of life was in her veins, turns pale as clay
From which the life has fled; the stars that stud
The midnight sky by thousands, glide away
Like foam-blown bells that burst within the ocean's bay.

The night—even like a fierce despotic king
That wraps the nation in a fearful shade,
Dark as the darkness which the death-glooms fling
Around the sepulchre where bones are laid;
The night departs—as when with power arrayed,
Some generous monarch from his throne has hurled
The gloomy tyrant, humbled and dismayed;
For now the gates of morning are unfurled,
And light, and loveliness, and joy, possess the world.

The dew-bent lilies, by the breezes kissed,
Awake in beauty on their grassy beds,
Like lovely infants from the mother's breast,
That joys to pillow their protected heads;
On Zion's holy hill the green-grape sheds
Its sweet perfume; the fig-tree is in blow;
On fertile Lebanon the corn-field spreads
Its store, and to the winds that o'er it go,
Heaves as the billows heave with undulating flow.

On Gilead's pastures green the bleating flocks
Disport, in Jordan's stream the fishes play;
The snow-white goats are gambolling on the rocks,
The insects dancing in the sunny ray;
The humming bees upon their early way
Are wandering happily from flower to flower;
And all unseen, where twilight shadows gray
Are lingering still, the wild birds in the bower
Pour out their choral song unto the matin hour.

And man comes from his dwelling forth—afar
He casts his eye o'er all the happy sight,
And lifts his heart to Him whose mercies are
Each morning new, whose faithfulness each night;
To Him who sends the sun in all his might
To bid the forests bud, the flowerets bloom;
Who fills the lower creatures with delight,
Who sweeps the shadows from the hearts of gloom,
And feeds the aspiring soul with hopes beyond the tomb.

KNOX.

NATURE.

How sweet at summer's noon, to sit and muse
Beneath the shadow of some ancient elm!
While at my feet the mazy streamlet flows
In tuneful lapse, laving the flowers that bend
To kiss its tide; while sport the finny throng
On the smooth surface of the crystal depth
In silvery circles, or in shallows leap,
That sparkle to the sunbeam's trembling glare.
Around the tiny jets, where humid bells
Break as they form, the water-spiders weave,
Brisk on the eddying pools, their ceaseless dance.
The wild bee winds her horn, lost in the cups
Of honeyed flowers, or sweeps with ample curve;
While o'er the summer's lap is heard the hum
Of countless insects sporting on the wing,
Inviting sleep. And from the leafy woods
One various song of bursting joy ascends,
While echo wafts the notes from grove to hill;
From hill to grove the grateful concert spreads,
As borne on fluttering plumes, encircling make
The happy birds flit through the balmy air,
Where plays the gossamer; and, as they felt
The general joy, bright exhalations dance;
And shepherd's pipe, and song of blooming maid,
Quick as she turns the odor-breathing swathes
Of new-mown hay, and children playing round
The ivy-clustered cot, and low of herds,
And bleat of lambs, that crop the verdant sward
With daisies spread, while smiles the heaven serene,
All wake to ecstacy, or melt to love,
And to the Source of goodness raise the soul—
Raise it to him, exhaustless Source of bliss!
That like the sun, best emblem of Himself,
For ever flowing, yet for ever full,
Diffuses life and happiness to all.

REV. W. GILLESPIE.

CONSOLATION.

PILGRIM burthened with thy sin,
Come the way to Zion's gate,
There, till mercy lets thee in,
Knock, and weep, and watch, and wait.
Knock!—He knows the sinner's cry;
Weep!—He loves the mourner's tears;
Watch!—for saving grace is nigh;
Wait—till heavenly light appears.

Hark! it is the bridegroom's voice:
Welcome, pilgrim, to thy rest;
Now within the gate rejoice,
Safe, and sealed, and bought, and blest.
Safe—from all the lures of vice,
Sealed—by signs the chosen know,
Bought by love, and life the price,
Blest—the mighty debt to owe.

Holy pilgrim! what for thee,
In a world like this remain?
From thy guarded breast shall flee,
Fear, and shame, and doubt, and pain.
Fear—the hope of heaven shall fly,
Shame—from glory's view retire,
Doubt—in certain rapture die,
Pain—in endless bliss expire

CRABBE.

TOO LATE.

Too late—too late! how heavily that phrase
Comes, like a knell, upon the shuddering ear,
Telling of slighted duties, wasted days;
Of privileges lost, of hopes once dear
Now quenched in gloom and darkness. Words like these
The worldling's callous heart must penetrate—
All that he might have been in thought he sees,
And sorrows o'er his present wreck too late.

Too late—too late! the prodigal who strays
Through the dim groves and winding bowers of sin;
The cold and false deceiver, who betrays
The trusting heart he fondly toiled to win;
The spendthrift, scattering his golden store,
And left in age despised and desolate,
All may their faults confess, forsake, deplore,
Yet struggle to retrieve the past too late.

Too late—too late! O dark and fatal ban,
Is there a spell thy terrors to assuage?
There is—there is! but seek it not from man:
Seek for the healing balm in God's own page;
Read of thy Savior's love, to him repair—
He looks with pity on thy guilty state;
Kneel at his throne in deep and fervent prayer—
Kneel and repent, ere yet it is too late.

Too late—too late! that direful sound portends
Sorrow on earth, but not immortal pain:
Thou mayst have lost the confidence of friends,
The love of kindred thou mayst ne'er regain;
But there is One above who marks thy tears,
And opes for thee salvation's golden gate.
Come, then, poor mourner, cast away thy fears.
Believe, and enter—it is not too late!

MRS. ABDY

PILATE'S QUESTION.

WHAT is truth? The fickle Roman
Asked, nor waited for reply.
Question of momentous omen!
Shall I also pass it by?
No, my Lord! I'll turn me to it,
Anxious all its depths to sound;
Let me humbly, closely, view it,
Till I have the answer found.

What is truth? The only token
Lent to guide our blinded race,
Is the Word which God hath spoken
By the heralds of his grace.
Thence we learn how helpless strangers,
Guilty rebels, such as we,
May escape ten thousand dangers,
Burst our fetters, and be free.

What is truth? That man is mortal,
Wretched, feeble, and depraved;
Dying still at mercy's portal,
Yet unwilling to be saved:
Oft to safety's path invited,
Prone from it to wander far;
In the blaze of noon benighted,
With himself and God at war.

What is truth? That He, who made us,
He, who all our weakness knows,
Stooped himself from heaven to aid us,
Bear our guilt, and feel our woes.
Like the lamb the peasant slaughters,
See him unresisting led;
'Midst the tears of Judah's daughters,
Mocked, and numbered with the dead!

Yes, my soul! thy lost condition
Brought the gentle Savior low;
Hast thou felt one hour's contrition
For those sins which pierced him so?
Dost thou bear the love thou owest
For such proof of grace divine?
Meek I answer, Lord, thou knowest,
That this heart is wholly thine!

Long, indeed, too long I wandered
From the path thy children tread;
Long my time and substance squandered,
Seeking that which was not bread.
Now—though flesh may disallow it,
Now—though sense no glory see,
In thy strength, my God! I vow it,
Ne'er again to turn from thee!

DR. HUIE

ADDRESS TO POETS.

Ye whose hearts are beating high
With the pulse of Poesy,
Heirs of more than royal race,
Framed by Heaven's peculiar grace,
God's own work to do on earth,
(If the word be not too bold),
Giving virtue a new birth,
And a life that ne'er grows old—

Sovereign masters of all hearts!
Know ye who hath set your parts?
He, who gave you breath to sing,
By whose strength ye sweep the string,
He hath chosen you to lead
His hosannas here below;—
Mount, and claim your glorious meed;
Linger not with sin and wo.

But if ye should hold your peace,
Deem not that the song would cease—
Angels round His glory-throne,
Stars, His guiding hand that own,
Flowers, that grow beneath our feet,
Stones, in earth's dark womb that rest,
High and low in choir shall meet,
Ere His name shall be unblest.

Lord, by every minstrel tongue
Be thy praise so duly sung,
That thine angels' harps may ne'er
Fail to find fit echoing here!
We the while, of meaner birth,
Who in that divinest spell
Dare not hope to join on earth,
Give us grace to listen well.

But should thankless silence seal
Lips that might half heaven reveal—
Should bards in idol-hymns profane
The sacred soul enthralling strain,
(As in this bad world below
Noblest things find vilest using),
Then, thy power and mercy show,
In vile things noble breath infusing.

Then waken into sound divine
The very pavement of thy shrine,
Till we, like heaven's star-sprinkled floor,
Faintly give back what we adore,
Childlike though the voices be,
And untunable the parts,
Thou wilt own the minstrelsey,
If it flow from childlike hearts. Keble.

THE METEOR.

A shepherd on the silent moor
Pursued his lone employ,
And by him watched, at midnight hour,
His loved and gentle boy.

The night was still, the sky was clear,
The moon and stars were bright;
And well the youngster loved to hear
Of those fair orbs of light.

When, lo! an earth-born meteor's glare
Made stars and planets dim;
In transient splendor through the air
Its glory seemed to swim.

No more could stars' or planets' spell
The stripling's eye enchant,
He only urged his sire to tell
Of this new visitant.

But ere the shepherd found a tongue,
The meteor's gleam was gone;
And in their glory o'er them hung
The orbs of night alone.

Canst thou the simple lesson read,
My artless muse hath given!
The only lights that safely lead,
Are those that shine from heaven!

Barton.

SAUL JOURNEYING TO DAMASCUS.

Whose is that sword—that voice and eye of flame—
That heart of unextinguishable ire?
Who bears the dungeon keys, and bonds of fire?
Along his dark and withering path he came—
Death in his looks, and terror in his name,
Tempting the might of heaven's Eternal Sire.
Lo! the light shone!—the sun's veiled beams expire—
A Savior's self, a Savior's lips proclaim!
Who is yon form, stretched on the earth's cold bed,
With smitten soul and tears of agony
Mourning the past? Bowed is the lofty head—
Rayless the orbs that flashed with victory.
Over the raging waves of human will
The Savior's spirit walked—and all was still!

Roscoe

HYMN FOR THE OPENING OF A CHURCH.

O Thou to whom, in ancient time,
The lyre of Hebrew bards was strung,
Whom kings adored in song sublime,
And prophets praised with glowing tongue

Not now, on Zion's height alone,
Thy favored worshipper may dwell,
Nor where, at sultry noon, thy Son
Sat, weary, by the Patriarch's well.

From every place below the skies,
The grateful song, the fervent prayer—
The incense of the heart—may rise
To heaven, and find acceptance there.

In this Thy house, whose doors we now
For social worship first unfold,
To Thee the suppliant throng shall bow,
While circling years on years are rolled.

To Thee shall Age, with snowy hair,
And Strength and Beauty, bend the knee,
And Childhood lisp, with reverent air,
Its praises and its prayers to Thee.

O Thou, to whom, in ancient time,
The lyre of prophet bards was strung,
To Thee, at last, in every clime,
Shall temples rise and praise be sung.

Pierpont

CHARACTER OF A HAPPY LIFE.

How happy is he born and taught,
That serveth not another's will;
Whose armor is his honest thought,
And simple truth his utmost skill!

Whose passions not his masters are,
Whose soul is still prepared for death;
Untied unto the worldly care
Of public fame, or private breath;

Who envies none that chance doth raise,
Or vice; who never understood
How deepest wounds are given by praise;
Nor rules of state, but rules of good;

Who hath his life from rumors freed;
Whose conscience is his strong retreat;
Whose state can neither flatterers feed,
Nor ruin make oppressors great;

Who God doth late and early pray
More of his grace than gifts to lend;
And entertains the harmless day
With a religious book or friend:—

This man is freed from servile bands
Of hope to rise, and fear to fall;
Lord of himself, though not of lands;
And having nothing, yet hath all.

Wotton.

THE HUGUENOT'S BATTLE HYMN.

Now glory to the Loid of Hosts, from whom all glories are!
And glory to our sovereign liege, King Henry of Navarre!
Now let there be the merry sound of music and of dance,
Through thy corn-fields green, and sunny vines, O pleasant land of France!
And thou, Rochelle, our own Rochelle, proud city of the waters,
Again let rapture light the eyes of all thy mourning daughters.
As thou wert constant in our ills, be joyous in our joy,
For cold, and stiff, and still, are they who wrought thy walls annoy.
Hurrah! hurrah! a single field hath turned the chance of war,
Hurrah! hurrah! for Ivry, and Henry of Navarre.

O! how our hearts were beating, when, at the dawn of day,
We saw the army of the League drawn out in long array;
With all its priest-led citizens, and all its rebel peers,
And Appenzel's stout infantry, and Egmont's Flemish spears.
There rode the brood of false Lorraine, the curses of our land;
And dark Mayenne was in the midst, a truncheon in his hand:
And as we looked on them, we thought of Seine's empurpled flood,
And good Coligni's hoary hair, all dabbled with his blood;
And we cried unto the living God, who rules the fate of war,
To fight for his own holy name, and Henry of Navarre!

The King is come to marshal us, in all his armor dressed,
And he has bound a snow-white plume upon his gallant crest.
He looked upon his people, and a tear was in his eye;
He looked upon the traitors, and his glance was stern and high.
Right graciously he smiled on us, as rolled from wing to wing,
Down all our line, a deafening shout, "God save our Lord the King!"
"And if my standard-bearer fall, as fall full well he may,
For never saw I promise yet of such a bloody fray—
Press where ye see my white plume shine amid the ranks of war,
And be your oriflamme to-day the helmet of Navarre!"

Hurrah! the foes are moving—hark to the mingled din
Of fife and steed, and trump and drum, and roaring culverin.
The fiery Duke is pricking fast across Saint Andre's plain,
With all the hireling chivalry of Guelders and Almayne.
Now by the lips of those we love, fair gentlemen of France,
Charge for the golden lilies—upon them with the lance!
A thousand spurs are striking deep, a thousand spears in rest,
A thousand knights are pressing close behind the snow-white crest;
And in they burst, and on they rushed, while like a guiding star,
Amid the thickest carnage blazed the helmet of Navarre!

Now, God be praised, the day is ours! Mayenne hath turned his rein!
D'Aumale hath cried for quarter! The Flemish Count is slain!
Their ranks are breaking like thin clouds before a Biscay gale!
The field is heaped with bleeding steeds, and flags, and cloven mail.
And then we thought on vengeance; and, all along our van—
"Remember Saint Bartholomew!" was passed from man to man:
But out spake gentle Henry—"No Frenchman is my foe—
Down, down, with every foreigner, but let your brethren go."
Oh! was there ever such a knight, in friendship or in war,
As our Sovereign Lord King Henry, the soldier of Navarre!

Ho! maidens of Vienna!—ho! matrons of Lucerne!
Weep, weep, and rend your hair for those who never shall return.
Ho! Philip, send, for charity, thy Mexican pistoles,
That Antwerp monks may sing a mass for thy poor spearmen's souls.
Ho! gallant nobles of the League, look that your arms be bright;
Ho! burghers of Saint Genevieve, keep watch and ward to-night,
For our God hath crushed the tyrant, our God hath raised the slave,
And mocked the counsel of the wise, and the valor of the brave.
Then glory to his holy name, from whom all glories are;
And glory to our Sovereign Lord, King Henry of Navarre!

T. B. Macauley.

LABORERS' NOON-DAY HYMN.

Up to the throne of God is borne
The voice of praise at early morn,
And he accepts the punctual hymn
Sung as the light of day grows dim.

Nor will he turn his ear aside
From holy off'rings at noon-tide;
Then, here reposing, let us raise
A song of gratitude and praise.

What though our burden be not light,
We need not toil from morn to night;
The respite of the mid-day hour
Is in the thankful creature's power.

Blest are the moments, doubly blest,
That, drawn from this one hour of rest,
Are with a ready heart bestowed
Upon the service of our God.

Why should we crave a hallowed spot?
An altar is in each man's cot,
A church in every grove that spreads
Its living roof above our heads.

Look up to heaven!—the industrious sun
Already half his race hath run;
He can not halt or go astray—
But our immortal spirits may.

Lord, since his rising in the east,
If we have faltered or transgressed,
Guide, from thy love's abundant source,
What yet remains of this day's course.

Help with thy grace, through life's short day,
Our upward and our downward way;
And glorify for us the west,
When we shall sink to final rest.

Wordsworth

CHRIST IN THE GARDEN.

A wreath of glory circles still His head—
And yet he kneels—and yet he seems to be
Convulsed with more than human agony;
On his pale brow the drops are large and red
As victim's blood at votive altar shed—
His hands are clasped, his eyes are raised in prayer:
Alas! and is there strife he can not bear,
Who calmed the tempest, and who raised the dead?

There is! there is! for now the powers of hell
Are struggling for the mastery—'tis the hour
When Death exerts his last permitted power,
When the dread weight of sin since Adam fell,
Is visited on him, who deigned to dwell
A man with men—that he might bear the stroke
Of wrath divine, and burst the captive's yoke—
But O! of that dread strife what words can tell?

Those—only those which broke with many a groan
  From his full heart—"O Father, take away
  The cup of vengeance I must drink to-day—
Yet, Father, not my will, but thine be done!"
It could not pass away—for he alone
  Was mighty to endure, and strong to save:
  Nor would Jehovah leave him in the grave;
Nor could corruption taint his Holy One.

DALE.

THE DYING CHRISTIAN.

DEATHLESS principle, arise!
Soar, thou native of the skies!
Pearl of price, by Jesus bought,
To his glorious likeness wrought,
Go, to shine before his throne—
Deck his mediatorial crown;
Go, his triumphs to adorn—
Born for God, to God return.

Lo, he beckons from on high!
Fearless to his presence fly;
Thine the merit of his blood,
Thine the righteousness of God!
Angels, joyful to attend,
Hovering round thy pillow bend;
Wait to catch the signal given,
And escort thee quick to heaven!

Is thy earthly house distrest?
Willing to retain its guest?
'Tis not thou, but it must die—
Fly, celestial tenant, fly!
Burst thy shackles, drop thy clay;
Sweetly breathe thyself away:
Singing, to thy crown remove,
Swift of wing, and fired with love.

Shudder not to pass the stream,
Venture all thy cares on him—
Him, whose dying love and power
Stilled its tossing, hushed its roar;
Safe in the expanded wave,
Gentle as a summer's eve;
Not one object of his care
Ever suffered shipwreck there!

See the haven full in view,
Love divine shall bear thee through;
Trust to that propitious gale,
Weigh thy anchor, spread thy sail!
Saints in glory perfect made,
Wait thy passage through the shade:
Ardent for thy coming o'er,
See! they throng the blissful shore!

Mount, their transports to improve,
Join the longing choir above,
Swiftly to their wish be given,
Kindle higher joy in heaven.
Such the prospects that arise
To the dying Christian's eyes!
Such the glorious vista Faith
Opens through the shades of death!

TOPLADY.

THE RESTORATION OF ISRAEL.

'Tis eventide; the golden teints are dying
  Along the horizon's glowing verge away;
Far in the grove the nightingale is sighing
  Her requiem to the last receding ray;
  And still thou holdest thy appointed way.
But Salem's light is quenched. Majestic sun!
  Her beauteous flock hath wandered far astray,
Led by their guides the path of life to shun:
Her orb hath sunk ere yet his wonted course was run.

In ages past all glorious was the land,
  And lovely were thy borders, Palestine!
The heavens were wont to shed their influence bland
  On all those mountains and those vales of thine;
  For o'er thy coasts resplendent then did shine
The light of God's approving countenance,
  With rapturous glow of blessedness divine.
And 'neath the radiance of that mighty glance,
Basked the wide-scattered isles o'er ocean's blue expanse.

But there survives a tinge of glory yet,
  O'er all thy pastures and thy heights of green,
Which, though the lustre of thy day hath set,
  Tells of the joy and splendor which hath been:
  So some proud ruin, 'mid the desert seen,
By traveller, halting on his path awhile,
  Declares how once beneath the light serene
Of brief posterity's unclouded smile,
Uprose in grandeur there some vast imperial pile.

O Thou, who through the wilderness of old
  Thy people to their promised rest didst bring,
Hasten the days by prophet-bards foretold,
  When roses shall again be blossoming
  In Sharon, and Siloa's cooling spring
Shall murmur freshly at the noontide hour;
  And shepherds oft in Achor's vale shall sing
The mysteries of that redeeming power
Which hath their ashes changed for beauty's sunniest bower.

Thou hadst a plant of thy peculiar choice,
  A fruitful vine from Egypt's servile shore;
Thou mad'st it in the smile of heaven rejoice;
  But the ripe clusters which awhile it bore
  Now purple on the verdant hills no more;
The wild-boar hath upon its branches trod;
  Yet once again thy choicest influence pour,
Transplant it from this dim terrestrial sod,
To adorn with deathless bloom the paradise of God.

T. G. NICHOLAS.

THE CRUCIFIXION.

BOUND upon the accursed tree,
Faint and bleeding—who is He?
By the eyes so pale and dim,
Streaming blood, and writhing limb,
By the flesh with scourges torn,
By the crown of twisted thorn,
By the side so deeply pierced,
By the baffled, burning thirst,
By the drooping, death-dewed brow,
Son of Man! 'tis thou, 'tis thou!

Bound upon the accursed tree,
Dread and awful—who is He?
By the sun at noon-day pale,
Shivering rocks, and rending veil;
By earth that trembles at his doom,
By yonder saints who burst their tomb,
By Eden, promised ere he died
To the felon at his side,
Lord! our suppliant knees we bow,
Son of God! 'tis thou, 'tis thou!

Bound upon the accursed tree,
Sad and dying—who is he?
By the last and bitter cry,
The ghost given up in agony;
By the lifeless body laid
In the chambers of the dead;
By the mourners come to weep
Where the bones of Jesus sleep:
Crucified! we know thee now—
Son of Man! 'tis thou, 'tis thou!

Bound upon the accursed tree,
Dread and awful—who is he?
By the prayer for them that slew—
"Lord! they know not what they do!"
By the spoiled and empty grave,
By the souls he died to save,
By the conquest he hath won,
By the saints before his throne,
By the rainbow round his brow,
Son of God! 'tis thou, 'tis thou!

MILMAN.

AN ALPINE HYMN.

Awake, my soul! not only passive praise
Thou owest! not alone these swelling tears,
Mute thanks and secret ecstasy! Awake,
Voice of sweet song! Awake, my heart, awake!
Green vales and icy cliffs, all join my hymn:
Thou first and chief, sole sovereign of the vale!
O struggling with the darkness all the night,
And visited all night by troops of stars,
Or when they climb the sky, or when they sink;
Companion of the Morning-star at dawn,
Thyself Earth's rosy star, and of the dawn
Co-herald! wake, O wake, and utter praise!
Who sank thy sunless pillars deep in earth?
Who filled thy countenance with rosy light?
Who made thee parent of perpetual streams?
And you, ye five wild torrents fiercely glad!
Who called you forth from night and utter death—
From dark and icy caverns called you forth,
Down those precipitous, black, jagged rocks,
For ever shattered, and the same for ever?
Who gave you your invulnerable life,
Your strength, your speed, your fury, and your joy,
Unceasing thunder, and eternal foam?
And who commanded (and the silence came)—
"Here let the billows stiffen, and have rest?"—
Ye icy-falls! ye that from the mountain's brow
Adown enormous ravines slope amain!
Torrents, methinks, that heard a mighty voice,
And stopped at once amid their maddest plunge!
Motionless torrents! silent cataracts!
Who made you glorious as the gates of Heaven
Beneath the keen full moon? Who bade the Sun
Clothe you with rainbows? Who, with living flowers
Of loveliest hue, spread garlands at your feet?
God! Let the torrents, like a shout of nations,
Answer! and let the ice-plains echo God!—
God! sing ye meadow-streams with gladsome voice!
Ye pine-groves, with your soft and soul-like sounds!
And they too have a voice, yon piles of snow,
And in their perilous fall shall thunder, God!—
Ye living flowers that skirt the eternal frost!
Ye wild-goats sporting round the eagle's nest!
Ye eagles, playmates of the mountain-storm!
Ye lightnings, the dread arrows of the clouds!
Ye signs and wonders of the element!
Utter forth God, and fill the hills with praise!—
Once more, hoar Mount! with thy sky-pointing peaks,
Oft from whose feet the avalanche, unheard,
Shoots downward glittering through the pure serene,
Into the depth of clouds that veil thy breast.—
Thou too, again, stupendous Mountain! thou
That, as I raise my head, awhile bowed low
In adoration, upward from thy base,
Slow-travelling, with dim eyes suffused with tears,
Solemnly seemest, like a vapory cloud,
To rise before me—Rise, O ever rise—
Rise like a cloud of incense, from the earth!
Thou kingly spirit throned among the hills—
Thou dread ambassador from Earth to Heaven.
Great hierarch! tell thou the silent sky,
And tell the stars, and tell yon rising sun,
Earth, with her thousand voices, praises God.

Coleridge.

HYMN.

Oh, blest were the accents of early creation,
When the word of Jehovah came down from above;
In the clouds of the earth to infuse animation,
And wake their cold atoms to life and to love!

And mighty the tones which the firmament rended,
When on wheels of the thunder, and wings of the wind,
By lightning, and hail, and thick darkness attended,
He uttered, on Sinai, his laws to mankind.

And sweet was the voice of the First-born of heaven,
(Tho' poor his apparel, tho' earthly his form,)
Who said to the mourner, "Thy sins are forgiven!"
"Be whole," to the sick, and "Be still" to the storm.

O Judge of the world! when arrayed in thy glory,
Thy summons again shall be heard from on high;
When nature stands trembling and naked before thee,
And waits on thy sentence to live or to die;

When the heavens shall fly fast from the sound of thy thunder,
And the sun, in thy lightnings, grow languid and pale,
And the sea yield her dead, and the tomb cleave asunder,
In the hour of thy terrors let mercy prevail!

Heber.

STANZAS.

I looked unto God in the season of anguish,
When earth and its trifles could charm me no more;
When pain and affliction had caused me to languish,
And the dream of my youthful existence was o'er:
I looked unto Him who alone can deliver,
Whose arm of omnipotence never shall yield;
And I prayed that his grace might support me for ever,
My rock and my refuge, my sun and my shield.

How bitterly then did my conscience upbraid me;
For the least of my crimes I had nothing to plead.
But I thought of the promise which Jesus had made me,
And I cried unto him in the time of my need.
Yes; he whose entreaties so oft I'd neglected,
And met all his kind invitations with scorn;
The Savior and Prince whom I thus had rejected,
Was my only relief when I wandered forlorn.

Yet still—oh! the baseness that reigns in my spirit—
I often forget thee my heavenly Friend,
And thankless for all which from thee I inherit,
Deny thee, and grieve thee,—ay times without end.
How oft when the worldling has dared me to trial,
Have I passed him in silence regardlessly by;
Was this like the courage, the boundless denial,
Which a sense of thy favor should ever supply?

O Father of mercies, assist me to cherish
The light of thy word in my innermost soul;
Without thine assistance I feel I must perish,
In the tempest of sin which I can not control:
But thou, who canst say to the foam crested ocean,
Thus far and no farther thy proud waves shall come;
Thou only canst curb each unhallowed emotion,
And guide me in peace to my glorious home.

John Buchanan

SONG OF THE STARS.

When the radiant morn of creation broke,
And the world in the smile of God awoke,
And the empty realms of darkness and death
Were moved through their depths by his mighty breath
And orbs of beauty and spheres of flame
From the void abyss by myriads came,
In the joy of youth as they darted away,
Through the widening waste of space to play,
Their silver voices in chorus rang,
And this was the song the bright ones sang:—

'Away, away, through the wide, wide sky,
The fair blue fields that before us lie;
Each sun with the worlds that round us roll,
Each planet poised on her turning pole,
With her isles of green, and her clouds of white
And waters that lie like fluid light.

"For the Source of glory uncovers his face,
And the brightness o'erflows unbounded space:
And we drink, as we go, the luminous tides
In our ruddy air and our blooming sides;
Lo, yonder the living splendors play!
Away, on our joyous path, away!

"Look, look through our glittering ranks afar
In the infinite azure, star after star,
How they brighten and bloom as they swiftly pass;
How the verdure runs o'er each rolling mass!
And the path of the gentle winds is seen,
Where the small waves dance and the young woods lean.

"And see where the brighter day-beams pour,
How the rainbows hang in the sunny shower:
And the morn and the eve, with their pomp of hues,
Shift o'er the bright planets and shed their dews,
And 'twixt them both, o'er the teeming ground,
With her shadowy cone, the night goes round.

"Away, away! In our blossoming bowers,
In the soft air wrapping these spheres of ours,
In the seas and fountains that shine with morn,
See love is brooding, and life is born,
And breathing myriads are breaking from night,
To rejoice, like us, in motion and light."

Glide on in your beauty, ye youthful spheres,
To weave the dance that measures the years:
Glide on in the glory, and gladness, sent
To the farthest wall of the firmament,
The boundless visible smile of HIM,
To the veil of whose brow our lamps are dim.

ANONYMOUS.

CHRIST STILLING THE TEMPEST.

FEAR was within the tossing bark,
When stormy winds grew loud,
And waves came rolling high and dark,
And the tall mast was bowed.

And men stood breathless in their dread,
And baffled in their skill—
But One was there, who rose and said
To the wild sea, "Be still!"

And the wind ceased—it ceased—that word
Passed through the gloomy sky;
The troubled billows knew their Lord,
And sank beneath his eye.

And slumber settled on the deep,
And silence on the blast,
As when the righteous falls asleep,
When death's fierce throes are past.

Thou that didst rule the angry hour,
And tame the tempest's mood,
Oh! send thy Spirit forth in power,
O'er our dark souls to brood!

Thou that didst bow the billow's pride,
Thy mandates to fulfil,—
So speak to passion's raging tide,
Speak and stay,—Peace, be still.

MRS. HEMANS.

MESSIAH'S ADVENT.

HE came not in his people's day,
Of miracle and might,
When awe-struck nations owned their sway,
And conquest crowned each fight;—
When nature's self with wonder saw,
Her ancient power, her boasted law,
To feeble man give way—
The elements of earth and heaven
For Israel stayed—for Judah riven!

Pillar and cloud Jehovah gave,
High emblems of his grace;
And clove the rock, and smote the wave,
Moved mountains from their place;—
But judgment was with mercy blent—
In thunder was the promise sent—
Fierce lightnings veiled his face;
The jealous God—the burning law—
Were all thy chosen people saw.

Behold them—pilgrim tribes no more—
The promised land their own;
And blessings theirs of sea and shore,
To other realms unknown:
From age to age a favored line,
Of mighty kings and seers divine,
A temple and a throne:
Not then, but in their hour of shame,
Wo, want, and weakness—then "He came."

Not in the earthquake's rending force,
Not in the blasting fire;
Not in the strong wind's rushing course,
Came He their soul's desire!
Forerunners of his coming these,
Proclaiming over earth and seas,
As God, his might and ire;
The still, small voice—the hovering dove,
Proved him Messiah—spoke him "Love!"

Of life the way, of life the spring
Eternal, undefiled;
Redeemer, Prophet, Priest, and King—
Yet came he as a child!
And Zion's favored eye grown dim,
Knew not her promised Lord in Him,
The lowly and the mild!
She saw the manger, and the tree,
And scornful cried—"Can this be He?"

ANONYMOUS.

BEST WISHES.

WHO art thou, stranger? Nay, read on,
I will not ask thy name or lot;
Whether thy days be well nigh gone
Or in their spring—it matters not;
Thou art my brother! and for thee
Stranger! shall my best wishes be.

Life is a sea of stormy pain;
Thou knowest it or thou soon *will* know:
Thine be the faith that braves the main,
When its most angry tempests blow:
Thine anchor cast within the veil;
None ever knew that mooring fail.

Thine be the love,—refined from sense,—
That seeks its object in the skies,
Draws all its warmth and brightness thence,
Its comfort, confidence, and joys;
And be thy best affections given,
To Him, who loved thee first, in heaven.

Thine be the refuge,—ever found
By them who seek in faith and prayer—
From all the trials that abound
Throughout this wilderness of care,
The faithfulness of Him, whose love
Storms can not quench, nor death remove.

Thine be the meekness of the flower
That bows its head before the blast;
Increase in wisdom and in power;
Be lowliness around thee cast;
Thy faith and love, like flames of fire
Trembling, the higher they aspire.

And when thy Master calls thee, thine,
Thine be the crown of endless joy,
Where heaven's eternal rivers shine
Beneath a bright and cloudless sky.
Those realms—how beautiful and fair,
Stranger! a blissful meeting there!

ANONYMOUS.

THE MERCIES OF REDEMPTION.

OH! can such charms be left to waste,
Unmarked by man's insensate taste?
Can beauty, use, and health,
Be spread before regardless eyes,
And not one thankful accent rise
For all creation's wealth?

Alas! in vain—if outward sense
Is claimed by Heaven's benevolence,
How shall it hope to reach
The callous bosom's inmost core,
And bid the heart with love run o'er,
That mocks the vent of speech?

Such love as lost and ruined man
Owes to redemption's wondrous plan;
Such love as He demands,

Who, clothed in poverty's disgrace,
Was given on earth no resting-place,
Save by his murderers' hands.

The Son of God descend from Heaven!
The Son of God to slaughter given
For man's offending race!
Oh! help us to conceive aright
The mysteries of that awful sight,
Oh! help us, guardian grace!

When all the heavenly host around
Heard the tremendous fiat's sound,
That man was doomed to die;
Each on the other gazed in dread,
Each hung his sad angelic head,
And silence filled the sky.

Then, like the light, first-born above,
And launched o'er earth by holy love,
Stood forth the all-gracious Son;
Eager to pay the appointed price,
Offered HIMSELF the sacrifice,
And man's redemption won.

Shot through the vast ethereal space,
Flew the bright messenger of grace
At heaven's appointed hour;
And o'er yon low Judean roof,
While human power stood far aloof,
Announced the Incarnate Power.

The Virgin hears, with holy awe,
The great fulfilment of the law,
Sprung from herself on earth;
And now the manifesting star
Calls wisdom from the east afar,
To hail the promised birth.

Ye nations, worship at the call!
Emmanuel comes, to rescue all
From death's relentless doom:
Thou slumbering world, awake and see
Thy life and immortality
In yon poor manger's gloom!

Lay down your worthy offerings here;
The myrrh he loves is sorrow's tear,
O'er conscious guilt distilled;
His frankincense the grateful sigh
Of guilt redeemed from misery—
Thus be his temple filled!

"Peace and good-will" to earth he brings,
And heaven that hears, in transport sings!
Oh! turn to him alone,
Turk, Heathen, Jew! till Heaven behold
One Shepherd, and one spotless fold
Surround Jehovah's throne.

HODGSON.

CHRISTIAN WARFARE.

SOLDIER, go, but not to claim
Mouldering spoils of earth-born treasure,
Not to build a vaunting name,
Not to dwell in tents of pleasure.
Dream not that the way is smooth,
Hope not that the thorns are roses;
Turn no wishful eye of youth
Where the sunny beam reposes;—
Thou hast sterner work to do,
Hosts to cut thy passage through:
Close behind thee gulfs are burning—
Forward! there is no returning.

Soldier, rest—but not for thee
Spreads the world her downy pillow;
On the rock thy couch must be,
While around thee chafes the billow
Thine must be a watchful sleep,
Wearier than another's waking;
Such a charge as thou dost keep
Brooks no moment of forsaking.
Sleep, as on the battle-field,
Girded—grasping sword and shield
Those thou canst not name nor number,
Steal upon thy broken slumber.

Soldier, rise—the war is done:
Lo! the hosts of hell are flying;
'Twas thy Lord the battle won;
Jesus vanquished them by dying.
Pass the stream—before thee lies
All the conquered land of glory
Hark what songs of rapture rise,
These proclaim the victor's story.
Soldier, lay thy weapons down,
Quit the sword, and take the crown
Triumph! all thy foes are banished,
Death is slain, and earth has vanished.

CHARLOTTE ELIZABETH.

A CHURCH-YARD SCENE.

How sweet and solemn, all alone,
With reverend step, from stone to stone,
In a small village church-yard lying,
O'er intervening flowers to move—
And as we read the names unknown,
Of young and old, to judgment gone,
And hear, in the calm air above,
Time onward, softly flying,
To meditate, in Christian love,
Upon the dead and dying!
Across the silence seem to go
With dream-like motion, wavery, slow,
And shrouded in their folds of snow,
The friends we loved long, long ago!
Gliding across the sad retreat,
How beautiful their phantom feet!
What tenderness is in their eyes,
Turned where the poor survivor lies,
Mid monitory sanctities!
What years of vanished joy are fanned
From one uplifting of that hand
In its white stillness! When the shade
Doth glimmeringly in sunshine fade
From our embrace, how dim appears
This world's life, through a mist of tears!
Vain hopes! Wild sorrows! Needless fears!
Such is the scene around me now:
A little church-yard, on the brow
Of a green pastoral hill:
Its sylvan village sleeps below,
And faintly, here, is heard the flow
Of Woodburn's summer rill;
A place where all things mournful meet,
And, yet, the sweetest of the sweet!—
The stillest of the still!
With what a pensive beauty fall,
Across the mossy, mouldering wall
That rose-tree's clustered arches! See
The robin-redbreast, warily,
Bright through the blossoms leaves his nest
Sweet ingrate! through the winter blest
At the firesides of men—but shy
Through all the sunny, summer hours,—
He hides himself among the flowers
In his own wild festivity.
What lulling sound, and shadow cool,
Hangs half the darkened church-yard o'er,
From thy green depths, so beautiful,
Thou gorgeous sycamore!
Oft hath the lonely wine and bread,
Been blest beneath thy murmuring tent,
Where many a bright and hoary head,
Bowed at the awful sacrament.
Now all beneath the turf are laid,
On which they sat, and sang, and prayed.
Alone that consecrated tree
Ascends the tapering spire, that seems
To lift the soul up silently
To heaven, with all its dreams!—
While in the belfry, deep and low,
From his heaved bosom's purple gleams
The dove's continuous murmurs flow,
A dirge-like song, half-bliss, half wo,—
The voice so lonely seems!

JOHN WILSON

PULPIT ELOQUENCE.

The day was declining—the breeze in its glee
Had left the fair blossoms to sing on the sea,
As the sun in its gorgeousness, radiant and still,
Dropped down like a gem from the brow of the hill,
One tremulous star in the glory of June
Came out with a smile and sat down by the moon,
As she graced her blue throne with the pride of a queen,
The smiles of her loveliness gladdened the scene.

The scene was enchanting! in distance away
Rolled the foam-crested waves of the Chesapeake bay,
While bathing in moonlight the village was seen
With the church in the distance that stood on the green,
The soft-sleeping meadows lay brightly enrolled,
With their mantles of verdure and blossoms of gold,
And the earth in her beauty, forgetting to grieve,
Lay asleep in her bloom on the bosom of eve.

A light-hearted child, I had wandered away
From the spot where my footsteps had gamboled all day;
And free as a bird's was the song of my soul,
As I heard the wild waters exultingly roll;
While lightening my heart as I sported along,
With bursts of low laughter and snatches of song,
I struck in the pathway half worn o'er the sod
By the feet that went up to the worship of God.

As I traced its green windings, a murmur of prayer
With the hymn of the worshippers rose on the air,
And drawn by the links of its sweetness along,
I stood unobserved in the midst of the throng.
For awhile my young spirit still wandered about
With the birds, and the winds, that were singing without;
But birds, waves, and zephyrs, were quickly forgot
In one angel-like being that brightened the spot.

In stature majestic, apart from the throng,
He stood in his beauty, the theme of my song!
His cheek pale with fervor—the blue orbs above
Lit up with the splendors of youth and of love,
Yet the heart-glowing rapture that beamed from those eyes
Seemed saddened by sorrow, and chastened by sighs,
As if the young heart in its bloom had grown cold
With its loves unrequited, its sorrows untold.

Such language as his may I never recall,
But his theme was salvation—salvation to all—
And the souls of a thousand in ecstasy hung
On the manna-like sweetness that dropped from his tongue.
Not alone on the ear his wild eloquence stole:
Enforced by each gesture, it sunk to the soul,
Till it seemed that an angel had brightened the sod,
And brought to each bosom a message from God.

He spoke of the Savior—what pictures he drew!
The scenes of his sufferings rose clear on my view—
The cross—the rude cross, where he suffered and died;
The gush of bright crimson that flowed from his side;
The cup of his sorrows—the wormwood and gall;
The darkness that mantled the earth as a pall;
The garland of thorns; and the demon-like crews
Who knelt as they scoffed him, "Hail, King of the Jews!"

He spoke, and it seemed that his statue-like form
Expanded and glowed, as his spirit grew warm;
His tone so impassioned—so melting his air,
As touched with compassion he ended in prayer;
His hands clasped above him—his blue orbs upthrown,
Still pleading for sins that were never his own,
While that mouth where such sweetness ineffably clung,
Still spoke, though expression had died on his tongue.

O God! what emotions the speaker awoke!
A mortal he seemed—yet a Deity spoke;
A man—yet so far from humanity riven;
On earth—yet so closely connected with heaven!
How oft in my fancy I've pictured him there
As he stood in that triumph of passion and prayer,
With his eyes closed in rapture—their transient eclipse
Made bright by the smiles that illumined his lips

2

There's a charm in delivery—a magical art
That thrills like a kiss, from the lip to the heart;
'Tis the glance—the expression—the well-chosen word,
By whose magic the depths of the spirit are stirred;
The smile—the mute gesture—the soul-startling pause,
The eye's sweet expression, that melts while it awes—
The lips soft persuasion, its musical tone:
O such was the charm of that eloquent one!

The time is long past—yet how clearly defined
That bay, church, and village, float up on my mind;
I see amid azure the moon in her pride,
With the sweet little trembler that sat by her side;
I hear the blue waves, as she wanders along,
Leap up in their gladness and sing her a song,
And I tread in the pathway half worn o'er the sod
By the feet that went up to the worship of God.

The time is long past—yet what visions I see!
The past, the dim past, is the present to me;
I am standing once more 'mid that heart-stricken throng,
A vision floats up—'tis the theme of my song—
All glorious and bright as a spirit of air,
The light, like a halo encircling his hair,
As I catch the same accents of sweetness and love,
He whispers of Jesus, and points us above.

How sweet to my heart is the picture I've traced!
Its chain of bright fancies seem almost effaced,
Till Memory, the fond one that sits in the soul,
Took up the frail links, and collected the whole.
As the dew to the blossom—the bud to the bee—
As the scent to the rose—are those memories to me.
Round the cords of my heart they have tremblingly clung,
And the echo it gives is the song I have sung.

Cor. of Louisville Journal.

THE DAISY.

Not worlds on worlds in phalanx deep,
  Need we to prove a God is here:
The daisy, fresh from winter's sleep,
  Tells of his hand in lines as clear.

For who but he that arched the skies,
  And pours the day-spring's living flood,
Wondrous alike in all he tries,
  Could rear the daisy's purple bud?

Mould its green cup, its wiry stem,
  Its fringed border nicely spin,
And cut the gold-embossed gem,
  That, set in silver, gleams within?

Then fling it, unrestrained and free,
  O'er hill and dale, and desert sod,
That man, where'er he walks, may see
  In every step, the stamp of God.

J. M. Good.

POWER AND BENEVOLENCE.

God is not *great* because *omnipotent!*
  But because power in him is understood,
And felt and proved, to be benevolent,
  And wise, and holy—thus it ever should!
  For what He wills, we know is pure and good,
And has in view the happiness of all:
  Hence love and adoration—never could
The contrite spirit at his footstool fall,
If power, and power *alone*, its feelings did appal!

If then divinest power be truly so,
  Because its object is to bless;
It follows, that all power which man can know,
  The highest even monarchs can possess,
  Displays alone, their "less than littleness,"
Unless it seek the happiness of man,
  And glory of the Highest:—nothing less
Than such a use of power one moment can
Make its possessor great, on wisdom's god-like plan

Barton.

TO THE RAINBOW.

Triumphal arch, that fill'st the sky,
  When storms prepare to part,
I ask not proud philosophy
  To teach me what thou art.

Still seem as to my childhood's sight,
  A midway station given
For happy spirits to alight
  Betwixt the earth and heaven.

Can all that optics teach, unfold
  Thy form to please me so,
As when I dreamed of gems and gold
  Hid in thy radiant bow?

When Science from creation's face
  Enchantment's veil withdraws,
What lovely visions yield their place
  To cold material laws.

And yet, fair bow, no fabling dreams,
  But words of the Most High,
Have told, why first thy robe of beams
  Was woven in the sky.

When o'er the green undeluged earth
  Heaven's cov'nant thou didst shine,
How came the world's gray fathers forth
  To watch thy sacred sign!

And when its yellow lustre smiled
  O'er mountains yet untrod,
Each mother held aloft her child
  To bless the bow of God.

Methinks thy jubilee to keep,
  The first-made anthem rang,
On earth delivered from the deep,
  And the first poet sang.

Nor ever shall the Muse's eye
  Unraptured greet thy beam:
Theme of primeval prophecy,
  Be still the poet's theme!

The earth to thee its incense yields,
  The lark thy welcome sings,
When glittering in the freshened fields
  The snowy mushroom springs.

How glorious is thy girdle cast,
  O'er mountain, tower, and town;
Or mirrored in the ocean vast,
  A thousand fathoms down!

As fresh in yon horizon dark,
  As young thy beauties seem,
As when the eagle from the ark
  First sported in thy beam.

For, faithful to its sacred page,
  Heaven still rebuilds thy span,
Nor lets the type grow pale with age,
  That first spoke peace to man.

T. Campbell.

THE DEAD SEA.

The wind blows chill across those gloomy waves;
  Oh! how unlike the green and dancing main!
The surge is foul as if it rolled o'er graves:
  Stranger! here lie the cities of the plain.

Yes, on that plain, by wild waves covered now,
  Rose palace once, and sparkling pinnacle;
On pomp and spectacle beamed morning's glow,
  On pomp and festival the twilight fell.

Lovely and splendid all—but Sodom's soul
  Was stained with blood, and pride, and perjury;
Long warned, long spared, till her whole heart was foul,
  And fiery vengeance on its clouds came nigh.

And still she mocked, and danced, and taunting, spoke
  Her sportive blasphemies against the Throne:
It came!—the thunder on her slumber broke—
  God spake the word of wrath!—Her dream was done

Yet, in her final night, amid her stood
  Immortal messengers, and pausing Heaven
Pleaded with man, but she was quite imbued,
  Her last hour waned—she scorned to be forgiven.

'Twas done! down poured at once the sulphurous shower
  Down stooped, in flame, the heaven's red canopy.
Oh! for the arm of God, in that fierce hour!
  'Twas vain, nor help of God or man was nigh.

They rush, they bound, they howl, the men of sin;
  Still stooped the cloud, still burst the thicker blaze;
The earthquake heaved!—then sank the hideous din!—
  Yon wave of darkness o'er their ashes strays.

Rev. G. Croly.

PARTED FRIENDS.

Parted friends may meet again,
  When the storms of life are past;
And the spirit freed from pain,
  Basks in friendship that will last.

Worldly cares may sever wide—
  Distant far their path may be;
But, the bond by Death untied,
  They shall once again be free.

Death—the end of care and pain—
  Death, the wretch's happiness meed,
Death can break the strongest chain,
  Death is liberty indeed.

Parted friends again may meet,
  From the toils of nature free;
Crowned with mercy, Oh! how sweet
  Will eternal friendship be!

C. W. Thomson.

THE STARS.

Oh 'tis lovely to watch ye at twilight rise,
When the last gleam fades in the distant skies
When the silver chime of the minster-bell,
And the warbling fount in the woodland dell,
And the viewless sounds in the upper air,
    Proclaim the hour of prayer!

Then ye shine in beauty above the sea,
Bright wanderers o'er the blue sky free!
Catching the tone of each sighing breeze,
And the whispering sound of the forest-trees,
Or the far-off voice, through the quiet dim
    Of some hamlet's hymn!

And the midnight, too, all still and lone!
Ye guard in beauty, from many a throne!
In your silver silence throughout the hour,
Watching the rest of each folded flower,
Gladdening with vision's each infant's sleep,
    Through the night hour deep!

Yes, ye look over Nature's hushed repose,
By the forest still where the streamlet flows,
By the breezeless hush of many a plain,
And the pearly flow of the silver main,
Or sweetly far o'er some chapel shrine
    Of the olden time!

Thus in shadeless glory ye onward roll,
Bright realms of beauty, from pole to pole!
'Mid the vaulted space where your bright paths lie,
In the hidden depths of the midnight sky,
To some far-off land—to some distant home,
    'Neath the ocean's foam!

But lo! the far voice of the waking sea,
And the dim dew rising o'er lawn and lea,
And the first faint tinge of the early day,
Shining afar o'er the ocean's spray!
Oh, ye that have been as a power and a spell,
    Through the dim midnight!—Farewell!

F. Muller.

THE ASPEN LEAF.

I WOULD not be
A leaf on yonder aspen tree;
In every fickle breeze to play,
Wildly, weakly, idly, gay,
So feebly framed, so lightly hung,
By the wing of an insect stirred and swung;
Thrilling ev'n to a redbreast's note,
Drooping if only a light mist float,
Brightened and dimmed like a varying glass,
As shadow or sunbeam chance to pass:—
I would not be
A leaf on yonder aspen tree.
It is not because the autumn sere
Would change my merry guise and cheer—
That soon, full soon, nor leaf, nor stem,
Sunlight would gladden, or dew-drop gem—
That I, with my fellows, must fall to the earth,
Forgotten our beauty and breezy mirth,
Or else on the bough where all had grown,
Must linger on, and linger alone;
Might life be an endless summer's day,
And I be for ever green and gay,
I would not be, I would not be,
A leaf on yonder aspen tree!

Proudly spoken, heart of mine,
Yet weakness and change perchance are thine,
More, and darker, and sadder, to see,
Than befall the leaves of yonder tree!
What if they flutter—their life is a dance;
Or toy with the sunbeam—they live in his glance;
To bird, breeze, and insect, rustle and thrill,
Never the same, never mute, never still—
Emblems of all that is fickle and gay,
But leaves in their birth, but leaves in decay—
Chide them not—heed them not—spirit, away!
In to thyself, to thine own hidden shrine,
What there dost thou worship? what deem'st thou divine?
Thy hopes—are they steadfast, and holy, and high?
Are they built on a rock? are they raised to the sky?
Thy deep, secret yearnings—oh! whither point they,
To the triumphs of earth, to the toys of a day?
Thy friendships and feelings—doth impulse prevail,
To make them, and mar them, as wind swells the sail?
Thy life's ruling passion—thy being's first aim—
What are they? and yield they contentment, or shame?
Spirit, proud spirit, ponder thy state,
If thine the leaf's lightness, not thine the leaf's fate,
It may flutter, and glisten, and wither, and die,
And heed not our pity, and ask not our sigh;
But for thee, the immortal, no winter may throw
Eternal repose on thy joy, or thy wo;
Thou must live—live for ever—in glory or gloom,
Beyond the world's precincts, beyond the dark tomb.
Look to thyself, then, ere past is Hope's reign,
And looking and longing alike are in vain;
Lest thou deem it a bliss to have been or to be,
But a fluttering leaf on yon aspen tree.

MISS JEWSBURY.

THE MANIAC.

To see the human mind o'erturned,
  Its loftiest heights in ruin laid,
And reason's lamp, which brightly burned,
  Obscured, or quenched in phrensy's shade:
A sight like this may well awake
Our grief, our fear—for nature's sake.

It is a painful, humbling thought—
  To know the empire of the mind,
With wit endowed, with science fraught,
  Is fleeting as the passing wind;
And that the richest boon of heaven
To man—is rather lent than given.

To-day he sits on reason's throne,
  And bids his subject powers obey:
Thought, memory, will—all seem his own,
  Come at his bidding, list his sway;
To-morrow—from dominion hurled—
Madness pervades the mental world!

Yet think not, though forlorn and drear
  The maniac's doom—*his* lot the worst:
There is a suffering more severe
  Than these sad records have rehearsed
'Tis his, whose virtue struggles still
In hopeless conflict with his will.

There are—before whose mental eye
  Truth has her chastest charms displayed;
But gaudier phantoms flut'ring by,
  The erring mind have still betrayed;
Till gathering clouds in awful night,
Have quenched each beam of heavenly light.

There are—whose mental ear has heard
  The "*the still small voice!*" yet prone to wrong,
Have proudly, foolishly preferred
  The sophist's creed, the syren's song;
And staked, upon a desperate throw,
Their hopes above—their peace below.

There are, in short, whose days present
  One constant scene of painful strife;
Who hourly for themselves invent
  Fresh conflicts—till this dream of life
Has made their throbbing bosoms ache,
And yet, alas! they fear to wake.

With theirs compared, the maniac's doom,
  Though abject, must be counted blest;
His mind, though often veiled in gloom,
  At times may know a vacant rest:
Not so, while thought and conscience prey
Upon the heart which slights their sway.

O Thou! whose cause they both espouse,
  In mercy bid such conflict cease;
Strengthen the wakening sinner's vows,
  And grant him penitence and peace;
Or else, in pity, o'er the soul
The dark'ning clouds of madness roll.

BARTON

THE CRIMINAL.

THE dungeon walls were dark and high,
  The narrow pavement bare,
No sunlight of the blessed sky
  Might ever enter there:
In all the melancholy weeks
  The prisoner chained had lain,
No breath of heaven had kissed his cheeks,
  Or cooled his fevered brain.

For him—awake—asleep—there came
  No vision of sweet rest;
Undying memory, like a flame,
  Burned in his guilty breast:
Dark as the weary gloom around
  His soul was dark within;
For, oh! he lived but in the sound
  Of shamelessness and sin.

His mother heard his final doom,
  With shrieks that thrilled through all—
Oh! could naught save him from the tomb?
  Must he—must he! *thus* fall?
The arrow pierced her aged head,
  With cold and deadly pain;
She tottered senseless to her bed,
  And never rose again!

His father spoke not—but the pale
  And quivering lip confessed,
The agonies which did assail
  His miserable breast;
His eyes were closed, as if the light
  Was loathsome to behold;
But tears burst *from the lids* to sight—
  They could not be controlled!

Fast flew the fatal hours—he trod
  Life's very brink, alone;
Yet had no hope—no fear—*no God!*
  His heart was turned to stone.

I saw him as he passed along,
A branded death to die;
Wild curses were upon his tongue—
Despair, and blasphemy!

If there be one these lines may teach
A moral, not in vain
Have I endeavored thus to reach
A more reflective strain;
The picture is from life—each day
As sad a tale records:
Virtue! may thy eternal ray
Light *all* our deeds and words!

CHARLES SWAIN.

VERSES WRITTEN AFTER RECOVERING FROM A DANGEROUS ILLNESS.

THOUGH taught by woes to mortals seldom known,
The humbling truth, that "man is not his own,"
That, till we live to Him for us who died,
All love is selfish, and all knowledge pride,
All happiness a momentary gleam,
All hope a meteor, and all peace a dream:
Though taught this truth by discipline severe,
(Such as health could not, life could scarcely bear),
Strong are the ties which still my mind entwine,
And counteract the work of love divine.
The world, the world, its glittering baits prepares,
Its friendship offers, and obtrudes its cares;
Still would intemperate fancy wildly stray,
Spite of the secret check, the secret ray;
Weak to withstand, and yet afraid to yield,
I neither keep, nor wholly quit the field.

Father of mercies, "till the day-spring rise,"
And thy salvation glad my longing eyes;
Till doubt and fear like "morning shadows flee,"
And all my griefs are lost in love of thee;
While through this cheerless wild I faintly strive,
Hope sore depressed, and Faith but just alive,
Teach me to dread all guidance but thy own,
And patient tread "in paths I have not known:"
Forgive my murmurings; let thy quickening power
Support my spirit in the gloomy hour;
And, when the host of household foes appal,
"Turn, thou beloved," at my feeble call.
Come "with the swiftness of the mountain roe,"
And strength, proportioned to my wants, bestow;
Teach me those wants more deeply still to feel,
And deeply feeling, suppliant when to kneel;
Oh! in my soul that ardent thirst renew,
Which naught can satiate but celestial dew;
Drive thou from thence unprofitable care,
Yea, all that mars it for a house of prayer;
Dislodge alike the abject and the proud,
Passion's low mist, and notion's airy cloud;
Whate'er thy power has shaken, shake again,
Till naught but things immovable remain.

Thus, gracious Father, break each false repose,
And unrelenting, "rule amidst thy foes,"
Till, every low propensity exiled,
"My soul is even as a weaned child,"
From mean self-love, or gross, or specious, free,
And all my treasures, all my springs in thee.

MARRIOT.

CHRIST'S NATIVITY.

WHEN Jordan hushed his waters still,
And silence slept on Zion's hill;
When Bethlehem's shepherds through the night,
Watched o'er their flocks by starry light;

Hark! from the midnight hills around,
A voice of more than mortal sound,
In distant hallelujah's stole,
Wild murmuring o'er the raptured soul.

Then swift to every startled eye,
New streams of glory light the sky;
Heaven bursts her azure gates to pour
Her spirits to the midnight hour.

On wheels of light, on wings of flame,
The glorious hosts of Zion came;
High heaven with songs of triumph rung,
While thus they struck their harps and sung;

O Zion! lift thy raptured eye,
The long expected hour is nigh;
The joys of nature rise again,
The Prince of Salem comes to reign.

See, Mercy, from her golden urn,
Pours a rich stream to them that mourn;
Behold she binds with tender care,
The bleeding bosom of despair.

He comes! to cheer the trembling heart,
Bids Satan and his host depart;
Again the day-star gilds the gloom,
Again the bowers of Eden bloom;

O Zion! lift thy raptured eye,
The long expected hour is nigh;
The joys of nature rise again,
The Prince of Salem comes to reign.

CAMPBELL.

CHRISTIAN TRIUMPHS.

THOUGH laurel crowns and victor wreaths
Be for the sons of triumph twined;
Though song her sweetest music breathes
For the destroyers of our kind;
Oh let them weep, for time shall sweep
Their perishable pomp away;
Oh let them mourn, for death shall turn
The proudest conqueror into clay

But here's a deathless coronet,
Wrought for the holy and the wise,
And here is music sweeter yet,
Which never faints and never dies!
The good may see earth's glory flee,
Heaven's ever living glory theirs;
Their path is peace and pleasantness,
And they are joy's immortal heirs.

JOHN BOWRING.

RECOLLECTION.

HAIL, gentle Echo, Music's softer daughter,
Reclining on thy deep romantic seat;
From cliff, or thick-set wood, or rocky water,
Springing to meet us on ethereal feet!

Yet in the soul doth softer Echo linger,
It seems the spirit of departed song;
When touch'd again by MEMORY's airy finger,
The harp note wanders lovelily along.

Such is the train of holy thought returning,
When sacred seasons long have passed away,
By memory rekindled, glowing, burning—
Indeed with fainter, but as sweet a ray.

So the lost sunbeam, in its soft reflection,
Beamed from the bosom of the Queen of night,
Sheds over nature's face a recollection,
More fair, more tender, though, indeed, less bright.

Thus will the touch of memory awaken,
And bid the sabbath shine along the week,
And bring again sweet moments long forsaken,
And altars which the spirit fain would seek—

Of holy converse, and of high communion,
Of praise celestial, and of ardent prayer,
Of sacred mystery, and the blessed union
Of hearts which glowed in our possession there.

How doubly blest? first in the full possessing,
And after in reflected life and light!
The past—the present—plenitude of blessing,
Which not eternity itself will blight!

JAMES EDMESTONE.

INFANT'S PRAYER.

O Thou! who mak'st the sun to rise,
Beam on my soul, illume mine eyes,
And guide me through this world of care:
The wandering atom thou canst see.
The falling sparrow's marked by thee,
Then, turning Mercy's ear to me,
Listen! listen!
Listen to an infant's prayer!

O Thou! whose blood was spilt to save
Man's nature from a second grave;
To share in whose redeeming care,
Want's lowliest child is not too mean,
Guilt's darkest victim too unclean,
Oh! Thou wilt deign from heaven to lean,
And listen, listen,
Listen to an infant's prayer.

O Thou! who wilt from monarchs part,
To dwell within the contrite heart,
And build thyself a temple there;
O'er all my dull affections move,
Fill all my soul with heavenly love,
And, kindly stooping from above,
Listen! listen,
Listen to an infant's prayer!

Neele.

THE PILGRIMS OF EMMAUS.

It happened on a solemn eventide,
Soon after He who was our surety died,
Two bosom friends, each pensively inclined,
The scene of all their sorrows left behind,
Sought their own village, busied as they went,
In musings worthy of the great event:
They spake of him they loved, of him whose life
Though blameless, had incurred perpetual strife,
Whose deeds had left, in spite of hostile arts,
A deep memorial graven on their hearts.
The recollection, like a vein of ore,
The further traced, enriched them still the more;
They thought him, and they justly thought him, one
Sent to do more than he appeared t' have done:
T' exalt a people, and to place them high
Above all else, and wondered he should die.
Ere yet they brought their journey to an end,
A stranger joined them, courteous as a friend,
And asked them, with a kind, engaging air,
What their affliction was, and begged a share.
Informed, he gathered up the broken thread,
And, truth and wisdom gracing all he said,
Explained, illustrated, and searched so well
The tender theme, on which they chose to dwell,
That reaching home, "The night," they said, "is near,
We need not now be parted—sojourn here."
The new acquaintance soon became a guest,
And made so welcome, at their simple feast
He blessed the bread, but vanished at the word,
And left them both exclaiming—"'Twas the Lord!
Did not our hearts feel all he deigned to say—
Did they not burn within us by the way?"

Cowper.

THE HOUR OF PRAYER.

Blest hour! when mortal man retires
To hold communion with his God,
To send to heaven his warm desires,
And listen to his sacred word.

Blest hour! when earthly cares resign
Their empire o'er his anxious breast;
While all around, the calm divine
Proclaims the holy day of rest.

Blest hour! when God himself draws nigh,
Well pleased his people's voice to hear;
To list the penitential sigh,
And wipe away the mourner's tear.

Blest hour!—for then where He resorts,
Foretastes of future bliss are given,
And mortals find his earthly courts
The House of God—the Gate of Heaven.

Hail! peaceful hour, supremely blest
Amid the hours of earthly care!
The hour that yields the spirit rest,
That sacred hour—the hour of prayer.

And when my hours of prayer are past,
Oh! may I leave these Sabbath days,
To find eternity at last
A never-ending hour of praise.

Rev. T. Raffles

PRAYER.

Prayer is the soul's sincere desire,
Uttered or unexpressed;
The motion of a hidden fire
That trembles in the breast.

Prayer is the burden of a sigh,—
The falling of a tear,—
The upward glancing of an eye
When none but God is near.

Prayer is the simplest form of speech
That infant lips can try;
Prayer the sublimest strains that reach
The Majesty on high.

Prayer is the Christian's vital breath—
The Christian's native air,
His watch-word at the gates of death,
He enters Heaven with prayer.

Prayer is the contrite sinner's voice
Returning from his ways,
While angels on their wings rejoice,
And say,—"Behold, he prays!"

The saints in prayer appear as one
In word, and deed, and mind,
When with the Father, Spirit, Son,
Sweet fellowship they find.

Nor prayer is made on earth *alone*,
The Holy Spirit pleads,
And Jesus on the eternal throne,
For sinners intercedes.

O thou, by whom we come to God!
The Life—the Truth—the Way!
The path of prayer thyself has trod,
Lord, teach us how to pray!

J. Montgomery

THE GRAVE.

O Grave, thou hast thy victory!
Beauty and strength are laid with thee;
Thus is it in each distant clime;
Thus was it in the ancient time.

The prophets of all former days;
All who win honour, love, and praise,
The eloquent tongue, the arm of might,
The bard whose soul is love and light,
The patriot king, the wise, the brave,
Are ever mouldering in the grave.

O Grave, thou hast thy victory!
The desert sands are sown by thee;
And years must pass in misery steeped,
Ere that dread harvest will be reaped;
The desert air is parched and dry,
And thousands have lain down to die;
The traveller's steps grow slow and faint,
His kind hear not his last complaint,
See not his last convulsive start,
As death is busy at his heart;
His grave is in the burning sand,
His memory in his native land.

Of old thou hadst thy victory!
And Cheops nobly built for thee;
Raising thy trophy in the pile,
That casts its shadow many a mile.
Thine was the gain when rose on high
The Egyptian's mother's midnight cry;
And when God's angel with the blast
Of death among the Assyrians passed;
When the unnumbered Persians lay
On Salamis at break of day;
And when mid revelry, came down
Darkness on the Italian town,—
O Grave, thou hadst thy victory!

Thine are the isles, and thine the sea
The hoary hills are all thine own,
With the gray cairn and cromlech-stone
And groves of oak and woods of pine,
And the dim ocean's caves are thine.
Thy ancient slumbers lie beneath
The untilled verdure of the heath:
And in the field thy ardent race
Outstrips the hunter in the chase;
The mariner finds no unknown bay,
But there thou lurkest for thy prey.

O Grave, what wo is wrought by thee!
What clouded years of misery!
What loving hearts hast thou bereft;
What joyless, hopeless mourners left;
Young innocence without a guide,
Beset with snares on every side;
Age, with white hairs and chilled blood,
Pining in friendless solitude!

Yet, than earth's mightiest mightier,
O Grave thou hast thy vanquisher!
Long in thy night was man forlorn,
Long didst thou laugh his hope to scorn:
Vainly Philosophy might dream,
Her light was but the meteor gleam,
Till rose the Conqueror of Death,—
The humble Man of Nazareth:
He stood between us and despair:
He bore, and gave us strength to bear;
The mysteries of the grave unsealed,
Our glorious destiny revealed;
Nor sage nor bard may comprehend
The heaven of rest to which we tend.
Our home is not this mortal clime;
Our life hath not its bounds in time;
And death is but the cloud that lies
Between our souls and paradise.

O Grave! well might each thoughtful race
Give thee the high and holy place:
Mountains and groves were meet for thee,
Thou portal of eternity!

MARY HOWITT.

THE DEATH OF THE RIGHTEOUS.

How fair and how lovely it is to behold
The sun in its splendor, approaching the west,
Its race is near run, and refulgent as gold,
It glides through the ether as hastening to rest.

It sinks,—but in sinking 'tis only to rise,
Its splendor and glory afresh to display;
It sets,—but in other and far distant skies,
It rises and reigns in the brightness of day.

Yet far more resplendent than this is the scene
Of the good man approaching the confines of time,
All loving, all peaceful, all calm and serene,
He passes away with a brightness sublime.

He dies,—but no pencil can ever display,
The splendor and glory that burst on his sight,
As guided by angels he speeds on his way,
Through the portals of praise to the temple of light.

J. HARRIS.

THE SABBATH.

WHAT spell has o'er the populous city past?
The wonted current of its life is stayed;
Its sports, its gainful schemes are earthward cast,
As though their vileness were at once displayed;
The roar of trade has ceased, and on the air
Come holy songs and solemn sounds of prayer.

Far spreads the charm; from every hamlet spire
A note of rest, and heavenward thought is pealed:
By his calm hearth reclines the peasant sire;
The toil-worn steed basks in the breezy field.
Within, without, through farm and cottage blest,
'Tis one bright day of gladness and of rest.

Down from the mountain dwellings, while the dew
Shines on the heath-bells, and the fern is bending
In the fresh breeze, in festive garbs I view
Childhood, and age, and buoyant youth descending.
God! who hast piled thy wonders, round their home,
'Tis in their love they to thy temple come.

A stately ship speeds o'er the mighty main—
Oh! many a league from our own happy land:
Yet from its heart ascends the choral strain;
For there its little isolated band,
Amid the ocean desert's awful roar
Praise Him whose love links shore to distant shore.

O'er palmy woods where summer radiance falls,
In the glad islands of the Indian main,
What thronging crowds the missionary calls
To raise to heaven the Christian's glorious strain.
Lo! where engirt by children of the sun,
Stands the white man, and counts his victories won.

In the fierce deserts of a distant zone,
'Mid savage nations, terrible and stern,
A lonely atom, severed from his own,
The traveller wends, death or renown to earn.
Parched, fasting, wearied, verging to despair,
He kneels, he prays—hope kindles in his prayer.

O'er the wide world, blest day, thine influence flies;
Rest o'er the sufferer spreads her balmy wings;
Love wakes, joy dawns, praise fills the listening skies;
The expanding heart from earth's enchantment springs
Heaven, for one day, withdraws its ancient ban,
Unbars its gates, and dwells once more with man.

WILLIAM HOWITT.

SPIRITUAL WORSHIP.

THOUGH glorious, O God! must thy temple have been,
On the day of its first dedication,
When the cherubim's wings, widely waving were seen
On high, o'er the ark's holy station;
When even the chosen of Levi, though skilled,
To minister, standing before Thee,
Retired from the cloud which the temple then filled,
And thy glory made Israel adore Thee:

Though awfully grand was thy majesty then;
Yet the worship thy gospel discloses,
Less splendid in pomp to the vision of men,
Far surpasses the ritual of Moses.
And by whom was that ritual for ever repealed?
But by Him unto whom it was given
To enter the Oracle, where is revealed,
Not the cloud, but the brightness of heaven.

Who, having once entered, hath shown us the way
O Lord, how to worship before thee;
Not with shadowy forms of that earlier day,
But in *spirit* and *truth* to adore thee!
This, this is the worship the Savior made known,
When she of Samaria found him,
By the patriarch's well, sitting weary, alone,
With the stillness of noontide around him.

How sublime, yet how simple the homage he taught
To her, who inquired by that fountain,
If Jehovah at Solyma's shrine would be sought?
Or adored on Samaria's mountain?

"Woman! believe me, the hour is near,
When He if ye rightly would hail him,
Will neither be worshipped *exclusively* here,
Nor yet at the altar of Salem.

"For God is a Spirit! and they, who aright
Would perform the pure worship he loveth,
In the heart's holy temple will seek with delight,
That spirit the Father approveth."
And many that prophecy's truth can declare,
Whose bosoms have livingly known it;
Whom God hath instructed to worship him there,
And convinced that his mercy will own it.

The temple that Solomon built to his name.
Now lives but in history's story;
Extinguished long since is its altar's bright flame,
And vanished each glimpse of its glory.
But the Christian, made wise by a wisdom divine,
Though all human fabrics may falter,
Still finds in his heart a far holier shrine,
Where the fire burns unquenched on the altar.

BARTON.

HYMN TO VIRTUE.

Ever lovely and benign,
Endowed with energy divine,
Hail, Virtue! hail! From thee proceed
The great design, th' heroic deed,
The heart that melts for human woes,
Valor, and truth, and calm repose.
Though fortune frown, though fate prepare
Her shafts, and wake corroding care,
Though wrathful clouds involve the skies,
Though lightnings glare and storms arise,
In vain to shake the guiltless soul,
Changed fortune frowns and thunders roll.

Pile, Avarice, thy yellow hoard;
Spread, Luxury, thy costly board.
Ambition, crown thy head with bays;
Let Sloth recline on beds of ease;
Admired, adored, let Beauty roll
The magic eye that melts the soul;
Unless, with purifying fires,
Virtue, the conscious soul inspires,
In vain, to bar intruding wo,
Wealth, fame, and power, and pleasure flow.

To me thy sovereign gift impart,
The resolute, unshaken heart,
To guide me from the flowery way
Where pleasure tunes her siren lay;
Deceitful path! where shame and care
The poisonous shaft, concealed, prepare!
And shield me with thy generous pride,
When fashion scoffs, and fools deride.

Ne'er let Ambition's meteor ray
Mislead my reason, and betray
My fancy with the gilded dream
Of hoarded wealth and noisy fame.
But let my soul, consenting flow,
Compassionate of others' wo.
Teach me the kind, endearing art
To heal the mourner's broken heart,
To ease the rankling wounds of care,
And sooth the phrensy of despair.

So, lovely virgin, may I gain
Admission to thy hallowed fane;
Where peace of mind, of eye serene,
Of heavenly hue, and placid mien,
Leads, smiling, thy celestial choir,
And strikes the consecrated lyre.
And may that minstrelsey, whose charm
Can rage, and care, and grief disarm,
Can Passion's lawless force control,
Sooth, melt, and elevate my soul!

ANONYMOUS.

THE BUDDING LEAF.

Now Nature wears her vernal hue;
Again will poets sing
Of "daisies pied, and violets blue,"
And all the charms of spring:
The budding leaves with joy we see,
And former bliss recall;
But oh! what may our feelings be,
When these young leaves shall fall?

Then hearts which now are throbbing high
With hopes that widely soar,
May heave sad disappointment's sigh,
And learn to hope no more:
The maid whose eyes, whose smile, whose bloom,
Are soft enchantment all,
May sink love's victim in the tomb,
When these young leaves shall fall.

The mind whose energy and fire
Shines through the sparkling eye,
May then—O fate forlorn and dire!
A wreck, a ruin lie;
Its reason fled, its judgment lost,
While fancied fears appal,
In whirls of stormy passion tossed
When these young leaves shall fall.

And many a one whose soul is twined
With soul of kindred truth,
Whose passion, ardent yet refined,
Survives the charms of youth,
May sadly mourn love's broken tie
Within the lonely hall,
And heave the solitary sigh,
When these young leaves shall fall.

O Man! thy date of joy is brief,
More brief is pleasure's hour;
It withers like the blighted leaf—
Fades like the gathered flower.
The view is awful, yet sublime,
Of earth's still changeful ball;
I shrink while musing on the time,
When these young leaves shall fall.

But hark! I hear an airy voice
Soft whispering in my ear—
"Thou who dost mourn when most rejoice,
And saddenest hope with fear,
Thy worldly cares and woes may rest
Within the church-yard wall,
And dark weeds wither on thy breast.
When these young leaves shall fall."

ANONYMOUS

THE FIRST GRAVE.

A SINGLE grave! the only one
In this unbroken ground,
Where yet the garden leaf and flower,
Are lingering around.

A single grave!—my heart has felt
How utterly alone
In crowded halls, where breathed for me
Not one familiar tone:

The shade where forest trees shut out
All but the distant sky;
I've felt the loneliness of night
When the dark winds passed by:

My pulse has quickened with its awe,
My lip has gasped for breath;
But what were they to such as this—
The solitude of death!

A single grave! we half forget
How sunder human ties,
When round the silent place of rest
A gathered kindred lies.

We stand beneath the haunted yew,
And watch each quiet tomb;
And in the ancient church-yard feel
Solemnity, not gloom:

The place is purified with hope,
  The hope that is of prayer;
And human love, and heavenward thought,
  And pious faith are there.

The wild flowers spring amid the grass;
  And many a stone appears,
Carved by affection's memory,
  Wet with affection's tears.

The golden chord which binds us all,
  Is loosed, not rent in twain;
And love, and hope, and fear unite
  To bring the past again.

But *this* grave is so desolate,
  With no remembering stone,
No fellow-graves for sympathy—
  'Tis utterly alone.

I do not know who sleeps beneath,
  His history or name—
Whether if, lonely in his life,
  He is in death the same:

Whether he died unloved, unmourned,
  The last leaf on the bough;
Or if some desolated hearth
  Is weeping for him now.

Perhaps this is too fanciful:
  Though single be his sod,
Yet not the less it has around
  The presence of his God.

It may be weakness of the heart,
  But yet its kindliest, best;
Better if in our selfish world
  It could be less repressed.

Those gentler charities which draw
  Man closer with his kind—
Those sweet humanities which make
  The music which they find.

How many a bitter word 'twould hush—
  How many a pang 'twould save,
If life more precious held those ties
  Which sanctify the grave!

MISS LANDON.

STANZAS.

DAYS of my youth! ye have glided away;
Hairs of my youth! ye are frosted and gray;
Eyes of my youth! your keen sight is no more;
Cheeks of my youth! ye are furrowed all o'er;
Strength of my youth! all thy vigor is gone;
Thoughts of my youth! your gay visions are flown,

Days of my youth! I wish not your recall;
Hairs of my youth! I'm content ye shall fall;
Eyes of my youth! you much evil have seen;
Cheeks of my youth! bathed in tears you have been;
Thoughts of my youth! ye have led me astray;
Strength of my youth! why lament thy decay?

Days of my age! ye will shortly be past;
Pains of my age; yet awhile ye can last;
Joys of my age! in true wisdom delight;
Eyes of my age! be religion your light;
Thoughts of my age! dread ye not the cold sod;
Hopes of my age! be ye fixed on your God.

TUCKER.

THERE IS A TONGUE IN EVERY LEAF.

THERE is a tongue in every leaf,
  A voice in every rill;
A voice that speaketh everywhere,
In flood and fire, through earth and air!
  A tongue that's never still.

'Tis the Great Spirit wide diffused
  Through everything we see,
That with our spirits communeth
Of things mysterious—Life and Death,
  Time and Eternity!

I see Him in the blazing sun,
  And in the thunder-cloud:
I hear Him in the mighty roar,
That rusheth through the forest hoar,
  When winds are piping loud.

I see Him, hear Him, *everywhere*,
  In *all things*—darkness, light,
Silence, and sound; but most of all,
When slumber's dusky curtains fall,
  At the dead hour of night.

I *feel* Him in the silent dews,
  By grateful earth betrayed;
I feel Him in the gentle showers,
The soft south wind, the breath of flowers,
  The sunshine and the shade.

And yet (ungrateful that I am),
  I've turned in sullen mood
From all these things, whereof He said,
When the great whole was finished,
  That they were "very good."

My sadness on the loveliest things
  Fell like the unwholesome dew;
The darkness that encompassed me,
The gloom I felt so palpably,
  Mine own dark spirit threw.

Yet was He patient—slow to wrath,
  Though every day provoked
By selfish, pining discontent,
Acceptance cold or negligent,
  And promises revoked;

And still the same rich feast was spread
  For my insensate heart!
Not always so—I woke again
To join Creation's rapturous strain,
  "O Lord, how good thou art."

The clouds drew up, the shadows fled,
  The glorious sun broke out,
And love, and hope, and gratitude,
Dispelled that miserable mood
  Of darkness and of doubt.

ANONYMOUS.

PRAYER.

O THOU Great Being! what thou art
  Surpasses me to know:
Yet sure I am, that, known to thee
  Are all thy works below.

Thy creature here before thee stands,
  All wretched and distressed:
Yet sure those ills that wring my soul
  Obey thy high behest.

Sure thou, Almighty, canst not act
  From cruelty or wrath!
Oh, free my weary eyes from tears,
  Or close them fast in death.

But if I must afflicted be,
  To suit some wise design;
Then man my soul with firm resolves
  To bear and not repine!

BURNS.

ODE TO DUTY.

STERN Daughter of the Voice of God!
O Duty! if that name thou love
Who art a Light to guide, a Rod
To check the erring, and reprove;
Thou who art victory and law,
When empty terrors overawe;
From vain temptations dost set free,
And calm'st the weary strife of frail humanity.

There are who ask not if thine eye
Be on them; who, in love and truth,
Where no misgiving is, rely
Upon the genial sense of youth:

Glad hearts! without reproach or blot!
Who do thy work, and know it not:
May joys be theirs while life shall last;
And thou, if they should totter, teach them to stand fast.

Serene will be our days, and bright,
And happy will our nature be,
When love is an unerring light,
And joy its own security.
And blest are they who in the main
This faith e'en now do entertain:
Live in the spirit of this creed;
Yet find that other strength, according to their need.

I, loving freedom, and untried;
No sport of every random gust,
Yet being to myself a guide,
Too blindly have reposed my trust;
Full oft, when in my heart was heard
Thy timely mandate, I deferred
The task imposed, from day to day;
But thee I now would serve more strictly, if I may.

Though no disturbance of my soul,
Or strong compunction in me wrought,
I supplicate for thy control;
But in the quietness of thought:
Me this unchartered freedom tires;
I feel the weight of chance desires:
My hopes no more must change their name,
I long for a repose which ever is the same.

Stern Lawgiver! yet thou dost wear
The Godhead's most benignant grace!
Nor know we anything so fair
As is the smile upon thy face:
Flowers laugh before thee on their beds;
And fragrance in thy footing treads;
Thou dost preserve the stars from wrong:
And the most ancient heavens through thee are fresh and strong.

To humbler functions, awful Power!
I call thee: I myself commend
Unto thy guidance from this hour;
Oh! let my weakness have an end!
Give unto me, made lowly wise,
The spirit of self-sacrifice;
The confidence of reason give;
And in the light of truth thy bondman let me live.

WORDSWORTH.

THE TOMB OF CYRUS.

A VOICE fram stately Babylon, a mourner's rising cry—
And Libya's marble palaces give back their deep reply;
And like the sound of distant winds o'er ocean billows sent,
Ecbatana, thy storied walls send forth the wild lament.

For he, the dreaded arbiter—a dawning empire's trust—
The eagle child of victory—the great, the wise, the just,
Assyria's famed and conquering sword, and Media's regal strength—
Hath bowed his head to earth beneath a mightier hand at length.

And darkly, through a sorrowing land, Euphrates winds along,
And Cyndus, with its silver wave, has heard the funeral song;
And through the wide and sultry East, and through the frozen North,
The tabret and the harp are hushed—the wail of grief goes forth.

There is a solitary tomb, with rankling weeds o'ergrown,
A single palm bends mournfully beside the mould'ring stone,
Amid whose leaves the passing breeze, with fitful gust and slow,
Seems sighing with a feeble dirge for him who sleeps below.

Beside its sparkling drops of foam a desert fountain showers,
And, floating calm, the lotus wreaths its red and scented flowers;
And lurks the mountain-fox, unseen, beside the vulture's nest,
And steals the wild hyena past in lone and silent quest.

Is this ambition's resting-place—the couch of fallen might?
And ends the path of glory thus, and fame's enshrining light?
Chief of a progeny of kings renowned and feared afar,
How is thy boasting name forgot, and dimmed thine honor's star?

Approach: what saith that graven verse? Alas, for human pride!—
"Dominion's envied gifts were mine—nor earth her praise denied:
Thou traveller, if a suppliant's voice find echo in thy breast,
Oh! envy not the little dust which hides my mortal rest!"

ANONYMOUS.

WHO LOVES ME BEST?

WHO loves me best?—My mother sweet,
Whose every look with love is replete;
Who held me, an infant on her knee—
Who hath ever watched me tenderly;
And yet I have heard my mother say,
That she sometime must pass away:
Who then shall shield me from earthly ill?
Some one must love me better still!

Who loves me best?—My father dear,
Who loveth to have me always near;
He whom I fly each eve to meet,
When passed away is the noontide heat;
Who from the bank where the sunbeam lies
Brings me the wild-wood strawberries.
Oh! he is dear as my mother to me—
But he will perish, even as she.

Who loves me best?—The gentle dove
That I have tamed with my childish love,
That every one save myself doth fear,
Whose soft coo soundeth when I come near:
Yet perhaps it but loves me because I bring
To its cage the drops from the clearest spring,
And hang green branches around the door:
Something, surely, must love me more!

Who loves me best?—My sister fair,
With her laughing eyes and clustering hair!
Who flowers around my head doth twine,
Who presseth her rosy lips to mine,
Who singeth me songs in her artless glee,
Can any love me better than she?
Yet, when I asked, that sister confessed,
Of all, she did not love me the best!

Who loves me best?—My brother young,
With his healthy cheek and his lisping tongue;
Who delighteth to lead me in merry play
Far down the green wood's bushy way;
Who showeth me where the hazel-nuts grow,
And where the fairest field-flowers blow;
Yet perhaps he loves me no more than the rest—
How shall I find who loves me best?

My mother loves me—but she may die;
My white dove loves me—but that may fly;
My father loves me—he may be changed;
I have heard of brothers and sisters estranged;
If they should forsake me, what should I do?
Where should I bear my sad heart to?
Some one, surely, would be my stay—
Some one must love me better than they.

Yes, fair child, there is One above,
Who loves thee with an unchangeable love;
He who formed those frail, dear things,
To which thy young heart fondly clings—
Even though all should forsake thee, still
He would protect thee through every ill.
Oh! is not such love worth all the rest?
Child! it is God who loves thee best!

MARY ANN BROWN.

THE SISTER'S VOICE.

O! MY sister's voice is gone away!
  Around our social hearth
We have lost its tones, that were so gay,
  So full of harmless mirth—
We miss the glancing of her eye,
  The waving of her hair,
The footsteps lightly gliding by,
  The hand so small and fair;
And the wild, bright smile that lit her face,
  And made our hearts rejoice—
Sadly we mourn each vanished grace,
  But most of all her voice.

For oh! it was so soft and sweet
  When uttered forth in words;
Such tones it had as hearts repeat
  In echoes on their chords;
And lovely when in measure soft
  She sung a mournful song,
And heavenly when it swelled aloft
  In triumph-chorus strong;
And dearest when its words of love
  Would sooth our bosoms' care,
And loveliest when it rose above
  In sounds of praise and prayer.

Oh, in my childhood I have sate,
  When that sweet voice hath breathed,
Forgetful of each merry mate—
  Of the wild flowers I had wreathed;
And though each other voice I scorned,
  That called me from my play,
If my sweet sister only warned,
  I never could delay,
'Twas she who sang me many a rhyme,
  And told me many a tale,
And many a legend of olden time
  That made my spirit quail.

There are a thousand pleasant sounds
  Around our cottage still—
The torrent that before it bounds,
  The breeze upon the hill,
The murmuring of the wood-dove's sigh,
  The swallow in the eaves,
And the wind that sweeps a melody
  In passing from the leaves;
And the pattering of the early rain,
  The opening flowers to wet—
But they want my sister's voice again,
  To make them sweeter yet.

We stood around her dying bed,
  We saw her blue eyes close;
While from her heart the pulses fled,
  And from her cheek the rose:
And still her lips in fondness moved,
  And still she strove to speak
To the mournful beings that she loved,
  And yet she was too weak;
Till at last from her eye came one bright ray,
  That bound us like a spell;
And as her spirit passed away,
  We heard her sigh, "Farewell!"

And oft since then that voice hath come
  Across my heart again;
And it seems to speak as from the tomb,
  And bids me not complain;
And I never hear a low, soft flute,
  Or the sound of a rippling stream,
Or the rich, deep music of a lute,
  But it renews my dream,
And brings the hidden treasures forth
  That lie in memory's store;
And again to thoughts of that voice gives birth,
  That voice I shall hear no more.

No more!—it is not so—my hope
  Shall still be strong in Heaven—
Still search around the spacious scope
  For peace and comfort given.
We know there is a world above,
  Where all the blessed meet,
Where we shall gaze on those we love,
  Around the Savior's feet;
And I shall hear my sister's voice,
  In holier, purer tone—
With all those spotless souls rejoice
  Before the Eternal Throne.

BROWNE.

GOD AN UNFAILING REFUGE.

THE smoothest seas will sometimes prove
To the confiding bark untrue;
And if she trust the stars above,
They can be treacherous too.

Th' umbrageous oak, in pomp outspread,
Full oft, when storms the welkin rend,
Draws lightning down upon the head
It promised to defend.

But thou art true, incarnate Lord!
Who didst vouchsafe for man to die;
Thy smile is sure, thy plighted word
No change can falsify!

I bent before thy gracious throne,
And asked for peace with suppliant knee;
And peace was given—nor peace alone,
But faith, and hope, and ecstasy!

WORDSWORTH.

THE CHRISTIAN POET.

ONE of this mood I do remember well—
In humbler dwelling born, retired, remote;
In rural quietude, 'mong hills, and streams,
And melancholy deserts, where the sun
Saw, as he passed, a shepherd only, here
And there, watching his little flock, or heard
The ploughman talking to his steers; his hopes,
His morning hopes, awoke before him, smiling,
Among the dews and holy mountain airs;
And fancy colored them with every hue
Of heavenly loveliness. But soon his dreams
Of childhood fled away: those rainbow dreams,
So innocent and fair, that withered age,
E'en at the grave, cleared up his dusty eye,
And passing all between, looked fondly back
To see them once again, ere he departed:
These fled away, and anxious thought, that wished
To go, yet whither knew not well to go,
Possessed his soul, and held it still awhile.
He listened, heard from far the voice of fame,
Heard and was charmed; and deep and sudden vow
Of resolution made to be renowned;
And deeper vowed again to keep his vow.
His parents saw—his parents whom God made
Of kindest heart—saw, and indulged his hope.

The ancient page he turned, read much, thought much,
And with old bards of honorable name
Measured his soul severely; and looked up
To fame, ambitious of no second place.
Hope grew from inward faith, and promised fair,
And out before him opened many a path
Ascending, where the laurel highest waved
Her branch of endless green. He stood admiring;
But stood, admired, not long. The harp he seized—
The harp he loved, loved better than his life—
The harp which uttered deepest notes, and held
The ear of thought a captive to its song.
He searched, and meditated much, and whiles,
With rapturous hand, in secret touched the lyre,
Aiming at glorious strains; and searched again
For theme deserving of immortal verse;
Chose now, and now refused, unsatisfied;
Pleased, then displeased, and hesitating still.

Thus stood his mind, when round him came a cloud—
Slowly and heavily it came; a cloud
Of ills we mention not. Enough to say,
'Twas cold, and dead, impenetrable gloom.
He saw its dark approach, and saw his hopes,
One after one, put out, as nearer still
It drew his soul; but fainted not at first,
Fainted not soon. He knew the lot of man
Was trouble, and prepared to bear the worst—
Endure whate'er should come, without a sigh—
Endure, and drink, e'en to the very dregs,
The bitterest cup that Time could measure out;
And, having done, look up, and ask for more.

He called Philosophy, and with his heart
Reasoned. He called Religion, too, but called
Reluctantly, and therefore was not heard.
Ashamed to be o'ermatched by earthly woes,
He sought, and sought, with eye that dimmed apace,
To find some avenue to light, some place
On which to rest a hope—but sought in vain.
Darker and darker still the darkness grew.
At length he sunk, and Disappointment stood
His only comforter, and mournfully
Told all was past. His interest in life,
In being, ceased: and now he seemed to feel,
And shuddered as he felt; his powers of mind
Decaying in the spring-time of his day.
The vigorous, weak became—the clear, obscure.
Memory gave up her charge, Decision reeled,
And from her flight, Fancy returned—returned
Because she found no nourishment abroad.
The blue heavens withered; and the moon, and sun,
And all the stars, and the green earth, and morn,
And evening, withered, and the eyes, and smiles,
And faces, of all men and women, withered;
Withered to him; and all the universe,
Like something which had been, appeared; but now
Was dead, and mouldering fast away. He tried
No more to hope, wished to forget his vow,
Wished to forget his harp; then ceased to wish.
That was his last. Enjoyment now was done.
He had no hope, no wish, and scarce a fear;
Or being sensible, and sensible
Of loss, he as some atom seemed, which God
Had made superfluously, and needed not
To build creation with; but back again
To nothing threw, and left it in the void,
With everlasting sense that once it was.

Oh! who can tell what days, what nights he spent,
Of tideless, waveless, sailless, shoreless wo!
And who can tell how many, glorious once,
To others and themselves of promise full,
Conducted to this pass of human thought,
This wilderness of intellectual death,
Wasted and pined, and vanished from the earth,
Leaving no vestige of memorial there!

It was not so with him. When thus he lay,
Forlorn of heart, withered and desolate,
As leaf of Autumn, which the wolfish winds
Selecting from its former sisters, chase
Far from its native grove, to lifeless wastes,
And leave it there alone to be forgotten
Eternally, God passed in mercy by,—
His praise be ever new! and on him breathed,
And bade him live, and put into his hands
A holy harp, into his lips a song,
That rolled its numbers down the tide of time:
Ambitious now but little, to be praised
Of men alone; ambitious most to be
Approved of God, the Judge of all, and have
His name recorded in the book of life.

Pollok.

TO-MORROW.

How sweet to the heart is the thought of To-morrow,
When Hope's fairy pictures bright colors display;
How sweet, when we can from futurity borrow
A balm for the griefs that afflict us to-day.

When wearisome sickness hath taught me to languish
For health, and the comforts it bears on its wing,
Let me hope (oh! how soon it will lessen my anguish!)
That To-morrow will ease and serenity bring.

When travelling alone, quite forlorn, unbefriended,
Sweet the hope, that To-morrow my wand'rings will
That at home, with all care sympathetic attended,
I shall rest unmolested, and slumber in peace.

Or, when from the friends of my heart long divided,
The fond expectation with joy how replete!
That from far distant regions, by Providence guided,
To-morrow will see us most happily meet.

When six days of labor each other succeeding,
With hurry and toil have my spirits oppressed,
What pleasure to think as the last is receding,
To-morrow will be a sweet sabbath of rest.

And when the vain shadows of time are retiring,
When life is fast fleeting, and death is in sight,
The Christian believing, exulting, expiring,
Beholds a To-morrow of endless delight.

J. Brown.

THE OFFERING.

With blood—but not his own—the awful sign
At once of sin's desert and guilt's remission,
The Jew besought the clemency divine,
The hope of mercy blending with contrition.
Sin must have death! Its holy requisition
The law may not relax. The opening tomb
Expects its prey! mere respite, life's condition;
Nor can the body shun its penal doom.
Yet, there is mercy: wherefore else delay
To punish! Why the victim and the rite?
But can the type and symbol take away
The guilt, and for a broken law requite?
The Cross unfolds the mystery: Jesus died:
The sinner lives: the law is satisfied!
With blood—but not his own—the Jew drew near
The mercy-seat, and heaven received his prayer.
Yet still his hope was dimmed by doubt and fear:
"If thou shouldst mark transgression, who might dare
To stand before Thee?" Mercy loves to spare
And pardon: but stern Justice has a voice,
And cries—our God is holy, nor can bear
Uncleanness in the people of his choice.
But now one Offering, ne'er to be renewed,
Hath made our peace for ever. This now gives
Free access to the Throne of Heavenly Grace.
No more base fear and dark disquietude.
He who was slain—the accepted Victim—lives,
And intercedes before the Father's face.

Josiah Conder.

ON THE NEW YEAR.

Another year! another year,
Is borne by time away;
Nor pauses yet his swift career,
Nor tires his wing, nor makes he here
E'en one short hour's delay—

But hurries on, and round, and round,
The wheel of life is sped;
Unnoted oft, until rebound,
Upon the ear, the startling sound,
Another year has fled!

Whoever said 'tis New Year's Day,
With unmixed care or glee?
For hope still paints the future gay,
And memory o'er the past will stray,
With sorrowing constancy.

Yet blest if they but there behold
The grave of well spent days;
The joy of gratitude that told
The tear, in patient trust that rolled—
The Christian's hallowed bays

Another year! so swift it flew,
We scarce had marked it ours;
Ere, fading from our backward view,
Tis but the past our eyes pursue;
Eternity's long hours!

'Tis New Year's Day! the coming year
All blank before us lies;
Oh! may no blot or stain appear,
To mar its history written here,
When published in the skies!

'Tis New Year's Day! how oft have I,
While yet a simple child,
Made it the goal from whence to try,
That race to run, which to the sky
Can guide through Time's dark wild.

The sky, that home of quiet rest,
When life's poor dream is o'er,
Where spirits mingle with the blest,
And sorrow, in the aching breast,
Shall reign, shall reign no more!

E. DICKINSON.

FAREWELL TO A DEPARTED FRIEND.

THOU art gone to the grave—but we will not deplore thee;
Though sorrows and darkness encompass the tomb,
The Savior has passed through its portals before thee,
And the lamp of his love is thy guide through the gloom.

Thou art gone to the grave—we no longer behold thee,
Nor tread the rough path of the world by thy side;
But the wide arms of mercy are spread to enfold thee,
And sinners may hope, since the sinless has died.

Thou art gone to the grave—and its mansion forsaking,
Perhaps thy tried spirit in doubt lingered long;
But the sunshine of heaven beamed bright on thy waking,
And the song which thou heardst was the seraphim's song.

Thou art gone to the grave—but 'twere wrong to deplore thee,
When God was thy ransom, thy guardian, thy guide;
He gave thee, and took thee, and soon will restore thee,
Where death hath no sting, since the Savior hath died.

HEBER.

THE CRUCIFIXION.

CITY of God! Jerusalem,
Why rushes out thy living stream?
The turbaned priest, the hoary seer,
The Roman in his pride are there!
And thousands, tens of thousands, still
Cluster round Calvary's wild hill.

Still onward rolls the living tide,
There rush the bridegroom and the bride—
Prince, beggar, soldier, Pharisee,—
The old, the young, the bond, the free;
The nation's furious multitude,
All maddening with the cry of blood.

'Tis glorious morn; from height to height
Shoot the keen arrows of the light:
And glorious, in their central shower,
Palace of holiness and power,
The temple on Moriah's brow
Looks a new risen sun below.

But wo to hill, and wo to vale!
Against them shall come forth a wail:
And wo to bridegroom and to bride!
For death shall on the whirlwind ride;
And wo to thee, resplendent shrine,
The sword is out for thee and thine.

Hide, hide thee in the heavens, thou sun,
Before the deed of blood is done!
Upon that temple's haughty steep
Jerusalem's last angels weep;
They see destruction's funeral pall
Blackening o'er Sion's sacred wall.

Like tempests gathering on the shore,
They hear the coming army's roar:
They see in Sion's halls of state,
The Sign that maketh desolate—
The idol standard, pagan spear,
The tomb, the flame, the massacre.

They see the vengeance fall; the chain,
The long, long age of guilt and pain:
The exile's thousand desperate years,
The more than groans, the more than tears;
Jerusalem, a vanished name—
Its tribes earth's warnings, scoff, and shame.

Still pours along the multitude,
Still rends the heavens the shout of blood;
But in the murderer's furious van
Who totters on? A weary man;
A cross upon his shoulder bound—
His brow, his frame, one gushing wound.

And now he treads on Calvary—
What slave upon that hill must die?
What hand, what heart, in guilt embrued,
Must be the mountain vulture's food?
There stand two victims gaunt and bare,
Two culprits emblems of despair.

Yet who the third? The yell of shame
Is phrensied at the sufferer's name.
Hands clenched, teeth gnashing, vestures torn,
The curse, the taunt, the laugh of scorn,
All that the dying hour can sting,
Are round thee now, thou thorn-crowned king

Yet cursed and tortured, taunted, spurned
No wrath is for the wrath returned;
No vengeance flashes from the eye;
The Sufferer calmly waits to die;
The sceptre-reed, the thorny crown,
Wake on that pallid brow no frown.

At last the word of death is given,
The form is bound, the nails are driven:
Now triumph, Scribe and Pharisee!
Now Roman, bend the mocking knee!
The cross is reared. The deed is done,
There stands MESSIAH'S earthly throne!

This was the earth's consummate hour;
For this hath blazed the prophet's power;
For this hath swept the conqueror's sword;
Hath ravaged, raised, cast down, restored;
Persepolis, Rome, Babylon,
For this ye sank, for this ye shone.

Yet things to which earth's brightest beam
Were darkness—earth itself a dream.
Foreheads on which shall crowns be laid
Sublime, when sun and star shall fade:
Worlds upon worlds, eternal things,
Hung on thy anguish, King of kings!

Still from his lip no curse has come,
His lofty eye has looked no doom!
No earthquake burst, no angel brand,
Crushes the black, blaspheming band:
What say those lips by anguish riven?
"God, be my murderers forgiven!"

He dies! in whose high victory
The slayer, Death, himself shall die:
He dies! by whose all conquering tread
Shall yet be crushed the serpent's head;
From his proud throne to darkness hurled,
The god and tempter of this world.

He dies! Creation's awful Lord,
Jehovah, Christ, Eternal word!
To come in thunder from the skies;
To bid the buried world arise;
The earth his footstool; heaven his throne;
Redeemer! may thy will be done.

ANONYMOUS.

THE OFFERING.

I SEE them fading round me,
The beautiful, the bright,
As the rose-red lights that darken
At the falling of the night.

I had a lute, whose music
Made sweet the summer wind,
But the broken strings have vanished,
And no song remains behind.

I had a lovely garden,
Fruits and flowers on every bough,
But the frost came too severely—
'Tis decayed and blighted now.

That lute is like my spirits—
They have lost their buoyant tone;
Crushed and shattered, they've forgotten
The glad notes once their own.

And my mind is like that garden—
It has spent its early store;
And wearied and exhausted,
It has no strength for more.

I will look on them as warnings,
Sent less in wrath than love,
To call the being homeward—
To its other home above.

As the Lesbian in false worship
Hung her harp upon the shrine,
When the world lost its attraction,
So will I offer mine:

But in another spirit,
With a higher hope and aim,
And in a holier temple,
And to a holier name.

I offer up affections,
Void, violent, and vain;
I offer years of sorrow
Of the mind, and body's pain:

I offer up my memory—
'Tis a drear and darkened page,
Where experience has been bitter,
And whose youth has been like age.

I offer hopes whose folly
Only after-thoughts can know,
For instead of seeking heaven
They were chained to earth below.

Saying, wrong and grief have brought me,
To thy altar as a home;
I am sad and broken-hearted,
And therefore am I come.

Let the incense of my sorrow
Be on high a sacrifice;
The worn and contrite spirit,
Thou alone would not despise? L. E. L.

THE PARTED SPIRIT.

"YE CAN NOT TELL WHENCE IT COMETH, OR WHITHER IT GOETH."

MYSTERIOUS in its birth,
And viewless as the blast;
Where hath the spirit fled from earth,
For ever past?

I ask the grave below—
It keeps the secret well;
I call upon the heavens to show—
They will not tell.

Of earth's remotest strand,
Are tales and tidings known;
But from the Spirit's distant land,
Returneth none.

Winds waft the breath of flowers,
To wanderer's o'er the wave,
But no message from the bowers
Beyond the grave.

Proud Science scales the skies
From star to star to roam,
But reacheth not the shore where lies
The Spirit's home.

Impervious shadows hide
This mystery of Heaven;
But, where all knowledge is denied,
To hope is given!

JOHN MALCOLM.

EARTH AND HEAVEN.

EARTH.

THERE is grief, there is grief—there is wringing of hands,
And weeping and calling for aid;
For sorrow hath summoned her group, and it stands,
Round the couch where the sufferer is laid.
And lips are all pallid, and cheeks are all cold,
And tears from the heart-springs are shed;
Yet who that looks on the sweet saint to behold,
But would gladly lie down in her stead!

There is grief, there is grief—there is anguish and strife,
See, the sufferer is toiling for breath;
For the spirit will cling, oh! how fondly, to life,
And stern is the struggle with death!
But the terrible conflict grows deadlier still,
Till the last fatal symptoms have birth;
And the eye-ball is glazed, and the heart-blood is chill;
And this is the portion of earth!

HEAVEN.

There is bliss, there is bliss in the regions above,
They have opened the gates of the sky;
A spirit has soared to those mansions of love,
And seeks for admittance on high.
And friends long divided are hasting to greet
To a land, where no sorrow may come,
And the seraphs are eager a sister to meet,
And to welcome the child to its home.

There is bliss, there is bliss at the foot of the throne,
See the spirit all purified bend;
And it beams with delight, since it gazes alone,
On the face of a father, a friend!
Then it joins in the anthems for ever that rise,
And its frailty or folly forgiven,
It is dead to the earth and new-born to the skies:
And this is the portion of Heaven!

C. F. RICHARDSON

THE WIZARD.

HE waved his wand! dark spirits knew
That rod—yet none obeyed its call;
And twice the mystic sign he drew,
And twice beheld them bootless all:
Then knew the seer Jehovah's hand,
And crushed the scroll and broke the wand;

"I feel Him like a burning fire,
When I would curse, my lips are dumb;
But from those lips, 'mid hate and ire,
Unchecked the words of blessing come;
They come and on his people rest.
A people by the curser blest!

"I see them from the mountain-top,
How fair their dwellings on the plain!
Like trees that crown the valley's slope,
Like waves that glitter on the main!
Strong, strong the lion slumbering there—
Who first shall rouse him from his lair?

"Crouch, Amalek—and thou, vain king!
Crouch by thine altars—vainer still!
Hear ye the royal shouts that ring
From Israel's camp beneath the hill?

They have a God amid their tents,
Banner at once, and battlements!

"A star shall break through yonder skies,
And beam on every nation's sight;
From yonder ranks a sceptre rise,
And bow the nations to its might:
I see their glorious strength afar—
All hail, mild sceptre! hail, bright Star!

"And who am I, for whom is flung
Aside the shrouding veil of time?
The seer whose rebel soul is wrung,
By wrath, and prophecy, and crime,
The future as the past I see—
Wo, then, for Moab! wo for me!"

On Peor's top the wizard stood,
Around him Moab's princes bowed;
He bade—and altars streamed with blood,
And incense wrapped him like a shroud!
But vain the rites of earth and hell—
He spake—a mastered oracle!

MISS JEWSBURY.

ADVENT HYMN.

THE chariot! the chariot! its wheels roll in fire,
As the Lord cometh down in the pomp of his ire;
Self-moving, it drives on its pathway of cloud,
And the heavens with the burden of Godhead are bowed.

The glory! the glory! around him are poured
The myriads of angels that wait on the Lord;
And the glorified saints and the martyrs are there,
And all who the palm-wreaths of victory wear.

The trumpet! the trumpet! the dead have all heard;
Lo, the depths of the stone-covered monuments stirred!
From ocean and earth, from the south pole and north,
Lo, the vast generations of ages come forth!

The judgment! the judgment! the thrones are all set,
Where the lambs and the white-vested elders are met;
All flesh is at once in the sight of the Lord,
And the doom of eternity hangs on his word.

Oh mercy! oh mercy! Look down from above,
Redeemer, on us, thy sad children, with love
When beneath to their darkness the wicked are driven,
May our justified souls find a welcome in heaven!

MILLMAN.

THE PILGRIMS HOME.

THERE are climates of sunshine, of beauty and gladness,
Where roses are flourishing all the year long;
Their bowers are despoiled not by wintry sadness,
And their echoes reply to the nightingale's song:
But coldly the Briton regards their temptations,
Condemned from his friends and his kindred to roam,
He looks on the brightness of lovelier nations,
But his heart and his wishes still turn to his home.

Oh! why is this duteous and home-loving feeling
So seldom displayed by the Pilgrim of Life?
While faith to his mind a bright scene is revealing,
He toils through a world of sin, sorrow, and strife:
Yet, lured by the paltry attractions around him,
Too oft he forgets the pure pleasure to come,
And wildly foregoes for the toys that surround him,
His hopes of a lasting, a glorious Home.

Not such is the Christian: devoted, believing,
Through storm and through sunshine his trust shall abide:
The way that he wends may be dark or deceiving,
But heaven is his shrine, and the Lord is his guide.
And when death's warning angel around him shall hover,
He dreads not the mandate that bids him to come;
It tells that his toils and temptations are over—
'Tis the voice of his Father: it calls to his Home.

ANONYMOUS.

THE MOTHER'S GRIEF.

To mark the sufferings of the babe
That can not speak its wo;
To see the infant tears gush forth,
Yet know not why they flow;
To meet the meek, uplifted eye,
That fain would ask relief,
Yet can but tell of agony—
This is a mother's grief.

Through dreary days and darker nights,
To trace the mark of death;
To hear the faint and frequent sigh,
The quick and shortened breath;
To watch the last dread strife draw near,
And pray that struggle brief;
Though all is ended with its close—
This is a mother's grief.

To see in one short hour decayed,
The hope of future years;
To feel how vain a father's prayers,
How vain a mother's tears;
To think the cold grave now must close
O'er what was once the chief
Of all the treasured joys on earth—
This is a mother's grief.

Yet, when the first wild throb is past,
Of anguish and despair,
To lift the eye of faith to heaven,
And think "my child is *there!*"
This best can dry the gushing tears—
This yield the heart relief;
Until the Christian's pious hope
O'ercomes a mother's grief.

REV. T. DALE.

THE RAISING OF LAZARUS.

'TIS still thine hour, O Death!
Thine, Lord of Hades, is the kingdom still;
Yet twice thy sword unstained hath sought its sheath,
Though twice upraised to kill;
And once again the tomb
Shall yield its captive prey;
A mightier arm shall pierce the pathless gloom,
And rend the prize away:
Nor comes thy Conqueror armed with spear or sword—
He hath no arms but Prayer—no weapon but his Word

'Tis now the fourth sad morn
Since Lazarus, the pious and the just,
To his last home by sorrowing kinsmen borne,
Hath parted, dust to dust.
The grave-worm revels now
Upon his mouldering clay—
And He, before whose car the mountains bow-
The rivers roll away
In conscious awe—He only can revive
Corruption's withering prey, and call the dead to live!

Yet still the sister's keep
Their sad and silent vigil at the grave,
Watching for Jesus—"Comes he not to weep?
He did not come to save!"
But now *one* straining eye
Th' advancing Form hath traced;—
And soon in wild, resistless agony
Have Martha's arms embraced
The Savior's feet—"O Lord! hadst thou been nigh—
But speak the word e'en now—it shall be heard on high!"

They led him to the cave—
The rocky bed, where now in darkness slept
Their brother, and his friend—then at the grave
They paused—for "JESUS WEPT."
O Love, sublime and deep!
O Hand and Heart divine!
He comes to rescue, though he deigns to weep—
The captive is not thine,
O Death! thy bands are burst asunder now—
There stands beside the grave a Mightier far than thou.

"Come forth," he cries, "thou dead!"
O God! what means that strange and sudden sound,
That murmurs from the tomb—that ghastly head,
With funeral fillets bound?
It is a LIVING FORM—
The loved, the lost, the won—
Won from the grave, corruption, and the worm—
"And is not this the Son
Of God!" they whispered—while the sisters poured
Their gratitude in tears; for they had known the Lord.

Yet now the Son of God—
For such he was in truth—approached the hour
For which alone the path of thorns he trod;—
In which to thee the power,
O Death! should be restored—
And yet restored in vain—
For though the blood of ransom must be poured,
The spotless Victim slain;
He shall but yield to conquer, fall to rise,
And make the cold dark grave a portal to the skies!

THOMAS DALE.

THE CLOUDS.

WHEN first the day-beam blessed the sky,
I marked the varied clouds on high—
The clouds through which the sun-light broke,
As if it came from heaven, and woke
Their sleepy shadows into smiles,
And wooed them with a thousand wiles.
Those at a distance yet, were cold
And dull and naked after night;
But on, toward the east, they rolled
And clad them in a robe of light.
Others, as if they loved to dwell
In darkness, moved but slowly on,
And when on them its brightness fell,
But little of their gloom had gone:
One, gloomier still, its course delays,
As though too heavy for the sky,
Then breaks and passes gayly by:
While some had gathered round the rays
That gave them hues and forms so fair,
As loath to leave that glorious place,
To lose their beauty and to trace
Their pathway through the murky air.
I marked, when day was at its height,
Others of many a varied die,
More fair of form, more purely bright
Than those that decked the morning sky,
And gazed, till over all on high
The sun held undisputed sway,
And chased from heaven all gloom away;
While the few clouds that o'er it past,
No beam obscured, no shadow cast.

But when the day was almost done,
The clouds were beautiful indeed,
When, from his daily duty freed,
Still in his glorious strength, the sun
Shone forth upon the twilight skies,
And graced them with his myriad dies.
I saw the clouds that onward drew,
From out the deep and distant blue,
Become all beautiful and bright,
As if to show the coming night
How great the radiance and the power,
E'en of the sun's departing hour.
They took all shapes, as Fancy wrought
Her web, and mingled thought with thought!
Some like familiar forms—the themes
Of early loves that fade to dreams—
Some were of rainbow shape and hues;
Some glistened, like our earth, with dews;
Some were like forests, seen afar;
Some like the restless wandering star;
While some appeared like coral caves
Half hidden by the ocean waves,
All covered with their snow-white spray;
Others were there, which seemed to be
Fair islands in a dark blue sea,
Which human eyes at eve behold;
But only then—unseen by day
Their shores and mountains all of gold.
They vanished as the night came on—
Those varied hues and forms were gone:
But in their stead, Reflection woke
To teach her lesson—thus she spoke:—

"Those very clouds, so bright, so gay,
So fair—are vapors which the earth
Flung, as diseased parts, away—
Foul mists, which owe their second birth
To him who keeps his throne on high,
To bless the earth and gild the sky.
Yes! 'tis the sun whose influence brings
A change to these degraded things—
That gives them lovely forms—and then
Deprives them of their baneful powers,
And sends to mother earth again,
In gentle dews and cheering showers,
What was her burden and her ban.
Man feels a change as great—when man
Feels that immortal spark within
Whose might no human tongue can tell,
Which shines to lighten and dispel
The darkness and the weight of sin:
When He, who formed Creation's whole,
To school and guide the human soul,
Bids o'er the intellectual skies
The Sun of Righteousness arise,
And things of heaven and earth assume
Their proper shape of light or gloom."

Now let the contemplative mind
Fill up the blank I leave behind;
And see through all Creation's plan
Some useful lesson taught to man:
Compare the changes wrought within,
And those without—by nature wrought:
Compare the man who lives in sin,
And him by virtue led and taught—
See how the Christian's shining light
Makes all that once was darkness, bright;
And see how, like the clouds on high,
His every feeling, every thought,
Adorn and bless the mental sky,
—And then his glories *never* die!

S. C. HALL.

THE LAND WHICH NO MORTAL MAY KNOW.

THOUGH Earth has full many a beautiful spot,
As a poet or painter might show,
Yet more lovely and beautiful, holy and bright,
To the hopes of the heart, and the spirit's glad sight,
Is the land that no mortal may know.

There the crystalline stream bursting forth from the throne,
Flows on, and for ever will flow;
Its waves, as they roll, are with melody rife,
And its waters are sparkling with beauty and life,
In the land which no mortal may know.

And there, on its margin, with leaves ever green,
With its fruits healing sickness and wo,
The fair Tree of Life, in its glory and pride,
Is fed by that deep, inexhaustible tide,
Of the land which no mortal may know.

There, too, are the lost! whom we loved on this earth,
With whose mem'ries our bosoms yet glow;
Their relics we gave to the place of the dead,
But their glorified spirits before us have fled,
To the land which no mortal may know.

There the pale orb of night, and the fountain of day,
Nor beauty nor splendor bestow;
But the presence of HIM, the unchanging I AM!
And the holy, the pure, the immaculate Lamb!
Light the land which no mortal may know.

Oh! who but must pine, in this dark vale of tears,
From its clouds and its shadows to go?
To walk in the light of the glory above,
And to share in the peace, and the joy, and the love,
Of the land which no mortal may know.

BERNARD BARTON.

A MOTHER'S LOVE.

HAST thou sounded the depth of yonder sea,
And counted the sands that under it be?
Hast thou measured the height of Heaven above?
Then mayest thou mete out a mother's love.

Hast thou talked with the blessed, of leading on
To the throne of God some wandering son?
Hast thou witnessed the angel's bright employ?
Then mayest thou speak of a mother's joy.

Evening and morn hast thou watched the bee
Go forth on her errands of industry?
The bee for herself hath gathered and toiled,
But the mother's cares are all for her child.

Hast thou gone with the traveller Thought afar?
From pole to pole, and from star to star?
Thou hast—but on ocean, earth, or sea,
The heart of a mother has gone with thee.

There is not a grand, inspiring thought,
There is not a truth by wisdom taught,
There is not a feeling pure and high,
That may not be read in a mother's eye.

And ever since earth began, that look
Has been to the wise, an open book,
To win them back from the lore they prize,
To the holier love that edifies.

There are teachings on earth, and sky, and air,
The heavens the glory of God declare!
But more loud than the voice beneath, above,
He is heard to speak through a mother's love.

EMILY TAYLOR.

EVENING TIME.

ZECH. xiv. 7.

AT evening time let there be light:
Life's little day draws near its close;
Around me fall the shades of night,
The night of death, the grave's repose:
To crown my joys, to end my woes,
At evening time let there be light.

At evening time let there be light:
Stormy and dark hath been my day;
Yet rose the morn divinely bright,
Dews, birds, and blossoms, cheered the way;
Oh for one sweet, one parting ray!
At evening time let there be light.

At evening time there *shall* be light;
For God hath spoken—it must be:
Fear, doubt, and anguish, take their flight,
His glory now is risen on me!
Mine eyes shall his salvation see:
—'Tis evening time, and there *is* light!

JAMES MONTGOMERY.

NIGHT.

NIGHT is the time for rest;
How sweet when labors close,
To gather round an aching breast
The curtain of repose,
Stretch the tired limbs, and lay the head
Upon our own delightful bed.

Night is the time for dreams;
The gay romance of life,
When truth that is, and truth that seems,
Blend in fantastic strife;
Ah! visions less beguiling far
Than waking dreams by daylight are.

Night is the time for toil;
To plough the classic field,
Intent to find the buried spoil
Its wealthy furrows yield;
Till all is ours that sages taught,
That poets sang, or heroes wrought.

Night is the time to weep;
To wet with unseen tears
Those graves of memory, where sleep
The joys of other years,
Hopes that were angels in their birth,
But perished young—like things on earth.

Night is the time to watch,
On ocean's dark expanse;
To hail the Pleiades, or catch
The full moon's earliest glance,
That brings into the home-sick mind
All we have loved and left behind.

Night is the time for care;
Brooding on hours mis-spent,
To see the spectre of despair
Come to our lonely tent;
Like Brutus, 'mid his slumbering host,
Startled by Cesar's stalwart ghost.

Night is the time to muse;
Then from the eye the soul
Takes flight, and with expanding views,
Beyond the starry pole
Descries, athwart th' abyss of night,
The dawn of uncreated light.

Night is the time to pray;
Our Savior oft withdrew
To desert mountains far away:
So will his followers do—
Steal from the throng to haunts untrod,
And hold communion there with God.

Night is the time for death;
When all around is peace,
Calmly to yield the weary breath
From sin and suffering cease,
Think of heaven's bliss, and give the sign
To parting friends—such death be mine!

MONTGOMERY

"WATCH YE."

MARK xiv. 38.

WHEN summer decks thy path with flowers,
And pleasure's smile is sweetest;
When not a cloud above thee lowers,
And sunshine leads thy happy hours,
Thy happiest and thy fleetest;
Oh! watch thou then, lest pleasure's smile
Thy spirit of its hope beguile.

When round thee gathering storms are nigh,
And grief thy days hath shaded;
When earthly joys but bloom to die,
And tears suffuse thy weeping eye,
And hope's bright bow hath faded;
Oh! watch thou then, lest anxious care
Invade thy *heart*, and rankle there.

Through all life's scenes—through weal and wo,
Through days of mirth and sadness,
Where'er thy wandering footsteps go—
Oh! think how transient here below
Thy sorrow and thy gladness:
And watch thou ALWAYS, lest thou stray
From Him who points the heavenward way.

ANONYMOUS.

THE CELESTIAL SABBATH.

THE golden palace of my God,
Towering above the clouds, I see;
Beyond the cherub's bright abode,
Higher than angel's thoughts can be.
How can I in those courts appear,
Without a wedding garment on?
Conduct me, thou Life-giver, there,
Conduct me to thy glorious throne!
And clothe me with thy robes of light,
And lead me through sin's darksome night,
My Savior and my God.

RUSSIAN POETRY

SONGS FOR THE SABBATH.

THE WORKS OF CREATION.

I PRAISED the Earth, in beauty seen
With garlands gay of various green;
I praised the Sea, whose ample field
Shone glorious as a silver shield;
And Earth and Ocean seemed to say,
"Our beauties are but for to-day."

I praised the Sun, whose chariot rolled
On wheels of amber and of gold;
I praised the Moon, whose softer eye
Gleamed sweetly through the summer sky;
And Moon and Sun in answer said,
"Our days of light are numbered."

O God! O good beyond compare!
If thus thy meaner works are fair,
If thus thy beauties gild the span
Of ruined earth and sinful man,
How glorious must the mansion be
Where thy redeemed shall dwell with thee!

THE WORLD.

UNTHINKING, idle, wild, and young,
I laughed, and talked, and danced and sung;
And proud of health, of freedom vain,
Dreamed not of sorrow, care, or pain:
Concluding, in those hours of glee,
That all the world was made for me.

But when the days of trial came,
When sickness shook this trembling frame,
When folly's gay pursuits were o'er,
And I could dance and sing no more,
It then occurred, how sad 'twould be,
Were this world, only, made for me!

LIFE FADING.

SWEET day, so cool, so calm, so bright,
  Bridal of earth and sky!
The dew shall weep thy fall to-night;
  For thou, alas! must die.

Sweet rose, in air whose odors wave,
  And color charms the eye!
Thy root is ever in its grave,
  And thou, alas! must die.

Sweet spring, of days and roses made,
  Whose charms for beauty vie!
Thy days depart, thy roses fade,
  Thou, too, alas! must die.

Be wise then, Christian, while you may,
  For swiftly time is flying;
The thoughtless man, that laughs to-day,
  To-morrow will be dying.

CHRISTIAN HOPE.

HOPE, with uplifted foot, set free from earth,
Pants for the place of its ethereal birth,
On steady wing, flies through the immense abyss,
Plucks amaranthine joys from bowers of bliss,
And crowns the soul while yet a sufferer here,
With wreaths like those angelic spirits wear.

EARLY PIETY.

BY cool Siloam's shady rill
  How sweet the lily grows!
How sweet the breath beneath the hill
  Of Sharon's dewy rose!
Lo! such the child whose early feet
  The paths of peace have trod,
Whose secret heart with influence sweet
  Is upward drawn to God!

By cool Siloam's shady rill
  The lily must decay;
The rose that blooms beneath the hill
  Must shortly fade away.
And soon, too soon, the wintry hour
  Of man's maturer age
Will shake the soul with sorrow's power,
  And stormy passion's rage!

O thou, whose infant feet were found
  Within thy Father's shrine!
Whose years with changeless virtue crowned
  Were all alike divine!
Dependant on thy bounteous breath,
  We seek thy grace alone,
In childhood, manhood, age, and death,
  To keep us still thy own!

HEAVEN AND EARTH.

ASK the bird that soars on high,
Midway between earth and sky
What he sees, when he is there,
Of the world's receding sphere.
He could teach, if he might say,
Heavenward as he bends his way,
How the wide world lessens fast,
In the growing distance lost.
Lesser objects lost to view,
Great ones are but little now—
All that once were bright and fair
Lose their teints and disappear.
Doubt you, then, why they who rise
Near and nearer to the skies,
See on earth's diminished sphere.
Little that is worth their care?
They whose bosoms once could joy
In the vain world's vainest toy—
They whose hearts could sometimes feel
E'en the slightest touch of ill—
From the world by sorrow riven,
Gone already half to heaven—
Look with calmness on a scene,
Scarcely now within their ken.
Deem not that the heart is chilled,
Which, though once with anguish filled,
Such emotions all forgot,
Smiles and says, "It matters not."

THE DAY OF JUDGMENT.

GREAT God! what do I see and hear!
  The end of things created:
The Judge of all men doth appear
  In clouds of glory seated;
The trumpet sounds, the graves restore
The dead which they contained before.
  Prepare, my soul, to meet him.

FRAILTY OF MAN.

LIKE to the falling of a star,
Or as the flights of eagles are,
Or like the fresh spring's gaudy hue,
Or silver drops of morning dew;

Or like a wind that chafes the flood,
Or bubbles which on water stood;
E'en such is man, whose borrowed light
Is straight called in, and paid to-night.

The wind blows out, the bubble dies:
The spring entombed in autumn lies;
The dew dries up, the star is shot;
The flight is past—and man forgot.

MAN IS VANITY.

WHAT is this passing scene?
A peevish April day!
A little sun—a little rain—
And then night sweeps along the plain,
And all things fade away:
Man (soon discussed)
Yields up his trust;
And all his hopes and fears lie with him in the dust!

And what is beauty's power?
It flourishes and dies;
Will the cold earth its silence break,
To tell how soft, how smooth a cheek
Beneath its surface lies?
Mute, mute is all
O'er beauty's fall:
Her praise resounds no more, when mantled in her pall.

The most beloved on earth
Not long survives to-day;
So music past is obsolete,
And yet 'twas sweet, 'twas passing sweet,
But now 'tis gone away;
Thus does the shade,
In memory fade,
When in forsaken tomb the form beloved is laid!

Then since this world is vain
And volatile and fleet,
Why should I lay up earthly joy,
Where rust corrupts and moths destroy,
And cares and sorrows eat?
Why fly from ill
With anxious skill,
When soon this hand will freeze, this throbbing heart lie still?

THE STAR OF THE EAST.

BRIGHTEST and best of the sons of the morning!
Dawn on our darkness, and lend us thine aid,
Star of the East, the horizon adorning,
Guide where our infant Redeemer is laid!

Cold on his cradle the dewdrops are shining,
Low lies his head with the beasts of the stall,
Angels adore him in slumber reclining,
Maker, and Monarch, and Savior of all.

Say, shall we yield him, in costly devotion,
Odors of Edom, and offerings divine?
Gems of the mountain, and pearls of the ocean,
Myrrh from the forest, or gold from the mine?

Vainly we offer each ample oblation,
Vainly with gifts would his favor secure:
Richer by far is the heart's adoration;
Dearer to God are the prayers of the poor.

Brightest and best of the sons of the morning!
Dawn on our darkness, and lend us thine aid,
Star of the East, the horizon adorning,
Guide where our infant Redeemer is laid!

RACHEL WEEPING.

O WEEP not o'er thy children's tomb,
O Rachel, weep not so!
The bud is cropped by martyrdom,
The flower in heaven shall blow!

Firstlings of faith! the murderer's knife
Has missed its deadliest aim!
The God for whom they gave their life,
For them to suffer came!

Though feeble were their days and few,
Baptized in blood and pain,
He knows them, whom they never knew,
And they shall live again.

Then weep not o'er thy children's tomb,
O Rachel, weep not so!
The bud is cropped by martyrdom,
The flower in heaven shall blow!

THE GUIDANCE OF GOD.

THE golden palace of my God
Towering above the clouds I see:
Beyond the cherub's bright abode,
Higher than angel's thoughts can be.
How can I in those courts appear
Without a wedding garment on?
Conduct me, thou Life-giver there,
Conduct me to thy glorious throne!
And clothe me with thy robes of light,
And lead me through sin's darksome night,
My Savior and my God.

THE WORKS OF GOD.

THE God of nature and of grace
In all his works appears;
His goodness through the earth we trace,
His grandeur in the spheres.

Behold this fair and fertile globe,
By him in wisdom planned;
'Twas he who girded, like a robe,
The ocean round the land.

Lift to the arch of heaven your eye,
Thither his path pursue;
His glory, boundless as the sky,
O'erwhelms the wondering view.

He bows the heavens—the mountains stand
A highway for their God;
He walks amidst the desert land—
'Tis Eden where he trod.

The forests in his strength rejoice:
Hark! on the evening breeze,
As once of old his solemn voice
Is heard among the trees.

Here on the hills he feeds his herds,
His flocks on yonder plains:
His praise is warbled by the birds,
O could we catch their strains:—

Mount with the lark, and bear our song
Up to the gates of light;
Or, with the nightingale, prolong
Our numbers through the night!

In every stream his bounty flows,
Diffusing joy and wealth;
In every breeze his spirit blows
The breath of life and health.

His blessings fall in plenteous showers
Upon the lap of earth,
That teems with foliage, fruit, and flowers,
And rings with infant mirth.

If God has made this world so fair
Where sin and death abound,
How beautiful, beyond compare,
Will paradise be found!

MAN'S FRAILTY.

How few and evil are thy days,
Oh, man, of woman born!
Trouble and peril haunt thy ways,
—Forth like a flower at morn,
The tender infant springs to light:
Youth blossoms with the breeze;
Age, withering age, is cropped ere night
—Man like a shadow flees.

And dost thou look on such a one?
Will God to judgment call
A worm, for what a worm hath done
Against the Lord of all?
As fall the waters from the deep,
As summer brooks run dry,
Man lieth down in dreamless sleep;
—Our life is vanity.

Man lieth down, no more to wake,
Till yonder arching sphere
Shall with a roll of thunder break,
And nature disappear.
—O hide me till thy wrath be past,
Thou, who canst kill or save;
Hide me, where hope may anchor fast,
In my Redeemer's grave.

EMBLEM OF A DEPARTING SAINT.

A cloud lay cradled near the setting sun,
A gleam of crimson tinged its braided snows:
Long had I watched the glory moving on,
O'er the still radiance of the lake below:
Tranquil its spirit seemed, and floated slow,
E'en in its very motion there was rest,
While every breath of eve that chanced to blow,
Wafted the traveller to the beauteous west.
Emblem methought, of the departed soul,
To whose white robe the gleam of bliss is given,
And by the breath of mercy made to roll
Right onward to the golden gates of heaven:
Where to the eye of faith it peaceful lies,
And tells to man his glorious destinies.

SUPERIORITY TO THE WORLD.

Ah! why should this immortal mind,
Enslaved by sense, be thus confined,
And never, never rise?
Why, thus amused with empty toys,
And soothed with visionary joys,
Forget her native skies!

The mind was formed to mount sublime,
Beyond the narrow bounds of time,
To everlasting things;
But earthly vapors cloud her sight,
And hang with cold oppressive weight
Upon her drooping wings.

The world employs its various snares,
Of hopes and pleasures, pains and cares,
And chained to earth I lie:
When shall my fettered powers be free,
And leave these seats of vanity,
And upward learn to fly!

Bright scenes of bliss, unclouded skies,
Invite my soul—O could I rise,
Nor leave a thought below!
I'd bid farewell to anxious care,
And say to every tempting snare,
Heaven calls, and I must go.

Heaven calls, and can I yet delay?
Can aught on earth engage my stay?
Ah, wretched, lingering heart!
Come, Lord, with strength, and life and light,
Assist and guide my upward flight,
And bid the world depart.

THE PROVIDENCE OF GOD.

Lo the lilies of the field,
How their leaves instruction yield!
Hark to nature's lesson given
By the cheerful birds of heaven!
Every bush and tufted tree
Warbles sweet philosophy;
"Mortal, fly from doubt and sorrow;
God provideth for the morrow!

"Say, with richer crimson glows
The kingly mantle than the rose?
Say, have kings more wholesome fare
Than we poor citizens of air?
Barns nor hoarded grain have we,
Yet we carol merrily.
Mortal, fly from doubt and sorrow,
God provideth for the morrow!

"One there lives whose guardian eye
Guides our humble destiny;
One there lives, who, Lord of all,
Keeps our feathers lest they fall:
Pass we blithely then, the time,
Fearless of the snare and lime,
Free from doubt and faithless sorrow:
God provideth for the morrow!"

THE CHRISTIAN WARRIOR TRIUMPHANT IN DEATH.

"Servant of God! well done;
Rest from thy loved employ;
The battle fought, the victory won,
Enter thy Master's joy."
—The voice at midnight came;
He started up to hear,
A mortal arrow pierced his frame;
He fell—but felt no fear.

Tranquil amidst alarms,
It found him in the field,
A veteran slumbering on his arms,
Beneath his red-cross shield:
His sword was in his hand,
Still warm with recent fight;
Ready that moment, at command,
Through rock and steel to smite.

It was a two-edged blade,
Of heavenly temper keen:
And double were the wounds it made,
Where'er it smote between:
'Twas death to sin;—'twas life
To all that mourned for sin;
It kindled, and it silenced, strife,
Made war, and peace, within.
Oft with its fiery force,
His arm had quelled the foe,
And laid, resistless in his course,
The alien-armies low.
Bent on such glorious toils,
The world to him was loss;
Yet all his trophies, all his spoils,
He hung upon the cross.

At midnight came the cry,
"To meet thy God prepare!"
He woke,—and caught his captain's eye;
Then, strong in faith and prayer,
His spirit, with a bound,
Burst its encumbering clay,
His tent, at sunrise on the ground,
A darkened ruin lay.

The pains of death are past,
Labor and sorrow cease,
And, life's long warfare closed at last,
His soul is found in peace.
Soldier of Christ, well done;
Praise be thy new employ;
And while eternal ages run,
Rest in thy Savior's joy.

HEAVEN.

Friend after friend departs,
  Who hath not lost a friend?
There is no union here of hearts,
  That finds not here an end;
Were this frail world our final rest,
Living or dying, none were blessed.

Beyond the flight of time,—
  Beyond the reign of death,—
There surely is some blessed clime
  Where life is not a breath;
Nor life's affections, transient fire,
Whose sparks fly upward and expire!

There is a world above,
  Where parting is unknown;
A long eternity of love,
  Formed for the good alone;
And faith beholds the dying, here,
Translated to that glorious sphere.

Thus star by star declines,
  Till all are passed away;
As morning high and higher shines,
  To pure and perfect day:
Nor sink those stars in empty night,
But hide themselves in heaven's own light.

LONGING FOR HEAVEN.

Rise, my soul, and stretch thy wings,
  Thy better portion trace;
Rise from transitory things,
  Toward heaven, thy native place.
Sun, and moon, and stars, decay,
  Time shall soon this earth remove;
Rise, my soul, and haste away
  To seats prepared above.

Rivers to the ocean run,
  Nor stay in all their course:
Fire ascending seeks the sun,
  Both speed them to their source.
So a soul new-born of God
  Pants to view his glorious face;
Upward tends to his abode,
  To rest in his embrace.

Cease, ye pilgrims, cease to mourn,
  Press onward to the prize:
Soon the Savior will return
  Triumphant in the skies.
Yet a season, and you know
  Happy entrance will be given,
All our sorrows left below,
  And earth exchanged for heaven.

GOD'S PREVENTING GRACE.

God of my life, how good, how wise,
  Thy judgments on my soul have been!
They were but mercies in disguise,
  The painful remedies of sin:
How different now thy ways appear,
  Most merciful, when most severe!

Since first the maze of life I trod,
  Hast thou not hedged about my way,
My worldly vain designs withstood,
  And robbed my passions of their prey,
Withheld the fuel from the fire,
And crossed my every fond desire?

How oft didst thou my soul withhold,
  And baffle my pursuit of fame,
And mortify my lust of gold,
  And blast me in my surest aim;
Withdraw my animal delight,
  And starve my grovelling appetite!

Thou wouldst not let the captive go,
  Or leave me to my carnal will;
Thy love forbade my rest below,
  Thy patient love pursued me still,
And forced me from my sin to part,
And tore the idol from my heart.

But can I now the loss lament,
  Or murmur at thy friendly blow?
Thy friendly blow my heart hath rent,
  From every seeming good below;
Thrice happy loss which makes me se[e]
My happiness alone in thee!

UNCERTAINTY OF LIFE.

What is life? 'tis but a vapor;
  Soon it vanishes away:
Life is like a dying taper:
  O, my soul, why wish to stay?
Why not spread thy wings and fly
Straight to yonder world of joy?

See that glory, how resplendent!
  Brighter far than fancy paints,
There, in majesty transcendent,
  Jesus reigns, the King of saints.
Spread thy wings, my soul, and fly
Straight to yonder world of joy!

Joyful crowds, his throne surrounding,
  Sing with rapture of his love:
Through the heavens his praises sounding,
  Filling all the courts above.
Spread thy wings, my soul, and fly
Straight to yonder world of joy!

Go and share his people's glory,
  'Midst the ransomed crowd appear;
Thine a joyful, wondrous story:
  One that angels love to hear.
Spread thy wings, my soul and fly
Straight to yonder world of joy!

JACOB WRESTLING WITH THE ANGEL.

PART FIRST.

Come, O thou traveller unknown,
Whom still I hold, but can not see
My company before is gone,
And I am left alone with thee;
With thee all night I mean to stay,
And wrestle till the break of day.

I need not tell thee who I am;
My misery and sin declare:
Thyself hast called me by my name
Look on thy hands, and read it then
But who, I ask thee, who art thou?
Tell me thy name, and tell me now.

In vain thou strugglest to get free,
I never will unloose my hold;
Art thou the Man that died for me?
The secret of thy love unfold:
Wrestling, I will not let thee go,
Till I thy name, thy nature know.

Wilt thou not yet to me reveal
Thy new unutterable name!
Tell me, I still beseech thee, tell?
To know it now, resolved I am:
Wrestling, I will not let thee go,
Till I thy name, thy nature know.

What though my shrinking flesh complain,
And murmur to contend so long,
I rise superior to my pain:
When I am weak, then I am strong:
And when my all of strength shall fail,
I shall with the God man prevail.

PART SECOND.

Yield to me now, for I am weak;
But confident in self despair:
Speak to my heart, in blessings speak;
Be conquered by my instant prayer:
Speak, or thou never hence shall move,
And tell me if thy name be Love.

'Tis Love! 'tis Love! Thou diedst for me;
I hear thy whisper in my heart:
The morning breaks, the shadows flee;
Pure, Universal Love, thou art;
To me, to all, thy bowels move;
Thy nature and thy name is Love.

My prayer hath power with God; the grace
Unspeakable I now receive;
Through faith I see thee face to face;
I see thee face to face, and live;
In vain I have not wept and strove;
Thy nature and thy name is Love.

I know thee, Savior, who thou art,
Jesus, the feeble sinner's friend:
Nor wilt thou with the night depart,
But stay and love me to the end:
Thy mercies never shall remove;
Thy nature and thy name is Love.

The Sun of Righteousness on me
Hath risen, with healing on his wings;
Withered my nature's strength; from thee
My soul its life and succor brings;
My help is all laid up above;
Thy nature and thy name is Love.

Contented now, upon my thigh
I halt, till life's short journey end;
All helplessness, all weakness, I
On Thee alone for strength depend;
Nor have I power from thee to move:
Thy nature and thy name is Love.

Lame as I am, I take the prey;
Hell, earth, and sin, with ease o'ercome;
I leap for joy, pursue my way,
And, as a bounding hart, fly home;
Through all eternity to prove,
Thy nature and thy name is Love.

A FATHER LEAVING HIS FAMILY TO GOD.

Amid the anguish and the strife,
That shrinking nature fears,
Look gently down, great Source of life,
And dry death's starting tears!

Serene, like Jacob, we would die,
And "gather up our feet;"
Would chide the lingering hours, and fly
Our Savior God to meet.

Our dearest comforts we could leave.
With glory in our eyes:
Would wipe the tears of those that grieve,
And point them to the skies.

Our trembling lips, if thou art nigh,
When life's sad hours are few,
With joy shall say—"Behold we die,
But God shall be with you."

A REFLECTION AT SEA.

See how beneath the moonbeam's smile
Yon little billow heaves its breast,
And foams and sparkles for awhile,
And murmuring then subsides to rest.

Thus man, the sport of bliss and care,
Rises on time's eventful sea,
And having swelled a moment there,
Thus melts into eternity.

THE HEAVENLY JERUSALEM.

Jerusalem! my happy home!
Name ever dear to me!
When shall my labors have an end,
In joy, and peace, and thee?

When shall these eyes thy heaven-built walls
And pearly gates behold?
Thy bulwarks, with salvation strong,
And streets of shining gold?

O when, thou city of my God,
Shall I thy courts ascend,
Where congregations ne'er break up,
And sabbaths have no end?

There happier bowers than Eden's bloom,
Nor sin nor sorrow know;
Blessed seats! through rude and stormy scenes
I onward press to you.

Why should I shrink at pain and wo?
Or feel, at death, dismay?
I've Canaan's goodly land in view,
And realms of endless day.

Apostles, martyrs, prophets, there,
Around my Savior stand;
And soon my friends in Christ below
Will join the glorious band.

Jerusalem! my happy home!
My soul still pants for thee;
Then shall my labors have an end,
When I thy joys shall see.

SELF-EXAMINATION.

At evening to myself I say,
My soul, where hast thou gleaned to-day,
Thy labors how bestowed?
What hast thou rightly said or done?
What grace attained, or knowledge won,
In following after God?

LITANY.

By thy birth and early years,
By thy human griefs and fears;
By thy fasting and distress;
In the lonely wilderness;
By thy victory, in the hour
Of the subtle tempter's power—
Jesus! look with pitying eye,
Hear our solemn litany.

By the sympathy that wept
O'er the grave where Lazarus slept;
By thy bitter tears that flowed
Over Salem's lost abode;
By the troubled sigh that told
Treason lurked within thy fold—
Jesus! look with pitying eye,
Hear our solemn litany.

By thine hour of dark despair;
By thine agony of prayer;
By the purple robe of scorn;
By thy wounds, thy crown of thorn,
Cross and passion, pangs and cries;
By thy perfect sacrifice—
Jesus! look with pitying eye,
Hear our solemn litany.

By thy deep expiring groan;
By the sealed sepulchral stone;
By thy triumph o'er the grave;
By thy power from death to save—
Mighty God! ascended Lord!
To thy throne in heaven restored
Prince and Savior! hear the cry
Of our solemn litany.

WHAT ARE MEETINGS, HERE, BUT PARTINGS?

WHAT are meetings, here, but partings?
What are ecstasies, but smartings?
Unions what, but separations?
What attachments, but vexations?
Every smile but brings its tear,
Love its ache, and hope its fear;
All that's sweet must bitter prove;
All we hold most dear—remove?

Foes may harm us; but the dearest,
Ever, here, are the severest:
Sorrows wound us; but we borrow
From delight the keenest sorrow:
'Tis to love our farewells owe
All their emphasis of wo;
Most it charms that most annoys;
Joys are griefs, and griefs are joys!

Heavenward rise!—'tis Heaven, in kindness
Mars our bliss, to heal our blindness:
Hope from vanity to sever;
Offering joys that bloom for ever,
In that amaranthine clime,
Far above the tears of time,
Where nor fear nor hope intrude,
Lost in pure beatitude!

A NEW YEAR.

COME, let us anew,
Our journey pursue,
Roll round with the year,
And never stand still,
Till the Master appear.

His adorable will
Let us gladly fulfill,
And our talents improve
By the patience of hope,
And the labor of love.

Our life is a dream,
Our time as a stream
Glides swiftly away;
And the fugitive moment
Refuses to stay.

The arrow is flown,
The moment is gone;
The millenial year
Rushes on to our view,
And eternity's here.

O that each in the day,
Of his coming may say,
"I have fought my way through;
I have finished the work
Thou didst give me to do."

O that each from his Lord,
May receive the glad word:
"Well and faithfully done!
Enter into my joy,
And sit down on my throne!"

THE BREVITY OF LIFE.

SWIFT as the arrow cuts its way
Through the soft yielding air:
Or as the sun's more subtle ray,
Or lightning's sudden glare;
Or as an eagle to the prey,
Or shuttle through the loom—
So haste our fleeting lives away,
So pass we to the tomb.

Like airy bubbles, lo! we rise,
And dance upon life's stream;
Till soon the air that caused, destroys
Th' attenuated frame.
Down the swift stream we glide apace,
And carry death within;
Then break, and scarcely leave a trace,
To show that we have been.

The man, the wisest of our kind,
Who length of days had seen,
To birth and death a time assigned,
But none to life between;—
Yet O! what consequences close
This transient state below!
Eternal joys: or, losing those,
Interminable wo!

THE LAW OF LOVE.

BLESSED is the man whose softening heart
Feels all another's pain;
To whom the supplicating eye
Was never raised in vain:

Whose breast expands with generous warmth,
A stranger's woes to feel;
And bleeds in pity o'er the wound
He wants the power to heal.

He spreads his kind, supporting arms,
To every child of grief;
His secret bounty largely flows,
And brings unasked relief.

To gentle offices of love
His feet are never slow;
He views, through mercy's melting eye,
A brother in a foe.

Peace from the bosom of his God,
My peace to him I give;
And when he kneels before the throne,
His trembling soul shall live.

To him protection shall be shown,
And mercy from above
Descend on those who thus fulfil
The perfect law of love.

TIME.

TIME *was*, is past; thou canst not it recall:
Time *is*, thou hast; employ the portion small:
Time *future* is not; and may never be:
Time *present* is the only time for thee.

FRAILTY OF MAN.

LET others boast how strong they be,
Nor death nor danger fear;
But we'll confess, O Lord, to thee,
What feeble things we are.

Fresh as the grass our bodies stand,
And flourish bright and gay;
A blasting wind sweeps o'er the land,
And fades the grass away.

Our life contains a thousand springs,
And dies if one go wrong;
Strange! that a harp of thousand strings
Should keep in tune so long.

'Tis God who made and keeps our frame,
In God alone we'll trust;
Salvation to the Almighty Name
That reared us from the dust.

SHORTNESS OF TIME.

The moments fly—a minute's gone!
The minutes fly—an hour is run!
The day is fled the night is here!
Thus flies a week—a month—a year.

A year—alas! how soon it's past;
Who knows but *this* may be my last!
A few short years, how soon they're fled,
And we are numbered with the dead.

INNOCENT EARTHLY PLEASURES.

Few rightly estimate the worth,
Of joys that spring and fade on earth;
They are not weeds we should despise,
They are not fruits of Paradise;
But wild flowers in the pilgrim's way
That cheer, yet not protract his stay;
Which he dare not too fondly clasp,
Lest they should perish in his grasp;
And yet may view, and wisely love,
As proofs and types of joys above.

RESIGNATION.

One prayer I have,—all prayers in one,—
When I am wholly thine:
Thy will, my God, thy will be done,
And let that will be mine.

All-wise, almighty, and all-good,
In thee I firmly trust:
Thy ways, unknown or understood,
Are merciful and just.

Is life with many comforts crowned,
Upheld in peace and health,
With dear affections twined around?
—Lord, in my time of wealth,—

May I remember, that to thee,
Whate'er I have I owe:
And back, in gratitude from me,
May of all thy bounties flow.

Thy gifts are only then enjoyed,
When used as talents lent;
Those talents only well employed,
When in thy service spent.

And though thy wisdom takes away.
Shall I arraign thy will?
No, let me bless thy name, and say,
"The Lord is gracious still."

A pilgrim through the earth I roam,
Of nothing long possessed,
And all must fall when I go home
For this is not my rest.

Write but my name upon the roll
Of thy redeemed above;
Then, heart, and mind, and strength, and soul,
Shall love thee for *thy* love.

DEPENDANCE ON GOD.

E'en as the needle, that directs the hour,
Touched with the loadstone, by the secret power
Of hidden nature, points upon the Pole;
E'en so the wavering powers of my soul,
Touched by the virtue of thy Spirit, flee
From what is earth, and point alone to thee.
When I have faith to hold thee by the hand,
I walk securely, and methinks I stand
More firm than Atlas; but when I forsake
The safe protection of thine arm, I quake
Like wind-shaked reeds, and have no strength at all,
But like a vine, the prop cut down, I fall.

FAMILY HARMONY.

Oh! sweet as vernal dews that fill
The closing buds on Zion's hill,
When evening clouds draw thither,—
So sweet, so heavenly 'tis, to see
The members of one family
Live peacefully together.

The children like the lily flowers,
On which descend the suns and showers,
Their hues of beauty blending;—
The parents, like the willow boughs,
On which the lovely foliage grows,
Their friendly shade extending.

But leaves the greenest will decay,—
And flowers the brightest fade away,
When autumn winds are sweeping,
And be the household e'er so fair,
The hand of death will soon be there,
And turn the scene to weeping.

Yet leaves again will clothe the trees,
And lilies wave beneath the breeze,
When spring comes smiling hither;
And friends who parted at the tomb,
May yet renew their loveliest bloom,
And meet in heaven together.

WATCHMAN! WHAT OF THE NIGHT.

Watchman! tell us of the night,
What its signs of promise are?
Traveller! o'er yon mountain's height,
See that glory-beaming star!
Watchman! does its beauteous ray
Aught of hope or joy foretell?
Traveller! yes: it brings the day,—
Promised day of Israel!

Watchman! tell us of the night;
Higher yet that star ascends;
Traveller! blessedness and light,
Peace and truth, its course portends.
Watchman! will its beams alone
Gild the spot that gave them birth?
Traveller! ages are its own,
And it bursts o'er all the earth.

Watchman! tell us of the night,
For the morning seems to dawn:
Traveller! darkness takes its flight,
Doubt and terror are withdrawn,
Watchman! let thy wanderings cease:
Hie thee to thy quiet home:
Traveller! lo! the Prince of peace,
Lo! the Son of God is come!

THE SEASONS.

How pleasing is the voice
Of God our heavenly King
Who bids the frosts retire,
And wakes the lovely spring!
Bright suns arise,
The mild wind blows,
And beauty glows
Through earth and skies.

The morn, with glory crowned,
His hand arrays in smiles;
He bids the eve decline,
Rejoicing o'er the hills:
The evening breeze
His breath perfumes:
His beauty blooms
In flowers and trees.

With life he clothes the spring,—
The earth with summer warms:
He spreads the autumnal feast,
And rides on wintry storms:
His gifts divine,
Through all appear;
And round the year
His glories shine.

THE HARMONY OF LOVE.

Lord, subdue our selfish will;
Each to each our tempers suit
By thy modulating skill,
Heart to heart, as lute to lute.
Sweetly on our spirits move;
Gently touch the trembling strings
Make the harmony of love
Music for the King of kings!

WHAT IS LIFE?

Oh! what is life? 'Tis like a flower
That blossoms—and is gone:
It flourishes its little hour,
With all its beauty on:—
Death comes—and like a wintry day,
It cuts the lovely flower away.

Oh! what is life?—'Tis like the bow
That glistens in the sky:
We love to see its colors glow—
But while we look they die;
Life fails as soon; to-day 'tis here—
To-morrow it may disappear.

Lord, what is life?—If spent with thee,
In humble praise and prayer,
How long or short our life may be,
We feel no anxious care:
Though life depart, our joys shall last
When life and all its joys are past.

THE WAVES.

When on the giddy cliff I stand,
I see the billows roar,
And, breaking on the coral strand,
Whiten with foam the shore.

But 'tis in vain they strive to break
Beyond the bounds decreed;
"No farther come," let God but speak,
No farther they proceed.

Though furiously their heads they rear,
And mingle sea and skies,
They smooth as polished glass appear,
If "Peace, be still," he cries.

Shall winds and waves their God obey,
And I refuse to hear?
Shall he that bounds the flowing sea,
Not bind me with his fear?

O Thou who rulest seas and skies,
Corruption's flood control;
Nor let the waves of passion rise
Within my troubled soul.

Then I, within thy sacred mound,
Shall, in obedience blest,
Calm, gently flowing, kiss the bound,
And wait eternal rest.

MORNING.

Hues of the rich unfolding morn,
That, ere the glorious sun be born,
By some soft touch invisible
Around his path are taught to swell;—
Thou rustling breeze so fresh and gay,
That danced forth at opening day,
And brushing by with joyous wing,
Wakenest each little leaf to sing;—
Ye fragrant clouds of dewy steam,
By which deep grove and tangled stream
Pay, for soft rains in season given,
Their tribute to the genial heaven;—
Why waste your treasures of delight
Upon our thankless, joyless sight;
Who day by day to sin awake,
Seldom of heaven, and you partake?
Oh! timely happy, timely wise,
Hearts that with rising morn arise!
Eyes that the beam celestial view,
Which evermore makes all things new!
New every morning is the love
Our wakening and uprising prove;
Through sleep and darkness safely brought,
Restored to life, and power, and thought.
New mercies each returning day,
Hover around us while we pray;
New perils past, new sins forgiven,
New thoughts of God, new hopes of heaven.
If on our daily course our mind
Be set to hallow all we find,
New treasure, still of countless price,
God will provide for sacrifice.
Old friends, old scenes, will lovelier be,
As more of heaven in each we see;
Some softening gleam of love and prayer
Shall dawn on every cross and care.
As for some dear familiar strain
Untired we ask, and ask again,
Ever, in its melodious store,
Finding a spell unheard before;
Such is the bliss of souls serene,
When they have sworn, and steadfast mean,
Counting the cost, in all t' espy
Their God, in all themselves deny.
O could we learn that sacrifice,
What lights would around us rise!
How would our hearts with wisdom talk
Along life's dullest, dreariest walk!
We need not bid for cloistered cell,
Our neighbor and our work farewell,
Nor strive to wind ourselves too high
For sinful man beneath the sky:
The trivial round, the common task,
Would furnish all we ought to ask;
Room to deny ourselves; a road
To bring us, daily, nearer God.

GOD UNSEARCHABLE.

Canst thou by searching find out God,
The Almighty to perfection trace?
And pierce the clouds whose darkness shrouds
The brightness of Jehovah's face?

Proud, daring man, this thought of thine
Proves thee the dupe of Satan's art:
The vain attempt must bring contempt
On thy rebellious head and heart.

First try the things thy senses reach,
Their nature, power, and essence tell;
If here thou fail, canst thou prevail
To find out the Unsearchable?

Go count the stars and call their names,
Sweep with the comet through the sky;
Fix thy bold gaze on the sun's blaze,
With an undazzled, tearless eye.

Go sleep upon the thunder-cloud,
Grasp the forked lightning in thy hand;
Proceed to find whence comes the wind,
And trace its path o'er sea and land.

Go and unbend the rainbow's arch,
Untwist its robes of various hues;
Then view the source, and trace the course,
Of rain, hail, vapors, and the dews.

Go view the everlasting snows
Moistening the axles of the poles;
Then boldly probe straight through the globe,
And span the line on which it rolls.

Should thy mind shrink from such attempts,
View the *least* work of Deity;
The blades of grass thy skill surpass,
And thou art baffled by a fly.

If *every* work of God is full
Of mysteries we can never scan,
His word 'tis plain, must then contain
Wonders above the powers of man.

Before the great Unsearchable
With lowliness and love I'll bend;
And gladly trace in Jesus face
My God, my Savior, and my Friend.

MY DYING MOTHER.

I do remember, and will ne'er forget,
The dying eye!—That eye alone was bright,
And brighter grew, as nearer death approached:
As I have seen the gentle little flower
Look fairest in the silver beam which fell,
Reflected from the thunder cloud that soon
Came down, and o'er the desert scattered far
And wide its loveliness. She made a sign
To bring her babe—'twas brought and by her placed;
She looked upon its face that neither smiled
Nor wept, nor knew who gazed upon it; and laid
Her hand upon its little breast, and sought
For it, with look that seemed to penetrate
The heavens, unutterable blessings, such
As God to dying parents only granted,
For infants left behind them in the world.
"God keep my child!" we heard her say, and heard
No more. The Angel of the Covenant
Was come, and faithful to his promise stood
Prepared to walk with her through death's dark vale.
And now her eyes grew bright, and brighter still,
Too bright for ours to look upon, suffused
With many tears; and closed without a cloud
They set as sets the morning star, which goes
Not down behind the darkened west, nor hides
Obscured among the tempests of the sky,
But melts away into the light of heaven.

BLESSED BE THY NAME FOR EVER.

Blessed be thy name for ever,
Thou of life the guard and giver:
Thou canst guard thy creatures sleeping;
Heal the heart long broke with weeping.
God of stillness and of motion,
Of the desert and the ocean,
Of the mountain, rock, and river,
Blessed be thy name for ever.

Thou who slumberest not nor sleepest,
Blessed are they thou kindly keepest;
God of evening's parting ray,
Of midnight's gloom, and dawning day,
That rises from the azure sea,
Like breathings of eternity;
God of life! that fade shall never,
Blessed be thy name for ever!

COMMITTING OUR WAYS UNTO THE LORD.

Commit thou all thy griefs
And ways into his hands,
To his sure truth and tender care,
Who heaven and earth commands:

Who points the clouds their course,
Whom winds and seas obey,
He shall direct thy wandering feet,
He shall prepare thy way.

Put thou thy trust in God,
In duty's path go on;
Fix on his word thy steadfast eye,
So shall thy work be done:

No profit canst thou gain
By self-consuming care:
To him commend thy cause, his ear
Attends the softest prayer.

Give to the winds thy fears,
Hope, and be undismayed;
God hears thy sighs, and counts thy tears,
God shall lift up thy head.

Through waves, and clouds, and storms,
He gently clears thy way:
Wait thou his time—thy darkest night
Shall end in brightest day.

PRAYER.

Prayer is the soul's sincere desire,
Uttered or unexpressed;
The motion of a hidden fire
That trembles in the breast.

Prayer is the burden of a sigh
The falling of a tear;
The upward glancing of an eye,
When none but God is near.

Prayer is the simplest form of speech
That infant lips can try;
Prayer the sublimest strains that reach
The Majesty on high.

Prayer is the Christian's vital breath,
The Christian's native air,
His watchword at the gates of death,
He enters heaven with prayer.

Prayer is the contrite sinner's voice,
Returning from his ways;
While angels in their songs rejoice,
And cry, "Behold he prays."

The saints, in prayer, appear as one,
In word, in deed, and mind,
While with the Father and his Son
Their fellowship they find.

Nor prayer is made on earth alone:
The Holy Spirit pleads;
And Jesus, on the eternal throne,
For mourners intercedes.

O thou, by whom we come to God,
The Life, the Truth, the Way;
The path of prayer thyself hast trod.
Lord, teach us how to pray.

THE HAPPINESS OF THE GODLY

Happy the men whose bliss supreme
Flows from a source on high,
And flows in one perpetual stream,
When earthly springs are dry.

Contentment makes their little—more;
And sweetens good possessed;
While faith foretastes the joys in store,
And makes them doubly blessed.

If Providence their comforts shroud,
And dark distresses lour;
Hope paints its rainbow on the cloud,
And grace shines through the shower.

What troubles can their hearts o'erwhelm,
Who view a Savior near?
Whose Father sits and guides the helm;
Whose voice forbids their fear?

Let tempests rage, and billows rise,
And mortal firmness shrink;
Their anchor fastens in the skies;
Their bark, no storm can sink!

God is their joy and portion still,
When earthly good retires;
And shall their hearts sustain and fill,
When earth itself expires.

WISDOM.

Ah! when did wisdom covet length of days?
Or seek its bliss in pleasure, wealth, or praise?
No: wisdom views, with an indifferent eye,
All finite joys, all blessings born to die.
The soul on earth is an immortal guest,
Compelled to starve at an unreal feast;
A spark that upward tends by nature's force,
A stream diverted from its parent source;
A drop dissevered from the boundless sea,
A moment parted from eternity!
A pilgrim panting for a rest to come;
An exile anxious for his native home.

THE WELCOME SABBATH.

Return, thou wished and welcome guest;
Thou day of holiness and rest!
Thou best, the dearest of the seven,
Emblem and harbinger of heaven!

YOUTH AND AGE.

The seas are quiet when the winds are o'er
So calm are we when passions are no more!
For then we know how vain it was to boast
Of fleeting things so certain to be lost.

Clouds of affection from her younger eyes,
Conceals that emptiness which age descries:
The soul's dark cottage, battered and decayed,
Lets in new light through chinks that time has made.

Stronger by weakness, wiser men become
As they draw near to their eternal home;
Leaving the old, both worlds at once they view,
That stand upon the threshold of the new.

SABBATH EVENING.

Is there a time when moments flow,
More peacefully than all beside?
It is of all the times below,
A sabbath eve in summer tide.
O then the setting sun smiles fair,
And all below, and all above
The different forms of nature wear
One universal garb of love.
And then the peace that Jesus beams,
The life of grace, the death of sin,
With nature's placid woods and streams,
Is peace without, and peace within.
Delightful scene! a world at rest,
A God all love, no grief nor fear;
A heavenly hope, a peaceful breast,
A smile unsullied by a tear.
If heaven be ever felt below,
A scene so heavenly sure as this
May cause a heart on earth to know
Some foretaste of celestial bliss.
Delightful hour! how soon will night
Spread her dark mantle o'er thy reign;
And morrow's quick returning light
Must call us to the world again.
Yet will there dawn at last a day,
A sun that never sets shall rise;
Night will not veil his ceaseless ray
The heavenly sabbath never dies!

IS THERE AN UNBELIEVER?

Is there an unbeliever?
One man who walks the earth,
And madly doubts that Providence
Watched o'er him at his birth?
He robs mankind for ever
Of hopes beyond the tomb;
What gives he as a recompense?
The brute's unhallowed doom.

In manhood's loftiest hour,
In health, and strength, and pride
Oh! lead his steps through valleys green,
Where rills mid cowslips glide:
Climb nature's granite tower,
Where man hath rarely trod:
And will he then, in such a scene,
Deny there is a God?

Yes—the proud heart will ever
Prompt the false tongue's reply!
An Omnipresent Providence
Still madly he'll deny.
But see the unbeliever
Sinking in death's decay;
And hear the cry of penitence!—
He never learned to pray!

OH, JUDAH!

Jerusalem mourneth.—*Jeremiah.*

Oh, Judah! thy dwellings are sad,
Thy children are weeping around,
In sackcloth their bosoms are clad
As they look on the famishing ground;
In the deserts they make them a home,
And the mountains awake to their cry;
For the frown of Jehovah hath come,
And his anger is red in the sky.

Thy tender ones throng at the brink,
But the waters are gone from the well;
They gaze on the rock, and they think
Of the gush of the stream from its cell;
How they came to its margin before,
And drank in their innocent mirth;
Away! it is sealed, and no more
Shall the fountain give freshness to earth.

The hearts of the mighty are bowed,
And the lowly are haggard with care;
The voices of mothers are loud,
As they shriek the wild note of despair.
Oh, Jerusalem! mourn through thy halls,
And bend to the dust in thy shame,
For the doom that thy spirit appals,
Is famine, the sword, and the flame!

SOUND AN ALARM!

My arms!—Against this Gorgias will I go!
The Dumean Governor shall know
How vain, how ineffective, his design
While rage his leader and Jehovah mine.

Sound an alarm!—Your silver trumpets sound,
And call the brave, and only brave, around!
Who listeth, follow to the field again—
Justice and courage is a thousand men!

ANGELS EVER BRIGHT AND FAIR.

Angels ever bright and fair,
Take, O take me to your care.
Speed to your own courts my flight,
Clad in robes of virgin white.

ROCKED IN THE CRADLE OF THE DEEP.

Rocked in the cradle of the deep,
I lay me down in peace to sleep;
Secure I rest upon the wave,
For thou, oh! Lord, hast power to save.

I know thou wilt not slight my call!
For thou dost mark the sparrow's fall!
And calm and peaceful is my sleep,
Rocked in the cradle of the deep.

And such the trust that still were mine,
Though stormy winds swept o'er the brine.
Or though the tempest's fiery breath
Roused from sleep to wreck and death!

In ocean cave still safe with thee,
The germe of immortality;
And calm and peaceful is my sleep,
Rocked in the cradle of the deep.

Mrs. Willard.

HAGAR IN THE DESERT.

O'er the desert, vast and dreary,
Hagar's fainting footsteps passed;
While her soul of life, nigh weary,
Shrank beneath the burning blast.
As her mournful journey wending,
Through that vale of death she strayed,
For the child her steps attending,
Thus, the outcast mother prayed!

"Lord! the fount is dry and failing,
"And my thirst-parched infant tries.
"Vainly now, mid tears and wailing,
"For its draught—he faints he dies.
"Pity, Lord! a mother's anguish,
"Close this pilgrimage of grief;
"Let me not behold him languish,
"Nor have power to yield relief.

"Cruel was the hand that turned us,
"Thus to wander in despair;
"Cruel was the hate that spurned us,
"Lord! in mercy hear my prayer!
"Ope the desert's hidden water
"To these vainly-searching eyes;
"Then shall Egypt's wretched daughter
"Bless the aid that Heaven supplies."

FRIENDSHIP WHICH NEVER SHALL FADE.

In the tempest of life when the wave and the gale,
Are around and above, if thy footing should fail,
If thine eye should grow dim, and thy caution depart,
Look aloft and be firm and be fearless of heart.

If the friend who embraced in prosperities glow,
With a smile for each joy and a tear for each wo,
Should betray thee; when sorrow like clouds are arrayed,
Look aloft to that friendship which never shall fade.

Should they who are dearest—the son of thy heart,
The wife of thy bosom, in sorrow depart,
Look aloft from the darkness and dust of the tomb,
To the soil where affection is ever in bloom.

And O! when death comes in terrors to cast,
His fears o'er the future, his pall o'er the past,
In that moment of darkness, with hope in thy heart
And a smile in thine eye, look aloft and depart.

CHARITY.

A poor wayfaring man of grief
Hath often crossed me on my way,
Who sued so humbly for relief
That I could never answer "nay,"
I had not power to ask his name,
Whither he went, or whence he came;
Yet there was something in his eye,
That won my love, I know not why.

Once when my scanty meal was spread,
He entered—not a word he spake;
Just perishing for want of bread;
I gave him all; he blessed it, brake
And ate,—but gave me part again—
Mine was an Angel's portion then;
For while I sped with eager haste,
That crust was manna to my taste.

I spied him where a fountain burst,
Clean from a rock—his strength was gone;
The heedless water mocked his thirst—
He heard it—saw it hurrying on;
I ran to raise the sufferer up;
Thrice from the stream he drained my cup,
Dipt, and returned it running o'er;
I drank, and never thirsted more.

Stripped, wounded, beaten, nigh to death,
I found him by the highway side;
I roused his pulse—brought back his breath,
Revived his spirit, and supplied
Wine, oil, refreshment—he was healed—
I had myself a wound concealed;
But from that hour forgot the smart,
And peace bound up my broken heart.

HYMN OF THE HEBREW MAID.

When Israel of the Lord beloved,
Out from the land of bondage came
Her father's God before her moved,
An awful guide in smoke and flame.

By day along the astonished lands
The cloudy pillar glided slow;
By night, Arabia's crimsoned sands
Returned the fiery pillar's glow.

There rose the choral hymn of praise,
And trump and timbrel answered keen,
And Zion's daughters poured their lays,
With priests' and warriors' voice between.
No portents now our foes amaze,
Forsaken Israel wanders lone;
Our fathers would not know thy ways,
And thou has left them to their own.

But present still, though now unseen,
When brightly shines the prosperous day,
Be thoughts of thee a cloudy screen,
To temper the deceitful ray.
And oh! when stoops on Judah's path,
In shade and storm the frequent night,
Be thou long-suffering, slow to wrath,
A burning and a shining light!

Our harps we left by Babel's streams
The tyrant's jest, the Gentiles' scorn;
No censer round our altar beams,
And mute are timbrel, trump, and horn.
But thou hast said, "The blood of goat,
The flesh of rams, I will not prize;
A contrite heart, an humble thought,
Are mine accepted sacrifice."

Sir Walter Scott.

THE STAR OF BETHLEHEM.

When marshalled on the nightly plain,
The glitt'ring host bestud the sky;
One star alone of all the train,
Can fix the sinner's wandering eye.

Hark! hark! to God the chorus breaks
From every host, from every gem;
But one alone the Savior speaks,
It is the Star of Bethlehem.

Once on the raging seas I rode,
The storm was loud, the night was dark,
The ocean yawned—and rudely blowed
The wind that tossed my found'ring bark.

Deep horrors then my vitals froze,
Death-struck—I ceased the tide to stem;
When suddenly a star arose,
It was the Star of Bethlehem.

It was my guide, my light, my all;
It bade my dark forebodings cease;
And through the storm, and danger's thrall,
It led me to the port of peace.

Now safely moored—my perils o'er,
I'll sing, first in night's diadem,
For ever and for evermore,
The Star!—the Star of Bethlehem!

Kirke White.

THE HEAVENLY JERUSALEM.

High in yonder realms of light,
Far above these lower skies,
Fair and exquisitely bright,
Heaven's unfading mansions rise;
Built of pure and massy gold,
Strong and durable are they;
Decked with gems of worth untold,
Subjected to no decay!

Glad within these blest abodes,
Dwell the raptured saints above,
Where no anxious care corrodes,
Happy in Emmanuel's love!
One, indeed, like us below,
Pilgrims in this vale of tears,
Torturing pain, and heavy wo,
Gloomy doubts, distressing fears ·

These, alas! full well they knew,
  Sad companions of their way;
Oft on them the tempest blew,
  Through the long and cheerless day!
Oft their vileness they deplored,
  Wills perverse and hearts untrue,
Grieved they could not love their Lord,
  Love him as they wished to do.

Oft the big unbidden tear,
  Stealing down the furrowed cheek,
Told, in eloquence sincere,
  Tales of wo they could not speak;
But these days of weeping o'er,
  Past this scene of toil and pain,
They shall feel distress no more,
  Never, never, weep again!

'Mid the chorus of the skies,
  'Mid the angelic lyres above,
Hark! their songs melodious rise,
  Songs of praise to Jesus' love!
Happy spirits! ye are fled,
  Where no grief can entrance find;
Lulled to rest the aching head,
  Soothed the anguish of the mind!

All is tranquil and serene,
  Calm and undisturbed repose;
There no cloud can intervene,
  There no angry tempest blows!
Every tear is wiped away,
  Sighs no more shall heave the breast;
Night is lost in endless day—
  Sorrow in eternal rest.—RAFLES.

THE DAY OF WRATH.

THE day of wrath, that dreadful day,
When heaven and earth shall pass away,
What power shall be the sinner's stay?
Whom shall he trust that dreadful day?

When shrivelling like a parched scroll,
The flaming heavens together roll;
When, louder yet, and yet more dread,
Swells the high trump that wakes the dead.

Oh, on that day, that wrathful day,
When man to judgment wakes from clay,
Be thou, O Christ! the sinner's stay,
Though heaven and earth shall pass away!
SIR WALTER SCOTT.

THE BURIAL ANTHEM.

BROTHER, thou art gone before us,
  And thy saintly soul is flown
Where tears are wiped from every eye,
  And sorrow is unknown.
From the burthen of the flesh,
  And from care and fear released,
Where the wicked cease from troubling,
  And the weary are at rest.

The toilsome way thou'st travelled o'er,
  And borne the heavy load,
But Christ hath taught thy languid feet
  To reach his blessed abode;
Thou'rt sleeping now, like Lazarus
  Upon his Father's breast,
Where the wicked cease from troubling,
  And the weary are at rest.

Sin can never taint thee now,
  Nor doubt thy faith assail,
Nor thy meek trust in Jesus Christ,
  And the Holy Spirit fail:
And there thou'rt sure to meet the good,
  Whom on earth thou lovedst best,
Where the wicked cease from troubling,
  And the weary are at rest.

"Earth to earth," and "dust to dust,"
  The solemn priest hath said,
So we lay the turf above thee now,
  And we seal thy narrow bed:
But thy spirit, brother, soars away
  Among the faithful blest,
Where the wicked cease from troubling,
  And the weary are at rest.—MILMAN

THE DAY OF JUDGMENT.

Lo! He comes, with clouds descending,
  Once for favored sinners slain,
Thousand, thousand saints attending,
  Swell the triumphs of his train;
Hallelujah!
Jesus now shall ever reign!

Every eye shall now behold him,
  Clothed in awful majesty;
Those who set at naught and sold him,
  Pierced and nailed him to the tree,
Deeply wailing,
Shall the great Messiah see!

Every island, sea, and mountain,
  Heaven and earth shall flee way;
All who hate Him must, confounded,
  Hear the trump proclaim the day,
"Come to judgment!
Come to judgment! Come away!"

Now, redemption, long expected,
  See in solemn pomp appear!
All his saints, by men rejected,
  Now shall meet him in the air!
Hallelujah!
See the day of God appear!

Answer thine own Bride and Spirit!
  Hasten, Lord, the general doom!
Promised glory to inherit,
  Take thy pining exiles home;
All creation
Travails, groans, and bids thee come.

Yea! Amen! Let all adore thee,
  High on thine exalted throne;
Savior! take the power and glory,
  Claim the kingdom for thine own!
O come quickly!
Hallelujah! Come, Lord, Come!

THE HOUR OF PRAYER.

CHILD, amid the flowers at play,
While the red light fades away;
Mother, with thine earnest eye,
Ever following silently;
Father, by the breeze of eve,
Called thy harvest work to leave:
Pray!—ere yet the dark hours be,
Lift the hand and bend the knee.

Traveller, in the stranger's land,
Far from thine own household band;
Mourner, haunted by the tone
Of a voice from this world gone;
Captive, in whose narrow cell
Sunshine hath not leave to dwell;
Sailor, on the darkening sea,
Lift the heart and bend the knee.

Warrior, that from battle won,
Breathest now at set of sun;
Woman, o'er the lowly slain,
Weeping on his burial plain;
Ye that triumph, ye that sigh,
Kindred by one holy tie;
Heaven's first star alike ye see—
Lift the heart and bend the knee.—HEMANS.

THE NATIVITY.

When Jordan hushed his waters still,
And silence slept on Zion hill;
When Bethlehem's shepherds through the night
Watched o'er their flocks by starry light;

Hark! from the midnight hills around,
A voice of more than mortal sound,
In distant hallelujahs stole,
Wild murm'ring o'er the raptured soul.

Then swift to every startled eye,
New streams of glory light the sky;
Heaven bursts her azure gates to pour
Her spirits to the midnight hour.

On wheels of light, on wings of flame,
The glorious hosts of Zion came;
High heaven with songs of triumph rung,
While thus they struck their harps and sung.

O Zion! lift thy raptured eye,
The long-expected hour is nigh
The joys of nature rise again,
The Prince of Salem comes to reign.

See, Mercy from her golden urn
Pours a rich stream to them that mourn;
Behold, she binds, with tender care,
The bleeding bosom of despair.

He comes, to cheer the trembling heart,
Bids Satan and his host depart;
Again the day-star gilds the gloom,
Again the bowers of Eden bloom!

O Zion! lift thy raptured eye,
The long expected hour is nigh;
The joys of nature rise again,
The Prince of Salem comes to reign.—Campbell.

GOD GLORIFIED IN ALL HIS WORKS.

The spacious firmament on high,
With all the blue ethereal sky,
And spangled heavens, a shining frame,
Their great Original proclaim.

Th' unwearied sun, from day to day,
Does his Creator's praise display,
And publishes to every land
The work of an Almighty hand.

Soon as the evening shades prevail,
The moon takes up the wondrous tale,
And nightly, to the list'ning earth,
Repeats the story of her birth;

While all the stars that round her burn,
And all the planets in their turn,
Confirm the tidings as they roll,
And spread the truth from pole to pole.

What though in solemn silence all
Move round the dark terrestrial ball,
What though nor voice nor minstrel sound
Among their radiant orbs be found:

With saints and angels they rejoice,
And utter forth their glorious voice;
For ever singing as they shine,
"The hand that made us is Divine!"—Addison.

THE RAINBOW.

When the floods of the deluge to ocean had rolled,
  And the green-mantled hills reappeared;
When the valleys unfolded their blossoms of gold,
And Noah, the patriarch, came forth from his hold,
  The voice of Jehovah was heard—
The voice of Jehovah brought tidings of bliss
To the world late entombed in the fearful abyss.

"The smoke of thine offering hath come up on high,
  Thou father of nations to be!
And now I my rainbow shall set in the sky,
When tempests are dark to thy terrified eye,
  That shall bring consolation to thee—
To thousands of thousands that after thee tread
The regions of life to the realms of the dead.

"It is for a sign that I never again
  With waters shall cover the earth;
And the birds in the arbors shall warble their strain,
And the cattle shall browse on the nourishing plain,
  And give to their progeny birth;
And die as they died by the curse that I spoke,
When my cov'nant of old by thy father was broke.

"And thou, Noah, thou art preserved for thy worth,
  To repeople the desolate world;
To the climes of the south, to the isles of the north,
To the east and the west, shall thy children go forth,
  With the white flags of ocean unfurled—
To publish my praises throughout every land,
And the judgments of vengeance that come from my hand.

"And seed-time and harvest shall duly be given
  To the hopes and the hands of mankind;
And summer and winter, and morning and even,
And the dew-drops of earth, and the light-rays of heaven,
  And the cloud, and the rain, and the wind,
While earth on her orbit is destined to run,
And give her green breast to the beams of the sun."
Knox.

THE COMMUNION OF SAINTS.

Not to the mount that burned with fire,
To darkness, tempest, and the sound
Of trumpet waxing higher and higher,
Nor voice of words that rent the ground,
While Israel heard, with trembling awe,
Jehovah thunder forth his law:

But to Mount Zion we are come,
The city of the living God,
Jerusalem, our heavenly home,
The courts by angel-legions trod,
Where meet, in everlasting love,
The church of the first-born above:

To God, the Judge of quick and dead,
The perfect spirits of the just,
Jesus, our great new-covenant Head,
The blood of sprinkling—from the dust,
That speaks better things than Abel's cries,
And pleads a Savior's sacrifice.

Oh, hearken to the healing voice,
That speaks from heaven in tones so mild!
To-day are life and death our choice,
To-day, through mercy reconciled,
Our all to God we yet may give;
Now let us hear his voice and live.
Montgomery.

THE EXEMPLARY WIFE.

O blest is he whose arms enfold
  A consort virtuous as fair!
Her price is far above the gold
  That worldly spirits love to share.
On her, as on a beauteous isle,
  Amid life's dark and stormy sea,
In all his trouble, all his toil,
  He rests with deep security.

Even in the night-watch, dark and lone,
  The distaff fills her busy hand;
Her husband in the gates is known
  Among the elders of the land;
Her household all delight to share
  The food and raiment she bestows—
Even she with a parent's care
  Regards their weakness and their woes.

Her pitying hand supplies the poor,
The widowed one, the orphan child,
Like birds assembled round her door,
When sweeps the winter tempest wild.
Her lips, with love and wisdom fraught,
Drop, like the honeycomb, their sweets;
The young are by her dictates taught,
The mourner her condolence meets.

Her lovely babes around her rise—
Fair scions of a holy stem!
And deeply shall her bosom prize
The blessings she receives from them.
Beauty is vain as summer bloom
To which a transient fate is given;
But hers awaits a lasting doom
In the eternal bowers of heaven.—Knox.

HYMN BEFORE THE SACRAMENT.

Bread of the world, in mercy broken!
Wine of the soul, in mercy shed!
By whom the words of life were spoken,
And in whose death our sins are dead!

Look on the heart by sorrow broken,
Look on the tears by sinners shed,
And be thy feast to us the token
That by thy grace our souls are fed!—Heber.

HYMN OF PRAISE.

Source of being, source of light,
With unfading beauties bright;
Thee, when morning greets the skies,
Blushing sweet with humid eyes;
Thee, when soft declining day
Sinks in purple waves away;
Thee, O parent, will I sing,
To thy feet my tribute bring!

Yonder azure vault on high,
Yonder blue, low, liquid sky;
Earth on its firm basis placed,
And with circling waves embraced;
All creating power confess,
All their mighty Maker bless;
Shaking nature with thy nod,
Earth and heaven confess their God.

Source of light, thou bidst the sun
On his burning axles run;
Stars like dust around him fly,
Strew the area of the sky;
Fills the queen of solemn night
From his vase her orb of light;
Lunar lustre, thus we see,
Solar virtue shines by thee.

Father, King, whose heavenly face
Shines serene upon our race;
Mindful of thy guardian care,
Slow to punish, prone to spare;
We thy majesty adore,
We thy well-known aid implore;
Not in vain thy aid we call,
Nothing want, for thou art all!—Wesley.

GOD VISIBLE IN HIS WORKS.

Above—below—where'er I gaze,
Thy guiding finger, Lord, I view.
Traced in the midnight planets' blaze,
Or glistening in the morning dew;
Whate'er is beautiful or fair,
Is but thine own reflection there.

I hear thee in the stormy wind,
That turns the ocean wave to foam;
Nor less thy wondrous power I find,
When summer airs around me roam;
The tempest and the calm declare
Thyself—for thou art everywhere.

I find thee in the noon of night,
And read thy name in every star
That drinks its splendor from the light
That flows from mercy's beaming car:
Thy footstool, Lord, each starry gem
Composes—not thy diadem.

And when the radiant orb of light
Hath tipped the mountain tops with gold,
Smote with the blaze my weary sight
Shrinks from the wonders I behold:
That ray of glory bright and fair,
Is but thy living shadow there.

Thine is the silent noon of night,
The twilight, eve—the dewy morn;
Whate'er is beautiful and bright,
Thine hands have fashioned to adorn:
Thy glory walks in every sphere,
And all things whisper, "God is here!"

A DOMESTIC SCENE.

'Twas early day—and sunlight streamed
Soft through a quiet room,
That hushed, but not forsaken seemed—
Still, but with naught of gloom;
For then, secure in happy age,
Whose hope is from above,
A father communed with the page
Of heaven's recorded love.

Pure fell the beam and meekly bright,
On his gray holy hair,
And touched the book with tenderest light
As if its shrine were there;
But oh! that patriarch's aspect shone
With something lovelier far—
A radiance, all the Spirit's own,
Caught not from sun or star.

Some word of light e'en then had met
His calm benignant eye,
Some ancient promise, breathing yet
Of immortality:
Some heart's deep language when the glow
Of quenchless faith survives,
For, every feature said—"I know
That my Redeemer lives."

And silent stood his children by,
Hushing their very breath,
Before the solemn sanctity
Of thought, o'er-sweeping death:
Silent—yet did not each young breast
With love and reverence melt?
Oh! blest be those fair girls—and blest
The home where God is felt.—Hemans.

THE SABBATH.

Lord of the sabbath and its light;
I hail thy hallowed day of rest;
It is my weary soul's delight,
The solace of my care-worn breast.

Its dewy morn—its glowing noon—
Its tranquil eve—its solemn night—
Pass sweetly; but they pass too soon,
And leave me saddened at their flight.

Yet sweetly as they glide along,
And hallowed though the calm they yield;
Transporting though their rapturous song,
And heavenly visions seem revealed:

My soul is desolate and drear,
My silent harp untuned remains;
Unless, my Savior, thou art near,
To heal my wounds and sooth my pains.

O ever, ever let me hail
Thy presence with thy day of rest!
Then will thy servant never fail
To deem thy sabbaths doubly blest.—East

A PRAYER TO JESUS.

WHEN our heads are bowed with wo,
When our bitter tears o'erflow;
When we mourn the lost, the dear,
Gracious Son of Mary hear!

Thou our throbbing flesh hast worn,
Thou our mortal griefs hast borne,
Thou hast shed the human tear;
Gracious son of Mary, hear!

When the sullen death-bell tolls
For our own departed souls;
When our final doom is near,
Gracious Son of Mary, hear!

Thou hast bowed the dying head;
Thou the blood of life hast shed;
Thou hast filled a mortal bier;
Gracious Son of Mary, hear!

When the heart is sad within,
With the thought of all its sin;
When the spirit shrinks with fear,
Gracious Son of Mary, hear!

Thou the shame, the grief, hast known,
Though the sins were not thine own,
Thou hast deigned their load to bear,
Gracious Son of Mary, hear!—HEBER.

THE REST OF THE GRAVE.

How still and peaceful is the grave!
Where, life's vain tumults past,
The appointed house, by Heaven's decree,
Receives us all at last.

The wicked there from troubling cease,
Their passions rage no more;
And there the weary pilgrim rests
From all the toils he bore.

There rest the prisoners, now released
From slavery's sad abode:
No more they hear the oppressor's voice,
Or dread the tyrant's rod.

There, servants, masters, small and great,
Partake the same repose;
And there, in peace, the ashes mix
Of those who once were foes.

All, levelled by the hand of Death,
Lie sleeping in the tomb;
Till God in judgment calls them forth,
To meet their final doom.

SATURDAY NIGHT.

AGAIN the week's dull labors close;
The sons of toil from toil repose;
And fast the evening gloom descends,
While home the weary peasant wends.
This night his eyes, in slumber sweet,
Shall droop their lids; to-morrow greet
A day of calm content and rest—
To Labor's aching limbs how blest!

Now, ere I seek my peaceful bed,
And on the pillow rest my head,
Oh, come, my soul, and wide display
The mercies of the week and day!
From danger who my frame hath kept,
While waking, and what time I slept?
Who hath my every want supplied,
And to my footsteps proved a guide?

Tis thou, my God!—to thee belong
Incense of praise, and hallowed song;
To Thee be all the glory given,
Of all my mercies under heaven.
From thee my daily bread and health,
Each comfort—all my spirit's wealth,
Have been derived; my sins alone,
And errings I can call my own.

Oh, when to-morrow's sun shall rise,
And light once more shall glad these eyes,
May I thy blessed Sabbath prove,
A day of holy rest and love.
May my Redeemer's praises claim
My constant thought; the Spirit's flame
Descend, my accents to inspire,
And fill my soul with rapture's fire.

And when the night of Death is come,
And I must slumber in the tomb,
Oh, then, my God, this faint heart cheer,
And far dispel the shades of fear,
And teach me, in thy strength, to tread
The path which leads me to the dead,
Assured, when life's hard toils are o'er,
Of rest with thee for evermore!—WALKER.

CHRIST A PRESENT HELP.

WHEN gathering clouds around I view,
And days are dark, and friends are few,
On Him I lean, who not in vain,
Experienced every human pain.
He sees my griefs, allays my fears,
And counts and treasures up my tears.

If aught should tempt my soul to stray
From heavenly wisdom's narrow way,
To fly the good I would pursue,
Or do the thing I would not do;
Still He, who felt temptation's power,
Shall guard me in that dangerous hour.

If wounded love my bosom swell,
Despised by those I prized too well;
He shall his pitying aid bestow,
Who felt on earth severer wo;
At once betrayed, denied, or fled,
By those who shared his daily bread.

When vexing thoughts within me rise,
And, sore dismayed, my spirit dies;
Yet He who once vouchsafed to bear
The sickening anguish of despair,
Shall sweetly sooth, shall gently dry,
The throbbing heart, the streaming eye.

When, mourning, o'er some stone I bend,
Which covers all that was a friend,
And from his voice, his hand, his smile,
Divides me for a little while;
Thou Savior, markst the tears I shed,
For thou didst weep o'er Lazarus dead.

And, oh, when I have safely past
Through every conflict but the last,
Still, still unchanging, watch beside
My painful bed—for thou hast died:
Then point to realms of cloudless day,
And wipe the latest tear away.—GRANT.

MARY MAGDALENE.

THERE is a tender sadness in that air,
While yet devotion lifts the soul above;
Mournful though calm, as rainbow-glories prove
The parting storm, it marks the past despair!
Heedless of gazers, once with flowing hair
She dried his tear-besprinkled feet, whose love,
Powerful alike to pardon and reprove,
Took from her aching heart its load of care,
Thenceforth nor time nor pain could e'er efface
Her Savior's pity; through all worldly scorn,
To her he had a glory and a grace,
Which made her humbly love and meekly mourn.
Till by his faithful care she reached the place—
Where his redeemed saints above all griefs are borne.
NOEL.

THE GERMAN WATCHMEN'S SONG.

Among the watchmen in Germany, a singular custom prevails, of chanting devotional hymns as well as songs of a national or amusing character, during the night. Of the former description of pieces, the following is a specimen, the several stanzas being chanted as the hours of the night are successively announced.

Hark! ye neighbors, and hear me tell—
Ten now strikes on the belfry bell!
Ten are the holy commandments given
To man below, from God in Heaven.

CHORUS.

Human watch from harm can't ward us,
God will watch and God will guard us;
He, through his eternal might,
Grant us all a blessed night.

Hark! ye neighbors, and hear me tell—
Eleven sounds on the belfry bell!
Eleven apostles of holy mind,
Taught the Gospel to mankind.
Human watch, &c.

Hark! ye neighbors, and hear me tell—
Twelve resounds from the belfry bell!
Twelve disciples to Jesus came,
Who suffered rebuke for their Savior's name,
Human watch, &c.

Hark! ye neighbors, and hear me tell—
One has pealed on the belfry bell!
One God above, one Lord indeed,
Who bears us forth in hour of need.
Human watch, &c.

Hark! ye neighbors, and hear me tell—
Two resounds from the belfry bell!
Two paths before mankind are free,
Neighbors choose the best for thee.
Human watch, &c.

Hark! ye neighbors, and hear me tell—
Three now sounds on the belfry bell!
Threefold reigns the Heavenly Host,
Father, Son and Holy Ghost!
Human watch, &c.

MISSIONARY HYMN.

From Greenland's icy mountains,
From India's coral strand,
Where Afric's sunny fountains
Roll down their golden sand;
From many an ancient river,
From many a balmy plain,
They call us to deliver
Their land from error's chain.

What though the spicy breezes
Blow soft on Ceylon's isle,
Though every prospect pleases,
And only man is vile;
In vain with lavish kindness,
The gifts of God are strown,
The heathen, in his blindness,
Bows down to wood and stone.

Shall we whose souls are lighted
With wisdom from on high,
Shall we to man benighted
The lamp of life deny?
Salvation! oh, salvation!
The joyful sound proclaim,
Till each remotest nation
Has learnt Messiah's name.

Waft, waft, ye winds, his story
And you, ye waters, roll;
Till like a sea of glory,
It spreads from pole to pole!
Till o'er our ransomed nature,
The Lamb for sinners slain,
Redeemer, King, Creator,
In bliss returns to reign.—Heber.

WHAT IS TIME?

I asked an aged man, a man of cares,
Wrinkled, and curved, and white with hoary hairs;
"Time is the warp of life," he said, "O tell
The young, the fair, the gay, to weave it well!"

I asked the ancient venerable dead,
Sages who wrote, and warriors who bled:
From the cold grave a hollow murmur flowed,
"Time sowed the seeds we reap in this abode!"

I asked a dying sinner, ere the stroke
Of ruthless death life's "golden bowl had broke;"
I asked him, What is time? "Time," he replied,
"I've lost it, Ah, the treasure!" and he died!

I asked the golden sun and silver spheres,
Those bright chronometers of days and years;
They answered, "Time is but a meteor's glare,"
And bade me for Eternity prepare.

I asked the seasons, in their annual round
Which beautify, or desolate the ground;
And they replied (no oracle more wise),
"'Tis folly's blank, and wisdom's highest prize."

I asked a spirit lost, but, O the shriek
That pierced my soul! I shudder while I speak!
It cried, "a particle! a speck! a mite
Of endless years, duration infinite!"

Of things inanimate, my dial I
Consulted, and it made me this reply,
"Time is the season fair of living well
The path to glory, or the path to hell."

I asked my Bible, and methinks it said,
"Thine is the present hour, the past is fled;
Live! live to-day! to-morrow never yet
On any human being rose or set!"

I asked old father Time himself at last;
But in a moment he flew swiftly past;
His chariot was a cloud, the viewless wind
His noiseless steeds, that left no trace behind.

I asked the mighty Angel, who shall stand
One foot on sea, and one on solid land;
"By heavens, great King, I swear the mystery's o'er!
Time was," he cried,—"but Time shall be no more!"
Marsden.

THE BETTER LAND.

I hear thee speak of the better land,
Thou call'st its children a happy band;
Mother! oh, where is that radiant shore—
Shall we not seek it and weep no more?
Is it where the flower of the orange blows,
And the fire-flies dance through the myrtle boughs?
"Not there, not there, my child."

Is it where the feathery palm-trees rise,
And the date grows ripe under sunny skies,
Or midst the green islands of glittering seas,
Where fragrant forests perfume the breeze,
And strange bright birds on their starry wings,
Bear the rich hues of all glorious things?
"Not there, not there, my child."

Is it far away in some region old,
Where the rivers wander o'er sands of gold—
Where the burning rays of the ruby shine,
And the diamond lights up the secret mine,
And the pearl gleams forth from the coral strand—
Is it there, sweet mother, that better land?
"Not there, not there, my child.

"Eye hath not seen it, my gentle boy!
Ear hath not heard its deep songs of joy,
Dreams can not picture a world so fair,
Sorrow and death may not enter there;
Time doth not breathe on its fadeless bloom,
For beyond the clouds, and beyond the tomb,
It is there, it is there, my child!"—Hemans.

THE SONGS AND BALLADS

OF

CHARLES DIBDIN.

POOR JACK.

Go patter to lubbers and swabs, do ye see,
'Bout danger, and fear, and the like;
A tight water-boat and good sea-room give me,
And it ent to a little I'll strike;
Though the tempest top-gallant masts smack smooth should smite,
And shiver each splinter of wood,
Clear the wreck, stow the yards, and bouse everything tight,
And under reefed foresail we'll scud:
Avast! nor don't think me a milksop so soft
To be taken for trifles aback;
For they say there's a Providence sits up aloft,
To keep watch for the life of poor Jack!

I heard our good chaplain palaver one day
About souls, heaven, mercy, and such;
And, my timbers! what lingo he'd coil and belay,
Why, 'twas just all as one as High Dutch:
For he said how a sparrow can't founder, d'ye see,
Without orders that come down below;
And a many fine things that proved clearly to me
That Providence takes us in tow:
"For," says he, "do you mind me, let storms e'er so oft
Take the topsails of sailors aback,
There's a sweet little cherub that sits up aloft,
To keep watch for the life of poor Jack!"

I said to our Poll, for, d'ye see, she would cry,
When last we weighed anchor for sea—
"What argufies sniv'ling and piping your eye?
Why, what a damned fool you must be!
Can't you see the world's wide, and there's room for us all,
Both for seamen and lubbers ashore?
And if to old Davy I should go, friend Poll,
You never will hear of me more:
What then? all's a hazard: come, don't be so soft;
Perhaps I may laughing come back,
For, d'ye see, there's a cherub sits smiling aloft,
To keep watch for the life of poor Jack!"

D'ye mind me, a sailor should be every inch
All as one as a piece of the ship,
And with her brave the world without offering to flinch,
From the moment the anchor's a-trip.
As for me, in all weathers, all times, sides, and ends,
Naught's a trouble from duty that springs,
For my heart is my Poll's, and my rhino's my friend's,
And as for my life, 'tis the king's:
Even when my time comes, ne'er believe me so soft
As for grief to be taken aback,
For the same little cherub that sits up aloft
Will look out a good berth for poor Jack

THE GOOD SHIP THE KITTY.

I sailed in the good ship the Kitty,
With a smart blowing gale and rough sea;
Left my Polly, the lads call so pretty,
Safe here at an anchor—Yo, Yea!

She blubbered salt tears when we parted,
And cried, "Now be constant to me!"
I told her not to be down-hearted,
So up went the anchor—Yo, Yea!

And from that time, no worse nor no better,
I've thought on just nothing but she;
Nor could grog nor flip make me forget her,
She's my best bower-anchor—Yo, Yea!

When the wind whistled larboard and starboard,
And the storm came on weather and lee,
The hope I with her should be harbored
Was my cable and anchor—Yo, Yea!

And yet, my boys, would you believe me?
I returned with no rhino from sea;
Mistress Polly would never receive me,
So again I heaved anchor—Yo, Yea!

THE JOLLY YOUNG WATERMAN.

And did not you hear of a jolly young waterman,
Who at Blackfriars bridge used for to ply?
He feathered his oars with such skill and dexterity,
Winning each heart, and delighting each eye.
He looked so neat and rowed so steadily,
The maidens all flocked to his boat so readily;
And he eyed the young rogues with so charming an air
That this waterman ne'er was in want of a fare.

What sights of fine folks he rowed in his wherry,
'Twas cleaned out so nice and so painted withal:
He was always first oars when the fine city ladies
In a party to Ranelagh went, or Vauxhall.
And oftentimes would they be giggling and leering,
But 'twas all one to Tom their gibing and jeering:
For loving or liking he little did care,
For this waterman ne'er was in want of a fare.

And yet but to see how strangely things happen,
As he rowed along thinking of nothing at all,
He was plied by a damsel so lovely and charming,
That she smiled, and so straightway in love he did fall.
And would this young damsel but banish his sorrow,
He'd wed her to-night, before to-morrow.
And how should this waterman ever know care,
When he's married and never in want of a fare?

FAREWELL AND RETURN.

THOUGH hard the valiant soldier's life,
They some sweet moments know;
Joy ne'er was yet unmixed with strife,
Or happiness with wo.
'Tis hard, when friend, when children, wife,
Reluctant from him part,
And fancy paints the muffled drum,
And plaintive fife,
And the loud volley o'er the grave,
That sounds sad requiems to the brave;
All this he hears,
And calms their fears
With smiles, though horror's in his heart.
But when the joyful hour shall come,
To bring him home at last,
How sweet his constant wife to greet,
His children, friends,
And in their circling arms to find amends
For all his sufferings past.

'Tis hard when, desolation spread,
Death whirls the rapid car;
And those invaded hear, and dread,
The thunder of the war.
Ah! then, indeed, friends, children, wife,
Have ye true cause to fear;
Too soon, alas! the muffled drum,
The mournful fife,
And the loud volley o'er the grave,
Shall sound sad requiems to the brave,
While those alive
Faint joy revive,
And blend hope's smile with pity's tear
But when the joyful hour shall come,
To bring him home at last,
How sweet his constant wife to greet,
His children, friends,
And in their circling arms to find amends
For all his sufferings past!

POOR TOM!

THEN farewell, my trim-built wherry!
Oars, and coat, and badge, farewell!
Never more at Chelsea ferry
Shall your Thomas take a spell.

But, to hope and peace a stranger,
In the battle's heat I'll go,
Where, exposed to every danger,
Some friendly ball may lay me low.

Then, mayhap, when homeward steering
With the news, my messmates come,
Even you, the story hearing,
With a sigh may cry—"Poor Tom!"

THE BUSY CREW.

THE busy crew, their sails unbending,
The ship in harbor safe arrived,
Jack Oakum, all his perils ending,
Had made the port where Kitty lived.

His rigging, no one dare attack it;
Tight fore and aft, above, below;
Long-quartered shoes, check shirt, blue jacket,
With trousers like the driven snow.

His honest heart, with pleasure glowing,
He flew like lightning to the side;
Scarce had he been a boat's length rowing,
Before his Kitty he espied.

A flowing pennant gayly fluttered
From her neat-made hat of straw;
Red were her cheeks when first she uttered
It was "her sailor" that she saw.

And now the gazing crew surround her,
While, secure from all alarms,
Swift as a ball from a nine-pounder,
They dart into each other's arms.

THE SIGNAL TO ENGAGE.

THE signal to engage shall be
A whistle and a hollow;
Be one and all but firm, like me,
And conquest soon will follow.
You, Gunnel, keep the helm in hand—
Thus, thus, boys, steady, steady,
Till right ahead you see the land,
Then, soon as we are ready,
The signal, &c.

Keep, boys, a good look-out, d'ye hear!
'Tis for your country's honor;
Just as you brought your lower tier
Broadside to bear upon her,
The signal, &c.

All hands then, lads, the ship to clear;
Load all your guns and mortars;
Silent as death th' attack prepare:
And, when you're all at quarters,
The signal, &c.

JACK RATLIN.

JACK RATLIN was the ablest seaman,
None like him could hand, reef, and steer;
No dangerous toil but he'd encounter
With skill, and in contempt of fear.
In fight, a lion: the battle ended,
Meek as the bleating lamb he'd prove:
Thus Jack had manners, courage, merit;
Yet did he sigh—and all for love.

The song, the jest, the flowing liquor,
For none of these had Jack regard:
He, while his messmates were carousing,
High sitting on the pendant-yard,
Would think upon his fair one's beauties,
Swear never from such charms to rove;
That truly he'd adore them living,
And, dying, sigh—to end his love.

The same express the crew commanded
Once more to view their native land,
Among the rest, brought Jack some tidings—
Would it had been his love's fair hand!
Oh, fate! her death defaced the letter;
Instant his pulse forgot to move;
With quiv'ring lips, and eyes uplifted,
He heaved a sigh—and died for love!

YO, HEAVE, HO!

THE boatswain calls, the wind is fair,
The anchor heaving,
Our sweethearts leaving,
We to duty must repair,
Where our stations well we know.
Cast off halliards from the cleets,
Stand by well, clear all the sheets;
Come, my boys,
Your handspikes poise,
And give one general huzza!
Yet sighing, as you pull away,
For the tears ashore that flow:
To the windlass let us go,
With yo, heave, ho!

The anchor coming now apeak,
Lest the ship, striving,
Be on it driving,
That we the tap'ring yards must seek,
And back the foretop-sail well we know.
A pleasing duty! From aloft
We faintly see those charms, where oft,
When returning,
With passion burning,
We fondly gaze, those eyes that seem,
In parting, with big tears to stream.
But come! lest ours as fast should flow,
To the windlass once more go,
With yo, heave, ho!

Now the ship is under weigh,
The breeze so willing
The canvass filling,
The pressed triangle cracks the stay,
So taught to haul the sheet we know.
And now in trim we gayly sail,
The massy beam receives the gale;
While freed from duty,
To his beauty
(Left on the less'ning shore afar)
A fervent sigh heaves every tar;
To thank those tears for him that flow,
That from his true-love he should go,
With yo, heave, ho!

WHEN LAST FROM THE STRAITS.

When last from the Straits we had fairly cast anchor,
I went Bonny Kitty to hail,
With quintables stored, for our voyage was a spanker,
And bran new was every sail:

But I knew well enough how, with words sweet as honey,
They trick us poor tars of our gold,
And when the sly gipsies have fingered the money,
The bag they poor Jack give to hold.

So I chased her, d'ye see, my lads, under false colors,
Swore my riches were all at an end,
That I'd sported away all my good-looking dollars,
And borrowed my togs of a friend.

O then, had you seen her—no longer "My honey"—
'Twas "Varlet, audacious, and bold,
Begone from my sight! now you've spent all your money,
For Kitty the bag you may hold."

With that I took out double handfuls of shiners,
And scornfully bade her good-by;
'Twould have done your heart good, had you then seen her fine airs,
How she'd leer, and she'd sob, and she'd sigh;

But I stood well the broadside; while jewel and honey
She called me, I put up the gold,
And bearing away, as I sacked all the money,
Left the bag for ma'am Kitty to hold.

LIFE'S TROUBLED SEA.

This life is like a troubled sea,
Where, helm a-weather or a-lee,
The ship will neither stay nor wear,
But drives, of every rock in fear.

All seamanship in vain we try,
We can not keep her steadily;
But just as fortune's wind may blow,
The vessel's tosticated to and fro;
Yet, come but love on board,
Our hearts with pleasure stored,
No storm can overwhelm,
Still blows in vain
The hurricane,
While love is at the helm.

THE HEART OF A TAR.

Yet though I've no fortune to offer,
I've something to put on a par;
Come, then, and accept of my proffer,
'Tis the kind honest heart of a tar.

Ne'er let such a trifle as this is,
Girls, be to my pleasure a bar,
You'll be rich, though 'tis only in kisses,
With the kind honest heart of a tar.

Besides, I am none of your ninnies;
The next time I come from afar
I'll give you a lapful of guineas,
With the kind honest heart of a tar.

Your lords, with such fine baby faces,
That strut in a garter and star,
Have they, under their tambour and laces,
The kind honest heart of a tar?

I've this here to say, now, and mind it,
If love, that no hazard can mar,
You are seeking, you'll certainly find it—
In the kind honest heart of a tar.

EACH BULLET HAS ITS COMMISSION.

What argufies pride and ambition?
Soon or late death will take us in tow:
Each bullet has got its commission,
And when our time's come we must go
Then be merry—hang pain and sorrow,
The halter was made for the neck;
He that's now 'live and lusty, to-morrow
Perhaps may be stretched on the deck.

There was little Tom Linstock of Dover
Got killed, and left Polly in pain;
Poll cried, but her grief was soon over,
And then she got married again.
Then be merry, &c.

Jack Junk was ill used by Bet Crocker,
And so took to guzzling the stuff,
Till he tumbled in old Davy's locker,
And there he got liquor enough.
Then be merry, &c.

For our prize-money then to the proctor,
Take of joy, while 'tis going, our freak;
For what argufies calling the doctor
When the anchor of life is a-peak?
Then be merry, &c.

SWEETHEARTS AND WIVES.

'Twas Saturday night, the twinkling star
Shone on the rippling sea;
No duty called the jovial tars,
The helm was lashed a-lee;
The ample can adorned the board—
Prepared to see it out,
Each gave the girl that he adored,
And pushed the can about.

Cried honest Tom, my Peg I'll toast,
A frigate neat and trim,
All jolly Portsmouth's favorite boast;
I'd venture life and limb—
Sail seven long years, and ne'er see land,
With dauntless heart and stout,
So tight a vessel to command;
Then push the can about.

I'll give, cried little Jack, my Poll,
Sailing in comely state,
Top-ga'nt sails set, she is so tall,
She looks like a first-rate;
Ah! would she take her Jack in tow,
A voyage for life throughout,
No better berth I'd wish to know;
Then push the can about.

I'll give, cried I, my charming Nan,
Trim, handsome, neat, and tight;
With joy so fine a ship to man,
She is my heart's delight!
So well she bears the storms of life,
I'd sail the world throughout,
Brave ev'ry toil for such a wife:
Then push the can about.

Thus to describe Poll, Peg, or Nan,
Each his best manner tried,
Till, summoned by the empty can,
They to their hammocks hied;
Yet still did they their vigils keep,
Though the huge can was out,
For, in soft visions, gentle sleep
Still pushed the can about.

THE SOLDIER'S GRAVE.

Of all sensations pity brings
  To proudly swell the ample heart,
From which the willing sorrow springs,
  In others' wo that bears a part;
Of all sad sympathy's delights,
  The manly dignity of grief,
A joy in mourning that excites,
  And gives the anxious mind relief:
Of these would you the feeling know,
  Most gen'rous, noble, greatly brave,
That ever taught a heart to glow—
  'Tis the tear that bedews a soldier's grave.

For hard and painful is his lot,
  Let dangers come, he braves them all;
Valiant perhaps to be forgot,
  Or undistinguished doomed to fall:
Yet wrapt in conscious worth secure,
  The world that now forgets his toil
He views from a retreat obscure,
  And quits it with a willing smile.
Then, trav'ller, one kind drop bestow—
  'Twere graceful pity, nobly brave;
Naught ever taught the heart to glow
  Like the tear that bedews a soldier's grave.

SATURDAY NIGHT.

'Tis said we vent'rous die-hards, when we leave the shore,
    Our friends should mourn,
    Lest we return
To bless their sight no more;
  But this is all a notion
    Bold Jack can't understand,
  Some die upon the ocean,
    And some upon the land.
      Then since 'tis clear,
      Howe'er we steer,
  No man's life's under his command;
      Let tempests howl,
      And billows roll,
    And dangers press:
  Of those, in spite, there are some joys
    Us jolly tars to bless,
  For Saturday night still comes, my boys,
    To drink to Poll and Bess.

One seaman hands the sails, another heaves the log,
    The purser swops
    Our pay for slops,
The landlord sells us grog:
  Then each man to his station,
    To keep life's ship in trim:
  What argufies no ration?
    The rest is all a whim.
      Cheerly, my hearts!
      Then play your parts,
  Boldly resolved to sink or swim;
      The mighty surge
      May ruin urge,
    And danger press:
      Of these in spite, &c.

For all the world just like the ropes aboard a ship
    Each man's rigged out,
    A vessel stout,
To take for life a trip.
  The shrouds, the stays, the braces,
    Are joys, and hopes, and fears;
  The halliards, sheets, and traces,
    Still, as each passion veers,
      And whim prevails,
      Direct the sails,
  As on the sea of life he steers.
      Then let the storm
      Heaven's face deform,
    And dangers press:
      Of these in spite, &c.

BONNY KATE.

The wind was hushed, the fleecy wave
Scarcely the vessel's sides could lave,
When in the mizen-top his stand
Tom Clueline, taking, spied the land.
Oh, sweet reward for all his toil!
Once more he views his native soil—
Once more he thanks indulgent Fate,
That brings him to his bonny Kate.

Soft as the sighs of Zephyr flow,
Tender and plaintive as her wo,
Serene was the attentive eve,
That heard Tom's bonny Kitty grieve.
"O what avails," cried she, "my pain?
He's swallowed in the greedy main;
Ah, never shall I welcome home,
With tender joy, my honest Tom!"

Now high upon the faithful shroud,
The land awhile that seemed a cloud,
While objects from the mist arise,
A feast presents Tom's longing eyes.
A riband near his heart which lay,
Now see him on his hat display,
The given sign to show that Fate
Had brought him safe to bonny Kate.

Near to a cliff, whose heights command
A prospect of the shelly strand,
While Kitty Fate, and Fortune, blamed,
Sudden with rapture she exclaimed,
"But see, oh Heaven! a ship in view—
My Tom appears among the crew;
The pledge he swore to bring safe home
Streams in his hat—'tis honest Tom!"

What now remains were easy told;
Tom comes, his pockets lined with gold;
Now rich enough no more to roam,
He serves his native land at home;
Recounts each toil, and shows each scar,
While Kitty and her constant tar
With rev'rence teach to bless their fates
Young honest Toms and Bonny Kates.

BEN BACKSTAY.

Ben Backstay loved the gentle Anna,
  Constant as purity was she,
Her honey words, like succ'ring manna,
  Cheered him each voyage he made to sea
One fatal morning saw them parting,
  While each other's sorrow dried,
They, by the tear that then was starting,
  Vowed to be constant till they died.

At distance from his Anna's beauty,
  While howling winds the sky deform,
Ben sighs, and well performs his duty,
  And braves, for love, the frightful storm.
Alas, in vain! The vessel battered,
  On a rock splitting, opened wide;
While, lacerated, torn, and shattered,
  Ben thought of Anna, sighed, and died.

The semblance of each charming feature
  That Ben had worn around his neck,
Where art stood substitute for nature,
  A tar, his friend, saved from the wreck.
In fervent hope, while Anna, burning,
  Blushed as she wished to be a bride,
The portrait came—joy turned to mourning—
  She saw, grew pale, sunk down, and died.

LITTLE BEN.

Resplendent gleamed the ample moon,
  Reflected on the glitt'ring lee,
The bell proclaimed night's awful noon,
  And scarce a ripple shook the sea,
When thus for sailors, nature's care,
  What education has denied,
Are of strong sense, a bounteous share,
  By observation well supplied

While thus, in bold and honest guise,
For wisdom moved his tongue,
Drawing from reason, comfort's drop,
In truth and fair reflection wise,
Right cheerfully sung
Little Ben that kept his watch in the main-top.

Why should the hardy tar complain?
'Tis certain true he weathers more,
From dangers on the roaring main,
Than lazy lubbers do ashore.
Ne'er let the noble mind despair,
Though roaring seas run mountains high;
All things are built with equal care,
First-rate, or wherry, man, or fly.
If there's a Power that never errs,
And certainly 'tis so—
For honest hearts what comforts drop—
As well as kings and emperors,
Why not take in tow
Little Ben that keeps his watch in the main-top?

What though to distant climes I roam,
Far from my darling Nancy's charms,
The sweeter is my welcome home,
To blissful moorings in her arms.
Perhaps she on that sober moon
A lover's observation takes,
And longs that little Ben may soon
Relieve that heart which sorely aches.
Ne'er fear; that power that never errs,
That guards all things below—
For honest hearts what comforts drop—
As well as kings and emperors,
Will surely take in tow
Little Ben that keeps his watch in the main-top.

THE SAILOR'S MAXIM.

Of us tars 'tis reported again and again,
That we sail round the world, yet know nothing of men;
And, if this assertion is made with a view
To prove sailors know naught of men's follies, 'tis true.
How should Jack practise treachery, disguise, or foul art,
In whose honest face you may read his fair heart?
Of that maxim still ready example to give,
Better death earned with honor than ignobly to live.

How can he wholesome Truth's admonitions defy,
On whose manly brow never sat a foul lie?
Of the fair-born protector, how Virtue offend?
To a foe how be cruel? how ruin a friend?
If danger he risk in professional strife,
There his honor is safe, though he venture his life;
Of that maxim still ready example to give,
Better death earned with honor than ignobly to live.

But to put it at worst, from fair truth could he swerve,
And betray the kind friend he pretended to serve,
While snares laid with craft his fair honor trepan,
Man betray him to error, himself but a man:
Should repentance and shame to his aid come too late,
Wonder not if in battle he rush on his fate;
Of that maxim still ready example to give.
Better death earned with honor than ignobly to live.

THE ANCHOR APEAK.

I be one of they sailors who think 'tis no lie,
That for every wherefore of life there's a why,
That fortune's strange weather, a calm or a squall,
Our berths, good or bad, are chalked out for us all;
That the stays and the braces of life will be found
To be some of 'em rotten, and some of 'em sound;
That the good we should cherish, the bad never seek,
For death will too soon bring each anchor apeak.

When astride on the yard the top-lifts they let go,
And I comed, like a shot, plump among 'em below,
Why I cotched at a halliard, and jumped upon deck,
And so broke my fall to save breaking my neck;
Just like your philosophers, for all their jaw,
Who less than a rope gladly catch at a straw;
Thus the good we should cherish, the bad never seek,
For death will too soon bring each anchor apeak.

Why, now, that there cruise that we made off the Banks,
Where I peppered the foe, and got shot for my thanks,
What then? She soon struck; and though crippled on shore,
And laid up to refit, I had shiners galore,
At length live and looking I tried the false main,
And to get more prize-money got shot at again;
Thus the good we should cherish, the bad never seek.
For death will too soon bring each anchor apeak.

Then just as it comes take the bad with the good;
One man's spoon's made of silver, another's of wood;
What's poison for one man's another man's balm,
Some are safe in a storm, and some lost in a calm;
Some are rolling in riches, some not worth a sous,
To-day we eat beef, and to-morrow lobs-scouse;
Thus the good we should cherish, the bad never seek
For death will too soon bring each anchor apeak

THE SOLDIER'S ADIEU.

Adieu, adieu, my only life!
My honor calls me from thee;
Remember thou'rt a soldier's wife,
Those tears but ill become thee:
What though by duty I am called
Where thund'ring cannons rattle,
Where Valor's self might stand appalled,
When on the wings of thy dear love
To heaven above
Thy fervent orisons are flown,
The tender prayer
Thou putt'st up there
Shall call a guardia[illegible]vn
To watch me in the bat[illegible]

My safety thy fair truth shall be,
As sword and buckler serving,
My life shall be more dear to me,
Because of thy preserving;
Let perils come, let horror threat,
Let thund'ring cannons rattle,
I'll fearless seek the conflict's heat,
Assured, when on the wings of love,
To heaven above, &c.

Enough; with that benignant smile
Some kindred god inspired thee,
Who knew thy bosom void of guile,
Who wondered, and admired thee;
I go assured, my life, adieu!
Though thund'ring cannons rattle,
Though murd'ring carnage stalk in view
When, on the wings of thy true love,
To heaven above, &c.

SOLDIER DICK.

Why, don't you know me by my scars?
I'm soldier Dick, come from the wars;
Where many a head without a hat
Crowds honor's bed—but what of that?
Beat drums, play fifes, 'tis glory calls,
What argufies who stands or falls?
Lord, what should one be sorry for?
Life's but the fortune of the war:
Then rich or poor, or well or sick,
Still laugh and sing shall soldier Dick.

I used to look two ways at once—
A bullet hit me on the sconce,
And dowsed my glim: d'ye think I'd wince?
Why, Lord, I've never squinted since.
Beat drums, &c.

Some distant keep from war's alarms,
For fear of wooden legs and arms,
While others die safe in their beds
Who all their lives had wooden heads.
Beat drums, &c.

Thus gout or fever, sword or shot,
Or something—sends us all to pot:
That we're to die, then, do not grieve,
But let's be merry while we live.
Beat drums, &c.

THE TAR FOR ALL WEATHERS.

I SAILED from the Downs in the Nancy,
My jib how she smacked through the breeze!
She's a vessel as tight to my fancy
As ever sailed on the salt seas.
So adieu to the white cliffs of Dover,
Our girls, and our dear native shore!
For if some hard rock we should split on,
We shall never see them any more.
But sailors were born for all weathers,
Great guns let it blow high or low,
Our duty keeps us to our tethers,
And where the gale drives we must go.

When we entered the Gut of Gibraltar,
I verily thought she'd have sunk,
For the wind so began for to alter,
She yaw'd just as thof she was drunk.
The squall tore the mainsail to shivers,
Helm a-wether the hoarse boatswain cries;
Brace the foresail athwart; see she quivers,
As through the rough tempest she flies.
But sailors, &c.

The storm came on thicker and faster,
As black just as pitch was the sky,
When truly a doleful disaster
Befell three poor sailors and I.
Ben Buntline, Sam Shroud, and Dick Handsail,
By a blast that came furious and hard,
Just while we were furling the mainsail,
Were every soul swept from the yard.
But sailors, &c.

Poor Ben, Sam, and Dick cried peccavi;
As for I, at the risk of my neck,
While they sank down in peace to old Davy,
Caught a rope and so landed on deck.
Well what would you have? We were stranded,
And out of a fine jolly crew
Of three hundred that sailed, never landed
But I and, I think, twenty-two.
But sailors, &c.

After thus we at sea had miscarried,
Another guess way set the wind,
For homeward I came, and got married
To a lass that was comely and kind.
But whether for joy or vexation,
We know not for what we were born
Perhaps I may find a kind station,
Perhaps I may touch at Cape Horn.
For sailors, &c.

HAPPY JERRY.

I WAS the pride of all the Thames,
My name was natty Jerry,
The best of smarts and flashy dames
I've carried in my wherry:
For then no mortal soul like me
So merrily did jog it;
I loved my wife and friend, d'ye see,
And won the prize of Doggett:
In coat and badge, so neat and spruce,
I rowed, all blithe and merry,
And every waterman did use
To call me happy Jerry.

But times soon changed—I went to sea;
My wife and friend betrayed me,
And in my absence treacherously
Some pretty frolics played me:
Returned, I used them like a man,
But still, 'twas so provoking,
I never could enjoy the can,
Nor even fancy smoking;
In tarnished badge, and coat so queer,
No longer blithe and merry,
Old friends now passed me with a sneer,
And called me Dismal Jerry.

At sea, as with a dangerous wound,
I lay under the surgeons,
Two friends each help I wanted found
In every emergence:
Soon after my sweet friend and wife
Into this mess had brought me,
These two kind friends who saved my life,
In my misfortune sought me:
We're come, cried they, that once again
In coat and badge so merry,
Your kind old friends, the watermen,
May hail you Happy Jerry.

I'm Peggy, once your soul's desire,
To whom you proved a rover,
Who since that time, in man's attire,
Have sought you the world over:
And I, cried t'other, am that Jack,
When boys, you used so badly,
Though now the best friend to your back—
Then prithee look not sadly.
Few words are be t: I seized their hands,
My grateful heart grew merry—
And now in love and friendship's bands
I'm once more Happy Jerry.

TACK AND TACK.

ADIEU, my gallant sailor, obey thy duty's call,
Though false the sea, there's truth ashore;
Till nature is found changing, thou'rt sure of constant Poll
And yet, as now we sever,
Ah, much I fear that never
Shall I, alas, behold thee more!

Jack kissed her, hitched his trousers, and hied him to begone,
Weighed anchor, and lost sight of shore:
Next day a brisk sou'wester a heavy gale brought on—
Adieu, cried Jack, for ever,
For much I fear that never
Shall I, sweet Poll, behold you more!

Poll heard that to the bottom was sunk her honest tar,
And for a while lamented sore;
At length, cried she, I'll marry; what should I tarry for?
I may lead apes for ever,
Jack's gone, and never, never
Shall I, alas, behold him more!

Jack, safe and sound returning, sought out his faithful Poll:
Think you, cried she, that false I swore?
I'm constant still as ever, 'tis nature's changed, that's all;
And thus we part for ever,
For never, sailor, never,
Shall I behold you more!

If, as you say, that nature like winds can shift and veer,
About ship for a kinder shore:
I heard the trick you played me, and so, d'ye see, my dear,
To a kind heart for ever
I've spliced myself—so never
Shall I, false Poll, behold you more.

TRUE-HEARTED SAILOR.

JACK dances and sings, and is always content,
In his vows to his lass he'll ne'er fail her;
His anchor's a-trip when his money's all spent—
And this is the life of a sailor.

Alert in his duty, he readily flies
Where the winds the tired vessel are flinging;
Though sunk to the sea-gods, or tossed to the skies,
Still Jack is found working and singing.

'Longside of an enemy, boldly and brave,
He'll with broadside on broadside regale her;
Yet he'll sigh to the soul o'er that enemy's grave,
So noble's the mind of a sailor.

Let cannons roar loud, burst their sides let the bombs,
Let the winds a dread hurricane rattle;
The rough and the pleasant he takes as it comes,
And laughs at the storm and the battle.

In a fostering Power while Jack puts his trust,
As Fortune comes, smiling he'll hail her;
Resigned, still, and manly—since what must be must—
And this is the mind of a sailor.

Though careless and headlong, if danger should press,
And ranked 'mongst the free list of rovers,
Yet he'll melt into tears at a tale of distress,
And prove the most constant of lovers.

To rancor unknown, to no passion a slave,
Nor unmanly, nor mean, nor a railer,
He's gentle as mercy, as fortitude brave—
And this is a true hearted sailor.

GREAVING'S A FOLLY.

SPANKING Jack was so comely, so pleasant, so jolly,
Though winds blew great guns, still he'd whistle and sing,
For Jack loved his friend, and was true to his Molly,
And, if honor gives greatness, was great as a king.
One night as we drove with two reefs in the main-sail,
And the scud came on low'ring upon a lee-shore,
Jack went up aloft for to hand the top-g'ant-sail—
A spray washed him off, and we ne'er saw him more:
But grieving's a folly,
Come let us be jolly;
If we've troubles on sea, boys, we've pleasures on shore.

Whiffling Tom still of mischief, or fun in the middle,
Through life in all weathers at random would jog;
He'd dance, and he'd sing, and he'd play on the fiddle,
And swig with an air his allowance of grog:
'Longside of a Don, in the Terrible frigate,
As yard-arm and yard-arm we lay off the shore,
In and out whiffling Tom did so caper and jig it,
That his head was shot off, and we ne'er saw him more:
But grieving's a folly, &c.

Bonny Ben was to each jolly messmate a brother,
He was manly and honest, good-natured and free;
If ever one tar was more true than another
To his friend and his duty, that sailor was he:
One day with the davit to weigh the kedge-anchor,
Ben went in the boat on a bold craggy shore—
He overboard tipped, when a shark and a spanker
Soon nipped him in two, and we ne'er saw him more:
But grieving's a folly, &c.

But what of it all, lads? shall we be downhearted
Because that mayhap we now take our last sup?
Life's cable must one day or other be parted,
And Death in safe moorings will bring us all up.
But 'tis always the way on't—one scarce finds a brother
Fond as pitch, honest, hearty, and true to the core,
But by battle, or storm, or some damned thing or other,
He's popped off the hooks, and we ne'er see him more!
But grieving's a folly, &c.

BLEAK WAS THE MORN.

BLEAK was the morn when William left his Nancy,
The fleecy snow frowned on the whitened shore,
Cold as the fears that chilled her dreary fancy,
While she her sailor from her bosom tore:
To his filled heart a little Nancy pressing,
While a young tar the ample trousers eyed,
In need of firmness in this state distressing,
Will checked the rising sigh, and fondly cried—
Ne'er fear the perils of the fickle ocean,
Sorrow's a notion,
Grief all in vain;
Sweet love, take heart,
For we but part
In joy to meet again.

Loud blew the wind, when, leaning on that willow
Where the dear name of honest William stood,
Poor Nancy saw, tossed by a faithless billow,
A ship dashed 'gainst a rock that topped the flood:
Her tender heart with frantic thrilling,
Wild as the storm that howled along the shore,
No longer could resist a stroke so killing—
'Tis he! she cried, nor shall I see him more!
Why did he ever trust the fickle ocean?
Sorrow's my portion,
Misery and pain!
Break, my poor heart,
For now we part
Never to meet again!

Mild was the eve, all nature was smiling,
Four tedious years had Nancy passed in grief,
When, with her children, the sad hours beguiling,
She saw her William fly to her relief!
Sunk in his arms with bliss he quickly found her,
But soon returned to life, to love, and joy,
While her grown young ones anxiously surround her
And now Will clasps his girl, and now his boy.
Did I not say, though 'tis a fickle ocean,
Sorrow's all a notion,
Grief all in vain?
My joy now sweet,
For now we meet
Never to part again!

POOR SHIPWRECKED TAR.

ESCAPED with life, in tatters,
Behold me safe ashore;
Such trifles little matters,
I'll soon get togs galore:
For Poll swore when we parted
No chance her faith should jar,
And Poll's too tender-hearted
To slight a Shipwrecked Tar.

To Poll his course straight steering,
He hastens on apace;
Poor Jack can't get a hearing—
She never saw his face.
From Meg, Doll, Sue, and Kitty,
Relief is just as far,
Not one has the least pity
For a poor Shipwrecked Tar.

This, whom he thought Love's needle,
Now his sad mis'ry mocks,
That wants to call the beadle
To set him in the stocks.
Cried Jack, "This is hard dealing;
The elements at war
Than this had kinder feeling—
They spared a Shipwrecked Tar.

But all their taunts and fetches
A judgment are on me;
I, for these hardened wretches,
Dear Nancy, slighted thee.
But see, poor Tray assails me,
His mistress is not far,
He wags his tail and hails me,
Though a poor Shipwrecked Tar."

'Twas faithful love that brought him—
Oh, lesson for mankind!
"'Tis one," cried she, "I taught him;
For on my constant mind
Thine image, dear, was graven;
And now, removed each bar,
My arms shall be the haven
For my poor Shipwrecked Tar."

'Heaven and my love reward thee!
I'm shipwrecked, but I'm rich;
All shall with pride regard thee—
Thy love shall so bewitch
With wonder each fond fancy,
That children near and far
Shall lisp the name of Nancy,
Who saved her Shipwrecked Tar."

TOM TACKLE.

TOM TACKLE was noble, was true to his word;
If merit bought titles, Tom might be my lord;
How gayly his bark through Life's ocean would sail!
Truth furnished the rigging, and Honor the gale:
Yet Tom had a failing, if ever man had,
That, good as he was, made him all that was bad;
He was paltry and pitiful, scurvy and mean,
And the sniv'lingest scoundrel that ever was seen;
For so said the girls and the landlords 'long shore:
Would you know what his fault was?—Tom Tackle was poor!

'Twas once on a time when we took a galloon,
And the crew touched the agent for cash to some tune,
Tom a trip took to jail, an old messmate to free,
And four thankful prattlers soon sat on his knee.
Then Tom was an angel, downright from heaven sent!
While they'd hands he his goodness should never repent:
Returned from next voyage, he bemoaned his sad case,
To find his dear friend shut the door in his face!
"Why d'ye wonder?" cried one, "you're served right, to be sure;
Once Tom Tackle was rich—now Tom Tackle is poor!"

I ben't you see, versed in high maxims and sich;
But don't this same honor concern poor and rich?
If it don't come from good hearts, I can't see where from,
And hang me, if e'er tar had a good heart 'twas Tom.
Yet, somehow or 'nother, Tom never did right:
None knew better the time when to spare or to fight;
He, by finding a leak, once preserved crew and ship,
Saved the commodore's life—then he made such rare flip!
And yet for all this, no one Tom could endure;
I fancies as how 'twas—because he was poor!

At last an old shipmate, that Tom might hail land,
Who saw that his heart sailed too fast for his hand,
In the riding of comfort a mooring to find,
Reefed the sails of Tom's fortune, that shook in the wind:
He gave him enough through Life's ocean to steer,
Be the breeze what it might, steady, thus, or no near;
His pittance is daily, and yet Tom imparts
What he can to his friends—and may all honest hearts,
Like Tom Tackle, have what keeps the wolf from the door,
Just enough to be generous—too much to be poor.

LOVELY NAN.

SWEET is the ship that, under sail,
Spreads her white bosom to the gale;
Sweet, oh! sweet the flowing can;
Sweet to poise the laboring oar,
That tugs us to our native shore
When the boatswain pipes the barge to man;
Sweet sailing with a fav'ring breeze;
But oh! much sweeter than all these,
Is Jack's delight—his lovely Nan!

The needle, faithful to the north,
To show of constancy the worth,
A curious lesson teaches man:
The needle time may rust, the squall
Capsize the binnacle and all,
Let seamanship do all it can;
My love in worth shall higher rise,
Nor time shall rust, nor squalls capsize
My faith and truth to lovely Nan.

When in the bilboes I was penned,
For serving of a worthless friend,
And every creature from me ran;
No ship performing quarantine
Was ever so deserted seen,
None hailed me, woman, child, nor man;
But though false friendship's sails were furled,
Though cut adrift by all the world,
I'd all the world in lovely Nan.

I love my duty, love my friend,
Love truth and merit to defend,
To mourn their loss who hazard ran:
I love to take an honest part,
Love beauty, with a spotless heart,
By manners love to show the man;
To sail through life by honor's breeze—
'Twas all along of loving these
First made me dote on lovely Nan.

TOM BOWLING.

HERE, a sheer hulk, lies poor Tom Bowling.
The darling of our crew;
No more he'll hear the tempest howling,
For death has broached him to.
His form was of the manliest beauty,
His heart was kind and soft,
Faithful, below, he did his duty,
But now he's gone aloft.

Tom never from his word departed,
His virtues were so rare,
His friends were many and true-hearted,
His Poll was kind and fair:
And then he'd sing so blithe and jolly,
Ah, many's the time and oft!
But mirth is turned to melancholy,
For Tom is gone aloft.

Yet shall poor Tom find pleasant weather,
When He who all commands,
Shall give, to call life's crew together,
The word to pipe all hands.
Thus Death, who kings and tars despatches,
In vain Tom's life has doffed,
For, though his body's under hatches,
His soul has gone aloft.

TRUE COURAGE.

WHY, what's that to you, if my eyes I'm a wiping?
A tear is a pleasure, d'ye see in its way;
'Tis nonsense for trifles, I own, to be piping;
But they that han't pity, why I pities they.
Says the captain, says he (I shall never forget it),
"If of courage you'd know, lads, the true from the sham,
'Tis a furious lion in battle, so let it,
But, duty appeased, 'tis in mercy a lamb."

There was bustling Bob Bounce, for the old one not caring,
Helter skelter, to work, pelt away, cut and drive;
Swearing he, for his part, had no notion of sparing,
And as for a foe, why, he'd eat him alive.
But when that he found an old prisoner he'd wounded,
That once saved his life as near drowning he swam,
The lion was tamed, and, with pity confounded,
He cried over him just all as one as a lamb.

That my friend Jack or Tom I should rescue from danger,
Or lay my life down for each lad in the mess,
Is nothing at all—'tis the poor wounded stranger,
And the poorer the more I shall succor distress:
For however their duty bold tars may delight in,
A peril defy, as a bugbear, a flam,
Though the lion may feel surly pleasure in fighting,
He'll feel more by compassion when turned to a lamb.

The heart and the eyes, you see, feel the same motion,
And if both shed their drops, 'tis all to the same end;
And thus 'tis that every tight lad of the ocean
Sheds his blood for his country, his tears for his friend.
If my maxim's disease, 'tis disease I shall die on—
You may snigger and titter, I don't care a flam!
In me let the foe feel the paw of a lion,
But, the battle once ended, the heart of a lamb.

FORGING THE ANCHOR.

LIKE Ætna's dread volcano see the ample forge,
Large heaps upon large heaps of jetty fuel gorge,
While, salamander-like, the pond'rous anchor lies
Glutted with vivid fire through all its pores that flies;
The dingy anchorsmiths, to renovate their strength,
Stretched out in death-like sleep are snoring at their length,

Waiting the master's signal when the tackle's force
Shall, like split rocks, the anchor from the fire divorce;
While, as old Vulcan's Cyclops did the anvil bang,
In deafening concert shall their pond'rous hammers clang,
And into symmetry the mass incongruous beat,
To save from adverse winds and waves the gallant British fleet.

Now, as more vivid and intense each splinter flies,
The temper of the fire the skilful master tries;
And, as the dingy hue assumes a brilliant red,
The heated anchor feeds that fire on which it fed:
The huge sledge-hammers round in order they arrange,
And waking anchorsmiths await the looked-for change,
Longing with all their force the ardent mass to smite,
When issuing from the fire arrayed in dazzling white;
And, as old Vulcan's Cyclops did the anvil bang,
To make in concert rude their pond'rous hammers clang,
So the misshapen lump to symmetry they beat,
To save from adverse winds and waves the gallant British fleet.

The preparations thicken: with forks the fire they goad;
And now twelve anchorsmiths the heaving bellows load;
While armed from every danger, and in grim array,
Anxious as howling demons waiting for their prey:
The forge the anchor yields from out its fiery maw,
Which, on the anvil prone, the cavern shouts hurraw!
And now the scorched beholders want the power to gaze,
Faint with its heat, and dazzled with its powerful rays;
While, as old Vulcan's Cyclops did the anvil bang,
To forge Jove's thunderbolts, their pond'rous hammers clang;
And, till its fire's extinct, the monstrous mass they beat,
To save from adverse winds and waves the gallant British fleet.

LOVE ME EVERMORE.

In either eye a lingering tear,
His love and duty well to prove,
Jack left his wife and children dear,
Impelled by honor and by love;
And as he loitered, wrapped in care,
A sapling in his hand he bore,
Curiously carved, in letters fair—
"Love me; ah, love me evermore!"

At leisure to behold his worth,
Tokens, and rings, and broken gold,
He plunged the sapling firm in earth,
And o'er and o'er his treasure told;
The letters spelt, the kindness traced,
And all affection's precious store,
Each with the favorite motto graced—
"Love me; ah, love me, evermore!"

While on this anxious task employed,
Tender remembrance all his care,
His ears are suddenly annoyed,
The boatswain's whistle cleaves the air,
'Tis duty calls his nerves are braced,
He rushes to the crowded shore,
Leaving the sapling in his haste,
That bids him love for evermore.

The magic branch thus unreclaimed,
Far off at sea, no comfort near,
His thoughtless haste he loudly blamed
With many a sigh and many a tear;
Yet why act this unmanly part?
The words the precious relic bore,
Are they not marked upon my heart?
"Love me; ah, love me, evermore!"

Escaped from treacherous waves and winds,
That three years he had felt at sea,
A wondrous miracle he finds—
The sapling is become a tree!
A goodly head that graceful rears,
Enlarged the trunk, enlarged the core!
And on the rind, enlarged, appears
"Love me; ah, love me, evermore!"

While gazing on the spell-like charms
Of this most wonderful of trees,
His Nancy rushes to his arms,
His children cling about his knees.
Increased in love, increased in size,
Taught from the mother's tender store,
Each little urchin, lisping, cries,
"Love me; ah, love me, evermore!"

Amazement seized the admiring crowd;
"My children," cried a village seer,
"These signs, though mute, declare aloud
The hand of Providence is here—
Whose hidden, yet whose sure decrees
For those its succor who implore,
Can still the tempest, level seas,
And crown true love for evermore."

HONESTY IN TATTERS.

This here's what I does—I d'ye see, forms a notion
That our troubles, our sorrows and strife,
Are the winds and the billows that foment the ocean,
As we work through the passage of life.
And for fear on life's sea lest the vessel should founder,
To lament, and to weep, and to wail,
Is a pop-gun that tries to outroar a nine-pounder,
All the same as a whiff in a gale.
Why now I, though hard fortune has pretty near starved me
And my togs are all ragged and queer,
Ne'er yet gave the bag to the friend who had served me,
Or caused ruined beauty a tear.

Now there t'other day, when my messmate deceived me,
Stole my rhino, my chest, and our Poll,
Do you think in revenge, while their treachery grieved me,
I a court-martial called?—Not at all.
This here on the matter was my way of arg'ing—
'Tis true they han't left me a cross;
A vile wife and false friend though are gone by the bargain
So the gain d'ye see's more than the loss:
For though fortune's a jilt, and has, &c.

The heart's all—when that's built as it should, sound and clever,
We go 'fore the wind like a fly,
But if rotten and crank, you may luff up for ever
You'll always sail in the wind's eye:
With palaver and nonsense I'm not to be paid off,
I'm adrift, let it blow then great guns,
A gale, a fresh breeze, or the old gemman's head off,
I takes life rough and smooth as it runs:
Content, though hard fortune, &c.

CONSTANCY.

The surge hoarsely murm'ring, young Fanny's grief mocking,
The spray rudely dashing as salt as her tears;
The ship's in the offing, perpetually rocking,
Too faithful a type of her hopes and her fears.
"'Twas here," she cried out, "that Jack's vows were so many,
Here I bitterly wept, and I bitterly weep:
Her heart-whole he swore to return to his Fanny,
Near the trembling pine that nods over the deep.

Ah! mock not my troubles, ye pitiless breakers;
Ye winds, do not thus melt my heart with alarms;
He is your pride and mine, in my grief then partakers;
My sailor in safety waft back to my arms.
They are deaf and ungrateful: these woes are too many,
Here, here, will I die, where I bitterly weep;
Some true lover shall write the sad fate of poor Fanny
On the trembling pine that hangs over the deep.

Thus, her heart sadly torn with its wild perturbation,
No friend but her sorrow, no hope but her grave;
Led on by her grief to the last desperation,
She ran to the cliff, and plunged into the wave.
A tar saved her life—the fond tale shall please many,
Who before wept her fate, now no longer shall weep:
'Twas her Jack, who, returning, had sought out his Fanny,
Near the trembling pine that hangs over the deep.

JACK COME HOME.

Jack come home, his pockets lined,
In search of Poll, his only pleasure,
To Pickle Stairs his course inclined,
In her fair lap to pour his treasure;
But scarce arrived at famed Rag-fair,
Where the keen Jew the clodpole fleeces.
His whistle turned into a stare
At "Come, who'll buy my water-cresses?"

He starts and trembles at the sound,
Which now is heard, and now obstructed;
And now his hopes are all aground,
And now 'tis to his ear conducted.
"Zounds!" cried out Jack, "I know that phiz—
But then, such togs—they're all to pieces!
Why, it can't be! my eyes it is—
'Tis Poll a-bawling water-cresses!"

And now she's in his arms, while he
Bids her relate fortune's reverses;
The world finds faithless as the sea,
And loads false friends, in troops, with curses.
"They took," cried she, "my very bed;
The sticks they seized, and sold in pieces;
So, to get a bit of honest bread,
I cries, who'll buy my water-cresses?"

"Still art thou rich, my girl," cried Jack,
"And still shalt taste each earthly pleasure;
Thou'rt true, though rags are on thy back,
And honor, Poll's a noble treasure.
In this gay tog-shop rigg'd so neat,
Ill fortune from this moment ceases;"
This said, he scattered in the street
Basket, and rags, and water-cresses.

NANCY.

You ask how it comes that I sing about Nancy
For ever, yet find something new;
As well may you ask why delight fills the fancy
When land first appears to the crew.
When, safe from the toils of the perilous ocean,
In each thanks of gratitude spring;
Feel this, and you'll have of my joy a faint notion
When with rapture of Nancy I sing.

You and I nature's beauties have seen the world over,
Yet never knew which to prefer;
Then why should you wonder that I am no rover,
Since I see all those beauties in her?
Why, you'll find about ships all you've known and been hearing,
On their different bearings to bring;
Though they all make their ports, they all vary in steering,
So do I when of Nancy I sing.

Could a ship round the world, wind and weather permitting,
A thousand times go and come back,
The ocean's so spacious, 'twould never be hitting
For leagues upon leagues the same tack:
So her charms are so numerous, so various, so clever,
They produce in my mind such a string,
That, my tongue once let loose, I could sing on for ever,
And vary the oftener I sing.

Shall I tell you the secret? you've but to love truly,
Own a heart in the right place that's hung;
And just as the prow to the helm answers duly,
That heart will lend words to the tongue.
No art do I boast of, no skill I inherit,
Then do not of my praises ring;
But to love and to nature allow all the merit
That taught me of Nancy to sing.

NATURE AND NANCY.

Let swabs, with their wows, their palaver, and lies,
Sly flattery's silk sails still be trimming,
Swear their Polls be all angels dropped down from the skies—
Your angels don't like—I loves women.
And I loves a warm heart, and a sweet honest mind,
Good as truth, and as lively as fancy;
As constant as honor, as tenderness kind;
In short, I loves Nature and Nancy.

I read in a song about Wenus, I thinks,
All rigged out with her Cupids and Graces:
And how roses and lilies, carnations and pinks,
Was made paint to daub over their faces.
They that loves it may take all such art for their pains—
For mine 'tis another guess fancy;
Give me the rich health, flesh and blood, and blue veins,
That pays the sweet face of my Nancy.

Why, I went to the play, where they talked well at least,
As to act all their parts they were trying;
They were playing at soldiers, and playing at feast,
And some they was playing at dying.
Let 'em hang, drown, or starve, or take poison, d'ye see,
All just for their gig and their fancy;
What to them was but jest is right earnest to me,
For I live and I'd die for my Nancy.

Let the girls then, like so many Algerine Turks,
Dash away, a fine gay-painted galley,
With their jacks, and their pennants, and gingerbread works,
All for show, and just nothing for value—
False colors throw out, decked by labor and art,
To take of pert coxcombs the fancy;
They are all for the person, I'm all for the heart—
In short, I'm for Nature and Nancy.

ANNA, ANNE, NAN, NANCE, OR NANCY

My love's a vessel trim and gay,
Rigged out with truth and stored by honor,
As through life's sea she cuts her way,
All eyes with rapture gaze upon her:
Built every wondering heart to please—
The lucky shipwrights, Love and Fancy;
From stem to stern she moves with ease,
And at her launch they called her Nancy.

When bearing up against life's gales,
So well she stems the dangerous trouble,
I call her Anna—as she sails,
Her form's so grand, her air's so noble.
When o'er the trembling wave she flies
That plays and sports as she advances,
Well said, my Nan! I fondly cries,
As my full heart in concert dances.

In studding-sails before life's breeze
So sweetly gentle is her motion,
She's Anne—for, as she moves with ease,
She seems the queen of all the ocean.
But when on Sundays rigged in stays,
Like beauty gay, and light as fancy,
She wins my heart a thousand ways;
I then delight to call her Nancy.

When laying on a tack so neat,
The breeze her milk-white bosom filling,
She skims the yielding waves so fleet,
I call her Nance, my bosom thrilling.
Thus is she precious to my heart,
By whate'er name comes o'er my fancy;
Graceful or gay, grand, neat, or smart,
Or Anna, Anne, Nan, Nance, or Nancy.

BROTHER JACK.

If the good old maxim's true,
That sons of Eve should all be brothers,
Tars have it to their hearts in view,
For their first good's the good of others;
Nay, Jack such narrow love derides,
'Midst every danger still contented,
He the whole family provides
With every good that Heaven invented;

And, leaving caution to the wind,
Risks every chance to serve mankind.

Away to India, cries the fair;
To Beauty's voice obedient listen!
The vessel cuts the yielding air,
And muslins wave, and diamonds glisten;
Should winter, in its bleak array,
With chilling frosts and winds alarm her,
Jack points the prow to Hudson's Bay,
And comely furs both deck and warm her;
And, gayly leaving care behind,
Ransacks the world to serve mankind.

Would cits the rich, voluptuous treat—
Amid the bustle and the hurry,
To make the bill of fare complete,
Jack brings the turtle and the curry;
He fetches tea for maiden aunts,
Finery and fashions for our spouses,
Feeds, clothes us, and supplies our wants,
And even furnishes our houses:
What thanks for those then shall we find,
Who thus adventure for mankind?

Then be the friendly toast we pass,
As honest hearts and Nature's freemen—
Excluding daylight from the glass—
Prosperity to English seamen!
On danger's brink who careless found,
For others make their lives a slavery;
The very wine that now goes round
We owe to their adventurous bravery.
Then drink to those, with grateful mind,
Who risk their lives to serve mankind.

THE MANES OF THE BRAVE.

Now that war has, in human distress, done its best;
Now that, glutted with mischief, fell slaughter's at rest;
Now that smiling content crowns the peasant's clean board,
And the industrious ploughshare takes place of the sword;
In this season what care o'er the fancy shall brood?
What sigh press for vent, or what tear shall intrude?
Ah! indulge and reflect on each glorious grave—
A sigh and a tear to the manes of the brave.

Now that loud acclamations expand through the air,
And the brows of the brave are adorned by the fair;
Now that bands of musicians so gayly advance,
In the concert to join or enliven the dance;
At one grateful idea the tumult shall end,
The soft flute the sad cadence alone shall suspend;
And, while fancy leads on to the cold hallowed grave,
Shall echo a sigh to the manes of the brave.

Proud award of those heroes for glory who burn,
Alike nobly honored the arch and the urn;
Surviving, or dying, such fame who achieve,
'Tis joy to regret, and 'tis pleasure to grieve.
Then our rapturous bosoms let gratitude swell,
While those sons of renown, who so gloriously fell,
Shall from heaven cheer those mourners who throng near each grave,
And dry up their tears for the manes of the brave.

SAILOR'S JOURNAL.

'Twas post meridian, half past four,
By signal I from Nancy parted,
At six she lingered on the shore,
With uplift hands and broken-hearted.
At seven, while taughtening the forestay,
I saw her faint, or else 'twas fancy;
At eight we all got under weigh,
And bade a long adieu to Nancy!

Night came, and now eight bells had rung,
While careless sailors, ever cheery,
On the mid watch so jovial sung,
With tempers labor can not weary.
I, little to their mirth inclined,
While tender thoughts rushed on my fancy,
And my warm sighs increased the wind,
Looked on the moon, and thought of Nancy!

Next morn a storm came on at four,
At six the elements in motion
Plunged me and three poor sailors more
Headlong within the foaming ocean.
Poor wretches! they soon found their graves:
For me—it may be only fancy—
But love seemed to forbid the waves
To snatch me from the arms of Nancy!

Scarce the foul hurricane had cleared,
Scarce winds and waves had ceased to rattle,
When a bold enemy appeared,
And, dauntless, we prepared for battle.
And now, while some loved friend or wife
Like lightning rushed on every fancy,
To Providence I trusted life,
Put up a prayer, and thought of Nancy!

At last—'twas in the month of May—
The crew, it being lovely weather,
At three, A. M., discovered day
And England's chalky cliffs together.
At seven up Channel how we bore,
While hopes and fears rushed on my fancy,
At twelve I gayly jumped ashore,
And to my throbbing heart pressed Nancy!

THE NANCY.

Mayhap you have heard that as dear as their lives
All true-hearted tars love their ships and their wives;
To their duty like pitch sticking close till they die,
And whoe'r wants to know it, I'll tell 'em for why:
One through dangers and storms brings me safely ashore,
Th' other welcomes me home when my danger is o'er;
Both smoothing the ups and the downs of this life,
For my ship's called the Nancy, and Nancy's my wife.

When Nancy my wife o'er the lawn scuds so neat
And so light, the proud grass scarcely yields to her feet,
So rigged out and so lovely, t'ent easy to trace
Which is reddest—her top-knight, her shoes, or her face;
While the neighbors to see her forget all their cares,
And are pleased that she's mine, though they wish she was theirs.
Marvel not, then, to think of this joy of my life—
I my ship calls the Nancy, for Nancy's my wife.

As for Nancy my vessel, but see her in trim,
She seems through the ocean to fly, and not swim;
'Fore the wind, like a dolphin, she merrily plays,
She goes anyhow well, but she looks best in stays.
Scudding, trying, or tacking, 'tis all one to she,
Mountain-high, or sunk low in the trough of the sea;
She has saved me from many hard squeaks for my life,
So I called her the Nancy, 'cause Nancy's my wife.

When so sweet in the dance careless glides my heart's queen,
She sets out, and sets in, far the best on the green;
So, of all the grand fleet, my gay vessel's the flower,
She outsails the whole tote by a knot in an hour.
Then they both sail so cheerful through life's varying breeze,
All hearts with such pilots must be at their ease;
Thus I've two good protectors to watch me through life,
My good ship the Nancy, and Nancy my wife.

Then these hands from protecting them who shall debar?
Ne'er ingratitude lurked in the heart of a tar;
Why, everything female from peril to save,
Is the noblest distinction that honors the brave.
While a rag, or a timber, or compass I boast,
I'll protect the dear creatures against a whole host;
Still grateful to both to the end of my life—
My good ship the Nancy, and Nancy my wife.

BEN BLOCK.

Would you hear a sad story of wo,
That tears from a stone might provoke?
'Tis concerning a tar, you must know,
As honest as e'er biscuit broke:
His name was Ben Block, of all men
The most true, the most kind, the most brave·
But harsh-treated by fortune—for Ben
In his prime found a watery grave.

His place no one ever knew more;
His heart was all kindness and love;
Though on duty an eagle he'd soar,
His nature had most of the dove.
He loved a fair maiden named Kate,
His father, to interest a slave,
Sent him far from his love, where hard fate
Plunged him deep in a watery grave.

A curse on all slanderous tongues!—
A false friend his mild nature abused,
And sweet Kate of the vilest of wrongs
To poison Ben's pleasure accused;
That she never had been truly kind;
That false were the tokens she gave;
That she scorned him, and wished he might find,
In the ocean a watery grave.

Too sure from this cankerous elf
The venom accomplished its end;
Ben, all truth and honor himself,
Suspected no fraud in his friend.
On the yard while suspended in air,
A loose to his sorrows he gave—
Take thy wish, he cried, false, cruel fair,
And plunged in a watery grave.

THE CANARY-BIRD.

Since fate of sailors hourly varies,
Lest doubts should wound my anxious breast,
This pretty bird from the Canaries
Jack brought, to set my heart at rest;
His life is charmed, and when with sadness,
Cried he, his notes he mournful gives,
Then cherish care,
Indulge despair;
But sweetly, if they thrill with gladness,
Rejoice, and know your lover lives;
Attentive mark!
Hark! hark!
Rejoice, and know your lover lives.

Each hour, while my poor bosom flutters,
Relying on my lover's word,
Anxious to hear the song he utters,
I listen to my pretty bird;
But, thanks to Heaven, never with sadness
Has he yet mourned; even now he gives
(To silence care,
And chase despair)
His sprightly notes with joy and gladness;
And thus I know my lover lives;
Attentive mark!
Hark! hark!
'Tis thus I know my lover lives.

But see, he's here! my heart's contented;
Sweet warbler, truly didst thou speak.
Dear love, cried Jack, 'twas all invented,
Lest thy poor heart my fate might break.
Love taught the cheat to cheer thy sadness,
And cheats of love true love forgives;
This anxious care
Healed thy despair;
Birds always sing with joy and gladness;
Thy love to thee and honor lives;
Attentive mark!
Hark! hark!
Thy love to thee and honor lives.

THE LADY'S DIARY.

Lectured by Pa and Ma o'er night;
Monday, at ten, quite vexed and jealous;
Resolved in future to be right,
And never listen to the fellows:
Stitched half a wristband, read the text,
Received a note from Mrs. Racket—
I hate that woman—she sat next,
All church-time, to sweet Captain Clackit

Tuesday got scolded—did not care;
The toast was cold, 'twas past eleven;
I dreamt the Captain through the air
On Cupid's wings bore me to heaven.
Pouted and dined, dressed, looked divine,
Made an excuse—got Ma to back it;
Went to the play—what joy was mine!
Talked loud and laughed with Captain Clackit.

Wednesday came down, no lark so gay;
The girl's quite altered, said my mother;
Cried dad, I recollect the day
When, dearee, thou wert such another.
Danced, drew a landscape, skimmed a play;
In the paper read that widow Flackit
To Gretna Green had run away—
The forward minx!—with Captain Clackit.

Thursday fell sick:—poor soul, she'll die!
Five doctors came, with lengthened faces;
Each felt my pulse:—Ah, me! cried I,
Are these my promised loves and graces?
Friday, grew worse—cried Ma, in pain,
Our day was fair—Heaven, do not black it:
Where's your complaint, love? In my brain.
What shall I give you? Captain Clackit.

Early next morn a nostrum came,
Worth all their cordials, balms, and spices—
A letter—I had been to blame:
The Captain's truth brought on a crisis.
Sunday, for fear of more delays,
Of a few clothes I made a packet,
And, Monday morn, stepped in a chaise,
And ran away with Captain Clackit.

RATIONAL VANITY.

Man, poor forked animal, why art thou vain?
Of thy form that so matchless the Deity owns,
Where beauty, proportion, and symmetry reign,
Adding grace to distinction, and splendor to thrones!
While, by folly and fashion, this form so divine
Is abused 'till all figures fantastic it wears,
Till, worn by diseases and bloated by wine,
Men, the Deity's image, turn monkeys and bears.
A mass of remorse, of reflection, of pain,
Man, poor forked animal, why art thou vain?

Art vain of thy mind? still, the Deity there,
Where virtues angelic their natures impress,
Pale anguish to chase, smooth the brow of despair,
And with charity's hand dry the tear of distress.
While this generous mind, on beneficence bent,
Fair gratitude's height shall in vain strive to climb,
And those lavished riches, so liberally meant,
'Stead of virtue rewarding shall sanctify crime.
While philanthropy gives disappointment to gain,
Man, poor restless animal, why art thou vain?

Take the rational mean: If thou'rt proud of thy form,
Let health given by temperance glow in thy face;
Let simplicity's hand, as it decks every charm,
To decorum add neatness, to decency grace.
Then to temper thy mind neither tower nor stoop,
Nor with sordidness grovel, nor arrogance ride;
Be not niggard nor lavish, a churl nor a dupe,
But let prudence the hand of benevolence guide.
Thus in form and in heart shall the Deity reign;
Thus reason shall teach, and thus man shall be vain.

EACH HIS OWN PILOT.

I WAS saying to Jack, as we talk'd t'other day
About lubbers and snivelling elves,
That if people in life did not steer the right way,
They had nothing to thank but themselves.
Now, when a man's caught by those mermaids the girls,
With their flatt'ring palaver and smiles,
He runs, while he's list'ning to their fal de rals,
Bump ashore on the Scilly Isles.
Thus in steering in life, as in steering with us,
To one course in your conduct resort,—
In foul winds, leaving luff and no near, keep her thus:
In honor's line ready,
When fair, keep her steady,
And neither to starboard incline nor to port.

If he's true in his dealings, life's wind to defy,
And the helm has a trim and right scope,
Not luffing, but keeping the ship full and by,
He may weather the Cape of Good Hope.
But if he steers wide in temptation's high sea,
And to pleasure gives too much head way,
Hard a-port goes the helm, the ship's brought by the lee,
And she founders in Botany Bay.
Thus in, &c.

In wedlock so many wrong courses are made,
They part convoy so oft and so fast,
Till so fond they are grown of that same Guinea-trade,
Cape Farewell is their anchorage at last.
Some men, I must own, to be dubb'd may be born;
But this, for the wives, I will say,
They seldom or ever bear down for Cape Horn
'Till the husbands have showed them the way.
Thus in, &c.

As to mutinous spirits that through the world roll,
If we had 'em aboard, Jack, with we,
They should make No Man's Land, and skulk through Lubber's Hole,
And at last be laid in the Red sea;
But fine honest fellows, to honor so dear,
Shall in this world by nothing perplexed,
Of False Bay get to windward, bring up in Cape Clear,
And bespeak a snug berth in the next.
Thus in, &c.

MOORINGS.

"I'VE heard," cried out one, "that you tars tack and tack,
And at sea what strange hardships befell you;
But I don't know what's mooring's." "What, don't you?" said Jack;
"Man you ear-tackle, then, and I'll tell you :—
Suppose you'd a daughter quite beautiful grown,
And, in spite of her prayers and implorings,
Some scoundrel abused her, and you knocked him down,
Why, d'ye see, he'd be safe at his moorings.

"In life's voyage should you trust a false friend with the helm,
The top-lifts of his heart all akimbo,
A tempest of treachery your bark will o'erwhelm,
And your moorings will soon be in limbo;
But if his heart's timbers bear up against pelf,
And he's just in his reckoning and scorings,
He'll for you keep a look-out the same as himself,
And you'll find in his friendship safe moorings.

"If wedlock's your port, and your mate, true and kind,
In all weathers will stick to her duty,
A calm of contentment shall beam in your mind,
Safe moored in the haven of beauty;
But if some frisky skiff, crank at every joint,
That listens to vows and adorings,
Shape your course how you will, still you'll make Cuckold's Point,
To lay up a beacon at moorings.

"A glutton's safe moored, head and stern, by the gout,
A drunkard's moored under the table,
In straws drowning men will Hope's anchor find out,
While a hair's a philosopher's cable:
Thus mankind are a ship, life a boisterous main,
Of Fate's billows where all hear the roarings,
Where for one calm of pleasure we've ten storms of pain,
Till death brings us all to our moorings."

THE LAST SHILLING.

As pensive one night in my garret I sate,
My last shilling produced on the table;
That advent'rer, cried I, might a hist'ry relate,
If to think and to speak it were able.
Whether fancy or magic 'twas played me the freak,
The face seemed with life to be filling,
And cried, instantly speaking, or seeming to speak,
Pay attention to me thy last shilling.

I was once the last coin of the law a sad limb,
Who in cheating was ne'er known to falter;
'Till at length, brought to justice, the law cheated him,
And he paid me to buy him a halter:
A Jack Tar, all his rhino but me at an end,
With a pleasure so hearty and willing,
Though hungry himself, to a poor distressed friend,
Wished it hundreds, and gave his last shilling.

'Twas the wife of his messmate, whose glistening eye
With pleasure ran o'er as she viewed me;
She changed me for bread as her child she heard cry,
And at parting with tears she bedewed me.
But I've other scenes known, riot leading the way,
Pale want their poor families chilling;
Where rakes, in their revels the piper to pay,
Have spurned me, their best friend and last shilling.

Though thyself hast been thoughtless, for profligates bail,
But to-morrow all care shalt thou bury,
When my little history thou offerest for sale;
In the interim, spend me and be merry!
Never, never, cried I, thou'rt my Mentor, my muse,
And, grateful thy dictates fulfilling,
I'll hoard thee in my heart:—thus men counsel refuse,
'Till the lecture comes from the last shilling.

THE STANDING TOAST.

[The last Song written by Mr. Dibdin.]

THE moon on the ocean was dimmed by a ripple,
Affording a checkered delight,
The gay jolly tars passed the word for the tipple
And the toast—for 'twas Saturday night:
Some sweetheart or wife that he loved as his life,
Each drank, while he wished he could hail her;
But the standing toast that pleased the most
Was—The wind that blows, the ship that goes,
And the lass that loves a sailor!

Some drank the king and his brave ships,
And some the constitution,
Some—May our foes and all such rips
Own English resolution!
That fate might bless some Poll or Bess,
And that they soon might hail her:
But the standing toast, &c.

Some drank our queen, and some our land,
Our glorious land of freedom!
Some that our tars might never stand
For heroes brave to lead 'em!
That beauty in distress might find
Such friends as ne'er would fail her:
But the standing toast, &c.

SONGS IN DIBDIN'S STYLE.

THE ORIGIN OF NAVAL ARTILLERY.

WHEN Vulcan forged the bolts of Jove
In Etna's roaring glow,
Neptune petitioned he might prove
Their use and power below;
But finding in the boundless deep
Their thunders did but idly sleep,
He with them armed fair Freedom's hand,
To guard from foes her chosen land.

Long may she own the glorious right,
And when through circling flame
She darts her thunder in the fight,
May justice guide her aim!
And when opposed in future wars,
Her soldiers brave and gallant tars
Shall launch her fires from every hand
On every foe to Freedom's land.

ALL'S WELL.

BY T. DIBDIN.

DESERTED by the waning moon,
When skies proclaim night's cheerless noon,
On tower, fort, or tented ground,
The sentry walks his lonely round;
And should some footstep haply stray
Where caution marks the guarded way:
"Who goes there? Stranger, quickly tell!"
"A friend!"—"The word?"—"Good-night! All's well!"

Or sailing on the midnight deep,
When weary messmates soundly sleep,
The careful watch patrols the deck,
To guard the ship from foes or wreck,
And while his thoughts oft homeward veer,
Some well-known voice salutes his ear:
"Who goes there? Brother, quickly tell!"
"Above! Below!"—"Good-night! All's well!"

THE CABIN-BOY.

BY T. DIBDIN.

THE sea was rough, the clouds were dark,
Far distant every joy,
When, forced by fortune to embark,
I went a Cabin-Boy.

My purse soon filled with foemen's gold,
I hastened back with joy,
When, wrecked in sight of port, behold
The hapless Cabin-Boy!

NAVAL PROMOTION.

BY T. DIBDIN.

THE Cabin-Boy's over the sea,
For his sister and mother weeps he;
Till good conduct prevails, and homeward he sails,
To land his full pockets with glee.

Next a Middy away o'er the wave,
'Tis his fortune in action to save
His officer's life, in the heat of the strife,
And he lands at home happy and brave.

Now an Officer over the main,
Fresh laurels on ocean to gain,
Till, commanding a prize, his friends see him rise,
And a Captain's commission obtain.

The Captain adventures once more,
Returning a bold Commodore;
And, his wishes to crown, he comes up to town
With an Admiral's flag at the fore.

WHO'LL SERVE?

BY T. DIBDIN.

"WHO'LL serve with me?" cried the sergeant aloud,
Roll went the drum, and the fife played sweetly.
"Here, master sergeant!" said I, from the crowd,
"Is a lad who will answer your purpose completely."
My father was a corporal, and well he knew his trade;
Of women, wine, and gunpowder, he never was afraid.
He'd march, fight, left! right!
Front flank! centre rank!
Storm the trenches, court the wenches,
Loved the rattle of a battle;
Died in glory, lives in story!
And, like him, I found a soldier's life, if taken smooth and rough,
A very merry, hey-down-derry, sort of life enough."

"Hold up your head!" cried the sergeant at drill,
Roll went the drum, and the fife played loudly.
"Turn out your toes, sir!"—Says I, "Sir, I will;"
For a nimble-wristed round rattan the sergeant flourished proudly.
My father died when corporal, but I ne'er turned my back,
Till promoted to a halbert, I was sergeant in a crack.
In sword and sash cut a dash;
Spurred and booted, next recruited,
Hob and Clob, awkward squad,
Then began my rattan!
When boys unwilling came to drilling,
Till made the colonel's orderly, then who but I so bluffy
Led a very merry, hey-down-derry, sort of life enough.

"Homeward, my lads!" cried the general—"huzza!"
Roll went the drum, and the fife played cheerly;
To quick time we footed, and sung all the way,
"Hey, for the pretty girls we all love dearly!"
My father lived with jolly boys in bustle, jars, and strife,
And, like him, being fond of noise, I mean to take a wife.
Soon as miss blushes y-i-s,
Rings, gloves, dears, loves,
Bells ringing, comrades singing,
Honeymoon finished soon;
Scolding, sighing, children crying!
Yet still a wedded life may prove, if taken smooth and rough,
A very merry, hey-down-derry, sort of life enough.

THE BAY OF BISCAY O!

BY ANDREW CHERRY.

LOUD roared the dreadful thunder,
The rain a deluge showers;
The clouds were rent asunder
By lightning's vivid powers!
The night both drear and dark;
Our poor deluded bark!
Till next day,
There she lay,
In the Bay of Biscay O!

Now, dashed upon the billow,
Her opening timbers creak;
Each fears a wat'ry pillow!
None stop the dreadful leak!—
To cling to slipp'ry shrouds
Each breathless seaman tries,
As she lay,
Till the day,
In the Bay of Biscay O!

At length the wished-for morrow
Broke through the hazy sky;
Absorbed in silent sorrow,
Each heaved a bitter sigh!—

The dismal wreck to view
Struck horror to the crew,
As she lay,
On that day,
In the Bay of Biscay O!

Her yielding timbers sever;
Her pitchy seams are rent!
When Heaven (all bounteous ever)
Its boundless mercy sent!
A sail in sight appears!
We hail her with three cheers!
Now we sail
With the gale
From the Bay of Biscay O!

BLACK-EYED SUSAN.

BY JOHN GAY.

All in the Downs the fleet lay moored,
The streamers waving in the wind,
When black-eyed Susan came on board—
Oh! where shall I my true love find?
Tell me, ye jovial sailors, tell me true,
If my sweet William sails among your crew.

William, who high upon the yard
Rocked with the billows to and fro,
Soon as her well-known voice he heard,
He sighed, and cast his eyes below.
The cord glides swiftly through his glowing hands,
And quick as lightning on the deck he stands.

So the sweet lark, high poised in air,
Shuts close his pinions to his breast,
If chance his mate's shrill call he hear,
And drops at once into her nest.
The noblest captain in the British fleet
Might envy William's lips those kisses sweet.

O Susan, Susan, lovely dear!
My vows shall ever true remain;
Let me kiss off that falling tear—
We only part to meet again.
Change as ye list, ye winds, my heart shall be
The faithful compass that still points to thee!

Believe not what the landmen say,
Who tempt with doubts thy constant mind;
They'll tell thee sailors, when away,
In every port a mistress find;
Yes, yes, believe them when they tell thee so,
For thou art present wheresoe'er I go!

If to far India's coast we sail,
Thy eyes are seen in diamonds bright,
Thy breath is Afric's spicy gale,
Thy skin is ivory so white:
Thus every beauteous object that I view
Wakes in my soul some charm of lovely Sue.

Though battle calls me from thy arms,
Let not my pretty Susan mourn;
Though cannons roar, yet, safe from harms,
William shall to his dear return;
Love turns aside the balls that round me fly,
Lest precious tears should drop from Susan's eye.

The boatswain gave the dreadful word,
The sails their swelling bosoms spread,
No longer must she stay on board;
They kissed, she sighed, he hung his head.
The lessening boat unwilling rows to land;
Adieu! she cried, and waved her lily hand.

STAND TO YOUR GUNS.

Stand to your guns, my hearts of oak,
Let not a word on board be spoke;
Victory is ours, 'mid fire and smoke,
Be silent and be ready.
Ram home the guns and sponge them well
Let us be sure the balls will tell;
The cannon's roar shall sound their knell:
Be steady, boys, be steady.

Nor yet, nor yet, nor yet:
Reserve your fire, I do desire.

Now the elements do rattle;
The gods amazed behold the battle.
A broadside, my boys!
See the blood in purple tide
Trickle down her battered side.
Winged with fate, the bullets fly—
Conquer, boys, or bravely die.
She sinks, she sinks, she sinks, huzza!
To the bottom down she goes!

OUR COUNTRY IS OUR SHIP.

BY JAMES COBB.

Our country is our ship, d'ye see,
A gallant vessel, too;
And of his fortune proud is he
Who's of our vessel's crew.
Each man, whate'er his station be,
When duty's call commands,
Should take his stand,
And lend a hand,
As the common cause demands.

And when our haughty enemies
Our noble ship assail,
Then all true-hearted lads despise
What peril may prevail;
But, shrinking from the cause we prize,
If lubbers skulk below,
To the sharks
Heave such sparks—
They assist the common foe.

Among ourselves, in peace, 'tis true,
We quarrel—make a rout;
And, having nothing else to do,
We fairly scold it out:
But once the enemy in view,
Shake hands, we soon are friends;
On the deck,
Till a wreck,
Each the common cause defends.

LOOSE EVERY SAIL TO THE BREEZE.

BY MICHAEL ARNE.

Loose every sail to the breeze,
The course of my vessel improve;
I've done with the toils of the seas—
Ye sailors, I'm bound to my love.

Since Emma is true as she's fair,
My griefs I fling all to the wind;
'Tis a pleasing return to my care,
My mistress is constant and kind.

My sails are all filled to my dear;
What tropic-bird swifter can move?
Who cruel shall hold his career
That returns to the nest of his love?

Hoist every sail to the breeze:
Come, shipmates, and join in the song:
Let's drink, while the ship cuts the seas,
To the gale that may drive her along.

WAPPING OLD STAIRS.

BY PERCY.

Your Molly has never been false, she declares,
Since last time we parted at Wapping Old Stairs,
When I swore that I still would continue the same,
And gave you the 'bacco-box marked with my name.

When I passed a whole fortnight between decks with you,
Did I e'er give a kiss, Tom, to one of your crew?
To be useful and kind to my Thomas I stayed,
For his trousers I washed, and his grog too I made.

Though you promised last Sunday to walk in the Mall
With Susan from Deptford, and likewise with Sall,
In silence I stood, your unkindness to hear,
And only upbraided my Tom with a tear.
Why should Sall, or should Susan, than me be more prized?
For the heart that is true, Tom, should ne'er be despised.
Then be constant and kind, nor your Molly forsake,
Still your trousers I'll wash, and your grog too I'll make.

HURRAH FOR THE SEA.

BY WILLES JOHNSON.

Your poets may sing of the pleasures of home,
Of the land and a bright sunny sky;
Give me the rough ocean, with bosom of foam,
And a bark, when in chase, that will fly:
Though aloft to the clouds on the billow we soar,
And then sink to the valley below,
We danger defy 'mid the hurricane's roar,
And reck not how hard it may blow!
Then, hurrah for the sea, boys! hurrah for the sea!
The mariner's life is the life for me.

The dear ones we love, when our pockets are lined,
Help to spend all our rhino on shore,
And when empty, "Up anchor!" we're sure soon to find
A prize that will furnish them more.
All friends we avoid as we roam on the wave:
The sail which we welcome's a foe;
And should Death heave us to, there's a ready-made grave,
And down to the bottom we go!
Then hurrah for the sea, boys! hurrah for the sea!
A mariner's life is the life for me!

THE STORM.

BY G. A. STEVENS.

Cease, rude Boreas, blustering railer!
List, ye landsmen, all to me;
Messmates, hear a brother sailor
Sing the dangers of the sea;
From bounding billows first in motion,
When the distant whirlwinds rise,
To the tempest-troubled ocean,
Where the seas contend with skies.

Hark! the boatswain hoarsely bawling:—
"By topsail-sheets and haulyards stand,
Down top-gallants, quick, be hauling,
Down your staysails, hand, boys, hand!
Now it freshens, set the braces,
The lee topsail-sheets let go;
Luff, boys, luff! don't make wry faces,
Up your topsails nimbly clew."

Now all you, on down beds sporting,
Fondly locked in beauty's arms,
Fresh enjoyments, wanton courting,
Safe from all but love's alarms:
Round us roars the tempest louder,
Think what fears our minds enthral;
Harder yet, it yet blows harder;
Hark! again the boatswain's call!—

"The topsail-yards point to the wind, boys,
See all clear to reef each course;
Let the foresheet go—don't mind, boys,
Though the weather should prove worse
Fore and aft the spritsail-yard get,
Reef the mizen, see all clear,
Hands up, each preventer-brace set,
Man the foreyard! Cheer, lads, cheer!"

Now the dreadful thunder rolling,
Peal on peal, contending, clash;
On our heads fierce rain falls pouring,
In our eyes blue lightnings flash:
One wide water all around us,
All above us one black sky,
Different deaths at once surround us;—
Hark! what means that dreadful cry!

"The foremast's gone!" cries every tongue out,
"O'er the lee, twelve feet 'bove deck;
A leak beneath the chest-tree's sprung out—
Call all hands to clear the wreck.
Quick! the lanyards cut to pieces;
Come, my hearts, be stout and bold!
Plumb the well, the leak increases,
Four feet water in the hold!

While o'er the ship wild waves are beating,
We for wives or children mourn:
Alas! from hence there's no retreating;
Alas! from hence there's no return.
Still the leak is gaining on us;
Both chain-pumps are choked below;
Heaven have mercy here upon us!
For only that can save us now.

O'er the lee-beam is the land, boys!
Let the guns o'erboard be thrown;
To the pump come every hand, boys!
See, our mizen-mast is gone!
The leak we've found, it can not pour fast;
We've lightened her a foot or more;
Up and rig a jury foremast:—
She rights! she rights, boys! we're off shore!

Now once more on joys we're thinking,
Since kind Fortune saved our lives;
Come, the can, boys! let's be drinking
To our sweethearts and our wives:
Fill it up, about ship wheel it,
Close to the lips a brimmer join.
Where's the tempest now? who feel it?
None! our danger's drowned in wine."

ON CHARLES DIBDIN'S MONUMENT AT GREENWICH.

BY T. DIBDIN.

Stop! shipmate, stop! He can't be dead,
His lay yet lives to memory dear;
His spirit, merely shot ahead,
Will yet command Jack's smile and tear!
Still in my ear the songs resound,
That stemmed rebellion at the Nore!
Avast! each hope of mirth's aground,
Should Charley be indeed no more!

The evening watch, the sounding lead,
Will sadly miss old Charley's line.
"Saturday Night" may go to bed,
His sun is set no more to shine!
"Sweethearts and Wives," though we may sing
And toast, at sea, the girls on shore;
Yet now 'tis quite another thing,
Since Charley spins the yarn no more!

"Jack Rattlin's" story now who'll tell?
Or chronicle each boatswain brave?
The sailor's kind historian fell
With him who sung the "Soldier's Grave!"
"Poor Jack!" "Tom Bowling!" but belay!
Starboard and larboard, aft and fore,
Each from his brow may swab the spray,
Since tuneful Charley is no more!

The capstan, compass, and the log,
Will oft his Muse to memory bring;
And when all hands wheel round the grog,
They'll drink and blubber as they sing.
For grog was often Charley's theme,
A double spirit then it bore;
It sometimes seems to me a dream,
That such a spirit is no more.

It smoothed the tempest, cheered the calm,
Made each a hero at his gun;
It even proved for foes a balm,
Soon as the angry fight was done.
Then, shipmate, check that rising sigh
He's only gone ahead before:
For even foremast men must die,
As well as Charley, now no more!

GEMS OF SCOTTISH SONG.

AULD ROBIN GRAY.

SCOTLAND has much honour by her female song writers. Some of the richest gems in her lyric crown are the productions of ladies. And it may be worthy of observation that, while the female song writers have, with few exceptions, been of "good family," the reverse is the case as regards the male lyrists, the great majority of whom have sprung from the lower classes. Lady Anne Lyndsay, the authoress of this universally admired ballad, was the daughter of the Earl of Balcarras. She was born in 1750, was married in 1793, and died in 1825. The ballad was written when the authoress was in her 21st year. The interest it created when first made public will best appear from her own pleasing communication made to Sir Walter Scott shortly before her death. "I longed," says Lady Anne, "to sing old Sophy's air to different words, and give to its plaintive tones some little history of virtuous distress in humble life, such as might suit it. While attempting to effect this, in my closet, I called to my little sister, now Lady Hardwicke, who was the only person near me, 'I have been writing a ballad, my dear; I am oppressing my heroine with many misfortunes. I have already sent her Jamie to sea—and broken her father's arm—and made her mother fall sick—and given her auld Robin Gray for her lover; but I wish to load her with a fifth sorrow within the four lines, poor thing! Help me to one.' 'Steal the cow, sister Anne,' said the little Elizabeth. 'The cow was immediately *lifted* by me, and the song completed." The ballad soon became a great favourite with the public; and a warm dispute arose among the learned whether it was an old or new composition. A reward of twenty guineas was offered to the person who would ascertain the point past doubt. The secretary to the Antiquarian Society was deputed to wait upon Lady Anne, but he offended her ladyship by trying to entrap the truth from her instead of putting the request direct. On this subject she facetiously remarks: "The annoyance, however, of this important ambassador from the Antiquaries, was amply repaid to me by the noble exhibition of the 'Ballet of Auld Robin Gray's Courtship,' as performed by dancing dogs, under my windows. It proved its popularity from the highest to the lowest, and gave me pleasure while I hugged myself in my obscurity." The air to which this ballad is now sung is the composition of the Rev. W. Levees; the old air to which the words were written is only sung to the first verse, as a recitative, which is now rarely done; and the first verse, accordingly, is very generally omitted.

WHEN the sheep are in the fauld, and the kye a' at hame,
When a' the weary world to sleep are gane;
The waes o' my heart fa' in showers from my ee,
While my gudeman lies sound by me.

Young Jamie lo'ed me weel, and sought me for his bride,
But saving a crown he had naething else beside;
To make the crown a pound, my Jamie went to sea,
And the crown and the pound were baith for me.

He had na been gane a week but only twa,
When my father brake his arm, and our cow was stown
My mither she fell sick and my Jamie at the sea, [awa',
And auld Robin Gray came a courting me.

My father couldna work and my mither couldna spin,
I toiled day and night but their bread I couldna win;
Auld Rob maintained them baith, and wi' tears in his ee
Said, Jenny, for their sakes, will ye marry me?
My heart it said nay, I looked for Jamie back;
But the wind it blew high, and the ship it was a wreck;
The ship it was a wreck, why didna Jenny die?
And why do I live to say, wae is me?

My father urged me sair, though my mither didna speak,
She looked in my face till my heart was like to break;
They gied him my hand, though my heart was on the sea,
And Auld Robin Gray is gudeman to me.
I hadna been a wife a week but only four,
When sitting sae mournfully at my ain door;
I saw my Jamie's wraith, for I couldna think it he,
Till he said, I'm come back, love, to marry thee.

O sair did we greet, and muckle did we say;
We took but ae kiss, and we tore ourselves away;
I wish I were dead, but I am no like to die:
And why do I live to say, wae is me?
I gang like a ghaist, and carena to spin;
I darena think on Jamie, for that would be a sin;
But I'll do my best a gude wife to be,
For auld Robin Gray is a kind man to me.

BLUE BONNETS OVER THE BORDER.

THIS first appeared in the romance of "The Monastery," by SIR WALTER SCOTT, 1820.

MARCH, march, Ettrick and Teviotdale,
Why, my lads, dinna ye march forward in order?
March, march, Eskdale and Liddesdale,
All the blue bonnets are over the border.
Many a banner spread, flutters above your head,
Many a crest that is famous in story,
Mount and make ready then, sons of the mountain glen
Fight for your Queen and the old Scottish glory.

Come from the hills where your hirsels are grazing,
Come from the glen of the buck and the roe;
Come to the crag where the beacon is blazing;
Come with the buckler, the lance, and the bow
Trumpets are sounding, war-steeds are bounding;
Stand to your arms, and march in good order;
England shall many a day tell of the bloody fray,
When the blue bonnets came over the border

THE ROSE OF ALLANDALE.

Words by C. Jefferys. Music composed by S. Nelson.

The morn was fair, the skies were clear,
No breath came o'er the sea,
When Mary left her Highland cot,
And wander'd forth with me;
Tho' flowers deck'd the mountain's side,
And fragrance fill'd the vale,
By far the sweetest flower there,
Was the rose of Allandale.

Where'er I wander'd, east or west,
Tho' fate began to lower,
A solace still was she to me,
In sorrow's lonely hour.
When tempests lash'd our gallant bark,
And rent her shiv'ring sail,
One maiden form withstood the storm,
'Twas the rose of Allandale.

And when my fever'd lips were parch'd
On Afric's burning sand,
She whisper'd hopes of happiness,
And tales of distant land:
My life had been a wilderness,
Unbless'd by fortune's gale,
Had fate not link'd my lot to hers,
The Rose of Allandale.

SAW YE MY WEE THING?

The author of this fine ballad was Hector Macniel. He was born in 1746, and terminated a life of much vicissitude and bodily suffering, in 1818. He was the author of many popular works, and was looked up to as Scotland's hope in song when Burns died. In the dramatic style of song-writing, of which this is a specimen, he stands unequalled.

Saw ye my wee thing? Saw ye my ain thing?
Saw ye my true love down on yon lea?
Cross'd she the meadow yestreen at the gloamin'?
Sought she the burnie whar flow'rs the haw tree?
Her hair it is lint-white; her skin it is milk-white;
Dark is the blue o' her saft rolling e'e;
Red, red her ripe lips, and sweeter than roses:—
Whar could my wee thing wander frae me?

I saw na your wee thing, I saw na your ain thing,
Nor saw I your true love down on yon lea;
But I met my bonnie thing late in the gloamin',
Down by the burnie whar flow'rs the haw tree.
Her hair it was lint-white; her skin it was milk-white;
Dark was the blue o' her saft rolling e'e;
Red were her ripe lips, and sweeter than roses:
Sweet were the kisses that she ga'e to me.

It was na my wee thing, it was na my ain thing,
It was na my true love ye met by the tree:
Proud is her leal heart! modest her nature!
She never lo'ed onie till ance she lo'ed me.
Her name it is Mary; she's frae Castle-Cary:
Aft has she sat, when a bairn, on my knee:—
Fair as your face is, war't fifty times fairer,
Young bragger, she ne'er would gi'e kisses to thee.

It was then your Mary; she's frae Castle-Cary,
It was then your true love I met by the tree;
Proud as her heart is, and modest her nature,
Sweet were the kisses that she ga'e to me.
Sair gloom'd his dark brow, blood-red his cheek grew,
Wild flash'd the fire frae his red rolling e'e!—
Ye's rue sair this morning your boasts and your scorning:
Defend ye, fause traitor! fu' loudly ye lie.

Awa' wi' beguiling, cried the youth, smiling:—
Aff went the bonnet; the lint-white locks flee;
The belted plaid fa'ing, her white bosom shawing,
Fair stood the loved maid wi' the dark rolling e'e!

Is it my wee thing! is it my ain thing!
Is it my true love here that I see!
O Jamie forgi'e me; your heart's constant to me;
I'll never mair wander, dear laddie, frae thee:

CRAZY JANE.

On the authority of Mr. Sinclair I ascribe this song to Mr. Lewis, the author of "The Monk," &c. He says Mr. Lewis wrote it while on a visit at Inverary Castle; that the incident it relates was real; and that the Duchess of Argyle was the "fair maid" addressed by the maniac. The writer of these remarks remembers a crazy creature, evidently the wreck of beauty, whom he frequently saw during a two years' residence in that neighbourhood. She occasionally carried a bundle of clothes, fancying it to be a baby. It is most touchingly sung by Miss M. A. Cumming.

Why, fair maid, in every feature
Are such signs of grief express'd;
Can a wandering, wretched creature
With such terror fill thy breast?
Do my phrensied looks alarm thee?
Trust me, sweet, thy fears are vain;
Not for kingdoms would I harm thee;
Shun not then poor Crazy Jane.

Dost thou weep to see my anguish?
Mark me, and avoid my wo:
When men flatter, sigh, and languish,
Think them false—I found them so;—
For I loved, oh! so sincerely,
None could ever love again—
But the youth I loved so dearly
Stole the heart of Crazy Jane.

Fondly my fond heart received him,
Which was doom'd to love but one;
He sigh'd, he vow'd, and I believed him,
He was false, and I, undone!
From that hour has reason never
Held her empire o'er my brain:
Henry fled—with him, forever,
Fled the wits of Crazy Jane.

Now forlorn and broken-hearted,
And with phrensied thoughts beset,
On that spot where last we parted,
On that spot where first we met,
Still I sing my love-lorn ditty,
Still I slowly pace the plain,
Whilst each passer-by, in pity,
Cries, "God help thee, Crazy Jane!"

THE FLOWER O' DUNBLANE.

This popular song, written by Tannahill, and set to music by R. A. Smith, was first introduced to the public in the year 1808. "The third stanza," says Smith, "was not written till several months after the others were finished. The poet," he adds, "had no particular fair one in his eye at the time, and Jessie was quite an imaginary personage." The truth is, Tannahill wrote the words to supplant the old coarse song, called "Bob o' Dunblane"—hence the title. He never was in Dunblane, but from his favourite Braes o' Gleniffer had often doubtless seen the sun go down o'er the lofty Ben Lomond.

The sun has gone down o'er the lofty Ben Lomond,
And left the red clouds to preside o'er the scene,
While lonely I stray, in the calm simmer gloamin',
To muse on sweet Jessie, the flower o' Dunblane.
How sweet is the brier, wi' its saft fauldin' blossom!
And sweet is the birk, wi' its mantle o' green;
Yet sweeter and fairer, and dear to this bosom,
Is lovely young Jessie, the flower o' Dunblane.

She's modest as onie, and blythe as she's bonnie;
For guileless simplicity marks her its ain;

And far be the villain, divested o' feeling,
  Wha'd blight in its bloom the sweet flower o' Dunblane.
Sing on, thou sweet mavis, thy hymn to the e'ening,
  Thou'rt dear to the echoes of Calderwood glen;
Sae dear to this bosom, sae artless and winning,
  Is charming young Jessie, the flower o' Dunblane.

How lost were my days till I met wi' my Jessie!
  The sports o' the city seemed foolish and vain:
I ne'er saw a nymph I could ca' my dear lassie,
  Till charm'd wi' sweet Jessie, the flower o' Dunblane.
Though mine were the station o' loftiest grandeur,
  Amidst the profusion I'd lavish in vain,
And reckon as naething the height o' its splendour,
  If wanting sweet Jessie, the flower o' Dunblane.

COME ALL YE JOLLY SHEPHERDS.

This sweetest of pastoral songs is the production of James Hogg, the Ettrick Shepherd. Mr. Clirehugh's spirited execution has rendered it a favourite with all classes.

Come all ye jolly shepherds
  That whistle through the glen,
I'll tell ye of a secret
  That courtiers dinna ken.
What is the greatest bliss
  That the tongue o' man can name?
'Tis to woo a bonnie lassie
  When the kye come hame.
    When the kye come hame,
      When the kye come hame,
    'Tween the gloamin and the mirk,
      When the kye come hame.

'Tis not beneath the burgonet,
  Nor yet beneath the crown,
'Tis not on couch of velvet,
  Nor yet on bed of down:
'Tis beneath the spreading birch,
  In the dell without a name,
Wi' a bonnie, bonnie lassie,
  When the kye come hame.

There the blackbird bigs his nest
  For the mate he loves to see,
And up upon the tapmost bough,
  Oh, a happy bird is he!
Then he pours his melting ditty,
  And love 'tis a' the theme,
And he'll woo his bonnie lassie
  When the kye come hame.

When the bluart bears a pearl,
  And the daisy turns a pea,
And the bonnie lucken gowan
  Has fauldit up his e'e,
Then the laverock frae the blue lift
  Draps down, and thinks nae shame
To woo his bonnie lassie
  When the kye come hame.

Then the eye shines sae bright,
  The hail soul to beguile,
There's love in every whisper,
  And joy in every smile;
O, who would choose a crown,
  Wi' its perils and its fame,
And miss a bonnie lassie
  When the kye come hame?

See yonder pawky shepherd
  That lingers on the hill—
His yowes are in the fauld,
  And his lambs are lying still;
Yet he downa gang to rest,
  For his heart is in a flame
To meet his bonnie lassie
  When the kye come hame.

Awa' wi' fame and fortune—
  What comfort can they gi'e?—
And a' the arts that prey
  On man's life and libertie!
Gi'e me the highest joy
  That the heart o' man can frame,
My bonnie, bonnie lassie,
  When the kye come hame.

ROW WEEL, MY BOATIE.

The author of these stanzas is unknown. The music is by R. A. Smith, and is remarkably beautiful.

Row weel, my boatie, row weel,
  Row weel, my merry men a',
For there's dool and there's wae in Glenfiorich's bowers,
  And there's grief in my father's ha'.

And the skiff it danced light on the merry wee waves,
  And it flew ower the water sae blue,
And the wind it blew light, and the moon it shone bright,
  But the boatie ne'er reach'd Allandhu.

Ohon! for fair Ellen, ohon!
  Ohon! for the pride of Strathcoe—
In the deep, deep sea, in the salt, salt bree,
  Lord Reoch, thy Ellen lies low

O'ER THE WATER TO CHARLIE.

This popular Jacobite song has been subjected to various alterations by different hands, so that few copies read alike. We give here Hogg's version, in his "Relics." The tune, "O'er the water to Charlie," is older than the '45, and it is probable that there was some old song with that burthen *before* the Jacobitical effusion.

Come, boat me ower, come, row me ower,
  Come, boat me ower to Charlie;
I'll gi'e John Ross another bawbee,
  To ferry me ower to Charlie.
    We'll over the water, and over the sea,
      We'll over the water to Charlie;
    Come weel, come woe, we'll gather and go,
      And live and die wi' Charlie.

It's weel I lo'e my Charlie's name,
  Though some there be that abhor him;
But O, to see Auld Nick gaun hame,
  And Charlie's faes before him!

I swear by moon and stars sae bricht,
  And the sun that glances early,
If I had twenty thousand lives,
  I'd gi'e them a' for Charlie.

I ance had sons, I now ha'e nane;
  I bred them, toiling sairly;
And I wad bear them a' again,
  And lose them a' for Charlie!

THE TEARS I SHED.

This elegant effusion was the production of Mrs. Dugald Stewart, wife of the celebrated philosopher. She was the daughter of the Hon. George Cranstoun, son of William, Lord Cranstoun; was born in 1765, and died in 1838. The first four lines of the last stanza were written by Burns, to suit the music, which requires double verses.

The tears I shed must ever fall:
  I mourn not for an absent swain;
For thoughts may past delights recall,
  And parted lovers meet again.
I weep not for the silent dead.
  Their toils are past, their sorrows o'er;
And those they loved their steps shall tread,
  And death shall join to part no more.

Though boundless oceans roll between,
 If certain that his heart is near,
A conscious transport glads each scene,
 Soft is the sigh, and sweet the tear.
E'en when by death's cold hand removed,
 We mourn the tenant of the tomb;
To think that e'en in death he loved,
 Can gild the horrors of the gloom.

But bitter, bitter are the tears
 Of her who slighted love bewails;
No hope her dreary prospect cheers,
 No pleasing melancholy hails.
Hers are the pangs of wounded pride,
 Of blasted hope, of wither'd joy;
The flatt'ring veil is rent aside,
 The flame of love burns to destroy.

In vain does memory renew
 The hours once tinged in transport's dye;
The sad reverse soon starts to view,
 And turns the past to agony.
E'en time itself despairs to cure
 Those pangs to ev'ry feeling due:
Ungenerous youth! thy boast how poor,
 To win a heart—and break it too!

No cold approach, no alter'd mien,
 Just what would make suspicion start;
No pause the dire extremes between,
 He made me blest—and broke my heart.
From hope, the wretched's anchor, torn;
 Neglected and neglecting all;
Friendless, forsaken, and forlorn;
 The tears I shed must ever fall.

THOU ART GANE AWA'.

The author of this song and his Mary were one evening at a ball, when they were paid an unexpected visit by an early friend; to pay him all possible respect, the intended bridegroom gave up his Mary as his partner for the night, when she eloped with the stranger in the morning; which ingratitude on the one part, and falsity on the other, left the author to die a melancholy death.

Thou art gane awa', thou art gane awa',
 Thou art gane awa' frae me, Mary!
Nor friends nor I could make thee stay—
 Thou hast cheated them and me, Mary!
Until this hour I never thought
 That ought could alter thee, Mary;
Thou'rt still the mistress of my heart,
 Think what you will of me, Mary.

Whate'er he said or might pretend,
 That stole the heart of thine, Mary,
True love, I'm sure, was ne'er his end,
 Or nae sic love as mine, Mary.
I spoke sincere, nor flatter'd much,
 Had no unworthy thoughts, Mary;
Ambition, wealth, nor naething such;
 No, I loved only thee, Mary.

Though you 've been false, yet while I live,
 I'll lo'e nae maid but thee, Mary;
Let friends forget, as I forgive,
 Thy wrongs to them and me, Mary;
So then, farewell! of this be sure,
 Since you've been false to me, Mary;
For all the world I'd not endure
 Half what I 've done for thee, Mary

THE HEATHER BELL.

This poetic trifle, though possessing no originality, either in music or words, became suddenly a great favourite. It is the production of Dr. Spittal, son of the late Lord Provost of Edinburgh.

Oh! deck thy hair wi' the heather bell,
 The heather bell alone;
Leave roses to the Lowland maid,
 The Lowland maid alone.
I've seen thee wi' the gay, gay rose,
 And wi' the heather bell,—
I love you much with both, fair maid;
 But wear the heather bell.
For the heather bell, the heather bell,
 Which breathes the mountain air,
Is far more fit than roses gay
 To deck thy flowing hair.

Away, away, ye roses gay!
 The heather bell for me;
Fair maiden, let me hear thee say,
 The heather bell for me.
Then twine a wreath o' the heather bell,
 The heather bell alone;
Nor rose, nor lily, twine ye there,
 The heather bell alone;
For the heather bell, the heather bell,
 Which breathes the mountain air,
Is far more fit than roses gay
 To deck thy flowing hair.

CONNEL AND FLORA.

Written by Alexander Wilson, of Paisley, the author of "Watty and Meg," and the great Ornithologist of America.

Dark lowers the night o'er the wide stormy main,
Till mild rosy morning rise cheerful again;
Alas! morn returns to revisit the shore;
But Connel returns to his Flora no more.

For see, on yon mountain the dark cloud of death
O'er Connel's lone cottage, lies low on the heath;
While bloody and pale on a far distant shore
He lies, to return to his Flora no more.

Ye light fleating spirits that glide o'er the steep
O, would you but waft me across the wild deep,
There fearless I'd mix in the battle's loud roar,
I'd die with my Connel, and leave him no more.

LAND O' THE LEAL.

The author of this touching lyric is unknown. It appeared shortly after the death of Burns, and has been commonly but erroneously attributed to him.

I'm wearing awa', Jean,
Like snaw when it is thaw, Jean;
I'm wearing awa', Jean,
 To the land o' the leal.
There's nae sorrow there, Jean,
There's neither cauld nor care, Jean,
The day is aye fair, Jean,
 In the land o' the leal.

Ye were aye leal and true, Jean,
Your task's ended now, Jean,
And I'll welcome you
 To the land o' the leal.
Our bonnie bairn's there, Jean,
She was baith guid and fair, Jean,
And we grudged her right sair
 To the land o' the leal.

Then dry that tearfu' e'e, Jean,
My soul langs to be free, Jean,
And angels wait on me
 To the land o' the leal.
Now fare ye weel, my ain Jean,
This warld's care is vain, Jean,
We'll meet and aye be fain
 In the land o' the leal.

THE LASS O' GOWRIE.

THE following is a modern version of a ballad by Mr. WILLIAM REID, of Glasgow; somewhat famous as an interpolator of good verses in old songs.

UPON a simmer afternoon,
A wee before the sun gade down,
My lassie, in a braw new gown,
Cam' o'er the hills to Gowrie.
The rose-bud, tinged with morning show'r,
Blooms fresh within the sunny bow'r;
But Katie was the fairest flower
That ever bloom'd in Gowrie.

Nae thought had I to do her wrang,
But round her waist my arms I flang,
And said, My dearie, will ye gang
To see the Carse o' Gowrie?
I'll tak' ye to my father's ha',
In yon green fields beside the shaw;
I'll mak' you lady o' them a',
The brawest wife in Gowrie.

Saft kisses on her lips I laid,
The blush upon her cheeks soon spread,
She whisper'd modestly, and said,
I'll gang wi' thee to Gowrie!
The auld folks soon ga'e their consent,
Syne for Mess John they quickly sent,
Wha ty'd them to their heart's content,
And now she's Lady Gowrie.

ANNIE LAURIE.

THIS is a modern version of an old song written by a Mr. DOUGLASS, of Finland, and lately introduced by the Misses Cumming, in their Scottish Concerts.

MAXWELTON braes are bonnie,
Where early fa's the dew,
And it's there that Annie Laurie
Gied me her promise true;
Gied me her promise true,
Which ne'er forgot will be;
And for bonnie Annie Laurie
I'd lay me down and dee.

Her brow is like the snaw-drift,
Her throat is like the swan,
Her face it is the fairest
That e'er the sun shone on;
That e'er the sun shone on,
And dark blue is her e'e;
And for bonnie Annie Laurie
I'd lay me down and dee.

Like dew on the gowan lying,
Is the fa' o' her fairy feet;
And like winds in summer sighing,
Her voice is low and sweet.
Her voice is low and sweet,
And she's a' the world to me;
And for bonnie Annie Laurie
I'd lay me down and dee.

MARY DHU.

WRITTEN by D. M. MOIR, the talented and amiable author of Mansie Waugh—the "Delta" of Blackwood's Magazine.

SWEET, sweet is the rose-bud
Bathed in dew;
But sweeter art thou,
My Mary dhu.
Oh! the skies of night,
With their eyes of light,
Are not so bright
As my Mary dhu.

Whenever thy radiant face I see,
The clouds of sorrow depart from me;
As the shadows fly
From day's bright eye,
Thou lightest life's sky,
My Mary dhu.

Sad, sad is my heart,
When I sigh, Adieu!
Or gaze on thy parting,
My Mary dhu!
Then for thee I mourn,
Till thy steps' return
Bids my bosom burn,—
My Mary dhu.
I think but of thee on the broom-clad hills,
I muse but on thee by the moorland rills·
In the morning light,
In the moonshine bright,
Thou art still in my sight,
My Mary dhu.

Thy voice trembles through me
Like the breeze,
That ruffles, in gladness,
The leafy trees;
'Tis a wafted tone
From heaven's high throne,
Making hearts thine own,
My Mary dhu.
Be the flowers of joy ever round thy feet,
With colours glowing, and incense sweet;
And when thou must away,
May life's rose decay
In the west wind's sway—
My Mary dhu!

THE HARPER O' MULL.

IN the island of Mull there lived a harper famed for his skill and beloved for his virtues. Rosie, the fairest girl on the island, became his bride. Soon after, when on a visit with her to some friends at a distance, they were overtaken in a snow-storm, and to save his Rosie's life he burned his beloved harp. On the next day she proved faithless, and the poor harper was left forlorn and distracted. On this story TANNAHILL composed his song.

WHEN Rosie was faithful, how happy was I!
Still gladsome as summer the time glided by;
I play'd my harp cheery, while fondly I sang
Of the charms of my Rosie the winter nights lang.
But now I'm as waefu' as waefu' can be,
Come simmer, come winter, 'tis a' ane to me,
For the dark gloom of falsehood sae clouds my sad soul,
That cheerless for aye is the Harper of Mull.

I wander the glens and the wild woods alane,
In their deepest recesses I make my sad mane,
My harp's mournful melody joins in the strain,
While sadly I sing of the days that are gane.
Though Rosie is faithless, she's no the less fair,
And the thought of her beauty but feeds my despair;
With painful remembrance my bosom is full,
And weary of life is the Harper of Mull.

As slumb'ring I lay by the dark mountain stream,
My lovely young Rosie appear'd in my dream;
I thought her still kind, and I ne'er was sae blest,
As in fancy I clasp'd the dear nymph to my breast
Thou false fleeting vision, too soon thou wert o'er;
Thou wak'dst me to tortures unequall'd before;
But death's silent slumbers my griefs soon shall lull,
And the green grass wave over the Harper of Mull.

WITHIN A MILE OF EDINBURGH.

THIS is an improved version of an old song supposed to have been written by JOHN D'URFEY, towards the close of the 17th century. The air is the composition of Mr.

JAMES HOOK, father of the late Theodore Hook. The words here given are from the first volume of Johnson's Museum, 1787.

'TWAS within a mile of Edinburgh town,
In the rosy time of the year;
Sweet flowers bloom'd, and the grass was down,
And each shepherd woo'd his dear.
Bonnie Jocky, blythe and gay,
Kiss'd sweet Jenny, making hay,
The lassie blush'd, and frowning, cried, "No, no, it will not do;
I canna, canna, winna, winna, manna buckle too."

Jocky was a wag that never would wed,
Though long he had follow'd the lass:
Contented she earn'd and eat her brown bread,
And merrily turn'd up the grass.
Bonnie Jocky, blythe and free,
Won her heart right merrily:
Yet still she blush'd, and frowning, cried, "No, no, it will not do;
I canna, canna, winna, winna, manna buckle too."

But when he vow'd he would make her his bride,
Though his flocks and herds were not few,
She gave him her hand, and a kiss beside,
And vow'd she'd forever be true.
Bonnie Jocky, blythe and free,
Won her heart right merrily:
At church she no more frowning cried, "No, no, it will not do;
I canna, canna, winna, winna, manna buckle too."

ON WI' THE TARTAN.

THIS spirited song is from the pen of a very able lyrist, HUGH AINSLIE, long a resident in Louisville, Ky., and the author of much good poetry and prose.

CAN ye lo'e, my dear lassie,
The hills wild and free,
Whar the sang o' the shepherd
Gars a' ring wi' glee?
Or the steep rocky glens,
Where the wild falcons bide?
Then on wi' the tartan,
And fy let us ride!

Can ye lo'e the knowes, lassie,
That ne'er war in rigs?
Or the bonnie loune lee,
Where the sweet robin biggs?
Or the sang o' the lintie,
Whan wooin' his bride?
Then on wi' the tartan,
And fy let us ride!

Can ye lo'e the burn, lassie,
That loups amang linns?
Or the bonnie green howmes
Where it cannilie rins?
Wi' a cantie bit housie,
Sae snug by its side?
Then on wi' the tartan,
And fy let us ride!

LOCHABER.

WRITTEN by ALLAN RAMSAY to the tune of "Lochaber no more." The air, at an earlier period, is said to have been called "King James's March to Ireland."

FAREWELL to Lochaber, farewell to my Jean,
Where heartsome wi' her I ha'e mony a day been;
To Lochaber no more, to Lochaber no more,
We'll maybe return to Lochaber no more.
These tears that I shed, they're a' for my dear,
And no for the dangers attending on weir;
Though borne on rough seas to a far bloody shore,
Maybe to return to Lochaber no more!

Though hurricanes rise, though rise every wind,
No tempest can equal the storm in my mind;
Though loudest of thunders on louder waves roar,
There's naething like leavin' my love on the shore
To leave thee behind me my heart is sair pain'd;
But by ease that's inglorious no fame can be gain'd:
And beauty and love's the reward of the brave;
And I maun deserve it before I can crave.

Then glory, my Jeanie, maun plead my excuse;
Since honour commands me, how can I refuse?
Without it, I ne'er can have merit for thee;
And losing thy favour I'd better not be.
I gae then, my lass, to win honour and fame;
And if I should chance to come glorious hame,
I'll bring a heart to thee with love running o'er,
And then I'll leave thee and Lochaber no more

I'LL LO'E THEE, ANNIE.

THIS song is the production of ROBERT HAMILTON, Esq., late editor of the "Ladies' Companion," now of Boston; author of "The Sea Nymph's Wake," and other productions, poetry and prose.

I'LL lo'e thee Annie, while the dew
In siller bells hings on the tree;
Or while the burnie's waves o' blue
Rin wimplin' to the rowin' sea.
I'll lo'e thee while the gowan mild
Its crimson fringe spreads on the lea;
While blooms the heather in the wild—
Oh! Annie, I'll be true to thee.

I'll lo'e thee while the lintie sings
His sang o' love on whinny brae;
I'll lo'e thee while the crystal springs
Glint in the gowden gleams o' day;
I'll lo'e thee while there's licht aboon,
And stars to stud the breast o' sky;
I'll lo'e thee till life's day is done,
And bless thee wi' my latest sigh

BONNIE PRINCE CHARLIE.

WRITTEN by JAMES HOGG. Composed and arranged for the Piano Forte by N. Gow, jun.

CAM' ye by Athol, lad wi' the philabeg,
Down by the Tummel, or banks of the Gary?
Saw ye our lads, wi' their bonnets an' white cockades,
Leaving their mountains to follow Prince Charlie?
Follow thee, follow thee, wha wadna follow thee?
Lang hast thou loved and trusted us fairly!
Charlie, Charlie, wha wadna follow thee?
King of the Highland hearts, bonnie Prince Charlie

I ha'e but ae son, my brave young Donald;
But if I had ten they should follow Glengarry:
Health to M'Donald and gallant Clan-Ronald,
For these are the men that will die for their Charlie
Follow thee, follow thee, &c.

I'll to Lochiel and Appin, and kneel to them;
Down by Lord Murray and Roy of Kildarlie;
Brave Mackintosh he shall fly to the field wi' them;
They are the lads I can trust wi' my Charlie.
Follow thee, follow thee, &c.

Down through the Lowlands, down wi' the whigamore,
Loyal true Highlanders, down with them rarely;
Ronald and Donald drive on wi' the braid claymore,
Over the necks of the foes of Prince Charlie.
Follow thee, follow thee, &c

JENNY DANG THE WEAVER

THIS humorous song is the production of SIR ALEXANDER BOSWELL, son of the biographer of Johnson, and the fatal partner in the duel with James Stuart, author of "Three Years in America." Boswell wrote many excellent poems, chiefly humorous.

At Willie's wedding on the green,
The lasses, bonnie witches,
Were a' dress'd out in aprons clean,
And braw white Sunday mutches:
Auld Maggie bade the lads tak' tent,
But Jock would not believe her;
But soon the fool his folly kent,
For Jenny dang the Weaver.
And Jenny dang, Jenny dang,
Jenny dang the Weaver;
But soon the fool his folly kent,
For Jenny dang the Weaver.

At ilka country dance or reel,
Wi' her he would be bobbing;
When she sat down—he sat down,
And to her would be gabbing;
Where'er she gaed baith butt and ben,
The coof would never leave her;
Aye kecklin' like a clocking hen,
But Jenny dang the Weaver.
Jenny dang, &c.

Quo' he, My lass, to speak my mind,
In troth I needna swither;
You've bonnie een, and if you're kind,
I'll never seek anither:
He humm'd and haw'd, the lass cried Peugh!
And bade the coof no deave her;
Syne snapt her fingers, lap and leugh,
And dang the silly weaver.
And Jenny dang, Jenny dang,
Jenny dang the Weaver;
Syne snapt her fingers, lap and leugh,
And dang the silly Weaver.

O SAFT IS THE BLINK O' THINE E'E.

On the author of this song, James Ballentyne, has fallen the mantle of Burns. He is the author of numerous poems in the Scottish dialect, all of distinguished merit. He is also the author of two novels, describing humble Scottish life—"The Gaberlunzie," and the "Miller o' Deanhaugh;" a path chosen by himself, and abounding in scenes of pathos and beauty.

O saft is the blink o' thine e'e, lassie,
Saft is the blink o' thine e'e;
An' a bonnie wee sun glimmers on its blue orb
As kindly it glints upón me.

The ringlets that twine round thy brow, lassie,
Are gowden as gowden may be;
Like the wee curly cluds that play round the sun
When he's just gaun to drap in the sea.

Thou hast a bonnie wee mou', lassie,
As sweet as a body may pree;
An' fondly I'll pree that wee hinny mou',
E'en though thou shouldst frown upon me.

Thou hast a lily white hand, lassie,
As fair as a body may see;
An' saft is the touch o' that wee genty hand,
At eve when thou partest wi' me.

Thy thoughts are sae haly and pure, lassie,
Thy heart is sae kind and sae free;
That the bright sun o' heaven is nae pleased wi' himsel',
Till he glasses himsel' in thine e'e.

O, thou art a' thing to me, lassie,
O thou art a' thing to me;
What care I although fortune should frown,
Gin I gain the blythe blink o' thine e'e.

THERE'S NAE LUCK ABOUT THE HOUSE.

This admirable ballad is from the pen of a poor schoolmistress, named Jean Adams. It has been ascribed to Mr. Meckle, the translator of the Lusiad, but with faint authority. The sixth stanza, beginning, "The cauld blasts," was an interpolation of Dr. Beattie, the celebrated author of the "Minstrel."

And are ye sure the news is true?
And are ye sure he's weel?
Is this a time to think o' wark?
Ye jauds, fling bye your wheel.
Is this a time to think o' wark,
When Colin's at the door?
Rax me my cloak,—I'll to the quay,
And see him come ashore.
For there's nae luck about the house,
There's nae luck at a';
There's little pleasure in the house,
When our gudeman's awa'.

And gi'e to me my biggonet,
My bishops' satin gown,
For I maun tell the baillie's wife
That Colin's come to town.
My Turkey slippers maun gae on,
My hose o' pearl blue;
'Tis a' to please my ain gudeman,
For he's baith leal and true.
For there's nae luck, &c.

Rise up and mak' a clean fireside;
Put on the muckle pot;
Gi'e little Kate her cotton gown,
And Jock his Sunday coat:
And mak' their shoon as black as slaes,
Their hose as white as snaw;
It's a' to please my ain gudeman,
For he's been lang awa',
For there's nae luck, &c.

There's twa fat hens upon the bauk,
They've fed this month and mair;
Mak' haste and thraw their necks about,
That Colin weel may fare;
And spread the table neat and clean,
Gar ilka thing look braw;
For wha can tell how Colin fared,
When he was far awa'.
For there's nae luck, &c.

Sae true his heart, sae smooth his speech
His breath like caller air;
His very foot has music in't,
As he comes up the stair.
And will I see his face again?
And will I hear him speak?
I'm downright dizzy wi' the thought,—
In troth I'm like to greet.
For there's nae luck, &c.

The cauld blasts o' the winter wind,
That thirl'd through my heart,
They're a' blown by, I ha'e him safe,
Till death we'll never part;
But what puts parting in my head?
It may be far awa';
The present moment is our ain,
The neist we never saw.
For there's nae luck, &c.

Since Colin's weel, I'm weel content,
I ha'e nae mair to crave;
Could I but live to mak' him blest,
I'm blest aboon the lave:
And will I see his face again?
And will I hear him speak?
I'm downright dizzy wi' the thought,—
In troth, I'm like to greet.
For there's nae luck, &c.

FOR LACK OF GOLD.

This song was composed by the late Dr. Austin, physician at Edinburgh. He had courted a lady, to whom he was shortly to have been married; but the Duke of Athole having seen her, became so much in love with her, that he made proposals of marriage; which were accepted of, and she jilted the doctor.—Although Dr. Austin says—

"No cruel fair shall ever move
My injured heart again to love,"

he afterwards married Miss Anne Sempill, sister of Lord Sempill, by whom he had a large family He died in 1774.

For lack of gold she has left me, O,
And of all that's dear she's bereft me, O;
She me forsook for Athole's duke,
And to endless woe she has left me, O.
A star and garter have more art
Than youth, a true and faithful heart;
For empty titles we must part—
For glittering show she has left me, O.

No cruel fair shall ever move
My injured heart again to love;
Through distant climates I must rove,
Since Jeany she has left me, O.
Ye powers above, I to your care
Resign my faithless, lovely fair;
Your choicest blessing be her share,
Though she has ever left me, O.

DRAW THE SWORD.

Words by J. R. Planché. Music altered and arranged by G. Herbert Rodwell.

Draw the sword, Scotland, Scotland, Scotland!
Over mountain and moor hath pass'd the war sign:
The pibroch is pealing, pealing, pealing,
Who heeds not the summons is nae son o' thine.
The clans they are gath'ring, gath'ring, gath'ring,
The clans they are gath'ring by loch and by lea;
The banners they are flying, flying, flying,
The banners they are flying that lead to victory.
Draw the sword, Scotland, Scotland, Scotland!
Charge as ye charged in the days o' langsyne;
Sound to the onset, the onset, the onset,
He who but falters is nae son o' thine.

Sheath the sword, Scotland, Scotland, Scotland!
Sheath the sword, Scotland, for dimm'd is its shine;
Thy foemen are fleeing, fleeing, fleeing,
And wha kens nae mercy is nae son o' thine!
The struggle is over, over, over,
The struggle is over!—the victory won!
There are tears for the fallen, the fallen, the fallen,
And glory for all who their duty have done!
Sheath the sword, Scotland, Scotland, Scotland!
With thy loved thistle new laurels entwine;
Time shall ne'er part them, part them, part them,
But hand down the garland to each son o' thine.

WHAT'S A' THE STEER, KIMMER?

The following are the words of the favourite duet introduced by the Misses Cumming, at their late Scottish Concerts. The music will soon appear in an edition of their songs preparing for publication.

What's a' the steer, kimmer?
What's a' the steer?
Charlie he is landed,
An', haith, he'll soon be here.
The win' was at his back, carle,
The win' was at his back;
I carena, sin' he's come, carle,
We were na worth a plack.

I'm right glad to hear't, kimmer,
I'm right glad to hear't;
I ha'e a gude braid claymore,
And for his sake I'll wear't.
Sin' Charlie he is landed,
We ha'e nae mair to fear;
Sin' Charlie he is come, kimmer,
We'll ha'e a jub'lee year.

OH, I LO'ED MY LASSIE WEEL.

This excellent lyric is the production of the late Robert Frazer, editor of the Fife Herald, author of a volume of poems, published at Cupar, Fifeshire, for the benefit of his widow.

Oh, I lo'ed my lassie weel,
How weel I canna tell—
Lang, lang ere ithers trow'd,
Lang ere I wist mysel'.
At the school amang the lave,
If I wrestled or I ran,
I cared nae for the prize
If she saw me when I wan.

Oh, I lo'ed my lassie weel,
When the gleesome days were gane,
Mang a' the bonnie an' the gude
To match her saw I nane;
Though the cauld warl' o'er me cam'
Wi' its cumber an' its toil,
My day-tide dool was a' forgot
In her blythe e'enin' smile.

Oh, I lo'ed, nor lo'ed in vain,
An' though mony cam' to woo,
Wha to won her wad been fain,
Yet to me she aye was true;
She grat wi' very joy
When our waddin' day was set,
An' though twal' gude years sinsyne ha'e fled,
She's my darling lassie yet.

HIGHLAND MARY.

These stanzas are the production of the gifted Hon Mrs. Norton.

I would I were the light fern growing
Beneath my Highland Mary's tread,
I would I were the green tree throwing
Its shadow o'er her gentle head!
I would I were a wild-flower springing
Where my sweet Mary loves to rest.
That she might pluck me while she's singing,
And place me on her snowy breast!

I would I were in yonder heaven
A silver star, whose soft dim light
Would rise to bless each summer even,
And watch my Mary all the night!
I would, beneath these small white fingers,
I were the lute her breath has fanned—
The gentle lute, whose soft note lingers
As loth to leave her fairy hand!

Ah, happy things! ye may not wander
From Scotland to some darker sky,
But ever live unchanging yonder,
To happiness and Mary nigh!
While I at midnight sadly weeping
Upon its deep transparent blue,
Can only gaze while all are sleeping,
And dream my Mary watches too!

WHEN I ROVED A YOUNG HIGHLANDER

Words by Lord Byron. Music by J. P. Knight.

When I roved a young Highlander o'er the dark heath,
And climb'd thy dark summit, O Morven, of snow!

To gaze on the torrent that slumber'd beneath,
Or the mist of the tempest that gather'd below;
Untutor'd by science, a stranger to fear,
And rude as the rocks where my infancy grew,
No feeling, save one, to my bosom was dear—
Need I say, my sweet Mary, 'twas centred in you?

I arose with the dawn, with my dog as my guide,
From mountain to mountain I bounded along;
I breasted the billows of Dee's rushing tide,
And heard at a distance the Highlander's song—
At eve, on my heath-cover'd couch of repose,
No dreams, save of Mary, were spread to my view;
And warm to the skies my devotions arose,
For the first of my prayers was a blessing on you.

Yet the day may arrive, when the mountains once more
Shall rise to my sight in their mantles of snow;
But while these soar above me, unchanged as before,
Will Mary be there to receive me? ah no!
Adieu! then, ye hills, where my childhood was bred—
Thou sweet flowing Dee, to thy waters adieu!
No home in the forest shall shelter my head,—
Ah, Mary! what home could be mine without you?

ROY'S WIFE OF ALDIVALLOCH

Was written by Mrs. Grant, of Carron, on the river Spey. Her maiden name was Grant, and she afterwards married Dr. Murray, of Bath. She was born about 1745, and died about 1814.

Roy's wife of Aldivalloch,
Roy's wife of Aldivalloch,
Wat ye how she cheated me,
As I cam' o'er the braes of Balloch?

She vow'd, she swore she wad be mine;
She said she lo'ed me best of onie;
But ah! the fickle, faithless quean,
She's ta'en the carle, and left her Johnnie.
Roy's wife, &c.

O, she was a cantie quean,
Weel could she dance the Highland walloch;
How happy I, had she been mine,
Or I been Roy of Aldivalloch.
Roy's wife, &c.

Her hair sae fair, her een sae clear,
Her wee bit mou' sae sweet and bonnie;
To me she ever will be dear,
Though she's for ever left her Johnnie.
Roy's wife, &c.

LOGAN BRAES.

The two first stanzas of this song are by John Mayne, author of the "Siller Gun," and other poems of distinction. The author of the other stanzas is unknown. Mayne was a native of Dumfries; was long connected with the London press, and died in 1836. The air "Logan Water," to which the song is sung, is of considerable antiquity.

"By Logan's streams that rin sae deep,
Fu' aft wi' glee I've herded sheep;
Herded sheep, or gather'd slaes,
Wi' my dear lad, on Logan braes.
But wae's my heart! thae days are gane,
And I, wi' grief, may herd alane;
While my dear lad maun face his faes,
Far, far frae me, an' Logan braes.

"Nae mair at Logan kirk will he
Atween the preachings meet wi' me;
Meet wi' me, or when it's mirk,
Convoy me hame frae Logan kirk.
I weel may sing thae days are gane—
Frae kirk an' fair I come alane,
While my dear lad maun face his faes,
Far, far frae me, an' Logan braes!"

While for her love she thus did sigh,
She saw a sodger passing by,
Passing by wi' scarlet claes,
While sair she grat on Logan braes:
Says he, "What gars thee greet sae sair,
What fills thy heart sae fu' o' care?
Thae sporting lambs hae blythesome days,
An' playfu' skip on Logan braes!"

"What can I do but weep and mourn?
I fear my lad will ne'er return,
Ne'er return to ease my waes,
Will ne'er come hame to Logan braes."
Wi' that he clasp'd her in his arms,
And said, "I'm free from war's alarms,
I now ha'e conquer'd a' my faes;
We'll happy live on Logan braes."

OH, DINNA ASK ME.

Dunlop.—Tune, "Comin' through the rye."

Oh! dinna ask me gin I lo'e thee;
Troth, I daurna tell:
Dinna ask me gin I lo'e ye;
Ask it o' yoursel'.

Oh! dinna look sae sair at me,
For weel ye ken me true;
O, gin ye look sae sair at me,
I daurna look at you.

When ye gang to yon braw braw town,
And bonnier lasses see,
O, Jamie, dinna, look at them,
Lest you should mind na me.

For I could never bide the lass,
That ye'd lo'e mair than me;
And O, I'm sure, my heart would break,
Gin ye'd prove false to me.

BIRD OF THE WILDERNESS.

This poetic gem of the Ettrick Shepherd has been set to music by Mr. Dempster, the well-known talented composer and pleasing vocalist.

Bird of the wilderness,
Blythesome and cumberless,
Sweet be thy matin o'er moorland and lea!
Emblem of happiness,
Bless'd is thy dwelling-place,
Oh! to abide in the desert with thee!

Wild is thy lay and loud,
Far in the downy cloud;
Love gives it energy, love gave it birth;
Where on the dewy wing,
Where art thou journeying?
Thy lay is in heaven, thy love is on earth

O'er fell and fountain sheen,
O'er moor and mountain green,
O'er the red streamer that heralds the day,
Over the cloudlet dim,
Over the rainbow's rim,
Musical cherub, hie, hie thee away.

Then when the gloaming comes,
Low in the heather blooms,
Sweet will thy welcome and bed of love be!
Bird of the wilderness,
Bless'd is thy dwelling-place,
Oh! to abide in the desert with thee.

WHAT AILS THIS HEART O' MINE?

This beautiful lyric is the production of Miss Blamire, whose poems have been lately collected by the erudite Mr. Maxwell, of Edinburgh.

What ails this heart o' mine?
 What ails this watery e'e?
What gars me a' turn cauld as death
 When I take leave o' thee?
When thou art far awa'
 Thou'lt dearer grow to me;
But change o' place and change o' face
 May gar thy fancy jee.

When I gae out at e'en,
 Or walk at morning air,
Ilk rustling bush will seem to say
 I used to meet thee there.
Then I'll sit down and cry,
 And live aneath the tree,
And when a leaf fa's i' my lap
 I'll ca't a word frae thee.

I'll hie me to the bower
 That thou wi' roses tied,
And where wi' mony a blushing bud
 I strove mysel' to hide.
I'll doat on ilka spot
 Where I ha'e been wi' thee;
And ca' to mind some kindly word
 By ilka burn and tree!

WHAT WILL A' THE LADS DO?

This is another of the Misses Cummings' popular duets. The words are by the Ettrick Shepherd.

O, what will a' the lads do
 When Maggie gangs away?
O, what will a' the lads do,
 When Maggie gangs away?
There's no a heart in a' the glen
 That disna dread the day.
O, what will a' the lads do
 When Maggie gangs away?

Young Jock has ta'en the hill for't—
 A waefu' wight is he;
Poor Harry's ta'en the bed for't,
 An' laid him doun to dee;
An' Sandy's gane unto the kirk,
 An' learning fast to pray.
And, O, what will the lads do
 When Maggie gangs away?

The young laird o' the Lang-shaw
 Has drunk her health in wine;
The priest has said—in confidence—
 The lassie was divine:
And that is mair in maiden's praise
 Than ony priest should say:
But, O, what will the lads do
 When Maggie gangs away?

The wailing in our green glen
 That day will quaver high;
'Twill draw the red-breast frae the wood,
 The laverock frae the sky;
The fairies frae their beds o' dew
 Will rise and join the lay:
An' hey! what a day 'twill be
 When Maggie gangs away!

EARL MARCH.

This is from the classic pen of Thomas Campbell, author of "The Pleasures of Hope."

Earl March look'd on his dying child,
 And smit with grief to view her—
The youth, he cried, whom I exiled
 Shall be restored to woo her

She's at the window many an hour,
 His coming to discover;
And her love look'd up to Ellen's bower,
 And she look'd on her lover.

But ah! so pale, he knew her not,
 Though her smile on him was dwelling,
And am I then forgot—forgot?—
 It broke the heart of Ellen

In vain he weeps, in vain he sighs,
 Her cheek is cold as ashes;
Nor love's own kiss shall wake those eyes
 To lift their silken lashes.

LOGIE O' BUCHAN.

This song has been till of late ascribed to the authoress of Auld Robin Gray; but it is now on good authority attributed to a Mr. George Halket, a schoolmaster in the north of Scotland, who died in 1756.

O Logie o' Buchan, O Logie the laird,
They ha'e ta'en awa' Jamie, that delved in the yard,
Wha play'd on the pipe, and the viol sae sma';
They ha'e ta'en awa' Jamie, the flower o' them a'.
 He said, Think na lang lassie, tho' I gang awa';
 He said, Think na lang lassie, tho' I gang awa';
 For simmer is coming, cauld winter's awa',
 And I'll come and see thee in spite o' them a'.

Tho' Sandy has ousan, has gear, and has kye;
A house and a hadden, and siller forbye;
Yet I'd tak' mine ain lad, wi' his staff in his hand,
Before I'd ha'e him, wi' his houses and land.
 He said, Think nae lang, &c.

My daddie looks sulky, my minnie looks sour,
They frown upon Jamie because he is poor:
Tho' I lo'e them as weel as a daughter should do,
They're nae hauf sae dear to me, Jamie, as you.
 He said, Think nae lang, &c.

I sit on my creepie, I spin at my wheel,
And think on the laddie that lo'ed me sae weel;
He had but ae saxpence, he brak it in twa,
And gi'ed me the hauf o't when he gade awa'.
 Then haste ye back, Jamie, and bide na awa'
 Then haste ye back, Jamie, and bide na awa',
 The simmer is coming, cauld winter's awa',
 Sae come soon and see me in spite o' them a'.

THE BANKS OF ALLAN WATER.

This very popular ballad was written by M. G. Lewis Esq., author of "The Monk," "Castle Spectre," &c.

On the banks of Allan Water,
 When the sweet spring-time did fall,
Was the Miller's lovely daughter,
 Fairest of them all!
For his bride a soldier sought her,
 And a winning tongue had he,
On the banks of Allan Water
 None so gay as she!

On the banks of Allan Water,
 When brown Autumn spread his store,
There I saw the Miller's daughter,
 But she smiled no more;
For the Summer, grief had brought her,
 And the soldier, false was he,
On the banks of Allan Water,
 None so sad as she!

On the banks of Allan Water,
 When the Winter snow fell fast,
Still was seen the Miller's daughter.
 Chilling blew the blast;

But the Miller's lovely daughter,
Both from cold and care was free!
On the banks of Allan Water,
There a corpse lay she!

SOME LOVE TO ROAM.

Charles Mackay, Esq., the author of this popular lyric, is the author of many excellent poetic and prose productions. The music is by Henry Russell.

Some love to roam o'er the dark sea's foam,
Where the shrill winds whistle free;
But a chosen band in a mountain land,
And a life in the woods for me.
When morning beams o'er the mountain streams,
Oh! merrily forth we go,
To follow the stag to his slippery crag,
And to chase the bounding roe.—Ho! ho! ho! ho!
Some love to roam, &c.

The deer we mark in the forest dark,
And the prowling wolf we track;
And for right good cheer, in the wild woods here,
Oh! why should a hunter lack?
For with steady aim at the bounding game,
And hearts that fear no foe,
To the darksome glade, in the forest shade,
Oh! merrily forth we go. Ho! ho! ho! ho!
Some love to roam, &c.

BONNIE JEANNIE GRAY.

The first and last stanzas of this popular song were written by W. Paul, Glasgow, and set to music by Richard Webster. The second stanza is an interpolation by William Thom, of Inverury.

Oh whar was ye sae late yestreen,
My bonnie Jeannie Gray?
Your mither miss'd you late at e'en,
And eke at break o' day.
Your mither look'd sae sour and sad,
Your father dull and wae,
Oh! whar was ye sae late yestreen,
My bonnie Jeannie Gray?

I've mark'd that lanely look o' thine,
My bonnie Jeannie Gray;
I've kent your kindly bosom pine,
This monie, monie day.
Ha'e hinnied words o' promise lured
Your guileless heart astray?
O! dinna hide your grief frae me,
My bonnie Jeannie Gray.

Dear sister, sit ye down by me,
And let nae body ken;
For I ha'e promised late yestreen
To wed young Jamie Glen;
The melting tear stood in his e'e,
What heart could say him nay?
As aft he vow'd, through life, I'm thine,
My bonnie Jeannie Gray.

LADDIE, OH! LEAVE ME.

Down whar the burnie rins whimplin' and cheery,
When love's star was smilin', I met wi' my dearie;
Ah! vain was its smilin', she wadna believe me,
But said wi' a saucy air, "Laddie, Oh! leave me,
Leave me, leave me, laddie, Oh! leave me."

"I've lo'ed thee o'er truly to seek a new dearie,
I've lo'ed thee o'er fondly, through life e'er to weary,
I've lo'ed thee o'er lang, love, at last to deceive thee.
Look cauldly or kindly, but bid me not leave thee."
Leave thee, leave thee, &c.

"There's nae ither saft e'e can fill me wi' pleasure,
There's nae ither rose-lip has half o' its treasure,
There's nae ither bower, love, shall ever receive me, [thee."
Till death break this fond heart—oh, then I maun leave
Leave thee, leave thee, &c.

The tears o'er her cheeks ran like dew frae red roses.
What hope to the lover one tear-drop discloses!
I kiss'd her, and blest her: at last, to relieve me,
She yielded her hand, and sigh'd, "Oh! never leave me."
Leave me, leave me, &c.

JOCK O' HAZELDEAN.

Written by Sir Walter Scott for Albyn's Anthology, a collection of Highland airs edited by Alex. Campbell. There is an old balled, called Jock o' *Hazelgreen*, from which the poet has borrowed several lines.

"Why weep ye by the tide, ladye—
Why weep ye by the tide?
I'll wed ye to my youngest son,
And ye shall be his bride;
And ye shall be his bride, ladye,
Sae comely to be seen:"
But aye she loot the tears down fa',
For Jock o' Hazeldean.

"Now let this wilful grief be done,
And dry that cheek so pale:
Young Frank is chief of Errington,
And lord of Langley dale;
His step is first in peaceful ha',
His sword in battle keen:"
But aye she loot the tears down fa',
For Jock o' Hazeldean.

"A chain o' gold ye shall not lack,
Nor braid to bind your hair,
Nor mettled hound, nor managed hawk,
Nor palfrey fresh and fair;
And you, the foremost o' them a',
Shall ride our forest queen:"
But aye she loot the tears down fa',
For Jock o' Hazeldean.

The kirk was deck'd at morning-tide,
The tapers glimmer'd fair;
The priest and bridegroom wait the bride,
And dame and knight were there:
They sought her baith by bower and ha';
The ladye was not seen!
She's o'er the border, and awa'
Wi' Jock o' Hazeldean!

DONALD AND FLORA.

This song refers to an incident which occurred during the war of independence. Donald, the lover, accompanied the British troops to America, and perished "on Saratoga's plain." The news of his death arrives, and reason forsakes the unhappy Flora. The words are by the author of "Saw ye my wee thing?" The air is very beautiful. Donald was a Captain Stewart, and Flora was a young lady in Athole.

When merry hearts were gay,
Careless of aught but play,
Poor Flora slipt away,
Sadd'ning to Mora.
Loose flow'd her yellow hair,
Quick heaved her bosom bare;
And thus to the troubled air
She vented her sorrow:

"Loud howls the northern blast,
Bleak is the dreary waste,
Haste then, O Donald, haste,
Haste to thy Flora!

Twice twelve long months are o'er,
Since on a foreign shore
You promised to fight no more—
But meet me in Mora.

"Come then, O come away!
Donald! no longer stay!
Where can my rover stray
From his loved Flora?
Ah! sure he ne'er could be
False to his vows and me!
Heavens! Is't not yonder he
Comes bounding o'er Mora?"

Never, O wretched fair!
(Sigh'd the sad messenger,)
Never shall Donald mair
Meet his loved Flora!
Cold as yon mountain's snow,
Donald, thy love, lies low!
He sent me to sooth thy wo,
Weeping in Mora!

Well fought his valiant men
On Saratoga's plain;
Thrice fled the hostile train
From British glory.
But, though his foes did flee,
Sad was the loss to thee;
Every fresh victory
Drown'd us in sorrow.

"Here, take this love-wrought plaid,
(Donald, expiring, said,)
Give it to yon dear maid,
Drooping in Mora.
Tell her, O, Allan, tell
Donald thus bravely fell;
And in his last farewell,
Thought on his Flora."

Mute stood the trembling fair,
Speechless with wild despair:
Striking her bosom bare,
She sigh'd, poor Flora!
Ah! Donald, ah! well-a-day!
Was all the fond heart could say,
And the sound died away
Forever on Mora!

THE FLOWERS OF THE FOREST.

Mrs. Cockburn, the author of this song, was daughter of Mr. Rutherford, of Fairnielie, in Roxburghshire. She was born in 17—, married to a Mr. Cockburn, Advocate, Edinburgh, in 1731, and died in 1794. The song refers to the disastrous battle of Flodden, fought in 1513, where King James IV., of Scotland, and the flower of his nobility, were slain. "The Forest" was the name given to a particular district of country noted for its fine archers, who, almost to a man, perished on the field, and the song laments their loss—"*The flowers of the forest are a' wede away.*" There is another song written about the same time, to the same air, and upon the same subject. It begins, "I've seen the lilting, at our yowe-milking." The author was Miss Jane Elliot, daughter of Sir Gilbert Elliot, of Minto. The air to which these songs are sung has been recently discovered in an old manuscript, written in 1620, and is much superior in its original simplicity to the sets of the air now in use.

I've seen the smiling of Fortune beguiling,
I've tasted her pleasures and found them decay;
Sweet was her blessing, and kind her caressing,
But now they are fled, they are fled far away.
I've seen the forest adorned the foremost,
Wi' flowers o' the fairest, baith pleasant and gay;
Sae bonny was their blooming, their scent the air perfuming,
But now they are wither'd, and a' wede away.

I've seen the morning with gold the hills adorning,
And loud tempest storming before middle day;
I've seen Tweed's silver streams, glittering in the sunny beams,
Grow drumlie and dark as they roll'd on their way.
O fickle fortune, why this cruel sporting,
Why thus perplex us poor sons of a day?
Nae mair thy frowns will fear me, nae mair thy smiles will cheer me,
Since the Flowers of the Forest are a' wede away.

THE BONNIE HOUSE O' AIRLY.

All who have heard Mr. Clirehugh's inimitable execution of this old ballad will be pleased to possess the words. There are different readings of the ballad, all of which are very imperfect; it is here rendered as sung by Mr. Clirehugh.

It fell on a day, a bonnie simmer day,
When the corn waved green and yellow,
There fell out a great dispute
Between Argyle and Airly!

Argyle has ta'en a hundred o' his men,
A hundred men and mairly,
An' he's awa' to the back o' Dunkeld,
To plunder the bonnie house o' Airly

Lady Ogilvie look'd o'er the high castle wa',
An' ah! but she sigh'd sairly.
When she saw Argyle an' a' his men
Come to plunder the bonnie house o' Airly.

Come down, come down, Lady Ogilvie, he cried,
Come down and kiss me fairly,
Or I swear by the sword I hold in my hand,
That I winna leave a stan'in' stane on Airly!

I'll no come down, ye fause Argyle,
Until ye speak mair fairly;
Nor would I kiss the proud Argyle
Tho' he leave na a stan'in' stane on Airly!

For if my brave lord was here this night,
As he's this night wi' Charlie,
There's no a Campbell in a' Argyle
Dare tread on the bonnie green o' Airly!

* * * * * * *

He has ta'en her by the middle sae sma',
But he has nae ta'en her fairly;
An' he's led her up to a high hill tap
Where she saw the burnin' o' Airly.

TAK YER AULD CLOAK ABOUT YE.

This ballad had found its way into England early in the reign of Queen Elizabeth, as we find it quoted by Shakspeare, in the tragedy of Othello. Its authorship is unknown, having been handed down by oral communication, like many other fine old Scottish ballads.

In winter, when the rain rain'd cauld,
And frost and snaw on ilka hill,
And Boreas, wi' his blasts sae bauld,
Was threat'nin' a' our kye to kill:
Then Bell, my wife, wha lo'es nae strife,
She said to me right hastilie,
Get up, gudeman, save Crummie's life,
And tak' yer auld cloak about ye.

My Crummie is a usefu' cow,
And she is come of a good kin';
Aft has she wet the bairns's mou',
And I am laith that she should tyne;
Get up, gudeman, it is fu' time,
The sun shines frae the lift sae hie;
Sloth never made a gracious end;
Gae, tak' your auld cloak about ye.

My cloak was ance a gude grey cloak,
  When it was fitting for my wear;
But now it's scantly worth a groat,
  For I have worn't this thretty year:
Let's spend the gear that we ha'e won,
  We little ken the day we'll die;
Then I'll be proud, since I have sworn
  To ha'e a new cloak about me.

In days when our King Robert rang,
  His trews they cost but half a croun,
He said they were a groat ower dear,
  And ca'd the tailor thief and loon:
He was the king that wore a croun,
  And thou the man of laigh degree:
It's pride puts a' the country doun;
  Sae tak' your auld cloak about ye.

Ilka land has its ain lauch,
  Ilk kind o' corn has its ain hool;
I think the world is a' gane wrang,
  When ilka wife her man wad rule:
Do ye no see Rob, Jock, and Hab,
  As they are girded gallantlie,
While I sit huyklin i' the aese?—
  I'll ha'e a new cloak about me.

Gudeman, I wat its thretty year
  Sin' we did ane anither ken;
And we ha'e had atween us twa
  Of lads and bonnie lassies ten:
Now they are women grown and men,
  I wish and pray weel may they be;
If you would prove a good husband,
  E'en tak' your auld cloak about ye.

Bell, my wife, she lo'es nae strife,
  But she would rule me, if she can;
And to maintain an easy life,
  I aft maun yield, though I'm gudeman:
Nocht's to be gain'd at woman's hand,
  Unless ye gi'e her a' the plea;
Then I'll leave aff where I began,
  And tak' my auld cloak about me.

I LO'ED NE'ER A LADDIE BUT ANE.

The first stanza of this song is attributed to the Rev. John Clunie; the remaining, are the composition of Hector Macniel. The air bears a striking resemblance to the Irish tune "My lodging is on the cold ground," but the emigration from Scotland to Ireland during the periods of religious persecution was so great that many of the old airs have long been familiar in both countries. We give only the stanzas that are generally sung.

I lo'ed ne'er a laddie but ane;
  He lo'ed ne'er a lassie but me;
He's willing to mak' me his ain;
  And his ain I am willing to be.
He has coft me a rokelay o' blue,
  And a pair o' mittens o' green;
The price was a kiss o' my mou';
  And I paid him the debt yestreen.

Let ithers brag weel o' their gear,
  Their land, and their lordly degree;
I carena for aught but my dear,
  For he's ilka thing lordly to me:
Our laird has baith honours and wealth,
  Yet see how he's dwining wi' care;
Now we, though we've naething but health,
  Are cantie and leal evermair.

O Marion! the heart that is true,
  Has something mair costly than gear;
Ilk e'en it has naething to rue—
  Ilk morn it has naething to fear.
Ye lasses wha lo'e to torment
  Your wooers wi' fause scorn and strife,
Play your pranks—I ha'e gi'en my consent
  And this night I am Jamie's for life.

THERE LIVES A YOUNG LASSIE.

This song has recently been introduced to an American audience by the Misses Cummings, and will no doubt become a favourite. The words are by John Imlah.

There lives a young lassie
  Far down in yon glen;
And I lo'e that lassie
  As nae ane may ken!
O! a saint's faith may vary,
  But faithful I'll be;
For weel I lo'e Mary,
  An' Mary lo'es me.

Red, red as the rowan
  Her smiling wee mou';
An' white as the gowan
  Her breast and her brow!
Wi' a foot o' a fairy
  She links o'er the lea;
O! weel I lo'e Mary,
  An' Mary lo'es me.

She sings sweet as onie
  Wee bird of the air,
She's blithe as she's bonnie,
  She's guid as she's fair;
Like a lammie sae airy
  And artless is she;
O! weel I lo'e Mary,
  And Mary lo'es me!

Where yon tall forest timmer,
  An' lowly broom bower,
To the sunshine o' simmer
  Spread verdure an' flower;
There, when night clouds the cary,
  Beside her I'll be;
For weel I lo'e Mary,
  And Mary lo'es me.

BONNIE MARY HAY.

Was written by Archibald Crawford, a native of Ayr. The music was composed by R. A. Smith.

Bonnie Mary Hay, I will lo'e thee yet;
For thy eye is the slae, and thy hair is the jet,
The snaw is thy skin, and the rose is thy cheek.
Oh! bonnie Mary Hay, I will lo'e thee yet.

Bonnie Mary Hay, will you gang wi' me,
When the sun's in the west, to the hawthorn tree?
To the hawthorn tree in the bonnie berry den?
And I'll tell you, Mary, how I lo'e you then.

Bonnie Mary Hay, it's haliday to me,
When thou art coothie, kind, and free:
There's nae clouds in the lift, nor storms in the sky,
My bonnie Mary Hay, when thou art nigh.

Bonnie Mary Hay, thou maunna say me nay;
But come to the bow'r by the hawthorn brae,
But come to the bow'r, an' I'll tell ye a' what's true,
How, Mary! I can ne'er lo'e ane but you.

SAW YE JOHNNY COMIN'.

Both words and music of this song are old, and their authors unknown.

Saw ye Johnny comin', quo' she,
  Saw ye Johnny comin';
Saw ye Johnny comin', quo' she,
  Saw ye Johnny comin;
Saw ye Johnny comin', quo' she,
  Saw ye Johnny comin';
Wi' his blue bonnet on his head,
  And his doggie rinnin', quo' she,
  And his doggie rinnin'?

Fee him, father, fee him, quo' she,
  Fee him, father, fee him;
Fee him, father, fee him, quo' she,
  Fee him, father, fee him;
For he is a gallant lad,
  And a weel-doin';
And a' the wark about the house,
  Gaes wi' me when I see him, quo' she,
  Wi' me when I see him.

What will I do wi' him, quo' he,
  What will I do wi' him?
He's ne'er a sark upon his back,
  And I ha'e nane to gi'e him.
I ha'e twa sarks into my kist,
  And ane o' them I'll gi'e him;
And for a merk o' mair fee
  Dinna stand wi' him, quo' she,
  Dinna stand wi' him.

For weel do I lo'e him, quo' she,
  Weel do I lo'e him;
For weel do I lo'e him, quo' she,
  Weel do I lo'e him.
O fee him, father, fee him, quo' she,
  Fee him, father, fee him;
He'll haud the pleugh, thrash in the barn,
  And crack wi' me at e'en, quo' she,
  And crack wi' me at e'en.

THE LAIRD O' COCKPEN.

This highly humorous and popular song is ascribed to Miss Ferrier, the accomplished authoress of "Destiny," "Marriage," and "Inheritance,"—three novels of distinguished merit.

The Laird o' Cockpen, he's proud an' he's great;
His mind is ta'en up wi' the things o' the state:
He wanted a wife his braw house to keep;
But favour wi' wooin' was fashious to seek

Doun by the dyke-side a lady did dwell.
At his table-head he thought she'd look well;
M'Clish's ae daughter o' Claverse-ha' Lee,
A pennyless lass wi' a lang pedigree.

His wig was weel pouther'd, as guid as when new,
His waistcoat was white, his coat it was blue;
He put on a ring, a sword, and cock'd hat—
And wha could refuse the Laird wi' a' that?

He took the grey mare, and rade cannilie—
And rapped at the yett o' Claverse-ha' Lee,
"Gae tell mistress Jean to come speedily ben:
She's wanted to speak wi' the Laird o' Cockpen."

Mistress Jean she was makin' the elder-flower wine;
"And what brings the Laird at sic a like time?"
She put aff her apron, and on her silk gown,
Her mutch wi' red ribbons, and gaed awa' down.

And when she cam' ben, he boued fu' low;
And what was his errand he soon let her know.
Amazed was the Laird when the lady said, Na,
And wi' a laigh curtsie she turned awa'.

Dumfounder'd he was, but nae sigh did he gi'e;
He mounted his mare, and rade cannilie;
And aften he thought, as he gaed through the glen,
"She's daft to refuse the Laird o' Cockpen."

LIZZY LINDSAY.

This is a new version of a very old ballad It has been recently introduced by the Misses Cumming, and become a favourite with the public.

Will ye gang wi' me, Lizzy Lindsay,
  Will ye gang to the Highlands wi' me?
Will ye gang wi' me, Lizzy Lindsay,
  My bride and my darling to be?

O ye are the bonniest maiden,
  The flower o' the west kintrie;
Will ye gang to the hielands, Lizzy Lindsay,
  My pride and my darling to be?

To gang to the Highlands wi' you, sir,
  I dinna ken how that may be;
For I ken nae the land that ye live in,
  Nor ken I the lad I'm gaun wi'.

O Lizzy, lass, ye maun ken little,
  If sae be ye dinna ken me;
My name is Lord Ronald MacDonald,
  A chieftain o' high degree.

I've goud and I've gear, Lizzy Lindsay,
  And a heart that lo'es only thee;
They a' shall be thine, Lizzy Lindsay,
  Gin ye my loved darling will be.

She has kilted her coats o' green satin,
  She has kilted them up to the knee,
And she's aff and awa' wi' Lord Ronald,
  His bride and his darling to be.

SCOTLAND YET.

Written by the Rev. H. S. Riddel. Set to music by Peter MacLeod.

Gae bring my gude auld harp ance mair,
  Gae bring it firm and fast—
For I maun sing anither sang,
  Ere a' my glee be past.
And trow ye as I sing, my lads,
  The burden o't shall be,
Auld Scotland's howes, and Scotland's knowes,
  And Scotland's hills for me!
I'll drink a cup to Scotland yet,
  Wi' a' the honours three.

The heath waves wild upon her hills,
  And, foaming frae the fells,
Her fountains sing o' freedom still,
  As they dance down the dells;
And weel I lo'e the land, my lads,
  That's girded by the sea;
Then Scotland's dales, and Scotland's vales,
  And Scotland's hills for me!
I'll drink a cup to Scotland yet,
  Wi' a' the honours three.

Her thistle waves upon the fields
  Where Wallace bore his blade,
That gave her foemen's dearest bluid
  To dye her auld grey plaid;
And looking to the lift, my lads,
  He sang this doughty glee,
Auld Scotland's right, and Scotland's might,
  And Scotland's hills for me!
Then drink a cup to Scotland yet,
  Wi' a' the honours three.

They tell o' lands wi' brighter skies,
  Where freedom's voice ne'er rang—
Gi'e me the hills where Ossian dwelt,
  And Coila's Minstrel sang;
For I've nae skill o' lands, my lads,
  That ken na to be free.
Then Scotland's right, and Scotland's might,
  And Scotland's hills for me!
We'll drink a cup to Scotland yet,
  Wi' a' the honours three.

O WHY LEFT I MY HAME.

This is one of the best songs which has been in modern times added to the National Lyrics of Scotland. The words are from the pen of R. Gilfillan, a poet of no mean celebrity; and the air is by P. McLeod, Esq. of Edinburgh It is supposed to be sung by an emigrant in the East Indies.

O WHY left I my hame, why did I cross the deep,
O why left I the land where my forefathers sleep!
I sigh for Scotia's shore, and I gaze across the sea,
But I canna get a blink o' my ain kintrie.

The palm-tree waveth high, and fair the myrtle springs,
And to the Indian maid the bulbul sweetly sings;
But I dinna see the broom with its tassels on the lea,
Nor hear the linties' sang o' my ain kintrie.

O here nae sabbath bell awakes the sabbath morn,
Nor song of reapers heard amang the yellow corn;
For the tyrant's voice is heard and the wail o' slaverie,
But the sun of freedom shines in my ain kintrie.

There's a hope for every wo, and a balm for every pain,
But the first days of our heart come ne'er back again;
There's a track upon the deep, and a path across the sea,
But the weary ne'er return to their ain kintrie.

JEAN LINN.

THIS admirable ballad is the production of W. WILSON, Esq., of Poughkeepsie. It was published many years ago in an Edinburgh literary publication, and was very highly appreciated as an excellent imitation of the old ballad style.

O HAUD na your noddle sae hie my doo,
O haud na your noddle sae hie;
The time that has been, may be yet again seen,
Sae look na sae lightly on me, my doo.

O geck na at hame, hoddin gray Jean Linn,
O geck na at hame, hoddin gray;
Your gutcher and mine, wad hae thocht themselves fine,
In siccan attire, bonny May.

Ye mind when we won in whin glen, Jean Linn?
Ye mind when we won in whin glen?
Your daddy, douse carle, was cottar to mine,
And our herd was your bonny sell, then, Jean Linn.

O then you were a' thing to me, Jean Linn,
O then you were a' thing to me;
An' the hours scour'd by, like birds thro' the sky,
When tenting the owsen wi' thee, Jean Linn.

I twin'd you a bower by the burn, Jean Linn,
I twin'd you a bower by the burn;
But dreamt na the hour, as we sat in the bow'r,
That fortune wad tak sic a turn, Jean Linn.

You busk noo in satins fu' braw, Jean Linn,
You busk noo in satins fu' braw;
Your daddie's a laird, mine's in the kirk yard,
And I'm your puir ploughman, Jock Law, Jean Linn.

THE MITHERLESS BAIRN.

THIS is the production of a true son of genius—WILLIAM THOM, a poor weaver, in Inverury, a small village in the north of Scotland.

WHEN a' ither bairnies are hush'd to their hame,
By aunty, or cousin, or frecky grand-dame,
Wha stands last an' lanely, an' sairly forfairn?
'Tis the puir dowie laddie—the mitherless bairn!

The mitherless bairnie creeps to his lane bed,
Nane covers his cauld back, or haps his bare head;
His wee hackit heelies are hard as the airn,
An' lithless the lair o' the mitherless bairn!

Aneath his cauld brow, siccan dreams hover there,
O' hands that wont kindly to kaim his dark hair!
But mornin' brings clutches, a' reckless an' stern,
That lo'e na the locks o' the mitherless bairn!

The sister wha sang o'er his saftly rock'd bed,
Now rests in the mools whare their mammie is laid;
While the father toils sair his wee bannock to earn,
An' kens na the wrangs o' his mitherless bairn.

Her spirit that pass'd in yon hour of his birth,
Still watches his lone lorn wand'rings on earth,
Recording in heaven the blessings they earn,
Wha couthilie deal wi' the mitherless bairn!

Oh! speak him na harshly—he trembles the while,
He bends to your bidding, and blesses your smile:—
In the dark hour o' anguish, the heartless shall learn,
That God deals the blow for the mitherless bairn!

LUCY'S FLITTIN'.

IT is of WILLIAM LAIDLAW, the author of this song, and the valued friend and steward of Sir W. Scott, that the following touching anecdote is related. Scott, on his return from Naples during his last illness, recognised few or none of his friends or relatives, and lay apparently insensible; but seeing Laidlaw near him, at his bed-side, his eyes brightened up as he said—"Is that you, Willie? I ken I'm hame noo." It is strange that he who wrote so well should have written so little—this is the only song the author has written.

'TWAS when the wan leaf frae the birk-tree was fa'in',
And Martinmas dowie had wound up the year,
That Lucy row'd up her wee kist wi' her a' in't,
And left her auld maister and neebours sae dear:
For Lucy had served i' the glen a' the simmer;
She cam there afore the flower bloom'd on the pea
An orphan was she, and they had been gude till her—
Oh, that was the thing brocht the tear to her e'e.

She gaed by the stable where Jamie was stannin';
Richt sair was his kind heart, the flittin' to see:
'Fare ye weel, Lucy!' quo' Jamie, and ran in;
The gatherin' tears trickled fast frae his e'e.
As down the burn-side she gaed slow wi' her flittin',
'Fare ye weel, Lucy!' was ilka bird's sang;
She heard the craw sayin't, high on the tree sittin',
And Robin was chirpin't the brown leaves amang

'O, what is't that pits my puir heart in a flutter?
And what gars the tears come sae fast to my e'e?
If I wasna ettled to be ony better,
Then what gars me wish ony better to be?
I'm just like a lammie that loses its mither;
Nae mither or friend the puir lammie can see;
I fear I hae tint my puir heart a'thegither,
Nae wonder the tear fa's sae fast frae my e'e.

Wi' the rest o' my claes I hae row'd up the ribbon,
The bonny blue ribbon that Jamie gae me;
Yestreen, when he gae me't, and saw I was sabbin',
I'll never forget the wae blink o' his e'e.
Though now he said naething but 'Fare ye weel, Lucy!'
It made me I neither could speak, hear, nor see:
He could nae say mair but just, 'Fare ye weel, Lucy!'
Yet that I will mind till the day that I dee.

The lamb likes the gowan wi' dew when its droukit;
The hare likes the brake and the braird on the lea;
But Lucy likes Jamie;—she turn'd and she lookit,
She thocht the dear place she wad never mair see.
Ah, weel may young Jamie gang dowie and cheerless!
And weel may he greet on the bank o' the burn!
For bonnie sweet Lucy, sae gentle and peerless,
Lies cauld in her grave, and will never return!

THE LONELY AULD WIFE.

THIS affecting lyric is the production of JULIAN CRAMER. The music is by Mr. DEMPSTER, and has been much admired.

BESIDE the old hearth she hath cherish'd for life,
Silent and sad sits the lonely auld wife;
Time hath left many a trace on her brow,
But grief hath not troubled her spirit till now

There are tears in her eyes, that are dim with age,
And she looketh in vain on the holy page;
But she canna see aught but an old oak chair,
That vacant and lonely is standing there.

Long ago, when her bosom was swelling wi' pride,
The lonely auld wife was a gay young bride;
And the rose on her cheek wore its richest bloom
When she gave her hand to the joyous groom.
Faded and worn is her beauty now,
Gray are the hairs on her wrinkled brow;
Silent she sits by the auld hearth stane—
Sad are her thoughts—she is there alane!

Her gudeman is gone to his dreamless rest,
And the lonely auld wife hath a troubled breast;
Yet not for the world would she banish away
The chair he hath sat in for many a day.
She speaketh not, save with a trembling breath,
But hopeth, and waiteth, and prayeth for death;
For joyless and dark are the days o' her life,
When the gudeman is gone frae the lonely auld wife.

MY AIN FIRESIDE.

This is another of the admirable duets introduced by the Misses Cumming, and is a very great favourite with the public. The words are a modern version of a song written by Hamilton, the friend of Allan Ramsay; the music is arranged by the Misses Cumming.

Oh, I hae seen great anes, and sat in great ha's,
Mang lords and mang leddies a' cover'd wi' braws;
But a sight sae delightful I trow I ne'er spied,
As the bonnie blythe blink o' my ain fireside;
My ain fireside, my ain fireside—
Oh, sweet is the blink o' ane's ain fireside.

Ance mair, Heaven be praised, round my ain heartsome [ingle,
Wi' the friends o' my youth I cordially mingle,
Nae forms to compel me to seem wae or glad,
I may laugh when I'm merry, and sigh when I'm sad.

Nae falsehood to dread, nae malice to fear,
But truth to delight me, and friendship to cheer;
O' a' roads to pleasure that ever were tried,
There's nane half so sweet as ane's ain fireside.

GLOSSARY OF THE LESS FAMILIAR WORDS.

Aese, Ashes.
Brag, Boast.
Bairns, Children.
Biggonet, Kind of head-dress.
Butt, } *Ben*, } Kitchen and parlour.
Bobbing, Bowing.
Bawbee, A coin, the value of a cent.
Burnie, Rivulet.
Biggs, Builds.
Braw, Fine looking.
Bluart, A flower that grows in corn.
Bauk, Bank.
Bucht, Sheep-pen.
Coof, Fool.
Clockin' hen, A hen hatching.
Caller, Fresh.
Claymore, Broadsword.
Cannilie, Carefully.
Cary, Sky.
Crack, Converse.
Cantie, Lively.
Couthilie, Kindly.
Dyke, Garden wall
Drumlie, Muddy.
Dowie, Fatigued.
Droukit, Wet.
Dang, Pushed.
Deave, Deafen.
Downa, Darenot.
Dhu, Black.
Dool, Grief.
Ettled, To try.
Fashious, Troublesome.
Fain, Glad.
Forfairn, Distressed.
Gabbing, Talking.
Glint, Glanced.
Gowden, Golden.
Grat, Weeped.
Gear, Riches
Geck, Scorn.
Gutcher, Sire.
Hinny, Honey.
Howmes, Rich undulating land.
Hool, Outer skin of seeds.
Huyklin, Hilching.
Howes, The hollows of undulating land.
Kackling, To cackle as a hen.
Kye, Cows.
Knowes, The high parts of undulating land
Kimmer, Goodwife or friend.
Ken, Know.
Kist, Clothes-chest.
Kaim, Comb.
Links, To trip lightly
Larthe, Loath.
Lift, Heavens.
Lauch, Lake.
Luigh, Low.
Leugh, To laugh.
Lap, To leap.
Lucken, Looken.
Laverock Lark.
Leal, True.
Loune, Rascal.
Loups, Leaps.
Linns, Cascades.
Lifted, Stolen.
Luck, Fortune.
Lave, What remains
Mutch, Lady's cap.
Mittens, Gloves.
Muckle, Much.
Mools, Dust.
Mirk, Dark.
Noddle, Head.
Owsen, Sheep.
Plack, A coin of little value.
Pleugh, Plough.
Peugh, An exclamation signifying distaste for any thing.
Pree, To taste.
Rax, To stretch.
Rokelay, An ornament for the bosom
Scantly, Scarcely.
Sark, Shirt.
Sodger, Soldier.
Shoon, Shoes.
Steer, Stir or bustle.
Trow'd, Believed.
Tyne, Go astray.
Tryste, Engagement.
Wraith, Ghost.
Wight, Stout fellow.
Wede, To wither or die away
Won, Dwelt.
Wist, Knew.
Weir, War.

THE

SONGS AND MISCELLANEOUS POEMS

OF

BARRY CORNWALL.

THE SEA.

THE sea! the sea! the open sea!
The blue, the fresh, the ever free!
Without a mark, without a bound,
It runneth the earth's wide regions round;
It plays with the clouds; it mocks the skies;
Or like a cradled creature lies.

I'm on the sea! I'm on the sea!
I am where I would ever be,
With the blue above, and the blue below,
And silence wheresoe'er I go:
If a storm should come, and awake the deep,
What matter? *I* shall ride and sleep.

I love, oh! *how* I love to ride
On the fierce, foaming, bursting tide,
When every mad wave drowns the moon,
Or whistles aloft his tempest tune,
And tells how goeth the world below,
And why the sou'west blasts do blow.

I never was on the dull tame shore,
But I loved the great sea more and more,
And backward flew to her billowy breast,
Like a bird that seeketh its mother's nest;
And a mother she *was*, and *is* to me;
For I was born on the open sea!

The waves were white, and red the morn,
In the noisy hour when I was born;
And the whale it whistled, the porpoise rolled,
And the dolphins bared their backs of gold;
And never was heard such an outcry wild
As welcomed to life the ocean-child!

I've lived since then, in calm and strife,
Full fifty summers a sailor's life,
With wealth to spend and a power to range,
But never have sought, nor sighed for change;
And Death, whenever he comes to me,
Shall come on the wild unbounded sea!

INDIAN LOVE.

TELL me not that thou dost love me,
Though it thrill me with delight:
Thou art like the stars, above me;
I, the lowly earth at night.

Hast thou (*thou* from kings descended)
Loved the Indian cottage-born;
And shall she, whom Love befriended,
Darken all thy hopeful morn?

Go; and, for thy father's glory,
Wed the blood that's pure and free:
'Tis enough to gild my story
That I *once* was loved by thee!

KING DEATH.

KING Death was a rare old fellow!
He sat where no sun could shine;
And he lifted his hand so yellow,
And poured out his coal-black wine.
Hurrah! for the coal-black wine!

There came to him many a Maiden,
Whose eyes had forgot to shine;
And Widows, with grief o'erladen,
For a draught of his sleepy wine.
Hurrah! for the coal-black wine!

The Scholar left all his learning;
The Poet his fancied woes;
And the Beauty her bloom returning,
Like life to the fading rose.
Hurrah! for the coal-black wine!

All came to the royal old fellow,
Who laugh'd till his eyes dropp'd brine,
As he gave them his hand so yellow,
And pledged them in Death's black wine.
Hurrah! hurrah!
Hurrah! for the coal black-wine!

THE COMMON LOT.

MOURN not thy daughter fading!
It is the common lot,
That those we love should come and go,
And leave us in this world of wo:
So, murmur not!

Her life was short, but fair,
Unsullied by a blot;
And now she sinks to dreamless rest—
(A dove, who makes the earth her nest);
So, murmur not!

No pangs, nor passionate grief,
Nor anger raging hot,
No ills shall ever harm her more;
She goes unto the silent shore,
Where pain is not.

Weep'st thou that none should mourn
For thee, and thy sad lot?
Peace, peace! and know that few e'er grieve
When Death, the tyrant, doth unweave
Life's little knot.

E'en *thou* scarce wept must fade!
It is the common lot,
To link our hearts to things that fly—
To love without return—and die,
And be—forgot!

THE HOME OF THE ABSENTEE.

THE weed mourns on the castle wall,
The grass lies on the chamber-floor,
And on the hearth, and in the hall,
Where merry music danced of yore!
And the blood-red wine no longer
Runs (how it used to run!)
And the shadows within, grown stronger,
Look black on the mid-day sun!
All is gone; save a Voice
That never did yet rejoice:
'Tis sweet and low; 'tis sad and lone;
And it biddeth us love the thing that's flown.

The Gardens feed no fruits nor flowers,
But childless seem, and in decay;
The traitor clock forsakes the hours,
And points to times—oh, far away!
And the steed no longer neigheth,
Nor paws the startled ground;
And the dun hound no longer bayeth;
But death is in all around!
All is gone; save a Voice
That never did yet rejoice:
'Tis sweet and low; 'tis sad and lone;
And it biddeth us love the thing that's flown.

The Lord of all the lone domain,
An undeserving master flies,
And leaves a land where he might reign,
For alien hearts and stranger skies:
And the peasant disdains the story,
He loved to recount of yore;
And the Name, that was once a glory,
Is heard in the land no more!
All is gone; save a Voice
That never did yet rejoice:
'Tis sweet and low; 'tis sad and lone;
And it biddeth us love the thing that's flown.

PAST TIMES.

OLD Acquaintance, shall the nights
You and I once talked together,
Be forgot like common things—
Like some dreary night that brings
Naught, save foul weather?

We were young, when you and I
Talked of golden things together—
Of love and rhyme, of books and men:
Ah! our hearts were buoyant *then*
As the wild-goose feather!

Twenty years have fled, we know,
Bringing care and changing weather;
But hath the heart no *backward* flights,
That we again may see those nights,
And laugh together?

Jove's eagle, soaring to the sun,
Renews the past year's mouldering feather:
Ah, why not you and I, then, soar
From age to youth—and dream once more
Long nights together?

TO MY LYRE.

SLEEP—sleep, my Lyre!
Untouched—unsought—unstrung!
No one now will e'er inquire
If poet to thee ever sung;
Nor if his spirit clung
To thy witching wire!—
Bid thy soul of music sleep,
As winds lie on the charmed deep,
When the mistress Moon doth chide
The tempest or the murmuring tide!
'Tis well to be a thing forgot!
Oblivion is a happy lot!
'Tis well that neither Love nor Wo,
Nor sad sweet thoughts of "long ago,"
Should 'waken again thy self-consuming fire!
Therefore, therefore, sleep my Lyre

A SERENADE.

AWAKE!—The starry midnight Hour
Hangs charmed, and pauseth in its flight:
In its own sweetness sleeps the flower;
And the doves lie hushed in deep delight!
Awake! Awake!
Look forth, my love, for Love's sweet sake!

Awake!—Soft dews will soon arise
From daisied mead and thorny brake;
Then, Sweet, uncloud those eastern eyes,
And like the tender morning break!
Awake! Awake!
Dawn forth, my love, for Love's sweet sake!

Awake!—Within the musk-rose bower
I watch, pale flower of love, for thee:
Ah, come and show the starry Hour
What wealth of love thou hid'st from me!
Awake! Awake!
Show all thy love, for Love's sweet sake!

Awake!—Ne'er heed, though listening Night
Steal music from thy silver voice;
Uncloud thy beauty, rare and bright,
And bid the world and me rejoice!
Awake! Awake!
She comes—at last for Love's sweet sake!

THE ONSET.—A BATTLE SONG.

SOUND an alarum! The foe is come.
I hear the tramp—the neigh—the hum,
The cry, and the blow of his daring drum—
Huzzah!

Sound! The blast of our trumpet blown
Shall carry dismay into hearts of stone,
What! shall we shake at a foe unknown?
Huzzah!—Huzzah!

Have we not sinews as strong as they?
Have we not hearts that ne'er gave way?
Have we not GOD on our side to-day?
Huzzah!

Look! They are staggered on yon black heath:
Steady awhile, and hold your breath!
Now is your time, men—down like death!
Huzzah!—Huzzah!

Stand by each other and front your foes!
Fight, while a drop of the red blood flows!
Fight, as ye fought for the old red rose!
Huzzah!

Sound! Bid your terrible trumpets bray!
Blow, till their brazen throats give way!
Sound to the battle! Sound, I say!
Huzzah!—Huzzah!

THE SEA-KING.

COME sing, come sing, of the great Sea-King,
And the fame that now hangs o'er him,
Who once did sweep o'er the vanquish'd deep,
And drove the world before him!
His deck was a throne, on the ocean lone,
And the sea was his park of pleasure,
Where he scattered in fear the human deer,
And rested—when he had leisure!
Come, shout and sing
Of the great Sea-King,
And ride in the track he rode in!
He sits at the head
Of the mighty dead,
On the red right-hand of Odin!

He sprang, from birth, like a God on earth,
And soared on his victor pinions,
And he traversed the sea, as the eagles flee,
When they look on their blue dominions.
His whole earth life was a conquering strife,
And he lived till his beard grew hoary,
And he died at last, by his blood-red mast,
And now—he is lost in glory!
So, shout and sing, &c.

SONG FOR TWILIGHT.

Hide me, O twilight air!
Hide me from thought, from care,
From all things, foul or fair,
Until to-morrow!
To-night I strive no more;
No more my soul shall soar;
Come, Sleep, and shut the door
'Gainst Pain and Sorrow!

If I must see through dreams,
Be mine Elysian gleams,
Be mine by morning streams
To watch and wander!
So may my spirit cast
(Serpent-like) off the past,
And my free soul at last
Have leave to ponder!

And shouldst thou 'scape control,
Ponder on love, sweet Soul,
On joy—the end—the goal
Of all endeavor!
But if earth's pains will rise,
(As damps will seek the skies),
Then, Night, seal thou mine eyes,
In sleep, for ever!

THE HUNTER'S SONG.

Rise! Sleep no more! 'Tis a noble morn;
The dews hang thick on the fringed thorn,
And the frost shrinks back, like a beaten hound,
Under the steaming, steaming ground.
Behold, where the billowy clouds flow by,
And leave us alone in the clear gray sky!
Our horses are ready and steady—So, ho!
I'm gone, like a dart from the Tartar's bow.
Hark, hark! Who calleth the maiden Morn
From her sleep in the woods and the stubble corn?
The horn, the horn!
The merry sweet ring of the hunter's horn.

Now—through the copse, where the fox is found,
And over the stream, at a mighty bound,
And over the high lands, and over the low,
O'er furrows, o'er meadows, the hunters go!
Away! as a hawk flies full at its prey,
So flieth the hunter, away—away!
From the burst at the cover till set of sun,
When the red fox dies and—the day is done!
Hark, hark! What sound on the wind is borne?
'Tis the conquering voice of the hunter's horn!
The horn, the horn!
The merry bold voice of the hunter's horn.

Sound! Sound the horn! To the hunter good
What's the gully deep or the roaring flood?
Right over he bounds, as the wild stag bounds,
At the heels of his swift, sure, silent hounds.
Oh! *what* delight can a mortal lack,
When he once is firm on his horse's back,
With his stirrups short, and his snaffle strong,
And the blast of the horn for his morning song?
Hark, hark! Now, home! and dream till morn,
Of the bold sweet sound of the hunter's horn!
The horn, the horn!
Oh, the sound of all sounds is the hunter's horn!

THE RECALL.

Come again! Come again!
Sunshine cometh after rain.
As a lamp fed newly burneth,
Pleasure, who doth fly, returneth,
Scattering every cloud of pain.
As the year, which dies in showers,
Riseth in a world of flowers,
Called by many a vernal strain,
Come *thou*—for whom tears were falling,
And a thousand tongues are calling!
Come again, O come again!
Like the sunshine after rain!

THE EXILE'S FAREWELL.

Farewell Old England's shores!
Farewell her rugged men!
Now, sailors, strain your oars
I ne'er will look again.
I've lived—I've sought—I've seen—
Oh, things I love too well,
Upon those shores of green:
So, England! long farewell!
Farewell!

I go; what matter where?
The Exile, when he flies,
Thinks not of *other* air,
Dreams not of *alien* skies:
He seeks but to depart
From the land he loves too well—
From thoughts that smite his heart:
So, England! long farewell!
Farewell!

O'er lands and the lonely main,
A lonelier man, I roam,
To seek some balm for pain—
Perhaps to find a home:
I go; but time nor tide,
Nor all that tongue may tell,
Shall e'er from thee divide
My heart: and so, farewell!
Old England! fare thee well.

THE WILD CHERRY-TREE.

Oh, there never was yet so fair a thing,
By racing river or bubbling spring,
Nothing that ever so gayly grew
Up from the ground when the skies were blue,
Nothing so brave, nothing so free
As *thou*, my wild wild Cherry-tree!

Jove! how it danced in the gusty breeze!
Jove! how it frolicked among the trees!
Dashing the pride of the poplar down,
Stripping the thorn of his hoary crown!
Oak or ash—what matter to *thee?*
'Twas the same to my wild wild Cherry-tree.

Never at rest, like one that's young
Abroad to the winds its arms it flung,
Shaking its bright and crowned head,
Whilst I stole up for its berries red—
Beautiful berries! beautiful tree!
Hurrah! for the wild wild Cherry-tree!

Back I fly to the days gone by,
And I see thy branches against the sky,
I see on the grass thy blossoms shed,
I see (nay I taste) thy berries red,
And I shout—like the tempest loud and free,
Hurrah! for the wild wild Cherry-tree!

THE LITTLE VOICE.

Once there was a little Voice,
Merry as the month of May,
That did cry "*Rejoice! rejoice!*"
Now—'tis flown away!

Sweet it was, and very clear,
Chasing every thought of pain:
Summer! shall I ever hear
Such a voice again?

have pondered all night long,
Listening for as soft a sound:
But so sweet and clear a song
Never have I found!

I would give a mine of gold,
Could I hear that little Voice—
Could I, as in days of old,
At a sound rejoice!

ON A MOTHER AND CHILD SLEEPING.

NIGHT gaze, but send no sound!
Fond heart, thy fondness keep!
Nurse Silence, wray them round!
Breathe low; they sleep, they sleep!

No wind! no murmuring showers!
No music, soft and deep!
No thoughts, nor dreams of flowers!
All hence; they sleep, they sleep!

Time's step is all unheard:
Heaven's stars bright silence keep:
No breath, no sigh, no word!
All's still; they sleep, they sleep!

O Life! O Night! O Time!
Thus ever round them creep!
From pain, from hate, from crime,
E'er guard them, gentle Sleep!

DARK-EYED BEAUTY OF THE SOUTH.

DARK-EYED beauty of the South!
Mistress of the rosy mouth!
Doth thy heart desert its duty?
Doth thy blood belie thy beauty?
Art thou false, and art thou cold?
Art thou sworn to wed for gold?

On thy forehead sitteth pride,
Crowned with scorn, and falcon-eyed;
But beneath, methinks, thou twinest
Silken smiles that *seem* divinest.
Can such smiles be false and cold?
Canst thou—*wilt* thou—wed for gold?

We, who dwell on Northern earth,
Fill the frozen air with mirth—
Soar upon the wings of laughter,
(Though we droop the moment after):
But, through all our regions cold,
None will sell their hearts for gold.

SHE WAS NOT FAIR NOR FULL OF GRACE.

SHE was not fair, nor full of grace,
Nor crowned with thought or aught beside;
Nor wealth had she, of mind or face,
To win our love or raise our pride;
No lover's thought her cheek did touch;
No poet's dream was 'round her thrown;
And yet we miss her—ah, too much,
Now—she hath flown!

We miss her when the morning calls,
As one that mingled in our mirth;
We miss her when the evening falls—
A trifle wanted on the earth!
Some fancy, small, or subtle thought,
Is checked 'ere to its blossom grown;
Some chain is broken that we wrought,
Now—she hath flown!

No solid good, nor hope defined,
Is marred now she hath sunk in night;
And yet the strong immortal Mind
Is stopped in its triumphant flight!
Perhaps some grain lost to its sphere
Might cast the great Sun from his throne;
For all we know is—"She was here,"
And—"She hath flown!"

A SONG FOR THE SEASONS.

WHEN the merry lark doth gild
With his song the summer hours,
And their nests the swallows build
In the roofs and tops of towers,
And the golden broom-flower burns
All about the waste,
And the maiden May returns
With a pretty haste—
Then, how merry are the times!
The Summer times! the Spring times!

Now, from off the ashy stone
The chilly midnight cricket crieth,
And all merry birds are flown,
And our dream of pleasure dieth;
Now the once blue laughing sky
Saddens into gray,
And the frozen rivers sigh,
Pining all away!
Now, how solemn are the times!
The Winter times! the Night times!

Yet, be merry; all around
Is through one vast change resolving;
Even Night, who lately frowned,
Is in paler dawn dissolving;
Earth will burst her fetters strange,
And in spring grow free;
All things in the world will change,
Save—my love for thee!
Sing then, hopeful are all times!
Winter, Summer, Spring times!

THE QUADROON.

SAY they that all beauty lies
In the paler maiden's hue?
Say they that all softness flies,
Save from eyes of April blue?
Arise thou, like a night in June,
Beautiful Quadroon!

Come—all dark and bright, as skies
With the tender starlight hung!
Loose the Love from out thine eyes!
Loose the Angel from thy tongue!
Let them hear Heaven's own sweet tune,
Beautiful Quadroon!

Tell them—Beauty (born above)
From no shade nor hue doth fly;
All she asks is Mind, is Love,
And both upon *thine* aspect lie—
Like the light upon the moon,
Beautiful Quadroon!

IS MY LOVER ON THE SEA.

Is my lover on the sea,
Sailing East, or sailing West?
Mighty Ocean, gentle be,
Rock him into rest!

Let no angry wind arise,
Nor a wave with whitened crest;
All be gentle as his eyes
When he is caressed!

Bear him (as the breeze above
Bears the bird unto its nest),
Here—unto his home of love,
And there bid him rest!

CONSTANCY.

I WOULD I were the bold March-wind,
The merry boisterous bold March-wind,
Who in the violet's tender eyes,
Casts a kiss—and forward flies!
Yet—no! No slight to thee!
O Constancy! O Constancy!

I would I were the soft West-wind,
The wandering sighing soft West-wind,
Who fondles 'round the hyacinth bells,
Then takes wing—as story tells!
Yet—no! No slight to thee!
O Constancy! O Constancy

No; rather will I be the breeze,
That blows straight on in Indian seas;
Or scents, which, in the rose's heart,
Live and love—and *ne'er* depart!
Love—Love—for aye to thee!
O Constancy! O Constancy!

THE MISTLETOE.

WHEN winter nights grow long,
  And winds without blow cold,
We sit in a ring round the warm wood-fire,
  And listen to stories old!
And we try to look grave (as maids should be),
When the men bring in boughs of the laurel-tree.
    O, the Laurel, the evergreen tree!
    The Poets have laurels—and why not we?

How pleasant, when night falls down,
  And hides the wintry sun,
To see them come in to the blazing fire,
  And know that their work is done;
While many bring in, with a laugh or rhyme,
Green branches of holly for Christmas time!
    O the Holly, the bright green Holly,
    It tells (like a tongue) that the times are jolly!

Sometimes—in *our* grave-house,
  Observe, this happeneth not;
But, at times, the evergreen laurel boughs
  And the holly are all forgot!
And then! what then? why, the men laugh low,
And hang up a branch of—the Mistletoe!
    Oh, brave is the Laurel! and brave is the Holly!
    But the Mistletoe banisheth melancholy!
    Ah, nobody knows, nor ever shall know
    What is done—under the Mistletoe!

A BACCHANALIAN SONG.

SING!—Who sings
To her who weareth a hundred rings?
  Ah, who is this lady fine?
  The VINE, boys, the VINE!
  The mother of mighty Wine.
    A roamer is she
    O'er wall and tree,
And sometimes very good company

Drink!—Who drinks
To her who blusheth and never thinks?
  Ah, who is this maid of thine?
  The GRAPE, boys, the GRAPE!
  O, never let her escape
  Until she be turned to Wine!
    For better is she,
    Than vine can be,
And very, very good company!

Dream!—Who dreams
Of the God who governs a thousand streams?
  Ah, who is this Spirit fine?
  'Tis WINE, boys, 'tis WINE!
  God Bacchus, a friend of mine.
    O better is he
    Than grape or tree,
And the best of all good company!

THE NIGHTS.

OH! the Summer Night
  Has a smile of light,
And she sits on a sapphire throne;
  While the sweet Winds load her
  With garlands of odor,
From the bud to the rose o'er-blown!

  But the Autumn Night
  Has a piercing sight,
And a step both strong and free;
  And a voice for wonder,
  Like the wrath of the Thunder,
When he shouts to the stormy sea!

  And the Winter Night
  Is all cold and white,
And she singeth a song of pain;
  Till the wild bee hummeth,
  And warm Spring cometh,
When she dies in a dream of rain!

  Oh, the Night, the Night!
  'Tis a lovely sight,
Whatever the clime or time;
  For sorrow then soareth,
  And the lover out-poureth
His soul in a star-bright rhyme.

  It bringeth sleep
  To the forests deep,
The forest-bird to its nest;
  To Care bright hours,
  And dreams of flowers,
And that balm to the weary—Rest!

THE STORMY PETREL.

A THOUSAND miles from land are we,
Tossing about on the roaring sea;
From billow to bounding billow cast,
Like fleecy snow on the stormy blast;
The sails are scattered abroad, like weeds,
The strong masts shake like quivering reeds,
The mighty cables, and iron chains,
The hull, which all earthly strength disdains,
They strain and they crack, and hearts like stone
Their natural hard proud strength disown.

Up and down! Up and down!
From the base of the wave to the billow's crown,
And amid the flashing and feathery foam
The Stormy Petrel finds a home—
A home, if such a place may be,
For her who lives on the wide wide sea,
On the craggy ice, in the frozen air,
And only seeketh her rocky lair
To warm her young, and to teach them spring
At once o'er the waves on their stormy wing!

O'er the Deep! O'er the Deep!
Where the whale, and the shark, and the sword-fish sleep,
Outflying the blast and the driving rain,
The Petrel telleth her tale—in vain;
For the mariner curseth the warning bird
Who bringeth him news of the storms unheard!
Ah! thus does the prophet, of good or ill,
Meet hate from the creatures he serveth still;
Yet *he* ne'er falters:—So Petrel! spring
Once more o'er the waves on thy stormy wing!

SONG OF THE SOLDIER TO HIS SWORD.

MY Sword! My friend! My noble friend!
  Champion fearless! Servant true!
Whom my fathers without end
  In their thousand battles drew—
    Come!
Let me bare thee to the light!
  Let me clutch thee in my hand!
Oh! how keen, how blue, how bright,
  Is my noble, noble brand!

Thou wast plucked from some base mine—
  Born 'mid stone and stubborn clay;
Ah! who dreamt that aught divine
  In that rugged aspect lay?
    Come!
Once we called and thou didst come
  Straight from out thy sleep didst start,
And the trump and stormy drum
  Woke at once thy iron heart!

Thou wast like the lightning, driven
  By the tempest's strength at speed!
Brazen shields and armor riven
  Told what thou couldst do, at need.
    Come!
Hark! again the trumpets bray!
  Hark! where rolls the stormy drum!
I am here to lead the way;
  Servant of my fathers—Come!

TO A NIGHTINGALE, AT MIDDAY.

THY voice is sweet—is sad—is clear,
And yet, methinks, 't should flow unseen,
Like hidden rivers that we hear
Singing among the forests green.

Delay, delay! till downy Eve
Into her twilight woods hath flown:
Too soon, musician, dost thou grieve;
Love bloometh best (like thought)—alone.

Cease, cease awhile! Thy holy strain
Should be among the silence born;
Thy heart may then unfold its pain,
Leaning upon its bridal thorn.

The insect noise, the human folly,
Disturb thy grave thoughts with their din;
Then, cease awhile, bird Melancholy,
And when the fond Night hears—begin!

EARTH AND AIR.

How bountiful, how wonderful
Thou art, sweet Air!
And yet, albeit thine odors lie
On every gust that mocks the eye,
We pass thy gentle blessings by
Without a care!

How bountiful, how wonderful
Thou art, sweet Earth!
Thy seasons changing with the sun—
Thy beauty out of darkness won!
And yet, whose tongue (when all is done)
Will tell thy worth?

The poet's!—He alone doth still
Uphold *all* worth!
Then love the poet;—love his themes,
His thoughts, half hid in golden dreams,
Which make thrice fair the songs and streams
Of Air and Earth.

HURRAH FOR MERRY ENGLAND.

HURRAH for the Land of England!
Firm-set in the subject sea;
Where the women are fair,
And the men (like air)
Are all lovers of liberty!
Hurrah! for merry England!
Long life, without strife, for England!

Hurrah, for the Spirit of England!
The merry, the true, the free;
Who stretcheth his hand,
With a king's command,
All over the circling sea!
Hurrah! for merry England!
Long life, without strife, for England!

Let tyrants rush forth on the nations,
And strive to chain down the free;
But do *thou* stand fast,
From the first to the last,
For "THE RIGHT"—wherever it be!
O merry, O merry England!
Long life to the Spirit of England!

Hurrah, for William of England!
Our friend—as a king should be;
Who casteth aside
Man's useless pride,
And leans on his people free!
Hurrah! for the King of England!
The boast of merry England!

Her King is the boast of England!
Her guards are her ships at sea;
But her beauty lies
In her women's eyes,
And her strength in her People free!
So, three cheers for merry England!
For the King and the Freemen of England!
Hurrah! Hurrah! Hurrah!

THE HAPPY HOURS.

O, THE Hours! the happy Hours!
When there shone the light of Love,
And all the sky was blue above,
And the earth was full of flowers!
Why should Time and Toil
The worth and beauty spoil
Of such happy Hours?

O, the Hours! the spring-time Hours!
When the soul doth forward bend
And dream the sweet world hath no end,
Neither spot, nor shade, nor showers!
Can we ne'er resume
The love, the light, the bloom,
Of those vernal Hours?

Ever do the year's bright Hours
Come, with laughing April, round,
And with her walk the grassy ground,
When she calleth forth the flowers:
But no new springs bear
To us thoughts half so fair
As the by-gone Hours!

PEACE! WHAT DO TEARS AVAIL?

PEACE! what do tears avail?
She lies all dumb and pale,
And from her eye
The spirit of lovely life is fading—
And she must die!
Why looks the lover wroth? the friend upbraiding?
Reply, reply!

Hath she not dwelt too long
'Midst pain, and grief, and wrong?
Then, why not die?
Why suffer again her doom of sorrow,
And hopeless lie?
Why nurse the trembling dream until to-morrow?
Reply, reply!

Death! take her to thine arms,
In all her stainless charms,
And with her fly
To heavenly haunts, where, clad in brightness,
The Angels lie!
Wilt bear her there, O Death! in all her whiteness?
Reply, reply!

THE WOOD-THRUSH.

WHITHER hath the Wood-thrush flown,
From our greenwood bowers?
Wherefore builds he not again,
Where the white-thorn flowers?

Bid him come! for on his wings,
The sunny year he bringeth;
And the heart unlocks its springs,
Wheresoe'er he singeth.

Lover-like the creature waits,
And when Morning soareth,
All his little soul of song
Tow'rd the dawn he poureth.

Sweet one, why art thou not heard
Now, where woods are stillest?
Oh, come back! and bring with thee—
Whatsoe'er thou willest:—

Laughing thoughts, delightful songs,
Dreams of azure hours,
Something, nothing—all we ask
Is to see thee ours!

'Tis enough that thou shouldst sing
For thy own pure pleasure!
'Tis enough that thou hast *once*
Sweetened human leisure!

COUNT BALTHAZAR.

"A famous man is Robin Hood:
But 'each land' hath a thief as good;
Then let us chant a passing stave
In honor of the Hero brave!"
WORDSWORTH'S ROB ROY.

COUNT BALTHAZAR reigns in his strong stone tower,
Girt round by his iron men;
And his strength, like the terrible Tempest's power,
Sweeps through each Alpine glen!

A hunter he *is*, though a monarch grim
He seems on his mountain throne;
But he hunts not the stag, nor the ermine slim,
Nor the wolf, nor the eagle lone.

He breedeth no cattle, he traineth no vine,
He hath naught that is bought or sold:
Yet his cellars are bursting with brave bright wine,
And his coffers are crammed with gold.

Whenever he lacketh or kine or corn,
He calls to his armed band;
And they hunt through the valleys, from night till morn,
And beg for him—sword in hand!

So he drinks and he revels, till daylight gleams:
But—nothing is free from pain!
For a Demon e'er watches his blood-red dreams,
(Whose laughter is deep
As the depths of sleep,)
And scares him to life again!

* * * * * *

So Balthazar lives, and so must he die,
However the seasons roll:
The visions of guilt must haunt his eye,
And the dread of the damn'd, his soul!

He arose, like a pillar of fire, whose head
Is borne up by the raving blast:
He will sink (like the fire), deserted—dead,
And be trodden in dust at last!

So—down with the tower, the old stone tower!
And, down with the iron men!
Let's summon our hearts, and unfetter our power,
And cleanse out the robber's den!

Where lieth their strength? In a vague false fame.
Where based? On our fear alone.
Then let *us* build a phantom, and forge us a name,
In a foundery of our own!

WHY DOTH THE BOTTLE STAND?

WHY doth the bottle stand, boys?
Let the glass run silent round!
Wine should go,
As the blood doth flow,
Its course, without pause or sound.
Scorn not Wine!—Truth divine!
And Courage dwell with noble Wine.
Send round the bottle quick, boys!
No reason ask, nor pause!
Wine should run,
Like a circling sun,
By its own unquestioned laws.
Scorn not Wine! &c.

Fill to the beaded brims, boys,
Let each glass, like a king, be crown'd!
Drink—"Joy, and Wealth,
And a mighty Health,
To ourselves and the world around!"
Scorn not Wine! &c.

WHEN FRIENDS LOOK DARK AND COLD.

WHEN friends look dark and cold,
And maids neither laugh nor sigh,
And your enemy proffers his gold,
Be sure there is danger nigh.
O, then 'tis time to look forward,
And back, like the hunted hare;
And to watch, as the little bird watches,
When the falcon is in the air.

When the trader is scant of words,
And your neighbor is rough or shy,
And your banker recalls his hoards,
Be sure there is danger nigh.
O, then 'tis time to look forward, &c.

Whenever a change is wrought,
And you know not the reason why,
In your own or an old friend's thought,
Be sure there is evil nigh.
O, then 'tis time to look forward, &c.

THE NIGHT IS CLOSING ROUND, MOTHER.

THE night is closing round, Mother!
The shadows are thick and deep!
All round me they cling, like an iron ring,
And I can not—can not sleep!

Ah, Heaven! thy hand, thy hand, Mother!
Let me lie on thy nursing breast!
They have smitten my brain with a piercing pain:
But 'tis gone!—and I now shall rest.

I could sleep a long long sleep, Mother!
So, seek me a calm cool bed:
You may lay me low, in the virgin snow,
With a moss-bank for my head.

I would lie in the wild wild woods, Mother!
Where naught but the birds are known;
Where nothing is seen, but the branches green,
And flow'rs on the greensward strewn.

No lovers there witch the air, Mother!
Nor mock at the holy sky:
One may live and be gay, like a summer day,
And at last, like the Summer—die!

MIDNIGHT RHYMES.

OH! 'tis merry when the stars are bright
To sing, as you pace along,
Of the things that are dreamt by night,
To the motion of some old song;
For the fancy of mortals teems,
Whether they wake or sleep,
With figures that shine like dreams,
Then—die in the darkness deep!
Oh! merry are Christmas times,
And merry the belfry chimes;
But the merriest things
That a man e'er sings,
Are his Midnight Rhymes.

'Tis night when the usurers feel
That their money is thrice repaid;
'Tis night when adorers kneel,
By scores to the sleeping maid;
'Tis night when the author deems
That his critics are all at bay,
And the gamester regains in dreams
The gold that he lost by day.
Oh! merry are Christmas times, &c.

At night, both the sick and the lame
Abandon their world of care;
And the creature that droops with shame
Forgetteth her old despair!
The boy on the raging deep
Laughs loud that the skies are clear;
And the murderer turns, in sleep,
And dreams that a pardon's near!
Oh! merry are Christmas times, &c.

At night, all wrongs are right,
And all perils of life grow smooth;
Then why cometh the fierce daylight,
When fancy is bright as truth?
All hearts, 'tween the earth and the moon,
Recover their hopes again;
Ah—'tis pity so sweet a tune
Should ever be jarred by pain!
Yet—merry are Christmas times, &c.

A LOVE SONG.

Give me but thy heart, though cold;
I ask no more!
Give to others gems and gold;
But leave *me* poor.
Give to whom thou wilt thy smiles;
Cast o'r others all thy wiles;
But let thy tears flow fast and free,
For *me*, with *me!*

Giv'st thou but *one* look, sweet heart!
A word—no more!
It is Music's sweetest part,
When lips run o'er!
'Tis a part I fain would learn,
So pr'ythee, *here* thy lessons turn,
And teach me, to the close,
All Love's pleasures—all its woes!

SONG IN PRAISE OF SPRING.

When the wind blows
In the sweet rose-tree,
And the cow lows
On the fragrant lea,
And the stream flows
All bright and free,
'Tis not for thee, 'tis not for me;
'Tis not for any *one* here, I trow:
The gentle wind bloweth,
The happy cow loweth,
The merry stream floweth,
For all below!
O the Spring! the bountiful Spring!
She shineth and smileth on everything.

Where come the sheep?
To the rich man's moor.
Where cometh sleep?
To the bed that's poor.
Peasants must weep,
And kings endure;
That is a fate that none can cure.
Yet Spring doeth all she can, I trow:
She brings the bright hours,
She weaves the sweet flowers,
She dresseth her bowers,
For all below!—*O the Spring, &c.*

BELSHAZZAR.

Belshazzar is King! Belshazzar is Lord!
And a thousand dark nobles all bend at his board;
Fruits glisten, flow'rs blossom, meats steam, and a flood
Of the wine that man loveth runs redder than blood:
Wild dancers are there, and a riot of mirth,
And the beauty that maddens the passions of earth;
And the crowds all shout,
Till the vast roofs ring—
"All praise to Belshazzar, Belshazzar the king!"

"Bring forth," cries the Monarch, "the vessels of gold,
Which my father tore down from the temples of old:
Bring forth, and we'll drink, while the trumpets are blown,
To the Gods of bright silver, of gold, and of stone:
Bring forth!"—and before him the vessels all shine,
And he bows unto Baal, and he drinks the dark wine;
While the trumpets bray,
And the cymbals ring—
"Praise, praise to Belshazzar, Belshazzar the king!"

Now what cometh—look, look!—without menace, or call?
Who writes, with the Lightning's bright hand, on the wall?
What pierceth the king, like the point of a dart?
What drives the bold blood from his cheek to his heart?
"Chaldeans! Magicians! the letters expound!"
They are read—and Belshazzar is dead on the ground!
Hark!—the Persian is come
On a conqueror's wing;
And a Mede's on the throne of Belshazzar the king!

THE BLOOD HORSE.

Gamarra is a dainty steed,
Strong, black, and of a noble breed,
Full of fire, and full of bone,
With all his line of fathers known;
Fine his nose, his nostrils thin,
But blown abroad by the pride within!
His mane is like a river flowing,
And his eyes like embers glowing
In the darkness of the night,
And his pace as swift as light.

Look! how 'round his straining throat
Grace and shifting beauty float!
Sinewy strength is on his reins,
And the red blood gallops through his veins—
Richer, redder, never ran
Through the boasting heart of man.
He can trace his lineage higher
Than the Bourbon dare aspire—
Douglas, Guzman, or the Guelph
Or O'Brien's blood itself!

He, who hath no peer, was born
Here, upon a red March morn:
But his famous fathers dead
Were Arabs all, and Arab bred,
And the last of that great line
Trod like one of a race divine!
And yet—he was but friend to one,
Who fed him at the set of sun,
By some lone fountain fringed with green:
With *him*, a roving Bedouin,
He lived—(none else would he obey
Through all the hot Arabian day)—
And died untamed upon the sands
Where Balkh amid the desert stands!

THE STRANGER.

A Stranger came to a rich man's door,
And smiled on his mighty feast;
And away his brightest child he bore,
And laid her toward the East.

He came next spring, with a smile as gay,
(At the time the East wind blows),
And another bright creature he led away,
With a cheek like a burning rose.

And he came once more, when the spring was blue,
And whispered the last to rest,
And bore her away—yet nobody knew
The name of the fearful guest!

Next year, there was none but the rich man left—
Left alone in his pride and pain,
Who called on the Stranger, like one bereft,
And sought through the land—in vain!

He came not; he never was heard nor seen
Again (so the story saith);
But, wherever his terrible smile had been,
Men shuddered, and talked of—Death!

THE HEART-BROKEN.

Gentle Mother, do not weave
Garlands for my forehead pale!
Unto hearts that e'er must grieve,
What do crowns avail?

Tell me not of bridal flowers!
What are they when life is past?
Tell me not of happy hours,
When they flee so fast!

Bind thy cypress round my heart!
Hide me in the mortal pall!
Show them, when all hopes depart,
What sad things befall!

I am—dead, a statue, left
Pointing perils out unknown,
Shorn of life, and love-bereft,
All my youth o'erthrown!
All o'erthrown!

SONG OF THE OUTCAST.

I WAS born on a winter's morn,
Welcomed to life with hate and scorn,
Torn from a famished mother's side,
Who left me here, with a laugh, and—died;
Left me here with the curse of life,
To be tossed about in the burning strife,
Linked to nothing but shame and pain,
Echoing nothing but man's disdain;
O, that I might *again* be born,
With treble my strength of hate and scorn!

I was born by a sudden shock—
Born by the blow of a ruffian sire,
Given to air, as the blasted rock
Gives out the reddening roaring fire.
My sire was stone; but *my* dark blood
Ran its round like a fiery flood,
Rushing through every tingling vein,
And flaming ever at man's disdain;
Ready to give back, night or morn,
Hate for hate, and scorn for scorn!

They cast me out, in my hungry need,
(A dog, whom none would own, nor feed,)
Without a home, without a meal,
And bade me go forth—to slay and steal!
What wonder, God! had my hands been red,
With the blood of a host in secret shed!
But no! I fought on the free sea-wave,
And perilled my *life* for my plunder brave,
And never yet shrank, in nerve or breath,
But struck, as the pirate strikes—to death!

A PHANTASY.

FEED her with the leaves of Love,
(Love, the rose, that blossoms here!)
Music, gently 'round her move!
Bind her to the cypress near!
Weave her round and round,
With skeins of silken sound!
'Tis a little stricken deer,
Who doth from the hunter fly,
And comes here to droop—to die,
Ignorant of her wound!

Sooth her with sad stories,
O poet, till she sleep!
Dreams, come forth with all your glories!
Night, breathe soft and deep!
Music, round her creep!
If she steal away to weep,
Seek her out—and, when you find her,
Gentle, gentlest Music, wind her
Round and round,
Round and round,
With your bands of softest sound;
Such as we, at night-fall, hear
In the wizard forest near,
When the charmed Maiden sings
At the hidden springs!

LIFE.

WE are born; we laugh; we weep;
We love; we droop; we die!
Ah! wherefore do we laugh, or weep?
Why do we live, or die?
Who knows that secret deep?
Alas, not I!

Why doth the violet spring
Unseen by human eye?
Why do the radiant seasons bring
Sweet thoughts that quickly fly?
Why do our fond hearts cling
To things that die?

We toil—through pain and wrong;
We fight—and fly;
We love: we lose; and then, ere long,
Stone-dead we lie.
O life! is *all* thy song
"Endure and—die?"

AN IRISH SONG.

AIR—KATHLEEN O'MORE.

HE is gone to the wars, and has left me alone,
The poor Irish soldier, unfriended, unknown,
My husband, my Patrick,
The bird of my bosom—though now he is flown!

How I mourned for the boy! yet I murmured the more,
'Cause we once were so happy in darlin' Lismore,
Poor Ellen and Patrick!
Perhaps he *now* thinks of poor Ellen no more!

A cabin we had, and the cow was hard by,
And a slip of a garden that gladden'd the eye:
And there was our Patrick—
Ne'er idle while light ever lived in the sky.

We married—too young, and it's likely too poor,
Yet no two were so happy in happy Lismore,
As Ellen and Patrick;
Till they tempted and took him away from our door.

He said he would bring me, ere Autumn should fall,
A linnet or lark that should come at my call:
Alas! the poor Patrick!
He has left me a bird that is sweeter than all.

'Twas born in a hovel, 'twas nourished in pain,
But it came in my grief, like a light on the brain,
(The child of poor Patrick),
And taught me to hope for bright fortune again.

And now—we two wander from door unto door,
And, sometimes we steal back to happy Lismore,
And ask for poor Patrick;
And dream of the days when all wars will be o'er.

HOME.—(A DUET.)

He. DOST thou love wandering? Whither wouldst thou go?
Dreamst thou, sweet daughter, of a land more fair?
Dost thou not love these aye-blue streams that flow?
These spicy forests? and this golden air?

She. O, yes, I love the woods and streams, so gay;
And, more than all, O father, I love *thee;*
Yet would I fain be wandering—far away,
Where such things never were, nor e'er shall be.

He. Speak, mine own daughter with the sunbright locks!
To what pale banished region wouldst thou roam?
She. O father, let us find our frozen rocks!
Let's seek that country of all countries—Home!

He. Seest thou these orange flowers? this palm that rears
Its head up toward heaven's blue and cloudless dome?
She. I dream, I dream; mine eyes are hid in tears;
My heart is wandering round our ancient home.

He. Why, then, we'll go. Farewell, ye tender skies,
Who sheltered us, when we were forced to roam!
She. On, on! Let's pass the swallow as he flies!
Farewell. kind land! Now, father, *now*—for Home!

THE EVENING STAR.

THE Evening Star, the lover's star,
The beautiful star comes hither!
He steereth his barque
Through the azure dark,
And brings us the bright blue weather—Love!
The beautiful bright blue weather.

The birds lie dumb, when the night stars come,
And silence broods o'er the covers;
But a voice now wakes
In the thorny brakes,
And singeth a song for lovers—Love!
A sad sweet song for lovers.

It singeth a song of grief and wrong,
A passionate song for others;
Yet its own sweet pain
Can never be vain,
If it 'wakeneth love in others'—Love!
It 'wakeneth love in others.

THE VINTAGE SONG.

O THE merry vintage-time!
The merry, matchless vintage-time!
What can vie
Beneath the sky
With the merry merry vintage-time?
What, though summer birds have fled,
Singing to some other clime;
We have tongues that music shed
Still, and a song for vintage-time!
Come!—O'er the hills the moon is glancing!
Now's the time for dancing, dancing!
Now's the time, Now's the time,
The merry merry vintage-time!

Now's the happy vintage-time,
The happy honor'd vintage-time!
E'en great Earth
Doth mix in mirth
With us, her sons, at vintage-time.
Not a storm doth vex her brow,
Flooding rain, nor frosty rime;
But the sunny Autumn now
Laugheth out—"'Tis vintage-time."—*Come &c.*

Praise, then, all the vintage-time,
Children of the vintage-time!
Girls and boys
Who know the joys
Of the merry fruitful vintage-time!
Leave to Spring the love-sweet flowers;
Winter still its song and rhyme;
Summer all her balmy hours;
Still we've our dance at vintage-time!—*Come &c.*

THE RETURN OF THE ADMIRAL.

How gallantly, how merrily,
We ride along the sea!
The morning is all sunshine,
The wind is blowing free:
The billows are all sparkling,
And bounding in the light,
Like creatures in whose sunny veins
The blood is running bright.
All nature knows our triumph:
Strange birds about us sweep;
Strange things come up to look at us
The masters of the deep.
In our wake, like any servant,
Follows even the bold shark—
Oh, proud must be our Admiral
Of such a bonny barque!

Proud, proud, must be our Admiral,
(Though he is pale to-day,)
Of twice five hundred iron men,
Who all his nod obey;
Who've fought for him, and conquered—
Who've won, with sweat and gore,
Nobility! which he shall have
Whene'er he touch the shore.
Oh! would I were our Admiral,
To order, with a word—
To lose a dozen drops of blood,
And straight rise up a lord!
I'd shout e'en to yon shark, there,
Who follows in our lee,
"Some day I'll make thee carry me,
Like lightning through the sea."

—The Admiral grew paler,
And paler as we flew:
Still talked he to his officers,
And smiled upon his crew;
And he looked up at the heavens,
And he looked down on the sea,
And at last he spied the creature,
That kept following in our lee.
He shook—'twas but an instant—
For speedily the pride
Ran crimson to his heart,
Till all chances he defied;
It threw boldness on his forehead;
Gave firmness to his breath;
And he stood like some grim warrior
New risen up from death.

That night, a horrid whisper
Fell on us where we lay;
And we knew our old fine Admiral
Was changing into clay;
And we heard the wash of waters,
Though nothing could we see,
And a whistle and a plunge
Among the billows in our lee!
Till dawn we watched the body
In its dead and ghastly sleep,
And next evening at sunset,
It was slung into the deep!
And never, from that moment—
Save *one* shudder through the sea,
Saw we (or heard) the shark
That had followed in our lee!

LOVE AND MIRTH.

WHAT song doth the cricket sing?
What news doth the swallow bring?
What doth laughing boyhood tell?
What calls out the marriage bell?
What say all?—Love and Mirth!
In the air, and in the earth:
Very, very soft and merry
Is the natural song of Earth.

Mark the Morn, when first she springs
Upward on her golden wings;
Hark, to the soaring, soaring lark!
And the echoing forests—hark!
What say they?—Love and Mirth, &c.

With the leaves the apples wrestle;
In the grass the daisies nestle;
And the sun smiles on the wall:
Tell us, what's the cause of all?
Mirth and Love—Love and Mirth, &c.

Is it Mirth? Then why will man
Spoil the sweet song all he can?
Bid him, rather, aye rejoice,
With a kind and a merry voice!
Bid him sing "Love and Mirth!"
To the air, and to the earth, &c.

SONG OVER A CHILD.

DREAM, Baby, dream!
The stars are glowing.
Hear'st thou the stream?
'Tis softly flowing.
All gently glide the Hours:
Above, no tempest lowers:
Below, are fragrant flowers
In silence growing.

Sleep, Baby, sleep,
'Till dawn to-morrow!
Why shouldst thou weep,
Who know'st not sorrow?
Too soon comes pains and fears
Too soon a cause for tears:
So, from thy future years
No sadness borrow!

Dream, Baby, dream!
Thine eyelids quiver.
Know'st thou the theme
Of yon soft river?
It saith, "Be calm, be sure,
Unfailing, gentle, pure:
So shall thy life endure,
Like mine, for ever!"

THE NIGHT BEFORE THE BRIDAL.

Now, what shady wreath wilt wear,
Maiden—Maiden ?
Bid them bind the veil with care,
'Round the sunshine of thy hair !
Let thy brow be free from scorn ;
Let thine eye have gentle light
On the gentle marriage morn ;
And so—Good Night !

It is now the youth of May,
Maiden—Maiden !
Choose thou, then, at blush of day,
Buds and blossoms, not too gay ;
And, behind their veiling sweets,
Bashful be, 'midst all their light,
When the tender lover greets :
And so—Good Night !

Soon To-morrow will be here,
Maiden—Maiden !
Then—as hopes aye mix with fears,
Mix thou smiles with pearled tears ;
So shall he who loves thee feel
Thrice his first sweet pure delight,
And nearer to thy bosom steal ;
And so—Good Night !

A DEEP AND A MIGHTY SHADOW

A DEEP and a mighty shadow
Across my heart is thrown,
Like a cloud on a summer meadow,
Where the Thunder-wind hath blown !
The wild-rose, Fancy, dieth,
The sweet bird, Memory, flieth,
And leaveth me alone—

Alone with my hopeless Sorrow :
No other mate I know !
I strive to awake To-morrow ;
But the dull words will not flow !
I pray—but my prayers are driven
Aside, by the angry Heaven,
And weigh me down with wo !

I call on the Past, to lend me
Its songs, to sooth my pain :
I bid the dim Future send me
A light from its eyes—in vain !
Naught comes ; but a shrill cry starteth
From Hope, as she fast departeth :—
"I go, and come not again !"

THE LANDSMAN'S SONG.

OH ! who would be bound to the barren Sea,
If he could dwell on Land—
Where his step is ever both firm and free,
Where flowers arise,
Like sweet girls' eyes,
And rivulets sing
Like birds in spring ?
For me—I will take my stand
On Land, on Land !
For ever and ever on solid Land !

[I've] sailed on the riotous roaring sea,
With an undaunted band :
[Bu]t my village home more pleaseth me,
With its valley gay
Where maidens stray,
And its grassy mead
Where the white flocks feed :
A[n]d so—I will take my stand
On Land, on Land !
F[o]r ever and ever on solid Land !

Some swear they could die on the salt salt sea.
(But have they been loved on Land ?)
Some rave of the Ocean in drunken glee—
Of the music born
On a gusty morn,
When the tempest is waking,
And billows are breaking,
And lightning flashing,
And the thick rain dashing,
And the winds and the thunders
Shout forth the sea-wonders !
—Such things may give joy
To a dreaming boy :
But for *me*—I will take my stand
On Land, on Land !
For ever and ever on solid Land !

PERDITA.

THE nest of the dove is rifled ;
Alas ! alas !
The dream of delight is stifled ;
And all that was
Of beauty and hope is broken ;
But words will flee,
Though truest were ever spoken :
Alas, for me !

His love was as fragrant ever,
As flowers to bees ;
His voice like the mournful river ;
But streams will freeze !
Ah ! where can I fly, deceived ?
Ah ! where, where rest ?
I am sick, like the dove bereaved,
And have no nest !

THE WEAVER'S SONG.

WEAVE, brothers, weave !—Swiftly throw
The shuttle athwart the loom,
And show us how brightly your flowers grow,
That have beauty but no perfume !
Come, show us the rose, with a hundred dyes,
The lily, that hath no spot ;
The violet, deep as your true love's eyes,
And the little forget-me-not.
Sing—sing, brothers ! weave and sing !
'Tis good both to sing and to weave ;
'Tis better to work than live idle ;
'Tis better to sing than grieve.

Weave, brothers, weave !—Weave, and bid
The colors of sunset glow !
Let grace in each gliding thread be hid !
Let beauty about ye blow !
Let your skein be long, and your silk be fine,
And your hands both firm and sure,
And time nor chance shall your work untwine ;
But all—like a truth—endure.
So—sing, brothers, &c.

Weave, brothers, weave !—Toil is ours ;
But toil is the lot of men ;
One gathers the fruit, one gathers the flowers,
One soweth the seed again !
There is not a creature, from England's king,
To the peasant that delves the soil,
That knows half the pleasures the seasons bring,
If he have not his share of toil !
So—sing brothers, &c.

SLEEP ON.

SLEEP on ! The world is vain :
All grief, and sin, and pain ;
If there be a dream of joy,
It comes in slumber, pretty boy !
So, sweet Sleep !
Hang upon his eyelids deep ;
Show him all that can not be,
Ere thou dost flee !

Sleep on ! Let no bad truth
Fall yet upon his youth ;
Let him see no thing unkind,
But live a little longer blind !
O sweet Sleep !
Hang upon his eyelids deep ;
Show him Love, without his wings,
And all fair things !

LOVE THE POET, PRETTY ONE!

LOVE the poet, pretty one!
He unfoldeth knowledge fair—
Lessons of the earth and sun,
And of azure air.

He can teach thee how to reap
Music from the golden lyre:
He can show thee how to steep
All thy thoughts in fire.

Heed not, though at times he seem
Dark and still, and cold as clay:
He is shadowed by his dream!
But 'twill pass away.

Then—bright fancies will he weave,
Caught from air and heaven above:
Some will teach thee how to grieve;
Others, how—to love!

How from sweet to sweet to rove—
How all evil things to shun:
Should I not then whisper, "Love—
Love *the poet*, pretty one"?

LUCY.

LUCY is a golden girl;
But a man—*a man* should woo her!
They who seek her shrink aback,
When they should, like storms, pursue her.

All her smiles are hid in light;
All her hair is lost in splendor;
But she hath the eyes of Night,
And a heart that's over-tender.

Yet, the foolish suiters fly
(Is't excess of dread or duty?)
From the starlight of her eye,
Leaving to neglect her beauty!

Men by fifty seasons taught,
Leave her to a young beginner,
Who, without a second thought,
Whispers, woos, and straight must win her.

Lucy is a golden girl!
Toast her in a goblet brimming!
May the man that wins her wear
On his *heart* the Rose of Women!

THE WOOING SONG.

O PLEASANT is the fisher's life,
By the waters streaming;
And pleasant is the poet's life,
Ever, ever dreaming;
And pleasant is the hunter's life,
O'er the meadows riding;
And pleasant is the sailor's life,
On the seas abiding!
But, oh! the merry life is wooing, is wooing;
Never overtaking, and always pursuing!

The hunter, when the chase is done,
Laugheth loud and drinketh;
The poet, at the set of sun,
Sigheth deep, and thinketh;
The sailor, though from sea withdrawn,
Dreams he's half seas over,
The fisher dreameth of the dawn,
But, what dreams the lover?
He dreams that the merry life is wooing, is wooing;
Never overtaking, and always pursuing!

Some think that life is very long,
And murmur at the measure;
Some think it is a syren song—
A short, false, fleeting pleasure;
Some sigh it out in gloomy shades,
Thinking naught, nor doing;
But *we'll* ne'er think it gloomy, Maids!
While there's time for wooing.
For, sure, the merry life is wooing, is wooing;
Never overtaking, and always pursuing!

HERMIONE.

THOU hast beauty bright and fair,
Manner noble, aspect free,
Eyes that are untouched by care:
What then do we ask from thee?
Hermione, Hermione?

Thou hast reason quick and strong,
Wit that envious men admire,
And a voice, itself a song!
What then can we still desire?
Hermione, Hermione?

Something thou dost want, O queen!
(As the gold doth ask alloy),
Tears, amid thy laughter seen,
Pity, mingling with thy joy.
This is all we ask from thee,
Hermione, Hermione!

THE OWL.

IN the hollow tree, in the old gray tower,
The spectral Owl doth dwell;
Dull, hated, despised, in the sunshine hour,
But at dusk—he's abroad and well!
Not a bird of the forest e'er mates with him;
All mock him outright, by day:
But at night, when the woods grow still and dim,
The boldest will shrink away!
O, when the night falls, and roosts the fowl,
Then, then *is the reign of the Horned Owl!*

And the Owl hath a bride, who is fond and bold,
And loveth the wood's deep gloom;
And, with eyes like the shine of the moonstone cold,
She awaiteth her ghastly groom!
Not a feather she moves, not a carol she sings,
As she waits in her tree so still;
But when her heart heareth his flapping wings,
She hoots out her welcome shrill!
O, when the moon shines, and dogs do howl!
Then, then *is the joy of the Horned Owl!*

Mourn not for the Owl, nor his gloomy plight!
The Owl hath his share of good:
If a prisoner he be in the broad daylight,
He is Lord in the dark green-wood!
Nor lonely the bird, nor his ghastly mate,
They are each unto each a pride:
Thrice fonder, perhaps, since a strange dark fate
Hath rent them from all beside!
So, when the night falls and dogs do howl,
Sing, Ho! for the reign of the Hornea Owl!
We know not alway
Who are kings by day,
But the King of the night is the bold brown Owl

THE HUMBER FERRY.

BOATMAN, hither! Furl your sail!
Row us o'er the Humber ferry!
Furl it close! The blustering gale
Seems as he would fain be merry.
Pleasant is he, when in fun
He blows about the bud or berry;
But his mirth we fain would shun
Out upon the Humber ferry!

Now, bold fisher, shall we go
With thee o'er the Humber river?
Hear'st thou how the blast doth blow?
See'st thou how thy sail doth shiver?
Wilt thou dare (dismayed by naught)
Wind and wave, thou bold sea-liver?
And shall *we*, whom Love hath taught,
Tremble at the rolling river?

Row us forth! Unfurl thy sail!
What care we for tempests blowing?
Let us kiss the blustering gale!
Let us breast the waters flowing!
Though the North rush cold and loud,
Love shall warm and make us merry;
Though the waves all weave a shroud,
We will dare the Humber ferry!

MARIAN.

Spirit of the summer breeze!
Wherefore sleep'st thou in the trees?
Come, and kiss the maiden rose,
That on Marian's bosom blows!

Come, and fawn about her hair!
Kiss the fringes of her eyes!
Ask her why she looks so fair,
When she heedeth not my sighs?

Tell her, murmuring summer air,
That her beauty's all untrue;
Tell her, she should not seem fair,
Unless she be gentle too!

A REPOSE.

She sleeps among her pillows soft,
(A dove, now wearied with her flight,)
And all around, and all aloft,
Hang flutes and folds of virgin white:
Her hair out-darkens the dark night,
Her glance outshines the starry sky;
But now her locks are hidden quite,
And closed is her fringed eye!

She sleepeth: wherefore doth she start?
She sigheth: doth she feel no pain?
None, none! the Dream is near her heart:
The Spirit of sleep is in her brain.
He cometh down like golden rain,
Without a wish, without a sound;
He cheers the sleeper (ne'er in vain)
Like May, when earth is winter-bound.

All day within some cave he lies,
Dethroned from his nightly sway—
Far fading when the dawning skies
Our souls with wakening thoughts array.
Two Spirits of might doth man obey;
By each he's wrought, from each he learns:
The one is Lord of life by day;
The other when starry Night returns.

THE REMONSTRANCE.

Thou'lt take me with thee, my love, my love?
Wherever thou'rt forced by fate to move?
Over the land, or over the sea?—
Thou know'st 'tis the same delight to *me.*
What say'st thou, dear?
Thy bride is here,
All ready to live and die with thee.
Her heart was in the song;
It murmured in the measure;
It touched the music, all along,
With a grave sweet pleasure.

Thou wilt not leave me behind, behind,
To the malice of fortune, harsh and blind?
I'll follow thy call, as a bird would flee,
And sing or be mute as thou biddest me.
What say'st thou, dear?
To my fond, fond fear?
Thou *canst* not banish thy love from thee!
Her heart was in the song;
It murmured in the measure;
It touched the music, all along,
With a grave sweet pleasure.

What say'st thou, my soldier, my love, my pride?
Thy answer? What, was I not *born* thy bride?
From thy cradle e'er cherished for love and thee,
And dar'st thou now banish or bid me flee?
Smil'st thou at my fear?
Ah, then, my dear,
I *know* I may love—live—die with thee!
Her heart was in the song;
It murmured in the measure;
It touched the music, all along,
With a grave sweet pleasure.

SING, MAIDEN, SING!

Sing, Maiden, sing!
Mouths were made for singing;
Listen—Songs thou'lt hear
Through the wide world ringing;
Songs from all the birds,
Songs from winds and showers,
Songs from seas and streams,
Even from sweet flowers.

Hearest thou the rain,
How it gently falleth?
Hearest thou the bird,
Who from forest calleth?
Hearest thou the bee
O'er the sunflower ringing?
Tell us, Maiden, *now*—
Shouldst thou not be singing?

Hearest thou the breeze
Round the rose-bud sighing?
And the small sweet rose
Love to love replying?
So shouldst *thou* reply,
To the prayer we're bringing;
So that bud, thy mouth,
Should burst forth in singing!

MAUREEN.

The cottage is here, as of old I remember;
The pathway is worn, as it ever hath been;
On the turf-piled hearth there still lives a bright ember;
But—where is Maureen?

The same pleasant prospect still shineth before me—
The river—the mountain—the valley of green,
And heaven itself (a bright blessing!) is o'er me!
But—where is Maureen?

Lost! Lost!—Like a dream that hath come and departed,
(Ah, why are the loved and lost ever seen?)
She hath fallen—hath flown with a lover false-hearted;
So, mourn for Maureen!

And She, who so loved her, is slain (the poor mother),
Struck dead in a day, by a shadow unseen!
And the home we now loved, is the home of another,
And—lost is Maureen!

Sweet Shannon! a moment by thee let me ponder;
A moment look back at the things that have been;
Then, away to the world where the ruined ones wander,
To look for Maureen!

WINE.

I love Wine! Bold bright Wine!
That maketh the Spirit both dance and shine!
Others may care
For water fare;
But give *me*—Wine!

Ancient Wine! Brave old Wine!
How it around the heart doth twine!
Poets may love
The stars above;
But *I* love—Wine!

Naught but Wine! Noble Wine,
Strong, and sound, and old, and fine.
What can scare
The devil Despair,
Like brave bright wine?

O brave Wine! Rare old Wine!
Once thou wast deemed a God divine!
Bad are the rhymes,
And bad the times,
That scorn old Wine!

So, brave old Wine! Dear old Wine!
Morning, Noon, and Night, I'm thine!
Whatever may be,
I'll stand by thee,
Immortal Wine!

UNEQUAL LOVE.

"Wailing for his dæmon lover."

Wilt not eat with me, my bride?
Wilt not drink my amorous wines?
Dainty meats are by thy side;
Mark how bright the Rhenish shines!
Come, be kind! What ills betide thee!
Is not he thou lov'st beside thee?

Wherefore sigh'st thou, maiden mine?
Must thou to the forest haste?
Nothing have I, meats or wine,
That thy fairy lips may taste?
Speak, love! must I vainly woo thee!
I—who gave my heart unto thee?

Dark one, thou hast bid me press
Human love upon thy lips;
But thou yieldst a cold caress,
And *thy* love is in eclipse!
Cold and dim while I am burning!
In Love is there no returning?

I have loved thee, sought—pursued—
Won thee from thy charmed springs.
O, that I, instead, had wooed
The humblest girl that laughs and sings!
From the dust thy beauty won me;
But, sweet Love!—He hath undone me!

SING! WHO MINGLES WITH MY LAYS?

Sing! Who mingles with my lays?
Maiden of the primrose days!
Sing with me, and I will show
All that thou in spring shouldst know,
All the names of all the flowers,
What to do with primrose hours!

Sing! who mingles with my song?
Soldier in the battle strong!
Sing, and thee I'll music teach,
Such as thunders on the beach,
When the waves run mad and white,
Like a warrior in the fight!

Sing! who loves the music tender?
Widow, who hath no defender!—
Orphan!—Scholar!—Mother wild,
Who hast loved (and lost) a child!
Maiden, dreaming of to-morrow!
Let us sing and banish sorrow!
Come!—Sweet music hath a smart,
And a balm for every heart!

I LOVE MY LOVE, BECAUSE HE LOVES ME.

Man, man loves his steed,
For its blood or its breed,
For its odor the rose, for its honey the bee,
His own haughty beauty
From pride or from duty;
But *I* love my love, because—*he* loves *me*.

Oh, my love has an eye,
Like a star in the sky,
And breath like the sweets from the hawthorn tree;
And his heart is a treasure,
Whose worth is past measure;
And yet he hath given all—*all* to me!

It crowns me with light
In the dead of the night,
It brightens my journey by land and sea;
And thus, while I wander,
I sigh and grow fonder,
For *my* love ever grows with *his* love for me

Why didst thou depart,
Thou sweet bird of my heart?
Oh, come back to my bosom, and never flee:
I never will grieve thee,
I'll never deceive thee,
But love thee for ever, as—*thou* lov'st *me*.

MIRIAM.

(RECITATIVE.)

Darkness and God's great wrath for many an age
Have lain on Israel! O what nights of wo!
What dreams of long and lonely banishment!
Spring cometh round, and Summer sweet returneth
Still to our father's land:—But where are We?
Still Siloa murmurs: but we hear her not!
Still the rose opens, and the lilies pale
Are born beneath the sun: but we have lost
All suns, all seasons—music—fragrance—flowers!

Peace—Darkness hath her share of good, like day;
Sleep and the world of dreams belong to her;
And, in our long dark exile, *we* have stars
That light us onward, and their beauty shed
Alone upon the sons of Israel!
Look—where one shines:—'tis—Miriam! Judah's child!
Her pride—her glory! Statelier than the palm,
Swift as the roe, dowered with love—she comes!
And thus I celebrate her grace in song!

(AIR.)

Oh, fairer than the fairest of the flowers!
Oh, sweeter than the bud when it blows!
Oh, brighter than the summer when it showers
Its riches on the red red rose!
Come—Show us that the color of the sky
Still lives in the Hebrew's eye,
Miriam!

Oh, show us there is truth in thy story;
That thy country is worthy of her fame!
Reappear—like the shadow of her glory!
Reappear—like the Spirit of her name!
Come—Show us all the starriness that lies
In the night of the Hebrew's eyes,
Miriam!

Look! Look! where a Spirit, like the lightning,
Comes flashing from her dark deep gaze!
Is the tempest e'er more terrible or blighting, in
The strength of its storm-bright days?
Quick!—Show us all the terror that may lie
In the flash of a Hebrew's eye,
Miriam!
Our pride, our glory—Miriam!

BABYLON.

(RECITATIVE.)

Pause in this desert! Here, men say, of old
Belshazzar reigned, and drank from cups of gold;
Here, to his hideous idols, bowed the slave,
And here—God struck him dead!
* * * * Where lies his grave?
'Tis lost!—His brazen gates? his soaring towers,
From whose dark tops men watched the starry hours!
All to the dust gone down! The desert bare
Scarce yields an echo when we question "*Where?*"
The lonely herdsman seeks in vain the spot;
And the black wandering Arab knows it not.
No brick, nor fragment lingereth now, to tell
Where Babylon (mighty city!) rose—and fell!

(AIR.)

O City, vast and old!
Where, where is thy grandeur fled?
The stream that around thee rolled,
Still rolls in its ancient bed!
But where, oh, where art Thou gone?
Oh, Babylon! Oh, Babylon!

The Giant, when he dies,
Still leaveth his bones behind,
To shrink in the winter skies,
And whiten beneath the wind!
But where, oh, where art Thou gone?
Oh, Babylon! Oh, Babylon!

Thou liv'st!—for thy name still glows,
A light in the desert skies;
As the fame of the hero grows
Thrice trebled because he dies!
Oh, Babylon! Oh, Babylon!

TALK NOT TO ME OF LOVE.

TALK not to me of love!
The deer that dies
Knows more of love than I,
Who seek the skies.
Strive not to bind my soul
With chains of clay!
I scorn thy poor control;
Away—Away!

Now wherefore dost thou weave
Thy falsehoods strange?
Sad words may make me grieve,
But never change.
A snake sleeps in thine eye;
It stirs thine heart:
Why dost thou vainly sigh?
Depart—Depart!

Thy dreams, when Fortune flew,
Did elsewhere range:
But love is *always* true,
And knows no change.
More firm in want, in strife,
Ay, firm through crime,
He looketh down on life,
The star of Time!

A DILEMMA.

WHICH is the maiden I love best?
Twenty now are buzzing round me;
Three in their milk-white arms have wound me,
Gently—yet I feel no rest!
One hath showered her black locks o'er me,
Ten kneel on the ground before me,
Casting forth such beams of blue,
That I'm pierced—oh, through and through!
Bacchus! Gods! what *can* I do?
Which *must* I love best?

Tell me—(ah, more gently take me,
Sweet one, in thy warm white arms!)
Tell me, which will ne'er forsake me
Through all life's ills and harms?
Is it *she*, whose blood's retreating
From that forehead crowned with pride?
Is it *she*, whose pulse is beating
Full against my unarmed side?
What do all these things betide?
Strong my doubts grow—strong—and stronger:
Quick! give answer to my call!
If ye pause a moment longer,
I shall love ye—ALL!

THE LAKE HAS BURST.

THE lake has burst! The lake has burst!
Down through the chasms the wild waves flee;
They gallop along
With a roaring song,
Away to the eager awaiting sea!

Down through the valleys, and over the rocks,
And over the forests the flood runs free;
And wherever it dashes,
The oaks and the ashes
Shrink, drop, and are borne to the hungry sea!

The cottage of reeds and the tower of stone,
Both shaken to ruin, at last agree;
And the slave and his master
In one wide disaster
Are hurried like weeds to the scornful sea!

The sea-beast he tosseth his foaming mane;
He bellows aloud to the misty sky,
And the sleep-buried Thunder
Awakens in wonder,
And the Lightning opens her piercing eye!

There is death above, there is death around,
There is death wheresover the waters be,
There is nothing now doing
But terror and ruin,
On earth, and in air, and the stormy sea!

HER LARGE DARK LUMINOUS EYES ARE ON ME.

HER large dark luminous eyes are on me!
I can not fly—I can not move!
The beauty that in boyhood won me
Wins me still—to look and love!

The tongue that wound its music 'round me,
And might have charmed aside all pain,
Again all bare and weak hath found me,
And stings me to the heart again!

O Beauty, who my soul subdueth!
What mean the lightnings of thine eye?
Why is it that thy scorn pursueth
My love—yet leaves it not to die?

Sweet Music, cease! Bright Eyes, all beaming
With light that makes me mad—ah, close!
Give back my colder, calmer dreaming!
Give back my dull dark old repose!

KILL THE LOVE THAT WINDS AROUND THEE.

KILL the love that winds around thee
With its snake-like death-like twine!
Where's the guardian steel that bound thee?
Where are all thy gifts divine?
Where is wisdom? Where is wine?
Where's the sad dark truth of story?
Where the Muse's mighty line?
Where the fame that burned before thee?

What is love, but life deformed
From its grand original aim?
Hero into slave transformed?
Worlds lost at a single game?
Whose the peril—whose the shame,
Shouldst thou die in love's fond slavery?
Rise! Earth's naught without its fame!
Rise! Life's naught without its bravery!

THE BEGGAR'S SONG.

I AM a merry beggar,
A beggar I was born,
Tossed about the wide world,
From evening till morn;
A plaything of the tempest,
A brother of the night,
A conqueror, a conjurer,
When 'tis merry star-light!

Oh! nothing can withstand me,
Whenever I do stoop,
From the warm heart of the housewife
To the chicken in the coop;
From the linen of the lady,
To the larder of the knight,
All come when I do conjure,
In the merry star-light!

I pay no tithes to parson,
Tho' I follow like his clerk;
For he takes his tenths by daylight,
I take mine in the dark;
I pay the king no window-tax;
From some it may be right,
But all *I* do beneath the blue,
Is by merry star-light!

I roam from lane to common,
From city unto town,
And I tell a merry story,
To gentleman or clown;
Each gives me bed or victuals,
Or ale that glitters bright,
Or—I contrive to borrow them
By merry star-light!

Oh, the tradesman he is rich, sirs,
The farmer well to pass,
The soldier he's a lion,
The alderman's an ass;
The courtier he is subtle, sirs,
And the scholar he is bright;
But who, like me, is ever free
In the merry star-light?

THE BLOODHOUND.

Come, Herod, my hound, from the stranger's floor!
Old friend—we must wander the world once more!
For no one now liveth to welcome us back:
So, come! let us speed on our fated track.
What matter the region—what matter the weather,
So you and I travel, till death, together?
And in death?—why, e'en *there* I may still be found
By the side of my beautiful black bloodhound.

We've traversed the desert, we've traversed the sea,
And we've trod on the heights where the eagles be;
Seen Tartar, and Arab, and swart Hindoo;
(How thou pull'dst down the deer in those skies of blue!)
No joy did divide us; no peril could part
The man from his friend of the noble heart;
Ay, his *friend;* for where, where shall there ever be found
A friend like his resolute fond bloodhound!

What, Herod, old hound! dost remember the day
When I fronted the wolves, like a stag at bay?
When downward they galloped to where we stood,
While I staggered with fear in the dark pine wood?
Dost remember their howlings? their horrible speed?
God, God! how I prayed for a friend in need!
And—he came! Ah! 'twas then, my dear Herod, I found
That the best of all friends was my bold bloodhound.

Men tell us, dear friend, that the noble hound
Must for ever be lost in the worthless ground:
Yet, "Courage"—"Fidelity"—"Love"—(they say)
Bear *Man*, as on wings, to his skies away.
Well, Herod—go tell them, whatever may be,
I'll hope I may ever be found by thee.
If in sleep—in sleep: if with skies around,
May'st thou follow e'en thither, my dear bloodhound!

THE FAREWELL OF THE SOLDIER.

I love thee, I love thee,
Far better than wine,
But the curse is above me;
Thou'lt never be mine!

As the blade wears the scabbard,
The billow the shore,
So sorrow doth fret me
For evermore.

Fair beauty, I leave thee,
To conquer my heart;
I'll see thee, I'll bless thee,
And then—depart.

Let me take, ere I vanish,
One look of thine eyes—
One smile for remembrance,
For life soon flies!

—And now for the fortune,
That hangeth above;
And to bury in battle,
My dream of love!

THE NIGHT-SHADE.

Tread aside from my starry bloom!
I am the nurse who feed the tomb
(The tomb, my child)
With dainties piled,
Until it grows strong as a tempest wild.

Trample not on a virgin flower!
I am the maid of the midnight hour;
I bear sweet sleep
To those who weep,
And lie on their eyelids dark and deep.

Tread not thou on my snaky eyes!
I am the worm that the weary prize,
The Nile's soft asp,
That they strive to grasp,
And one that a queen has loved to clasp!

Pity me! I am she whom man
Hath hated since ever the world began;
I sooth his brain,
In the night of pain,
But at morning he waketh—and all is vain!

THE POET'S SONG TO HIS WIFE.

How many Summers, love,
Have I been thine?
How many days, thou dove,
Hast thou been mine?
Time, like the winged wind
When't bends the flowers,
Hath left no mark behind,
To count the hours!

Some weight of thought, though loath,
On thee he leaves;
Some lines of care round both
Perhaps he weaves;
Some fears—a soft regret
For joys scarce known;
Sweet looks we half forget:
All else is flown!

Ah! with what thankless heart
I mourn and sing!
Look, where our children start,
Like sudden Spring!
With tongues all sweet and low,
Like a pleasant rhyme,
They tell how much I owe
To thee and Time!

TO SOPHIE.

Wilt thou be a nun, Sophie?
Nothing but a nun?
Is it not a better thing
With thy friends to laugh and sing?
To be loved and sought?
To be woo'd and—won?
Dost thou love the shadow, Sophie,
Better than the sun?

I'm a poor lay-brother, Sophie;
Yet, I this may say—
Thou hadst better bear with love,
Than dwell here, a prison'd dove,
Weeping life away.
Oh!—*I'd* bear love's pangs, rather,
Fifty times a day!

WHAT SAY THE CLOUDS ON THE HILL AND PLAIN?

What say the clouds on the hill and plain?
"We come, we go."
What say the springs of the dreaming brain?
"We shrink, we flow."
What say the maids in their changeful hours?
"We laugh, we cry."
What say the budding and fading flowers?
"We live, we die."
And thus all things go ranging,
From riddle to riddle changing,
From day into night, from life into death,
And no one knows why, my song saith.

A fable is good, and a truth is good,
And loss, and gain;
And the ebb and the flood, and the black pine wood,
And the vast bare plain;
To wake and to sleep, and to dream of the deep,
Are good, say I;
And 'tis good to laugh, and 'tis good to weep;
But who knows why?
Yet thus all things go ranging, &c.

We cumber the earth for a hundred years;
We learn, we teach;
We fight amid perils, and hopes, and fears,
Fame's rock to reach.
We boast that our fellows are sages wrought
In toil and pain;
Yet the common lesson by Nature taught,
Doth vex their brain!
Oh! all things here go ranging, &c.

THE

SONGS AND MISCELLANEOUS POEMS

OF

BARRY CORNWALL.

PART II.

TO A FLOWER.

Dawn, gentle flower,
  From the morning earth!
We will gaze and wonder
  At thy wondrous birth!

Bloom, gentle flower!
  Lover of the light,
Sought by wind and shower,
  Fondled by the night!

Fade, gentle flower!
  All thy white leaves close;
Having shown thy beauty,
  Time 'tis for repose.

Die, gentle flower,
  In the silent sun!
So—all pangs are over,
  All thy tasks are done!

Day hath no more glory,
  Though he soars so high;
Thine is all man's story,
  Live—and love—and die!

THE LEVELLER.

The king he reigns on a throne of gold,
  Fenced round by his "power divine;"
The baron he sits in his castle old,
  Drinking his ripe red wine:
But below, below, in his ragged coat,
The beggar he tuneth a hungry note;
And the spinner is bound to his weary thread,
And the debtor lies down with an aching head.
So the world goes!
So the stream flows!
Yet there is a fellow, whom nobody knows,
Who maketh all free
On land and sea,
And forceth the rich like the poor to flee!

The lady lies down in her warm white lawn,
  And dreams of her pearled pride;
The milkmaid sings to the wild-eyed dawn,
  Sad songs on the cold hill-side:
And the saint he leaves (while he prattles of faith)
Good deeds to the sinner, as scandal saith,
And the scholar he bows to the face of brass,
And the wise man he worships the golden ass!
So the world goes &c.

SOFTLY WOO AWAY HER BREATH.

Softly woo away her breath,
  Gentle Death!
Let her leave thee with no strife,
  Tender mournful, murmuring Life!
She hath seen her happy day;
  She hath had her bud and blossom;
Now she pales and shrinks away,
  Earth, into thy gentle bosom!

She hath done her bidding here,
  Angels dear!
Bear her perfect soul above,
  Seraph of the skies—sweet Love!
Good she was, and fair in youth,
  And her mind was seen to soar,
And her heart was wed to truth;
  Take her, then for evermore—
  For ever—evermore!

HIDDEN THOUGHTS.

Some joys we loudly tell;
  Some thoughts we keep apart,
Fenced round, and bid them dwell
  In inmost heart.

Close in that heart (their den)
  The tiger passions sleep:
There, too, shut out from men,
  Resolve lies deep.

There dreams repose—so fair,
  So frail, that but to sigh
Their names unto the air,
  Would force them die.

These give, like violets hid,
  A perfume to the mind—
Give sight, as once they did,
  To poet blind!

THE FISHERMAN.

A perilous life, and sad as life may be,
Hath the lone fisher on the lonely sea,
O'er the wild waters laboring, far from home,
For some bleak pittance e'er compelled to roam.
Few hearts to cheer him through his dangerous life,
And none to aid him in the stormy strife.
Companion of the sea and silent air,
The lonely fisher thus must ever fare;
Without the comfort, hope—with scarce a friend,
He looks through life and only sees—its end!

TRUE LOVE.

Is'T true the false poor beauty flies
From thee? oh, 'tis well—'tis right!
My love shall now adorn thine eyes,
With brightness like the unclouded night!
The poet sheds, on herb and flower,
His fancies, till they breathe and shine:
And shall *I*, in thy drooping hour,
Neglect to hallow aught of *thine?*

Love shall flow along,
Singing like a gentle river;
Its saddest, still its sweetest song
For ever—for ever!

Come to me—dearer, fairer far,
Than when men's smiles did round thee fawn.
Look on me—as the last pale star
Looks round upon the glowing dawn!
Yet, fly not! Stay, and smile, sweet heart,
On whate'er chance may now befall;
My love, though every good depart,
Shall make thee dear amends for all!

True love reigns on high,
Like the constant stars, that quiver
And look bright from every sky,
For ever—for ever!

FORBIDDEN LOVE.

I LOVE thee! Oh, the strife, the pain,
The fiery thoughts that through me roll!
I love thee! Look—again, again!
O Stars! that thou couldst read my soul:
I would thy bright bright eye could pierce
The crimson folds that hide my heart;
Then wouldst thou find the serpent fierce,
That stings me—and will *not* depart!

Look love upon me, with thine eyes!
Yet, no—men's evil tongues are nigh:
Look pity, then, and with thy sighs
Waste music on me—till I die!
Yet, love not! sigh not! Turn (thou *must*)
Thy beauty from me, sweet and kind;
'Tis fit that I should burn to dust—
To death: because—I am not blind!

I love thee—and I live! The Moon
Who sees me from her calm above,
The Wind who weaves her dim soft tune
About me, know how *much* I love!
Naught else, save Night and the lonely Hour,
E'er heard my passion wild and strong:
Even *thou* yet deemst not of thy power,
Unless—thou readst aright my song!

A BRIDAL DIRGE.

WEAVE no more the marriage chain!
All unmated is the lover;
Death has ta'en the place of Pain;
Love doth call on love in vain;
Life and years of hope are over!

No more want of marriage bell!
No more need of bridal favor!
Where is she to wear them well?
You beside the lover tell!
Gone—with all the love he gave her!

Paler than the stone she lies:
Colder than the winter's morning!
Wherefore did she thus despise
(She with pity in her eyes)
Mother's care, and lover's warning?

Youth and beauty—shall they not
Last beyond a brief to-morrow?
No: a prayer, and then forgot!
This the truest lover's lot;
This the sum of human sorrow!

THE RHINE.

WE'VE sailed through banks of green,
Where the wild waves fret and quiver,
And we've down the Danube been,
The dark deep thundering river!
We've thridded the Elbe and Rhone,
The Tyber and blood-died Seine,
And have watched where the blue Garonne
Goes laughing to meet the main;
But what is so lovely, what is so grand,
As the river that runs through Rhine-land?

On the Rhine-river were we born,
Midst its flowers and famous wines,
And we know that our country's morn,
With a treble-sweet aspect shines.
Let other lands boast their flowers,
Let other men dream wild dreams;
Let them hope they've a land like ours,
And a stream, like our stream of streams;
Yet, what is half so bright or so grand,
As the river that runs through Rhine-land?

Are we smit by the blinding sun,
That fell on our tender youth?
Do we coward-like shrink and shun
The thought-telling touch of truth?
On our heads be the sin, then, set!
We'll bear all the shame divine;
But we'll never disown the debt,
That we owe to our noble Rhine!
O, the Rhine! the Rhine! the broad and the grand
Is the river that runs through Rhine-land!

SWEET FRIEND, WHERE SLEEPS THY SONG?

SWEET friend! where sleeps thy song?
Ah, wherefore hath it lain so long
In idle slumbers!
Quick thou, the ancient bondage break,
And bid its dreaming soul awake
In airy numbers!

Bid it burst forth, like Spring,
When first the youthful rivers sing—
That small bright river,
That runneth laughing from the earth,
And thinketh, in its new-born mirth,
To live for ever!

Bid it come forth, like Spring,
When brooks and trees their music bring,
And fields their flowers;
And we will hearken all, and hoard
Thy sweet sweet thoughts, like riches stored,
For after hours!

SONG OF WOOD-NYMPHS.

COME here, come here, and dwell
In forest deep!
Come here, come here, and tell
Why thou dost weep!
Is it for love (sweet pain!)
That thus thou darest complain
Among our pleasant shades, our summer leaves
Where naught else grieves?

Come here, come here, and lie
By whispering stream!
Here no one dares to die
For love's sweet dream;
But health all seek, and joy,
And shun perverse annoy,
And race along green paths till close of day,
And laugh—alway!

Or else, through half the year,
On rushy floor,
We lie by waters clear,
While sky-larks pour
Their songs into the sun!
And when bright day is done,
We hide 'neath bells of flowers, or nodding corn,
And dream—till morn!

THE CONVICT'S FAREWELL.

A Boat is rowed along the sea,
Full of souls as it may be;
Their dress is coarse, their hair is shorn,
And every squalid face forlorn
Is full of sorrow, and hate, and scorn!
What is't?—It is the Convict Boat,
That o'er the waves is forced to float,
Bearing its wicked burden o'er
The ocean, to a distant shore:
Man scowls upon it; but the sea
(The same with fettered as with free)
Danceth beneath it heedlessly!

Slowly the boat is borne along;
Yet they who row are hard and strong,
And well their oars keep time,
To one who sings (and clanks his chain,
The better thus to hide his pain)
A bitter, banished rhyme!
He sings: and all his mates in wo
Chant sullen chorus as they go!

SONG.

Row us on, a felon band,
Farther out to sea,
Till we lose all sight of land,
And then—we shall be free!
Row us on, and loose our fetters;
Yeo! the boat makes way:
Let's say "Good-by" unto our betters.
And, hey for a brighter day!

CHORUS.

Row us fast! Row us fast!
Trial's o'er and sentence past:
Here's a whistle for those who tried to blind us,
And a curse on all we leave behind us!

Farewell, juries, jailers, friends,
(Traitors to the close!)
Here the felon's danger ends.
Farewell, bloody foes!
Farewell, England! We are quitting
Now thy dungeon doors:
Take our blessing, as we're flitting—
"A curse upon thy shores!"

Farewell, England—honest nurse
Of all our wants and sins!
What to thee's the felon's curse?
What to thee who wins?
Murder thriveth in thy cities,
Famine through thine isle:
One may cause a dozen ditties,
But t'other scarce a smile.

Farewell, England—tender soil,
Where babes who leave the breast,
From morning into midnight toil,
That pride may be proudly drest!
Where he who's right and he who swerveth
Meet at the goal the same;
Where no one hath what he deserveth,
Not even in empty fame!

So, fare thee well, our country dear!
Our last wish, ere we go,
Is—May your heart be never clear
From tax, nor tithe, nor wo!
May they who sow e'er reap for others,
The hundred for the one!
May friends grow false, and twin-born brothers
Each hate his Mother's son!

May pains and forms still fence the place
Where justice must be *bought!*
So he who's poor must hide his face,
And he who thinks—his thought!
May Might o'er Right be crowned the winner,
The head still o'er the heart,
And the Saint be still so like the Sinner,
You'll not know them apart!

May your traders grumble when bread is high,
And your farmers when bread is low,
And your pauper brats, scarce two feet high,
Learn more than your nobles know!
May your sick have foggy or frosty weather,
And your convicts all short throats,
And your blood-covered bankers e'er hang together,
And tempt ye with one-pound notes!

And so—with hunger in your jaws,
And peril within your breast,
And a bar of gold, to guard your laws,
For those who *pay* the best;
Farewell to England's wo and weal!
. . . For our betters, so bold and blythe,
May they never want, when they want a meal
A Parson to take their Tithe!

THE SECRET OF SINGING.

Lady, sing no more!
Science all is vain,
Till the heart be touched, lady,
And give forth its pain.

'Tis a hidden lyre,
Cherished near the sun;
O'er whose witching wire, lady,
Faery fingers run.

Pity comes in tears,
From her home above;
Hope, and sometimes Fears, lady,
And the wizard—Love!

Each doth search the heart,
To its inmost springs;
And when they depart, lady,
Then the Spirit sings!

THE HIRLAS HORN.

Fill high, fill high the Hirlas horn,
Rimmed, with sunlight, like the morn!
Deep, and vast, and fit to drown
All the troubles of a crown;
Deep, and vast, and crowned with mead,
'Tis a cup for kings indeed,
Full of courage, full of worth,
Making man a god on earth!
Warriors, Heroes, Cambrian-born,
Drink—from the Hirlas horn!

Hide with foam the golden tip;
Make it rich for a prince's lip!
Here's to the fame of Roderick dead!
Bards! why do your harps not shed
Music? Come a mighty draft
To dead Roderick's name be quaffed!
Tell us all the hero won,
All he did, from sun to sun!
Bards, and Heroes, Cambrian-born,
Drink—from the Hirlas horn!

Fill the horn to Madoc's name,
First in the mighty race of fame,
Eagle-hearted, eagle-eyed,
All hearts shuddered when he died!
Yet, why so? for Tudor rose
Like a lion upon our foes;—
Like the wild storm-smitten ocean,
When he puts his strength in motion!
Come, brave Spirits, Cambrian-born,
Drink—from the Hirlas horn!

Cambrian people—Cambrian mountains,
Back into your wizard fountains
(Where the Druid seers are dwelling)
Shout unto the crowned Llewellin!
Patriot! Hero! Monarch! Friend!
Wreathed with virtues without end!
First of men 'tween Earth and Sky!
The sword and the shield of Liberty!
Drink, all Spirits, Cambrian born,
Drink to the good, great crowned Llewellin
Drink—from the Hirlas horn!

AN EPISTLE TO CHARLES LAMB,

ON HIS EMANCIPATION FROM CLERKSHIP.

(WRITTEN OVER A FLASK OF SHERRIS.)

Dear Lamb, I drink to thee—*to thee*
Married to sweet Liberty!

What! old friend, and art thou freed
From the bondage of the pen?
Free from care and toil, indeed?
Free to wander among men
When and howsoe'er thou wilt?
All thy drops of labor spilt
On those huge and figured pages,
Which will sleep unclasped for ages,
Little knowing who did wield
The quill that traversed their white field?

Come—another mighty health!
Thou hast earn'd thy sum of wealth—
Countless ease—immortal leisure—
Days and nights of boundless pleasure,
Checker'd by no dream of pain,
Such as hangs on clerk-like brain
Like a nightmare, and doth press
The happy soul from happiness.

Oh! happy thou—whose all of time
(Day and eve, and morning prime)
Is fill'd with talk on pleasant themes—
Or visions quaint, which come in dreams
Such as panther'd Bacchus rules,
When his rod is on "the schools,"
Mixing wisdom with their wine—
Or, perhaps, thy wit so fine
Strayeth in some elder book
Whereon our modern Solons look,
With severe ungifted eyes,
Wondering what thou seest to prize.
Happy thou, whose skill can take
Pleasure at each turn, and slake
Thy thirst by every fountain's brink,
Where less wise men would pause to shrink:
Sometimes 'mid stately avenues
With Cowley thou, or Marvel's muse,
Dost walk; or Gray, by Eton towers;
Or Pope, in Hampton's chestnut bowers;
Or Walton, by his loved Lea stream;
Or dost thou with our Milton dream
Of Eden and the Apocalypse,
And hear the words from his great lips?

Speak—in what grove or hazel shade,
For "musing meditation made,"
Dost wander?—or on Penshurst lawn,
Where Sidney's fame had time to dawn
And die, ere yet the hate of Men
Could envy at his perfect pen?
Or, dost thou, in some London street
(With voices fill'd and thronging feet)
Loiter, with mien 'twixt grave and gay—
Or take, along some pathway sweet,
Thy calm suburban way?

Happy beyond that man of Ross,
Whom mere content could ne'er engross,
Art thou—with hope, health, "learned leisure,"
Friends, books, thy thoughts—an endless pleasure!
—Yet—yet—(for when was pleasure made
Sunshine all without a shade?)
Thou, perhaps, as now thou rovest
Through the busy scenes thou lovest,
With an Idler's careless look,
Turning some moth-pierced book,
Feel'st a sharp and sudden wo
For visions vanished long ago!
And then, thou think'st how time has fled
Over thy unsilvered head,
Snatching many a fellow mind
Away, and leaving—what?—behind!
Naught, alas! save joy and pain
Mingled ever, like a strain
Of music where the discords vie
With the truer harmony.

So, perhaps, with thee the vein
Is sullied ever—so the chain
Of habits and affections old,
Like a weight of solid gold,
Presseth on thy gentle breast,
Till sorrow rob thee of thy rest.

Aye: so't must be! E'en I (whose lot
The fairy Love so long forgot),
Seated beside this Sherris wine,
And near to books and shapes divine,
Which poets and the painters past
Have wrought in lines that aye shall last—
E'en I, with Shakspere's self beside me,
And one whose tender talk can guide me
Through fears, and pains, and troublous themes,
Whose smile doth fall upon my dreams
Like sunshine on a stormy sea—
Want *something*—when I think of thee!

THE FALCON.

(AFTER A PAINTING BY TITIAN

The Falcon is a noble bird,
And when his heart of hearts is stirred,
He'll seek the eagle, though he run
Into his chamber near the sun.
Never was there brute or bird,
Whom the woods or mountains heard,
That could force a fear or care
From him—the Arab of the air!

To-day he sits upon a wrist,
Whose purple veins a queen has kissed,
And on him falls a sterner eye
Than he can face where'er he fly,
Though he scale the summit cold
Of the Grimsel, vast and old—
Though he search yon sunless stream,
That thrids the forest like a dream.

Ah, noble Soldier! noble Bird!
Will your names be ever heard—
Ever seen in future story,
Crowning it with deathless glory?
—Peace, ho!—the master's eye is drawn
Away unto the bursting dawn!
Arise, thou bird of birds, arise,
And seek thy quarry in the skies!

BUILD UP A COLUMN TO BOLIVAR!

Build up a column to Bolivar!
Build it under a tropic star!
Build it high as his mounting fame!
Crown its head with his noble name!
Let the letters tell, like a light afar,
"*This is the column of Bolivar!*"

Soldier in war, in peace a man,
Did he not all that a hero can?
Wasting his life for his country's care,
Laying it down with a patriot prayer,
Shedding his blood like the summer rain,
Loving the land, though he loved in vain

Man is a creature, good or ill,
Little or great, at his own strong will;
And *he* grew good, and wise, and great,
Albeit he fought with a tyrant fate,
And showered his golden gifts on men,
Who paid him in basest wrongs again!

Raise the column to Bolivar!
Firm in peace, and fierce in war!
Shout forth his noble, noble name!
Shout till his enemies die, in shame!
Shout till Columbia's woods awaken,
Like seas by a mighty tempest shaken—
Till pity, and praise, and great disdain,
Sound like an Indian hurricane!
Shout, as ye shout in conquering war,
While ye build the column to Bolivar!

THE FIRE-FLY.

Tell us, O Guide! by what strange natural laws
This winged flower throws out, night after night,
Such lunar brightness? *Why?* for what grave cause
Is this earth-insect crown'd with heavenly light?
Peace! Rest content! See where, by cliff and dell,
Past tangled forest paths and silent river,
The little lustrous creature guides us well,
And where we fail, his small light aids us ever.

Night's shining servant! Pretty star of earth!
I ask not why thy lamp doth ever burn.
Perhaps it is thy very life—thy mind;
And thou, if robbed of that strange right of birth,
Might be no more than Man—when Death doth turn
His beauty into darkness, cold and blind!

TO THE SINGER PASTA.

Never till now—never till now, O Queen
And Wonder of the enchanted world of sound!
Never till now was such bright creature seen,
Startling to transport all the regions round!
Whence com'st thou—with those eyes and that fine mien,
Thou sweet, sweet singer? Like an angel found
Mourning alone, thou seem'st (thy mates all fled)
A star 'mong clouds—a spirit 'mid the dead.

Melodious thoughts hang round thee! Sorrow sings
Perpetual sweetness near—divine despair!
Thou speak'st—and Music, with her thousand strings,
Gives golden answers from the haunted air!
Thou mov'st—and round thee Grace her beauty flings!
Thou look'st—and Love is born! O songstress rare!
Lives there on earth a power like that which lies
In those resistless tones—in those dark eyes?

Oh, I have lived—how long!—with one deep treasure,
One fountain of delight unlocked, unknown;
But *thou*, the prophetess of my new pleasure,
Hast come at last, and struck my heart of stone;
And now outgushes, without stint or measure,
The endless rapture—and in places lone
I shout it to the stars and winds that flee,
And *then* I think on all I owe to thee!

I see thee at all hours—beneath all skies—
In every shape thou tak'st, or passionate path:
Now art thou like some winged thing that cries
Over a city flaming fast to death;
Now, in thy voice, the mad Medea dies:
Now Desdemona yields her gentle breath:—
All things thou art by turns—from wrath to love;
From the queen eagle to the vestal dove!

Horror is stern and strong, and death (unmasked
In slow pale silence, or 'mid brief eclipse);
But what are they to *thy* sweet strength, when tasked
To its height—with all the God upon thy lips?
Not even the cloudless days and riches, asked
By one who in the book of darkness dips,
Vies with that radiant wealth which they inherit
Who own, like thee, the Muse's deathless spirit.

Would I could crown thee as a king can crown!
Yet, what are kingly gifts to thy fair fame,
Whose echoes shall all vulgar triumphs drown—
Whose light shall darken every meaner name?
The gallant courts thee for his own renown;
Mimicking thee, he plays love's pleasant game:
The critic brings thee praise, which all rehearse;
And I—alas!—I can but bring my verse!

COME! LET US TO THE LAND.

Come—let us go to the land
Where the violets grow!
Let's go thither, hand in hand,
Over the waters, over the snow,
To the land where the sweet sweet violets blow!

There—in the beautiful South,
Where the sweet flowers lie,
Thou shalt sing, with thy sweeter mouth,
Under the light of the evening sky,
That Love never fades, though violets die!

FULLER'S BIRD.

"I have read of a bird, which hath a face like, and yet will prey upon, a man; who coming to the water to drink, and finding there by reflection that he had killed one like himself, pineth away by degrees, and never afterward enjoyeth itself."—Fuller's Worthies.

The wild-winged creature, clad in gore,
(His bloody human meal being o'er,)
Comes down to the water's brink:
'Tis the first time he there hath gazed,
And straight he shrinks—alarmed—amazed,
And dares not drink.

"Have I till now," he sadly said,
"Preyed on my brother's blood, and made
His flesh my meal to-day?"
Once more he glances in the brook,
And once more sees his victim's look;
Then turns away.

With such sharp pain as human hearts
May feel, the drooping thing departs
Unto the dark wild wood;
And, where the place is thick with weeds,
He hideth his remorse, and feeds
No more on blood.

And in that weedy brake he lies,
And pines, and pines, until he dies;
And, when all's o'er—
What follows? Naught! his brothers slake
Their thirst in blood in that same brake,
Fierce as before!

—So fable flows!—But would you find
Its moral wrought in human kind,
Its tale made worse;
Turn straight to *Man*, and in his fame
And forehead read "*The Harpy's*" name;
But no remorse!

THE SEA—IN CALM.

Look what immortal floods the sunset pours
Upon us!—Mark! how still (as though in dreams
Bound) the once wild and terrible Ocean seems!
How silent are the winds! No billow roars:
But all is tranquil as Elysian shores!
The silver margin which aye runneth round
The moon-enchanted sea, hath here no sound:
Even Echo speaks not on these radiant moors!

What! is the Giant of the ocean dead,
Whose strength was all unmatched beneath the sun?
No; he reposes! Now his toils are done,
More quiet than the babbling brooks is he.
So mightiest powers by deepest calms are fed,
And sleep, how oft, in things that gentlest be!

A CHAMBER SCENE.

Tread softly through these amorous rooms:
For every bough is hung with life,
And kisses in harmonious strife,
Unloose their sharp and wing'd perfumes!
From Afric, and the Persian looms,
The carpet's silken leaves have sprung,
And heaven, in its blue bounty, flung
These starry flowers, and azure blooms.

Tread softly! By a creature fair
The deity of love reposes,
His red lips open, like the roses
Which round his hyacinthine hair
Hang in crimson coronals;
And Passion fills the arched halls;
And Beauty floats upon the air.

Tread softly—softly, like the foot
Of Winter, shod with fleecy snow,
Who cometh white, and cold, and mute,
Lest he should wake the Spring below.
Oh, look! for here lie Love and Youth,
Fair Spirits of the heart and mind:
Alas! that one should stray from truth;
And one—be ever, ever blind!

THE PAST.

This common field, this little brook—
What is there hidden in these two,
That I so often on them look,
Oftener than on the heavens blue?
No beauty lies upon the field;
Small music doth the river yield;
And yet I look and look again,
With something of a pleasant pain.

'Tis thirty—*can't* be thirty years,
Since last I stood upon this plank,
Which o'er the brook its figure rears,
And watch'd the pebbles as they sank?
How white the stream! I still remember
Its margin glassed by hoar December,
And how the sun fell on the snow:
Ah! *can* it be so long ago?

It cometh back;—So blythe, so bright,
It hurries to my eager ken,
As though but one short winter's night
Had darken'd o'er the world since then.
It is the same clear dazzling scene;—
Perhaps the grass is scarce as green;
Perhaps the river's troubled voice
Doth not so *plainly* say—"Rejoice."

Yet Nature surely never ranges,
Ne'er quits her gay and flowery crown;
But, ever joyful, merrily changes
The primrose for the thistle-down.
'*Tis we* alone who, waxing old,
Look on her with an aspect cold,
Dissolve her in our burning tears,
Or clothe her with the mists of years!

Then, why should not the grass be green?
And why should not the river's song
Be merry—as they both have been
When I was here an urchin strong?
Ah, true—too true! I *see* the sun
Through thirty winter years hath run,
For grave eyes, mirrored in the brook,
Usurp the urchin's laughing look!

So be it! I have lost—and won!
For, once, the past was poor to me—
The future dim; and though the sun
Shed life and strength, and I was free,
I *felt* not—*knew* no grateful pleasure:
All seemed but as the common measure:
But NOW—the experienced Spirit old
Turns all the leaden past to gold!

THE PAUPER'S JUBILEE.

Hurrah! Who was e'er so gay,
As we merry folks to-day?
Brother Beggars, do not stare,
But toss your rags into the air,
And cry, "No work, and better fare!"
Each man, be he saint or sinner,
Shall to-day have—Meat for *Dinner!!*

Yesterday, oh, Yesterday!
That indeed was a bad day;
Iron bread, and rascal gruel,
Water drink, and scanty fuel,
With the beadle at our backs,
Cursing us as we beat flax,
Just like twelve Old Bailey varlets,
Among ochre-picking harlots!

Why should we such things endure?
Though we be the parish Poor,
This is usage bad and rough.
Are not age and pain enough?
Lonely age, unpitied pain?
With the Ban that, like a chain,
To our prison bare hath bound us,
And the unwelcomed Winter 'round us?

Why should we for ever work?
Do we starve beneath the Turk,
That, with one foot in the grave,
We should still toil like the slave?
Seventy winters on our heads,
Yet we freeze on wooden beds!
With one blanket for a fold,
That lets in the horrid cold,
And cramps and agues manifold!

Yet—sometimes we're merry people,
When the chimes clang in the steeple:
If't be summer-time, we all
(Dropsied, palsied, crippled) crawl
Underneath the sunny wall:
Up and down like worms we creep,
Or stand still and fall asleep,
With our faces in the sun,
Forgetting all the world has done!

If't be May, with hawthorn blooms
In our breasts, we sit on tombs,
And spell o'er, with eager ken,
The epitaphs of *older* men,
(Choosing those, for some strange reasons,
Who've weather'd ninety—a hundred seasons,)
Till forth at last we shout in chorus,
"We've thirty good years *still* before us!"

But to-day's a bonny day!
What shall we be doing?
What's the use of saving money,
When rivers flow with milk and honey?
Prudence is our ruin.
What have we to do with care?
Who, to be a pauper's heir,
Would mask his false face in a smile,
Or hide his honest hate in guile?

But come—why do we loiter here?
Boy, go get us some small beer:
Quick! 'twill make our blood run quicker,
And drown the devil Pain in liquor!
March so fierce is almost past,
April will be here at last,
And May must come,
When bees do hum,
And Summer over cold victorious!
Hurrah! 'tis a prospect glorious!
Meat! small beer! and *warmer weather!*
Come boys—let's be mad together!

A THOUGHT ON A RIVULET.

Look at this brook, so blithe, so free!
Thus hath it been, fair boy, for ever—
A shining, dancing, babbling river;
And thus 'twill ever be.
'Twill run, from mountain to the main,
With just the same sweet babbling voice
That now sings out, "Rejoice—rejoice!"
Perhaps 'twill be a chain
That will a thousand years remain—
Ay, through all times and changes last,
And link the present to the past.
Perhaps upon this self-same spot,
Hereafter, may a merry knot
(My children's children!) meet and play,
And think on *me*, some summer day;
And smile (perhaps through youth's brief tears,
While thinking back through wastes of years,)
And softly say—
"'Twas here the old man used to stray,
And gaze upon the sky; and dream
(Long, long ago!) by this same stream.
He's in his grave! Ungentle Time
Hath dealt but harshly with his rhyme:
But *We* will ne'er forget, that he
Taught us to love this river free."

A STORM.

The Spirits of the mighty Sea,
  To-night are 'wakened from their dreams,
And upward to the tempest flee,
  Baring their foreheads where the gleams
Of lightning run, and thunders cry,
Rushing and raining through the sky!

The Spirits of the sea are waging
  Loud war upon the peaceful Night,
And bands of the black winds are raging
  Through the tempest blue and bright;
Blowing her cloudy hair to dust
With kisses, like a madman's lust!

What Ghost now, like an Até, walketh
  Earth—ocean—air? and aye with Time,
Mingled, as with a lover talketh?
  Methinks their colloquy sublime
Draws anger from the sky, which raves
Over the self-abandoned waves!

Behold! like millions mass'd in battle,
  The trembling billows headlong go,
Lashing the barren deeps, which rattle
  In mighty transport till they grow
All fruitful in their rocky home,
And burst from phrensy into foam.

And look! where on the faithless billows
  Lie women, and men, and children fair;
Some hanging, like sleep, to their swollen pillows,
  With helpless sinews and streaming hair,
And some who plunge in the yawning graves!
Ah! lives there no strength beyond the waves?

'Tis said, the Moon can rock the Sea
  From phrensy strange, to silence mild—
To sleep—to death:—But where is *She*,
  While now her storm-born giant child
Upheaves his shoulder to the skies?
Arise, sweet planet pale—arise!

She cometh—lovelier than the dawn
  In summer, when the leaves are green—
More graceful than the alarmed fawn,
  Over his grassy supper seen:
Bright quiet from her beauty falls,
Until—again the tempest calls!

The supernatural storm—he 'waketh
  Again, and lo! from sheets all white,
Stands up unto the stars, and shaketh
  Scorn on the jewell'd locks of Night.
He carries a ship on his foaming crown,
And a cry, like Hell, as he rushes down!

And so still soars from calm to storm,
  The stature of the unresting Sea:
So doth desire or wrath deform
  Our else calm humanity—
    Until at last we sleep,
  And never 'wake nor weep,
(Hush'd to death by some faint tune,)
In our grave beneath the Moon!

THE SONG OF A FELON'S WIFE.

The brand is on thy brow,
  A dark and guilty spot;
'Tis ne'er to be erased!
  'Tis ne'er to be forgot!

The brand is on thy brow!
  Yet *I* must shade the spot:
For who will love thee now,
  If *I* love thee not?

Thy soul is dark—is stained—
  From out the bright world thrown;
By God and man disdained,
  But not by *me*—thy own!

Oh! even the tiger slain
  Hath *one* who ne'er doth flee,
Who sooths his dying pain!
  -That one am I to thee!

I LOVED HER WHEN SHE LOOKED FROM ME.

I loved her when she looked from me,
  And hid her stifled sighs:
I loved her too when she did smile
  With shy and downcast eyes,
The light within them rounding "like
  The young moon in its rise."

I loved her!—Dost thou love no more,
  Now she from thee is flown,
To some far distant—distant shore,
  Unfetter'd, and alone?
Peace, peace! I know her: she will come
  Again, and be mine own.

A kiss—a sigh—a little word
  We changed, when we did part;
No more: yet read I in her eyes
  The promise of her heart;
And Hope (who from all others flies)
  From *me* will ne'er depart.

So here I live—a lover lone,
  Contented with my state,
More sure of love, if she return,
  Than others are of hate:
And if she die?—I too can die,
  Content still with my fate.

PARENTS' LOVE.

Young Love! what have thy dreams above
  Thy hope, thy gladness, thy despair,
That with the *parent's* painful love
  May dare compare?

Thy hopes are like the misty cloud;
  Thy gladness like the shrinking stream;
Thy loud despair all over-loud;
  Thy life—a dream!

But deeper than the unfathomed Main,
  The parent's voiceless love e'er lies;
And oh! the dread, the *death*, the pain,
  When all hope dies!

THE VAIN REGRET.

Oh! had I nursed, when I was young,
The lessons of my father's tongue,
(The deep laborious thoughts he drew,
From all he saw and others knew,)
I might have been—ah, me!
Thrice sager than I e'er shall be.
  For what saith Time?
Alas! he only shows the truth
Of all that I was told in youth!

The thoughts now budding in my brain—
The wisdom I have bought with pain—
The knowledge of life's brevity—
Frail friendship—false philosophy—
And all that issues out of wo—
Methinks, were taught me long ago!
  Then what says Time?
Alas! he but brings back the truth
Of all I heard (and lost!) in youth!

Truths!—hardly learned, and lately brought
  From many a far forgotten scene!
Had I but listened, as I ought,
  To your voices, sage—serene,
Oh! what might I not have been
  In the realms of thought!

HIS LOVE IS HIDDEN.

His love is hidden, like the springs
  Which lie in Earth's deep heart below;
And murmur there a thousand things,
  Which naught above may hear or know.

'Tis hid, not buried! Without sound,
  Or light or limit, night and day,
It (like the dark springs underground)
  Runs, ebbs not, and ne'er *can* decay.

THE FIGHT OF RAVENNA.

He is bound for the wars,
He is armed for the fight,
With iron-like sinews,
And the heart of a knight:
All hidden in steel,
Like the sun in a cloud,
And he calls for his charger,
Who neigheth aloud;
And he calls for his page,
Who comes forth like the light:
And they mount and ride off,
For the Brescian fight.

Count Gaston de Foix
Is the heir of Narbonne,
But his page is an orphan,
Known—link'd unto none;
The master is young,
But as bold as the blast;
The servant all tender—
Too tender to last:
A bud that was born
For the summer-soft skies,
But, left to wild winter,
Unfoldeth, and dies!

"Come forward, my young one,
Ride on by my side:
What, child, wilt thou quell
The Castilian pride?"
Thus speaks the gay soldier,
His heart in his smile,
But his page blushes deep—
Was it anger?—the while.
Was it anger? Ah, no:
For the tender dark eye
Saith—"Master, for thee
I will live, I will die!"

They speed to the field,
Storm-swift in their flight,
And Breschia falleth,
Like fruit in a blight;
Scarce a blow for a battle
A shout for her fame:
All's lost—given up
To the sound of a name!
But Ravenna hath soldiers,
Whose hearts are more bold,
Whose wine is all Spanish,
Whose pay is all gold.

So he turns, with a laugh
Of contempt for his foe,
And now girdeth his sword,
For a weightier blow.
Straight forward he rideth
'Till night's in the sky,
When the page and the master
Together must lie.
Where loiters the page?
Ha! he hangeth his head,
And, with forehead like fire,
He shunneth the bed!

"Now rest thee, my weary one;
Drown thee in sleep.
The great sun himself
Lieth down in the deep;
The beast on his pasture,
The bird on his bough,
The lord and the servant,
Are slumberers now."
"I am wont," sighed the page,
"A long watching to keep;
But my lord shall lie down,
While I charm him to sleep."

Soon (cased in his armor)
Down lieth the knight,
And the page he is tuning
His cittern aright:
At last through a voice
That is tender and low,
The melody mourns
Like a stream at its flow—
Sad, gentle, uncertain,
As the life of a dream:
And thus the page singeth,
With love for his theme:—

SONG.

I.

There lived a lady, long ago;
Her heart was sad and dark—ah, me!
Dark with a single secret wo,
That none could ever see!

II.

She left her home, she lost her pride,
Forgot the jeering world—ah, me!
And followed a knight, and fought, and died,
All for the love of—chivalry!

III.

She died—and when in her last dull sleep,
She lay all pale and cold—ah, me!
They read of a love as wild and deep
As the dark deep sea!

The song's at an end!
But the singer, so young,
Still weeps at the music
That fell from his tongue:
His hands are enclasped,
His cheeks are on fire,
And his black locks, unloosened,
Lie mixed with the wire:
But his lord—*he* reposes
As calm as the night,
Until dawn cometh forth
With her summons of light.

Then—onward they ride
Under clouds of the vine;
Now silent, now singing
Old stories divine;
Now resting awhile,
Near the cool of a stream;
Now wild for the battle,
Now lost in a dream:
At last—they are thridding
The forest of pines,
And Ravenna, beleaguer'd
By chivalry, shines!

• • • •

Ravenna! Ravenna!
Now "God for the right!"
For the Gaul and the Spaniard
Are full in the fight.
French squadrons are charging,
Some conquer, some reel;
Wild trumpets are braying
Aloud for Castile!
Each cannon that roareth
Bears blood on its sound,
And the dead and the dying
Lie thick on the ground.

Now shrieks are the music
That's borne on the gust,
And the groan of the war-horse
Who dies in the dust:
Now Spaniards are cheered
By the "honor" they love;
Now France by the flower
That bloometh above;
And, indeed, o'er the riot,
The steam, and the cloud,
Still the Oriflamme floateth—
The pride of the proud!

What ho! for King Louis!
What ho! for Narbonne!
Come, soldiers! 'tis Gaston
Who leadeth ye on!

'Tis Gaston, your brother,
Who waveth his hand;
Who fights, as *ye* fight,
For the vine-covered land!
'Tis Gaston! 'tis Gaston!
The last of his name,
Who fights for sweet France,
And will die for her fame!

'Come forward! Come"—— Ha!
What is doing? He stops!
Why? why? By Saint Denis!
He staggers—he drops!
'Twas something—'twas nothing—
A shot and a sound:
Yet the ever-bright hero
Lies low on the ground!
He loseth his eye-sight—
He loseth his breath—
He smiles—Ah! his beauty
Is darkened by death!

No pause—not an instant—
For wailing or wo!
For the battle still rageth;
Still fighteth the foe;
Again roar the cannon—
Again flies the ball—
And the heart of the Spaniard
Spouts blood on the Gaul!
Strong armor is riven,
Proud courage laid low,
And Frenchmen and foemen
Are dead at a blow!

Oh, the bellowing thunders!
The shudders—the shocks!
When thousands 'gainst thousands
Come clashing like rocks!
When the rain is all scarlet,
And clouds are half fire,
And men's sinews are snapped
Like the threads of a lyre!
When each litter's a hearse,
And each bullet a knell—
When each breath is a curse,
And each bosom—a hell!

• • • •

Mourn, Soldiers—he's dead!
The last heir of Narbonne!
The bravest—the best!
But the battle is won!
The Spaniards have flown
To their fosse-covered tent;
And the victors are left
To rejoice and lament!
They still have proud leaders,
Still chivalry brave;
But the *first* of their heroes
Lies dumb in the grave!

They bear him in honor;
They laurel his head:
But, who meets the pale burthen,
And drops by the dead?
The Page? No—the Woman!
Who followed her love,
And who'll follow him still
(If it *may* be)—above;
Who'll watch him, and tend him,
On earth, or in sky;
Who was ready to live for him—
Ready to die!

. . . A month has flown by,
On the wings of the year;
And a train of sad maidens
Droop after a bier:
No crown on the coffin—
No name on the lid—
Yet the flow'r of all Provence
Within it is hid!

Blanche—Countess—and heiress—
Who loved like the sun,
Lies at last by the side
Of the heir of Narbonne!

. . . Oh Courage! dost *always*
Pay blood for a name?
True Love! must thou *evermore*
Die for thy fame?
'Twere sweet—could it be—
That the lover should dwell
In the bosom (a heaven!)
He loveth so well:
But, if *not*—why then, Death,
Be thou just to his worth,
And sweep him at once
From the scorn of the earth!

COURAGE.

Courage!—Nothing can withstand
Long a wronged, undaunted land;
If the hearts within her be
True unto themselves and thee,
Thou freed giant, Liberty!
Oh! no mountain-nymph art thou,
When the helm is on thy brow,
And the sword is in thy hand,
Fighting for thy own good land!

Courage!—Nothing e'er withstood
Freemen fighting for their good;
Armed with all their father's fame,
They will win and wear a name
That shall go to endless glory,
Like the gods of old Greek story,
Raised to heaven and heavenly worth,
For the good they gave to earth.

Courage!—There is none so poor,
(None of all who wrong endure,)
None so humble, none so weak,
But may flush his father's cheek;
And his Maidens dear and true,
With the deeds that he may do.
Be his days as dark as night,
He may make himself a light.
What! though sunken be the sun,
There are stars when day is done!

Courage!—Who will be a slave,
That hath strength to dig a grave,
And therein his fetters hide,
And lay a tyrant by his side?
Courage!—Hope, howe'er he fly
For a time, can *never* die!
Courage, therefore, brother men!
Cry "*God!* and to the fight again!"

SIT DOWN, SAD SOUL.

Sit down, sad soul, and count
The moments flying:
Come—tell the sweet amount
That's lost by sighing!
How many smiles?—a score?
Then laugh, and count no more,
For day is dying!

Lie down, sad soul, and sleep,
And no more measure
The flight of Time, nor weep
The loss of leisure;
But here, by this lone stream,
Lie down with us, and dream
Of starry treasure!

We dream: do thou the same:
We love—for ever;
We laugh; yet few we shame—
The gentle, never.
Stay, then, till Sorrow dies:
Then—hope and happy skies
Are thine for ever!

A HYMN OF EVIL SPIRITS.

THE Moon is shining on her way,
  The planets, yet undimmed by sleep,
Drink light from the far-flaming day,
  Who still is hid beyond the deep:
But *here* both men and Spirits weep,
  And earth all mourneth unto air,
Because there liveth nothing fair,
  Nor great, save on the azure steep.

And on that hill of Heaven, none
  Of human strength or thought may climb;
For there bright Angels lie alone,
  Reposing since the birth of Time.
They bask beneath HIS looks sublime;
  But naught of ease or hope is here,
Where sleep is linked to dreams of fear,
  And error to the pains of crime.

The moon is come—but she shall go;
  The stars are in their azure nest;
The jaded wind shall cease to blow;
  But when shall WE have hope or rest?
Now some are sad, and some are blessed;
  But what to us is smile or sigh?
Though Peace, the white-winged dove, be nigh,
  It ne'er must be the Spirit's guest!

Behold! The young and glistening Hour
  Comes riding through the gate of morn,
And we awhile must quit our power.
  And vanish from the world we scorn.
Look! Flattering sin begins to dawn
  From man's false lips and woman's eyes,
And hopes and hearts are racked and torn
  In God's green earthly paradise!

THE VIOLET.

I LOVE all things the seasons bring,
All buds that start, all birds that sing,
    All leaves, from white to jet;
All the sweet words that Summer sends,
When she recalls her flowery friends,
    But chief—the Violet!

I love, how *much* I love the rose,
On whose soft lips the South-wind blows,
    In pretty amorous threat;
The lily paler than the moon,
The odorous wondrous world of June,
    Yet more—the Violet!

She comes—the first, the fairest thing
That Heaven upon the earth doth fling,
    Ere Winter's star has set:
She dwells behind her leafy screen,
And gives, as angels give, unseen:
    So, love—the Violet!

What modest thoughts the Violet teaches,
What gracious boons the Violet preaches,
    Bright maiden, ne'er forget!
But learn, and love, and so depart,
And sing thou, with thy wiser heart,
    "*Long live the Violet!*"

A REPROACH.

Look gently on me! Thou dost move
  (Yet why?) thine eyes away!
Dost dream that I could harm thee, Love,
  Or thy sweet soul betray?

Know better! Some may seek their end,
  Through all bad deeds that be:
But *I*—beyond the world thy friend—
  Can never injure *thee!*

My love, my wo, I not deny;
  And I *can not* from them flee:
But—if thou biddest—I can die
  Far—far away from thee!

BEAUTY.

PAINTERS—Poets—who can tell
What Beauty is—bright miracle?
Sometimes brown and sometimes white,
She shifts from darkness into light,
Swimming on with such fine ease,
That we miss her small degrees,
Knowing not that she hath ranged,
Till we find her sweetly changed.

They are poets false who say
That Beauty must be fair as day,
And that the rich red rose
On her cheek for ever glows,
Or that the cold white lily lieth
On her breast, and never flieth.
Beauty is not so unkind,
Not so niggard, not so blind,
As yield her favor but to one,
When she may walk unconfined,
Associate with the unfettered Wind
And wander with the sun.
No; she spreads her gifts, her grace,
O'er every color, every face.
She can laugh, and she can breathe
Freely where she will—beneath
Polar darkness, tropic star,
Impoverished Delhi, dark Bahár,
And all the regions bright and far,
Where India's sweet-voiced women are!

SYBILLA.

SYBILLA! Dost thou love?
  Oh, swear! Oh, swear!
By those steadfast stars above!
  By this pure sweet air!
  By all things true, and deep, and fair!
By hearts made rich with love,
  Made wise by care!

Sybilla! I love *thee!*
  I swear, I swear—
By all bright things that be!
  By thyself, my fair!
By thine eyes, and motions free!
By thy *sting*, thou honey-bee!
By thy angel thoughts that flee
  Singing through the golden air,
  I swear, I swear!

Sybilla! dost thou frown?
  Beware, beware!
If scorn thy beauty crown,
  I fly—yet where?
Why are thine eyes withdrawn?
Why dost thou turn, thou fawn?
Look on me, like the dawn
  On weeping air!
She smiles—Oh, Beauty bless'd,
Take—take me to thy breast,
  And cure all care!

THOU HAST LOVE WITHIN THINE EYES.

THOU hast love within thine eyes,
  Though they be as dark as night;
And a pity (shown by sighs)
  Heaveth in thy bosom white;
  What is all the azure light
Which the flaxen beauties show,
  If the scorn be sharp and bright,
Where the tender love should glow?

Do I love thee?—Lady, no!
  I was born for other skies,
Where the palmy branches grow,
  And the unclouded mornings rise;
  There—(when sudden evening dies)
I will tell of thee, before
  The beauty of Dione's eyes,
And she shall love thee evermore!

A MIDSUMMER FANCY.

Come hither! Let thou and I
Mount on the dolphin, Pleasure,
And dive through the azure air!
Would't not be fine—would't not be rare,
To live in that sweet, sweet sea, the air—
That ocean which hath no measure,
No peril, no rocky shore,
(But only its airy, airy streams,
And its singing stars, and its orbed dreams,)
For ever and evermore!

Of its wild and its changing weather
What matter—how foul or fair?
We will ever be found together:
Ah! then, sweet Love, what care,
Whether we haunt on the earth or air?
In ocean or inland stream?
Or are lost in some endless, endless dream?
Or are bodiless made, like the tender sprite
Of Love, who watch'd me but yesternight,
With moon-flowers white on her whiter brow,
And smiled and sighed,
In her sad sweet pride,
As *Thou*, fair girl! dost now.

PAST AND PRESENT.

In earlier days, in happier hours,
I watched and wandered with the Sun:
I saw him when the East was red;
I saw him when the day was dead—
All his earthly journey done!
Looks of love were in the West,
But he passed—and took no rest!

O'er the immeasurable blue,
Across the rain, amid the blast,
Onward and onward, like a God,
Through the trackless air he trod,
Scattering bounties as he passed
By the portals of the West—
And never shut his eyes in rest!

Oh, how—in those too happy hours—
How deeply then did I adore
The bright unwearied sleepless Sun,
And wish, just thus, my course to run—
From sea to sea, from shore to shore,
My deeds thus good, thus known, thus bright,
Thus undisturbed by rest or night.

But *now*—since I have heard and seen
The many cares that trouble life,
The evil that requiteth good,
The benefits not understood,
Unfilial, unpaternal strife,
The hate, the lie, the bitter jest—
I feel how sweet are night and rest!

And, oh! what morning ever look'd
So lovely as the quiet eve,
When low and fragrant winds arise,
And draw the curtains of the skies,
And gentle songs of summer weave—
Such as between the alders creep,
Now, and sooth my soul to sleep!

ON SOME HUMAN BONES, FOUND ON A HEADLAND IN THE BAY OF PANAMA.

Vague Mystery hangs on all these desert places!
The fear which hath no name, hath wrought a spell!
Strength, courage, wrath—have been, and left no traces!
They came—and fled: but whither? Who can tell?

We know but that they *were*—that once (in days
When ocean was a bar 'twixt man and man)
Stout spirits wandered o'er these capes and bays,
And perished where these river waters ran,

Methinks they should have built some mighty tomb,
Whose granite might endure the century's rain—
Cold winter, and the sharp night winds, that boom
Like Spirits in their purgatorial pain.

They left, 'tis *said*, their proud unburied bones
To whiten on this unacknowledged shore:
Yet naught beside the rocks and worn sea-stones,
Now answer to the great Pacific's roar!

A mountain stands where Agamemnon died,
And Cheops hath derived eternal fame,
Because he made his tomb a place of pride:
And thus the dead Metella earned a name.

But *these*—they vanished as the lightnings die
(Their mischiefs over) in the affrighted earth;
And no one knoweth underneath the sky,
What heroes perished here, nor whence their birth!

'TIS BETTER WE LAUGH THAN WEEP.

Why, why doth your music grieve
In passion so grave and deep?
Ah! sweet Musicians, believe,
'Tis better we laugh than weep.
Say, say—both grave and gay,
Should we not laugh, whene'er we may?
Thro' day and night, thro' night and day?

Life, life has its share of pain;
Yet for *ever* why weep or fear?
Since the Past ne'er cometh again,
And To-morrow is not yet here?

All, all that is quite our own,
Is the minute we touch to-day,
And that, while we speak, is flown,
And beareth its ills away!

So, let not your music grieve
In melodies grave nor deep;
For, dear Musicians, believe,
'Tis better we laugh than weep!

A DRINKING SONG.

Drink, and fill the night with mirth!
Let us have a mighty measure,
Till we quite forget the earth,
And soar into the world of pleasure.
Drink, and let a health go round,
('Tis the drinker's noble duty,)
To the eyes that shine and wound,
To the mouths that bud in beauty!

Here's to Helen! Why, ah! why
Doth she fly from my pursuing?
Here's to Marian, cold and shy!
May she warm before thy wooing!
Here's to Janet! I've been e'er,
Boy and man, her stanch defender,
Always sworn that she was fair,
Always *known* that she was tender!

Fill the deep-mouthed glasses high!
Let them with the champaign tremble.
Like the loose wrack in the sky,
When the four wild winds assemble!
Here's to all the love on earth,
(Love, the young man's, wise man's, treasure!)
Drink, and fill your throats with mirth!
Drink, and drown the world in pleasure!

SISTER, I CAN NOT READ TO-DAY.

Sister, I can not read to day!
Before my eyes the letters stream;
Now—one by one—they fade away,
Like shadows in a dream:
All seems a fancy, half forgot;
Sweet sister, do I dream or not?

I can not work; I can not rest;
I can not sing—nor think, to day;
The wild heart panteth in my breast,
As though 'twould break away.
Why—wherefore—Ah, girl! ease my wo,
And tell me—*why* he tarrieth so!

RIVER OF THE MORN.

River of the morn!
Fast thou flowest and bright;
From the sundered East thou flowest,
Bearing down the Night:
Every cloud thy beauty drinketh;
Darkness from thy current shrinketh;
Leaving the Heavens empty quite,
For the conquering Light!

O, the Thought new-born!
Lovely 'tis, and bright;
Like some jewel of the morn,
Nursed in frozen night.
But it trembleth soon and groweth
And dissolved in splendor floweth,
(Like the flooding dawn that pours
O'er and o'er the cloudy shores,)
Till blind Ignorance wings her flight
From the conquering Light!

O, ye Thoughts of youth,
Long since flown away!
What ye want in truth,
Ye in love repay!
Though in shadowy forests hidden,
Like the bird that's lost and chidden,
Back again with all your songs,
Ye do come and sooth our wrongs,
Till the unburthened heart doth soar
Wiser than before!

SONG SHOULD BREATHE.

Song should breathe of scents and flowers;
Song should like a river flow;
Song should bring back scenes and hours
That we loved—ah, long ago!

Song from baser thoughts should win us;
Song should charm us out of wo;
Song should stir the heart within us,
Like a patriot's friendly blow.

Pains and pleasures, all man doeth,
War and peace, and right and wrong—
All things that the soul subdueth
Should be vanquished, too, by Song.

Song should spur the mind to duty;
Nerve the weak, and stir the strong:
Every deed of truth and beauty
Should be crowned by starry Song!

I DIE FOR THY SWEET LOVE.

I die for thy sweet love! The ground
Not panteth so for summer rain,
As I for one soft look of thine:
And yet—I sigh in vain!

A hundred men are near thee now—
Each one, perhaps, surpassing me:
But who doth feel a thousandth part
Of what I feel for thee?

They look on thee, as men will look
Who 'round the wild world laugh and rove:
I only think how sweet 'twould be
To *die* for thy sweet love!

WHAT USE IS ALL THE LOVE I BEAR THEE?

What use is all the love I bear thee,
Without thy sweet return?
What use in Fate's cold patient lesson,
Which *my* soul can not learn?

I love thee—as, they tell in story,
Men love in burning climes:
And I let loose my wild heart before thee,
In burning, burning rhymes!

Were't not for this, my chafed Spirit
Would burst its bonds and flee!
And *Thou?* Ah, yes, thy gentle heart
Would *still* give a thought to *me!*

SONG FOR OUR FATHER LAND.

Hurrah! Here's a health to the land,
Brave brothers, wherein we were born;
Here's a health to the friend that we love!
Here's a heart for the man that's forlorn!
Let us drink unto all,
Who help us or lack us,
From the child and the poor man,
To Ceres and Bacchus;
And to Plenty (thrice over!) not forgetting her horn!

Here's a health to the Sun in the sky;
To the corn—to the fruit in the ground;
To the fish—to the brute—to the bird;
To the vine—may it spread and abound!
To good fellows and friends
Whom we love or who love us,
Far off us, or near us,
Below, or above us;
For a friend is a gem, wheresoever he's found!

Here's a curse on bad times that are past!
Were they better—but now they're no more.
So here's to all *Good*—may it last!
And a health to THE FUTURE—thrice o'er!
May the hope that we look upon
Never deceive us!
May the Spirit of good
Never fail us or leave us;
But stand up like a friend that is true to the core

Ambition—oh lay it in dust!
Revenge—'tis a snake; let it die!
And for Pride—let it feed on a crust,
Though sweet Pity look out from the sky!
But Wisdom and Hope,
And the *honest* endeavor—
May they smile on us *now*,
And stand by us for ever,
Fast friends, wheresoever the tempest shall fly!

TO THE SNOW-DROP

Pretty firstling of the year!
Herald of the host of flowers,
Hast thou left my cavern drear,
In the hope of summer hours?
Back unto my earthern bowers!
Back to thy warm world below,
Till the strength of suns and showers
Quell the now relentless snow!

Art *still* here?—Alive? and blythe?
Though the stormy night hath fled,
And the Frost hath passed his scythe
O'er thy small unsheltered head?
Ah!—some lie amid the dead,
(Many a giant stubborn tree,—
Many a plant, its spirit shed,)
That were better nursed than thee!

What hath saved thee? Thou wast not
'Gainst the arrowy winter furred,—
Armed in scale—but all forgot
When the frozen winds were stirred
Nature, who doth clothe the bird,
Should have hid thee in the earth,
Till the cuckoo's song was heard,
And the Spring let loose her mirth.

Nature—deep and mystic word,
Mighty mother, still unknown!
Thou didst sure the Snow-drop gird
With an armor all thine own!
Thou, who sent'st it forth alone
To the cold and sullen season,
(Like a thought at random thrown,)
Sent it thus for some grave reason!

If 'twere but to pierce the mind
With a single gentle thought,
Who shall deem thee harsh or blind?
Who that thou hast vainly wrought?
Hoard the gentle virtue caught
From the Snow-drop—reader wise!
Good is good, wherever taught,
On the ground or in the skies!

WILT THOU LEAVE ME?

Wilt thou leave me? I did give
  All my fond true heart to *thee*,
Dreaming thou might'st scorn it not;
  And canst thou abandon me?

I have loved—oh, word of love,
  Bear me to thy star of bliss,
Let me know if worlds above
  Can requite the pain of this?

I have loved—oh lover, why
  Must I all my fondness tell?
Do not—do not bid me die
  At thy cruel word—"Farewell."

IN COMMEMORATION OF HAYDN.

Come forth, victorious Sounds—from harp and horn,
From viol, and trump, and echoing instruments!
  A hundred years have flown! A hundred years,
  Of toil and strife, of joys and tears,
Have risen to life, and died 'mid vain laments,
  Since that harmonious morn,
  Whereon the Muse's mighty Son was born!

Sound—Immortal Music, sound!
Bid the golden words go 'round!
Every heart and tongue, proclaim
Haydn's power! Haydn's fame!
Sing—how well he earned his glory!
Sing—how he shall live in story!
Sing—how he *doth* live in light;
  Shining like a star above us,
  Bending down to cheer and love us
Crowned with his own divine delight!
Sound—Immortal Music, sound!
Bid thy golden words go 'round!

Every grand and gentle tone,
Every truth he made his own;
Gathering from the human mind
All the bloom that poets find—
Gathering, from the winds and ocean,
Dreams, to feed his high emotion.
When the Muse was past control—
Gathering, from all things that roll
Within Time's vast and starry round,
The thoughts that give a Soul to sound!

ON THE PORTRAIT OF A CHILD.

A year—an age shall fade away,
  (Ages of pleasure and of pain)
And yet the face I see to-day
  For ever shall remain—
In my heart and in my brain!
Not all the scalding tears of care
Shall wash away that vision fair;
Not all the thousand thoughts that rise,
Not all the sights that dim mine eyes,
  Shall e'er usurp the place
  Of that little angel face!
  But here it shall remain
For ever; and if joy or pain
Turn my troubled winter gaze
Back unto my hawthorn days,
There—among the hoarded past,
I shall see it to the last;
The only thing, save poet's rhyme,
That shall not own the touch of Time!

INSCRIPTIONS.

I. FOR A FOUNTAIN.

Rest! This little Fountain runs
  Thus for aye:—It never stays
For the look of summer suns,
  Nor the cold of winter days.
Whosoe'er shall wander near,
  When the Syrian heat is worst,
Let him hither come, nor fear
  Lest he may not slake his thirst:
He will find this little river
Running still as bright as ever.
Let him drink, and onward hie,
Bearing but in thought that I,
Erotas, bade the Naiad fall,
And thank the great god Pan for all!

II. FOR A TEMPLE OF ÆSCULAPIUS.

In this high nook, built all by mortal hand,
An Epidaurian Temple, here I stand
Sacred to him who drives away disease,
And gives to all who seek him health and ease!
I stand devoted to the God of health—
To Æsculapius old; built by the wealth
Of grateful men, who owe to his rare skill,
Life, ease, and all that Fortune spares them still.

III. FOR A STREAMLET.

Traveller, note! Although I seem
But a little sparkling stream,
I come from regions where the sun
Dwelleth when his toil is done—
From yon proud hills in the West.
Thence I come, and never rest,
Till (curling round the mountain's feet)
I find myself 'mid pastures sweet,
Vernal, green, and ever gay;
And then I gently slide away,
A thing of silence—till I cast
My life into the sea at last!

IV. FOR AN ANTIQUE DRINKING CUP.

Drink! If thou find'st my round all filled with wine,
Which lifts men's creeping thoughts to dreams divine,
Drink, and become a God! Anacreon old
Once quenched his mighty thirst from out my gold:
Rich was I, red, and brimming;—but he laughed,
And (tasting sparely) drained me at a draught.
Bacchanal! If thou lov'st the Teian's fame,
Take courage—grasp me fast—and strait do Thou the same!

SHE SATE BY THE RIVER SPRINGS.

She sate by the river springs,
  And bound her coal-black hair;
And she sang, as the cuckoo sings,
  Alone—in the Evening air,
  With a patient smile, and a look of care,
  And a cheek that was dusk, not fair:
She sate, but her thoughts had wings,
  That carried her sweet despair
Away to the azure plains,
  Where Truth and the angels are:
She sang—but she sang in vain:
Ah! why doth she sing again?

She mourns, like the sweet wind grieving in
  The pines on an autumn night;
She will fade, like the fading Evening,
  When Hesper is blooming bright:
  And her song?—it must take its flight!
    So pretty a song
    Must die ere long,
  Like a too, too sharp delight!

She *was*—like the rose in summer;
  She *is*—like the lily frail;
Yet, they'll welcome the sweet new-comer,
  Below, in the regions pale!
And the ghost will forget his pain,
  As he roams through the dusk alone:
And *We?*—We will mourn in vain,
  O'er the Shadow of beauty flown!

WILT THOU GO?

Wilt thou go? Thou'lt come again?
Swear it, Love, by love's sweet pain!
Swear it, by the stars that glisten
In thy brow as thou dost listen!
Swear it, by the love-sick air,
Wandering, murmuring, here and there,
Seeking for some tender nest,
Yet, like thee, can never rest.
Swear!—and I shall safer be
Amid love's sweet mutiny!

GOLDEN-TRESSED ADELAIDE.

A SONG FOR A CHILD.

SING, I pray, a little song,
Mother dear!
Neither sad nor very long:
It is for a little maid,
Golden-tressed Adelaide!
Therefore let it suit a merry, merry ear,
Mother dear!

Let it be a merry strain,
Mother dear!
Shunning e'en the thought of pain:
For our gentle child will weep,
If the theme be dark and deep;
And *We* will not draw a single single tear,
Mother dear!

Childhood should be all divine,
Mother dear!
And like an endless summer shine;
Gay as Edward's shouts and cries,
Bright as Agnes' azure eyes:
Therefore, bid thy song be merry:—dost thou hear,
Mother dear?

LOVE FLYING.

LOVE flies, fond wretch, across the desert air;
Pursued by passionate thoughts and phantom fears,
His tender heart, though young, the home of care,
His eyes (now hidden) blind with many tears:
To what less hopeless region can he flee,
Sweet and gentle Iole!

Tell *me*, and bid me fly; and tell me, too,
Why Love goes weeping when he looks at thee?
Why do his eyes, like mine, forsake Heaven's blue?
Why can we nothing see,
Save that one spot of earth where *Thou* mayst be?

Give me *one* smile, sweet heart!—for my eyes now
Grow dim, like Love's, with tears; and I could fade
Beneath the beauty of thy gentle brow,
Into the everlasting fatal shade,
Where cold Oblivion near pale Death is laid,
Could I but win one tender thought from *thee*,
Sweet—sweet Iole!

A DREAMER'S SONG.

I DREAM of thee at morn,
When all the earth is gay,
Save I, who live a life forlorn,
And die thro' a long decay.

I dream of thee at noon,
When the summer sun is high,
And the river sings a sleepy tune,
And the woods give no reply.

I dream of thee at eve,
Beneath the fading sun,
When even the winds begin to grieve;
And I dream till day is done.

I dream of thee at night,
When dreams, men say, are free;
Alas, thou dear—too dear delight!
When dream I *not* of thee?

WISHES.

SWEET be her dreams, the fair, the young!
Grace, beauty, breathe upon her!
Music, haunt thou about her tongue!
Life, fill her path with honor!

All golden thoughts, all wealth of days,
Truth, Friendship, Love, surround her
So may she smile till life be closed,
And Angel hands have crowned her!

A POET'S THOUGHT.

TELL me, what is a poet's thought?
Is it on the sudden born?
Is it from the star-light caught?
Is it by the tempest taught?
Or by whispering morn?

Was it cradled in the brain?
Chained awhile, or nursed in night?
Was it wrought with toil and pain?
Did it bloom and fade again,
Ere it burst to light?

No more question of its birth:
Rather love its better part!
'Tis a thing of sky and earth,
Gathering all its golden worth
From the Poet's heart.

TO A LADY ATTIRING HERSELF.

FOR whom—(too happy for the earth or skies!)
Dost thou adorn thee with such restless care?
Or veil the star-light beauty of thine eyes?
Or bind in fatal wreaths thy golden hair?

He dies who looks on thee—as *I* have died,
(Love's ghost and victim) slain by thy cold pride!
He dies, oh! he *must* die—but will he wander
(As *I* have done) for ever round thy door?
Or on thy deadly beauty dream and ponder,
(As I still dream) for ever and evermore?

WILT THOU REMEMBER ME?

WILT thou remember me when I am gone—
Gone to that leaden darkness, where men lie,
Shut out from friends, in chambers all of stone—
Waiting my summons from the awful sky?

Think of me, *sometimes*, sweet!—all cold, all pale,
Beyond the power of pain—a Spirit taken
By Death to regions where no hearts awaken;
Where no hopes haunt us—no wild sorrows wail—
Where even *thy* love itself can then no more avail!

I GO, AND SHE DOTH MISS ME NOT!

I GO—and she doth miss me not!
So shall I die, and be forgot—
Forgot, as is some sorrow past,
Or cloud by fleeting sickness cast.

Death, and the all-absorbing tomb,
Will hide me in eternal gloom;
And she will live—as gay—alone,
As though I had been never known!

'Tis well, perhaps, that this should be;
'Tis surely well sad thoughts should flee!
Nor would I wish—when I am hid
Underneath the coffin's lid—
That thou shouldst spoil *one* blooming thought for me,
Fair and for-aye-beloved Iole!

A PETITION TO TIME.

TOUCH us gently, Time!
Let us glide adown thy stream
Gently—as we sometimes glide
Through a quiet dream!
Humble voyagers are We,
Husband, wife, and children three—
(One is lost—an angel, fled
To the azure overhead!)

Touch us gently, Time!
We've not proud nor soaring wings,
Our ambition, *our* content,
Lies in simple things.
Humble voyagers are We,
O'er Life's dim unsounded sea,
Seeking only some calm clime;—
Touch us *gently*, gentle Time!

NAPOLEON.

HARK! the world is rent asunder:
Nations are aghast; and kings
(Mingling in the common wonder)
Shake, like humbler things.
Only thou art left alone,
Napoleon! Napoleon!

Plague, from out her trance awaking,
Quits her ancient hot domain;
And War, the statesman's fetters breaking,
Shouts to thee—in vain!
Both to thee are now unknown,
Napoleon! Napoleon!

He who rode War's fiery billows
Once, and ruled their surges wild,
Now beneath Helena's willows
Sleepeth—like a child!
All thy soaring spirit flown:
Napoleon! Napoleon!

In his grave the warrior sleepeth,
Humbly laid, and half forgot,
And naught, besides the willow, weepeth
O'er that silent spot!
Calm it is, and all thine own;
Napoleon! Napoleon!

But—what columns teach his merit?
What rich ermines wrap him round?—
None;—His proud and plumed Spirit
Crowns alone the ground!
Proud and pale, and all alone,
Lies the dead Napoleon!

A PRAYER IN SICKNESS.

SEND down thy winged angel, God!
Amid this night so wild;
And bid him come where now we watch,
And breathe upon our child!

She lies upon her pillow, pale,
And moans within her sleep,
Or wakeneth with a patient smile,
And striveth *not* to weep.

How gentle and how good a child
She is, we know too well,
And dearer to her parents' hearts,
Than our weak words can tell.

We love—we watch throughout the night,
To aid, when need may be;
We hope—and have despaired, at times;
But *now* we turn to Thee!

Send down thy sweet-souled angel, God!
Amid the darkness wild,
And bid him sooth our souls to-night
And heal our gentle child!

TO A VOYAGER.

MY Love is journeying o'er the sea,
God guard her on the deep!
And force the Ocean harms to flee,
And bid the tempests sleep.
To-night she leaves our English strand,
To sail unto the Indian land!

She goes, all ignorant of my love!
And fit it thus should be!
For why should waves or winds above
Bear hopeless sighs from me?
'Tis better I should bear—in vain,
Than *she* should answer—pain for pain!

Bright Stars, look gently on her sleep!
Sweet guardian Heaven, enfold her round;
And quell all madness in the deep;
And banish from the air its sound!
Oh! guard her from all ill—all strife;
And bless her through the bloom of life!

ON THE DEATH OF A CHILD.

HITHER come, at close of day,
And o'er this dust, sweet Mothers, pray!
A little infant lies within,
Who never knew the name of sin,
Beloved—bright—and all our own;
Like morning fair—and sooner flown!

No leaves or garlands wither here,
Like those in foreign lands;
No marble hides our dear one's bier,
The work of alien hands:
The months it lived, the name it bore,
The silver telleth—nothing more!

No more;—yet Silence stalketh round
This vault so dim and deep,
And Death keeps watch without a sound.
Where all lie pale and sleep;
But palest here and latest hid,
Is *He*—beneath this coffin-lid.

How fair he was—how *very* fair—
What dreams we pondered o'er,
Making his life so long and clear,
His fortune's flowing o'er;
Our hopes—(that he would happy be,
When we ourselves were old,)
The scenes we saw, or hoped to see—
They're soon and sadly told.

All was a dream!—it came and fled,
And left us here, among the dead!
Pray, Mothers, pray, at close of day,
While we, sad parents, weep alway!
Pray, too (and softly be't and long),
That all *your* babes, now fair and strong,
May blossom like—*not* like the rose,
For that doth fade when summer goes—
('Twas thus *our* pretty infant died,
The summer and its mother's pride!)
But, like some stern enduring tree,
That reacheth its green century,
May grow, may flourish—then decay,
After a long, calm, happy day,
Made happier by good deeds to men,
And hopes in heaven to meet again!

Pray!—From the happy, prayer is due;
While we—('tis all we now can do!)
Will check our tears, and pray with you.

SONG FROM A PLAY.

WHY art thou, Love! so fair, so young
Why is that sad sweet music hung,
For ever, on thy gentle tongue?

Why art thou fond? Why art thou fair?
Why sitteth, in thy soft eye, Care?
Why smil'st thou in such sweet despair?

Youth, beauty, fade—like summer roses;
Sad music sadder love discloses;
Dark Care in darker death reposes!

All's vain! the rough world careth not
For thee—for me—for our dark lot.
We love, Sweet, but to be forgot!

We love—and meet the world's sharp scorn;
We live—to die some common morn—
Unknown, unwept, and still forlorn!
Why, dear one, why—*why* where we born?

TO A POETESS.

DREAD'ST thou lest thou shouldst die unknown
What matter? All the strength of Fame
And Death have this poor power alone-
To give thee an uncertain fame.

The critic dull and envious bard
Will quarrel o'er thine ashes dear;
That past—thy single sad reward
Must be some lonely lover's tear!

A NIGHT SONG.

'Tis Night! 'tis Night! the Hour of hours,
When Love lies down with folded wings,
By Psyche in her starless bowers,
And down his fatal arrows flings—
Those bowers whence not a sound is heard,
Save only from the bridal bird,
Who 'mid that utter darkness sings:
This her burthen soft and clear—
Love is here! Love is here!

'Tis Night! The moon is on the stream·
Bright spells are on the soothed sea
And Hope, the child, is gone to dream,
Of pleasures which may never be!
And now is haggard Care asleep;
Now doth the widow Sorrow smile;
And slaves are hushed in slumber deep,
Forgetting grief and toil awhile!

What sight can fiery morning show
To shame the stars or pale moonlight?
What bounty can the day bestow,
Like that which falls from gentle Night
Sweet Lady, sing I not aright?
Oh! turn and tell me—for the day
Is faint and fading fast away;
And now comes back the Hour of hours,
When Love his lovelier mistress seeks,
And sighs, like winds 'mong evening flowers,
Until the maiden Silence speaks!

Fair girl, methinks—nay, hither turn
Those eyes, which 'mid their blushes burn—
Methinks, at such a time one's heart
Can better bear both sweet and smart—
Love's look—the first—which never dieth,
Or Death—who comes when Beauty flieth,
When strength is slain, when youth is past,
And all, save Truth, is lost at last!

TO ADELAIDE.

Child of my heart! My sweet beloved Firstborn!
Thou dove who tidings bring'st of calmer hours!
Thou rainbow who dost shine when all the showers
Are past—or passing! Rose which hath no thorn—
No spot, no blemish—pure, and unforlorn!
Untouched, untainted! O, my Flower of flowers!
More welcome than to bees are summer bowers,
To stranded seamen life-assuring morn!
Welcome—a thousand welcomes! Care, who clings
'Round all, seems loosening now its serpent fold:
New hope springs upward; and the bright world seems
Cast back into a youth of endless springs!
Sweet mother, is it so?—or grow I old
Bewildered in divine Elysian dreams?
November, 1825.

A CONCEIT.

Sweet sights, sweet scents, sweet sounds,
All to my sweet Love hie:
Some go their viewless rounds;
Some sail before her eye;
But the sweetest—oh! the sweetest,
Deep in her bosom lie!

The violet comes to woo her,
With an eye like Heaven above;
Night's sweet bird mourns unto her;
Soft winds all round her rove;
And tender—tenderest thoughts pursue her,
With a voice as sweet as love!

SEASHORE STANZAS.

Methinks, I fain would lie by the lone Sea,
And hear the waters their white music weave!
Methinks it were a pleasant thing to grieve,
So that our sorrows might companioned be,
By that strange harmony
Of winds and billows, and the living sound
Sent down from Heaven when the Thunder speaks,
Unto the listening shores and torrent creeks, as
When the swoll'n sea doth strive to bursts his bound!

Methinks, when tempests come and kiss the Ocean,
Until the vast and terrible billows wake,
I see the writhing of that curled snake,
Which men of old believed—and my emotion
Warreth within me, till the fable reigns
God of my fancy, and my curdling veins
Do homage to that serpent old,
Which clasped the great world in its fold,
And brooded over earth, and the charmed sea,
Like endless, restless, drear Eternity!

AN EPITAPH.

He died, and left the world behind!
His once wild heart is cold!
His once keen eye is quelled and blind!
What more?—His tale is told.

He came, and, baring his heaven-bright thought,
He earned the base World's ban:
And—having vainly lived and taught,
Gave place to a meaner man!

A QUESTION AND REPLY

"What is there on this dark cold bank,
That thou so long hast sought?
Methinks these briers and rushes dank—
This hollow, with the wild grass rank,
Show nothing worth a thought!"

"I seek what thou canst value not,
What thou canst never see—
Soft eyes, by all but me forgot,
Which here—ay, on this dark cold spot,
Bent their last look on *me!*"

A PARTING SONG.

Wilt thou leave thy home so kind,
For the Ocean wild?
Canst thou leave *me*, old and blind,
Untender child?

Dost thou think the storms above thee
Will respect my son?
Dost thou dream the world will love thee
As *I* have done?

Boy, through nights and years I've nursed thee,
How—thy heart should tell,
And (come what will) I have not cursed thee:
And so—farewell!

A FAREWELL.

Farewell!—Now Time must slowlier move
Than e'er since this dark world began;
And thou wilt give thy heaven of love
Unto another, happier man!

And *then*—I never more will see
Those eyes—but hide, far off, my pain:
And thou wilt have forgotten *me*,
Or smile thou see'st me not again.

Live happy, in thy happier lot:
And I will strive (if't so must be)
To think 'tis well to be forgot,
Since it may keep a pang from *thee!*

INTRODUCTORY REMARKS TO PINKNEY'S POEMS.

WHAT poetry would be in a world where Toil were not the Siamesed twin of Excellence—(in other words, where man had not fallen)—"is a curious question, coz!" The wild horse runs very well in the prairie, but we give our admiration to the "good continuer" by toilsome training. Whether the *fainéant* angels, who "sit in the clouds," admire most the objectless careerings of he wild steed, or the arrowy endurance of the winner of the sweepstakes—whether the fragmentary poetry dashed off while the inspiration is on, and checked, ill-finished, when the whim evaporates, be more celestial than the smooth and complete product of painful toil and disciplined concentration—I have had my luxurious doubts. Pinkney's genius, as evidenced on paper, has all the impulsive abandonment which marked his character and course of life. He was a born poet—with all needful imagination, discrimination, perception, and sensibility; and he had besides the flesh-and-bloodfulness necessary to keep poetry on terra firma. Several of his productions have become common air—known and enjoyed by everybody, but without a name. The songs beginning—

"I fill this cup to one made up of loveliness alone,"

"We break the glass whose sacred wine
To some beloved health we drain,
Lest future pledges, less divine,
Should e'er the hallow'd toy profane;
And thus I broke a heart that pour'd
Its tide of feelings out for thee," etc.—

These and two or three others of Pinkney's "entire and perfect chrysolites" should be re-graven with his name, for the world owes his memory a debt for them. The small volume of his poetry from which the Mirror Library edition is copied, was printed in 1825, and has been long lost sight of. It contains—not the stuff for a classic—but a delicious bundle of heart-touching passages, fresh, peculiar, and invaluable more especially to lovers, whose sweetest and best interpreter Pinkney was. Every man or woman who has occasion to embroider a love-letter with the very essence-flowers of passionate verse, should possess a copy of Pinkney's Poems

THE

MISCELLANEOUS POEMS

OF

EDWARD C. PINKNEY.

ITALY.

I.

Know'st thou the land which lovers ought to choose?
Like blessings there descend the sparkling dews;
In gleaming streams the crystal rivers run,
The purple vintage clusters in the sun;
Odours of flowers haunt the balmy breeze,
Rich fruits hang high upon the vernant trees;
And vivid blossoms gem the shady groves,
Where bright-plumed birds discourse their careless loves.
Beloved!—speed we from this sullen strand
Until thy light feet press that green shore's yellow sand.

II.

Look seaward thence, and naught shall meet thine eye
But fairy isles, like paintings on the sky;
And, flying fast and free before the gale,
The gaudy vessel with its glancing sail;
And waters glittering in the glare of noon,
Or touched with silver by the stars and moon,
Or flecked with broken lines of crimson light
When the far fisher's fire affronts the night.
Lovely as loved! towards that smiling shore
Bear we our household gods, to fix for evermore.

III.

It looks a dimple on the face of earth,
The seal of beauty, and the shrine of mirth;
Nature is delicate and graceful there,
The place's genius, feminine and fair:
The winds are awed, nor dare to breathe aloud;
The air seems never to have borne a cloud,
Save where volcanoes send to heaven their curled
And solemn smokes, like altars of the world.
Thrice beautiful!—to that delightful spot
Carry our married hearts, and be all pain forgot.

IV.

There Art too shows, when Nature's beauty palls,
Her sculptured marbles, and her pictured walls;
And there are forms in which they both conspire
To whisper themes that know not how to tire:
The speaking ruins in that gentle clime
Have but been hallowed by the hand of Time,
And each can mutely prompt some thought of flame—
The meanest stone is not without a name.
Then come, beloved!—hasten o'er the sea
To build our happy hearth in blooming Italy.

THE INDIAN'S BRIDE.

I.

Why is that graceful female here
With yon red hunter of the deer?
Of gentle mien and shape, she seems
For civil halls designed,
Yet with the stately savage walks
As she were of his kind.
Look on her leafy diadem,
Enriched with many a floral gem:
Those simple ornaments about
Her candid brow, disclose
The loitering Spring's last violet,
And Summer's earliest rose:
But not a flower lies breathing there,
Sweet as herself, or half so fair.
Exchanging lustre with the sun,
A part of day she strays—
A glancing, living, human smile,
On nature's face she plays.
Can none instruct me what are these
Companions of the lofty trees?—

II.

Intent to blend with his her lot,
Fate formed her all that he was not;
And, as by mere unlikeness thoughts
Associate we see,
Their hearts from very difference caught
A perfect sympathy.
The household goddess here to be
Of that one dusky votary,—
She left her pallid countrymen,
An earthling most divine,
And sought in this sequestered wood
A solitary shrine.
Behold them roaming hand in hand,
Like night and sleep, along the land;
Observe their movements:—he for her
Restrains his active stride,
While she assumes a bolder gait
To ramble at his side:
Thus, even as the steps they frame,
Their souls fast alter to the same.
The one forsakes ferocity,
And momently grows mild;
The other tempers more and more
The artful with the wild.
She humanizes him, and he
Educates her to liberty.

III.

Oh, say not they must soon be old,
Their limbs prove faint, their breasts feel cold!
Yet envy I that sylvan pair,
More than my words express,
The singular beauty of their lot,
And seeming happiness.
They have not been reduced to share
The painful pleasures of despair:
Their sun declines not in the sky
Nor are their wishes cast,
Like shadows of the afternoon,
Repining towards the past:
With naught to dread, or to repent,
The present yields them full content.
In solitude there is no crime;
Their actions are all free,
And passion lends their way of life
The only dignity;
And how should they have any cares?—
Whose interest contends with theirs?

IV.

The world, or all they know of it,
Is theirs:—for them the stars are lit;
For them the earth beneath is green,
The heavens above are bright;
For them the moon doth wax and wane,
And decorate the night;
For them the branches of those trees
Wave music in the vernal breeze;
For them upon that dancing spray
The free bird sits and sings,
And glitt'ring insects flit about
Upon delighted wings;
For them that brook, the brakes among,
Murmurs its small and drowsy song;
For them the many-coloured clouds
Their shapes diversify,
And change at once, like smiles and frowns,
Th' expression of the sky.
For them, and by them, all is gay,
And fresh and beautiful as they:
The images their minds receive,
Their minds assimilate,
To outward forms imparting thus
The glory of their state.
Could aught be painted otherwise
Than fair, seen through her star-bright eyes?
He too, because she fills his sight,
Each object falsely sees;
The pleasure that he has in her,
Makes all things seem to please.
And this is love;—and it is life
They lead,—that Indian and his wife.

A PICTURE-SONG.

How may this little tablet feign the features of a face,
Which o'er-informs with loveliness its proper share of space;
Or human hands on ivory enable us to see
The charms, that all must wonder at, thou work of gods, in thee!

But yet, methinks, that sunny smile familiar stories tells,
And I should know those placid eyes, two shaded crystal wells;
Nor can my soul, the limner's art attesting with a sigh,
Forget the blood that decked thy cheek, as rosy clouds the sky.

They could not semble what thou art, more excellent than fair,
As soft as sleep or pity is, and pure as mountain-air;
But here are common, earthly hues, to such an aspect wrought,
That none, save thine, can seem so like the beautiful of thought.

The song I sing, thy likeness like, is painful mimicry
Of something better, which is now a memory to me,
Who have upon life's frozen sea arrived the icy spot,
Where men's magnetic feelings show their guiding task forgot.

The sportive hopes, that used to chase their shifting shadows on,
Like children playing in the sun, are gone—forever gone;
And on a careless, sullen peace, my double-fronted mind,
Like Janus when his gates were shut, looks forward and behind.

Apollo placed his harp, of old, awhile upon a stone,
Which has resounded since, when struck, a breaking harp-string's tone;
And thus my heart, though wholly now from early softness free,
If touched, will yield the music yet, it first received of thee.

THE VOYAGER'S SONG.

"A tradition prevailed among the natives of Puerto Rico, that in the Isle of Bimini, one of the Lucayos, there was a fountain of such wonderful virtue, as to renew the youth and recall the vigour of every person who bathed in its salutary waters. In hopes of finding this grand restorative, Ponce de Leon and his followers ranged through the islands, searching with fruitless solicitude for the fountain, which was the chief object of the expedition." [*Robertson's America.*

I.

Sound trumpets, ho!—weigh anchor—loosen sail—
The seaward flying banners chide delay;
As if 'twere heaven that breathes this kindly gale,
Our life-like bark beneath it speeds away.
Flit we, a gliding dream, with troublous motion,
Across the slumbers of uneasy ocean;
And furl our canvass by a happier land,
So fraught with emanations from the sun,
That potable gold streams through the sand
Where element should run.

II.

Onward, my friends, to that bright, florid isle,
The jewel of a smooth and silver sea,
With springs on which perennial summers smile
A power of causing immortality.
For Bimini;—in its enchanted ground,
The hallowed fountains we would seek, are found;
Bathed in the waters of those mystic wells,
The frame starts up in renovated truth,
And, freed from Time's deforming spells,
Resumes its proper youth.

III.

Hail, better birth!—once more my feelings all
A graven image to themselves shall make,
And, placed upon my heart for pedestal,
That glorious idol long will keep awake
Their natural religion, nor be cast
To earth by Age, the great Iconoclast.
As from Gadara's founts they once could come,
Charm-called, from these Love's genii shall arise,
And build tneir perdurable home,
Miranda, in thine eyes.

IV.

By Nature wisely gifted, not destroyed
With golden presents, like the Roman maid,—
A sublunary paradise enjoyed,
Shall teach thee bliss incapable of shade;—
An Eden ours, nor angry gods, nor men,
Nor star-clad Fates, can take from us again.
Superior to animal decay,
Sun of that perfect heaven, thou'lt calmly see
Stag, raven, phenix, drop away
With *human* transiency.

V.

Thus rich in being,—beautiful,—adored,
Fear not exhausting pleasure's precious mine;
The wondrous waters we approach, when poured
On passion's lees, supply the wasted wine:
Then be thy bosom's tenant prodigal,
And confident of termless carnival.
Like idle yellow leaves afloat on time,
Let others lapse to death's pacific sea,—
We'll fade nor fall, but sport sublime
In green eternity.

VI.

The envious years, which steal our pleasures, thou
Mayst call at once, like magic memory, back,
And, as they pass o'er thine unwithering brow,
Efface their footsteps ere they form a track.
Thy bloom with wilful weeping never stain,
Perpetual life must not belong to pain.
For me,—this world has not yet been a place
Conscious of joys so great as will be mine,
Because the light has kissed no face
Forever fair as thine.

LINES

FROM THE PORTFOLIO OF H——.

No. I.

We met upon the world's wide face,
When each of us was young—
We parted soon, and to her place
A darker spirit sprung;
A feeling such as must have stirred
The Roman's bosom when he heard,
Beneath the trembling ground,
The god, his genius, marching forth
From the old city of his mirth,
To lively music's sound.

A sense it was, that I could see
The angel leave my side—
That thenceforth my prosperity
Must be a falling tide;
A strange and ominous belief,
That in spring-time the yellow leaf
Had fallen on my hours;
And that all hope must be most vain,
Of finding on my path again
Its former, vanished flowers.

But thou, the idol of my few
And fleeting better days—
The light that cheered when life was new
My being with its rays—
And though, alas!—its joy be gone,
Art yet, like tomb-lamps, shining on
The phantoms of my mind—
The memories of many a dream
Floating on thought's fantastic stream,
Like storm-clouds on the wind!

Is thy life but the wayward child
Of fever in the heart,
In part a crowd of fancies wild,
Of ill-made efforts part?
Are such accurst familiars thine,
As by thee were made early mine?
And is it as with me—
Doth hope in birthless ashes lie,
And seems the sun a hostile eye
Thy pains well-pleased to see?

I trust, not so:—though thou hast been
An evil star to mine,
Let all of good the world has seen
Hang ever upon thine.
May thy suns those of summer be,
And time show as one joy to thee,
Like thine own nature pure:
Thou didst but rouse, within my breast,
The sleeping devils from a rest
That could not long endure.

The firstlings of my simple song
Were offered to thy name:
Again the altar, idle long,
In worship rears its flame.
My sacrifice of sullen years,
My many hecatombs of tears,
No happier hours recall—
Yet may thy wandering thoughts restore
To one who ever loved thee more
Than fickle fortune's all.

And now, farewell!—and although here
Men hate the source of pain,
I hold thee and thy follies dear,
Nor of thy faults complain.
For my misused and blighted powers,
My waste of miserable hours,
I will accuse thee not:—
The fool who could from self depart,
And take for fate one human heart,
Deserved no better lot

I reck of mine the less, because
In wiser moods I feel
A doubtful question of its cause,
And nature, on me steal—
An ancient notion, that time flings
Our pains and pleasures from his wings
With much equality—
And that, in reason, happiness
Both of accession and decrease
Incapable must be.

LINES

FROM THE PORTFOLIO OF H——

No. II.

By woods and groves the oracles
Of the old age were nursed;
To Brutus came in solitude
The spectral warning first,
When murdered Cesar's mighty shade
The sanguine homicide dismayed,
And fantasy rehearsed
The ides of March, and, not in vain,
Showed forth Philippi's penal plain.

In loneliness I heard my hopes
Pronounce, "Let us depart!"
And saw my mind—a Marius—
Desponding o'er my heart:
The evil genius, long concealed,
To thought's keen eye itself revealed,
Unfolding like a chart—
But rolled away, and left me free
As Stoics once aspired to be

It brought, thou spirit of my breast,
And Naiad of the tears
Which have been welling coldly there,
Although unshed, for years!
It brought, in kindness or in hate,
The final menaces of fate,
But prompted no base fears—
Ah, could I with ill feelings see
Aught, love, so near allied to thee?

The drowsy harbinger of death,
That slumber dull and deep,
Is welcome, and I would not wake
Till thou dost join my sleep.
Life's conscious calm,—the flapping sail,—
The stagnant sea nor tide nor gale
In pleasing motion keep,—
Oppress me; and I wish release
From this to more substantial peace.

Star of that sea!—the cynosure
Of magnet-passions, long!—
A ceaseless apparition, and
A very ocular song!—
My skies have changed their hemisphere
And forfeited thy radiant cheer:
Thy shadow still is strong;
And, beaming darkness, follows me,
Far duskier than obscurity.

Star of that sea!—its currents bear
My vessel to the bourne,
Whence neither busy voyager
Nor pilgrim may return.
Such consummation I can brook,
Yet, with a fixed and lingering look,
Must anxiously discern
The far horizon, where thy rays
Surceased to light my night-like days

Unwise, or most unfortunate,
My way was; let the sign,
The proof of it, be simply this—
Thou art not, wert not, mine!
For 'tis the want of chance to bless
Pursuit, if patient, with success;
And envy may repine,
That, commonly, some triumph must
Be won by everlasting lust.

How I have lived imports not now
I am about to die,
Else I might chide thee that my life
Has been a stifled sigh:
Yes, life; for times beyond the line
Our parting traced, appear not mine,
Or of a world gone by;
And often almost would evince,
My soul had transmigrated since.

Pass wasted powers; alike the grave,
To which I fast go down,
Will give the joy of nothingness
To me, and to renown:
Unto its careless tenants, fame
Is idle as that gilded name,
Of vanity the crown,
Helvetian hands inscribe upon
The forehead of a skeleton.

List the last cadence of a lay,
That, closing as begun,
Is governed by a note of pain,
Oh, lost and worshipped one!—
None shall attend a sadder strain,
Till Memnon's statue stand again
To mourn the setting sun,—
Nor sweeter, if my numbers seem
To share the nature of their theme.

ON PARTING.

Alas! our pleasant moments fly
On rapid wings away,
While those recorded with a sigh,
Mock us by long delay.

Time,—envious time,—loves not to be
In company with mirth,
But makes malignant pause to see
The work of pain on earth.

ELYSIUM.

FROM AN UNFINISHED POEM.

She dwelleth in Elysium; there,
Like Echo, floating in the air;
Feeding on light as feed the flowers,
She fleets away uncounted hours,
Where halcyon Peace, among the blest,
Sits brooding o'er her tranquil nest.

She needs no impulse; one she is,
Whom thought supplies with ample bliss:
The fancies fashioned in her mind
By heaven, are after its own kind;
Like sky-reflections in a lake,
Whose calm no winds occur to break.

Her memory is purified,
And she seems never to have sighed:
She hath forgot the way to weep,
Her being is a joyous sleep;
The mere imagining of pain
Hath passed, and cannot come again.

Except of pleasure most intense
And constant, she hath lost all sense;
Her life is day without a night,
An endless, innocent delight;
No chance her happiness now mars,
Howe'er Fate twine *her* wreaths of stars.

And palpable and pure, the part,
Which pleasure playeth with her heart;
For every joy that seeks the maid,
Foregoes its common painful shade,
Like shapes that issue from the grove
Arcadian, dedicate to Jove.

EVERGREENS.

To ——.

When Summer's sunny hues adorn
Sky, forest, hill, and meadow,
The foliage of the evergreens,
In contrast, seems a shadow.

But when the tints of Autumn have
Their sober reign asserted,
The landscape that cold shadow shows,
Into a light converted.

Thus thoughts that frown upon our mirth
Will smile upon our sorrow,
And many dark fears of to-day
May be bright hopes to-morrow

And thine unfading image thus
Shall often cheer my sadness,
Though now its constant looks reprove
A momentary gladness.

SONG.

We break the glass, whose sacred wine
To some beloved health we drain,
Lest future pledges, less divine,
Should e'er the hallowed toy profane
And thus I broke a heart, that poured
Its tide of feelings out for thee,
In draughts, by after-times deplored,
Yet dear to memory.

But still the old impassioned ways
And habits of my mind remain,
And still unhappy light displays
Thine image chambered in my brain
And still it looks as when the hours
Went by like flights of singing birds,
Or that soft chain of spoken flowers,
And airy gems, thy words.

SERENADE.

Look out upon the stars, my love,
And shame them with thine eyes,
On which, than on the lights above,
There hang more destinies.
Night's beauty is the harmony
Of blending shades and light;
Then, Lady, up,—look out, and be
A sister to the night!—

Sleep not!—thine image wakes for aye,
Within my watching breast:
Sleep not!—from her soft sleep should fly,
Who robs all hearts of rest.
Nay, Lady, from thy slumbers break,
And make this darkness gay,
With looks, whose brightness well might make
Of darker nights a day.

SONG.

I need not name thy thrilling name,
Though now I drink to thee, my dear,
Since all sounds shape that magic word,
That fall upon my ear,—Mary;
And silence, with a wakeful voice,
Speaks it in accents loudly free,
As darkness hath a light that shows
Thy gentle face to me,—Mary.

I pledge thee in the grape's pure soul,
With scarce one hope, and many fears,
Mixed, were I of a melting mood,
With many bitter tears,—Mary—
I pledge thee, and the empty cup
Emblems this hollow life of mine,
To which, a gone enchantment, thou
No more wilt be the wine,—Mary.

A HEALTH.

I FILL this cup to one made up of loveliness alone,
A woman, of her gentle sex the seeming paragon;
To whom the better elements and kindly stars have given
A form so fair, that, like the air, 'tis less of earth than heaven.

Her every tone is music's own, like those of morning birds,
And something more than melody dwells ever in her words;
The coinage of her heart are they, and from her lips each flows
As one may see the burthened bee forth issue from the rose.

Affections are as thoughts to her, the measures of her hours;
Her feelings have the fragrancy, the freshness, of young flowers;
And lovely passions, changing oft, so fill her, she appears
The image of themselves by turns,—the idol of past years!

Of her bright face one glance will trace a picture on the brain,
And of her voice in echoing hearts a sound must long remain;
But memory such as mine of her so very much endears,
When death is nigh my latest sigh will not be life's but hers.

I filled this cup to one made up of loveliness alone,
A woman, of her gentle sex the seeming paragon—
Her health! and would on earth there stood some more of such a frame,
That life might be all poetry, and weariness a name.

PROLOGUE,

Delivered at the Greek Benefit, in Baltimore—1823.

"ILLE, NON EGO."

I.

As one, who long upon his couch hath lain
Subdued by sickness to a slave of pain,
When time and sudden health his strength repair,
Springs jocund to his feet, and walks the air;
So Greece, through centuries a prostrate land,
At length starts up—forever may she stand

II.

Since smiling Liberty, the sun thrice blest,
That had its rising in our happy west,
Extends its radiance, eastward, to that shore,
The place of gods whom yet our hearts adore;
And, hailed by loud acclaim of thousands, hath
Been worshipped with a more than Magian faith,
With slain Barbarian hosts for sacrifice,
And burning fleets for holocausts of price:
Shall we, who almost placed it in the sky,
Fail to assist the magnanimity,
With which, regardless of much pressing want,
They greet their fair and heavenly visitant?
Forbid it, Justice! we detest the state,
Which, knowing that mortality must rate
By mere comparison things dark or bright,—
Would make its fame as painters form a light,
By circumjacent blackness—we are free,
And so could wish the total earth to be.
Greece *shall*,—Greece *is*,—each old. heroic shade,
Draws, with her living sons, his spectral blade,
And combats, proud of times so like his own,
Like Theseus' ghost at storied Marathon.

III.

"The Last of Grecians,"—is become a phrase,
Improper in these new triumphant days:
The swords well wielded against Turkish bands,
Are not unworthy of those mighty hands
Which overthrew the haughty Persian, when
Pausanias and Leonidas were men.

IV.

To-night, the useful and the pleasing claim,
Still more than commonly, to seem the same;
For, pleasing you, we aid, "in our degree,"
A struggling nation's strife for liberty,—
The strife whose voice from this great world demands,
What mine of you beseeches—"clap your hands!"

THE WIDOW'S SONG.

I BURN no incense, hang no wreath,
On this, thine early tomb:
Such cannot cheer the place of death,
But only mock its gloom.
Here odorous smoke and breathing flower
No grateful influence shed;
They lose their perfume and their power,
When offered to the dead.

And if, as is the Afghaun's creed,
The spirit may return,
A disembodied sense, to feed
On fragrance, near its urn—
It is enough, that she, whom thou
Didst love in living years,
Sits desolate beside it now,
And falls these heavy tears.

TO ——.

With Wordsworth's, "She was a phantom of delight," &c.

ACCEPT this portraiture of thee,
Revealed to Wordsworth in a dream—
One less immortal stays with me,
Whose airy hues thine own may seem:
Mental reflection of thy light,
A rainbow beautiful and bright;
A shining lamp of constant ray,
To which my fancy shall be slave;
A shaping that cannot decay,
Until it moulder in my grave.—
The image-breaker, Time, may mar
All meaner sculpture of my mind,
But in its darkness, like a star,
Thy semblance shall remain enshrined
Nor would I that the sullen thing
Its place in being should resign,
While, like a casket rich with gems,
It treasures forms so fair as thine.

TO ——.

'Twas eve; the broadly shining sun
Its long, celestial course, had run;
The twilight heaven, so soft and blue,
Met earth in tender interview,
Ev'n as the angel met of yore
His gifted mortal paramour,
Woman, a child of morning then,—
A spirit still,—compared with men.
Like happy islands of the sky,
The gleaming clouds reposed on high,
Each fixed sublime, deprived of motion,
A Delos to the airy ocean.
Upon the stirless shore no breeze
Shook the green drapery of the trees,
Or, rebel to tranquillity,
Awoke a ripple on the sea.
Nor, in a more tumultuous sound,
Were the world's audible breathings drowned;
The low strange hum of herbage growing,
The voice of hidden waters flowing,
Made songs of nature, which the ear
Could scarcely be pronounced to hear;
But noise had furled its subtle wings,
And moved not through material things,
All which lay calm as they had been
Parts of the painter's mimic scene.
'Twas eve; my thoughts belong to thee,
Thou shape of separate memory!
When, like a stream to lands of flame,
Unto my mind a vision came.
Methought, from human haunts and strife
Remote, we lived a loving life;
Our wedded spirits seemed to blend
In harmony too sweet to end,
Such concord as the echoes cherish
Fondly, but leave at length to perish.
Wet rain-stars are thy lucid eyes,
The Hyades of earthly skies,
But then upon my heart they shone,
As shines on snow the fervid sun.
And fast went by those moments bright,
Like meteors shooting through the night;
But faster fleeted the wild dream,
That clothed them with their transient beam
Yet love can years to days condense,
And long appeared that life intense;
It was,—to give a better measure
Than time,—a century of pleasure.

SONG.

Those starry eyes, those starry eyes,
Those eyes that used to be
Unto my heart as beacon-lights
To pilgrims of the sea!—

I see them yet, I seem them yet.
Though long since quenched and gone—
I could not live enlumined by
The common sun alone.

Could they seem thus, could they seem thus,
If but a memory?——
Ah, yes! upon this wintry earth,
They burn no more for me.

SONG.

Day departs this upper air,
My lively, lovely lady;
And the eve-star sparkles fair,
And our good steeds are ready.
Leave, leave these loveless halls,
So lordly though they be;—
Come, come—affection calls—
Away at once with me!

Sweet thy words in sense as sound,
And gladly do I hear them;
Though thy kinsmen are around,
And tamer bosoms fear them.
Mount, mount,—I'll keep thee, dear,
In safety as we ride;—
On, on—my heart is here,
My sword is at my side!

THE OLD TREE.

FROM THE NOTE-BOOK OF A TRAVELLER

And is it gone, that venerable tree,
The old spectator of my infancy!—
It used to stand upon this very spot,
And now almost its absence is forgot.
I knew its mighty strength had known decay,
Its heart, like every old one, shrunk away,
But dreamt not that its frame would fall, ere mine
At all partook my weary soul's decline.

The great reformist, that each day removes
The old, yet never on the old improves—
The dotard, Time, that like a child destroys,
As sport or spleen may prompt, his ancient toys,
And shapes their ruins into something new—
Has planted other playthings where it grew.
The wind pursues an unobstructed course,
Which once among its leaves delayed perforce;
The harmless Hamadryad, that, of yore,
Inhabited its bole, subsists no more;
Its roots have long since felt the ruthless plough
There is no vestige of its glories now!
But in my mind, which doth not soon forget,
That venerable tree is growing yet;
Nourished, like those wild plants that feed on air
By thoughts of years unconversant with care,
And visions such as pass ere man grows wholl
A fiendish thing, or mischief adds to folly
I still behold it with my fancy's eye,
A vernant record of the days gone by:
I see not the sweet form and face more plain,
Whose memory *was* a weight upon my brain.
—Dear to my song, and dearer to my soul,
Who knew but half my heart, yet had the whole
Sun of my life, whose presence and whose flight
Its brief day caused, and never-ending night!
Must this delightless verse, which is indeed
The mere wild product of a worthless weed,
(But which, like sun-flowers, turns a loving face
Towards the lost light, and scorns its birth and place,)
End with such cold allusion unto you,
To whom, in youth, my very dreams were true?
It must; I have no more of that soft kind,
*My age is not the same, nor is my mind

* Horace.

RODOLPH,

A FRAGMENT.

"Call these forms from under ground,
With a soft and happy sound."

Fletcher.

"There is an order
Of mortals on the earth, who do become
Old in their youth, and die ere middle age,
Without the violence of warlike death;
Some perishing of pleasure—some of study—
Some worn with toil—some of mere weariness,
Some of disease—and some insanity—
And some of withered, or of broken hearts;
For this last is a malady which slays
More than are numbered in the lists of fate,
Taking all shapes, and bearing many names."

Lord Byron.

DEDICATION.

Sweet Promiser!—if now to thee
(No halcyon on the wintry sea
Of troubled feeling yet)
I dedicate this idle rhyme,
Woven to cheer the laggard time,
Though wisdom would forget;
Learn that when as a funeral train
The mournful moments crossed my brain,
I could not but remember hours,
Which wore bright coronals of flowers,
And came successively to me,
Like notes of heart-felt melody.
Learn further, that with these was shown
A phantom fairer far—thine own—
An apparition none can know,
Or guess of, saving only *thou.*
As for this story of an age
That saw life fanciful as dreams,
Thy gem-like eye will scan its page;
And if, with sounds of sleepy streams,
Thy voice make music of my lays—
Could they obtain a dearer praise?

PART I.

I.

The Summer's heir on land and sea
Had thrown his parting glance,
And Winter taken angrily
His waste inheritance.
The winds in stormy revelry
Sported beneath a frowning sky;
The chafing waves with hollow roar
Tumbled upon the shaken shore,
And sent their spray in upward shower
To Rodolph's proud ancestral tower,
Whose station from its mural crown
A regal look cast sternly down

II.

At such a season, his domain
The lord at last arrived again,
Changed to the sight, and scarce the same,
Grown old in heart, infirm of frame.
His earlier years had been too blest
For anguish not to curse the rest:
Men, like the Dioscuri, dwell
Alternately in heaven and hell.
Let those, whose lives are in their prime,
Use to the uttermost the time;
For as with the enchanted thrall
Of Eblis and his fatal hall,
When a short period departs,
The flame shall kindle in their hearts.
Thou only, mighty Love!—canst will
Much herald good, much after-ill;
Thou holdest human hearts in fee,
And art the Second Destiny.
He loved—he won—and whom?—he sighed
First *for*, next *with*, another's bride:
To both extremes of feeling,—strong
Or feeble,—the same signs belong,
And sighs may the expression be
Of ecstasy or agony.
* * * * *

III.

Like rarest porcelain were they,
Moulded of accidental clay:
She, loving, lovely, kind, and fair—
He, wise, and fortunate, and brave—
You'll easily suppose they were
A passionate and radiant pair,
Lighting the scenes else dark and cold,
As the sepulchral lamps of old,
A subterranean cave.
'Tis pity that their loves were vices,
And purchased at such painful prices;
'Tis pity, and Delight deplores
That grief allays her golden stores.
Yet if all chance brought rapture here,
Life would become a ceaseless fear
To leave a world, then rightly dear.
Two kindred mysteries* are bright,
And cloud-like, in the southern sky;
A shadow and its sister-light,
Around the pole they float on high,
Linked in a strong though sightless chain,
The types of pleasure and of pain.

IV.

There was an age, they tell us, when
Eros and Anteros dwelt with men,
Ere selfishness had backward driven
The wrathful deities to heaven:
Then gods forsook their outshone skies,
For stars mistaking female eyes;
Woman was true, and man, though free,
Was faithful in idolatry.
No dial needed they to measure
Unsighing being—Time was Pleasure

* The Magellan clouds

And lustres, never dimmed by tears,
Were not misnamed from lustrous years.
Alas! that such a tale must seem
The fiction of a dreaming dream!—
Is it but fable?—has that age
Shone only on the poet's page,
Where earth, a luminous sphere portrayed,
Revolves not both in sun and shade?
No!—happy love, too seldom known,
May make it for a while our own.

V.

Yes, although fleeting rapidly,
It sometimes may be ours,
And he was gladsome as the bee*
Which always sleeps in flowers.
Might this endure?—her husband came
At an untimely tide,
But ere his tongue pronounced her shame
Slain suddenly, he died.
'Twas whispered by whose hand he fell,
And Rodolph's prosperous loves were gone.
The lady sought a convent-cell,
And lived in penitence alone;
Thrice blest, that she the waves among
Of ebbing pleasure staid not long,
To watch the sullen tide, and find
The hideous shapings left behind.
Such, sinking to its slimy bed,
Old Nile upon the antique land,
Where Time's inviolate temples stand,†
Hath ne'er deposited.
Happy, the monster of that Nile,
The vast and vigorous crocodile;
Happy, because his dying day
Is unpreceded by decay:
We perish slowly—loss of breath
Only completes our piece-meal death.

VI.

She ceased to smile back on the sun,
Their task the Destinies had done;
And earth, which gave, resumed the charms,
Whose freshness withered in its arms:
But never walked upon its face,
Nor mouldered in its dull embrace,
A creature fitter to prepare
Sorrow, or social joy to share:
When her the latter life required,
A vital harmony expired;
And in that melancholy hour,
Nature displayed its saddest power,
Subtracting from man's darkened eye
Beauties that seemed unmeant to die,
And claiming deeper sympathy
Than even when the wise or brave
Descend into an early grave.
We grieve when morning puts to flight
The pleasant visions of the night;
And surely we shall have good leave,
When a fair woman dies, to grieve.
Whither have fled that shape, and gleam
Of thought—the woman, and the dream?—

* The Florisomnus. † The Pyramids.

Whither have fled that inner light,
And benefactress of our sight?—
Nothing in answer aught can show,
Only thus much of each we know—
The dream may visit us again,
She left for aye the sons of men!—
Death may in part discharge its debt,
Half render back its trust—
Life may redeem her likeness yet,
Reanimate her dust;
But both will bear another name,
Nor, like the dream, appear the same.

VII.

While Hope attends her sacred fire,
All joy rejoices in its pyre:
Once quenched, what ray the flame renews?
What but calamity ensues?
When ill-report disgraced his name,
And turned to infamy his fame,
Bearing from home his blighted prime,
He journeyed to some distant clime,
Where babbling rumour could not trace
His footsteps to a resting-place.
Meanwhile, the quest of happiness
He made, despairing of success;
Unhoped, but not pursued the less,
It urged around the world its flight
Away from him, like day from night.
There are, who deem of misery
As if it ever craved to die:
They err; the full of soul regard,
More than the calm, their graves with hate;
The loss of such a life is hard,
And, ending their eventful fate,
From so much into nothing must
The change be pain—from *this* to dust!
To fill the chasms of the breast,
'Tis happiness they seek, not rest,
Wishing for something to amend
Existence, they must shun its end;
And this the princely will betrays
To many sufferings and days.

VIII.

As sunk, avoiding mortal touch,
The Cabalist's discovered treasure,
So met his sight, escaped his clutch,
Many appearances of pleasure,
Deceitful as that airy lie,
The child of vapour and the sky,*
Which cheats the thirsty Arab's eye,
Only the palm, heat-loving tree,
Or bird of happy Araby,
May burn, and not to die:
Philosophy has lost the power†
From ashes to reform a flower;
Magic and alchymy no more
Men's primal strength and youth restore,
Nor could those great and dream-like arts,
While flourishing, revoke their hearts:
The feelings rise regenerate never,
But, once consumed, are gone forever.

*   *   *   *   *
*   *   *   *   *

* The Mirage. † Palingenesy.

RODOLPH,

PART II.

I.

How feels the guiltless dreamer, who
With idly curious gaze
Has let his mind's glance wander through
The relics of past days?—
As feels the pilgrim that has scanned,
Within their skirting wall,
The moonlit marbles of some grand
Disburied capital;
Masses of whiteness and of g.oom,
The darkly bright remains
Of desolate palace, empty tomb,
And desecrated fanes:—
For in the ruins of old hours,
Remembrance haply sees
Temples, and tombs, and palaces,
Not different from these.

II.

But such mere musings could not now
Move Rodolph's lip, or curl his brow:
His countenance had lost its free
And former fine transparency,
Nor would, as once, his spirit pass
Its fleshly mask, like light through glass.
In his sad aspect seemed to be
Troubled reflections of a life,
Nourished by passion, spent in strife—
Gleams, as of drowned antiquity
From cities underneath the sea
Which glooms in famous Galilee.

III.

In the calm scene he viewed was aught
That might disturb a froward thought?
He saw, new-married to the air,
The tranquil, waveless deep,
Reposing in a night as fair
As woman's softest sleep:
Peaceful and silent, were met all
The elements in festival,
And the wide universe seemed to be
One clear obscure transparency.
Could such a quiet Fancy wake?
And doth she from her slumbers break,
As drowsy mortals often will,
When lamps go out, or clocks fall still?
No less than when the Wind-god's breath
Blackens the wilderness beneath,
Until contrasted stars blaze bright
With their own proper heavenly light,
And almost make the gazer sigh,
For our unseen mythology.
Motion or rest, a sound, a glance,
Alike rouse memory from its trance.

IV.

Perhaps, presentiment of ill
Might shake him—hearts are prophets stil..
What though the fount of Castaly
Not now stains leaves with prophecy?
What though are of another age
Omens, and Sybil's boding page?—
Augurs and oracles resign
Their voices—fear can still divine:
Dreams and hand-writings on the wall
Need not foretell our fortune's fall;
Domitian in his galleries,*
The soul all hostile advents sees,
As in the mirror-stone;
Like shadows by a brilliant day
Cast down from falcons on their prey;
Or watery demons, in strong light,
By haunted waves of fountains old,
Shown indistinctly to the sight
Of the inquisitive and bold.
The mind is capable to show
Thoughts of so dim a feature,
That consciousness can only know
Their presence, not their nature;
Things which, like fleeting insect-mothers,
Supply recording life to others,
And forthwith lose their own.

V.

He backed his steed, and took his way
Where a large cemetery lay,
Beaming beneath the star-light gay,
A white spot in the greenery,
Semblant of what it well might be—
A blossom unto which the earth
As a spring-favour yielded birth.
They looked for his return in vain,
Homeward he never rode again.
What boots it to protract the verse,
In which his story I rehearse?
He had won safely through the past,
The growing sickness smote at last:
His vassals found him on the morn,
Senseless beside his lady's urn;
And they beheld with wonderment
His visage—like a bow unbent,
From the distorting mind unstrung,
By painful thought no longer wrung,
It offered once more to their gaze
The cheerful mien of former days,
And on it the fix'd smile had place,
Which lights the Memnon's marble face.

VI.

Hot fever raged in Rodolph's brain,
Till tortured reason fled,
And madness a delirious reign
Asserted in its stead;
And then he raved of many crimes,
Achieved in shadows of all climes;
Of Indian islands, tropic seas,
Ships winged before the flying breeze;
Of peace, of war, of wine, of blood,
Of love, and hate, of changing mood,
Or changing scenery;
And often on his language hung
The accents of an alien tongue,
But still they circled one dark deed,
As charmed men that magic weed,

* Vide Suetonius.

The herb of Normandy.*
He spoke of one too dearly loved,
And one unwisely slain,
Of an affection hardly proved
By murder done in vain—
Affection which no time could tire,
Constant as emeralds in fire,
Like that which weds insanity
To the sole truth that earth may see.
Some fragments of his speech my rhyme
Shall rescue from the grasp of time,
As trophies, by the march of song,
In tuneless triumph borne along.

VII.

"The evil hour in which you traced
"Your name upon my heart, is past,
"And hidden fires or lightning-flashes
"Have since reduced it into ashes;
"Yet oft will busy thought unroll
"That fragile, scorched, and blackened scroll,
"And shrink to find the spell, your name,
"A legend uneffaced by flame.

VIII.

"Who spoke that lawless, sounding word,
"So early hushed, so long unheard?—
"Its syllables came o'er my brain,
"Like the last trumpet's call;
"And, starting from their graves again,
"My buried thoughts, in fear and pain,
"Are gathering one and all.
"The pictured memories hid by grief
"Come forth in beautiful relief,
"Freed from their former thrall—
"As, through the torch-touched rust of years,
"A waxen painting reappears
"On a sepulchral wall.

IX.

"Thy face revives the face of one
"That *lived* in other days—
"Whose fading phantom had begun
"To fail my fancy's gaze;
"Though shadowed forth too long and well,
"As my sad history may tell.
"Thy face revives the face of one,
"That *loved* in other days—
"Of whom or thought or speech was none
"Less passionate than praise:
"So much she beautified the place
"Replete with her in time and space.
"Thy face revives the face of one,
"That *died* in other days—
"Who bought, not borrowed, from the sun
"Its scarcely needed rays;
"And thousand charms could not concur
"To make thee fair,—yet unlike her.
"It is herself!—the gods in pity
"Restore her from the silent city!—
"Now, where are they, that falsely said,
"Her form in stirless dust was laid?
"Who reared the lying pyramid,
"Whose epitaph, and lamp, and flame,
"Told that her heavenward home lay hid
"In its sky-pointing frame?
"She is not dead—behold her eye,
"That portion of a summer sky:
"She is not dead—her cheeks are rife
"With rosy clouds of blooming life:
"She is not dead—the shining hair
"Is wreathed about her forehead fair,
"As when I saw in better hours
"Her gentle shape of living mirth,
"And trod with her upon all flowers
"Worn by the festive earth.
"Time interposed—it was not Death,
"He could not stop her spicy breath—
"But hearts and hands have met once more
"We will be happy as before;
"And my crime-sullied memory
"Like a rewritten code* shall be,
"Full of the poetry of truth,
"The annals of a second youth,
"Illuminations blazoned bright
"With sun-born tints of golden light.

X.

"If, memory, on thy silent shore
"The stream of time hath left
"Some broken hopes, plans quick no more,
"And thoughts of breath bereft;
"The strong belief in happiness,
"It could but half destroy;
"The now dead generous carelessness,
"That hung around the boy;
"And feelings which the subtile wave
"Bore not through later years—
"Such wrecks the smiles of wisdom crave
"Not less than passion's tears.—
"But thou, the sweetest of Eve's daughters,
"Genius† of that shore, and those waters!—
"A music visible, a light
"Like lamps unto an infant's sight!—
"A temple of celestial soul,
"Too lovely for aught ill to mar,
"Which Love from Beauty's planet stole,
"The morn and evening star!—
"Come thou, and pass away with me
"From haunts unworthy of thy smile,
"And find, in some far, sunny sea,
"A lonely, laughing isle,
"Where we may through all pleasures rove
"And live like votaries of love,
"Drinking the sparkling stream of years,
"Pure, and unmixed with wormwood tears.
* * * * *

XI.

"Why have I, speaking thus to thee,
"Vague sense that these things may not be?—
"Strange flitting fires each other chase,
"Like meteors, through a cheerless space:
"My sight grows heavy, and my breast
"By something mountainous is pressed;
"And, in my veins, the lazy blood
"Is not that eager, rushing flood,
"It was when thou wert nigh,

* "L'Herbe Maudite."

* "Codex rescriptus." † "Genius Loci."

"Nor will my limbs avail to bear
"My feeble, sickly body, where
"Thou standest moveless by.
"I feel a weary wish to close
"Mine eyelids in a long repose;
"But fear that thou wilt fly,
"And let me wake alone to sigh
"That one so beautiful *could* die!—

XII.

"Author of my unhappiness!
"Let me thy lip and small hand press.
"Since love increases when the day
"Its object's presence makes is done,
"And takes from night a warmer ray,
"As did the Fountain of the Sun,*
"Thine, so long absent, should forgive
"The death of one I slew for thee—
"Resentment cannot bid him live,
"Pardon perchance may me.
"Obdurate Lady, even thine eye
"To my fond prayer makes no reply;
"And hast thou come then from afar,
"A coldly reappearing star?—
"Thou never lov'dst:—thy constancy
"Would answer else aright to mine:
"In one so lovely, love must be
"Preserved still fresh, like grapes in wine.
"Thy smiles were but a shining mask,
"Thy vows no more than vocal air,
"If thou canst, let me vainly ask
"Relief from this despair.
"By all that I have borne and bear,
"She fades to unsubstantial air!—
* * * * *

XIII.

The perturbation of my soul
Subsides as I approach the goal;
"Yet dreamt I one was here but now,
"Whose brow was like her ivory brow.
"When shall we two meet again,
"And not, as last, to part in pain?
"Spring shall leave to rear the flowers,
"And Autumn to let fall the showers;
"Summer shall forbear to glow,
"And Winter doff its veil of snow;
"Man shall know no more to mourn,
"The age of miracles return;
"Woman shall forget to range,
"And fortune and the moon to change;
"Tears and tides shall cease to flow,
"The sea and life their storms forego:
"Opportunity shall stay
"The wings on which it flies away
"Memory the past shall scan,
"Yet see not, like a drowning man,
"Fast upon the bitter wave
"The ship depart, that ought to save;
"Noon and midnight shall have met,
"The stars have risen where they set;
"Ere, though but in sleep, we twain
"Can dream one hope to meet again.—
"She lies amid the sluggish mould,
"Her ardent heart has long been cold:
"Above it wave the idle weeds,
"On it the sordid earth-worm feeds.
"Mine too is buried there—her knell
"Served also for its passing bell;
"It died—and would have known 'twas time
"Without that melancholy chime.
"That knell!—I feel its strokes again,
"Like stunning blows upon my brain
"I listen yet the dissonant laughter
"Of the same bell, some moments after;
"And now the frequent ding-dong hear,
"With which it mimics hope and fear.

XIV.

"Ay, wrapt around a whiter breast,
"The shroud her body doth invest;
"But in that other world, her grave,
"My soul and body both inter,
"There to enjoy the rest they crave,
"And, if at all, arise with her:
"Never may either wake, unless
"To her, and former happiness!—
"Yet how am I assured that rest
"Will ever bless the aching breast,
"Which passion has so long possessed?—
"At baffled Death's oblivious art
"This love perchance will mock,
"Deep dwelling in my festering heart,
"A reptile in its rock:
"The warm and tender violet
"Beside the glaciers grows,
"Although with frosty airs beset,
"And everlasting snows;
"So, lying in obstruction chill,
"This stronger flower may flourish still.
"Oh, in the earth, ye Furies, let
"My thoughtful clay all thought forget.
"Suffer no sparkles of hot pain
"Among mine ashes to remain:
"Give, give me utterly to prove
"Insentient of the pangs of love!—
"—Why waver thus these forms?—there is
"A palpable blackness on mine eyes;
"And yet the figures gleam
"With the impressive energy,
"Which clothes the phantoms that we see
"Shown by a fever-dream.
"How the air thickens—all things move—
"'Tis night—'tis chaos—my lost love!—"

XV.

He perished. None wept o'er his bier,
Although above such things we weep,
And rest obtains the useless tear,
Due rather to the state of sleep;
For why?—because the common faith
Of passion is averse from death;
Yet Jove, the sages all declare,
Granted the Argive mother's* prayer.

* "Fons Solis."

* Cydippe. See Herod.

BIOGRAPHICAL NOTICE

OF

EDWARD COATE PINKNEY,

BY THE LATE

WILLIAM LEGGETT.

(WRITTEN IN 1827.)

A BIOGRAPHICAL account of eminent men, who still exist among us, must generally be brief and imperfect. Many interesting anecdotes of their private lives are forgotten by friendship, until the grave gives a new impulse to memory; and such as are recollected, are communicated with reluctance, and must be used with cautious delicacy. Of the poet, in particular, it is difficult to acquire biographical materials; his life glides along in unobtrusive and unnoticed seclusion; and a narrative, disclosing the place and time of his birth, his opportunities of education, and the nature and merits of the different productions of his genius, is, very often, all that can be furnished, even after death has unlocked the sources of information. In the present instance, our space will not allow us to be diffuse; and the necessary paucity of data forbids minuteness of accuracy: yet, in speaking of this distinguished individual, whatever we relate may be relied on as true, and whatever is true of him cannot but be interesting.

EDWARD COATE PINKNEY, the third of ten children of the illustrious William Pinkney, was born in London, in the month of October, 1802, while his father was Minister of the United States at the Court of St. James. His mother, who is still living, is the sister of Commodore Rogers. Nearly nine years of the infancy of Mr. Pinkney were passed in England, at the expiration of which time his parents returned with him to this country, and established again their residence in Baltimore.

At an early period of his life, Mr. Pinkney exhibited evidences of genius which awakened the fondest hopes of his future eminence—hopes that one of his parents has lived to see fully realized. Between ten and eleven years of age, he was placed a student in Baltimore College, where the rapidity of his progress excited the surprise of his classmates, and the warm encomiums of his instructors. When about fourteen, his father procured for him the appointment of Midshipman, in the navy of the United States; and bidding adieu, in the course of a few months after, to the walls of a college, he entered, full of hope and gayety, into the active performance of the duties of his office. He continued in the service nine years, during which he necessarily had many and advantageous opportunities of visiting various parts of the globe; and a long Mediterranean cruise made him intimately acquainted with some of the most interesting scenes of classic story. The beautiful poem entitled Italy, of which we shall speak anon, sufficiently shows that he looked upon those scenes with a poet's eye.

On the death of his father, from a desire to be with his bereaved mother, he resigned his appointment in the navy: and soon after, animated with a noble ambition to tread in the path which had led his parent to greatness, he commenced the practice of the law, in which he has since continued with unabated ardor, and with such closeness of application as has prevented the exercise of that brilliant poetic genius which nature has bestowed upon him in an unusual degree. In 1824 he was married to Miss Georgiana M'Causland, who must indeed have been a beautiful and accomplished young lady, if she sat for the por trait (as we suspect) which her husband has drawn in the two exquisite poems, called a Picture Song, and the Health.

In the following year, the volume of poems which bears his name was published in Baltimore, by Joseph Robinson. Rodolph, the only poem of any great length in the collection, had been previously before the public, printed separately and anonymously; but as only a very small edition was struck off, few had an opportunity of deciding on its merits. The opinions of such, however, as did peruse it, were highly favourable, and induced the author to consent to another edition being printed, with several additional shorter pieces, some of which are rich in beauties of a peculiar nature, and are not surpassed by any productions, of a similar character, in the English language.

Rodolph, the principal poem, contains many undeniable evidences of a fine genius and a cultivated mind; but it is also disfigured with many faults, both in sentiment and execution. Were this our only criterion of Mr. Pinkney's poetic merits, we should still be inclined to award to him a high rank among the eminent poets of this country; but we could not accord to him that unmixed praise which his other effusions deserve. The story is neither novel, interesting, nor moral; and the meaning of the language is often obscured by an affected use of obsolete expressions, when such as are in frequent use would not only have been better understood, but also more appropriate. It commences beautifully—and here we are led to remark the author's happy and original fertility in illustrations, which abound on every page of the work, and yet are always so apt and so new, that in no single instance are we fatigued by them. His use of classical allusions, too, is remarkably felicitous, showing that he has attentively read and properly appreciated the ancient authors for himself, and not drawn his resources from a Lempriere's Dictionary, or the hackneyed quotations of others.

The poem, entitled Italy, written after the manner of Goethe's *Kennst du das Land*, is a production of uncommon sweetness and spirit; and the first and third stanzas possess such rare excellence that we cannot forbear copying them:

"Know'st thou the land which lovers ought to choose?
Like blessings there descend the sparkling dews;
In gleaming streams the crystal rivers run,
The purple vintage clusters in the sun;
Odours of flowers haunt the balmy breeze,
Rich fruits hang high upon the vernant trees;
And vivid blossoms gem the shady groves,
Where bright-plumed birds discourse their careless loves
Beloved!—speed we from this sullen strand
Until thy light feet press that green shore's yellow sand

It looks a dimple on the face of earth,
The seal of beauty and the shrine of mirth;
Nature is delicate and graceful there,
The place's genius, feminine and fair:
The winds are awed, nor dare to breathe aloud;
The air seems never to have borne a cloud,
Save where volcanoes send to heav'n their curled
And solemn smokes, like altars of the world.
Thrice beautiful!—to that delightful spot
Carry our married hearts, and be all pain forgot."

The four lines, beginning "The winds are awed," are not surpassed by any four lines of description in the whole range of English poetry.

"Exchanging lustre with the sun,
A part of day she strays—
A glancing, living, human smile,
On nature's face that plays."

Who has ever read a more animated and poetical description of a lovely female than this? But it will not answer for us to occupy our space by quoting the beauties of Mr. Pinkney's volume; for, did we once commence the task, we should scarcely be able to leave it, without extracting nearly all its contents. We sincerely hope that another edition of it will shortly be put to press, so that the many who are still unfurnished, may have it in their power to obtain a copy; and we should be still better pleased if it were enlarged with a few more effusions from a mind well capable of advancing, by its single effort, the literary reputation of this country to a still higher elevation.

Edward Coate Pinkney died in 1828, at Baltimore.

www.ingramcontent.com/pod-product-compliance
Lightning Source LLC
LaVergne TN
LVHW021220110826
845150LV00002B/208

* 9 7 8 1 4 2 5 5 6 4 2 3 0 *